THE OXFORD HANDB

ROMAN EGYPT

Roman Egypt is a critical area of interdisciplinary research, which has steadily expanded since the 1970s and continues to grow. Egypt played a pivotal role in the Roman empire, not only in terms of political, economic, and military strategies, but also as part of an intricate cultural discourse involving themes that resonate today—east and west, old world and new, acculturation and shifting identities, patterns of language use and religious belief, and the management of agriculture and trade. Roman Egypt was a literal and figurative crossroads shaped by the movement of people, goods, and ideas, and framed by permeable boundaries of self and space.

This handbook is unique in drawing together many different strands of research on Roman Egypt, in order to suggest both the state of knowledge in the field and the possibilities for collaborative, synthetic, and interpretive research. Arranged in seven thematic sections, each of which includes essays from a variety of disciplinary vantage points and multiple sources of information, it offers new perspectives from both established and younger scholars, featuring individual essay topics, themes, and intellectual juxtapositions.

Christina Riggs is Chair in the History of Visual Culture at the Department of History, Durham University.

Praise for *The Oxford Handbook of Roman Egypt*

'This is a comprehensive, balanced, critically engaged and eminently useful introduction for anyone approaching Roman Egypt today, irrespective of one's methodical point of departure.'

David M. Ratzan, *Near Eastern Archaeology*

'Riggs presents a succinct introduction to the study of Roman Egypt followed by a historical overview of the period, providing a firm background from which 45 papers, and the specific topics covered within them, can branch out.... [T]his volume is highly useful to those readers delving into initial research, making the diverse study of the history and culture of Roman Egypt more easily accessible.'

Emily Millward, *Rosetta*

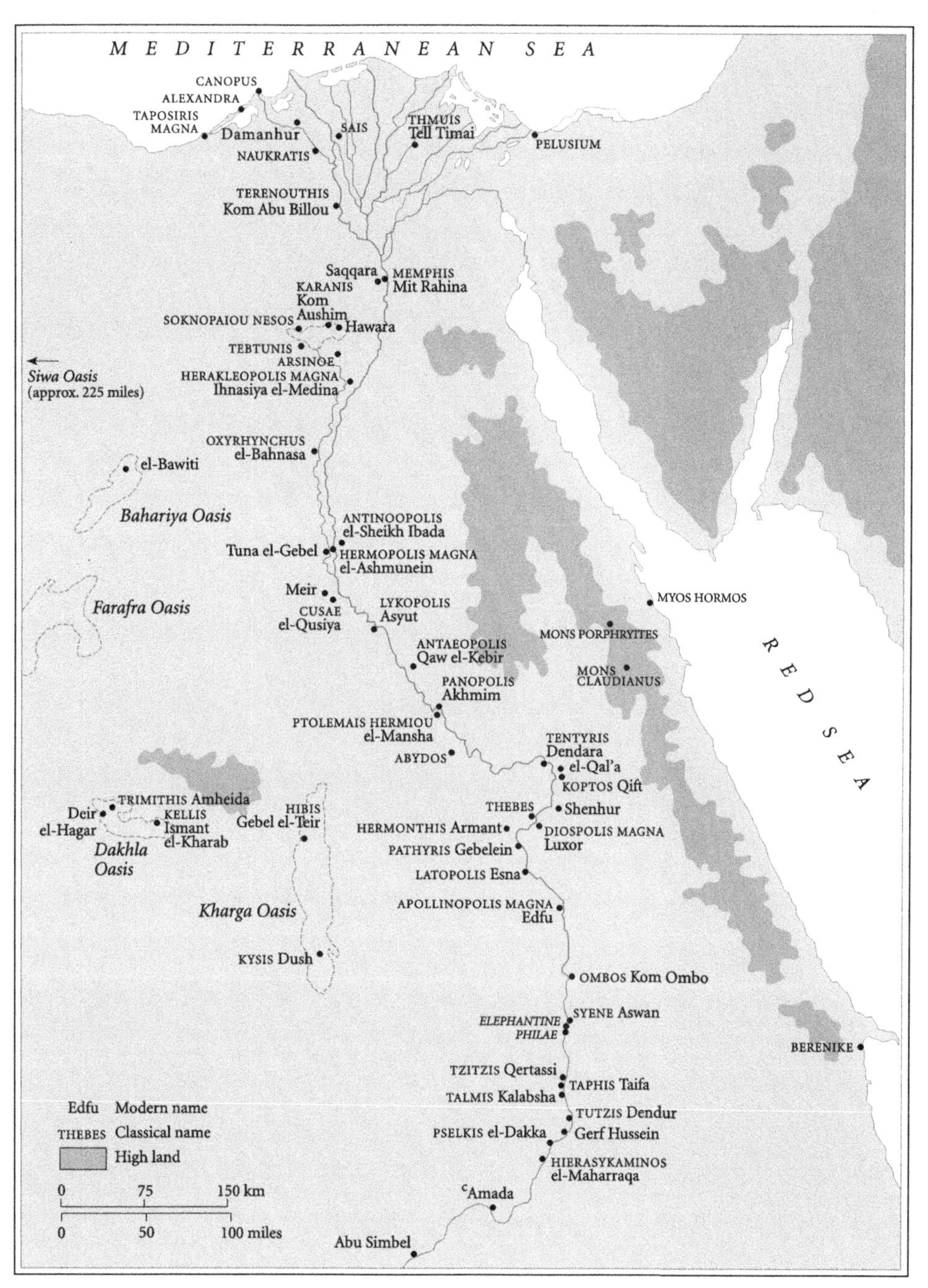

Map of Egypt in the Roman Period, showing key sites mentioned in the text.

THE OXFORD HANDBOOK OF

ROMAN EGYPT

Edited by

CHRISTINA RIGGS

OXFORD
UNIVERSITY PRESS

Great Clarendon Street, Oxford, OX2 6DP,
United Kingdom

Oxford University Press is a department of the University of Oxford. It furthers the University's objective of excellence in research, scholarship, and education by publishing worldwide. Oxford is a registered trade mark of Oxford University Press in the UK and in certain other countries

First published 2012
First published in paperback 2019

Published in the United States of America by Oxford University Press
198 Madison Avenue, New York, NY 10016, United States of America

British Library Cataloguing in Publication Data
Data available

Library of Congress Cataloging in Publication Data
Data available

ISBN 978–0–19–885490–6 (Pbk.)

Contents

List of Figures xi
List of Tables xvii
List of Contributors xviii
List of Abbreviations and Conventions xxi

Introduction 1
Christina Riggs

PART I LAND AND STATE

1. *Aegypto Capta*: Augustus and the Annexation of Egypt 11
Friederike Herklotz

2. Between Water and Sand: Agriculture and Husbandry 22
Katherine Blouin

3. Manufacture, Trade, and the Economy 38
Matt Gibbs

4. Government, Taxation, and Law 56
Andrea Jördens

5. The Roman Army in Egypt 68
Rudolf Haensch

6. The Imperial Cult in Egypt 83
Stefan Pfeiffer

PART II CITY, TOWN, AND *CHORA*

7. Alexandria 103
Marjorie S. Venit

8. Settlement and Population 122
Laurens E. Tacoma

9. Archaeology in the Delta 136
Penelope Wilson

10. The Archaeology of the Fayum 152
PAOLA DAVOLI

11. The Theban Region under the Roman Empire 171
ADAM ŁAJTAR

12. Classical Architecture 189
DONALD M. BAILEY

13. City of the Dead: Tuna el-Gebel 205
KATJA LEMBKE

14. The University of Michigan Excavation of Karanis (1924–1935): Images from the Kelsey Museum Photographic Archives 223
T. G. WILFONG

PART III PEOPLE

15. Status and Citizenship 247
ANDREA JÖRDENS

16. Identity 260
KATELIJN VANDORPE

17. The Jews in Roman Egypt: Trials and Rebellions 277
ANDREW HARKER

18. Families, Households, and Children 288
MYRTO MALOUTA

19. Age and Health 305
WALTER SCHEIDEL

PART IV RELIGION

20. Religious Practice and Piety 319
DAVID FRANKFURTER

21. Coping with a Difficult Life: Magic, Healing, and Sacred Knowledge 337
JACCO DIELEMAN

22. Egyptian Temples 362
MARTINA MINAS-NERPEL

23. Funerary Religion: The Final Phase of an Egyptian Tradition 383
MARTIN ANDREAS STADLER

24. Oracles 398
Gaëlle Tallet

25. Isis, Osiris, and Serapis 419
Martin Bommas

26. Imported Cults 436
Gaëlle Tallet and Christiane Zivie-Coche

27. Egyptian Cult: Evidence from Temple Scriptoria and Christian Hagiographies 457
Martin Andreas Stadler

28. Christianity 474
Malcolm Choat

PART V TEXTS AND LANGUAGE

29. Language Use, Literacy, and Bilingualism 493
Mark Depauw

30. Papyri in the Archaeological Record 507
Arthur Verhoogt

31. Latin in Egypt 516
T. V. Evans

32. Greek Language, Education, and Literary Culture 526
Amin Benaissa

33. Hieratic and Demotic Literature 543
Friedhelm Hoffmann

34. Egyptian Hieroglyphs 563
David Klotz

35. Coptic 581
Malcolm Choat

PART VI IMAGES AND OBJECTS

36. Funerary Artists: The Textual Evidence 597
Maria Cannata

37. Portraits 613
Barbara E. Borg

38. Terracottas 630
SANDRA SANDRI

39. Pottery 648
JENNIFER GATES-FOSTER

40. Mummies and Mummification 664
BEATRIX GESSLER-LÖHR

41. Nilotica and the Image of Egypt 684
MOLLY SWETNAM-BURLAND

PART VII BORDERS, TRADE, AND TOURISM

42. Travel and Pilgrimage 701
IAN C. RUTHERFORD

43. The Western Oases 717
OLAF E. KAPER

44. The Eastern Desert and the Red Sea Ports 736
JENNIFER GATES-FOSTER

45. Between Egypt and Meroitic Nubia: The Southern Frontier Region 749
LÁSZLÓ TÖRÖK

Index 763

List of Figures

1.1 Silver denarius of Octavian, later the emperor Augustus, commemorating the annexation of Egypt 18
2.1 Fields near Timai el-Amdid (ancient Thmuis) 23
5.1 Front and back of the first tablet of an incised bronze document known as a military diploma, 3 March 179 CE 70
5.2 The most important fortified settlement in the stone-quarrying district of Mons Claudianus 71
5.3 Mummy portrait of a Roman soldier, *c.*160–70 CE 78
6.1 The temple of Augustus on the island of Philae 88
6.2 Architrave fragment from the temple of Augustus on the island of Philae 89
6.3 Imperial cult chapel in front of the first pylon of Karnak temple 90
7.1 The harbour of Alexandria, as viewed from the Metropole Hotel in 1994 103
7.2 Plan of Alexandria in the Roman period 105
7.3 Column of Diocletian ('Pompey's Pillar'), erected in 293 CE 106
7.4 Early twentieth-century postcard of the Column of Diocletian ('Pompey's Pillar'), erected in 293 CE 106
7.5 'Cleopatra's needle': New Kingdom obelisk of Thutmose II, reinscribed by Ramesses II, from Heliopolis. Erected in Alexandria under Augustus, and now in Central Park, New York City 111
7.6 Mosaic emblema of a Medusa head, *c.*150 CE 115
7.7 Moustapha Pasha Tomb 1, doorway to *kline* and burial rooms, with Egyptianizing sphinxes 116
7.8 Kom el-Shuqafa, 'Hall of Caracalla', Persephone Tomb 2, late first to early second century CE 117
7.9 Tigrane Tomb, painting on the back wall of the left niche above the sarcophagus, second century CE 118
9.1 Kom el-Ahmar in the western Delta, an example of a 'typical' settlement site continuing from the Ptolemaic to the Roman period 137
9.2 Map with 'Roman' period sites, mostly as identified on the Egypt Exploration Society Delta Survey, to show the potential abundance of Roman period archaeology 142
9.3 Sketch map of Naukratis with areas of Roman sherding indicated after fieldwalking 144
9.4 Plan of the Roman villa at Athribis (Tell Atrib) 147
9.5 Sketch map of Athribis (Tell Atrib) with Roman find spots and the sites of Polish excavations, to show the possible form of the Roman city against the small areas excavated 148

10.1 Satellite view of the Fayum, with the main sites of the Graeco-Roman period 153
10.2 Plan of Philadelphia, drawn in 1924 159
10.3 The present state of preservation at Philadelphia 160
10.4 Plan of Soknopaiou Nesos, based on fieldwork up to 2009 162
10.5 The ruins at Soknopaiou Nesos 165
11.1 Map of the Theban region, indicating Roman period sites and settlements 172
11.2 The small Serapeum outside Luxor temple, with a statue of Isis set up inside 174
11.3 The last dated stela commemorating a Buchis bull, from the Bucheum at Armant 181
11.4 The colossi of Memnon 184
12.1 Edmé Jomard's map of Antinoopolis, 1799 191
12.2 Reconstruction of the centre of Hermopolis Magna in the Roman period 198
12.3 Drawings of el-Bahnasa and the site of Oxyrhynchus, 1798, by Vivant Denon 200
12.4 Doric peristyle and eastern gateway of Oxyrhynchus 201
12.5 Red granite columns at Herakleopolis Magna, photographed in 1996 202
13.1 General plan of the site Tuna el-Gebel 206
13.2 Plan of the excavated area of the necropolis of Tuna el-Gebel 208
13.3 Temple-tombs T 12/SE (left), T 11/SE (behind T 12), and T 14/SE (right) at Tuna el-Gebel 211
13.4 Façade of temple-tombs T 4/SS (right) and T 5/SS (left) at Tuna el-Gebel 212
13.5 Relief on the tomb enclosure of temple-tomb T 5/SS at Tuna el-Gebel 212
13.6 One of the main streets at Tuna el-Gebel, with tombs T 9/SE (pillar) and M 11/SS (building in the foreground) 213
13.7 Façade of house-tomb M 12/SS at Tuna el-Gebel 215
13.8 House-tomb M 3/SS at Tuna el-Gebel: main burial 216
13.9 House-tomb M 5/SE at Tuna el-Gebel: main burial 217
14.1 Excavation of Karanis: A view from the east over the central area excavated by the *sebakhin* 224
14.2 Excavation of Karanis: Cross-section of the walls of X100 in the path of the *sebakhin* 226
14.3 Excavation of Karanis: A view looking north along Street CS46 227
14.4 Excavation of Karanis: Part of house 5002 after excavation 227
14.5 Excavation of Karanis: A view looking west over the roofing covering B109A-D, on top of C57 228
14.6 Excavation of Karanis: Part of mummified crocodile in inner sanctuary of Northern Temple 229
14.7 Excavation of Karanis: January 2, 1930. A view looking northwest at the gateway to T4 230

14.8 Excavation of Karanis: Rolls of papyrus as found in the threshold of doorway between rooms D and E of 5026 231
14.9 Excavation of Karanis: Division of Papyrus. 1927 papyri 232
14.10 Excavation of Karanis: Semi-profile view of black statue of priest 233
14.11 Excavation of Karanis: Wall fresco in a house on the western side, southeastern corner 234
14.12 Excavation of Karanis: Pots in a cross wall between the passage and room A2 of house 100 235
14.13 Excavation of Karanis: Pot in situ in the northeastern corner of C37K 235
14.14 Excavation of Karanis: Five pots as found 236
14.15 Excavation of Karanis: Division of Toys 1929–30 237
14.16 Excavation of Karanis: Wooden toy horses, D, as found in BC72K 238
14.17 Excavation of Karanis: Group of bronze bells as found in CS48 239
14.18 Excavation of Karanis: Division of Natural objects, 1935 239
14.19 Excavation of Karanis: Skeleton in Tomb 100 240
14.20 Excavation of Karanis: Division of Baskets, 1935 241
18.1 Ground-plan of a house, in *P Oxy*. XXIV 2406 296
18.2 Wooden toy horse on wheels from Karanis 299
19.1 Distribution of ages recorded in census documents from Roman Egypt 306
19.2 Smoothed age distribution of the adult urban metropolitan census population of Roman Egypt (excluding lodgers and slaves) compared with model life tables 307
19.3 Smoothed age distribution of the female census population of villages in Roman Egypt compared with model life tables 307
19.4 Seasonal mortality in Upper Egypt and Nubia according to Greek and Coptic funerary inscriptions and adjusted dates on Greek mummy labels 308
20.1 Terracotta figurine of Harpocrates as a nude infant with hand in pot and extended phallus, from Karanis 323
20.2 Painted wall-niche altar from a domestic structure at Karanis, House C119E 323
20.3 Watercolour reproduction of a mural of Isis *lactans*, from a domestic structure at Karanis, House B50 324
20.4 Haematite gem (obverse), with two-headed god (snake and ibis heads) holding an Egyptian *was* sceptre and *ankh* symbol, standing over a crocodile with a solar disk 329
20.5 Painted wooden *cippus* of Harpocrates standing on crocodiles, surmounted by a large Bes head, dated to the Late or Ptolemaic period 330
21.1 Gem of heliotrope (bloodstone) showing the rooster-headed anguipede and the sun-child, second century CE 340

21.2 Gem of quartz showing Chnoubis as a lion-headed snake with, on the reverse side, the Jewish name IAŌ, second century CE 341

21.3 Recipe to mollify an angry overseer. The incantation is given in Greek first and then in Demotic Egyptian, late second to third century CE 347

21.4 Greek papyrus amulet inscribed for a certain Artemidora, from Oxyrhynchus, third century CE 348

21.5 Protective design to be inscribed on amulet, from Thebes, third century CE 349

21.6 Assemblage of a female figurine of clay pierced with thirteen needles, lead tablet inscribed with Greek curse, and clay vessel in which the former two were found, from Middle Egypt, second to third century CE 351

21.7 Design to be inscribed on a gold or silver *lamella* and worn as a wrath-restraining amulet, as explained in its recipe, fourth century CE 352

22.1 Plan of the temple complex at Dendara 365

22.2 Temple of Hathor and north gateway, Dendara 366

22.3 Temples of Hathor and Isis at Dendara, from the south-east 367

22.4 Naos on the rear wall of the temple of Hathor at Dendara: Cleopatra VII and Ptolemy XV Caesarion offer to the deities of Dendara at both ends of the wall 368

22.5 *Wabet* and open court at the temple of Hathor, Dendara 369

22.6 Plan of the temple of Sobek and Haroeris at Kom Ombo 372

22.7 The Emperors' Corridor at the temple of Sobek and Haroeris, Kom Ombo 377

23.1 Mummy breastplate inscribed for a man named Hor, late Ptolemaic to early Roman period 384

24.1 Icosahedron (twenty-sided die) used in oracular practice 402

24.2 The Book of the *Sortes Astrampsychi*, third century CE 404

24.3 Oracular statue of Horus, second to third century CE 406

24.4 Stela of the oracular god Tutu with the griffin of Petbe-Nemesis. From the Fayum, Roman period 410

25.1 Faience figure of Isis and the infant Horus, dated to the Late or Ptolemaic period 420

25.2 Bronze figure of Osiris, dated to the Late or Ptolemaic period 421

25.3 Dedication mentioning a priest of Osiris, island of Delos, Greece 425

25.4 Sanctuary for Egyptian gods at Dion, Greece, early third century CE 429

26.1 Framed wooden panel depicting Heron and the god with the double axe 445

26.2 Wall paintings of the god with the double axe and the god Heron, from Theadelphia 447

26.3 Bronze figure of Zeus Helios Megas Serapis 448

26.4 Terracotta figure of the solar child 450

26.5 Stone relief representing the god Sobek in human form, with solar rays 451

32.1 The wall of a schoolroom painted by a teacher with short epigrams addressed to his students, first half of the fourth century CE 529

32.2 Portrait on the mummy of a woman from the Fayum, identifying her as 'Hermione *grammatike*', first century CE 531

33.1 List of quarries and mountains, written in hieratic with Demotic and Old Coptic supralinear glosses 544

33.2 A Demotic papyrus with one of the Inaros and Petubastis tales ('The Contest for the Armour of Inaros') 544

34.1 Relief of Trajan, from the birth house at Dendara 568

34.2 Detail of a hymn to Amun from Karnak, from the reign of Domitian 569

36.1 Framed portrait of a woman, found leaning against a mummy in a burial at Hawara 598

36.2 A sketch on a wooden panel with annotations by the artist, from Tebtunis 602

36.3 Set of paint pots found in a grave at Hawara 603

37.1 Honorific marble statue of a woman, from Oxyrhynchus, first quarter of the second century CE 616

37.2 Marble funerary monument of a reclining man, from Abusir el-Meleq, second century CE? 617

37.3 Marble grave stela of Aurelius Sabius, a Roman soldier from *legio II Germanica*, which used the cemetery at Alexandria where the stela was found between 213 and 235 CE 619

37.4 Mummy mask from Tuna el-Gebel (?) with a hairstyle typical of the second half of the third century CE 622

37.5 Painted mummy portrait from the Severan era 623

38.1 Terracotta figure of a child-god with a pot 633

38.2 Terracotta figure of a child-god with goose, pot, and round loaf 634

38.3 Terracotta figure of Isis nursing (Isis *lactans*) 636

38.4 Terracotta figure of a dancer with a boy 639

38.5 Terracotta figure of cult servant with features of dwarfism, with an altar for incense and a round loaf of bread 640

38.6 Terracotta figure of a musician with syrinx and bagpipes 642

39.1 Imported early Roman sigillatas and their Egyptian imitations 654

39.2 Examples of Egyptian early Roman finewares, tablewares, and cooking and storage vessels 656

39.3 Common imported and Egyptian amphora types of the early Roman period 658

40.1 Mummy of a boy aged 4 to 6 years, in a six-layered rhomboid-patterned wrapping, second half of the first century CE 665

40.2 Gold foil eye and tongue plates from a mummy 676

41.1 The Nile Mosaic (reconstructed), Palestrina, last quarter of the second century BCE to first quarter of the first century BCE 686

41.2 Montecitorio Obelisk, 26th dynasty, brought to Rome in 10 BCE 690
41.3 The Vatican Nile, front view, second century CE 691
41.4 The Vatican Nile, rear detail with pygmies 692
42.1 Inscriptions on the foot and ankle of one of the Memnon colossi 706
42.2 Graffiti near the first pylon of the Temple of Isis at Philae 708
43.1 Reconstruction drawing of a relief at Ain Birbiya from the time of Augustus, depicting the local god Amunnakht 723
43.2 The mammisi of Kellis (Ismant el-Kharab), west wall, showing a decorative scheme with classical and Egyptian paintings 724
43.3 A clay tablet from Trimithis (Amheida), inscribed in Greek 726
43.4 A wooden *ba* bird found at Kellis (Ismant el-Kharab), North Tomb 2 727
43.5 Large pyramid superstructure over a tomb at Trimithis (Amheida) 728
44.1 The Wadi Sikait 737
44.2 Early Roman ostraca and reed pen from Berenike 740
44.3 The early Roman *praesidium* near ad-Dweig (ancient Phalacro) 743
45.1 Lantern slide view of Philae in the nineteenth century, with the remains of mud-brick structures around the Isis temple 752
45.2 Detail of a screen wall from the pronaos of the Temple of Mandulis and Isis at Talmis (Kalabsha), early first century CE 757
45.3 Kiosk with Hathor head capitals at Kertassi, dating to the early first century CE 758

List of Tables

2.1 Mendesian agro-fiscal typology under the principate, according to papyri 25

2.2 Agro-fiscal typology and land vocation in the Mendesian nome under the principate, according to papyri 27

2.3 Diversification in the Mendesian nome under the principate, in the light of the fiscal terminology 30

28.1 Christian literary papyri dated to the second century CE 478

28.2 Numbers of Christian literary papyri dated to the turn of the second/third or early third centuries CE 479

28.3 Christian literary papyri from the third and turn of the third/fourth century CE 484

30.1 Deposition of objects in the lifecycle of domestic structures 512

34.1 Common unilateral (alphabetic) signs used in hieroglyphic texts of the Roman period, especially in renderings of imperial titularies 570

35.1 Egyptian texts in Greek characters before *c.*300 CE 584

39.1 Important sites for the study of early Roman pottery in Egypt, first to third centuries CE 650

List of Contributors

†**Donald M. Bailey**, formerly a curator in the Greek and Roman Department of the British Museum.

Amin Benaissa, Associate Professor and Tutorial Fellow at Lady Margaret Hall, Oxford.

Katherine Blouin, Associate Professor in Greek and Roman History, University of Toronto.

Martin Bommas, Senior Lecturer in Egyptology and Curator of the Eton Myers Collection, University of Birmingham.

Barbara E. Borg, Professor of Classical Archaeology at the University of Exeter and Extraordinary Professor of Ancient Studies, Stellenbosch University.

Maria Cannata is a specialist in Demotic, who has taught most recently at the University of Wales, Swansea and Peking University, Beijing.

Malcolm Choat, Associate Professor in the Department of Ancient History and Director of the Ancient Cultures Research Centre at Macquarie University, Sydney.

Paola Davoli, Associate Professor of Egyptology at the University of Salento (Lecce), co-director of the archaeological mission at Dime (Soknopaiou Nesos), and archaeological director at Amheida, Dakhla Oasis, New York University.

Mark Depauw, Professor in Ancient History at the Katholieke University, Leuven, and director of the interdisciplinary online platform Trismegistos.

Jacco Dieleman, formerly Associate Professor of Egyptology at the University of California, Los Angeles.

T. V. Evans, Associate Professor in the Department of Ancient History and member of the Ancient Cultures Research Centre at Macquarie University, Sydney.

David Frankfurter, William Goodwin Aurelio Chair of the Appreciation of Scripture, Boston University.

Jennifer Gates-Foster, Associate Professor of Classics and Archaeology, University of North Carolina, Chapel Hill.

Beatrix Gessler-Löhr, Research Associate at the Egyptological Institute, Heidelberg University.

Matt Gibbs, Associate Professor in the Department of Classics at the University of Winnipeg, Manitoba.

Rudolf Haensch, Scientific Director of the Kommission für Alte Geschichte und Epigraphik at the German Archaeological Institute, and Professor at Ludwig-Maximilians-Universität, Munich.

Andrew Harker, Teacher of Classics in Hertfordshire.

Friederike Herklotz, member of the Institut für Klassische Philologie at Humboldt University, Berlin.

Friedhelm Hoffmann, Professor of Egyptology at Ludwig-Maximilians-Universität, Munich.

Andrea Jördens, Professor of Papyrology at Ruprecht-Karls-Universität Heidelberg.

Olaf E. Kaper, Professor of Egyptology at Leiden University, and member of the Dakhleh Oasis Project.

David Klotz, Associate Research Fellow, Eikones Project, University of Basel.

Adam Łajtar, Professor of Greek epigraphy and papyrology at the University of Warsaw.

Katja Lembke, Director of the Lower Saxony State Museum, Hanover.

Myrto Malouta, Assistant Professor of Greek Papyrology at the Ionian University, Corfu.

Martina Minas-Nerpel, Professor of Egyptology at Trier University, Germany.

Stefan Pfeiffer, Professor for the Ancient World and Europe at Chemnitz Technological University.

Christina Riggs, Chair in the History of Visual Culture, Department of History, Durham University.

Ian C. Rutherford, Professor of Greek at the University of Reading.

Sandra Sandri, Postdoctoral researcher at the Institut für Ägyptologie und Altorientalistik at the Johannes Gutenberg University, Mainz.

Walter Scheidel, Dickason Professor in the Humanities at Stanford University.

Martin Andreas Stadler, Professor of Egyptology at the Julius-Maximilians-Universität, Würzburg.

Molly Swetnam-Burland, Adina Allen Term Distinguished Associate Professor of Classical Studies at the College of William and Mary, Virginia.

Laurens E. Tacoma, Lecturer in Ancient History at Leiden University.

Gaëlle Tallet, Assistant Professor in Greek History at the University of Limoges and director of the archaeological excavations at el-Deir, Kharga Oasis.

László Török, Research Professor at the Archaeological Institute of the Hungarian Academy of Sciences and a member of the Hungarian Academy of Sciences and the Norwegian Academy of Science and Letters.

Katelijn Vandorpe, Professor of Ancient History at the Katholieke Universiteit, Leuven.

†Marjorie S. Venit, Emerita Professor of Ancient Mediterranean Art and Archaeology in the Department of Art History and Archaeology at the University of Maryland.

Arthur Verhoogt, Arthur F. Thurnau Professor Professor of Papyrology and Greek, Department of Classical Studies, University of Michigan.

T. G. Wilfong, Curator for Graeco-Roman Egypt at the Kelsey Museum of Archaeology and Professor of Egyptology in the Department of Near Eastern Studies at the University of Michigan.

Penelope Wilson, Associate Professor in Egyptian Archaeology in the Department of Archaeology at Durham University.

Christiane Zivie-Coche, Director of Studies and Chair of Ancient Egyptian Religion at the École Pratique des Hautes Études, Paris.

List of Abbreviations and Conventions

This Handbook avoids abbreviations as much as possible, but some shortened forms are essential tools that scholars use to refer to published versions of the material they study, especially where textual sources are concerned. The quantity of inscribed material found in Egypt can look like an alphabet soup of letters and numbers, used to cite individual texts like papyri, ostraca, or graffiti. Throughout *The Oxford Handbook of Roman Egypt* abbreviated citations for papyri and ostraca adhere to the formats set out in John F. Oates, Roger S. Bagnall, Sarah J. Clackson, Alexandra A. O'Brien, Joshua D. Sosin, Terry G. Wilfong, and Klaas A. Worp, *Checklist of Greek, Latin, Demotic and Coptic Papyri, Ostraca and Tablets*, <http://scriptorium.lib.duke.edu/papyrus/texts/clist.html>, last accessed March 2011. Objects in museums, including some papyri, are identified by museum name and inventory number.

Classical authors are cited according to the conventions of S. Hornblower and A. Spawforth (eds), *Oxford Classical Dictionary*, 3rd edition (Oxford: Oxford University Press, 1996). Translations of many Greek and Latin texts are freely available online.

In addition, a number of abbreviations and acronyms in the Handbook refer to published series, epigraphic sources, text editions, and other reference works. These may be either ongoing projects or completed projects that resulted in multi-volume compilations of ancient textual sources. Some of the works can be abbreviated in different ways, and the following list provides a key for the format adopted in this Handbook.

AE	*L'Année Épigraphique*
BE	*Bulletin Épigraphique*
BGU	*Ägyptische Urkunden aus den Staatlichen Museen zu Berlin: Griechische Urkunden*
BL	*Berichtigungsliste der griechischen Papyrusurkunden aus Ägypten*
CEL	*Corpus Epistularum Latinarum: Papyris Tabulis Ostracis Servatarum*, ed. P. Cugusi, 3 vols. Florence: Gonnelli, 1992–2002.
CIL	*Corpus Inscriptionum Latinarum*. Berlin: Reimerum and de Gruyter, 1862–.
C Pap. Jud.	*Corpus Papyrorum Judaicarum* I–III, ed. V. A. Tcherikover, A. Fuks, and M. Stern. Cambridge, Mass.: Harvard University Press, 1957–64.
CPL	*Corpus Papyrorum Latinarum*, ed. R. Cavenaile. Wiesbaden: Harrassowitz, 1956–8.
DAI	Deutsches Archäologisches Institut
FHN	T. Eide, T. Hägg, R. H. Pierce, and L. Török, *Fontes Historiae Nubiorum: Textual Sources for the History of the Middle Nile Region* II and III. Bergen: University of Bergen, 1996–8.

FIRA — S. Riccobono, J. Baviera, C. Ferrini, et al., *Fontes Iuris Romani Antejustiniani*, 3 vols. Florence: Barbèra, 1940–3.

I Alex. — F. Kayser, *Recueil des inscriptions grecques et latines (non funéraires) d'Alexandrie impériale (Ier–IIIe s. apr. J.-C.)*. Cairo: Institut Français d'Archéologie Orientale, 1994.

I Fay. — É. Bernand, *Recueil des inscriptions grecques du Fayoum* I. Leiden: Brill, 1975; II–III. Cairo: Institut Français d'Archéologie Orientale, 1981.

IGLCM — A. Bernand and É. Bernand, *Les Inscriptions grecques et latines du Colosse de Memnon*. Cairo: Institut Français d'Archéologie Orientale, 1960.

IGP — A. Bernand and É. Bernand, *Les Inscriptions grecques de Philae*. Paris: Centre National de la Recherche Scientifique, 1969.

IGR — R. Cagnat et al., *Inscriptiones Graecae ad Res Romanas Pertinentes*, 3 vols. Paris: Leroux, 1911–27.

I Hibis — H. G. Evelyn White and J. H. Oliver, *The Temple of Hibis in el Khargeh Oasis*, pt II: *Greek Inscriptions*. New York: Metropolitan Museum of Art, 1938.

ILS — H. Dessau, *Inscriptiones Latinae Selectae*. Berlin: Weidmann, 1892–1916.

IMEGR — É. Bernand, *Inscriptions métriques de l'Egypte gréco-romaine: Recherches sur la poésie épigrammatique des grecs en Égypte*. Paris: Belles Lettres, 1969.

I Syringes — J. Baillet, *Inscriptions grecques et latines des Tombeaux des Rois ou Syringes*, 3 vols. Cairo: Institut Français d'Archéologie Orientale, 1920–7.

I Th. Sy. — A. Bernand, *De Thèbes à Syène*. Paris: Centre National de la Recherche Scientifique, 1989.

LDAB — Leuven Database of Ancient Books. <http://www.trismegistos.org/ldab/index.php>

M Chr. — L. Mitteis and U. Wilcken, *Grundzüge und Chrestomathie der Papyruskunde*, vol. 2: *Juristischer Teil*, pt II: *Chrestomathie*. Leipzig: Teubner, 1912.

New Docs — *New Documents Illustrating Early Christianity*. North Ryde, NSW: Eerdmans, 1981–.

OGIS — W. Dittenberger, *Orientis Graeci Inscriptiones Selectae: Supplementum sylloges inscriptionum graecarum* I–II. Leipzig: Hirzel, 1903–5.

PDM — H. D. Betz (ed.), *The Greek Magical Papyri in Translation, including the Demotic Spells*. Chicago: University of Chicago Press, 1986.

PGM — K. Preisendanz (ed.), *Papyri Graecae Magicae: Die griechischen Zauberpapyri*, 2 vols. Leipzig: Teubner, 1928–41; 2nd edn, ed. A. Henrichs. Stuttgart: Teubner, 1973–4.

PSI — *Papiri greci e latini*, 15 vols. Florence: Ariani, 1912–79.

REM — J. Leclant, A. Heyler, C. Berger-el Naggar, and C. Rilly, *Répertoire d'épigraphie Méroïtique: Corpus des inscriptions publiées*, 3 vols. Paris: de Boccard, 2000.

RIGLE — M. Letronne, *Recueil des inscriptions grecques et latines de l'Égypte*, 3 vols. Paris: Imprimerie Royale, 1842–8.

RMD	M. Roxan, *Roman Military Diplomas*, vols 1–3: London: Institute of Archaeology; vol. 4: London: Institute of Classical Studies, School of Advanced Study, 1978–2003; vol. 5: ed. P. Holder, London, 2006.
SB	*Sammelbuch griechischer Urkunden aus Ägypten*
Sel. Pap.	*Select Papyri*, 3 vols. Cambridge, Mass.: Harvard University Press, 1932–.
SPP	C. Wessely (ed.), *Studien zur Palaeographie und Papyruskunde*. Leipzig: Haessel and Avenarius, 1901–24.
Suppl. Mag.	*Supplementum Magicum*, ed. R. W. Daniel and F. Maltomini, I: nos 1–51; II: nos 52–100. Opladen: Westdeutscher, 1990–2.
TAM	*Tituli Asiae Minoris* I–III. Vienna: Hoelder; IV. Vienna: Apud Academiam Scientiarum Austriacam; V. Vienna: Österreichische Akademie der Wissenschaften, 1901–.
UPZ	U. Wilcken (ed.), *Urkunden der Ptolemäerzeit (ältere Funde)*, 2 vols. Berlin: de Gruyter, 1927–57.
WB	A. Erman and H. Grapow (eds), *Wörterbuch der ägyptischen Sprache*, 5 vols. Berlin: Akademie, 1926–61.
W Chr.	L. Mitteis and U. Wilcken, *Grundzüge und Chrestomathie der Papyruskunde*, vol. 1: *Historischer Teil*, pt II: *Chrestomathie*. Leipzig: Teubner, 1912.

INTRODUCTION

CHRISTINA RIGGS

TWENTY years ago, undergraduate curiosity found me browsing the Brown University library for something to fill the considerable gaps between my classes in Egyptology on the one hand, and in Roman art and archaeology on the other. There was Naphtali Lewis's *Life in Egypt under Roman Rule*, from 1983, but beyond his readable, papyrology-based account, which had few illustrations, introductory information on Roman Egypt was elusive. Alan Bowman's *Egypt after the Pharaohs* (first edition 1986) had only just appeared ('on order' in the library); the excavation reports from Karanis were perfunctory, and decades old; and in the few exhibition catalogues available in English, visual material was shoe-horned into discussions of 'late' or 'Coptic' art, whose 'provincial' character was remarked and as quickly dismissed. Knowing some German made it possible to tackle the astonishing array of material collected in Klaus Parlasca's *Mumienportäts und verwandte Denkmäler* (1966), and Günter Grimm's *Die römischen Mumienmasken aus Ägypten* (1974). But who were these people in plaster and paint, and what factors affected their lives, once Egypt was on the less powerful side of the Mediterranean?

The Oxford Handbook of Roman Egypt is the book I wish I had found in the library back then, but there was a good reason such a work didn't yet exist. Over the past two decades, scholarship on Roman Egypt has witnessed a remarkable expansion, branching out in terms of the kinds of evidence it considers and the questions it feels confident to pose. The number of researchers working in the area has increased, and with it the diversity of approaches they have adopted. Once the preserve of Greek papyrology, and consigned to the fringes of classical archaeology and Egyptology, the study of Roman Egypt is inherently multidisciplinary. It is often, though by no means always, interdisciplinary, in the sense of fully integrating the methods and results of different academic disciplines. This development parallels a much larger trend in the humanities since the 1980s, whereby many disciplines began to question their own boundaries, foundations, and methodologies. In classics and classical archaeology, topics such as local administration and artistic production were no longer off limits, and in fact became central to fresh considerations of imperialism, colonization, and Romanization in both the western and eastern reaches of the empire (for instance, Millett 1990; Alcock 1993; Woolf 1994; Webster and Cooper 1996; Mattingly 1997; Laurence and Berry 1998; Wiseman 2002; Whitmarsh 2010).

Although a smaller and in some ways less self-reflexive discipline, Egyptology too has broadened the scope of its subject matter, resulting in the growth of object-based studies and archaeological fieldwork addressing the Roman period. At the same time, there has been an increase in focus on Demotic texts from the period, which number in the thousands but have fewer scholars working on them than the Greek papyri. The history of ancient religions is another field where Roman Egyptian evidence has been put to ever more, and better, use, from studies of religious syncretism and the Isis cult in the 1970s (e.g. Dunand and Lévêque 1975) to the adaptation and transformation of religious practices in late antiquity (Frankfurter 1998; Dijkstra 2008). These developments are in part a response to new material becoming available, such as editions of papyri, and excavations at important Roman sites in the Fayum and the Western Oases. They are also due to the increased visibility of objects that had languished in the proverbial cupboard, sometimes for a century of more. Most notably, in the late 1990s a series of museum exhibitions in the United Kingdom and Europe coincided with renewed research on mummy portraits, encouraging scholars to view some of the artistic output of Roman Egypt in a fresh light (see Riggs 2002). In early 2011, with the manuscript for this volume completed, the time certainly seems right not only to present new evidence in detail, but, crucially, to see how these details fit it into a bigger picture. To this end, in *The Handbook of Roman Egypt* more than forty researchers working in this area have tried to consider what are the right questions to ask right now, and how to go about answering them.

The Structure of the Handbook

The organization of this volume has tried to blur disciplinary boundaries, although it could not claim to have erased them altogether. Such an erasure would, in fact, be counterproductive, because seeing how different scholars approach a subject in different ways, depending on their own training or specialization, is informative in itself. Some of the authors in the Handbook disagree with each other, or with me, but intense debate signals a healthy and thriving research area. It also indicates that researchers are reading and engaging with each other's work, so that the field continues to move forward rather than becoming set in stone. The work of younger scholars is central to this process, and several chapters were commissioned with that in mind.

The Handbook is divided into seven themed parts: Land and State; City, Town, and *Chora*; People; Religion; Texts and Language; Images and Objects; and Borders, Trade, and Tourism. Almost every section includes chapters by authors with different disciplinary profiles and approaches, and throughout the volume, chapters have combined textual, visual, and archaeological evidence wherever it suits the subject matter. Part I, Land and State, considers administrative functions of the Roman state in Egypt, from the ruler cult to the day-to-day running of the province's key source of income, agriculture. Part II, City, Town, and *Chora*, looks at the evidence for urban life in Roman Egypt, as well as in the countryside and its villages. In Part III, People, the social structure of Roman Egypt comes under scrutiny in complementary chapters by Andrea Jördens and Katelijn Vandorpe. This part also considers family life, patterns of health and life expectancy, and the experience of Egypt's important Jewish communities under Roman rule.

Part IV, devoted to religion, is the largest, reflecting the number of different approaches to this theme, and its wide reach. Starting with a chapter by David Frankfurter, this is a key part for considering issues of identity and the transformation of ideas and images as well. In Part V,

Texts and Languages, Mark Depauw discusses the implications of bilingualism in Roman Egypt, and several scholars examine the array of texts and scripts that were in use, as well as the preservation of papyri in the archaeological record. Part VI, Images and Objects, covers types of object (terracottas, pottery) as well as genres of imagery (such as portraits). Images do not 'reflect' an ancient view of the world: they helped create it, as Molly Swetnam-Burland's chapter on Roman *nilotica* demonstrates. In Roman Egypt mummification and funerary art were privileged arenas of display in local communities, and this part also gathers evidence for how these trades were practised. Finally, Part VII, Borders, Trade, and Tourism, looks at activities related to the movement of people within Egypt and around its borderlands: the Western Oases, the Eastern Desert and Red Sea coast, and the southern frontier.

A few words on conventions adopted in the Handbook. Each chapter ends with a paragraph of suggested reading, which points readers to key publications for exploring the subject further; the suggestions place an emphasis on sources available in English, but knowledge of other modern languages, especially German and French, is essential for all higher-level study in the field. To make the chapters as accessible as possible to entry-level readers, the text uses minimal abbreviations and offers English translations of ancient texts. The expression 'Graeco-Roman' does not imply that there was no difference between Greek and Roman culture, or between the Hellenistic and Roman periods in Egypt. Instead, it refers to the Greek or Hellenic identity and character of many cultural phenomena in the eastern Roman empire, including Egypt. Similarly, some authors use the adjective 'Hellenized' or 'hellenistic' to describe Greek influence on social norms and cultural forms. Like the words 'classical' (as in classical archaeology) or 'pharaonic', 'hellenistic' in this sense starts with a lower-case letter. Written with an initial upper case, 'Hellenistic' refers to the time period of Alexander and his successors, which in Egypt is identical to the Ptolemaic period, and 'Pharaonic' refers to the period of rule by sequential Egyptian dynasties prior to Alexander's conquest in 332 BCE.

Historical Overview: Egypt Under Roman Rule

Chronological boundaries can be as arbitrary, and permeable, as any other kind, but the parameters of the Handbook are set roughly between the annexation of Egypt by Octavian in 30 BCE and the reign of Diocletian, around 300 CE. Some authors use earlier, Hellenistic developments as a precursor to the Roman material they discuss, and others use late Roman or early Byzantine evidence to illuminate phenomena from the first three centuries of the empire. The cut-off point around the start of the fourth century CE takes into account not only the effects of Diocletian's extensive reforms, but also the ramifications of Christianity, whose adoption and influence gathered pace under Constantine in the 320s. Thus, the chronological spread of this volume approximates the coverage of Roman Egypt in the second edition of *The Cambridge Ancient History* (Bowman 1996, 2008).

Octavian entered Alexandria in August of 30 BCE, ten months after he defeated Mark Antony and Cleopatra at the battle of Actium. Annexing Egypt as a province, Octavian put in place an administrative system that would remain fundamentally unchanged for the next 300 years. He also set in motion a sequence of events that saw the Roman senate award him the titles Augustus and Princeps from 27 BCE, when he took sole command of the fledgling empire. Unlike in other provinces, which had governors of senatorial rank, the Roman administration in Egypt was headed by a prefect of equestrian rank; they averaged about three years in post and used the role as a stepping stone in their careers, sometimes advancing to the praetorian prefecture. For all the changes it brought about, Roman rule in Egypt was essentially stable and, given Egypt's sizeable grain output earmarked for Rome, in some respects prosperous, especially during the first and second centuries. The new administration encouraged urban settlements and Hellenic cultural forms by granting certain privileges to the citizens of Greek cities and to a class registered as residents of the district towns, known as *metropoleis*, hence the metropolite class. Regular censuses and the use of legal documents known as status declarations helped control who was who and, at least in the early empire, put a brake on social mobility, since status was normally based on parentage. In effect, the Romans were probably codifying a stratification that had developed during the Ptolemaic period, as Greeks settled in Egypt and married Egyptians, while Egyptians adopted Greek language and acculturated to advance themselves. The towns of the nome districts were pivotal owing to their close relationship with the *chora*, or countryside, Egypt's agricultural heart. During the Roman period, private enterprise and landownership increased, with around half of the land estimated to be in private hands in the first and second centuries, rising to almost all of it by the early fourth century. In addition to the yield of wheat produced for export, agriculture supported a population of around 5 million; more generous estimates place it at 7.5 million at its peak, but any estimate should allow for a drop due to the Antonine plague in the mid-second century. Papyrus and flax were also key crops, processed into paper and linen for the market at home and abroad.

Important as it was in the founding of the empire, Egypt also played a role in imperial politics on other occasions, and several emperors visited the province. Under the prefect Tiberius Julius Alexander, who was from one of the leading Jewish families of Alexandria, the Roman army in Egypt proclaimed Vespasian emperor in 69, and he spent several months in the country before returning to Rome. The Jewish revolt in 115–17 affected not just Alexandria but the whole province, sparked off by pressures in the Alexandrian Jewish community and the influx of Jews into Egypt after the Roman sack of Jerusalem in 70 CE. Hadrian made an extended tour of Egypt in 130–1, when the death of his companion Antinoos led to the founding of a fourth *polis* in the province, Antinoopolis, often shortened to Antinoe. Avidius Cassius, a leading general and the son of a past prefect, was responsible for suppressing an uprising in 172, known as the revolt of the Boukoloi, and in 175 he briefly ruled Egypt after proclaiming himself emperor while Marcus Aurelius was still in power. Septimius Severus visited Egypt in 199/200, and finally granted town councils to Alexandria and the other cities, as well as the *metropoleis*; the absence of such councils had been an anomaly in Egypt, although the cities had a degree of self-governance through the system of magistrate offices known as *archai*. After Septimius Severus' death in 211, his son and successor Caracalla granted Roman citizenship to free men and women throughout the empire, in an edict of 212 known as the Constitutio Antoniniana. This marked a considerable change for Egypt, where previously few people had qualified as Roman citizens. But there are hints that some communities in Egypt, notably the citizens of Alexandria, were sometimes dissatisfied with imperial power. When the Alexandrians produced a satire implicating Caracalla in his brother Geta's death, the emperor used his visit to Egypt in 215 to retaliate, removing the prefect from office and ordering the city's youth to be slaughtered. Caracalla was also said to have been the last Roman emperor to visit the embalmed corpse of Alexander, just as Octavian-Augustus had done more than two centuries earlier.

The mid-third century witnessed further unrest in Egypt and elsewhere, and in the 260s and 270s the eastern Mediterranean was caught up in conflicts between the Sassanid rulers of Persia and the wealthy city of Palmyra in Syria, which in turn rebelled against Rome. The Palmyrene queen Zenobia and her son Vaballathus occupied Alexandria from 270 to 272, until the emperor Aurelian reasserted Roman rule. At the end of the third century, Egypt was also the base for an unsuccessful revolt by the Roman general Lucius Domitius Domitianus, which was put down by Diocletian. Diocletian recaptured Alexandria in 298 and travelled up the Nile to the southern border at Philae. Diocletian introduced economic reforms such as the Maximum Price Edict (in 301) and changed the administrative structure of the province, and eventually the empire as a whole, with the aim of restoring stability and securing tax revenue. In a similar vein, however, he issued repressive edicts against Christians, leading to such persecutions that the Egyptian Church referred to his reign as the Era of the Martyrs (Anno Martyri) and began counting calendrical years from his accession in 284. The successors of Diocletian continued to adapt his reforms and institute further changes, most likely, as Bowman (2008) observes, in response to long-standing issues rather than the 'crisis' conjectured in earlier scholarship. The financial burden of the liturgical system, which required individuals to perform, and pay for, civic offices; the practicalities of tax collection, which in Egypt seems to have been made the responsibility of the town councils; and the logistics of supplying the army across such vast territories, were three such issues that were crucial in the third century but had much earlier origins. Egyptian towns and cities witnessed the emergence of an expanded urban elite during the third century as well (Tacoma 2006), and although later than the formation of similar elites in Asia Minor, for instance, this too was the continuation of the trend instigated in the early empire (see Bowman and Rathbone 1992). With the extensive information offered by documentary papyri, Egypt is a unique source for financial transactions, population data, and legal and administrative matters during the Roman period. Current opinion rejects the view of early twentieth-century scholarship that Egypt held a special, anomalous position in the Roman empire, but at the same time cautions that the documentation available for Egypt is distinct to Egypt, and not necessarily applicable to other imperial provinces. The history of Roman Egypt has been just as subject to fresh interpretations as any other area, revising the conclusions of earlier research and developing alternative perspectives on the social, political, and economic life of Augustus' prize catch.

Conclusion: Roman Egypt in the Twenty-First Century

The questioning of old assumptions and incorporation of new information characterize all the chapters in the Handbook, and to conclude this Introduction, it is worth highlighting some of the core issues and debates that recur throughout the volume. One issue is the question of personal and communal identity, and social mobility. The legal and administrative regimes sketched above, and discussed in more detail in the Handbook, affected how people lived their lives, from the language they used to whom they married, and from their standard of living to their status within their local community, which are not intrinsically the same thing. Those who were already ahead, or wanted to get or stay there, had recourse to the Greek heritage inculcated in the Ptolemaic period, speaking Greek, attending the gymnasium, and reading Homer (see Cribiore 2001). This did not preclude a self-conscious conservatism, however, as some groups emphasized a connection to the Egyptian past, creating a distinctive identity that both complemented and countered pressures from the Roman regime.

Developments in religious beliefs, practices, and cult organizations are important throughout the Roman period, especially in light of the interactions between Egyptian, Greek, and Roman religion, and the presence of other religions in Egypt, like Mithraism, Judaism, and nascent Christianity. As Jacco Dieleman points out in his chapter for Part IV, most people in Roman Egypt lived precariously, whether through financial and social disadvantages or the ever-present threat of ill health and difficult life transitions. 'Magic' was once a pejorative term in scholarship, but the use of magic, oracles, and astrology is now better understood as a rational response to such life experiences. Christianity may have changed some of the forms such practices took, but not their underlying aims.

The juxtaposition of continuity and change is a theme that recurs throughout the Handbook, especially among authors approaching the Roman period from an Egyptological background. What needs to be borne in mind, though, is that 'continuity' is not a foregone conclusion. To borrow the expression of Hobsbawm and Ranger (1983), traditions are invented. 'Traditional' practices and cultural forms are made, not born, whether by ancient actors who selected something from the past to preserve or revive, or by researchers who see an unbroken line rather than a series of meaningful dots and dashes. Mummification is a case in point. While it was a distinctive Egyptian practice, and had been applied to a wider spectrum of the population over time, it was never the only process used to treat corpses, and was performed selectively. In Roman Egypt the extraordinary care taken over mummification and the decoration of mummies suggests a purposeful emphasis on the Egyptian past, affirming local roles and ranks in the process. At some point in the Roman period, if not before, the time came when the old temples, the masked mummies, and the conventional images of the Egyptian gods looked 'old-fashioned', which fit certain uses but could not fulfil every requirement. Visuality, which is the acculturated experience of vision, had some shared similarities in Egyptian, Greek, and Roman society, for instance in terms of imbuing images with sacred power (compare Elsner 2000). But there were crucial differences as well, for instance in the apprehension of space, the quality of mimesis, and the social context of seeing an image. The old gods needed new tricks, or at least new visual manifestations, and that is one reason why the terracotta figures produced for boisterous and popular religious festivals, and repurposed for domestic use, almost exclusively show Egyptian deities like Isis and Harpocrates in contemporary, Graeco-Roman form.

The scope of the Handbook encompasses these debates, and more, not to offer the final word on any subject but to provide a critical look at where scholarship stands in the early twenty-first century, and where it might go from here. There will always be new material to study, but there is also more to do in terms of framing and reframing the questions asked of the material. Moreover, it would be illusory to think that the editing of texts, publication of excavations, or presentation of museum objects is ever a straightforward account of 'facts' or data. Every approach to the past is an interpretation of the past, mediated through current scholarship and informed by the concerns of the present. The Roman Egypt readers will encounter in this volume is not the Roman Egypt that I encountered as an undergraduate, and, as its editor, I hope that this Handbook helps create yet another Roman Egypt, which I look forward to encountering at some future date.

Acknowledgements

Alan Bowman, whose work was my own introduction to Roman Egypt, offered invaluable guidance at the planning stages of this volume, and I am grateful for his encouragement and advice. Martina Minas-Nerpel gave helpful feedback and suggested possible topics and authors to include, as did the late Traianos Gagos, whose impact on the field can be seen in the number of contributors connected to the University of Michigan.

At the University of East Anglia, Nick Warr was indispensable in producing several of the figures. The work of translators Tomas Derikovsky, Maria Cannata, and Helen Strudwick, with input from Susanne Bickel, has made several of the chapters available to an English-speaking audience.

Bibliography

Alcock, S. E. 1993. *Graecia Capta: The Landscapes of Roman Greece*, 1st edn. Cambridge: Cambridge University Press.

Bowman, A. K. 1986. *Egypt after the Pharaohs, 332 BC–AD 642: From Alexander to the Arab Conquest*. London: British Museum Press.

—— 1996. 'Egypt', in A. K. Bowman, E. Champlin, and A. Lintott (eds), *The Cambridge Ancient History*, vol. 10, 2nd edn. Cambridge: Cambridge University Press, 676–702.

—— 2008. 'Egypt from Septimius Severus to the Death of Constantine', in A. K. Bowman, A. Cameron, and P. Garnsey (eds), *The Cambridge Ancient History*, vol. 12, 2nd edn. Cambridge: Cambridge University Press, 313–26.

—— and D. W. Rathbone. 1992. 'Cities and Administration in Roman Egypt', *Journal of Roman Studies* 82: 107–27.

Cribiore, R. 2001. *Gymnastics of the Mind: Greek Education in Hellenistic and Roman Egypt*. Princeton: Princeton University Press.

Dijkstra, J. H. F. 2008. *Philae and the End of Ancient Egyptian Religion: A Regional Study of Religious Transformation (298–642 CE)*. Leuven: Peeters.

Dunand, F., and P. Lévêque (eds) 1975. *Les Syncrétismes dans les religions de l'antiquité: Colloque de Besançon, 22–23 octobre 1973*. Leiden: Brill.

Elsner, J. 2000. 'Between Mimesis and Divine Power: Visuality in the Greco-Roman World', in R. Nelson (ed.), *Visuality before and beyond the Renaissance: Seeing as Others Saw*. Cambridge: Cambridge University Press, 45–69.

Frankfurter, D. 1998. *Religion in Roman Egypt: Assimilation and Resistance*. Princeton: Princeton University Press.

Grimm, G. 1974. *Die römischen Mumienmasken aus Ägypten*. Wiesbaden: Steiner.

Hobsbawm, E., and T. Ranger (eds) 1983. *The Invention of Tradition*. Cambridge: Cambridge University Press.

Laurence, R., and J. Berry (eds) 1998. *Cultural Identity in the Roman Empire*. London: Routledge.

Lewis, N. 1983. *Life in Egypt under Roman Rule*. Oxford: Clarendon Press.

Mattingly, D. J. 1997. *Dialogues in Roman Imperialism: Power, Discourse, and Discrepant Experience in the Roman Empire*. Portsmouth, RI: Journal of Roman Archaeology.

Millett, M. 1990. *The Romanization of Britain: An Essay in Archaeological Interpretation*. Cambridge: Cambridge University Press.

Parlasca, K. 1966. *Mumienporträts und verwandte Denkmäler*. Wiesbaden: Steiner.

Riggs, C. 2002. 'Facing the Dead: Recent Research on the Funerary Art of Ptolemaic and Roman Egypt', *American Journal of Archaeology* 106: 85–101.

Tacoma, L. E. 2006. *Fragile Hierarchies: The Urban Elites of Third-Century Roman Egypt*. Leiden: Brill.

Webster, J., and N. J. Cooper (eds) 1996. *Roman Imperialism: Post-Colonial Perspectives*. Leicester: School of Archaeological Studies.

Whitmarsh, T. (ed.) 2010. *Local Knowledge and Microidentities in the Imperial Greek World*. Cambridge: Cambridge University Press.

Wiseman, T. P. (ed.) 2002. *Classics in Progress: Essays on Ancient Greece and Rome*. Oxford: Oxford University Press.

Woolf, G. 1994. 'Becoming Roman, Staying Greek: Culture, Identity and the Civilizing Process in the Roman East', *Proceedings of the Cambridge Philological Society* 40: 116–43.

PART I

LAND AND STATE

CHAPTER 1

AEGYPTO CAPTA

Augustus and the Annexation of Egypt

FRIEDERIKE HERKLOTZ

'I HAVE added Egypt to the ruling area of the Roman people.' With this short assertion, Caesar Augustus described the amalgamation of Egypt into the Roman empire in the twenty-seventh chapter of his record of achievements. The annexation of Egypt was, de facto, a long drawn-out process, which began in the middle of the second century and was completed with the conquest of Alexandria in 30 BCE.

THE PTOLEMAIC LEGACY AND EGYPTIAN INDEPENDENCE

From having been a world power in the third century BCE, the Ptolemaic empire fell into crisis in the course of the second century BCE. Almost all of its external possessions were lost and central authority became weaker because there were often two, or even three, kings or queens ruling together. Finally, for about twenty years at the beginning of the second century a separate state, with a native pharaoh, arose in the Theban area (Pestman 1995; McGing 1997; Veïsse 2004). In 168 BCE Egypt was under threat from the Seleucid king Antiochos IV, who had already trodden Egyptian soil and planned to conquer the land of the Nile. It was only possible to expel this invader from Egypt with the help of the Romans (Livy, *Per.* 45.12; Polyb. 29.27; Diod. Sic. 31.2). This proved to be the prelude to Egypt's increasingly strong dependence on Rome. After Rome had conquered a great many Mediterranean regions, it was feared that Egypt too might become a province of the Roman empire (Lampela 1998; dealt with in detail in Hölbl 1994, 2001, and Huß 2001).

The father of Cleopatra, Ptolemy XII Neos Dionysos (80–51 BCE), presided over the task of securing the independence of his country. Although the prospects for this were extremely poor, using skilful negotiations and a cleverly applied policy of bribery, he achieved recognition from the Roman state as an *amicus et socius populi Romani* ('friend and partner of the Roman people'). Within the country, he stabilized his rule by strenuously maintaining a good relationship with the Egyptian priesthood. This is demonstrated not least by the numerous temple structures erected or decorated in his name. The image of a feeble king, as suggested by the Greek and Latin sources, and as appears in older research literature, can no longer be supported (Herklotz 2009).

In his will, Ptolemy XII sought to secure the beneficial relationships of his country in perpetuity. He installed his daughter Cleopatra as ruler, together with his eldest son, Ptolemy XIII, who was at that time 10 years old. The Romans were supposed to ensure that the terms of his will were observed (Caes. *B Civ.* 3.108.4–6; *B Alex.* 33.1; Cass. Dio 42.35.4).

Cleopatra VII had to deal with a difficult legacy. Moreover, her status in the country was threatened because her brother strove to rule alone. She found support in Julius Caesar, who, after the Alexandrian War, managed the situation in Egypt to his own benefit; Cleopatra was to rule with her younger brother, Ptolemy XIV. Caesar left three legions in Egypt, which he put under the control of a trustworthy officer named Rufio (Schäfer 2006: 40–106). Hölbl (1994: 212; 2001: 237) rightly points out that this set-up can be seen as a precursor to the rule of Octavian, who likewise left behind as governor of the country an *eques* who had supported him during the conquest of Egypt.

From her liaison with Caesar, Cleopatra bore a son, Ptolemy XV Caesarion. Heinen has demonstrated that Cleopatra wished to set her son up as the founder of a Ptolemaic–Roman dynasty (Heinen 1998; 2007: 186–7). After Caesar's murder, the queen needed to find a new ally, and she found one in Mark Antony, to whom it had fallen to renew the organization of the eastern part of the Roman empire and to conquer the Parthian empire. By virtue of its favourable position in the eastern Mediterranean, Egypt formed a good starting point for this campaign. It also had access to numerous raw materials useful for weapons of war. In recent research the land grants made to Cleopatra are seen as being part of the reorganization of the east (Schrapel 1996; Benne 2001: 28–53; Schäfer 2006: 151–62). With the defeat of the Parthians, however, Mark Antony's fall from power began. His rival Octavian was able to record several successes in the west at this time, and relations between the two triumvirates, who had once been close allies, deteriorated rapidly. The famous naval battle of Actium took place in 31 BCE. Defeated, Mark Antony and Cleopatra fled to Alexandria.

The Annexation of Egypt

In the spring of 30 BCE Octavian went to Asia Minor in order to advance towards Pelusium from Syria. In the meantime, C. Cornelius Gallus, who later became prefect, had already taken the western border fortress of Paraitonion from Cyrenaica; nothing else now stood in the way of the conquest of Alexandria. After Mark Antony's suicide, Cleopatra took her own life in August 30 BCE (Skeat 1953). Caesarion was executed because he was the last of the Ptolemaic dynasty, and also, as a true son of Caesar, he represented a threat to Octavian.

Very little is known about Octavian's residency in Egypt (Herklotz 2007: 103–8). In his own record of his achievements, Augustus referred to the conquest in the single sentence quoted above, even though it had such far-reaching consequences. The reports of Suetonius

(*Aug.* 18.1) and Cassius Dio (51.16–17; see Dundas 2002) are also extremely brief, and not contemporary. The difficulty of reconstructing the events is that both authors write from the perspective of the victor, Augustus.

The ancient geographer Strabo lived during the reign of Augustus (between 64 BCE and 26 CE). He had accompanied the prefect Aelius Gallus on his journey through Egypt in 25/24 BCE and lived in Alexandria for a long time (Strabo 2.5.2, 2.3.5). His work provides not only important information about Egyptian culture but also evidence about the administration of the province of Egypt. He also reported extensively on the military conflict between the first prefect and the kingdom of Meroe.

Unfortunately, there are no accounts from the Egyptians about Octavian's stay in Egypt. Augustus left no hieroglyphic inscriptions on temple walls or stelae to enumerate and extol his deeds. The only hieroglyphic inscription that can be cited is on the stela of the first prefect, C. Cornelius Gallus (Cairo, Egyptian Museum CG 9295). This is a traditional Egyptian 'historical' text, which also contains contemporary references (Hoffmann, Minas-Nerpel, and Pfeiffer 2009: 173). The stela was found in 1896 on the northern part of the island of Philae in front of the temple of Augustus. The inscription appears in Egyptian, Greek, and Latin, and is dated 16 April 29 BCE. On the stela are described the deeds of the first prefect during the suppression of rebellions in Nubia and the Thebaid.

What can be reconstructed about Octavian's sojourn in Egypt? Cassius Dio (51.16.3) emphasizes that no wrong was done to the Egyptians because this sizeable population might be useful to the Roman empire. As a pretext for his kindness, Octavian cites the god Serapis, Alexander the Great, the founder of the capital city, and the philosopher Arius, Octavian's teacher. The relationship with Alexander also becomes clear during Octavian's visit to his tomb (Suet. *Aug.* 18.1; Cass. Dio 51.16.5; Kienast 1969). As a great conqueror, Alexander was above all a role model for Octavian. He refused, however, to visit the tombs of the Ptolemies, his immediate precursors, for he wanted to see kings, but not dead ones. Here the break with the past is very clear.

Like Alexander, Octavian subsequently visited Memphis, the ancient Egyptian royal city, where the god Ptah and the Apis bull had been revered since the 1st dynasty. During the Ptolemaic period, the priesthood in Memphis maintained a very close relationship with the Ptolemaic dynasty (Crawford 1980; Thompson 1988). Furthermore, it was here that the so-called high priest of Ptah carried out the coronation of the ruler during the Ptolemaic period. The coronation, which took place sometime after the pharaoh's actual accession to the throne, represented the mythological protection of the king's rule through the gods. It was on this occasion that the king received his titulary (Barta 1980). It is reported of Alexander that he made a sacrifice to the Apis bull at Memphis and was crowned pharaoh. However, this coronation only appears in the fictional account of Alexander (Callisthenes 1.34.1), although it is tacitly accepted by most researchers (Hölbl 1994: 9; 2001: 9–10; Winter 2005: 206; for a contrary view, Burstein 1991; see also Suet. *Aug.* 93; Cass. Dio 51.16.5). Augustus refused the veneration of Apis, saying that he would make offerings to gods, but not to beasts. Nothing is known about an Egyptian coronation of Octavian, which in any case would have been contrary to his position at Rome since he was, at that time, only a representative of the Roman state provided with special powers. Octavian wanted to consolidate his status in Rome, and being crowned an Egyptian pharaoh would have made his recognition by the senate impossible. In addition, Egypt would thereby have attained a prominent position among the other provinces (Herklotz 2007: 106).

Egyptian sources, however, paint a different picture. Here we draw on the grave stelae of a high priest named Imouthes-Petubastis and those of a 'chantress of Ptah' named Tneferos, which are preserved in hieroglyphic and Demotic language (British Museum EA 188 and 184, respectively: Quaegebeur 1972; Young 1982: 70–4; Herklotz 2007: 294–7). The high priest of Ptah, Imouthes-Petubastis III, died two days before the conquest of Egypt (British Museum EA 188, lines 4–5). He was mummified, but not buried. A successor was not immediately appointed, which could indicate turbulence at the beginning of Roman rule. Possibly the Romans had a poor relationship with the priesthood, which had had a close association with the Ptolemies. Two and a half years later, Octavian (now named Augustus) named a successor, Psenamun, who was the cousin of his predecessor and therefore came from a different family (British Museum EA 184, line 5). The new priest was even given the title 'prophet of Caesar' and was thus possibly responsible for the cult of Augustus in Memphis. For the award of the title, the new high priest received a crown of gold and many gifts, and construction of a chapel was also authorized (British Museum EA 184, line 6). This shows that Augustus sought good relations with the house of the high priest of Ptah at Memphis and that he did in fact understand the importance for the monarchy of the cult performed there. Imouthes-Petubastis was finally buried in year 7 of the reign of Augustus, together with the mummy of the chantress of Ptah, Tneferos (British Museum EA 188, line 6). After the death of Psenamun, no further high priest is attested.

A coronation cannot, however, be established from these documents. Nevertheless, the Egyptian priests recognized Octavian as ruler in the first year of his reign in Egypt. On the Gallus stela, his name is written in a cartouche, and thus Octavian was named as the reigning pharaoh. Like every Egyptian pharaoh, Augustus received a titulary that can be found on various temples and stelae. The priesthood in Memphis probably formulated it, because the titulary contains many references to Ptah. Grenier (1987, 1989a, b, 1995) analysed the titles and worked out fundamental changes in form and content. Augustus' titulary was reduced to three elements, and consisted only of the Horus name, the 'dual king' (*nswt-bity*) title, and the 'son of Re' title (Grenier 1989a). Augustus' dual king name was formed on the basis of a completely new model. The name developed over the early years of Roman rule (Hölbl 1996: 100–5; 2000–5: I 18–22). First, the Egyptian word *hrmys* ('the Roman') appeared inside the cartouche, a reference to the origin of Augustus. But by no later than year 9 of his reign, it was replaced by *autokrator*, transcribed into hieroglyphs (*Awtkrtr*). The 'son of Re' part of the titulary was formed from his own name, *Kysrs* (Caesar). This emphasizes that Augustus received his office not from the Egyptian gods, but from the *imperium* granted to him by the senate and people of Rome. This is a novelty, because normally Egyptian pharaohs exercised their role as the earthly representative of the god Re, and were placed in that role by the gods.

A striking feature of the titulary is the Horus name, which became very long and was maintained in this form for the later emperors. The full version is recorded in seven places; additionally, an abbreviated form can be recognized in another twenty-three places (Grenier 1989a; Herklotz 2007: 413–21). The Horus name of Augustus contained elements of Egyptian royal ideology, praising the ruler as an ideal Egyptian pharaoh. Augustus was portrayed as conquering the country with his mighty arm, protecting it from enemies internally and externally, ensuring law and order, looking after the welfare of the population, and striving to maintain a good relationship with the Egyptian gods. Inscribing the texts on temple walls or on stelae was intended to create, by magic, a reality that did not actually exist. The Horus name also includes components of the royal titulary of the Ptolemaic period that, above all, indicate the king's relationship to Ptah. Finally, it is made clear in the Horus name that Augustus resided not in Egypt but in Rome, and that his dominion, and the justice he dispensed, extended over the whole earth. For the Egyptians this was completely new, because it is the first time an Egyptian text records that the residence of the ruler was outside Egypt. The formulation acknowledges the fact that Egypt was an important province of the Roman empire, but only one of many.

Octavian left Egypt in the autumn of 30 BCE. Shortly before his departure, he ordered his soldiers to repair the dams and dikes that were vital for irrigation (Cass. Dio 51.18.1; Suet. *Aug.* 18.2; Strabo 17.1.3). Egypt was now owned by the Roman state, since Octavian was at this time only a representative of the Roman republic who had been provided with special powers. However, he could freely command the country. He passed on the *imperium* to C. Cornelius Gallus, a member of the equestrian class who had excelled himself in the conquest of Egypt (Jördens 2009: 10). As prefect, he was the true representative of Rome and also the highest authority in the land; only the distant emperor himself was above him (Jördens 2009: 11). Cassius Dio (51.17.1) delivers further action to secure the regime:

> For in view of the populousness of both the cities and the country, the facile, fickle character of the inhabitants, and the extent of the grain supply and of the wealth, so far from daring to entrust the land to any senator, he [Augustus] would not even grant a senator permission to live in it, except as he personally made the concession to him by name.

Tacitus (*Ann.* 2.59.3) also reports on this ban. Similar travel bans existed in other provinces of the empire; in Egypt, however, they were handled in a particularly restrictive way. The reason for this was that Egypt's wealth and geostrategic position made it an ideal power base for a usurper (Jördens 2009: 40–1).

With the beginning of Roman rule, a completely new era dawned in Egypt. This is also clear from the way Octavian's regnal years were counted. In Egypt the years were dated by ruler. The first year of a ruler's reign, which was also the last year of the reign of his predecessor, lasted from the date of his accession until the end of the solar year. However, the first year of Octavian did not begin on the day of Cleopatra's death, in August 30 BCE, but on the next New Year's Day, the first day of Thoth in 30/29 BCE (Skeat 1953; Herklotz 2007: 309–10; Jördens 2009: 32–3). A new era was also introduced, known as *kaisaros kratesis theou huiou* ('dominion of Caesar, the son of a god'), which dated from the conquest of Egypt (Cass. Dio 51.19.6). It has even been suggested that, in the first five years of Roman rule, New Year's Day was brought forward to 1 August, the day of the conquest of Alexandria (Skeat 1994; Jördens 2009: 29–32; for a sceptical view, see Herklotz 2007: 312–13). In any event, by the fifth year of Augustus' reign at the latest, this unusual way of dating (if one follows Skeat and Jördens) had been abandoned (*SB* XVI 12469).

The existing administrative structure was not torn down but was modified according to the requirements of the new rulers; thus, the old moulds were filled with new contents. The new administration did not suddenly come into being but was gradually adapted to fit the new conditions. The first signs, however, can be detected very early. Some posts disappeared completely, such as all the functions of the Ptolemaic royal court and the eponymous priesthoods (see Jördens 2009: 27–8). Next came tighter controls within government, the revision of some duties, shorter terms for some officials, and the introduction of several new posts, with Romans holding higher offices (Huzar 1988: 359). Another important factor was that these posts were not filled by men who lived in proximity to the king, but by officials who were paid for their work and who had a fairly high degree of autonomy (Sartre 1991: 422).

All the state officials of Egypt were subordinate to the prefect; however, the most senior administrative posts were appointed by the emperor. The country was divided into three, and later four, *epistrategoi*, which were also administered by Roman officials appointed by the emperor (Thomas 1982). The most important administrative unit, however, was the so-called *nomos* (district, or nome), which consisted of several villages and a more important urban centre, the *metropolis*. In Roman times, this town became a city-like entity with a civic administration that remained dependent on central government. The *nomoi* were controlled by the *strategoi* ('governors'), but they had no military power (Dirscherl 2002; for a detailed list, Whitehorne 2006). Closely associated with the *strategos* was the *basilikos grammateus* (literally, 'royal scribe'), who could replace the *strategos* if necessary (Kruse 2002). All these officials had only very short periods of office, usually not exceeding three years. The Greek cities—of which there were only three in the Augustan period, Alexandria, Naukratis, and Ptolemais Hermiou—had a greater degree of autonomy, were more independent of central government, and had a municipal government, although Octavian banned the *boule* (council) of the Alexandrians (*PSI* X 1160). At the village level, the local Egyptians were ultimately responsible for managing administrative affairs.

The old upper class, the priests, were essentially the maintainers of indigenous tradition and ancient Egyptian culture (Hölbl 1994: 29; 2001: 27). It should be noted that this was a heterogeneous group: even a simple lighter of candles was an Egyptian priest. In the early years of Roman rule, temple land was largely nationalized, asylum and priestly privileges were restricted, and the remaining temple land was strictly controlled (*P Tebt.* II 302). But it is possible that this picture, promulgated for a long time in the research literature, is too one-sided. Unfortunately, an overall view of Egyptian priests in the Roman period is lacking; the work of Otto (1905–8) is largely obsolete, and Glare (1993) relies on Greek rather than Demotic sources. The priests continued to have certain privileges, because the Roman emperors were dependent on them in managing the country and maintaining the support of the provincial elite. Although there is no proof that the priesthood received financial support from the state, the construction of several new Egyptian temples carried out under Augustus must at least have been approved by the Romans. Others were restored and enlarged, for example at Kom Ombo, Shenhur, Koptos, el-Qal'a, and Dendara, and in the temples of Khonsu and Opet at Karnak (Hölbl 2000–5: I; Herklotz 2007: 170–201; and see Chapter 22).

The First Roman Prefects in Egypt

It would appear that some people in Egypt resisted Roman rule at first. Dio Cassius (51.17.4) may have alluded to this unrest when he wrote, 'Thus was Egypt enslaved. All the inhabitants *who resisted for a time* were finally subdued, as, indeed, heaven very clearly indicated to them beforehand.' Strabo (17.1.53) reports that the first prefect, C. Cornelius Gallus, put down a rebellion in the Thebaid and in the eastern Nile Delta, sparked by the burden of levies. The uprisings in Upper Egypt are also reported on the stele of C. Cornelius Gallus, which states that the Thebaid had seceded (lines 2–3 of the Latin text or lines 12–13 of the Greek text). Gallus was able to subdue the rebels within fifteen days and captured five towns in the Thebaid. The domination of this area was very important because it gave access to transport routes used to reach reserves of raw materials in the Eastern Desert, and ultimately the ports of the Red Sea. From the ports, ships sailed to southern Arabia, India, and Ceylon, and, as Strabo writes, trading activities in this area increased significantly under Augustus (Strabo 17.1.45; Sidebotham 1986; Rathbone 2002; Lembke, Fluck, and Vittman 2004: 81–4).

In addition, the stela of C. Cornelius Gallus records activities in Lower Nubia (lines 5–6/14–15; 7–8/16–18). The northern part of Lower Nubia, the Twelve Mile Land (Dodekaschoinos), formed a cultural and political border between Egypt and Nubia. It was also a passage from the Mediterranean to the interior of Africa. Many trading caravans passed through the area and there was also access from here to the deposits of natural resources in the Eastern Desert (Török 1997: 432; Locher 1999: 230–3). At the time of Octavian's conquest of Egypt, there was a culturally, economically, and at times politically important empire in Nubia named after its capital, Meroe (Hölbl 1994: 54; 2001: 55). During the late second and early first centuries BCE, Egypt gradually withdrew from Nubia, probably because of the general weakness of the Ptolemaic empire (Hölbl 1994: 190–1; 2001: 211; Hoffmann, Minas-Nerpel, and Pfeiffer 2009: 143). The Romans attempted to bring this important area back under their control. The Gallus stela reports that the prefect undertook a campaign to Lower Nubia, received Meroitic envoys on the island of Philae, and installed a Roman vassal prince, a *tyrannos*, over the Thirty Mile Land that stretched as far as the Second Cataract (Hoffmann, Minas-Nerpel, and Pfeiffer 2009: 157). Gallus must have been in agreement with Octavian, who pursued a policy of conquest on a grand scale (Kienast 1969: 333; Stickler 2002: 21–4; Hoffmann, Minas-Nerpel, and Pfeiffer 2009: 141–2). In their study of the stela, Hoffmann, Pfeiffer, and Minas-Nerpel (2009) have very clearly shown that the prefect in no way exceeded his powers. The Greek inscription emphasizes that Gallus had Octavian's authority to carry out his political and military activities, because the latter had appointed him (line 11). Nonetheless, only two years later Gallus was removed from office and committed suicide (Cass. Dio 53.23.5–7).

Gallus had not brought lasting peace to the Thirty Mile Land, and in the years that followed disputes arose with the Meroites, which were only ended by the Treaty of Samos in 21/20 BCE. Augustus led the negotiations himself. The border was set at Hierasykaminos, 110 km south of Aswan; the Romans waived the payment of tribute by the Meroites (Strabo 17.1.54; Locher 2002). Although not an ideal outcome for the Romans, the treaty helped secure peace in this region for the next 300 years (see Chapter 45).

Probably because it was both so important and contested, there is evidence of a lively building programme in this region in the Augustan period. The Ptolemaic temple of Kalabsha was replaced by a huge new building, the largest temple in Nubia, with a length of 77 metres. In all these temples Augustus is shown in the guise of an Egyptian pharaoh making offerings to the gods. By means of these representations, the priests integrated Augustus into Egyptian royal ideology, which allowed them to come to an accommodation with the Roman regime. For Augustus, in turn, a cooperative relationship with the priests and the elite of the country, and the support of Egyptian religion, were important means of legitimizing his power and maintaining internal peace. Hölbl repeatedly emphasizes in his work (2000–5) that the images in the temples only represented a 'cult' pharaoh and had no historical background because Augustus never made offerings to the gods. One must agree. It is noticeable, however, that there was an extensive programme of temple building in his reign (Herklotz 2007: 137–209). This was obviously planned and thought out with care, as most of these temples were constructed in strategic areas of the country; therefore, it appears that Octavian-Augustus countenanced the programme.

Conclusion

In contrast to earlier changes of ruler, the annexation of Egypt by Octavian represents a particularly lasting break in the country's history. Octavian was quickly able to stabilize Roman authority in the newly created province. As in the other provinces of the empire, a new, well-designed, and effective administration was speedily introduced. It was headed by the prefect, the direct representative of the emperor. To secure his rule, Octavian-Augustus also sought engagement with the priests, the elite of the country. This is evident in the numerous temples that were built, particularly in areas of strategic and economic importance. On the temple walls Augustus is indeed shown as a pharaoh acting in a cultic role, but the inscriptions make it clear that he received his office not from the Egyptian gods but through his *imperium*. Similarly, there is no proof of his coronation as pharaoh, which represents a break with the past for Egypt. In political terms, Egypt did not hold any special position in relation to the other provinces of the Roman empire. Without question, however, the land by the Nile was a significant province for the Romans, both for its financial benefits and for its key location in the eastern Mediterranean. As the coins Octavian issued to proclaim his victory decreed, Egypt, the powerful crocodile, had been captured and tamed (Fig. 1.1).

FIG. 1.1 Silver denarius of Octavian, later the emperor Augustus, commemorating the annexation of Egypt with the phrase [*A*]*egypto capta* around the figure of a crocodile. Minted in Italy, 28 BCE

Courtesy of the Trustees of the British Museum.

Suggested Reading

The most detailed overviews of the history of the Ptolemaic period are Hölbl (1994, 2001) and Huß (2001); Huß provides a comprehensive list of sources and reference for historical events. The latest research on Cleopatra is summarized in Schäfer (2006). For the conquest of Egypt, consult Geraci (1983, 1988), Heinen (1995), and Herklotz (2007: 103–8). The question of the special position of Egypt in the Roman empire is discussed by Lewis (1970, 1984), Geraci (1983), and Jördens (2009: 24–58). The titulary of Augustus in Egypt has been treated extensively by Grenier (1987, 1989a, b), Hölbl (1996: 100–5; 2000–5: I 18–22), and Herklotz (2007: 117–36, 413–21). Hölbl (2000–5) and Herklotz (2007: 137–209) analyse the programme of temple building, with detailed references. For the imperial administration and the activities of the prefect, see Jördens (2009). The topography and history of the area around the First Cataract is dealt with by Locher (1999). This work explores the activities of the first prefects in this region as well, as do Stickler (2002), Herklotz (2007: 139–45), and Hoffmann, Minas-Nerpel, and Pfeiffer (2009), as part of their translation and commentary on the trilingual stela of C. Cornelius Gallus.

Bibliography

Barta, W. 1980. 'Thronbesteigung und Krönungsfeier als unterschiedliche Zeugnisse königlicher Herrschaftsübernahme', *Studien zur Altägyptischen Kultur* 8: 33–53.

Benne, S. 2001. *Marcus Antonius und Kleopatra* VII: *Machtaufbau, herrscherliche Repräsentation und politische Propaganda*. Göttingen: Duehrkohp & Radicke.

Burstein, S. M. 1991. 'Pharao Alexander: A Scholarly Myth', *Ancient Society* 22: 139–45.

Crawford, D. J. 1980. 'Ptolemy, Ptah and Apis in Hellenistic Memphis', in Crawford (ed.), *Studies on Ptolemaic Memphis*. Leuven: Peeters, 1–42.

Dirscherl, H.-C. 2002. *Der Gaustratege im römischen Ägypten: Seine Aufgaben am Beispiel des Archiv-, Finanz- und Bodenwesens und der Liturgien: Entstehung—Konsolidierung—Niedergang? 30 v. Chr.–300 n. Chr.* St Katharinen: Scripta Mercaturae.

Dundas, G. S. 2002. 'Augustus and the Kingship of Egypt', *Historia* 51: 433–48.

Geraci, G. 1983. *Genesi della provincia romana d'Egitto*. Bologna: CLUEB.

—— 1988. '*Eparchia de nun esti*: La concezione augustea del governo d'Egitto', in H. Temporini (ed.), *Aufstieg und Niedergang der römischen Welt* II 10.1. Berlin: de Gruyter, 383–411.

Glare, P. M. 1993. 'The Temples of Egypt: The Impact of Rome', doctoral dissertation, Cambridge University.

Grenier, J.-C. 1987. 'Le protocole pharaonique des empereurs romains: Analyse formelle et signification historique', *Revue d'Égyptologie* 38: 81–104.

—— 1989a. *Les titulatures des empereurs romains dans les documents en langue égyptienne*. Brussels: Fondation Égyptologique Reine Élisabeth.

—— 1989b. 'Traditions pharaoniques et réalités impériales: Le nom de couronnement du pharaon à l'époque romaine', in L. Criscuolo and G. Geraci (eds), *Egitto e storica antica dall'Ellenismo all'èta araba: Bilancio di un confronto*. Bologna: CLUEB, 403–20.

—— 1995. 'L'empereur et le pharaon', in W. Haase and H. Temporini (eds), *Aufstieg und Niedergang der römischen Welt* II 18.4. Berlin: de Gruyter, 3181–94.

Heinen, H. 1995. 'Vorstufen und Anfänge des Herrscherkultes im römischen Ägypten', in W. Haase and H. Temporini (eds), *Aufstieg und Niedergang der römischen Welt* II 18.4. Berlin: de Gruyter, 3144–80.

—— 1998. 'Eine Darstellung des vergöttlichten Julius Caesar auf einer ägyptischen Stele? Beobachtungen zu einem mißverstandenen Denkmal (SB I 1570 = IG Fay. I 14)', in P. Kneissl and V. Losemann (eds), *Imperium Romanum: Studien zu Geschichte und Rezeption: Festschrift für Karl Christ zum 75. Geburtstag*. Stuttgart: Steiner.

—— 2007. 'Ägypten im römischen Reich: Beobachtungen zum Thema Akkulturation und Identität', in S. Pfeiffer (ed.), *Ägypten unter fremden Herrschern zwischen persischer Satrapie und römischer Provinz*. Frankfurt: Antike, 186–207.

Herklotz, F. 2007. *Prinzeps und Pharao: Der Kult des Augustus in Ägypten*. Frankfurt: Antike.

—— 2009. 'Ptolemaios XII: Versager oder siegreicher Pharao', in M. Fitzenreiter (ed.), *Das Ereignis: Geschichtsschreibung zwischen Vorfall und Befund*. London: Golden House, 137–54.

Hoffmann, F., M. Minas-Nerpel, and S. Pfeiffer. 2009. *Die dreisprachige Stele des C. Cornelius Gallus: Übersetzung und Kommentar*. Berlin: de Gruyter.

Hölbl, G. 1994. *Geschichte des Ptolemäerreiches*. Darmstadt: Wissenschaftliche Buchgesellschaft. Trans. as Hölbl (2001).

—— 1996. 'Ideologische Fragen bei der Ausbildung des römischen Pharaos', in M. Schade-Busch (ed.), *Wege öffnen: Festschrift für Rolf Gundlach zum 65. Geburtstag*. Wiesbaden: Harrassowitz, 98–109.

—— 2000–5. *Altägypten im römischen Reich: Der römische Pharao und seine Tempel* I–III. Mainz: von Zabern.

—— 2001. *A History of the Ptolemaic Empire*. London: Routledge. Trans. of Hölbl (1994).

Huß, W. 2001. *Ägypten in hellenistischer Zeit. 332–30 v. Chr*. Munich: Beck.

Huzar, E. G. 1988. 'Augustus: Heir of the Ptolemies', in H. Temporini (ed.), *Aufstieg und Niedergang der römischen Welt* II 10.1. Berlin: de Gruyter, 343–82.

Jördens, A. 2009. *Statthalterliche Verwaltung in der römischen Kaiserzeit: Studien zum praefectus Aegypti*. Stuttgart: Steiner.

Kienast, D. 1969. 'Augustus und Alexander', *Gymnasium* 76: 430–56.

Kruse, T. 2002. *Der königliche Schreiber und die Gauverwaltung: Untersuchungen zur Verwaltungsgeschichte Ägyptens in der Zeit von Augustus bis Philippus Arabs (30 v. Chr.–245 n. Chr.)*. Munich: Saur.

Lampela, A. 1998. *Rome and the Ptolemies of Egypt: The Development of their Political Relations 273–80* B.C. Helsinki: Societas Scientiarum Fennica.

Lembke, K., C. Fluck, and G. Vittmann. 2004. *Ägyptens späte Blüte: Die Römer am Nil*. Mainz: von Zabern.

Lewis, N. 1970. '"Greco-Roman Egypt": Fact or Fiction?', in D. H. Samuel (ed.), *Proceedings of the Twelfth International Congress of Papyrology*. Toronto: Hakkert, 3–14.

—— 1984. 'The Romanity of Roman Egypt: A Growing Consensus', in *Atti del XVII Congresso Internazionale di Papirologia, Napoli, 19–26 maggio 1983*, vol. 3. Naples: Centro Internazionale per lo Studio dei Papiri Ercolanesi, 1077–84.

Locher, J. 1999. *Topographie und Geschichte der Region am Ersten Nilkatarakt in griechisch-römischer Zeit*. Stuttgart: Teubner.

—— 2002. 'Die Anfänge der römischen Herrschaft in Nubien und der Konflikt zwischen Rom und Meroe', *Ancient Society* 32: 73–132.

McGing, B. C. 1997. 'Revolt Egyptian Style: Internal Opposition to Ptolemaic Rule', *Archiv für Papyrusforschung* 43: 273–314.

Otto, W. 1905–8. *Priester und Tempel im hellenistischen Ägypten*. Leipzig: Teubner.

Pestman, P. W. 1995. 'Haronnophris and Chaonnophris: Two Indigenous Pharaohs in Ptolemaic Egypt (205–186 B.C.)', in S. P. Vleeming (ed.), *Hundred-Gated Thebes: Acts of a Colloquium on Thebes and the Theban Area in the Graeco-Roman Period*. Leiden: Brill, 101–37.

Quaegebeur, J. 1972. 'Contribution à la prosopographie des prêtres memphites à l'époque ptolémaïque', *Ancient Society* 3: 77–109.

Rathbone, D. W. 2002. 'Koptos the Emporion: Economy and Society, I–III AD', in M.-F. Boussac (ed.), *Autour de Coptos: Actes du colloque organisée au Musée des Beaux Arts de Lyon (17–18 mars 2000)*. Paris: de Boccard; Lyon: Topoi, 179–98.

Sartre, M. 1991. *L'orient romain: Provinces et sociétés provinciales en Méditerranée orientale d'Auguste aux Sévères (31 avant J.-C.–235 après J.-C.)*. Paris: Seuil.

Schäfer, C. 2006. *Kleopatra*. Darmstadt: Wissenschaftliche Buchgesellschaft.

Schrapel, T. 1996. *Das Reich der Kleopatra: Quellenkritische Untersuchungen zu den 'Landschenkungen' Mark Antons*. Trier: Trierer Historische Forschungen.

Sidebotham, S. E. 1986. *Roman Economic Policy in the Erythra Thalassa, 30 BC–AD 217*. Leiden: Brill.

Skeat, T. C. 1953. 'The Last Days of Cleopatra', *Journal of Roman Studies* 43: 98–100.

—— 1994. 'The Beginning and the End of the Kaisaros Kratesis Era in Egypt', *Chronique d'Égypte* 69: 308–12.

Stickler, T. 2002. *'Gallus amore peribat'? Cornelius Gallus und die Anfänge der römischen Herrschaft in Ägypten*. Rahden, Westphalia: Leidorf.

Thomas, J. D. 1982. *The Epistrategos in Ptolemaic and Roman Egypt*, pt 2: *The Roman Epistrategos*. Opladen: Westdeutscher Verlag.

Thompson, D. J. 1988. *Memphis under the Ptolemies*. Princeton: Princeton University Press.

Török, L. 1997. *The Kingdom of Kush: Handbook of the Napatan-Meroitic Civilization*. Leiden: Brill.

Veïsse, A.-E. 2004. *Les 'révoltes égyptiennes': Recherches sur les troubles intérieurs en Égypte du règne de Ptolémée III à la conquête romaine*. Leuven: Peeters.

Whitehorne, J. 2006. *Strategy and Royal Scribes of Roman Egypt (Str. R. Scr. 2)*. Florence: Gonnelli.

Winter, E. 2005. 'Alexander der Große', in H. Beck, P. C. Bol, and M. Bückling (eds), *Ägypten, Griechenland, Rom: Abwehr und Berührung*. Frankfurt: Städel, 204–15.

Young, T. 1982. *Hieroglyphics Collected by the Egyptian Society*. Wiesbaden: LTR.

CHAPTER 2

BETWEEN WATER AND SAND

Agriculture and Husbandry

KATHERINE BLOUIN

Over the past twenty years, on the heels of the emergence of environmental history, the topic of agriculture and husbandry has been of rising interest among historians and archaeologists of the ancient Mediterranean (Horden and Purcell 2000; Banaji 2002; Clavel-Lévêque and Hermon 2004; Bowman and Wilson forthcoming), and notably of Roman Egypt. Indeed, in addition to Schnebel's (1925) study of agriculture in Hellenistic Egypt, we benefit nowadays from the results of several regional studies (Rathbone 1991 and Schubert 2007 (on the Arsinoite nome); Rowlandson 1996 (Oxyrhynchite nome); Bousquet 1996 and Bagnall 1997 (Western Oases); Blouin forthcoming a (Mendesian nome)); from diachronic studies (Bowman and Rogan 1999; Moreno García 2005); and from quantitative studies (Bowman 2009; forthcoming). These deal with a variety of issues such as local environments and micro-ecologies, population and settlement patterns, water management and food production, agrarian and fiscal policies, landscapes, and religion.

Our knowledge of Roman Egypt's rural life relies heavily on documentary papyri. Their abundance and the wealth of information they contain allow unparalleled insights into the socio-economic life of a Roman province. Studies of the rural economy also incorporate literary, archaeological, and, increasingly, palaeo-environmental evidence. To that effect, multidisciplinary initiatives contribute more and more to a holistic and diachronic understanding of past socio-environmental dynamics, while highlighting the crucial role of local enquiries (on the importance of local studies, see Rowlandson 1999: 138; Bowman forthcoming: 1). From this perspective, this chapter presents an overview of agriculture and husbandry in Roman Egypt which, while using the results of the research mentioned above, will focus more specifically on a district of the north-eastern Nile Delta called the Mendesian nome (district, from the Greek *nomos*).

Throughout most of antiquity, the Mendesian nome was traversed by the Mendesian branch of the Nile. This fluvial tributary, which apparently began to silt up in the Hellenistic period, disappeared at some point in Roman times (Blouin 2008). The nome, which borders part of today's Lake Menzaleh, was also rich in marshy zones and had direct access to the Mediterranean. These hydric features allowed Mendes and Thmuis, the successive capitals of the nome, to become major commercial centres (Blouin 2008; Leclère 2008: 313–61).

FIG. 2.1 Fields near Timai el-Amdid (ancient Thmuis)

Author's photograph.

The region is also one of the very few deltaic zones documented with a significant papyrological corpus, most of which consists in the so-called carbonized archives from Thmuis. These archives were found in Thmuis, the Roman *metropolis* of the nome (Fig. 2.1). They contain fiscal reports, and cadastral (land survey) and tax arrears registers, all of which date from the end of the second to the beginning of the third century CE, a time of regional socio-economic crisis (Kambitsis 1985; Blouin 2007a). These archives have their limits. First, they deal essentially with specific types of land (dry, *P Thmouis*; vineyards, orchards, and gardens, *P Ryl.* II 216). Secondly, the nome's toparchies (administrative subdivisions) are unevenly represented, which means that some activities, such as husbandry, were much more widespread than the papyri show. Work organization within villages, and practices such as fallow intervals, crop rotation, and mixed cropping, are not documented, while some crops attested in the third century BCE (papyrus, lotus, and sesame) do not figure in the Roman papyri (Blouin 2007b).

Nevertheless, owing to the exhaustive and explicit cadastral and fiscal data they contain, these papyri provide us with an invaluable deltaic sample that can be compared with what is known of the situation that prevailed elsewhere in Egypt at the time. Since comprehensive coverage of all aspects dealing with the subject is impossible here, three main issues will be discussed: agro-fiscal management policies, land use and food production, and religious landscapes.

The State and the Land: The Agro-Fiscal Management of Roman Egypt

Although they adapted the Egyptian agrarian 'model' to their needs (notably by intensive development of the Fayum Oasis), the Ptolemies retained most of the pharaonic land categories. There were three main types of land: royal (*basilike*), the chief source of revenue; sacred (*hiera*), which belonged to the temples; and gifted (*en dorea*) (Crawford 1971; Thompson 1999; Manning 2003).

After Egypt's annexation to the Roman empire, Augustus introduced an important reform of the land tenure system. The Ptolemaic terminology was retained, but it was classified according to a distinction between private property—which until then had been rather marginal—and the public domain. Consequently, a more complex agro-fiscal terminology developed, to which papyri testify (see especially Wallace 1938: 1–19; Kehoe 1992; Rowlandson 1996: 27–69). Thus, more than forty different categories of land are attested in the Mendesian nome. Although not exhaustive, this sample generally fits with what is found elsewhere in the province, while some regional peculiarities may also be noted. Overall, it shows how the Roman management of Egypt's agrarian territory rested upon three main criteria: the juridical status of the land, its purpose, and its relative level of moisture. What follows is based on Blouin (2007a: 167–201).

Private and Public Land

In Roman Egypt there was less private than public land. Because of this, and the fact that private land was subject to lower taxation rates, it contributed less to the revenues of the province. Regional discrepancies must, however, be taken into account. For instance, the carbonized archives from Thmuis mostly concern private land categories (Table 2.1). This may result in part from the nature of the registers, which deal mostly with uninundated and dry parcels, but it may also hint at the abundance of private domains (notably in marginal areas) in the nome.

Private Land

In Roman Egypt private land (*idiotike ge*) was essentially made of former clerouchic (*klerouchike*) and catoechic (*katoikike*) land (Rowlandson 1996: 41–55). Yield quantities were measured by artaba (1 artaba = 30–40 litres), and land by aroura (1 aroura = 2756.25 m ^{2}). The generally low taxation rates (between 3/4 and 2 artabas per aroura, usually about 1 artaba/aroura) granted to cleruchs (native army or police veterans), katoichs (Greek army veterans), and their descendants under the Ptolemies were maintained by the Romans, but thereafter attached to the land itself. The fact that many clerouchic denominations had in reality become toponyms (fossilized *kleroi*) testifies to this. Mendesian papyri, and notably the *P Mendesius Genevensis* (*SPP* XVII S 13–29), reveal how widespread this phenomenon was in this nome (Martin 1967). In addition to former *kleroi*, many other land categories were considered private property, several of which appear in Mendesian papyri.

Although most of the time managed as public land, non-confiscated 'sacred land' (*hiera ge*) was sometime considered private property (Martin 1967: 39). The same goes for *idioktetos* land, whose exact nature remains unclear (Kambitsis 1985: 21; Rowlandson 1996: 42–3), whereas 'bought land' (*eonemene ge*) corresponded to unproductive or confiscated parcels that were sold by the state at a fixed price or through auction (Wallace 1938: 5). 'Inferior land' (*hypologos ge*) included uncultivated parcels that were sold at a fixed—generally very low—price, and that could be assigned to forced cultivation. The new owner benefited from a three-year tax exemption. Such incentives find a parallel in those promulgated in Africa through the *lex Manciana* and the *lex Hadriana de rudibus agris* as well as in Gaul in the

Table 2.1 Mendesian agro-fiscal typology under the Principate, according to papyri*

Private Land	Public Land
ἰδιωτική	ἱερὰ ἐν ἐκφορίῳ
ἰδιω[τικ	ἱερὰ (διάρταβος) μεμισθωμένη may belong to ἱερὰ ἐν ἐκφορίῳ
(μονάρταβος)	
αd	ἱερὰ (μεμισθωμένη) may belong to ἱερὰ ἐν ἐκφορίῳ
ας' χερσάμπελος	
(ἡμιτεταρταβίας) (δεκαρούρων)	ἐν ἐκφορίῳ δημοσία γῆ
(δεκαρούρων)	διοικήσεως
λιμνιτικὴ (δεκαρούρων)	βασιλικὴ γῆ διοικήσεως
(δεκαρούρων) 'Ιετηριτῶν	διοικήσεως ἐν ἐκφορίῳ
ει (δεκαρούρων) 'Ιετηριτῶν	οὐσιακή
ει (δεκαπενταρούρων)	ἱερα(τικῆς) θεοῦ ε.[?] (*ousia?*)
(ἑπταρούρων)	νομαὶ κτηνῶν
[.](ἀρταβ) ῥαβδοφόρων	πλεονασμός
ἡμι[.....]ιως	
βs ἀπογρ()	
πρότερον κληρουχικῆς	
ας' ἰδιόκτητος	
ἰδιόκτητος ἐκ (δρ.) κ	
ἐωνημένη ἰδιωτικὴ γῆ	
(μονάρταβος) ἐωνημένη	
λιμνιτικὴ (μονάρταβος) ἐωνημένη	
ἐωνημένη	
(μονάρταβος) ἐωνημένη	
ἐωνημένη ἀπὸ ἱερατικοῦ ὑπολόγου	
ἐωνημένη ἀπὸ βασιλικοῦ ὑπολόγου	
ὠνήσασθαι ἀπὸ ὑπολόγου χερσαμπέλου	
ἐωνημένη ἀπὸ λιμνιτικῆς προσόδου	
χέρσου ὑπολόγου	
ἀπὸ ἱερατικοῦ ὑπολόγου	
ἀπὸ βασιλικοῦ ὑπολόγου	
ἀπὸ λιμνιτικοῦ ὑπολόγου	
χερσαμπέλου = ~ χερσαμπέλου ὑπολόγου	
ἱερὰ ἐπὶ καθήκουσι	
~ ἱερὰ = ~ ἱερὰ ἐπὶ καθήκουσι	
χερσάμπελος, χέρσος ἐπὶ ναυβίῳ, χέρσος	
λιμνιτική	

*~: possibly

cadastre B d'Orange (Blouin 2007b: 155). In all cases, the aim was obviously for the Roman administration to encourage the extension of farmed land. Productive plots—for the most part land confiscated either from debtors of the state or from intestate owners—were auctioned. Given their fertility, they did not benefit from exemptions and were sold at considerably higher prices than *hypologos ge*. The status of 'revenue land' (*prosodou ge*) remains uncertain. It may have corresponded to confiscated land waiting for sale or assignation (*P Bour.* 42, introduction; *P Phil.* 9, introduction), and may have included sequestered plots whose yield was paid to the state until full reimbursement of the debt. Finally, one must mention 'limnitic' land (*limnitike ge*), a category that is so far attested only in the Mendesian nome and which, as its name suggests, included parcels originally located by a *limne* (lake or marsh). Owing, in all likelihood, to its peculiarity, it was administered by a specific department and was subject to low taxation rates (Blouin forthcoming b).

Public Land

Public land was much more profitable to the fisc. Indeed, while private parcels were taxed at an average rate of 1 artaba per aroura, public ones could be taxed at 2–7 artabas/aroura, with an average of 3 artabas/aroura (Rowlandson 1996: 71–80; 1999: 148). Most of Egypt's public domain was made up of former royal land, still commonly called *basilike ge* in papyri at least until the end of the third century CE. The expression *demosia ge*, which equates with the Latin *ager publicus*, often seems to be used as a synonym for *basilike ge*. Mendesian papyri refer to the following public categories:

- plots whose category included *dioikesis* (i.e. were administered by the *dioikesis*, or government treasury department);
- parts of the sacred domain (*hiera ge*) that were also public, as well as sacred plots that had been confiscated under the last Ptolemies and Augustus;
- the *ousiai*, former imperial domains and estates belonging to the family, friends, and freedmen of the emperors, that had been made public properties (Crawford 1976; Parássoglou 1978; Kehoe 1992: 1–57);
- *nomai ktenon* (state pastures);
- land called *pleonasmos* and other unproductive public parcels that were assigned to forced cultivation. These were generally attached to private properties, and are also referred to as *epibole*, *georgia*, *epimerismos*, *chalasma* (see Blouin 2007b: 156).

In addition to the distinction between private and public land, plots were also categorized according to their purpose. Here, too, a fundamental duality can be observed: that between grain land and orchards/gardens.

Cereal Land, Orchards, and Gardens

A fundamental difference existed between these grain lands and orchards/gardens (Table 2.2). Grain land was mostly taxed in kind, that is, in artabas per aroura (the same went for legume land). However, as can be seen, for instance, in *P Thmouis* 1, which deals

Table 2.2 Agro-fiscal typology and land vocation in the Mendesian nome under the Principate, according to papyri

Land Category	Grain Land	Vineyard	Pastures
ἰδιωτική	X		
ἰδιω[τικ	X		
(μονάρταβος)	X		
αd	X		
ας' χερσάμπελος	X		
(ἡμιτεταρταβίας) (δεκαρούρων)	X		
(δεκαρούρων)	X		
λιμνιτικὴ (δεκαρούρων)	X		
(δεκαρούρων) 'Ιετηριτῶν	X		
εΙ (δεκαρούρων) 'Ιετηριτῶν	X		
εΙ (δεκαπενταρούρων)	X		
(ἑπταρούρων)	X		
[.](ἀρταβ) ῥαβδοφόρων	X		
ἡμι[.....]ιως	X		
βs ἀπογρ()	X		
πρότερον κληρουχικῆς	X		
ας' ἰδιόκτητος	X		
ἰδιόκτητος ἐκ (δρ.)		X	
(μονάρταβος) ἐωνημένη	X		
λιμνιτικὴ (μονάρταβος) ἐωνημένη	X		
ἐωνημένη	X		
(μονάρταβος) ἐωνημένη	X		
ἐωνημένη ἀπὸ ἱερατικοῦ ὑπολόγου	X		
ἐωνημένη ἀπὸ βασιλικοῦ ὑπολόγου	X		
ἐωνημένη ἀπὸ ὑπολόγου χερσαμπέλου	X	X	
ἐωνημένη ἀπὸ λιμνιτικῆς προσόδου	X		
χέρσου ὑπολόγου			X
ἀπὸ ἱερατικοῦ ὑπολόγου	X		
ἀπὸ βασιλικοῦ ὑπολόγου	X		
ἀπὸ λιμνιτικοῦ ὑπολόγου	X		
χερσαμπέλου = ~ χερσαμπέλου ὑπολόγου	X		
ἱερά = ~ ἱερὰ ἐπὶ καθήκουσι	X		
χερσάμπελος, χέρσος ἐπὶ ναυβίῳ, χέρσος		X	
ἱερὰ ἐν ἐκφορίῳ	X		
ἱερὰ (διάρταβος) μεμισθωμένη may belong to ἱερὰ ἐν ἐκφορίῳ			
ἱερὰ (μεμισθωμένη) may belong to ἱερὰ ἐν ἐκφορίῳ		X	
διοικήσεως	X		
βασιλικὴ γῆ διοικήσεως	X		
διοικήσεως ἐν ἐκφορίῳ	X		
οὐσιακή			X
νομαὶ κτηνῶν			X
πλεονασμός	X		

exclusively with tax arrears in cash, it was also subject to monetary taxes. Apart from the common payments in wine and olive oil, orchards and gardens were taxed in money. This general rule, which is by no means exclusive to Egypt, arose out of practical considerations. Cereals (and legumes) were easy to preserve for long periods, and could be stored in large quantities and transported over long distances. This, of course, is not the case with fresh fruit and vegetables, hence the preference for taxation in money. As for pastures, taxes and rents were most often calculated by head of cattle.

Grain land made up the great bulk of Egypt's agrarian land. A papyrus from Oxyrhynchus (*P Oxy.* XXIV 3205) provides us with a useful Mendesian example. This land register informs us that at the turn of the fourth century CE more than 75 per cent of the agrarian land of the toparchy of Phernouphites was dedicated to grain cultivation. Viticulture, gardens, legumes, and reeds occupied about 20 per cent of the land, with the remainder being made up of sandy scrubland (Blouin 2007b: 151–6). This results from the suitability of most of the land to cereal crops, Egyptian and Mediterranean dietary habits, the key role played by Egypt's wheat in imperial and Mediterranean food supply networks, and the great profitability of cereals within the context of speculation. Therefore, whenever and wherever the land was deemed suited for it, cereals, and especially wheat, were a prime choice for tenants and landowners (including the State) alike. In all cases, however, the use of any parcel of land was ultimately dependent on its access to water (see Thompson 1999: 125).

From Dry to Flooded

Before the construction of the Aswan High Dam in 1964, Egypt's annual yield was inextricably linked to the quality of the annual flood of the Nile, and also to the proper functioning of the irrigation system (Bonneau 1993). Like their predecessors, the Macedonian and Roman authorities were aware of the need to adjust tax rates at least roughly to the fertility of the soil, which was dependent on access to water. Papyri testify to the development during this period—in direct continuity with the Egyptian fiscal tradition—of a Greek terminology of land fertility. This descriptive vocabulary covers the whole range of levels of moisture, from permanently dry to submerged land. At the centre of the range stood the 'perfectly' inundated soil (*bebregmene ge*), while the two most agriculturally unproductive types of land, namely land either dry (*chersos*) or submerged (*limne*) for many years figured at its extremities (Bonneau 1971: 66–82).

Among the numerous terms used in Egypt to render the subtle effects of the flood on the land, the most common ones in the Mendesian papyri are (from the driest to the wettest): *chersos* (dry for many years), *abrochos* (not flooded for one year), *epentlemene* or *antlemene* (artificially irrigated), and *limnitike* (submerged for many years). All of these refer to agriculturally marginal soils that, because of a lack or a surplus of water, were subject to total (*chersos, abrochos*) or partial (*epentlemene, limnitike*) tax relief. This reflects the abundance of marginal zones in the nome, the nature of our evidence, and the general context of socio-economic crisis of the time in the region.

The official fertility of every parcel, and hence any possible tax relief, were at first determined during the general land *episkepsis*. From the second century CE, probably from the reign of Marcus Aurelius, only plots declared as inundated either severely or not at all were inspected (Bonneau 1971: 184–8). This new rule, which arose out of the administration's wish to reconnect with the agrarian reality, paradoxically led to an increased disconnection between the fiscal management of Egyptian agricultural land and agrarian reality. Consequently, as the tense socio-economic context evident in the carbonized archives from Thmuis illustrates, taxpayers ended up feeling greater fiscal pressure.

This pressure was notably dealt with through a diversity of property patterns and landowner–tenant dynamics. *Papyrus Mendes Geneva* (*SPP* XVII S 13–29) documents this in the Mendesian nome (Blouin 2009). This papyrus, which belongs to the carbonized archives of Thmuis, contains a list of public and private wheat parcels declared as uninundated or artificially irrigated. All the parcels were located in the same, unidentified village. The information preserved in the document shows that a little more than half the declarations dealt with one parcel, whereas almost the same proportion concerned two plots or more. Further, apart from a small number of large owners, most declarants were apparently small to medium landowners. In all cases, plots often happen to have been widespread and of diverse categories. Such heterogeneous data, which parallel those from the Fayum and the Nile Valley (Bowman forthcoming), testify to a land tenure system based on the delegation of fiscal responsibility among tenants and farmers (who themselves often sub-let their plots), as well as on family patterns of farming.

Land Use and Food Production

Recent work has shown that by far the main crop cultivated in the Fayum and the Nile Valley was wheat. It was followed by a variety of foodstuffs and husbandry including barley, fodder, legumes, vine, olives, fruit and vegetables, livestock, poultry, and fish. The relative importance of each of these depended on local environmental and socio-economic conditions and was motivated by a search for subsistence, a quest for autarky, or the generation of profits (Rathbone 1991: 212–64; Rowlandson 1996: 19–26; Bowman forthcoming).

The situation was generally similar in the Mendesian nome, though some regional peculiarities can be observed. A total of over 100 taxes and royalties—mostly in cash, but also in kind—are preserved in the Mendesian papyri. These come mostly from the carbonized archives from Thmuis and date from the second half of the second century CE. Thanks to the descriptive and specific nature of their fiscal terminology, the main food production activities practised in the nome can be identified and their relative importance gauged (Table 2.3).

Most of Mendesian agrarian land was dedicated to wheat cultivation. Taxes on wheat land are so far attested in twelve out of the fifteen, or perhaps sixteen, known toparchies of the nome. Interestingly, cereal culture was even practised on 'limnitic' (originally submerged) plots. Since wheat is intolerant of humidity, at some point these parcels must have been drained, either artificially and/or geomorphologically, perhaps in the context of the silting up of the Mendesian branch (Blouin forthcoming b).

Barley is also documented in the nome. In Roman Egypt barley was used mainly as animal fodder, but also for human consumption. Bagnall (1993: 25) estimates that about 20 per cent of all grain land was sown with barley. It was not as prevalent as wheat, which was worth twice as much, but since barley is more resistant to drought and salinity than wheat, it provides a better yield when sown on marginal land or following an average flood (Bonneau 1987: 189; Thanheiser 1992). As for taxes on and general references to beans and lentils, these underscore the conspicuous role played by legumes in ancient Mediterranean diets (Garnsey 1998).

Table 2.3 Diversification in the Mendesian nome under the Principate, in the light of the fiscal terminology

Sector	Crop/Animal	Tax or Royalty (source in the case of non-fiscal or general attestation)
Agriculture	Grain (wheat and barley)	ἀλλαγή
		εἰκοστή
		ἡμιαρταβία ποδώματος
		[κοσ]κινία ἀλώνων
		[ ]ν κοσκινίας ἀλώνων
		ναύβιον
		παράναυλον
		πελωχικόν
		χωματικόν
		BGU III 976–980
	Beans	*P Oxy.* XXIV 3205
	Lentils	τέλος φακοῦ ἐρείξεως
	Vines	ἀλλαγή
		ἀπόμοιρα
		β. τριώβ. Ἀλεξανδρέων
		γεωμετρία
		~δεκάδραχμος
		ἑξάδραχμος Φιλαδέλφου
		ἐπαρούριον
		ναύβιον
		οἴνου τέλος
		ὀκτάδραχμος
		τέλεσμα ἀμπέλου
		τρίδραχμος / τρίδραχμος μητροπολιτῶν
		φόρος ἀμπέλου
	Fruit and vegetables (general)	ἀπόμοιρα
		β. τριώβ. Ἀλεξανδρέων
		γεωμετρία
		~δεκάδραχμος
		ἐπαρούριον

(*cont.*)

Sector	Crop/Animal	Tax or Royalty (source in the case of non-fiscal or general attestation)
		~πεντάδραχμος
		τρίδραχμος/ τρίδραχμος μητροπολιτῶν
	Olive trees	ἐλαϊκή
		τέλος ἐλαιουργικῶν/τέλεσμα τῶν ὀργάνων
	Flax	μερισμὸς ἐνδεήματος ὀθονιηρᾶς/ ὀθονιηρά
		τιμὴ λινοκαλάμης
	Ricin	κικιουργικοῦ ὀργάνου
	Reeds	*P Oxy.* XXIV 3205
Husbandry	Livestock (general)	δερματηρὰ νομοῦ
		τιμὴ θρεμμάτων
		φόρος νομῶν καὶ ἄλλων
		[ζ]ῴων
		[......] ποιμένων
	Pigs	ὑική
	Sheep and goats	ἐννόμιον
		ὑποκείμενον ἐννομίου
		[ ]ὴ προβάτων
		φόρος προβάτων
	Goats (sacred context)	λύτρωσις αἰγῶν
	Calf (sacred context)	μόσχου τέλος
	Donkeys	(ἑξαδραχμία) τῶν ὄνων
	Poultry (general)	τοκαδεία
		ὑποκείμενον τοκαδείας
		ὑποκείμενον καὶ κηρυκικὸν τοκαδείας
	Geese and chickens	τοκαδεία χ[ηνῶ]ν καὶ ὀρνείθων
	Pigeons	τρίτη περιστερεώνων
Hunting and Fishing		Θωνειτικὰ καὶ λιμνιτικά
		φόροι (λιμνιτικά)
		χειρωνάξιον ἀμφιβολέων

Fodder, which was an important crop in the Arsinoite and Oxyrhynchite nomes, is not referred to explicitly in Mendesian fiscal terminology. This is certainly due to the incomplete nature of the evidence. Rathbone (1991: 214) believes that, after wheat and barley, hay was the third most important crop cultivated on Appianus' estate in Theadelphia, whereas Rowlandson (1996: 20–1; 1999: 146) claims that it came second in the Oxyrhynchite nome, after wheat. Given the general need for animal fodder, its customary use as a fallow crop, and its suitability for marginal land (Rowlandson 1999: 149–51), these estimates might well be representative of what was going on in the Mendesian nome.

Many taxes on fruit and vegetables appear in the Mendesian papyri. Since most of them are general, they give us no hint of what specific crops were grown on each parcel (for a general overview, see Bagnall 1993: 31), except for taxes concerning vineyards and olive trees. This may be due to the fact that, unlike cereals, fruit and vegetables (as well as flowers) were usually cultivated on a small scale and destined for domestic or local consumption. They were nevertheless an interesting investment for farmers, who could make considerable profits out of the sale of fresh produce in local markets. The close economic relationships that existed (and still exist) between rural peripheries and urban centres explain the great profitability of these commodities.

There were vineyards in at least nine Mendesian toparchies. In Egypt vines have to be planted above the flood line, on hills that are less well suited for grain cultivation. Vine growing required artificial irrigation and considerable care, but these efforts were compensated by the profitability of wine (Schnebel 1925: 239–92; Rathbone 1991: 212–13; Brun 2004: 143–68). In Egyptian papyri, vineyards are sometimes associated with trees (fruit or other) and mixed cropping. Such practices are attested elsewhere in the Roman empire (Bousquet 1996; Rowlandson 1996: 19–20; Brun 2004: 144). This could explain why many taxes dealt with gardens, orchards, and vineyards together.

Oil crops were also taxed (Schnebel 1925: 197–203; Sandy 1989; Bagnall 1993: 29–31; Brun 2004: 169–84). Mendesian papyri contain references to the payment of taxes on olive and castor oil presses as well as on flax. Olive production appeared as a regular practice only in the Roman period. However, the fact that there are overall few attestations to olive growing in the Mendesian nome, and in the province in general, could be due to the relative marginality of this activity in Egypt (Rathbone 1991: 244–7; Rowlandson 1996: 24; Thompson 1999: 131–3). Indeed, like grape vines, olive trees are not suited to the flood-plains of the Nile Delta and valley. Consequently, they can only be planted on higher ground, which, apart from villages and towns, is relatively rare. Ricin oil, also known in Ptolemaic sources as *croton* or under its Egyptian name *kiki*, was used exclusively for lighting because of its toxicity (Plin. *HN* 15.7). As for flax, its cultivation—essentially for textiles—continued to be an important sector of activity in the northern Delta throughout antiquity and the medieval period (Blouin 2007a: 249–56).

According to the numerous occurrences in the papyri of the so-called *uike*, *ennomion*, and *tokadeia* (the latter being to date unique to the Mendesian nome), Mendesian husbandry consisted of a combination of pig, sheep, goat, and poultry breeding (*P Ryl.* II 213, introduction). Pigeons, whose droppings were a coveted fertilizer, were also commonly raised in Roman Egypt, as they are today (Husselman 1953). The existence of a tax on pigeons documents this practice in the Mendesian nome. Mentions of royalties on donkeys remind us that these animals, together with oxen and mules, were (and still are) commonly used as modes of transportation. Although no Mendesian tax refers specifically to cattle breeding, literary sources on the *Boukoloi* (cattle breeders who inhabited marshy areas) tend to show that this activity was widespread in the marginal zones of the Delta (Blouin 2010). Several Mendesian references to pasture royalties document the existence of public pastures in the nome. These were most probably located in arid, salty, or damp plots unsuitable for grain cultivation.

Finally, we can mention some practices associated with lacustrine, palustrine, lagoonal, and coastal environments, in addition to flax cultivation and animal husbandry. Commercial exploitation of papyrus and lotus, which were widespread in the Delta, is attested in the Mendesian nome in the Ptolemaic period, whereas hunting, fishing, and fish farming, which were (and remain) important activities in the Lake Menzaleh region (Henein 2010: 18–19), are mentioned in the carbonized archives from Thmuis. To these can be added pickling and, in the eastern Lake Menzaleh, salt pan exploitation (Blouin 2007a: 239–44). The centrality of these activities in the Mendesian nome shows vividly through the identity and attributes of the fish-goddess Hatmehyt, whose worship shaped the sacred landscape of the nome.

Sacred Landscapes: The Case of Hatmehyt

It is a cliché but it is true: ancient Egyptian religion was inextricably linked to Nilotic environments. The Nile, its annual flooding, and all living and non-living things were seen by the ancient Egyptians as manifestations of a superior force that was embodied in a myriad of deities. In addition to the pan-Egyptian Nilotic cults of Osiris and Isis, Hapy, and, in the Hellenistic and Roman periods, Neilos, many local cults existed. Centred around village and town sanctuaries, they were at the heart of Egypt's spiritual life. The fundamental role of local religious practices in the identity and socio-economic organization of Egyptian society is inseparable from the varied micro-ecologies that made up its landscape. The association of a river, a village, a nome, and so forth with a deity transformed the landscape into a sacred web in which societies connected the features of their environment to a network of omniscient and omnipotent interlocutors who, in return for acts of devotion, were expected to watch over the well-being of those under their protection. To that effect, the case of Hatmehyt, the fish-goddess of Mendes, is exemplary.

Hatmehyt (literally 'She who is at the head of the fishes'; *WB* 3.21.15) was the first tutelary deity of Mendes, as can be seen by the nome's pisciform standard (Montet 1957: 143). The identity of the 'Mendes fish' (*itn* in Egyptian) has been much debated. While it was thought by many to be a dolphin (Meeks 1973), it is now accepted that it was a schilbe (a kind of catfish) (Gamer-Wallert 1970: 100–1; Brewer and Friedman 1990: 65; Redford 1995; Sahrhage 1998: 137). The schilbe figures on Egyptian bas-reliefs from the Old Kingdom onwards (Brewer and Friedman 1990: 64). This freshwater fish inhabits the Nile and Senegal rivers as well as the Great Lakes and favours sandy shallows and low-current bodies of water. The damp environments of the Mendesian nome were thus perfectly suited for this species, and its association with Hatmehyt must have ensued from its presence in the region. Consumption of the schilbe was considered taboo in the nome, although this was not necessarily followed in practice (Meeks 1973: 209–13).

Hatmehyt was the only Egyptian deity whose avatar was a fish. Her cult being attested almost exclusively in Mendes, she seems to have been in essence a regional goddess, whose roots can be sought in the importance of fishing in the nome. Although from an early date she was paired with, and later superseded by, the ram god Banebdjeb, Hatmehyt retained a strong position in the Mendesian religious landscape throughout antiquity. Together with their son Harpocrates, Banebdjed and Hatmehyt formed the Mendesian triad. Epithets such as 'Divine spouse at the head of the Ram house', 'Eye of Ra', 'Mistress of the Sky', 'Queen of all Gods', and 'Powerful' express what a central figure she was (de Meulenaere 1976: 178). Hatmehyt was also assimilated with Isis as 'She who makes the flood come' (Bonneau 1964: 254), and associated with Nephthys, with whom she was said to have gathered together Osiris' limbs after his body was torn to pieces and scattered by his brother. Finally, the goddess was also the patron of Mendesian perfumery (de Rodrigo 2000; Blouin 2007a: 256–61). All these links are symptomatic of the clear and close connection that existed between the fish-goddess and the Mendesian fluvial environment, from the Nile flood to the Mendesian branch's commercial potential (de Meulenaere 1976).

Archaeological remains found in Mendes show that in the Ramesside period, the site of Nepherites' funerary complex hosted a temple to Hatmehyt. This temple was located at the easternmost edge of the city, close to the harbour, a setting that further testifies to the fluvial and commercial patronage of the goddess. Excavations in the area of Nepherites' tomb discovered ceramic vessels containing immature specimens of schilbe, sometimes wrapped in linen. Fragments of twenty-nine stelae covered with incised fishes have also been found, which have been interpreted as votive offerings (Redford 1995; 2004: 32–3). Hatmehyt's continued popularity in the Roman period is evident through local onomastics as well as the presence of reliefs of fishes (probably schilbe) on libation tables from Thmuis, used to pray for good Nile floods. The association between Hatmehyt, fishes, and the fertilizing property of the Nile is once again clear (Bonneau 1964: 294–6; Hibbs 1985: 83–6).

In her roles as the wife of Banebdjed, fertilizing mother goddess, manifestation of Isis and Nephthys, and patron of the Mendesian perfumery, Hatmehyt appears as the protector of all activities associated with the hydric environments of the nome, including agriculture, certainly, but also fishing and related practices, as well as commercial activities. As such, her cult incarnates splendidly the fundamental links that existed in ancient Egypt between spirituality and the landscape.

Conclusion

The agro-fiscal management of Roman Egypt was oriented towards the maximization of its agrarian yields and, hence, fiscal revenues. In this regard, particular attention was dedicated to the promotion of agriculturally marginal land, as Mendesian agrarian terminology shows. Overall, the province's agricultural life was mainly dedicated to wheat cultivation. This is clear from the documentary papyri, notably those from the Arsinoite, Oxyrhynchite, and Mendesian nomes, and seems to have been general throughout the province. It was a result of the crucial role played by wheat in Egyptian and Mediterranean diets, as well as the speculative profitability of this staple. The cultivation of barley, fodder, legumes, fruit and vegetables (including grapes and olives), as well as husbandry, are also commonly attested. Although these appear in smaller proportions in our sources, their importance and profitability should not be underestimated. Such diversified practices were the result of an opportunistic adaptation to local environments, as is also observed in the Fayum and the Nile Valley. Hunting, fishing, fish breeding, husbandry, flax, and possibly papyrus cultivation and picking seem to have been more prevalent in marshy zones such as the ones that abounded in the northern Nile Delta. For these practices, the Mendesian data stand out, and might well denote local or, more generally, northern deltaic specificities.

The cult of Hatmehyt vividly illustrates the fundamental role played by the relationship between society and the environment in ancient Egyptian religious schemes. The dual process of 'sacralization of the animal' and 'animalization of the sacred', which led to the identification of Hatmehyt with the schilbe, resulted from a representational system that saw all components of the environment as manifestations of the religious sphere. This system, which was still very much alive in the Roman period, was an integrative model in which human beings stood on a level with all the other elements of their surroundings. As such, the palpable world was part of the divine realm and vice versa. The inhabitants of the Mendesian nome, like all Egyptians, thus belonged to a spiritual universe that was based upon the relationships that existed between them and their environment. This universe was as complex as the microecologies in which they lived were diverse. Egyptian and Mendesian religious and agro-fiscal data alike, however, highlight a common preoccupation with the maintenance of the fertility of the land, the prosperity of its inhabitants, and, ultimately, the stability of the Roman state.

Suggested Reading

Rathbone (1991) and Rowlandson (1996) provide fundamental insights into the regional rural economy of Roman Egypt, drawing primarily on papyri from the Fayum and the Oxyrhynchite nome. In a wider chronological and geographical perspective, Bowman and Rogan (1999) offers comparisons over a long period of time from antiquity to the present day, whereas the agricultural economy of the Roman empire, for which Egypt is an important source of documentation, is the subject of a multi-author volume edited by Bowman and Wilson (forthcoming). This includes evidence specific to the Mendesian nome (Blouin forthcoming a).

Bibliography

Banaji, J. 2002. *Agrarian Change in Late Antiquity: Gold, Labour and Aristocratic Dominance.* Oxford: Oxford University Press.

Bagnall, R. S. 1993. *Egypt in Late Antiquity.* Princeton: Princeton University Press.

—— (ed.) 1997. *The Kellis Agricultural Book.* Oxford: Oxbow.

Blouin, K. 2007a. 'Homme et milieu dans le nome mendésien à l'époque romaine (1er au 6e s.)', doctoral dissertation, Québec: Université Laval; Nice: Université de Nice.

—— 2007b. 'Environnement et fisc dans le nome mendésien à l'époque romaine: Réalités et enjeux de la diversification', *Bulletin of the American Society of Papyrologists* 44: 135–66.

Blouin, K. 2008. 'De Mendès à Thmouis (delta du Nil, Égypte): Hydrologie mobile, société mobile?', in E. Hermon (ed.), *L'Eau comme patrimoine: De la Méditerranée à l'Amérique du Nord*. Québec: Presses de l'Université Laval, 107–28.

—— 2009. 'Diversification foncière dans le nome mendésien: Le cas du *P. Mendes. Genev.*', *Bulletin of the American Society of Papyrologists* 46: 97–108.

—— 2010. 'La révolte des *Boukoloi* (delta du Nil, *ca.* 166–172 de notre ère): Regard socio-environnemental sur la violence', *Phoenix* 64/3–4: 386–422.

—— forthcoming a. 'The Agricultural Economy of the Mendesian Nome during the Roman Period', in A. K. Bowman and A. I. Wilson (eds), *The Agricultural Economy of the Roman Empire*. Oxford: Oxford University Press.

—— forthcoming b. 'Régionalisme fiscal dans l'Égypte romaine: Le cas des terres limnitiques mendésiennes', in F. de Angelis (ed.), *Proceedings of the Conference Regionalism and Globalism in Antiquity*. Leuven: Peeters.

Bonneau, D. 1964. *La crue du Nil, divinité égyptienne, à travers mille ans d'histoire*. Paris: Klincksieck.

—— 1971. *Le fisc et le Nil*. Paris: Cujas.

—— 1987. 'Les hommes et le Nil dans l'antiquité', in A. de Réparaz (ed.), *L'eau et les hommes en Méditerranée*. Paris: Centre National de la Recherche Scientifique, 187–98.

—— 1993. *Le régime administratif de l'eau du Nil dans l'Égypte grecque, romaine et byzantine*. Leiden: Brill.

Bousquet, B. 1996. *Tell-Douch et sa région: Géographie d'une limite de milieu à une frontière d'Empire*. Cairo: Institut Français d'Archéologie Orientale.

Bowman, A. K. 2009. 'Quantifying Egyptian Agriculture', in A. K. Bowman and A. I. Wilson (eds), *Quantifying the Roman Economy: Methods and Problems*. Oxford: Oxford University Press, 177–204.

—— forthcoming. 'Agricultural Production and Consumption in Egypt', in A. K. Bowman and A. I. Wilson (eds), *The Agricultural Economy of the Roman Empire*. Oxford: Oxford University Press.

—— and E. Rogan (eds) 1999. *Agriculture in Egypt from Pharaonic to Modern Times*. Oxford: British Academy.

—— and A. I. Wilson (eds) forthcoming. *The Agricultural Economy of the Roman Empire: Methods and Problems*. Oxford: Oxford University Press.

Brewer, D., and R. F. Friedman. 1990. *Fish and Fishing in Ancient Egypt*. Cairo: American University in Cairo Press.

Brun, J. P. 2004. *Archéologie du vin et de l'huile dans l'Empire romain*. Paris: Errance.

Clavel-Lévêque, M., and E. Hermon (eds) 2004. *Espaces intégrés et ressources naturelles dans l'Empire romain*. Besançon: Presses Universitaires de Franche-Comté.

Crawford, D. J. 1971. *Kerkeosiris: An Egyptian Village in the Ptolemaic Period*. Cambridge: Cambridge University Press.

—— 1976. 'Imperial Estates', in M. Finley (ed.), *Studies in Roman Property*. Cambridge: Cambridge University Press, 35–70.

de Meulenaere, H. 1976. 'Mendes in Antiquity', in E. Swan Hall and B. V. Bothmer (eds), *Mendes II*. Warminster: Aris and Phillips, 14–190.

de Rodrigo, A. D. 2000. 'An Ancient Mendesian Industry', in Z. Hawass (ed.), *Egyptology at the Dawn of the Twenty-First Century*. Cairo: American University in Cairo Press, 455–9.

Dixon, M. 1969. 'A Note on Cereals in Ancient Egypt', in P. J. Ucko and G. W. Dimbleby (eds), *The Domestication and Exploitation of Plants and Animals*. London: Duckworth, 131–42.

Gamer-Wallert, I. 1970. *Fische und Fischkult im alten Ägypten*. Wiesbaden: Harrassowitz.
Garnsey, P. 1998. 'The Bean: Substance and Symbol', in W. Scheidel (ed.), *Cities, Peasants and Food in Classical Antiquity*. Cambridge: Cambridge University Press, 214–25.
Henein, N. 2010. *Pêche et chasse au lac Manzala*. Cairo: Institut Français d'Archéologie Orientale.
Hibbs, V. A. 1985. *The Mendes Maze*. New York: Garland.
Horden, P., and N. Purcell. 2000. *The Corrupting Sea*. Malden, Mass.: Blackwell.
Husselman, E. M. 1953. 'The Dovecotes of Karanis', *Transactions of the American Philological Association* 84: 81–91.
Kambitsis, S. 1985. *Le papyrus Thmouis 1: Colonnes 68–160*. Paris: Sorbonne.
Kehoe, D. P. 1992. *Management and Investment on Estates in Roman Egypt during the Early Empire*. Bonn: Habelt.
Leclère, F. 2008. *Les villes de Basse Égypte au Ier millénaire av. J. C.* Cairo: Institut Français d'Archéologie Orientale.
Manning, J. G. 2003. *Land and Power in Ptolemaic Egypt: The Structure of Land Tenure*. Cambridge: Cambridge University Press.
Martin, V. 1967. 'Un document administratif du nome de Mendès', *Studien zur Paläographie und Papyruskunde* 17: 9–48.
Meeks, D. 1973. 'Le nom du dauphin et le poisson de Mendès', *Revue d'Égyptologie* 25: 209–16.
Montet, P. 1957. *Géographie de l'Égypte ancienne*, vol. 1. Paris: Klincksieck.
Moreno García, J. C. (ed.) 2005. *L'agriculture institutionnelle en Égyte ancienne*. Lille: CRIPEL 25.
Parássoglou, G. M. 1978. *Imperial Estates in Roman Egypt*. Amsterdam: Hakkert.
Rathbone, D. W. 1991. *Economic Rationalism and Rural Society in Third-Century A.D. Egypt*. Cambridge: Cambridge University Press.
Redford, D. B. 1994. 'Some Observations on the Northern and North-Eastern Delta in the Late Predynastic Period', in B. M. Bryan and D. Lorton (eds), *Essays in Egyptology in Honor of Hans Goedicke*. San Antonio, Tex.: van Siclen, 201–10.
—— 1995. 'The Fifth Season of Excavation at Mendes', *Akhenaton Temple Project Newsletter* 1995/4: 1–3.
—— 2004. *Excavations at Mendes*, vol. 1. Leiden: Brill.
Rowlandson, J. 1996. *Landowners and Tenants in Roman Egypt*. Oxford: Clarendon Press.
—— 1999. 'Agricultural Tenancy and Village Society in Roman Egypt', in A. Bowman and E. Rogan (eds), *Agriculture in Egypt from Pharaonic to Modern Times*. Oxford: British Academy, 139–58.
Sahrhage, D. 1998. *Fischgang und Fischkult im altem Ägypten*. Mainz: von Zabern.
Sandy, D. B. 1989. *The Production and Use of Vegetable Oils in Ptolemaic Egypt*. Atlanta: Scholars Press.
Schnebel, M. 1925. *Die Landwirtschaft im hellenistischen Aegypten*. Munich: Beck.
Schubert, P. 2007. *Philadelphie: Un village égyptien en mutation entre le IIe et le IIIe siècle ap. J.-C.* Basel: Schwabe.
Thanheiser, U. 1992. 'Plant Remains from Minshat Abu Omar: First Impressions', in E. C. M. Van den Brink (ed.), *The Nile Delta in Transition*. Cairo: Brink, 167–70.
Thompson, D. J. 1999. 'Irrigation and Drainage in the Early Ptolemaic Fayum', in A. K. Bowman and E. Rogan (eds), *Agriculture in Egypt from Pharaonic to Modern Times*. Oxford: Oxford University Press, 107–38.
Wallace, S. L. 1938. *Taxation in Egypt from Augustus to Diocletian*. New York: Greenwood.

CHAPTER 3

MANUFACTURE, TRADE, AND THE ECONOMY*

MATT GIBBS

THIS chapter considers the nature of manufacture, trade, and the economy in Egypt during the first three centuries of Roman rule. The human element of trade and manufacture is considered here, in combination with an overview of the organization of labour and production. The chapter also considers the markets within and beyond the province, which affected the movement of information, people, and goods.

Two issues should be considered at the outset, given that they have, in the past, directly impinged on the study of the economy of Roman Egypt. The first is the supposed uniqueness of Egypt, often stressed in earlier studies; this seems largely based on the idea that Egypt was not a typical Roman province (whatever that may be), and that it was peripheral to the imperial economic structure. As Bagnall has recently noted (2005: 188), this view can no longer stand. The argument has been significantly weakened, not only by the discovery of similar forms of ancient documentation in other parts of the empire (e.g. Bowman and Thomas 1994; Cotton, Cockle, and Millar 1995; Koenen 1996; Pollard 2000: 1, 9–11), but also by the use of papyri to consider significant issues in the broader context of the Roman economy (e.g. Rathbone 1989; Bagnall 2005). The second issue concerns the difficulties arising from the enduring myth of the unchanging character of agriculture in Egypt, which severely hampers the recognition—and the study—of periods of significant economic change (Bowman and Rogan 1999: 1; Rathbone 2007: 698).

It should be no surprise that these factors are occasionally compounded by problems with the papyri: the primary form of evidence that contain the majority of our economic data. The published corpus of papyrological material (including ostraca) provides us with evidence that can be used to study the economy of Roman Egypt, which also admits to quantification. Even here, however, there are problems. Abundant as they may be, the papyri are skewed both chronologically and geographically, providing less evidence for the late Ptolemaic and early

* I should like to thank Colin Adams, Jennifer Cromwell, Jitse Dijkstra, Georgy Kantor, Ben Kelly, Pauline Ripat, and Conor Whately for their advice and helpful comments.

Roman periods than for the early Ptolemaic and later Roman periods. Moreover, references to certain areas, most notably the Delta—the region where both Alexandria and Egypt's second Mediterranean port, Pelusium, were situated—are conspicuously sparse (Bowman 2009: 178; Habermann 1998: 144–60). The consequence is, then, that constructing a picture of economic life in the communities of Roman Egypt—from the villages to the *metropoleis*—is problematic. Despite these problems, the gaps in the evidence may, at least to some degree, be modelled to allow historians to build approximations (Bagnall 2009: 206), and recent work on carbonized papyri does provide data for communities in the Delta (see Chapter 2). Unfortunately, the archaeology of the Roman period in Egypt, often central to the study of patterns of trade, remains in its infancy; until the late twentieth century, none of the nome capitals or Greek cities of Egypt had been subject to a full-scale excavation. More recently, the increase in both excavations and surveys has yielded an abundance of new material, most notably from the Delta and the Eastern Desert regions, with particular reference to manufacture and trade: Berenike, Myos Hormos, and Pelusium have been subjected to several investigations since the 1990s with significant results (e.g. Grzymski et al. 1994; Sidebotham and Wendrich 2000; Abdal-Maqsoud, Taba'i, and Grossmann 2001; Peacock et al. 2006).

The Economy of Roman Egypt

Tradesmen, their trades, and manufacture had already had a lengthy history in Egypt prior to Octavian's victory at Actium and the subsequent fall of the Ptolemaic dynasty. The Ptolemies (323–30 BCE) had inherited a country that was already active in the Mediterranean basin, and had been for some time. During the Saite and Persian periods (650–332 BCE), Egypt had already begun to transform and adapt to the changing political and economic climate, with long-distance trade and an ever-increasing focus on the Mediterranean (Manning 2007: 442, 458).

With the annexation of Egypt, the Roman administration introduced several changes, modifying the remnants of the Ptolemaic administration and its interventionist methods (Rathbone 2000b: 52; Bagnall 2005: 198). These changes, however, appear to have been based on the Ptolemaic agrarian economic framework. The economy of early Roman Egypt was already integrated to a significant degree because of these earlier fiscal structures; this integration developed further during the early first century CE, and, importantly for our purposes here, appears to have allowed a free market (Temin 2001: 169–81; Rathbone 2007: 712). Political unity and peace, achieved through Roman conquest, and movements that attempted to standardize the legal and judicial system, all stimulated the economy (Woolf 1992: 290; Rathbone 2007: 712). The institutional, commercial, and behavioural impact of integration into the empire, and the consequent success of this economic environment, was perhaps reflected in aggregate and per capita growth during the first two centuries. There may have been some aggregate decline in production following the Antonine plague, but renewed, albeit differentiated, per capita growth—attributed largely to internal socio-economic changes—appears to have continued afterwards (Rathbone 2007: 700; but note Kehoe 1997: 16; cf. Alston 2002: 346–60; Kehoe 2007: 559; Rathbone 2007: 705–6 and n. 28).

Such major economic trends were accompanied by social and cultural developments but the most important change was in the land tenure system. The Ptolemaic system was severely modified, and land was turned over to private ownership on a much greater scale, falling into line with patterns in the rest of the eastern empire (Rowlandson 1996: 68–9, 102–201; Bagnall 2005: 198; Frier and Kehoe 2007: 141). In addition to ownership, individuals could increase their earning potential by renting land, and as a result, for landowners in Roman Egypt, tenancy played an important role, particularly where arable land seems to have been concerned (Rowlandson 1996: 202–79). Typically, however, capital-intensive fruit and wine crops were managed directly, with larger operations run for profit. The rural areas were also home to 'mid-range' landowners, who appear to have operated well above the level of subsistence, and who were often very closely linked to the operations of the urban economy. Moreover, the productive capacity of the agricultural sector during the Roman period seems to have been high, but notably also appears to have risen during the first three centuries CE.

By the Roman period, the burgeoning trade had resulted in permanent and semi-permanent markets at which crafts- and tradesmen gathered to sell their wares (*SB* XVI 12695 (143 CE)), while the state administration used some of the products made by them to supply their legions in other Egypt and other provinces. Beyond this, however, the Roman state's attitude to trade appears to have been impartial (Rathbone 2007: 717). Its interest was in the revenues that could be drawn from tax duties and licence fees that replaced Ptolemaic monopolies, as well as imports and exports; imports were taxed highly at frontiers (25 per cent in kind), but internally, customs duties were low (Cottier 2010: 147–8; compare Sijpesteijn 1987 and Cottier 2005 generally) Local retail networks appear to have flourished into regional systems of distribution, underpinned by the Nile itself and overland routes, which were part of a system of transport (Adams 2007: 17–46). Land routes connected imperial concerns in the east of the province, such as the mines and quarries, and also linked the Nile Valley to the Red Sea ports, where, among a huge variety of commodities, traders also dealt in 'luxury' goods (Sidebotham 1986: 13–47; Rathbone 2000a, 2003; Adams 2007: 22–40). These routes also connected imperial interests in the west of the province: the Oases, where olive oil was produced, were linked to the Nile, and this allowed the entire province to operate as a collective unit. Moreover, these routes, and the associated attempt to suppress banditry (Alston 1995: 81–6; McGing 1998; Wolff 2003: 157–76), facilitated the movement of products and producers, allowing trade associations, their members, and individual traders opportunities outside their own communities and regions. In fact, by the mid-first century CE, Egypt had become famous for its linen production, which was apparently in great demand in Eastern trade, and later for the cultivation of flax in the late third and fourth centuries CE (Plin. *HN* 19.13–14; SHA *Gallienus* 6.4; Rowlandson 1996: 236–40; Mayerson 1997: 202–3 nn. 11–12; Erdkamp 2005: 102; Rathbone 2007: 707). This economic environment provided a setting in which traders and craftsmen could flourish.

Manufacture and the Organization of Production

A vast number of trades and crafts are attested in the papyri, in both the villages and the cities, including professions and service occupations that appear in other parts of the Roman empire: from carpenters, farmers, and grocers, through to bankers, prostitutes, and wet-nurses, although textile workers dominate the papyrological record.

Tradesmen may have worked independently, with other family members, and with other unrelated workers; in fact, different trading activities in the family are well known from later pre-industrial societies (Mitterauer 1984), and, not surprisingly, can be seen in Roman Egypt (e.g. *BGU* I 115 = *W Chr.* 203 (189 CE); Wipszycka 1965: 33–4). This was not, however, always the case: the collectives that operated around the Red Sea were made up of family members and unrelated workers. An example can be found in the archive of Nikanor, which concerns a collective engaged in the transportation of commodities between the Nile Valley and the Red Sea. The ostraca indicate that the business included Nikanor himself, his two brothers Philostratos and Apollos, Nikanor's two sons Miresis and Peteharpocrates; two other individuals involved—Isidora, daughter of Menodoros, and Peteasmephis, son of Herakles—were probably unrelated (*O Petr.* 244 (36 CE), 208 (44 CE), 224 (6 CE); cf. Sidebotham 1986: 83 and nn. 17–18, 176–7; Young 2001: 64 and n. 208; Adams 2007: 221 n. 3).

Moreover, formal associations of traders and craftsmen certainly did exist in Roman Egypt (see San Nicolò 1972: 1.66–194; Gibbs 2008; Venticinque 2009), although participation in these collectives appears to have largely been voluntary, at least until after the Diocletianic reforms, when compulsory membership may have been introduced (Łajtar 1991: 63 n. 12; Fikhman 1994: 25–6; Carrié 2002: 315–18). It is worth noting that pressure could be put upon independent tradesmen not only by association members, but also by particular statutes included in their ordinance; for instance, the *halopolai* (salt merchants) of Tebtunis refused to sell salt to other merchants (*P Mich.* V 245 (47 CE)). In Roman Egypt these groups offered members both social and religious opportunities, from holding symposia and dinners through to the celebration of births and contributions towards funeral costs, and also provided sureties in case members had legal difficulties (e.g. *P Mich.* V 243 (14–37 CE); V 245 (47 CE); *P Ryl.* II 94 (14–37 CE)). These collectives offered economic benefits to their members: as unified groups, they dealt with state officials, and it was often through these associations that both the *laographia* (the poll tax) and the *cheironaxia* (trade taxes) were paid collectively (*P Mich.* V 245 (47 CE); *P Tebt.* II 359 (127 CE)). They also appear to have arranged licence fees and trading areas, and played a role in providing and perhaps organizing state requisitions (*P Ryl.* II 189 (128 CE); *BGU* VII 1564 (138 CE); VII 1572 (139 CE); perhaps, *P Oxy.* XIX 2230 (119 CE)).

Despite the relative wealth of evidence for traders, craftsmen, and their institutions, even taken alongside the data from the available censuses and poll tax lists, any serious quantification of those individuals involved in professional trades and crafts is difficult. The scale of manufacture, production, and trade, however, is illustrated in several other ways, although all seem to have varied considerably owing to constraints such as state interest, technological capability, and the availability of raw materials. Nevertheless, much can be gained from the papyrological record: a mid-third century CE document (probably a customs register) from the Oxyrhynchite nome illustrates that, over a period of five days in the month of Hathyr, 1,956 items of clothing (predominantly children's chitons) were exported from the *metropolis* or from the nome itself (*P Oxy. Hels.* 40 (*BL* VIII 274–5; X 157–8); van Minnen 1986, 1987: 78; Bagnall 1995: 80–1). These data may well suggest an annual figure of 80,000–100,000 pieces of cloth exported from Oxyrhynchus, or (more likely) the Oxyrhynchite nome, during a period when the activity at the market in the Serapeum of Oxyrhynchus was apparently close to its slowest point (van Minnen 1986: 92; see especially Bagnall 1995: 80–1, who raises important questions about this papyrus). Comparable evidence is found in *O Wilck.* II 150: in the month of Mesore 129 CE, when 2,000 jars (or flasks) were exported from the Theban region (cf. *W Chr.* 291 = *O Wilck.* II 43 (95–6 CE) where 1,500 jars were produced).

Some cities and towns had quarters that were named after types of craftsman, trader, or area of production: Oxyrhynchus had quarters apparently named after gooseherds and shepherds (*P Oxy.* XIV 1634 (222 CE); I 99 (55 CE)), while Arsinoe and Karanis had linen workshops' quarters (*P Fay.* 59 (178 CE); *P Tebt.* II 321 (147 CE); *BGU* XV 2471 (*c.*158 CE); *SB* VI 9554 2c (147 CE)). Particular villages may have specialized in one type of commodity or product that could then be sold in larger communities (van Minnen 1987: 77), and there are some suggestive data, albeit in a register from the earlier Ptolemaic period: here the *tapiduphantai* (carpet weavers) form one of the largest groups, but are only found in two villages (*P Count* 3v iii 58 (229 BCE)). This may well suggest centralized production carried out in community workshops (Clarysse and Thompson 2006: 1.112), but definitive evidence, unfortunately, remains elusive: besides the names relating to city quarters or markets, or references to loose groupings of craftsmen, there is little to suggest that specific concentrations of trades were more prominent in specific areas or communities (Alston 2002: 155). Consequently, determining the extent of this productivity and whether it was aimed at external markets or internal ones (particularly given the relevant custom duties) is very difficult, but certainly some of the goods sold abroad, like linen and papyrus, were likely produced in the nomes of the *chora*.

Traders and craftsmen may have leased collective premises to produce, and perhaps even sell, their wares. A series of third-century documents from Oxyrhynchus provides an example where three potters leased out a pottery and the necessary equipment for one or two years (*P Oxy.* L 3595 (243 CE); L 3596 (240–55 CE); L 3597 (260 CE); Cockle 1981; cf. Mayerson 2000). For associations of traders and craftsmen, using collective premises would not only cut costs and facilitate production, but would also provide a location for the more social aspects of collective life that are attested in their regulations (e.g. *P Mich.* V 244 (43 CE); V 245 (47 CE)). Unfortunately, there is little definitive evidence for this, apart from a mid-third-century instance of a collective of *elaiourgoi* (oil manufacturers) who apparently owned a *thesauros* (a storehouse), probably some form of storage room or warehouse (*P Ryl.* II 110 (259 CE); cf. San Nicolò 1972: 2.144–5). On the other hand, the case of the *halopolai* of mid-first-century CE Tebtunis suggests an interesting, and rather novel, alternative: that goods produced or purchased for resale by these groups could have been kept at the premises of a nominated member. Gypsum purchased by any member of the *halopolai* was to be kept at the 'place' of Orseus, from where it would later be resold once 'he takes it outside and sells it' (*P Mich.* V 245.31–4 (47 CE)).

There are also several examples of linen *ergasteria* (workshops) in Egypt: one from the late second century appears in a text containing judicial proceedings and a petition of Isidorus; he was a foreman weaver who employed a number of workers in his *ergasterion*, probably in Alexandria (*P Oxy.* XXII 2340; Jones 1960: 189; van Minnen 1987: 47; Rathbone 2007: 708). The second appears in accounts concerning the estate of Valerius Titanianus in the Fayum during the mid-third century; the estate itself seems to have leased out a number of weaving *ergasteria*, often to several weavers (*P Mich.* XI 620; cf. el-Fakharani 1983: 178–81; Rathbone 1991: 166–74). Although it is worth noting that, in this case, weaving was a secondary economic pursuit that took place in the background of agricultural activity, these large workshops broadly reflect the *Verlagssystem*—the 'putting-out system'—through which a large-scale merchant provided individual artisans with materials and paid them for each garment they produced. In this system, the workers had no direct contact with customers, and did not play any role in acquiring raw materials (Kehoe 2007: 566). There is, however, not a great deal of evidence for this type of arrangement in Egypt, except perhaps the earlier Ptolemaic monopolies (which are unlikely to have been 'full' monopolies in any sense).

Most commonly, production would have occurred in individual workshops (particularly in the case of the textile industry), and these formed the basic units of production (Kehoe 2007: 561, 565; Rathbone 2007: 708). Most trades required the cooperation of few, if any, hired or independent workers. There are several examples of these individual workshops and premises: the brothers Petesouchos and Sochotes leased a bakery from Herakleides for two years (*P Mich.* X 586 (*c.*30 CE)). A second-century petition may indicate that Heras, a weaver, had a domestic workshop (*P Oxy.* X 1272 (144 CE)). In the third century, a weaver contracted a lease for two-thirds of a house in Herakleopolis from a former *agoranomos* (who was also a *bouleutes*) for 160 drachmas, with provisions not only to restrict weaving activity to the pylon (gateway, perhaps courtyard) of the house, but also to limit the establishment to three looms, or four if the tenant was making garments for his own use (*SPP* XX 53 (246 CE)).

The available evidence for the organization of production in Roman Egypt also provides invaluable information for the division of labour. There are numerous divisions of labour in ancient and modern society (skill, age, gender, and occupation), and divisions of trade and occupation are usually obvious in the papyri. References to various professions and their activities are common, and more general categories such as gender, status, and age can also be found.

Women were involved in many areas of business and trade, and occasionally worked in what appear to have been male-dominated occupations: Aurelia Libouke worked as a weaver in the Arsinoite nome (*SB* XVIII 13305 (271 CE)), and Aurelia Cyrilla was a practising member of the *entaphiastai* (undertakers), as was her future husband (*P Oxy.* XLIX 3500 (third century CE)). They were subject to the relevant taxes upon the trades that they practised, although they were free from other liabilities such as the poll tax: for instance, a female weaver from Oxyrhynchus can be seen paying the relevant trade tax to the *nomarch* (*PSI* IX 1055b (265 CE)).

The picture concerning slavery in Roman Egypt is rather unusual. Slaves and freedmen were present in startlingly low numbers: the percentage of slaves in the non-Alexandrian population has been estimated at *c.*10 per cent (Biezunska-Malowist 1977: 156–8), and the percentage of slaves in the population of the villages and *metropoleis* has been posited at 8–8.5 per cent or 13–13.4 per cent (Hombert and Préaux 1952: 13, 170; Bagnall and Frier 1994: 70–1 n. 69). The exploitation of the lower classes, through tenancy and renting, gave landowners a much more effective return (Lewis 1999: 57). The relatively small number of slaves was found mainly in households, where they supplemented the domestic workforce (Biezunska-Malowist 1977: 158; Rathbone 1991: 89–91; Bagnall and Frier 1994: 49; Bowman 1996: 130–1), and occasionally appear as apprentices (*P Oxy.* XIV 1647 (late second century CE); *BGU* IV 1021 (third century CE)). The small number of slaves meant fewer freedmen, but they do appear as traders as well as manual labourers: an apprenticeship contract from Oxyrhynchus shows that Thonis, freedman of Harpocration, was trading as a *ktenistes* (perhaps a wool carder or a hairdresser) (*P Oxy.* XLI 2977 (239 CE)), and Dioscoros, freedman of Sarapion, also of Oxyrhynchus, notified the city scribe Diogenes that he was going to begin practising as a *ergates potamou* (river worker) (*P Oxy.* X 1263 (128–9 CE)).

There are numerous examples of children under the age of 14, whether slave or freeborn, participating in trade as active workers and apprentices. Apprenticeship was not uncommon in Roman Egypt, and was, by all accounts, of interest to the state administration (*P Oxy.* VII 1029 (107 CE); *SB* XX 15023 (second century CE); cf. Bülow-Jacobsen 1989: 125–6). Training in skilled crafts may have been largely hereditary, as in pre-industrial societies generally, but there are several instances of minors being contracted as apprentices outside the family (*P Oxy.* II 322 (36 CE); II 275 (66 CE); IV 724 (155 CE); IV 725 (183 CE); *P Tebt.* II 442 (113 CE); II 385 (117 CE)). In Roman Egypt, as elsewhere, apprenticeships were carried out under the direction of a skilled trades- or craftsman, whether freeborn or slave. The master tradesman could apparently have more than one apprentice in his charge at any one time (*P Oxy.* IV 725 13–15 (183 CE)), and although in several cases masters had to furnish little besides training (*P Oxy.* IV 724 (155 CE); *BGU* IV 1021 (third century CE)), there were certainly occasions when they were required to feed and clothe their apprentices (*P Wisc.* I 4 (53 CE); *P Tebt.* II 385 (117 CE)). Apprentices were, however, liable for trade taxes, and these costs could be paid by their masters, by their parents or guardians, or even by themselves (*P Oxy.* XIV 1647 (late second century CE); *P Tebt.* II 384 (10 CE); II 385 (117 CE); *SB* X 10236 (36 CE); *P Oxy.* II 275 (66 CE); XXXVIII 2875 (third century CE)).

From the contracts it appears that any of the parties involved could seek these positions. In terms of economic rationality, at the heart of the system of apprenticeship there may have been vested interests, most notably in relation to production and relative independence. Certainly, in instances where slave minors were apprenticed, both the slave owner and the slave had a vested interest: the slave owner would profit from the skills and knowledge the slave acquired, and the slave could benefit from a form of training that might lead to relative independence, which would be of direct benefit if they were freed (*SB* XVIII 13305 (271 CE); *P Oxy.* XLI 2977 (239–40 CE)). In cases where minors were free, the notion of economic independence (or perhaps the idea of 'good employment') becomes much more significant. The system of apprenticeship may also have increased productive output, benefiting the master tradesman: a large number of apprentices, especially once partially trained, offered a cost advantage through the number of additional workers, at a lower cost than fully trained tradesmen; presumably, in these instances the master provided the apprentice with training in return for a gain in output. Moreover, on occasion these contracts note 'compensation' for the master tradesperson, when elements of the contract were not met by the parties involved (*P Oxy.* II 275 (66 CE); *P Tebt.* II 385 (117 CE); cf. perhaps *P Mich.* V 322 (48–56 CE)). Finally, there are examples of contracts in which the master was paid for taking on an apprentice: according to *P Oxy.* IV 724 (155 CE), Panechotes, an ex-*cosmetes* of Oxyrhynchus, apprenticed his slave Chaerammon to Apollonius, a shorthand writer, for two years; Apollonius was apparently paid 120 drachmas in three equal instalments.

Several observations can be made regarding 'specialization' resulting from the division of labour in the production process (see Wilson 2008). Specialization may refer to a change in production in response to consumer demand, as tradesmen could shift their efforts to the production of this item alone. This differentiation of craftsman by product can result in several different specific crafts falling under one more general trade. Specialization, however, can also denote the differentiation in the process of production: the production process can be split, creating specialists in the process, as opposed to the final product: here, workers 'specialize' according to their method of production (Weber 1947: 225; Harris 2002: 70–81, esp. 70–1). Both notions of specialization appear to have existed in Roman Egypt, but the available data suggest that differentiation in the production process was the more common, and most often in the fields of textile production and metalworking.

Textile production had several specializations that moved through the entire production process, from raw materials to finished goods: notable examples include the *eriokartes*, who was involved in both carding wool and shearing sheep (*P Mil. Vogl.* IV 212r v (109 CE)); the *bapheis*, who dyed textiles (*P Tebt.* II 287 (161–9 CE)); the specialist trouser makers, the *brakarioi* (e.g. *P Oxy.* X 1341 (4th century CE)); the *gnapheis*, who fulled finished garments and refurbished and washed old clothes (*P Lond.* II 286 (88–9 CE); *P Phil.* 1 (103–24 CE)); the *linouphos*, a weaver who specialized in linen (*P Oxy.* XXII 2340 (192 CE); XII 1414 (270–5 CE)); the *sakkoplokoi*, who produced sacks from coarse textile (*P Giss.* I 10 (118 CE)); the *eriemporoi*, or *eriopolai*, who acted as wool merchants and were presumably responsible for the supply and sale of the final product (*P Fouad* I 77 (second century CE); *P Mich.* II 123r vi 25 (45–6 CE); *SB* XX 15024 (second century CE); *P Giss.* I 10 (118 CE)); and finally, the *himatiopolai*, dealers who traded in textiles (*P Oxy.* XIX 2230 (119 CE); *P Amh.* II 76 (second/third century CE)). There are also rare examples of single individuals involved in several specialized trades: one individual notes that he was not only a *linouphos*, but also a *histonarches*, an *orthouphos*, and a *linepsos* (*BGU* XV 2471 (158 CE); cf. *P Bub.* I 2 i 2 (224 CE)).

In metalworking, workers were typically divided into specialist fields according to the metal they worked with: copper- and bronze-smiths (*SB* XVI 12648 ii 26 (338 CE); *P Laur.* IV 155 (283–92? CE); cf. *BL* VIII 167) and ironworkers are all attested (*P Oxy.* I 84 (316 CE)). The papyri also refer to specialists for precious metals, such as goldsmiths and silversmiths (*P Mert.* II 73 18 (163–4 CE); *P Giss. Apoll.* 6 (117 CE; cf. *BL* V 85; X 79)). Furthermore, there is evidence for specialists who manufactured specific metal products, notably nail-smiths and locksmiths (*BGU* IV 1028 (second century CE); *P Lips.* I 3 i 10 (256 CE)).

These forms of specialization in the division of labour are important, particularly from an economic standpoint, as they show that labour processes were split into separate elements. The particular tasks and roles increase the productivity of labour, and generally it seems that the growth of a more complex division of labour is closely related to the growth of total output and trade.

Trade: Markets, Transfers of Information, and Mobility

The evidence for markets in Roman Egypt is relatively plentiful: they could apparently be found at Ptolemais Euergetis, Ptolemais Hermiou, Tebtunis, Alexandrou Nesos, at Philadelphia, Theadelphia, Soknopaiou Nesos, Arsinoe, Kerkesoucha, Oxyrhynchus, and perhaps at Karanis (van Lith 1974: 151–3; Rea 1982; Pintaudi 1987: 46–7; Litinas 1997; Alston 1998). At the end of the third and through the fourth century, we have evidence that animals were traded at markets in the Oxyrhynchite and Upper Cynopolite nome (Jördens 1995, esp. 49–52; Adams 2007: 91–134, esp. 94–9). Of course, markets were not the only medium in which crafts- and tradesmen could sell their produce. Accounts of personal and institutional expenditure, such as those of Kronion, the supervisor of the record office of Tebtunis in the mid-first century, or those of the estate owner Sarapion in the early second century, show a daily routine of small-scale purchases for cash that may suggest the existence of permanent local retail networks built not only on the back of markets, but also on smaller retail premises (Rathbone 2007: 709 n. 38; *P Mich.* II 123v (45–6 CE); II 127 (45–7 CE); *P Sarap.* 55 (128 CE); 56 (128 CE); 66 (90–133 CE); 68 (90–133 CE); cf. Bandi 1937: 382–419). These 'shops' are attested in the papyri, but appear more often in the cities and larger villages: in Oxyrhynchus in 222 CE, an individual registered a vegetable seller's shop in Broad Street (*P Oxy.* XII 1461; cf. perhaps *SPP* XX 53 (246 CE)), and in a series of directions from Hermopolis, there is an isolated reference to a basket-weaving shop (*P Oxy.* XXXIV 2719 (third century CE); cf. generally *Dig.* 14.3.5.4, 9; Hor. *S.* 2.3.225–30).

Nevertheless, markets were not simply places that allowed people to sell their goods and services, or to purchase necessary materials and products. From an economic perspective, the purpose of these concentrations of trade is clear: they facilitated 'market' transactions, such as the production of goods, transfers from buyer to seller, and guarantees of quality (Frier and Kehoe 2007: 119 and n. 21). In this context, sellers and buyers were not only able to operate in a competitive setting, but were also able to establish a link in the network of relationships that would arise in regular markets. Given that these links were based on patterns of trust and reliance that were, in turn, based on prior experiences, it seems entirely possible that traders and craftsmen who visited both recurring and temporary markets had access to a vast network of links around the province. Consequently, the cultivation of long-term relational contacts may well have been more important than simply finding the lowest price (Frier and Kehoe 2007: 119; *P Oxy.* XLI 2983–4 (second/third century CE)).

The Nile provided a medium and focus of a network of communications that facilitated the movement and mobility of individuals, information, and items (Bagnall 2006: 340, 345). These networks, and the information carried within them, were central to the continued existence and integration of the markets. Since the networks depended almost entirely on reliable flows of information, judging their place in Roman Egypt requires some consideration of how information about 'prices' moved. These transfers of information, products, and services involved movement of the traders themselves or written or verbal accounts concerning market conditions through the networks to which the traders belonged (e.g. *BGU* XVI 2611 (10 BCE); *SB* XII 11127 = *P Mich. Mchl.* 25 (88 CE); *P Oslo* II 49 (second century CE); *SB* XVI 12559 (155 CE)). Related are issues of mobility (movement around the nomes) and the transfer of money (and actual credit or 'money').

To deal with the latter issue first, it is generally accepted that by pre-industrial standards Egypt enjoyed an extensively monetized economy in the Ptolemaic period (von Reden 2006, 2007; Manning 2008), a situation that increased during the Roman period (Rathbone 1991: 318–30, 393, 397–8; 2007: 714; Kehoe 1997: 16; van Minnen 2008). The economy nonetheless remained agrarian in nature. Agricultural products, such as wheat, were still used to store wealth and could operate as a medium of exchange, although this appears to have occurred mainly in smaller communities in terms of land taxation in kind, specific payments (notably as rations for long-term employees on private estates), and as deposits in state granaries (Rathbone 1991: 307–18; 2007: 714 n. 55). Even here, these payments in kind were often combined with payments in cash. This fluidity should come as no surprise: Ptolemaic coinage continued to be used, and the Roman administration clearly saw benefits to maintaining it. The taxation scheme introduced by the Romans, itself a considerable source of revenue for the state, seems to have presumed a significant liquidity at all levels of society (Rathbone 2007: 718). So cash, as coinage, became a prime lubricant in local and regional economies, flowing between village, town, and *metropolis* (Bowman 1996: 116; Christiansen 2004: 138), facilitating the exchange of commodities.

Moreover, the credit and banking system illustrated by the papyri allowed the transfer of credit and 'money' between buyer and seller, and individual and state (e.g. *P Oxy.* XLI 2983 (second/third century CE)). Typically, the existence of a credit system requires a high amount of reliable means of payment available in cash on demand (Christiansen 2004: 138), but credit transactions could, of course, take place without the physical movement of coinage (Howgego 2009: 288). A system of private and public, or state, banks—the latter were responsible for the collection and payment of sums due from or to the state—could be found in major centres of the province, as well as villages (Andreau 1999: 32; Bogaert 2000: 135–6, 213–14; Rathbone 2007: 715; Geens 2008: 134). These phenomena were not solely urban developments; the rural economy too was highly monetized and closely tied to the *metropoleis* and towns through leasing, credit, and marketing (Bagnall 2005: 198).

The other issue concerns the movement, or mobility, of crafts- and tradesmen in Egypt during the Roman period. Professional traders and craftsmen not only moved around their own communities to work, but also travelled across their own nomes practising their trade: for instance, in the mid-first century, the apprentice Harmiysis was required to accompany his master everywhere 'around the nome' (*P Mich.* V 355 11 (48–56 CE); cf. Wipszycka 1965: 21 n. 36; van Minnen 1987: 69–70). Even movement between nomes can be found: in the mid-third century, Aurelius son of Asklas, from Athribis, offered his services for gilding part of the gymnasium in Antinoopolis (*P Köln* I 52 (263 CE), with *BL* VIII 155). Caracalla's edict from the early third century, concerning recent disturbances at Alexandria and calling for the removal of all 'Egyptians' from the city, may reveal a movement of *linouphoi* to Alexandria from other areas of Egypt, who had migrated perhaps for employment (*P Giss. Lit.* 6.3 = *Sel. Pap.* II 215 (*c.*215 CE); Buraselis 1995: 167 n. 5, 185).

Perhaps one of the most interesting, however, is the example of the donkey trader Aurelius Theodorus, apparently from Oxyrhynchus (cf. Aurelius Apollonius in Adams 2007: 94–6; *P Oxy.* XLIII 3143 (305 CE); *P Corn.* I 13 (311 CE); *P Oxy.* XLIII 3144 (313 CE); XLIII 3145 (early fourth century)). His movements, and the movement of the individuals with whom he conducted business, were perhaps dictated through the occurrences of animal markets in both Oxyrhynchus and the Upper Cynopolite nome. Theodorus' activity is noted in several texts. In one, Aurelius Ophelius, from the village of Isieion Kato in the Oxyrhynchite nome, records that he sold a young donkey to Theodorus for 5 talents and 1,000 drachmas (*P Oxy.* LXIX 4748 (307 CE)); a second, conceivably a donkey sale, records an agreement between Aurelius Severus, from Hermopolis, and Theodorus (*P Oxy.* LXIX 4749 (307 CE)); a third preserves a transaction in which Aurelius Horion, from the Hermopolite nome, sold a colt to Theodorus for 9 talents and 3,000 drachmas (*P Oxy.* LXIX 4752 (311 CE)); a fourth records Theodorus' purchase of a donkey (or an ass) from Aurelius Hierax, an inhabitant of a village in the Hermopolite nome, for 6 talents and 3,500 drachmas (*P Berl. Leihg.* I 21 (309 CE)); in a fifth, Theodorus purchased an ass for 10 talents and 4,000 drachmas, from a seller of the village of Penne in the Herakleopolite nome (*P Oxy.* XIV 1708 (311 CE)). All of the payments were apparently made in cash. Through his activities and movement, between several nomes and several markets, Theodorus and the individuals he did business with influenced the physical movement of money and goods.

Several ports that played a significant role in trade with the east were situated on the Red Sea coast: Ptolemy states that there were six (*Geog.* 4.5.8), although both the *Periplus Maris Erythraei* (1.19) and Strabo (17.1.45) note only two, Berenike and Myos Hormos. Trade with

Arabia and India continued throughout the first three centuries CE (Raschke 1978; Sidebotham 1986: 13–33; Young 2001: 24–122). Evidence for this, as well as the presence of Indians at Berenike and Myos Hormos, appears in the form of Tamil-Brahmi graffiti, and imports of pottery, beads of South Indian origin, gems, ivory, teak wood, textiles, and botanical remains, including spices such as peppercorns, coconut, and Job's tear (Salomon 1991; Mahadevan 1996; Cappers 1998, 2006; Begley and Tomber 1999; Wendrich et al. 2003, esp. 62–72; Tomber 2004, 2008: 71–87; Parker 2008: 147–202). Exports included gold and silver bullion (although it began as coinage), and, on occasion, wine and textiles (Rathbone 2007: 710). The magnitude of this trade is, perhaps, most strikingly observed in the mid-second-century 'Muziris' papyrus (*SB* XVIII 13167), which records the return cargo of one ship from India. After the requisite 25 per cent import duty in kind had been paid, the cargo's value was worth almost 7 million drachmas, and represents nearly 770,000 artabas of wheat (more than 23,000 tonnes), the product of over 75,000 arouras of land, which therefore amounts to almost 1 per cent of the productive arable land of Egypt in the mid-second century (Rathbone 2000a: 49). How unusual this particular cargo actually was is almost impossible to determine (see Whittaker 2004: 163–80); other maritime loans perhaps procured for similar voyages are much smaller (e.g. *SB* XIV 11850 = VI 9571 (149 CE), with *BL* VIII 375; the loan in this case was 47,160 drachmas). Earlier examples, however, suggest that similar journeys were made under the Ptolemies (*SB* III 7169 (second century BCE); Rathbone 2002: 181), and Strabo notes that merchants from Alexandria were sailing fleets between the Red Sea ports in Egypt, the Arabian Gulf, and India (2.5.12, 17.1.13). Even if Strabo exaggerates the scale of this activity, the Muziris papyrus certainly illustrates the potential of trade with India, but only the extremely wealthy would have been able to operate on this scale (Adams 2007: 229–30).

The city of Koptos gained a reputation as the *emporion* for the trade between Rome and India, and linked the Nile to Myos Hormos and Berenike. Here merchants and traders could first have the tax assessed on their respective shipments and then cleared through customs (Rathbone 2002: 184). This eastern trade not only brought to Koptos the interests of the richer financiers and merchants, but also generated employment for a variety of traders and craftsmen, albeit for some only on a seasonal basis: independent ship-owners, pilots, merchants, shipbuilders, and porters, alongside camel and donkey drivers and owners (*OGIS* II 674 = *IGR* I 1183; Rathbone 2002: 188–9, 191–2). One of the most important archives relating to Koptos concerns the commercial activities of the family of Nikanor. They were involved in transporting goods between Berenike, Myos Hormos, and Koptos, which appears to have been their base of operations (Adams 2007: 221–2). It is difficult to reconstruct the size of Nikanor's operation, but a recent estimate has suggested that it consisted of around thirty-six camels, or that he was able to hire additional animals to supplement his own when needed (Adams 2007: 222–3 with nn. 7 and 8). This represents a sizeable operation: the largest herd at Soknopaiou Nesos, an important village for the camel trade, had twenty-six animals (Jördens 1995: 66 n. 138; cf. Adams 2007: 106–9). Furthermore, the ostraca in the archive provide information about several individuals involved in trading activities in the ports, who held accounts with Nikanor; they were probably agents of landowners or merchants who lived in the Nile Valley or Alexandria. Roman citizens are also attested: four ostraca record deliveries made for the agents of Marcus Julius Alexander, brother of the future prefect of Egypt, Tiberius Julius Alexander (*O Petr.* 266 (43 CE); 267 (43 CE); 268 (44 CE); 271 (43/4 CE)), while another records a transaction between Nikanor and Tiberius Claudius Epaphroditus, who may have been a freedman of Claudius (*O Petr.* 290 (62 CE)).

Conclusion

It is worth noting from the outset that manufacture, production, and trade had a long history in Egypt, but the economy in which these processes operated, as well as those who worked in them, developed significantly in the Roman period. Although agrarian in nature, the economy was supplemented by manufacture, production, and trade, which could, and arguably did, flourish with socio-economic and cultural change. In this setting, crafts- and tradesmen worked either independently, in family groups, in loose collectives, or even in more formal associations. Typically, smaller workshops formed the basic unit of production, although larger establishments are attested. Those involved, at least according to the evidence, were usually male, but the papyri indicate that both women and children—slave and free—played a role in production and manufacture, as did apprentices, working as general and eventually skilled workers, increasing productive output for little outlay.

Markets not only offered an environment in which commodities and wares were sold, but also provided a setting in which personal relationships and links to local and provincial networks could be exploited. Moreover, these networks likely played a role in the movement of crafts- and tradesmen locally and across the province, and this may well have caused a movement of information, money, products, and services between rural and urban communities. The ports on the east coast served as emporia for trade with Arabia and India, and, like the west of the province, were linked to the Nile through a transport system created to satisfy state concerns; nevertheless, trade appears to have flourished on the back of these interests. In the Nile Valley, Koptos played an important role in the transport of products between the Red Sea ports, Lower Egypt, and the Mediterranean coast, albeit on a seasonal basis. The majority of crafts- and tradesmen in these ports and Koptos may well have been Graeco-Egyptian, but foreign workers and agents are attested too.

In the broader context, although the Roman administration's attitude to manufacture and trade was largely impartial, its interest in facilitating the movement of goods and services (for instance, for the supply of the Roman army) provided not only a framework upon which trade and production was cultivated, but also indirect economic benefit for the state in the form of taxation. Once this system was in place, it was at the level of the market, borne on the backs of crafts- and tradesmen through manufacture, production, and trade, that one of the main stimuli to Egypt's economic development was carried: the *pax Romana* supported a Mediterranean-wide emporium, and created a demand for products that were both manufactured in, and transported through, Roman Egypt.

Suggested Reading

For a general survey of the economy in Roman Egypt, see Rathbone (2007). For Roman economic policy and trade on the Red Sea coast, Sidebotham (1986) remains the central text. For transport in Egypt, with reference to the economy, Adams (2007) is essential. On the *metropoleis* and concentrations of trade in them, see the relevant discussions in Alston

(2002) and earlier scholarship of Calderini and Daris (1935–2003: 3.203 and suppl. 1; Daris 1981). On women in Roman Egypt, with reference to non-agricultural professions, see van Minnen (1998) and the relevant parts of Rowlandson (1998); on apprenticeship, the recent scholarship by Bergamasco (1995, 1998 (with *P Kellis* I 19a appendix), 2004, 2006) replaces Johnson (1936), although the latter remains useful. For broader treatments of the economy in the Roman empire, Bowman and Wilson (2009) and the relevant chapters in Manning and Morris (2005) provide both specific treatments of Egypt and other Roman provinces, and aspects of the economy.

Bibliography

Abdal-Maqsoud, M., A. Taba'i, and P. Grossmann. 2001. 'New Discoveries in Pelusium (Tall al-Faramã), with a Contribution of H.-Chr. Noeske on the Coins Found at Pelusium', *Bulletin de la Société d'Archéologie Copte* 40: 11–34.

Adams, C. E. P. 2007. *Land Transport in Roman Egypt: A Study of Economics and Administration in a Roman Province.* Oxford: Oxford University Press.

Alston, R. 1995. *Soldier and Society in Roman Egypt: A Social History.* London: Routledge.

—— 1998. 'Trade and the City in Roman Egypt', in H. Parkins and C. Smith (eds), *Trade, Traders and the Ancient City.* London: Routledge, 168–202.

—— 2002. *The City in Roman and Byzantine Egypt.* London: Routledge.

Andreau, J. 1999. *Banking and Business in the Roman World.* Cambridge: Cambridge University Press.

Bagnall, R. S. 1995. *Reading Papyri, Writing Ancient History.* London: Routledge.

—— 2005. 'Evidence and Models for the Economy of Roman Egypt', in J. G. Manning and I. Morris (eds), *The Ancient Economy: Evidence and Models.* Stanford, Calif.: Stanford University Press, 187–204.

—— 2006. 'Egypt and the Concept of the Mediterranean', in W. V. Harris (ed.), *Rethinking the Mediterranean.* Oxford: Oxford University Press, 339–47.

—— 2009. 'Response to Alan Bowman', in A. K. Bowman and A. I. Wilson (eds), *Quantifying the Roman Economy: Methods and Problems.* Oxford: Oxford University Press, 205–9.

—— and B. W. Frier. 1994. *The Demography of Roman Egypt.* Cambridge: Cambridge University Press.

Bandi, L. 1937. 'I conti privati nei papyri dell'Egitto greco-romano', *Aegyptus* 17: 349–451.

Begley, V., and R. Tomber. 1999. 'Indian Pottery Sherds', in S. E. Sidebotham and W. Z. Wendrich (eds), *Berenike 1997: Report of the 1997 Excavations at Berenike (Egyptian Red Sea Coast) and the Survey of the Eastern Desert.* Leiden: CNWS, 161–81.

Bergamasco, M. 1995. 'Le didascali nella ricerca attuale', *Aegyptus* 75: 95–167.

—— 1998. 'P. Kell. G. 19.A, Appendix', *Zeitschrift für Papyrologie und Epigraphik* 121: 193–6.

—— 2004. 'Tre note a tre *διδασκαλικαί*', *Studi di Egittologia e di Papirologia: Rivista Internazionale* 1: 31–43.

—— 2006. 'La *διδασκαλική* di P. Col. inv. 164', *Zeitschrift für Papyrologie und Epigraphik* 158: 207–12.

Biezunska-Malowist, I. 1977. *l'esclavage dans l'Égypte gréco-romaine*, vol. 2: *Période romaine.* Warsaw: Zakład Narodowy im. Ossolinskich.

Bogaert, R. 2000. 'Les opérations des banques de l'Égypte romaine', *Ancient Society* 30: 135–269.

Bowman, A. K. 1996. *Egypt after the Pharaohs: 332 BC–AD 642: From Alexander to the Arab Conquest* 2nd edn. London: British Museum Press.

—— 2009. 'Quantifying Egyptian Agriculture', in A. K. Bowman and A. I. Wilson (eds), *Quantifying the Roman Economy: Methods and Problems*. Oxford: Oxford University Press, 177–204.

—— and E. Rogan. 1999. 'Agriculture in Egypt from Pharaonic to Modern Times', in A. K. Bowman and E. Rogan (eds), *Agriculture in Egypt from Pharaonic to Modern Times*. Oxford: Oxford University Press, 1–32.

—— and J. D. Thomas. 1994. *The Vindolanda Writing-Tablets (Tabulae Vindolandenses II)*. London: British Museum Press.

—— and A. I. Wilson (eds) 2009. *Quantifying the Roman Economy: Methods and Problems*. Oxford: Oxford University Press.

Bülow-Jacobsen, A. 1989. 'Two Greek Papyri Carlsberg from Tebtunis', *Zeitschrift für Papyrologie und Epigraphik* 78: 125–31.

Buraselis, K. 1995. 'Zu Caracallas Strafmaßnahmen in Alexandrien (215/6): Die Frage der Leinenweber in *P. Giss*. 40 II und der Syssitia in *Cass. Dio* 77 (78). 23. 3', *Zeitschrift für Papyrologie und Epigraphik* 108: 166–84.

Calderini, A., and S. Daris. 1935–2003. *Dizionario dei nomi geografici e topografici dell'Egitto greco-romano*, vols 1–4 and suppls 1–4. Cairo: Società Reale di Geografia d'Egitto.

Cappers, R. T. J. 1998. 'Archaeobotanical Remains', in S. E. Sidebotham and W. Z. Wendrich (eds), *Berenike 1996: Report of the 1996 Excavations at Berenike (Egyptian Red Sea Coast) and the Survey of the Eastern Desert*. Leiden: CNWS, 289–330.

—— 2006. *Roman Foodprints at Berenike: Archaeobotanical Evidence of Subsistence and Trade in the Eastern Desert of Egypt*. Los Angeles: Cotsen Institute of Archaeology.

Carrié, J.-M. 2002. 'Les associations professionnelles à l'époque tardive: Entre *munus* et convivialité', in J.-M. Carrié and R. Lizzi Testa (eds), *Humana Sapit: Études d'antiquité tardive offertes à Lellia Cracco Ruggini*. Turnhout: Brepols, 309–32.

Christiansen, E. 2004. *Coinage in Roman Egypt: The Hoard Evidence*. Aarhus: Aarhus University Press.

Clarysse, W., and D. J. Thompson. 2006. *Counting the People in Hellenistic Egypt*, 2 vols. Cambridge: Cambridge University Press.

Cockle, W. H. M. 1981. 'Pottery Manufacture in Roman Egypt: A New Papyrus', *Journal of Roman Studies* 71: 87–97.

Cottier, M. 2005. 'The Organisation of Customs Duties in Ptolemaic and Roman Egypt (circa 332 BC to AD 284)', doctoral dissertation, University of Oxford.

—— 2010. 'The Customs Districts of Roman Egypt', in T. Gagos (ed.), *Proceedings of the 25th International Congress of Papyrology*. Ann Arbor: Scholarly Publishing Office, University of Michigan Library, 141–8.

Cotton, H. M., W. E. H. Cockle, and F. Millar. 1995. 'The Papyrology of the Roman Near East: A Survey', *Journal of Roman Studies* 85: 214–35.

Daris, S. 1981. 'I quartieri di Arsinoe in età romana', *Aegyptus* 61: 143–54.

el-Fakharani, F. 1983. 'Recent Excavations at Marea in Egypt', in G. Grimm, H. Heinen, and E. Winter (eds), *Das römisch-byzantinische Ägypten: Akten des Internationalen Symposions 26.–30. September 1978 in Trier*, vol. 2. Mainz: von Zabern, 175–86.

Erdkamp, P. 2005. *The Grain Market in the Roman Empire: A Social, Political and Economic Study*. Cambridge: Cambridge University Press.

Fikhman, I. 1994. 'Sur quelques aspects socio-économiques de l'activité des corporations professionelles de l'Égypte byzantine', *Zeitschrift für Papyrologie und Epigraphik* 103: 19–40.

Frier, B. W., and D. P. Kehoe. 2007. 'Law and Economic Institutions', in W. Scheidel, I. Morris, and R. Saller (eds), *The Cambridge Economic History of the Greco-Roman World*. Cambridge: Cambridge University Press, 113–43.

Geens, K. 2008. 'Financial Archives of Graeco-Roman Egypt', in K. Verboven, K. Vandorpe, and V. Chankowski (eds), *Pistoi dia tèn technèn: Bankers, Loans and Archives in the Ancient World: Studies in Honour of Raymond Bogaert*. Leuven: Peeters, 133–51.

Gibbs, M. A. 2008. 'Professional and Trade Associations in Ptolemaic and Roman Egypt', doctoral dissertation, University of Oxford.

Grzymski, K., et al. 1994. 'Canadian–Egyptian Excavations at Tell el-Farama (Pelusium) West: Spring 1993', *Cahier de Recherches de l'Institut de Papyrologie et d'Égyptologie de Lille* 16: 109–21.

Habermann, W. 1998. 'Zur chronologischen Verteilung der papyrologischen Zeugnisse', *Zeitschrift für Papyrologie und Epigraphik* 122: 144–60.

Harris, E. M. 2002. 'Workshop, Marketplace and Household: The Nature of Technical Specialization in Classical Athens and its Influence on Economy and Society', in P. Cartledge, E. E. Cohen, and L. Foxhall (eds), *Money, Labour and Land: Approaches to the Economies of Ancient Greece*. London: Routledge, 67–99.

Hombert, M., and C. Préaux. 1952. *Recherches sur le recensement dans l'Égypte romaine (P. Bruxelles inv. E. 7616)*. Leiden: Brill.

Howgego, C. 2009. 'Some Numismatic Approaches to Quantifying the Roman Economy', in A. K. Bowman and A. I. Wilson (eds), *Quantifying the Roman Economy: Methods and Problems*. Oxford: Oxford University Press, 287–95.

Johnson, A. C. 1936. *Roman Egypt to the Reign of Diocletian: An Economic Survey of Ancient Rome*, ed. T. Frank, vol. 2. Baltimore: Johns Hopkins University Press.

Jones, A. H. M. 1960. 'The Cloth Industry under the Roman Empire', *Economic History Review*, 2nd ser., 13: 183–92.

Jördens, A. 1995. 'Sozialstrukturen im Arbeitstierhandel des Kaiserzeitlichen Ägypten', *Tyche* 10: 37–100.

Kehoe, D. P. 1997. *Investment, Profit, and Tenancy: The Jurists and the Roman Agrarian Economy*. Ann Arbor: University of Michigan Press.

—— 2007. 'The Early Roman Empire: Production', in W. Scheidel, I. Morris, and R. Saller (eds), *The Cambridge Economic History of the Greco-Roman World*. Cambridge: Cambridge University Press, 543–69.

Koenen, L. 1996. 'The Carbonized Archive from Petra', *Journal of Roman Archaeology* 9: 177–88.

Łajtar, A. 1991. 'Proskynema Inscriptions of a Corporation of Iron-Workers from Hermonthis in the Temple of Hatshepshut in Deir El-Bahari: New Evidence for Pagan Cults in Egypt in the 4th Cent. AD', *Journal of Juristic Papyrology* 21: 53–70.

Lewis, N. 1999. *Life in Egypt under Roman Rule*. Atlanta: Scholars Press.

Lith, S. M. E. van. 1974. 'Lease of Sheep and Goats/Nursing Contract with Accompanying Receipt', *Zeitschrift für Papyrologie und Epigraphik* 14: 145–62.

Litinas, N. 1997. 'Market-Places in Graeco-Roman Egypt: The Use of the Word ἀγορά in the Papyri', in B. Kramer et al. (eds), *Akten des 21. Internationalen Papyrologenkongresses, Berlin 13.–19. 8. 1995*. Stuttgart: Teubner, 2.601–6.

McGing, B. C. 1998. 'Bandits, Real and Imagined, in Greco-Roman Egypt', *Bulletin of the American Society of Papyrologists* 35: 159–83.

Mahadevan, I. 1996. 'Tamil-Brahmi Graffito', in S. E. Sidebotham and W. Z. Wendrich (eds), *Berenike 1995: Report of the 1995 Excavations at Berenike (Egyptian Red Sea Coast) and the Survey of the Eastern Desert.* Leiden: CNWS, 205–8.

Manning, J. G. 2007. 'Hellenistic Egypt', in W. Scheidel, I. Morris, and R. Saller (eds), *The Cambridge Economic History of the Greco-Roman World.* Cambridge: Cambridge University Press, 434–59.

—— 2008. 'Coinage as "Code" in Ptolemaic Egypt', in W. V. Harris (ed.), *The Monetary Systems of the Greeks and Romans.* Oxford: Oxford University Press, 84–111.

—— and I. Morris (eds) 2005. *The Ancient Economy: Evidence and Models.* Stanford, Calif.: Stanford University Press.

Mayerson, P. 1997. 'The Role of Flax in Roman and Fatimid Egypt', *Journal of Near Eastern Studies* 56: 201–7.

—— 2000. 'The Economic Status of Potters in P. Oxy. L 3595–3597 & XVI 1911, 1913', *Bulletin of the American Society of Papyrologists* 37: 97–100.

Mitterauer, M. 1984. 'Familie und Arbeitsorganisation in städtischen Gesellschaften des späten Mittelalters und der frühen Neuzeit', in A. Haverkamp (ed.), *Haus und Familie in der spätmittelalterlichen Stadt.* Cologne: Böhlau, 1–36.

Parker, G. 2008. *The Making of Roman India.* Cambridge: Cambridge University Press.

Peacock, D. P. S., et al. 2006. *Myos Hormos—Quseir al-Quadim: Roman and Islamic Ports on the Red Sea.* Oxford: Oxbow.

Pintaudi, R. 1987. 'L'attività degli esattori dell'mercato di Alexandru Nesos', *Archiv für Papyrusforschung* 33: 43–7.

Pollard, N. 2000. *Soldiers, Cities, and Civilians in Roman Syria.* Ann Arbor: University of Michigan Press.

Raschke, M. G. 1978. 'New Studies in Roman Commerce with the East', in H. Temporini (ed.), *Aufstieg und Niedergang der römischen Welt* II 9.2. Berlin: de Gruyter, 604–1378.

Rathbone, D. W. 1989. 'The Ancient Economy and Graeco-Roman Egypt', in L. Criscuolo and G. Geraci (eds), *Egitto e storia antica dall'ellenismo all'età araba: A: Bilancio di un confronto.* Bologna: CLUEB, 159–76.

—— 1991. *Economic Rationalism and Rural Society in Third Century* A.D. *Egypt.* Cambridge: Cambridge University Press.

—— 2000a. 'The "Muziris" Papyrus (*SB* XVIII 13167): Financing Roman Trade with India', in M. Abd-el-Ghani, S. Z. Bassiouni, and W. A. Farag (eds), *Alexandrian Studies II: In Honour of Mostafa el-Abbadi*, Bulletin 46. Alexandria: Société d'Archéologie d'Alexandrie, 39–50.

—— 2000b. 'Ptolemaic to Roman Egypt: The Death of the Dirigiste State?', in E. Lo Cascio and D. W. Rathbone (eds), *Production and Public Powers in Classical Antiquity.* Cambridge: Cambridge Philological Society, 44–54.

—— 2002. 'Koptos the Emporion: Economy and Society, I–III AD', in K.-F. Boussac (ed.), *Autour de Coptos: Actes du colloque organisé au Musée de Beaux-Arts de Lyon (17–18 mars 2000).* Paris: de Boccard; Lyon: Topoi, 179–98.

—— 2003. 'The Financing of Maritime Commerce in the Roman Empire, I–II AD', in E. Lo Cascio (ed.), *Credito e moneta nel mondo romano: Atti degli Incontri Capresi di Storia dell'Economia Antica (Capri 12–14 ottobre 2000).* Bari: Edipuglia, 197–229.

—— 2007. 'Roman Egypt', in W. Scheidel, I. Morris, and R. Saller (eds), *The Cambridge Economic History of the Greco-Roman World.* Cambridge: Cambridge University Press, 698–719.

Rea, J. R. 1982. 'P. Lond. inv. 1562 verso: Market Taxes in Oxyrhynchus', *Zeitschrift für Papyrologie und Epigraphik* 46: 191–209.

Rowlandson, J. 1996. *Landowners and Tenants in Roman Egypt*. Oxford: Clarendon Press.

—— (ed.) 1998. *Women and Society in Greek and Roman Egypt: A Sourcebook*. Cambridge: Cambridge University Press.

Salomon, R. 1991. 'Epigraphic Remains of Indian Traders in Egypt', *Journal of the American Oriental Society* 3: 731–6.

San Nicolò, M. 1972. *Ägyptisches Vereinswesen zur Zeit der Ptolemäer und Römer*, 2 vols. Munich: Beck.

Sidebotham, S. E. 1986. *Roman Economic Policy in the Erythra Thalassa, 30 BC–AD 217*. Leiden: Brill.

—— and W. Z. Wendrich. 2000. *Berenike 1998: Report of the 1998 Excavations at Berenike and the Survey of the Egyptian Eastern Desert, including Excavations at Wadi Kalalat*. Leiden: CNWS.

Sijpesteijn, P. J. 1987. *Customs Duties in Graeco-Roman Egypt*. Zutphen: Terra.

Temin, P. 2001. 'A Market Economy in the Early Roman Empire', *Journal of Roman Studies* 91: 169–81.

Tomber, R. S. 2004. 'Roman and South Arabia: New Artefactual Evidence from the Red Sea', *Proceedings of the Seminar for Arabian Studies* 34: 351–60.

—— 2008. *Indo-Roman Trade: From Pots to Pepper*. London: Duckworth.

van Lith, S. M. E. 1974. 'Lease of Sheep and Goats/Nursing Contract with Accompanying Receipt', *ZPE* 14: 145–62.

van Minnen, P. 1986. 'The Volume of the Oxyrhynchite Textile Trade', *Münsterische Beiträge zur Antiken Handelsgeschichte* 5: 88–95.

—— 1987. 'Urban Craftsmen in Roman Egypt', *Münsterische Beiträge zur Antiken Handelsgeschichte* 6: 31–88.

—— 1998. 'Berenice, a Business Woman from Oxyrhynchus: Appearance and Reality', in A. M. F. W. Verhoogt and S. P. Vleeming (eds), *The Two Faces of Graeco-Roman Egypt: Greek and Demotic and Greek-Demotic Texts and Studies presented to P. W. Pestman*. Leiden: Brill, 59–70.

—— 2008. 'Money and Credit in Roman Egypt', in W. V. Harris (ed.), *The Monetary Systems of the Greeks and Romans*. Oxford: Oxford University Press, 226–41.

Venticinque, P. F. 2009. 'Common Causes: Guilds, Craftsmen and Merchants in the Economy and Society of Roman and Late Roman Egypt', doctoral dissertation, University of Chicago.

von Reden, S. 2006. 'The Ancient Economy and Ptolemaic Egypt', in P. F. Bang, M. Ikeguchi, and H. G. Ziche (eds), *Ancient Economies, Modern Methodologies: Archaeology, Comparative History, Models and Institutions*. Bari: Edipuglia, 161–78.

—— 2007. *Money in Ptolemaic Egypt: From the Macedonian Conquest to the End of the Third Century BC*. Cambridge: Cambridge University Press.

Weber, M. 1947. *The Theory of Social and Economic Organization, Wirtschaft und Gesellschaft*, pt 1, ed. with introd. by T. Parsons, trans. A. M. Henderson and T. Parsons. New York: Free Press.

Wendrich, W. Z., et al. 2003. 'Berenike Crossroads: The Integration of Information', *Journal of the Economic and Social History of the Orient* 46: 46–87.

Whittaker, C. R. 2004. *Rome and its Frontiers: The Dynamics of Empire*. London: Routledge.

Wilson, A. I. 2008. 'Large-Scale Manufacturing, Standardization, and Trade', in J. P. Oleson (ed.), *The Oxford Handbook of Engineering and Technology in the Classical World*. Oxford: Oxford University Press, 393–417.

Wipszycka, E. 1965. *L'industrie textile dans l'Égypte romaine*. Warsaw: Zakład Narodowy im. Ossolinskich.

Wolff, C. 2003. *Les brigands en Orient sous le Haut-Empire romain*. Rome: École Française de Rome.

Woolf, G. 1992. 'Imperialism, Empire and the Integration of the Roman Economy', *World Archaeology* 23: 283–93.

Young, G. K. 2001. *Rome's Eastern Trade: International Commerce and Imperial Policy, 31 BC–AD 305*. London: Routledge.

CHAPTER 4

GOVERNMENT, TAXATION, AND LAW

ANDREA JÖRDENS

GOVERNMENT

Because of its geography Egypt had always been a country of two parts, but it was able to develop into an important state entity only after the unification of Upper and Lower Egypt. Politics, of course, had hardly any bearing on nature, and the differences between the two regions continued to exist; thus, the thin strip of arable land in the Nile Valley, hundreds of kilometres long, was used mainly for cereal cultivation, while in the Nile Delta animal husbandry prevailed. A third factor that came into play after 331 BCE was the new capital, Alexandria, founded by Alexander the Great on an arid limestone spur at the furthest western point, outside the Nile Delta and therefore not strictly speaking part of Egypt itself.

The history of Egypt, stretching back for millennia, shows that it was almost inevitable that the government should take account of these two and later three distinct parts, and the resulting differences were reflected in the administration. Still, the former heartlands of the Ptolemaic empire remained under central control for the first three centuries of Roman rule, until Diocletian eventually divided Egypt into separate provinces. Until then, the correct title of the governor, who was usually designated simply as *praefectus Aegypti*, or *eparchos Aigyptou* in Greek, was accordingly *praefectus Alexandreae et Aegypti* (Geraci 1995; Bastianini 1988 for the titles more specifically). As he had a high profile in the Egyptian hinterland too, the *fasti* (official calendar) of the prefect can be reconstructed with very few gaps (Bastianini 1975).

Among the major provinces of the Roman empire, Aegyptus was the only one that was administered by a governor from the equestrian order, directly appointed by the emperor. In terms of authority, the prefect had basically the same powers as governors from the senatorial class, as a *lex* accorded him an *imperium ad similitudinem proconsulis*, which ended as soon as his successor entered Alexandria (*Dig.* 1.17.1). Not least, this initially included command of three legions, and later, from the time of Tiberius, two, something that was normally restricted to senators alone. The prefect also had unlimited power in the civilian sector. Thus, like a Roman magistrate, he enjoyed the *ius edicendi* (the power to make edicts), as attested by more than five dozen edicts (Katzoff 1980). Similarly, as was customary, he also had supreme judicial powers in the country, including capital punishment granted by the *ius gladii* (Liebs 1981). In contrast to other governors, a focal point of the prefect's duties was in the area of finance, as he was responsible for levying various taxes, as well as for corn deliveries from Egypt. A prerequisite for this was a tightly organized administration over which constant control was exercised. It was for this reason that at the yearly *conventus*, which the governor made from January to April in varying locations, and apparently every second year in Upper Egypt as well (Haensch 1997), not only were trials held, but the administrative practice of subordinate officials was assessed (hence the Greek term *dialogismos*). Deeply impressed by the example of the emperor, the prefect perceived his official status and duties on the model of the imperial *providentia* and *aequitas*; there is no evidence that any special modification was made for the specific characteristics of the province (Jördens 2009).

From its inception the governorship of Egypt belonged to the most important offices open to members of the second tier of Roman society and, from the beginning of the second century, it acted as a springboard to the highest office of the equestrian *cursus honorum*, the praetorian prefecture (Brunt 1975). Like the *praefectus praetorio*, the *praefectus Aegypti* held at least a ducenarian post; that is, he was paid an annual salary of 200,000 sesterces and was thus one of the best-paid officials in the Roman empire. Several other procurators were also appointed in Egypt by the emperor. These officials were subordinate to the *praefectus Aegypti* and, like the prefect himself, resided at Alexandria. From the beginning, these included the *dikaiodotes* or *iuridicus*, who was in charge of jurisdiction (Kupiszewski 1953–4; Elia 1990), and the head of the so-called *Idios Logos* (Swarney 1970), responsible for special revenues such as *bona caduca*, property that became vacant for various reasons. Control over financial affairs of the province and overall control of the temples, however, rested with the prefect and were transferred only in Hadrianic times to specific procurators—in this case the *dioiketes* (Hagedorn 1985) or the *archiereus* (Stead 1981; Demougin 2006). Without exception, these officers came from the equestrian order and also had ducenarian rank, although perhaps only from the time of Commodus onwards (Habermann 2004). Thus, they could, if necessary, act as the representative of the prefect; however, fixed rules governing such deputizing do not seem to have existed (Mitthof 2002a), contrary to earlier assumptions.

In addition, separate procuratorships were set up for individual areas of activity, which at first were often occupied by imperial freedmen and were only incorporated into the equestrian offices on occasion and over the course of several decades. Most important among these was the *procurator usiacus*, who was in charge of state-owned lands (Parássoglou 1978; Beutler 2007), but there were also procurators with responsibility for the Alexandrian storage facilities (*procurator Neaspoleos*), for permits to leave and probably also for export controls from Egypt (*procurator Phari*), for overseeing the cultivated land (*procurator episkepseos*), or the *procurator ad Mercurium*, entrusted with farming out certain monopolies (Beutler-Kränzl 2007). For many of these lower offices, however, we know little more than what they were called, and the names of a handful, at most, of people who held the office (for a review, see Pflaum 1960–1: 3.1083–92). In any case, we are hardly better informed about the detailed organization of the central administration than in other provinces, because the transmission of records in Alexandria was particularly unfavourable (Haensch 2008).

Compared with that, the situation in the hinterland, known as the *chora*, is much better known, though the documentary evidence is quite unevenly distributed over the territory. Probably owing to its enormous expanse, the country was divided into a few larger administrative units. If there were perhaps only two of these at the outset, in line with the ancient dichotomy of Upper and Lower Egypt, the areas immediately to the south of Memphis, together with the large semi-oasis of the Fayum, were soon to form an epistrategy in its own right, the 'Seven nomes and the Arsinoite nome'. Moreover, it seems that the Delta was at times under the control of two of the so-called *epistrategoi*, literally 'senior *strategoi*'. They were again Roman procurators and held sexagenarian posts, that is, they received only 60,000 sesterces a year. Unlike the other procurators, they were responsible for general tasks and not tied to a particular field of activity, although liturgical matters received special attention. Although once again superior to the local authorities, the *epistrategoi* should be seen as having had a limited role as regular intermediaries between the prefect and the nome administration, because it would appear that they were only marginally concerned with everyday administrative duties (Thomas 1982).

Day-to-day administration was for the most part in the hands of the local authorities, specifically the heads of the roughly four dozen districts, the so-called *nomoi*, or nomes, into which Egypt had been divided from time immemorial. These heads, called *strategoi*, acted as the highest representatives of state power on the local level. They were members of the provincial upper class and, in the first century in particular, preferably Alexandrian citizens; despite their titles, they had purely civilian powers. They owed their appointment to the prefect and had frequent and direct contact with him, as he directed most of the business of administration to them (Thomas 1999). Thus, they acted as intermediaries between the population of the villages as well as that of the nome capitals and the prefect (Jördens 1999, 2006); also, they exercised minor local jurisdiction on the prefect's behalf. The three years' service decreed by the prefect Tiberius Julius Alexander (*I Hibis* 4.34–5 §10 (6 July 68 CE)) was probably a guideline and not a fixed rule.

Even after they had completed their service, the *strategoi* might need to answer for the way they conducted their administration and so usually took some of their files home with them. For this reason a few reports have survived from the second century onwards about the administration of the otherwise little-known nomes of the Delta (Daris 1983). The papers of the *strategos* Apollonios, a well-to-do landowner in the Hermopolite nome, who from 113 to 120 CE administered the Apollonopolite Heptakomias nome 120 km further south, are particularly illustrative in this regard, especially since they include numerous letters as well as official documents. The correspondence that arose during his time in office not only provides valuable information about the duties and social background of such officials but also represents one of our most important sources for the great Jewish revolt, which rocked Egypt to its foundations during that period.

Assisting the *strategos* in each nome there was a so-called *basilikos grammateus*, literally 'royal scribe', who could act as his proxy and who was, above all, responsible for financial matters at the nome level. This entailed control of the inhabitants and their property, as well as administration of the land and its revenue, including the temples; in its intricacy and attention to detail, his records and files are second to none in ancient sources (Kruse 2002). He had to report on his areas of accountability to the central administration in Alexandria, where the nomes were represented by financial secretaries who were individually responsible for only one specific nome each, that is the *eklogistes* in the general financial administration, and the *graphon ton nomon*, who was probably assigned to the department of the *Idios Logos* (Mitthof 2002b: 18–20; Jördens 2009: 99–102).

At the village level, a similar central position was held by the village scribe (Greek *komogrammateus*), who was responsible for the registration of all land and of all the inhabitants, along with their status. As the person most familiar with the individual capabilities of the villagers, it fell to him to propose to the *strategos*, and, in the case of higher-level duties, to the *epistrategos*, the names of potential liturgists who were capable of undertaking unpaid public duty for a limited time. While liturgists selected in this way usually served in their own community, the village clerks themselves, and the higher officials too, were apparently assigned to places away from their home, undoubtedly with the intention of avoiding potential conflicts of interest. Unlike the other liturgists, they seem to have been remunerated for carrying out their tasks, although we still lack certain evidence for this. We are informed about their manifold tasks by the archive of Petaus, who was scribe for several villages in the south-eastern Arsinoite nome in the late 180s. To him we owe a plethora of interesting detailed information—including the fact that Petaus could write only with difficulty, notwithstanding holding this office (Hagedorn et al. 1969; in general, see also Derda 2006: 147–261).

In contrast to the office of *komogrammateus*, which was mostly held for three years, the other liturgists were engaged for one year, as a rule. The best known of these are certainly the *praktores*, responsible for the collection of various taxes in cash or in kind, and the many officials concerned with the transport of state grain on land and water, such as granary officials (*sitologoi*), public cattle drivers (*demosioi ktenotrophoi*), and cargo supervisors (*epiplooi*), and, in addition to these, various security guards and police squads. Moreover, there were also liturgical officials who were charged with narrowly defined tasks, such as ensuring the food supply during the prefect's official visits, where they were each responsible for bread, wine, oil, poultry, hay, barley, wood, vegetables, and so forth, respectively (*P Petaus* 45–7 (January 185 CE)). Owing to the state of transmission of documents, we are as a rule best acquainted with this lowest level of administration, so that here too we are able to detect developments over time. For reasons of space, rather than describe this in detail, reference may be made to the most relevant studies on liturgies (Oertel 1917; Lewis 1997).

The sources provide rich evidence of the administrative work associated with these liturgies, and also of the seemingly constant, and often successful, efforts the people made to escape the burdens imposed on them. For this reason, too, the liturgy system may be seen as one of the characteristic traits of Roman Egypt, with its first attestations under Tiberius, and gradually expanding over the course of the first century until, by the time of Trajan, it was used extensively to cover, if not all, at least the main areas of everyday administrative duties.

Taxation

Most of the officials in the province of Egypt worked in the financial sector, specifically with the collection and management of state income (detailed in Sharp 1999). As in the other provinces, in addition to the cash to be paid regularly as a *tributum capitis*, the state imposed a *tributum soli*, which in the case of Egypt consisted of the vast grain supplies earmarked for Rome. On a more or less frequent basis, the government also required additional payments, again in money or in kind, among which the best known is probably the *aurum coronarium*, paid to the emperor on special occasions. Moreover, a plethora of major and minor taxes was imposed on income of various kinds, derived from land, business, working animals, or any other source, but there were also fees to be paid on completion of certain legal procedures. The various import duties were a large sector in themselves.

The poll tax (*laographia*) was levied on all male Egyptians aged 14 to 62 years, and its collection from taxpayers was assured through a fourteen-year cycle of census declarations (Bagnall and Frier 2006; Jördens 2009: 62–94). The level of the poll tax depended on the district, with the inhabitants of the Arsinoite nome probably having to pay most, at 40 drachmas a year. Privileged groups enjoyed reduced rates or could even be completely excluded (see Chapters 15 and 16). Also collected per capita was the Jewish tax introduced after the destruction of the temple in Jerusalem in 70 CE; it applied to the entire Jewish population between 3 and 62 years of age, regardless of sex. The rate of 2 (Attic) drachmas applicable throughout the empire was based, according to Josephus (*BJ* 7.218), on the amount that previously every Jew had to pay to the temple in Jerusalem, and which now went instead to the Roman temple of Jupiter Capitolinus (Cass. Dio 65.7.2). Accordingly, this *Ioudaikon telesma* was also designated the 'price for two denarii' (*time denarion duo*); as denars and Attic drachmas were worth 4 Egyptian drachmas, each person had to pay 8 drachmas, plus 2 obols' conversion fee. Another poll tax, which was referred to as such at least in the Arsinoite nome, is the *zytera kat'andra*, but this seems to have been a sequel to the Ptolemaic monopoly on private brewery, converted into a licence fee (Reiter 2004: 145–64). For smaller per capita taxes, like the tax on salt (*halike*) or pork (*hyike*), it was barely worth listing them individually in the tax receipts, which is why they were entered together with the *laographia* under the generic term *syntaximon*.

The land tax was based on categories of land that were taken over from the Ptolemaic period. The highest rates were paid by the cultivators of public lands, which of course included both taxes and rent, unlike other categories (Rowlandson 1996: 27–62). Since the annual Nile flood moved property boundaries again and again, setting an appropriate level of taxation required an extensive surveying process, and the same was true of the traditional tax reductions granted in the case of an inadequate or excessive flood which resulted in significantly smaller harvests. The various attempts by the Roman administration to limit the administrative burden and simplify the system proved to be practicable only to a limited extent, and only under Diocletian was the situation resolved when, for the first time, the tax was linked definitively to the crops (*P Cair. Isid.* 1 (16 March 297 CE); see Jördens 2009: 96–120).

In the first century the collection of both the *tributum capitis* and the *tributum soli* was often farmed out for many years to a tax collector, but with Trajan's reforms the liturgical appointments that are so characteristic of Roman Egypt became the rule. For the numerous types of business tax, however, the system of tax farming remained in force much longer. The diversity of the charges and fees that were applied to this sector are known particularly from the many documents from the office of the nomarch of the Arsinoite nome (Reiter 2004). No matter what the activity—weaving, milling, the use of work animals, grazing, fishing, or the certifying of sacrificial bulls—the state took a small portion, at least. As can be seen especially from the well-documented weaving taxes, there were many regional variations in the annual taxation rate, with different amounts recorded even within one nome (Reiter 2004: 131–44). Moreover, at times the *strategoi* seem to have been empowered to levy additional taxes at the local level, at least in the early years of the empire, as is shown by the example of the *katakrimata* condemned by Tiberius Julius Alexander (*I Hibis* 4.45–50 §13 (6 July 68 CE); see Kruse 1999; Jördens 2009: 136–42).

Import and export duties, which were imposed not only at the provincial borders but also at the nome and epistrategy boundaries, were also farmed out (Jördens 2009: 355–96). The highest rate was levied on imported goods from the southern and eastern trade, where the tax attested in the papyri, the *tetarte* (literally 'quarter part', or 25 per cent), seems to have applied throughout the empire. Farming out all of these duties was in the hands of the prefect, who apparently acted also as head of the independent Egyptian customs district. A similar independence can be observed regarding the customs tariffs that were applicable only in one single nome. On the basis of the sources we have available it is hard to decide whether the process of farming out could be delegated to lower authorities, as is easy to imagine in the case of nome customs duties. The fact that in Julio-Claudian times we also encounter interested parties from the west as tax farmers—like the well-known case of P. Annius Plocamus, who farmed out from the fisc all the tax income from the Red Sea (Plin. *HN* 6.84)—might suggest that at least the auction of the *tetarte* was actually held in Rome. However, all other contractors that we know of so far had come from the local elite, and their official title, which according to inscriptions was *arabarches*, shows such unmistakably regional associations that, in all likelihood, the 25 per cent customs levy too was farmed out by the prefect.

Liturgists appointed ad hoc were, as a rule, in charge of the recovery of any special taxes. This is most evident with the so-called *praktores stephanikon*, who had to collect the *stephanikon* or *aurum coronarium*, the tax imposed on the population for wreaths. These tokens of honour were customarily given to the imperial family on special occasions, and were funded, at least in Egypt, by means of a levy (Jördens 2009: 139–59). A similar system existed for matters relating to public construction, as can be seen especially from the Upper Egyptian documents (Palme 1989: 44–8). It is hard to gain an oversight of the plethora of fees and charges, however, and for this reason the one summary work on the subject, although over 70 years old, is still in large measure authoritative (Wallace 1938).

Law

Not only the nation-state as such, but also the idea of law that applies equally to all the residents of a country, are modern concepts, completely alien to antiquity. Just as it was usual in ancient states for various members of different ethnic groups to live side by side, so there was a variety of different laws, graduated in rank in certain cases, which were each tied to a person's ethnicity or origin. The respecting of these jurisdictions as separate from each other, which was also reflected in establishing different courts, seems generally to have been one of the tenets in all the Hellenistic monarchies, though we have most detailed knowledge of Ptolemaic Egypt merely because of the state of transmission of documents. This fundamental separation of the various jurisdictions in general conceptions of the law, and above all in the practice of law, does not affect the fact that, over the course of time, convergences and even adoptions can be observed. In the final analysis one has to recognize that this was merely a natural consequence of close coexistence in a multicultural society (see Wolff 2002: 23–98).

This basic structure was largely preserved after the end of the Ptolemaic period. However, with the exception of *cives Romani* and citizens of the three, later four, Greek *poleis*, the Romans considered all the residents of the country to be Egyptians, who lacked a binding system of law that might have been in competition with the Roman law. Thus, in the Egyptian *chora* there was, as it were, a legal vacuum which the new rulers were willing and able to fill by any available means.

Yet, to do so in a systematic way would have gone against all customs, and there is no evidence of any interest at all in standardization of whatever kind, let alone any attempt by the Romans to impose their own concepts of law by force. Although in all likelihood they were never positively confirmed, essentially the customary forms of law continued to remain in force in practice; indeed, they persisted well into late antiquity. Not even the Constitutio Antoniniana seems to have brought about any fundamental changes; with this legislation, Caracalla gave Roman citizenship to all free inhabitants of the Roman empire in the year 212, with the exception of the mysterious group of the so-called *dediticii*. Although the entire population of the Imperium Romanum was now under the reign of the *ius civile*, the body of common laws that applied to Roman citizens, there was no radical alteration of the public or private law system; perhaps the only generally perceptible change was the fact that, from that time, even ordinary inhabitants were permitted to use the imperial name Aurelius or Aurelia. The discrimination that existed in taxation continued uninterrupted, in any case, and in contract law, too, there is at best a change in the formal aspect, but hardly in content. There does seem to have been a terminological change towards Romanization in the following period (see especially Wolff 2002: 191–200), and contracts were supplemented with new Roman elements, namely the stipulation clause, now ubiquitous. Yet these features that were adopted are often only superficial ones, while the practice of law remained more or less the same until the last years of Roman Egypt.

Admittedly the *ius civile* had not been nearly as important as would have been expected from the proportion of Roman citizens in the total population. Rather, the citizens generally merged with their immediate environment, as they were free to determine the way their legal matters were handled, in both form and content. This was all the less problematic for the mass of new citizens, as they came from this foreign milieu anyway, and, as is well known, there are few areas that make people act as conservatively as law of persons and family and law of succession. If even before 212 Roman law was only the special law of the *cives Romani*, and thus of rather marginal importance in the network of various systems of law customary in Egypt, it was even less successful after 212 in establishing itself and determining the legal climate of the province.

However, provincial law developed alongside Roman law through the effect of Roman courts on the local legal traditions in the area of administration and justice. Jurisdiction, in particular, had a pioneering role here, especially when magistrates from abroad made judgments that resulted in supplementing, modifying, and even in some cases replacing the local laws and customs, and thus laid the foundations for an autonomous tradition of law in this province. This was done particularly by the *iuridicus*, who performed broad activities in judicial matters, the procurator of the *Idios Logos*, also appointed by the emperor to the court of special revenues, and not least by the prefect himself and his respective *iudices delegati*, auxiliary judges appointed by him for specific cases to be examined and decided upon. This was all the more possible as the population were able at any time to approach the Roman officials and even the governor with submissions of any kind, and request assistance and legal protection from individuals as well as officials—apparently an option that the people liked to use, and, in the case of the prefect, the *conventus*, in particular, provided an opportunity. Thus, in one case, 1,804 petitions were received in less than three days (*P Yale* I 61 (208–11 CE)), and this onslaught required ever more sophisticated means of dealing with it (Haensch 1994). The general trust in the judicial institutions was to all appearances great, which presumably may be ascribed not least to the obviously low zeal for law reform of the new lords of the land—no matter whether this came from negligence or indifference.

An additional source of the provincial law was legislation by the prefect that was promulgated in edicts and in circulars to the *strategoi* (though these were put in the form merely of administrative guidelines: Jördens 1997; for a general overview, see Katzoff 1980). In principle, he was free to act at his own discretion. Yet, for major measures of all kinds, consultation with the emperor seems to have been obligatory (see also *I Hibis* 4.8–9 (6 July 68 CE)). The edict form was in no way reserved for general directives, but could also be used for special cases like the promulgation of a letter from the emperor (*P Lond.* VI 1912.1–13 (10 November 41 CE)) or even the search for a sole refugee liturgist (*P Berl. Leihg.* II 46.41–51 (1 April 136 CE)). Although both forms of enactment mostly confirmed, inculcated, or defined more closely practices and regulations that were already in force, occasionally new directives were promulgated, such as an amnesty given by the emperor to returned absconders who were willing to reintegrate (*BGU* II 372 (29 August 154 CE)) or the institution of a further central documentary archive (*P Oxy.* I 34 (22 March and 20 August 127 CE)).

Archiving was in any case the one area of administration where we meet the most active interventions (Wolff 2002: 178–9), as the rule of law was a matter of particular importance to the prefect (Jördens 2010). Individual proclamations were quoted in petitions decades later, so they seem in practice to have had unlimited binding force; a well-known example of this is the petition by Dionysia, who supported her position with, among other things, three edicts by prefects, as well as extracts from the official diaries of two other prefects, of a *iuridicus*, and of an *epistrategos* (*P Oxy.* II 237 (after 27 June 186 CE, with documents from the years 89, 109, 128, 133, and 142 CE)). However, as all these dispositions could be set aside at any time, they must be thought of only as precedents (Katzoff 1980: 822–4).

In principle, the senate (as stated explicitly by *BGU* V 1210.3–4 (after 149 CE)) and the emperor, of course, were authorized to intervene at any time in the law of the province (Wolff 2002: 181–7). However, right from the outset such cases were few, and direct intervention by means of ordinances occurred only exceptionally. Rather, we must assume that here, too, decisions made in other contexts were adduced as precedents (Katzoff 1972). Significant if atypical examples are the pronouncements given by Septimius Severus and Caracalla during their visit to Alexandria from 14 to 16 March 200, parts of which were copied by an interested lawyer (the so-called Apokrimata; *SB* VI 9526). No matter how highly they ranked, imperial dispositions played a subsidiary role, at best, in the formation of provincial law; a further factor was that the prefect was usually the intermediary, at least, if not the absolute initiator of all such activities.

All in all, a legal policy that would bring the law more closely into line with Roman legal principles, and thus, in the long term, would have resulted in the complete restructuring of the law or, more precisely, the different laws of the land, apparently did not exist. Rather, one would search in vain for a clear will determining the shape of the law in this sense, and one can speak even less of any standardization instigated, let alone imposed, from above. As previously under the Ptolemies, the chief principle seems to have been the preservation of a generally accepted system of law, as the maintenance of order in the province seemed easiest by these means. However, the Romans were not troubled about asserting their absolute authority if the laws in force were diametrically opposed to their own and the need arose. This may have been the case when it came to the repeated intervention in the sphere of moneylending, particularly the lowering of the lending rate to 12 per cent, which was one of the few attested innovations of the Roman period (Wolff 2002: 189–91). The significance of this dictate, introduced at an early date and with lasting success, is pointed up not least in the strikingly high fines of half or quarter of the fortune imposed on the lender or borrower by the so-called Gnomon of the *Idios Logos* (*BGU* V 1210.235–6 §105 (after 149 CE)). The general guidance of the *aequum et iustum* principle, which is shown here no less than elsewhere, gave the Roman rule of law the necessary flexibility to deal again and again with the changed needs of the time, clearly in a manner that was universally satisfactory.

Conclusion

The most striking feature of the Egyptian provincial government remains its overall structure, in particular the geographically defined division into many smaller, relatively independent, but nevertheless tightly run administrative units, and above all the strict hierarchy of offices with a proper chain of appeal and the prefect at the top (for a schematic overview, see Bowman 1986: 67). However, these characteristics should not obscure the fact that the principles of administration were in line with general parameters, and thus there can be no notion that the former Ptolemaic kingdom had any special standing within the Roman empire as compared with the other provinces.

This is certainly one of the most pressing issues in current research: how far can inferences be drawn from the rich Egyptian sources of evidence about possible parallel developments in other parts of the empire? The more so because one must, on the basis of general considerations, recognize certain structural similarities throughout the earlier Hellenistic kingdoms. Yet, attempts to apply the result obtained here to other regions are the exception, not the rule. This has been easiest to do in the context of the army, particularly in relation to the *beneficiarii*, who were deployed throughout the empire (Ott 1995), or in the *kolletiones*, who brought loathing upon themselves under the early Severans in Asia Minor and Egypt by manipulating documentation (Rea 1983: 97–100). According to a new study, remarkable commonalities that could hardly be coincidental also appear among the so-called eirenarchs who were responsible for security (Sänger 2010).

In the area of taxation, as has been shown, there was a plethora of varieties in Egypt itself. This is why it is by no means easy to determine which structural features (if any) may also be observed in other regions of the Roman empire. Because the points of comparison are rare, we can only occasionally discover things in common, as has been the case with the *tetarte*. Here, the continuation of given practices, varying according to the time and place in which they were established, seems to have been the rule.

Much the same applies in the field of jurisdiction, where the Romans apparently refrained from intervening too rigidly in the law and customs of the population. Even if they did not impose their own concepts of law, their steady concern for jurisdiction had its own effect on the local legal traditions and eventually helped to develop the specific forms of provincial law. Again, we grasp the parts of a process that without doubt could be observed in other parts of the empire if we had similar documentation from there. All in all, we may be confident that there are many more unexpected discoveries to be made if we look with fresh and unbiased eyes at all the relevant sources of any type and origin.

Suggested Reading

For a comprehensive introduction to Hellenistic and Roman Egypt, see Bowman (1986). On the prefect, see Brunt (1975) and Jördens (2009), where topics of more general relevance are also treated. The changes that took place during Augustan times are now best summarized in Haensch (2008); on financial matters, see Rathbone (1993), while on taxation in general, Wallace (1938) is still fundamental. The same applies to Wolff (1978, 2002) for the whole area of law and lawmaking; for the role of the prefect, compare Katzoff (1980). Several articles on different topics are collected in Eck (1999), where related evidence from other parts of the Roman empire may also be found.

Bibliography

Bagnall, R. S., and B. W. Frier. 2006. *The Demography of Roman Egypt*, 2nd edn. Cambridge: Cambridge University Press.

Bastianini, G. 1975. 'Lista dei prefetti d'Egitto del 30a a 299p', *Zeitschrift für Papyrologie und Epigraphik* 17: 263–328.

—— 1988. '*Ἔπαρχος Αἰγύπτου* nel formulario dei documenti da Augusto a Diocleziano', in W. Haase and H. Temporini (eds), *Aufstieg und Niedergang der römischen Welt* II 10.1. Berlin: de Gruyter, 581–97.

Beutler, F. 2007. 'Wer war ein *Procurator Usiacus*? Die Verwaltung des Patrimoniums in Ägypten in der ersten Hälfte des 2. Jahrhunderts', *Cahiers du Centre Gustave-Glotz* 18: 67–82.

Beutler-Kränzl, F. 2007. 'Procurator ad Mercurium', in B. Palme (ed.), *Akten des 23. Internationalen Papyrologenkongresses, Wien 22.–28. Juli 2001*. Vienna: Verlag der Österreichischen Akademie der Wissenschaften, 53–56.

Bowman, A. K. 1986. *Egypt after the Pharaohs: 332 BC–AD 642*. London: British Museum Press.

Brunt, P. A. 1975. 'The Administrators of Roman Egypt', *Journal of Roman Studies* 65: 124–47; repr. in Brunt, *Roman Imperial Themes*. Oxford: Clarendon Press, 1990, 215–54.

Daris, S. 1983. 'Papiri non ossirinchiti ad Ossirinco', *Studia Papyrologica* 22: 121–33.

Demougin, S. 2006. '*Archiereus Alexandreae et Totius Aegypti*: Un office profane', in A. Vigourt et al. (eds), *Pouvoir et religion dans le monde romain: En hommage à Jean-Pierre Martin*. Paris: Presses de l'Université Paris-Sorbonne, 513–19.

Derda, T. 2006. *Arsinoites Nomos: Administration of the Fayum under Roman Rule*, *Journal of Juristic Papyrology*, suppl. 7. Warsaw: Warsaw University.

Eck, W. (ed.) 1999. *Lokale Autonomie und römische Ordnungsmacht in den kaiserzeitlichen Provinzen vom 1. bis 3. Jahrhundert*. Munich: Oldenbourg.

Elia, F. 1990. 'I iuridici Alexandreae', *Studi in memoria di S. Mazzarino III = Quaderni Catanesi* 2: 185–216.

Geraci, G. 1995. '*Praefectus Alexandreae et Aegypti*: Alcune riflessioni', *Simblos* 1: 159–75.

Habermann, W. 2004. 'Publius Marcius Crispus, Epistratege und Iuridicus in Ägypten unter Antoninus Pius', in J. M. S. Cowey and B. Kramer (eds), *Paramone: Editionen und Aufsätze von Mitgliedern des Heidelberger Instituts für Papyrologie zwischen 1982 und 2004*. Munich: Saur, 241–50.

Haensch, R. 1994. 'Die Bearbeitungsweisen von Petitionen in der Provinz Aegyptus', *Zeitschrift für Papyrologie und Epigraphik* 100: 487–546.

—— 1997. 'Zur Konventsordnung in Aegyptus und den übrigen Provinzen des römischen Reiches', in B. Kramer et al. (eds), *Akten des 21. Internationalen Papyrologenkongresses, Berlin 13.–19. 8. 1995*. Stuttgart: Teubner, 1.320–91.

—— 2008. 'Die Provinz Aegyptus: Kontinuitäten und Brüche zum ptolemäischen Ägypten: Das Beispiel des administrativen Personals', in I. Piso (ed.), *Die römischen Provinzen: Begriff und Gründung*. Cluj-Napoca: Mega, 81–105.

Hagedorn, D. 1985. 'Zum Amt des διοικητής im römischen Ägypten', *Yale Classical Studies* 28: 167–210.

—— et al. 1969. *Das Archiv des Petaus (P. Petaus)*. Opladen: Westdeutscher Verlag.

Jördens, A. 1997. 'Erlasse und Edikte: Ein neuer Erlaß des Präfekten M. Sempronius Liberalis und die Frage der statthalterlichen Rechtsetzungskompetenz', in G. Thür and J. Vélissaropoulos-Karakostas (eds), *Symposion 1995: Vorträge zur griechischen und hellenistischen Rechtsgeschichte, Korfu, 1.–5. September 1995*. Cologne: Böhlau, 325–52.

—— 1999. 'Das Verhältnis der römischen Amtsträger in Ägypten zu den "Städten" in der Provinz', in W. Eck (ed.), *Lokale Autonomie und römische Ordnungsmacht in den kaiserzeitlichen Provinzen vom 1. bis 3. Jahrhundert*. Munich: Oldenbourg, 141–80.

—— 2006. 'Der Praefectus Aegypti und die Städte', in A. Kolb (ed.), *Herrschaftsstrukturen und Herrschaftspraxis: Konzeption, Prinzipien und Strategien der Administration im römischen Kaiserreich*. Berlin: Akademie, 191–200.

—— 2009. *Statthalterliche Verwaltung in der römischen Kaiserzeit: Studien zum Praefectus Aegypti*. Stuttgart: Steiner.

—— 2010. 'Öffentliche Archive und römische Rechtspolitik', in K. Lembke, M. Minas-Nerpel, and S. Pfeiffer (eds), *Tradition and Transformation: Egypt under Roman Rule*. Leiden: Brill, 159–79.

Katzoff, R. 1972. 'Precedents in the Courts of Roman Egypt', *Zeitschrift der Savigny-Stiftung für Rechtsgeschichte, Romanistische Abteilung* 89: 256–92.

—— 1980. 'Sources of Law in Roman Egypt: The Role of the Prefect', in W. Haase and H. Temporini (eds), *Aufstieg und Niedergang der römischen Welt* II 13. Berlin: de Gruyter, 807–44.

Kruse, T. 1999. '*Κατάκριμα*—Strafzahlung oder Steuer? Überlegungen zur Steuererhebung im römischen Ägypten in iulisch-claudischer Zeit anhand von P. Oxy. XLI 2971, SB XIV 11381, SPP IV p. 70–71, BGU VII 1613 und OGIS II 669', *Zeitschrift für Papyrologie und Epigraphik* 124: 157–90.

—— 2002. *Der Königliche Schreiber und die Gauverwaltung: Untersuchungen zur Verwaltungsgeschichte Ägyptens in der Zeit von Augustus bis Philippus Arabs (30 v. Chr.–245 n. Chr.)*. Munich: Saur.

Kupiszewski, H. 1953–4. 'The *Iuridicus Alexandreae*', *Journal of Juristic Papyrology* 7–8: 187–204.

Lewis, N. 1997. *The Compulsory Public Services of Roman Egypt (Second Edition) (ICS^3)*. Florence: Gonnelli.

Liebs, D. 1981. 'Das *Ius Gladii* der römischen Provinzgouverneure in der Kaiserzeit', *Zeitschrift für Papyrologie und Epigraphik* 43: 217–23.
Mitthof, F. 2002a. 'Munatidius Merula, ritterlicher Procurator und stellvertretender Dioiket der Provinz Ägypten im Jahre 201 n. Chr.?', *Tyche* 17: 121–27.
—— 2002b. *Neue Dokumente aus dem römischen und spätantiken Ägypten zu Verwaltung und Reichsgeschichte (1.–7. Jh. n. Chr.)*. Vienna: Hollinek.
Oertel, F. 1917. *Die Liturgie: Studien zur ptolemäischen und kaiserlichen Verwaltung Ägyptens*. Leipzig: Teubner.
Ott, J. 1995. *Die Beneficiarier: Untersuchungen zu ihrer Stellung innerhalb der Rangordnung des römischen Heeres und zu ihrer Funktion*. Stuttgart: Steiner.
Palme, B. 1989. *Das Amt des ἀπαιτητής in Ägypten*. Vienna: Hollinek.
Parássoglou, G. M. 1978. *Imperial Estates in Roman Egypt*. Amsterdam: Hakkert.
Pflaum, H.-G. 1960–1. *Les carrières procuratoriennes équestres sous le Haut-Empire romain*, 4 vols. Paris: Geuthner.
Rathbone, D. W. 1993. 'Egypt, Augustus and Roman Taxation', *Cahiers du Centre Gustave Glotz* 4: 81–112.
Rea, J. R. 1983. 'Proceedings before Q. Maecius Laetus, Praef. Aeg., etc.', *Journal of Juristic Papyrology* 19: 91–101.
Reiter, F. 2004. *Die Nomarchen des Arsinoites: Ein Beitrag zum Steuerwesen im römischen Ägypten*. Paderborn: Schöningh.
Rowlandson, J. 1996. *Landowners and Tenants in Roman Egypt*. Oxford: Clarendon Press.
Sänger, P. 2010. 'Zur Organisation des Sicherheitswesens im Kaiserzeitlichen Kleinasien und Ägypten', *Tyche* 25: 99–122.
Sharp, M. 1999. 'Shearing Sheep: Rome and the Collection of Taxes in Egypt, 30 BC–AD 200', in W. Eck (ed.), *Lokale Autonomie und römische Ordnungsmacht in den kaiserzeit lichen Provinzen vom 1. bis 3. Jahrhundert*. Munich: Oldenbourg, 213–41.
Stead, M. 1981. 'The High Priest of Alexandria and All Egypt', in R. S. Bagnall et al. (eds), *Proceedings of the Sixteenth International Congress of Papyrology, New York, 24–31 July 1980*. Chico: Scholars Press, 411–18.
Swarney, P. R. 1970. *The Ptolemaic and Roman Idios Logos*. Toronto: Hakkert.
Thomas, J. D. 1982. *The Epistrategos in Ptolemaic and Roman Egypt*, pt 2: *The Roman Epistrategos*. Opladen: Westdeutscher Verlag.
—— 1999. 'Communication between the Prefect of Egypt, the Procurators and the Nome Officials', in W. Eck (ed.), *Lokale Autonomie und römische Ordnungsmacht in den kaiserzeitlichen Provinzen vom 1. bis 3. Jahrhundert*. Munich: Oldenbourg, 181–95.
Wallace, S. L. 1938. *Taxation in Egypt from Augustus to Diocletian*. Princeton: Princeton University Press.
Wolff, H. J. 1978. *Das Recht der griechischen Papyri Ägyptens in der Zeit der Ptolemaeer und des Prinzipats*, vol. 2: *Organisation und Kontrolle des privaten Rechtsverkehrs*. Munich: Beck.
—— 2002. *Das Recht der griechischen Papyri Ägyptens in der Zeit der Ptolemaeer und des Prinzipats*, vol. 1: *Bedingungen und Triebkräfte der Rechtsentwicklung*. Munich: Beck.

CHAPTER 5

THE ROMAN ARMY IN EGYPT

RUDOLF HAENSCH

The topic of the Roman army in imperial Egypt has two faces. Structurally, the army was certainly one of the most homogeneous organizations in the Roman empire—if not the most homogeneous. Much of what there is to say about it therefore applies equally to the formations stationed in other regions of the empire. For instance, we find in the whole empire the same types of unit with the same strength of numbers and the same structure: the large infantry divisions of the Roman army, the legions, which in the early principate still consisted fundamentally of Roman citizens, and the units recruited originally from non-Romans, namely the auxiliary troop formations (*auxilia*), whether cavalry (*ala*), infantry (*cohors*), or mixed (*cohors equitata*). There were general, empire-wide rules concerning the length of service for soldiers, their pay, and the privileges that they were entitled to at the end of their service, though the members of different types of unit did receive different benefits (*FIRA* III 171). Furthermore, their senior officers consistently came from the two small and relatively exclusive leadership classes: the army and legion commanders normally came from the approximately 700 senatorial families of the empire, and the majority of the other senior officers, particularly the commanders of auxiliary units, came from the second rank of the empire, the equestrian order, which numbered about 10,000 men in the whole Roman world. An important factor in preventing the various provincial armies from drifting apart was the fact that these senior officers often originated in other provinces than Egypt and had served in further provinces—something that applied only to some of the middle-ranking officers, the centurions and decurions. The more varied experience of the senior officers helped to enforce consistency across the empire, as did the constant transfer of whole units or major parts of such units from one province to another (from the time of Hadrian only by way of exception in the case of legions).

This chapter concentrates on the characteristics specific to the Roman army in Egypt, providing an overview of the subject and emphasizing the developing insights of scholarship. The first element specific to the province of Aegyptus, as was also the case in every province of the empire, was the composition of the garrison, and in particular the units stationed there and their military engagements. Also specific to the *exercitus Aegyptiacus* (the Latin designation for the 'army of Egypt') were a few institutional regulations dating from Octavian's conquest and the form he gave to the province's administration. And finally, two kinds of source, namely the papyri and ostraca, are specific to the province. Although there are bodies of evidence of this kind from other parts of the empire—for instance, from Dura Europos, a few forts in northern Africa, and particularly Vindolanda on Hadrian's Wall—there is not nearly as much evidence as for Egypt.

The Garrison

The history of the garrison in the province, and of the military engagements in which it was involved, has been an essential part of research on the Roman army in Egypt since it began (Lesquier 1918: 1–114; Daris 1988, 2000a, b, 2005; Speidel 1988). Papyri tend to come from villages in Middle Egypt, particularly at the peak of the empire, and therefore only rarely reflect political-military events beyond the local level. Thus, our knowledge of military events in this province has increased little beyond the first comprehensive study by Lesquier, despite all the additional papyri published in the course of the last century. Inscriptions, too, rarely give information about such events. Therefore, it is not surprising that even in the case of legions stationed in the province, a number of important questions remain unanswered: for instance, during Augustan times, which legion, apart from the *legiones III Cyrenaica* (Wolff 2000) and *XXII Deiotariana* (Daris 2000b), was stationed in the province, at what place, and when was it withdrawn? This is significant, as answers to these questions would make it clear for how long after the administration of the first two prefects, C. Cornelius Gallus and Aelius Gallus, the Romans were thinking of a policy of further expansion, and where, during the early years of the province, the Romans saw the greatest danger.

By 23 CE at the latest, the core of the province's garrison was reduced to the two legions named above. They were stationed together in Nikopolis near Alexandria. Under Augustus, the three and then two legions had been stationed at Nikopolis, at Babylon (Sheehan 1996), and perhaps Thebes (Maxfield 2009: 66; see in this context *I Syringes* 1733). At the beginning of the second century, the number of legions stationed in Egypt was further reduced: shortly after August 119, the *legio III Cyrenaica* was transferred out of the province (*BGU* I 140), and the same papyrus provides the last piece of evidence for the existence of the *legio XXII Deiotariana*. No later than 127/8, the *legio II Traiana* arrived in the province, and constituted the core of the provincial army for the next two centuries (Daris 2000b; Sänger 2009). The reason our knowledge of these legions' history is so incomplete is that only a few papyri from Alexandria survive. Likewise, we know so little of the archaeology of the legionary and auxiliary camps at the peak of the empire because they were built over or flooded, in addition to the lack of archaeological interest that prevailed for many years with regard to Roman period sites.

For the history of the auxiliary units stationed in Egypt, the key sources are documents that scholars refer to as military diplomas (Fig. 5.1). These are inscriptions on bronze recording the award granted to auxiliary soldiers after their period of service of twenty-five or twenty-six years, whereby they received Roman citizenship and the so-called *connubium*, the right to a form of marriage that gave children of the union the status of Roman citizens (see Chapter 18). The wording of the diplomas includes a list of all the units whose soldiers were entitled to privileges, which was usually all or almost all the auxiliary units in a province (sometimes there were no soldiers with twenty-five or twenty-six years of service in a unit). Six such documents concerning soldiers of the Egyptian army have been published, covering the period between 83 and 206 CE (in chronological order: *CIL* XVI 29; *RMD* I 9; *CIL* XVI 184; Eck 2011; see further the very fragmentary diplomata *RMD* III 185; V 341). These documents show that in the late first and the second century, the total number of *auxilia* stationed in the province remained fairly constant, though it was perhaps raised slightly in the last quarter of the second century: there were three to four *alae* (cavalry units with a full strength of approximately 500 men) and about seven to ten *cohortes* (units of about 500 infantry, or, in the case of the so-called *cohortes equitatae*, about 600 men, of which about 120 were cavalry). On the basis of all the relevant documentation, it is evident that a number of units were part of the garrison of the province for decades, or even centuries (see also Stoll 2009: 424). Thus, for instance, we can trace the *ala Apriana* from the years 37/40 CE (*P Lips.* II 133) until 268/70 (*SPP* XX 71), and the *cohors II Ituraerorum equitata* from 39 CE (*ILS* 8899) up to the *Notitia Dignitatum*, an administrative handbook of the late fourth or fifth century (Eastern part: XXVII 44).

Such an unchanging composition of the auxiliary garrison is not found in the first decades of the principate, when some of the auxiliary units had not even been firmly established and troops were moved in the course of the conquest of large areas. After the first decades of Roman rule, however, there is relative consistency in military concentration, with Nikopolis near Alexandria (Stoll 2009: 421) taking prime place. At first two legions were garrisoned there, then one, together with auxiliary units, mostly *alae*; in addition, there was the Alexandrian fleet, the *classis Alexandrina*. The choice of this centre appears to have had two aims (Alston 1995: 36–7). On the one hand, it meant that the prefect had a reserve at his main place of residence, ready to be put into action; cavalry in particular could be sent out quite easily in

FIG. 5.1 Front and back of the first tablet of an incised bronze document known as a military diploma, for an infantryman of the *cohors II Thracum* named Plution, son of Tithoes. From Koptos. Dated 3 March 179 CE. 14.5 × 11.2 cm; weight 170 grams

RMD III 185; Römer (1990).

all directions. On the other hand, it meant that troops were available to suppress uprisings in the city of Alexandria, which was regarded with suspicion, and with good reason (Haensch 1997: 219–21). When seen in this context, the 8,000 soldiers stationed at such a megalopolis in the second and third centuries were not a large force.

A second important centre, though by no means so heavily guarded, was the southern entry point to Egypt, the region of the First Cataract around Syene and Philae (see Chapter 45). It appears that at least three auxiliary units were permanently stationed in this region (Speidel 1988; see also Locher 1999: 280–1; Maxfield 2000, 2009: 67–9; primary sources: especially Strabo 17.1.12, 53; *ILS* 8907). In addition to protecting Egypt from enemy attack from the south, they were probably also intended to prevent possible uprisings in the Thebaid.

We have little precise information about where the remaining units were stationed (Alston 1995: 33–6; Maxfield 2009). We cannot even tell whether all the units were actually garrisoned in specific military installations. It is in any case clear that a significant number of the soldiers from these units were detailed for service in smaller outposts. How far such outposts were sent has recently been shown by an inscription found on the island of Farasan at the outlet of the Red Sea (*AE* 2004: 1643 = 2005: 1639; most recently Speidel 2009c: 633–49). The life of these soldiers in their outposts (*praesidia*) has been greatly elucidated through the numerous finds and the publication of ostraca by Hélène Cuvigny (2003, 2005 in particular). These finds are the result of surveys and excavations on the road from Koptos to Myos Hormos and the Red Sea, and in the quarries of Mons Claudianus, carried out by Cuvigny and her team (Fig. 5.2). The ostraca illustrate very clearly the daily life of these soldiers, who were charged with protecting the road from attacks by nomads, and with controlling the quarry

FIG. 5.2 The most important fortified settlement in the stone-quarrying district of Mons Claudianus

Photo: Adam Bülow-Jacobsen.

labourers and giving them technical help. We know less about the soldiers, particularly the *beneficiarii* and the *centuriones*, whose task it was to maintain peace and order in the settlements of the Nile Valley. From the beginning of the second century, they were additional representatives of state authority alongside the competent officials of the civil administration, in particular the *strategos*, who governed each nome or district (see particularly Rankov 1994; Nelis-Clément 2000: 214–17, 227–43, 413–14; Palme 2006, 2008).

The Origin of Roman Soldiers and Officers in Egypt

The origin of the soldiers serving in the various military units seems to be, *mutatis mutandis*, analogous to other provinces. As we see particularly from the work of Forni (1953, 1992), throughout the empire in the second and beginning of the third century there was a tendency to recruit a significant proportion of the men for the units in one province from that province itself. This does not apply only to the auxiliary units, but also to the legions, in which only Roman citizens were supposed to serve; therefore, to facilitate local recruitment, the recruits first needed to be given Roman citizenship. As is shown in particular by two lists of legionaries, preserved as inscriptions, local recruitment for the Egyptian legions increased over time: according to *ILS* 2483, an inscription possibly from Flavian times, the largest group after those recruited in Asia Minor were those born in the province, particularly in Alexandria (in a ratio of 2:1). In Severan times local recruitment was even more predominant, as might be expected: according to a list of discharged legionaries published as *CIL* III 6950, three-quarters of all those legionaries named were born in Egypt. Two-thirds of these were children of soldiers (so-called *castrenses*) born in the *canabae*, that is, the civil settlement near Nikopolis; the recruits born as citizens of Alexandria were only about one-eighth of the total. None of this is significantly different from what can be observed for the recruitment of legions in the rest of the empire (Speidel 2009a: 219; see also Alston 1995: 39–52; Stoll 2009: 433–4).

Despite their small number, for methodological reasons the military diplomas mentioned above are another important source for the origin of auxiliary soldiers in the Egyptian army, since the conditions under which they were transmitted were almost identical throughout the empire. Thus, we get for all provinces the same amount of information. On the contrary, in the case of the papyri and ostraca that document the Egyptian origin of a soldier, it remains an open question to what extent these documents, typical only of Egypt, make these soldiers appear much more numerous than they actually were, owing to the unique conditions of their preservation.

Therefore, alongside lists of entire groups of soldiers in one unit, with their places of origin, the military diplomas are methodologically a more reliable criterion for the origin of the majority of these soldiers than the numerous individual attestations from Egypt itself (Cavenaile 1970; Criniti 1973, 1979). At least two of the six diplomas were found in Egypt, suggesting that an auxiliary soldier and a *centurio* of the auxiliary unit, who came from Chios, in all likelihood lived in Egypt after the end of their period of service. In addition, one of the diplomas explicitly mentions Koptos as a soldier's place of origin. Egyptian place names predominate in a list of fourteen soldiers in an auxiliary unit at the end of the second century (among these, *castrensis* is mentioned six times as their origin; *P Mich.* III 162 = *Rom. Mil. Rec.* 39). Alongside Egypt itself the three neighbouring regions, Africa, Syria, and Asia Minor, are singled out: a military diploma from Trajan's time mentions a soldier from Hippo (probably Hippo Regius in North Africa, rather than Hippos in Judaea). Of the two diplomas not originating in Egypt, one was found in Syria, and another most likely was, since it attests to a soldier from Apamea, which is probably the Syrian town of that name.

If, in a batch of six receipts issued in September 117 by the *signiferi* (standard-bearers) *cohortis I Lusitanorum*, there are 126 *tirones Asiani* (new recruits from Asia) attested (*PSI* IX 1053 = *Rom. Mil. Rec.* 74), then the conspicuous feature is probably only the extent of the recruitment drive carried out in Asia Minor, rather than the place of origin of the recruits. Recruitment from Asia Minor may have been due to population reduction in Egypt and Syria caused by the Jewish uprising under Trajan. As in other provincial armies, the army in Egypt seems to have had recourse to the southern Balkans as a reservoir for recruitment as well: if many auxiliary soldiers with Dacian names (many of them cavalrymen, some not) appear in ostraca from Trajan's time, this is probably explained by the particular situation of the conquest of Dacia, especially as these Dacians were apparently removed from the province later (Cuvigny 2003: 278, 289; 2005: 166–7; Dana and Matei-Popescu 2009: 210, 237–8). The recruitment of Thracians, frequently attested in other provinces (Speidel 2009a: 232), seems to have occurred in the Egyptian army too, judging by the find spot of one military diploma. In all, therefore, the recruitment of soldiers for the provincial army, from the end of the first century at the latest, is comparable to what happened in other provinces: a considerable proportion made up from residents of the province, plus recruits from the neighbouring regions, and finally a certain proportion of recruits from the southern Balkans. To a rather unusual extent, compared with other provinces, the new soldiers seem to have been given typical Roman names. In the armies of Germania Inferior or of Syria, for example, indigenous names are frequently attested, but they are almost entirely absent in the case of the Egyptian army. Even an Alexandrian called Ptolemaios, son of Ptolemaios, was constrained to call himself C. Julius Saturnilus upon his entry to the Roman army (*P Oxy.* XXII 2349 (70 CE); cf. *BGU* II 423; *P Oxy.* XLI 2978).

As for the officers, in comparison with the army units stationed in neighbouring Syria, it is conspicuous how many equestrian officers come from the province of Egypt, particularly in the second century. Seven out of eighteen known officers of the Egyptian army came from the province itself (mostly from Alexandria), while among the forty-one known equivalent officers in the Syrian army, not a single one was of local origin. Was the equestrian upper class of Egypt or Alexandria prepared to enter Roman military service to a much greater extent than the corresponding Syrian class? And was one of the reasons for this that they were required to carry out only administrative duties during their years of service, as Devijver (1981) suggested? The problematic nature of such a conclusion becomes clear when one examines the sources for the origins of these officers, however. In a great majority of cases, the information comes from a type of document which is quite formulaic, used when individuals wanted to collect debts. Such petitions needed to be made to Alexandrian notables who held the office of *archidikastes*, and each time the supplicants listed all the important titles of these notables, including those of their military careers (*P Oxy.* XLI 2978; *P IFAO* III 11; *M Chr.* 116; *PSI* VIII 962; compare also *SB* IV 7362.2–3.209). Such papyri survive from Egypt but not elsewhere, skewing the picture. If all that was available to us were the inscriptions, as is typical for other provinces, then we would know of only two equestrian officers from Egypt (*IGR* I 1044; *IGR* I 1200 = *IGLCM* 20), and there would be practically no difference from the army in Syria, for instance. Thus, there is no reason to make assumptions about quiet desk jobs for equestrian officers in Egypt, or the popularity of military adventure holidays among the Alexandrian notables.

Distinctive Features of the Egyptian Army

In many respects, what can be said about the Roman army in the province of Egypt is only a local adaptation of what was typical of the Roman army in general. But the army in this province did quite clearly exhibit certain individual features: while the highest military commanders throughout the empire—that is, the governors and the commanders of the largest military units, the legions—came from the senatorial class, in Egypt these commanders, were members of the second rank of the empire, the equestrian order. As with the office of prefect, Octavian, who feared a power challenge or usurpation, decided that the government of this province would fall to men of the equestrian order and not, as was customary, the senatorial class. He probably saw in this ruling, promulgated in the most formal way as a *lex*, an additional guarantee that Egypt could not once again be made into a centre of resistance to him—and for a time, this was undoubtedly correct (Eich 2007: 382–3; Jördens 2009: 46–51). But it would have gone against all notions of the relations between ranks, on the part of both *ordines*, if he had put senatorial legion commanders under an equestrian governor. Thus, the legion commanders could only come from the *ordo equester*.

This provision caused differences not only in rank and prestige among these high-ranking commanders, but also in the extent of their experience. These legion commanders had had very different military careers from those of the senatorial legion commanders, who could appeal at best to experience which they had obtained during their very short tours of duty as military tribunes, when they were frequently not in sole command. But the equestrian commanders of the legions in Egypt were raised to equestrian rank apparently only after lengthy careers as *centurio* and *primipilus II*, the highest centurion rank (for an early example, see *AE* 1978: 286; cf. *AE* 1954: 163). It remains an open question whether this difference in social origin and military experience caused differences in military leadership of the large units, because neither in Egypt nor in other provinces do we have insight into everyday military leadership, in the narrow sense. In these questions, Egypt does not offer more insight into everyday reality than other provinces, because the legions were soon concentrated in Nikopolis and were thus in a part of the province for which we have papyri only in exceptional cases. We therefore know almost nothing about the ways in which the prefect and the high-ranking equestrian officers under him went about their military functions—to what extent, for instance, they carried out manoeuvres.

We do, however, know that the army in this province had a more Greek-speaking character than those in other provinces: in the first century, when two legions were still stationed in Egypt, at least one of the commanders in charge of both legions, and also presumably of all the auxiliary formations in the province, was designated in an official Latin inscription as *praefectus stratopedarches*, Latinizing the Greek term for the head of the camp (*AE* 1954: 163;

cf. *P Wisc.* II 48). The same function could apparently also be designated *praef(ectus) ex[er]citu qui est in Aegypto* (*CIL* III 6809 = *ILS* 2696).

We also find two other cases where the titles of officers in this provincial army mix Greek and Latin. In Egypt, as in other provinces, the prefect relied on soldiers detailed from the army as an essential part of his staff. In the second century there was an equestrian official with the title *archistrator* at the head of the *stratores*, those responsible for the horses of the prefect's staff (*AE* 1929: 125 = *TAM* III 52). We also find a very similar title for the head of another department of the prefect's office, at this same time: there was an equestrian commander titled *archistator* in charge of a formation of apparently several hundred men, so-called *statores*-soldiers who, on the basis of their designation, were prepared to take on tasks of all kinds (*AE* 1958: 156; cf. *P Oxy.* II 294; XXXVI 2754). We know of no parallels for such Latin–Greek titles elsewhere in the Roman army. It is of fundamental importance that we find these titles in memorial inscriptions erected in provinces other than Egypt. Documentation specific to this individual province therefore has no relevance, and thus one cannot argue that we find no comparable peculiarities merely on account of the poorer state of preservation in other provinces. Titles where Greek and Latin are mixed can probably only be explained by the fact that in the *exercitus Aegyptiacus*, and especially in the staff of the *praefectus Aegypti*, Greek was significantly more common than in other provinces, even eastern ones (Haensch 2008).

The *statores* were an exceptional institution in another respect as well. Only the *praefectus Aegypti*, among all the governors of the principate, had at his disposal a body of soldiers of this kind. In the Republican period, one does find *statores*, but under quite different officials. In the imperial army they only survived either as a unit of the troops of the city of Rome, in which case they were commanded by the praetorian prefects, or as individual functionaries (there may have been two or three of them) assisting equestrian auxiliary commanders, that is, commanders of smaller units in the Roman army. Clearly the fact that the functions of prefect of Egypt and of praetorian prefect originated from the middle equestrian officer corps meant that these functionaries retained conditions typical of equestrian officers, although they had become much more important than them. The equestrian rank of *archistrator* (and *archistator*) is equally exceptional and may be explained only in terms applicable to the province of Egypt and to the city of Alexandria. In all other provinces the head of a governor's *stratores* was only a *centurio*. Presumably the great number of equestrian officials in Egypt and the many Alexandrian notables of equestrian rank meant that it was felt necessary to raise the rank of important *officiales* serving under the prefect. A third unique institution—the existence of an *agrimensor* (land surveyor) *praefecti Aegypti* (*SB* III 7183 = *FIRA* III 142), for whom there was no known parallel in any other provincial governor's staff—may be explained by the need for a surveyor of this type in a province where the arable land changed with each flooding of the Nile.

A Soldier's Life

Even in the case of Egypt, with its exceptional range of sources, papyri, and ostraca, we have only a limited insight into the day-to-day service of the soldiers. The problems of survival mentioned above, in the case of the camps generally and the Nikopolis camp in particular, means that the sources we have are those that, for some reason or other, were taken to the *chora* (see, for instance, the duty rosters in *Rom. Mil. Rec.* 9–10, and a court judgment by a *centurio*, *P Mich.* III 159 = *CPL* 212). Only for the case of the soldiers stationed in the *praesidia* on the roads to the Red Sea and on the Mons Claudianus is the situation completely different, as Cuvigny's work has revealed. We also have a little more day-to-day documentation about the Roman army administration, such as tables of manpower at certain key dates (*pridiana*), staff lists, lists of cavalry units' horses, official letters, tables of pay and the *deposita* of individual soldiers at particular times, and receipts from individual soldiers for pay or payment in kind, either for themselves or for supplies obtained locally (on this, see *Rom. Mil. Rec.* with, for example, Speidel 2009b and Stauner 2004). On the basis of the last-mentioned documents Mitthof (2001) has reconstructed the system of logistics in the third and the following centuries, a system that was typical not only of Egypt but also of the whole empire during these times.

But in a number of respects, even the exceptional preservation of Egyptian documents does not always improve upon what we know about other provinces from literary sources and individual epigraphic evidence. This is also true of the private life of individual soldiers. Although there are several dossiers relating to soldiers, veterans, or families of soldiers (Alston 1995: 117–42; Schubert 2007; Strassi 2008; Sänger 2011), only rarely do we glimpse their personal feelings; instead, the dossiers offer a clearer picture of the soldiers' financial situation, and the social networks on which they relied, than what we can reconstruct in the case of other provinces (Alston 1995: 126–37; Mitthof 2000).

However, in other respects the transmission of documents from Egypt does provide sources for areas that cannot be elucidated in the case of any other province. Thus, the ostraca from the road to Myos Hormos reveal the scale of prostitution and the circumstances surrounding it, as it affected the Roman army, a subject for which there are no other sources at all (Cuvigny 2003: 374–98).

In addition to papyri and ostraca, valuable sources specific to Egypt are the so-called proskynemata, which provide insight into a religious world that otherwise remains completely closed to us, namely that of the simple auxiliary soldiers. Proskynemata are inscriptions that visitors to sanctuaries were permitted to inscribe (or have inscribed) by painting or carving on the temple walls. With these they sought to make supplication to the relevant god for protection for themselves and those close to them. Proskynemata by auxiliary soldiers are preserved in numbers in several places in Egypt and Nubia, including Darka, Hierasykaminos, Pselkis, Abu Duruah near Pselkis, the wadis of Foakhir and Hammamat, and above all the sanctuary of the god Talmis in Kalabsha, where over fifty such inscriptions have been found (for a general view, see Stoll 2009: 450–1, 453–5). In contrast, in the rest of the empire there are almost no religious monuments endowed by single auxiliary soldiers acting individually. Irrespective of whether such soldiers lacked money or whether they never became accustomed to writing inscriptions, it is very rare to find altars endowed by individual *auxiliarii*. Even in the case of legionaries, such attestations of individual religious practice are extremely rare and occur only from the middle of the second century. In the proskynemata, however, we find evidence of such individual religious practice, specifically for the late first and early second centuries, when setting up consecrated altars was by no means a common practice in other provinces.

The proskynemata of Talmis are a good example to consider more closely: all of them are in the Greek language and are addressed to the deity of the temple, the god Mandulis, who is sometimes designated 'greatest' god or 'lord'. The soldiers, who have common, typically Roman names as discussed above, regularly state the unit to which they belonged—almost without exception they were auxiliary cohorts—and its subsection, that is, the *centuria* or *turma* with the name of the commanding officer. At least eight different auxiliary units are attested: the *cohortes I Hispanorum*, *I Thebaeorum*, *I Lusitanorum*, *I* and *II Thracum*, and *II* and *III Ituraeorum*, and the *ala Commagenorum*. The fact that the soldiers' own praenomina are always spelled out and not abbreviated may be an indication of how unfamiliar the soldiers were with such names. A formula like 'the proskynema was written by those active in the *prasidium Talmis*' (*SB* V 8514), and both the location of the sanctuaries and several indications that these soldiers were *stationarii* (that is, soldiers stationed at a certain place for a longer period), suggest that these soldiers had been detailed to these places or visited the sanctuary for religious reasons, but in any case were not from that district. However, only one soldier mentioned in these proskynemata explicitly names his place of origin: Halikarnassos in Asia Minor (*SB* I 4607). This soldier is also the only one who departs from the practice of his comrades by addressing not only the god of the sanctuary concerned, but all other gods as well. The conspicuous feature of all these proskynemata is that they revere only the particular local god. Other gods—including those of the Roman state—are not mentioned. None of the proskynemata have the formulation so common in dedicatory inscriptions elsewhere, whereby the religious act is said to be performed 'for the salvation and protection of the emperor'. The religious structure of the Roman state was apparently of no importance in the personal religious practice of these soldiers, who stated their Roman military affiliation so precisely.

Exactly the same thing can be observed in another body of sources for which there are no parallels elsewhere in the empire: these are the religious statements of individual soldiers, not in the medium of inscriptions conceived from the perspective of the wider world and eternity, but simply as casual, everyday writing. For understandable reasons, such statements are found only in letters preserved on papyrus. Among the Michigan papyri, for instance, we find a number of letters from the family and friends of a certain Claudius Tiberianus, a veteran and former *speculator*, and of a certain Claudius Terentianus, a soldier of the *classis Alexandrina*, who constantly refers to Tiberianus as 'father' but was probably a younger friend rather than this man's son (*P Mich.* VIII; on this circle of friends, see Strassi 2008). Among the correspondents there were also two people called Apollinarius. One, Julius Apollinarius, served as *librarius legionis* and then as *principalis* in the *legio III Cyrenaica* stationed in Arabia; the other served as a naval soldier in the *classis Misenatis*. These men living at the beginning of the second century were thus members of quite different military formations in places far distant from each other in the empire. But they all came from the Fayum, as far as we can tell (Fig. 5.3). In this case, too, Latin or Latinized names should not deceive us: the soldiers, or at least their ancestor who was recruited as the first army member in a family, were probably given these names only when they were inducted into the Roman army. Ethnically and socially they were from the middle class of the village of Karanis, and thus not from a Roman but from a Graeco-Egyptian milieu. In the letters of this circle we repeatedly find statements of the kind 'let there be prayers' to a certain god or gods 'for the welfare of the correspondent', or 'a certain event met with success thanks to' a god. In all these cases not one Roman god is named. Instead, the soldiers turned either to Serapis—and in some cases his associated gods—or to a plethora of gods not specified by name. These references to unnamed gods or a god are sometimes more specific to the extent that they mention 'all' the gods or, often, the 'local gods', or else the gods 'among whom I dwell'. Thus, a certain Apion, for example, thanked Serapis and not Neptune, for instance, for his crossing of the Mediterranean to Misenum without suffering harm (*BGU* II 423 = *W Chr.* 480). In circumstances like promotions, too, where one would most expect reference to the Roman gods that were closely connected to the army, the soldiers mention only Egyptian gods. For example, in the years 84 to 86 a certain Petronius Valens hoped, thanks to Serapis, to 'rise' in the military hierarchy (*P Turner* 18; see further *IMEGR* 169).

No other province of the empire has sources even remotely as numerous as those from Egypt. But there is considerable evidence that the behaviour of simple auxiliary soldiers and

FIG. 5.3 Mummy portrait of a Roman soldier wearing a green *sagum* cloak (usually dyed red) draped over his left shoulder, and a red leather, metal-studded sword strap (the *balteus*) across his white tunic. Encaustic and tempera paint on a hard wood. Date: *c.*160–70 CE. Height 43 cm

Acquired at el-Rubaiyat in the Fayum. British Museum EA 65345. Courtesy of the Trustees of the British Museum.

legionaries, so evident in Egypt, was typical of other provinces as well, in structural terms. Throughout the empire we observe great reverence for the main local god, the vast number of dedications to the *genius loci* providing the most unambiguous example. To offer just another example, the ordinary legionaries of the *I Minervia* stationed in Germania Inferior addressed the most important local (female) gods, the *matronae*, in their private dedications, and the cult of the emperor was of no significance in this context either (Haensch 2001). Once more, it is clear that what can be observed in the case of the army in Egypt is mostly in line with what applied in other provinces. Truly unique features are rare, but many details were adapted to the specific conditions in Egypt.

Conclusion

The Roman empire would not have existed without its army, but the might of the military was only part of its role in sustaining the expanded territories. With very few exceptions, the structure and operation of the Roman army in Egypt was consistent with military organization in other provinces. At the same time, the evidence of papyri, ostraca, and proskynemata make Egypt stand out as a rich source of more personal information about the soldiers who served there, bringing their backgrounds, family, financial relationships, and religious practices into much sharper focus.

Suggested Reading

The work of Lesquier (1918) remains fundamental, although many new sources have since appeared; in this context one has to mention especially Cuvigny's work on papyri and ostraca from the Eastern Desert. For an interpretation of the Roman army in Egypt from the perspective of social history, see Alston (1995), but aspects of this work have not been without controversy (see Bagnall 1997). For the Roman army throughout the empire, see Cosme (2007), Erdkamp (2007), and Sabin, van Wees, and Whitby (2007), which have differing approaches and emphases.

Bibliography

Adams, C. E. P. 1999. 'Supplying the Roman Army: Bureaucracy in Roman Egypt', in A. Goldsworthy and I. Haynes (eds), *The Roman Army as a Community*. Portsmouth, RI: Journal of Roman Archaeology, 119–26.

Alston, R. 1995. *Soldier and Society in Roman Egypt: A Social History*. London: Routledge.

Angeli Bertinelli, M. G. 1983. 'I centurioni della "Legio II Traiana"', in *Studi in onore di Arnaldo Biscardi*, vol. 4. Milan: Istituto Editoriale Cisalpino—La Goliardica, 143–99.

Bagnall, R. S. 1997. 'A Kinder, Gentler Roman Army?', *Journal of Roman Archaeology* 10: 504–12.

Brunt, P. A. 1975. 'The Administrators of Roman Egypt', *Journal of Roman Studies* 65: 124–47.
Cavenaile, R. 1970. 'Prosopographie de l'armée romaine d'Égypte d'Auguste à Diocletien', *Aegyptus* 50: 213–312.
Cosme, P. 2007. *L'armée romaine: VIIIe s. av. J.-C.–Ve s. ap. J.-C.* Paris: Colin.
Criniti, N. 1973. 'Supplemento alla prosopografia dell'esercito romano d'Egitto da Augusto a Diocleziano', *Aegyptus* 53: 93–158.
—— 1979. 'Sulle forze armate romane d'Egitto: Osservazioni e nuove aggiunte prosopografiche', *Aegyptus* 59: 190–261.
Cuvigny, H. (ed.) 2003. *La route de Myos Hormos: L'armée romaine dans le désert oriental d'Égypte*, 2 vols. Cairo: Institut Français d'Archéologie Orientale.
—— 2005. *Ostraca de Krokodilô: La correspondance militaire et sa circulation.* Cairo: Institut Français d'Archéologie Orientale.
Dana, D., and F. Matei-Popescu. 2009. 'Soldats d'origine dace dans les diplômes militaires', *Chiron* 39: 209–56.
Daris, S. 1988. 'Le truppe ausiliarie romane in Egitto', in H. Temporini (ed.), *Aufstieg und Niedergang der römischen Welt* II 10.1. Berlin: de Gruyter, 743–66.
—— 2000a. 'Legio II Traiana Fortis', in Y. Le Bohec and C. Wolff (eds), *Les légions de Rome sous le Haut-Empire.* Lyon: de Boccard, 359–67.
—— 2000b. 'Legio XXII Deiotariana', in Y. Le Bohec (ed.), *Les légions de Rome sous le Haut-Empire: Actes du Congrès de Lyon (17–19 septembre 1998)*, 2 vols. Lyon: de Boccard, 365–67.
—— 2005. 'Note per la storia dell' esercito romano in Egitto III', *Studi di Egittologia e Papirologia*, 57–74.
Devijver, H. 1974. 'The Roman Army in Egypt (with special reference to the Militiae Equestres)', in W. Haase and H. Temporini (eds), *Aufstieg und Niedergang der römischen Welt* II 1 Berlin: de Gruyter, 452–92.
—— 1975. *De Aegypto et Exercitu Romano, sive, Prosopographia Militiarum Equestrium quae ab Augusto ad Gallienum seu statione seu origine ad Aegyptum pertinebat.* Leuven: no publisher.
—— 1981. 'Eine neue Lesung des Papyrus IFAO, III, 11', *Anagennesis* 1: 205–18.
—— 1989. 'L'Égypte et l'histoire de l'armée romaine', in L. Criscuolo and G. Geraci (eds), *Egitto e storia antica dell' ellenismo all' età araba: Bilancio di un confronto.* Bologna: CLUEB, 37–54.
Dobson, B. 1978. *Die Primipilares: Entwicklung und Bedeutung, Laufbahnen und Persönlichkeiten eines römischen Offiziersranges.* Cologne: Rheinland.
Eck, W. 2011. 'Septimius Severus und die Soldaten: Das Problem der Soldatenehe und ein neues Auxiliardiplom', in B. Onken and D. Rohde (eds), *In Omnia Historia Curiosus: Studien zur Geschichte von der Antike bis zur Neuzeit: Festschrift für Helmuth Schneider zum 65. Geburtstag.* Wiesbaden: Harrassowitz, 63–77.
Eich, P. 2005. *Zur Metamorphose des politischen Systems in der römischen Kaiserzeit: Die Entstehung einer 'personalen Bürokratie' im langen dritten Jahrhundert.* Berlin: Akademie.
—— 2007. 'Die Administratoren des römischen Ägyptens', in R. Haensch and J. Heinrichs (eds), *Herrschen und Verwalten: Der Alltag der römischen Administration in der Hoher Kaiserzeit.* Cologne: Böhlau, 378–99.
Erdkamp, P. (ed.) 2007. *A Companion to the Roman Army.* Oxford: Blackwell.
Forni, G. 1953. *Il reclutamento delle legioni da Augusto a Diocleziano.* Milan: Fratelli Bocca.
—— 1992. *Esercito e marina di Roma antica: Raccolta di contributi.* Stuttgart: Steiner.

Franke, T. 2005. 'Legio XV Apollinaris unter Traian in Ägypten?', in W. Spickermann, K. Matijević, and H. H. Steenken (eds), *Rom, Germanien und das Reich: Festschrift zu Ehren von Rainer Wiegels anlässlich seines 65. Geburtstages*. St Katharinen: Scripta Mercaturae, 318–28.

Gatier, P.-L. 2000. 'La Legio III Cyrenaica et l'Arabie', in Y. Le Bohec and C. Wolff (eds), *Les légions de Rome sous le Haut-Empire*. Lyon: Centre d'Études et de Recherches sur l'Occident Romain, 341–9.

Haensch, R. 1997. *Capita provinciarum*. Mainz: von Zabern.

—— 2001. 'Inschriften und Bevölkerungsgeschichte Niedergermaniens: Zu den Soldaten der legiones I Minervia und XXX Ulpia Victrix', *Kölner Jahrbuch* 33: 89–134.

—— 2008. 'Typisch römisch? Die Gerichtsprotokolle der in Aegyptus und den übrigen östlichen Provinzen tätigen Vertreter Roms: Das Zeugnis von Papyri und Inschriften', in H. Börm, N. Ehrhardt, and K. Wiesehöfer (eds), *Monumentum et instrumentum inscriptum: Beschriftete Objekte aus Kaiserzeit und Spätantike als historische Zeugnisse*. Stuttgart: Steiner, 117–25.

Hölbl, G. 1990. 'Das römische Militär im religiösen Leben Nubiens', in H. Vetters and M. Kandler (eds), *Akten des 14. Internationalen Limeskongresses 1986 in Carnuntum*. Vienna: Österreichische Akademie der Wissenschaften, 233–47.

Jördens, A. 2009. *Statthalterliche Verwaltung in der römischen Kaiserzeit: Studien zum praefectus Aegypti*. Stuttgart: Steiner.

Lesquier, J. 1918. *L'armée romaine d'Égypte d'Auguste à Dioclétien*. Cairo: Institut Français d'Archéologie Orientale.

Locher, J. 1999. *Topographie und Geschichte der Region am Ersten Nilkatarakt in griechisch-römischer Zeit*. Stuttgart: Teubner.

Mann, J. C. 1983. *Legionary Recruitment and Veteran Settlement during the Principate*. London: Institute of Archaeology.

Maxfield, V. A. 2000. 'The Deployment of the Roman Auxilia in Upper Egypt and the Eastern Desert during the Principate', in G. Alföldy, B. Dobson, and W. Eck (eds), *Kaiser, Heer und Gesellschaft in der römischen Kaiserzeit: Gedenkschrift für Eric Birley*. Stuttgart: Steiner, 407–42.

—— 2009. '"Where Did They Put the Men?" An Enquiry into the Accommodation of Soldiers in Roman Egypt', in W. S. Hanson (ed.), *The Army and Frontiers of Rome*. Portsmouth, RI: Journal of Roman Archaeology, 63–82.

Mitthof, F. 2000. 'Soldaten und Veteranen in der Gesellschaft des römischen Ägypten (1.–2. Jh. n. Chr.)', in G. Alföldy, B. Dobson, and W. Eck (eds), *Kaiser, Heer und Gesellschaft in der römischen Kaiserzeit: Gedenkschrift für Eric Birley*. Stuttgart: Steiner, 377–405.

—— 2001. *Annona militaris: Die Heeresversorgung im spätantiken Ägypten*. Florence: Gonnelli.

Nelis-Clément, J. 2000. *Les Beneficiarii: Militaires et administrateurs au service de l'empire (Ier s. a. C.–VIe s. p. C.)*. Bordeaux: Ausonius.

Palme, B. 2006. 'Zivile Aufgaben der Armee im kaiserzeitlichen Ägypten', in A. Kolb (ed.), *Herrschaftsstrukturen und Herrschaftspraxis: Konzeption, Prinzipien und Strategien der Administration im römischen Kaiserreich*. Berlin: Akademie, 299–328.

—— 2008. 'Militärs in der Rechtsprechung des römischen Ägypten', in E. Harris and G. Thür (eds), *Symposion 2007: Vorträge zur griechischen und hellenistischen Rechtsgeschichte (Durham, 2.–6. Sept. 2007)*. Vienna: Österreichische Akademie der Wissenschaften, 279–94.

Rankov, B. 1994. 'Die Beneficiarier in den literarischen und papyrologischen Texten', in E. Schallmayer et al. (eds), *Der römische Weihebezirk von Osterburken*, vol. 2: *Kolloquium 1990 und paläobotanische-osteologische Untersuchungen*. Stuttgart: Theiss, 219–32.

Reinmuth, O. W. 1935. *The Prefect of Egypt from Augustus to Diocletian*. Leipzig: Dieterich.

Ritterling, E. 1924–5. 'Legio', in G. Wissowa et al. (eds), *Paulys Realencyclopädie der classischen Altertumswissenschaften*, new edn, vol. 12/1–2: 1211–1829.

Römer, C. 1990. 'Diplom für einen Fußsoldaten aus Koptos vom 23. März 179', *Zeitschrift für Papyrologie und Epigraphik* 82: 137–53.

Sabin, P., H. van Wees, and M. Whitby. 2007. *The Cambridge History of Greek and Roman Warfare*, vol. 2: *Rome from the Late Republic to the Late Empire*. Cambridge: Cambridge University Press.

Sänger, P. 2009. 'Die Nomenklatur der legio II Traiana Fortis im 3. Jh. n. Chr.', *Zeitschrift für Papyrologie und Epigraphik* 169: 277–86.

—— 2011. *Veteranen unter den Severern und frühen Soldatenkaisern: Die Dokumentensammlungen der Veteranen Aelius Sarapammon und Aelius Syrion*. Stuttgart: Steiner.

Schubert, P. 2007. *Philadelphie: Un village égyptien en mutation entre le IIe et le IIIe siècle ap. J.-C.* Basel: Schwabe.

Sheehan, P. 1996. 'The Roman Fortress of Babylon in Old Cairo', in D. M. Bailey, *Archaeological Research in Roman Egypt*. Ann Arbor: Journal of Roman Archaeology, 95–8.

Speidel, M. A. 2009a. 'Rekruten für fremde Provinzen: Der Papyrus ChLA X 422 und die kaiserliche Rekrutierungszentrale', in Speidel, *Heer und Herrschaft im römischen Reich der Hohen Kaiserzeit*. Stuttgart: Steiner, 213–34.

—— 2009b. 'Einheit und Vielfalt in der römischen Heeresverwaltung', in Speidel, *Heer und Herrschaft im römischen Reich der Hohen Kaiserzeit*. Stuttgart: Steiner, 283–304.

—— 2009c. 'Ausserhalb des Reiches? Zu neuen lateinischen Inschriften aus Saudi Arabien und zur Ausdehnung der römischen Herrschaft am Roten Meer', in Speidel, *Heer und Herrschaft im römischen Reich der Hohen Kaiserzeit*. Stuttgart: Steiner, 633–49.

Speidel, M. P. 1988. 'Nubia's Roman Garrison', in H. Temporini (ed.), *Aufstieg und Niedergang der römischen Welt* II 10.1. Berlin: de Gruyter, 768–98.

Stauner, K. 2004. *Das offizielle Schriftwesen des römischen Heeres von Augustus bis Gallienus (27 v. Chr.–268 n. Chr.)*. Bonn: Habelt.

Stoll, O. 2009. 'Integration und doppelte Identität: Römisches Militär und die Kulte der Soldaten und Veteranen in Ägypten von Augustus bis Diokletian', in R. Gundlach and C. Vogel (eds), *Militärgeschichte des pharaonischen Ägypten*. Paderborn: Ferdinand Schöningh, 419–58.

Strassi, S. 2008. *L'archivio di Claudius Tiberianus da Karanis*. Berlin: de Gruyter.

Strobel, K. 1995. 'Rangordnung und Papyrologie', in Y. Le Bohec (ed.), *La Hiérarchie (Rangordnung) de l'armée romaine sous le Haut-Empire*. Paris: de Boccard, 93–111.

Wolff, C. 2000. 'La legio III Cyrenaica au Ier siècle', in Y. Le Bohec and C. Wolff (eds), *Les légions de Rome sous le Haut-Empire*. Lyon: Centre d'Études et de Recherches sur l'Occident Romain, 339–40.

CHAPTER 6

THE IMPERIAL CULT IN EGYPT

STEFAN PFEIFFER

THROUGHOUT the Roman empire, the living emperor was the subject of worship and also, in part, the object of a cult that was often very similar, if not identical, to the cult of the gods. This also applies to the Roman province of Aegyptus. Here the worship of the living ruler as a god was already a 300-year-old Ptolemaic tradition (see Pfeiffer 2008). This chapter presents the institutional structures of the cult of the emperor in Roman Egypt.

DEFINITIONS

To understand the cult of the emperor in Egypt, some preliminaries must be set out. The first question to be asked is what exactly the cult of the emperor is. Secondly, a wider consideration of the entire Roman empire is needed to show how the imperial cult developed throughout its territories. That is to say, it is only by considering the worship of the emperor empire-wide that an understanding of the specifically Egyptian construct of imperial cult is possible.

The Emperor as God: The Distinction between Imperial Cult and Emperor Worship

Although the title of this chapter refers to the 'imperial cult in Egypt', researchers are not entirely agreed about what an imperial cult actually is. The word 'cult' implies that the emperor was venerated as or like a god. Many see a solution to the problem in the difference between 'cult' and 'worship': cult is the honour reserved for the gods (e.g. offerings); worship can be given to mortals as well (e.g. prayer to a deity for the welfare of a person). Many researchers have a problem in assigning the emperor the status of a deity and would rather see him as a person especially venerated by his contemporaries, or else they attribute him a status between man and god (Fishwick 1987–2004); hence, problems of terminology arise, because the emperor was the recipient of a cult like a god in many parts of the empire. Gradel (2002) nevertheless avoids using the term 'imperial cult' and speaks instead of 'emperor worship'. For Gradel the divine cult of the emperor is nothing more than an *aspect* of emperor worship. Divinity in the ancient sense is, in his view, a 'distinction of status between the respective beings, rather than a distinction between their respective natures' (Gradel 2002: 26). The worshipped emperor was not a god in an 'absolute sense', but he had a 'divine status... in relation to the worshippers' (2002: 29). The person performing the cult ritual sought merely to ensure that the emperor ruled effectively: 'by receiving such honours, the emperor was morally obliged to return benefactions, that is, to rule well' (2002: 369).

Following this line of research, one may ultimately draw a clear distinction between the immortal gods and mortal emperor. This strict separation is not followed in a different line of research, however. Clauss (2001: 470) took the following view: 'At a time when the divine could be imagined in anything and everything, when each person themselves could become a deity in a mystery cult, why should the emperor, who was not just any man, not be seen as a deity?' (my translation).

It is indeed very likely that a person whom his ancient contemporaries addressed as a god, and who was provided with a cult, *could* be considered a god, and the definition formulated by Gradel is therefore too shallow. We do not know the personal beliefs of the ancient people when they made a dedication to the emperor as a deity, so it is not for us to decide that they did not consider him as a deity. Since the pagan concept of god has only the word 'god' in common with Judaeo-Christian tradition (otherwise both mean something completely different by 'god'), it should be assumed that, in fact, an emperor could always be a god in the ancient sense if he was given the same worship and addressed in the same way as a god—and this was often the case. The emperor was at that moment a present and powerful god residing in the world. Of course, he then had to behave as such, and that was exactly how offerings were meant to affect him. The same rules about a binding act of communication affected him as the gods—this was the ancient *do ut des* principle: 'If I perform a cult for you as a god, you have to behave like a god'.

Thus, if the emperor appears as a god, we may speak of an imperial *cult* after all—and cult is therefore to be understood here in the sense used by Cicero (*Nat. D* 2.3.8), as *cultus deorum pius*. The essential characteristics that comprise a cult for the emperor and his family are:

- temples, groves, and altars dedicated to the emperor and his family;
- the establishment of a priesthood for the emperor;
- rites or rituals for the emperor that are only accorded to gods;
- celebrating festivals for the emperor that are identical with festivals for the gods;
- the equivalence of the emperor with deities, a cult shared with other gods.

However, emperor *worship*, which can be found much more frequently in the sources, is always present when it is a question of honours that could be paid to particularly deserving people without placing them on a level with the gods. The most common expression of emperor worship was when subjects showed their gratitude and/or loyalty to the ruler by means of dedications or an offering for his safety (Latin: *pro/pro salute*; Greek: *ὑπέρ* plus genitive). These dedications went in the cultic sense to a deity (e.g. Zeus or Apollo), who was to guarantee the salvation of the emperor and, ultimately, his subjects. So, in my eyes, emperor worship is qualitatively something completely different from emperor cult, but both together could be called, as Fishwick (1987–2004) points out, 'imperial religion'.

Different Forms of Imperial Cult in the Roman Empire

Imperial Cult in the Provinces

In the east of the Roman empire, especially in Asia Minor, the establishment of the imperial cult emerged from the provinces. In 30/29 BCE Octavian, later Augustus, had already allowed cities to institute his divine worship in Asia Minor (see Friesen 1993: 7–15). The Koinon of Asia, which was the federation of Greek cities in the province of Asia, practised the official imperial cult. At their provincial parliament, representatives of all the Greek cities of the province met to discuss common issues and to perform the imperial cult (Price 1984: 56). For this reason we may talk about a provincial imperial cult of Augustus and the goddess Roma. Accordingly, the provincial priest of Asia had the title of 'chief priest of the goddess Roma and the emperor Caesar, son of god, Augustus' (Fayer 1976: 112–23).

The provincial cult in Asia Minor was the model Augustus and his successors used to establish the imperial cult in the west of the empire (Fishwick 1987–2004). Following the example of the Koinon of Asia, similar provincial parliaments were created in provinces that were still vulnerable in the west, with the particular objective of pacifying and building up the loyalty of local elites to the emperor. The beginning of this was the installation of a provincial cult around the *ara Romae et Augusti* in 12 BCE in Lyons, serving the Tres Galliae ('Three Gauls'), and before 7 BCE around the *ara Ubiorum* at Cologne. As Wlosok (1978: 47) observed, the purpose of establishing these cults was to promote the 'Romanization' of the provinces and consolidate the loyalty of local elites, whose members were responsible for both the priesthood and the provincial administration. However, the old senatorial provinces, long under Roman domination, did not have an imperial cult at the outset. Only under Vespasian were provincial cults introduced into these provinces.

Unofficial Imperial Cult

In addition to the imperial cult officially sanctioned by Rome, there were two other opportunities in the east to provide the emperor with a cult. First, there was the so-called municipal imperial cult, which was the responsibility of each Greek municipality (Kienast 1999: 251, with further references in n. 150). Secondly, there was the possibility of a private imperial cult, which did not have to be located within, or tied to, an institution. Even prayers and vows to the emperors can sometimes be found—evidence, therefore, of the existence of private piety focused on the ruler (Fishwick 1990; Chaniotis 2003: 19).

The Research Problem: What Kind of Cult Existed in Egypt?

In his examination of the imperial cult in Egypt, which still remains an important study, Blumenthal (1913: 325–7) maintained that there was no official provincial imperial cult of a Roman type in Egypt, because it would not have been possible, as was the case in Asia Minor, for a koinon of cities to have organized a cult of this kind. He believed that the cult, as comprehended through the *sebasteia* (as the temples of the imperial cult were called), was a purely urban cult, constitutionally on the same level as the municipal cults mentioned above; therefore, no imperial cult, organized by the emperor or by Rome, existed in Egypt. This would mean that the Roman rulers had no political interest in the veneration of their person in Egypt, but rather left it to their conquered subjects to decide whether to provide the emperor with a cult or not. An important proof of this would be the fact that in Egypt, Augustus was not worshipped together with Roma, as he was everywhere else in the empire.

Dunand (1983: 51–3) reinforced Blumenthal's view that the cult was in the hands of the local authorities and was dependent upon their goodwill. Dunand saw the establishment of imperial temples, in their Egyptian form, as a series of sporadic gestures. In her opinion, however, there were no indications that any official guidance or interference, either by the emperor or by a representative of Rome, was involved. However, Rigsby (1985: 284) takes exactly the opposite view, which assumes that Rome adopted a strictly neutral stance towards other religions and that it simply had a different appearance in Egypt: 'Unlike imperial cult elsewhere, this was a creature of imperial policy and represents a decision by some emperor that he must sponsor emperor worship in Egypt.' Similarly, Dundas (1994: 119) believes that the Roman administration did institutionalize the imperial cult at a local level, in the *metropoleis*. Although neither Rigsby nor Dundas provide clear evidence for their opinion, or adequately address the opposing viewpoint, they are undoubtedly correct: an imperial cult did exist in Egypt and it was official, that is, instituted by Rome. The resolution to this research problem is set out in the following analysis of the structures and institutions that were associated with the imperial cult in Egypt.

Institutions of the Imperial Cult in Egypt

The Imperial Temples

In the whole of Egypt there are archaeological and papyrological references to imperial temples called *sebasteia* (from the Greek translation of the name Augustus) or *caesarea* (from the Latin title 'caesar', hence *caesareum*, both derived from the cognomen of Julius Caesar). In addition to their administrative functions, these temples were assigned the responsibility for emperor worship or the imperial cult.

The Sebasteion (Caesareum) in Alexandria

The biggest *sebasteion* in Egypt was, of course, in Alexandria (Herklotz 2007: 267–72). This is a construction begun by Cleopatra VII that was subsequently rededicated to Augustus and referred to as the 'temple' or 'shrine', variously *Καίσαρος νεώς*, *Caesaris templum*, or *Caesareum Magnum*, as well as *ὁ ναὼς τοῦ Σεβαστοῦ* (Plin. *HN* 36.69; *C Pap. Jud.* II 153.60–1; *W Chr.* 463 II 7). If we want to try to deduce the appearance of this complex, we have to resort to the Jewish writer Philo of Alexandria, who reports that throughout the world, Augustus received honours equivalent to those of the Olympian gods (Philo, *Leg.* 149–51). To give one example of that, Philo describes the Alexandrian Caesareum as follows:

> Nowhere is there a holy place comparable to the so-called Sebasteion... great and famous, filled with offerings like nowhere else, surrounded with paintings and statues of silver and gold, a vast sacred precinct with covered ambulatories, libraries, rooms, sacred groves, gates, large open spaces, open courts, all decorated in the most extravagant manner.

The sanctuary was built in an elevated location and hence was clearly visible to all (Philo, *Leg.* 151). Although the archaeological record in Alexandria is generally extremely poor, we do know more about the location and layout of the Alexandrian Caesareum. Two obelisks survive, which are now in London and New York and which marked the location of the temple until the nineteenth century. The sanctuary of Augustus was indeed, as Pliny describes, *ad portum*, right on the harbour (Plin. *HN* 36.69; Strabo 17.1.9; Philo, *Leg.* 151). On a bronze sculpture of a crab placed beneath it, one of the obelisks bore the dedicatory inscription 'Year 18 [13/12 BCE] of Caesar, Barbarus erected it under the overall supervision of Pontius' (*OGIS* II 656 = *I Alex.* 2). Hence, the completion of the imperial cult complex was the responsibility of a Roman official named Pontius, and likewise its facilities, in this case the erection of an obelisk, were financed by a representative of the power of the state, Barbarus.

In a convincing interpretation, Alföldy successfully demonstrated that a third obelisk, now in St Peter's Square in Rome, also belonged to the temple of Augustus. Before its erasure, the Latin inscription on the base of the object read: 'By order of the Emperor Caesar, son of god, Caius Cornelius Gallus, son of Gnaeus, the *praefectus fabrum*, constructed the *forum Iulium* for Caesar, the son of god' (*Iussu Imp(eratoris) Caesaris Divi f(ili) C(aius) Cornelius Cn(aei) f(ilius) Gallus praef(ectus) fabr(um) Caesaris Divi f(ili) forum Iulium fecit*; Alföldy 1990: 18). Alföldy was able to show that the *forum Iulium* could only have been located in Alexandria and must have been a monumental complex of open spaces, which may be identical to the *Σεβαστὴ ἀγορά*, or the *forum Augusti*, known from papyri. It must therefore have been an open space located at the temple of Augustus (Alföldy 1990: 41–2).

The *forum Iulium* was renamed the *forum Augusti* after 27 BCE, when Octavian received the name Augustus. Thus, Gallus, the first prefect of Egypt, completed work on the space around the Caesareum that had in fact been begun by Cleopatra.

Furthermore, archaeological research quite plausibly suggests that the appearance of the temple of Augustus in Alexandria resembled official buildings of the city of Rome (Tuchelt 1981: 173). Ruggendorfer (1996: 218–19) points to the porticus of Octavia, the porticus of Pompey, and the Saepta Julia as comparanda. A complex based on a model from the city of Rome or a Romanizing model also accords rather well with Roman supervision of the design.

In summary, the Alexandrian sanctuary of Augustus was an institution with a direct imperial connection, since a Roman administrator was involved in erecting obelisks at the complex and the overseer of the project was also a Roman. It is therefore likely that the central Roman authority for establishing a cult for Augustus was at work in Alexandria. However, the cult was supported by the citizens of Alexandria, who chose the *neokoroi*—the cult officials designated as 'temple guardians'—from among their ranks. A letter from the emperor Claudius to the Alexandrians set out a lottery process for electing these cult officials, which eliminated the possibility of certain parties obtaining more influence and prestige by permanent occupation of the office (*C Pap. Jud.* II 153). The fact that it was Claudius who stipulated this procedure once again shows the direct connection between this complex and the emperor.

The Imperial Temple on Philae

On the island of Philae in Upper Egypt, which marked the southern border of the province, there was also a temple of Augustus (Herklotz 2007: 273–5). Its architrave bore the dedicatory inscription 'For the emperor Caesar Augustus, saviour and benefactor, in the 18th year [13/12 BCE], during the term of office of the (*praefectus Aegypti*) Publius Rubrius Barbarus' (*Αὐτοκράτορι Καίσαρι Σεβαστῶι σωτῆρι καὶ εὐεργέτῃ, (ἔτους) ιη ἐπὶ Ποπλίου Ῥοβρίου Βαρβάρου*; *OGIS* 657 = *IGP* II 140).

The temple is thus from the same year in which the foundation sculpture of a crab was placed under the obelisk in the Caesareum at Alexandria. In the open space in front of the cult building the foundations of a sacrificial altar can be detected (Fig. 6.1). A staircase occupies the middle half of the front of the temple and leads up to the tetrastyle pronaos *in antis*. The cult building stood on a podium, 9.7 × 16.7 metres in area and about 1.25 metres high—a feature that identifies this sanctuary as a Roman podium temple (Hänlein-Schäfer 1985: 220).

The naos itself had a floor area of 7.8 × 10.1 metres. The surviving architrave fragment with the inscription shows the remains of a Doric triglyph (Fig. 6.2). In addition, there were Corinthian capitals; these may have terminated the sanctuary's pillars, which had no fluting and stood on Attic bases. It is a mixed Doric–Corinthian temple, a composite style consistent with

FIG. 6.1 The temple of Augustus on the island of Philae

Author's photograph.

the period. This form is similar to what was known elsewhere from hellenistic culture; however, Schenk (1997: 143) points out that the beams have a parallel in the Arch of Augustus at Rome.

Thus, in Upper Egypt, on the border with ancient Ethiopia, stands a temple of a very unusual design for Egypt. On whose initiative the sanctuary was built cannot be determined from the building inscription. The idea that the sanctuary was dedicated by the local inhabitants is based on a misinterpretation of an inscription from the time of Vespasian (*IGP* II 161 = *OGIS* II 670; *pace* Herklotz 2007: 282). This inscription merely states that the residents of the area donated a statue of the emperor, which reveals nothing about the initiative behind the construction of the sanctuary itself.

The Imperial Chapel at Karnak

Another imperial temple, probably also from the time of the emperor Augustus, was located in Karnak, next to the causeway of the temple of Amun. It stood just to the right in front of the first pylon, with its entrance aligned towards the dromos. Just like the temple at Philae, this sanctuary was located outside the enclosure wall of the Egyptian temple. Because of its location by the sacred way of the temple, however, this temple was directly related to the Egyptian temple and, in the fullest possible way, its public worship, which was always enacted on the temple approach (Fig. 6.3).

FIG. 6.2 Architrave fragment from the temple of Augustus on the island of Philae

Author's photograph.

FIG. 6.3 Imperial cult chapel in front of the first pylon of Karnak temple

Author's photograph.

The structure is in the form of a prostyle tetrastyle temple. The columns were of Corinthian design, since a column capital of that type was found, which can almost certainly be attributed to the architecture of the building (Pensabene 1993). However, it is no longer possible to reconstruct whether the sanctuary was a *templum in antis*, as at Philae, or whether the antae were replaced by two columns (Lauffray 1971, figs 2 and 31). Its small size—only 8.6 × 14 metres—seems to warrant calling the structure a chapel. Just like its much larger counterpart at Philae, it had a small staircase that occupies roughly the middle half of the façade, leading up to the podium temple.

It is revealing that the bases from a total of fourteen emperors' statues were found close together in the almost square cella. Not all of the statues have inscriptions, but two can be ascribed to Augustus and three to Claudius. At Narona, Dalmatia, a free-standing imperial cult building with similar features survives, in the form of archaeological remains. On the west side of the forum there, a nearly square room contained the remains of up to sixteen statues of the emperors and their family members, which date from the first century to the time of Trajan (Marin 1999).

Sebasteia and Caesarea in the Chora, Known from Papyri

Besides the three archaeologically documented examples, there are several records from Egyptian papyri of *sebasteia* or *caesarea* in the *chora*, of which the earliest is that at Canopus

(41 CE; *C Pap. Jud.* 153.60–1). It was under the administration of the Alexandrian citizenship, as attested by the previously mentioned letter from Claudius to the Alexandrians. Additionally, the existence of *caesarea* and *sebasteia* can be proved for Antinoopolis, Arsinoe, Elephantine, Heptakomia, Herakleopolis, Hermopolis, Lykopolis (probably), Oxyrhynchus, and Philadelphia (listed in Kunderewicz 1961: 124 and Strassi 2006: 236–43; for individual examples, see Dundas 1994: 135–77; Herklotz 2007: 275–82). Buildings of this kind appear to have existed especially in nome capitals; however, there is evidence from the villages of Philadelphia and Heptakomia (Strassi 2006: 224–5) that the cult of Augustus and his successors, and particularly the civic administration, was centred on a *caesareum* in other places, too.

Roman Podium Temples to the Emperor

It is highly significant that the imperial cult temples known from the Egyptian archaeological record were sanctuaries of Roman design. In Egypt the construction of Roman temples to the emperor, especially in the extreme south of the *imperium*, should be seen as an anomaly, otherwise attested only in the case of a few later sanctuaries to Serapis (Mons Claudianus, Tehne, Ras el-Soda (Alexandria)). Unlike in other provinces of the east, classical architectural forms, in particular following hellenistic trends, were not usually adopted for the sanctuaries of the gods; instead, temples in the ancient Egyptian tradition continued to be constructed for the indigenous deities.

As for the propagation of the imperial cult and emperor worship, the following observation should be made: the *caesareum* at Alexandria was situated at the 'most visible' (as Philo said) point in the city, and the temples of Philae and Karnak were in locations clearly visible to everyone. It is most likely that the other *sebasteia*, as well as those of Asia Minor, were also built where people came together for ritual, political, economic, ceremonial, and private reasons. As in Asia Minor, the Egyptian imperial cult complexes were closely linked to public and religious life.

The Regional High Priesthood: The 'High Priest of the City'

Like the cult of the gods in an Egyptian nome capital, the imperial cult was in the hands of a city official, who, from the mid-second century, is frequently encountered in the papyri with the title 'high priest of the city' (*ἀρχιερεὺς τῆς πόλεως*; Oertel 1917: 335–8; Drecoll 1997: 104–5).

Unfortunately, information is very sparse about the activities associated with the civic 'obligatory' and 'honorary' functions of a high priest. It is certain that the office was only held by members of the wealthiest families, because there was a great financial burden associated with assuming a magistracy of this kind. Indeed, it can be assumed that no small part of the public cult festivities was the responsibility of this man. His specific responsibility for the imperial cult can be seen from his official titles. From papyrus *P Merton* I 18, dated 161 CE, the full title of the priest is recorded 'as high priest of the Lords Augusti and all the gods' (*ἀρχιερεὺς τῶν κυρίων Σεβαστῶν καὶ θεῶν ἁπάντων*). If this indicates that the high priest of the emperors was responsible for all the gods, then it is understandable that his title could simply be 'high priest of the city'. Since he is probably identical to the high priest of the Augusti, or high priest of the Lords Augusti, his main task probably lies in his imperial cult function. This is to be expected simply because all the other cults of a city had a local tradition with local priesthoods, whereas the imperial cult, as a cult form that had not grown up organically from Egyptian or Greek society, had no regional priesthood.

Let us turn now to the question of when the high priesthood of the city began. The specific difficulty is that the high priests of the city appear in papyri in increasing numbers only from the second century onwards. This would suggest that the office only existed from that time, although imperial temples in Egypt are known from archaeological evidence already from the time of Augustus. An Alexandrian inscription (*I Alex.* 29) may possibly help to fill this gap in our records: there we meet an Apollon, the 'current high priest of the Lords Augusti' from the time of Marcus Aurelius (ruled 161–80). Apollon also enumerates his genealogy, from which we can see that almost all of his ancestors and relatives were also priests of the Augusti. Therefore, the office must have been in the hands of this family since the mid-50s of the first century CE (Kruse 2002: 924).

The High Priests of Alexandria and the Whole of Egypt

An official known as the 'high priest of Alexandria and Egypt' (*ἀρχιερεὺς Ἀλεξανδρείας καὶ Αἰγύπτου πάσης*) is known to us from numerous documents; the man serving as this priest had to hold the rank of a Roman *eques*. In contrast to the regional high priest, he is of Roman origin. Although the high priest of Alexandria and Egypt is certainly not to be confused with the regional high priests of the city just discussed, who served in the towns and cities of the *chora* as well as for Alexandria, it is proving difficult for researchers to reconstruct his areas of responsibility.

The Research Problem

Research on this problem generally starts from the premiss that there is no evidence that the high priest of Alexandria and all Egypt was a high priest of the imperial cult for the province. The general view is that, while it is true that the high priest had administrative oversight for all the cults in the country, despite his official title he did not function as an imperial priest. Stead (1980: 418), for instance, concludes that this priest, 'despite his title, was a bureaucrat'.

From the evidence in the papyri, the main task of the 'high priest of Alexandria and Egypt' was to control access to the Egyptian priesthood, because the circumcision of candidates for the priesthood had to be approved by him. Furthermore, he acted as a link between the people and the Egyptian temples, and mediated in disputes (Stead 1980: 415; Kruse 2002: 728–50; Demougin 2006: 515). This purely administrative function of the high priest is attested from the second century onwards. Furthermore, no one questions his responsibility for Greek cults in the province, even though there is no explicit evidence for it. Consequently, the high priest was responsible for the administrative oversight of all cult activities in Egypt, which means also the imperial cult. In a papyrus from the early third century (*P Harr.* I 69), he appears to have even had jurisdictional competence in a dispute about an inheritance with a temple-related background (it concerned the release of a sum of money from the estate of a priest, on which there were earlier claims).

Although the general opinion of scholarship assumes that the office was set up under Hadrian, there are a few voices that have a different viewpoint. Wilcken (1912: 127) believed it was possible that the highest supervisory office had already been introduced by Augustus, which would then have been analogous to what happened to the high priesthood in Syria, since the first *archiereus* there was also a contemporary of Augustus (*BE* 1976: 718). Capponi also thought along those lines (2005: 41–2; in contrast Herklotz 2007: 300), drawing attention to *P Oxy*. XII 1434.9–10 and the former high priest Gaius Julius Theon, who is named there. Although the relevant papyrus dates to 107/8 CE, it relates to land that had formerly been in the possession of Theon. As the editors of the text note, Theon himself was a contemporary of Gaius Julius Aquila, the prefect of Egypt in 10–11 CE.

Rigsby (1985: 284–6) is also of the opinion that the high priest of Alexandria and all Egypt had existed quite early on, probably before 39/40 CE, because at that time a local 'high priest of Gaius Caesar Augustus Germanicus' appears in the Fayum (*P Merton* I 11; *P Ryl.* II 149). According to Rigsby, ever since then there had also been the generic 'high priest of Alexandria and all Egypt' to whom the regional high priests were subordinate. However, this is based on the premiss that the 'high priest of Alexandria and all Egypt' was actually responsible for the cult of the emperor, and that regional high priests had to be under the control of a central Alexandrian high priest—Rigsby assumes both of these without discussion. He also thinks that the office of 'high priest of Alexandria and Egypt' was set up by Tiberius for his late predecessor, and that under Caligula it was eventually extended to the cult of the living ruler.

The Duties of the High Priest of Alexandria and All Egypt

Varied opinions have appeared in research literature about whether, in addition to his administrative duties, the high priest of Alexandria and Egypt also had primary responsibility for the cult of the emperor, and whether he was, moreover, the cultic head of all the other high priests of the emperor in Egypt. A renewed debate on this issue is necessary, given that the title 'high priest' indicates a sacred office. In the other provinces of the empire, high priests of the imperial cult, with sacred duties, had already been installed in the reign of Augustus, so it is right to ask why exactly the high priest of Egypt should have held no sacred office.

The following points should be noted:

- It is not acceptable to conclude, solely based on the silence of the papyri, that the high priest was not accorded any ritual function.
- The very fact that the high priest held a sacred title suggests he had a sacred responsibility.
- Similar titles in other parts of the *imperium*, where the priests were undoubtedly responsible for the emperor worship, suggest that the high priest in Egypt was likewise responsible for the cult of the emperor.

First, therefore, the full title of the high priest needs to be considered: it was 'high priest of the gods Augusti and the Great Serapis and the one who is responsible for the temples of Egypt and the whole country'. Unlike the regional priest, who carried out the cult for the 'Lords Augusti', the high priest of Alexandria and Egypt was thus responsible for the cult of the 'gods Augusti'—this variation enables us to distinguish between the two priesthoods. The title of the Alexandrian high priest had no fixed formula and could certainly be shortened. In the applications for circumcision by candidates for the Egyptian priesthood he was called both ἀρχιερεὺς καὶ ἐπὶ τῶν ἐν Αἰγύπτῳ ἱ[ε]ρῶν ('high priest and overseer of the temples in Egypt'; *SB* I 15.28, 16.17, 17.16) or simply ἀρχιερεὺς καὶ ἐπὶ τῶν ἱερῶν ('high priest and overseer of the temples'; *W Chr.* 76.15–16). From the full title of the high priest, it is clear, however, that the administrative aspect, here expressed by the phrase ἐπὶ τ[ῶ]ν [κατὰ Ἀλεξάνδ]ρε[ιαν καὶ κατὰ Αἴγυ]πτον ἱερῶν, '*the one who is responsible* for the temples in Alexandria and all of Egypt', was an additional task of the high priest rather than his principal duty. His main responsibility lay rather in the care and management of the pan-Egyptian cult of the emperors, as well as the cult of Serapis.

The title 'high priest of Alexandria and Egypt', always abbreviated in other documents, thus needs to be looked at carefully. The role holder was, on the one hand, the high priest and, on the other, the head of the governmental administration (*procurator*) of all the cult complexes in Egypt. From this it is clear that the Romans made a precise distinction between cultic and administrative duties, and the high priest, just like the comparable high priest in other provinces, was responsible for the imperial cult. It is also important that the cult of Serapis was under the control of the most senior management of the same Roman priest, which underlines the importance of that deity for Roman rule in Egypt.

In addition, it is likely that the high priests carried out different duties in various provinces of the empire as part of their *cursus honorum*. Thus, Lucius Julius Vestinus, mentioned above, was *ab epistulis* Hadrian and responsible for the Latin and Greek libraries in Rome, but was also ἀρχιερεὺς Ἀλεξανδρίας καὶ Αἰγύπτου πάσης ('high priest of Alexandria and all Egypt'; *OGIS* II 679). In addition to his possible activities as high priest in 55–9 CE, Tiberius Claudius Balbillus was *praefectus Aegypti* (Stein 1950: 33–4; Pflaum 1960–1, no. 15). Because of this *cursus* it is safe to assume that the high priests, like all the procurators, were of equestrian rank.

To summarize this line of argument, the full title 'chief (or high) priest of the gods Augusti and the Great Serapis and the one who is responsible for the temples of Egypt and the whole country' shows that the high priesthood covered both the Augusti and Serapis. The term high priest, *archiereus*, was chosen because it genuinely related to a sacred area of responsibility. Furthermore, the highest administrative responsibility of this man for the ritual aspects of Egyptian temples is recorded definitively in papyrological sources—which clearly demonstrates the second component of the full title. All the high priests of this title who are known by name were Roman citizens, and were probably of equestrian rank. The high priests were appointed by the emperor, as we learn from one of Hadrian's decrees of appointment (*SB* XII 11236). And lastly, we can also learn from these titles that, as well as the cult for the Augusti, which was to be performed throughout Egypt, the cult of Serapis must have held a central position in Roman times. Otherwise almost no Romans would have attained this position in the priesthood or, to put it another way, Rome would certainly not have been so interested in the supervision, and thus also the control, of the cult of Serapis.

A Provincial Imperial Cult in Egypt

As we have seen, there is archaeological evidence for temples of Augustus in Egypt that are of Roman design. There is, however, not the slightest trace of parts of a temple of Augustus together with the goddess Roma, unlike the other provinces of the empire. This was possibly because the senate, as the main representative of Rome, had no access to the province. In Karnak there is also evidence that the successors of Augustus were represented by statues in the Caesareum there, and there is a strong possibility that a cult of Augustus was already being performed in the *sebasteia* of Egypt during his lifetime—the temples were, after all, dedicated to him. Whether the other emperors received a cult in these temples cannot be established for certain, but since there were priests of Tiberius and Gaius at the level of the nomes, it seems quite possible.

Not taken into account in the literature so far is the fact that two of the three remaining imperial cult complexes in Egypt chose a design based on a Roman model, namely a podium temple. Although the podiums of the two complexes was not particularly high, they exhibited a foreign character to the Egyptians and Greeks living in Egypt. The foreignness of the imperial cult expressed in this way is also brought into stark relief by the fact that the imperial cult complexes in Asia Minor were constructed using what were, for the Greeks, familiar architectural forms, signalling the close relationship between divine cult and emperor worship (Zanker 2003: 295). In contrast, the podium temple was not a familiar form of building for either the Egyptians or the Greeks in Egypt. The acculturation of the imperial cult in Asia Minor is largely explained by the fact that the cult primarily emerged from the initiative of Greek cities and koina, who also built the temples. However, when a foreign design began to be used in Egypt, it seems likely that the initiative for such cult complexes came from the foreign power. The aim was to make a clear break with the Ptolemaic period (Pfeiffer 2009). If there were *sebasteia* in every nome from that time onwards, as Blumenthal (1913: 322) and Dundas (1994: 176) believe, then these temples must have been established immediately after Egypt became a province. In that case, the *sebasteia* in question must have been set up by the ruling power. At the very least, it is unlikely that members of the local elites would have taken the initiative to establish imperial cult places in the nome capitals, because it was not possible for them to take jointly coordinated action—there was no city council or similar body at that level. Instead, it is possible that a short time after Egypt became a province, the first *princeps* or the prefect of Egypt issued a decree to provide the whole of Egypt with *sebasteia*.

Besides the architectural argument for a Roman directive for establishing an imperial cult in Egypt, there are some other indications that this was the case. From the surviving evidence, the imperial cult temples, called *caesarea* or *sebasteia*, were the central places of administration within the nomes from the second century onwards, and must therefore have had very close official links with the Roman authorities. The imperial priesthood of the individual nomes was, furthermore, part of the public offices of the regional metropolitan administration, which means that the priests of the emperor were recruited from the local elite and involved in municipal government. It is highly likely that all the metropolitan regional imperial priests were subordinate to the 'high priest of Alexandria and all Egypt'. And lastly, the 'high priest of Alexandria and all Egypt' was a procurator-like official, appointed by Rome, and a Roman *eques*, who was also responsible for administrative oversight of all the cults in Egypt. Since the high priesthood of the Lords Augusti had no precedent in the form of a similar type of institution from Ptolemaic Egypt that might have been continued, it is hardly likely that the high priesthood was established in the whole of Egypt through the initiative of local elites without the assistance of the government; in fact, it is more likely that a higher authority ensured its establishment in Egyptian *metropoleis*, and this higher authority can only have been the emperor himself or his local representative, the *praefectus Aegypti*.

The Impact of the Imperial Cult in Egypt

In the non-government sector, in other words outside the precincts of the imperial cult, there is evidence of the emperor cult in the form of a handful, at most, of imperial cult *collegiae* (clubs or associations) (cf. *W Chr.* 112 = *BGU* IV 1137). It is also noteworthy that the Egyptian priests, in contrast to the Ptolemaic period, played almost no role in the imperial cult (see Pfeiffer 2004). The Roman emperor—unlike the Ptolemaic kings (see Pfeiffer 2008)—was not a god in Egyptian sanctuaries, and the existence of a private imperial cult practised by the populace, outside the official imperial cult, cannot be established. In the private context of his subjects, the emperor almost never achieved the position of a divinity who could receive a cult, or for whom one might gratefully fulfil a vow. This is quite remarkable, especially compared with the Greek east, where there were multiple forms of the imperial cult at a local level. In Egypt the explanation for this, at least in part, is the fact that there was no major impetus for it: there was none of the competitive situation between the Greek cities vying with each other for the attention of the emperor and the bestowal of so-called *neokoriai* (which were granted to cities in Asia Minor).

At the non-governmental level, emperor worship, rather than cult, was the dominant and prevalent way of demonstrating loyalty, especially by making offerings to the emperor. Whatever their ethnic, cultural, or religious background, his subjects made many donations directed towards their own divinities, asking the gods to guarantee the well-being of the ruler. In this, the Romans, Greeks, and Egyptians were alike; even Jews offered entire sacrifices to their supreme god for the emperor's sake (Philo, *Leg.* 357). Consequently, offerings *for the benefit of* the emperor was the unifying 'prescribed terminology' of emperor worship in Egypt. A similar situation existed in Rome, in the western empire, and in the Greek east.

The question of whether and to what extent the Roman emperor was able to persuade the hearts and minds of his subjects in Egypt to accept his sovereignty, and the special venerability of his person, is a different matter. Did the imperial cult strengthen the legitimization of Roman rule? The question is difficult to answer because we do not know what his subjects were thinking when they worshipped the emperor or provided him with a cult. For the mindset of the Alexandrian population at least, the viewpoint found in the so-called *Acta Alexandrinorum* is very revealing (see Chapter 17). If the citizens were interested in the deification of the emperor, as one is led to believe from their official statements (*C Pap. Jud.* II 153), the documents reveal this merely as an effort to secure goodwill, privileges, and benefits from him (on this, see Harker 2008). Despite all the loyalty it proclaimed to the emperor in inscriptions and oaths, the city's elite had serious clashes with the imperial house—clashes in which the Alexandrians were the losers. Whether the processes described in the *Acta Alexandrinorum* are historically documented conflicts or not is of secondary importance in this context. What is important is the insight that the texts provide into the almost anti-imperial mentality of the Greek upper-middle class in Alexandria. The discovery of copies of the documents throughout the country may further indicate that similar views were widely held among Greeks living there, including the Hellenized Egyptians. Apparently, Rome had not managed to get the elite, or at least important parts of the Greek middle class, entirely on its side.

Conclusion

After an almost total break from the traditions of the cult of rulers as it had been shaped by the Ptolemies, organized around the cult of Alexander and the Egyptian temples (Pfeiffer 2008), Augustus had already introduced into Egypt his own form of worship for the rulers. The state imperial cult in Egypt was fundamentally different from all the other official provincial cults in the empire in that the goddess Roma was of no importance here. The cult was institutionalized in the imperial temples of the nome capitals. Here, the office of high priest was exercised by liturgical officials from the metropolitan elite. Overall supervision of Egyptian emperor worship was the responsibility of the high priest of Alexandria and Egypt, who, as a Roman, was also the priest of the pan-Egyptian cult of the emperors and Serapis, as well as procurator of all cult matters in Egypt. The absence of the goddess Roma is due to the special importance that the province of Egypt without doubt attained in the overall structure of the *imperium*. In Egypt, the Roman senate had no power of control de jure or de facto here. The worship of Roma was closely connected with the senate, which is why Augustus did not introduce it in Egypt.

Let us therefore return to the starting point of this analysis—to the various possible cults of the emperor in the *imperium*: the material analysed does not allow any other possibility than to expand or differentiate the distinction of the imperial cult in the *imperium*. In Egypt the imperial cult was neither purely provincial, nor purely urban. Instead, it was a provincial imperial cult that was set up from above and locally organized, and which was subject to central supervision. The Egyptian form of the imperial cult directed from Rome differed only in part from other provincial cults. There was no Egypt-wide meeting of all provincial supervisors at an *ara Augusti*; this seems not to have been desired officially (Dundas 1994: 107). Here we have the most significant difference from the west of the empire. On the other hand there were *sebasteia* in Galatia, in other words in the east of the empire, as well as in Egypt, throughout the country, each having an altar to Augustus where his subjects were to demonstrate their loyalty to Augustus. How little, however, the imperial cult may have appealed to the subjects is apparent, on the one hand, from the solid Alexandrian criticism of the Roman emperors, and also from the existence of only very little evidence of the imperial cult from private individuals.

Suggested Reading

A number of recent works have re-evaluated the imperial cult throughout the Roman empire, such as Price (1984), Clauss (2001), Gradel (2002), or the still important work of Taeger (1960). For the imperial cult in Egypt, Blumenthal's (1913) early study remains valuable, but see also Dundas (1994), Heinen (1995), Herklotz (2007), and Pfeiffer (2010). For the Caesareum in Alexandria, see McKenzie (2007).

Bibliography

Alföldy, G. 1990. *Der Obelisk auf dem Petersplatz in Rom: Ein historisches Monument der Antike*. Heidelberg: Winter.

Blumenthal, F. 1913. 'Der ägyptische Kaiserkult', *Archiv für Papyrusforschung* 5: 317–45.

Capponi, L. 2005. *Augustan Egypt: The Creation of a Roman Province*. London: Routledge.

Chaniotis, A. 2003. 'Der Kaiserkult im Osten des römischen Reiches im Kontext der zeitgenössischen Ritualpraxis', in H. Cancik and K. Hitzl (eds), *Die Praxis der Herrscherverehrung in Rom und seinen Provinzen*. Tübingen: Wachsmuth, 3–28.

Clauss, M. 2001. *Kaiser und Gott: Herrscherkult im römischen Reich*, 2nd edn. Darmstadt: Wissenschaftliche Buchgesellschaft.

Demougin, S. 2006. '*Archiereus Alexandreae et Totius Aegypti*: Un office profane', in A. Vigourt et al. (eds), *Pouvoir et religion dans le monde romain: En hommage à Jean-Pierre Martin*. Paris: Presses de l'Université Paris–Sorbonne, 513–19.

Drecoll, C. 1997. *Die Liturgien im römischen Kaiserreich des 3. und 4. Jh. n. Chr. Untersuchungen über Zugang, Inhalt und wirtschaftliche Bedeutung der öffentlichen Zwangsdienste in Ägypten und anderen Provinzen*. Stuttgart: Steiner.

Dunand, F. 1983. 'Culte royal et culte impérial en Égypte: Continuités et ruptures', in G. Grimm, H. Heinen, and E. Winter (eds), *Das römisch byzantinische Ägypten: Akten des Internationalen Symposions, 26.–30. September 1978 in Trier*. Mainz: von Zabern, 47–56.

Dundas, G. S. 1994. 'Pharaoh, Basileus and Imperator: The Roman Imperial Cult in Egypt', doctoral dissertation, University of California, Los Angeles.

Fayer, C. 1976. *Il culto della dea roma: Origine e diffusione nell'Impero*. Pescara: Trimestre.

Fishwick, D. 1987–2004. *The Imperial Cult in the Latin West: Studies in the Ruler Cult of the Western Provinces of the Roman Empire*. Leiden: Brill.

—— 1990. 'Votive Offerings to the Emperor?', *Zeitschrift für Papyrologie und Epigraphik* 80: 121–30.

Friesen, S. J. 1993. *Twice Neokoros: Ephesus, Asia and the Cult of the Flavian Imperial Family*. Leiden: Brill.

Gradel, I. 2002. *Emperor Worship and Roman Religion*. Oxford: Oxford University Press.

Hänlein-Schäfer, H. 1985. *Veneratio Augusti: Eine Studie zu den Tempeln des ersten römischen Kaisers*. Rome: Bretschneider.

—— 1996. 'Die Ikonographie des Genius Augusti im Kompital- und Hauskult der frühen Kaiserzeit', in A. Small (ed.), *Subject and Ruler: The Cult of the Ruling Power in Classical Antiquity*. Ann Arbor: Journal of Roman Archaeology, 73–98.

Harker, A. 2008. *Loyalty and Dissidence in Roman Egypt: The Case of the Acta Alexandrinorum*. Cambridge: Cambridge University Press.

Heinen, H. 1995. 'Vorstufen und Anfänge des Herrscherkultes im römischen Ägypten', in W. Haase and H. Temporini (eds), *Aufstieg und Niedergang der römischen Welt* II 18.5. Berlin: de Gruyter, 3144–80.

Herklotz, F. 2007. *Prinzeps und Pharao: Der Kult des Augustus in Ägypten*. Frankfurt: Antike.

Kienast, D. 1999. *Augustus: Prinzeps und Monarch*, 3rd edn. Darmstadt: Wissenschaftliche Buchgesellschaft.

Kruse, T. 2002. *Der königliche Schreiber und die Gauverwaltung: Untersuchungen zur Verwaltungsgeschichte Ägyptens in der Zeit von Augustus bis Philippus Arabs (30 v. Chr.–245 n. Chr.)*. Munich: Saur.

Kunderewicz, C. 1961. 'Quelques Remarques sur le rôle des *ΚΑΙΣΑΡΕΙΑ* dans la vie juridique le l'Égypte romaine', *Journal of Juristic Papyrology* 13: 123–9.

Lauffray, J. 1971. 'Abords occidentaux du premier pylône de Karnak: Le dromos, la tribune et les aménagements portuaires', *Kêmi* 21: 77–144.

McKenzie, J. 2007. *The Architecture of Alexandria and Egypt, c.300* B.C. *to* A.D. *700*. New Haven: Yale University Press.

Marin, E. 1999. 'Découverte d'un Augusteum à Narona', in E. Marin et al. (eds), *Narona*. Zagreb: Naro Naklada, 63–74.

Nock, A. D. 1934. 'The Institution of Ruler-Worship', in A. K. Bowman, E. Champlin, and A. Lintott (eds), *The Cambridge Ancient History*, vol. 10. Cambridge: Cambridge University Press, 481–9.

Oertel, F. 1917. *Die Liturgie: Studien zur ptolemäischen und kaiserlichen Verwaltung Ägyptens*. Leipzig: Teubner.

Pensabene, P. 1993. *Repertorio d'arte dell'Egitto greco-romano C*, vol. 3: *Elementi architettonici di Alessandria e di altri siti egiziani*. Rome: 'L'Erma' di Bretschneider.

Pfeiffer, S. 2004. *Das Dekret von Kanopos (238 v. Chr.): Kommentar und historische Auswertung eines dreisprachigen Synodaldekretes der ägyptischen Priester zu Ehren Ptolemaios' III. und seiner Familie*. Munich: Saur.

—— 2008. *Herrscher- und Dynastiekulte im Ptolemäerreich: Systematik und Einordnung der Kultformen*. Munich: Beck.

—— 2009. 'Octavian-Augustus und Ägypten', in A. Coskun et al. (eds), *Repräsentation von Identität und Zugehörigkeit im Osten der griechisch-römischen Welt*. Frankfurt: Peter Lang, 173–210.

—— 2010. *Der römische Kaiser und das Land am Nil: Kaiserverehrung und Kaiserkult in Alexandria und Ägypten von Augustus bis Caracalla (30 v. Chr.–217 n. Chr.)*. Stuttgart: Steiner.

Pflaum, H.-G. 1960–1. *Les carrières procuratoriennes équestres sous le Haut-Empire romain*, 4 vols. Paris: Geuthner.

Price, S. R. F. 1984. *Rituals and Power: The Roman Imperial Cult in Asia Minor*. Cambridge: Cambridge University Press.

Rigsby, K. J. 1985. 'On the High Priest of Egypt', *Bulletin of the American Society of Papyrology* 22: 279–89.

Ruggendorfer, P. 1996. 'Zum Kaisareion von Alexandria', in F. Blakolmer et al. (eds), *Fremde Zeiten: Festschrift für Jürgen Borchardt zum sechzigsten Geburtstag am 25. Februar 1996 dargebracht von Kollegen, Schülern und Freunden*, vol. 2. Vienna: Phoibos-Verlag, 213–23.

Schenk, R. 1997. *Der korinthische Tempel bis zum Ende des Prinzipats des Augustus*. Espelkamp: Leidorf.

Stead, M. 1980. 'The High Priest of Alexandria and All Egypt', in R. S. Bagnall et al. (eds.), *Proceedings of the Sixteenth International Congress of Papyrology, New York, 24–31 July 1980*. Chico, Calif.: Scholars Press, 411–18.

Stein, A. 1950. *Die Präfekten von Ägypten in der römischen Kaiserzeit*. Bern: Francke.

Strassi, S. 2006. '*Οἱ ἐκ τοῦ Καισαρεί ου*: Diffusione e valore simbolico dei Kaisareia nell'Egitto romano', *Archiv für Papyrusforschung* 52: 218–43.

Taeger, F. 1960. *Charisma: Studien zur Geschichte des antiken Herrscherkultes*, vol. 2. Stuttgart: Kohlhammer.

Tuchelt, K. 1981. 'Zum Problem "Kaisareion-Sebasteion": Eine Frage zu den Anfängen des römischen Kaiserkultes', *Mitteilungen des Deutschen Archäologischen Instituts: Abteilung Istanbul* 31: 167–86.

Wilcken, U. 1912. *Grundzüge und Chrestomathie der Papyruskunde*, vol. 1/1: *Historischer Teil: Grundzüge*. Leipzig: Teubner.

Wlosok, A. 1978. 'Einführung', in Wlosok (ed.), *Römischer Kaiserkult*. Darmstadt: Wissenschaftliche Buchgesellschaft, 1–52.

Zanker, P. 2003. *Augustus und die Macht der Bilder*, 4th edn. Munich: Beck.

PART II

CITY, TOWN, AND *CHORA*

CHAPTER 7

ALEXANDRIA

MARJORIE S. VENIT

Distinguished in the first century BCE as 'the first city of the civilized world' (Diod. Sic. 17.52.5), Alexandria still wore the accolade 'crown of all cities' as late as the fourth century CE (Amm. Marc. 22.16.7). After Egypt's annexation by Rome in 30 BCE, the luminous city that had been the capital of Ptolemaic Egypt was transformed into the seat of the *praefectus Alexandreae et Aegyptii*, appointed by the Roman emperor, the prefect's administrative title at once privileging Alexandria while concurrently recalling the city's geographical siting on Egypt's edge (Fig. 7.1).

Founded in 331 BCE by Alexander the Great on the north coast of Egypt just west of the Canopic branch of the Nile, Alexandria ad Aegyptum ('Alexandria by, or near, Egypt') was conceived as a Greek city. It was laid out on a grid plan with broad streets and avenues, and it

FIG. 7.1 The harbour of Alexandria, as viewed from the Metropole Hotel (looking west) in 1994

Author's photograph.

contained the Greek elements of an agora (Arr. *Anab*. 3.1.5), a theatre, a council hall (bouleuterion) (see Delia 1991: 115), law courts, a gymnasium, a hippodrome, temples to Greek gods (Strabo 17.1.9–10), and an armoury (Philo, *In Flacc*. 92) (see Fig. 7.2). Though the incorporation of Egypt into the Roman empire changed the political governance of Egypt and the administration of Alexandria (the *boule*, for example, was dissolved until reinstated between 199–201 CE; Delia 1991: 120–1), and the three centuries of Roman rule that followed added monuments with a contemporary cast to the urban landscape of the city, the language, ethnic priority, intellectual life, and identity of the city remained culturally—though not necessarily ethnically—Greek. For almost from its foundation, Alexandria was a multi-ethnic city, and by the late first or early second century CE, Dio Chrysostom (*Or*. 32.40), speaking to an unruly crowd, reprimanded not only Greeks and Italians in his audience, but Syrians, Libyans, Cilicians, Ethiopians, Arabs, Bactrians, Scythians, Persians, and Indians, as well. Yet, fittingly, he addressed this ethnically diverse crowd in Greek, and as late as the third century CE, the monument raised after the victory by the emperor Diocletian in 297 took the form of a Corinthian column (Figs 7.3, 7.4).

Social Structure

As well as replicating Greek cultural institutions, Ptolemaic rulers also incorporated a political and social framework based on the model of Athens: in addition to establishment of the *boule* and (possibly) the *ecclesia* (assembly), Alexandrian citizens were divided into tribes (*phylai*) and demes. Upon his conquest of Egypt, Augustus reorganized the demes (Delia 1991: 63), and under Roman rule, the tribes were renamed (Delia 1991: 64–8), but throughout the period of Roman rule, tribal and deme membership still formed the basis of Alexandrian citizenship. Alexandrian citizens, like those of the Greek cities of Ptolemais and Naukratis (and, after its foundation by Hadrian, Antinoopolis), enjoyed special privileges. Most notably they were exempted from the poll tax that burdened other inhabitants of Roman Egypt (and that also acted to designate the latter's lower social status) (Delia 1991: 30–4). Most significant, however, was that until the third century CE, Alexandrian citizens were the only inhabitants of Egypt who could claim Roman citizenship (Rowlandson and Harker 2004: 82, 103; queried by Delia 1991: 39–46).

Alexandrian citizenship was a hereditary institution, though it was also granted to a small minority of Egyptians: Pliny's masseur was one (Plin. *Ep*. 10.7); Apion, a Graeco-Egyptian intellectual named after the Egyptian deity Apis, was another (van der Horst 2002: 208). Nevertheless, Chaeremon, a mid-first-century CE Egyptian priest with Stoic philosophical leanings, who was head of the Alexandrian school of grammarians and, perhaps, keeper of the museum (van der Horst 1984, p. ix), was probably never granted citizenship. It is unclear whether Jews could attain Alexandrian citizenship: the erudition of Philo, the elevated social and political position of his brother the alabarch Alexander Lysimachus, and the administrative and military role played by his nephew Tiberius Julius Alexander (who, as prefect of Egypt, led Roman troops against the city's Jewish population in 68 CE) indicate that some Jews were permitted to earn a gymnasium education, but whether they could aspire to citizenship as well is still an open question (see Chapter 17).

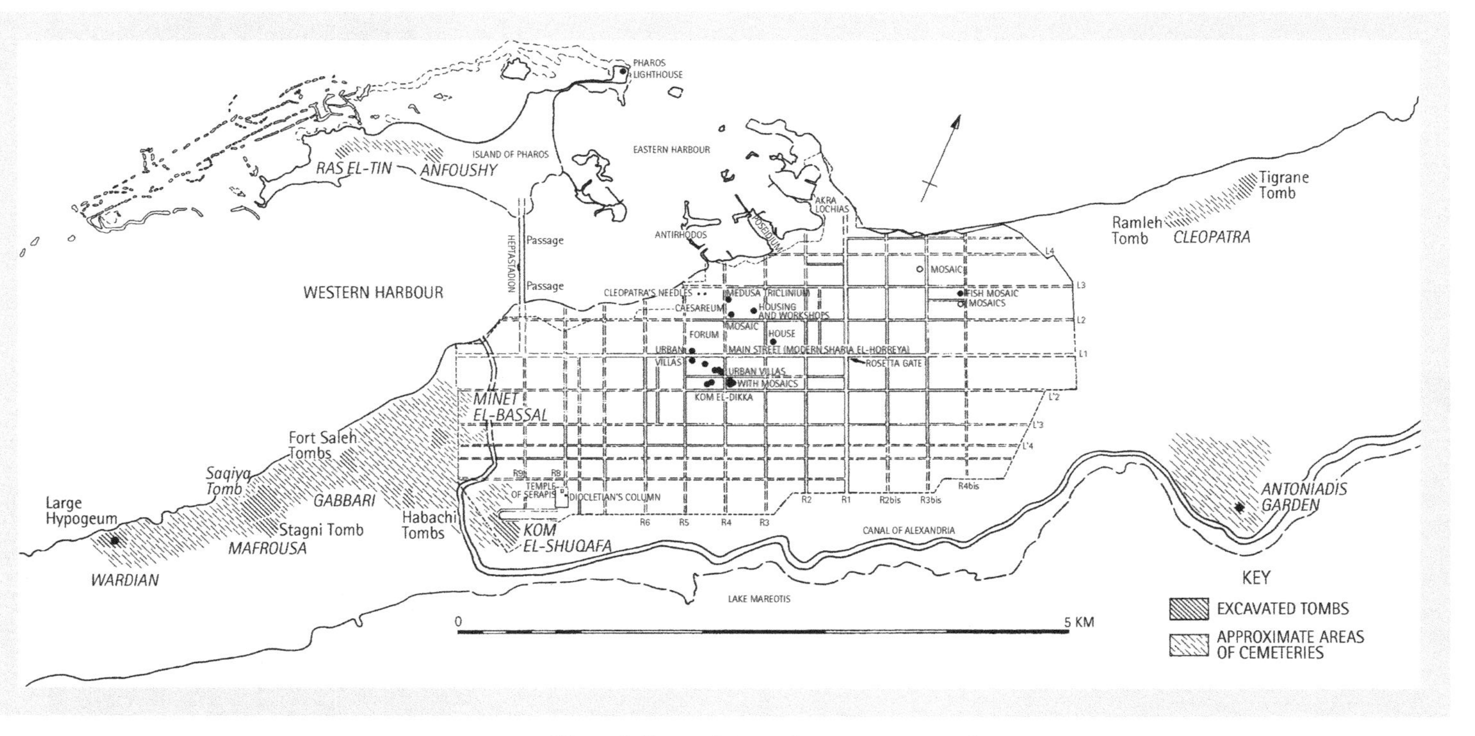

FIG. 7.2 Plan of Alexandria in the Roman period

After McKenzie (2007, figs. 29 and 299).

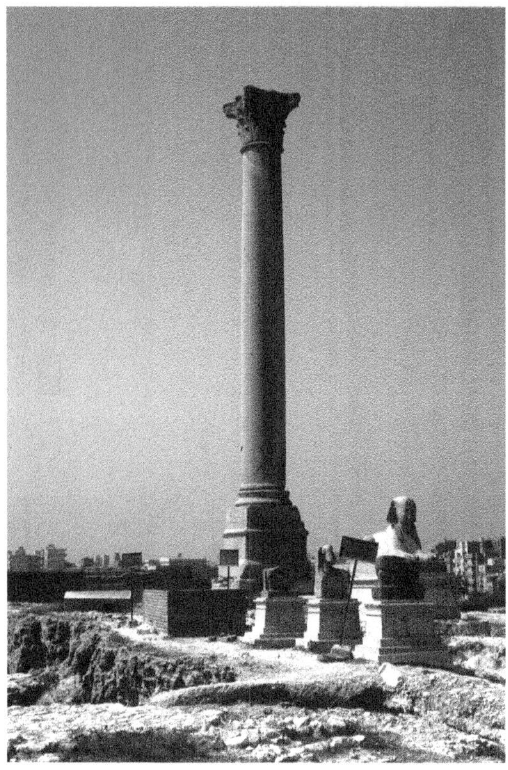

FIG. 7.3 Column of Diocletian ('Pompey's Pillar'), erected in 293 CE

Author's photograph.

FIG. 7.4 Early twentieth-century postcard of the Column of Diocletian ('Pompey's Pillar'), erected in 293 CE, seen beyond a Muslim cemetery

Author's photograph.

Economy

In the late Ptolemaic and Roman Imperial period, Alexandria was considered 'the greatest emporium of the inhabited earth' (Strabo 17.1.13). Its foundation on a narrow spit of limestone poised between the Nile-fed lake Mareotis to its south and the Mediterranean to the north established Alexandria as auspiciously sited to channel goods streaming from both eastern emporiums and the Egyptian *chora* to the greater Mediterranean world. Egypt became the proverbial bread-basket of Rome, but, in addition to grain, the port of Alexandria supplied Rome with Egyptian papyrus, glass, and flax. Yet it also served as a transfer point for lucrative international trade. Strabo (17.1.13), who had visited Egypt in the 20s CE, emphasizes that in his day 'great fleets are dispatched even so far as India and the limits of Ethiopia, from which the most precious cargo is brought to Egypt and from there, then, sent out to other places... with these things, Alexandria... abundantly supplies the outside world'. Christopher Haas (1997: 42) estimates that during the height of the Roman empire 'over thirty-two fully loaded vessels would have sailed weekly from Alexandria'. The economy of Alexandria flourished through its shipping trade, and the life of the city prospered not only financially, but intellectually and socially, through the sophistication and taste for the exotic that internationalism necessarily generates.

Topography

In the mid-second century CE, the Alexandrian novelist Achilles Tatius (*Leucippe and Clitophon* 5.1–5.2.1) has Clitophon exclaim:

> As I was coming up to the city entrance whose gates are dedicated to Helios suddenly the beauty of the city struck me like a flash of lightning. My eyes were filled to the brim with pleasure. A double row of columns led straight across the entire city.... Between the columns there lay the city's open area. Crossing it is such a long journey that you would think that you were going abroad, though you are staying at home.

Clitophon concludes,

> The things to see outstripped my sight; the prospects lured me on. Turning round and round to face all the streets, I grew faint at the sight and at last exclaimed, like a luckless lover, 'Eyes, we have met our match.' (Reardon 1989: 233; trans. Jack Winkler)

Clitophon's hyperbolic style notwithstanding, Alexandria must have presented a radiant cityscape to its visitors as well as its inhabitants.

Rising ground-water and the encroaching sea, the post-Roman period habitation, and the extent of the modern city have hampered archaeological investigation of Alexandria, and much of the soundest (though not entirely uncontroversial) evidence for the city is provided by descriptions or the chance remarks preserved in literary sources. Nevertheless, though difference of opinion still exists concerning the extent of Alexandria and the precise placement of its walls in the Ptolemaic period, the city's eastern expansion in the Roman period to encompass the eastern Ptolemaic cemeteries at Chatby and Hadra has been confirmed by excavation, as has its grid plan, first identified in modern times by Mahmoud Bey el-Falaki (McKenzie 2007: 19–24; but see Majcherek 2010: 76–7). Alexandria's major east–west street, the Canopic Way, which reached from the Gate of the Sun to the Gate of the Moon and formed the vista that stupefied Clitophon, acted as the Decumanes Maximus of the Roman city, and Clitophon (5.1) notes its intersection with a second colonnaded street, which formed the north–south Cardo (see also Strabo 17.1.8). The city itself was divided into five districts named for the first five letters of the Greek alphabet. According to Strabo (17.1.8), initially a quarter or even one-third of the city was given over to the royal palaces, which also housed the museum and the royal library; two of the named districts, Philo tells us (*In Flacc.* 55), were largely inhabited by Jews, though Josephus seems to limit Jews to the Delta quarter (*BJ* 2.495). However, although Jews apparently retained some presence in the city after the massacre of 117 CE (Horbury and Noy, for example, note two late Roman synagogue dedications from the city; 1992: 22–3, no. 15, and 23–5, no. 16), by the end of the first quarter of the second century their number had diminished significantly.

Civic Buildings

Almost nothing of the civic or commercial buildings recorded by ancient visitors to the city remains. Archaeology has yet to recover the theatre, gymnasium, bouleuterion, hippodrome (recorded in the nineteenth century; McKenzie 2007: 23), warehouses, ship sheds, armoury, or other public buildings noted by ancient chroniclers of the city.

The Pharos

The most famous monument in Alexandria and one of the ancient world's seven wonders, the great lighthouse—the Pharos—presented the tallest tower in the ancient world. Standing between 120 and 140 metres high (Pfrommer 1999: 11), it was erected between 297 and 283/2 on an island connected to the mainland by the man-made Heptastadeion. According to Poseidippus (Page 1942: 446–7, no. 104a), it was designed by Sostratos of Knidos, though Strabo (17.1.6) records that Sostratos acted solely as the dedicator. The Pharos became a symbol for the city itself, reproduced on Alexandrian coinage (see, for instance, Pfrommer 1999: 10, fig. 10) and replicated in a tomb at Taposiris Magna, about 45 km west of Alexandria. Its fame illuminated the ancient Roman world, and it was probably the inspiration for the lighthouse at Ostia, the port of Rome, and other lighthouses throughout the empire.

Underwater excavations near the site of the Pharos have yielded a substantial number of blocks that can be associated with the lighthouse as well as fragmentary sculpture, primarily from the Pharaonic period, with a few of Ptolemaic date (Pfrommer 1999: 13–16). Some early sculpture was refabricated to be reused as building material; the remainder may have added an Egyptian embellishment to the Pharos, but Strabo's silence on Egyptian elements in Alexandria presents a problem for this interpretation, and the material may have been dumped to serve as a 'makeshift breakwater' (Ashton 2004: 17–19).

The Royal Quarter

No small part of the fame of Alexandria resides in its intellectual achievements, which were initiated by the first Ptolemaic rulers, who made Alexandria a centre for learning. Within the acreage given over to the royal palaces, which were set out on Cape Lochias in the north-east section of the city, the early Ptolemies constructed the museum, which incorporated the royal library. The Sema, the tomb of Alexander, which became a key tourist or pilgrimage attraction, was notably visited by Julius Caesar (Luc. 10.19–24) and Octavian, who famously (and apocryphally) knocked off the nose of Alexander's embalmed corpse (Cass. Dio 51.16). The tombs of the Ptolemies were also contained within the palace precinct (e.g. Strabo 17.1.8).

The Museum and the Library

Founded under Ptolemy I Soter with the advice of Demetrius of Phaleron, and enlarged by the emperor Claudius (Suet. *Div. Claud.* 42; see Fraser 1972: 315), the museum was a cult centre dedicated to the Muses, and as such, a sacred space. In the Roman period, the priest of the museum was appointed by the emperor. Because it contained the great library, the museum was provided with communal arrangements for study: an exedra with seating and a large building that contained a common dining hall were at the disposal of the eminent intellectuals, and a promenade served the public as well (Strabo 17.1.8).

Alexandria's enduring fame, as well as much of its Greek identity, is based on the library contained within the museum precinct. Yet despite its renown, almost everything about the library—the date of its inception, the date of its destruction, the originality of its scholarship, and its intellectual imprint on the Roman period—is unclear. The earliest reference to the library is contained in the *Letter of Aristeas* (Bagnall 2002: 349) in its discussion of the Hebrew Bible's translation into Greek under Ptolemy II Philadelphus, but the *Letter* includes glaring inconsistencies, and most scholars agree that the library was almost certainly founded by Soter (el-Abbadi 1990: 79–82; but see Bagnall 2002: 346–51). The holdings of the library were vast: though ancient numerical accounts are unreliable (see Delia 1992: 1458–9; Bagnall 2002: 351–2), Aulus Gellius (*NA* 7.17.3), writing in the second century, gives the quantity of works as 700,000, as does Ammianus Marcellinus (22.16.13) in the fourth. The twelfth-century poet and grammarian Tzetzes numbers the volumes in the palace library as 400,000 rolls containing multiple works and 90,000 more devoted to a single work (Fraser 1972: 329). The date of the destruction of the museum's library is clouded by the presence of other libraries in Alexandria—the 'daughter' library in the Serapeum and the Roman period library in the Caesareum—because it is difficult to untangle with confidence to which library most ancient sources refer.

The three different culprits normally blamed for the destruction of the royal library are: Julius Caesar in 48 BCE during the Alexandrian War; the bishop of Alexandria Theophilus in 391 CE, upon the order of the Christian emperor Theodosius; and ʾAmr ibn al-ʿAsi during the Arab conquest of Alexandria in 642. The last possible perpetrator is given little credence by contemporary scholars, because the account preserved by ibn al-Qifti does not bear close scrutiny (el-Abbadi 1990: 168–70). Julius Caesar is the offender most often vilified, but the story is confusing. Caesar (*B Civ.* 3.111) only allows that in his attempt to conquer Alexandria for Cleopatra VII in 48 BCE, he burned the Alexandrian fleet, including those ships in the docks. Lucan in *De Bello Civile* (10.486–505) and Dio Cassius (42.38.2) agree that Caesar set fire to the ships in the harbour and that the conflagration spread to the buildings at the harbour's edge, but Dio Cassius adds that it also destroyed the book storehouses (*apothikai...ton biblion*). These sources leave the story there. Plutarch (*Caes.* 49.3), however, advises that Caesar destroyed the 'great library'. Scholars debate the accuracy of Plutarch's account, suggesting that Caesar's destruction only involved either quayside depots that held scrolls waiting to be accessioned (e.g. Fraser 1972: 326; Delia 1992: 1461–2) or partial destruction of the library's contents (Empereur 2008: 76, 87–8). They also explain variously the silence of Strabo, who visited Alexandria *c.*20 BCE and failed to acknowledge the library, though Mostafa el-Abbadi (1990: 154) sees this point as crucial to support its destruction by Caesar. Jean-Yves Empereur (2008: 75–88) proposes a fourth possibility for the end of the royal library. Citing the destruction of two villas in the Bruchion quarter near the palaces in the second half of the third century CE—a destruction he associates with the battles that consumed Alexandria from 269 until its final Roman recapture in 297—he postulates that the library may also have been destroyed during these attacks (see also Casson 2001: 47).

Despite the copious amount of scholarly ink invested in the problem, it is primarily the romance of the great library (and doubtless the romance of Julius Caesar and Cleopatra) that has fuelled the debate. Regardless of the date of the destruction of the museum's library, scholars in Alexandria—the grammarians Didymus and Tryphon and Theon the lexicographer, for example—still had the resources of a library in the late first century BCE, as did the rhetorician Theon Aelius in the first century CE. Galen, the court physician to Marcus Aurelius, who studied medicine in Alexandria in the mid-second century; Ptolemy, the mathematician, astronomer, and geographer, who wrote in Alexandria in the third quarter of the second century; a third Theon, another mathematician and the father of Hypatia; and Hypatia herself, all made use of Alexandrian textual resources in the fourth century; and lecture halls discovered at Kom el-Dikka (Majcherek 2008) also indicate that intellectual life was alive in Alexandria until at least the fourth century CE, if not considerably later (Majcherek 2010: 83–6).

Religious Alexandria

In addition to the opportunity it provided for intellectual enterprise, Alexandria was well positioned to honour the religious activities of its inhabitants. The Syriac *Urbis Notitia Alexandriae* of Michael bar Elias (the original of which is dated by P. M. Fraser to before the mid-fourth century CE) counts 2,478 temples in Alexandria, though in order for this number to bear any accuracy, it must include private shrines as well (see Fraser 1951: 105, 106–7). With the exception of the Hellenized Serapis and his consort, Isis, who were admitted into the Greek pantheon, temples to Egyptian deities were, for the most part, relegated to the fringes of the city (Haas 1997: 145), though the Tychaion, a classical temple in the city centre, held statues of both Greek and Egyptian gods (Haas 1997: 143). Consonant with the Graeco-Roman architectural and intellectual landscape of the city, Alexandria's town centre contained temples primarily honouring classical deities and Ptolemaic and Roman rulers (see Fraser 1972: 215–46). Alexander was honoured as *archegetes* (founder of a city) and his tomb functioned as a site of reverence, as did temples the Ptolemies erected to their cult (McKenzie 2007: 51–2; Pfeiffer 2008: 398–400). The Caesareum, or Sebasteion, a late Ptolemaic period temple Cleopatra built to honour Mark Antony (completed by Augustus as a monument to himself), is described by Philo (*Leg.* 151) as a large temple within a vast precinct, crowded with votive offerings and sumptuously embellished with porticoes, libraries, chambers, groves, *propylaea* (gateways), and wide, open terraces. In front of the Caesareum, Augustus placed the two New Kingdom obelisks (now found on the Thames Embankment in London and in New York's Central Park: Fig. 7.5) he had rescued from the ruins at Heliopolis that added an Egyptian cast to the complex while declaring Augustus' conquest of Egypt.

FIG. 7.5 'Cleopatra's needle': New Kingdom obelisk of Thutmose II, reinscribed by Ramesses II, from Heliopolis. Erected in Alexandria under Augustus, and now in Central Park, New York City

Author's photograph.

Sanctuaries and Temples to Greek Gods

No temples to traditional Greek gods have survived, and their identification is embedded only in the textual and epigraphic record. Among Greek gods worshipped, Strabo (17.1.9 –10) records that Poseidon had a temple set above the harbour near the theatre and Pan a sanctuary built on a height to resemble a rocky hill with a spiralling path leading to its summit. Another temple to Poseidon stood on Pharos Island, as did a temple to a Hellenized Isis-Pharia (Haas 1997: 144). Polybius, who visited Alexandria in 140 BCE, mentions the temple of Demeter (15.27) and, later, the Thesmophorium (15.29.8, 33.8–9), which undoubtedly refers to the same landmark. Françoise Dunand (2007: 256) obliquely suggests that the Alexandrian suburb of Eleusis may have accommodated a sanctuary to celebrate the mysteries, though P. M. Fraser (1972: 201) had emphatically denied the possibility. Suetonius (*Aug.* 18.2) records that Augustus enlarged an ancient temple to Apollo, and Satyrus adds a public temple to Leto (Fraser 1972: 196). Aphrodite was honoured in the Caesareum and also had another temple near the Heptastadeion (Haas 1997: 144). Athenaeus (7.276a–b), quoting Eratosthenes, librarian under Ptolemy III Euergetes, mentions sacrifices to Dionysos. A temple, given the Ptolemies' association with Dionysos, would not be unexpected, and Sozomen (*Hist. Eccl.* 7.15) mentions Theophilus' destruction of a temple of Dionysos in the last decade of the fourth century.

Fraser, who notes that many of the Greek gods attested in Alexandria are connected with a chthonic cult, identifies evidence for Zeus Soter and Hera Teleia (Fraser 1972: 196, 194), and Clitophon (Ach. Tat. 5.2) describes a chthonic Zeus Melchios also worshipped as Zeus Orania—a celestial Zeus—but given the context and the chthonic associations of Serapis, he may have been referencing the latter deity. A temple to Nemesis, another chthonic deity, that stood 'near the city' was destroyed during the Jewish revolt of 115–16 (App. *B Civ.* 2.90), and Herakles Soter, a chthonic version of the hero, is figured in a late Ptolemaic tomb at Ras el-Tin (Venit 2002: fig. 54).

A number of northern European and western Asian deities were also worshipped in Alexandria, especially in Hellenized versions, and at least one of them, Bendis, originally a Thracian goddess, was awarded a temple (Callisthenes 1.31). Cybele, the Phrygian Great Mother goddess, was known in Alexandria as early as the third century BCE (Fraser 1972: 244), and in at least one Mithraeum, destroyed in the late fourth century CE under the bishop Theophilus (Socrates, *Hist. Eccl.* 3.2, 5.16), mysteries were enacted to the Persian Mithras.

Places of Worship of Jews and Christians

Alexandria's Jewish populace, which first probably entered Alexandria in the third century BCE and which formed a major population group, was served by a great number of synagogues throughout the city (Philo, *Leg.* 132–4), and inscriptions confirm that synagogues were not limited to the traditional Jewish quarters (Horbury and Noy 1992: 13–15, no. 9; 19–21, no. 13; 23–6, nos 16 and 17; 30–2, no. 19). Among these synagogues, one was so large and so splendidly appointed that it is referenced in the Talmud (*Sukkah* 5: 1, 55*a*–*b*; Paget 2004: 143–4).

Christianity in Alexandria found its genesis in the philosophical inclination of Alexandrian Judaism (see Paget 2004: 156–62). Yet despite the fame of the Alexandrian church fathers Clement and Origen, and though tombs of Christians can be identified, the *Notitia* does not appear to include any churches (Fraser 1951: 106), and few Christian places of worship that date earlier than the late fourth century have yet come to light in the city (see Haas 1997: 206–11).

Isis

The major deities connected with the city of Alexandria are Serapis and Isis, who are considered here in turn. Although Arrian (*An.* 3.1.5) records Alexander founding a temple to Isis, modern scholars disagree on whether an independent temple to Isis existed before the late Ptolemaic period. The goddess was certainly worshipped alongside Serapis in the Serapeum, where Ptolemy IV Philopator also dedicated a temple to their son Harpocrates (McKenzie, Gibson, and Reyes 2004: 84–5, 90).

Goddio and Fabre postulate a late Ptolemaic period sanctuary to Isis on Antirhodos Island on the basis of two sphinxes and a statue of a priest holding an Osiris-Canopus vase (Goddio and Fabre 2008: 38), but this identification seems premature, and the statues appear to be of Roman date (Ashton 2004: 30). Plutarch (*Vit. Ant.* 74.1), however, notes that Cleopatra had her tomb built near the temple of Isis, and on that basis, a late Ptolemaic temple to the deity on Cape Lochias has been postulated. A little Roman period temple at Ras al-Soda that incorporated the cults of Isis, Hermanoubis, Harpocrates, and Osiris-Canopus, as well as the decoration of the Tigrane Tomb (Venit 2002: 146–59), permits the possibility that the mysteries of Isis were also practised in (or near) Alexandria during the Roman period.

Serapis and the Serapeum

Despite Plutarch's description of Ptolemy I Soter's dream (*De Is. et Os.* 28; see also Tac. *Hist.* 4.83–4), in which the colossal statue of Pluto of Sinope exhorts the king to transport him to Alexandria, scholars agree that Soter's Serapis was instead based on the Egyptian deity Osir-Apis—a combination of the Egyptian god of the dead Osiris and the sacred Apis bull worshipped at Memphis. The Greek sculptor Bryaxis is credited with devising the statue of the god, and images show Serapis as a bearded deity, a *kalathos*, or basket (his distinguishing attribute), on his head, and his hair dressed like that of Hades with strands hanging down onto his forehead. Serapis was an Alexandrian deity, but his cult spread throughout much of the Graeco-Roman world, and from the first to the third centuries CE, papyrological evidence points to all Egyptians supplicating his beneficence and Roman emperors paying homage at his sanctuary (Rowlandson and Harker 2004: 87–8).

In his encomium to Alexandria, Ammianus Marcellinus (22.16.12) ranks the Serapeum second only to the Capitolium in Rome, praising it for its 'impressive columned public rooms (*atria*)', its 'breathing forms of statues', and 'the rest of the multitude of [its] works'. Excavation has uncovered sculpture executed in a classical style, dating from the Ptolemaic and Roman periods, and in traditional pharaonic style, constituting both antiques wrested from other Delta sites and those carved in the Ptolemaic period (McKenzie, Gibson, and Reyes 2004: 100–1). Both types must have decorated the Serapeum complex celebrated by Ammianus.

Private dedications record the worship of Serapis on the site as early as the late reign of Ptolemy I Soter or the early reign of Ptolemy II Philadelphus (Fraser 1972: 268; McKenzie,

Gibson, and Reyes 2004: 84; Pfeiffer 2008: 394–5), and though foundation plaques date the temple to the reign of Ptolemy III Euergetes, an earlier shrine might have marked the site (McKenzie, Gibson, and Reyes 2004: 81, 83–4). The temple was in the Corinthian order and formed the focal point of a complex bordered by stoas on the south and west, a library, and the temple to Harpocrates. The Ptolemaic temple stood until a conflagration in 181 CE, which also claimed the temple to Harpocrates (McKenzie, Gibson, and Reyes 2004: 86, 111). The Serapeum was then rebuilt between 181 and 217 in an even more monumental form (McKenzie, Gibson, and Reyes 2004: 98), and it remained active until its final destruction by Theophilus in the late fourth century.

The Serapeum Library

The Serapeum library may have been initiated by Ptolemy III Euergetes (Fraser 1972: 323), though its first mention is not until the late second century CE (McKenzie, Gibson, and Reyes 2004: 99). The south stoa was identified by its excavator Alan Rowe as housing the library (supported by Fraser 1972: 323), but McKenzie judges this possibility implausible for the later period at least (McKenzie, Gibson, and Reyes 2004: 99). Recognizing that Roman period fireplaces in the south stoa's lower level would have militated against the nearby storage of easily perishable rolls, she suggests that the west stoa could have equally served as a book depository.

Houses for the Living

Excavation has revealed remains of houses from the Ptolemaic through the Roman period in a style seemingly unique to Alexandria. Roman period houses most often combine the *prostas-oikos* plan (a house with a porch and a wide reception room), known from elsewhere in the Greek world, with a pseudo-peristyle courtyard discrete to Alexandria (Majcherek 2001: 32). The pseudo-peristyle—a peristyle courtyard defined by engaged rather than free-standing columns—is best seen preserved in the tomb Moustapha Pasha 1, but houses excavated at Kom el-Dikka leave no doubt as to its domestic employment.

Houses dating between the first and mid-third century CE indicate a wealthy populace residing in at least two areas of the city: the Bruchion region near the royal palaces and the area excavated at Kom el-Dikka. These houses could rise to two storeys and could contain kitchens, wells and cisterns for fresh water, and bathrooms, lavatories, and latrines served by sewers (Majcherek 2010: 80). At least one house boasted two triclinia (dining rooms); another had a room whose doorway was flanked by granite columns and Corinthian pilasters (Majcherek 1998: 39); a third, the Villa of the Birds, contained a sundial in the pseudo-peristyle court (Rodziewicz 1976: 177). Wall decoration followed Greek masonry style, best exemplified at Delos but also seen in the court of the Ptolemaic period Moustapha Pasha Tomb 1 (Venit 2002: 53–4 and fig. 39), with high orthostats set above a low socle (Majcherek 2001: 42), and the main rooms are paved with figured, floral, and geometric bichrome and polychrome tessellated mosaics or polychrome *opus sectile* (inlay).

FIG. 7.6 Mosaic emblema of a Medusa head, *c*.150 CE

Courtesy of the Centre d'Études Alexandrines.

The high-quality figural mosaics that decorated the floors of these houses accord well with examples of the genre from other parts of the empire. One, from the triclinium of a villa dated to 150 CE excavated in the Bruchion quarter near the royal palaces, has an emblema (central panel) with a head of Medusa set on a terracotta disc for insertion into the floor (Fig. 7.6). The emblema centred a geometric framework that defined the placement of the banquettes and permitted the identification of the room (Empereur 2002: 14; Guimier-Sorbets 2002). Similarly, a house at Kom el-Dikka preserved a very fine emblema of Dionysos, constructed in tiny tesserae and set on a ceramic disc (Majcherek 2003: 34).

The most extensive corpus of mosaics in Alexandria emerges from the Villa of the Birds. The building's construction is dated to the mid-first century CE (Rodziewicz 1976: 179), but the mosaics are part of a reconstruction of the building in the first half of the second century (Kołątaj, Majcherek, and Parandowska 2007: 26). The house takes its name from the theme of its most lavishly decorated room. Probably a cubiculum, the room preserves a polychrome mosaic of nine guilloche-bordered squares, each enclosing an image of a bird amid fruit or flowers set against a white ground (Rodziewicz 1976: 179). In one square, two pigeons drink from a skyphos-shaped cup, recalling perhaps the doves in the mosaic attributed to Sosos (Plin. *NH* 36.60.182–4), though lacking its remarkable quality. The triclinium of the villa combines an *opus tesselatum* carpet, defining the position of the *klinai* (couches), with a central field in *opus sectile* (Kołątaj, Majcherek, and Parandowska 2007: 28–34). A small corner room tucked between the cubiculum and the triclinium had a central rosette in bichrome *opus tesselatum*, and other rooms around the court also preserve bichrome and polychrome tessellated mosaic floors (Kołątaj, Majcherek, and Parandowska 2007: 26–8, 38–41).

Houses for the Dead

Best preserved of all ancient monuments in Alexandria are the monumental tombs cut deep into the nummulitic limestone that underlies the city. Though they owe a debt to Egypt for their loculi and perhaps their open courts, the tombs are classical in their architectural detail. Almost from their inception, they extol classical architectural elements and everyday appurtenances appropriated from the quotidian world—engaged columns, friezes, altars, *klinai*—fashioning a statement of verisimilitude based on trompe l'œil technique. Tomb A at Chatby, for example, one of the earliest monumental tombs extant, cuts window frames and half-open shutters in stone and uses a light blue paint to indicate the airy landscape behind the windows and between the appliquéd columns of its court (Venit 2002, fig. 12). But from early on, Alexandrian tombs also admitted Egyptian iconographic motifs. Egyptianizing sphinxes in the otherwise entirely classical Tomb 1 at Moustapha Pasha are an early example of this practice (Fig. 7.7; see also Venit 2002, fig. 41). Strabo (17.1.10) coined the word 'necropolis' to explain the cemeteries of Alexandria, and the term reflects both the tombs' magnitude and the visibility their open courts provide to herald their similitude to the world of the living.

Only the Alabaster Tomb in the eastern part of the city is in the Macedonian manner. It is the single extant tomb built above ground and the only one seemingly covered with a

FIG. 7.7 Moustapha Pasha Tomb 1, doorway to *kline* and burial rooms, with Egyptianizing sphinxes

Author's photograph.

tumulus. Only one room of the original two-room configuration survives, but the immense slabs of alabaster from which the tomb is constructed also set it apart, and it must have been a royal monument (Venit 2002: 8–9) constructed within the palaces (*pace* Grimm 1996: 60, who places it outside the city walls). A second tomb that must have been above-ground (and two-storeyed), if the tale related by Plutarch offers any accuracy, is that of Cleopatra VII. Plutarch reports that Cleopatra stood at a window in her tomb, and, the doors being locked, she hauled Mark Antony up by ropes to reach her (*Vit. Ant.* 77.1); Proculeius later entered with a ladder (*Vit. Ant.* 79.1).

Roman period tombs follow the general plan of their Ptolemaic predecessors but substitute triclinium-shaped chambers for the Ptolemaic kline room and admit a richer variety of Egyptian decorative and narrative elements into their classical fabric. The most extensive of these tombs, the Great Catacomb at Kom el-Shuqafa, marries Egyptian architectural and iconographic details to classical formal spaces—exedrae, a triclinium, and a burial chamber in triclinium form, in which Roman garland sarcophagi are cut to form niches that carry sculpted scenes depicting Egyptian deities (Venit 2002: 124–45). Two other tombs show variations on this bicultural theme. A catacomb adjoining the Great Catacomb contains two tomb niches that combine the scene of the lustration of the mummy (painted in Egyptianizing style) in the upper frieze with the abduction of Persephone (painted in a classical style) in the lower, engendering a bilingual reading (Fig. 7.8; see Guimier-Sorbets and Seif el-Din

FIG. 7.8 Kom el-Shuqafa, 'Hall of Caracalla', Persephone Tomb 2, late first to early second century CE

Painting by Mary-Jane Schumacher. Photo: André Pelle, Centre National de la Recherche Scientifique, Paris. Courtesy of the Centre d'Études Alexandrines.

FIG. 7.9 Tigrane Tomb, painting on the back wall of the left niche above the sarcophagus, second century CE

Author's photograph.

1997). Another, the Tigrane Tomb, couples classical features—a Hadrianic-inspired painted dome centred on a classical gorgoneion, and a triclinium-shaped burial chamber formed by rock-cut classical sarcophagi—with Egyptian-derived narratives in the sarcophagus niches, which may reference Isiac initiation, their Eyptianizing style having been chosen to connote their esoteric content (Fig. 7.9; see Venit 2002: 148–59).

Jews and early Christians were also buried in the loculi and chambers of monumental tombs. Identifiable only by inscription or iconography, their burials are found within the same tomb complexes as those of their polytheistic neighbours (see Venit 2002: 20–1, 181–6).

Conclusion

Everything points to Roman Alexandria as an extraordinary city: economically powerful, visually breathtaking, and intellectually vibrant. Dio Chrysostom (*Or.* 32.35), in the second century CE, places Alexandria second only to Rome in size and situation; Herodian (7.6.1), in the third century, who adds wealth as a criterion, vacillates between Alexandria and Carthage for second spot. Through the seventh century, Alexandria held its place among the greatest cities in the Mediterranean world.

Echoing Strabo, Dio Chrysostom (*Or.* 32.35) places Roman Alexandria at the economic crossroads of the world, citing its monopoly on Mediterranean shipping achieved by the beauty of its harbours, the great size of its fleet, and the products it imported and exported. Physically the city combined the Ptolemaic underpinning (and many of the Ptolemaic monuments) with those raised in Roman times, and intellectually it continued the tradition established by the Ptolemies. As late as the fourth century, Ammianus Marcellinus (who celebrated Alexandria as the 'crown of all cities') extolled its balmy climate, its temples with ostentatiously high pediments, its skilled engineering exemplified by the Pharos and the Heptastadeion, its splendid library, and the intellectual climate—especially regarding music, mathematics, astronomy, and medicine—that the library and the city propagated (Amm. Marc. 22.16.7–13, 15–18). Gleaming golden in the rising sun, blushed with the setting sun of evening, Alexandria still existed as a major city for centuries after its old gods had been replaced by those of the new religion.

Suggested Reading

No handbook in English specifically addresses Roman Alexandria, but for German readers two magnificently illustrated books are available (Grimm 1998; Pfrommer 1999). Evidence for the topography and architecture of Alexandria is laid out by McKenzie's volume (2007), and the city's ancient tombs, which constitute the greatest part of its archaeological remains, are covered in Venit (2002). Recent underwater excavations in the eastern harbour are discussed and illustrated by Goddio and Fabre (2008), and see Empereur (1998) for a summary of the underwater excavations near Fort Qait Bey, as well as rescue operations in Alexandria conducted by the Centre d'Études Alexandrines. Hassan (2002) contains excellent images of the most important monuments in the Graeco-Roman Museum, most of which were found in Alexandria. Though the book's title suggests it treats only late antique Alexandria, glimpses into the social, economic, and political history of Roman Alexandria can be found in Haas (1997).

Bibliography

Ashton, S.-A. 2004. 'Ptolemaic Alexandria and the Egyptian Tradition', in A. Hirst and M. Silk (eds), *Alexandria, Real and Imagined*. Aldershot: Ashgate, 15–40.

Bagnall, R. S. 2002. 'Alexandria: Library of Dreams', *Proceedings of the American Philosophical Society* 146: 348–62.

Casson, L. 2001. *Libraries in the Ancient World*. New Haven: Yale University Press.

Delia, D. 1988. 'The Population of Roman Alexandria', *Transactions of the American Philological Association* 118: 275–92.

—— 1991. *Alexandrian Citizenship during the Roman Principate*. Atlanta: Scholars Press.

—— 1992. 'From Romance to Rhetoric: The Alexandria Library in Classical and Islamic Tradition', *American Historical Review* 97: 1449–67.

Dunand, F. 2007. 'The Religious System at Alexandria', in D. Ogden (ed.), *A Companion to Greek Religion*. Malden, Mass.: Blackwell, 253–63.

el-Abbadi, M. 1990. *The Life and Fate of the Ancient Library of Alexandria*. Paris: Unesco.

Empereur, J.-Y. 1998. *Alexandria Rediscovered*, trans. Margaret Maehler. New York: Braziller.

—— 2002. 'Découvertes récentes à Alexandrie', in *Greek Archaeology without Frontiers*. Athens: National Hellenic Research Foundation, 13–20.

—— 2008. 'The Destruction of the Library of Alexandria: An Archaeological Viewpoint', in M. el-Abbadi and O. M. Fathallah (eds), *What Happened to the Ancient Library of Alexandria?* Leiden: Brill, 75–88.

Fraser, P. M. 1951. 'A Syriac *Notitia Urbis Alexandrinae*', *Journal of Egyptian Archaeology* 37: 103–8.

—— 1972. *Ptolemaic Alexandria*. Oxford: Clarendon Press.

Goddio, F., and D. Fabre (eds) 2008. *Egypt's Sunken Treasures*. Munich: Prestel.

Grimm, G. 1996. 'City Planning?', in K. Hamma (ed.), *Alexandria and Alexandrianism*. Malibu, Calif.: J. Paul Getty Museum, 55–74.

—— 1998. *Alexandria: Die erste Königsstadt der hellenistischen Welt*. Mainz: von Zabern.

Guimier-Sorbets, A.-M. 2002. 'Nouvelles recherches sur les mosaïques d'Alexandrie', in *Greek Archaeology without Frontiers*. Athens: National Hellenic Research Foundation, 21–8.

—— and M. Seif el-Din. 1997. 'Les Deux Tombes de Perséphone dans la nécropole de Kom el-Chougafa à Alexandrie', *Bulletin de la Correspondance Hellénique* 121: 355–410.

Haas, C. 1997. *Alexandria in Late Antiquity: Topography and Social Conflict*. Baltimore: Johns Hopkins University Press.

Hassan, F. (ed.) 2002. *Alexandria: The Graeco-Roman Museum: A Thematic Guide*. Cairo: National Center for Documentation of Cultural and Natural Heritage and the Supreme Council of Antiquities.

Horbury, W., and D. Noy. 1992. *Jewish Inscriptions from Graeco-Roman Egypt*. Cambridge: Cambridge University Press.

Kołątaj, W., G. Majcherek, and E. Parandowska. 2007. *Villa of the Birds: The Excavation and Preservation of the Kom al-Dikka Mosaics*. Cairo: American University in Cairo Press.

McKenzie, J. 2007. *The Architecture of Alexandria and Egypt c.300 BC to AD 700*. New Haven: Yale University Press.

—— S. Gibson, and A. T. Reyes. 2004. 'Reconstructing the Serapeum in Alexandria from the Archaeological Evidence', *Journal of Roman Studies* 94: 73–121.

Majcherek, G. 1998. 'Kom el-Dikka Excavations, 1997/98', *Polish Archaeology in the Mediterranean: Reports* 10: 29–39.

—— 2001. 'Kom el-Dikka Excavations, 2001/2002', *Polish Archaeology in the Mediterranean: Reports* 13: 31–43.

—— 2003. 'Kom el-Dikka Excavations, and Preservation Work, 2002/2003', *Polish Archaeology in the Mediterranean: Reports* 15: 25–38.

—— 2008. 'Academic Life of Late Antique Alexandria: A View from the Field', in M. el-Abbadi and O. M. Fathallah (eds), *What Happened to the Ancient Library of Alexandria?* Leiden: Brill, 191–206.

—— 2010. 'Discovering Alexandria: Archaeological Update on the Finds from Kom el-Dikka', in D. Robinson and A. Wilson (eds), *Alexandria and the North-Western Delta*. Oxford: School of Archaeology, University of Oxford, 75–89.

Page, D. L. 1942. *Greek Literary Papyri* I. Cambridge, Mass.: Harvard University Press.

Paget, J. C. 2004. 'Jews and Christians in Ancient Alexandria from the Ptolemies to Caracalla', in A. Hirst and M. Silk (eds), *Alexandria, Real and Imagined*. Aldershot: Ashgate, 143–66.

Pfeiffer, S. 2008. 'The God Serapis, his Cult and the Beginnings of the Ruler Cult in Ptolemaic Egypt', in P. McKechnie and P. Guillaume (eds), *Ptolemy II Philadelphus and his World*. Boston: Brill, 387–408.

Pfrommer, M. 1999. *Alexandria: Im Schatten der Pyramiden*. Mainz: von Zabern.

Reardon, B. P. (ed.) 1989. *Collected Ancient Greek Novels*. Berkeley: University of California Press.

Rodziewicz, M. 1976. 'Un quartier d'habitation gréco-romain à Kôm el-Dikka (Sondage R, 1970–1973)', *Études et Travaux* 9: 169–210.

Rowlandson, J., and A. Harker. 2004. 'Roman Alexandria from the Perspective of the Papyri', in A. Hirst and M. Silk (eds), *Alexandria, Real and Imagined*. Aldershot: Ashgate, 79–111.

van der Horst, P. W. 1984. *Chaeremon: Egyptian Priest and Stoic Philosopher*. Leiden: Brill.

—— 2002. 'Who Was Apion?', in van der Horst (ed.), *Japheth in the Tents of Shem*. Leuven: Peeters, 207–21.

Venit, M. S. 2002. *The Monumental Tombs of Ancient Alexandria: The Theater of the Dead*. Cambridge, Mass.: Cambridge University Press.

CHAPTER 8

SETTLEMENT AND POPULATION*

LAURENS E. TACOMA

THIS chapter is based on two simple assumptions: first, that Roman Egypt had a relatively large population, and secondly, that it had a large number of settlements. The aim is then to analyse how the population was distributed over these settlements, and by what methods we may perform such an analysis. Who lived where, and how can we know?

The seemingly simple question 'who lived where?' is of real historical importance, for it has a bearing on debates about urbanization. Cities formed a constituent element of the Graeco-Roman world. It is probable that ancient society was heavily urbanized, at least by pre-industrial standards. However, quantitative data are for the most part lacking to support the large claims that ancient historians have made. There is a clear need for substantiation.

Roman Egypt has an important role to play in this debate. Egypt provides sources unavailable elsewhere, allowing a combination of quantitative and qualitative approaches. The archaeology of urban sites is not as good as one would like, but for the study of smaller settlements the archaeological evidence is crucial (Bowman 1996, app. 3). The papyri offer data that are not matched by sources from elsewhere, concerning phenomena as diverse as population size, population structure, occupational structure, and distribution of landholding. The richness of the Egyptian sources also allows one to probe deeper, and analyse the relation between demography and settlement patterns. Over the past decades, the general outlines of the size and structure of the population of Roman Egypt have become reasonably clear (Bagnall and Frier 1994; Scheidel 2001a). This raises the question of how our demographic knowledge affects the interpretation of settlement patterns, and vice versa.

These questions and debates underlie the analysis in this chapter. In the first section, I shall start to discuss the validity of the standard typology of dividing Egyptian settlements into cities, towns, and villages. In the second section, I shall discuss the various (and rather controversial) population estimates that have been put forward. I shall argue that, despite the

* My thanks to Miriam Groen-Vallinga, Brian Muhs, and Christina Riggs for suggesting improvements in content and style.

uncertainties involved, they imply that levels of urbanization were relatively high. In the third section, I shall consider in more detail the criteria that have been employed to determine what constitutes a city. They show that instead of a clear-cut dichotomy between city and village, a spectrum of settlements existed. In the fourth section, I shall discuss the implications of this spectrum for the study of population structure. To what extent is it legitimate to differentiate demographically between rural and urban populations? In the fifth and last section, several broader theories will be discussed that may be helpful in analysing settlement patterns.

The focus of the chapter will be deliberately theoretical. Given the fragmentary state of the sources, the question 'how can we know?' is perhaps even more important than the question 'who lived where?' There are, of course, risks involved in such an approach (Morley 2004). In any type of generalization the details of the sources are inevitably lost. However, the sources still need to be interpreted and do not speak for themselves. There is a clear need for a theoretical framework that allows comparison with other times and places.

Cities, Towns, and Villages

The conventional distinction between settlements in Roman Egypt is based on their administrative status. Three types of settlement existed: *poleis*, *metropoleis*, and *komai*, which are normally translated as cities, towns, and villages respectively. The major advantage of this threefold categorization is that in almost all cases the status of a settlement is known. But to what extent is the categorization also helpful as a typology of settlements? It might be useful to look at each of the three categories in turn.

Metropoleis were the administrative capitals of the districts, the nomes. It was from the *metropoleis* that the surrounding villages were administered, and as such the *metropoleis* were the seat of the *strategos*. In many cases nome and capital carried similar names: the Oxyrhynchite nome had as its capital Oxyrhynchus, the Hermopolite nome Hermopolis, and so on. The nome system itself went back to time immemorial, when Egypt consisted of a fixed number of nomes, each with a capital. Although in Roman times alterations were made through the creation and dissolution of nomes and capitals, the system was relatively stable. By the Roman period the number of *metropoleis* may have been slightly over fifty.

All settlements that were not *metropoleis* (or, in a few exceptional cases to be discussed below, *poleis*) were categorized as villages, normally styled *komai*, though other terms were also in use for the smaller settlements. Excavations have brought to light many such villages, and the papyri have preserved village names by the hundreds. They varied greatly in size and importance. Some of these will have been one-donkey towns; others, such as Karanis, were quite substantial (see Chapter 14).

Outside the system of *metropoleis* and *komai*, there were three, later four, Greek *poleis*: Naukratis, Alexandria, Ptolemais, and Antinoopolis. They possessed autonomy in their internal affairs and had their own constitutions. Naukratis had started life as a Greek *emporion* well before the Ptolemaic period. Alexandria, one of a larger number of homonymous foundations of Alexander the Great, had grown to be one of the most important cities of the

Mediterranean world soon after its foundation, and in the Roman period became the second city of the empire, after Rome (see Chapter 7). Ptolemais in Upper Egypt was created in the early Ptolemaic period. Antinoopolis was founded by Hadrian in 130 CE as a tribute to his lover Antinoos, who had drowned in the Nile.

To some extent the conventional distinction between cities, towns, and villages is helpful, if only because it is so easy: there are hardly any uncertainties about the status of most settlements. But on closer reflection problems occur. Modern typologies are normally based on two, not three, categories: city and village. The point is all too obvious, but immediately shows where the problem lies—in the classification of the intermediate category of *metropoleis*. For discussions of urbanization it makes all the difference whether we have only four or more than fifty cities in Roman Egypt.

This might seem no more than an academic question, but the application of the word 'town' to *metropoleis* easily leads to the notion that *metropoleis* were less urban than *poleis*, or even not urban at all (so Finley 1985: 203–4). However, the available sources show that *metropoleis* were anything but insignificant. In addition, it can be pointed out that the institutional roles of *poleis* and *metropoleis* converged in the Roman period. The *metropoleis* adopted various Greek civic institutions, a process that culminated in the introduction of councils at the turn of the third century (Bowman and Rathbone 1992). Conversely, with the exception of Alexandria the *poleis* gradually came to function as nome capitals. *Poleis* and *metropoleis* should therefore be seen as structurally equivalent: both should be classified as cities. The use of the word 'town' for *metropoleis* is only to be retained for conventional purposes.

Population Size and Levels of Urbanization

If we want to people these settlements, we ought to have population figures. Demography consists of two components, size and structure. The major advances of the past decades in the field of ancient demography have caused (or are in fact caused by) a shift in the discussion from the former to the latter: there is more to historical demography than just population size. However, both elements remain important.

Roman Egypt offers data about both the size and the structure of the population, but the sources are different in each case. The census declarations that are so fundamental to studies of population structure have surprisingly little to tell about population size. Population totals have to be derived in other ways. Literary sources provide some figures about the size of the total population and may also help in estimating the size of Alexandria. Papyri generated by the taxation process offer some data that can be turned into estimates of the population size of particular settlements. The importance of these data should be neither overestimated nor underestimated. On close inspection the hard figures of Roman Egypt have a tendency to become softer, but the simple fact remains that in many respects the evidence available for Roman Egypt is much better than elsewhere.

With respect to the total population, prolonged discussion has essentially only increased the extent of our ignorance. Whereas it was previously thought that ancient sources offered a reasonably reliable estimate for a total population of 7 million inhabitants at the beginning of the Roman period, now there are strong reasons for doubt. We are left with a broad band of possible population sizes ranging from 3 to 7 million inhabitants, with perhaps a greater likelihood for the higher part of the range, but without the possibility to narrow the figures down (Rathbone 1990).

Estimating the population of specific settlements involves similar uncertainties. In the case of Alexandria, an estimate between 200,000 and 500,000 is normally employed, again with a greater likelihood for the higher part of the range (Delia 1988). The estimates of the population sizes of specific settlements are based on extrapolation of smaller figures found in the papyri. These reconstructed data indicate urban population sizes in the order of 10,000 to 50,000, and village populations running from several hundreds to a couple of thousand, with 10,000 as a reasonable upper limit for the very largest villages (Alston and Alston 1997: 202).

All these data then are in fact not figures but broad bands of possibilities, and any attempt at greater precision is vulnerable to substantial criticism. These uncertainties obviously hinder quantification of levels of urbanization. As the number of people living in cities is of real importance for cross-cultural comparison, it is nevertheless important to make some attempt at quantification. I have argued elsewhere that if the broad band of possibilities is accepted, it is very difficult to argue for levels of urbanization below 10 per cent. More likely they were in the order of 20 per cent (Tacoma 2006: 21–36). The finding, no matter how tentative, is important, because it is relatively high in comparative perspective (compare de Vries 1984).

To sum up: several scholars over the past decade have argued for the relatively urbanized character of Roman Egypt (Bowman 2000). The first conceptual step has been to consider the *metropoleis* as urban centres. The second has been to explore the implications of the available figures. The sources do not provide us with as hard evidence for population figures as one may think. Nevertheless, they do suggest that levels of urbanization were comparatively high.

Defining the City

Thus far, the distinction between city and village has been based on administrative status. However, there is no guarantee that this criterion corresponds completely to other criteria. The problem is well known: in the ancient world, city status could be conferred on very small settlements. To what extent do the administrative criteria of Roman Egypt match with other criteria?

The subject is best approached through discussions about the definition of the city. Scholars have long tried to find uniformly applicable criteria to determine what constitutes a city. Next to administrative status a host of other criteria can be applied: institutional, social, economic, cultural, and demographic, each of which can be considered in turn.

Institutional criteria comprise the presence or absence of political institutions (most notably city councils), of civic institutions (for example, gymnasia), or of particular offices (see Mueller 2006: 102–4 for the Ptolemaic period). A difficulty with an institutional approach is that in many cases the possession of an institution is a consequence of the assigned administrative status of a settlement. The approach is therefore primarily useful to differentiate between settlements that fall within the same administrative category. This might also bring out anomalous cases where institutions do not follow administrative status; for instance, in the case of Alexandria, the absence of a city council up until the third century, and, in the case of the villages, the fact that some possessed gymnasia.

It is also possible to use social criteria, on the (somewhat crude but in principle no doubt correct) assumption that more important settlements show greater social complexity and a lesser degree of homogeneity. Social differentiation is not always easy to analyse, however, as status is a relative and subjective phenomenon that does not lend itself to easy recording. Consequently, there is a natural tendency to analyse social differentiation through social institutions, and in these cases the boundary between institutional and social criteria tends to become blurred. A first, relatively visible element might be the presence of a local elite that sets itself apart from the rest of the population. The best-known example is constituted by the town councils of the *metropoleis* that were instituted at the turn of the third century (Bowman 1971; Tacoma 2006), but such elites can also be found in other settlements and in other periods. One may also look at the presence of other social groups that intersect with the elite, such as the gymnasial class. Again it is useful to keep in mind that many such groups came into existence as a consequence of the administrative status of a settlement.

Then there are economic criteria that can be used, offering three major lines of inquiry. The first one concerns the degree of occupational specialization, which is supposed to be larger in more important settlements. Such specialization can be charted in a rudimentary but fairly straightforward way by compiling and analysing lists of attested occupations (see Alston and Alston 1997: 204–6). A second issue is the part of the population not involved in agriculture. In the case of Roman Egypt this is difficult to measure, as it requires independent estimates for population size and the number of landowners within that population, and, in addition, some estimate of the people who are engaged in agriculture without owning land (Tacoma 2008). Lastly, the degree of differentiation in wealth can be measured, which is assumed to be higher in the more important settlements. This can be achieved through the study of the distribution of landholdings among urban and rural landowners (Bowman 1985; Bagnall 1992). In such studies, the underlying assumption is that differences in landholdings among the inhabitants of a settlement form a representative reflection of differences in income in general.

Cultural criteria can also be employed. These comprise potentially an extremely broad range. One may think of the presence of monumental architecture and the availability of the standard Graeco-Roman amenities of urban life. Some caution in the application of such criteria as straightforward indications of urbanity is needed, however. A scheme of a unilateral process of ever-increasing hellenistic urban civilization is simplistic, if only for the fact that Egyptian culture was certainly not averse to city life.

A last set of criteria is demographic. It consists of two major lines of inquiry. The first is population size and has been discussed already in the previous section. It is very often used by urban historians of all periods, primarily for practical reasons: single figures lend themselves to easy comparison. The requirement is of course that figures are available, and, as we have seen, in the case of Roman Egypt their establishment is hardly without problems, though a relative order of magnitude is available. A second demographic criterion is formed by population densities, expressed in persons per hectare or km^2. The problem for the ancient world is that estimating population density requires knowledge of two figures: inhabited area and population size. In practice, independent figures for both are seldom obtainable, and there has been a natural tendency among ancient historians to work the other way round, and estimate from inhabited areas the population size by using a fixed figure for population density (so Hansen 2006 for classical Greece). The sometimes ignored danger in this is that cities have three instead of two dimensions: larger cities might have higher buildings rather than a larger inhabited area, and therefore have a larger population density. In the case of Roman Egypt this reverse method has not been employed systematically, no doubt because of the relative paucity of urban excavations. A less precise but certainly rewarding approach is to look at the extent to which there is evidence for multi-storey housing (Alston and Alston 1997: 208–9).

As the discussion of these criteria demonstrates, each method has its risks and possibilities. Moreover, some criteria lend themselves more easily to quantification than others. The importance assigned to each of these criteria has varied from scholar to scholar. Some have used population size alone, based on the assumption that other criteria are likely to match (Tacoma 2006: 37–68, working with a range of estimated sizes of *metropoleis*). Others have advocated more complex methods, combining a number of criteria (Alston and Alston 1997). In all cases a balance has to be found between what is deemed important in theory and what is feasible in practice.

A closer consideration of the nature of the criteria and their possible quantification also reveals that in almost all cases a spectrum rather than a clear-cut dichotomy exists. For example, as one ascends the settlement hierarchy, one can expect a gradual decrease in the number of people engaged in agriculture. But in order to decide which settlements are regarded as cities, a cut-off point needs to be established. Ideally the threshold is chosen at the point where there is a real change in the graph, but any cut-off point remains to some extent arbitrary and is bound to create ambiguities around it.

In the case of the settlements of Roman Egypt, in many cases there is a demonstrably close correlation between the various criteria and the assigned administrative status. This applies in particular to the *metropoleis*, which are by almost any standard urban. Institutionally and socially they present complex landscapes. The acquisition of councils at the beginning of the third century completed a process by which *polis* and *metropolis* gradually become structurally equivalent (Bowman and Rathbone 1992). Economically, significant differences in the degree of occupational specialization between village and *metropolis* can be found (Alston and Alston 1997). Registers of landholding can be used to show that in the *metropoleis* the number of people engaged in agriculture was relatively small (Tacoma 2008), and that significant differences in distribution patterns of wealth existed between village and *metropolis* (Bagnall 1992). Culturally, the *metropoleis* can be shown to be eager to employ the type of monumental architecture that was a standard feature of Graeco-Roman cities (see Chapter 12). In terms of population, the available evidence indicates sizes between 10,000 and 50,000 inhabitants (with significant variation between them), well above the attested sizes of villages.

In the case of the *metropoleis* the correlation between the criteria and the assigned status is comforting. But perhaps just as important for the understanding of the urban landscape is the degree of differentiation *between* the settlements. This occurs both within those settlements that are classified as urban and within those that are classified as rural. Not all cities were as important as Oxyrhynchus or Hermopolis (Tacoma 2006: 37–68). Not all villages conformed to some average model village. In fact, a continuum of settlements existed that straddled the boundary between village and city. Any settlement landscape is bound to consist of such a spectrum, but what is striking is the degree of differentiation, with the spectrum running all the way from Alexandria to the most insignificant hamlet.

The findings are then seemingly contradictory: there exist good reasons to uphold a dichotomy between village and city, yet at the same time we find a spectrum of settlements. The problem can be rephrased, however: as predicted, the main problems occur around the thresholds constructed to distinguish village from city. Some large villages may be considered urban in all but name. Some of these may have a relatively large population, perhaps, in the largest cases, approaching the threshold of 10,000 inhabitants. More importantly, the social and economic complexity of such settlements was great.

The existence of some borderline cases has potential consequences for the calculations of levels of urbanization discussed in the previous section. But the problem is less important than it may seem, for the most likely implication is simply that in the calculations of urbanization cities are underrepresented. In consequence, such estimates should be regarded as minimum estimates—not a real source for worry.

Population Structure: Urban–Rural Differentials

The findings of the previous sections might also have repercussions for our understanding of the population structure of the settlements. Historical demography shows that in urbanized societies substantial differences can exist between the demographic regimes of villages and cities. In Roman Egypt, the marked hierarchy in the spectrum of settlements raises the question, to what extent is it possible to show such differences?

The basic contours of the demographic regime of Roman Egypt have been reconstructed by Bagnall and Frier on the basis of the census documents (Bagnall and Frier 1994). This constitutes one of the truly important advances in the study of ancient history of the past decades. Nevertheless, it is also important to keep in mind the limitations of the sources. So, it is impossible to *prove* with the help of the census data that the application is warranted of the standardized model life tables that ancient historians use to model patterns of mortality (Parkin 1992; Scheidel 2001b,c; Woods 2007), though the rough match between the tables and the census data is surely comforting. Dividing the data into smaller subsets, such as those for villages and cities, is therefore bound to increase the number of uncertainties.

Despite the difficulties, the question of such differential demography is worth considering, for it has a wider significance, potentially bearing on the so-called urban graveyard theory. This theory has been formulated on the basis of evidence from early modern Europe (London in particular), but has found wide application in urban history in general, including studies of the city of Rome (e.g. Lo Cascio 2000; Jongman 2003). According to the theory, urban populations were unable to reproduce themselves and therefore needed an influx of migrants in order to remain at a stable size.

The theory comes in two varieties. The classic version of the urban graveyard theory was formulated to explain the spectacular and exceptional growth of London between 1650 and

1750 (Wrigley 1967). At the basis of this model were differences in rural and urban mortality: levels of mortality in London were significantly higher than in the countryside. But despite London's natural decrease, the city grew at a spectacular rate. The only possible explanation was that the very high levels of urban mortality were compensated by even higher levels of immigration. A major attempt at revision of the theory was made by Sharlin in 1978. Sharlin did not deny the importance of migration for urban growth, but reversed the underlying causative mechanism. According to him the key was fertility, not mortality. He distinguished between two groups, namely a resident core population and an envelope of temporary migrants. The core population had normal demographic characteristics. The migrants, by contrast, had a very different demographic profile: they consisted of young men and women who were hindered by institutional barriers to marry. In consequence, their fertility lagged behind. Migrants therefore offered their fair share to levels of mortality, but hardly contributed to fertility. Paradoxically, cities were able to grow thanks to the influx of migrants, but at the same time the migrants also produced a much higher level of urban mortality. Migrants were therefore both the cause of and solution to the problem (Sharlin 1978).

Two major issues have structured the ensuing debate among historians of early modern Europe. One is (unsurprisingly) the question to which of the two theories is correct, the problem being that the empirical evidence is too imprecise to make an authoritative choice (Woods 1989, 2003). The other is the problem of general applicability. Urban historians have warned against the risk of applying the graveyard theory as a mechanistic law (de Vries 1984: 183), and it is hard to avoid the impression that this is precisely what has happened.

In principle, the cities that are covered by the census documents of Roman Egypt had a population size and population density that was sufficient for urban graveyard effects to occur. We may then envisage them as being surrounded by feeder settlements from which migrants moved into the city. However, testing the theory with the help of the census documents is far from easy. The evidence is tantalizing, but consists only of indirect pointers. Differences between village and city cannot be established in two fundamental areas of the demographic regime, mortality and fertility (Bagnall and Frier 1994: 164). The one demographic area where it has been possible to establish differences is that of households. In the cities, nuclear families are found much more frequently than in villages, where complex and extended family forms dominate (Bagnall and Frier 1994: 66–7). The finding is very important, yet it is difficult to proceed from there as there is no obvious connection to the urban graveyard theory.

There is one area of analysis that has a direct bearing on the theory, and that is migration. The census documents do not allow a direct analysis of migration patterns, but offer indirect pointers. The fact that renting of houses occurred more often in cities than in villages, the presence of many freeborn lodgers in those cities, and the fact that proportionately more men than women lived in cities can all at least partly be explained by rural–urban migration of young men (Bagnall and Frier 1994: 69–70, 160–9). There is a strong possibility that such mobility occurred on a structural scale.

The conclusion, then, is mixed. Bagnall and Frier have established beyond doubt that some demographic differences existed between city and village, and that is an important finding in itself. But the differences occur in an area that has no direct bearing on the theory of urban graveyards, which is so important to our understanding of the population structure in any settlement. With regard to the latter's applicability, there are strong hints at significant levels of rural–urban migration. This type of migration may be interpreted in the context of the theory, but it is not possible to go further than that at present. Even the census evidence has its limits.

Modelling Settlement Patterns

To complete this discussion, the findings might be turned into more generalizing models of settlement patterns. Four such models merit attention: the consumer city model, central place theory, rank–size distributions, and urban network theory. There are some dangers involved in the use of such models—not because they are simplifying, for that is what models are by definition. The danger is that, given the imperfections of the sources, the models cannot be tested. In fact, they may in some cases even be used to fill in the gaps of our knowledge. On a more moderate stance, they should rather be seen as tools that may help our understanding of settlement patterns. The question is thus not so much whether they are correct (there is no means of testing that anyway), but to what extent they are helpful.

The first theory that merits attention is Finley's theory of the consumer city (Finley 1977). In his view, ancient cities were places in which people lived off the exploitation of the surrounding countryside, where they had their landholdings. Cities were in that sense consumer cities. Urban production certainly occurred, but was not meant for export. Town and country were inextricably linked to each other. The main focus is thus on the character of the cities and the exploitative nature of the relations with their hinterlands.

For Finley, the theory of the consumer city was part of a wider model describing the functioning of the ancient economy, which in contrast to more optimistic evaluations he painted in primitivist terms (Finley 1985). It is this wider model that has sparked an immense debate (see e.g. Scheidel and von Reden 2002). Although it is not entirely possible to disentangle the two, there are some problems with the theory of the consumer city itself that merit attention (compare Morley 2004: 7–14). First, methodologically it is essentially a statement of principle rather than something that can be subjected to further analysis. Contrary indications are relegated to the margins or deemed exceptional. Secondly, the model is a negative one: it tells what the ancient city was not—it was not a producer city. The model does not help in further analysis. Thirdly, there is the problem that the model was essentially created with the classical Greek *polis* in mind, leaving later hellenistic and Roman developments out. Increasing differentiation in settlement hierarchies, socio-economic complexity within the settlements themselves, and their incorporation into wider political and economic units are all left unaccounted for.

Given these problems, the application of the consumer city model to the settlements of Roman Egypt essentially means formulating responses to it. The existence of a landowning elite that lives in the city is certainly in line with the basic ideas of the consumer city model, and the same applies to the fact that the cities lived off the agricultural produce of the countryside. But beyond these simple observations Egypt also shows the complexities of urban landowning. Not only was the number of urban landowners very limited, but there were also a high differentiation in wealth, a significant number of urban smallholders, and a high turnover rate of land, and patterns of leasing could be extremely complex (Tacoma 2008). One might also point to the complexities of village life: a strict dichotomy between exploited poor peasants in the villages and greedy landowners in the cities does not hold. The resulting picture is much more nuanced than a crude application of the theory would suggest.

A second important theory is central place theory, a theory that seeks to explain the size, number, and location of settlements. Whereas the consumer city model makes statements about the nature of the city and the ties with its hinterland, central place theory focuses primarily on location. It derives its name from the idea that centres functioned as central places providing goods and services for their surrounding territory. In a theoretical model of an open limitless space with completely homogeneous characteristics, the predicted outcome (the optimized location) is a series of hexagons with a centre in each of them. Between these centres, differences come into existence as goods and services have different threshold values and ranges: some need a larger territory than others. The outcome is the creation of a hierarchy of settlements, with a small number of important centres that can be found in the middle of wider areas, surrounded by lower-order settlements in the periphery.

Despite its fame in geography, application of central place theory to the settlement structure of historical societies has proven difficult. The main obstacle is the highly theoretical nature of the model: mathematical elegance is combined with highly unrealistic assumptions. Actual settlement patterns that correspond exactly to the predictions of the theory are difficult to find, if only because in reality no landscape consists of an open homogeneous space without boundaries.

It is therefore hardly surprising that the theory has found little application to the settlements of Roman Egypt (compare Butzer 1976 for an earlier period). However, it is certainly possible to use some of the elements of the theory at nome level. At least for some nomes in Middle Egypt the location of the more important settlements is reasonably well established—which, to be sure, is a vital requirement for the application of the theory. In these nomes it is possible to investigate the extent to which settlements functioned as a central place for the surrounding area, offering goods and services not available elsewhere. The virtue of the approach would be that more stress would be put on the hierarchies within the settlements than purely on city–country dichotomies. In particular, it would highlight the importance of sub-centres within the nome.

Thirdly, there are rank–size distributions (de Vries 1984: 81–172). Just as in central place theory, this approach starts from a ranking of settlements. The difference is that in the case of rank–size distributions the ranking occurs not on the basis of the availability of goods and services, but on the basis of population sizes. Usually the sizes are categorized in various orders, say a first order consisting of settlements with a population of over 100,000 inhabitants, a second order with populations of 50,000–100,000 inhabitants, a third with 10,000–50,000 inhabitants, and so on. Such ranking and categorization might be used as a descriptive tool, for instance to state how many settlements there were in each category. But it might also be used in a more active way. According to an established rule, in a normal rank–size distribution, second-order settlements are half the size of the main settlement, third-order settlements one-third, and so on (Mueller 2006: 94–5). One can measure the extent to which settlement patterns conform to that rule. A directly related issue is that of 'primacy': how large was the largest settlement relative to the other settlements?

The theory focuses solely on population size, not on location (as with central place theory), or on the nature of the settlements (as in the consumer city model). An obvious condition is that data for population size should be known. This is a major challenge for all pre-industrial societies (compare the painstaking efforts of de Vries 1984 for early modern Europe). These problems may be avoided by classifying settlements without estimating their population size, for a rough order of magnitude can often be determined.

Studies have been carried out both for Egypt (Tacoma 2006; Mueller 2006 for the Ptolemaic period) and for other parts of the empire (see de Ligt 2008 for northern Italy). Application to Egypt reveals two points. First, as already mentioned, the larger villages are hard to classify. Secondly, and more importantly, it points to an unevenness in the urban system. By any estimate primacy was large. The wide variation reflects the uncertainties in the estimates, but Alexandria (200,000–500,000 inhabitants) must have been larger by a factor of 4 to 10 than the largest *metropolis* (say 50,000 inhabitants). A category of cities with sizes in between Alexandria and the large *metropoleis* is lacking. This also implies that a normal rank–size distribution does not apply in the Roman period (compare Mueller 2006).

The last theory that might be applied is that of urban networks, which sees settlements as nodal points in a web of ties that relate them to each other. The emphasis is not so much on the character, location, or size of the settlements (though all can be taken into account) as on the nature of the ties between the nodes. It analyses the type of relations between settlements and the extent to which they are integrated in the network.

Network theory is often used as a statement of principle, a perspective, not in more formalized approaches that can be subjected to further analysis. However, it should certainly be possible to measure the level of integration of settlements in the wider world and their degree of connectedness according to different criteria. The virtue of such an approach would be that it is not necessarily the nearest neighbour that is the closest in the network, since physical proximity and other types of relation may or may not correlate.

With regard to Roman Egypt, networks could be studied at the level of district capitals, analysing in particular their external contacts. Such research would have to differentiate between the specific types of relation. Through its taxation Egypt was closely tied to the rest of the empire and to Rome, but in other respects the geographical horizons of the *metropoleis* seem to have been much more limited. The Nile had the potential to connect settlements that were far apart, but urban settlements did not necessarily value or exploit this potential. While some contacts certainly existed between neighbouring nome capitals, the *metropoleis* devoted far more attention to Alexandria, and paid little attention to the world outside Egypt.

All four models have something to offer, even in cases where critical responses are formulated. The consumer city model points to the complexities of the relations between city and countryside, central place theory to the existence of sub-centres next to the district capitals, rank–size distributions to the high degree of primacy of Alexandria, and network theory to the skewed external relations of district capitals with the outside world.

Conclusion

By way of conclusion, it may be useful to summarize the findings of this chapter, and then formulate some further thoughts on their implications.

Traditionally, settlements are classified on the basis of administrative criteria into cities (*poleis*), towns (*metropoleis*), and villages (*komai*). The distinction has its uses, especially because the status of a settlement is usually known. In studying settlement patterns, it is important to realize that *metropoleis* are just as urban as the *poleis*. Quantifying levels of urbanization is difficult. Some figures are available both for the general population and for a number of cities, but all have wide margins of error. What can be ascertained is that at least 1 in 10 inhabitants lived in cities, and perhaps as many as 1 in 5. For pre-industrial societies these figures are high. On closer inspection, potential difficulties arise with definitions of what exactly constitutes a city. Apart from administrative status, a host of institutional, social, economic, cultural, and demographic criteria can also be taken into consideration. The discussion of these criteria suggests, first, that the pool of settlements to be classified as cities might be widened, and secondly, that there existed a spectrum of settlements, with a wide variation between them. Both the relatively high levels of urbanization and the existence of a steep settlement hierarchy have implications for the study of demography. Differences in the demographic regimes of cities and villages can to some extent be observed in the census population. However, whether—and if so in what form—an urban graveyard mechanism applied should remain open. Turning the findings about settlements into broader models reveals the complexities of the relations between city and countryside, the existence of sub-centres next to the district capitals, the high degree of primacy of Alexandria, and the somewhat skewed external relations of district capitals with the outside world.

Egypt was a highly urbanized part of the Roman world. But what does that statement mean? How should future research be conducted? A comparison with another region of the Roman empire might be helpful. In an important study of Roman Greece, Alcock raised a number of issues that may be relevant to the study of the settlements of Roman Egypt (Alcock 1993). She suggested that in Roman Greece a relatively empty, depopulated landscape went hand in hand with relatively large cities. A process of nucleation had taken place, which she connected to the coming of the Romans. Their direct interventions in the landscape were limited, while by contrast much more subtle processes of interaction between Romans and Greeks were at work.

Although the sources from Roman Greece did not allow quantification, Alcock's combination of a depopulated countryside with relatively large cities might imply relatively high levels of urbanization. The figures for Roman Greece may have been as high as those of Egypt, but the underlying situation seems to have been quite different. Alcock's study serves as a warning that identical levels of urbanization may capture different realities. Studying population figures is clearly not sufficient.

Alcock's book also raises questions of agency, for she interpreted changes in the urban landscape as responses to the incorporation of the region into the Roman world. These responses were mainly indirect: who did what is by and large irrecoverable. Just as in the case of Roman Egypt, Roman Greece shows relatively few direct interventions in the settlement structure, but the changes in the landscape were nevertheless profound. The question of agency (direct and indirect) should likewise be posed for Roman Egypt: to what extent is the hierarchical settlement pattern of Egypt a Roman product? This is, of course, a large issue that can hardly be analysed directly with the available sources. But the question should certainly be addressed.

A comparison with Roman Greece also demonstrates that the position of Roman Egypt in these debates is somewhat odd. Given the scarcity of ancient figures, the quantification that Egypt offers is very welcome indeed, but it is clearly not sufficient. As the example of Roman

Greece shows, similarly high levels of urbanization may capture quite different situations. The wealth of sources from Roman Egypt allows researchers to probe more deeply, and to use several approaches at once. Ironically, in a way this richness also obscures the analysis. Comparisons are hindered by the simple fact that no other areas of the Roman empire offer similar sources. In the case of Roman Egypt, riches can become an embarrassment.

Suggested Reading

An introductory survey of urbanization in Roman Egypt is offered by Bowman (2000); Alston and Alston (1997) covers the theoretical side of the topic. See further Alston (2002) and Tacoma (2006, 2008). Population sizes are discussed by Rathbone (1990). The essential publication on the population structure of Roman Egypt is Bagnall and Frier (1994) (see further Bagnall, Frier, and Rutherford 1997), and Scheidel has offered a wide range of additional demographic studies, e.g. Scheidel (2001b). Parkin (1992) provides a general introduction to ancient demography. For comparative purposes, the classic and highly influential study of de Vries (1984) on the cities of early modern Europe offers the best starting point.

Bibliography

Alcock, S. E. 1993. *Graecia Capta: The Landscapes of Roman Greece*. Cambridge: Cambridge University Press.

Alston, R. 2002. *The City in Roman and Byzantine Egypt*. London: Routledge.

——and R. D. Alston. 1997. 'Urbanism and the Urban Community in Roman Egypt', *Journal of Egyptian Archaeology* 83: 199–216.

Bagnall, R. S. 1992. 'Landholding in Late Roman Egypt: The Distribution of Wealth', *Journal of Roman Studies* 82: 128–49; repr. in R. S. Bagnall (ed.), *Later Roman Egypt: Society, Religion, Economy and Administration*. Aldershot: Ashgate, 2003.

——and B. W. Frier. 1994. *The Demography of Roman Egypt*. Cambridge: Cambridge University Press.

——and I. C. Rutherford. 1997. *The Census Register P.Oxy. 984: The Reverse of Pindar's Paeans*. Brussels: Fondation Égyptologique Reine Élisabeth.

Bowman, A. K. 1971. *The Town Councils of Roman Egypt*. Toronto: Hakkert.

——1985. 'Landholding in the Hermopolite Nome in the Fourth Century A.D.', *Journal of Roman Studies* 75: 137–63.

——1996. *Egypt after the Pharaohs 332 BC–AD 642*, 2nd edn. London: British Museum Press.

——2000. 'Urbanization in Roman Egypt', in E. Fentress (ed.), *Romanization and the City: Creation, Transformation and Failure*. Portsmouth, RI: Journal of Roman Archaeology, 173–87.

——and D. W. Rathbone. 1992. 'Cities and Administration in Roman Egypt', *Journal of Roman Studies* 82: 107–27.

Butzer, K. W. 1976. *Early Hydraulic Civilization in Egypt: A Study in Cultural Ecology*. Chicago: University of Chicago Press.

Delia, D. 1988. 'The Population of Roman Alexandria', *Transactions of the American Philological Association* 118: 275–92.

de Ligt, L. 2008. 'The Population of Cisalpine Gaul in the Time of Augustus', in L. de Ligt and S. Northwood (eds), *People, Land and Politics: Demographic Developments and the Transformation of Roman Italy 300 B.C.–A.D. 14*. Leiden: Brill, 139–83.
de Vries, J. 1984. *European Urbanization, 1500–1800*. London: Methuen.
Finley, M. I. 1977. 'The Ancient City from Fustel de Coulanges to Max Weber and Beyond', *Comparative Studies in Society and History* 19: 305–27.
——1985. *The Ancient Economy*, 2nd edn. London: Hogarth Press.
Hansen, M. H. 2006. *The Shotgun Method: The Demography of the Ancient Greek City-State Culture*. Columbia: University of Missouri Press.
Jongman, W. M. 2003. 'Slavery and the Growth of Rome: The Transformation of Italy in the Second and First Centuries BCE', in C. Edwards and G. Woolf (eds), *Rome the Cosmopolis*. Cambridge: Cambridge University Press, 100–22.
Lo Cascio, E. 2000. 'La popolazione', in E. Lo Cascio (ed.), *Roma imperiale: Una metropolis antica*. Rome: Carocci, 17–69.
Morley, N. 2004. *Theories, Models and Concepts in Ancient History*. London: Routledge.
Mueller, K. 2006. *Settlements of the Ptolemies: City Foundation and New Settlement in the Hellenistic World*. Leuven: Peeters.
Parkin, T. G. 1992. *Demography and Roman Society*. Baltimore: Johns Hopkins University Press.
Rathbone, D. W. 1990. 'Villages, Land and Population in Graeco-Roman Egypt', *Proceedings of the Cambridge Philological Society*, new ser. 36: 103–42.
Scheidel, W. 2001a. 'Progress and Problems in Roman Demography', in W. Scheidel (ed.), *Debating Roman Demography*. Leiden: Brill, 1–81.
——2001b. *Death on the Nile: Disease and the Demography of Roman Egypt*. Leiden: Brill.
——2001c. 'Roman Age Structure: Evidence and Models', *Journal of Roman Studies* 91: 1–26.
——and S. von Reden (eds) 2002. *The Ancient Economy*. New York: Routledge.
Sharlin, A. 1978. 'Natural Decrease in Early Modern Cities: A Reconsideration', *Past and Present* 79: 126–38.
Tacoma, L. E. 2006. *Fragile Hierarchies: The Urban Elites of Third-Century Roman Egypt*. Leiden: Brill.
——2008. 'Urbanization and Access to Land in Roman Egypt', in R. Alston and O. van Nijf (eds), *Feeding the Ancient Greek City*. Leuven: Peeters, 85–108.
Woods, R. I. 1989. 'What Would One Need to Know to Solve the "Natural Decrease in Early Modern Cities" Problem?', in R. Lawton (ed.), *The Rise and Fall of Great Cities*. London: Belhaven Press, 80–95.
——2003. 'Urban–Rural Mortality Differentials: An Unresolved Debate', *Population and Development Review* 29: 29–46.
——2007. 'Ancient and Early Modern Mortality: Experience and Understanding', *Economic History Review* 60: 373–99.
Wrigley, E. A. 1967. 'A Simple Model of London's Importance in Changing English Society and Economy', *Past and Present* 37: 47–70.

CHAPTER 9

ARCHAEOLOGY IN THE DELTA

PENELOPE WILSON

THE idealized Roman image of the Nilotic landscape of Egypt consisted of verdant papyrus swamps and lotus marshes, populated by lusty pygmies in papyrus skiffs and rampaging hippopotami and crocodiles (Versluys 2002). The Delta was certainly swampy, especially during the annual flood, and some of the representations of villas beside lakes may well have represented the area around Lake Mareotis or at Canopus. The archaeology, however, presents a different, urbanized area, with Roman institutions gradually replacing the intense agricultural development of the marshlands carried out under the Ptolemies.

The topography of the Nile Delta in Roman times varied considerably from that of the modern era. The coastline has changed, with areas in the Canopic basin on the west submerged since antiquity and other areas extending, as at the Rosetta and Damietta promontories. There were five major Nile branches across the Delta floodplain with significant distributaries and a system of irrigation canals. The inland lakes and swampy marshlands of lakes Mareotis (Maryut), Idku, Burullus, and Menzaleh formed a natural buffer zone around the northern crown of the Delta, with thin fingers of land creating a landscape with lacustrine, fluvial, and marine interconnections. The Ptolemaic programme of land reclamation around the major administrative centres and, in particular, the emphasis on a food supply network south-east of Alexandria had led to the foundation of 'new' farm estates, which in turn became small towns (Shafei 1952; Wilson 2010). It is likely that the policy continued under Roman rule and focused on the area in the centre and north of the Delta, with marshy land being drained, waterways managed, and towns secured to ensure that the new farms were cultivated and produce, especially grain, was shipped onward as efficiently as possible (Fig. 9.1). Production may have peaked in the first century CE, with up to 16,000 km^2 of cultivable Delta land (Butzer 1976: 83, Ptolemaic period; Bagnall 1993: 20) producing a good proportion of the 20 million *modii* or around 135,000 tonnes of wheat sent from Egypt to Rome under Augustus (Aur. Vict. *Caes.* 1.6, in Festy 1999). Other writers recorded the richness of vineyards, market gardens, orchards, and vegetable plots.

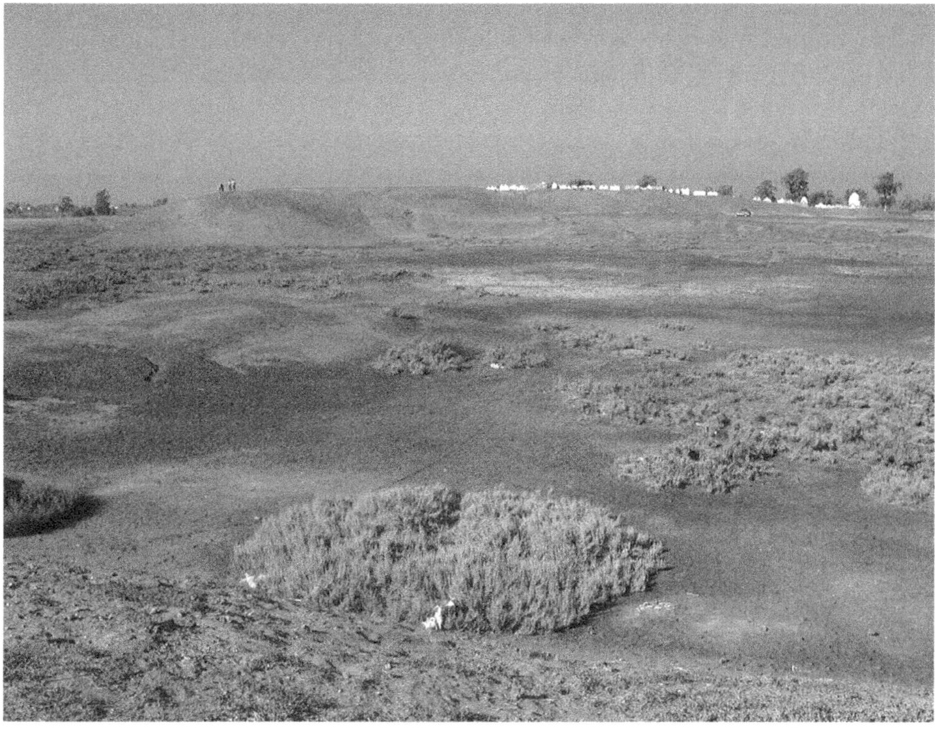

FIG. 9.1 Kom el-Ahmar in the western Delta, an example of a 'typical' settlement site continuing from the Ptolemaic to the Roman period. The site used to consist of one large mound, but has been reduced to three smaller mounds, a flat area, and a bath house after *sebakhin* digging

Author's photograph.

Problems of Archaeological Work in the Delta

Although there is information available in order to trace the process of agricultural, social, and administrative development in the archaeological record, the Roman archaeology of the Delta has not been the primary focus of Egyptologists interested in Pharaonic remains, or of Romanists, who have been reliant upon textual material. There is little of the latter directly pertaining to the Delta, except for some finds of carbonized papyri, including those from Tell Timai relating to a brief administrative period, 158–70 CE (Kambitsis 1985). Inscribed monuments, such as funerary stelae, have been emphasized if they are unusual in content, for example those from the so-called Jewish cemetery at Tell el-Yahudiyeh (Leibovitch 1942).

Egyptologists have not been insensitive to Roman archaeological material, recording it as it has been found within their excavations. Petrie was comparatively assiduous in the work he carried out among 'Roman period' houses and cemeteries at Tanis (Petrie 1885). The overall context of such material has proved difficult to establish—whether they were genuine urban developments of the Imperial period or traces of those who were living at the site in order to dismantle the Pharaonic stone monuments. The limited archaeological excavations in Roman period sites have shown the complexity of the stratigraphy of such sites, with Roman layers sandwiched between Pharaonic and later Roman and Islamic layers, as well as the large quantities of pottery sherds, smashed stonework, and small finds that have to be recorded and analysed. In order to deal physically and conceptually with the amount of potential material and with the kinds of useful information it can provide, a strategy needs to be developed against the background of a lack of large-scale project funding, the continuing rapid disappearance of the sites themselves, and the ability to understand sites subsumed already underneath towns and agriculture.

In recent years, however, the Supreme Council of Antiquities in Egypt has encouraged excavation work in the north of Egypt, and classical archaeologists have initiated projects such as that at Schedia, the port of Alexandria. Some of the logistical problems are being addressed by the holistic recording by Uppsala University of the *tell* and its environs at Tell el-Khawalid (Phragonis) and the gathering of basic information about as many sites as possible by the Delta Survey of the Egypt Exploration Society. A focus upon the Roman archaeology of such sites will play a key role in understanding the processes of cultural change in Egypt from a Pharaonic to Christian then Islamic society.

Previous Work in the Delta

Previous knowledge of the Roman Delta has been driven by chance finds that were then investigated by the Egyptian Antiquities Organization (now SCA). Some of the reports were published in the *Annales du Service des Antiquités de l'Égypte* (Foucart 1901), but the results of other excavations have not yet been made available. At the end of the nineteenth and into the twentieth century, finds were often made by workers digging out ancient earth for use as fertilizer on fields on behalf of land companies. The finds were largely without context and the site from which they came was actually in the process of being destroyed. Where projects have been able to locate and describe material with more purpose, such as at Terenouthis (McCleary 1987), only some of the inscribed finds have been assessed and published (for example, Hooper 1961; Winnicke 1992). Furthermore, the settlements nearest to the cemetery have not been surveyed and further rescue work has had to be undertaken in the cemetery itself, so that attempts to understand the broader regional and social development of the population from the first century onwards have only recently been undertaken (Dhennin 2009: 49–82).

Certain types of chance find have been used to identify sites as dating to the Imperial Roman period, in particular bath houses, cemeteries and burials, coins, statuary, metalwork, and mosaics. In *sebakhin* digging, work would stop if a significant find were made and then the authorities would be called in to carry out more controlled excavations. Each of the categories above was, however, only a very small part of an often much larger archaeological site, yet they can still be helpful in understanding aspects of Roman life in the Delta. Bath houses, found throughout Egypt and the Roman world, have been found in twenty-six Delta sites so far, including Alexandria. Bath houses with a circular *tholos* of individual foot-baths (or hip tubs) were introduced during the Hellenistic period, but they were refurbished throughout the Imperial period to transform them into plunge or immersion baths for Roman-style bathing and, eventually, in the fourth century hypocausts were introduced to heat the water for bathing, much later than elsewhere in the eastern Mediterranean (Trümper 2009). At Xois (Kom Sakha), for example, there were large public as well as private bath houses (el-Khashab 1949, 1978), while at Sersena and Kom Doshen in the central south Delta, two fine examples of Imperial period baths were found, with complete sets of pipework, cisterns, and drains—including lead pipes, amphora-neck pipes, and limestone-lined watercourses. The bath house at Kom el-Ahmar in the western Delta was built to accommodate men and women separately, from the reign of Claudius until the late Roman period (el-Khashab 1949), and probably contained mosaic floors, as did the bath house at Schedia (Abd el-Fattah and Gallo 1998). Although it seems that in Roman Egypt public bathing in plunge baths was not so popular as washing in individual sinks and then individual bathing in tubs (Trümper 2009: 159–61), whether a person was in Gortys in Greece or in Sais, they could enjoy the same bathing experience.

Finds of stone objects, especially statuary, have also suffered from a lack of context. The style, subject matter, and the fact that many statues were made from marble seemed to suggest that they were most likely commissioned from Italy and shipped to Egypt and perhaps were also linked to Alexandrian workshops. The types of statue include private individuals, such as a statue in blue-white marble of an old woman wearing a long tunic, from Tell Moqdam (Leontopolis) and dated to the end of the first century–beginning of the second (Cairo, Egyptian Museum CG 27477; Graindor 1937: 120–2, no. 61, pls 53–4). A tradition of locally produced works in classical style may be suggested by examples in limestone, such as that of a man standing next to a tree or papyrus roll box from Abiar near Kafr el-Zayet (Alexandria, Graeco-Roman Museum GRM 24061, 17041B) and the headless statue of Hercules leaning on his club, wrapped in his lion skin, from Kom el-Tawil (Cairo, Egyptian Museum JE 46212). Whether the sculptures were intended for private houses, shrines, or tombs is unknown, although the Serapis boy-priest marble statue (Cairo, Egyptian Museum JE 39468) from Terenouthis may well have been placed in his tomb last of all (Graindor 1937: 56, no. 15, pl. 15). The torso of a red granite statue, identified as Caracalla and represented as a bearded Egyptian pharaoh, is a rare find from the Delta. Its find spot in the River Nile, however, raises interesting questions about what that statue might have meant and whether it could have been a ritual deposit for the Nile flood (Hawass 1997).

The burial of the dead in the Delta was a problem because many major towns did not have access to suitable desert edge environments. Terenouthis, however, was on the western Delta edge and with a cemetery for a large town whose inhabitants perhaps were involved in the operation of the natron quarries in Wadi Natrun and included military men protecting the western Delta fringe. In the course of several excavations, up to 8,000 tombs may have been excavated in all, and they show a range of architectural styles ranging from pits in the ground, to barrel-vaulted chambers, to tombs surmounted by a truncated pyramid, all made out of mud-brick (el-Nasseri and Wagner 1978). The focal part of the funerary cult of the dead was a limestone stela with inscriptions, mostly in Greek, but a few in Demotic and Latin, showing the dead in the architectural setting of their tomb, reclining on a couch at the funerary banquet, or praying in the presence of Anubis and Horus, represented by a jackal and falcon respectively. The grave goods were not rich, including pottery and glass vessels as well as terracotta statuettes of gods. Coins show that the floruit of the cemetery was in the third to fourth century and that some of the coinage was provided to pay the ferryman Charon for the journey across the River Styx, in a neat fusion of Egyptian and hellenistic funerary culture in Roman Egypt (McCleary 1987). Other local topographic features could be used for cemeteries on the Delta floodplain. The presence of a natural sand hill at Quesna, some 25 km to the north of Athribis (Tell Atrib) across the river, was a natural place for the burial of families from the Late period onwards, but Roman terracotta double-jar burials have also been found there (Gomaa and Hegazy 2001). Minshat Abu Omar on the eastern Delta edge provides an area of high, sandy ground that had been a predynastic necropolis, but was used again for over 800 burials from the Ptolemaic to the Roman period. The burials were often made in pits in the sand, sometimes with mud-brick surrounds or with mud floors, and occasionally in terracotta coffins. Even though, in a few cases, people were provided with coins and gold-leaf eye, mouth, and abdominal incision coverings, or with gold earrings or other basic grave goods, the burials were of ordinary townspeople, perhaps from the nearby city of Imet (Kroeper and Wildung 1985, pp. x–xii). In other towns, such as Tanis, Heroonpolis, and Buto (Tell Fara'in), outlying areas of the towns were brought into use for poor adult burials in terracotta vessels and children in amphoras (Cotelle-Michel 2004).

From the Roman period in particular, the best dating evidence found by chance on sites is coins, which can help to pinpoint dates for other types of material if found in controlled excavations. Coin hoards have been found in the north of Egypt in some numbers, although the exact quantity of material recovered is hard to establish because of the speed with which some hoards were dug out, divided, sold, and removed from Egypt. Often the find spots are unknown or obscured, but in 1905 an estimated 20,000 billion Alexandrian coins were found in seven jars somewhere in the Delta; the more controlled 1909 excavation in the bath house at Athribis yielded around 3,500 bronze coins; and in 1930 at Xois thousands of Roman *aurei* were found dating to between the reigns of Nero and Commodus (Christiansen 2004: 36–85). The mass of evidence shows that the Roman era was certainly more monetized than the Ptolemaic period, but also that people buried their money perhaps for safekeeping, although why and under what individual circumstances is not clear. It is noticeable that a large proportion of coin hoards date to the fifty years after Caracalla, when there was much strife and civil disturbance. These may be 'emergency' hoards, debasement hoards (people storing coins in case their value increased later), or tax-evading hoards (Christiansen 2004: 140). The presence of such material was also an unwelcome inducement to illicit excavation.

Other small finds of often unprovenanced Roman material have made their way into museum collections because of the intrinsically attractive qualities of the chance finds, such as metalwork, terracotta figures, lamps, jewellery, and glassware, but whole assemblages have clearly suffered as a result.

Current Research and Survey

In order to begin to address the gaps in our knowledge of Roman period Delta archaeology—and the Delta as a whole—survey work and large multi-period site excavations have formed the basis of research in the Delta for the last forty years. Survey work includes the visual assessment, mapping, surface pottery study, and sometimes geophysical and drill auger analysis of sites, while excavation builds up stratigraphic layers, detailed planning of structures and features, and analysis of all of the material culture and environmental data from sites. The aim has been to create a wider picture of sites, their location, and type against the detailed examination of particular sites in order to understand their development over time, often from the Pharaonic into the Byzantine or Islamic periods. The dynamic interactions between the cultural phases may in themselves have a unique flavour for each place, depending upon the constituent population or purpose of the town/site. 'Roman' period sites are identified in survey principally through five types of archaeological evidence:

1. 'Roman' period pottery, including *terra sigillata* finewares, amphora bases and necks from the whole Mediterranean as well as Egypt, and coarseware domestic vessels, including *saqiya* pots and casserole dishes.
2. Coins, either as surface finds or in hoards as described above.
3. Structures made of fired red brick. This identifier is more problematic because although fired brickwork is known from the Pharaonic period, it was used more regularly in the Ptolemaic period and seems to have been the material of choice for constructions requiring waterproofing in the Imperial Roman period, that is, baths, wineries, and cisterns. In this case the finding of fired brick, mortar, and waterproof concrete refers to the type of building, not to its date. Red brick also lasts longer than the mud-brick from which other houses and buildings were made, a fact that was evident to *sebakhin* diggers, resulting in the large number of bath houses reported during such activities.
4. Inscribed material such as funerary stelae.
5. 'Roman' period terracotta sarcophagi, though often in relation to other types of find.

All such material also depends upon its context for dating, as it could have been reused, deposited later, or dumped in earth from elsewhere.

Survey and Recording

The Egypt Exploration Society Delta Survey has logged a total of around 730 sites in the Delta, combining the results of all work carried out in the past (Delta Survey website). Around 230 sites, not all extant and including the large administrative towns, have been identified as having 'Roman' material, through visits, chance finds, survey, and excavation. The term 'Roman' may include material from the 'Graeco-Roman' period (that is, from the beginning of the Ptolemaic dynasty to the Arab invasion, 323 BCE–641 CE), the late Roman (that is, fifth to seventh centuries), or the Coptic–Byzantine period (that is, around the fourth to seventh centuries). When the sites are mapped, a number of aspects become clear (Fig. 9.2). There are apparent clusters of sites in the north-west, namely, the Alexandrian hinterland; the east, covering the regions of the Menzaleh–Pelusiac branches together with the main route and Trajan Canal through the Wadi Tumilat; and in the north centre of the Delta. The

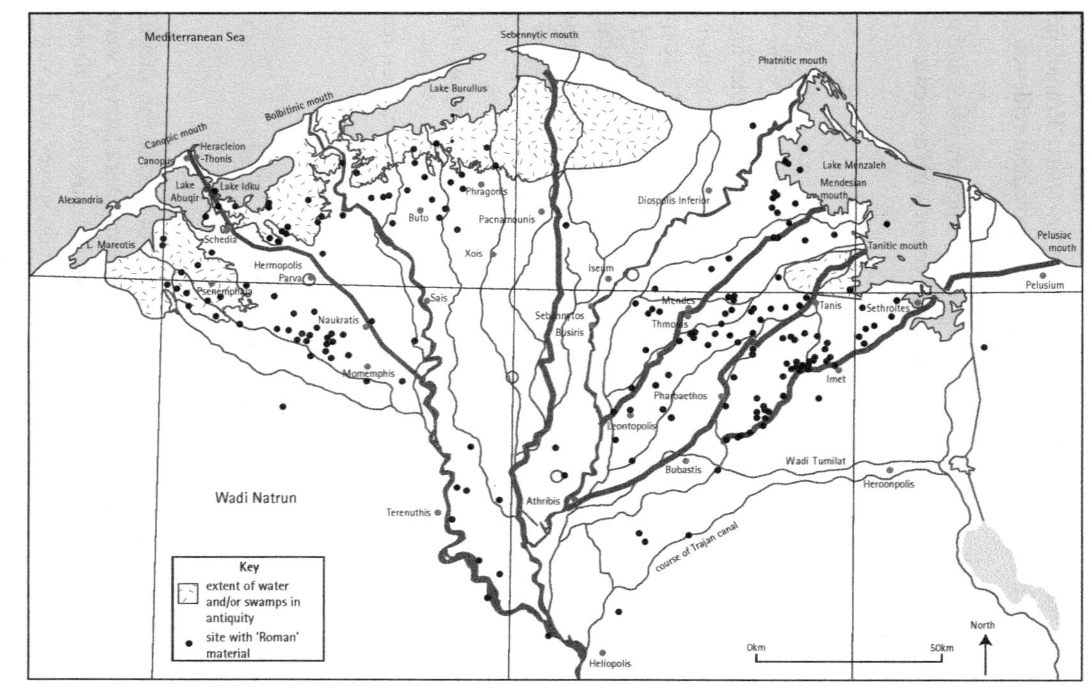

FIG. 9.2 Map with 'Roman' period sites, mostly as identified on the Egypt Exploration Society Delta Survey, to show the potential abundance of Roman period archaeology

By P. Wilson and J. R. Dickinson; adapted from Bietak (1975: 175, fig. 42), Goddio (2007: 25, fig. 1.24), and Wilson and Grigoropoulos (2009: 31, map 10).

clusters have been identified by focused survey work, so the results should be seen to reflect modern archaeological activity and are only indicative of an ancient reality. There is a noticeable lack of sites in the centre of the Delta, and it is likely that this is because no systematic survey work has been carried out there yet; it does not necessarily mean that there are no sites there. Even with the gaps, the map suggests that the Delta was a well-settled and inhabited area during the Roman period.

The West Delta Regional Survey attempted to put the results of low-level survey work into some kind of broader context and in doing so identified several areas of Roman development that had not been suspected (Wilson and Grigoropoulos 2009). The survey work showed a strong link, as in the case of the old nome capitals, between Ptolemaic institutions and Roman towns, especially in the immediate Alexandrian hinterland. It is noticeable that in the comparison of survey data from the north-west Delta, 73.5 per cent of the sites surveyed and dated by pottery collection had Ptolemaic roots—some even had late Dynastic material—and continued into the Roman period, apparently ending around the seventh to eighth century. In the northern central part of the Delta, 22 per cent of the sites surveyed had a Ptolemaic foundation date onwards, but 78 per cent ranged from the Roman period into the ninth or tenth century (Wilson and Grigoropoulos 2009: 287–8). There was also considerable disparity between the better-preserved north-central sites and the more destroyed north-western sites. Although such results should be used with caution, they may suggest that there was a Ptolemaic emphasis on new agricultural foundations in the north-west in the Alexandrian hinterland, whereas in the Roman period, the desire for more agricultural land resulted in drainage of the northern central areas and foundation of new towns to take advantage of the expansion in farmlands. The resulting influx of people may then have led to the rejuvenation of the large cities of Athribis, as well as Buto with its vast manufacturing industries, creating a regional production centre and leading to the Romanization of places such as Xois, with its bath house, coin hoards, and statuary. The events of the third century, when people fled their new towns and tried to escape taxation and pestilence, may be represented at Xois by the displacement of population to a nearby site at Kafr el-Sheikh. The archaeological evidence may help to identify such fractures in settlement elsewhere, as, for example, at Tell Daba-Tida and Casaba-Disuq in the same area, and expand the historical narrative.

The only site in the Delta that has been the focus of a fieldwalking and pottery survey is Naukratis. The results of the work have interesting implications for how the taphonomic processes affecting sites are to be understood and the implications for discussing settlement development into the Roman period. Naukratis was the Saite inland port and continued to be of importance during the Ptolemaic period as it was on the Canopic branch and allowed access through Lake Mareotis to Alexandria or to Schedia and thence to Alexandria or Canopus and out of Egypt. The main *tell* here was destroyed by *sebakhin* in the 1880s when Petrie and Gardner carried out rescue excavations (Leclère 2008: 113–57). No further work was conducted at the site until the work of Coulson and Leonard (1981), who carried out a field survey, collecting pottery around the main area of the ancient *tell* in order to discern the spread of the settlement (Coulson 1996: 5). The problem for the survey was that material dredged from the local canals was spread onto the fields, and because the main *tell* had been dug over by *sebakhin* and left as a water-filled lake, it was unclear whether the topsoil was a fair representation of what might be underneath it, as is usually the case in less disturbed European fieldwalking conditions. If the pottery from the fieldwalking is mapped (Fig. 9.3), it seems clear that the strips bordering the north and west of the lake area contained Roman and Hellenistic period pottery, with a concentration of sherds along the western edge of the lake dating to the second to fourth centuries. There is also a relative concentration to the south of the lake area and a lesser spread to the north-east. Although Gardner reported finding two 'burnt-brick' Roman tombs, one with traces of fresco painting, on a cemetery mound north of Naukratis, the finds from the burials as a whole suggest a Ptolemaic date, so it seems unlikely that this was the main Roman period cemetery, which may be underneath a modern village (Gardner 1888: 11, 23). The city may have developed on the north and east sides of the lake in Ptolemaic times, then spread to the west and possibly south in Roman times, with a consistent material culture across the city, rather than the 'zoned' organization of the Late period material (Coulson 1996: 11). The results of the survey,

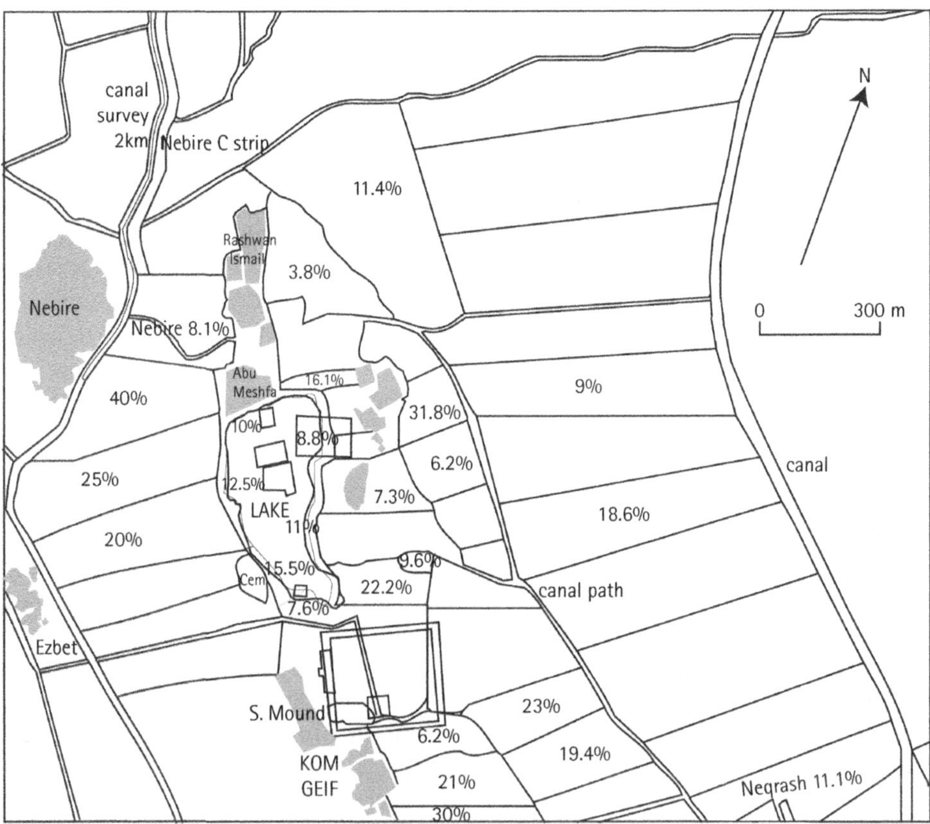

FIG. 9.3 Sketch map of Naukratis with areas of Roman sherding indicated after fieldwalking. The percentages are percentages of Roman period pottery from the total diagnostic sherds found in each area

By P. Wilson; compiled and adapted from Coulson (1996: 8, fig. 5, 173, fig. 68, and data *passim*).

however, may be due to the spread of material from the top of the original *tell* or come from outlying satellite or daughter towns at Neqrash and Nebire, and may also be determined by the exact position of the waterways at Naukratis, either to the west (Leclère 2008: 141) or east of the main city (Coulson 1996: 171–4). Nevertheless, despite the difficulty of reading the survey data and mapping it onto unknown buried features, the results represent a useful attempt to extend the methods of investigation available to archaeologists in the Delta. Further refinement of pottery dating would fine-tune the results even further, along with re-evaluation of the earlier excavations.

At the other end of the scale, a sophisticated array of underwater survey equipment has been used to rediscover the submerged cities of Canopus and Herakleion-Thonis (Goddio 2007). Although preliminary results have focused more on the Ptolemaic and late Roman periods, detailed work is uncovering the functioning and development of this great trading centre in Roman times. Further use of such techniques will be of value in targeting excavations throughout Egypt and improving predictions of what will be found.

Excavation

Evidence from individual sites suggests that large towns and administrative units, active from the Pharaonic into the Ptolemaic period, continued to function into the Roman period, but that there were also Roman period foundations, often for strategic reasons. The Romanization of Egyptian towns in general has been discussed in administrative terms, often based on texts (Bowman and Rathbone 1992; Alston 2002), but in material culture (archaeological) terms the process has been less easily detected.

At Diospolis Parva (Tell el-Balamun) the processional route of the main temple remains of the Pharaonic period was built over by a Roman street during the reigns of Vespasian and Hadrian, using limestone paving slabs, red brick, and pink mortar. The modification suggests to some extent that the ancient towns of the Delta were enhanced to become curiously vibrant places in the Roman period (Spencer 2005, 2009: 9–26, 109).

Athribis has provided some of the most detailed plans of buildings and complex stratigraphy for one of the four greatest towns in Egypt, according to Ammianus Marcellinus, writing in the fourth century (22.16.4; Rolfe 1963). The city was already an important central Delta capital from the Late period, and, although much of it is now beneath the modern city of Benha, excavations by Polish missions have focused on understanding how the city had developed (Leclère 2008: 258–61). They investigated two main areas of the site, one to the north and centre of the main antiquities area (Michałowski 1962, 1964a, b) and the other to the west of the village of Atrib, south of the tomb of Sheikh Yussef (Myśliwiec and Sztetyłło 2000). The excavations showed how the Ptolemaic town had been gradually subsumed into the Roman town, perhaps covering up to 140 hectares altogether (Leclère 2008: 582), but that new buildings had been constructed at the edges of the older town as it expanded to the north-east. In particular, several fine bath houses were excavated, along with a villa (Fig. 9.4). The latter contained an imposing entrance up a flight of steps into a hallway with an *impluvium* (a pool for collecting rainwater). The water and drainage facilities of the building were of the highest quality, made of fired brick and limestone, and it seems that the villa had its own bath house and perhaps winery. The wall plaster in the villa was refurbished at least six times, with new layers of plaster covering the old and fresh frescos and murals painted on the walls in the current style, mostly consisting of veined marble and floral motifs. Over time, changes were made every so often to enhance the building and its rooms in some way. The servants' quarters around the main villa effectively created a small urban estate (Myśliwiec and Sztetyłło 2000: 9–37). The complex pattern of small, narrow streets, organic urban development, and constant reconstruction makes understanding each part of the building's lifespan difficult, never mind individual people's lives. Reconstructions of the city suggest that the old Pharaonic temple area lay on a levee on the east near the river, with the town spreading out to the west (Fig. 9.5). In order to create a focus in the Roman town, Dąbrowski (1962) suggested that an axial road was constructed through the suburbs to create a town with four quarters. By the fifth century, a monumental gateway probably stood at the crossroads. A colossal marble head of Augustus (Graindor 1937: 44, no. 3, pl. III), as well as one of Hadrian (Alexandria, Graeco-Roman Museum GRM 20885) found in the centre of the *kom* areas, and large columns with a variety of classical capital styles suggest that a Roman temple stood in the city, stamping the imperial presence there. In addition, domestic quarters with kilns and hearths were located, as well as possible storage facilities, and there may also have been an elaborate quay with warehousing, and perhaps even a circus at the north of the site. The small proportion of the town investigated hints at the complex nature of the street plans and crowded nature of some of the quarters.

At Schedia was the inland harbour serving Alexandria, on the western side of the Delta on the Canopic branch. Linked by a canal to Alexandria, the harbour enabled ships coming from Egypt to tranship cargoes onward. Excavations at Schedia (Kom el-Giza and Kom Hammam) have located the position of buildings associated with the town here, including a villa with bath house and what seems to have been a large storage facility built in the Ptolemaic period, refurbished and made larger in the Roman period and falling out of use and becoming a farmhouse in the seventh century (Bergmann and Heinzelmann 2007). In the Roman period, it is tempting to see this building as a store where grain was kept for shipment directly to the river mouth at Canopus and thence to Ostia or to Alexandria through the Cleopatra Canal. The strata here, with intercutting layers, pits, and pottery dumps, as well as the magnetometer survey showing regular roomed magazines, suggest that the archaeology at Schedia is difficult but rewarding, and the main problem lies in peeling back the modern topography of fields, villages, modern waterways, and roads in order to reconstruct the ancient natural and urban landscapes.

At better-preserved sites such as Buto, the Roman development of the site may have followed a similar trajectory to Athribis (Leclère 2008: 210–16), but it is the industrial quarters that may prove to be more fruitful. The large site, covering up to 65 hectares, includes a Pharaonic temple enclosure (Kom B) to the east, which was converted into an industrial zone and settlement area between the first and fourth centuries. At Kom C, to the south-west of the temenos, a bath house of the circular *tholos* type, dating from the late Ptolemaic to the Roman period, was found, along with a cover of slag on the mounds. Resistivity survey of Kom A to the north-west has found the magnetic signature of over thirty kilns, most likely

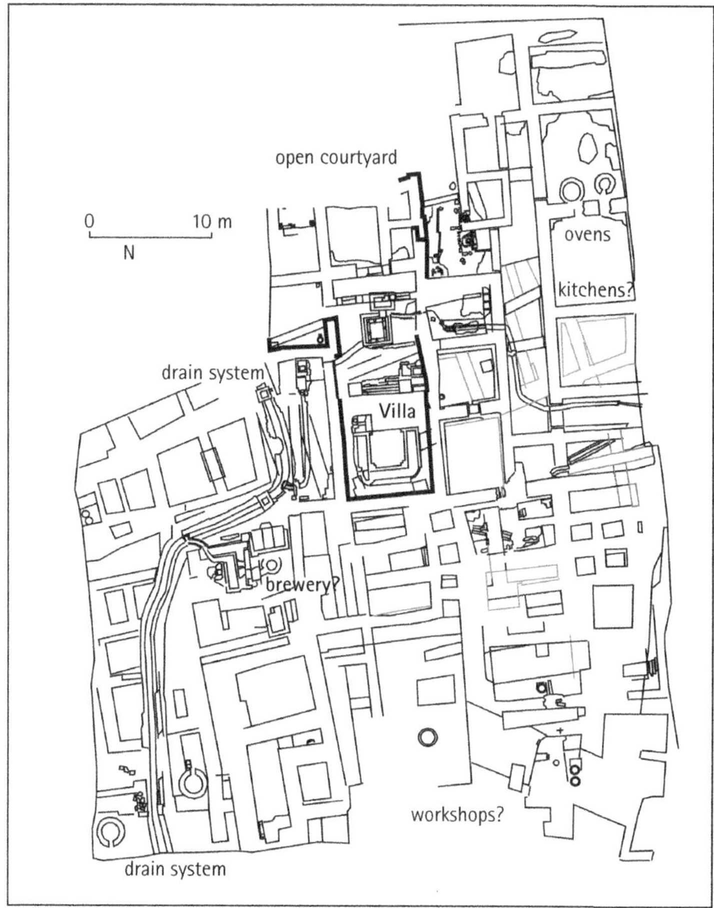

FIG. 9.4 Plan of the Roman villa at Athribis (Tell Atrib), with the villa outlined, showing the complexity of the buildings and their relationships

By P. Wilson; after Myśliwiec and Sztetyllo (2000).

for pottery, perhaps dating to the second to third century (Ballet 2004; Dixneuf and Lecuyot 2007). The prospect of locating production centres is of importance for the identification and dating of pottery, including both finewares and amphoras. Kom A was also a focus for the Roman settlement, with a hellenistic-style bath house, a cellular foundation for an administrative building or magazine, and a large cemetery which seems to have been used from the Saite period into the late Roman era. The Roman burials in it were mostly in terracotta sarcophagi consisting of the double vessel type in superimposed layers. The picture is of a settlement full of manufacturing activity, although it is not clear which areas were exactly contemporary; thus, there could be further refinement of the nature of, and relationship between, the busy industrial, settlement, and burial areas.

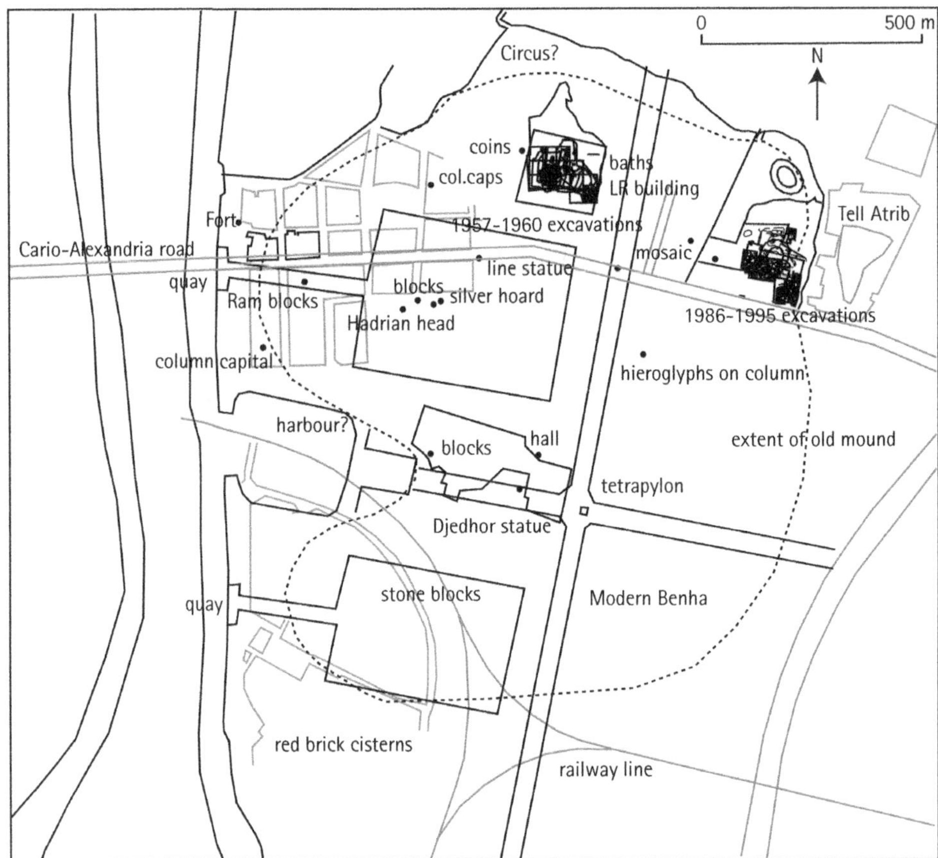

FIG. 9.5 Sketch map of Athribis (Tell Atrib) with Roman find spots and the sites of Polish excavations, to show the possible form of the Roman city against the small areas excavated

By P. Wilson; compiled and adapted from Dąbrowski (1962, pls. 1 and 2); Michałowski (1962, pl. 1); Myśliwiec and Sztetyłło (2000: 14, fig. 3 and plans 1–4); Benha Survey of Egypt, map 1:25,000 series; GoogleEarth™ satellite image 16 January 2008.

CONCLUSION

The Nilotic landscape of Egypt was a fantasy place in the Roman imagination. For the people who lived there, the archaeological remains suggest a vibrant society with new towns springing up to manage the agricultural lands. The old Pharaonic temple cities were reinvigorated as *metropoleis*, with all of the trappings of Roman life from a monetized economic system to marble statuary brought from Italy, and with industrial areas manufacturing goods for local consumers and visitors. Even in death, although some chose the expense of mummification, many did not bother, preferring or only able to afford terracotta coffins for the protection of their bodies and leaving coins for the travel expenses of their souls. The main cultural disjuncture occurred between Roman and late Roman material, with new pottery forms and decoration appearing in the archaeological record around the fourth century. In terms of material culture, there is more continuity from Ptolemaic into Roman society than Roman to late Roman (or Late Antique, as the period is sometimes known). Although the temple ceased to be the focus for the towns, it seems that bath houses provided a social link, even until the Islamic period.

Suggested Reading

For detailed information and bibliographies about all Delta sites, consult the Egypt Exploration Society's Delta Survey website: <http://www.ees.ac.uk/deltasurvey/ds-home.html>. See also Wilson and Grigoropolous (2009), for the western Delta, and Blue (2010) for the Mareotis area next to Alexandria. For ten of the main cities of the Delta, Leclère (2008) has collected all the material, from all periods, in one place. For background on urban settlement, although not specifically about the Delta, see Alston (2002).

Bibliography

Abd el-Fattah, A., and P. Gallo. 1998. 'Aegyptiaca Alexandrina: Monuments pharaoniques découverts récemment à Alexandrie', in J.-Y. Empereur (éd.), *Alexandrina* I. Cairo: Institut Français d'Archéologie Orientale, 7–19.

Alston, R. 2002. *The City in Roman and Byzantine Egypt*. London: Routledge.

Bagnall, R. S. 1993. *Egypt in Late Antiquity*. Princeton: Princeton University Press.

Ballet, P. 2004. 'The Graeco-Roman Pottery Workshops of Buto', *Egyptian Archaeology* 24: 18–19.

Bergmann, M., and M. Heinzelmann. 2007. 'Schedia, Alexandrias Hafen am Kanopischen Nil: Zwischen Bericht zu den Arbeiten 2003–2007', *Hefte des Archäologischen Seminars der Universität Bern* 20: 65–77.

Bietak, M. 1975. *Tell el-Dab'a* II: *Der Fundort im Rahmen einer archäologisch-geographischen Untersuchung über das Ägyptische Ostdelta*. Vienna: Österreichischen Akademie der Wissenschaften.

Blue, L. (ed.) 2010. *Lake Mareotis: Reconstructing the Past: Proceedings of the International Conference on the Archaeology of the Mareotic Region held at Alexandria University, Egypt, 5th–6th April 2008*. Oxford: Archaeopress.

Bowman, A. K., and D. W. Rathbone. 1992. 'Cities and Administration in Roman Egypt', *Journal of Roman Studies* 82: 107–27.

Butzer, K. W. 1976. *Early Hydraulic Civilization in Egypt: A Study in Cultural Ecology*. Chicago: University of Chicago Press.

Christiansen, E. 2004. *Coinage in Roman Egypt: The Hoard Evidence*. Aarhus: Aarhus University Press.

Cotelle-Michel, L. 2004. *Les sarcophages en terre cuite en Égypte et en Nubie de l'époque prédynastique à l'époque romaine*. Dijon: Faton.

Coulson, W. D. E. 1996. *Ancient Naukratis*, vol. 2, pt 1: *The Survey at Naukratis*. Oxford: Oxbow.

—— and A. Leonard, Jr. 1981. *Naukratis: Preliminary Report on the 1977–78 and 1980 Seasons*. Malibu, Calif.: Undena.

Dąbrowski, L. 1962. 'Topography of Athribis in the Roman Period', *Annales du Service des Antiquités de l'Égypte* 57: 19–31.

Dhennin, S. 2009. 'De Kôm Abou Billou à la Ménoufieh: Recherche historique et archéologique dans le Delta égyptien', doctoral dissertation, Université Charles-de-Gaulle, Lille 3.

Dixneuf, D., and G. Lecuyot. 2007. 'Note préliminaire sur les amphores découvertes par la mission "Recherches sur les ateliers hellénistiques et romains de Bouto" (2002–2003)', *Cahiers de la Céramique Égyptienne* 8, special issue: *Amphores d'Égypte de la Basse Époque à l'époque arabe*, ed. S. Marchand and A. Marangou, 135–41.

el-Khashab, A. 1949. *Ptolemaic and Roman Baths of Kôm el-Ahmar*, *Annales du Service des Antiquités de l'Égypte* 10, suppl.

—— 1978. *ΤΑ ΣΑΡΑΠΕΙΑ: À Sakha et au Fayum, ou, Les bains thérapeutiques*, *Annales du Service des Antiquités de l'Égypte*, suppl. 25.

el-Nasseri, S., and G. Wagner. 1978. 'Nouvelles stèles de Kom Abu Bellou', *Bulletin de l'Institut Français d'Archéologie Orientale* 78: 231–58.

Festy, M. 1999. *Aurelius Victor: Epitome de Caesaribus*. Paris: Belles Lettres.

Foucart, G. 1901. 'Extraits des rapports adressés pendant une inspection de la Basse-Égypte en 1893–1894', *Annales du Service des Antiquités de l'Égypte* 2: 44–83, 258–64.

Gardner, E. A. 1888. *Naukratis, Part II*. London: Egypt Exploration Fund.

Goddio, F. 2007. *The Topography and Excavation of Heracleion-Thonis and East Canopus (1996–2006)*. Oxford: Oxford Centre for Maritime Archaeology.

Gomaa, F., and E.-S. Hegazy. 2001. *Die neuentdeckte Nekropole von Athribis*. Wiesbaden: Harrassowitz.

Graindor, P. 1937. *Bustes et statues-portraits d'Égypte romaine*. Cairo: Grenier and Barbey.

Hawass, Z. 1997. 'A Statue of Caracalla Found in the Nile by a Fisherman', in J. Phillips (ed.), *Ancient Egypt, the Aegean and the Near East: Studies in Honour of Martha Rhoads Bell*, vol. 1. San Antonio, Tex.: van Siclen, 227–33.

Hooper, F. 1961. *Funerary Stelae from Kom Abou Billou*. Ann Arbor: Kelsey Museum of Archaeology.

Kambitsis, S. 1985. *Le papyrus Thmouis 1: Colonnes 68–160*. Paris: Sorbonne.

Kroeper, K., and D. Wildung. 1985. *Minshat Abu Omar: Ein vor- und frühgeschichtlicher Friedhof im Nildelta* I. Munich: Staatliche Sammlung Ägyptischer Kunst.

Leclère, F. 2008. *Les villes de Basse Égypte au Ier millénaire av. J.-C.* Cairo: Institut Français d'Archéologie Orientale.

Leibovitch, J. 1942. 'Stèles funéraires de Tell el-Yahoudieh', *Annales du Service des Antiquités de l'Égypte* 41: 41–6.

McCleary, R. 1987. *Portals to Eternity: The Necropolis at Terenouthis in Lower Egypt*. Ann Arbor: Kelsey Museum of Archaeology.

Michałowski, K. 1962. 'Fouilles polonaises à Tell Atrib en 1960', *Annales du Service des Antiquités de l'Égypte* 57: 68–77.

—— 1964a. 'Les fouilles polonaises à Tell Atrib (Saison 1961)', *Annales du Service des Antiquités de l'Égypte* 58: 235–44.

—— 1964b. 'Sixième campagne de fouilles à Tell Atrib (Saison 1962)', *Annales du Service des Antiquités de l'Égypte* 58: 245–54.

Myśliwiec, K., and Z. Sztetyłło. 2000. *Tell Atrib 1985–1995 I: Pottery Stamps: Rescue Excavations*. Warsaw: Neriton.

Petrie, W. M. F. 1885. *Tanis* I. London: Egypt Exploration Fund.

Rolfe, J. C. 1963. *Ammianus Marcellinus* II. London: Heinemann.

Shafei, A. 1952. 'Lake Mareotis: Its Past History and its Future Development', *Bulletin de l'Institut Fouad 1er du Désert* 2: 71–101.

Spencer, A. J. 2005. 'Main Street, Diospolis Inferior', in N. Crummy (ed.), *Image, Craft and the Classical World: Essays in Honour of Donald Bailey and Catherine Johns*. Montagnac: Mergoil, 233–41.

—— 2009. *Excavations at Tell el-Balamun 2003–2008*. <http://www.britishmuseum.org/research/research_projects/excavation_in_egypt/reports_in_detail.aspx>.

Trümper, M. 2009. 'Complex Public Bath Buildings of the Hellenistic Period: A Case Study in Regional Differences', in M.-F. Boussac, T. Fournet, and B. Redon (eds), *Le bain collectif en Égypte*. Cairo: Institut Français d'Archéologie Orientale, 139–79.

Versluys, M. J. 2002. *Aegyptiaca Romana: Nilotic Scenes and the Roman Views of Egypt*. Leiden: Brill.

Wilson, P. 2010. 'Recent Survey Work in the Southern Mareotis Area', in L. Blue (ed.), *Lake Mareotis: Reconstructing the Past: Proceedings of the International Conference on the Archaeology of the Mareotic Region held at Alexandria University, Egypt, 5th–6th April 2008*. Oxford: Archaeopress, 119–25.

—— and D. Grigoropoulos. 2009. *The West Delta Regional Survey, Beheira and Kafr el-Sheikh Provinces*. London: Egypt Exploration Society.

Winnicke, J. K. 1992. 'Demotische Stelen aus Terenuthis', in J. Johnson (ed.), *Life in a Multi-Cultural Society: Egypt from Cambyses to Constantine and Beyond*. Chicago: Oriental Institute, 351–8.

CHAPTER 10

THE ARCHAEOLOGY OF THE FAYUM

PAOLA DAVOLI

THE Fayum region lies in a natural depression in Egypt's Western Desert, about 80 km southwest of Cairo (Fig. 10.1). Around 2,200 km^2, it is one of the country's most fertile regions thanks to the abundance of water and of fertile soil of Nilotic origin. It is unique in that it is not a true oasis but rather a pseudo-oasis, because it is connected to the Nile Valley by a natural channel, the Bahr Yusuf, which enters the depression via the el-Lahun corridor, or Hawara Canal. This corridor was formed during the phase known as the Prenile (Embabi 2004: 44), when the Nile waters turned the depression into a huge lake, about 44 metres above sea level. The lake levels have varied over time both because of natural causes and, from the Middle Kingdom onwards, through human intervention. The area itself has no other outlet, and the water is trapped inside without possibility of escaping, except through evaporation. The deepest point is located at the bottom of the present lake, the Birket Qarun, at 52.9 metres below sea level. The ancient lake has left its traces in the desert surrounding the fertile area in the form of beaches, or terraces, located at different heights, which testify to the continuous fluctuation of its levels. This riverine environment favoured the appearance and development of Palaeolithic and then Neolithic communities, as well as the presence of a rich fauna.

The present lake represents the last stage in the development of the ancient lake of Moeris, as Herodotus identified it (2.149.1–2, 4–5; 150.1–4), artificially maintained at 45 metres below sea level. Over the millennia, water evaporation, and the subsequent accumulation of salts, has caused the present high salinity of the lake, though it remains unknown exactly when its waters turned brackish and thus unsuitable for drinking and for agricultural purposes. The original lake formed during the Prenile left a thick layer of alluvial sediments over which lay the more recent deposits of Nile silt. Such deposits create a deltaic cone from the point where the water of the Bahr Yusuf enters the ancient lake, forming what has been termed the Fayum delta. Its fan-like surface extends towards the centre of the region, gently sloping down from 18 metres to about 5 metres, resulting in a vast terrace where the region's capital, Medinet el-Fayum, stands; its ancient Egyptian name was Shedet, and in Greek it was called Krokodilopolis and Ptolemais Euergetis and then, in the Roman period, Arsinoiton Polis (Arsinoe). The

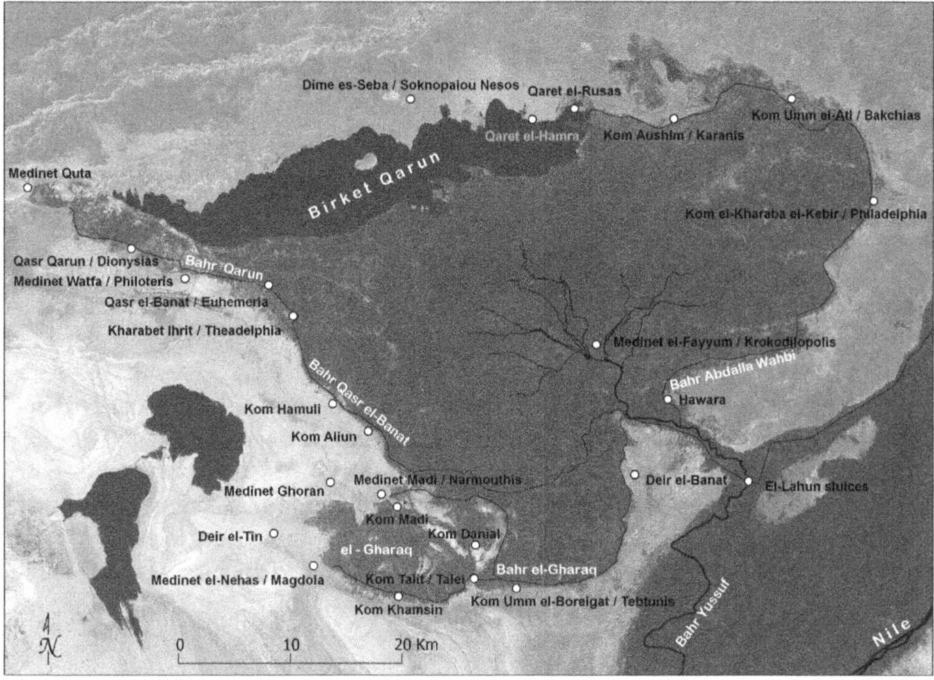

FIG. 10.1 Satellite view of the Fayum, with the main sites of the Graeco-Roman period

Copyright B. Bazzani.

location of the region's main city, one of the oldest in Egyptian history, has never changed since it is strategically situated for control of the central hydraulic system.

It is clear that the habitability and wealth of the region greatly depend on this connection with the Nile, and on the careful management of the amount of water that is fed into the depression through the Bahr Yusuf: too much water would raise the lake level, thus reducing the amount of cultivable land, while too little water would not be sufficient to irrigate the vast agricultural area. It is therefore a question of negotiating a careful balance, which was achieved between the third century BCE and the third century CE. During this time, the Fayum periodically reached peaks of productivity and demography, alternating with less productive phases.

Projects of Land Reclamation

The first attempt to control the waters and the amount of land cultivated took place during the 12th dynasty, with the so-called first land reclamation project. Works probably started during the reign of Senwosret I and were completed by Amenemhat III. Senwosret II and Amenemhat III (*c.*1880–1808 BCE) chose, perhaps significantly, el-Lahun and Hawara as the location for their burials, with both royal pyramids located to the right of the el-Lahun corridor. The locks that regulate the amount of water flowing into the depression are still located there. These, together with the connected canal system, were most likely among the first works undertaken during the Middle Kingdom, although there is no archaeological or textual evidence that sheds light on the exact extent of the works carried out at this period. On the basis of practical and geographical considerations, given that this is the only entrance point to the depression, it is clear that it is the only place where effective water control could be implemented through a system that would allow in only the quantity of water needed, with the excess flowing out northward through an artificial canal, the modern Bahr el-Giza. In this way it is possible to keep a check on the lake levels, which in turn is essential for any plan concerning a vast territory.

Various Middle Kingdom settlements and monuments are still preserved in the Fayum, but they do not provide us with any information regarding the type of works carried out during the first land reclamation project, or the extent reached at this time by the cultivable area. The latter depends on the presence of a capillary distribution of the waters over the territory through a series of natural channels and, above all, artificial canals, and on the management of the natural slopes and gorges that would cause the water to flow rapidly towards the lower areas of the depression without allowing it to be used for agricultural purposes. Such gorges are deep natural valleys dug into the deltaic sediments, unconnected with the hydraulic system of the Bahr Yusuf, which branches out at Medinet el-Fayum into a series of canals with a fan-like shape. In addition, at present there are three artificial canals running from the Bahr Yusuf at the end of the el-Lahun corridor, bordering the region: the one flowing northwards is called Bahr Abdalla Wahbi, the southern one is the Bahr el-Gharaq, while the western one is the Bahr Qasr el-Banat and Bahr Qarun. They provide water to the lands located at the margins of the depression, thus maximizing its agricultural expansion. However, it is not known when these canals, or rather the precursors of the current canals, which result from the ninteenth-century land reclamation campaign, were created. It is generally thought that they are part of the second land reclamation undertaken in the Fayum at the beginning of the Hellenistic period by Ptolemy I and Ptolemy II. Some information about these works is provided by a number of papyri from the archive of Kleon (also known as the Petrie Papyri), the engineer who, together with Petheconsis and Theodorus, was in charge of the works in the Arsinoite nome. It is not by chance that these papyri were recovered from cartonnage mummies found at Medinet Ghurob, which is located on the opposite bank from el-Lahun.

Besides the hundreds of kilometres of artificial canals built or repaired during this important territorial project, hundreds of settlements were also created. The study of toponyms known through papyri suggests that the campaign of land reclamation started in the eastern area of the Fayum, in the *meris* (a sub-territorial division of the Arsinoite nome) of Herakleides, then continued in the southern area, corresponding to the *meris* of Polemon, and then onto the western area in the *meris* of Themistos (Clarysse 2007: 78–9). Of these settlements only a few have left traces in the archaeological record, for reasons that will be discussed below.

During the Roman period the whole canal system and the settlements continued to function as before, with periods of high population density and agricultural productivity, particularly of wheat. It is very likely that the canal system was repaired at the beginning of the Imperial period, and the productivity of the land system optimized, so much so that the

Fayum became the granary of Egypt. The lake levels in the Graeco-Roman period were probably similar to or lower than that of today (Davoli 2001), since the remains of two settlements, Qaret el-Hamra and Qaret el-Rusas, have been discovered at the eastern end of its shore (39 metres below sea level). Like other possible settlements that were originally located by the lake shore in the Graeco-Roman period, these were probably destroyed by the waters as the lake height increased in late antiquity because of mismanagement of the canals, many of which were abandoned and silted up (Davoli 2001: 354–5). The causes of such a hydraulic and/or administrative crisis, which started in the fourth century CE, are not entirely clear. The result was a progressive depopulation of settlements, which decreased in size and number until they were completely abandoned, at least those located along the borders of the region.

It is these that, until the twentieth century, were the best-preserved sites, both because they were rapidly and completely covered over with sand, and because of their distance from agricultural land and human activity (Davoli 2001). On the other hand, settlements in the hinterland have disappeared through continuous human activity, and because of excessive wetness—conditions similar to those found in the Nile Delta. An exception is represented by the ancient capital, a site known as Kiman Fares, which, despite its hinterland location, remains to the north of Medinet el-Fayum, and had been largely preserved up to the beginning of the 1900s.

During Muhammad Ali's reign (1805–48), what could be termed the third land reclamation campaign in the Fayum began, part of a process of renewal of the country and its economy. With agriculture being the state's main economic resource, an attempt was made to intensify production and to make it more efficient through the reclamation of desert areas and an overhaul of the hydraulic system, with the aim of better exploiting and controlling the Nile waters (Marsot 1984: 149–50). The new system involved both the construction of dams on the Nile, so as to create water reserves to be used throughout the year, in order to increase the number of harvests, and the creation of a capillary network of artificial canals that, thanks also to mechanical pumps, brought the waters to areas located some distance away from the river basin. Thus was introduced a type of perennial irrigation that even today allows for intensive agricultural production. These works concerned the Fayum too, where, at the beginning of the twentieth century, the extent of desert land reclaimed for agricultural purposes was almost the same as that reached by the Ptolemaic land reclamation campaign.

Discoveries and Archaeological Excavations

It was in the course of the late nineteenth- and early twentieth-century land reclamation process that the ancient Fayum settlements, abandoned and still preserved, were found by the new inhabitants, who started exploiting the mounds (*kiman*) for materials to reuse, these being easy to recover and freely available. The *sebakhin*—individuals who collected *sebakh* (an organic deposit that can be used both as fertilizer and to obtain saltpetre)—sought out other material as well: stone, baked and unbaked bricks, wood, and potsherds were all needed for the construction of new settlements, bridges, and cemeteries. Artefacts, papyri, and monuments were found in some quantities during this activity, which, at the beginning, was not regulated or controlled by the Service des Antiquités de l'Égypte (Davoli 2008). The process of land reclamation reached the western side of the Fayum in 1900, later than in the rest of the region, with the new canals, the Bahr Qasr el-Banat and the Bahr Qarun, once more bringing water to areas near Theadelphia, Euhemeria, and Dionysias, settlements that had been abandoned between the fourth and the sixth centuries probably because of the lack of water. As a result, these archaeological sites were heavily destroyed by the *sebakhin*; important discoveries were made in the period between 1901 and 1911, such as the archives of Heroninus and of Sakaon (1903) and two Greek stelae mentioning the temple of the god Pnepheros and the Bubasteion at Theadelphia. Gustav Lefebvre, at that time the inspector of the Service des Antiquités, relates that in 1908 Theadelphia and its cemeteries had been almost completely turned over to cultivation (Davoli 2008: 112–13).

A large number of the Fayum sites still well preserved at the end of the nineteenth century were razed by the end of the 1930s (for example, Theadelphia, Euhemeria, and Philadelphia), while others were only partly destroyed (for example, Bacchias, Dionysias, Soknopaiou Nesos, and Tebtunis). The capital, at Kiman Fares, after being heavily damaged at the beginning of the twentieth century by *sebakhin*, was almost totally obliterated by the new districts of Medinet el-Fayum in the 1960s and 1970s (Davoli and Nahla 2006).

At the end of the nineteenth century the archaeology of the Fayum was still largely unknown to scholars, since little had been published on this region by travellers and explorers—the first, albeit limited, study of its geography being that published in the *Description de l'Égypte* in 1822 (Jomard 1822a, b). In 1823 Rifaud was the first European to explore the remains of Krokodilopolis and to undertake an excavation that could be defined as 'stratigraphic', if not for the excavation methods used, then because he was able to distinguish four levels of occupation that he recorded in a simplified, yet indicative, section plan (Rifaud 1829). In 1843, during the Prussian expedition in Egypt, Lepsius undertook a series of quick excavations and recordings at el-Lahun, Hawara, Soknopaiou Nesos, Krokodilopolis, and Dionysias. The published plates and the description of the sites are today of great importance for determining the state of preservation of these sites and their monuments, which, in some cases, were lost in the following years. A dramatic improvement in the knowledge of Kiman Fares came from the works done in 1887 by Schweinfurth, who was the first and only person to publish a plan of the ruins (Schweinfurth 1887, pl. 2).

The first survey of the region with the aim of locating archaeological sites was undertaken by Petrie in 1890. He was able to identify about twenty sites, which he dated on the basis of the ceramic assemblages present on the surface. These he recorded on a crude map, which he drew himself. They are located along the eastern perimeter canal, in the el-Lahun corridor, and in el-Gharaq (Petrie 1891, pl. 30).

Petrie's discoveries at Hawara—among which were the many tombs of the Hellenistic and Roman periods with well-preserved cartonnage masks, shrouds, and mummy portraits, and Greek literary papyri—and, above all, at Medinet Ghurob—where he found cartonnage composed of Hellenistic papyri that Sayce immediately recognized as the oldest yet known—prompted the British papyrologists Grenfell and Hunt to begin fieldwork in the Fayum in 1895, under the aegis of the Egypt Exploration Fund. Their work produced the first coherent picture of Fayum ancient topography based on a series of papyrological discoveries made until 1900 (Grenfell, Hunt, and Hogarth 1900). They were able to identify toponyms with actual archaeological sites, thanks to the recovery of papyri during their excavations, which were, nonetheless, rapid, often lasting just a few weeks or days, and not accurate in terms of archaeological recording. In fact, their stated aim was that of recovering quickly the largest possible number of papyri. This prevented the systematic exploration of sites, or even of individual buildings, which were often destroyed only a few years later by *sebakhin*, and thus lost for ever. The evidence recovered by Grenfell and Hunt seldom has a find context, other than a generic indication of the place or of the area of a discovery (temple, house, or necropolis).

From 1895 to 1901 Grenfell and Hunt undertook excavations in sixteen sites,[1] all of which are located in the desert along the region's border, where the preservation of papyrus, and of organic materials in general, was more likely. Not all sites were equally productive in terms of finds, which, despite the technique and the methodologies developed by the two scholars, were still left to chance, and dependent upon the area chosen for investigation. In fact, numerous and important recoveries of papyri were made in the following years in the areas they had already explored, both by *sebakhin* and by other papyrologists. The difficult living and working conditions, together with the obvious need for rapid action so as to pre-empt the destructive activity of robbers and *sebakhin*, were, understandably, the main factors influencing the excavations of that time. Between 1900 and 1914, following the example of Grenfell and Hunt, using the same methodologies and with the same aims, other papyrologists began excavating in the Fayum. Between 1900 and 1902 Jouguet excavated at Medinet Madi (Narmouthis), Medinet Ghoran, and Medinet el-Nehas (Magdola), on behalf of the French Ministry of Public Education. Notable in terms of both numbers and importance are the mummy cartonnages that he found in the necropolis of Medinet Ghoran, and which yielded about 300 Greek papyri. In 1902, together with Lefebvre, he explored Magdola, which he described as a village of some importance in his slim report on the work carried out. Today the area is completely covered over by a series of moving dunes that prevent the location of the temple, the settlement, and the cemetery seen and excavated by the French scholars. In this case, as elsewhere, the wealthier tombs were those of the Hellenistic period, with cartonnage made from discarded papyri.

In 1902 Otto Rubensohn carried out excavations at Kharabet Ihrit (Theadelphia) and Kom Umm el-Boreigat (Tebtunis) on behalf of the royal museums in Berlin. Rubensohn published the first study of the houses he investigated (Rubensohn 1905), although, as he himself cautions, they were not always thoroughly excavated, since the aim of the excavations was to recover papyri, and not to record archaeological contexts. Yet, for a long time, this article remained the only evidence for domestic architecture of the Graeco-Roman period in the Fayum.

Between 1908 and 1910 the Berlin-run excavations continued under the direction of Zucker at Philadelphia, Narmouthis, and Soknopaiou Nesos. The good state of preservation of the remains of Philadelphia at this time can be evinced from the published reports, although, again, the various structures investigated were not properly recorded (Viereck 1928). The sketch plan of the site (Fig. 10.2), a few plans of a temple and two houses, together with a few published photographs, represent the only documentation available on the ancient settlement. The site plan, in particular, is of great interest since a few years later the entire archaeological area was completely razed (Fig. 10.3), and this is, therefore, the only document that gives an idea of the spatial organization of the town. However, it is important to note that this plan was not made at the time of the excavation, whose true extent is

[1] More than one campaign was undertaken at some of these sites. In chronological order by campaign date, they are: Karanis, Bacchias, Euhemeria, Theadelphia, Philoteris, Dionysias, Tebtunis, Soknopaiou Nesos, Qasr el-Sagha, Medinet Quta, Philadelphia, Manashinshana, Seila, Kom Kamsin, Talit, and el-Lahun.

unknown, but only later, in 1924, by Ludwig Borchardt. Given that it is known that in the period between Zucker's excavations and 1924, *sebakhin* were particularly active at Philadelphia (witness the recovery around 1915 of the well-known Zenon archive), it is clear that the topographical plan is not truly indicative of the archaeological remains at the time of the original excavations. The negative effects of these papyrus 'excavations' were soon evident to Rostovtzeff (1929), who criticized the lack of documentation of, and attention to, the archaeological context. In the meantime, and particularly during the period before the First World War, *sebakhin* were more than ever active in the Fayum, and in some instances were even well organized by landowning companies, which also employed the decauville, or light rail, in order to remove large quantities of *sebakh* more easily from the archaeological areas.

The chance discovery at Theadelphia, in 1908, of two stelae inscribed in Greek (Bernand 1981, nos 116 and 117) prompted first Lefebvre and later Breccia to undertake excavation at the site in the hope of discovering the temple of the god Pnepheros, the Bubasteion, and the crocodile necropolis mentioned in the inscriptions. The temple, which was still standing, was indeed discovered by Breccia in 1912, who had its stone elements dismantled and reassembled in the Graeco-Roman Museum at Alexandria (Davoli 1998: 283–6).

In 1924 the *sebakhin* were at work at Karanis, where they had been authorized to remove 200 m^3 of *sebakh* per day. Such quarrying was restricted by the presence of the University of Michigan expedition, which conducted archaeological excavations at the site from 1924 to 1934. Their work represents the main intervention carried out with systematic archaeological methodologies in the Fayum at that time (see Chapter 14). The settlement was explored quite extensively at all its levels. The ensuing publications, which include excavation reports and artefact catalogues, make it the best-known site of the Fayum, even today (Davoli 1998: 73–116). The same archaeological mission excavated in two areas at Dime es-Seba (Soknopaiou Nesos) in 1931–2, where the same methodologies already tested at Karanis were applied. Unfortunately, the logistical difficulties linked to the location of the site, north of Lake Qarun, prevented further seasons of work (Boak 1935).

Sebakh digging and looting for antiquities dealers were also responsible for the destruction of a large residential quarter at Tebtunis between 1920 and 1930, which produced a large number of papyri and private archives, sold mainly to American and European collections (Gallazzi 1989: 182–5). This did not stop entirely, even after the intervention at the site of the Società Italiana per la Ricerca dei Papiri in Egitto under the direction of Breccia, and later Anti, in 1929–35. Unfortunately, the important results of these excavations were never extensively published. Another archaeological mission of the University of Milan, directed by Vogliano, began excavating at nearby Medinet Madi (1934–9) following the recovery of a considerable number of Manichaean texts there in 1930. Also very important was the discovery of a temple dedicated to the goddess Renenutet (Thermouthis), which had been built in the 12th dynasty and was then enlarged during the Ptolemaic and Roman periods (Davoli 1998: 224–32).

Following the Second World War and the post-war period, few foreign archaeological missions returned to the Fayum. In 1948 and 1950 Schwartz directed the excavations of the Franco-Swiss mission at Qasr Qarun (Dionysias), whose findings were published in two volumes (Schwartz and Wild 1950; Schwartz 1969). Besides the archaeological recording of the excavated structures and of the Roman fortress unearthed in 1950, the first general plan of the site, with the still-visible buildings and roads, was also produced at this time. Built in stone, baked bricks, and mud-bricks, a fortress at the site was known to have housed the *ala V*

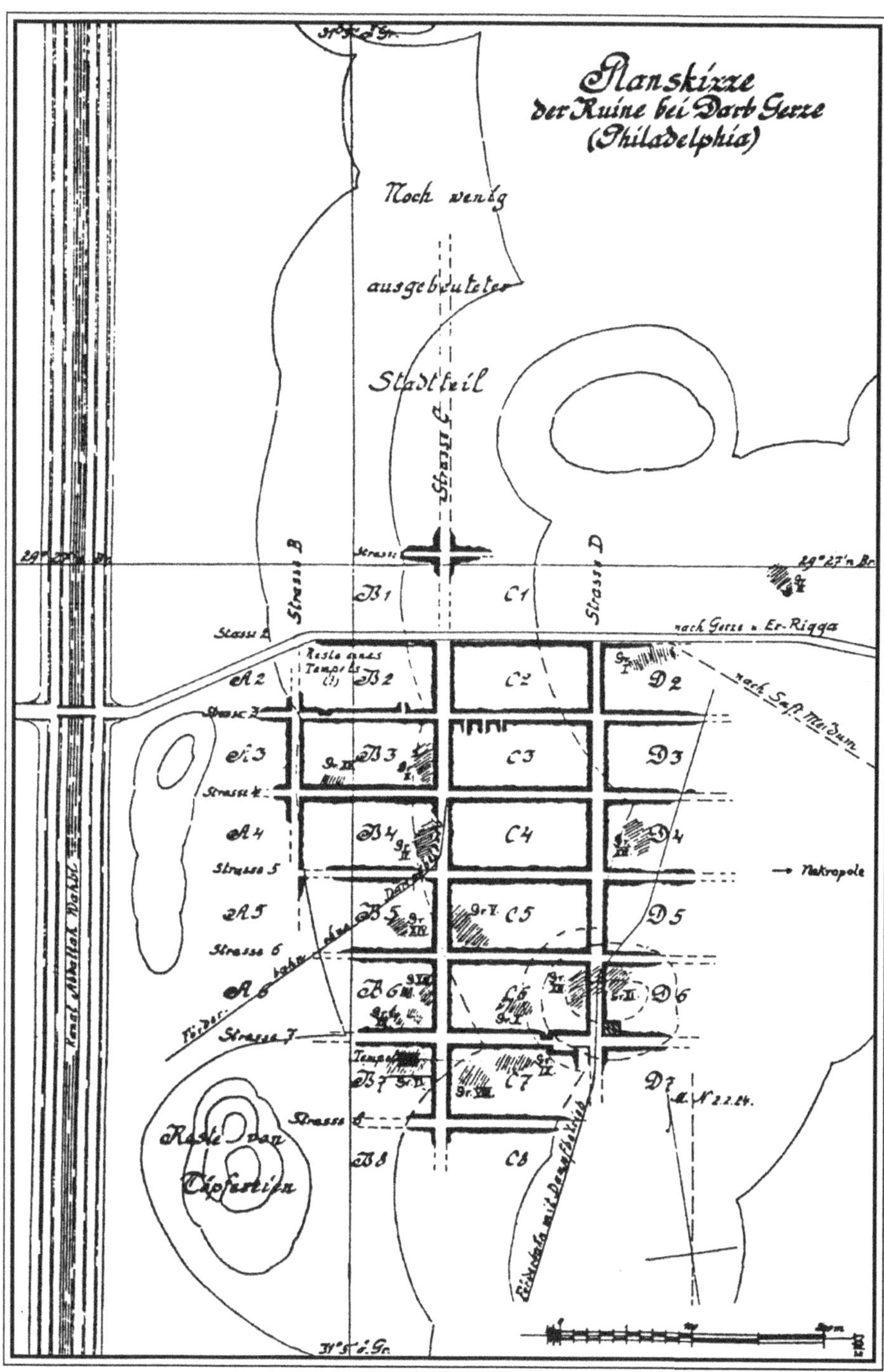

FIG. 10.2 Plan of Philadelphia, drawn in 1924

After Viereck (1928, pl. 1).

FIG. 10.3 The present state of preservation at Philadelphia

Author's photograph.

Praelectorum, according to the *Notitia Dignitatum* detailing the organization of the empire in the late Roman period. It is a small fort preserved to a height of about 2 metres, with a rectangular plan (83 × 70 metres), corner ramparts, and median towers, which was accessed from the north. Schwartz proposed a date in the Diocletian era, later rejected by Carrié (1974), according to whom only the restoration of the fort dates to the beginning of the fourth century.

Archaeological investigations of Graeco-Roman sites gradually resumed after the Second World War break. A brief survey of the el-Gharaq basin, carried out in 1964 and 1965 by Dieter Arnold (1966), recorded the state of preservation of a number of sites, and identified two new ones, Kom Danial and Tell el-Ma'raka, of which unfortunately very little remained. From 1966 a mission of the University of Milan, and then the University of Pisa, excavated at Medinet Madi under the direction of Edda Bresciani, a project that is ongoing (Bresciani et al. 2006). Numerous private and public buildings have been excavated in the past forty years or so. Among them are the temple dromos with two kiosks, a Ptolemaic temple dedicated to two crocodile deities, the so-called stoa (a large space surrounded by columns and located in front of the contra-temple), ten churches built between the fourth and the fifth centuries, a series of domestic buildings east and west of the dromos, and a late Roman fortress. The latter, according to the *Notitia Dignitatum*, housed the *cohors IV Numidarum*. It is a building constructed mainly from mud-brick, with some parts in stone and fired bricks; it has a square plan (50 × 50 metres), four square corner towers, and two entrances, the main one being located on the north side. Next to the south entrance was a water cistern fed by a canal dug into the bedrock (Bresciani and Pintaudi 2007).

Between 1967 and 1975 a mission from Cairo University returned to Kom Aushim (Karanis), where they excavated a number of houses and discovered a public bath (Davoli 1998: 87–9). The latter was a small thermae complex built in fired and unfired bricks, with two rooms provided with a hypocaust, and which was in use during the fourth until possibly the sixth century (Castel 2009).

From the end of the 1980s to the present day, the number of archaeological missions working on Graeco-Roman sites has increased, as has the number of publications on various historical, archaeological, and papyrological issues, and, as a result, our understanding of the Fayum during the Hellenistic and Roman periods is constantly improving. An Italo-French mission, present at Tebtunis since 1988, is obtaining important results through excavations, using up-to-date methodologies, a review of the findings of previous excavations, and archival studies. The temple area and the dromos have been re-excavated and their stratigraphy re-examined (Rondot 2004), as has also been the case with numerous public and private buildings, including a *thesauros* (granary), public baths (Hadji-Minaglou 2009: 181–90), *deipneteria* (dining rooms connected with temple activities), and houses (Gallazzi and Hadji-Minaglou 2000; Hadji-Minaglou 2007).

Excavations at Kom Umm el-Atl (Bacchias) were resumed in 1993 by the joint mission of the universities of Bologna and Lecce, and continued until 2004. The site is currently being excavated by the University of Bologna. Three temples have been unearthed there in a fairly good state of preservation, houses over different stratigraphic levels (Davoli 2005a), a *thesauros* (Tassinari 2008), a bath (Giorgi 2007), and a church (Buzi 2007).

Thanks to the Fayum Survey Project, carried out from 1993 to 2006, and directed first by Dominic Rathbone and subsequently by Dirk Obbink and Cornelia Römer, important data about the ancient topography of individual sites have been collected (Rathbone 1996; Römer 2004); the information pertains to sites located on the southern and western sides of the Fayum depression, as well as the territorial organization of settlements located in and around the el-Gharaq basin (Rathbone 2001). The survey discovered lacustrine sediments of an ancient lake that appears to have covered the entire el-Gharaq depression during the Graeco-Roman period. On its shores were built a series of small settlements, including Magdola, Tell el-Ma'raka, Kom el-Khamsin, and Kom Medinet Ghoran. The decrease in the lake levels has been dated to the third century CE (Bailey 2007: 232).

Annual excavation campaigns and topographical surveys have also been carried out since 2003 at Dime (Soknopaiou Nesos), by the Centro di Studi Papirologici dell'Università del Salento (Lecce) (Capasso and Davoli forthcoming). The topographical survey has documented the paving of the dromos, the cemeteries, and other visible structures in surrounding areas, besides those visible within the residential area (Fig. 10.4). Excavations have shed light on the developmental stages of the temple dedicated to Soknopaios and Isis Nepherses, and brought to light a new temple built in a second phase of the Ptolemaic period. It was built at the centre of the temenos using local limestone blocks (Davoli 2010a).

A new settlement, in use between the first and ninth centuries, and comprising a monastery, two churches, and an extensive necropolis, has been located at Deir el-Banat, a couple of kilometres north of Naqlun. This has been excavated since 2003 by a mission of the Russian Academy of Science (Krol 2005).

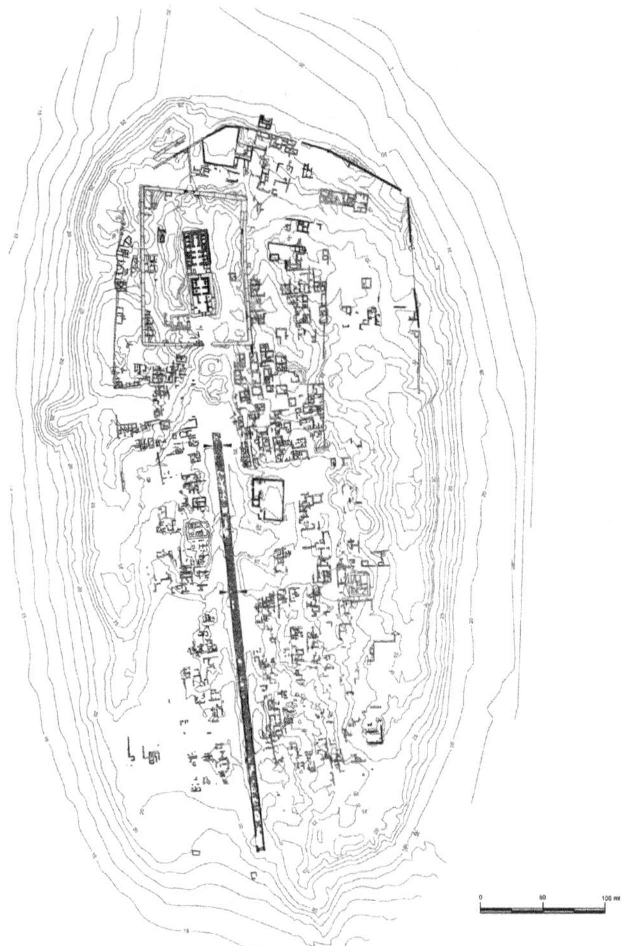

FIG. 10.4 Plan of Soknopaiou Nesos, based on fieldwork up to 2009

Courtesy of Centro di Studi Papirologici, Salento University.

Layout of Graeco-Roman Settlements

As can be gathered from the above history of excavations, today there are few Graeco-Roman settlements in the Fayum that are well preserved and well understood in terms of their urban, architectural, and historical development. It is only through modern excavations that it is possible to obtain reliable data on urbanism and stratigraphy. These excavations are ongoing, and our understanding is constantly improving through the publication of their findings.

On the basis of the ongoing work and current state of knowledge, I do not believe it is yet possible to write a history of urbanism in the Fayum. Much still remains to be done in terms of archaeological investigation and re-examination of the findings of previous excavations. In addition, many important settlements have been destroyed, and much is still being lost because of modern land reclamation and the considerable population increase in the Fayum, even before sites can be documented. The data available for evaluating the complete plans of individual sites are often misleading or extremely limited. Indeed, existing planimetric drawings record only the state of preservation of structures visible on the surface at the time the plan was made. These structures could belong to different strata, or occupation phases, and therefore may not be contemporary with one another. This is the case, for example, for those sites exposed by *sebakhin*, such as Bacchias, whose stratigraphy is very difficult to interpret owing to the presence of large craters where the exposed structures belong to the Hellenistic levels but are located next to hills with buildings of the Roman period.

The vast majority of the Fayum settlements bordering agricultural land, thus originally already close to the desert, display the kind of stratigraphy characteristic of *kom* and *tell*, consisting of several superimposed occupation levels, often interspersed with strata of wind-blown sand. A continuous and progressive sanding-up is a phenomenon characteristic of these settlements, where architectural devices are often in place to protect against the predominant north/north-west wind. Therefore, the activity of *sebakhin*, even where it has not completely destroyed the sites, has greatly altered their stratigraphy, uncovering buildings belonging to different periods. Some settlements do not appear to have developed over more than one level, as, for example, Philadelphia, Theadelphia, Euhemeria, Philoteris, and Dionysias, because, although near the margins, they were located within the area of cultivable land and thus were less exposed to wind-blown sand. In the case of the first three sites, this can no longer be verified, since they were completely razed at the beginning of the 1930s, although traces of canals and of cultivation plots in the desert surrounding these towns testifies to the presence in antiquity of cultivation around them. In these instances, the settlements developed horizontally, that is, over a single level, presumably with buildings being modified, demolished, and reconstructed. The excavations carried out at these sites in the past do not provide much data, though enough to support such a theory (Davoli 1998: 343).

It is clear that settlements evolved continuously in size, as well as in terms of number and density of houses, and of buildings in general. A diachronic reconstruction is possible only in a few cases or for limited areas, where all the levels were excavated stratigraphically, as, for example, at Karanis (Husselman 1979), Soknopaiou Nesos (Boak 1935), Bacchias (Davoli 2005a: 218–19), and Tebtunis (Hadji-Minaglou 2007). The shape of the settlements is not known, but it seems possible that it would vary depending on the orography, and on their position with respect to the canals and the agricultural areas. It is clear that settlements of the Imperial period were more extensive and more densely populated than those of the Hellenistic and Byzantine periods. Their enlargement was often influenced by the presence of a reference axis, which could be a dromos, a natural feature, or a canal.

Philadelphia has often been defined as a Hippodamian type of settlement because of its orthogonal, or grid-like, plan (Fig. 10.2). It has been suggested that the layout was therefore not of Egyptian origin, but settlements with regular and orthogonal plans are in fact present even in Pharaonic Egypt, as, for example, at Kahun (el-Lahun, 12th dynasty) and Amarna East (end of the 18th dynasty). Such an interpretation is based on a single, rather schematic, plan, drawn by Borchardt in 1924, and on an aerial photograph from 1925 (Davoli 1998, figs 60–1). However, it represents only a small part of the settlement, which had a much greater extent, as can be seen from the actual traces on the ground, and from satellite images. The road system seems to surround blocks that are rectangular in shape and of the same size (100 × 50 metres). Two temples are reported, both small in size, located within these blocks and lacking a dromos. They appear to be minor temples, while the main one with its dromos has not yet been located, although this does not mean that it never existed. The settlement has an axial alignment determined by the local perimeter canal, which here flows in a south–north direction and with which roads were aligned. It would appear that there were no town walls, or other type of perimeter barriers, but the settlement's expansion, if it did occur over time, was mainly to the north and the south, with the necropolis being located immediately east of the town centre (Fig. 10.3).

Another settlement oriented following the local main canals is Dionysias, where roads were parallel and orthogonal to the two canals that bordered the town on its north-east and south-west sides, as can be gathered from the plan made by Schwartz and Wild in 1950, and from satellite images. The temple, dating to the Ptolemaic period, is located virtually in the centre of the town, and has a south-east alignment, with a dromos and a kiosk for religious processions. On satellite images the settlement appears to be quite densely built, and divided into blocks along the main roads that crossed the town centre from the north-west to the south-east. The late Roman fortress does not entirely follow this alignment, but appears to be located on the margins, in an area apparently devoid of buildings. There are no traces of walls delimiting the perimeter of the settlement.

A third settlement that developed along a main axis (the dromos) is Soknopaiou Nesos, probably originally built around the main temple, which is located over a low hill reached by a raised dromos with a slight incline (Fig. 10.5; see Davoli 1998: 359–70 on the orientation of temples in the Fayum). In this case, too, the settlement has a north–south orientation, influenced in this instance by the presence of the lake to the south, which was used by the inhabitants to reach the agricultural area. The dromos at Soknopaiou Nesos is a paved processional way preserved over a distance of 329 metres, flanked by two parallel roads; it was built over a foundation wall standing at least 3 metres above road level. Therefore, the dromos represented a real barrier within the settlement, besides being a striking monumental way that effectively divided the town centre into two districts. Side stairs gave access to the dromos, while tunnels through its foundation walls linked the two side roads. On the basis of our current knowledge, it appears that the dromos was extended to the south as the settlement expanded in the same direction. Unlike Philadelphia, Soknopaiou Nesos developed around an axial road to which minor roads are aligned so as to form a grid, which is quite orthogonal, though not regular. Residential blocks seem to have developed during the Roman period with the construction of new buildings within the space previously left empty between the houses of the Hellenistic period. It is still unknown when the north perimeter wall was built, and whether it surrounded the entire site.

At Tebtunis a clear urban change can also be detected between the end of the Hellenistic period and the beginning of the Roman period, with the construction of new houses and the restoration of the dromos (Hadji-Minaglou 2008). In this case, the main temple and the dromos are located on the south-west side of the town, with only a very small part of the settlement developing west of the religious complex, while the vast majority of the buildings are located to its east and appear to follow a slightly different alignment. The temple and the dromos are oriented to the north, that is, towards the cultivation area, and are orthogonal to the

FIG. 10.5 The ruins at Soknopaiou Nesos

Courtesy of the Centro di Studi Papirologici, Salento University.

local main canal. A similar case is that of nearby Narmouthis, whose temple, founded in the 12th dynasty and then enlarged in the Hellenistic and Roman periods, is located to one side of the settlement. It is oriented to the south, with a long dromos that extends towards the cultivable area. The road system visible on the surface, thus likely to date to the Roman or late Roman period, consists of orthogonal roads forming an apparently regular grid aligned to the cardinal points and the dromos (Bresciani et al. 2006: 257).

Within the urban picture of the Fayum, Karanis appears to have a completely different urban layout: two main roads have been identified, both with north–south alignment—that is, towards the canal. The better-preserved and -recorded layer has been dated to the Roman period (Level C, late first to mid-second century CE), and consists of a series of irregular blocks separated by orthogonal roads that do not form a square grid, most of which end in T-junctions. Two temples have been found, both built in stone and apparently devoid of a dromos extending outside the temple enclosure, although it is important to note that this central area has been totally razed. However, the settlement developed well beyond the central area investigated by the University of Michigan, for which we still have no chronological data. Karanis also preserves public and semi-public buildings, such as granaries, dovecotes, and baths (Husselman 1979; Castel 2009), whose presence in other settlements is attested from papyri and the occasional chance discoveries.

One of the main characteristics of these settlements, therefore, is the presence of a dromos, stone-paved, with one or two kiosks. The dromos was where processions took place fairly frequently throughout the year, during the celebration of festivals dedicated to the main god and its *synnaoi theoi*. In the case of Soknopaiou Nesos, it is clear that the dromos did not serve any secular function, given that it stood much higher than the nearby roads. The better-preserved dromoi, with their associated structures and monuments, are those of Tebtunis, which is 210 metres long, and Narmouthis, at 230 metres long (Bresciani and Giammarusti 2009). Three different building phases have been identified at Tebtunis, dating from the beginning of the Hellenistic period to Augustan times (Rondot 2004). In these settlements the main temple was surrounded by a wide temenos, not always preserved, that enclosed chapels, workshops, and priests' accommodation. The location of the main temple at the Fayum settlements varies with respect to the residential area of the town, although it is not possible to determine the temples' position during single phases of occupation because these sites were not completely excavated. In at least three cases the temple appears to have occupied a central position (Dionysias, Karanis, and Bacchias), while in others it stands on one side of the settlement (Tebtunis, Narmouthis, and Soknopaiou Nesos). At Soknopaiou Nesos the temple is located at the northern end of the site, although it still retains a central, dominating position, since it stands on higher ground and because its dromos represents the central axis of the settlement (Davoli 2010a). Smaller temples have been identified along dromoi, for example at Tebtunis, Narmouthis, and Soknopaiou Nesos, but also occur within the residential areas, such as at Philadelphia.

Houses of the Roman Period

The architectural typology, the materials, and the building techniques employed in the settlements of the Fayum are quite uniform throughout the region, even during different historical periods. Dwellings of the Roman period are built using unfired bricks, sometimes over foundations of local stone chips, with three basic plans: rectangular, square, and L-shaped or irregular (Davoli 1998: 355–8). They consist of individual family units, each self-contained, with an external courtyard, where, generally, cooking installations were located. Houses developed over several floors. Those with a rectangular or a square plan generally have quite deep foundations, inside of which are small, unconnected cellars, roofed with barrel vaults, and accessed via narrow trapdoors. These types of house were generally at least two storeys high, with the upper floors accessed via a staircase built around a central pillar. The number and layout of the rooms vary considerably. Rooms above ground have flat roofs made of palm beams, reeds, and unfired bricks. Windows are generally narrow openings with slanting sills, placed just below the roofline so as to allow the sunlight in from above. Rooms were furnished with niches of various dimensions: some were provided with shelves and used as storage, while others were decorated, sometimes quite richly, with modelled plaster and used as a place for private worship (Husselman 1979: 47–8). A particular type of house, well attested in documents, is the tower house, or *pyrgos*, which was characterized by a square floor-plan and load-bearing walls; the latter suggest the presence of several floors, thus giving this type of house the appearance of a tower. Only three of these are attested in the archaeological record: two at Tebtunis and one at Soknopaiou Nesos (Hadji-Minaglou 2008). Houses with an L-shaped or irregular plan are generally large and richly decorated with stone architectural elements in the classical style, and sometimes with painted plaster in the same style. They are also characterized by the presence of a large reception room, perhaps for banquets, with one open side on which there are two pillars. This house type is attested at Dionysias, Theadelphia, and Narmouthis in levels dating from the Roman or late Roman period (Davoli 1998: 281, fig. 136; 233, fig. 112; Bresciani et al. 2006: 245–6). Because of their lavish decoration, these buildings have been understood as having had a public function, although such an interpretation is not corroborated by specific findings. They could equally be large private houses, like those of the third and fourth centuries, with elaborate painted decoration, that have been discovered at Trimithis and at Kellis in the Dakhla Oasis (Bagnall et al. 2006; Hope and Whitehouse 2006). At present, only one peristyle building is known, found at Tebtunis, but even in this instance the plan does not follow exactly that of houses elsewhere in the Greek and Roman world (Hadji-Minaglou 2008).

There are numerous Greek and Demotic papyri, such as sale contracts, that mention houses, stating not only their cost but also the dimensions and number of rooms and storeys. From these documents it appears that houses were sometimes divided into smaller units, owing to inheritance, which could then be sold individually (Maehler 1983). To my knowledge, no archaeological evidence has been found for partitioning inside houses, from which one could infer a clear division of space creating separate areas, possibly unconnected. The division of ownership thus reflects probably not an actual division of space but part-ownership of the property's value.

Conclusion

The Fayum was developed in Hellenistic and Roman times to maximize agricultural output, which also led to the foundation and development of several settlements. Although many sites were known by name following the discovery of papyri in the late nineteenth century, early explorations were not well documented or published by the excavators, and considerable damage was wrought by illicit digging and *sebakhin* activity. Fortunately, a number of ongoing projects, combining archaeology, papyrology, and archival research, are constantly improving our knowledge of Fayum settlements, and in particular the interrelationship between the temple, its dromos, and the residential areas of the towns and villages. This important research promises to provide excellent evidence for the day-to-day life of Egypt's farming and priestly communities in the Roman period.

Suggested Reading

Bagnall and Rathbone (2004) is a useful archaeological guide to the major sites of Ptolemaic, Roman, and Byzantine Egypt, well documented and updated with new discoveries and bibliography. Davoli (1998) is dedicated to the study of Graeco-Roman archaeological sites in the Fayum, through the critical analysis of a wide bibliography and a good knowledge of the archaeological remains. On the Roman administration of the Fayum, see the fundamental work of Tomasz Derda (2006), which analyses papyrological sources for the development and administration of the region.

Bibliography

Arnold, D. 1966. 'Bericht über Fahrten in das el-Gharaq-Becken (Faijûm)', *Mitteilungen des Deutschen Archäologischen Instituts, Abteilung Kairo* 21: 101–9.

Bagnall, R. S., and D. W. Rathbone. 2004. *Egypt from Alexander to the Copts: An Archaeological and Historical Guide*. London: British Museum Press.

—— et al. 2006. 'Roman Amheida: Excavating a Town in Egypt's Dakhleh Oasis', *Minerva* (Nov.–Dec.), 10–13.

Bailey, D. M. 2007. 'A Form of Amphores Egyptiennes 3 from the South-West Fayum', *Cahiers de la Céramique Égyptienne* 8, special issue: *Amphores d'Égypte de la Basse Époque à l'époque arabe*, ed. S. Marchand and A. Marangou, 227–37.

Bernand, E. 1981. *Recueil des inscriptions grecques du Fayoum*, vol. 2. Cairo: Institut Français d'Archéologie Orientale.

Boak, A. E. R. 1935. *Soknopaiou Nesos: The University of Michigan Excavations at Dimê in 1931–32*. Ann Arbor: University of Michigan Press.

Bresciani, E., and A. Giammarusti. 2009. 'I chioschi e il dromos di Medinet Madi', *Egitto e Vicino Oriente* 32: 271–312.

—— and R. Pintaudi. 2007. 'Medinet Madi: Site of the Castrum Narmoutheos', *Egyptian Archaeology* 31: 30–2.

—— et al. (eds) 2006. *Medinet Madi: Venti anni di esplorazione archeologica 1984–2005*. Pisa: University of Pisa.

Buzi, P. 2007. 'Nuove considerazioni sul complesso ecclesiastico del Kom sud', *Ricerche di Egittologia e di Antichità Copte* 9: 93–103.

Capasso, M., and P. Davoli (eds) Forthcoming. *Soknopaiou Nesos Project I (2003–2009)*. Pisa: Fabrizio Serra.

Carrié, J.-M. 1974. 'Les castra Dionysiados et l'évolution de l'architecture militaire romaine tardive', *Mélanges d'Archéologie et d'Histoire de l'École Française de Rome, Antiquité* 86: 819–50.

Castel, G. 2009. 'Bain nord de Karanis', in M.-F. Boussac, T. Fournet, and B. Redon (eds), *Le Bain collectif en Egypte*. Cairo: Institut Français d'Archéologie Orientale, 229–45.

Clarysse, W. 2007. 'Toponomy of Fayum Villages in the Ptolemaic Period', in M. Capasso and P. Davoli (eds), *New Archaeological and Papyrological Researches on the Fayum*. Galatina: Congedo, 67–81.

Davoli, P. 1998. *L'archeologia urbana nel Fayum di età ellenistica e romana*. Naples: Generoso Procaccini Editore.

—— 2001. 'Aspetti della topografia del Fayum in epoca ellenistica e romana', in I. Andorlini et al. (eds), *Atti del XXII Congresso Internazionale di Papirologia, Firenze, 23–29 agosto 1998*, vol. 1. Florence: Istituto Papirologico G. Vitelli, 353–9.

—— 2005a. 'Examples of Town Planning in the Fayum', *Bulletin of the American Society of Papyrologists* 42: 213–33.

—— 2005b. *Oggetti in argilla dall'area templare di Bakchias (el-Fayyum, Egitto)*. Pisa: Giardini.

—— 2008. 'Papiri, archeologia e storia moderna', *Atene e Roma*, new 2nd ser., 1–2: 100–24.
—— 2010a. 'Archaeological Research in Roman Soknopaiou Nesos: Results and Perspectives', in K. Lembke, M. Minas-Nerpel, and S. Pfeiffer (eds), *Tradition and Transformation: Egypt under Roman Rule*. Leiden: Brill, 53–77.
—— 2010b. 'Settlements: Distribution, Structure, Architecture: Graeco-Roman', in A. B. Lloyd (ed.), *A Companion to Ancient Egypt*, vol. 1. Oxford: Wiley-Blackwell, 350–69.
—— and Nahla Mohammed Ahmed. 2006. 'On Some Monuments from Kiman Fares (Medinet el-Fayyum)', *Studi di Egittologia e di Papirologia* 3: 81–109.
Derda, T. 2006. *Arsinoites Nomos: Administration of the Fayum under Roman Rule*, *Journal of Juristic Papyrology*, suppl. 7.
Embabi, N. S. 2004. *The Geomorphology of Egypt: Landforms and Evolutions*, vol. 1: *The Nile Valley and the Western Desert*. Cairo: Egyptian Geographical Society.
Gallazzi, C. 1989. 'Fouilles anciennes et nouvelles sur le site de Tebtynis', *Bulletin de l'Institut Français d'Archéologie Orientale* 89: 179–91.
—— and G. Hadji-Minaglou. 2000. *Tebtynis* I: *La reprise des fouilles et le quartier de la chapelle d'Isis-Thermouthis*. Cairo: Institut Français d'Archéologie Orientale.
Giorgi, E. 2007. 'Bakchias XVI: La Campagna di scavo 2007', *Ricerche di Egittologia e di Antichità Copte* 9: 47–92.
Grenfell, B. P., A. S. Hunt, and D. G. Hogarth. 1900. *Fayûm Towns and their Papyri*. London: Kegan Paul and Egypt Exploration Fund.
Hadji-Minaglou, G. 2007. *Tebtynis* IV: *Les habitations à l'est du temple de Soknebtynis*. Cairo: Institut Français d'Archéologie Orientale.
—— 2008. 'L'habitat à Tebtynis à la lumière des fouilles récentes: Ier s. av.–Ier s. apr. J.-C.', in S. Lippert and M. Schentuleit (eds), *Graeco-Roman Fayum: Texts and Archaeology*. Wiesbaden: Harrassowitz, 123–33.
—— 2009. 'L'établissement thermal de Tebtynis (Fayoum)', in M.-F. Boussac, T. Fournet, and B. Redon (eds), *Le bain collectif en Egypte*. Cairo: Institut Français d'Archéologie Orientale, 181–90.
Hope, C. A., and H. Whitehouse. 2006. 'A Painted Residence at Ismant el-Kharab (Kellis) in the Dakhleh Oasis', *Journal of Roman Archaeology* 19: 312–28.
Husselman, E. M. 1979. *Karanis: Excavations of the University of Michigan in Egypt 1928-1935, Topography and Architecture*. Ann Arbor: University of Michigan Press.
Jomard, E. 1822a. *Description des antiquités du nome arsinoite, aujourd'hui le Fayoum*, in *Description de l'Égypte*. Paris: Panckoucke, text IV, 437–527.
—— 1822b. *Mémoire sur le lac de Moeris comparé au lac du Fayoum*, in *Description de l'Egypte*. Paris: Panckoucke, text VI, 155–226.
Krol, A. 2005. 'The RIEC Archaeological and Anthropological Surveys at the Site of Dayr al-Banat', in G. Gabra (ed.), *Christianity and Monasticism in the Fayoum Oasis: Essays from the 2004 International Symposium of the Saint Mark Foundation and the Saint Shenouda the Archimandrite Coptic Society in Honor of Martin Krause*. Cairo: American University in Cairo Press, 209–16.
Maehler, H. 1983. 'Häuser und ihre Bewohner im Fayûm in der Kaiserzeit', in G. Grimm, H. Heinen, and E. Winter (eds), *Das römisch-byzantinische Ägypten: Akten des Internationalen Symposions 26.–30. September 1978 in Trier*, vol. 2. Mainz: von Zabern, 119–37.
Marsot, A. L. S. 1984. *Egypt in the Reign of Muhammad Ali*. Cambridge: Cambridge University Press.
Petrie, W. M. F. 1891. *Illahun, Kahun, and Gurob*. London: Aris and Phillips.

Rathbone, D. W. 1996. 'Kom Talit: The Rise and Fall of a Greek Town in the Faiyum', *Egyptian Archaeology* 8: 29–31.

——2001. 'Mapping the South-West Fayum: Sites and Texts', in I. Andorlini et al. (eds), *Atti del XXII Congresso Internazionale di Papirologia, Firenze, 23–29 agosto 1998*, vol. 2. Florence: Istituto Papirologico G. Vitelli, 1109–17.

Rifaud, J. J. 1829. 'Description des fouilles et des découvertes faites par M. Rifaud, dans la partie est de la butte Koum-Medinet-el-Farès, accompagnée du dessin, des coupes et du plan des constructions inférieures, lue à la Société de Géographie le vendredi 19 juin 1829', *Bulletin de la Société de Géographie* 12: 73–90.

Römer, C. E. 2004. 'Philoteris in the Themistou Meris: Report on the Archaeological Survey Carried out as Part of the Fayum Survey Project', *Zeitschrift für Papyrologie und Epigraphik* 147: 281–305.

Rondot, V. 2004. *Le temple de Soknebtynis et son dromos*. Cairo: Institut Français d'Archéologie Orientale.

Rostovtzeff, M. 1929. Review of P. Viereck and F. Zucker, *Papyri, Ostraka und Wachstafeln aus Philadelphia im Fayum* (Berlin, 1926), *Gnomon* 5: 435–40.

Rubensohn, O. 1905. 'Aus griechisch-römischen Häusern des Fayum', *Jahrbuch des deutschen archäologischen Institut* 20: 1–25.

Schwartz, J. 1969. *Fouilles franco-suisses: Rapports* II: *Qasr-Qârûn/Dionysias 1950*. Cairo: Institut Français d'Archéologie Orientale.

——and H. Wild. 1950. *Fouilles franco-suisses: Rapports* I: *Qasr-Qârûn/Dionysias 1948*. Cairo: Institut Français d'Archéologie Orientale.

Schweinfurth, G. 1887. 'Zur Topographie der Ruinenstätte des alten Schet (Krokodilopolis-Arsinoë)', *Zeitschrift des Gesellschaft für Allgemeine Erdkunde* 22: 54–79.

Tassinari, C. 2008. *Il thesauros di Bakchias: Rapporto definitivo*. Imola: La Mandragora.

Viereck, P. 1928. *Philadelpheia: Die Gründung einer hellenistischen militärkolonie in Ägypten*. Leipzig: Hinrichs.

CHAPTER 11

THE THEBAN REGION UNDER THE ROMAN EMPIRE

ADAM ŁAJTAR

THE Theban region refers to a portion of the Nile Valley north and south of the site of Thebes (modern Luxor), in Upper Egypt. The borders of the region are not clear-cut, but for the purpose of this study, we can set them at Kerameia (modern Medamud) in the north and Pathyris (modern Gebelein) in the south (Fig. 11.1). In the Pharaonic period, this area formed the fourth Upper Egyptian nome, designated the 'nome of the sceptre' (*W3s.t*). The early Ptolemaic rulers included it as a toparchy with the name Perithebas (*Περὶ Θήβας*) within a larger administrative unit called Thebais, the capital of which was the newly founded *polis* Ptolemais Hermiou, some 120 km north of Thebes. In the second century BCE, probably in the 170s, Thebais was upgraded to an epistrategy, overseen by an official called the *epistrategos*. In the frame of this new administrative arrangement, which remained valid until late antiquity, the Theban region was subdivided into two nomes: Perithebas and Pathyrites, the latter eventually called Hermonthites after the transfer of the nome capital to Hermonthis (Armant) caused by the devastation of Pathyris during the rebellion of 90–88 BCE. The Peritheban nome included the entire east bank territories of the region and a portion of the west bank territories north of Djeme (the Memnoneia), while Pathyrites (Hermonthites) was composed of only west bank territories, extending from Pathyris north to Djeme. The nome capital (*metropolis*) of Perithebas officially bore the name *Διόσπολις ἡ Μεγάλη* (Diospolis the Great, or Diospolis Magna), but the nome itself may have never been called *Διοσπολείτης* or *Διοπολείτης* (Diospoleites or Diopoleites) (Thomas 1964).

THE SOURCES

The study of the Theban region in both Ptolemaic and Roman times benefits from exceptionally rich and multifaceted source material, which can be divided into two categories: archaeological sources and written sources. The first category comprises sites and artefacts of mostly sacral and sepulchral character, and to the second category belong texts in Egyptian

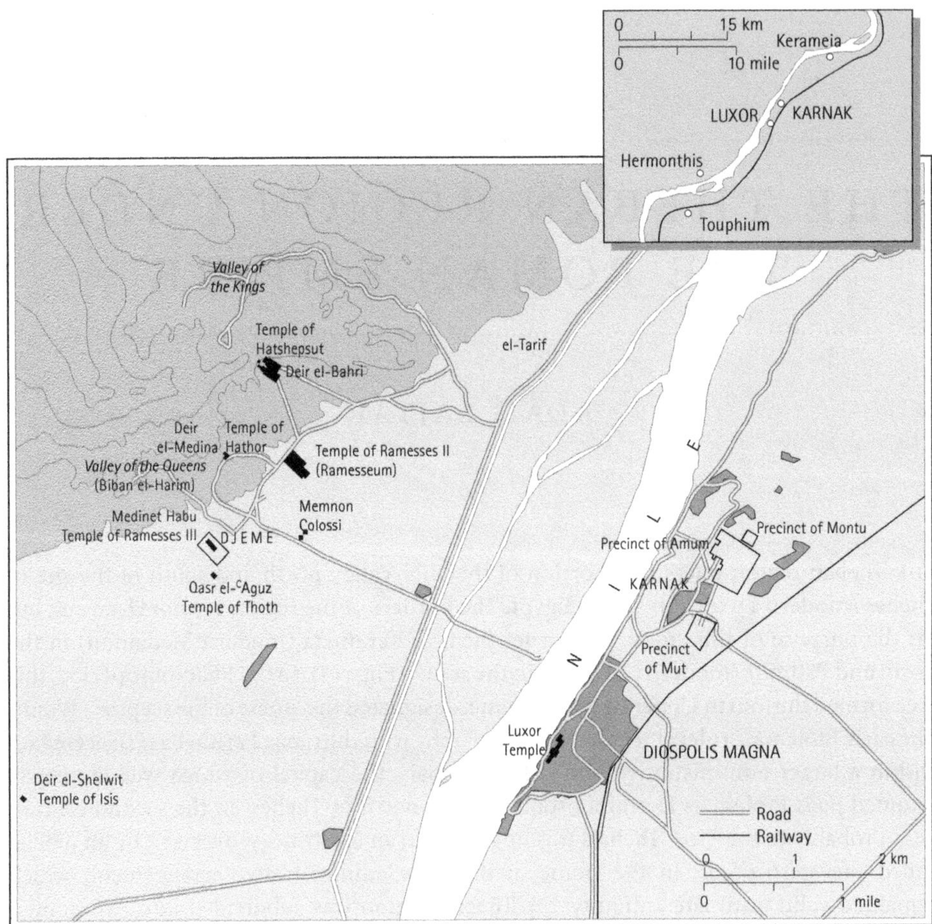

FIG. 11.1 Map of the Theban region, indicating Roman period sites and settlements

(in hieroglyphic, hieratic, and Demotic script), Greek, and Latin. Hieroglyphic texts occur in temple inscriptions and some coffins (see Chapter 34). Hieratic is restricted to religious papyri, including funerary papyri, while Demotic is found in literary papyri, documentary texts on papyrus and ostraca, and in inscriptions, either on stone stelae or on the walls of buildings (see Chapter 33). Texts in Demotic are common in the Ptolemaic and early Roman periods, until the middle of the first century CE, but later their number diminishes considerably, aside from several items in a Greek and Demotic magical archive, dating to the early fourth century CE (Dieleman 2005). Greek sources from the Roman period are almost exclusively on ostraca, rather than papyri as in the Ptolemaic period, and while the Ptolemaic documents in Greek are quite varied, those of the Roman period are predominantly receipts for different kinds of tax. In the Theban region, the term 'ostracon' encompasses texts inscribed not only on potsherds but also on limestone splits, a writing support not found elsewhere in Egypt. In addition to papyri and ostraca, Greek occurs in inscriptions, both monumental and casual, such as visitors' graffiti (Criscuolo 1995; see Chapter 42). Latin is restricted to visitors' graffiti on the Memnon colossi and in the Valley of the Kings, mostly left by soldiers and Roman officials.

The Historical Background

During Egypt's long dynastic history, Thebes was a capital city under the 11th dynasty and in the New Kingdom. Even though the centre of power moved north after the end of the 21st dynasty, Thebes kept its essential role as the main town of Upper Egypt and a vital religious centre, preserving old traditions and serving as a focus for the hopes and identity of the local population. This role was largely due to the power of the clergy of the local god Amun, whose temple at Karnak retained its economic and cultural sway.

Ptolemaic rule over Egypt apparently brought little change to the position of Thebes. In the third to second centuries BCE the town and its region saw large-scale building activity, not infrequently financed from royal donations, which was expressed in the renovation and decoration of old temples and the construction of new sanctuaries (see below). But at the same time, Thebes was the stage for several rebellions by the local population against foreign rule. Emerging in the unstable political situation caused by dynastic quarrels over the throne in Alexandria, the rebellions eventually led to the Ptolemies' temporary loss of control over this part of the country (Veïsse 2004). Among these uprisings, the most serious for the Ptolemaic state was that of the years 205–186 BCE, when a local leader, Harwennefer (Greek: Haronnophris), was crowned in Thebes as a king, as was his successor, Ankhwennefer (Channophris). The experience of this revolt led the Ptolemies to establish military garrisons at the southern border of the Theban region, a smaller one in Pathyris, and a larger one in neighbouring Krokodilopolis. Situated at a strategic point, where the Nile Valley narrows considerably, these garrisons could control the movement of people from the south to the north in order to prevent a possible invasion of Thebes from that direction. For the town of Thebes itself, still more fateful was the uprising of the years 90–88 BCE. It broke out to the south of Thebes, in Latopolites and Pathyrites, and quickly extended north. The town of Pathyris, which remained faithful to the crown, was damaged by rebels and never recovered. After suppressing the revolt, the victorious Ptolemy IX applied repressive policies towards the rebels, especially the Thebans. According to Pausanias (1.9.3), he 'treated them so cruelly that they were left not even a memorial of their former prosperity'.

Roman rule over the Theban region also started with a revolt, reportedly provoked by severe fiscal orders issued by the new government. The revolt was rapidly suppressed by Caius Cornelius Gallus, the first Roman prefect of Egypt. In his trilingual, Greek–Latin–hieroglyphic, inscription set up in Philae on 16 April 29, he claims to have subordinated the 'towns' of Keramike, Diospolis Magna, and Ophieion in just fifteen days (Hoffmann, Minas-Nerpel, and Pfeiffer 2009). In order to exercise control over the Theban region, the Romans sited a legion there, one of the three that formed the Egyptian garrison immediately after the conquest. These pacification efforts must have brought immediate results, as the legion was withdrawn and sent on to the Rhine during the reign of Tiberius (14–37). In place of the legion, an auxiliary unit was installed whose camp was situated in the neighbourhood of Luxor temple (Ophieion). Legionaries appeared in Thebes again in the time of Diocletian (284–305), during the reorganization carried out in connection with threats from the south.

FIG. 11.2 The small Serapeum outside Luxor temple, with a statue of Isis set up inside
Photo: Christina Riggs.

The size of the Theban garrison of the late third and early fourth centuries is unclear; it may have consisted of one or two legions. The legionaries were garrisoned in a newly built camp, the main axis of which was the temple of Luxor. One chamber of the temple was converted to the chapel of the standards, its reliefs being plastered and painted over with representations of the tetrarchs (see Deckers 1979; el-Saghir et al. 1986).

In the Roman period, Thebes lost any remaining political and economic importance. The administrative centre of the area moved to Koptos to the north, which had grown, thanks to its role in the Red Sea trade and the exploitation of the Eastern Desert. However, there is evidence that the Peritheban nome and its *metropolis* were still symbolically considered to be at the centre of southern Upper Egypt. If a document mentions several nomes, Perithebas was listed in priority before the others, and the poll tax (*laographia*) paid by the inhabitants of Thebes was considerably lower than that in other *metropoleis* of this part of Egypt, at 10 versus 16 drachmas (Thomas 1964).

Very little is known about the functioning of the state apparatus in the Theban region, and only a few of the nome governors (*strategoi*) of Perithebas and Hermonthites are known by name for the period. The only well-documented sphere, thanks to tax receipts written on ostraca, is the collection of taxes and the control of finances from the level of a village up to that of a *metropolis* (Bogaert 1984; Heilporn 2009). The municipal institutions of the *metropoleis* are also poorly understood. One of the few metropolitan officials known by name is Soter, the main figure of a family buried in the first–second century CE in a reused tomb on the west bank (van Landuyt 1995; Herbin 2002; Riggs 2006). In the Greek inscription on his coffin, he is designated as 'archon of Thebes', which may mean that he belonged to the ruling class of the *metropolis*. A proskynema inscription in the temple of Amenhotep and Imhotep in Deir el-Bahri mentions a certain Apollonides, who was gymnasiarch, *exegetes*, and *agoranomos*, apparently in Hermonthis (Łajtar 2006, no. 123).

Temples and Towns of the Theban Region

The centre of the Theban region was the agglomeration of Thebes, straddling both sides of the Nile. On the east side, it stretched along the river from Luxor temple in the south to Karnak in the north, and on the west bank, along the border of the cultivation from Deir el-Shelwit in the south to el-Tarif in the north. Although scholarship (and tourism) often contrasts the two banks today, treating the east as a 'city of the living' and the west as a 'city of the dead', it is important to note that the west bank had town and village settlements in addition to its cemeteries.

In Roman times, even if Thebes formed a unity in a cultural sense, it was sharply divided in administrative terms, for the opposing banks belonged to two different nomes (see above). The eastern part of the agglomeration, probably together with the north end of the west bank, formed the city of Thebes, which was the *metropolis* of the Peritheban nome. The Egyptian name of the city used in the period under consideration was *N(ỉ)w.t*, literally 'the town'. The official Greek name read Diospolis Magna, owing to the equating of Amun, the patron god of Thebes, with the Greek god Zeus. The name Thebes (*Θῆβαι*), of unknown origin, was used only in literary language.

Egyptian temples dominated the town, in both visual and cultural terms. Built successively from the Middle Kingdom until Roman times, the most important temples were located in the area of modern Karnak and formed three sacred precincts dedicated to three Theban gods: Amun, his divine consort Mut, and Montu, a warrior god who was an early patron of the Theban nome (Quaegebeur 1974, 1975–6; Vandorpe 1995: 212–18; 2004: 186–92; Coppens 2007b).

The precinct of Amun took the central position. It boasted the magnificent temple of Amun-Re, called the Ammonieion (*Ἀμμωνιεῖον*) in Greek. The temple was accessible from the west through a huge pylon preceded by a processional way leading to the Nile harbour. In addition to the temple of Amun-Re, several smaller temples stood within the enclosure walls of the precinct. Perhaps the most important of them was the temple of Khonsu, the offspring of Amun and Mut. Located in the south-western corner of the precinct and accessible by a processional way of its own, this temple, called the Xesebaieon or Herakleion (*Χεσεβαιῆον* or *Ἡρακλεῖον*) in Greek sources, played an important role in the legal life of Graeco-Roman Thebes. In front of its gate (the modern Bab el-Amara), verdicts were pronounced and oaths sworn, according to local judicial custom. Numerous examples of such oaths are preserved in Demotic and, less often, Greek from the Ptolemaic and early Roman period (Kaplony-Heckel 1960). Other temples within the precinct of Amun were dedicated to 'Opet the Great' (*Ip.t-wr.t*) (Demeter) (Greek: Demetrion or Papoerieion, *Δημητρῖον* or *Παποηριεῖον*), Ptah (Greek: Hephaesteion, *Ἡφαιστεῖον*), and Osiris of Koptos.

The precinct of Mut was situated to the south of Amun's domain and was connected with it by a processional way flanked by ram-headed sphinxes. It boasted the temple of the main goddess (Greek: Heraion, *Ἡραῖον*) and, in addition, the temple of Khonsu 'the Child' (*Ḫnsw-p3-ẖrd*) and the chapel of Mut and Sekhmet. The precinct was connected with the river by a wide road. The precinct of Montu neighboured the Amun precinct from the north and was called the Apolloneion (*Ἀπολλονεῖον*) in Greek.

Several further temples stood outside the three great precincts. They are attested either archaeologically or textually, or both. The list includes the temple of Thoth (Hermes), the temple of Khonsu, 'who governs at Thebes', the chapel of Neferhotep, the temple of Isis (*Ἰσιῆον*), the temple of Khnum, and many others.

Another important sacred complex was the temple of Amun at the present-day site known as Luxor temple, situated around 3 km south of Karnak. The two complexes were connected by a processional way flanked by human-headed sphinxes. The Luxor temple was called *ỉp.t-rsj.t*, 'the southern sanctuary', in hieroglyphic sources and *ỉpj* in Demotic. This was transcribed in Greek as Apis (*Ἆπις*) or Ophieon (*Ὠφιῆον*), although some scholars question whether the two names refer to the same thing (Vandorpe 1995: 218). At some point, the latter name came to encompass the entire area south of Karnak. A small Serapeum in classical style was built in front of the Luxor temple by Gaius Julius Antoninus, formerly *decurio* and *neokoros* of Sarapis, and consecrated to the emperor Hadrian on the occasion of his *dies natalis* on 24 January 126 (see Fig. 11.2; Golvin et al. 1981). A Roman auxiliary unit was garrisoned in the neighbourhood of the temple in the first to third centuries, and the temple must have fallen out of use by the time a legionary camp was constructed around the sanctuary itself, in the reign of Diocletian.

Residential quarters concentrated around the seats of gods. In the Ptolemaic period, as in previous times, the settlement centred on present-day Karnak and formed two clusters separated by the Amun temple, of which the northern is called the 'Town of the Cow' in Demotic sources and Chrysopolis in Greek ones. However, damage during and after the uprising of 90–88 BCE must have changed the character of the settlement considerably. In Roman times, according to the frequently quoted description of Strabo (17.1.46), Thebes was no longer a town but a conglomerate of villages only loosely connected with each other. These 'villages' should probably be identified with the 'districts' (*λαῦραι*) mentioned in sources, mostly innumerable tax receipts preserved on ostraca, from the mid-first century BCE to the mid-third century CE (Heilporn 2009: 33–69). These districts include Xarax, Agorai, Borras, Notos, Lips, Notos kai Lips, Ophieon, and perhaps also Notos kai Apeliotes. Of these, Notos kai Lips was probably situated on the west bank, the rest on the east. Ophieon should probably be identified with the settlement around the Luxor temple, while the other east bank districts were around the Amun precinct at Karnak. Little is known about what the residential areas of Thebes looked like in the Roman period. Archaeological remains are preserved only in the area of Karnak North, identified with the 'Town of the Cow' (Chrysopolis), but Greek and Demotic papyri of the Ptolemaic period reveal that houses could reach a considerable height, up to five storeys (Pestman 1992). Between the houses were spacious 'royal roads' (*ῥῦμαι βασιλικαί*) as well as narrow alleys and irrigation channels.

The west part of the Theban agglomeration was called 'the mound of Djeme' (*I3.t Ṯ3mt*) or simply Djeme (*Ṯ3mt*, *Ḏ3mt*) in hieroglyphic sources from the 21st dynasty onwards; this corresponds to *Ḏm3* in Demotic texts. The Greek sources use Memnonia (*Μεμνόνεια*), a name that is attested between the mid-third century BCE and the eighth century CE (Bataille 1952). The origin of the Egyptian name, which was also the name of the patron god of the town of Djeme, is unknown. Before it started to be used as a toponym, the Greek name was probably a collective designation for the New Kingdom royal mortuary temples on the west bank, and initially might have referred only to those temples of kings who bore a throne name that sounded the name of Memnon to the Greeks (Amenhotep III (*Nb-m3ʿ.t-Rʿ*), Seti I (*Mn-m3ʿ.t-Rʿ*), and Ramesses VI (*Nb-m3ʿ.t-Rʿ*)). It is important to observe that the name Djeme (Memnoneia) could have been used in three different ways (as established by Pestman 1993: 411–15). In a narrow sense it designated the town within and around the enclosure wall of the Ramesses III temple at Medinet Habu. In a broader sense it referred to the entire area of western Thebes. Thirdly, it was also the name of a fiscal district within the Hermonthite nome, encompassing Djeme.

The cultural landscape of the Theban west bank had once been dominated by the large New Kingdom temples. Diodorus (1.46.7), who might have had local informants among the priests, states that there were as many as forty-seven temples at the high point of Theban history, but by the time of Ptolemy I, the number of sanctuaries still functioning amounted to seventeen, diminishing to only a few by the first half of the first century BCE. By that time, the most magnificent of all the temples on the west bank, that of Amenhotep III, was non-existent. All that remained of it were two colossal statues of the king, the so-called Memnon colossi, which were a tourist attraction in Roman times (see below). The majority of the royal temples met similar fates, and among those that remained standing, the huge temple of Ramesses III at Medinet Habu was apparently in the best condition. However, its role had changed to become an administrative centre and site of the village of Djeme. The main cult place at Medinet Habu was the smaller temple neighbouring the Ramesses III temple from the east. Built under the 18th dynasty and enlarged into Roman times, this temple, dedicated to two forms of Amun—Amun in Djeme (or Amun with the Ogdoad) and Amun of Ipet in Djeme—was the focus of a pilgrimage made every ten days by the statue of Amun from his temple at Karnak. This event and other cult activity are documented by Demotic graffiti left on the walls and roof of the temple by Theban clergy (Thissen 1989). As in the Khonsu temple on the east bank, the local population of Djeme swore oaths in front of the temple pylon, samples of which have also been preserved (Kaplony-Heckel 1960). The fate of the temple of Ramesses II (the Ramesseum) in the Roman period is unclear. The lack of archaeological traces from these times seems to suggest that it was abandoned, but the occurrence of the proper name Zmanres (*Ζμανρῆς*, a transcription of the Egyptian (*Wsr-m3ʿ.t-Rʿ*) in the onomastics of the west bank may testify to the existence of a popular cult of Amun-Re centred in this very temple, built by a king with the name User-maat-re (Quaegebeur 1985a). The temple of Hatshepsut at Deir el-Bahri, with its three distinctive terraces, was filled up with sand to the level of the middle terrace. On its upper terrace, the cult of the local saint Amenhotep son of Hapu was installed at the beginning of the Ptolemaic period. An important official under Amenhotep III, Amenhotep son of Hapu was deified and worshipped as a healer and oracle giver. Under Ptolemy VIII, perhaps between 124 and 117 BCE, the cult place was remodelled and extended (Laskowska-Kusztal 1984), and it is probably then that another Egyptian healer-saint, Imhotep, was added to the cult, which endured into the Roman period (Łajtar 2006). The chapel of Hathor, situated in the middle terrace of the Hatshepsut temple, was probably also accessible and used for cult purposes.

In addition to these old temples, several new cult buildings were constructed in Ptolemaic and Roman times. At Deir el-Medina, more or less halfway between Deir el-Bahri and Medinet Habu, a temple for Hathor was built under Ptolemy IV and decorated under Ptolemy VI and VIII (du Bourguet and Gabolde 2002). Another new building was the temple of Thoth-the-Ibis in Qasr el-Aguz, south-east of Medinet Habu, built during the reign of Ptolemy VIII

(Mallet 1909). The god was worshipped there as an oracle giver, hence his epithets 'Thoth listens' (*Ḏḥwtj-sḏm*), *Θοτσύτμις*, Thotsytmis) and 'The face of the ibis has spoken' (*Ḏd-ḥr-p3-hb*), *Τεεφῖβις*, Teephibis) (Volokhine 2002). Finally, a temple of Isis was developed at Deir el-Shelwit, at the south end of the west bank settlements, around 3 km south of Medinet Habu (Zivie 1982–92).

The main residential area of the west bank was the town of Djeme at Medinet Habu. The houses were situated within the inner enclosure wall of the Ramesses III temple and between this wall and the lower outer wall (Vandorpe 1995: 223). The inner space, together with the temple itself, was called the phrourion Memnoneion (*φρούριον Μεμνονείων*), and the outer should probably be identified with Pakeis (*Πάκεις*; Egyptian: (*P3-ḳs*). The results of the American excavations of the 1930s, even if they refer mainly to the late antique period, give a good idea of what the town looked like (Hölscher 1954; Wilfong 2003). The mud-brick houses were several storeys high and stood cramped along narrow streets. Outside Medinet Habu there was a smaller settlement site at Deir el-Medina, in connection with the temple of Hathor (Montserrat and Meskell 1997).

Several important settlements were located outside the Theban agglomeration. On the east bank, the village of Kerameia (modern Medamud) situated about 8 km north of Thebes, was an age-old cult place of Montu, where the Ptolemies built two temples of the god in place of an older sanctuary. The village possessed its own *thesauros* (public granary) in the Roman period, attested by ostraca with tax receipts. Another temple of Montu was in Touphium (Tod), some 20 km south of Thebes. On the west bank, Hermonthis (modern Armant), which replaced Pathyris as a nome capital, had been a regionally important settlement and cult centre since Predynastic times. The main element of the town was the sacred precinct of Montu, built successively from the Middle Kingdom until Roman times. Cleopatra VII constructed a birth temple (*mammisi*), whose decoration depicted the queen with her son Caesarion in her arms. To the north-west of the Montu precinct was the Bucheum, the necropolis of the sacred Buchis bulls, bordered on the east by the necropolis for the sacred cows who were the mothers of the Buchis (Mond and Myers 1934). Remains of habitation were discovered in the neighbouring village of Bakaria and in Armant itself. In the late Roman period, the centre of the town moved into the precinct of Montu. Through the papyrological evidence we know the names of several hamlets, such as Nesoi, Senyris, Terkythis, Pentakomia, and many more; however, their exact location remains unknown.

During the Ptolemaic period, building activity at Thebes was focused predominantly on the construction of huge enclosure walls and gates for the sacred precincts on the east bank, but also on the erection of some new temples on both the east and the west banks of the river. In contrast to Ptolemaic times, the Roman period added little to Thebes in terms of Egyptian temple construction, owing to both the loss of the great Amun temple's economic power and the lack of interest in Thebes from the Roman authorities. Building activity was mainly restricted to repairs or the rebuilding of older constructions, not infrequently done with cheaper material (red brick rather than stone), and to secondary elements such as processional ways or the decoration of already existing buildings. Only a few original constructions are known from the Roman period, including the forecourt to the 18th dynasty temple at Medinet Habu, the temple of Isis at Deir el-Shelwit, and the small Serapeum at the Luxor temple (Fig. 11.2). There is little or no evidence for classical architectural remains in the region.

Population

In the Ptolemaic period, the population of Thebes stood at approximately 50,000, of which around 10 per cent were Greeks who had immigrated between the end of the fourth and the middle of the second centuries BCE (Clarysse 1995). These Greeks were largely, though not exclusively, part of an upper class in Theban society, attested in the state apparatus, army, police, as owners of banks, and so forth. By the early Ptolemaic times, however, Greek immigrants had accommodated to Egyptian ways of life, as the newcomers married women from the local elites, a classic example being Dryton, an officer of the Ptolemaic garrison in Pathyris, whose second wife was an Egyptian woman with the dual Greek and Egyptian name Apollonia, also called Senmonthis (Vandorpe 2002). Greeks acted legally according to local customs, worshipped Egyptian gods, and participated in Egyptian funerary practices. But acculturation to the dominant Greek culture took place at the same time. Egyptians started to speak Greek and Egyptian scribes to write it, so that a Greek-speaking upper class, in large part of Egyptian background, had taken shape by the end of the Ptolemaic period. As Clarysse (1995: 19) has observed, members of this social stratum 'could act in two ways according to the circumstances: as Greeks in the administration, the army and the gymnasium, as Egyptians in the temple and within the family'.

One can suppose that a similar situation continued in the Roman period, with the difference that the Greek-speaking Egyptians were much more numerous. Not only members of the elites but also common people used Greek in everyday communication while the knowledge of the epichoric language disappeared steadily. In the middle of the first century CE, scribes largely stopped drafting documents in Demotic. The Roman presence in Thebes, except for a short period under Augustus, was too insignificant to influence essentially local ethnic and cultural relations. Isolated testimonies indicate the existence of a small Jewish minority.

Religion

Originally, the main god of the Theban region was Montu, but his cult was overshadowed in the New Kingdom and Third Intermediate period by that of Amun, king of the gods and the patron of Thebes. Amun retained his dominant position in the Theban region until Roman times, although the cult of Montu rose to importance again from the 25th dynasty (712–657 BCE) onwards, especially on the west bank. The centre of the Amun cult was his temple in the area of present-day Karnak. Its subordinate was the temple in Luxor, which was attended by the cult personnel of the Karnak temple. Amun was also worshipped on the west bank as 'Amun in *Ỉpj*', or Amenopet, Greek Amenophis (Quaegebeur 1986). Although the Amun priesthood had lost its political power in the Ptolemaic period, it retained its high cultural and economic position into Roman times. Either the Ptolemies or their predecessors (the kings of the 30th dynasty) had revived the priestly office of first prophet of Amun, abolished by the Persians, and this title continued until 180 CE (Quaegebeur 1974: 43).

Nothing is known about the daily ritual in the Amun temple at Karnak, but we are much better informed about festivals during which a statue of the god left the temple in his sacred boat and visited other cult places in the area. One such festival, celebrated in the month of Pauni, was the so-called Beautiful Feast of the Valley, during which the Amun procession crossed over the Nile and visited various temples on the west bank. It may be this very festival that is referred to as a *διάβασις τοῦ μεγίστου θεοῦ Ἄμμωνος εἰς τὰ Μεμνόνεια* in the papyrological sources of the Ptolemaic period, and it may have continued in the Roman period as well. It is also possible, however, that this Greek designation covers the feast held every ten days when a statue of Amun visited the small temple at Medinet Habu to pay homage to the eight primeval gods known as the Ogdoad, who were considered to be his forefathers. This decadary feast flourished in Ptolemaic and Roman times, and may have taken over some of the elements of the Beautiful Feast of the Valley (Herbin 1984).

Montu had as many as three important cult places on the east bank, at Karnak, Medamud, and Tod, and was the true lord of the west bank with his main temple at Hermonthis. These four sanctuaries were closely related to each other, giving rise to the concept of the Four Montus, expressed in both iconography and onomastics. The sacred animal of Montu was a bull called Buchis (Goldbrunner 2004). The dead Buchis bulls were buried in a subterranean gallery founded by Nectanebo II (the so-called Bucheum) in Hermonthis. The importance of Montu in the Theban region is testified by the frequent occurrence of theophoric names derived from the name of the Buchis bull, from his name or his epithets, or from the name of Apollo, who, by *interpretatio Graeca*, was the counterpart of Montu: Pamonthes, Phthomonthes, Apollonios, Apollonides, Plenis, and Petesorbuchis, to name a few male examples (de Meulenaere 1962; Clarysse 1984). The last Buchis bull died and was buried in the Bucheum in 340 CE, complete with an epitaph in hieroglyphics which is the youngest surely dated text in this script (Fig. 11.3; Grenier 1983).

The goddess Hathor occupied an important place in the religious life of Graeco-Roman Thebes. She had at least two cult places on the west bank, one at Deir el-Medina and another at Deir el-Bahri, in both of which she was worshipped as the patroness of the surrounding cemeteries and the dead.

One characteristic trait of the religious landscape of Graeco-Roman Thebes is the presence of small temples or shrines, frequently boasting an oracular or healing cult, in which believers had direct contact with gods. Such were the sanctuary of Amenhotep and Imhotep at Deir el-Bahri and the temple of Thoth at Qasr el-Aguz, but the temple of Hathor at Deir el-Medina and the temple of Ptah at Karnak also had a similar character. Believers expressed their piety by leaving inscriptions of the proskynema type on the walls of temples, paying homage to the relevant god (Geraci 1971; see Chapter 42). These inscriptions substituted for the writer's worshipful presence before the god and perpetuated the name of the visitor, so that he (rarely, she) could possess the eternal blessing of the place. Interestingly, the greatest number of proskynemata recorded in the Theban region occurs in the sanctuary of Amenhotep and Imhotep at Deir el-Bahri (Łajtar 2006).

Another important element of Theban religious life in the Roman period, as elsewhere in Egypt, is the rise of animal cults, attested by the vitality of the cult of the Buchis bull and innumerable burials of sacred animals throughout the region. The Theban cemeteries have yielded mummified ibises, hawks, other birds, snakes, crocodiles, dogs and other canines, gazelles, hippopotami, cats, cattle, fish, apes, sheep, small mammals, small reptiles, and beetles—all of which are more likely to represent religious practices rather than

FIG. 11.3 The last dated stela commemorating a Buchis bull, from the Bucheum at Armant

Courtesy of the Egypt Exploration Society.

'pet' burials (Kessler 1989: 159–93). In a similar vein, magical practices were also vital to religious practice at Roman Thebes, and an archive dating to the first half of the fourth century CE contained a number of papyri in Greek and Demotic. The texts resemble working handbooks, and perhaps represent the personal library of a magic practitioner (Tait 1995; Dieleman 2005).

In the Roman period, the institutionalized religion centred in the temples gradually died out, so that priestly offices like first prophet of Amun (last mentioned in 180 CE) may have been little more than symbolic. The proskynemata in the Deir el-Bahri sanctuary of Amenhotep and Imhotep stop at more or less the same time. The end of temple religion, however, did not equal a complete disappearance of pagan beliefs; religion only changed its forms, becoming a private matter practised in close circles of relatives, friends, and members of an occupational or cult association (Bagnall 1993: 261–73; Frankfurter 1998). A good illustration of these tendencies are the inscriptions left in the temple of Hatshepsut at Deir el-Bahri by a corporation of ironworkers from Hermonthis. At the turn of the third to fourth century CE, members of the corporation came regularly to Deir el-Bahri, using the space previously dedicated to the cult of Amenhotep and Imhotep. Here, they celebrated the beginning of the new year in the Egyptian calendar (1 Tybi, around 27 December) with an offering of a donkey and a drinking feast (Łajtar 2006: 94–104).

Burial Practices

Burial activity took place throughout the entire Theban necropolis on the west bank with the exception of the Valley of the Kings (Riggs 2003; Strudwick 2003). In the Ptolemaic period, burials concentrated in the Asasif and the neighbouring Dra Abu el-Naga. The centre of this area boasted familial graves of the elite, situated either in earlier rock-cut tombs or in newly constructed structures of mud-brick, while the peripheries were occupied by collective burials. In the Roman period, more activity is observed in the south, in the area north-west of Medinet Habu, and in the Valley of the Queens. This part of the necropolis, perhaps used by the inhabitants of Djeme, is characterized by mass burials in reused rock-cut tombs, with as many as several dozen bodies, although more elite burials in brick graves are also known from there. The late Roman period is best represented by finds from Deir el-Bahri, for which the most typical are pit burials with mummies, sometimes provided with plaster-and-linen masks, placed directly in the ground with the head occasionally covered by a basket or a piece of pottery; some were buried in reused coffins (Riggs 2000; 2003: 198–9; 2005: 232–43). Similar burials were found at Medinet Habu, among the graves of the earlier Roman cemetery.

A constant element of Theban burial practices in the Roman period is the secondary use of earlier Middle Kingdom through Late period rock-cut tombs, and the adaptation of older funerary material. A good example of this phenomenon is the tomb opened in 1857 by the Scottish antiquarian Alexander Henry Rhind in Sheikh Abd el-Qurna, which is no longer identifiable (Riggs 2003: 191–3). This structure, most probably of New Kingdom date, was remodelled in the first years of Roman rule to house ten or so mummies of persons belonging to the family of local noblemen, priests of various Theban gods, and state officials. One of these mummies was placed in the usurped sarcophagus of Ankhnesneferibre, a divine adoratrice of Amun in the time of the 26th dynasty. Another reused tomb is that of Djehutymose from the time of Ramesses II (TT 32) in el-Khokha, used for the burials of Soter, members of his family, and probably other individuals in the first and second centuries CE (Kákosy 1995; Riggs 2003: 193–5; 2005: 182–205). The burials of the Pebos family (late second century CE) occupied the basement of an abandoned house at Deir el-Medina (Montserrat and Meskell 1997: 186–93; Riggs 2003: 195–8; 2005: 205–17).

Mortuary practices at Thebes show strong conservative tendencies, with changes taking place under the Romans on a more limited scale than in other parts of Egypt. Funerary adornment in classical style like the stele of the athlete Plenis found in Deir el-Bahri (Parlasca 2003) is extremely rare. Mummification was in use throughout the entire period, although not all bodies were embalmed, by any means. Some mummified bodies have gilded skin, and there is a custom of placing a wooden stick down the spine as an additional support for the body. Bodies were rarely provided with a painted portrait or a mask. The majority of bodies, both mummified and not, did not receive further adornment. Only a small proportion was wrapped in shrouds, which could be richly painted, or placed in coffins. Two types of coffin can be distinguished: anthropoid and vaulted. The former were made, as a rule, of terracotta, the latter of wood, shaped as a vaulted lid supported by four corner posts. The vaulted coffins of the Soter family are noteworthy for their rich decoration, which includes the signs of the zodiac (inside the vaulted lid) and the transit of the sun-god, as well as other scenes from Egyptian mythology (Beinlich-Seeber 1998; Riggs and Depauw 2002; Riggs

2006). Some mummies were provided with a mummy label that could assume the form of a *tabla* of considerable dimensions (Quaegebeur 1985b). Grave goods are poorly represented: rarely a funerary papyrus, as in the Soter burials and the Rhind tomb, and sometimes a wreath made of flowers or a more durable material (linen, metal), vessels, glass, baskets, lamps, and terracotta or wax figurines. An exceptional element is a wooden canopy found in the Rhind tomb, perhaps to fit over the wrapped or coffined body during the funeral procession (Riggs 2003: 192, with fig. 1).

In the Ptolemaic period, mummification was carried out by *taricheutai* and *paraschistai*, priests belonging to the lower classes of clergy, who were considered impure because of their direct contact with the dead. Mummified bodies were handed over to *choachytai* (*w3ḥ-mnw*), literally 'water pourers', who took care of the funerary cult, *inter alia* presenting offerings at the tomb on fixed days. The activity of the *choachytai* is relatively well known to us thanks to the rich papyrological source material from the third–second centuries BCE (Pestman 1992, 1993; Vleeming 1995). The *choachytai* founded an association under the patronage of Amenophis, the local form of Amun worshipped on the Theban west bank. With the beginning of the Roman period, however, *paraschistai* and *choachytai* disappear from the documentation. Either *taricheutai* took over the duties of the two other groups, or all three groups started to be called by the same designation.

The west bank cemeteries were used by all inhabitants of the Theban area (including Thebes and Djeme), irrespective of their social or economic status. Mummy labels indicate that people from more distant areas, up to 10 km or so away, also buried their dead there. The choice of burial place may have been dictated by family traditions, as well as the perceived sanctity of this ancient necropolis.

Tourists

André Bataille (1952: 346) called the Thebes of Ptolemaic and Roman times a 'museum-city', full of magnificent monuments of a glorious past but, in effect, dead. Although this negative appraisal is belied by the ongoing occupation of the area and the active engagement with the Theban past, it seems that the ancient Greeks and Romans shared Bataille's view, at least in part. The Roman poet Juvenal (second half of the first century CE), who spent some time in Upper Egypt as the officer of an auxiliary unit, describes Thebes in his Satire 15 as a town 'where the magic harmonies resonate from the truncated statue of Memnon and where ancient Thebes of the hundred gates lies buried' (*magicae resonant ubi Memnone chordae atque uetus Thebe centum iacet obruta portis*). This literary and romantic picture of Thebes, shaped in classical culture since the time of Homer, together with the remoteness of the town, imparted an atmosphere of mystery to it.

Lured by this picture, Greeks and Romans came to Thebes to confront the reality. Literary sources, papyri, and inscriptions transmit information about some famous visitors. Among them were the Greek writer Strabo, who visited the town with his friend Aelius Gallus, one of the first prefects of Egypt; Germanicus, Tiberius' adopted son; and the emperors Hadrian and Septimius Severus, and perhaps also Caracalla, the latter's son. Many other visitors are known only by name, where they left a graffito or proskynema to record their visit (Foertmeyer 1989).

We are unable to reconstruct a typical itinerary for a Graeco-Roman tourist in Thebes, but it probably included most of the monumental temples of the east bank, or at least those parts accessible to outsiders. On the west bank, two places were almost obligatory: the royal tombs in the Valley of the Kings and the so-called Memnon colossi. From among sixty-three tombs known to modern Egyptologists in the Valley of the Kings, around ten were accessible in Ptolemaic and Roman times. These inclined, corridor-like structures, cut into the cliff rock, were called *syringai* in Greek because of their resemblance to the Pan flute, and their magnificent decoration in paint and relief inspired admiration. Fascinated visitors left over 2,000 inscriptions in Greek, Latin, and Demotic, either painted or scratched on the walls of the tombs (*I Syringes*). As a rule they contain the name of the visitor, sometimes supplemented with the statement 'I saw and I admired' (*εἶδον καὶ ἐθαύμασα*).

In contrast to the royal tombs, the Memnon colossi, two gigantic statues once standing in front of the Amenhotep III temple, were not only a cultural attraction but also a natural one (Fig. 11.4). From the time of Augustus onwards, the north colossus produced at daybreak a sound resembling singing, probably evoked by the heating of air in cracks that formed in the statue during the earthquake of 27 BCE. The sounds were interpreted as the crying of Memnon addressed to his mother, Eos. The identification of King Amenhotep III with Memnon, the hero known from myths about the Trojan War, was possible thanks to the previous application of the term Memnoneia to the royal mortuary temples of the west bank. A total of 108 inscriptions in Greek and Latin on the surface of the colossus, dating between the time of Tiberius and the beginning of the third century, commemorate visits paid to admire the acoustic phenomenon (Bernand and Bernand 1960). The people mentioned in these inscriptions are mainly representatives of the Roman state apparatus in Egypt, including prefects,

FIG. 11.4 The colossi of Memnon

Photo: Christina Riggs.

lesser officers of the provincial administration, and soldiers. Among the inscriptions are four metric texts composed by the poet Julia Balbilla on the occasion of the visit of Hadrian and his wife, Sabina, to the colossus (Corey Brennan 1988). At some time in the third century, repairs to the colossus stopped its 'singing', and thus the inscriptions ceased.

Conclusion

The life of Thebes and its region in Roman times developed in the shadow of the town's glorious past. Once the capital of Egypt, Roman Thebes retained symbolically the position of the main cultural and religious centre in Upper Egypt, at the same time losing the majority of its political and economic power. The cultural milieu of Thebes in the time under consideration shows local Egyptian traits, only vaguely modified by the influence of Hellenism. This is seen especially in the religion, with the dominant cults of Amun and Montu, and in burial practices applied in the vast necropolis of western Thebes.

Suggested Reading

A monograph discussing Thebes and its region in Roman times is lacking, although Bataille's classic study (1952) examined all aspects of western Thebes. In the absence of a dedicated book, articles by Katelijn Vandorpe (1995, 2004) and Philipp Coppens (2007a,b) are concise and helpful. The topography of the city of Thebes is discussed in Paul Heilporn's excellent introduction to a publication of fiscal ostraca (Heilporn 2009). On the religion of Roman Thebes, several interesting articles by Quaegebeur (1974, 1975–6) are relevant, and one can especially recommend his 1974 discussion of Theban temples and cults on the basis of Greek and Egyptian texts. The cult of Buchis, the bull of Montu, is the subject of a book by Goldbrunner (2004), while Łajtar (2006) studies a small oracular and healing sanctuary of Amenhotep and Imhotep in Deir el-Bahri, and presents all the relevant Greek texts. Burial practices in the Theban necropolis are presented in a series of works by Christina Riggs (see especially Riggs 2003, 2005), to which the article by Nigel Strudwick (2003) can be added.

Bibliography

Bagnall, R. S. 1993. *Egypt in Late Antiquity*. Princeton: Princeton University Press.

Bataille, A. 1951. 'Thèbes gréco-romaine', *Chronique d'Égypte* 26: 325–53.

—— 1952. *Les Memnonia: Recherches de papyrologie et d'épigraphie grecque sur la nécropole de la Thèbes d'Égypte aux époques hellénistiques et romaine*. Cairo: Institut Français d'Archéologie Orientale.

Beinlich-Seeber, C. 1998. 'Ein römerzeitliches Sargfragment in Marseille', in A. Brodbeck (ed.), *Ein ägyptisches Glasperlenspiel: Ägyptologische Beiträge für Erik Hornung aus seinem Schülerkreis*. Berlin: Mann, 9–40.

Bernand, A., and É. Bernand. 1960. *Les inscriptions grecques et latines du Colosse de Memnon*. Cairo: Institut Français d'Archéologie Orientale.

Bogaert, R. 1984. 'Banques et banquiers à Thèbes à l'époque romaine', *Zeitschrift für Papyrologie und Epigraphik* 57: 241–96; repr. in Bogaert, *Trapezitica Aegyptiaca*. Florence: Gonnelli, 1994, 153–203.

Clarysse, W. 1984. 'Theban Personal Names and the Cult of Buchis', in H.-J. Thissen and K.-T. Zauzich (eds), *Grammata Demotica: Festschrift für Erich Lüddeckens zum 15. Juni 1983*. Würzburg: Zauzich, 25–39.

—— 1995. 'Greeks in Ptolemaic Thebes', in S. P. Vleeming (ed.), *Hundred-Gated Thebes: Acts of a Colloquium on Thebes and the Theban Area in the Graeco-Roman Period*. Leiden: Brill, 1–19.

Coppens, P. 2007a. 'Ptolemaic and Roman Thebes', in J. Mynárová and P. Onderka (eds), *Thebes: City of Gods and Pharaohs*. Prague: Národni Museum, 197–205.

—— 2007b. 'The Theban Temples in the Ptolemaic and Roman Periods', in J. Mynárová and P. Onderka (eds), *Thebes: City of Gods and Pharaohs*. Prague: Národni Museum, 207–9.

Corey Brennan, T. 1988. 'The Poets Julia Balbilla and Damo at the Colossus of Memnon', *Classical World* 91: 215–34.

Criscuolo, L. 1995. 'L'epigrafia greca a Tebe', in S. P. Vleeming (ed.), *Hundred-Gated Thebes: Acts of a Colloquium on Thebes and the Theban Area in the Graeco-Roman Period*. Leiden: Brill, 21–30.

Deckers, J. G. 1979. 'Die Wandmalereien im Kaiserkultraum von Luxor', *Jahrbuch des Deutschen Archäologischen Instituts* 94: 600–52.

de Meulenaere, H. 1962. 'Recherches onomastiques III: πλῆνις et ⲡⲗⲏⲓⲛⲉ en égyptien', *Kemi* 16: 35–7.

Dieleman, J. 2005. *Priests, Tongues, and Rites: The London–Leiden Magical Manuscripts and Translation in Egyptian Ritual (100–300 CE)*. Leiden: Brill.

du Bourguet, P., and L. Gabolde. 2002. *Le temple de Deir el-Médina*. Cairo: Institut Français d'Archéologie Orientale.

el-Saghir, M., et al. 1986. *Le camp romain de Louqsor*. Cairo: Institut Français d'Archéologie Orientale.

Foertmeyer, V. A. 1989. 'Tourism in Graeco-Roman Egypt', doctoral dissertation, Princeton University.

Frankfurter, D. 1998. *Religion in Roman Egypt: Assimilation and Resistance*. Princeton: Princeton University Press.

Geraci, G. 1971. 'Ricerche sul Proskynema', *Aegyptus* 51: 3–211.

Goldbrunner, L. 2004. *Buchis: Eine Untersuchung zur Theologie des heiligen Stieres in Theben zur griechisch-römischen Zeit*. Turnhout: Brepols.

Golvin, J.-C., et al. 1981. 'Le petit Sarapieion romain de Louqsor', *Bulletin de l'Institut Français d'Archéologie Orientale* 81: 115–48.

Grenier, J.-C. 1983. 'La stèle funéraire du dernier taureau Bouchis', *Bulletin de l'Institut Français d'Archéologie Orientale* 83: 197–208.

Heilporn, P. 2009. *Thèbes et ses taxes: Recherches sur la fiscalité en Égypte romaine (Ostraca de Strasbourg II)*. Paris: de Boccard.

Herbin, F.-R. 1984. 'Une liturgie des rites décadaires de Djéme: Papyrus Vienne 3865', *Revue d'Égyptologie* 35: 105–27.

—— 2002. *Padiimenipet fils de Sôter: Histoire d'une famille dans l'Égypte romaine*. Paris: Réunion des Musées Nationaux.

Hoffmann, F., M. Minas-Nerpel, and S. Pfeiffer. 2009. *Die dreisprachige Stele des C. Cornelius Gallus: Übersetzung und Kommentar*. Berlin: de Gruyter.
Hölscher, U. 1954. *The Excavations of Medinet Habu V: Post-Ramesside Remains*. Chicago: Oriental Institute.
Kákosy, L. 1995. 'The Soter Tomb in Thebes', in S. P. Vleeming (ed.), *Hundred-Gated Thebes: Acts of a Colloquium on Thebes and the Theban Area in the Graeco-Roman Period*. Leiden: Brill, 61–7.
Kaplony-Heckel, U. 1960. *Die demotischen Tempeleide*. Wiesbaden: Harrassowitz.
Kessler, D. 1989. *Die heiligen Tiere und der König*. Wiesbaden: Harrassowitz.
Łajtar, A. 2006. *Deir el-Bahari in the Hellenistic and Roman Periods: A Study of an Egyptian Temple Based on Greek Sources*. Warsaw: Warsaw University and the Raphael Taubenschlag Foundation.
Laskowska-Kusztal, E. 1984. *Le sanctuaire ptolémaïque de Deir el-Bahari*. Warsaw: PWN.
Mallet, D. 1909. *Le Kasr el-Agoûz*. Cairo: Institut Français d'Archéologie Orientale.
Mond, R., and O. H. Myers. 1934. *The Bucheum*, 3 vols. London: Egypt Exploration Society.
Montserrat, D., and L. Meskell. 1997. 'Mortuary Archaeology and Religious Landscape at Graeco-Roman Deir el-Medina', *Journal of Egyptian Archaeology* 83: 179–97.
Parlasca, K. 2003. 'Das Grabrelief eines Athleten aus Theben-West im British Museum', *Chronique d'Égypte* 78: 241–7.
Pestman, P. W. 1992. *Il processo di Hermias e altri documenti dell' archivio dei choachiti (P. Tor. Choachiti): Papiri greci e demotici conservati a Torino e in altre collezione d'Italia*. Turin: Museo Egizio.
—— 1993. *The Archive of Theban Choachytes (Second Century B.C.): A Survey of the Demotic and Greek Papyri Contained in the Archive*. Leuven: Peeters.
Quaegebeur, J. 1974. 'Prêtres et cultes thébains à la lumière de documents égyptiens et grecs', *Bulletin de la Societé Française d'Égyptologie* 70–1: 37–55.
—— 1975–6. 'Les appellations grecques des temples de Karnak', in P. Naster et al. (eds), *Miscellanea in Honorem J. Vergote*. Leuven: Peeters, 463–78.
—— 1985a. 'Les noms de trois temples funéraires thébains en écriture démotique', in S. F. Bondi (ed.), *Studi in onore di Edda Bresciani*. Pisa: Giardini, 461–73.
—— 1985b. 'Tablai de Thèbes au Musée de Birkenhead (GB)', *Chronique d'Égypte* 60: 263–74.
—— 1986. 'Aménophis, nom royal et nom divin: Questions méthodologiques', *Revue d'Égyptologie* 37: 97–106.
Riggs, C. 2000. 'Roman Period Mummy Masks from Deir el-Bahri', *Journal of Egyptian Archaeology* 86: 121–44.
—— 2003. 'The Egyptian Funerary Tradition at Thebes in the Roman Period', in N. Strudwick and J. H. Taylor (eds), *The Theban Necropolis: Past, Present and Future*. London: British Museum Press, 189–201.
—— 2005. *The Beautiful Burial in Roman Egypt: Art, Identity, and Funerary Religion*. Oxford: Oxford University Press.
—— 2006. 'Archaism and Artistic Sources in Roman Egypt: The Coffins of the Soter Family and the Temple of Deir el-Medina', *Bulletin de l'Institut Français d'Archéologie Orientale* 106: 315–32.
—— and M. Depauw. 2002. '"Soternalia" from Deir el-Bahari, including Two Coffin Lids with Demotic Inscriptions', *Revue d'Égyptologie* 53: 75–90.
Strudwick, N. 2003. 'Some Aspects of the Archaeology of the Theban Necropolis in the Ptolemaic and Roman Periods', in N. Strudwick and J. H. Taylor (eds), *The Theban Necropolis: Past, Present and Future*. London: British Museum Press, 167–88.

Tait, J. 1995. 'Theban Magic', in S. P. Vleeming (ed.), *Hundred-Gated Thebes: Acts of a Colloquium on Thebes and the Theban Area in the Graeco-Roman Period*. Leiden: Brill, 169–82.

Thissen, H.-J. 1989. *Die demotischen Graffiti von Medinet Habu: Zeugnisse zu Tempel und Kult im ptolemäischen Ägypten*. Sommerhausen: Zauzich.

Thomas, J. D. 1964. 'The Theban Administrative District in the Roman Period', *Journal of Egyptian Archaeology* 50: 139–43.

Vandorpe, K. 1995. 'City of Many a Gate, Harbour for Many a Rebel', in S. P. Vleeming (ed.), *Hundred-Gated Thebes: Acts of a Colloquium on Thebes and the Theban Area in the Graeco-Roman Period*. Leiden: Brill, 203–39.

—— 2002. *The Bilingual Family Archive of Dryton, his Wife Apollonia and their Daughter Senmouthis (P.Dryton)*. Brussels: Koninklijke Vlaamse Academie van België voor Wetenschappen en Kunsten.

—— 2004. 'The Theban Region', in R. S. Bagnall and D. W. Rathbone (eds), *Egypt from Alexander to the Copts: An Archaeological and Historical Guide*. London: British Museum Press, 184–208.

van Landuyt, K. 1995. 'The Soter Family: Genealogy and Onomastics', in S. P. Vleeming (ed.), *Hundred-Gated Thebes: Acts of a Colloquium on Thebes and the Theban Area in the Graeco-Roman Period*. Leiden: Brill, 69–82.

Veïsse, A.-E. 2004. *Les 'révoltes égyptiennes': Recherches sur les troubles intérieurs en Égypte du règne de Ptolémée III à la conquête romain*. Leuven: Peeters.

Vleeming, S. P. 1995. 'The Office of a Choachyte in the Theban Area', in Vleeming (ed.), *Hundred-Gated Thebes: Acts of a Colloquium on Thebes and the Theban Area in the Graeco-Roman Period*. Leiden: Brill, 241–55.

Volokhine, Y. 2002. 'Le dieu Thot au Qasr el-Agoûz', *Bulletin de l'Institut Français d'Archéologie Orientale* 102: 405–23.

Wilfong, T. G. 2003. *Women of Jeme: Lives in a Coptic Town in Late Antique Egypt*. Ann Arbor: University of Michigan Press.

Zivie, C. M. 1982–92. *Le temple de Deir Chelouit*. Cairo: Institut Français d'Archéologie Orientale.

CHAPTER 12

CLASSICAL ARCHITECTURE

DONALD M. BAILEY

MOST administrative capitals of the Pharaonic provinces (known as nomes) were retained as such during Ptolemaic and Roman times, with a *strategos* and a gymnasiarch in periodic residence. It is likely that their Roman public buildings were built employing classical styles of architecture, although this has survived in only a few cases.

This chapter looks at the evidence for classical architecture in stone in the urban centres of Middle Egypt, including one new Greek city and three *metropoleis*. In the order in which they are discussed, these are:

- *Antinoopolis*, the city of the deified Bithynian youth Antinoos, which is known mainly from the illustrations and descriptions compiled by Edmé Jomard and the Napoleonic expedition, the *Description de l'Égypte* (1821: 197–283; and pls 53–61);
- *Hermopolis Magna*, the great city of the god Hermes (Egyptian Thoth), known from surviving structures and the evidence of the Napoleonic expedition (*Description* 1821: 159–96; and pls 50–2);
- *Oxyrhynchus*, the city of the sacred mormyrus fish, which is known from sketches by Vivant Denon, leader of the Napoleonic expedition (which are now in the British Museum), from Jomard's description (*Description* 1821: 391–401), and from a few extant buildings or photographs of ruins;
- *Herakleopolis Magna*, the great city of the Greek god Herakles, which is known from two surviving groups of buildings, Jomard's notes (*Description* 1821: 403–10), and some modern plans.

Writing in the first century CE, Strabo (17.1.39–41) mentions the sacred animal cults of Hermopolis (baboon), Oxyrhynchus (mormyrus fish), and Herakleopolis (mongoose). In addition, all four centres are known from references in the papyri (brought together in Łukaszewicz 1986; see also Bowman and Rathbone 1992: 107–27 and Bagnall 1993: 45–109). The following discussion relies chiefly on the evidence of the Napoleonic expedition as well as excavations from the late nineteenth century to the present day, although it is important to keep in mind that archaeological methods and the level of record keeping and site publication vary widely.

The other *metropoleis* of Roman Egypt have yielded very little in terms of surviving classical architecture, often only single blocks of masonry, overlooked by stone robbers (see Bailey 1990; Pensabene 1993; McKenzie 2007). Larger structures preserved elsewhere include a triumphal arch and a temple of Rome and Augustus at the temple site of Philae; a temple of Serapis and a tetrastyle at Diospolis Magna (Thebes); and two theatres at Pelusium. How different were the *metropoleis* from each other? So very few remain that generalizations are hazardous, but most, like Athribis in the Delta, appear to have followed the *cardo–decumanus* layout based on Ptolemaic Alexandria, the *cardo* being the main north–south street of an urban grid, and the *decumanus* the east–west axis. *Metropoleis* near Antinoopolis were probably also influenced by that city, after its founding in 130 CE, but *metropoleis* south of Diospolis Magna may have been adorned by very few classical structures.

Antinoopolis

The emperor Hadrian ordered a city to be built near the spot where, in 130 CE, his companion Antinoos drowned in the Nile. It was named 'the city of Antinoos': Antinoopolis, often shortened to Antinoe. To populate the new city, which was the third Greek *polis* in the *chora* (after Naukratis and Ptolemais Hermiou), people registered as being of Greek origin—the 'New Hellenes'—from the settlement of Ptolemais Euergetis (?) and the Fayum were invited or persuaded to become its citizens. Citizens benefited from tax advantages and other inducements: they did not have to pay the poll tax, received child allowances, and had privileges denied to the other Greek *poleis*, such as being allowed to marry Egyptian women. In the middle years of the second century, the emperor Antonius Pius settled army veterans at Antinoopolis, further adding to the population. The new city concentrated wealth in the surrounding Hermopolite nome: although there was not much cultivable land in the area, surviving documents show that, by the fourth century CE, much of the land in the nome was owned by Antinoites. At the end of the third century, the emperor Diocletian made Antinoopolis the capital of its own nome, and it later became the capital of the Lower Thebaid, including both Middle and much of Upper Egypt; the duke of the Thebaid had his seat there in Byzantine times.

Antinoopolis was not far removed from Hermopolis Magna but lay on the opposite, east bank of the Nile. For most of the time, Hermopolis Magna remained the nome capital, occasionally ceding its administrative role to Antinoopolis. The public architecture of Antinoopolis was wholly Roman, except for a surviving temple of Ramesses II, which had a classical courtyard built in front of its lost pylon. Most of the architecture used different forms of the Corinthian order, but some buildings sported Ionic capitals and the colonnades along the paved streets had Doric elements. The Antinoopolis of the middle decades of the second century CE was a planned city, laid out rather like Alexandria, with one major thoroughfare running parallel with the Nile and crossed by other main streets at right angles to it. The city walls had a circumference of around 5 km, and the city itself was divided into four quarters (*grammata*) and at least thirteen blocks of buildings (*plinthia*). The two main streets were 16 metres wide with 2 metre colonnades on each side, so that the residents could walk in the shade.

The New City and its Topography

The city is known mainly from Jomard's work at the very end of the eighteenth century. By 1819 most of the splendid buildings he saw were gone, demolished by Muhammad Ali to provide stone for a palace at Asyut and other structures. The nineteenth century also saw destruction of the mound to feed a saltpetre factory at the north of the site, which was derelict by 1914. Thus, it is especially fortunate that Jomard's plan is very detailed, clearly showing the placement of buildings and roads (Fig. 12.1; see also Aufrère and Golvin 1997: 226–7; Manfredi and Pericoli 1998–9).

A small Egyptian village, Sheikh Abada, remains on the site, dwarfed by the ancient mound. The mound is about 600 metres wide and stretches more than 2 km along the east bank of the Nile, from the possible site of the temple-tomb of Antinoos to the south cemetery of the city. The city as seen by Napoleon's savants was laid out with a north-west–south-east colonnaded street, the *cardo*, which was about 1.8 km long and flanked by more than 750 Doric columns. The *cardo* runs from the temple-tomb of Antinoos straight to the theatre, passing several important structures. There were two main cross-streets, one of which had a *tetrastylon* (a group of honorific columns, one still standing until about 1819) dedicated to the third-century emperor Alexander Severus and his mother, Julia Mamaea. The other street, probably the *decumanus*, also had a Doric colonnade and ran along a large structure, perhaps a bath building. Its *tetrastylon* was completely collapsed and anonymous when the French expedition recorded it, although a *tetrastylon* of Antinoos is known from a papyrus of 176 CE. After crossing the *cardo*, the *decumanus* extended to the river gate, which was a triumphal arch. The *cardo* continued south-east, crossing the naturally formed Wadi Abada

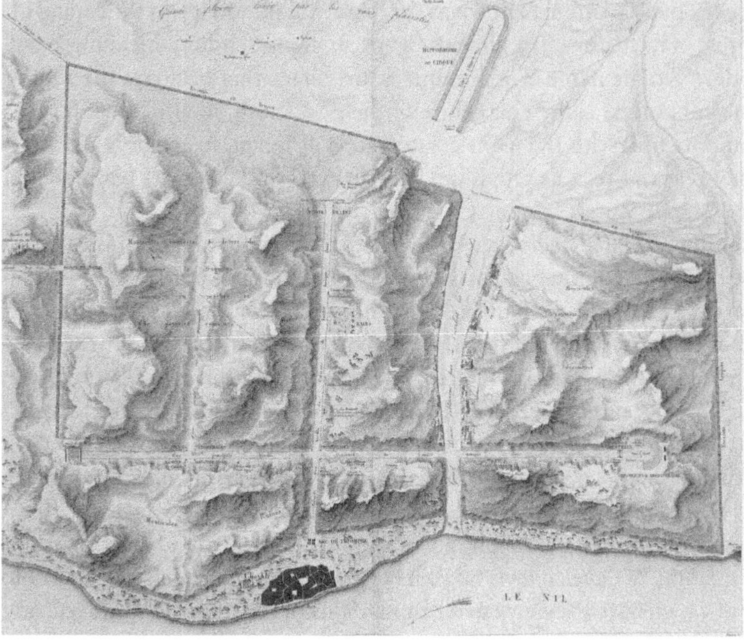

FIG. 12.1 Edmé Jomard's map of Antinoopolis, 1799

Description de l'Égypte (pl. 53). Courtesy of the Trustees of the British Museum.

and extending via the theatre gate (a Corinthian edifice) to the theatre itself. Various papyri mention a *caesareum* (for the ruler cult), baths, a gymnasium, a stoa, and a *praitoreion* (judicial hall). The two main rectangular areas of the mound depicted in the *Description*'s map were surrounded by a substantial mud-brick wall, probably dating to the third century. Outside the walls, to the north, lies the hippodrome; it remains unexcavated. In addition, the Via Hadriana was a new road to the Red Sea coast and its India trade, extending from Antinoopolis to the port of Berenike, far to the south; long stretches of it have only recently been traced (Tomber 2008: 59, fig. 12).

The French archaeologist Albert Gayet worked at Antinoopolis for many years in the early twentieth century, locating the temple of Ramesses II and examining numerous graves dating from the third to fifth centuries (Calament 2005). The burials included painted shrouds and distinctively shaped wooden mummy portraits, which are among the finest from Egypt (see Aubert et al. 2008: 169–227, 264–70, 275–8, 285–95, 298–308). Many subsequent excavators were anxious to locate papyrus documents; others have concentrated on Christian structures. Monasteries, churches, and tombs have been located in the north of the site by recent Italian excavations, indicating the potential for still further excavation (Pintaudi 2008).

Hermopolis Magna

Hermopolis Magna (known as Hermopolis) is situated about 200 km south of Cairo, on the west bank of the Nile roughly opposite Antinoopolis. Hermopolis was within the fifteenth Upper Egyptian nome, known as the 'hare' nome, and it was the capital of the nome through most of its history. The ancient Egyptian name Schmun, meaning 'eight', survives in the modern Arabic name el-Ashmunein, the village that occupies the southern end of the site. Hermopolis was the cult centre of the god Thoth, identified with the Greek god Hermes, and its link with the eight creator-gods of Egyptian religion yielded its ancient name. Pliny referred to it as Oppidum Mercurium, since Hermes was equated with the Roman god Mercury.

The monument that attracted early travellers to the site was the impressive pronaos of the temple of Thoth, commenced by Nectanebo I of the 30th dynasty, but inscribed under Alexander the Great and his half-brother Philip III Arrhidaeus. The temple was largely destroyed in Roman times, but the pronaos remained until it was destroyed and burned for lime in 1826. It was about 38 metres long and its columns stood more than 17 metres high (for views by early travellers, see Snape and Bailey 1988; for reconstructions, see Arnold 1994; 1999: 111–13).

Edmé Jomard, a scholar attached to Napoleon's invading army, made a map of Hermopolis in about 1799. The remains of the city lie about 4 km from the Nile, which once flowed past its walls. The mound is about 1.5 km long and about 1 km wide. Around the turn of the twentieth century, a quantity of Greek papyri (as well as Coptic and Arabic papyri) came onto the market, many of which have relevance to the topography of Hermopolis. More recently, the British Museum conducted archaeological research at the site from 1980 to 1990, revealing large areas of the Pharaonic city as well as aspects of the Roman remains (Spencer 1984, 1989, 1993; Bailey 1991). This work forms the basis for the following discussion.

The Sphinx Gate and the Sphinx Gate Temple

A temple of the second century CE, first examined in 1985, lies near the centre of the city, close to the crossing of the main north–south and east–west streets. Adjacent to the temple are the 30th dynasty Sphinx Gate and its flanking obelisks, excavated in the late 1930s (Roeder 1959). Part of the inner core of the east podium wall of a Roman temple also survives, built in the Corinthian order with plain red granite columns and limestone capitals, two of which lie close to their fallen columns; a third capital rolled to a stop within the jambs of the Sphinx Gate. The temple was about 28 by 12.3 metres with steps at the south end. It was hexastyle and peripteral, like so many temples in the eastern empire. The setting-out lines for the podium were cut into the pavement, and the podium engulfed the western obelisk of the Sphinx Gate and was thus at least 3.5 metres high. Such a high podium may point to this temple being the *capitolium* of the Roman city, for the state cult of Rome centred on Jupiter.

The *Komasterion*

We turn to what is perhaps the most interesting building surviving on the site: the *komasterion*, where sacred processions assembled. The building was some 40.66 metres wide and 31.5 metres long, without its steps. The podium at the front was about 2.6 metres high, with about seventeen steps projecting to the north. At the rear of the building, a similar limestone podium fronted Antinoe Street; this podium had only half a dozen steps, projecting into the street. To the west, most of the structure was supported by a series of vaulted brick piers running north and south, forming a cryptoporticus under much of the building. To the east, instead of the vaulting, the building was supported by the remains of the 30th dynasty enclosure wall of the Sacred Area, made of mud-brick that had been cut down and levelled off. A considerable number of red granite column shafts and their limestone bases and capitals were present, which, together with the foundation piers, show this remarkable building to be a basilica with no fewer than four aisles on each side of the main hall. It is unequalled and exemplifies the imagination that Roman architects brought to bear on their buildings.

The order is Corinthian and dates to the Antonine period, in the mid-second century CE. The red granite column shafts were ready-made at Aswan, hundreds of kilometres to the south. They vary remarkably in height, with the largest columns at the front and the rear of the building differing by up to half a metre and the seven smallest complete shafts by over 20 cm. The capitals and bases are of local limestone and were made on the spot, and these too are of various heights in order that the masons would, with much fudging, end up with a level entablature. When complete with bases and capitals, the large columns average 8.2 metres high and the small ones 6 metres.

If this structure is in fact the *komasterion*, it is situated in an ideal position for its role in processions. As late as the fourth century, a papyrus apparently from Hermopolis says that during the Sacred Month of Pharmuthi 'many processions take place without stop and in due order' (Rees 1964, no. 2), but the building may have become redundant with the rise of Christianity. Whether the *komasterion* was eventually used for some purpose other than as a procession house is impossible to say, but by the fifth century robbing of stone and brick had begun. Most of the columns of the *komasterion* probably still stood for a while after much of the walling and the steps were removed, but other buildings of second-century date were demolished to supply columns for the Great Basilica Church, built in the mid-fifth century.

To the north-east of the *komasterion* lay a large rectangular mud-brick structure, separated from the enclosure wall by a narrow passage. The structure measures 44 by 35 metres, and although very eroded, it survives at one point to a height of 6 metres. It had two storeys, and a series of chambers opens on each side of a central passageway extending from a stone porch on the west side. The chambers of the upper storey had windows, traces of which remain. This building may be a storehouse or treasury (*bastion*), and a Ptolemaic date is likely. The putative *bastion* and the *komasterion* fronted onto a large paved area, which is of Ptolemaic and Roman date and is made up of re-reused blocks from the Amarna era of the 18th dynasty.

The Great Tetrastylon

At the main city crossroads was a *tetrastylon*, one of three mentioned in the repair papyrus of Aurelius Appianus (see below), and from its prime position and the size of the few remains, it was very likely the one known as the Great Tetrastylon. Such structures consisted of honorific columns supporting bronze statues of emperors, placed at the four corners of street crossings. They are known from Antinoopolis, Oxyrhynchus, and elsewhere, including two within the late third-century Roman legionary fortress that enclosed the temple of Luxor (el-Saghir et al. 1986, pls 16–20).

According to Jomard's 1799 map of Hermopolis, a Greek inscription, now lost, was situated close to the point where the Sacred Way of Hermes is presumed to have crossed Antinoe Street. The inscription, which was nearly 4 metres high, was dedicated to Marcus Aurelius and Commodus, and must have been part of the pedestal of one of the columns of a *tetrastylon*. Close to the same crossing lies a sizeable Corinthian capital, of which only the lower part remains; it measures about 2.5 metres high and 3.5 metres across the top. If the lost inscribed pedestal belonged to a column with this size of capital, the height of the *tetrastylon* can be estimated to be about 26 metres, or as high as 29 metres. A column-drum noticed in 1987 and cleared in 1988 must also have come from this group of honorific columns. Both the large capital and the drum have Lewis holes for lifting them with a crane. If this estimated size is correct, the Great Tetrastylon at Hermopolis was not much smaller than the largest and best-known honorific column in Egypt, that of Diocletian at Alexandria ('Pompey's Pillar'; see Figs 7.3 and 7.4).

The Dromos of Hermes, Antinoe Street, and Aspects of the City

When Nectanebo I and his successors added to the Great Temple of Thoth, the Sacred Way may have run from the axis of the temple to the Sphinx Gate, passing through intermediate halls, courts, and the New Kingdom pylons, some of which may have already been demolished. But in 1982 the British Museum expedition found a paved road well to the east of this line, which is very likely to be the Dromos of Hermes, a stone-paved sacred way first mentioned in a papyrus of 89 BCE, leading to the Great Hermaion, as the Thoth temple was known in Ptolemaic and Roman times (Spencer 1989, pls 33, 92, 111). If projected south, this road passes along the western edge of the *komasterion* and the paved area in front of it, and crosses over Antinoe Street. To the north it passes along the eastern side of the Thoth temple, perhaps leading straight on to the north gate in the enclosure wall. The building of this road, perhaps in the Ptolemaic period, would have involved at minimum the destruction of the east side of the Ramesside pylon, from which the Amarna blocks in the paved area came. Thus, in the Roman period, Hermopolis had a sacred way passing the temple of Hermes Trismegistos ('Thoth the three-times-great') and the *komasterion*, fronting on a wide paved area, all very suitable for the formation of processions. Participants could enter the *komasterion* from the city through the south door, costume themselves and collect their equipment, and emerge from the north door onto the paved area. The Dromos of Hermes crossed the main east–west road (Antinoe Street) and continued southwards into the secular part of the city. Partly colonnaded and with shaded pavements, Antinoe Street passed across the rear of the *komasterion* and also along one side of a vast sacred area dating to Ptolemaic times.

Two main thoroughfares thus divided the city: the north–south Dromos of Hermes and the east–west Antinoe Street, which was possibly called Serapis Street prior to the foundation of Antinoopolis in 130 CE. It may have led westwards, ultimately to the Serapis temple at Tuna el-Gebel, the city's necropolis (see Chapter 13). It appears that in Ptolemaic times the area of the city enclosed by the 30th dynasty wall was known as the Citadel of the Great Hermaion, which, around 55 BCE, was also known as the King's Citadel. The term 'citadel' was used throughout the centuries of Roman rule for the area north of Antinoe Street, and by the middle of the first century CE, if not before, it was divided into two districts, the West Citadel quarter and the East Citadel quarter. A Jewish quarter is mentioned in a papyrus of the second century CE as being in the West Citadel quarter, but it may have been destroyed in one of the Jewish revolts. South of Antinoe Street were the two districts known as the West City quarter and the East City quarter. These four quarters are mentioned in papyri at least as late as the Arab conquest in the seventh century CE. It must be presumed that both the citadel quarters extended eastward and westward, spilling outside the enclosure wall, where domestic mounds still survive. While there must have been considerable tracts of housing within the enclosure wall, large parts of the Sacred Area were kept clear until the end of the fourth century for the benefit of the temples and their ceremonies. In the Christian period, houses, workshops, and churches were built all over the Sacred Area, burying the Thoth temple and a temple dedicated to Thoth's consort, Nehmetawy, probably erected in the 30th dynasty by Nectanebo I, but largely rebuilt by the Roman emperor Domitian.

No private house of the Roman period has been recorded archaeologically at Hermopolis Magna, although hundreds must have been cleared away by *sebakh* diggers, papyrus hunters, and excavators. We must imagine them to be like those excavated at Karanis, several with many storeys, the lower rooms often falling out of use with rising road levels (Husselman 1979). Four water towers have been identified, perhaps serving the four quarters of the city. Three of them were built on top of the enclosure wall to give them height; the fourth was high on the mound known as Kom el-Kenissa (the Mound of the Church).

A Roman Crane Operator

A metrical Greek epitaph of the early third century CE, from a tomb at the Tuna el-Gebel necropolis, offers a glimpse of how impressive the architecture of Hermopolis Magna was—and how it informed the identity of the city's residents. The epitaph takes the form of a dialogue between the tomb and a passer-by, and commemorates a crane operator named Harpalus, who helped erect the Antonine buildings in Hermopolis (Bailey 1996):

TOMB: I am the tomb of Harpalus.

PASSER-BY: Of which Harpalus?

TOMB: That Harpalus, you must know, who was highly skilled in the many arts of cunning wisdom.

PASSER-BY: I understand, you Fates: inventive Art is passed away.

TOMB: What other living man was like Harpalus? It was he who adorned the lofty walls of temples, supported colonnades with pillars as high as the roof, and oft-times led the crests of mountains with poles as thin as spills by persuasive force of slender ropes.

PASSER-BY: So once Amphion, so Orpheus by charm of their minstrelsy led rocks without effort.

TOMB: Achilles, too, son of Harpalus, lies here: a common urn hides the dust of both.

PASSER-BY: Nay, but I marvel not: the threads spun by the Fates are too strong, and against death the mightiest engine cannot prevail.

(Translation adapted from Skeat 1942)

The 'lofty walls' of Hermopolis were a point of personal as well as civic pride.

The 'Repair Papyrus' of Aurelius Appianus

A certain amount is known about the structures flanking Antinoe Street, from the Gate of the Sun at the east to the Gate of the Moon at the west. In a papyrus dating to about 263 CE, during the reign of Gallienus, a man named Aurelius Appianus reports to the senate of the Hermopolis on a series of buildings that were repaired at great cost (Wessely 1905, no. 127 (12565); Schmitz 1934; Kiessling 1971 = *SB* 10299). The buildings may have been damaged in 'the abominable riots' that had recently taken place, as another papyrus of the time put it (Bailey 1991: 56–9). These buildings included some of the structures mentioned above as well as two fountain houses. The fountain houses probably looked like the second-century CE examples at Dendara, where one is on each side of the sacred way outside the north gate of the temple of Hathor (Castel et al. 1984). The Aurelius Appianus repair papyrus comes from the archives of the senate, consisting of about 100 surviving documents from the third century CE. Several of these papyri detail public works, and this building activity has led some commentators to suggest that during Gallienus' reign there was a 'mania' for public works, despite the general impoverishment of the empire at this time. Most large-scale Roman construction of public buildings at Hermopolis took place during the reigns of Hadrian and Antoninus Pius in the second century CE, perhaps in conjunction with, or in response to, the construction of Antinoopolis nearby. At Hermopolis some of this building work may also have been necessary to replace buildings damaged or destroyed during the Jewish revolts of 115–18 and 132–5. Large sums were indeed spent during the reign of Gallienus, but they were used not for new structures, but to repair existing buildings, probably damaged during the anarchy of the time of Macrianus and Quietus (260–1).

Although many fine buildings in the central area of Hermopolis were robbed and destroyed in late Roman times, in particular as their use for pagan religious purposes declined, other public buildings continued to be built, this time for Christian worship. These include the Great Basilica Church (the cathedral of Hermopolis Magna; Wace et al. 1959) and the so-called South Church (Grossmann and Bailey 1994). Although the South Church had newly carved masonry, the Great Basilica Church mainly employed second-century CE and Ptolemaic era *spolia*. The Fatimid mosque of el-Ashmunein was also built with Roman *spolia*, on top of a church, and around it are scattered marble column shafts and capitals, which were imported into Egypt, perhaps from Constantinople.

The Great Basilica Church was constructed in the mid-fifth century, south-east of the crossing of Antinoe Street and the Sacred Way of Hermes. It uses an immense amount of second-century CE *spolia* and architectural elements from destroyed Ptolemaic temples of all three classical orders (Doric, Ionic, and Corinthian). A Doric frieze beneath the church has a dedication to Ptolemy III Euergetes and his queen, Berenike II, from a cavalry detachment stationed in Hermopolis. The Great Basilica Church itself may not have survived for more than a couple of hundred years. The excavators found many of its columns fallen southwards in orderly rows, caused by earthquake action. This same earthquake may have finally demolished the Sphinx Gate Temple and also what remained of the *komasterion*, many of whose columns fell neatly to the north at the front, and to the south across Antinoe Street at the rear. Pottery evidence suggests a date in the seventh or eighth century for the fall of these columns.

Reconstructing Hermopolis Magna

Can this archaeological and architectural evidence, together with information supplied by the many surviving papyri, give an idea of what the Roman city of Hermopolis Magna was like? The basic layout of the city has been known from ancient written documents since the early years of the last century, and information continues to be added. Many public buildings are mentioned by Aurelius Appianus as being repaired in 263. The papyrus is damaged and is ambiguous as to where these structures were placed; several commentators have attempted to work out their positions along Antinoe Street, but most were hampered by assuming erroneously that the enclosure wall running alongside Antinoe Street still survived to its full height, that the Sacred Way of Hermes ran through the Sphinx Gate, and that the agora was where it is now known that the Great Basilica Church and its underlying Ptolemaic temples still stood. Two of the structures mentioned by Aurelius Appianus can now be placed archaeologically: the *komasterion* (Procession House) and the Great Tetrastylon, the former having been partially built on the cut-down enclosure wall. The position of the eastern fountain house is also almost certain (Bailey 1991, pl. 109), and it is possible to reconstruct the centre of the city (Fig. 12.2). Although it is not possible to locate the marketplace (the 'agora', 'an excellent ornament of our city', as a mid-third-century senate document described it) with certainty, I believe it to have been in the West City quarter, within the south-west quadrant formed by the crossing of Antinoe Street and the Sacred Way of Hermes.

In the Roman period, probably to the end of the fourth century CE, the Sacred Area north of Antinoe Street contained the Great Hermaion, commenced in the New Kingdom; a temple of Thoth's consort, Nehemetawy, reconstructed by Domitian; the 19th dynasty Amun/Thoth temple; the temple by the Sphinx Gate; and the *komasterion*. Other public buildings known from the papyri and inscriptions, but unlocated (and not necessarily of classical

FIG. 12.2 Reconstruction of the centre of Hermopolis Magna in the Roman period
Drawing by Sue Bird (1991). Copyright Sue Bird and D. M. Bailey.

style) include a *makellon* (market building), baths and stoas, and temples of Apollo, Asklepios, Bast, the Dioskouroi, Serapis (apparently three, including that near the Temple of the Nile, and also the Great Serapis Temple in the gymnasium). The existence of a temple of Mithras can be inferred from a bull-slaying relief in Cairo. Another inference is a temple of Athena, since the *tetrastylon* of Athena was probably named after a nearby shrine. A temple of Isis might be expected, and one is mentioned in a second-century BCE papyrus; Roman period statues of priestesses in Berlin and Alexandria may be from this shrine or from a Serapis temple (see Bailey 1991: 59 nn. 75–6). Buildings devoted to the imperial cult are also known from the papyri.

Other public buildings include the Council House, council offices and a library, the Baths of Hadrian, and the gymnasium, all in one architectural complex that also contained the Great Temple of Serapis. Other baths, both public and private, are mentioned in the papyri. There was a triumphal arch, which may be the same as the 'tetrapylon of the town' mentioned in a Coptic life of Pamin, a Christian holy man. In later Roman times and well into the Arab period, many of the main public buildings were churches.

Because of the wholesale removal of the upper levels of much of the mound, the extent of the Arab occupation will never be determined: it seems very likely that by the eleventh century whole areas of the city were abandoned and it became not much more than a village situated where el-Ashmunein now stands. An earthquake during the seventh or eighth century must have accelerated its decline. The twelfth-century battle of el-Ashmunein, during the Crusades, probably took place in an almost wholly ruinous site, with a few columns of the Basilica Church still standing and, in the north, the pronaos of the Great Hermaion. Thereafter came the continual search for stone to burn for lime. After 5,000 years very little remains of the Pharaonic nome capital or of the Ptolemaic and Roman urban centre, described by its proud citizens in many surviving papyri by the fulsome formula 'The Great, Ancient, Illustrious and Most August City of Hermopolis'.

Oxyrhynchus

Oxyrhynchus was the nome capital (*metropolis*) of the nineteenth Upper Egyptian nome, in the Roman period referred to by its residents as the 'Glorious and Most Glorious City of the Oxyrhynchites'. The walled city lies on the left bank of the Bahr Yusuf, a branch of the Nile leading to the Fayum basin; the modern village of el-Bahnasa marks the ancient site, and there is a direct road west to the Bahariya Oasis. Much is known about the Roman city from the wealth of papyrus documents found in its rubbish heaps by the British papyrologists Bernard Grenfell and Arthur Hunt in the 1890s (Bowman et al. 2007; Rathbone 2007). The work of the Oxyrhynchus Papyri project is ongoing, and a number of writers have used the papyri to discuss the urban topography of the site (Rowlandson 1996: 1–26; Alston 2002; Bagnall and Rathbone 2004: 158–61; Parsons 2007: 46–60).

Classical Buildings

The Roman architecture of this *metropolis* can be retrieved through historic drawings and photographs and some extant remains. Vivant Denon, leader of the Napoleonic expedition, drew the city's remains during a visit in 1798 (British Museum 1936.1-9.33a–b, engraved in Denon 1802, pls 31.1–31.2). The drawings show a panoramic view of the village of el-Bahnasa, with minarets, domed saints' tombs, and the upper part of a Corinthian honorific column, complete with its statue base on top (Fig. 12.3). The lower part of this column still survives (Coles 2007, pl. 3; Parsons 2007, pl. 5). Scholars searching for papyri, like Grenfell and Hunt, did little to record archaeological finds or architecture, but other researchers have concentrated on the excavation of the city. These include the British archaeologist W. M. F. Petrie, who worked briefly on the cemeteries, colonnaded streets, and gigantic theatre, the largest surviving in North Africa (Petrie 1925: 12–16; Bailey 2007), and more recently the wide-ranging work of a Catalan–Egyptian mission (Padró 2007).

Various individuals and expeditions have attempted to map the city and the areas of their work, with different degrees of accuracy (Petrie 1925, pls 38–9; Bowman et al. 1983, p. ix; 2007, pl. 5; Thomas 2000, fig. 60; Bagnall and Rathbone 2004: 158; Coles 2007: 12, figs 1, 8; Padró 2007: 131, 137). Surviving features noted on the ground include the edifices excavated by Petrie and the east gate, topped by the spectacular minaret of the Zain el-'Abidin mosque (Fig. 12.4; see Padró 2007, pls 19–21). Padró's map suggests locations for the hippodrome, the north-west gate, the theatre, colonnades, a Doric peristyle, and the honorific column drawn by Denon, which may be a surviving column of the *tetrastylon* of Thoeris. Denon himself remarked on the *spolia* at the site, including numerous columns in different varieties of marble, possibly imported to Egypt (Denon 1803: 157). In addition, the papyri mention many structures that cannot be located with certainty: a *kapitoleion*, a *caesareum*, a *sebasteion*, a *hadrianeion*, and many other named temples, a *praetorion*, a *palation*, a *komasterion* (perhaps), a *nympheion*, a gymnasium, a *makellon*, a bouleuterion, baths, libraries, various stoas, a nilometer, and an area known as the Jewish quarter (Łukaszewicz 1986).

FIG. 12.3 Drawings of el-Bahnasa and the site of Oxyrhynchus, 1798, by Vivant Denon

British Museum, Department of Prints and Drawings, 1836.1-9.33a–b. Photo: Catherine Johns, courtesy of the Trustees of the British Museum.

Herakleopolis Magna

The *metropolis* of the twentieth Upper Egyptian nome is at Ehnasiya el-Medina, situated on the east bank of the Bahr Yusuf. The city received its Greek name from the equation of the local ram-headed god Herishef with the hero Herakles. Despite stone-robbing activity, and the presence of two saltpetre factories in the nineteenth century, the surviving ancient mounds are still of considerable height and width (see the plans drawn by Adolf Erman: Naville 1894, pl. 13; and by Ulrich Wilcken and Heinrich Schäfer: Petrie 1905, pl. 45). There are considerable remains in Egyptian style of the temple of the local god, largely built by Ramesses II. Other temples, edifices, and tombs abound (Aufrère and Golvin 1997: 206–9).

Herakleopolis Magna is a typical example of a nome capital where, although almost certainly once present, classical architecture has largely vanished, probably before the visit of the Napoleonic expedition at the end of the eighteenth century. Jomard does not mention

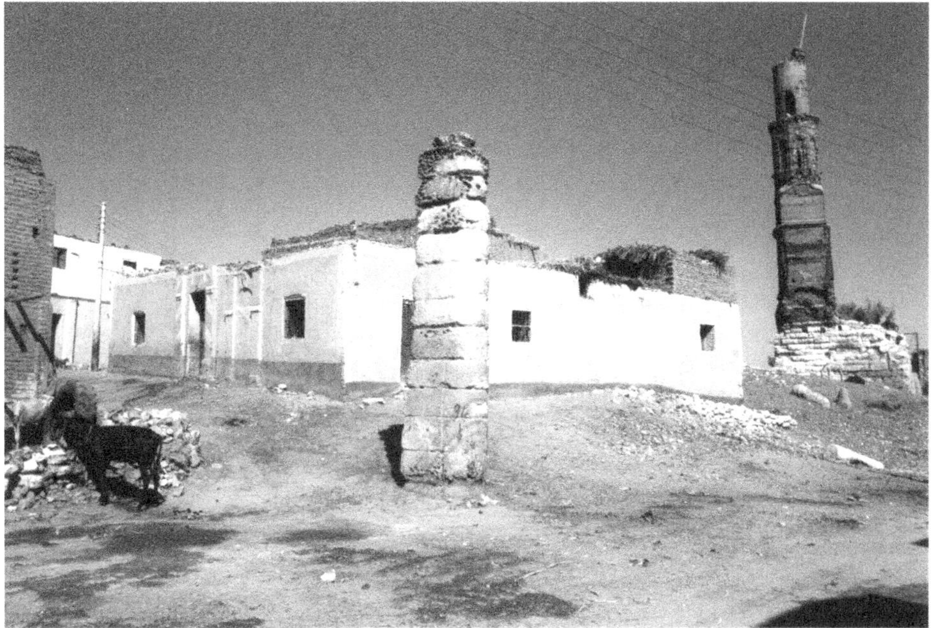

FIG. 12.4 Doric peristyle and eastern gateway of Oxyrhynchus

Author's photograph.

any classical architecture in the text of the *Description de l'Égypte* aside from granite columns near Beni-Suif, which may have been Egyptian or Greek (1821: 403–12). However, classical architecture does remain on the surface at Herakleopolis, in the form of a large area of collapsed masonry where four large columns stand in line amid many fallen fragments and Corinthian capitals, all carved with much effort from Aswan red granite (Fig. 12.5). Although marked in the plans mentioned above as 'Kenisseh', or 'Church', this group of structures dates to the second century (reign of Hadrian or Antoninus Pius) and was once a splendid mass of public buildings, rather than a church. Excavating for the Egypt Exploration Fund, Naville likewise dismissed the suggestion of a church, proposing instead that the remains belonged to a Roman temple (Naville 1894: 32). Fine Roman stonework also survives from the gate of the city's south wall, hinting at the kind of monumental classical architecture that once featured at Herakleopolis Magna (Padró 1999: 304, pl. 4). Similarly, papyri mention a bath building, gymnasium, theatre, *palaestra*, and stoas, which may suggest that the city had a grid layout with a *cardo* and *decumanus*, as we have seen from the other Middle Egyptian nome capitals considered in this chapter (Łukaszewicz 1986).

CONCLUSION

In the major towns and cities of Roman Egypt, classical architecture coexisted with pharaonic features, with the exception of the new foundation of Antinoopolis. Papyrological evidence augments archaeological work, of which too little was recorded in the early days of fieldwork,

FIG. 12.5 Red granite columns at Herakleopolis Magna, photographed in 1996

Author's photograph.

making records like the *Description* an invaluable source as well. What survives at different sites suggests that the urban environments shared many similarities in terms of city layout and types of building, in keeping with the widespread use of classical architecture in the Roman Near East and the relationship between architectural projects, building types, and the social and political infrastructure of the Roman empire.

Suggested Reading

Judith McKenzie's study of architecture in Alexandria and Egypt, covering the period from 300 BCE to 700CE, includes a chapter on classical architecture outside Alexandria, richly illustrated by drawings, photographs, plans, and reconstructions (McKenzie 2007: 151–72). In addition, Bagnall and Rathbone (2004) offers a brief overview of archaeological sites, including town and city remains, while Alston (2002) presents the urban environment of Roman Egypt in a broader social and economic context. For detailed architectural studies of buildings at Hermopolis Magna, see Bailey (1990, 1991), and at Oxyrhynchus, Bailey (2007). Peter Parsons (2007) has written an enjoyable book on the town of Oxyrhynchus, which presents a lively account based on the rich evidence of the town's papyri.

Bibliography

Alston, R. 2002. *The City in Roman and Byzantine Egypt*. London: Routledge.

Arnold, D. 1994. 'Zur Rekonstruktion des Pronaos von Hermopolis', *Mitteilungen des Deutschen Archäologischen Instituts, Abteilung Kairo* 50: 13–22.

—— 1999. *Temples of the Last Pharaohs*. New York: Oxford University Press.

Aubert, M.-F., et al. 2008. *Portrait funéraires de l'Égypte romaine: Cartonnage, linceuls et bois*. Paris: Musée du Louvre and Institut Khéops.

Aufrère, S., and J.-C. Golvin. 1997. *L'Égypte restituée*, vol. 3. Paris: Errance.

Bagnall, R. S. 1993. *Egypt in Late Antiquity*. Princeton: Princeton University Press.

—— and D. W. Rathbone (eds) 2004. *Egypt, from Alexander to the Copts: An Archaeological and Historical Guide*. London: British Museum Press.

Bailey, D. M. 1990. 'Classical Architecture in Roman Egypt', in M. Henig (ed.), *Architecture and Architectural Sculpture in the Roman Empire*. Oxford: Oxford University Committee for Archaeology, 121–37.

—— 1991. *Hermopolis Magna: Buildings of the Roman Period*. London: British Museum Press.

—— 1996. 'Honorific Columns, Cranes, and the Tuna Epitaph', in Bailey (ed.), *Archaeological Research in Roman Egypt, Journal of Roman Archaeology*, suppl. ser. 19: 167–8.

—— 2007. 'The Great Theatre', in A. K. Bowman et al. (eds), *Oxyrhynchus: A City and its Texts*. London: Egypt Exploration Society, 70–90.

Bowman, A. K., and D. W. Rathbone. 1992. 'Cities and Administration in Roman Egypt', *Journal of Roman Studies* 82: 107–27.

—— et al. (eds) 1983. *The Oxyrhynchus Papyri*, vol. 50. London: Egypt Exploration Society.

—— et al. (eds) 2007. *Oxyrhynchus: A City and its Texts*. London: Egypt Exploration Society.

Calament, F. 2005. *La révélation d'Antinoé par Albert Gayet: Histoire, archéologie, muséographie*. Cairo: Institut Française d'Archéologie Orientale.

Castel, G., et al. 1984. *Dendara: Les fontaines de la porte nord*. Cairo: Institut Français d'Archéologie Orientale.

Coles, R. A. 2007. 'Oxyrhynchus: A City and its Texts', in A. K. Bowman et al. (eds), *Oxyrhynchus: A City and its Texts*. London: Egypt Exploration Society, 3–16.

Denon, D. V. 1802. *Voyage dans la basse et la Haute Égypte*. Paris: Institut Français d'Archéologie Orientale.

—— 1803. *Travels in Upper and Lower Egypt*. London: Langman.

Description de l'Égypte. 1821 [etc.]. Plates, various edns, incl. 1809. Paris: Imprimerie Impériale. Texts, 2nd edn, IV. Paris: Panckoucke, 1821.

el-Saghir, M., et al. 1986. *Le camp romain de Louqsor*. Cairo: Institut Français d'Archéologie Orientale.

Grossmann, P., and D. M. Bailey. 1994. 'The South Church at Hermopolis Magna (Ashmunein): A Preliminary Account', in K. Painter (ed.), *'Churches Built in Ancient Times': Recent Studies in Early Christian Archaeology*. London: Society of Antiquaries, 49–71.

Husselman, E. M. 1979. *Karanis: Topography and Architecture*. Ann Arbor: University of Michigan Press.

Kiessling, E. 1971. *Sammelbuch griechischer Urkunden aus Ägypten*, vol. 10. Wiesbaden: Harrassowitz.

Łukaszewicz, A. 1986. *Les edifices publiques dans les villes de l'Égypte romaine: Problèmes administratifs et financiers*. Warsaw: University of Warsaw Press.
McKenzie, J. 2007. *The Architecture of Alexandria and Egypt, c.300 BCE–CE 700*. New Haven: Yale University Press.
Manfredi, M., and A. Pericoli. 1998–9. *Carta di Antinoupolis*. Florence: Istituto Papirologico G. Vitelli.
Naville, E. 1894. *Ahnas el Medineh (Heracleopolis Magna)*. London: Egypt Exploration Fund.
Padró, J. 1999. *Études historico-archéologiques sur Héracléopolis Magna: La nécropole de la muraille méridionale*. Barcelona: University of Barcelona.
—— 2007. 'Recent Archaeological Work', in A. K. Bowman et al. (eds), *Oxyrhynchus: A City and its Texts*. London: Egypt Exploration Society, 129–38.
Parsons, P. 2007. *City of the Sharp-Nosed Fish: Greek Lives in Roman Egypt*. London: Weidenfeld and Nicolson.
Pensabene, P. 1993. *Elementi architettonici di Alessandria e di altri siti egiziani*. Rome: 'L'Erma' di Bretschneider.
Petrie, W. M. F. 1905. *Ehnasya 1904*. London: Egypt Exploration Fund.
—— 1925. *Tombs of the Courtiers and Oxyrhynchus*. London: British School of Archaeology in Egypt.
Pintaudi, R. 2007. 'The Italian Excavations', in A. K. Bowman et al. (eds), *Oxyrhynchus: A City and its Texts*. London: Egypt Exploration Society, 104–8.
—— (ed.) 2008. *Antinoupolis* I. Florence: Istituto Papirologico G. Vitelli.
Rathbone, D. W. 2007. 'Grenfell and Hunt in Oxyrhynchus and in the Fayum', in P. Spencer (ed.), *The Egypt Exploration Society: The Early Years*. London: Egypt Exploration Society, 199–229.
Rees, B. R. 1964. *Papyri from Hermopolis*. London: Egypt Exploration Society.
Roeder, G. (ed.) 1959. *Hermopolis 1929–1939*. Hildesheim: Gebrüder Gerstenberg.
Rowlandson, J. 1996. *Landowners and Tenants in Roman Egypt*. Oxford: Clarendon Press.
Schmitz, H. 1934. 'Die Bau-Urkunde in P. Vindob. Gr. 12565 im Lichte der Ergebnisse der deutschen Hermopolis-Expedition [= *SB* 10299]', in W. Otto and L. Wenger (eds), *Papyri und Altertumswissenschaft: Vorträge des 3. Internationalen Papyrologentages in München vom 4. bis 7. September 1933*. Munich: Beck, 406–28.
Skeat, T. C. 1942. 'An Epitaph from Hermopolis', *Journal of Egyptian Archaeology* 68: 68–9.
Snape, S., and D. M. Bailey. 1988. *British Museum Expedition to Middle Egypt: The Great Portico at Hermopolis Magna: Present State and Past Prospects*, Occasional Paper 63. London: British Museum Press.
Spencer, A. J. 1984. *The Topography of the Site*. London: British Museum Press.
—— 1989. *The Temple Area*. London: British Museum Press.
—— 1993. *The Town*. London: British Museum Press.
Thomas, T. K. 2000. *Late Antique Egyptian Funerary Sculpture*. Princeton: Princeton University Press.
Tomber, R. 2008. *Indo-Roman Trade: From Pots to Pepper*. London: Duckworth.
Wace, A. J. B., et al. 1959. *Hermopolis Magna, Ashmunein: The Ptolemaic Sanctuary and the Basilica*. Alexandria: Alexandria University Press.
Wessely, C. 1905. *Corpus Papyrorum Hermopolitanorum* I. Leipzig: Eduard Avenarius.

CHAPTER 13

CITY OF THE DEAD
Tuna el-Gebel[*]

KATJA LEMBKE

The History of Excavations and Exploration at Tuna el-Gebel

Although many of the unprovenanced funerary masks housed in museums worldwide were probably found at Tuna el-Gebel in the nineteenth century (Grimm 1974: 33), archaeological exploration of the site only officially began at the beginning of the twentieth century. After a first season led by Gombert from the Institut Français d'Archéologie Orientale in 1902–3 (Griffith 1902–3), a survey for the Deutsche Orient-Gesellschaft by Walter Honroth followed in 1913 (Borchardt 1913; Grimm 1975; Lembke et al. 2007: 75–80). In only ten days of exploratory excavation, he found different types of tomb dating from the Roman period. Most important was the discovery of several house-tombs with painted decoration consisting of up to four floors. In 1919 the tomb of Petosiris was found, excavated, and reconstructed over the course of two years (Lefebvre 1924).

From 1931 to 1952 Sami Gabra, professor at Cairo University, excavated at Tuna el-Gebel. In his first years he concentrated his investigations on the necropolis south of the tomb of Petosiris, while in the 1940s he started to explore the underground galleries full of animal burials (Gabra 1932, 1971; Gabra et al. 1941; Gabra and Drioton 1954). Further excavations were carried out by Alexander Badawy from 1949 (Badawy 1956, 1958, 1960). They focused on the temple of Thoth (?) with a *saqiya* in its second court and on the south-eastern area of the necropolis, discovering among other things the now destroyed Graffiti Chapel.

In the 1970s two German teams started to work at Tuna el-Gebel. While Dieter Kessler from Munich University explored the northern sector, concentrating on the underground

[*] The author is grateful for financial support for the survey of the Graeco-Roman necropolis granted by the Deutsche Forschungsgemeinschaft. I thank Ulrike Fauerbach (DAI Cairo) for providing information about the architecture of T 1/CP and T 4/SS. Special acknowledgements for their cooperation go to the Faculties of Architecture and of Land Surveying at Cottbus University and to the Faculty of Geophysics at Kiel University.

FIG. 13.1 General plan of the site Tuna el-Gebel

By C. Wilkening, T. Meyer, R. Haberland, and A. Druszynski-von Boetticher. Copyright Brandenburg Technical University Cottbus.

galleries and their structures above ground, the team of Grimm, Krause, and Sabottka from Trier University surveyed the southern sector with the necropolis around the tomb of Petosiris. The results of this project have remained unpublished. Since 2005 another German team, from the Roemer- und Pelizaeus-Museum, Hildesheim, guided by me, has continued the work of Trier University (Lembke et al. 2007; Helmbold-Doyé 2010; Lembke 2010a).

Thanks to the assistance of land surveyors and architects from Cottbus University and geophysicists from Kiel University, the team has been able to map the entire site, including the unexcavated areas and a detailed plan of the architectural development (Fig. 13.1).

The Site

The site of Tuna el-Gebel is situated in Middle Egypt about 270 km south of Cairo and 10 km west of the ancient *metropolis* of Hermopolis Magna, as the crow flies. The main structures include a large sacred area of the god Thoth, dating from the Late period at the latest. It flourished under the Ptolemies and was still functioning in the Roman period. Apart from temple structures above ground, it consists of a wide system of underground galleries where animals of different kinds were buried (Kessler and Nur el-Din 2002, 2005; Driesch et al. 2005). According to Kessler, there were at least two sanctuaries: a temple of Osiris the Baboon in the north and a temple of Serapis in the south (Kessler 1990). The latter was excavated by Badawy, who also explored a large *saqiya* in the second court of the sanctuary (Badawy 1956). According to his interpretation, the sacred area was used as a holy zoo for breeding animals, especially ibises, the sacred bird of Thoth. Another temple, still unexplored, lies on the edge of the western mountain on a cliff overlooking the site of Tuna el-Gebel.

Next to these sacred places a large cemetery is situated in the southern area. It consists of temple-like tombs built of local stone and house-like tombs built of mud-brick. Tomb pits and pillars contain further burials. A balustrade was constructed at its western side to divide the cemetery from the holy temple precinct with the *saqiya* (Fig. 13.2).

A recent geomagnetic survey by the Institute of Geophysics of Kiel University has provided new information about the area (see Fig. 13.1). While in the northern sector two broad streets with several small by-roads lead from the Nile Valley to the sanctuary of Thoth and its underground galleries, the southern sector, the so-called necropolis of Petosiris, is situated south of a processional way leading to the temple with the *saqiya* (Lembke 2010a, pl. 27). The survey came to the conclusion that only about 10 per cent of the area has been excavated and that the unexplored area of the necropolis measures about 400–500 m^2. It is therefore the largest Graeco-Roman necropolis in Egypt known so far.

The Necropolis of Tuna el-Gebel before Roman Rule

The first monumental tombs were built around 300 BCE by the high priests of Thoth. The most famous and best-preserved tomb belongs to Petosiris, a *lesonis* (the Egyptian *mr-sn* priest) of Thoth (Lefebvre 1924). Approximately of the same date is the tomb of his brother Djed-Thoth-iu-ef-ankh about 200 metres north of the tomb of Petosiris (Sabottka 1983). Also of an early Ptolemaic date, according to the architecture and the inscriptions, is the tomb of another priest called Padikam (Gabra et al. 1941: 11–37). They are all built of local shell limestone and

FIG. 13.2 Plan of the excavated area of the necropolis of Tuna el-Gebel

By C. Wilkening, T. Meyer, R. Haberland, and A. Druszynski-von Boetticher. Copyright Brandenburg Technical University Cottbus.

have a temple-like structure. Whereas the tomb of Djed-Thoth-iu-ef-ankh consisted in its first phase of one room with a small anteroom only (Sabottka 1983: 147–50), the tombs of Petosiris and Padikam have a short dromos leading to a T-shaped building with a wide hall at the front and an almost quadrangular main room. Other new features are the altars in front of the entrance; these places of worship seem to be a Greek interpretation of Egyptian offering tables (see below). The burials were laid in underground rooms accessible only by deep shafts (Lefebvre 1924, 17–21 and pl. 2; Gabra et al. 1941, pl. 5). All these buildings were at least partially decorated with reliefs and painted in vivid colours (Lefebvre 1924; Gabra and Drioton 1954, pl. 1). As Lefebvre realized, Petosiris was venerated during the third and second centuries BCE as a 'wise man among wise men' (Lefebvre 1924: 21–5), and it was probably in this period that the tomb was given a balustrade-like fence to divide this holy place from other tombs around it.

After the initial period of building single 'temple-tombs' like these, the cemetery was enlarged, and over the centuries it came to resemble a proper town: main streets led from the eastern fertile land into the western necropolis, while the streets from north to south were narrow and often closed off afterwards by new buildings. In general, however, we observe a more or less orthogonal structure in the layout of the area (see Fig. 13.2).

Considering the difference in building techniques, it seems probable that there was a considerable gap between the first buildings of the early Ptolemaic period and the later Ptolemaic and Roman stone tombs. First, the later constructions consist of smaller stones; therefore, construction ramps were not needed any more. Secondly, the first tombs were built with monumental stones and no mortar at the joints, while a reddish mortar was used excessively for the later stone buildings. Thirdly, the façades and walls of the later buildings were not cleaned and decorated with reliefs, but were left intentionally unfinished with bosses. Only the temple of Renenutet at Medinet Madi shows the same features in the Ptolemaic period (Arnold 1999: 160, fig. 106). It will be an aim of further investigations to understand the significance of this change; for instance, whether it had technical or religious implications. The later stone tombs also had a different layout. Instead of a T-shape, they consisted of two small rooms forming a rectangular outline. The architectural decoration with Egyptian-style capitals or cornices was limited to the façades, but in general this type was still a copy of temples. Another interesting feature is the reduction of the columnar hall to screen walls and the wall of the first room to one level (Gabra et al. 1941, pl. 19; Lembke 2010a, fig. 8). The burials were placed either in deep shafts, as in the early Ptolemaic tombs, or in pits below the floor.

According to Gabra, the tombs built of local nummulitic limestone belonged to the Ptolemaic period, while the tombs built of mud-brick were not earlier than the Roman period (Gabra and Drioton 1954: 13). Recent investigations, however, have shown that this theory is only partly true: there are certainly tombs built of stone belonging to the Roman period, and it is also possible that the first mud-brick tombs were already built during the reign of the Ptolemies (Lembke et al. 2007: 80–1, fig. 7). Unfortunately, the documentation of the earlier excavations does not usually make it possible to fix the date of the constructions. Furthermore, the temple-tombs were reused, with the result that inscriptions of the Roman period were found in Ptolemaic buildings. For example, the epitaph on a large marble slab honouring a certain Marcus Aurelius Ammonius, a Hermopolitan athlete, was found in a mud-brick wall of the tomb of Djed-Thoth-iu-ef-ankh, according to Gabra's unpublished documentation (no. 1545 from March 1945; cf. Bernand 1999: 138–43, no. 49, with incorrect provenance). Although the inscription dates from the beginning of the third century CE, the temple-tomb was certainly constructed in the Ptolemaic period; the slab, therefore, documents a reuse of the monument in the Roman period. As a consequence, the only clues to the period of construction of the uninscribed temple-tombs are architectural ornaments like lily capitals, which probably date to the second or first century BCE (e.g. temple-tombs T 1/CP and T 4/SS).

The Development of the Urban Structure in the Early Roman Period

The early Roman period, if not before, saw the building of the first mud-brick tombs at the site. The change of building technique may have been combined with a change of religious thought, since the Egyptians traditionally preferred stone for tombs, associating mud-brick with domestic architecture. Although this material had found its way into cemeteries before, for instance in the pyramid chapels at New Kingdom Deir el-Medina and the above-ground structures in the Theban Asasif in the Late period, the decorations of the tombs at Tuna el-Gebel combined mud-brick architecture with a more house-like character, which led Gabra to term them 'houses' (French: *maisons*). With the exception of house-tomb M 21/SE (see below), the tombs have either two rooms like most of the late stone temple-tombs or, at a later date, only one room.

As a result of the new building technique, the urbanization of the cemetery increased and more and more people were buried there. Instead of stone monuments for a single person of high social rank, the mud-brick buildings now offered a cheaper (and faster) alternative, with burial space for multiple individuals. The use of different building material therefore had not only a religious significance but also a social one. As a consequence, the necropolis developed in a city-like structure from north to south, with the tomb of Petosiris at its core.

In the Roman period three different types of tomb were used: stone 'temples', 'houses' of mud-brick, and tomb pillars built of stone or mud-brick. In addition, there are buildings in a mixed technique, built of stone in combination with mud-brick (e.g. M 11/SS, in Fig. 13.6). There is little information to date the later stone tombs precisely to either the late Ptolemaic or early Roman period, as discussed above. However, temple-tombs T 12/SE and T 5/SS are typically Roman constructions, although they are quite different. At first glance, T 12/SE is a copy of a Roman podium temple with a columnar hall at the front, an anteroom, and a cella (Fig. 13.3; see Gabra et al. 1941: 65–6, pl. 29). An unusual feature is the crypt in the podium. Although Gabra and, more recently, Naerebout both interpreted the building as a real temple because of its similarity to Roman places of worship (Gabra et al. 1941: 65–6; Naerebout 2007: 512, 526), it seems more reasonable to assume that this type, represented so far by the Ptolemaic building T 1/CP and the Roman 'temple' T 12/SE, ultimately has an Egyptian origin. It was probably modelled on the Ptolemaic temple for Opet at Karnak, begun under Nectanebo I, continued under Ptolemy III, and finished under Ptolemy VIII (Arnold 1999: 164–6, 197, figs 110–11). According to this example, the crypt of T 12/SE may be interpreted as the crypt of Osiris in a primordial hill. This idea also fits perfectly with the identification of the dead person as Osiris.

In contrast, T 5/SS consists of one room only, built against the eastern wall of T 4/SS (Fig. 13.4; see Gabra et al. 1941: 60–3, pls 24 and 26; Lembke 2010a: 248–9). As it was also built on a podium, we may conclude that T 5/SS is of a considerably later date than its neighbour. Furthermore, the façade of T 5/SS shows architectural ornaments in the Graeco-Roman style, like an Ionian door

FIG. 13.3 Temple-tombs T 12/SE (left), T 11/SE (behind T 12), and T 10/SE (right) at Tuna el-Gebel

Photo: Sami Gabra, courtesy of Günter Grimm, Trier University.

frame or Corinthian capitals, while the earlier temples followed the Egyptian style. Even more interesting is the decoration inside, where we find a burial enclosure decorated with an Egyptian-style relief showing the procession of several Egyptian gods towards Osiris (Fig. 13.5). As the smaller frieze in the upper register shows strong similarities to the decoration of the early Roman house-tomb M 21 (discussed below), this stone temple certainly is of a later date and was probably built around 100 CE. Another interesting feature in this tomb are two small niches in the interior western wall (Lembke 2010a, fig. 16). As they were originally closed by slabs, they can be interpreted as *loculi*, but their meaning remains uncertain. Either they were containers for canopic jars, which were rarely used during the Roman period, or else they contained cinerary urns, which would appear to be the more likely explanation. It cannot be excluded that the Greek custom of cremation was in use at Tuna el-Gebel during the Roman period, and there is other evidence from the site in support of this view, including objects that may be interpreted as urns and recesses in the interior of tomb pillars that are too small to contain mummies (Lembke 2010a, fig. 15).

Beginning in the early Roman period, mud-brick buildings became more and more numerous in the necropolis, and the interior as well as the façades of the tombs were plastered and painted. The earliest decorated example known so far is house-tomb M 21/SE (Gabra et al. 1941: 39–50, pls 8–17). Its ground-plan, with three rooms across a transverse front and a quadrangular burial room behind, is strongly related to the early Ptolemaic stone tombs like those of Petosiris or Padikam. Since the transverse hall of the tomb of Petosiris was transformed into three rooms at the end of the Ptolemaic period (Lefebvre 1924: 25–7), it seems possible that the architecture of M 21/SE was based on this model. As in the Ptolemaic buildings, the burials were placed in a deep shaft situated in the middle of the burial chamber. Furthermore, the anteroom and the burial chamber were richly decorated with paintings. Like the transverse hall in the tomb of Petosiris, the anteroom seems to communicate

FIG. 13.4 Façade of temple-tombs T 4/SS (right) and T 5/SS (left) at Tuna el-Gebel

DAI Cairo, negative F 9976. Photo: Dieter Johannes, courtesy of Deutsche Archäologisches Institut, Cairo.

FIG. 13.5 Relief on the tomb enclosure of temple-tomb T 5/SS at Tuna el-Gebel

Drawing from the papers of Sami Gabra, courtesy of Günter Grimm, Trier University.

in its decoration between this world and the next, while the scenes of the second room centre on illustrations from the Book of the Dead (Lembke forthcoming).

As a third alternative besides temple-tombs and house-tombs, pillars of different sizes were constructed with either stone or mud-brick. Although all known examples date to the Roman period, an earlier appearance cannot be excluded. Three types of pillar have been differentiated so far. The first one is built like a monumental stone sarcophagus, for one body only. A row of these tombs is situated along the balustrade that divides the necropolis from the sacred area associated with Thoth to the west, while others were placed near the main streets (Bernand 1999: 149, no. 59, pl. 27; Lembke 2010a, fig. 10). The second type is a high pillar made of mud-brick, also used for one burial only (Lembke 2010a, fig. 9). Because of their small dimensions it seems most probable that this type contained urns instead of mummies. Moreover, an inscription on one of these pillars refers to the burial of a 'sweet-smelling deceased', where the passer-by is not bothered by 'the stench of unpleasant cedar resin' (Bernand 1969: 377–86, no. 97; 1999: 160–2, no. 71), emphasizing the fact that the body of the dead person was not mummified. In addition, the inscriptions indicate that only boys or unmarried young men who died before their parents were buried in these pillars (Bernand 1999, nos 71, 72, 75, 76, 80).

The third type of tomb pillar is a temple-like stone construction with one small room and a pyramidal roof. While two of these pillars are situated near the tomb of Petosiris, an intact example was recently excavated in the northern area near the tomb of Djed-Thoth-iu-ef-ankh, containing the burials of five people and two animals (Kessler and Brose 2008;

FIG. 13.6 One of the main streets at Tuna el-Gebel, with tombs T 9/SE (pillar) and M 11/SS (building in the foreground)

DAI Cairo, negative F 9972. Photo: Dieter Johannes, courtesy of Deutsche Archäologisches Institut, Cairo.

Flossmann and Schütze 2010). In spite of its small dimensions, it was obviously a group burial, perhaps a family tomb, dating to the second century CE. Its construction technique resembles the late temple-tombs, while the wooden beds on which the mummies were placed copy the *klinai* in the house-tombs of the high Imperial period. All three types of tomb pillar are generally placed along the main east–west streets in the necropolis. The second type, the high pillars consisting of mud-brick, were usually surrounded by a small open court (Bernand 1999, pls 29 and 34). There is some overlap between types of pillar and buildings, too. For instance, structure T 9/SE is more like a tomb pillar of the third type than a temple-tomb (Fig. 13.6). Instead of a pyramidal roof, it has a classical façade and a small, niche-like cella on a podium that opens to the street. There was probably a statue inside the cella, an arrangement shown in the graffiti sketches in house-tombs M 1/CP and M 13/SS (Gabra et al. 1941: 68, 91). The dead bodies were placed in the podium of this structure, as in the case of temple-tomb T 12/SE discussed above.

To sum up, the early Roman period saw increasing building activity at Tuna el-Gebel. The use of mud-brick, rather than more expensive and time-consuming stone, enabled a larger community to build tombs that were then plastered and in some cases also decorated with paintings. Hieroglyphs were still common in this period, as the inscriptions in the house-tombs M 18/CP and M 21/SE illustrate. The burials were placed in deep shafts as in the early Ptolemaic period, or in pits below the floor. Nevertheless, we may also assume that the Greek custom of cremation was practised at Tuna el-Gebel at the end of the first century CE. In this period we observe an increasing use of classical iconography as well. The changing character of the cemetery's art and architecture points to the changing identity of the Graeco-Egyptian population and their interest in using both classical and Egyptian forms of cultural expression, especially in the wake of the Roman administration's status reforms (see Chapter 15).

The Tombs of the Second and Third Centuries CE

In addition to the horizontal expansion of the necropolis, we can also observe a vertical extension of the buildings, since most of the mud-brick 'houses' were constructed with more than one storey. It is obvious that the upper floors were not usually planned when the ground floor was built, because there are only a few houses with an internal staircase on the ground floor (Badawy 1958). To reach the upper floor, an external staircase was generally built against the façade instead. This staircase rests on a vault that framed the entrance to the ground floor while allowing access to the upper storey (Fig. 13.7). Later walls built against the sand around the ground-floor entrances demonstrate that cultic worship in the older parts of the tombs continued.

Some houses have an internal staircase on the first floor. In these cases, either the roof was in use as a terrace or a second floor was already planned when the first one was added. Honroth has documented at least one tomb with four storeys (Grimm 1975; Lembke et al. 2007: 75–80), but the state of preservation does not allow the reconstruction of the upper parts of most houses. The sequence of construction of the house-tombs suggests that the necropolis expanded from north to south in this period. For instance, house-tomb M 13/SS certainly

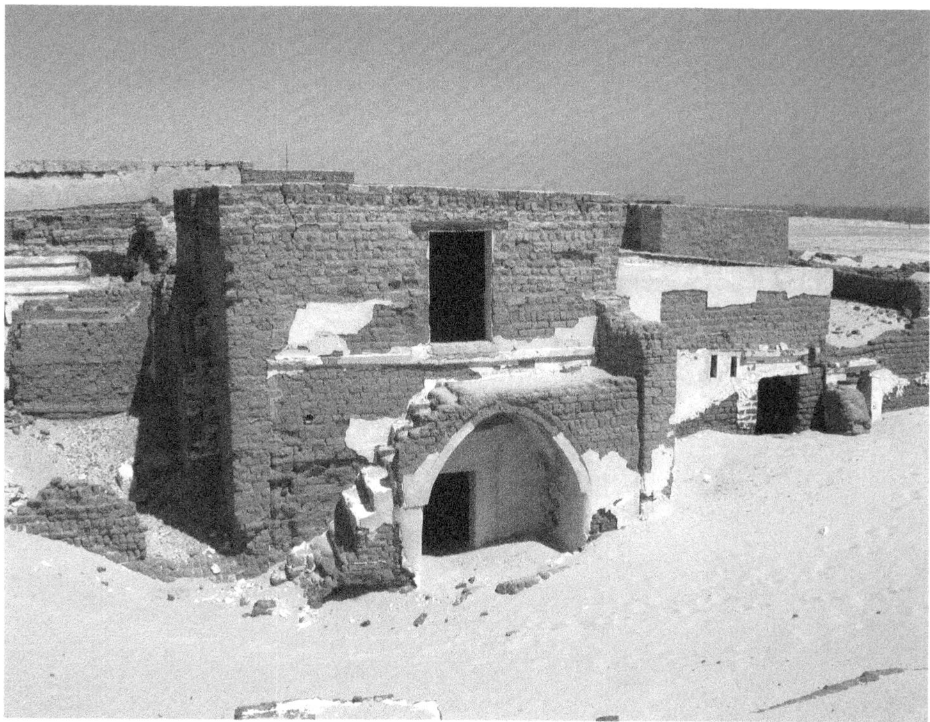

FIG. 13.7 Façade of house-tomb M 12/SS at Tuna el-Gebel

Author's photograph.

dates no earlier than the second century and is situated south of M 18/CP, M 20/SE, and M 21/SE, which had already been constructed and decorated in the first century.

On the upper floors of house-tombs, it was not usually possible to bury the dead in deep shafts or in pits below the floor, as on the ground floor. In a handful of cases, such as M 3/SS and M 22/SS, open spaces behind the tomb were used to enlarge the upper floor with an alcove where burials were placed, as if it were a shaft. Generally, however, brick walls were built at the back of the second room of the upper storey as an enclosure for burials. The walls were plastered and painted to imitate a *kline* with legs and a mattress. As holes in the walls indicate, this enclosure was covered by a wooden construction resembling an actual bed or couch (Fig. 13.8). Above this *kline* a baldachin was erected. The back wall was either decorated with paintings or had a shell sculpted in plasterwork. In some cases, mummies were found lying on the *kline* instead of inside the enclosure (M 1/CP and M 10; Lembke 2007: 31, fig. 6). As the Terenouthis funerary stelae demonstrate, placing the dead on the *kline* allowed them to take part simultaneously in an eternal *symposion* banquet and an eternal *prothesis*, the laying out of the dead for mourning (Lembke 2010b). During the third century CE, the situation altered somewhat, so that instead of *klinai* built of mud-brick, wooden beds were placed against the back wall. They were put under baldachin-like constructions as in M 5/SS (Fig. 13.9) or in arcosolia as in M 9/SE (Lembke et al. 2007: 86, fig. 17).

FIG. 13.8 House-tomb M 3/SS at Tuna el-Gebel: main burial

Author's photograph.

In summary, in the stone 'temples' as well as in the tomb-houses, we observe a more frequent tendency not to cover the mummies in shafts, but to present them openly on *klinai*. Like the tombs made of mud-brick, this aspect does not fit with the Egyptian idea of hiding and preserving the body for eternity. It indicates, on the contrary, an increasing influence of Roman ideas on Egyptian funerary habits.

The Development of the Decoration from Ptolemaic to Roman Times

When the tomb of Petosiris was published in 1923 and 1924 (Lefebvre 1924), it was not only the quality of the reliefs and the perfect preservation of the colours that attracted attention, but also the unusual combination of Greek and Egyptian iconography in different styles. Indeed, it was most surprising to find this unique mixture already at the beginning of the Ptolemaic period. Further excavations by Gabra and others brought to light more examples of this type of decoration, especially the reliefs from the tombs of Djed-Thoth-iu-ef-ankh and Padikam (Gabra and Drioton 1954, pl. 1). The reliefs suggest a school of artists well versed in the Egyptian representational system, but also influenced by the Greek imagery that circulated in the cosmopolitan environment of a city like Memphis, where similar works have

FIG. 13.9 House-tomb M 5/SE at Tuna el-Gebel: main burial

Author's photograph.

been described as being in the 'neo-Memphite' style. These richly decorated tombs are among the earliest at Tuna el-Gebel, dating to the early Ptolemaic period, but during the middle and probably also the late Ptolemaic period, reliefs or paintings went out of fashion and ornaments were restricted to architectural features like capitals, windows, or cornices. These later temple-tombs were intentionally left unfinished.

At the end of the Ptolemaic period or the beginning of the Roman period, decorated tombs appeared again, though instead of reliefs sculpted in stone, the mud-brick houses had plastered and painted interiors as well as façades. The earliest examples are the house-tombs M 21/SE, M 18/CP, and M 20/SE. In M 21/SE, decorated at the beginning of the first century CE, paintings appear in the entrance room and in the main room with the burial shaft (Riggs 2005: 129–39; Lembke forthcoming). The first room shows two mourning women on the entrance wall (Gabra et al. 1941, pl. 10 *bis*), and the other walls are arranged in two Egyptian registers over a dado of imitation stone orthostats. The paintings depict the purification of the dead girl or woman and a procession of gods and goddesses, which culminates in the presentation of the deceased to the other world (Gabra et al. 1941, pls 10–14, 15.1). On the entrance wall of the main room, which has only one, larger-scale register of decoration, Nephthys and Isis appear next to Nekhbet and Buto (Gabra et al. 1941, pls 15.2 and 16.1), while on the opposite, southern wall is the traditional scene of Anubis attending a mummy, accompanied by Isis and Nephthys (Gabra et al. 1941, pl. 17.1). The eastern wall of this room is decorated with a representation of chapter 16 from the Book of the Dead (Gabra et al. 1941, pl. 17.2), and on the western wall is an extraordinary representation of the goddess Nut seated on the ground, weeping over a mummy, which rests on her legs (Gabra et al. 1941, pl. 16). The Horus-falcon, grasping a feather, hovers protectively over the body, and Anubis, with Isis and Nephthys, offers a libation. Only in the entrance room, which is a threshold between two worlds, is the naturalistic style of Greek art present, in the equally liminal representations of the mourning women and the deceased being purified by Horus and Thoth (Riggs 2005: 129–39; Lembke forthcoming).

In later tombs, such Egyptian-themed decoration became rare, with only single scenes or motifs rather than larger compositions with a narrative structure. In M 18/CP, for example, the gods Nephthys, Osiris, and Isis appear without any context (Gabra and Drioton 1954, pl. 13), and in M 20/SE a falcon protects a mummy on a bier (Gabra et al. 1941, pl. 48). Furthermore, hieroglyphs were hardly used: only M 21/SE and M 18/CP have columns expressing Egyptian names and epithets. Demotic, which was not normally used in tomb decoration, does appear in a partly preserved column bearing the name of the deceased in M21/SE (Riggs 2005: 130–1), and in a few graffiti in M 21/SE (Gabra et al. 1941: 47) and M 22/SS (unpublished), but otherwise, Greek is the best-attested language among inscriptions at the site.

Around 100 CE the temple-tomb T 5/SS was built in the southern area of the necropolis (Lembke and Wilkening-Aumann forthcoming). This building is extraordinary because of its Greek façade combined with an Egyptian-style interior (see Fig. 13.4). In the single chamber we find a burial enclosure with the Egyptian gods Horus, Anubis, Isis, Shu, Tefnut, Khnum, and Neith in a procession towards Osiris, who is accompanied by Nephthys (see Fig. 13.5). Three aspects are remarkable in this relief: first, the absence of the local god Thoth in the procession; secondly, the absence of the tomb owner as adorant in front of Osiris; and thirdly, the inclusion of Shu, Tefnut, Khnum, and Neith in addition to the usual gods of the underworld. Above this scene is another, smaller register outlined in red and left unfinished. Here a person is shown in the same kneeling position as the figure presenting Maat to Osiris in the main room of the earlier house-tomb M 21/SE (Gabra et al. 1941, pl. 17.2). It seems quite probable that the artist who executed the relief in T 5/SS knew the older representation and copied it, which suggests that tombs continued to be accessible. Unlike the decoration in M 21/SE, however, the columns next to the gods in T 5/SS do not contain inscriptions, and the few signs in the upper register indicate the writer's uncertainty with the Egyptian script.

As Egyptian paintings fell out of fashion, the tombs of the second and third centuries CE began to favour classical iconography. The ground floor of M 12/SS, for example, has paintings in a floral design originally combined with a vintaging and erotic scene that is now lost (Gabra and Drioton 1954, pl. 12), while M 13/SS is richly decorated with stucco and paintings in Roman style (Lembke et al. 2007: 83, fig. 15). The close similarity to architectural ornaments from Hermopolis and the chapel in the temple of Tutu in Dakhla Oasis fix the date of this decoration at the beginning of the second century. In the second century we also find the first painted decoration on the first floors of house-tombs, including M 1/CP, M 2/SS, and shortly afterwards in M 3/SS (see Fig. 13.8). None of the upper storeys bear Egyptian decoration; instead we find painted orthostats imitating rare and costly materials like alabaster or porphyry in the first room (Gabra and Drioton 1954, pls 4, 21–2), while the second room has a richly decorated *kline* for the main burial (see above). The stone imitations certainly reflect the decoration in well-appointed houses at Hermopolis and are related to Roman paintings in the northern Mediterranean. Furthermore, classical myths like the story of Oedipus, the

Trojan horse, the Oresteia, or the rape of Persephone are well represented (Gabra and Drioton 1954, pls 14–16). These legends compare to painted decoration and mosaics in villas, thus displaying the knowledge and culture of the tomb owner, while the rape of Persephone is especially suited to a funerary context; similar scenes appear on Roman sarcophagi and in the Kom el-Shuqafa catacomb in Alexandria (see Chapter 7). Garlands painted in several house-tombs reflect the flowers used during the burial itself and may illustrate, like the *kline*, the eternal *prothesis* of the dead (Gabra and Drioton 1954, pls 3, 6, 11, 18; Lembke 2010b).

Burial Ceremonies and Visitors at the Tomb

Like the Asasif tombs of the Late period at Thebes, the tombs at Tuna el-Gebel show the continuing practice of venerating the dead. Although we have little information about the burials themselves and the objects found with them, the house-tombs were probably built not for one person only, although they had a main burial place. At least some of them were occupied by females, e.g. in M 1/CP, M 21/SE, and possibly in M 2/SS and the second floor of M 20/SE (Lembke et al. 2007: 110–11), but archaeological remains and inscriptions also clearly indicate the presence of male burials in these tombs, specifically in the first room of M 1/CP (Gabra 1932: 66), or in a niche of M 3/SS (Graindor 1932: 112–15; Bernand 1969: 109–15, no. 21; 1999: 165–6, no. 74). Therefore, it seems evident that these tombs were built as collective burial places, quite possibly for families. In addition, the stone tombs of the Ptolemaic period were reused in Roman times, and some of the mud-brick tombs were reused over time as well. These mass graves may have lost their familial association, or the deposit of bodies may have been decided by necropolis workers and priests (Lembke et al. 2007: 110).

Finds of kitchen pottery, amphoras, and fireplaces outside the tombs suggest that families met at the tomb not only to bury the deceased, but also to hold annual feasts in honour of their ancestors, up until the late Roman period (Lembke et al. 2007: 97–103; Helmbold-Doyé 2010: 134–5). Altars for food and drink offerings, placed opposite the entrances of the tombs, are a common feature at Tuna el-Gebel since the early Ptolemaic period and seem to have been adopted from Greek practice; several *thymiateria* (incense burners) and miniature altars were found inside the tombs as well (Helmbold-Doyé 2010: 142–3). Nevertheless, Egyptian offering tables at the site indicate that offerings could be made in the traditional manner as well. Other objects were not used for the funerary service of the families, but belonged to the burials themselves. Sarcophagi of clay or wood, wooden beds and boxes, *shabti* (mummiform servant) figures of faience or clay, different kinds of glass vessel like unguentaria, mummy masks, and coins to pay the ferryman, Charon, are typical tomb equipment or gifts for the deceased (Helmbold-Doyé 2010: 135–42). The lack of documented excavations makes it difficult to understand if the objects found in the tombs belonged to the original owners or to secondary burials. Furthermore, during the recent geomagnetic survey approximately thirty kilns for glass production were located (Helmbold-Doyé 2010: 146–7); further investigations will analyse whether the production was reserved for funerary use only or if at least some of the ovens were also used to meet a market beyond the necropolis.

Conclusion

Archaeological remains as well as inscriptions clearly indicate that Tuna el-Gebel was the cemetery of a thriving metropolis during the Roman period. Originating by the early Ptolemaic period, it developed from an exclusive place for burials of high priests of Thoth to a common burial place for the Hermopolitan elite, with its peak in the second and third centuries CE. Mass graves of a later period lead to the conclusion that in late antiquity poorer people were also buried there. Although some of the objects found in the Tuna el-Gebel necropolis, especially the pottery, were produced in late antiquity (Lembke et al. 2007: 79–80; Helmbold-Doyé 2010: 133–5), no specific traces of Christian belief appear at the site. At the latest, the use of the pagan necropolis came to an end during the fourth or fifth centuries CE, no doubt related to the spread of Christianity.

Suggested Reading

Although Tuna el-Gebel is the largest known cemetery of the Graeco-Roman period, it is still under-represented in larger studies. Bagnall and Rathbone (2004) provides a short introduction, while Riggs (2005: 129–39) considers house-tomb M 21/SE. Lembke (2010a) presents an overview of the history of the necropolis in the light of new fieldwork results. Since the excavations and surveys were conducted by Egyptian, French, and German teams, the primary publications are not in English but in other languages. Among them the books by Gabra et al. (1941) and Gabra and Drioton (1954) are fundamental reports on the excavations conducted since the 1930s by Cairo University. Grimm (1975) presents the German excavation in 1913, and Lembke et al. (2007) reports on the first results of the Hildesheim Museum project, started in 2004. Considering the so-called temple-tombs, the study of Pensabene (1993) offers an important insight into the development of specific architectural features, especially in relation to the city of Hermopolis. In two extensive studies, Bernand (1969, 1999) published the corpus of Greek inscriptions from Tuna el-Gebel, with French translations and commentaries.

Bibliography

Arnold, D. 1999. *Temples of the Last Pharaohs*. New York: Oxford University Press.

Badawy, A. 1956. 'Le grand temple greco-romain à Hermoupolis Ouest', *Chronique d'Égypte* 62: 257–66.

——1958. 'The Cemetery at Hermoupolis West: A Fortnight of Excavation', *Archaeology* 11: 117–22.

——1960. 'Une campagne de fouilles dans la nécropole d'Hermoupolis-Ouest', *Revue Archéologique* 1: 91–101.

Bagnall, R. S., and D. W. Rathbone (eds) 2004. *Egypt from Alexander to the Copts: An Archaeological and Historical Guide*. London: British Museum Press.

Bernand, É. 1969. *Inscriptions métriques de 1'Égypte greco-romaine: Recherches sur la poésie épigrammatique des Grecs en Égypte*. Paris: Belles Lettres.

—— 1999. *Inscriptions grecques d'Hermoupolis Magna et de sa nécropole*. Cairo: Institut Français d'Archéologie Orientale.

Borchardt, L. 1913. 'Ausgrabungen in Tell el-Amarna 1912/13: Vorläufiger Bericht', *Mitteilungen der Deutschen Orient-Gesellschaft zu Berlin* 52: 51–5.

Driesch, A. von den, et al. 2005. 'Mummified, Deified and Buried at Hermopolis Magna: The Sacred Birds from Tuna el-Gebel, Middle Egypt', *Egypt and the Levant* 15: 203–44.

Flossmann, M., and A. Schütze. 2010. 'Ein römerzeitliches Pyramidengrab und seine Ausstattung in Tuna el-Gebel: Ein Vorbericht zu den Grabungskampagnen 2007 und 2008', in K. Lembke, M. Minas-Nerpel, and S. Pfeiffer (eds), *Tradition and Transformation: Egypt under Roman Rule*. Leiden: Brill, 79–110.

Gabra, S. 1932. 'Rapport préliminaire sur les fouilles de l'Université Égyptienne à Touna (Hermopolis Ouest)', *Annales du Service des Antiquités de l'Égypte* 32: 56–77.

—— 1971. *Chez les derniers adorateurs du Trismegiste: La nécropole d'Hermopolis—Touna el-Gebel*. Cairo: al-Hayah al-Misriyah al-<ayn>Ammah.

—— and É. Drioton. 1954. *Peintures à fresques et scènes peintes à Hermoupolis-Ouest (Touna el-Gebel)*. Cairo: Institut Français d'Archéologie Orientale.

—— et al. 1941. *Rapport sur les fouilles d'Hermoupolis Ouest (Touna al Gebel)*. Cairo: Institut Français d'Archéologie Orientale.

Graindor, P. 1932. 'Inscriptions de la nécropole de Touna el-Gebel (Hermopolis)', *Bulletin de l'Institut Français d'Archéologie Orientale* 32: 97–119.

Griffith, F. L. 1902–3. 'Progress of Egyptology, A: Archaeology, Hieroglyphic Studies, etc.', *Archaeological Reports* 10–37.

Grimm, G. 1974. *Die römischen Mumienmasken aus Ägypten*. Wiesbaden: Harrassowitz.

—— 1975. 'Tuna el-Gebel 1913–1973: Eine Grabung des deutschen Architekten W. Honroth und neuere Untersuchungen in Hermopolis-West (Tanis Superior)', *Mitteilungen des Deutschen Archäologischen Instituts, Abteilung Kairo* 31: 221–36.

Helmbold-Doyé, J. 2010. 'Tuna el-Gebel: Fundgruppen, Werkplätze und Öfen: Ein Zwischenbericht', in K. Lembke, M. Minas-Nerpel, and S. Pfeiffer (eds), *Tradition and Transformation: Egypt under Roman Rule*. Leiden: Brill, 133–48.

Kessler, D. 1990. 'Der Serapeumsbezirk und das Serapeum von Tuna el-Gebel', in R. Schulz and M. Görg (eds), *Lingua Restituta Orientalis: Festgabe für Julius Assfalg*. Wiesbaden: Harrassowitz, 183–9.

—— and P. Brose. 2008. *Ägyptens letzte Pyramide: Das Grab des Seuta(s) in Tuna el-Gebel*. Haar: Brose.

—— and M. Abd el-Halim Nur el-Din. 2002. 'Inside the Ibis Galleries of Tuna el-Gebel', *Egyptian Archaeology* 20: 36–8.

———— 2005. 'Tuna al-Gebel: Millions of Ibises and Other Animals', in S. Ikram (ed.), *Divine Creatures: Animal Mummies in Ancient Egypt*. Cairo: American University in Cairo Press, 120–63.

Lefebvre, G. 1924. *Le tombeau de Petosiris* I–III. Cairo: Institut Français d'Archéologie Orientale.

Lembke, K. 2007. 'Tod und Bestattung im kaiserzeitlichen Ägypten', in G. Brands and A. Preiss (eds), *Verborgene Zierde: Spätantike und islamische Textilien aus Ägypten in Halle*. Leipzig: Scan Color, 24–33.

—— 2010a. 'The Petosiris-Necropolis of Tuna el-Gebel', in K. Lembke, M. Minas-Nerpel, and S. Pfeiffer (eds), *Tradition and Transformation: Egypt under Roman Rule*. Leiden: Brill, 231–54.

Lembke, K. 2010b. 'Terenuthis and Elsewhere: The Archaeology of Eating, Drinking and Dying in Ptolemaic and Roman Egypt', in D. Robinson and A. Wilson (eds), *Alexandria and the North-Western Delta*. Oxford: Oxbow, 259–67.

—— Forthcoming. 'Das Grab des Siamun in der Oase Siwa', *Mitteilungen des Deutsches Archäologisches Instituts, Abteilung Kairo*.

—— C. Fluck, and G. Vittmann. 2004. *Ägyptens späte Blüte: Die Römer am Nil*. Mainz: von Zabern.

—— M. Minas-Nerpel, and S. Pfeiffer (eds) 2010. *Tradition and Transformation: Egypt under Roman Rule*. Leiden: Brill.

—— et al. 2007. 'Vorbericht über den Survey in der Petosiris-Nekropole von Hermupolis/ Tuna el-Gebel (Mittelägypten)', *Archäologischer Anzeiger*, 71–127.

—— and C. Wilkening-Aumann. Forthcoming. 'Egyptian in Disguise: Ein römisches Tempelgrab in Tuna el-Gebel', in M.G. Witkowski (ed.), *Études et Travaux*.

Naerebout, F. G. 2007. 'The Temple at Ras el-Soda: Is it an Isis Temple? Is it Greek, Roman, Egyptian, or Neither? And So What?', in L. Bricault, M. J. Versluys, and P. G. P. Meyboom (eds), *Nile into Tiber: Egypt in the Roman World*. Leiden: Brill, 506–54.

Pensabene, P. 1993. *Elementi architettonici di Alessandria e di altri siti egiziani*, vol. 3: *Repertorio d'Arte dell'Egitto greco-romano C*. Rome: 'L'Erma' di Bretschneider.

Riggs, C. 2005. *The Beautiful Burial in Roman Egypt: Art, Identity, and Funerary Religion*. Oxford: Oxford University Press.

Sabottka, M. 1983. 'Tuna el-Gebel, Grab des Djed-Thot-jw-ef-ankh: Vorbericht', *Annales du Service des Antiquités de l'Égypte* 69: 147–51.

CHAPTER 14

THE UNIVERSITY OF MICHIGAN EXCAVATION OF KARANIS (1924–1935)

*Images from the Kelsey Museum Photographic Archives**

T. G. WILFONG

THE 1924–35 University of Michigan excavation of the Fayum site of Karanis (modern Kom Aushim) was neither the first nor the last archaeological project there, but remains the most extensive investigation of the site to date. The material from the Michigan Karanis excavation is an extraordinarily rich resource for the study of life in Roman Egypt, but its sheer volume proved a mixed blessing to the excavators both during and after the project. It is clear that the excavators were entirely unprepared for the amounts and kinds of artefacts they would find and the amount of data they would have to record. Earlier reports had suggested that Kom Aushim was a largely exhausted site in terms of finds and, although the Michigan team approached the excavation with optimism, the results of the first season of 1924–5 greatly taxed the resources of the excavation team as well as the support staff back in Michigan. When artefacts and archival records began to reach Ann Arbor after the initial division of finds, the need for facilities in which to house, store, conserve, study, and display the material from Karanis became acute. This led to the establishment of a permanent museum in Newberry Hall on the University of Michigan campus, what is now the Kelsey Museum of Archaeology, where the Karanis artefacts and archival records are housed to this day (excepting the papyri, which were either returned to Cairo or transferred to the University Library to form part of what is now the library's Papyrology Collection).

* This chapter would not have been possible without the efforts of Sebastián Encina, Kelsey Museum Coordinator of Museum Collections, whose photographic expertise, archival knowledge, and generosity with his time and efforts were crucial to this work. I also thank Michelle Fontenot, Kelsey Museum Collections Manager, for her help, and Robin Meador-Woodruff, former Kelsey Museum Curator of Photographs, who was my initial guide to the Karanis archival material when I first came to the Kelsey Museum. This chapter is dedicated to the memory of my dear friend and colleague Traianos Gagos, with whom I had so many discussions about the Karanis material.

Although ambitious plans for the publication of the Michigan Karanis excavation existed from the beginning, the amount of the material from the site and the complexities of its interpretation, combined with financial constraints and changing priorities at the University of Michigan in the 1930s, worked against the projected large-scale publication of the results of the excavation. Volumes publishing the architecture and topography of the site, a series of corpora of artefact types, and several volumes of papyri from the excavation have appeared over the years (see the bibliography in Gazda and Wilfong 2004: 47–50), but much remains to be done in terms of publication of artefacts, as well as large-scale interpretation of the archaeology of the site.

This chapter is an attempt to present a small sampling of unpublished material from the Kelsey Museum archives relating to the Michigan excavation of Karanis and its finds in the form of a photographic essay. The images it offers consist of field photography of the site as well as staged photographs of artefacts. Most of the latter were made for the purposes of the division of finds, intended for the extensive 'Division Albums' that remain such an important resource for the study of the Karanis material, documenting as they do the artefacts that came to Michigan, as well as those that stayed in Egypt, in something close to their original condition at discovery. The photographs were chosen for what they illustrate about daily life at Karanis and also for what they show of the processes and challenges of the archaeological excavation of the site.

The majority of the photographs from the Michigan Karanis excavation were taken by the project photographer George R. Swain, who had a long history of archaeological field photography for Francis W. Kelsey and his successors. Many of the uncredited photographs are likely to be by Swain as well. Photographs from the 1926–7 season, including a number of general views of the site (one of which is reproduced as Fig. 14.1), were taken by J. Anthony

FIG. 14.1 A view from the east over the central area excavated by the *sebakhin*

Photo: J. Anthony Chubb.

Chubb, the British artist and photographer attached to the Karanis project for the 1926–7 season (his name incorrectly given as 'D. Anthony Chubb' in the site report Boak 1933).

The twenty photographs presented here are a small fraction of the nearly 8,000 archival images from the Karanis excavation currently in the Kelsey Museum archives, themselves a subset of even more extensive archival materials including notes, plans, indexes, and maps. The 2009 opening of the William Upjohn wing of the Kelsey Museum of Archaeology has permitted a greatly expanded permanent installation of artefacts from the Karanis excavation, as well as improved storage, conservation, and study facilities for artefacts and archival material. In addition, initiatives are currently under way to make the archival material from the Karanis excavation freely available electronically, allowing researchers all over the world a chance to explore and study this unparalleled archive.

The site of Karanis as seen by the Michigan excavators in the earliest stages of the project was literally shaped by the activities of the *sebakhin*, local farmers who dug through ruins for *sebakh*, a combination of deteriorating organic material and mud-brick, gathered and used for fertilizer. Fayum sites such as Karanis were particularly rich fields for *sebakh* digging, and resulted in substantial destruction of Graeco-Roman remains in the nineteenth century (Cuvigny 2009: 34–5). Thus, the site of Karanis itself had already had several sections carved out of it by the activities of the *sebakhin*, as documented in Figure 14.2, and seen in the frequent legend 'destroyed by the *sebakhin*' found throughout the Karanis excavation maps. Unfortunately, *sebakh* digging was most extensive at some of the oldest areas of the site and also in the areas where non-residential buildings might have been expected, potentially skewing the results of the Michigan excavation as well as those of subsequent projects on the site. Most of the southern half of the town was destroyed, as was a substantial section of the centre. The view in Fig. 14.1 from 1926–7 gives a sense of the destruction caused by the *sebakhin*, but also shows the still-extensive remains that survived for excavation (itself an often destructive process).

Sebakh digging not only affected the site of Karanis as initially seen by the excavators, but also remained an ongoing threat in the years of the excavation. There was little active regulation of the activities of the *sebakhin*, and the Michigan excavators periodically had to deal with destruction of the very site they were trying to excavate. The *sebakh* digging cut through the mud-brick structures on the site without regard for architecture or plans, and sometimes even provided neat cross-sections of complex structures, as in the photograph in Fig. 14.2 from the 1929 season. The structure here, designated X100, shows the typical architecture of the multi-storey Karanis houses. Only a few finds, mostly papyri and ostraca, were recorded from this otherwise unplanned building. For the excavators, such structures illustrated the ongoing dangers of unrestricted *sebakh* digging on the site: although interesting to look at as a sectional view, much valuable information was lost. The 1928–31 seasons in particular saw extensive *sebakh* digging activity; the numerous finds from these seasons designated X (for surface find) or SG (for 'summer guards') were mostly material churned up during the destruction of the site while the Michigan team was away—in some cases very valuable material, but deprived of its context. Finally, in 1931, near the end of active excavation by the Michigan team, a Department of Antiquities rule was instituted whereby *sebakh* could only be dug in areas designated by excavators (Boak 1933: 54–5), a move that helped bring the destruction of the site under control, although coming almost too late to help the Michigan team.

The published photographs from the Michigan Karanis excavation tend to concentrate on the site as a pristine, uninhabited landscape, a sort of ghost town from which living humans

FIG. 14.2 Cross-section of the walls of X100 in the path of the *sebakhin*

Photo: George R. Swain.

have largely been excluded. Aside from the rare presence of a worker for scale, living people do not appear in the published images. The unpublished images in the photographic archives from the excavation, though, reveal many 'action' shots of the excavation, with the site full of workers digging and carrying dirt and debris to be sieved and discarded. Although photographs of workers on the excavation can be problematic (some appear staged, and all underline the issues inherent in the relationships between foreign archaeologists and the local inhabitants who work for them), such representations are invaluable for showing Karanis as an inhabited landscape. At a minimum, these peopled images can give useful impressions of the spatial relationships of the built town and its inhabitants. Thus, the photograph in Fig. 14.3 of the street designated CS46 shows how the space might have functioned in this narrow side street on a busy day.

Just as the published excavation photographs tend to show Karanis as an uninhabited space, they also tend to show to show the site as pristine, in terms of being unmarked by the processes of excavation. But the excavators did, in fact, literally mark up the site, as seen in the photograph in Fig. 14.4 of part of house 5002, in which structure number and room letter designation ('A') are marked on the mud-brick wall in white paint. Such marks were used partly for the excavators on the ground, in terms of keeping track of structures as excavated. But the markings were also used for their visibility in the photographs, to allow quick identification of the structures in images. The absence of such markings in the published images was accomplished partly by creative cropping, but also by retouching of photographs or even (in some cases) negatives.

FIG. 14.3 A view looking north along Street CS46

Photo: George R. Swain.

FIG. 14.4 Part of house 5002 after excavation

Photo: George R. Swain.

FIG. 14.5 A view looking west over the roofing covering B109A-D, on top of C57

Photo: George R. Swain.

The photograph in Fig. 14.5 is an excavation view, showing the complex interrelationships of Karanis structures and the levels assigned to them by excavators. The mud-brick roofing of B109 is shown here in the process of dismantling as the excavators go down further into the underlying structure C57, with walls of structures C50, C51, and C53 already visible. Photographs such as this one give a much more immediate understanding of the closeness and interconnected nature of the built environment at Karanis than do the maps and plans of the site. Such photographs also highlight the problems the excavators faced in assigning discrete 'layers' to a site where occupation was continuous and where stages in the use of structures overlapped in ways hard to separate out systematically. The excavators assigned dates to the layers they identified based mostly on datable coins and papyri found in these layers, but this system did not take into account how such dated material might shift and move over time, or explain wide date ranges within individual structures and even rooms. It is becoming increasingly clear now (and was already hinted at by the original excavators themselves) that both the assignment of structures and elements to layers and the dates accordingly assigned to them require substantial revision and even rethinking.

FIG. 14.6 Part of mummified crocodile in inner sanctuary of Northern Temple
Photo: George R. Swain.

The site of Karanis is anchored by its two surviving temples: the well-documented southern temple of Pnepheros and Petesouchos and the more enigmatic North Temple. Both were planned and excavated by the Michigan team, which made many discoveries in connection with both temples. The photograph in Fig. 14.6 is the only specific record of crocodile mummies at the site of the North Temple at Karanis, a partial crocodile mummy found inside the inner sanctuary of the temple. Although the excavators noted the discovery of 'a number of crocodile mummies' to the south-west of the temple, below the original ground level, these are otherwise unrecorded in the excavation records. The excavators further declared these mummies as unrelated to the cult of the North Temple, having been found at a level well below it, and suggested that they may instead have been connected with the earlier temple of Pnepheros and Petesouchos to the south (Boak 1933: 13). But the existence of this photograph and its attestation of a crocodile mummy within the North Temple sanctuary suggest that these mummies may indeed be connected with the North Temple itself. The find of crocodile mummies beneath the level of the North Temple may well imply the existence of a subterranean crypt for the interment of such mummies, not an uncommon feature of animal cults in Graeco-Roman Egypt.

FIG. 14.7 January 2, 1930. A view looking northwest at the gateway to T4
Photo: George R. Swain.

Fig 14.7 gives an alternative view to the well-known picture of the entrance to the 'Banquet Hall' (*deipneterion*) built under Vespasian to serve the temple of Pnepheros and Petesouchos (the 'South Temple') at Karanis. The most frequently published view of this gateway shows it head-on, with little relationship to surrounding structures; the present view shows the gateway more in its context (and also gives a much better sense of its thickness and monumentality).

The temple of Pnepheros and Petesouchos was home to the cult of these two crocodile gods and served as the main cult centre at Karanis after its initial foundation under Nero

FIG. 14.8 Rolls of papyrus as found in the threshold of doorway between rooms D and E of 5026

Photo: George R. Swain.

in 59/60 CE. The stone temple was surrounded by related mud-brick structures that show activity into the third century CE, after which the temple is presumed to have been abandoned.

Fig. 14.8 is an alternative view of the well-known image (Negative 5.1800) of the 1925 find of a group of early second-century CE papyri in a door threshold of structure 5026 at Karanis (see Cuvigny 2009: 38–9 for the other image and brief discussion). In spite of the thousands of papyri discovered during the excavations, *in situ* photographs of papyrus finds are rare in the Karanis archival material. In large part, this is because the majority of papyri were not found in such specific circumstances or in such good condition: most papyri at Karanis were fragmentary and found in room debris rather than in deliberately cached deposits. The archaeological context of papyri at Karanis, though, is extremely important in a number of respects. Dated or datable papyri have been crucial for establishing dates of structures and layers, although such information needs to be used with caution. Spatial relationships between the find spots of papyri and other artefacts, or between different papyri as in Fig.14.9 found in the same room or structure, can be used to establish connections that might not otherwise be made.

FIG. 14.9 Division of Papyrus. 1927 papyri

Photo: uncredited.

Pre-conservation photographs of papyri from the Michigan Karanis excavations from the Division Albums show the original condition of recently discovered papyri, as in Fig. 14.9. Although many well-preserved and complete sheets and rolls of papyrus were found at Karanis, the majority of papyri from the site looked more like the documents in this photograph, one of many recording papyri from the division of finds. Crumbling, fragmentary papyri painstakingly gathered from debris in rooms and streets make up the majority of papyrus finds at Karanis, and the role and importance of the papyrus conservator cannot be underestimated.

The well-known black basalt statue of a priest from the Michigan Karanis excavation is seen in Fig. 14.10 in an unpublished Division Album photograph, apparently soon after discovery in 1928 and before the statue was fully cleaned. This statue is one of the most important pieces of art from the Karanis excavation: a late first-century CE example of an Egyptian-style figure of some significance. Similar figures are known from other Fayum sites, including another very striking parallel from Soknopaiou Nesos, although not from the Michigan excavation there (Bianchi 1992: 18–19, and see also Lembke 1998). These figures represent an important phase in the last manifestations of indigenous Egyptian style in sculpture.

Aside from this figure, practically none of the published material from the Michigan excavation of Karanis reflects indigenous Egyptian culture, and this could be taken as an indication that very little such material existed at Karanis in the first place. In fact, the situation is more complicated; texts in hieroglyphs, hieratic, Demotic, and Coptic survive from Karanis, including unpublished material from the Michigan excavation, and some indigenous-style images do exist from the site. More common, though, are representations that combine Egyptian and Graeco-Roman styles and visual vocabularies: statues, terracottas, murals, and other images that show how indigenous culture manifested and transformed itself in the Roman period.

FIG. 14.10 Semi-profile view of black statue of priest

Photo: George R. Swain.

Several wall paintings were found during the Michigan Karanis excavations; the mural images of Heron, Isis and Harpocrates, Harpocrates and a sphinx, and a possible Mithraic sacrifice scene have been published and are well known (Boak and Peterson 1931: 32–4). The photograph in Fig. 14.11 shows an unpublished mural from House 5046, Room A, *in situ*: a complex scene spread across two adjacent walls that shows a range of standing and seated divinities combining Egyptian and Graeco-Roman features. Fragments of other murals were also recorded from the excavation. The larger and better-preserved murals were copied in facsimile in watercolour by the artist Hamzeh Carr on a visit to the site in 1925. Most of Carr's facsimiles were painted over black-and-white photographs, but in many cases preserve details not visible in the photographs. Most of the better-preserved murals were removed from the site during the course of the excavation and preserved in the Cairo Museum, but even these have deteriorated over time. Hamzeh Carr's facsimiles, now in the Kelsey Museum of Archaeology, are valuable records of these paintings in their original condition and colour.

Pottery is the most ubiquitous form of artefact to survive from Graeco-Roman Egypt, and the Michigan Karanis excavation yielded thousands of complete or near-complete ceramic vessels, as well as masses of pottery fragments. The more complete pottery and diagnostic fragments were recorded and, of these, both typical and unusual examples were retained by the excavators in the division of finds. The great majority of pottery found in the course of the excavation was designated 'N.T.H.' in the records—for 'not taken home'. The excavators began compilation of a complete typology of the Karanis pottery as early as the 1924–5 season, but this work was never completed. A summary of some of the Karanis pottery was published in 1981 by Barbara Johnson, but to date no complete corpus of the Karanis pottery

FIG. 14.11 Wall fresco in a house on the western side, southeastern corner

Photo: George R. Swain.

has appeared. Such a publication is both daunting and necessary, given the importance of the pottery for the dating of levels and structures at the site and also the interrelation between the pottery and the explicitly dated artefacts.

Fig. 14.12 shows a find of amphoras concealed within a wall. The amphoras from Karanis are particularly of interest for what they can tell about trade and dating. Many bear notations with evidence as to contents, provenance, and date, while the forms of the amphoras have good parallels with others from throughout the Roman world. A preliminary study of the Karanis amphoras (Pollard 1998) proposes dates for some of them that are well beyond the traditional mid-fifth-century CE date of the abandonment of Karanis. Although the textual and numismatic evidence from Karanis appears largely to disappear at this point, the amphoras and other artefactual material suggest further occupation into the sixth century CE (see the discussion in Keenan 2003: 122–9).

Fig. 14.13 shown an alternative view of the dovecote in structure C37. Six dovecotes or parts of dovecotes were found during the Michigan Karanis excavation, and this may only represent a fraction of the total originally in the area that Michigan excavated, let alone in the site as a whole (Husselman 1953: 81). Dovecotes were typically built in the upper storey of a house or even in a tower above the level of the house roof, and these were areas often already destroyed before the excavators reached them. The Karanis dovecotes consisted of specially constructed nesting pots set into mud-brick walls; the photograph gives a clear sense of how the pots are incorporated into the walls, while also giving a feel for how high up the dovecote was in regard to surrounding structures. Structure C37 contained at least 1,000 nesting pots

FIG. 14.12 Pots in a cross wall between the passage and room A2 of house 100

Photo: George R. Swain.

FIG. 14.13 Pot in situ in the northeastern corner of C37K

Photo: George R. Swain.

FIG. 14.14 Five pots as found

Photo: George R. Swain.

as excavated, and perhaps 1,500 originally, suggesting a substantial commercial operation for the raising of pigeons, with the substantial side benefit of their guano for fertilizer (Husselman 1953: 87). Papyri from Karanis record properties with associated dovecotes as well as tax paid on dovecotes, but none of the papyrologically attested dovecotes can be tied directly to specific archaeological remains (Husselman 1953: 90).

Fig. 14.14 shows a find of pottery, basketry, and wooden objects made in 1927 in structure 216, room A. These objects were found in a hole below floor level. Many of the groups of artefacts found at Karanis were found below floor level, typically consisting of material stored in pottery *pithoi*, or brick bins. The reasons behind these deposits vary widely—intentional abandonment or disposal, temporary or long-term storage, accidental deposits created by building collapse—but at least some of the deposits from later levels at Karanis may reflect conditions around the time of the total or partial abandonment of the site.

The painted pottery from Karanis, such as the examples in Fig. 14.14, is among the finest to survive from Roman Egypt, and reflects the often high levels of craftsmanship found in the artefacts from Karanis. The frequent characterization of Karanis as a 'farming village' may technically be correct, but often gives a misleading impression of the wide range of its material culture and the economic levels of its inhabitants.

The Division Album photographs show the extraordinary range of artefacts recovered from the Karanis excavation and also suggest the sheer abundance of this material. Objects were arranged roughly by category and material for the division of finds and documenting photographs, and the resulting Division Albums are quick guides to the types and ranges of artefacts from Roman Egypt.

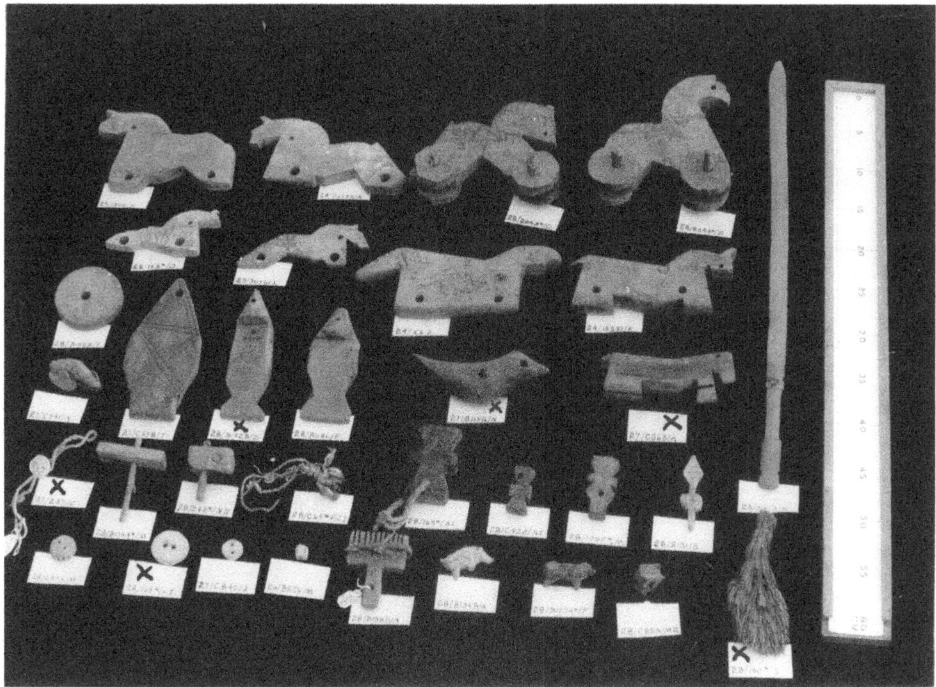

FIG. 14.15 Division of Toys 1929–30

Photo: George R. Swain.

Fig. 14.15 shows something of the wide variety of toys found during the Michigan Karanis excavation—one of several images of toys in many materials. Here are clay buzzers (some made of broken plates), simple clay images of farm animals, wooden dolls and miniatures (including hammers and a weaver's comb), and a range of wooden animal pull-toys. In particular, a large number of wheeled horse pull-toys were found at Karanis, the best-preserved retaining painted decoration, wheels and axels, and even the pull-cord. These toys raise interesting questions about their manufacture; the clay objects are, for the most part, clearly home-made, but many of the wooden toys would have required the use of tools that most Karanis inhabitants would not necessarily have had in their homes. The great regularity in shape and form of the wheeled wooden horses in particular suggests standardized workshop practice.

Fig. 14.16 is an extraordinary *in situ* photograph of a mass of wheeled wooden horses of the sort seen in the preceding image, found in 1926 on the floor near the wall of structure BC72, Room K. At least seven of these toys can be identified, and there may be more present. All look intact, with wheels in place, but the condition of these toys may not have been as good as the photograph suggests. None of these horses seem to have come to Michigan, or were retained by Cairo, and it is likely that they may have been beyond preservation once removed.

Finds such as this raise questions about why so many of a given type of artefact would be found together. Unlike accumulations of typical daily life objects like pottery or coins, a large group of toy horses is more difficult to explain. A few other groups of toy horses were found at Karanis and are now preserved in the Kelsey Museum of Archaeology. Preliminary

FIG. 14.16 Wooden toy horses, D, as found in BC72K

Photo: George R. Swain.

study of the related finds for at least one of these groups shows associated wooden objects of other types, suggesting that, in this particular case at least, the horses were part of the stock of a woodworker or merchant, rather than a specialized accumulation of toys.

The artefactual material can give tantalizing hints as to the intangible, sensual elements of life at Karanis—the tastes, smells, and sounds of daily life are hinted at by archaeological finds. Thus, the cluster of bronze bells seen in Fig. 14.17 is a sample of the many objects that would have produced sound, either intentionally, such as of musical instruments or noise-making toys, or unintentionally, such as objects of daily life (hammers, glass, doors, coins) that would have secondarily produced sound through their primary use. As scholars increasingly seek to reconstruct the auditory, olfactory, and other sensual experiences of the ancient world, archaeological sites like Karanis will play an important role in this effort. I am currently at work on a study (with the artist John Kannenberg) of the sonic world of Karanis as seen from the textual and archaeological evidence; preliminary research suggests that Karanis may indeed have been a very noisy place.

Extensive samples of faunal and botanical remains from the Karanis excavation were collected by the excavators with an eye to documenting animal and plant life on the site, especially as used for food (see Fig. 14.18). A report on such material from the earliest seasons of the excavation appeared in the published report (Boak 1933: 87–93), but was a cursory summary, mostly identifications with little detail, and did not cover finds from later seasons. The range of material recorded from the site was consistent with what would be expected. Plant remains include mostly food plants: durum wheat and barley, along with a range of fruits, nuts, and vegetables (to the listing in the published report should be added at least the coriander seeds, garlic, peas, and poppy seeds found in later seasons). Processed plant materials include traces of wine preserved

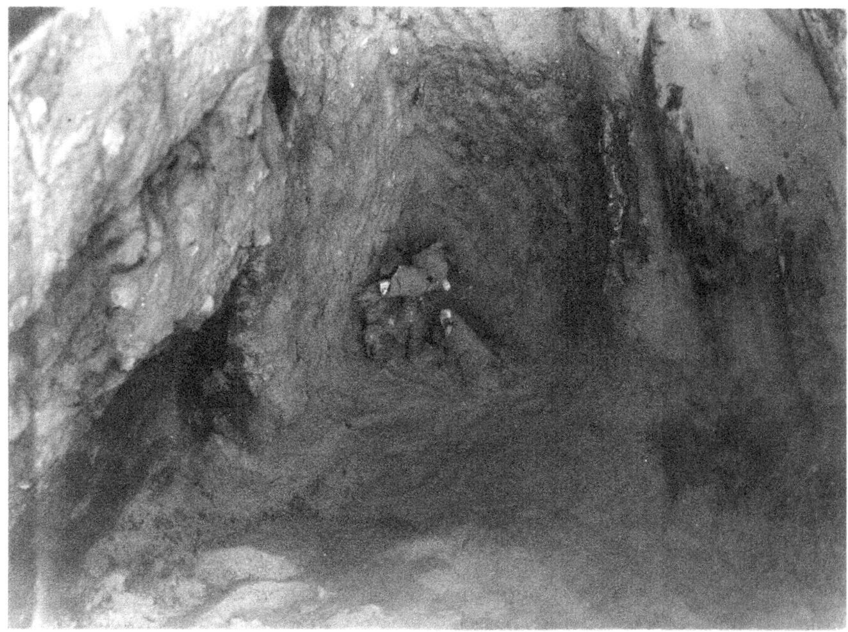

FIG. 14.17 Group of bronze bells as found in CS48

Photo: George R. Swain.

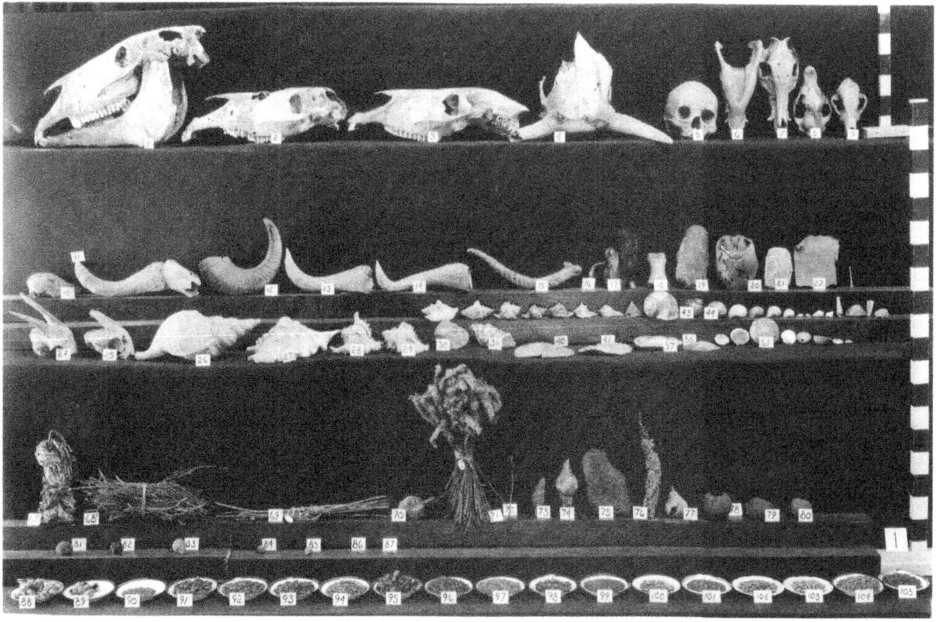

FIG. 14.18 Division of Natural objects, 1935

Photo: uncredited.

in a glass decanter, fragments of wheat bread, and cakes of olive pressings. Wild animals include gazelles, hartebeest, crocodiles, lizards, and three kinds of fish, while domesticated animals attested at the site included goats, sheep, dogs, donkeys, horses, cattle, and, especially, pigs.

One thing the publication of the faunal and (especially) the botanical remains did not make clear was the sheer volume of material found, nor was any clear indication given of the extent of material preserved by the excavators and brought back to Ann Arbor. In particular, large quantities of wheat, barley, legumes, and seeds are held in storage at the Kelsey Museum, while samples of most of the plant remains are part of the museum's permanent installation. To the published animal remains should also be added a collection of over 300 animal bones bearing designs in red ochre, probably magical in nature; most of these come from a single large deposit and are currently being prepared for publication by Andrew Wilburn.

As the Division Album photograph in Fig. 14.18 attests, human remains also survived from the Michigan Karanis excavation; most of these come from burials excavated early in the project, illustrated in the following photograph (Fig. 14.19).

Six burials were excavated at Karanis by the Michigan team near the beginning of the project, in the 1924–5 season. Very little was recorded of these graves; even their location on the site is unclear. Only four archival photographs (of which Fig. 14.19 was a typical example) document the burials *in situ*, while a further set of images from the division of finds record the human skeletal remains from the burials. At least some of the human skeletal remains are now in the Kelsey Museum of Archaeology, where they are currently the object of research by Thomas Landvatter.

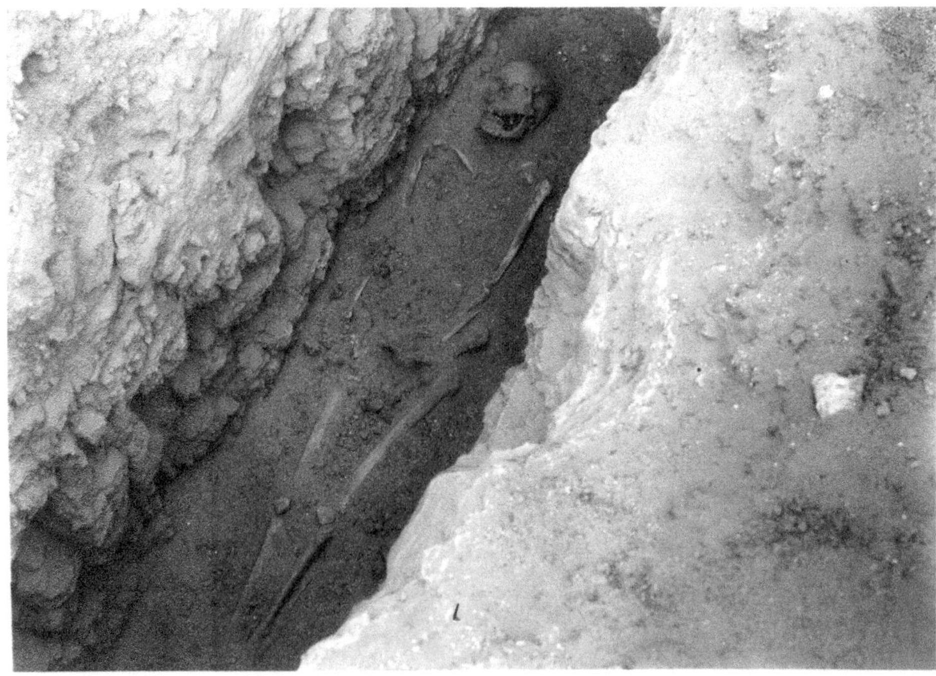

FIG. 14.19 Skeleton in Tomb 100

Photo: George R. Swain.

From the scant records, though, it is clear that the burials contained no grave goods or other evidence of mortuary practice beyond simple burial. And this is almost certainly why the Michigan project did not pursue excavation of further burials at Karanis. Francis Kelsey did have a strong interest in the finding of artefacts and contexts to provide illustrative material for funerary practices in Graeco-Roman Egypt, and the apparent lack of such material in these test excavations of Karanis graves must have led Michigan to abandon the idea of further investigation of the Karanis cemeteries. The Michigan project had to wait until the end of its time in Egypt to excavate a cemetery site that fulfilled its needs: Michigan's month-long 1935 season at Kom Abu Billou (ancient Terenouthis) yielded an enormous amount of material, including the well-known funerary stelae from second- to third-century CE cenotaphs and the lesser-known remains of nearly 200 later Roman burials.

The cemeteries of Karanis, however, remain largely unexcavated and unrecorded, and this could be a major priority for future work at the site. Analysis of the human remains, burial patterns, and practices there could tell much about the make-up of the population of Karanis.

Fig. 14.20 is a Division Album photograph showing mostly items made of palm fibre and reeds: baskets and sandals. The preservation of organic material at Egyptian sites in general tends to be good, but the level of preservation at abandoned Fayum sites like Karanis is exceptional even by Egyptian standards, or at least this was the case when the Michigan team excavated Karanis. Increasing human activity in the region and changes in the water level

FIG. 14.20 Division of Baskets, 1935

Photo: uncredited.

have posed an increasing threat to the arid conditions and overall preservation of Fayum sites in recent years, and this situation will only get worse in the future.

The basketry seen in this image is mostly workaday material, and the high state of preservation allows examination of traces of use and wear in the baskets that can give clues to function. The sandals from the Karanis excavation, many of which are preserved at the Kelsey Museum of Archaeology, provide some of the most eloquent traces of wear of any artefact from the site: several still bear the impressions of the feet that wore them.

Suggested Reading

For a general survey of the Michigan project at Karanis and an overview of its findings, see Gazda and Wilfong (2004). The exhibition catalogue Thomas (2001) is a useful look at a specific body of material (textiles) from the Michigan excavation and how such material can be used. The original excavations reports (Boak and Peterson 1931; Boak 1933), along with Elinor Husselman's summary of the later seasons (1979), are still essential starting points.

Bibliography

Bianchi, R. S. 1992. 'The Cultural Transformation of Egypt as Suggested by a Group of Enthroned Male Figures from the Faiyum', in J. H. Johnson (ed.), *Living in a Multi-Cultural Society: Egypt from Cambyses to Constantine and Beyond*. Chicago: Oriental Institute of the University of Chicago, 15–40.

Boak, A. E. R. 1933. *Karanis: The Temples, Coin Hoards, Botanical and Zoölogical Reports, Seasons 1924–1931*. Ann Arbor: University of Michigan Press.

—— and E. E. Peterson. 1931. *Karanis: Topographical and Architectural Report of the Excavations during the Seasons 1924–1928*. Ann Arbor: University of Michigan Press.

Cuvigny, H. 2009. 'The Finds of Papyri: The Archaeology of Papyrology', in R. S. Bagnall (ed.), *The Oxford Handbook of Papyrology*. Oxford: Oxford University Press, 30–58.

Gazda, E. K., and T. G. Wilfong. 2004. *Karanis: An Egyptian Town in Roman Times*, 2nd edn. Ann Arbor: Kelsey Museum of Archaeology.

Husselman, E. M. 1953. 'The Dovecotes of Karanis', *Transactions of the American Philological Association* 84: 81–91.

—— 1979. *Karanis Excavations of the University of Michigan in Egypt 1928–1935: Topography and Architecture*. Ann Arbor: Kelsey Museum of Archaeology.

Johnson, B. 1981. *Pottery from Karanis: Excavations of the University of Michigan, Ann Arbor*. Ann Arbor: Kelsey Museum of Archaeology.

Keenan, J. G. 2003. 'Deserted Villages: From the Ancient to the Medieval Fayyum', *Bulletin of the American Society of Papyrologists* 40: 119–39.

Lembke, K. 1998. 'Private Representation in Roman Times: The Statues from Dimeh/Fayum', in N. Bonacasa et al. (eds), *L'Egitto in Italia dall'antichità al medioevo: Atti del III Congresso Internazionale Italo-Egiziano, Roma, CNR-Pompei, 13–19 Novembre 1995*. Rome: Consiglio Nazionale delle Ricerche, 289–95.

Pollard, N. 1998. 'The Chronology and Economic Condition of Late Roman Karanis: An Archaeological Reassessment', *Journal of the American Research Center in Egypt* 35: 147–62.

Thomas, T. K. 2001. *Textiles from Karanis, Egypt, in the Kelsey Museum of Archaeology: Artefacts of Everyday Life*. Ann Arbor: Kelsey Museum of Archaeology.

PART III

PEOPLE

CHAPTER 15

STATUS AND CITIZENSHIP

ANDREA JÖRDENS

The mere fact that Roman Egypt had only a few of the *poleis* that were so typical of the rest of the Greek world made it an exception among the eastern Greek provinces. When the Romans incorporated the former Ptolemaic kingdom into the Roman empire, they found only three cities whose citizenry was constituted on the Greek model of *phylai* and demes, with a popular assembly and election of its own officials. In addition to the capital of Alexandria, founded by Alexander the Great, there was the ancient mercantile centre of Naukratis, which had first flourished under the pharaohs, and Ptolemais Hermiou in Upper Egypt, which was founded by Ptolemy I.

If we concentrate exclusively on political organization, we admittedly run the risk of giving a very skewed picture of the degree of urbanization. Despite the small number of *poleis*, some of which did not even have a council (*boule*), and despite the great significance of agriculture and particularly grain farming, Egypt was far from being a purely agricultural country. Rather, from the earliest times there had been numerous settlements with an urban character, with affluent inhabitants and individual traditions, as in the case of the principal towns of the nome districts. These offered all the amenities of city life, and in some cases were cultural centres of the first rank. The active settlement policy of the Ptolemies also brought about the founding, particularly in the Fayum, of a number of other towns that easily satisfied the high expectations of the Greek settlers, with grid pattern streets, generously proportioned markets, theatres, and gymnasia. There was a rapid development of bustling business, which in no way lagged behind the cities of the motherland in its unmistakably Greek character, and whose inhabitants were just as familiar with Greek culture and education as those in Greece—only they did not have political bodies or administrative autonomy.

In contrast to the provinces instituted in north-western Europe during these same decades, in Egypt the Romans found firmly established urban structures and a class of notables that would have been in no essential way different from the population of other new cities of the Greek east. And yet in the case of Egypt they failed for a long time to use this great potential for the administration of the province; indeed, they even took various measures in the area of civil rights policy that predictably offended the local elites, reduced their willingness to cooperate, and finally led to considerable internal conflicts. We shall probably never understand why the Romans departed so markedly from their usual successful practice of not offending the indigenous elites, but rather letting them carry out certain profitable activities, such as collecting taxes. One factor may have been that there was a functioning administrative apparatus already available, which could be taken over with little modification. This is probably the reason why autonomous urban administrative bodies had not developed in Ptolemaic times either.

The absence of municipal organization caused Theodor Mommsen (1887–8: 2.859) to deny, erroneously, that Egypt had the status of a province. We cannot completely exclude the possibility that the Romans themselves considered this absence as evidence of a lack of political maturity in the Graeco-Egyptian ruling class. In any case, Roman reservations about Egypt and its people were considerable, as expressed in Tacitus' succinct and scathing assessment of Egypt as 'a province so difficult of access, so productive of corn, ever distracted, excitable, and restless through the superstition and licentiousness of its inhabitants, knowing nothing of laws, and unused to civil rule' (Tac. *Hist.* 1.11.1; trans. A. J. Church and W. J. Brodribb). Not even the population of the capital city made a more edifying impression, as Strabo had observed one hundred years earlier. Unlike Tacitus, Strabo knew the city, the country, and the people at first hand. He had stopped in Alexandria in 26 BCE at the invitation of Aelius Gallus, who had recently been appointed governor of the newly established province, and accompanied his friend on his tour of inspection of the interior. This undoubtedly gives particular merit to Strabo's description of Egypt and Ethiopia, to which he devotes the whole of book 17 of his *Geographika*. Yet, his description of Alexandrian society relies heavily on Polybius, who had visited an allegedly tripartite city and was disgusted with the current state of things; under the last Ptolemies, things had even changed for the worse. We may easily suspect that this presentation is based not so much on Strabo's own experience as on the division of the *polis* into the three classes of farmers and artisans, warriors, and the educated upper class, customary since the time of Plato. Strabo persists with the idea that only the seizure of power by Augustus led to a radical change in the city, as the Romans undertook to reorder both Alexandria and the general administration of the country and replaced the old officials with new and capable ones. This reinforces the supposition that the purpose of a negative picture like Strabo's was above all to serve as a foil for the dynamic and rewarding exploits of the new Roman overlords.

All in all, Strabo is not very explicit in describing the internal conditions in the new province, particularly in the cities. Concerning the old capital of Memphis, for instance, he merely notes, 'The city is both large and populous, the second after Alexandria, and consists of mixed races of people, like those who have settled together there' (Strabo 17.1.32: C 807). Not even in the case of Alexandria itself, which in this period of upheaval was in a politically and legally very precarious situation, does he go into much greater detail; rather, he is content with a relatively superficial list of a few distinguished functionaries:

> Of the native officials in the city, one is the Interpreter (*exegetes*), who is clad in purple, has hereditary prerogatives, and has charge of the interests of the city; and another the Recorder (*hypomnematographos*); and another the Chief Judge (*archidikastes*); and the fourth the Night Commander (*nyktostrategos*). Now these officers existed also in the time of the kings, but, since the kings were carrying on a bad government, the prosperity of the city was also vanishing on account of the prevailing lawlessness. (Strabo 17.1.12: C 797; trans. Jones)

The lingering impression made by the kingly demeanour of the exegetes in Strabo may indeed have given the contemporary reader an idea of the rank and fascination of Alexandria. But we can trust this picture only to a limited extent, as the gymnasiarch, of all people, is absent from the list, though according to all other sources he was the most important of the Alexandrian dignitaries. We learn nothing at all about the civic organization, for instance the delicate question of the council, nor do we find out what the previously mentioned reforms consisted of, or how this process occurred in detail. Most notably, however, the most significant interventions in political life are passed over in complete silence: the radical reordering of all the social structures that came in the wake of the changes the Romans made in legal status.

Status and Citizenship: The Roman Reforms

The question of citizenship came to the foreground with the Roman annexation of Egypt, but it had been of some importance even before the Romans came to power. Yet, it had always been possible for members of the local elite in the service of the Hellenistic rulers to rise to respected positions at the Ptolemaic court—providing they were willing and able to take on a Greek mode of life and adopt the Greek language and culture. The essential condition for this was therefore Greek education rather than birth: those who had been educated, particularly in the gymnasium and *ephebia*, and were capable of mingling with the cultured upper classes, that is to say, they were socially confident and were accepted as full members of society, regardless of their origins. The self-esteem of these Hellenized circles was correspondingly high, as seen in the picture Strabo paints.

This was now no longer the case. Contact between the Romans and the local population was determined by legal status alone. This presented a particular problem, in that the Romans were prepared to recognize only three variants of legal status: Roman citizens, citizens of the Greek *poleis*, or non-citizens. According to these very clear principles, from a Roman perspective there were only a few Romans scattered in the former Ptolemaic kingdom and a number of *polis* citizens who enjoyed citizenship of the three Greek cities of Alexandria, Naukratis, and Ptolemais Hermiou mentioned above. The vast majority of the population were in the last category—non-citizens—and were classified without distinction as peregrines or, as the documentation in the Greek language so bluntly calls them, Egyptians (Mélèze Modrzejewski 1985, esp. 257–9).

The Greek inhabitants of the country must have felt this particularly keenly, as did the descendants of military settlers in the *chora*, whose social and economic precedence had until then been unchallenged. Admittedly factors like marriage with Egyptian women, the attraction of cultural activities found even in the hinterland, and, not least of all, the abovementioned upward mobility through education had brought about a gradual Hellenization of the local elites, so that the original barriers between the newly arrived Greeks and the indigenous population were lowered. The status decreed by the state now threatened to cause the painstakingly levelled barriers to be raised again.

Nonetheless, the Romans depended on the indigenous elite's willingness to cooperate, as only a few Roman officials occupied key positions in the new administration. This form of rule, with minimal personnel requirements, was characteristic of Rome, and could be made secure in the long term only if the provincial populace could be encouraged to participate actively. For this reason the Romans provided privileges for the cultural and social upper class; these were to distinguish them from the broad masses of the population. Significant in this regard was preferential treatment when it came to the Roman introduction of the poll tax, always considered to be discriminatory: citizens of the Greek *poleis* were completely exempt from the tax, and certain groups within the nome populations were at least partly so. This principle of carefully gradated legal relations was successful in taming not only Egypt in general, but also, finally, Alexandria. For almost the entire Imperial period it was free of uprisings, and Egypt—a province of strategic and economic importance, which the Romans once feared would be a centre of disquiet—instead evolved into a linchpin of stability in the empire.

Roman Citizens

All these developments did not affect the situation of those few Roman citizens who had settled in Egypt, concentrated in Alexandria, and scattered throughout the countryside. In the papyri we find, as a rule, that they can be recognized only by their names, though this is not always a reliable indicator; only the rare listing of the *tribus* removes all doubts. This is the case with M. Aemilius, son of Marcus, from the *tribus* Callidia (or Claudia?), who in February 13 BCE made a contract with a (probably) Jewish woman named Theodote, for her to act as nursemaid (*BGU* IV 1106 = *C Pap. Gr.* I 5). As we know him only from this one contract, as is so often the case, it remains unknown why he had gone to Alexandria and what business he had there. The latter also applies to M. Cottius Atticus and a certain Canuleius, who had been named through a formal Roman testament as legal guardians for L. Pomponius Rufus, son of L. Pomponius from the *tribus* Pollia, and who now were discharged by their former ward; as in the previous case, the papyrus takes the form of a document notarized before the Alexandrian *archidikastes* (*BGU* IV 1113 = *M Chr.* 169 (dated 1 November 14 CE)). Cases of these kinds attesting to the presence of 'authentic' Romans who had apparently settled in the province were an exception, however.

More frequently we find cases of individuals who were born in Egypt and had been granted Roman citizenship on the basis of special circumstances, commonly in recognition of certain meritorious service. This might be the case with the family of the Julii Theones, attested from Augustan times, who held high Alexandrian offices over the centuries; apart from papyri concerning their ownership of land in Middle Egypt, the family is known from literary sources and inscriptions (Sijpesteijn 1976). This was probably also the case with the brothers Tiberius Claudius Demetrius and Tiberius Claudius Isidorus, sons of Bion from the *tribus* Quirina; the former was a gymnasiarch and enjoyed lifelong board in the Museion, with the exemption from taxes that this entailed (*P Oxy.* XVII 2471 (*c.*50 CE)). The arabarch and former *strategos* Tiberius Julius Apollonius, son of a Ptolemaios who had also functioned as arabarch, presumably received his citizenship through the good offices of the prefect Tiberius Julius Alexander, who had been his superior as *epistrategos* of the Thebais district decades earlier (Jördens 2009: 361 n. 24). Tiberius Julius Alexander also provides the best example for the rise of an Alexandrian in Roman service. His father, the famous arabarch C. Julius Alexander, 'who surpassed all his fellow citizens both in ancestry and wealth' (Joseph, *AJ* 20.100), was the brother of the great Jewish hellenistic philosopher Philo. Among other activities, he was financier to the royal family of Judaea and conducted the business of Antonia Minor in Egypt; thus, he was given Roman citizenship in all probability by the emperor himself (Turner 1954).

The largest group of Roman citizens, at least in the Egyptian *chora*, was doubtless composed of members of the military, particularly veterans, some of whom crop up as early as the first century CE (Whitehorne 1990). Permanent military or veteran settlements of any size occurred only from the turn of the century, though this was probably never in any systematic fashion. From the beginning, the preferred region was clearly the Fayum, as attested in the 'archive' of L. Bellienus Gemellus and his administrator Epagathos (Rodney Ast, personal communication), found at Euhemeria. Philadelphia and Karanis in particular expanded from this influx (see Alston 1995). Veterans were also among the first settlers in Antinoopolis, the new *polis* founded by Hadrian (Schubert 1990). The papers of the veterans Aelius Syrion and Aelius Sarapammon, dating from Severan times, attest for the first time veteran settlements in the Herakleopolite nome as well (Sänger 2011). Finally, as late as the mid-fourth century CE we encounter Flavius Abinnaeus, the well-known commander of the fortress at Dionysias, who retired to Philadelphia following his time of service (Bell et al. 1962).

Regardless of how they acquired it, the holders of Roman citizenship, including the freed slaves discussed below, were strictly segregated in the eyes of the law from all other groups of the Egyptian population. Thus, special censuses were taken from Roman citizens, of which a declaration from the year 47/8 CE is the first and only instance (*PSI* XI 1183; Rathbone 2001). They were the only people required to register officially the birth of their legitimate children in so-called *tabulae professionis* (Sánchez-Moreno Ellart 2001). In the second century, if not before, there was also a status check called the *epikrisis*, under the auspices of the prefect himself (Nelson 1979: 40–6; on both matters, see also Haensch 1992: 283–93). Their special status is further shown in the so-called Gnomon of the *Idios Logos*, the handbook of the finance procurator responsible for special revenues, kept without interruption since Augustan times; the Gnomon lists legal provisions relating to status and, not least, the many sanctions that offences against Roman law incurred (*BGU* V 1210 (after 149), with Uxkull-Gyllenband 1934: 28–43, 48–58).

As indicated by the often laborious identification of such Roman citizens, however, in most cases the Romans were fully integrated in the daily life of the province, juridical matters included. At Rome, any litigation was a major action, because lawsuits were to be conducted according to the praetor's edict in a highly specialized formulary procedure. Thus, nobody could present his claim in court without the help of legal experts. In Egypt, Romans, just as any other person in the province, could apply in any form they wished to any judge, whether they disputed among themselves or with peregrines. It may be that Romans preferred conducting lawsuits before Roman officials, specifically either the prefect or *iuridicus* (Wolff 2002: 163), but the poor state of transmission of Alexandrian documents prevents us from proving it. Accordingly, the existence of the *edictum provinciale*, which should correspond to the praetor's edict at Rome, may be questioned (see Katzoff 1980: 825–33). The few exceptions where Roman law plays a major part are limited almost exclusively to the law of persons and family and the law of succession (details in Wolff 2002: 153–62), as is attested in the above-mentioned *tabulae professionis* and testaments (Migliardi Zingale 1997).

The fact that birth registrations are among those documents in which the special laws for Romans are most evident also indicates the great interest of many of these Roman citizens of Egypt in securing for their descendants the privileges associated with citizenship. One will hardly be mistaken in assuming that for persons from the peregrine milieu, such as the veterans, this was the essential aspect of Roman citizenship. Roman citizenship conferred, first and foremost, exemption from the poll tax and probably also from burdensome liturgies. An impressive letter from the *strategos* of the Koptite nome shows how this affected relations: the *strategos* complained bitterly to the prefect about the Romans, Alexandrians, and veterans in his nome who refused to support him in his duties (*BGU* III 747 = *W Chr.* 35 (before 30 March 139 CE)). The prefect replied in favour of the *strategos* in this instance, but reading between the lines, it would appear that the groups in question had succeeded often enough in avoiding such odious responsibilities.

Citizens of the Greek *Poleis*

By long-standing tradition, one of the other privileged groups in the population were the citizens of the three Greek *poleis* (and from 130 CE, Antinoopolis), who were completely exempt from paying the poll tax and enjoyed many other prerogatives as well. Like the Roman citizens, these *astoi* were, according to the Gnomon of the *Idios Logos*, subject to strict regulations regarding status, which prohibited marriage with members of other groups in the population, in some cases entirely, in others with serious consequences for children born of such unions.

In this connection the Alexandrians once again had special status in many respects, if we can trust the relevant literary sources, according to which only they, among all the inhabitants of Egypt, had direct access to Roman citizenship (Plin. *Ep.* 10.5–7, 10); they also enjoyed certain criminal law privileges (Philo, *In Flacc.* 78). In addition, only Alexandrians and Romans had their *epikrisis* (status declaration) carried out by the prefect himself, which may explain why they appear as a separate group in formulas of oaths from the *chora*. Yet, at first there were serious disputes about who was to be classified as an Alexandrian in this sense, as shown in the conflicts with the Jewish inhabitants of the city. With rare exceptions, the essential precondition for acquiring citizenship was that both parents were Alexandrian and enrolled in the *phylai* and demes, reformed once more in Nero's time. There was also great, if not decisive, weight given to service in the *ephebia* (Delia 1991; Whitehorne 2001).

Although the character of Alexandria as a Greek *polis* was unquestionable, and the city was actually the addressee of imperial letters, one central element of the *polis* constitution was denied it: the *boule*. Despite assiduous efforts and repeated embassies to Rome, the request for a council was rejected every time by the emperor, until Septimius Severus granted councils to all the Egyptian nome capitals, and thus also Alexandria, in 200 CE. How much the *gerousia* (council of elders), attested in literature, was able to fill the gap cannot be determined. In all other respects the city was organized according to the customary Greek model; together with division into *phylai* and demes, and the occasional appearance of a board of *prytaneis*, it is above all the titles of the Alexandrian officials that attest to this. In documents from the *chora*, too, we find gymnasiarchs, exegetes, kosmetes, hypomnematographs, euthe-niarchs, imperial priests, agoranomes, and various epimeletes from Alexandria, charged with special duties (Delia 1991: 88–113). More often than not we do not know exactly what these officials were responsible for. Still, it is notable that these offices do not correspond very well to Strabo's list, which I shall return to below.

It is not possible to establish with absolute certainty what other privileges the Alexandrians enjoyed. They were exempt from the poll tax and from liturgies in the *chora*, as Tiberius Julius Alexander asserted in his great edict of 6 July 68 CE, as well as from taxes on old Alexandrian land, an exemption that had been in place from time immemorial (*I Hibis* 4, §§9 and 14). Likewise, the Alexandrians may have had a dispensation from certain import duties, but note also a general responsibility on the part of the prefect for the city's food supply (Jördens 2009: 225–32).

There is even less information concerning Naukratis or Ptolemais Hermiou, aside from a few remarks that Athenaios made about the former, which was his home city (Ath. 4.149d–150b). In contrast, we know much more about Antinoopolis, which is the best attested of all the Greek *poleis* in Egypt. One reason for this is its better-preserved location in Middle Egypt. Even more important, however, is the composition of the new citizenry, who were recruited from the upper class of the *chora*. Among them, we find members of the so-called '6,475 Greek men of the Arsinoite nome' and military veterans who not infrequently received the citizenship of Antinoopolis along with Roman citizenship. As many of these men refused to resettle in the new city, and often remained for generations with their families at their old places of residence, there were constant conflicts with local authorities, who tended to doubt the privileges of Antinoite citizenship or even ignore them entirely. The collections of documents that accumulated in connection with these altercations offer a valuable insight into the multiplicity and variety of rights at issue, some of which applied even to citizens residing outside the city.

Most of these privileges could be traced back to Hadrian, who had ordered the planning of the city as the fourth *polis* during his journey to Egypt, at the place where his lover Antinoos died such a mysterious death. This seems to be true of the games instituted in honour of Antinoos, which, like the city itself, bore his name, just as of the designations of the city's newly established *phylai* and demes, which were so rich in allusions (Zahrnt 1988: 688 n. 74). Again, it may have been Hadrian who ordered the new foundation to adopt the constitution of Naukratis, though the marriage laws for the Antinoites were more liberal: as an exception, the Antinoites were granted the right to marry 'Egyptians', so that children from such mixed marriages retained their status as citizens (*W Chr.* 27 (after 161 CE)). Right from the beginning, Antinoopolis was provided with a council and a board of archontes; that the city treasury was ranked under the preferential creditors, having the right of first payment immediately after the fiscus, probably leads back to Hadrian as well. Yet the city continued to receive other favours from later emperors, for instance the expansion of the council by twenty-five members granted by Gordian III (*SB* XVIII 13776 (241/2 CE)).

Among the personal privileges of the citizens of Antinoopolis were, once again, exemption from the poll tax and liturgies in the *chora*, as well as additional rights, such as having opponents summonsed to court in the city. Such privileges could even be exercised by non-Antinoite spouses, provided the marriage had produced children. Other benefits, however, were apparently enjoyed only by those who resided in the city, for instance the dispensation from sales taxes or import duties on consumer goods. Hadrian also established a fund to feed Antinoite citizen children, provided the infants had been registered within thirty days of birth, and perhaps established the distribution of grain to citizens, attested in the middle of the second century (Zahrnt 1988: 690–7). These benefits may have been designed to encourage citizens to resettle.

Alongside such concrete advantages, questions of rank had great importance, and the city council repeatedly appealed to the *epistrategos* in the interests of the Antinoites. The *epistrategos*, who was a Roman procurator, was involved in various legal processes concerning status, such as the registration of ephebes, and the fact that the Antinoites petitioned him suggests that they did not come under nome regulations, and thus did not recognize the *strategos* as the highest local state official. Instead, as at Naukratis, a nomarch conducted the district's business, and accordingly the territory was called a 'nomarchia' (Jördens 1999: 160–4). Similar provisions may have applied in the other Greek *poleis*, excepting Alexandria, which, as the seat of the prefect and the entire central administration, probably had separate conditions in force.

Non-Citizens

The Romans classified all the other inhabitants of the country, without distinction, as Egyptians, regardless of their origin or education. Unlike the citizens of the Greek *poleis*, these non-citizens thus had to pay the poll tax, which dealt a heavy blow in particular to the pride of the Hellenized elites of the countryside. In order to avoid putting long-term strain on relations, a system of graduated taxes was therefore developed early on, it seems, taking account of the vital need for social distinction, and thus promising to encourage the acceptance of the new structures, and above all the essential willingness to cooperate with the Roman administration.

From the inhabitants of the nome capitals, the so-called *metropoleis*, a significantly lower rate of poll tax was exacted. Most paid only half of the amount, which varied with the nome, and accordingly they were designated more precisely as *metropolitai oktadrachmoi* ('metropolites at 8 drachmas') in the Hermopolite nome or *dodekadrachmoi* ('at 12 drachmas') in the Oxyrhynchite nome. In the Arsinoite nome, where the sum was 20 drachmas, the simple phrase *apo metropoleos* was sufficient to make a distinction between metropolites and the villagers assessed at the full amount, that is to say, 40 drachmas. In contrast, 'the members of the gymnasium' were a much smaller group, who defined themselves primarily through their membership of this typically Greek educational institution. For a long time, these were considered the elite among the metropolites; they seem to correspond to the above-mentioned '6,475 Greek men' in the Arsinoite nome, from whom the citizen-settlers of Antinoopolis were later recruited (Nelson 1979: 26–39).

Like the citizens of the Greek *poleis*, the members of these superior status groups in the *chora* had to undergo an *epikrisis* process, though in this case it was conducted by local officials, that is to say without the participation of Roman authorities (Nelson 1979: 10–25). The precondition again was that both parents should originate from the required milieu.

Metropolites needed to prove this only for their grandfathers, while applications made by the members of the gymnasium for *epikrisis* of their 13-year-old sons, as late as the end of the third century CE, set out their antecedents' membership of this privileged circle over many generations, and in exhaustive detail. We learn not only what year each of them underwent his *epikrisis*, but also when these status groups first appeared. In the case of Oxyrhynchus this can be traced back to the year 4/5 CE, as a list compiled at that time apparently had significance in constituting the original metropolite class; only in the year 72/3 CE were the gymnasial families finally determined, just as the evolution of these status groups was for the most part completed only under the Flavians (Montevecchi 1975).

Even if we are dealing with a significantly longer process than often thought, it is unquestionable that the foundation was laid with the graduated poll tax system in Augustan times. Even this attenuated form of privilege had its desired effect, for in this way the Romans had remarkably rapid success in reconciling the local elites with the new administration, conferring upon them an increasing number of honorary duties and securing their participation in the governance of the country. Thus, in the *chora*, forms of civic autonomy gradually evolved, which consciously took the Greek *polis* as their model, with their typically Greek official titles—gymnasiarchs, exegetes, and kosmetes.

Contrary to earlier assumptions, we cannot be sure that there were continuities of any kind with Ptolemaic practice. Rather, there was a transitional phase during which these civic offices were introduced into the nome capitals at different times over the course of the first century CE (Hagedorn 2007). Admittedly quite a few of the official titles occur in Julio-Claudian times, but although the titles are the same, these early Roman office-holders are not to be confused with the later city magistrates. For example, the exegetes was subordinate to the *strategos* until the 60s at least (Hagedorn 2007: 198–200), and the original gymnasiarchs were presidents of private associations of Greeks that still followed the tradition of the Ptolemaic village gymnasia (Hagedorn 2007: 203; see also Habermann 2004: 347–8). There are no certain attestations before the time of Trajan for the board of archontes, which later became the norm, its members holding office in yearly rotation and always contributing financially to the community. The earliest evidence is an account for the water supply of Arsinoe from the year 113 CE, which is unique in many respects (*SB* XXVI 16652; Habermann 2000). These gradual changes may also lie behind the discrepancies that have been noted between the Alexandrian magistrates in Strabo's list and those we encounter in documents from the *chora*.

The fact that they took on such duties, as honourable as they were costly, reveals the enhanced commitment of the local elites, which in the course of time was increasingly rewarded by the Romans. Thus, under Trajan we first find not just Alexandrians but members of the local upper class serving as nome *strategoi*, as is shown by the example of the well-known Apollonios, whose papers were found in his home city of Hermopolis. Another novelty were letters from prefects to the nome capitals, though they may have been restricted to certain established cases, such as recognition of particular investments in the city infrastructure (Jördens 2006: 197–9). In the earliest case, the prefect already uses the honorific 'city of the Oxyrhynchites', which also indicates that it was perceived as a civic body (*P Oxy.* XLII 3088 (21 March 128 CE?); Grocholl 1991: 268–9). Increasingly this corresponded to the self-image of the inhabitants, who used this honorific form of the city's name to designate their officials from the middle of the second century CE onwards (Hagedorn 1973).

This development finally reached its peak in the establishment of the town councils, which Septimius Severus granted to Alexandria and the nome capitals during his visit to Egypt. How these newly established *boulai* were constituted is unknown, as is the origin of those who were called to be councillors. This is noteworthy, for in accordance with recent thinking, initially only the inhabitants of the nome capitals acquired privileged status, not the gymnasial members, who were in no way a 'super-elite' (Mélèze Modrzejewski 1985: 263) but an independent group with their own criteria. Thus, in contrast to the metropolites, children from Graeco-Egyptian mixed marriages were admitted to the gymnasium if considered suitable, but not slaves or freedmen, who according to Roman principles shared the status of their (former) masters, which could be quite privileged (van Minnen 2002). Such differences, however, can be interpreted as phenomena of transition, and at the time the *boulai* were established in 200 CE, they had lost much of their significance. Instead, the authoritative example of the Greek *polis* and the marked awareness of tradition among the gymnasial families became more and more important. Thus, one may well find the core of the new leadership class in the gymnasial group, but this need not entail the idea of an elite consisting of only a few dozen members (Ruffini 2006; see also Tacoma 2006).

Admittedly the nome capitals were not the equal of the Greek *poleis*, even after the granting of a council constitution; rather, distinctions between the two were maintained in essential points. Above all, there was no change in the fulfilment of public duties. Thus, even after the Constitutio Antoniniana of 212, which made all the inhabitants of the empire Roman citizens, poll taxes and liturgies continued to be exacted. Nor did the newly created *phylai* receive their own names; they were simply numbered (Mitthof 2002: 202–4). So it is hardly surprising that the need for distinction continued undiminished: in fact, it increased with the renewed levelling of status, which made everyone Roman. It is conspicuous that *epikrisis* applications continue in the third century, and the so-called registrations of birth flourished as never before, although their function in this system requires further clarification (see most recently Sánchez-Moreno Ellart 2010).

A more decisive turning point came with the establishment of the councils, for which the surviving minutes of meetings in Oxyrhynchus and Hermopolis indicate a plethora of tasks and approvals. The council had its own treasury, instituted and maintained public facilities, staged festivals, and undertook to honour the participants in the various sporting and musical contests. The council *prytaneis* represented the interests of the city and the nome to higher authorities (Bowman 1971). This development greatly expanded, in space and content, the competencies of the civic bodies, notably in the area of taxes and liturgies. But taking on essential duties in tax collection, in particular, did not mean an increase in freedom of action for town councils as much as a shifting of burdens. Like the other inhabitants of the nome, the metropolites remained subject to the *strategos* as the highest state official at nome level; he continued to be the focus of the essential functions of administration. The reforms under Diocletian were to prove much more significant in that they brought about a change for the whole of Egypt (Bagnall 1993, esp. 54–62).

Still, one must not lose sight of the fact that the developments sketched here affected only a very small part of the population of Egypt. Most people had no privileged status of any kind, and certainly did not have citizenship. In the case of a few small groups, one can nevertheless ask whether they did not, at least for limited periods of time, consider themselves as separate status groups. The Jews, for instance, were the only group in the country, in fact in the empire, who were assessed for a tax specially devised for them. In the Gnomon of the *Idios Logos*, we find a group of 'Greeks' who are apparently identified neither with the '6,475 Greek men of the Arsinoite nome' nor with the citizens of Antinoopolis, who were designated 'New Greeks'. According to one appealing explanation, there may be a connection with the 'Greeks who died without heirs', whose lands crop up alongside those of 'liquidated Jews' in a number of texts from the high Imperial period. The ethnic and cultural affiliation may have been significant when it proved expedient, for political reasons, to differentiate between *bona vacantia*, estates without any heir under a will or by intestacy, and *bona damnatorum*, property confiscated from persons condemned to capital punishment, after the great Jewish uprising of the years 115–17 CE (Mélèze Modrzejewski 1989).

Apart from those in the cities, the largest status group was without doubt the priests, who were also subject to an *epikrisis*; indeed, they provide the earliest evidence of such a procedure (Nelson 1979: 60–2). As with the nome capitals, the central question was the obligation to pay poll tax, as the temples always counted a certain number of priests who were exempt from it. Here too the situation was formalized only over a period of time, yet for priests, unlike for urban centres, the restrictions seem to have constantly increased without compensation of any kind being offered (Jördens 2009: 338–43).

Conclusion

There can be no doubt that fiscal interests were mainly at stake in the rigid status policy of the Romans, with its division of the population into *cives Romani*, citizens of a *polis*, and non-citizens. These thoroughly self-serving intentions, apart from producing all the paperwork that epitomizes Roman Egypt, set in train an overall restructuring of society in Augustan times, where the legal implications, whether intentionally or not, gave the local elite a new consciousness of their status. This proved fundamental for all the ensuing developments, as this consciousness was the leavening for a gradual process of municipalization, which came to an interim conclusion with the introduction of town councils in the nome capitals in 200 CE.

We shall presumably never establish the extent to which this push towards the formation of urban elites was actually intended from the outset (thus Bowman and Rathbone 1992). There is much to support the idea that this was an unexpected but welcome side effect that received more and more support from Rome as time progressed. In recent years there are increased indications that—whether in the formation of urban elites or in the municipal offices—the Flavian period actually was a time of consolidation and change, and that the 'typical' structure of Imperial Egypt only later became manifest in its full extent. Problematic as the availability of sources for the Julio-Claudian period is, we must re-examine the hundred-year transition period for this very reason, because it is only in this way that the genesis of Roman Egypt will become clear.

Suggested Reading

Bowman and Rathbone (1992) present the key points of argument and evidence, but compare Jördens (1999). On municipal offices, see Hagedorn (2007), and on the introduction of town councils, see Bowman (1971). Delia (1991) discusses Alexandrian citizenship; on

Antinoopolis, see Zahrnt (1988), while Nelson (1979) is the classic study of status declaration documents from Roman Egypt. Recent engagements with issues of status and elite formation include van Minnen (2002), Ruffini (2006), and Tacoma (2006).

Bibliography

Alston, R. 1995. *Soldier and Society in Roman Egypt: A Social History*. London: Routledge.

Bagnall, R. S. 1993. *Egypt in Late Antiquity*. Princeton: Princeton University Press.

Bell, H. I., et al. 1962. *The Abinnaeus Archive: Papers of a Roman Officer in the Reign of Constantius II*. Oxford: Clarendon Press.

Bowman, A. K. 1971. *The Town Councils of Roman Egypt*. Toronto: Hakkert.

—— and D. W. Rathbone. 1992. 'Cities and Administration in Roman Egypt', *Journal of Roman Studies* 82: 107–27.

Delia, D. 1991. *Alexandrian Citizenship during the Roman Principate*. Atlanta: Scholars Press.

Grocholl, E.-M. 1991. 'Bemerkungen zur Datierung von Bezeichnungen und Epitheta der Stadt Oxyrhynchos', *Zeitschrift für Papyrologie und Epigraphik* 85: 268–70.

Habermann, W. 2000. *Zur Wasserversorgung einer Metropole im kaiserzeitlichen Ägypten: Neuedition von P. Lond. III 1177: Text, Übersetzung, Kommentar*. Munich: Beck.

—— 2004. 'Gymnasien im ptolemäischen Ägypten: Eine Skizze', in D. Kah and P. Scholz (eds), *Das hellenistische Gymnasion*. Berlin: Akademie, 335–48.

Haensch, R. 1992. 'Das Statthalterarchiv', *Zeitschrift der Savigny-Stiftung für Rechtsgeschichte, Romanistische Abteilung* 109: 209–317.

Hagedorn, D. 1973. 'Ὀξυρύγχων πόλις und ἡ Ὀξυρυγχιτῶν πόλις', *Zeitschrift für Papyrologie und Epigraphik* 12: 277–92.

—— 2007. 'The Emergence of Municipal Offices in the Nome-Capitals of Egypt', in A. K. Bowman et al. (eds), *Oxyrhynchus: A City and its Texts*. London: Egypt Exploration Society, 194–204.

Jördens, A. 1999. 'Das Verhältnis der römischen Amtsträger in Ägypten zu den "Städten" in der Provinz', in W. Eck (ed.), *Lokale Autonomie und römische Ordnungsmacht in den kaiserzeitlichen Provinzen vom 1. bis 3. Jahrhundert*. Munich: Oldenbourg, 141–80.

—— 2006. 'Der praefectus Aegypti und die Städte', in A. Kolb (ed.), *Herrschaftsstrukturen und Herrschaftspraxis: Konzeption, Prinzipien und Strategien der Administration im römischen Kaiserreich*. Berlin: Akademie, 191–200.

—— 2009. *Statthalterliche Verwaltung in der römischen Kaiserzeit: Studien zum praefectus Aegypti*. Stuttgart: Steiner.

Katzoff, R. 1980. 'Sources of Law in Roman Egypt: The Role of the Prefect', in W. Haase and H. Temporini (eds), *Aufstieg und Niedergang der römischen Welt* II 13. Berlin: de Gruyter, 807–44.

Mélèze Modrzejewski, J. 1985. 'Entre la cité et le fisc: Le statut grec dans l'Égypte romaine', in F. J. Fernández Nieto (ed.), *Symposion 1982: Actas de la Sociedad del Derecho Griego y Helenístico, Santander, 1–4 septiembre 1982*. Valencia: Universidad de Valencia, 241–80; repr. as *Droit impérial et traditions locales dans l'Égypte romaine*. Aldershot: Variorum, 1990, I.

—— 1989. 'Ἰουδαῖοι ἀφῃρημένοι: La fin de la communauté juive d'Égypte (115–117 de n.è.)', in G. Thür (ed.), *Symposion 1985: Vorträge zur griechischen und hellenistischen Rechtsgeschichte, Ringberg, 24.–26. Juli 1985*. Cologne: Böhlau, 337–61.

Migliardi Zingale, L. 1997. *I testamenti romani nei papiri e nelle tavolette d'Egitto: Silloge di documenti dal I al IV secolo d.C.*, 3rd edn. Turin: Giappichelli.

Mitthof, F. 2002. *Neue Dokumente aus dem römischen und spätantiken Ägypten zu Verwaltung und Reichsgeschichte (1.-7. Jh. n.Chr.)*. Vienna: Hollinek.

Mommsen, T. 1887–8. *Römisches Staatsrecht*, 3rd edn, 3 vols in 5. Leipzig: Hirzel.

Montevecchi, O. 1975. 'L'*epikrisis* dei Greco-Egizi', in *Proceedings of the XIV International Congress of Papyrologists, Oxford, 24–31 July 1974*. London: Egypt Exploration Society, 227–32; repr. in S. Daris (ed.), *Scripta Selecta*. Milan: Vita e Pensiero, 1998, 215–21.

Nelson, C. A. 1979. *Status Declarations in Roman Egypt*. Amsterdam: Hakkert.

Rathbone, D. 2001. '6. *PSI* XI 1183: Record of a Roman Census Declaration of A.D. 47/8', in T. Gagos and R. S. Bagnall (eds), *Essays and Texts in Honor of J. David Thomas*. Oakville, Conn.: American Society of Papyrologists, 99–113.

Ruffini, G. 2006. 'Genealogy and the Gymnasium', *Bulletin of the American Society of Papyrologists* 43: 71–99.

Sánchez-Moreno Ellart, C. 2001. *Professio Liberorum: Las declaraciones y los registros de nacimientos en derecho romano, con especial atención a las fuentes papirológicas*. Madrid: Dykinson.

—— 2010. '*ὑπομνήματα ἐπιγεννήσεως*: The Greco-Egyptian Birth Returns in Roman Egypt and the Case of P. Petaus 1–2', *Archiv für Papyrusforschung* 56: 91–129.

Sänger, P. 2011. *Veteranen unter den Severern und frühen Soldatenkaisern: Die Dokumentensammlungen der Veteranen Aelius Sarapammon und Aelius Syrion*. Stuttgart: Steiner.

Schubert, P. 1990. *Les Archives de Marcus Lucretius Diogenes et textes apparentés*. Bonn: Habelt.

Sijpesteijn, P. J. 1976. *The Family of the Tiberii Iulii Theones*. Amsterdam: Hakkert.

Tacoma, L. E. 2006. *Fragile Hierarchies: The Urban Elites of Third-Century Roman Egypt*. Leiden: Brill.

Turner, E. G. 1954. 'Tiberius Julius Alexander', *Journal of Roman Studies* 44: 54–64.

Uxkull-Gyllenband, W. 1934. *Der Gnomon des Idios Logos*, vol. 2: *Der Kommentar*. Berlin: Weidmannsche Buchhandlung.

van Minnen, P. 2002. '*αἱ ἀπὸ γυμνασίου*: "Greek" Women and the Greek "Elite" in the Metropoleis of Roman Egypt', in H. Melaerts and L. Mooren (eds), *Le rôle et le statut des femmes en Égypte hellénistique, romaine et byzantine*. Leuven: Peeters, 337–53.

Whitehorne, J. E. G. 1990. 'Soldiers and Veterans in the Local Economy of First Century Oxyrhynchus', in M. Capasso et al. (eds), *Miscellanea Papyrologica in occasione del bicentenario dell'edizione della Charta Borgiana*, 2 vols. Florence: Gonnelli, 543–57.

—— 2001. 'Becoming an Alexandrian Citizen', *Comunicazioni* 4: 25–34.

Wolff, H. J. 2002. *Das Recht der griechischen Papyri Ägyptens in der Zeit der Ptolemaeer und des Prinzipats*, vol. 1: *Bedingungen und Triebkräfte der Rechtsentwicklung*. Munich: Beck.

Zahrnt, M. 1988. 'Antinoopolis in Ägypten: Die hadrianische Gründung und ihre Privilegien in der neueren Forschung', in W. Haase and H. Temporini (eds), *Aufstieg und Niedergang der römischen Welt* II 10.1. Berlin: de Gruyter, 669–706.

CHAPTER 16

IDENTITY

KATELIJN VANDORPE

IDENTITY has become a hot topic in sociology, political sciences, anthropology, and philosophy. Opposite forces are responsible for our urge to explore 'identities': governments seek to unify people in the twin contexts of European integration and expanding globalization, while at the same time, on a personal level, there is a tendency towards fragmentation of identities, visible in the proliferation of social structures and the increase in ethnic and cultural diversity (Giddens 1995; Bauman 2001).

Were things simpler in Roman times? In some ways, perhaps. Bonding to a kinship group was more important, and individualism was less prominent. People bothered less about questions like 'who am I?' But ethnic and cultural diversity became important features of society as well, and unifying forces were even stronger, leading to the successful expansion of the Roman empire.

The identity debate among historians and archaeologists of the eastern Mediterranean focuses on the delicate balance between Greek and Roman characteristics of society in the Greek east (e.g. Woolf 1994; Hall 1997, 2002). In Graeco-Roman Egypt the identity problem is more complex, because the new rulers encountered a society with a long-established civilization, which could not be easily ignored. The example of Apion, a provincial from Egypt who left us some Greek letters on papyrus, illustrates the complex situation. Apion is a Greek anthroponym, built on the name of the Egyptian Apis bull. When he joined the Roman fleet at Misenum, Apion took on a Roman name, Antonius Maximus, although he could only expect to receive Roman citizenship upon completion of service. In a moment of danger, he invoked the Graeco-Egyptian god Serapis. Is Apion an Egyptian, a Greek, or a Roman in the making (Heinen 2007)?

COLLECTIVE IDENTITIES

For a long time, sociological research on identity focused on the formation of the 'me', the individual's sense of self. More recently, scholarly attention has refocused from the site of the individual to that of the collective, discussing family bonds, gender, race, nation, social classes, and ethnic, cultural, religious, and occupational groups. Collective entities deal with the 'we-ness' of a group, and its members should adopt certain core characteristics. People identify themselves with a broad range of micro- and macro-collectivities and assume multiple identities (Cerulo 1997; Pakulski and Tranter 2000). Through interviews and surveys modern research examines why, how, and to what degree someone develops a collective identity (such as a religious identity), which identities prevail, or how they were intermingled. For antiquity, we only have markers by which individuals reveal their identity. Such identifiers may be retrieved in an archaeological context (e.g. burial customs) or in written sources (e.g. names, ethnics, language). The 'why', 'how important', and 'to what degree' questions are thus more difficult to answer.

Among the kinds of identity negotiated in Roman Egypt, we can distinguish among bonds that are natural (family, gender), groupings that grew out of private initiative (cultural, religious, and occupational groups), and collective entities, for which admission and characteristics were strictly controlled by the Romans (nationality, social class). Ethnicity is a complex concept, touching on several of these collective identities.

Race is a concept that emerged in eighteenth-century European discourse, and although earlier scholarship sometimes applied it to Roman Egypt, race is now widely recognized as a constructed and anachronistic category, without biological foundation. As a form of identity, race has been based on physical differences in human phenotypes, to which cultural features or characteristics were then attached, often in a pejorative way. In ancient literature some 'proto-racist' patterns have been adduced (Isaac 2004), such as 'jealousy is part of the Egyptian nature' (Philo, *In Flacc.* 29) or 'true to her nature as a woman and an Egyptian, Cleopatra suddenly turned to flight' (Cass. Dio 50.33), but these are better described as ethnic prejudices (Millar 2005). As Smedley (1998: 693) observes, 'No structuring of inequality was associated with people because of their skin colour.'

State Identity

State and ethnic identities are linked, in that national identity usually emerges from preexisting ethnic identity. In complex civilizations, the state is considered central to referents of identities (Cerulo 1997). Most people of a modern nation-state, such as Australia, have a 'we' feeling, some rather because they have absorbed the core elements of its cultural traditions, others because they have the same commitments to the core institutions of society (Pakulski and Tranter 2000).

Did Egypt's inhabitants have a 'we' feeling when they became part of the Roman empire? Only a minority of the people living in the province of Aegyptus et Alexandria were Roman citizens. Coins, taxes, and the regnal year of the emperor, recorded in every official document, represent the most tangible contacts between the ordinary person and emperor or government. Although Egypt kept its closed currency system based on the Alexandrian silver tetradrachm, the coins carried the emperor's image and propaganda.

Some efforts were put in to make Egypt's inhabitants familiar with their emperor, but these were tailored to the army and elite groups. Vespasian was the first emperor to visit Alexandria, the city to which he owed his emperorship. The visits of Hadrian and Septimius Severus in the countryside resulted in major reforms privileging the Hellenic upper classes. Efforts to please the priestly elite, notably in strategic regions like the south and the areas where trade routes started, resulted in the restoration and building of temples. The imperial cult was a means for the local elite to express their loyalty.

Social Classes and Legal Categories

The basic class distinction is between the powerful and the powerless. Social classes with a great deal of power are usually viewed as the elites within their own societies. The Romans imposed a legal interpretation of the elites, using a strict hierarchical system of 'Romans', 'Greeks of the city-states', and 'Egyptians'. These labels are no longer linked to ethnic origin (Bagnall 2006): among the 'Romans' and the so-called 'Egyptians' we find numerous people we would label Greek. These are legal categories and fixed rules determined membership. The Gnomon of the *Idios Logos*, a set of regulations from the Augustan era but revised afterwards, shows how weak the ethnic basis of these classes was: a Roman could be married to a Greek or Egyptian 'without knowing', or a Greek citizen could live together with an Egyptian 'without knowing' (*BGU* V 1210.111–14 (§39 and comment, pp. 46–7); Rowlandson 1998, no. 131). As they led to social stratification and reflected different degrees of privileged position, these legal categories had a considerable impact on the social classes.

Roman Citizens

Few Romans emigrated to Egypt, and they rarely settled in the countryside (Legras 2004: 66–8). This small group was gradually broadened by individual grants of citizenship to prominent families, whereas Egyptian soldiers received Roman citizenship after their service (Rowlandson 2004: 153).

The citizens' names are identifiers of their class. Romans carried two or three names: the success of the *tria nomina* pattern (praenomen–nomen–cognomen) was limited in time, and in the Imperial age a two-name pattern became more common (praenomen–nomen or nomen–cognomen) (Salway 1994). The 'old' Roman citizens added the praenomen of their father and their *tribus* to their *duo* or *tria nomina*. New citizens had their old Graeco-Egyptian name as cognomen, but often did not (yet) have a *tribus* or were attributed to the Pollia *tribus*. There may have been a distinction between old and new citizens in that the former had more privileges, such as complete exemption from taxes and liturgies, whereas the latter still had to perform local liturgies (Dietze-Mager 2007). One should, though, be careful about using Roman names as identifiers for citizenship, since some Graeco-Egyptians entering the army assumed a Roman name before they actually received citizenship, like the recruits of the *cohors III Ituraeorum* (*P Oxy*. VII 1022). Even the children and grandchildren of veterans sometimes adopted a Roman name, although from 140 CE they were no longer entitled to do so (Alston 1995: 64–5, 129–32).

Greeks of the City-States

The *cives peregrini* or *astoi* were citizens of one of the four Greek *poleis* (Alexandria, Ptolemais, Naukratis, and Antinoopolis, founded in 130 CE; see Capponi 2005: 66–9). As under the Ptolemies, one became 'Alexandrian' by having citizen parents on both sides and after being registered in a deme (district), the number of which increased under Roman rule. In the reign of Nero a new administrative level was added, the tribe, or *phyle*. Identifiers were *Alexandreus* in administrative documents, whereas in private documents, the deme and later the tribe was the diacritic identifier (Delia 1991: 27, 45, 63–8; Dietze-Mager 2009).

Egyptians

For Roman law the culturally mixed population of Graeco-Egyptian inhabitants of the countryside were all considered 'Egyptians', *peregrini Aegyptii* or *Aigyptioi*, although their legal system was Greek in nature (Mélèze Modrzejewski 1988), with clear Egyptian influences (Yiftach-Firanko 2009). They were all subject to the new poll tax (*laographia*, or *capitatio*). Within the large subaltern mass of Egyptians, two elite groups were demarcated, who obtained a reduction in taxes: the priestly and the urban class.

Priestly Class

Under Roman rule, the clergy lost its preferential bond with the Ptolemaic king. Control over this class became tighter, and from Hadrian onwards was supervised by the *archiereus*, a Roman procurator. No hereditary priesthood was created, but access to the group was supervised by the Romans. Priests had privileges 'comparable to or better than those of the urban elites and they too practiced endogamy' (Hickey 2009: 506). They were exempted from some taxes and liturgies, and had prime access to temple lands (Clarysse 2010). Priestly and urban elite members of the *chora* formed networks (Hickey 2009). Eventually, some wealthy priestly families associated themselves with Hellenic culture and became members of the urban elite, like the family of Aurelius Ammon (281–366 CE: *P Ammon*; Geens 2007).

Urban Class or Gymnasial-Metropolite Order

The forty or so nomes of Egypt could not be governed solely through the three (and later four) Greek *poleis*. The Romans had to appeal to the local upper classes, which were turned into an elite group.

The creation of the gymnasial class was a private initiative by people who considered themselves Greeks. It was a continuation of a Ptolemaic group, which was attached to a gymnasium and whose members carried Greek ethnics. In Roman Egypt the gymnasium was still the point of entry into the Greek community and constituted its educational and recreational centre. At the same time, a distinct group who lived in the nome *metropoleis* was marked off from the villagers by government. The metropolites and 'those of the gymnasium' were fiscally privileged (Bowman and Rathbone 1992). As argued by van Minnen (2002), the two groups overlapped and represented the Greek population of the nome *metropoleis*. Geens (2007) summarizes the situation well: 'The metropolite order was created after Roman social practice, the gymnasial order after Greek social practice.' In the Fayum, the elite group is known as the '6,475 *katoikoi*', referring to a fixed (and probably imagined) number of settlers in Ptolemaic times.

Initially, the metropolite group was composed of Greek and Hellenized Egyptian residents of the *metropoleis*, whereas gymnasial status could be accorded to all those with a father of the gymnasial class and a freeborn (Greek or Egyptian) mother. Around 72/3 CE rules for admission were tightened: for the metropolite order, boys had to prove that both father and maternal grandfather were of metropolite status. The gymnasium administration had to list both father's and mother's gymnasial status (van Minnen 2002). The metropolite and gymnasial groups became exclusive orders. Social changes resulted in an 'increased attention for one's pedigree', since the name of the mother and the grandfather's name on the mother's side came to be systematically added in Greek documents (Depauw 2009). Other measures taken by government in the same period point to the administration's growing interest in Egypt's countryside and its elite in the mid- to late first century. The Fayum, for instance, was reorganized around 60–70 CE (Derda 2006).

The Romans made intermarriage between the urban class and Egyptian peasants unattractive, even though, ironically, the metropolites still belonged to the legal category of 'Egyptians'. The question arises whether the categories as designated under Augustus were adequate and to what extent people could identify themselves with the class of 'Egyptians'. In the early principate, there was still an influx of provincial Egyptians in the urban class, since gymnasial members were allowed to marry Egyptian women. Late in the reign of Nero or under Vespasian, when rules of admission became stricter, intermarriages with Egyptian peasants were no longer allowed if one wanted to produce legal offspring.

Gradually, the top layer of the urban class tried to compete with the elite of the Greek *poleis*. Civic benefaction surfaced in Egypt's *metropoleis*, as shown by liturgies like the maintenance of buildings and running of cults, which were local but expensive. Benefaction on a higher level, like the sponsoring of new public buildings or athletic games, was initially only found in the Greek *poleis* (Frisch 1986: 12). From about 120 CE, however, civic benefaction flourished as never before and led to a boom in new building projects, for instance in Hermopolis. The metropolites even managed to encroach on Alexandria's administrative primacy, when some of them were promoted nome *strategos* (Rathbone and Bowman 1992: 122–6).

It seems strange that the metropolite order was still part of the legal category of 'Egyptians', otherwise shorthand for administrative, fiscal, and cultural inferiority. This anomaly was partly removed when Hadrian founded Antinoopolis in 130 CE. Antinoite citizenship was open, among others, to the urban elite. The foundation must have been 'a psychological boost for the metropoleis' (Bowman and Rathbone 1992: 127). New citizens of the *polis* received numerous privileges (Hoogendijk and van Minnen 1987; *P Diog*. 26–9), and their new status involved residence in the *polis*. The 'Egyptian' anomaly was removed altogether in 202, when Septimius Severus granted all *metropoleis* the same political status as Greek *poleis*, so that they received a *boule*, or city council, the Greek equivalent of a Roman municipal senate. Economic power was translated into political power (Tacoma 2006). As in the case of Antinoite citizens, the landowning elite were drawn to the cities in larger numbers (Schwartz 1992).

The Constitutio Antoniniana and Roman Nationality

With Severus' reform of 202, the metropolites were no longer Egyptian 'barbarians', but a decade later neither were the freeborn Egyptian peasants: through the avenue of the empire-wide Constitutio Antoniniana, they all became Roman citizens. The previous classes disappeared and most 'barbarians' in the Greek east assumed the *nomen gentilicium* Aurelius. In addition, some Romans adopted the name Aurelius as a second nomen, 'apparently to advertise their loyalty to Caracalla' (Rathbone 1991: 48–9). Whereas before 212 a Roman name was already a status marker in itself, after the Constitutio Antoniniana, new status markers were created through onomastic practice. The praenomen Marcus in combination with Aurelius distinguished persons whose family had received citizenship before 212 from the simple Aurelii (without praenomen) (Hagedorn 1979).

The establishment of a *boule*, or city council, in Alexandria and in the nome capitals gave birth to a new elite group representing the wealthiest Hellenized urban residents: the bouleutic, or curial, class, formed by councillors (*bouleutai*) and their families and selected on the basis of their wealth (Tacoma 2006; Geens 2007). Membership of the council was a status marker, and even sons and daughters referred to their deceased father as a 'former councillor'. Those of the bouleutic class who wanted to compete with their colleagues had to accept financial burdens and perform heavy liturgies (compulsory public services), including the most prestigious magistracies. However, bouleutic liturgies could also be performed by wealthy outsiders. Members of the bouleutic class not only sought to rival other councillors; there was also an inter-city competition. As a result, panhellenic festivals became an essential part of civic life in the *metropoleis* (Frisch 1986). In Panopolis games in honour of Perseus were inaugurated in 264 CE (van Rengen 1971).

Roman citizens could be promoted to equestrian status by the mere possession of the requisite census, without holding a military or procuratorial post. The large landowner Aurelius Appianus may have been such an equestrian: identifiers for his status are the title *hippikos* and the honorific title *axiologotatos* ('the most worthy'), the Greek equivalent of *honestissimus* (Rathbone 1991: 46).

Shifts in Collective Identity: Social Mobility versus Compartmentalization

In Ptolemaic Egypt, upward mobility by serving in the army or by working in the administration was a realistic option for local people (Clarysse 1965). Local women could gain social promotion by marrying a Greek of the *chora*; their children assumed the father's ethnicity. Under Roman rule, descent was crucial to belonging to the upper classes, but some alternative ways for social promotion are attested within the civilian and military milieu for men, women, and their children.

Among the civilians, wealthy *euergetai* (benefactors) could move up from the metropolite to the Alexandrian class and, eventually, become Roman. According to Pliny's letters (10.6–7), Alexandrian citizenship was an essential preliminary stage of Roman citizenship, at least in the early principate (Dietze-Mager 2009). It is possible that after the Constitutio Antoniniana, Alexandrian citizenship facilitated promotion to the equestrian order. In any case, the metropolite elite still aspired to become Alexandrians (Rowlandson 1996: 113).

Egyptians from the countryside were more or less cut off from social promotion: they could no longer enter the metropolite group when more stringent rules were introduced around 72/3 CE. At the same time, marriages between full brother and sister surface. This exceptional phenomenon may be due to the desire to keep real property within wealthy families (Pomeroy 1988). The sibling marriages have been doubted (Huebner 2007), but conclusive arguments show that it was popular in Roman Egypt (Remijsen and Clarysse 2008; Rowlandson and Takahashi 2009). After the reforms of 72/3, Egyptian women occasionally had at their disposal 'sideways' routes to move up the social hierarchy: citizens of Antinoopolis received extensive privileges, among them, the *epigamia*, or right to be married to a woman of whatever origin.

The army was an alternative gateway to Roman citizenship, but restrictions hindered upward mobility for the soldiers' wives and children (Vandorpe and Waebens 2010). Alexandrians who enlisted in a legion became Romans, but legionaries were not allowed to marry during service (Phang 2001). Their 'wives' had no rights and their illegitimate children did not obtain Roman citizenship, nor could they inherit from their fathers. Some measures by Hadrian partly resolved the inheritance problems and, finally, Septimius Severus abolished the marriage ban in 197 (see Chapter 18).

Most Egyptians were never enlisted in a legion and served their whole careers in the auxiliary forces or the fleet. After twenty-five years (for the auxiliary forces) or twenty-six and later twenty-eight years of service (for the fleet), they became Roman citizens and received the *conubium*, the right to enter a legal Roman marriage with one woman of whatever origin. Their children, born during or after service, obtained the *civitas* as well. Social mobility was a reality for the ordinary man and his family. But things deteriorated in 140 CE. Antoninus Pius' policy resulted in strict rules: the *conubium* right was retained, but children born during service no longer became Roman citizens (Waebens forthcoming). Marrying an auxiliary soldier became less attractive for local women. There may have been some compensation, since in 148 and later, numerous veterans were granted Antinoite citizenship.

Roman rule also had its impact on daily life. Whereas, in Ptolemaic times, Greek immigrants often settled in the countryside, where they established their gymnasia, under Roman rule, compartmentalization was a fact of daily life: members of the urban elite were supposed to live in the city, and gymnasia were now only found there. The elite had their rural estates administered through managers. Some papyri suggest that the elite groups disdained the Egyptian masses. An Alexandrian called Egyptians 'inhuman' beings (*Sel. Pap.* I 152), and for one Greek, all Egyptians were 'dull' (*P Ups. Frid* 10).

Gender

Gender is the sum of characteristics that a society considers suitable for a sex and some of these characteristics are fixed by law. Gender is part of one's identity. In Ptolemaic times, upward mobility for women was possible by marrying a member of the elite, such as a Greek immigrant, but under Roman rule, local women could hardly marry into an elite class after stricter rules were introduced around 72/3 and in 140, as discussed above. The impact of Roman rule was to the disadvantage of Egypt's women, whereas after the Constitutio Antoniniana their position improved considerably.

In private legal affairs, however, women could continue indigenous Egyptian practices, which tended to be more favourable to them. Major changes nevertheless occurred in Roman Egypt, because the Ptolemaic bipartite administration and bilingual legislative mechanism was replaced by a single system, Greek in nature, though with Egyptian influences. Demotic contracts and, with them, Egyptian customs largely disappeared in the first century CE. Private affairs were Hellenized. While under the Ptolemies they could act independently, Egyptian women now needed a *kyrios*, or male guardian, for their transactions. The Hellenization was so well established that, when all women in Egypt became Roman citizens after 212 and needed a *tutor* (male guardian) only in a minority of cases, the Greek *kyrios* system remained in use until about 235. Thereafter, women in Egypt still recorded that their husband was present when a transaction was concluded (Vandorpe and Waebens 2010), but, in general, they gradually adapted to the less demanding Roman *tutor* system. Women who obtained the *ius trium liberorum* could act without a male guardian when they had borne three children. Thus, the legal capacity to act independently was restored to Egypt's women almost 600 years after the Ptolemies introduced the *kyrios* sytem (Pomeroy 1988).

The law of succession had become a mixture of Greek and Egyptian customs: daughters were entitled to a dowry (Greek custom) or a part of the inheritance (Egyptian custom) or both. Whereas the dowry had been designed by Greeks (except the Spartans) to avoid fragmentation of family property, the right for every child to inherit, as was customary in ancient Egypt, paved the way for extensive fragmentation. Only the eldest son was entitled to a larger portion of the property. As a result, about one-third to two-fifths of real estate was owned by women in Fayum villages (Hobson 1983). In a tax list of the Panopolite nome (197 CE) women often possessed vineyards and orchards, but their holdings were smaller than those of their male colleagues (*P Achm.* 9; Geens 2007). The situation is reminiscent of the Spartan *gynaikokratia* (women in power) criticized by Aristotle (*Pol.* $1269^{b}12$–$1270^{a}6$): women there could inherit as well (Hodkinson 1988) and two-fifths of Spartan land was in their hands. Some scholars ascribe the possession of real property by women in Egypt to the liturgical system: as women were not liable to liturgies, their husbands put land into their wives' names. But research shows that unmarried women owned the same amount of land as married women (Hobson 1983). The fragmentation of property due to the local law of inheritance is typical of Roman Egypt (Hobson 1985), and may be one of the reasons why sibling marriages in elite groups were popular (Pomeroy 1988). Though women could inherit and had economic opportunities, they are not prominently present in economic activities like lending (Hobson 1983).

Wealthy women throughout the Greek east came to the fore in public life in the early Roman period. They assume offices like *demiourgos* (mayor) or gymnasiarch for oil supplies, sponsor buildings, and receive statues and inscriptions in memory of their beneficence. These women continue family traditions, like Menodora from Sillyon and Plancia Magna from Perge (van Bremen 1996). Such prominent women are not well attested in Egypt, however: only in the third century do women step into the limelight, owning large estates in their own right and securing status for their descendants. They have their own archives and their own titles of rank (Rowlandson 1996: 114). The high status of Claudia Isidora, alias Apia, from Oxyrhynchus (214–37 CE), who acted as gymnasiarch, is shown by epithets like *kratiste* ('most excellent') and *lamprotate* ('most illustrious') (Rowlandson 1996: 114–15, 224–5). *Matrona stolata* referred to a woman of equestrian status.

Ethnicity and Cultural–Religious Identity

Defining ethnicity is a challenging task. Anthropologically and sociologically inspired research defines ethnicity as a social construct by the group itself, based on self-image (Hall 1997, 2002; Jones 1997; Riggs 2005). For the ancient past, the meaning of ethnic labels may vary depending on the institution, group, or individual who uses the label (member of the group, an outsider or adversary, ancient government, modern researcher). To understand the use of ethnics in the documentation of Roman Egypt, it is convenient to distinguish between (*a*) ethnic labelling by government ('I am an Egyptian according to law'), (*b*) ethnic labelling by the group itself (ethnic self-ascription: 'I consider myself a Greek'), and (*c*) ethnic labelling of particular religious and cultural features ('She has a Roman hairstyle'). These three types of ethnic label largely overlapped in classical Greece (an individual who was an Athenian according to law also considered himself an Athenian or a Greek), but in the multicultural society of Graeco-Roman Egypt, discrepancies arose (members of the gymnasium who were 'Egyptians' according to Roman law considered themselves 'Greeks').

When recorded in ancient documents, ethnics are usually of type *a*, which are official labels or legal categories, controlled by government. In classical Greece, for instance, an 'Athenian' had to be born of an Athenian father and mother from the time of Pericles, and this gave him political rights and the ability to own real estate. Naturalization was possible, but difficult. In Hellenistic Egypt, more than 200 Greek ethnics are found, like 'Athenian', 'Macedonian', 'Cretan', alongside non-Greek ethnics like 'Persian' (La'da 2002; Vandorpe 2008). These labels are still controlled by law, and in Greek contracts people had to mention their ethnic. In tax registers people with Greek ethnicity were listed under the heading 'Greeks' (Hellenes), since they were entitled to privileges like tax reduction. But the link to the original nation or home town was no longer literal in any sense, since social mobility and mixed marriages brought Egyptians into the Greek classes: an Egyptian who entered the army could become a 'Cyrenaean'. Ethnicity gradually became a legal category and status marker, without reference to origin or descent. The Romans abolished this elaborate system of ethnicity. They no longer considered Cretan 'immigrants', descended from those who settled in Egypt under the first Ptolemies, to be Cretans. Roman law created simple new categories, using terms with an ethnic connotation, as discussed above: 'Roman citizens', 'Egyptians', and Greek citizens of the four *poleis* like 'Alexandrians' or 'Antinoites'.

Most recent studies on ethnicity are anthropologically and sociologically informed and see ethnicity as a social construct defined by the group itself (type *b*). People may have feelings of a common descent, a common territorial homeland (current or ancestral), a common religion, or common cultural icons, including a similar language (Hall 1997; Whittaker 2009). They may apply ethnic self-ascription based on these ethnic identifiers. Festivals and processions reached a wide community of Greek- or Egyptian-minded people, whereas like-minded people who lived in adjacent locations might form an association or be attached to a common institution. Under the Ptolemies and Romans gymnasia were the educational centres for Greek-minded people, who considered themselves the social elite, though membership came under control of government (see Chapter 32). Egyptian-minded individuals were in some way connected to the local temple, where ancient Egyptian literature continued, or they were organized in cult guilds or religious associations (Clarysse 2010). These two spheres (gymnasium and temple) were, though, no longer mutually exclusive in late Ptolemaic and Roman Egypt: Greeks also frequented Egyptian temples, Egyptian religion was 'Hellenized', and some priests became part of the urban elite. As a result, the Greek identity persisted, but had an Egyptian colour: Greek-minded people probably realized that they were 'Greeks of Egypt', assuming names like Harpocration, a Greek derivation of an Egyptian god. Ethnic self-ascription by Egyptians is more difficult to trace, since many Egyptians adopted Greek or Roman characteristics in their pursuit of upward mobility. They still had a common language and may have had feelings of a common past, since pride in their pharaonic past was still part of their life through literature and monuments.

Graeco-Roman Egypt produced some smaller group associations with an ethnic label, grown out of private initiative. In Ptolemaic times, *politeumata* of Jews, Idumaeans, or other groups were organizations with a military background, and some were run based on the law of their ancestors. They gave immigrant soldiers a sense of identity in their new country. *Politeumata* survived into the Roman period, but only as organizations with a purely cultic role, cut off from their military origin. Some remained homogeneous ethnic communities, while others were held together by their religious character (Honigman 2003; Winnicki 2009). A more hybrid form of association, of a social, religious, and economic nature, is the corporation or guild (*koinon*) of craftsmen performing the same specialization and living in the same area. They were subject to craftsmen's taxes. Owing to increasing specialization, such guilds became common in late antiquity (van Minnen 1987).

A third level of ethnicity (type *c*) are ethnic labels attached to cultural or religious features of society: anthroponyms, toponyms, hairstyles, traditions, and so on, may have connotations of being Greek, Egyptian, or Roman. In daily life, borders were blurred owing to cultural hybridity, and it can be difficult to ascertain what meanings the people themselves ascribed to these features. For instance, mummy portraits of the local Fayum elite, who considered themselves Hellenized, are executed in a classical style but are found in an Egyptian funerary context (Bagnall 2006; Uytterhoeven 2009: 468–558; Riggs 2010). The combination of features—Egyptian mummy, Greek clothing, Roman hairstyle—conveyed the local prestige and at the same time Hellenized identity of these individuals. Certain cultural or religious habits became the focus of negative connotations, using ethnic designations: Philo, consciously defaming the Greeks of Alexandria, called them 'Egyptians', since they worshipped animals, a typical Egyptian custom (Pfeiffer 2009).

In general, Roman Egypt tends towards Hellenization. The reasons are multiple, but here two far-reaching policies are discussed: the language policy of the government and the socio-economic policy of the priestly elite. Spoken language is difficult to trace, but the transformation of Demotic into Coptic shows that Egyptian did persist, though interspersed with Greek words and written with largely Greek characters. The native language remained one of the strongest pillars of Egyptian identity. In written documentation, Roman rule ended the bilingual Ptolemaic administration and retained Greek. This language policy had a devastating impact on the Demotic script. As they now needed a Greek summary and subscription, Demotic contracts wasted away at the end of the first century CE (Depauw 2003; and see Chapter 29). Along with Greek contracts, some Greek customs were taken over by the Egyptians. For instance, Egyptian women used a *kyrios*, or guardian, for transactions, even after the law no longer required it. Hellenization went far beyond language borders.

Under Roman rule, the priestly elite was privileged in the same order as the urban elite. Networking between the two elite groups of the *chora* was an important catalyst for cultural exchange, both groups being 'desirous of signs that would further distinguish them from the mass of "inhuman" Egyptians' (Hickey 2009: 504–6). Though they had always been the keepers of indigenous traditions, priests were not averse to Greek culture. Religion was outwardly Hellenized, but Hellenism was not necessarily 'antithetical to local or indigenous cultural traditions' (Bowersock 1990). Greek hymns were written on the doorposts of the sanctuary of Narmouthis. Fragments of Homer and Euripides were found in the priestly houses near Fayum temples (Clarysse 2010). The *interpretatio Graeca* of Egyptian gods under the Ptolemies was given visual expression: Neith was pictured as Athena, and for the popular Nile-god a new, hellenistic iconography was designed. 'Indigenous Egyptian culture in a Hellenic disguise' lasted well into the fifth century (Geens 2007).

The Ethnic Identity of Egyptian Jews

I focus here on one ethnic label, which had a range of connotations: *Ioudaios/Ioudaia* (Tomson 1986; Kraemer 1989; Williams 1997). It can refer to ethnicity, religious belief, or geographic origin, or a combination of these. In the course of the unfortunate events of Roman times (see Chapter 17), *Ioudaios*, an official ethnic label, became a status marker with a notion of inferiority. Under the Ptolemies, some Jews operated within the Greek elite; others had obtained equal rights to those of the Alexandrian Greeks (*isopoliteia*) or were part of a *politeuma* with its own authority and separate organization. But after the Roman conquest, most Alexandrian Jews became de jure 'Egyptians' and could only secure some privileges of a religious nature (Mélèze Modrzejewski 1997; Pfeiffer 2009). The Jew Helenos, for instance, whose father had been a citizen under Cleopatra VII and who enjoyed the same status for some time, was deprived of Alexandrian citizenship under Augustus (*C Pap. Jud.* II 151). The *epikrisis* documents, dealing with the selection of members of the urban elite in the *chora*, do not record any Jewish name (Mélèze Modrzejewski 1997). Apparently, Jews were no longer part of the privileged class of the foreign conquerors or Hellenes, either in Alexandria or in the countryside. Only individuals who were ready to renounce the Jewish faith could obtain a better status, like the arabarch Alexander, who was granted Roman citizenship (Mélèze Modrzejewski 1997: 186–7; Winnicki 2009: 180–259).

Jews did not tacitly accept their inferior position. Their persistent claim for the right to Alexandrian citizenship, rather than their strict monotheism, led to anti-Jewish riots by the Alexandrian Greeks in the years 38–41 CE (Harker 2008; Pfeiffer 2008, 2009). The Roman administration did not intervene, and the *Epistula Claudiana* noted that Jews should be content with the privileges they formerly possessed and be happy to share the advantages of the city (*C Pap. Jud.* II 153). When the Temple of Jerusalem was destroyed in 70 CE, at the end of the Jewish War, Vespasian introduced the Jewish tax (Salvaterra 2000). It replaced the contribution the Jews had formerly paid for the upkeep of their temple and was destined for the temple of Jupiter Capitolinus in Rome instead. Whereas the old tax was a 'symbol of Jewish unity', the new tax became 'a mark of defeat and humiliation' (Mélèze Modrzejewski 1997: 214). The existence of such a tax implies that the government maintained lists of Jews: the ethnic *Ioudaios* had become an outsider's identity, though Jews were still allowed to practise their religion. After a fresh rebellion, which spread to Egypt (114–17), their identity was further disgraced. The Jews were slaughtered wholesale, and their property was confiscated (*C Pap. Jud.* II 448). Owing to the pejorative overtones, the ethnic *Ioudaios* was to a large extent replaced by *Hebreos* in Byzantine times.

The Rise of a New Religious Identity: Christianity

Egypt came into contact with Christianity at an early stage (see Chapter 28). Christians rarely revealed their identity in texts from Roman Egypt (*New Docs.* II 173; III 128–39; Luijendijk 2008). The most explicit identifier, *chres(t)ianos*, was invented by outsiders (Acts 11: 26) and taken over by Christians; it is attested for the first time in 256 CE (*P Oxy.* XLII 3035). Onomastic changes due to religious conversion are better attested in the post-Constantinian period (Bagnall 1982, 1987). Christian identity can be retrieved from earlier documents through atypical visual markers, such as Christian symbols (cross, christogram), *nomina sacra* (sacred names), or through the phenomenon of *isopsefia* (numbers replacing a word or expression, like 99, which substitutes 'amen'). In times of persecution, Christians concealed their identity, and under Decius some of them denied it in a *libellus*, certifying performance of pagan sacrifices (Rives 1999).

Names as Identifiers of Kinship Bonds and of Other Collectivities

In every society, names and name systems are identifiers par excellence, marking several aspects of identity: gender, family, social class, ethnicity, religion, and cultural identity (Luijendijk 2008: 41). Kinship has always been an important diagnostic of identity. In the Mediterranean, every person was identified by who his or her father was. In Egypt, where women had a better position, individuals also referred to their mothers. Children were often named after their grandfather or grandmother.

Family bonds could also be expressed by double names. Egypt produced this particular phenomenon of the double name: already in the Old Kingdom, a second name could be added to the first one through a stereotypic formula meaning 'alias' (Quaegebeur and Vandorpe 1995). In the Ptolemaic period, the most popular type were Graeco-Egyptian double names, reflecting the two faces of society. As an individual could use either both names or just one of his names, this system enabled people to manipulate their identity and be a Greek or an Egyptian, depending on the context. In Roman Egypt new combinations surface (Roman–Roman, Greek–Greek) and are more popular than ever before. The reason why people assumed two names needs further research, but preliminary conclusions are possible. In the Fayum town of Soknopaiou Nesos, with its limited onomastic pool, one type of double name adds a nickname to the first name in order to distinguish this person from others bearing the same name (Hobson 1989). Double names are also attested in wealthy families. The double name may link the individual to the high-ranking families of his parents or grandparents on both sides. The well-known Appianus has a daughter called Aurelia Appiana Diodora alias Posidonia. The first part of her name refers to her father's family, whereas her alias is taken from her maternal grandfather (Rathbone 1991: 51). Elsewhere in the Greek east, the second name is added as an additional cognomen, not as a double name. In Sagalossos the *eques* T. Flavius Severianus Neon built a library in memory of his father (Devijver 1993). His cognomen, Severianus, refers to the family of his grandmother, Neon to that of his grandfather.

Furthermore, names or name systems offer information about cultural identity. The choice of a Greek or Egyptian name may reflect cultural preferences (Colin 2001). After the reform of 202 CE, well-to-do metropolites gave their children a Greek name, indicating the change of status (van Minnen 1986): Hierax replaced Pbikis, referring to Horus the falcon. Onomastic evidence demonstrates a degree of Hellenization, even in the countryside (Geens 2007). Women, though, more often continued to bear Egyptian names, reflecting their inferior social status (Bingen 1991).

Theophoric names may be instructive for the religious identity of a family (Bagnall 1998; Colin 2001), though they may simply follow local fashion (Rowlandson 2004: 156). Some names were popular all over Egypt, such as Psansnos, which honoured the twin crocodile gods, sons of Neith (Quaegebeur 1992). Other names refer to local cults. The Panopolite nome produced numerous anthroponyms derived from the local triad Min, Triphis, and Kolanthes and from Min's consort, Thmesios, goddess of birth (Geens 2007).

Conclusion

What was the impact of Roman rule on the identity of people living in Egypt, notably in the *chora*? Identity is about one's place in society. As under the Ptolemies, descent was crucial to belonging to an elite group, and upward mobility was possible. Through wealth, civic donations, and networking, members of the elite were candidates for social promotion. But compared with Ptolemaic times, there was a downturn for the ordinary Egyptian man, woman, and their children, whose path towards the elite groups was limited in many respects. Compartmentalization gained the upper hand. After the Constitutio Antoniniana, wealth replaced descent as the crucial criterion to belonging to the elite.

Identity is also about one's cultural and religious preferences and traditions. In these more private spheres, Roman rule is usually less invasive. Already under the Ptolemies, elite status was closely linked to Greekness, but Roman policy and other developments led to a more uniform society, which was at least outwardly Hellenized, though it incorporated many cultural and religious features of Egyptian society. Ptolemaic identity in Egypt's *chora* had two faces (Greek and Egyptian), whereas Roman identity had one, which was to a larger or lesser extent Hellenized and bore some Roman features.

Suggested Reading

An instructive introduction to the problem of ethnic identity in Roman Egypt is provided by Bagnall (2006). Hall (1997, 2002) deals with Greek identity in general. Social classes and elite groups are dealt with by Bowman and Rathbone (1992), Tacoma (2006) (third century), and (on the priestly class) Hickey (2009) and Clarysse (2010). Studies by Hobson (1983, 1985), Pomeroy (1988), Rowlandson (1996, 1998, 2004), and Vandorpe and Waebens (2010) focus on gender. A comprehensive account of Christian identity is found in Luijendijk (2008). Names and name systems as markers of several aspects of identity are discussed by Salway (1994) (Roman names in general), Colin (2001) (Graeco-Roman Egypt), and Hobson (1989) (double names).

Bibliography

Alston, R. 1995. *Soldier and Civilian in Roman Egypt: A Social History*. London: Routledge.

Bagnall, R. S. 1982. 'Religious Conversion and Onomastic Change in Early Byzantine Egypt', *Bulletin of the American Society of Papyrologists* 19: 105–24.

—— 1987. 'Conversion and Onomastics: A Reply', *Zeitschrift für Papyrologie und Epigraphik* 69: 243–50.

—— 1998. 'Cults and Names of Ptolemais in Upper Egypt', in W. Clarysse, A. Schoors, and H. Willems (eds), *Egyptian Religion: The Last Thousand Years: Studies Dedicated to the Memory of J. Quaegebeur*, vol. 2. Leuven: Peeters, 1093–101.

—— 2006. 'The People of the Roman Fayum', in Bagnall, *Hellenistic and Roman Egypt: Sources and Approaches*. Aldershot: Ashgate, XIV.

Bauman, Z. 2001. *The Individualized Society*. Cambridge: Polity Press.

Bingen, J. 1991. 'Notables hermopolitains et onomastique féminine', *Chronique d'Égypte* 66: 324–9.

Bowersock, G. W. 1990. *Hellenism in Late Antiquity*. Cambridge: Cambridge University Press; Ann Arbor: University of Michigan Press.

Bowman, A. K., and D. W. Rathbone. 1992. 'Cities and Administration in Roman Egypt', *Journal of Roman Studies* 82: 107–27.

Capponi, L. 2005. *Augustan Egypt: The Creation of a Roman Province*. New York: Routledge.

Cerulo, K. A. 1997. 'Identity Construction: New Issues, New Directions', *Annual Review of Sociology* 23: 385–409.

Clarysse, W. 1985. 'Greeks and Egyptians in the Ptolemaic Army and Administration', *Aegyptus* 65: 57–66.

—— 2010. 'Egyptian Temples and Priests: Graeco-Roman', in A. B. Lloyd (ed.), *The Blackwell Companion to Ancient Egypt*, vol. 1. Oxford: Wiley-Blackwell, 274–90.

Colin, F. 2001. 'Onomastique et société: Problèmes et méthodes à la lumière des documents de l'Égypte hellénistique et romaine', in M. Dondin-Payre and M.-T. Raepsaet-Charlier (eds), *Noms, identités culturelles et romanisation sous le Haut-Empire*. Brussels: Timperman, 3–15.

Delia, D. 1991. *Alexandrian Citizenship during the Roman Principate*. Atlanta: Scholars Press.

Depauw, M. 2003. 'Autograph Confirmation in Demotic Private Contracts', *Chronique d'Égypte* 78: 66–111.

—— 2009. 'Do Mothers Matter? The Emergence of Metronymics in Early Roman Egypt', in T. V. Evans and D. D. Obbink (eds), *The Language of the Papyri*. Oxford: Oxford University Press, 120–39.

Derda, T. 2006. *Arsinoites Nomos: Administration of the Fayum under Roman Rule*, *Journal of Juristic Papyrology*, suppl. 7.

Devijver, H. 1993. 'The Inscriptions of the Neon-Library of Roman Sagalassos', in M. Waelkens and J. Poblome (eds), *Sagalassos* II. Leuven: Peeters, 107–17.

Dietze-Mager, G. 2007. 'Der Erwerb römischen Bürgerrechts in Ägypten: Legionaire und Veteranen', *Journal of Juristic Papyrology* 37: 96–103.
——2009. 'Die Beziehung zwischen römischen Bürgerrecht und Alexandrinischem Stadtrecht bis zur Constitutio Antoniniana (212)', in P. van Nuffelen (ed.), *Faces of Hellenism: Studies in the History of the Eastern Mediterranean (4th Century* B.C.*–5th Century* A.D.*)*. Leuven: Peeters, 217–75.
Frankfurter, D. 1998. *Religion in Roman Egypt: Assimilation and Resistance*. Princeton: Princeton University Press.
Frisch, P. 1986. *Zehn agonistische Papyri*. Opladen: Westdeutscher Verlag.
Geens, K. 2007. *Panopolis: A Nome Capital in Egypt in the Roman and Byzantine Period*, doctoral dissertation, 2 vols. Katholieke Universiteit, Leuven.
Giddens, A. 1995. *Modernity and Self-Identity: Self and Society in the Late Modern Age*. Cambridge: Polity Press.
Hagedorn, D. 1979. 'Marci Aurelii in Ägypten nach der Constitutio Antoniniana', *Bulletin of the American Society of Papyrologists* 16: 47–59.
Hall, J. M. 1997. *Ethnic Identity in Greek Antiquity*. Cambridge: Cambridge University Press.
——2002. *Hellenicity: Between Ethnicity and Culture*. Chicago: University of Chicago Press.
Harker, A. 2008. *Loyalty and Dissidence in Roman Egypt: The Case of the Acta Alexandrinorum*. Cambridge: Cambridge University Press.
Heinen, H. 2007. 'Ägypten im römischen Reich: Beobachtungen zum Thema Akkulturation und Identität', in S. Pfeiffer (ed.), *Ägypten unter fremden Herrschern von der persischen Satrapie bis zur römischen Provinz*. Frankfurt: Antike, 186–207.
Hickey, T. M. 2009. 'Writing Histories from the Papyri', in R. S. Bagnall (ed.), *The Oxford Handbook of Papyrology*. Oxford: Oxford University Press, 495–520.
Hobson, D. 1983. 'Women as Property Owners in Roman Egypt', *Transactions of the American Philological Association* 113: 311–21.
——1985. 'House and Household in Roman Egypt', *Yale Classical Studies* 28: 211–29.
——1989. 'Naming Practices in Roman Egypt', *Bulletin of the American Society of Papyrologists* 26: 157–74.
Hodkinson, S. 1988. 'Inheritance, Marriage and Demography: Perspectives upon the Success and Decline of Classical Sparta', in A. Powell (ed.), *Classical Sparta: Techniques behind her Success*. Norman: University of Oklahoma Press, 79–121.
Honigman, S. 2003. 'Politeumata and Ethnicity in Ptolemaic and Roman Egypt', *Ancient Society* 33: 61–102.
Hoogendijk, F. J. A., and P. van Minnen. 1987. 'Drei Kaiserbriefe Gordians III und die Bürger van Antinoopolis', *Tyche* 2: 41–74.
Huebner, S. R. 2007. '"Brother–Sister" Marriage in Roman Egypt: A Curiosity of Humankind or a Widespread Family Strategy?', *Journal of Roman Studies* 97: 21–49.
Isaac, B. 2004. *The Invention of Racism in Classical Antiquity*. Princeton: Princeton University Press.
Jones, S. 1997. *The Archaeology of Ethnicity: Constructing Identities in the Past and Present*. London: Routledge.
Kraemer, S. 1989. 'On the Meaning of the Term "Jew" in Graeco-Roman Inscriptions', *Harvard Theological Review* 82: 35–53.
La'da, C. 2002. *Foreign Ethnics in Hellenistic Egypt*. Leuven: Peeters.
Legras, B. 2004. *L'Égypte grecque et romaine*. Paris: Collin.

Luijendijk, A. 2008. *Greetings in the Lord: Early Christians and the Oxyrhynchus Papyri*. Cambridge, Mass.: Harvard University Press.

Mélèze Modrzejewski, J. 1988. '"La loi des Égyptiens": Le droit grec dans l'Égypte romaine', in B. G. Mandilaras (ed.), *Proceedings of the XVIII International Congress of Papyrology, Athens, 25–31 May 1986*, vol. 2. Athens: Greek Papyrological Society, 383–99.

—— 1997. *The Jews of Egypt: From Rameses II to Emperor Hadrian*, 2nd edn. Princeton: Princeton University Press.

Millar, F. 2005. 'Review: The Invention of Racism in Antiquity', *International History Review* 27/1: 85–8.

Pakulski, J., and B. Tranter. 2000. 'Civic, National and Denizen Identity in Australia', *Journal of Sociology* 36: 205–22.

Pfeiffer, S. 2008. 'Die alexandrinischen Juden im Spannungsfeld von griechischer Bürgerschaft und römischer Zentralherrschaft: Der Krieg des Jahres 66 n. Chr. in Alexandria', *Klio* 90: 387–402.

—— 2009. 'The Alexandrian Jews and their Agon for Affiliation: The Conflict of the Years 38–41 AD', in A. Gestrich, L. Raphael, and H. Uerlings (eds), *Strangers and Poor People: Changing Patterns of Inclusion and Exclusion in Europe and the Mediterranean World from Classical Antiquity to the Present Day*. Frankfurt: Peter Lang, 113–34.

Phang, S. E. 2001. *The Marriage of Roman Soldiers (13 BC–AD 235): Law and Family in the Imperial Army*. Leiden: Brill.

Pomeroy, S. B. 1988. 'Women in Roman Egypt: A Preliminary Study Based on Papyri', in W. Haase and H. Temporini (eds), *Aufstieg und Niedergang der römischen Welt* II 10.1. Berlin: de Gruyter, 708–23.

Quaegebeur, J. 1992. 'Greco-Egyptian Double Names as a Feature of a Bi-Cultural Society: The Case of *Ψοσνευς ὁ καὶ Τριάδελφος*', in J. H. Johnson (ed.), *Life in a Multi-Cultural Society: Egypt from Cambyses to Constantine and Beyond*. Chicago: Oriental Institute of the University of Chicago, 265–72.

—— and K. Vandorpe. 1995. 'Ancient Egyptian Onomastics', in *Namenforschung/Proper Name Studies/Les Noms propres*. Berlin: de Gruyter, 841–51.

Rathbone, D. W. 1991. *Economic Rationalism and Rural Society in Third-Century A.D. Egypt*. Cambridge: Cambridge University Press.

Remijsen, S., and W. Clarysse. 2008. 'Incest or Adoption? Brother–Sister Marriage in Roman Egypt Revisited', *Journal of Roman Studies* 98: 53–61.

Riggs, C. 2005. *The Beautiful Burial in Roman Egypt: Art, Identity, and Funerary Religion*. Oxford: Oxford University Press.

—— 2010. 'Tradition and Innovation in the Burial Practices of Roman Egypt', in K. Lembke, M. Minas-Nerpel, and S. Pfeiffer (eds), *Tradition and Transformation: Egypt under Roman Rule*. Leiden: Brill, 343–56.

Rives, J. B. 1999. 'The Decree of Decius and the Religion of Empire', *Journal of Roman Studies* 89: 135–54.

Rowlandson, J. 1996. *Landowners and Tenants in Roman Egypt*. Oxford: Clarendon Press.

—— (ed.) 1998. *Women and Society in Greek and Roman Egypt: A Sourcebook*. Cambridge: Cambridge University Press.

—— 2004. 'Gender and Cultural Identity in Roman Egypt', in F. McHardy and E. Marshall (eds), *Women's Influence on Classical Civilization*. London: Routledge, 151–66.

—— and R. Takahashi. 2009. 'Brother–Sister Marriage and Inheritance Strategies in Greco-Roman Egypt', *Journal of Roman Studies* 99: 104–39.

Salvaterra, C. 2000. 'L'amministrazione fiscale in una società multietnica: Un esempio dall' Egitto romano sulla base di *P. Carlsberg* 421', in L. Mooren (ed.), *Politics, Administration and Society in the Hellenistic and Roman World.* Leuven: Peeters, 287–348.

Salway, B. 1994. 'What's in a Name? A Survey of Roman Onomastic Practice from *c.*700 B.C. to A.D. 700', *Journal of Roman Studies* 84: 124–45.

Schwartz, J. 1992. 'Du village à la ville en Égypte romaine', in E. Frézouls (ed.), *La Mobilité sociale dans le monde romain.* Strasbourg: AECR, 223–30.

Smedley, A. 1998. '"Race" and the Construction of Human Identity', *American Anthropologist* 100/3: 690–702.

Tacoma, L. E. 2006. *Fragile Hierarchies: The Urban Elites of Third-Century Roman Egypt.* Leiden: Brill.

Tomson, P. J. 1986. 'The Names Israel and Jew in Ancient Judaism and in the New Testament', *Bijdragen: Tijdschrift voor Filosofie en Theologie* 47: 120–40, 266–89.

Uytterhoeven, I. 2009. *Hawara in the Graeco-Roman Period: Life and Death in a Fayum Village.* Leuven: Peeters.

van Bremen, R. 1996. *The Limits of Participation: Women and Civic Life in the Greek East in the Hellenistic and Roman Periods.* Amsterdam: Gieben.

Vandorpe, K. 2008. 'Persian Soldiers and Persians of the Epigone: Social Mobility of Soldiers-Herdsmen in Upper Egypt', *Archiv für Papyrusforschung* 54: 87–108.

——and S. Waebens. 2010. 'Women and Gender in Roman Egypt: The Impact of Roman Rule', in K. Lembke, M. Minas-Nerpel, and S. Pfeiffer (eds), *Tradition and Transformation: Egypt under Roman Rule.* Leiden: Brill, 415–35.

van Minnen, P. 1986. 'A Change of Names in Roman Egypt after A.D. 202? A Note on P. Amst. I 72', *Zeitschrift für Papyrologie und Epigraphik* 62: 87–92.

—— 1987. 'Urban Craftsmen in Roman Egypt', *Münstersche Beiträge zur Antiken Handelsgeschichte* 6: 31–88.

—— 2002. '*αἱ ἀπὸ γυμνασίου*: "Greek" Women and the Greek "Elite" in the Metropoleis of Roman Egypt', in H. Melaerts and L. Mooren (eds), *Le rôle et le statut de la femme en Égypte hellénistique, romaine et byzantine.* Leuven: Peeters, 337–53.

van Rengen, W. 1971. 'Les jeux de Panopolis', *Chronique d'Égypte* 46: 136–41.

Waebens, S. Forthcoming. 'Reflecting the "Change in A.D. 140": The Veteran Categories of the *epikrisis* Documents Revisited', *Zeitschrift für Papyrologie und Epigraphik.*

Whittaker, D. 2009. 'Ethnic Discourses on the Frontiers of Roman Africa', in T. Derks and N. Roymans (eds), *Ethnic Constructs in Antiquity: The Role of Power and Tradition.* Amsterdam: Amsterdam University Press, 189–205.

Williams, M. H. 1997. 'The Meaning and Function of *Ioudaios* in Graeco-Roman Inscriptions', *Zeitschrift für Papyrologie und Epigraphik* 116: 249–62.

Winnicki, J. K. 2009. *Late Egypt and her Neighbours: Foreign Population in Egypt in the First Millennium* BC, *Journal of Juristic Papyrology*, suppl. 12.

Woolf, G. 1994. 'Becoming Roman, Staying Greek: Culture, Identity and the Civilizing Process in the Roman East', *Proceedings of the Cambridge Philological Society* 40: 116–43.

Yiftach-Firanko, U. 2009. 'Law in Graeco-Roman Egypt: Hellenization, Fusion, Romanization', in R. S. Bagnall (ed.), *The Oxford Handbook of Papyrology.* Oxford: Oxford University Press, 541–60.

CHAPTER 17

THE JEWS IN ROMAN EGYPT

Trials and Rebellions

ANDREW HARKER

THIS chapter will examine the status, history, and development of the Jewish communities in Alexandria and Egypt during the Roman period, using the evidence from literary writings of Philo and Josephus, sub-literary texts (the *Acta Alexandrinorum* and the Oracle of the Potter), and documentary papyri. The chapter will examine the violence in Alexandria in 38–41 (all dates are CE unless stated otherwise), the two Jewish rebellions against Rome in Egypt in 66–70 and 115–17, and how the Jews were portrayed in the popular literature of the time.

Jewish communities lived in both the cities and the villages of Roman Egypt, the largest one living in Alexandria and estimated to number between a fifth and a third of the city's population (Delia 1988: 286–88). Following his conquest, Augustus had imposed a social hierarchy upon Egypt with political, administrative, fiscal, and legal privileges for the highest classes, the Roman citizens and the citizens of the Greek cities in Egypt (Alexandria, Ptolemais, Naukratis, and Antinoopolis). The other inhabitants of the *chora*, including Jews, were legally classed as 'Egyptians', the lowest free-born social group in the province, although the residents of nome capitals, the metropolites, enjoyed a slightly higher status and paid a reduced rate of the poll tax.

THE STATUS OF THE ALEXANDRIAN JEWS

The status and position held by the Jews in Alexandria was a contentious issue in antiquity and was a major factor behind the fighting between the Alexandrian Greeks and Jews. The ancient evidence is polemical. Jewish writers, such as Josephus and Philo, an Alexandrian Jew himself, imply that the Jews were Alexandrian citizens, and were consequently among the highest social group in the province. However, both writers refer to the Alexandrian Jews as *polites* and 'Alexandrian', terms that officially mean 'citizen' but informally can mean 'resident', and they discuss the Jews' *politeia*, which can range in meaning from 'citizenship' or 'civic rights' to 'way of life' (e.g. Philo, *Leg.* 183, 193–4, 349, 363, 371; *In Flacc.* 53–4, 80; Joseph, *Ap.* 2.35–7; *BJ* 2.487; *AJ* 12.8, 14.188). In contrast Greek writers, such as Apion, Chaeremon, and the authors of the *Acta Alexandrinorum*, vehemently deny this claim, and instead equate the Jews to the 'Egyptians', i.e. the lowest social group in the province (e.g. Joseph, *Ap.* 2.33–78; on the *Acta Alexandrinorum*, see below). Some documents, such as a letter of Claudius to the Alexandrians, preserved on a papyrus (*C Pap. Jud.* II 153) and in Josephus' histories (*AJ* 19.279–85), and a petition from a Jew named Helenus also refer to the status of the Alexandrian Jews, but this evidence can be interpreted in different ways (Harker 2008: 25–8, 212–20).

Over the course of the twentieth century it was widely speculated whether the Jews as a body enjoyed the citizenship of Alexandria or if they held the position of privileged residents, and, if the latter of these was the case, whether they were content with this or vying to improve their lot. At the start of the twentieth century the general consensus, based solely on the writings of Philo and Josephus, was that the Alexandrian Jews were all Alexandrian citizens (Bell 1924: 10–16). After the publication of Claudius' letter (*C Pap. Jud.* II 153) in 1924, in which Claudius referred to the Jews as living in a city that was not their own, the prevalent view was that the Alexandrian Jews were not citizens but were actively pressing for this privilege to be granted (Bell 1924: 16). More recently it has been argued that the Alexandrian Jews were organized into a political association called a *politeuma*, as other diasporan Jews were. An Alexandrian *politeuma* is referred to in one literary source (*Letter of Pseudo-Aristeas* 308–10), although this term is never used in Philo or Josephus. However, a Ptolemaic *politeuma* of Jews is attested in documents from Herakleopolis in Egypt from the second century BCE (Cowey and Maresch 2001), and this makes the existence of an Alexandrian *politeuma* more probable. It has also been argued that the Alexandrian Jews did not strive for Alexandrian citizenship and would not have wanted it, as participating in civic cults was prohibited by Judaism. The Jews therefore strove to protect their *politeuma* rights and to make them equal to those of the Greek citizen body (Smallwood 1976: 227–30; Kasher 1985).

The Alexandrian Jews, whether they were termed a *politeuma* or not, were granted significant and extensive privileges by Augustus in recognition of the services and aid which the community had provided for the Romans in the preceding years, such as the aid to Gabinus in 55 BCE (Joseph, *AJ* 14.99; *BJ* 1.175), to Julius Caesar (*AJ* 14.127–36, 193), and to Octavian himself (*BJ* 1.187–92; *Ap.* 2.61). These privileges, which were consistently upheld by Augustus' successors and which were allegedly inscribed on a bronze stela in the city (Joseph, *BJ* 14.188), included a measure of independence and autonomy. As well as being permitted to follow their ancestral customs, the Alexandrian Jews were allowed a governing body of elders. This body was initially headed by an ethnarch, who Josephus states governed his people as if he were the head of a sovereign state (*AJ* 14.117). When the first ethnarch died in 10–11, Augustus allowed a council of elders (*gerousia*) to replace him (Philo, *In Flacc.* 74). The Jews had their own record office (*BGU* IV 1151.7–8) and were allowed to send their own embassies to Rome. Philo reveals that the Jews shared the 'privilege' of Alexandrian citizens of being beaten with the flat of a sword rather than flogged (*In Flacc.* 78–9). The writer of one example of the *Acta Alexandrinorum* has Isidorus arguing that the Alexandrian Jews *should* pay the poll tax, which suggests that they shared the exemption from the poll tax enjoyed by the Alexandrian citizens (*C Pap. Jud.* II 156c 25–7). Another privilege may have been the potential to acquire Roman citizenship. Egyptians needed to gain Alexandrian citizenship before they could become Roman citizens (Plin. *Ep.* 10.5–7). However, as they enjoyed a higher status than the Egyptians, it is likely that emperors could award Roman citizenship to Alexandrian Jews. Philo's brother Alexander, for example, was a Roman citizen and passed this status on to his son (Turner 1954). It is likely that the Alexandrian Jews were registered in a similar way to Alexandrian citizens in order to prevent Jews from the *chora* from claiming the same privileges.

The community of Alexandrian Jews therefore enjoyed significant privileges, which were guaranteed and upheld by the emperors. The Alexandrian Greeks may have resented the fact that the Jews had acquired their privileged status through betraying the city to the Romans in the first century BCE. It seems likely that they also were aggrieved that the Jews were allowed a council (*gerousia*) to administer their affairs, while Augustus denied the Alexandrian Greeks the right to convene a *boule* (Cass. Dio 51.17.2). Also, whereas the Jews wanted to play a role in the running of the cities in which they resided, to enjoy a Greek education, and attend Greek institutions such as the theatre, they did not participate in civic cults or the imperial cult, hence Apion's objections that the Jews could call themselves Alexandrians when they did not worship the Alexandrian gods (Joseph, *Ap.* 2.65). There are several examples of Jews holding offices in Alexandria (e.g. *C Pap. Jud.* II 428). Philo himself attended banquets, frequented the theatre, watched horse races at the hippodrome, boxing, and wrestling matches (Philo, *Legum Allegoriae* 3.155–9; *De Ebrietate* 177; *Quod Omnis Probus Liber* 141; *De Providentia* 2.58; *Quod Omnis Probus Liber* 26). In his writings he also refers to Jews who took part in civic festivals, intermarriage between Greeks and Jews, and Jews who received a Greek gymnasial education, confirming that these activities, attested elsewhere in the Greek east of the Roman empire, also occurred at Alexandria (*De Agricultura Noë* 110–21; *De Specialibus Legibus* 3.29; *Legum Allegoriae* 3.167; *De Migratione Abrahami* 89–93; *De Specialibus Legibus* 2.229–30; *De Providentia* 2.44–6). Greeks in the east were not unwilling to admit Jews into their gymnasia. Even in Alexandria, Jews could not have enrolled in the ephebate without the approval of the Greek magistrates responsible for supervising entry.

What inflamed the situation in Alexandria was the fact that the status and position of the Alexandrian Jews was ultimately dependent on the goodwill of the Roman emperor. In the first century CE the Alexandrian Greeks witnessed Jewish expulsions from Rome (Suet. *Tib.* 36), Gaius' attempt to desecrate the Jewish temple (Philo, *Leg.* 184–337), and the brutal crushing of two Jewish revolts in 66–70 and 115–17, the first of which ended with the destruction of the Jewish temple and the imposition of the Jewish tax. This, not unnaturally, suggested to them that the imperial authorities could be persuaded to remove the privileges of the Jews and downgrade them to the status of 'Egyptians'.

The Alexandrian Riots, 38–41 CE

The first attested period of violence between the Greeks and the Jews in Alexandria occurred in 38. This prompted both sides to send embassies to the emperor Gaius, which he met with shortly before his death in 41. It was Claudius who finally dealt with the issues that lay behind the violence, his judgment sent to Alexandria in the form of a letter in October 41, preserved in *C Pap. Jud.* II 153. Philo provides a contemporary account of these events in the *In Flaccum*, which concentrates on the role of the prefect Flaccus during the rioting, and the *Legatio ad Gaium*, which tells the story of the Jewish embassy sent to Gaius shortly afterwards, of which Philo himself was a member. Philo aimed to demonstrate divine providence by showing what happened to those who persecuted the Jews, not to present a balanced or historical account. His treatises are supplemented by Josephus, who wrote a generation later in the Flavian period, in his historical works (the *Jewish Antiquities* and the *Jewish War*) and in his apologetic treatise the *Contra Apionem*, written in response to anti-Jewish statements made by Greek writers, principally Apion. The earliest *Acta Alexandrinorum* stories also refer to the characters and history of this period.

The violence of 38 has been discussed many times by modern scholars, yet many aspects remain controversial (Smallwood 1976: 220–56; Kasher 1985; Schwartz 1990: 77–89; Kushnir-Stein 2000; van der Horst 2003; Kerkeslager 2006; Harker 2008: 9–47). The serious rioting began shortly after a visit to Alexandria by the Jewish king Agrippa I in the summer of 38. The Alexandrian Jews triumphantly paraded Agrippa through the city and the sight of 'his bodyguard of spearmen, decked in armour gilded with gold and silver' stunned the Alexandrian Greeks (Philo, *In Flacc.* 27–30). In response, the Alexandrian Greeks congregated at the gymnasium and staged a parody of this parade, with a madman, Carabas ('Cabbage'), playing the role of king (*In Flacc.* 36–9). Following this the Greeks burnt many synagogues and desecrated others by erecting images of Gaius in them. According to a belligerent Philo, Flaccus turned a blind eye to this disorder; in return for this the Alexandrian politicians were to give Gaius no pretext to recall or prosecute him. Flaccus then issued an edict that destroyed the Jews' *politeia* by declaring them 'aliens and foreigners' (Philo, *In Flacc.* 22–3, 54). The Jews were herded into a section of the city and thirty-eight members of their council were marched to the theatre, where they were scourged (a punishment usually reserved only for Egyptians), tortured, hanged, or even crucified amid a Greek celebratory festival. Further atrocities followed until the violence was quelled by the Roman authorities (*In Flacc.* 29–96; *Leg.* 120–37).

It is unlikely that events proceeded in the exact way that Philo relates. It would be odd for Flaccus to allow the rioting to continue for any length of time, as losing control of his province would certainly lead to his recall; this was now imminent anyway after seven years in charge of Egypt. Flaccus probably used the legion stationed at Nikopolis to end the initial riot, but it seems evident that retaliatory violence from both sides created further serious incidents. It was not just the Alexandrian Greeks who attacked the Jews during the rioting; Philo refers to involvement by Egyptians on several occasions, and Flaccus may have lost control of the situation owing to this (*In Flacc.* 29; *Leg.* 132–9). In the aftermath of later riots in the city, prefects often restored order by issuing edicts expelling 'aliens and foreigners' (cf. *P Giss. Lit.* 6.3 (215 CE) and the routine expulsion orders in *Sel. Pap.* II 220 (104 CE) and *BGU* II 372 (154 CE)). It may have been the Alexandrian Greeks' interpretation of Flaccus' edict that led to the treatment of the Jews. Flaccus was arrested in September 38 (Philo, *In Flacc.* 116) and tried by Gaius early in 39, perhaps under the pretext of maladministration, his prosecutors including some of the Alexandrian Greeks with whom he was allegedly in alliance (*In Flacc.* 125–6). He was found guilty, exiled to Andros, and later executed (*In Flacc.* 151, 181–4).

Flaccus' successor Vitrasius Pollio referred the complicated and delicate legal, social, and religious issues that lay behind the rioting to Gaius. Greek and Jewish embassies sailed from Alexandria in the middle of a stormy winter (Philo, *Leg.* 190). On arrival in Rome, the Jews briefly met with Gaius in some imperial gardens before arguing their case fully, opposite a Greek embassy, at a later date (*Leg.* 181, 349–67). The date of this first meeting is unknown, but Philo clearly states that the second meeting took place in Rome after Gaius' German expedition (*Leg.* 356–7), i.e. between September 40 and Gaius' assassination on 24 January 41.

The purpose of the Jewish embassy, which Philo himself led (*Leg.* 371), was to discuss their 'sufferings' (during the rioting of 38) and their 'claims' (*Leg.* 178). One of these 'claims' was Jewish exemption from the imperial cult, as both Philo's and Josephus' accounts of the meeting with Gaius focus heavily on this (Philo, *Leg.* 355–67; Joseph, *AJ* 18.257–60). Philo also mentions that one of the 'claims' was 'showing that we are Alexandrians', and reports that Gaius asked the Jews to speak about their *politeia* (*Leg.* 193–4, 363). The purpose of the Greek embassy, of which Apion and Isidorus were members (Joseph, *AJ* 18.257; Philo, *Leg.* 355), was to defend their part in the rioting of 38 and to ensure that the Jews did not return to, or improve upon, the status that they had enjoyed before the riots.

Gaius' judgment is not preserved. According to Philo, although Gaius was initially critical and condescending towards the Jewish embassy, he did listen to their arguments. According to Philo, Gaius' verdict was that the Jews were 'not so much criminals as lunatics in not believing that I have been given a divine nature', and this, combined with Philo's preceding phrases ('God took pity on us and turned Gaius' heart to mercy' and Gaius 'became gentler'), suggests that Gaius confirmed the Jews' exemption from the imperial cult. Other sources suggest that the Alexandrian Greek embassy was successful. Josephus states that Gaius refused to listen to Philo, dismissed him angrily, and promised to punish the Jews (*AJ* 18.259–60). An *Acta Alexandrinorum* story cites a letter of Gaius to Alexandria in which he sides with the Alexandrian Greeks against their 'accusers', following the advice of Isidorus (*P Giss. Lit.* 4.7 iii.27–35), although no independent evidence of a written verdict exists.

The Jews in Alexandria rioted in February 41 upon hearing of Gaius' assassination (Joseph, *AJ* 19.278). New Greek and Jewish embassies were then dispatched to Rome. This Greek delegation was led by Tiberius Claudius Balbillus and consisted of eleven other men (*C Pap. Jud.* II 153 16–20). Both embassies had the formal purpose of congratulating Claudius on his accession and returned to the issues on which Gaius had not given a formal ruling. From Claudius' response it would appear that the Greeks, after requesting permission to institute honours for Claudius, asked for permission to convene a council (*boule*) to run the city and to prevent non-citizens from obtaining Alexandrian citizenship by enrolling in ephebic training. Claudius heard the new embassies at some point after March–April 41, and his response was published in Alexandria on 10 October that year (*C Pap. Jud.* II 153 11–13).

Claudius' response was issued with the aim of preventing further civic disturbances, and both sides partially gained their aims. Claudius agreed to some of the Alexandrian requests but refused to convene a *boule* or to hold an inquiry into the Jewish rioting of 41. He also warned the Greeks to behave kindly to their Jewish neighbours, referring to the rioting of 38 as 'the war against the Jews'. He did not censure the Alexandrian Jews for their recent rioting and restored their pre-38 legal, social, and religious privileges. However, he gave a series of prohibitions to the Jews: he warned them not to seek to improve their status because they already enjoyed many things in a city which is 'not their own', not to send two embassies to him, not to 'pour into' the games at the gymnasium, perhaps prohibiting them from gaining Alexandrian citizenship by means of the *ephebeia*. The Jews were also not to invite other Jews from Syria into the city as they had in the 41 CE riots. If they disobeyed, Claudius would proceed against them as though they were stirring up a plague for the whole world. He ends his letter by warning both sides about their future conduct: 'If both sides change their present ways and are willing to live in gentleness and kindness with one another, I for my part will do my utmost for the city, as one which has long been closely connected to the house of my ancestors' (*C Pap. Jud.* II 153 73–107).

Jewish Revolts in the Roman Empire

Claudius was only partially successful in preventing further disturbances. The Jews across the empire revolted three times against Rome: in 66–70, 115–17, and 132–5. The Alexandrian Jews were involved in the first two of these and the Egyptian Jews were involved in 115–17 CE. The revolt in 66 began in Caesarea, ignited by growing tensions between the Greeks and Jews living there (Joseph, *BJ* 2.14.5). Fighting broke out in Alexandria when the Greeks discovered and killed some Jewish spies at a meeting in the theatre while they were deliberating sending an embassy to the emperor Nero. Seeking revenge, the Jews began a sustained attack against the Greeks. The prefect Tiberius Julius Alexander sent in the legions after negotiations with Jewish leaders failed. Although Josephus' figure of 50,000 Jewish casualties is probably an exaggeration, the Alexandrian Jewish community lost a large number of men (Joseph, *BJ* 2.487–98). All the Jews in the empire were punished for this revolt by the imposition of the *fiscus Judaicus*, a poll tax payable to Rome (*BJ* 7.218).

In 115–16 the Jews of Cyrenaica, Egypt, Cyprus, Mesopotamia, and Judaea began to revolt against the Roman empire, led by messianic leaders. In Cyrenaica they rallied behind one Lucuas, or Andreas, who had ordered the Jews to destroy pagan temples; in Cyprus they rallied under Artemion. The sources do not agree with the date of the revolt, or even where it first broke out. According to an excerpt of Dio it began in Cyrenaica in the last months of 116 (Cass. Dio 68.32.1–2), although Christian sources suggest that the revolt broke out in Alexandria in 115 (Euseb. *Hist. Eccl.* 4.2.1–4; Oros. 7.12.6–7, 7.27.6). The lack of consistency in the various sources could well suggest that the revolts broke out more or less contemporaneously in these places (Pucci 2005: 259–62).

Several texts from the *Acta Alexandrinorum* literature offer a glimpse into the events in Alexandria in this period. *C Pap. Jud.* II 435 purports to be a copy of an edict of the prefect Rutlius Lupus dated 14 October 115, written in response to serious violence between Greeks and Jews in Alexandria. *C Pap. Jud.* II 158a and b reports a trial in the imperial court during the course of which an emperor questions Alexandrian Greeks and Jews about the events that led up to this violence before at least one Alexandrian Greek is led away for torture and execution (Harker 2008: 56–9, 73–9, 82–98).

The Alexandrian ambassadors suggest that the violence had been caused by an incident at the theatre and a triumphal parade through Alexandria. The scene is perhaps similar to the mocking of King Agrippa in 38, although on this occasion an actor may have played the role of one of the messianic figures around whom the Jews were gathering: 'Paulus gave evidence concerning the "king" whom they paraded and how he proclaimed "year one"(?), and Theon read the edict of Lupus in which he ordered them to bring to him the man from the stage and from the mime mocking the "king" ...' (*C Pap. Jud.* II 158a i.1–7, 435 ii.24). The Alexandrians also complain that the prefect 'had ordered the impious Jews to transfer their residence to a place from which they could easily attack and ravage our well-named city' (*C Pap. Jud.* II 158a vi.11–18). The only reference we have to a prefect 'settling' the Jews in any single area of the city is Flaccus' herding the Jews into a section of the city in 38, and the ambassadors may be alleging that Lupus did the same.

The edict of Lupus shows that the Romans had sided with the Alexandrian Greeks against the Jews, as they had in 38 and 66, but subsequently took steps to prevent the Greeks from continuing the violence (in *C Pap. Jud.* II 158a ii.8–9 the Jews accuse the Greeks of seizing Jewish prisoners from jails and wounding them). The edict was directed against the 'few' Alexandrian Greeks who were continuing to make retaliatory attacks on the Jews. The prefect acknowledges that most of the troublemakers are slaves, but holds their masters responsible for their actions and announces that a special judge is to be sent by the emperor to punish those who are guilty of retaliatory violence, and urges order to be restored to the city:

> Let there be an end of people saying, some truthfully, some falsely, that they have been wounded and demand justice violently and unjustly. For it was not necessary to be wounded. Some of these mistakes could perhaps have had an excuse before the battle between the Romans and the Jews, but now however such courts of judgment are useless and have never before been permitted. (*C Pap. Jud.* II 435 iii.20–iv.3)

The decision of the 'special judge' is alluded to in a damaged section of *C Pap. Jud.* II 158a, which is tentatively restored on the basis of a later copy, *C Pap. Jud.* II 158b: sixty Alexandrians and their slaves were punished: '[Paulus(?)]: Emperor, the Alexandrians did not [...] many were punished; sixty [Alexandrians and their] slaves. The Alexandrians [were exiled and their slaves(?)] beheaded' (*C Pap. Jud.* II 158a ii.23–7, 158b 5–9). It may even be the case that the 'Alexandrians, [their slaves having been crucified,] were beheaded', as Paulus later refers to mourning, 'the tears shed for all men' (*C Pap. Jud.* II 158a iii.1–2).

Further fighting in Alexandria was to follow in 116 CE (Euseb. *Hist. Eccl.* 4.2.3). Buildings in Alexandria were destroyed at this time (e.g. the Nemesion temple; App. *B Civ.* 2.90), and Eusebius hints at the scale of the damage by claiming 'Hadrian rebuilt Alexandria after it was destroyed by the Jews' (Euseb. *Chron.* Hadrian year 1). The Jews in Egypt did not revolt until the spring of 116, as several tax receipts show that the Jewish tax and other taxes were still being paid then by Jews (*C Pap. Jud.* II 227–9, 369; 227 bears the latest date, 18 May 116). Letters preserved on papyri from the archive of Apollonius, a *strategos* from the district of Apollinopolis-Heptakomias, offer a unique insight into the revolt (collected in *C Pap. Jud.* II 436–50; Pucci 2005, papyri nos 15–41). His mother, Eudaimonis, frequently writes of her hopes that her son will be safe and not defeated by the 'impious Jews' (e.g. *C Pap. Jud.* II 437), and his wife, Aline, shows her concerns too (e.g. *C Pap. Jud.* II 436). Egyptian villagers themselves became involved in the fighting. In one battle near Hermopolis Magna the Egyptian force was 'beaten and many were killed' (*C Pap. Jud.* II 438). In November 117 Apollonius resubmitted a request to the prefect for leave to attend several of his properties that had been damaged in the revolt (*C Pap. Jud.* II 443), suggesting that the revolt ended in the summer of 117 and had lasted just over a year. The Roman army in Egypt suffered a high number of casualties at this time, attesting the ferocity of the revolt (Fink 1971, nos 34 and 74).

The Jewish revolt had dire consequences for the Jews in Egypt. The Alexandrian Jews sustained heavy casualties in 115–17. Although the trial of *C Pap. Jud.* II 158a suggests that the community survived this incident to protest to the emperor, there was further fighting within the city during 116. There was also violence in the city in the early years of Hadrian's reign, which prompted Hadrian to write a strongly worded letter to the city (SHA *Hadr.* 12.1–2; cf. Cass. Dio 69.8.1a), and the Jews may have been involved in this. After this time the Alexandrian Jews leave little impact on the historical record. The fact that they did not join the Jewish revolt of 132–5 suggests that there were few left in the city. Papyri of the second century attest individual Jews but not communities. In Karanis, for example, a tax register of over a thousand men in the mid-second century reveals that there was only one Jew there at that time (*C Pap. Jud.* II 460; Kasher 1981). No receipts for the Jewish tax dating to after 117 have been found at Edfu, where around seventy receipts from the period 71–116 were discovered (*C Pap. Jud.* II 160–229). A 'Jewish account', set up to register land formerly owned by the Jews for the purposes of confiscation, is mentioned in documents (*C Pap. Jud.* II 445, 448; *P Köln* II 97; *SB* XII 10892, 10893). Almost a century later the Oxyrhynchites attempted to secure imperial favour by reminding Severus and Caracalla that they had aided the Romans in the war against the Jews. This document also reveals that the Oxyrhynchites still celebrated the day of the Jewish defeat as a festival (*C Pap. Jud.* II 450).

The *Acta Alexandrinorum* and the Oracle of the Potter

The literature read in Roman Egypt after the Jewish revolt portrayed the Jews as enemies. The *Acta Alexandrinorum*, which tell the stories of the deaths of Alexandrian Greek nobles and are presented as the official minutes (*acta*) of their trial in the imperial court, cast the Jews in the role of accusers. In the stories rival delegations of Alexandrian Greeks and Jews travel to Rome. The Jews persuade the emperor to ally himself with them against the Greeks and, consequently, after bitter exchanges between the emperor and the Alexandrian Greeks, some are led away to execution. There is no attempt in the stories to portray the trials in a fair and balanced way. The Jews are only individually named in one story (*C Pap. Jud.* II 157 13–16), and the speeches of the Jewish ambassadors are considerably shorter than those of the Greeks. Some of the stories have a historical and perhaps a documentary basis, and use historical personages, but all surviving examples have been fictionalized to some extent. The best-preserved examples featuring the Jews tell the story of the trial of Isidorus and Lampon before Claudius (*C Pap. Jud.* II 156a–d), Hermaiscus before Trajan (*C Pap. Jud.* II 157), and Paulus and Antoninus before either Trajan or Hadrian (*C Pap. Jud.* II 158a) (Musurillo 1954; Harker 2008).

The Alexandrian Greek ambassadors frequently insult the Jews. Isidorus retorts to Claudius: 'My Lord Caesar, what do you care for a three-obol Jew like Agrippa?' (*C Pap. Jud.* II

156b 17–19). The most likely meaning of this term is 'worthless'. In another section, Isidorus responds to being called 'the son of an actress (i.e. prostitute)' by Claudius by declaring that Claudius is 'a cast-off son of the Jewess Salome!' (*C Pap. Jud.* II 156d 7–12). Later Isidorus claims that the Jews wish to 'stir up the entire world' and asserts that the Jews' lack of culture should make them liable to pay the poll tax: 'I accuse them of wishing to stir up the entire world... We must consider every detail in order to judge the whole people. They are not of the same nature as the Alexandrians, but live rather in the same manner as the Egyptians. Are they not equal to those who pay the poll-tax?' (*C Pap. Jud.* II 156 22–7). In a different story Hermaiscus tells Trajan: 'It grieves us to see your imperial council filled with impious Jews' and 'is the name of the Jews not offensive? You should therefore help your own people (i.e. nobles) rather than play advocate for the impious Jews!' (*C Pap. Jud.* II 157 41–3, 47–50).

The Jewish ambassadors in the stories are portrayed as insidious and deceitful. In *C Pap. Jud.* II 157 the narrator relates how the Jews influenced the empress in order to win Trajan's favour for themselves:

> Plotina approached the senators so that they might oppose the Alexandrians and support the Jews. The Jews were the first to enter and greet the emperor Trajan, who greeted them most cordially in return, having already been won over by Plotina. The Alexandrian ambassadors entered next and greeted the emperor. He, however, did not receive them kindly but said: 'Do you say "hail" to me as though you deserved to receive a greeting—when you are guilty of such outrages against the Jews!' (*C Pap. Jud.* II 157 26–37)

In *C Pap. Jud.* II 158a they successfully persuade the emperor to punish some of the Alexandrian ambassadors, and in *C Pap. Jud.* II 156a, b, and d the emperor's friendship with the Jewish king Agrippa is stressed. The historicity of this alleged imperial favour towards the Jews is difficult to uphold as whenever there was violence in the city, the Roman army sided with the Greeks against the Jews.

These stories must have thrived in Alexandria. However, all the surviving examples come from the *chora* and, where the owners can be identified, they belonged to a class of 'upwardly mobile' Hellenized Egyptians. Reading these stories about Alexandria and its heroic citizens was a vehicle for socially ambitious Egyptians to lay a claim on a Greek identity, which allowed them subsequently to gain status and prominence in their local communities (Harker 2008: 112–19). One example is Nemesion, a Hellenized Egyptian tax collector from the substantial village of Philadelphia who copied Claudius' letter to the Alexandrians (Hanson 1984: 1107–18).

The Jews are portrayed in an equally negative light in the Oracle of the Potter, which stands in a long literary tradition of Egyptian nationalistic propaganda (Koenen 1968). The extant versions of the oracle, in which a potter from the Pharaonic period delivers a prophecy concerning the bleak future of Egypt, are written in Greek, and they were presumably read by educated, Hellenized Egyptians. However, the readers rejected the Greek identity coveted by the readers of the *Acta Alexandrinorum* in favour of an Egyptian identity drawn from its pharaonic heritage. The Oracle labels the Greeks 'Typhonians' (followers of Seth) and 'the girdle wearers', perhaps referring to the Greek dress worn in the army or police, and looks forward to a time when Alexandria ('the city by the sea') will be abandoned and become a 'fisherman's drying place' (Clarysse 1991).

The Oracle of the Potter was a fluid tradition, and several further fragments reveal how it was updated in the Roman period (*C Pap. Jud.* III 520 and some Oxyrhynchus fragments published in Koenen 2002). In these fragments hostility is shown towards the Romans, whose cavalry exercise in the grounds of old Egyptian temples, as well as the Greeks, but the main enemy is now the Jews; they are perhaps even to be identified with the Typhonians: 'The temples [will belong] to the horses [because of the] factions of the troops. Attack the Jews! Do not allow your city to become abandoned! Your largest temple will be a sandy exercise court for horses! They (the Jews) will commit injustice' (*C Pap. Jud.* II 520 3–6; Koenen 2002, fr. I 12–16). If the Jewish offences are to be taken as literal, rather than metaphorical, these sections may have been written in response to the Jewish revolt under Trajan (Frankfurter 1992).

Conclusion

Little is heard of the Jews after the revolt of 115–17, and it is to be hoped that further finds of papyri will help to redress both this void and the lack of evidence for the involvement of the Jews in the spread of Christianity in Roman Egypt. Jews no longer appear in the *Acta Alexandrinorum* stories set under the Antonine or Severan emperors. Nonetheless, the fortunes of the Jews slowly began to recover and communities were re-established, helped undoubtedly by immigration. Under the Severans their status in Alexandria and elsewhere in Egypt was improved. Between 198 and 211 Severus and Caracalla passed a law (or perhaps even ratified a pre-existing one) that allowed Jews to hold municipal offices without imposing obligations that affected their *superstitio* (*Dig.* 50.2.3.3). In Alexandria this should have stopped the objections to Jews gaining Alexandrian citizenship. With the Constitutio Antoniniana in 212, all Jews in the empire gained Roman citizenship. By the end of the third century a synagogue is attested in Oxyrhynchus, suggesting that a community had developed there once again (*C Pap. Jud.* III 473).

Suggested Reading

The plight of the Jews in Alexandria during this period is explored further in Collins (2005) and in Mélèze Modrzejewski's wide-ranging diachronic study of Judaism in Egypt, now translated into English (1995). The Jews in Egypt and Alexandria are also considered in Gruen (2002) and Schäfer (1997), along with the Jews in other provinces of the Roman empire.

Bibliography

Bell, H. 1924. *Jews and Christians in Egypt: The Jewish Troubles in Alexandria and the Athanasian Controversy (P. Lond. VI)*. London: British Museum Press.

Clarysse, W. 1991. 'The City of the Girdle-Wearers and a New Demotic Document', *Enchoria* 18: 177–8.

Collins, J. 2005. 'Anti-Semitism in Antiquity? The Case of Alexandria', in C. Bakhos (ed.), *Ancient Judaism in its Hellenistic Context*. Leiden: Brill, 9–29.

Cowey, J. M. S., and K. Maresch. 2001. *Urkunden des Politeuma der Juden von Heracleopolis [144/3–133/2 v. Chr] (P. Polit. Iud.)*. Wiesbaden: Westdeutscher.

Delia, D. 1988. 'The Population of Roman Alexandria', *Transactions of the American Philological Association* 118: 275–92.

Fink, R. O. 1971. *Roman Military Records on Papyrus*. Cleveland: Case Western Reserve University.

Frankfurter, D. 1992. 'Lest Egypt's City Be Deserted: Religion and Ideology in the Egyptian Response to the Jewish Revolt (116–117 CE)', *Journal of Jewish Studies* 43: 203–20.

Gruen, E. S. 2002. *Diaspora: Jews amidst Greeks and Romans*. Cambridge, Mass.: Harvard University Press.

Hanson, A. 1984. 'Caligulan Month-Names at Philadelphia and Related Matters', in *Atti del XVII Congresso Internazionale di Papirologia, Napoli, 19–26 maggio 1983*, vol. 3. Naples: Centro Internazionale per lo Studio dei Papiri Ercolanesi, 1107–18.

Harker, A. 2008. *Loyalty and Dissidence in Roman Egypt: The Case of the Acta Alexandrinorum*. Cambridge: Cambridge University Press.

Kasher, A. 1981. 'The Jewish Community of Oxyrhynchus in the Roman Period', *Journal of Jewish Studies* 32: 150–7.

—— 1985. *The Jews in Hellenistic and Roman Egypt: The Struggle for Equal Rights*. Tübingen: Mohr.

Kerkeslager, A. 2006. 'Agrippa and the Mourning Rites for Drusilla in Alexandria', *Journal for the Study of Judaism in the Persian, Hellenistic and Roman Period* 37: 367–400.

Koenen, L. 1968. 'Die Prophezeiungen des "Töpfers"', *Zeitschrift für Papyrologie und Epigraphik* 2: 178–209.

—— 2002. 'Die Apologie des Töpfers an König Amenophis, oder das Töpferorakel', in A. Blasius and B. U. Schipper (eds), *Apokalyptik und Ägypten: Eine kritische Analyse des relevanten Texte aus dem griechisch-römischen Ägypten*. Leuven: Peeters, 139–87.

Kushnir-Stein, A. 2000. 'On the Visit of Agrippa I to Alexandria in AD 38', *Journal of Jewish Studies* 51: 227–42.

Mélèze Modrzejewski, J. 1995. *The Jews of Egypt: From Rameses II to Emperor Hadrian*, trans. R. Cornman. Edinburgh: Edinburgh University Press.

Musurillo, H. 1954. *The Acts of the Pagan Martyrs: Acta Alexandrinorum*. Oxford: Clarendon Press.

Pucci, M. 2005. *Diaspora Judaism in Turmoil, 116/117 CE: Ancient Sources and Modern Insights*. Leuven: Peeters.

Schäfer, P. 1997. *Judeophobia: Attitudes towards the Jews in the Ancient World*. Cambridge, Mass.: Harvard University Press.

Schwartz, D. 1990. *Agrippa I: The Last King of Judaea*. Tübingen: Mohr.

Smallwood, E. 1976. *The Jews under Roman Rule from Pompey to Diocletian: A Study in Political Relations*. Leiden: Brill.

Turner, E. G. 1954. 'Tiberius Julius Alexander', *Journal of Roman Studies* 44: 54–64.

van der Horst, P. W. 2003. *Philo's Flaccus: The First Pogrom, Introduction, Translation and Commentary*. Leiden: Brill.

CHAPTER 18

FAMILIES, HOUSEHOLDS, AND CHILDREN*

MYRTO MALOUTA

More than any other part of the Roman empire, Egypt offers data such as census returns, contracts, and tax receipts that reveal much about family relationships and household structures—but also raise a number of questions and may present some situations unique to Egypt. This chapter draws chiefly on papyrological sources to discuss family matters in Roman Egypt, but also incorporates some of the archaeological and art-historical evidence.

Marriage and Divorce

Sources

Papyri from Roman Egypt are abundantly illustrative of various aspects of marriage. Most informative, especially on the procedural sides of the institution and the provisions taken in case it should fail, are the marriage documents themselves (see Yiftach-Firanko 2003: 9–32). Other types of papyrus texts also expose the lives of spouses and the problems they encountered or caused each other. In some petitions one spouse complains about the other, for reasons that may lead to divorce. There are also petitions following a decision to dissolve a marriage, mostly relating to the dowry and the care of children. Documents making provision in case of divorce or death of one of the spouses are also mostly involved with the material aspects of the union, as are those that record transfer of property between spouses. Various other types of document elucidate the process of getting married and carrying out administrative tasks such as registering children. There are also hybrid documents, such as marriage contracts combined with loans and wills (Montevecchi 1936; McNamee 1982; Gagos, Koenen, and McNellen 1992; Sijpesteijn 1996; Yiftach-Firanko 2003: 152, on the *syngraphodiatheke*).

* This chapter was written during the year 2010, when I held a scholarship from the Botsaris Foundation at the Institute of Greek and Roman Antiquity, National Hellenic Research Foundation. I wish to thank both for their support.

Form and Legal Aspects of Marriage

The act of marriage consisted mainly of the *ekdosis*, 'handing over', of the woman to be married, and the grant of the dowry. The 'handing over' was not just symbolic, since marriage in Egypt was virilocal, so the wife left her home and moved into her husband's household. A particularity of the *ekdosis* in Egypt, as opposed to Athenian practice, is that it was not contracted exclusively between men, but women could also participate, usually the mother of the bride and on occasion also the bride herself (Yiftach-Firanko 2003: 41–3). This practice was the basis of the act of marriage, and was occasionally recorded in a corresponding marriage document, though the specific *ekdosis* clause is rarely used in the Roman period and only according to local custom (Yiftach-Firanko 2003: 45).

The function of the document was just to record the marriage and commit to writing certain practical provisions, usually to do with property; it was not a constitutive element of the marriage itself (Yiftach-Firanko 2003: 260). Depending on whether such a document was composed or not, marriages were called *eggraphoi* or *agraphoi*. Recording the marriage did not affect its status or validity or impinge upon potential claims between the spouses or their children (Wolff 1939: 58–60; Yiftach-Firanko 2003: 45, 81–94). Often such a document was composed several years after the marriage had been contracted, and only when practical necessity arose (Yiftach-Firanko 2003: 104, 259). Accordingly, marriage documents in sibling marriages are very rare, since there was no urgent need to record in writing provisions the family would make anyway (Hopkins 1980: 323; Yiftach-Firanko 2003: 99–102). One exception that indicates that the document was not entirely devoid of legal ramifications relates to the power fathers exercised over their offspring: in an *agraphos gamos* the father's power (*exousia*) over his children and their property continued past puberty, as opposed to the *eggraphos gamos*, where it ceased (Montevecchi 1936: 10–11).

There are important differences in the practice and form of concluding a marriage in the *chora* of Egypt and in Augustan Alexandria, which suggests independent development of the same legal institution in different regions (Wolff 1939: 34–47; Allam 1990; Yiftach-Firanko 2003: 72–9; also Erdmann 1940, 1941; Burkhalter 2004). Nonetheless, the predominant characteristic of marriage in Roman Egypt was its informality. Its formation and termination was a private agreement between the spouses and their families, requiring no state intervention, while its legal consequences mostly concerned the legitimacy of the children resulting from the union (Bagnall and Frier 1994: 111–12).

The Dowry

The main type of dowry was the *pherne*. It is attested until the second century, but only the value is recorded, not the composition (for a list of dowry attestations in the papyri, see Krause 1994–5: II 256–63). New types of dowry are also attested from the beginning of the Roman period in Egypt, the *parapherna* and *prosphora*. As opposed to the *pherne*, the *parapherna* stayed in the wife's possession, while the *prosphora* conveyed to the husband the right to use assets, such as land and slaves, without bestowing ownership, thus restricting the husband's power over the dowry (Yiftach-Firanko 2003: 180–1). Some documents from Roman Egypt give a glimpse of the woman's point of view in planning her marriage provisions (Mélèze Modrzejewski 1981; Kutzner 1989).

Matrimonial Property

Although a daughter left home once she married, she went on being connected to her family through property she received through inheritance or dowry. This could cause problems, since she occasionally found her loyalties divided between father and husband. Even her own possessions put her in an ambiguous position, since landownership increased her dependence on her husband, who had to cooperate if she sold or leased it out, while her approval was required in the case of movables (Pomeroy 1988: 713–14). Within the landed classes, Bagnall suggests that women's independence, as well as the need to handle business on their own, was accentuated by long absences of their husbands, as attested by the papyri (Bagnall 2007: 189–90).

Until the time of Diocletian no formal provision for spouses in case of intestate death is attested, just as in classical Greek law, which covered the inheritance rights of relatives, but not of spouses. No documents refer specifically to the practice followed in such eventuality, and there is no evidence of property acquisition from either spouse when the other died intestate. It follows that when a husband died intestate, his widow had the following options: stay in the house, which now belonged not to her but to her children; return to her own family home; or remarry. It has been assumed that, in the absence of institutional provision, there must have been an acknowledged right of use by the widow of her children's inheritance (Rupprecht 1985: 291–2; see also Kreller 1919; Häge 1968). Krause deduces that most widows did not remarry and stayed in their children's homes, since this is where we find them in the census (Krause 1994–5: II 98). But remarried widows living in their new husbands' homes are not unambiguously visible as they often appear just as wives with children from someone other than their current husband.

Accordingly, in the surviving testaments careful provision is made for the care of a potential widow, unless she is already dead herself or no longer the testator's wife. Usually the widow received household items, jewellery, clothes, and the right to continue residing in the house. There is often the limitation that her residence right and any financial support are to cease if she remarries. Only very rarely is a wife nominated as heiress (Rupprecht 1985: 292–3). Krause (1994–5: II 97–100) provides a detailed list of testamentary bequests to widows.

To be sure, women in Egypt inherited and owned property throughout the Roman period, if not so much from their husbands then from their parents, both movables and real estate, and this includes Egyptian, Greek, and Roman women (Hobson 1983: 319). It has consequently been suggested that the husband may not have often bequeathed property to the wife because she already owned property through dowry or inheritance, so his will aimed at extending his main responsibility towards his wife, which was her maintenance during her lifetime (Hobson 1983: 320). It is difficult to draw conclusions from this, since in none of these cases do we know what property the wife herself may have owned. Besides, in women's wills husbands are only occasionally mentioned, and in donations and property divisions to take effect after death, spouses are regularly not included (Rupprecht 1985: 294). Regardless of the personal assets of either spouse, however, a preference for bequests to descendants is exhibited by both sexes, a phenomenon found in economics literature today as 'intergenerational altruism' (see Kolm and Ythier 2006).

Establishing the social and psychological situation of widows is much more complex. Tibiletti (1984) found evidence of women suffering badly, though these cases are mostly found in petitions and the suffering may have been exaggerated to gain the sympathy of the addressee. But he also found widowed women who prospered, managed their affairs competently, and raised their children unaided (Tibiletti 1984: 989–90; Bagnall 2007: 189–91).

Social and Demographic Aspects of Marriage

Marital practice in Roman Egypt was based on monogamy and virilocality. The census returns yield abundant information on the demographic aspects of marriage, not only isolated data on specific instances of married couples, but also on some long-term, stable marriages (Bagnall and Frier 1994: 121–2).

According to the census data, women started getting married at 12 years old or soon after. By age 20, 60 per cent or more had married. By their late twenties almost all free women had married at least once (Bagnall and Frier 1994: 111–16). Early marriage for women ensured better fertility and a better chance of virginity, which was important in proving paternity and sometimes also a requirement in marriage documents (Montserrat 1996: 81–2). Conversely, men rarely married before their late teens. Many did so in their early twenties and about half had married by 25. The rate of marriage slows substantially after that age, but by their early fifties all men were or had been married (Bagnall and Frier 1994: 116).

The pattern of data suggests that the husband was usually older. In two-thirds of recorded marriages the range is from zero to fifteen years and the overall mean age gap is seven and a half years. Occasionally we encounter an older wife, while the largest recorded gap is thirty-one years, the husband being senior (Bagnall and Frier 1994: 119).

Divorce

Either spouse in Roman Egypt had the right to demand the dissolution of their marriage, according to both Roman and Egyptian law (Bagnall 1987: 54). A husband initiating the divorce was obliged to restore to his wife without delay whatever type of dowry he had received. If a wife initiated it, different rules applied to the various dowry types (Yiftach-Firanko 2003: 208).

As was the case with marriage, divorce was also a strictly private affair. No third party with constitutive power was involved, and the divorce document had declaratory character, usually just acknowledging receipt of the dowry and stating any future obligations of the spouses (Arnaoutoglou 1995: 19–21). The husband's obligation to provide for his wife continued after divorce only if the wife was pregnant at the time of divorce. Then he had to offer a subsidy for childbirth and subsequently be responsible for the child's support (Adam 1983: 16).

According to the census, divorce was quite common among the general population, though probably not equally among all classes of the population; especially among the lower classes, frequency of divorce is a matter of debate. Since children were often attested, the issue probably was not the wife's infertility or inability to produce a male heir. Divorce frequently occurred at a young age and was followed by remarriage. Close-kin marriages seem to have ended in divorce more often than exogamous unions (Bagnall and Frier 1994: 123–4).

Remarriage after divorce is widely attested, especially for men, as is incorporation of children from previous marriages into new families (Bagnall and Frier 1994: 126). Conversely, remarriage after the death of a spouse is more common for women (Krause 1994–5: I 97).

The marriage documents from Roman Egypt do not contain explicit references to previous marriages for either party. Krause (1994–5: I 95–6) offers a list of such documents where it is known from other sources that the marriage in question is a second marriage for at least one party. The lack of reference to previous marriages or to the present being a second marriage suggests it was irrelevant for the purposes of a marriage contract and that the status of the second marriage was considered no different from that of the first marriage.

Beyond the formal and legal aspects, the process by which spouses reached the point of divorcing is illustrated by petitions from spouses reproaching their other halves, as well as documents illustrating procedural matters arising from the spouses' decision to separate, occasionally requiring an enforced resolution (Arnaoutoglou 1995: 14–17). The petitions, submitted by one of the spouses and less often by one of their parents, usually concern property affairs and the dowry. Where the outcome is known, it was either the dowry's return or a court decision to seize the husband's property instead (Arnaoutoglou 1995: 22–8). It follows that a husband had to provide material goods to the wife according to his means, and respect her personality, property, and rights, and both spouses must maintain fidelity and sexual exclusivity; failing these obligations often led to divorce (Arnaoutoglou 1995: 17–18).

Similar options were available to a divorcée as to a widow, though the former often ended up alone, since children usually stayed with their father (Bagnall 2007: 190). Returning to her family home was not always straightforward, especially if she wholly or partly owned the house in which she lived, as well as in the case of brother–sister marriage (see below). In the former case it is likely that it was the husband who had to leave the house, and indeed according to the census many divorced women owned their own house, though perhaps those houses were ceded to them by their parents after the divorce. Furthermore, when a brother–sister marriage ended, census evidence suggests that some previously married siblings continued to cohabit, an indication that there may have been little choice where to go in such cases (Barker 1997: 59–60).

Imperial legislation on divorce remained unchanged until the time of Constantine, who tried to make unilateral divorce more difficult, an attempt reversed by Julian (Bagnall 1987: 43–4). Thereafter, the tendency was increasingly to limit divorce, which culminated in Justinian's ban of divorce by mutual consent in 542 (Bagnall 1987: 45). This development is usually interpreted as Christian influence, but Bagnall attributes it to concern for family property and the property rights of children (Bagnall 1987: 52–3).

Brother–Sister Marriage

Brother–sister marriage in Roman Egypt has been a thorny issue not just for Roman historians and papyrologists, but also for anthropologists and biologists. The phenomenon has been traditionally considered an isolated instance in the history of humankind (but see Goody 1990: 321–3; Scheidel 1996a: 9; Frandsen 2009: 33) and a unique breach of the incest taboo, though recent discussions have emphasized the many possible definitions of incest according to the exact boundary between what is and is not allowed; after all, unions between children and parents were definitely prohibited in Egypt (Frandsen 2009: 18; Rowlandson and Takahashi 2009: 106–7). Hopkins (1980: 306, 326), adopting a similar argument, also explained the biological ramifications of endogamy over several generations (for which, see Scheidel 1996a: 9–51, in more detail).

The usual explanations suggested for brother–sister marriage have to do with the dowry and family property, tradition, or primacy of lineage. Most scholars nowadays tend to agree that no one explanation is enough to account for the phenomenon, but that a combination of the ramifications of virilocal marriage, partible inheritance, as well as Roman emphasis on status, could have led to endogamy. Moreover, the fact that endogamy was generally prohibited by Roman law and allowed by special dispensation in Egypt may have encouraged its dissemination as a distinctive custom (Rowlandson and Takahashi 2009). The brother–sister marriage debate was recently rekindled by an article expressing doubts about whether we are indeed dealing with biological siblings, or rather a widespread adoption practice, so far overlooked in the sources (Huebner 2007; see Kuryłowicz 1983 on adoption in the papyri). This theory has not been met with universal approval, but it raised important points and engendered valuable responses (Remijsen and Clarysse 2008; Rowlandson and Takahashi 2009).

Evidence of marriage of extremely close kin is widespread in the census and attested in successive generations (Hopkins 1980: 322; Scheidel 1996a: 11–12). Kinship between spouses is detectable, since the lineage of household members is usually stated in census documents. The first examples of sibling marriage in the census come from 103/4, by which time it was already a widespread phenomenon, attested in birth and status registrations, marriage and divorce settlements, tax and sale documents, wedding invitations, and so forth. In these documents sibling marriages are more visible than more distant endogamous unions (Alston 2005: 139). The evidence suggests that nearly one in six marriages was between full siblings, and the great majority of them obtained several children (Bagnall and Frier 1994: 127–8). The phenomenon continued until 212, when the applicability of Roman law to all inhabitants of Egypt suppressed it, though there is papyrological evidence for tolerance for a few years after the Constitutio Antoniniana, presumably for unions and children that predated it (Montevecchi 1979: 140–2).

It is difficult to determine whether the origins of the phenomenon lie in Hellenistic or Pharaonic Egypt, and in the period under examination names are of no help in determining whether the majority of those practising full sibling marriage were of Greek or Egyptian ancestry. The consensus is that the phenomenon spread in early Roman Egypt from north to south and from the *metropoleis* to the countryside; indeed, it was much more common in urban areas and *metropoleis*, especially in the Arsinoite nome (Bagnall and Frier 1994: 129–30). Nevertheless, the papyrological evidence may be misleading, since attestations of sibling marriage in the documents follow the overall pattern of documentation, so perhaps the ostensible chronological and geographical restrictions of the phenomenon are in fact imposed by the limitations of the documentation (Huebner 2007: 25). For example, Bussi's conclusions regarding a sharp rise in endogamy in the first two centuries, that the phenomenon is mostly attested among privileged metropolites, and that marriage of cousins is rarely attested and therefore probably not often practised, tend to take the evidence too much at face value (Bussi 2002: 3).

Marriage of Soldiers

Another idiosyncratic family form, though not peculiar to Egypt, was that of Roman soldiers. All soldiers were banned from contracting legal marital unions, probably from the time of Augustus until 197, when the marriage ban was lifted (Campbell 1978: 153; Alston

1995: 54–5; Phang 2001: 345). The reasons behind the ban are not explicitly stated in the sources, and theories usually aim at explanations that are financial or political, or pertaining to military administration. But many scholars attempting to explain the ban of the *matrimonium iustum* for soldiers follow a line of reasoning that assumes it banned formation of families—which it did not.

Notwithstanding the ban, there is ample evidence that soldiers formed de facto unions with women, both Roman and peregrine, had children, and shared their assets with them. The complications arising from such unions involved the status of the offspring, who were illegitimate; intestate succession, to which the soldier's family had no recourse for a long time; and property that exchanged hands between the couple.

The illegitimacy of soldiers' children was of no social consequence, and in Roman Egypt, according to the papyrological data, soldiers and veterans produced large households (Phang 2001: 296–9, 305). Legally, it has been a matter of debate whether those children became legitimate after their father's discharge, especially given the seemingly anomalous possibility that they might be Roman citizens (if both parents were Roman) but still illegitimate (Campbell 1978: 154; Phang 2002: 354). Phang has convincingly averred that only offspring produced after the father's discharge could ever be legitimate. In fact, legitimacy was not necessarily as sought after then as the weight of the word 'illegitimacy' might suggest today; indeed, there were also some advantages to it, such as being free from *patria potestas* (Phang 2001: 307, 318–19).

Admittedly illegitimacy caused some complications in inheritance law, so the children of soldiers had no claim to their father's estate if he died intestate, until Hadrian made this possible. But, even before, their father was free to make suitable testamentary arrangements, based on privileges conferred to soldiers already by Julius Caesar, which allowed them to bequeath any proportion of their estate to anyone (Alston 1995: 59).

Exchange of goods within a *matrimonium iustum* had, as we saw, the form of dowry. In the military unions in question women could only offer dowry in the form of 'deposit'. A deposit, unlike the dowry, could not be reclaimed in case of divorce, which severely limited the legal rights of a soldier's wife compared with a legitimate wife (Phang 2002: 355, 363). The union gained legitimacy at the time of the soldier's discharge, though any children already born remained illegitimate. A non-citizen soldier obtained Roman citizenship for himself and his children, but not his wife (Phang 2002: 357).

The authorities zealously kept the letter of the law regarding the ramifications of illegitimacy in the unions of soldiers, but seem not to have attempted outright prohibition of the actual formation of such unions (Campbell 1978: 154–6). It seems, therefore, that the ban did not reflect an objection to a soldier's enjoying the benefits of family life; the point was probably to avoid legal impediments to the dissolution of such unions and to ensure that any ties between father and children were only on the emotional level, unless the father made specific provisions to the contrary. In this way the state did not get involved in messy cases of inheritance claims from long-gone fathers once the legions moved on. Otherwise surely prohibitive measures, including punishment, would be taken in advance against such unions, rather than legal consequences that were only felt after the formation of the union. Especially since testamentary arrangements could be made, these consequences might hardly have mattered. Indeed, a cynical view is that the marriage ban was not a hindrance but a privilege for soldiers: it did nothing to prevent them from forming families and supporting them, while it removed all legal and financial constraints that obliged the rest of the population to do right by their families (Wells 1998: 189–90).

Houses and Households

Integration of Papyrology and Archaeology: Housing in Roman Egypt

The first extensive attempt to integrate papyrological and archaeological data about housing in Roman Egypt was made a century ago by Luckhard (1914), and, as both bodies of evidence grow, so does our understanding of the subject. The papyri are particularly useful in preserving language describing various aspects of housing, especially physical structures and their components. Husson (1983) is the main reference for the private house in Graeco-Roman Egypt, organized as lexical entries of terms for parts of the house as attested in the papyri. Papyrus texts also preserve information about the lives of the occupants, their identity, and social situation, and furnish details concerning urban housing, for which the archaeological evidence is scant. Excavations in the Fayum have revealed whole complexes of village housing where the form and architecture of the structures themselves can be studied. In particular, Roman Karanis preserves contemporaneous layers of dense structures, mostly houses, built without clear planning (see Chapter 14). The housing pattern in Karanis is similar to Soknopaiou Nesos, and it seems that the village, though probably more Hellenized than average, must have been representative of its kind (Alston 1997: 26, 28; van Minnen 1994: 230, 233, 237–49, for a reconstruction of a Karanis house).

The ground-plans of Karanis indicate great variation in house sizes: there were structures of under 40 m^2 and some of up to 200 m^2. The average was about 70 m^2, but usually houses comprised several storeys, not only in cities but also in villages, and had access to the roof. They usually also had a small yard, which could be sold separately from the rest of the house, as evidenced by the sale documents preserved on papyrus. Room division is attested in most houses, even small ones, though in no standard pattern (Alston 1997: 28–9).

The papyri imply that there were significant differences between urban and rural houses, though there must have been some overlap. Characteristic of an urban house was the *aithrion*, an internal courtyard. A type of house often attested in urban areas and typical of *metropoleis* was the *oikia dipurgia*, with two towers built onto the front (Alston 1997: 29–30). But, as in village houses, so in urban ones, there was great variation in shape and size, and explicit reference to stone houses in the papyri signifies that not all urban houses were made of stone. The mud-brick houses associated with villages must have been ubiquitous in towns too (Alston 1997: 39).

A typical case must have been that of Roman Oxyrhynchus, for which papyrological evidence is more forthcoming than archaeology (Fig. 18.1). All sorts of papyri mention housing, mostly juridical and administrative texts, but also private documents. They preserve names and topographical information on various quarters of the city. Stone structures are mentioned in the papyri more often than the much more common brick buildings (Husson 1976: 9–10). The *oikia dipurgia* is often attested in Oxyrhynchus, and houses of up to three storeys are common (*P Oxy*. XXXIV 2719 mentions a seven-storey house). Papyri sometimes note the condition of the exterior of the house as new, old, or ruined. Roofing

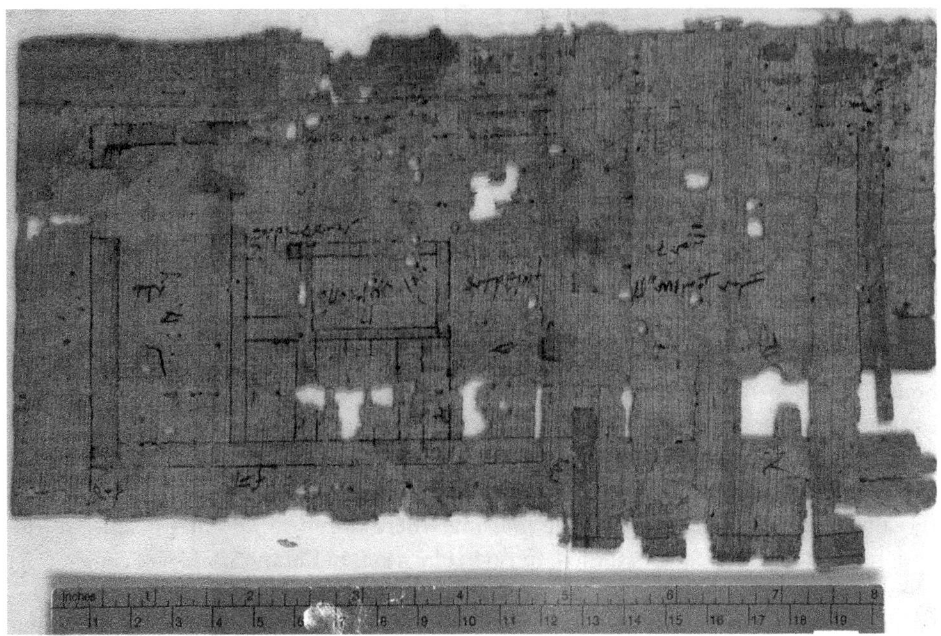

FIG. 18.1 Ground-plan of a house, in *P Oxy*. XXIV 2406

Courtesy of the Egypt Exploration Society and the Digital Imaging Project, Oxford University.

is hardly ever mentioned in the papyri, but stables, chicken pens, and camel pens are (Husson 1976: 13–14, 22).

Size and Composition of Households

Correlating the size of a house with the status and financial situation of the residents is difficult. Larger houses were often shared between two or more families or households, so it does not follow that a larger house meant more affluent residents. Social considerations could affect the distribution of social groups in urban settlements (Alston and Alston 1997: 211–15), and neighbourhoods could be arranged by occupation (Bagnall 2007: 184–5). So the key unit for understanding residential patterns is neither the house nor the family, since a family regularly shared a house with non-relatives, and was not necessarily confined to one house. Besides, evidence of a thriving housing market suggests a fluid relationship between houses and occupants (Alston 1997: 37). The Egyptian system of partible inheritance further contributed to the fragmentation of property ownership (see Hobson 1985: 213 n. 3).

The best point of reference therefore is the household, by which we understand a co-resident group of kin and non-kin, possibly also slaves, living in a house or part of a house. Village housing, in particular, was often shared between multiple nuclear families, as opposed to urban houses, the basis of which was usually a single family, but usually containing more slaves (Bagnall and Frier 1994: 60, 66–7, tables 3.1, 3.2; Alston 2005: 130). Extended families that occupied more than one house are difficult to trace, since tax lists and the census were organized by household, but they can occasionally be discerned in archival and epistolary material (Alston 2005: 141–2).

Consolidation of the census material in order to examine family structure was first undertaken by Calderini (1923, 1932a, b). By now approximately 300 returns are known, 167 of which are complete or near complete. One member in each household registered him- or herself and all other members of that household, stating their relationship to each other. But a rough sketch of the typical household is the best we can hope for, since the concept of 'household' was clear neither to census takers nor to declarants (Bagnall and Frier 1994: 57–8). The census documents must also be treated with some caution regarding the bias of age records and sex ratio (Scheidel 1996a: 53–91; 1996b).

Bagnall and Frier calculate the average size of the main resident family in a household as 4.3 persons, based on the 167 near-complete returns (4.0 if only the 136 complete are used), while families in villages are somewhat larger than urban families. Using the tax lists rather than census documents, Alston arrives at a slightly higher average (Bagnall and Frier 1994: 67–8; Alston 1997: 33–4). Slaves make up 11 per cent of the total census population, and are attested in slightly under one-sixth of households, mostly in the *metropoleis*, since most were domestic servants rather than workers. In both villages and cities most households that had slaves at all only had one or two, and few had more than six or seven (Bagnall and Frier 1994: 70–1).

Reproduction, Parents, and Children

Sex and Birth Control

Not much is known about the sex lives of married couples in Roman Egypt. There is evidence of sex for pleasure as opposed to procreation in the magical papyri, but it is doubtful whether these referred to married couples (Montserrat 1996: 86). At any rate, the evidence found therein cannot be considered representative, or it would suggest obsessive interest in sex in the society of Graeco-Roman Egypt, which is not supported by any other form of evidence (Whitehorne 1979: 242).

The methods of birth control potentially available to the population of Roman Egypt were contraception, abortion, and exposure of unwanted infants. There is more evidence of exposure, secondarily of abortion, and much less of contraception. There are, however, attestations in the Graeco-Roman world of potions as well as mechanical methods meant to prevent conception, some quite rational and possibly effective, and some ruled by magic and superstition (Eyben 1980–1: 9). Similar methods are mentioned as abortive practices, and surgical abortion is also attested (Eyben 1980–1: 11–12), while the distinction between contraception and abortion is not always clear in some medical sources (Hopkins 1965: 136–7).

In Egypt exposure is said to have been introduced by the Greeks. Evidence is found in the papyri, and in the Gnomon of the *Idios Logos* (a legal code followed in Roman Egypt) the adoption of exposed infants is penalized (Eyben 1980–1: 25–6). Exposure could aim either at the infant's discovery and 'rescue' or at its demise. Death was presumably the lot of most exposed infants, but many must have survived, especially in areas where there was great demand for slaves (Harris 1994: 9). The harsh reality of many people's lives meant that altruism might not have been enough of a reason for rescue, given the expenses involved in raising an exposed infant (calculated in Bagnall 1997: 135–7).

The extent to which birth control was practised in Graeco-Roman Egypt, the degree to which it was effective, and whether it was confined to certain classes of the population, have divided scholars. Eyben (1980–1: 7) attributes the small size of families in the Graeco-Roman world not just to social and biological problems, and Riddle (1992; Riddle, Worth Estes, and Russell 1994) argues for widespread usage of contraception in Egypt since before the Ptolemies. However, Frier (1994: 331) believes that such arguments do not stand in the light of demographic considerations, as they disregard the high mortality rates. Harris (1982) combined both schools of thought (ancient text-based and demographic–anthropological) in reviewing the debate on the demographic impact of infanticide in the Roman empire.

There is a distinction between birth control in general and birth control used by married couples to stop procreating after having a sufficient number of children. Frier claims that assuming such behaviour in Roman Egypt is both anachronistic and unsubstantiated, as there is not enough evidence for widespread family limitation in antiquity, while birth control, as attested in literature, is practised mostly in a non-marital context, namely prostitution, adultery, and sexual relations between or with slaves. At the most, family limitation may have been practised in some upper-class Roman families, and there may have been some attempt at birth spacing among the lower classes, in which cases contraception and abortion may have supplemented breast-feeding and post-partum abstinence (Frier 1994: 318–19, 332–3).

Harris (1994) conversely sees exposure as a way of limiting family size, and Hopkins (1965: 124, 136) takes it for granted that upper-class Romans wanted to limit the size of their families. To do so, they must have practised abortion on a large scale, while probably also using contraception quite extensively but not with consistent effectiveness, a fact that may also be reflected in the Severan legislation on birth control (Eyben 1980–1: 28–9).

Children and Parents: Legal Positions, Social Roles

Before 212 a peregrine child in Roman Egypt ceased to be a minor at the age of 14, and boys were then enrolled in the poll tax lists. For a Roman citizen, the age of legal majority was 25. After the promulgation of the Constitutio Antoniniana, the Roman age of 25 became the norm in Egypt, and under that both men and women were legally under age (Lewis 1979: 117).

For peregrines in Egypt, *patria potestas* was considered just a form of guardianship. For boys it ended with their coming of age at 14. For girls it was modified when they got married, but did not cease, since a father retained the right to intervene and take his daughter away from her husband—not, however, against her own will (Lewis 1970: 256). An unmarried adult daughter presumably remained under her father's control, while a divorced or widowed daughter probably reverted to it (Lewis 1970: 258).

References to missing parents are often found in the papyri from Roman Egypt; Krause (1994–5: III 255–64) discusses attestations of orphans in the papyri. A special category of children recorded as fatherless is that of the *apatores*, whose fatherlessness is a legal formality regarding official self-identification, rather than actual absence of a father. For some time, scholars thought the *apatores* were the children of soldiers, who, as discussed above, could not be considered legal offspring of their fathers (see Calderini 1953; Youtie 1975). The bulk of attestations of *apatores*, however, start long after the instigation of the marriage ban and go on for more than a century after the ban was lifted, so, while it is plausible that some *apatores* were indeed the children of soldiers, the extent to which this explanation can be applied may be quite limited (Malouta 2009: 121).

The visibility of children in the sources differs from that of adults. Regarding archaeology, the excavations at Karanis yielded ample material evidence of their presence in the form of toys and dolls (Fig. 18.2; see van Minnen 1994: 233). But since children paid no taxes and did not partake in economic transactions, they are much under-represented in the papyrological documentation. In literary texts a few attestations of child labour are found. In particular, children from families with low economic status were expected to work in the house and presumably also on the farm. An extension of this practice was to hire a child out as an apprentice, evidence of which is also found in the papyrological sources (Mirković 2005: 139–40), and children could be used as low-wage labourers in large-scale agriculture as well (Mirković 2005: 143–7).

Children, mostly those of higher social standing, appear in the papyri when registered by their parents (Nelson 1979). Notices of the birth of children of either sex were the same in structure, but they varied according to their provenance, especially those from the Arsinoite nome, Antinoopolis, and Oxyrhynchus (Mertens 1958: 48–65; Sánchez-Moreno Ellart 2010: 98–114). Registration was not demanded by the government, but sought to inform the authorities of a child's status and gave its lineage in order to prove it, so that the child could be included in the right tax lists and enjoy any privileges and other benefits its status might warrant (Cohen 1996: 389). Occasionally such notices were submitted long after the birth of a child, but before the age of legal maturity (see *P Ups. Frid* 6, introduction). In current

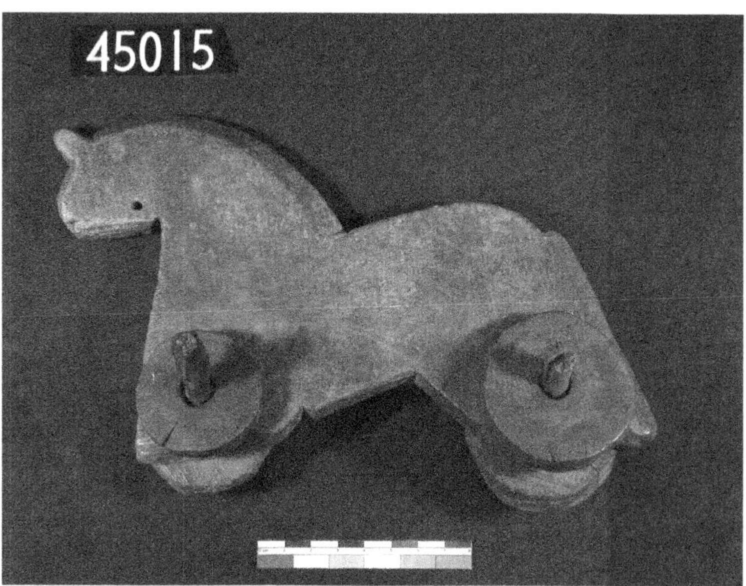

FIG. 18.2 Wooden toy horse on wheels from Karanis. Height *c*.15 cm

Petrie Museum of Egyptian Archaeology, UC 45015. Copyright the Petrie Museum of Egyptian Archaeology, University College London.

scholarship the term 'registration' of a child has become more popular than 'notice of birth' to reflect this (see Jördens 2000: 391; Sánchez-Moreno Ellart 2010: 93–5).

Beyond the scope of the papyrological evidence presented in this chapter, it is worth noting that children are well represented in the funerary art and archaeology of the Roman period, where great expense and care were seemingly taken to commemorate a premature death. Children's mummies among the burials of the Soter and Pebos families at Thebes were as elaborately embalmed and wrapped as the associated adults (e.g. Riggs 2005: 209–10, figs 102–3), as were children's burials at Hawara, and a number of mummy portraits from the Fayum represent children and adolescents. Several of these portraits depict boys with tufts of hair on otherwise shaved scalps, which has been interpreted as possibly being a mark of divine protection, perhaps sought in conjunction with healing (Ikram 2003), or else boys may have their hair arranged in a sidelock, or 'Horus lock', indicating their young age—the locks were cut off at the coming-of-age ceremony, or *mallokouria* (Montserrat 1991). Coming-of-age rites for girls, known as *therapeuteria*, are also attested; Huebner (2009) has recently suggested that this rite, which was celebrated with a party for family and friends, indicated that a girl had been circumcised, as a precondition for marriage and motherhood.

Conclusion

Documentary and material evidence from Roman Egypt allows us to identify the structures and institutions that govern life within the family and the household, and the position of those units within the wider social fabric. It also offers us a glimpse into the roles of parents and children; the experience of childhood is seldom evoked, but the responsibilities and obligations of parents are widely documented, as are the options available in cases of unwanted children. While some circumstances revealed in the papyri and in the archaeological evidence may be peculiar to Egypt, there is a wealth of information that can be extrapolated to complement our knowledge about Roman family law, the history of sexuality and reproduction, demography, and urban geography.

Suggested Reading

Recently, scholarship on the family in the ancient world has enjoyed a resurgence, linked to interests in childhood studies and gender studies: *The Oxford Handbook of Children in the Ancient World*, edited by Judith Evans Grubbs, is in preparation, and *A Companion to Families in the Greek and Roman Worlds* (Wiley-Blackwell), edited by Beryl Rawson, appeared in 2011, after this chapter was completed. Alston (1997, 2005) are useful entry points, and van Minnen (1994) is notable for its attempt to combine papyrological and archaeological sources. Parsons (2007) is a highly readable account of social life in Roman Oxyrhynchus, including a vivid description of what houses must have looked like (2007: 52–4). For sexuality in Graeco-Roman Egypt, Montserrat (1996) is thought-provoking and well illustrated; Yiftach-Firanko (2003) is the most up-to-date study of marriage documents.

Bibliography

Adam, S. 1983. 'La femme enceinte dans les papyrus', *Anagennesis* 3: 9–19.

Allam, S. 1990. 'Note sur le marriage par deux contrats dans l'Égypte gréco-romaine', *Chronique d'Égypte* 65: 323–3.

Alston, R. 1995. *Soldier and Society in Roman Egypt: A Social History*. London: Routledge.

—— 1997. 'Houses and Households in Roman Egypt', in R. Laurence and A. Wallace-Hadrill (eds), *Domestic Space in the Roman World: Pompeii and Beyond*. Portsmouth, RI: Journal of Roman Archaeology, 25–39.

—— 2005. 'Searching for the Romano-Egyptian Family', in M. George (ed.), *The Roman Family in the Empire: Rome, Italy, and Beyond*. Oxford: Oxford University Press, 129–58.

—— and Alston, R. D. 1997. 'Urbanism and the Urban Community in Roman Egypt', *Journal of Egyptian Archaeology* 83: 199–216.

Arnaoutoglou, I. 1995. 'Marital Disputes in Greco-Roman Egypt', *Journal of Juristic Papyrology* 25: 11–28.

Bagnall, R. S. 1987. 'Church, State and Divorce in Late Roman Egypt', in K.-L. Selig and R. Somerville (eds), *Florilegium Columbianum: Essays in Honor of P. O. Kristeller*. New York: Italica Press, 41–61.

—— 1997. 'Missing Females in Roman Egypt', *Scripta Classica Israelica* 16: 121–38.

—— 2007. 'Family and Society in Roman Oxyrhynchus', in A. K. Bowman et al. (eds), *Oxyrhynchus: A City and its Texts*. London: Egypt Exploration Society.

—— and B. W. Frier. 1994. *The Demography of Roman Egypt*. Cambridge: Cambridge University Press.

Barker, D. C. 1997. 'The Place of Residence of the Divorced Wife in Roman Egypt', in B. Kramer et al. (eds), *Akten des 21. Internationalen Papyrologenkongresses, Berlin, 13.–19. 8. 1995*, vol. 1. Stuttgart: Teubner, 59–66.

Burkhalter, F. 2004. 'Les hiérothytes alexandrins: Une magistrature grecque dans la capitale lagide', in W. V. Harris and G. Ruffini (eds), *Ancient Alexandria between Egypt and Greece*. Leiden: Brill, 99–114.

Bussi, S. 2002. 'Mariages endogames en Égypte hellénistique et romaine', *Revue Historique de Droit Français et Étranger* 80: 1–22.

Calderini, A. 1923. *La composizione della famiglia secondo le schede di censimento dell'Egitto romano*. Milan: Società Editrice 'Vita e Pensiero'.

—— 1932a. *Le schede di censimento dell'Egitto romano secondo le scoperte più recenti*. Rome: Istituto Poligrafico dello Stato.

—— 1932b. 'Nuove schede del censimento romano d'Egitto', *Aegyptus* 12: 346–54.

—— 1953. 'Apatores', *Aegyptus* 33: 358–69.

Campbell, B. 1978. 'The Marriage of Soldiers under the Empire', *Journal of Roman Studies* 68: 153–66.

Cohen, N. 1996. 'A Notice of Birth of a Girl', in R. Katzoff, Y. Petroff, and D. Schaps (eds), *Classical Studies in Honor of David Sohlberg*. Ramat Gan: Bar-Ilan University Press, 385–98.

Erdmann, W. 1940. 'Die Eheschließung im Rechte der graeco-ägyptischen Papyri von Besetzung bis in die Kaiserzeit', *Zeitschrift der Savigny-Stiftung für Rechtsgeschichte, Romanistische Abteilung* 60: 151–84.

—— 1941. 'Die Ehescheidung im Rechte der graeco-ägyptischen Papyri', *Zeitschrift der Savigny-Stiftung für Rechtsgeschichte, Romanistische Abteilung* 61: 44–57.

Evans Grubbs, J. Forthcoming. *The Oxford Handbook of Children in the Ancient World*. Oxford: Oxford University Press.

Eyben, E. 1980–1. 'Family Planning in Graeco-Roman Antiquity', *Ancient Society* 11–12: 5–82.

Frandsen, P. J. 2009. *Incestuous and Close-Kin Marriage in Ancient Egypt and Persia*. Copenhagen: Museum Tusculanum Press.

Frid, B. 1981. *Ten Uppsala Papyri*. Bonn: Habelt.

Frier, B. W. 1994. 'Natural Fertility and Family Limitation in Roman Marriage', *Classical Philology* 89: 318–33.

Gagos, T., L. Koenen, and B. E. McNellen. 1992. 'A First Century Archive from Oxyrhynchos or Oxyrhynchite Loan Contracts and Egyptian Marriage', in J. H. Johnson (ed.), *Life in a Multicultural Society*. Chicago: Oriental Institute, 181–205.

Goody, J. 1990. *The Oriental, the Ancient, and the Primitive*. Cambridge: Cambridge University Press.

Häge, G. 1968. *Ehegüterrechtliche Verhältnisse in den griechischen Papyri Ägyptens bis Diokletian*. Cologne: Böhlau.

Harris, W. V. 1982. 'The Theoretical Possibility of Extensive Infanticide in the Graeco-Roman World', *Classical Quarterly*, new ser. 32: 114–16.

—— 1994. 'Child-Exposure in the Roman Empire', *Journal of Roman Studies* 84: 1–22.

Hobson, D. 1983. 'Women as Property Owners in Roman Egypt', *Transactions of the American Philological Association* 113: 311–21.

—— 1985. 'House and Household in Roman Egypt', *Yale Classical Studies* 28: 211–29.

Hopkins, K. 1965. 'Contraception in the Roman Empire', *Comparative Studies in Society and History* 8: 124–51.

—— 1980. 'Brother–Sister Marriage in Roman Egypt', *Comparative Studies in Society and History* 22: 303–54.

Huebner, S. R. 2007. '"Brother–Sister" Marriage in Roman Egypt: A Curiosity of Humankind or a Widespread Family Strategy?', *Journal of Roman Studies* 97: 21–49.

—— 2009. 'Female Circumcision as a *rite de passage* in Egypt: Continuity through the Millennia?', *Journal of Egyptian History* 2: 149–71.

Husson, G. 1976. 'La maison privée à Oxyrhynchos aux trois premiers siècles de notre ère', *Ktema* 1: 5–27.

—— 1983. *Oikia: Le vocabulaire de la maison privée en Égypte d'après les papyrus grecs*. Paris: Sorbonne.

Ikram, S. 2003. 'Barbering the Beardless: A Possible Explanation for the Tufted Hairstyle Depicted in the "Fayum" Portrait of a Young Boy (J. P. Getty 78.AP.262)', *Journal of Egyptian Archaeology* 89: 247–51.

Jördens, A. 2000. 'Registrierungsgesuch aus Oxyrhynchos (sog. Geburtsanzeige)', in H. Melaerts (ed.), *Papyri in Honorem Johannis Bingen Octogenarii (P. Bingen)*. Leuven: Peeters, 389–400.

Kolm, S.-C., and J.-M. Ythier. 2006. *Handbook of the Economics of Giving, Altruism and Reciprocity*. Amsterdam: Elsevier.

Krause, J.-U. 1994–5. *Witwen und Waisen im römischen Reich I–IV*. Stuttgart: Steiner.

Kreller, H. 1919. *Erbrechtliche Untersuchungen auf Grund der gräko-ägyptischen Papyrusurkunden*. Leipzig: Teubner.

Kuryłowicz, M. 1983. 'Adoption on the Evidence of the Papyri', *Journal of Juristic Papyrology* 19: 61–75.

Kutzner, E. 1989. *Untersuchungen zur Stellung der Frau im römischen Oxyrhynchos*. Frankfurt: Lang.

Lewis, N. 1970. 'On Paternal Authority in Roman Egypt', *Revue Internationale des Droits de l'Antiquité* 17: 251–8.

Lewis, N. 1979. 'ΑΦΗΛΙΞ: Before and After the Constitutio Antoniniana', *Bulletin of the American Society of Papyrologists* 16: 117–20.
Luckhard, F. 1914. *Das Privathaus im ptolemäischen und römischen Aegypten*, doctoral dissertation, University of Bonn.
McNamee, K. 1982. 'Marriage Agreement with Property Division to Take Effect after Death', *Bulletin of the American Society of Papyrologists* 19: 149–57.
Malouta, M. 2009. 'Legitimate Paternity and Personal Identification in Roman Egypt', in S. Hübner and D. Ratzan (eds), *Growing up Fatherless in Antiquity*. Cambridge: Cambridge University Press.
Mélèze Modrzejewski, J. 1981. 'Le Mariage et la condition de la femme mariée dans l'Égypte grecque et romaine', *Annuaire de l'École Pratique des Hautes Études, IVe section III: 1978–1979*: 299–316.
Mertens, P. 1958. *Les services de l'état civil et la contrôle de la population à Oxyrhynchus*. Brussels: Palais des Académies.
Mirković, M. 2005. 'Child Labour and Taxes in the Agriculture of Roman Egypt: *Pais* and *aphelix*', *Scripta Classica Israelica* 24: 139–49.
Montevecchi, O. 1936. 'Ricerche di sociologia nei documenti dell'Egitto greco-romano II: I contratti di matrimonio e gli atti di divorzio', *Aegyptus* 16: 3–83.
—— 1979. 'Endogamia e cittadinanza romana in Egitto', *Aegyptus* 59: 137–44.
Montserrat, D. 1991. '*Mallokouria* and *therapeuteria*: Rituals of Transition in a Mixed Society?', *Bulletin of the American Society of Papyrologists* 28: 43–9.
—— 1996. *Sex and Society in Graeco-Roman Egypt*. London: Kegan Paul International.
Nelson, C. A. 1979. *Status Declarations in Roman Egypt*. Amsterdam: Hakkert.
Parsons, P. 2007. *City of the Sharp-Nosed Fish: Greek Lives in Roman Egypt*. London: Weidenfeld and Nicolson.
Phang, S. E. 2001. *The Marriage of Roman Soldiers (13 B.C.–A.D. 235): Law and Family in the Imperial Army*. Leiden: Brill.
—— 2002. 'The Families of Roman Soldiers (First and Second Centuries A.D.): Culture, Law, and Practice', *Journal of Family History* 27: 352–73.
Pomeroy, S. B. 1988. 'Women in Roman Egypt: A Preliminary Study Based on Papyri', in W. Haase and H. Temporini (eds), *Aufstieg und Niedergang der römischen Welt* II 10.1. Berlin: de Gruyter, 708–23.
Rawson, B. (ed.) 2011. *A Companion to Families in the Greek and Roman Worlds*. Oxford: Wiley-Blackwell.
Remijsen, S., and W. Clarysse. 2008. 'Incest or Adoption? Brother–Sister Marriage in Roman Egypt Revisited', *Journal of Roman Studies* 98: 53–61.
Riddle, J. M. 1992. *Contraception and Abortion from the Ancient World to the Renaissance*. Cambridge, Mass.: Harvard University Press.
—— J. Worth Estes, and J. C. Russell. 1994. 'Birth Control in the Ancient World', *Archeology* 47: 29–35.
Riggs, C. 2005. *The Beautiful Burial in Roman Egypt: Art, Identity, and Funerary Religion*. Oxford: Oxford University Press.
Rowlandson, J., and R. Takahashi. 2009. 'Brother–Sister Marriage and Inheritance Strategies in Greco-Roman Egypt', *Journal of Roman Studies* 99: 104–39.
Rupprecht, H.-A. 1985. 'Zum Ehegattenerbrecht nach den Papyri', *Bulletin of the American Society of Papyrologists* 22: 291–5.
Sánchez-Moreno Ellart, C. 2010. '*ὑπομνήματα ἐπιγεννήσεως*: The Greco-Egyptian Birth Returns in Roman Egypt and the Case of P. Petaus 1–2', *Archiv für Papyrusforschung* 56: 91–129.

Scheidel, W. 1996a. *Measuring Sex, Age and Death in the Roman Empire: Explorations in Ancient Demography*. Ann Arbor: Journal of Roman Archaeology.

—— 1996b. 'What's in an Age? A Comparative View of Bias in the Census Returns of Roman Egypt', *Bulletin of the American Society of Papyrologists* 33: 25–59.

Sijpesteijn, P. J. 1996. 'Marriage Agreement with Property Division to Take Effect after Death and Other Documents', *Zeitschrift für Papyrologie und Epigraphik* 111: 163–70.

Tibiletti, G. 1984. 'Le vedove nei papiri greci d'Égitto', in *Atti del XVII Congresso Internazionale di Papirologia*, vol. 3. Naples: Centro Internazionale per lo Studio dei Papiri Ercolanesi, 985–94.

van Minnen, P. 1994. 'House-to-House Enquiries: An Interdisciplinary Approach to Roman Karanis', *Zeitschrift für Papyrologie und Epigraphik* 100: 227–51.

Wells, C. M. 1998. 'Celibate Soldiers: Augustus and the Army', *American Journal of Ancient History* 14/2: 180–90.

Whitehorne, J. E. G. 1979. 'Sex and Society in Graeco-Roman Egypt', in J. Bingen and G. Nachtergael (eds), *Actes du XVe Congrès International de Papyrologie*, vol. 4. Brussels: Fondation Égyptologique Reine Élisabeth, 240–6.

Wolff, H. J. 1939. *Written and Unwritten Marriages in Hellenistic and Postclassical Roman Law*. Haverford, Pa.: American Philological Association.

Yiftach-Firanko, U. 2003. *Marriage and Marital Agreements: A History of the Greek Marriage Document in Egypt, 4th Century* BCE*–4th Century* CE. Munich: Münchener Beiträge zur Papyrusforschung und Antiken Rechtsgeschichte.

Youtie, H. C. 1975. 'Apatores: Law vs. Custom in Roman Egypt', in J. Bingen (ed.), *Le monde grec: Pensée, littérature, histoire, documents: Hommage à Claire Préaux*. Brussels: University of Brussels, 723–40; repr. in Youtie, *Scriptiunculae Posteriores*, vol. 1. Brussels: Habelt, 1981, 179–201.

CHAPTER 19

AGE AND HEALTH

WALTER SCHEIDEL

Age Structure and Life Expectancy

Roman Egypt is the only part of the ancient world where documentary evidence for the age composition of the general population has survived. Pertinent information is provided by extant census returns from the first three centuries of Roman rule. Gathered every fourteen years, these documents list the members of individual households with their names, familial status, and ages. Some 850 records have become known to date (Bagnall, Frier, and Rutherford 1997: 57–88; Bagnall and Frier 2006: 179–325). Knowledge of the age distribution enables us to track mortality rates and infer average life expectancy, which is a critical measure of overall well-being. In practice, however, the raw data reveal numerous deficiencies that interfere with straightforward demographic analysis (Fig. 19.1).

In 1994 Roger Bagnall and Bruce Frier's study (Bagnall and Frier 2006) of this material transformed our understanding of Roman Egyptian population history by exploiting the census data with the help of modern demographic techniques. Drawing on 710 age records available at the time, they reconstructed the age distributions of the male and female populations and estimated mean life expectancy at birth. This procedure entailed several assumptions. Because urban data are over-represented in the record, the raw data had to be adjusted to give due weight to evidence from the countryside. Gender rather than location was considered to be the crucial variable in accounting for differences in survival rates. Moreover, owing to the relative paucity of records for small children, average life expectancy at birth could not be directly measured and had to be derived by fitting the weighted and smoothed data to modern life tables (Bagnall and Frier 2006: 75–110). Implied life expectancy at birth was very low, in the low to mid-twenties for women and in the mid- to late twenties for men. These values resemble those documented for China in the first millennium CE, in eighteenth-century France, in nineteenth-century Spain and Russia, and in India in the late nineteenth and early twentieth centuries (Scheidel forthcoming a).

Despite their ostensible plausibility, these findings are open to a number of criticisms. One is that modern life tables, which are primarily based on fairly recent census data, may not capture the full range of the mortality experience of premodern populations (Scheidel

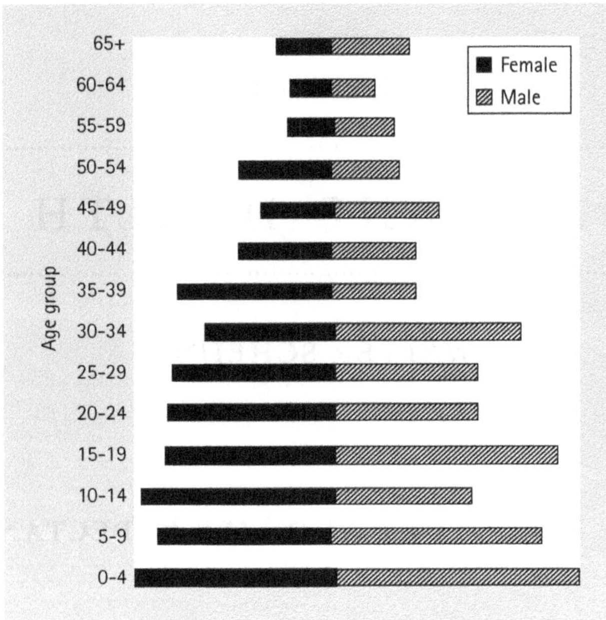

FIG. 19.1 Distribution of ages recorded in census documents from Roman Egypt (n = 847)

Bagnall and Frier (2006: 314–23, 348–50); Bagnall, Frier, and Rutherford (1997: 100)

2001a: 123–42; 2001b). More specifically, they tend to overstate deaths in childhood relative to those among adults. Alternative models have been developed to address this problem (Woods 2007). This raises the question with which, if any, modern model the Egyptian census data might best be compared. Another problem concerns the nature of the data: it has been argued that records for many male villagers are too corrupted by selective underreporting to be of much demographic value (Scheidel 2001a: 156–60). A third issue is that location may be a more significant determinant of mortality than gender. Urban census data fall into a pattern that differs from standard models by showing elevated rates of attrition among young and middle-aged adults (Fig. 19.2). If this divergence reflects reality, it may be interpreted as evidence of urban excess mortality driven by density-dependent disease (Scheidel 2001a: 144–56). A similar pattern is visible in a data set from an unknown city, probably Lykopolis, that was not initially available to Bagnall and Frier (*P Oxy.* 984A, in Bagnall, Frier, and Rutherford 1997). Census records for female villagers appear to be largely free from systematic distortions but remain insufficiently numerous to support firm estimates beyond a fairly wide range from twenty to more than thirty years of mean life expectancy at birth (Fig. 19.3; Scheidel 2001a: 160–2, 174–5).

Owing to commemorative biases, the numerous ages recorded on tombstones and mummy labels do not provide usable information on life expectancy (Boyaval 1975, 1976). Yet even if reconstructions built on the census records are not as robust as initially surmised, they nevertheless point to very high mortality rates overall (Scheidel forthcoming c). This notion is consistent with conditions in Egypt in the early twentieth century and may be explained with reference to environmental factors and unusually high population densities (Scheidel 2001a: 178; Chapter 8).

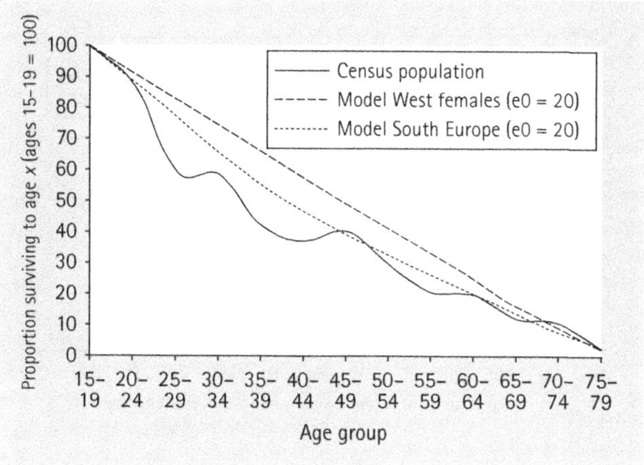

FIG. 19.2 Smoothed age distribution of the adult urban metropolitan census population of Roman Egypt (excluding lodgers and slaves) compared with model life tables

Coale and Demeny (1983: 55); Scheidel (2001a: 155); Woods (2007: 379).

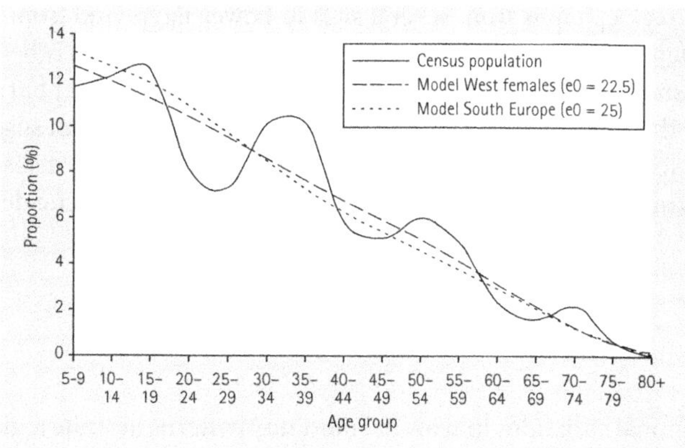

FIG. 19.3 Smoothed age distribution of the female census population of villages in Roman Egypt compared with model life tables

Coale and Demeny (1983: 56); Scheidel (2001a: 161); Woods (2007: 379).

Mortality Patterns

Dates of death recorded on tombstones and mummy labels help us gauge monthly variation in mortality. Most of this evidence comes from the Nile Valley south of the Delta, both in Egypt and in Nubia farther south. Greek epitaphs from the period of Roman rule as well as later Coptic records reveal a strong concentration of deaths in the spring. Months mentioned on mummy labels fall into a very similar pattern: previously misunderstood as dates of death, they refer to the completion of mummification ten weeks later (Scheidel 1998). Adjusted accordingly, these records match the epigraphic profile (Fig. 19.4; Scheidel 2001a: 4–19).

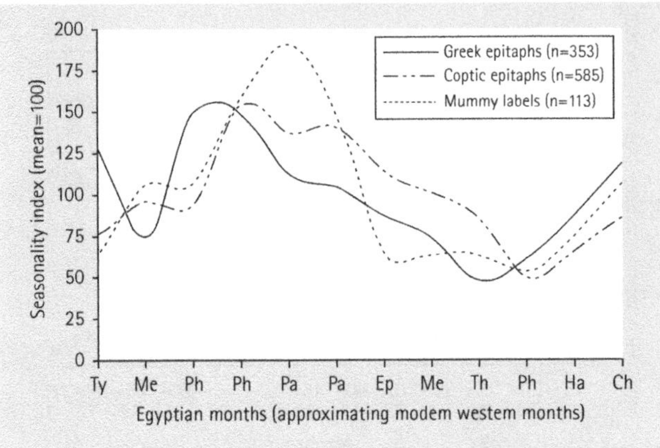

FIG. 19.4 Seasonal mortality in Upper Egypt and Nubia according to Greek and Coptic funerary inscriptions and adjusted dates on Greek mummy labels

Scheidel (2001a: 6, 13).

By contrast, Greek epitaphs from several sites in Lower Egypt and from the coast reveal substantially different distributions. Thus, data from Terenouthis and other sites in or near the Delta region show an increase in mortality in the autumn and winter but a comparatively low incidence in the spring. Data from Alexandria are scarce but do not suggest any significant seasonal concentrations (Scheidel 2001a: 19–25). Surviving death declarations also frequently list dates of death but fail to contribute reliable information (Scheidel 1999).

Causes of Death

The observed regional variations in seasonal mortality patterns indicate regional differences in the dominant causes of death. As in premodern societies more generally, infectious diseases can be expected to have accounted for the majority of deaths at most ages. Different infections flourished and affected people at different times of the year. The connection between the disease environment and seasonal mortality is visible in epitaphs from the city of Rome in late antiquity. They show a surge in the death rate during the late summer and early autumn, at a time when malaria, which appears to have been endemic, used to flare up and exacerbate other diseases (Scheidel forthcoming b). In Roman Egypt, by contrast, it is more difficult to establish a clear connection between seasonality profiles and particular diseases. Nevertheless, comparative data support the notion that the pattern documented for the Nile Valley reflected actual health conditions. Travellers' accounts from the sixteenth to the early nineteenth centuries consistently point to a concentration of fatal infections in the spring, variously reporting diarrhoea, dysentery, typhus, typhoid, relapsing fever, jaundice, malaria, tuberculosis, smallpox, plague, and cholera, as well as severe conditions that cannot be properly identified (Scheidel 2001a: 110). With only few exceptions—cholera and perhaps smallpox and typhus—these diseases were already present in antiquity. Acting concurrently, they would have been powerful enough to skew mortality patterns in the observed fashion.

As recently as in Cairo in 1859–60, 'typhoid fevers' peaked at that time of the year (Schnepp 1862: 552–3). It is also worth noting that funerary inscriptions from late Roman Palestine show a comparable spike in deaths during the spring (Patlagean 1977: 92–4).

In Lower Egypt, by contrast, elevated death rates in the late autumn and early winter may have been boosted by respiratory diseases precipitated by a somewhat cooler and wetter climate. If a large sample of seasonal mortality data from Terenouthis in Lower Egypt is disaggregated according to age, we find that the elderly were particularly vulnerable during the winter months, in much the same way as they were in the late antique city of Rome (Scheidel 2001a: 29; forthcoming b). The notion that the annual inundation caused epidemics, already featured in incantations in *P Edwin Smith* from the sixteenth century BCE (Westendorf 1999: 16–21), appears to be borne out by the observed increase in deaths in both Upper and Lower Egypt during the last three months of the year, as the waters of the Nile receded from their peak in September. Malaria may well have been the principal culprit.

Thanks to its coastal location, Alexandria appears to have fared better (see also below), similar to late Roman Carthage, which witnessed comparably aseasonal mortality. All this supports the notion that regional differences in the timing of mortality were a function of different disease regimes. It was only by the early twentieth century that seasonal mortality peaks in both Upper and Lower Egypt had shifted to the late spring and early summer. This suggests that causes of death changed in the very long term. We know that the presence and prevalence of diseases such as plague and smallpox varied over time. More generally, secular shifts in pathogen ecology seem to have been responsible for discontinuity between ancient or 'archaic' conditions and a more recent premodern disease regime that took shape in the nineteenth century (Sandwith 1905; Jagailloux 1986; Kuhnke 1990; Scheidel 2001a: 109–17).

Disease and Physical Well-Being

It is far easier to document the presence of certain diseases than to assess the relative importance of different causes of death. A wide range of techniques from textual study to biomolecular analysis have been brought to bear on the record. Thanks to the preservation of numerous mummified corpses and the exceptional time depth of the textual tradition, medically relevant evidence from ancient Egypt is particularly rich by premodern standards. This fortunate situation allows us not only to explore health conditions in the Roman period but also to place them in a broader context.

Medical and magical texts from the Dynastic period contain a wealth of information about different diseases (Westendorf 1999: 101–459). These include heart ailments; headaches; skin diseases; various eye problems such as glaucoma, cataracts, and blindness; bone fractures, wounds, and other injuries; paralysis; respiratory ailments; worm infection, gastro-intestinal and urinary tract problems; fevers; bites (with most attention paid to snake bites but also featuring those by fellow humans, dogs, pigs, lions, hippos, and crocodiles), as well as scorpion stings; and swellings and tumours. Symptoms indicative of mental illnesses are also reported. Medical investigation of mummies has primarily focused on the Dynastic period (e.g. Rose 1996; Cockburn, Cockburn, and Reyman 1998: 15–117; Westendorf 1999:

460–3; David 2008). Iconographic evidence further supplements the bio-anthropological record (Westendorf 1999: 463–5).

Texts from the Roman period itself also shed light on medical conditions (Marganne 1981; Hirt Raj 2006: 264–78). A number of magical spells were designed to heal, prevent, or induce various illnesses (Bonner 1950; Betz 1992). In this genre, fever, often accompanied by shivering fits, is the most commonly mentioned affliction, followed by headaches, eye problems, haemorrhage, fractures, coughs, cysts, inflammations, swollen testicles, hardened breasts, breast and abdominal pain, tumours, ulcers, angina, scrofula, epilepsy, strangury, insomnia, scorpion stings, and what is often termed elephantiasis. These and other texts likewise betray anxiety about reproductive health. In addition, papyri preserve information about the medical profession in Roman Egypt (Marganne-Mélard 1996; Hirt Raj 2006).

Rare glimpses of actual cases of illness in the second century CE are afforded by ostraca from the Mons Claudianus mines in the Eastern Desert that report workers' health problems (Cuvigny 1992, 1997). 'Hurt' tops the rankings, accompanied by fevers, eye ailments, scorpion stings, and inflammations of the uvula and tonsils. Unfortunately, generic sick lists that do not specify causes dominate this record. Surviving correspondence from the same site deals with the dispatch of assorted medical supplies.

In the most general terms, gastro-intestinal diseases such as diarrhoea, dysentery, and typhoid must have been pervasive and the most common causes of death for young children (Scheidel 2001a: 62–75). These infections still dominated several cause-of-death statistics from Cairo and Alexandria in the late nineteenth and early twentieth centuries. Just as in medical writings from antiquity, however, they receive scant attention in Egyptian sources and are hard or impossible to trace in physical remains.

Malaria also played an important role (Scheidel 2001a: 75–91). All manifestations of malaria that used to be endemic in the Mediterranean—quotidian, tertian, and quartan fevers, associated with *Plasmodium falciparum*, *vivax*, and *malariae*—are explicitly attested in charms from Graeco-Roman Egypt (Betz 1992: 255, 267, 310–11). Hints at the occurrence of malaria can already be found in earlier periods, such as a warning in a temple inscription at Dendara not to leave home after sunset in the weeks following the inundation (when mosquitoes would have proliferated), reported strategies of mosquito evasion that are typical of malarial areas (Hdt. 2.95), and, possibly, reference to the 'disease of the three days' (Westendorf 1999: 327, 460). *P. falciparum* is by far the most pernicious kind of malaria known from the region: both the antigen to that parasite and the actual parasite's DNA have been extracted from Dynastic period mummies (Miller et al. 1994; Nerlich et al. 2008). The same type of malaria was still common in Egypt in the 1930s, suggesting continuity in the long term. Comparative evidence makes it seem likely that the marshy Fayum would have been particularly exposed to endemic malaria. This must be taken into account in demographic evaluations of the census returns, many of which originate from that part of the country. Ancient claims that Alexandria was free from marsh vapour diseases (i.e. malaria) may be correct but should nevertheless be treated with caution (Strabo 17.1.7; Galen 1821–33: 16.363).

The incidence of tuberculosis in ancient Egypt has been the subject of considerable debate, in the first instance because physical evidence used to be limited to bone lesions suggestive of extrapulmonary tuberculosis (Pott's disease). Many reported cases remain uncertain (Buikstra, Baker, and Cook 1993: 38–45), and in any case only a tiny proportion of patients can be expected to develop bone lesions before they die. More recently, the discovery of molecular evidence of pulmonary tuberculosis has profoundly changed the state of our knowledge. The first reported extraction of *Mycobacterium tuberculosis* DNA from lung tissue in a New Kingdom mummy (Nerlich et al. 1997) has since been followed by much richer findings drawn from a series of tombs ranging from 3500 to 500 BCE (Zink et al. 2004; see also Donoghue et al. 2010). Specimens dating from 1500 to 500 BCE have been characterized as modern *M. tuberculosis* strains (Zink et al. 2007), which implies that patients would have exhibited familiar pathologies. Although no DNA data from the Roman period have so far been published, we may safely assume that pulmonary tuberculosis was present and, if the earlier molecular evidence is representative, potentially quite widespread. Even so, we also must allow for significant variation over time (Scheidel 2001a: 91–3).

A related pathogen, *Mycobacterium leprae*, is now equally solidly attested in Roman Egypt. Evidence of leprosy in the Dynastic period remains tenuous (Nunn 1996: 74–5; Westendorf 1999: 312). Very late antique physical evidence from a sixth-century CE Coptic body has been recognized for a long time (Sandison and Tapp 1998: 42), later followed by the tentative identification of leprosy in Ptolemaic skeletons in Dakhla Oasis in the Western Desert (Dzierzykray-Rogalski 1980). The same site has more recently yielded richer skeletal evidence from the fourth century CE. While studies of bone lesions have suggested only a few probable or possible cases (Molto 2002), DNA analysis has yielded a higher rate of leprosy infection, repeatedly coinciding with tuberculosis (Donoghue et al. 2005). This meshes well with the fact that Roman authors regarded elephantiasis (actually leprosy: Grmek 1989: 168–9) as a native disease of Egypt (Lucr. 6.1114–15; Plin. *HN* 26.5). In the second century CE the famous physician Galen considered it to be rife in Alexandria (Galen 1821–3: 11.142).

Pulmonary afflictions discovered in Dynastic period mummies include anthracosis (Walker et al. 1987) and fibrosis of the lung caused by the inhalation of sand particles (Sandison and Tapp 1998: 53), and would also have been present in the Roman period. Intestinal parasites added to the mix: Guinea worm disease was ascribed to Egypt by Greek and Roman authorities (Adamson 1988). Schistosomiasis has been common throughout Egyptian history (Miller et al. 1992; Westendorf 1999: 469–71; Lambert-Zazulak, Rutherford, and David 2003). The detection of schistosome antigen in New Kingdom mummies quite strikingly documents the spread of this condition, otherwise historically associated with farmers, even into elite circles (Deelder et al. 1990; Ziskind 2009). According to the second-century CE medical writer Aretaios (1.9.3–5), diphtheria was very common in Egypt and known as 'Egyptian ulcers'. What the Elder Pliny called *lichen*, or *mentagra*, a pustulous skin eruption spreading from the mouth, was likewise reportedly well known in Roman Egypt (*HN* 26.2–3; cf. *P Vindob.* 6257). Gout has likewise been observed (Sandison and Tapp 1998: 48–9; Hirt Raj 2006: 275–6).

Our knowledge of the history of smallpox in ancient Egypt depends to a significant extent on the answer to the question whether lesions on the mummy of the pharaoh Ramesses V (d. 1145 BCE) were indeed caused by this disease (Hopkins 2002: 14–15). Possible evidence is both scarce and ambiguous. It now seems likely that in antiquity smallpox did not commonly occur west of India (Li et al. 2007: 15790). The so-called 'Antonine Plague' of the late second century CE is often considered to have been a smallpox pandemic. Given high population densities, this disease might well have become endemic in Egypt at the time, but we lack positive evidence for this assumption (Scheidel 2001a: 94–7). Convincing accounts do not appear until the early seventh century CE, when Aaron of Alexandria described smallpox and measles. From the ninth century CE onward, smallpox was known as an endemic disease of childhood in the Near East (Hopkins 2002: 166–8).

Bubonic plague, on the other hand, was already ascribed to North Africa in the Hellenistic period and portrayed as prevalent in Libya, Egypt, and Syria in the second century CE (Thüry 1977; cf. Panagiotakopulu 2004). However, specific outbreaks are not documented prior to the great plague pandemic of the sixth to eighth centuries CE (Stathakopoulos 2004). While *Yersinia pestis* DNA has already been recovered from European skeletons from that period, it has yet to be identified in ancient Egyptian remains.

Dental studies suggest changes in the very long run. Thus, the incidence of enamel hypoplasia (a marker of developmental stress in children) in Graeco-Roman finds from Mendes is considerably lower than in specimens from the Old Kingdom (Lovell and Whyte 1999). A more wide-ranging diachronic study of Egyptian samples has found significantly lower levels of occlusal tooth wear and higher rates of caries in the Graeco-Roman period than in previous periods of Egyptian history. This may have been a function of changes in cereal consumption such as access to better grains or improved sieving techniques and of increasing use of sweeteners (Miller 2008: 68).

As already noted in the discussion of tuberculosis and leprosy, in recent years the skeletal remains from Dakhla Oasis have been subject to very fruitful scientific analysis. One study found a lower incidence of *cribra orbitalia* (skull lesions associated with chronic iron deficiency anaemias and other disorders) in Roman remains than in those from earlier periods, although the Roman rate is nevertheless fairly high even by ancient standards (Fairgrieve and Molto 2000; compare Scheidel forthcoming a). Another study failed to find evidence of bone infections in a sizeable sample from the same site (Cook, Molto, and Anderson 1989). One local female Roman period skeleton indicates hyperparathyroidism (Cook, Molto, and Anderson 1988). Isotopic analysis of teeth has shed new light on child feeding practices: while supplemental foods began to be provided from the age of 6 months onward, breastfeeding was not completed until the age of 3 years, in keeping with textual references to prolonged breastfeeding (Dupras et al. 2001; Dupras and Tocheri 2007). Extended breastfeeding would have conferred health benefits, and contrasts favourably with isotopic evidence of much earlier weaning in Portus near Rome (Prowse et al. 2008). More recent work on the Graeco-Roman remains of Bahariya Oasis further north has focused on spinal health. In addition to evidence for degenerative arthritis and degenerative bone lesions, researchers found an extremely high rate of *spina bifida occulta*, a congenital malformation that may have resulted from high levels of consanguinity in the isolated oasis population (Hussien et al. 2009).

This last point raises questions about the medical consequences of brother–sister marriage as it is documented in numerous Roman Egyptian census returns. Provided that this custom was real and did not merely entail notional sibling unions created through adoption (see Chapter 18), it ought to have had significant deleterious effects (Scheidel 1996: 9–51). However, empirical evidence is lacking. This calls for further study.

On occasion, extraordinary epidemics would have further added to the overall disease load (Casanova 1984). The severity of the first of the two best-known cases from the Roman period, the Antonine Plague of the late second century CE (probably smallpox), cannot be measured directly. Modern assessments rely on indirect indicators such as drops in population registers and subsequent changes in the value of land and labour. The plague pandemic of the sixth to eighth centuries CE appears to have had greater impact (Scheidel 2002, forthcoming c).

Conclusion

Herodotus' sweeping claim that 'the Egyptians are the healthiest of men, next to the Libyans' (2.77.3) is impossible to reconcile with evidence from antiquity or any other known historical period. On the contrary, for millennia Egypt appears to have been a hotbed of disease. Life was short even by premodern standards, and seasonal infections ravaged even people in the prime of life. Locational differences—between city and countryside and between different parts of the country—are discernible in the record. Observed mortality patterns can only tentatively be linked to evidence of particular diseases, and it is even more difficult to gauge the consequences of major epidemics.

The scientific study of human remains has made enormous progress in recent years and already greatly enriched our knowledge of medical conditions in ancient Egypt. Even so, much more work needs to be done to give us a better sense of the relative prevalence of particular diseases and of change over time. We also need to bear in mind that the most common health problems, caused by gastro-intestinal bacillary infections, are among the most difficult ones to document in the physical record. At the same time, analysis of dental structure and osseous lesions is capable of elucidating health and overall living conditions with respect to diet, work conditions, and class and gender inequality (e.g. Zaki, Hussien, and El Banna 2009). A steady progression from the study of disease to a more comprehensive history of well-being is the most promising path for the future.

Suggested Reading

Bagnall and Frier (2006) remains the basis for the study of age structure and life expectancy in Roman Egypt, to be consulted alongside the critical reassessment by Scheidel (2001a: 118–80). Scheidel (2001a: 1–117) discusses seasonal mortality and causes of death from a comparative perspective. Surveys of disease and medical evidence from Egypt tend to focus on the pre-Roman period but are nevertheless of relevance: Buikstra, Baker, and Cook (1993); Nunn (1996: 64–95); Sandison and Tapp (1998); and Westendorf (1999). Grmek's magisterial 1989 study of ancient diseases also takes account of Roman Egypt. Hirt Raj (2006) covers the medical profession. Technical studies published in scientific journals keep transforming our knowledge of Egyptian living conditions: while this chapter seeks to note at least the most pertinent recent studies up to the date of writing (early 2010), any bibliographical survey is bound to become outdated over time.

Bibliography

Adamson, P. B. 1988. 'Dracontiasis in Antiquity', *Medical History* 32: 204–9.

Bagnall, R. S., and B. W. Frier. 2006. *The Demography of Roman Egypt*, rev. edn. Cambridge: Cambridge University Press; first pub. 1994.

—— —— and I. C. Rutherford. 1997. *The Census Register P. Oxy. 984: The Reverse of Pindar's Paeans*. Brussels: Fondation Égyptologique Reine Élisabeth.

Betz, H. D. 1992. *The Greek Magical Papyri in Translation, including the Demotic Spells*, 2nd edn. Chicago: University of Chicago Press.

Bonner, C. 1950. *Studies in Magical Amulets, Chiefly Graeco-Egyptian*. Ann Arbor: University of Michigan Press.

Boyaval, B. 1975. 'Remarques à propos des indications d'âges des etiquettes de momies', *Zeitschrift für Papyrologie und Epigraphik* 18: 49–74.

—— 1976. 'Remarques sur les indications d'âges de l'épigraphie funéraire d'Égypte', *Zeitschrift für Papyrologie und Epigraphik* 21: 217–43.

Buikstra, J. E., B. J. Baker, and D. C. Cook. 1993. 'What Diseases Plagued the Ancient Egyptians? A Century of Controversy Considered', in W. V. Davies and R. Walker (eds), *Biological Anthropology and the Study of Ancient Egypt*. London: British Museum Press, 24–53.

Casanova, G. 1984. 'Epidemie e fame nella documentazione greco d'Egitto', *Aegyptus* 64: 163–201.

Coale, A. J., and P. Demeny. 1983. *Regional Model Life Tables and Stable Populations*, 2nd edn. New York: Academic Press.

Cockburn, A., E. Cockburn, and T. A. Reyman (eds) 1998. *Mummies, Disease, and Ancient Cultures*, 2nd edn. Cambridge: Cambridge University Press.

Cook, M., E. L. Molto, and C. Anderson. 1988. 'Possible Case of Hyperparathyroidism in a Roman Period Skeleton from the Dakhleh Oasis, Egypt, Diagnosed Using Bone Histomorphometry', *American Journal of Physical Anthropology* 75: 23–30.

—— —— —— 1989. 'Fluorochrome Labelling in Roman Period Skeletons from Dakhleh Oasis, Egypt', *American Journal of Physical Anthropology* 80: 137–43.

Cuvigny, H. 1992. 'La mort et la maladie', in J. Bingen et al. (eds), *Mons Claudianus: Ostraca graeca et latina* I. Cairo: Institut Français d'Archéologie Orientale, 75–109.

—— 1997. 'La mort et la maladie (191–223)', in J. Bingen et al. (eds), *Mons Claudianus: Ostraca graeca et latina* II. Cairo: Institut Français d'Archéologie Orientale, 19–41.

David, A. R. (ed.) 2008. *Egyptian Mummies and Modern Science*. Cambridge: Cambridge University Press.

Deelder, A. M., et al. 1990. 'Detection of Schistosome Antigen in Mummies', *The Lancet* 335: 724–5.

Donoghue, H. D., et al. 2005. 'Mycobacterium Leprae in Human Archaeological Samples: A Co-infection of Mycobacterium Tuberculosis and Possible Explanation for the Historical Decline of Leprosy', *Proceedings of the Royal Society B: Biological Sciences* 272: 389–94.

—— et al. 2010. 'Tuberculosis in Dr Granville's Mummy: A Molecular Re-examination of the Earliest Known Egyptian Mummy To Be Scientifically Examined and Given a Medical Diagnosis', *Proceedings of the Royal Society B: Biological Sciences* 277: 51–6.

Dupras, T. L., and M. W. Tocheri. 2007. 'Reconstructing Infant Weaning Histories at Roman Period Kellis, Egypt, Using Stable Isotope Analysis of Dentition', *American Journal of Physical Anthropology* 134: 63–74.

—— et al. 2001. 'Infant Feeding and Weaning Practices in Roman Egypt', *American Journal of Physical Anthropology* 115: 204–12.

Dzierzykray-Rogalski, T. 1980. 'Paleopathology of the Ptolemaic Inhabitants of Dakleh Oasis (Egypt)', *Journal of Human Evolution* 9: 71–4.

Fairgrieve, S. I., and J. E. Molto. 2000. 'Cribra Orbitalia in Two Temporally Disjunct Population Samples from the Dakhleh Oasis, Egypt', *American Journal of Physical Anthropology* 111: 319–31.

Galen. 1821–33. *Claudii Galeni Opera Omnia*, ed. C. G. Kühn, 20 vols in 22. Leipzig: Cnobloch.

Grmek, M. D. 1989. *Diseases in the Ancient Greek World.* Baltimore: Johns Hopkins University Press.

Hirt Raj, M. 2006. *Médecins et maladies de l'Égypte romaine: Étude socio-légale de la profession médicale et de ses praticiens du Ier au IVe siècle ap. J.-C.* Leiden: Brill.

Hopkins, D. R. 2002. *The Greatest Killer: Smallpox in History.* Chicago: University of Chicago Press.

Hussien, F. H., et al. 2009. 'Spinal Pathological Findings in Ancient Egyptians of the Greco-Roman Period Living in Bahriyah Oasis', *International Journal of Osteoarchaeology* 19: 613–27.

Jagailloux, S. 1986. *La médicalisation de l'Égypte au XIXe siècle (1798–1918).* Paris: Éditions Recherche sur les Civilisations.

Kuhnke, L. 1990. *Lives at Risk: Public Health in Nineteenth-Century Egypt.* Berkeley: University of California Press.

Lambert-Zazulak, P. I., P. Rutherford, and A. R. David. 2003. 'The International Ancient Egyptian Mummy Tissue Bank at the Manchester Museum as a Resource for the Palaeoepidemiological Study of Schistosomiasis', *World Archaeology* 35: 223–40.

Li, Y., et al. 2007. 'On the Origin of Smallpox: Correlating Variola Phylogenics with Historical Smallpox Records', *Proceedings of the National Academy of Sciences* 104: 15787–92.

Lovell, N. C., and I. Whyte. 1999. 'Patterns of Dental Enamel Defects at Ancient Mendes, Egypt', *American Journal of Physical Anthropology* 110: 69–80.

Marganne, M.-H. 1981. *Inventaire analytique des papyrus grecs de médicine.* Geneva: Droz.

Marganne-Mélard, M.-H. 1996. 'La médicine dans l'Égypte romaine: Les services et les méthodes', in H. Temporini (ed.), *Aufstieg und Niedergang der römischen Welt* II 37.3. Berlin: de Gruyter, 2709–40.

Miller, J. 2008. *An Appraisal of the Skulls and Dentition of the Ancient Egyptians, Highlighting the Pathology and Speculating on the Influence of Diet and Environment.* Oxford: Archaeopress.

Miller, R. L., et al. 1992. 'Palaeoepidemiology of Schistosoma Infection in Mummies', *British Medical Journal* 304: 555–6.

—— et al. 1994. 'Diagnosis of *Plasmodium falciparum* Infections in Mummies using the Rapid Manual *Para*SightTM-F Test', *Transactions of the Royal Society of Tropical Medicine and Hygiene* 88: 31–2.

Molto, J. E. 2002. 'Leprosy in Roman Period Skeletons from Kellis 2, Dakhleh, Egypt', in C. A. Roberts, M. E. Lewis, and K. Manchester (eds), *The Past and Present of Leprosy.* Oxford: Archaeopress, 179–92.

Nerlich, A. G., et al. 1997. 'Molecular Evidence for Tuberculosis in an Ancient Egyptian Mummy', *The Lancet* 350: 1404.

—— et al. 2008. '*Plasmodium falciparum* in Ancient Egypt', *Emerging Infectious Diseases* 14: 1317–19.

Nunn, J. F. 1996. *Ancient Egyptian Medicine.* London: British Museum Press.

Panagiotakopulu, E. 2004. 'Pharaonic Egypt and the Origins of Plague', *Journal of Biogeography* 31: 269–75.

Patlagean, E. 1977. *Pauvreté économique et pauvreté sociale à Byzance, 4e–7e siècles.* Paris: Mouton.

Prowse, T. L., et al. 2008. 'Isotopic and Dental Evidence for Infant and Young Child Feeding Practices in an Imperial Roman Skeletal Sample', *American Journal of Physical Anthropology* 137: 294–308.

Rose, J. C. 1996. *Bioarchaeology of Ancient Egypt and Nubia: A Bibliography.* London: British Museum Press.

Sandison, A. T., and E. Tapp. 1998. 'Disease in Ancient Egypt', in A. Cockburn, E. Cockburn, and T. A. Reyman (eds), *Mummies, Disease, and Ancient Cultures*, 2nd edn. Cambridge: Cambridge University Press, 38–58.

Sandwith, F. M. 1905. *The Medical Diseases of Egypt*. London: Henry Kimpton.

Scheidel, W. 1996. *Measuring Sex, Age and Death in the Roman Empire: Explorations in Ancient Demography*. Ann Arbor: Journal of Roman Archaeology.

—— 1998. 'The Meaning of Dates on Mummy Labels: Seasonal Mortality and Mortuary Practice in Roman Egypt', *Journal of Roman Archaeology* 11: 285–92.

—— 1999. 'The Death Declarations of Roman Egypt: A Re-appraisal', *Bulletin of the American Society of Papyrologists* 36: 53–70.

—— 2001a. *Death on the Nile: Disease and the Demography of Roman Egypt*. Leiden: Brill.

—— 2001b. 'Roman Age Structure: Evidence and Models', *Journal of Roman Studies* 91: 1–26.

—— 2002. 'A Model of Demographic and Economic Change in Roman Egypt after the Antonine Plague', *Journal of Roman Archaeology* 15: 97–114.

—— Forthcoming a. 'Physical Wellbeing', in Scheidel (ed.), *The Companion to the Roman Economy*. Cambridge: Cambridge University Press.

—— Forthcoming b. 'Disease and Death', in P. Erdkamp (ed.), *The Companion to Ancient Rome*. Cambridge: Cambridge University Press.

—— Forthcoming c. 'Roman Wellbeing and the Economic Consequences of the Antonine Plague', in E. Lo Cascio (ed.), *L'impatto della 'peste antonina'*. Bari: Edipuglia.

Schnepp, M. B. 1862. 'Considérations sur le mouvement de la population en Égypte', *Mémoires ou travaux originaux présentés et lus à l'Institut Egyptien* 1: 525–600.

Stathakopoulos, D. C. 2004. *Famine and Pestilence in the Late Roman and Early Byzantine Empire: A Systematic Survey of Subsistence Crises and Epidemics*. Aldershot: Ashgate.

Thüry, G. E. 1977. 'Zur Infektkette der Pest in hellenistisch-römischer Zeit', in *75 Jahre Anthropologische Staatssammlung München 1902–1977*. Munich: Anthropologische Staatssammlung, 275–83.

Walker, R., et al. 1987. 'Tissue Identification and Histologic Study of Six Lung Specimens from Egyptian Mummies', *American Journal of Physical Anthropology* 72: 43–8.

Westendorf, W. 1999. *Handbuch der altägyptischen Medizin*, vol. 1. Leiden: Brill.

Woods, R. I. 2007. 'Ancient and Early Modern Mortality: Experience and Understanding', *Economic History Review* 60: 373–99.

Zaki, M. E., F. H. Hussien, and A. E.-S. El Banna. 2009. 'Osteoporosis among Ancient Egyptians', *International Journal of Osteoarchaeology* 19: 78–89.

Zink, A. R., et al. 2004. 'Molecular Identification and Characterization of Mycobacterium Tuberculosis Complex in Ancient Egyptian Mummies', *International Journal of Osteoarchaeology* 14: 404–13.

—— et al. 2007. 'Molecular History of Tuberculosis from Ancient Mummies and Skeletons', *International Journal of Osteoarchaeology* 17: 380–91.

Ziskind, B. 2009. 'Urinary Schistosomiasis in Ancient Egypt', *Nephrologie et Therapeutique* 5: 658–61.

PART IV

RELIGION

CHAPTER 20

RELIGIOUS PRACTICE AND PIETY

DAVID FRANKFURTER

TRADITIONAL Egyptian religion involved much more than temples, priests, and processions. The rhythms of agriculture, the experience of the landscape, and the perpetuation and fortune of family and village all involved ritual interactions with diverse gods and spirits: in the home, in local shrines, and at festivals. Using papyri and epigraphical documentation, historians of Egyptian religion can track the fortunes of the temples through the Roman period from, first, two centuries of imperial munificence, then through financial decline (third to fourth century CE), and then imperial repression (fifth to sixth century CE) (see Bagnall 1988, 1993). However, we must be careful not to confuse the decline of temple cults with the end of Egyptian religion itself, a complex and subtle element in Egyptian life. Sources from the fourth and later centuries suggest, in fact, that the religious practices that sustained family and economic fortune shifted centrifugally from temple cult to village and domestic rites and even influenced some of the forms that Christianity itself assumed, in the home: the saint's shrine, the festival, the workshop, and the village (see Frankfurter 1998, 2003, 2005).

TEMPLES IN CONTEXT: FESTIVALS AND HELLENIZATION

Egyptian religion was not a monolithic thought system and therefore is ill-served by the term 'paganism'. Indeed, to conceptualize Egyptian religion of the Roman period requires the abandonment of simplistic binary categories like 'Christian/pagan' or 'Jewish/pagan', which misleadingly collapse temple cult with private rites, hybrid intellectual piety, and even ancient authors' interpretations of Egyptian religion, in order to provide a foil to 'Christian' or 'Jewish' religion. For accuracy's sake the student of religion must instead attend to the various social dimensions in which temple cult, local shrine, and domestic practices functioned. As with many premodern cultures, Egyptian religion in the Roman period predominantly involved local cults: that is, cults to local forms of more well-known deities like Isis, Sobek, and Horus, and even to lesser-known regional gods like Rattawy, Renenoutet, Montu, and Mandulis, each of which invited particular traditional practices of deep resonance to local people. Many such local gods might be recognizable to travellers, or outsiders, as forms of the principal royal gods (like Isis or Horus, to which they would be assimilated and standardized in temple reliefs). But Roman Egypt had become so thoroughly Hellenized that these principal gods themselves were often represented in Graeco-Roman form as well, in stone or wood or terracotta: Isis as a robed goddess; Horus as a solar-crowned emperor, armoured warrior, or even (in poetry) a cosmic *pantocrator*.

Egyptian religion of the Roman period involved a continual shifting across these three—local, royal (or pan-Egyptian), and hellenistic—dimensions of gods. Workshops created Hellenized figurines of local protector gods, and visitors to frontier shrines commissioned metrical Greek poetry to exalt a local deity. A single shrine might serve Egyptian devotees to the well-known crocodile-god Sobek and Roman devotees to the twin Dioscuri (Quaegebeur 1983). Yet distinctively hellenistic titles (Aion, Sun) and iconographic forms (frontality, nudity, armour) did not obliterate the local character of a deity in religious life; rather, such hellenistic forms served to convey, in new media, the particular features and powers of the deity in her local world. Alongside a profusion of cults and shrines to explicitly Graeco-Roman deities (Serapis, Demeter, Agathos Daimon), reflecting the increasing integration of non-Egyptian cults in the landscape, it is often difficult to tell whether devotees took a shrine's god as Graeco-Roman or Egyptian, or both (see Dunand 1975, 1979; Bowersock 1990; Dunand and Zivie-Coche 2004: 267–76). In a typical combination of Roman identity and allegiance to Egyptian gods, a letter-writer of the third century assures his father he makes devotions 'before the gods of the region' (*P Oxy*. VI 936). As a further example of such combinations of local, pan-Egyptian, and hellenistic religion we might note a small mud-brick shrine of the second century CE dedicated to Serapis just outside the great Luxor temple complex, which features a large marble statue of Isis in the classical form of her fringed, knotted mantle. The shrine represents both a Hellenized alternative to the traditional statuary in the Luxor Amun temple and a more intimate space for directing popular devotions (Golvin et al. 1981). Such shrines, minor as compared with the great temples but well attested in papyri, not only provided opportunities for the Hellenization and reconceptualization of gods but also allowed the gods a continual place in the practical life of the religion (see in general Frankfurter 1998: 97–144; Dunand and Zivie-Coche 2004: 299–306).

To be sure, the great regional temples at Luxor, Esna, Dendara, and elsewhere continued to sponsor traditional festival processions through at least the second century. The temple of Khnum at Esna, refurbished over the course of the third century, records its annual processional rites out of the temple and through the landscape to various smaller shrines, fructifying the fields and regenerating the cosmos; and we find similarly generative processions reflected in inscriptions and papyri for temples in the Kharga Oasis and the Fayum. Papyri record the activities of several temples to forms of Sobek in the Fayum, like Soknobraisis, Soknopaios, and Soknebtunis (Frankfurter 1998: 37–58, 97–111; Alston 2002: 196–218; Dunand and Zivie-Coche 2004: 116–19, 289–94). Some lives of Christian holy men recall, in credible if ironic terms, smaller-scale processions continuing in the fourth century (*Historia Monachorum in Aegypto* 8.25; *Vita Pachomii* 4). Those outside the temple not only gained the blessings of the procession (and the beneficent gaze of the god's image) but, as Plutarch describes, celebrated actively themselves, conducting special animal slaughters and preparing festival cakes stamped with festival marks (Plut. *De Is. et Os.* 50, 68), and they might purchase figurines representing the procession itself (see Dunand 1979: 93–100; Bailey 2008).

By the Roman period the temple festival, its formal procession and traditional expressions, represented only the focus—in some areas perhaps merely the pretext—for civic ceremony of a multicultural nature, and new hellenistic festivals for Greek gods and Roman emperors (and even the defeat of the Jewish rebellion in 117CE; *C Pap. Jud.* 450) had also entered the civic calendar (Perpillou-Thomas 1993; Alston 2002: 245–7; Dunand and Zivie-Coche 2004: 285–9). Temple processions did not simply involve the circuit of the god through his lands but also celebrated the urban elite and the patronage and social prominence of religious *synodoi*. A gold processional crown found at the Serapis temple of Kysis in the Kharga Oasis exemplifies the public religious status of the town notable for whom it must have been intended (Reddé 1992). By the Roman period many festivals had come to culminate in spectacles, games, and displays of hellenistic culture: they were *panegyreis* (see Bagnall 1993: 101–2, 104–5; Frankfurter 1998: 58–62). Reflecting the common discourse of Roman ceremony, these extra-temple festivals came to feature *thusia*—public libations and ritual animal slaughter—even of pigs, a once impure animal now associated with Isis devotion (see Bagnall and Rives 2000 on *thusia*; Perpillou-Thomas 1993: 203–9 on pork). While drawing public ritual life away from the temple and its processional displays, the elaboration of hellenistic processions, festivals, and *thusia* over the Roman period allowed local, non-priestly elites an increasingly prominent role in civic religion, both as ceremonial officiants and as patrons.

The economic decline of the empire in the later third century had a devastating effect on the staffing and performance of such traditional temple functions, since Roman administration had initially deprived the temples of financial independence and instead made them dependent on local, and to some extent imperial, munificence. This economic crisis provides the context for the obvious decline in evidence for temple building, maintenance, or even priestly activities after the mid-third century CE (Bagnall 1988). However, there is enough sporadic evidence for activities around smaller Egyptian shrines and temples thereafter that we can infer that some sort of ritual life continued around Egypt despite the dwindling of major temples and the establishment of Christianity.

Saints' lives, for example, a notoriously fantastic genre that typically mentioned traditional religion simply to caricature and demonize it (Frankfurter 2006b), nevertheless offer several credible accounts of local shrines and cults still maintained by their communities in the fifth century: one for Agathos Daimon (Egyptian: Shai) north of Panopolis (Frankfurter 2007), another for Isis east of Alexandria (Sansterre 1991), and in a dilapidated temple in fifth-century Abydos the popular protective and oracular god Bes was apparently still regarded as a numinous presence (Frankfurter 1998: 40–1, 128–31, 162–5). Furthermore, some formal religious activities continued at the southern Isis temple of Philae at least through the fifth century, owing partly to the patronage of Nubian peoples (Dijkstra 2008; and see Chapter 45). And the fiery late fourth-century abbot Shenoute of Atripe trumpeted his demolition of at least one functioning temple in the vicinity of his monastery (Emmel 2008; Frankfurter 2008a). These diverse witnesses reflect the centrifugal developments mentioned earlier: that as economic decline, imperial repression, and sporadic Christian persecution eliminated the larger, regional temples that depended on greater staffs and patronage, the ritual practices that linked family, community, landscape, and agriculture shifted to local shrines and domestic rites.

Religion in the Domestic Sphere

Excavations over several centuries have produced great numbers of terracotta figurines of Egyptian gods, Hellenized in such a way as to emphasize their protective or generative powers. These figurines point to the importance and self-determination of the private or domestic sphere for which the figurines were produced. (This sphere naturally extended to the private tombs in which many figurines were found.) The great diversity of forms in which one could purchase Isis, Harpocrates, Serapis, and Bes must reflect the desire, on the part of individuals and households, to choose images of a god that reflected family hopes and concerns, whether to leave in a tomb or *ex voto* at a shrine or to bring back for a domestic altar (Fig. 20.1; see Dunand 1979; Frankfurter 1998: 132–4, 140–1). Such altars have been found in the form of niches in Roman era houses in the Fayum town of Karanis (Fig. 20.2; Husselman 1975: 35–6, 47–8); and papyri refer to ritual devotions at such altars. Aelius Theon assures his brother that 'every day I make devotion on [your daughter's] behalf before the god... the lord Serapis' (*P Oxy*. 3992), while Apollonia and Epons ask their sisters to 'Please light a lamp for the shrines and spread the cushions' (*P Athen*. 60). An increasing corpus of painted images of Egyptian gods, some portable, others applied directly to house walls (Fig. 20.3), and all combining Graeco-Roman style and Egyptian details, show another way that people brought the mediating presence of regional deities into the home—and the corresponding creativity of workshops in developing new ways of miniaturizing religion for the home (Mathews 2001).

Still in the fifth century Shenoute of Atripe complains about householders who light lamps in their homes to proclaim the festival of the regional god Shai, and others who 'worship wood and stone or anything made by man's handiwork (with) wood and stone, or (moulded by putting) clay inside them' (*The Lord Thundered*; trans. Frankfurter 1998: 63–4, 78; Timbie and Zaborowski 2006); and a Christian saint's life recalls that traditional devotees to Shai maintained niches for an image of the god in their homes, before which they would bow their heads in veneration (see Frankfurter 2007: 179–82). All these testimonies reflect the home's traditional function as a site for religious practices, some interconnected with local or regional temples and their festivals (as long as these continued), while others addressed familial concerns for protection, procreative fertility, and contact with ancestors (Frankfurter 1998: 131–42; 2008b; Alston 2002: 92–6).

It is important not to juxtapose domestic and temple religion as discrete zones, even if the former would eventually outlast the latter. The terracotta figurines described here were sold at temples, moulded by artisans in consultation with temple priests, and they interpreted the traditional temple iconography in classical forms, using nudity, dress, body shape, and specific accoutrements (cornucopias, animals, swords) to draw out the authority and relevance of a god. An Isis lantern might indicate participation in the festival of Isis Pharia, while a jug with Bes' face might be carried full from a Bes festival (such as the one attested in second-century Dendara: *SB* VI 9127). A figurine of the toddler Harpocrates with his hand in a pot (see Fig. 20.1) may reflect the distribution of sweets at the Harpocrateia festival. Domestic

FIG. 20.1 Terracotta figurine of Harpocrates as a nude infant with hand in pot and extended phallus, from Karanis. Height 14 cm, width 10.5 cm

Kelsey Museum of Archaeology, KM 6514. Courtesy of the Kelsey Museum, University of Michigan.

FIG. 20.2 Painted wall-niche altar from a domestic structure at Karanis, House C119E. Height 2.15 m, width 1.5 m

Courtesy of the Kelsey Museum of Archaeology, University of Michigan.

FIG. 20.3 Watercolour reproduction of a mural of Isis *lactans*, from a domestic structure at Karanis, House B50

Kelsey Museum of Archaeology, KM 2003.2.2. Courtesy of the Kelsey Museum, University of Michigan.

religious artefacts of these types thus signify participation in regional cults and calendar, even a home's religious identity with a particular shrine and its god (Frankfurter 2008b).

Other materials point to the distinctive concerns of the family: nude, sometimes pregnant female figurines, to be left at shrines or in tombs to assure the pregnancy of a member of the domestic sphere. A remarkable first- or second-century letter from a woman in an early form of Coptic, meant to be read aloud before an ancestor's tomb (or the Osiris shrine among the tombs), complains in intimate terms about her husband's inattention and her desire to be pregnant:

> It is Esrmpe, the (daughter) of Kllaouč, who is complaining about Hor, the (son) of Tanesneou. My lord Osiris, (Lord) of Hasroē! I complain to you, do justice to me and Hor, the (son) of Tanesneou, concerning what I have done to him and what he has done to me. Namely, he does not have sex with me, I having no power, I having no protector-son. I am unable to help (myself), I am childless (?). There is no one who could complain concerning me before you [literally: him] because of Hor.... I complain to [you...]... Osiris, listen to my calls!... what he has done to me. (*P Schmidt*; see Satzinger 1975)

Here is one of the authentic voices of Egyptian domestic piety in the Roman period. As it extended to tombs and shrines, the Egyptian domestic sphere thus represented not only social space but also religious space, and it mediated procreative fertility, safety from hostile spirits and sorcery, festival participation, and food production. The artefacts of domestic religion, from figurines and interior niches to papyri and literary testimonies, show both the continuing concern for such ritual matters and the self-determination and creativity of family members in addressing them—through their efforts at festivals, on pilgrimages, with ritual specialists, or simply through the solitary determination of concerned mothers, as one fifth-century Christian writer complains:

> some of them ablute their children in polluted water and water from the arena, from the theatre, and moreover they pour all over themselves water with incantations (spoken over it), and they break their clay pots claiming it repels the evil eye. Some tie amulets on their children, hand-crafted by men—those (men) who provide a place for the dwelling of demons—while others anoint themselves with oil that is evil and incantations and such things that they tie on their heads and necks. (Pseudo-Athanasius, *Homily on the Virgin*; see Frankfurter 1998: 29)

We cannot label such ritual efforts 'Christian' or 'pagan' or even link them clearly with prevailing cults. Domestic religion involves a perpetual bricolage of ancestral traditions and new idioms of power. But even more importantly, what such testimonies illustrate is the effort and agency that keep such ritual traditions going for the sake of the home: to assure procreation, to protect inhabitants and family members, and to maintain some contact with ancestors and memories.

Divination and Magic in Roman Egypt: An Age of Insecurity and Superstition?

The religious world of Roman Egypt comprised a range of ritual practices and artefacts that seem to lie between the temple and the home: magical texts that combine Egyptian, Roman, Jewish, and other Mediterranean traditions; divination rites at shrines, private spaces, and even books; bizarre 'magical' iconographies on stelae and gems; and, of course, the wizards who purveyed these materials, with hybrid self-designations: priest, *magos*, prophet. Such materials show neither the intimacy of domestic religion nor the mythic conservatism and cosmic concerns of temple liturgy, yet they seem to partake in both spheres (Smith 2004). The very profusion of this hybrid data in the Roman period, especially when set against the staid remains of classical or pharaonic Egyptian religion, has long led ancient historians and classicists to infer a crisis of faith, a loss of centre and tradition, an age of anxiety, or—in the antiquarian Alphonse Barb's inimitable metaphor—the wholesale contamination of delicate traditions by alien teachings, like food poisoning from ethnic fare (Barb 1963: 99–100; cf. Dodds 1965). Such models and metaphors for the diversity of religious materials in Roman Egypt have naturally served to frame the success of Christianity: as either a triumph of spiritual clarity or the further perpetuation of neurotic obsessions. But do such conclusions, based solely on the data for magical and oracular practices and on fictional images of wizards, have any historical merit?

In fact, each of these hybrid religious phenomena can be easily understood in the context of Egyptian temple religion and of Hellenism itself. Egyptian temples, for example, had long addressed social needs for guidance—in justice, in agriculture, in crisis—through various types of divination. A palette of random elements would be set up to receive a god's message: for example, the god's statue on its processional barque, which could be felt to move on the shoulders of its priestly bearers; or written notes placed in the temple, near the altar, in such a way that one would be chosen; or even the body asleep in a holy place after ritual preparations, to receive divine messages in dreams. The particular configuration resulting from the palette—movements of the statue, chosen ticket, dream symbols—would constitute the omen and would require professional interpretation to turn into an oracle, a socially or institutionally authoritative instruction.

Such methods are well documented and indeed central to the administration and function of Egyptian religion from at least the New Kingdom. Hellenism hardly changed the social importance of temple divination; and thus great numbers of oracle 'tickets'—alternative answers to questions inscribed and submitted together to the god for his choice and guarantee—have been found in connection with the Sobek temples of the Fayum and many other temples through the third century, inscribed in Demotic Egyptian and Greek (Brashear 1995: 3448–56). Processional oracles, in which the image's movements on the priests' shoulders are observed at some designated point in the festival procession, are likewise attested at the Philae temple of Isis and the Tebtunis temple of Sobek; and an edict of Septimius Severus attempts to proscribe 'oracles... in writings as it were divinely delivered or through the procession of images' (*P Coll. Youtie* I 30; see Ritner 1995: 3355–6). Even dreams were sought in temple spaces as divine omens: initially by priests and kings, but increasingly through the Greek and Roman periods as a popular therapeutic pursuit at designated spaces in temples like Abydos and Deir el-Bahri. Against the rich history of Egyptian divination, the developments (and, as we shall see, diversification) of the Roman period seem largely perpetuations of indigenous traditions and their spaces.

One important example of divination's continuing vitality well into the fourth century occurred at the ancient Osiris temple at Abydos. This temple was transformed into a Serapis shrine in the Ptolemaic period and then, in the early Roman period, a site for dream revelations from Bes, a popular god of procreative fertility and protection with few known cult centres. The Abydos Bes cult received so many visitors as to gain international renown: individuals across the Mediterranean sent written oracle requests (Amm. Marc. 19.12.3–4; see Dunand 1997), and priests even developed mobile Bes-incubation rituals in Greek, to procure dreams anywhere (*PGM* VII 222–49, VIII 64–110, CII 1–17). Thus, the Bes oracle flourished until, in 359 CE, an imperial agent discovered subversive inquiries among the cult's archives and had the oracle shut down (Amm. Marc. 19.12.5–16). Yet still in the fifth century the *Life of Moses of Abydos*, about a holy man who established a convent in the Abydos temple complex, recalls its prior haunting by a 'demon Bes' (Frankfurter 1998: 169–74; 2005).

While most such evidence for divination practices in Roman Egypt shows continuity with older traditions, it is clear that Hellenism and the democratizing effects of Greek literacy contributed to a popularization, diversification, and even centrifugal shift in divination, from temples out to various potential sites. The development of therapeutic incubation cults in temples reflects a shift already from priestly dream cultivation for divine instruction to popular dream cultivation for healing—a shift attributable partly to a larger trend in Egyptian religion (from the late Pharaonic period) of democratizing royal and priestly ritual traditions (see Assmann 1997), and partly to Greek notions of divine control over the body (see in general Ritner 1995: 3346–8; Dunand 2006). Even more clearly, the numerous divination rituals described in the Greek and Demotic Magical Papyri, not only for gaining dream-visions but also for using mirrors, bowls, and the lucid eyes of children, reflect a distinctively hellenistic shift to private spaces (Betz 1986). The sacred—and, for many in Roman Egypt, exotic—mysteries of the Egyptian temple could be ostentatiously transferred to and miniaturized in more accessible sites for paying clients (Smith 1995).

Perhaps the clearest example of Hellenism's effect on the diversification of divination media is the Greek (and eventually Latin and Coptic) *sortes* books, each of which contained a list of questions, with several possible answers for each question scattered among a series of columns. The expert owner would produce the 'true' answer for the paying client by locating the column and then the correct answer according to a number chosen by the client—a procedure that allowed the appearance of supernatural intervention. This divination procedure took the authority behind mantic guidance from the temple, its god, and the hidden rites of the ticket oracle, and placed it entirely in the book (and its pedigree, often of a legendary sage). The questions—'will I beget children?', 'will I sell my cargo?', etc.—point not to the culture's pervasive anxiety but to the owners' and editors' sense of what they might be asked: the quotidian concerns and typical crises of a premodern society and its various classes (Frankfurter 1998: 179–84; Hansen 1998: 285–324, with translation and discussion). Divination is a perennial aspect of cultures, a way of gaining certainty and authority in decision making at every social level, and hardly a sign of cultural decadence.

Beyond rituals for private divination and revelation, the Greek and Demotic Magical Papyri (and later, analogous corpora in Coptic) provide spells and charms for gaining lovers (sometimes by interrupting existing relationships), cursing rivals, securing health and pregnancies, controlling spirits, and—especially in Christianized documents—repelling demons (Betz 1986; Brashear 1995; Meyer and Smith 1994). Unearthed from Egyptian sites and reflecting a consistent grounding in Egyptian religion (and often Egyptian language), alongside a deliberate eclecticism of Mediterranean gods and myths, these magical texts fundamentally belong to Egyptian religion of the Roman period and its various Hellenizing trends (Ritner 1995; Dieleman 2005).

Some texts are in the form of ritual manuals or compendiums of sometimes great length; others consist merely of amulets or inscribed charms to be worn or buried. How do we interpret these materials, especially those of an aggressive nature? In the most basic sense, rituals for maintaining relationships, gaining health, or securing helpful spirits are perennial features of local cultures, and Roman Egypt was no different in this respect. As anthropologists have long recognized, frustration, jealousy, anxiety, and suspicion will inevitably be negotiated through curses and amulets, even when legal means are available (Malinowski 1948). The most blood-chilling curse spells and erotic charms (like the assemblage in the Louvre that included a figurine of a bound woman pierced with pins) can be situated amid the rivalries of social life in village or city (see Winkler 1990; Frankfurter 2001, 2006a). By use of powerful names, sounds, commands, symbols, gestures, and liminal places, combined in consultation with a designated expert, a situation of powerlessness and frustration could be transformed into one of agency.

And who were these designated experts? The construction of pedigrees and ingredients in spell manuals like the following from Leiden seems to address a cultural world of exoticism and staged authenticity from the point of view of priests guarding secrets. A list of ingredients and their codes is prefaced as

> interpretations that the temple scribes employed, from the holy writings, in translation. Because of the curiosity of the masses they [the scribes] inscribed the names of the herbs and other things that they employed on the statues of the gods, so that they [the masses], since they do not take adequate precaution, might not [perform such rites] due to the consequence of their misunderstanding. But we have collected the explanations [of these names] from many copies [of the sacred writings], all of them secret. (*PGM* XII 401–9; Betz 1986: 167)

What is distinctive about the Greek and Demotic Magical Papyri is the self-conscious cosmopolitanism and exoticism in their presentation, addressing the realities of everyday crises like erotic passion or rivalry with both a staged mysteriousness and an ostentatious Hellenism: metrical hymns, Greek divine names and places, Homeric references, etc. (e.g. *PGM* IV 154, 885–6, 2006, 2124–5, 2967, 3007; V 96; see Faraone 2000). The self-presentation of these documents presumably reflects a similar self-presentation on the part of those who purveyed the spells in practice. Indeed, the magical papyri point to trends in the developing self-conceptions and public roles of Egyptian priests—from the Ptolemaic period but especially in the Roman period (Frankfurter 2000a; Dieleman 2005; and more broadly Fowden 1986).

It was a world, after all, that had long held Egyptian priests in exotic allure—a motif of many novels and hagiographies of the Roman period. And for this world, individual priests clearly appropriated the stereotypes projected upon them—in Alexandria and the *chora*, at temples and marketplaces—in an effort to elaborate their changing authority in hellenistic terms and to profit financially at a time when the temple infrastructure was dwindling (Frankfurter 2000a: 162–83). Of course, ritual expertise remained a vital role in local religious culture, whether in the person of the local priest or of the wise woman, but urban culture in particular expected exotic figures, *magoi* ('wizards')—whose spells seemed to come not from shared lore but from inaccessible temple libraries and cosmopolitan incantations (Frankfurter 1998: 217–37; 2002; see also Fowden 1986).

We may not need to attribute to this Hellenized priestly world another bizarre feature of the magical papyri, their invocation and iconographic depiction of hybrid and ambivalent deities: for example, the aggressive Seth-Typhon, the 'headless god', the whip-bearing anguipede god, and many figures found on magical gems (Fig. 20.4; see Bonner 1950). Much has been made of the apparent speculative interest of 'magicians' in dark or monstrous forces, their bottomless occult predilections and abandonment of proper public gods (see Barb 1963). It is therefore important not only to note that the preponderance of spells in the Greek and Demotic Magical Papyri address well-known cosmic deities like Hermes, Selene, Helios, and Serapis, but also to put the crafting of hybrid deities for ritual efficacy in Egyptian context: specifically, the tradition of developing apotropaic iconography out of the divine attributes of major gods and even out of the 'demons' of the mortuary passage, originally to safeguard the king in his various divine forms.

Well before the Ptolemaic period, priestly iconographers were combining traditional divine images (often in frontal form, like Bes or Harpocrates) with animals symbolic of demonic forces, to produce visual assemblages of supreme efficacy against cosmic dangers (see Sauneron 1960, 1970; Assmann 1997; Quack 2006). In learned circles these images had explicit sources in theological speculation, but their popular reproductions in local shrines and homes offered familiar and effective protection against liminal and threatening spirits (Frankfurter 1998: 111–20). Among the most popular types of such 'monstrous' images still crafted in the Roman period were the stone or wood Horus *cippi*, which depicted Harpocrates standing on crocodiles, holding serpents and antelopes in his hands, his head surmounted by a mask of Bes, an elaborate bricolage of the dangerous and the apotropaic (see Fig. 20.5; Ritner 1989; Gasse 2004). Another powerful image was the figure of Bes, armoured and brandishing a sword; and another was the sphinx-god Tutu, depicted on stone stelae with multiple animal heads (see Fig. 24.4 in Chapter 24; Sauneron 1960; Kaper 2003). Few Horus *cippi* remain from the Roman period, yet their iconography is reproduced in magical gems and seems even to have influenced forms of apotropaic Christian art. Much of magical crafts-

FIG. 20.4 Haematite gem (obverse), with two-headed god (snake and ibis heads) holding an Egyptian *was* sceptre and *ankh* symbol, standing over a crocodile with a solar disc. Height 2.4 cm, width 1.9 cm

Kelsey Museum of Archaeology, KM 26059. Courtesy of the Kelsey Museum, University of Michigan.

manship in Roman Egypt drew on priestly traditions, and protection and healing depended on the perpetuation and hybridization of efficacious iconographies.

Magic and divination remained central features of religious practice in Roman Egypt, both in the quotidian, domestic sphere and, in the case of divination, in the public sphere, where political (and even agricultural) guidance was sought in temple performances: the movements of statues, uses of the written word, and even priestly observation of the nilometer. But magic and divination also served as vehicles of Hellenization: for priests to reconstruct themselves as wizards, for oracles to employ new media, and for craftsmen of magical images to explore new meanings and hybrids of familiar gods.

Religious Practices across Class and Culture

Magic, divination, domestic altars and their rites—did everybody share such practices in Roman Egypt? The pictures of elite intellectual culture and of philosophical schools, especially in Alexandria, that authors like Philo, Clement, Eunapius, and Damascius provide have occasionally given historians licence to imagine two tiers of religion in Egypt: one rural, Egyptian, superstitious, and decadent, clinging to the defunct old gods, and

FIG. 20.5 Painted wooden *cippus* of Harpocrates standing on crocodiles, surmounted by a large Bes head, dated to the Late or Ptolemaic period

British Museum EA 60958. Courtesy of the Trustees of the British Museum.

another erudite and abstract 'Egyptian spirituality' (e.g. Heliod. *Aeth.* 3.16, 6.14). But the criticisms that Peter Brown (1981) levelled against such a two-tier model in the study of the Christian cults of saints pertain even more to religious practices in Roman Egypt: the model ignores the general commitment to these various traditions across classes and subcultures—and perpetuates the notion of a cultural division in religious practices for romantic (if not theological) reasons. In fact, what we glean of the lives of the intellectual elite and urban literati in Roman Egypt shows considerable participation in the diverse religious practices reviewed so far in this chapter.

For one thing, these same social classes displayed their prestige through patronage of festivals, providing wine and animals for feasting, and dramatic and athletic displays—and as often for temple-based events as for imperial holidays (see Perpillou-Thomas 1993: 226–37). Munificence and patronage shifted increasingly from communities to individuals over the Roman period, so even when public festivals lost explicit connections with temple processions, their patrons continued to engage with civic religion and its symbols and practices. In late fourth-century Syria as well, Libanius describes the regional patron as the linchpin of festival practice (30.19), while the fourth–fifth-century abbot Shenoute's tirades against a local notable, Gesios, enumerate his (private) protective efforts towards the remains of the local temple cult (see Frankfurter 1998: 77–82, with historical emendations in Emmel 2008).

Other literate elite showed more explicit investments in temple and private religion. A philosopher picked up in the inquisition following the imperial crackdown on the Abydos Bes oracle in 359 CE confessed to having practised devotions to Bes 'from early youth . . . to propitiate the deity' (Amm. Marc. 19.12.12). Indeed, the fact that this same oracle was solicited from afar for information on political matters illustrates the investment in traditional oracles (and popular gods) on the part of some elite. In the late fifth century a member of an Alexandrian philosophical school went out to an Isis temple in the village of Menouthis for assistance in procreation. (Public doubts about the baby he acquired there, according to the Christian author, precipitated riots between Hellene and Christian students and finally the destruction of the temple itself; see Zachariah of Mytilene, *Vita Severi*; Frankfurter 2000a: 189–91; Watts 2010: 63–71, 142–52.) For some intellectual Hellenes, of course, the gulf between their dedication to traditional religion and actual practices in and around the temples (even in the moribund state of most fourth- and fifth-century cults) was so great that we can only call their investment a staged authenticity. And yet, they did view their Hellenic and Egyptian identity as linked to these monuments and their gods, and the traditional practices that invoked these gods (Athanassiadi 1993a; Frankfurter 2000a: 184–93).

Primary documents also show a continuity between literate, cosmopolitan classes and the range of traditional and hybrid practices I have been reviewing. Many of the Greek and Demotic Magical Papyri, for example, derive from deeply Hellenized and cosmopolitan milieus (see Dieleman 2005), and the *sortes* books, described earlier, presume some 'learned' respect for the mysterious hybrid tome on the part of the client. While the ritual innovations particular to elite classes in Roman Egypt remain a rich topic for synthetic discussion (using sources like the *PGM* and *PDM*, Iamblichus, and Damascius; see Athanassiadi 1993a,b), it is clear that religious practices lay on a continuum across classes, both in the observance of traditional religion and, ultimately, in Christian practices as well.

Christianizing Religious Practice in Roman and Late Antique Egypt

What, then, of Christianity? As elsewhere in the empire, the religion gained most adherents for its promises of healing power and protection from demonic forces, both fields especially of ritual performance and practice (rather than theology or intellection). But in this case healing and protection were framed—rendered authoritative—by means of new sacred texts like the Gospels. In fact, a good number of the earliest (third- to fourth-century) fragments of Gospel texts on papyri appear to have been inscribed as protective or healing amulets (Judge 1987). Thus, Christianity's holy text was itself deemed magical from an early stage. Other materials, from the *Life of Antony* by Athanasius to inscriptions and stonework, show the predominant function of the cross as a protective symbol, highlighting both the enormity of Satanic danger in the Christian institutional world-view and Christianity's central identity in repelling demons. And just as early Christian literature stressed the authoritative actions of Jesus and the Apostles as paradigms for exorcism and healing, so the stories and documents of holy men in late antique Egypt stress their own performative abilities in healing, protection, and even cursing (see Frankfurter 2003). Abbot Shenoute describes first-hand

> the snake's head tied on someone's hand, another one with the crocodile's tooth tied to his arm, and another with fox claws tied to his legs—especially since it was an official who told him that it was wise to do so! Indeed, when I demanded whether the fox claws would heal him, he answered, 'It was a great monk who gave them to me, saying "Tie them on you (and) you will find relief."' (Acephalous Work A14)

If Christianity came eventually to serve as an institution permeating Egyptian society (see Bagnall 1993: 283–93), its initial impact on people and its ongoing influence was in the area of religious practice. Discourse, in the sense of communication *about* practice, devotion, and divinity, does not seem to have changed among ordinary people (Choat 2006).

By the fifth century religious practice had come to revolve around the shrine of the Christian saint, often a martyr, and its festivals. A phenomenon with roots in late third-century Christian martyr-cults at tombs (see Frankfurter 1994), Christian shrines gradually usurped the regional status that Egyptian temples had held, as social, economic, and cultic centres—as *axes mundi* in their architectural mediation of a divinity's presence. People would visit the shrines for healing and intercession. They would deposit, *ex voto*, or bring home as a souvenir one of the many terracotta figurines of pregnant or nursing women manufactured at shrines like Apa Mena, or a clay ampoule of holy oil stamped with the saint's image. They would follow processions, bring animals to feast, play musical instruments, and flirt. And they would even consult the saint's oracular powers using dual inscribed oracle tickets, much as had their forebears at the cults of Sobek three centuries earlier (Frankfurter 1998: 193–5; and in general Papaconstantinou 2001). Indeed, divination was one of the most popular functions of the saint's shrine in late antique Egypt, with various cults offering incubation, *sortes* consultation, ticket oracles, and even oracles from the mouths of the spirit-possessed (see Papaconstantinou 2001: 336–9; Frankfurter 2005, 2010).

Christianity thus progressed much as Hellenism had done: as an authoritative, mythic framework for healing, protective power, sacred landscape, and religious movement among shrines—a framework with cosmic or global resonance for people, but also a powerfully local resonance. If the ideology of Christianity was fundamentally intolerant of so-called 'heathen practices' and could thus mobilize violent iconoclastic acts, the forceful repression of traditional cults and buildings was sporadic and idiosyncratic to particular emperors, bishops, and regions, and it seldom affected private and local ritual practices (see Frankfurter 2000b, 2008b; Emmel 2008; Grossmann 2008). More illuminating than the stories and remains of iconoclasm are the references, in sermons and hagiographies, to local people's perpetuation of traditions and practices: holiday lamp-lighting in the home, a 'demon' still haunting a temple, divination at tombs and shrines, amuletic concoctions by holy men, and magical texts in Coptic to heal, protect, and bind rivals (Meyer and Smith 1994). These practices are not 'pagan survivals', as often described, but the basic elements of cultural expression, of habitus and memory, and of interaction with religious institutions that had comprised Egyptian religion through the Roman period.

Suggested Reading

Principal discussions of the nature, persistence, and decline of religion in Roman Egypt include Bagnall (1993), Frankfurter (1998), Dunand and Zivie-Coche (2004), and the essays in *Aufsteig und Niedergang der römischen Welt* II 18.5 (1995). New developments in priestly and intellectual subcultures (which led to the hybrid collections of Hermetica and magical papyri) are discussed by Fowden (1986), Athanassiadi (1993a), Frankfurter (2000a), and Dieleman (2005). The dynamics of Christianization in late antique Egypt are discussed in Frankfurter (2003, 2005, 2010), as well as Choat (2006) and Dijkstra (2008).

Bibliography

Alston, R. 2002. *The City in Roman and Byzantine Egypt*. London: Routledge.
Assmann, J. 1997. 'Magic and Theology in Ancient Egypt', in P. Schäfer and H. G. Kippenberg (eds), *Envisioning Magic: A Princeton Seminar and Symposium*. Leiden: Brill, 1–18.
Athanassiadi, P. 1993a. 'Persecution and Response in Late Paganism: The Evidence of Damascius', *Journal of Hellenic Studies* 113: 1–29.
—— 1993b. 'Dreams, Theurgy and Freelance Divination: The Testimony of Iamblichus', *Journal of Roman Studies* 83: 115–30.
Bagnall, R. 1988. 'Combat ou vide: Christianisme et paganisme dans l'Égypte romaine tardive', *Ktema* 13: 285–96.
—— 1993. *Egypt in Late Antiquity*. Princeton: Princeton University Press.
—— and J. B. Rives. 2000. 'A Prefect's Edict Mentioning Sacrifice', *Archiv für Religionsgeschichte* 2: 77–86.
Bailey, D. M. 2008. *Catalogue of Terracottas in the British Museum*, vol. 4: *Ptolemaic and Roman Terracottas from Egypt*. London: British Museum Press.
Barb, A. A. 1963. 'The Survival of the Magic Arts', in A. Momigliano (ed.), *The Conflict between Paganism and Christianity in the Fourth Century*. Oxford: Clarendon Press, 100–25.
Betz, H. D. (ed.) 1986. *The Greek Magical Papyri in Translation, including the Demotic Spells*. Chicago: University of Chicago Press.
Bonner, C. 1950. *Studies in Magical Amulets, Chiefly Graeco-Egyptian*. Ann Arbor: University of Michigan Press.
Bowersock, G. W. 1990. *Hellenism in Late Antiquity*. Ann Arbor: University of Michigan Press.
Brashear, W. 1995. 'The Greek Magical Papyri: An Introduction and Survey', in W. Haase and H. Temporini (eds), *Aufstieg und Niedergang der römischen Welt* II 18.5. Berlin: de Gruyter, 3380–684.
Brown, P. 1981. *The Cult of the Saints: Its Rise and Function in Latin Christianity*. Chicago: University of Chicago Press.
Choat, M. 2006. *Belief and Cult in Fourth-Century Papyri*. Turnhout: Brepols.
Dieleman, J. 2005. *Priests, Tongues, and Rites: The London-Leiden Magical Manuscripts and Translation in Egyptian Ritual (100–300 CE)*. Leiden: Brill.

Dijkstra, J. H. F. 2008. *Philae and the End of Ancient Egyptian Religion: A Regional Study of Religious Transformation (298–642 CE)*. Leuven: Peeters.
Dodds, E. R. 1965. *Pagan and Christian in an Age of Anxiety*. New York: Norton.
Dunand, F. 1975. 'Les syncrétismes dans la religion de l'Égypte romain', in F. Dunand and P. Lévêque (eds), *Les syncrétismes dans les religions de l'antiquité*. Leiden: Brill, 152–85.
—— 1979. *Religion populaire en Égypte romaine: Les terres cuites isiaques du Musée du Caire*. Leiden: Brill.
—— 1997. 'La consultation oraculaire en Égypte tardive: L'oracle de Bès à Abydos', in J.- G. Heintz (ed.), *Oracles et prophéties dans l'antiquité: Actes du Colloque de Strasbourg*. Paris: de Boccard, 65–84.
—— 2006. 'La guérison dans les temples (Égypte, époque tardive)', *Archiv für Religionsgeschichte* 8: 4–24.
—— and C. Zivie-Coche. 2004. *Gods and Men in Egypt: 3000 BCE to 395 CE*. Ithaca: Cornell University Press.
Emmel, S. 2008. 'Shenoute of Atripe and the Christian Destruction of Temples in Egypt: Rhetoric and Reality', in J. Hahn, S. Emmel, and U. Gotter (eds), *From Temple to Church: Destruction and Renewal of Local Cultic Topography in Late Antiquity*. Leiden: Brill, 161–201.
Faraone, C. A. 2000. 'Handbooks and Anthologies: The Collection of Greek and Egyptian Incantations in Late Hellenistic Egypt', *Archiv für Religionsgeschichte* 2: 195–214.
Fowden, G. 1986. *The Egyptian Hermes: A Historical Approach to the Late Pagan Mind*. Cambridge: Cambridge University Press.
Frankfurter, D. 1994. 'The Cult of the Martyrs in Egypt before Constantine: The Evidence of the Coptic Apocalypse of Elijah', *Vigiliae Christianae* 48: 25–47.
—— 1998. *Religion in Roman Egypt: Assimilation and Resistance*. Princeton: Princeton University Press.
—— 2000a. 'The Consequences of Hellenism in Late Antique Egypt: Religious Worlds and Actors', *Archiv für Religionsgeschichte* 2: 162–94.
—— 2000b. '"Things Unbefitting Christians": Violence and Christianization in Fifth-Century Panopolis', *Journal of Early Christian Studies* 8: 273–95.
—— 2001. 'The Perils of Love: Magic and Counter-Magic in Coptic Egypt', *Journal of the History of Sexuality* 10: 480–500.
—— 2002. 'Dynamics of Ritual Expertise in Antiquity and Beyond: Towards a New Taxonomy of "Magicians"', in P. Mirecki and M. Meyer (eds), *Magic and Ritual in the Ancient World*. Leiden: Brill, 159–78.
—— 2003. 'Syncretism and the Holy Man in Late Antique Egypt', *Journal of Early Christian Studies* 11: 339–85.
—— 2005. 'Voices, Books, and Dreams: The Diversification of Divination Media in Late Antique Egypt', in S. I. Johnston and P. Struck (eds), *Mantikē: Studies in Ancient Divination*. Leiden: Brill, 233–54.
—— 2006a. 'Fetus Magic and Sorcery Fears in Roman Egypt', *Greek, Roman, and Byzantine Studies* 46: 37–62.
—— 2006b. 'Hagiography and the Reconstruction of Local Religion in Late Antique Egypt: Memories, Inventions, and Landscapes', *Church History and Religious Culture* 86: 13–37.
—— 2007. 'Illuminating the Cult of Kothos: The *Panegryic on Macarius* and Local Religion in Fifth-Century Egypt', in J. E. Goehring and J. A. Timbie (eds), *The World of Early Egyptian Christianity: Language, Literature, and Social Context*. Washington, DC: Catholic University of America Press, 176–88.

—— 2008a. 'Iconoclasm and Christianization in Late Antique Egypt: Christian Treatments of Space and Image', in J. Hahn, S. Emmel, and U. Gotter (eds), *From Temple to Church: Destruction and Renewal of Local Cultic Topography in Late Antiquity*. Leiden: Brill, 135–59.

—— 2008b. 'The Interpenetration of Ritual Spaces in Late Antique Religions: An Overview', *Archiv für Religionsgeschichte* 10: 211–22.

—— 2010. 'Where the Spirits Dwell: Possession, Christianization, and Saint-Shrines in Late Antiquity', *Harvard Theological Review* 103: 27–46.

Gasse, A. 2004. *Les stèles d'Horus sur les crocodiles*. Paris: Réunion des Musées Nationaux.

Golvin, G., et al. 1981. 'Le petit Sarapeion romain de Louqsor', *Bulletin de l'Institut Français d'Archéologie Orientale* 81: 115–48.

Grossmann, P. 2008. 'Modalitäten der Zerstörung und Christianisierung pharaonischer Tempelanlagen', in J. Hahn, S. Emmel, and U. Gotter (eds), *From Temple to Church: Destruction and Renewal of Local Cultic Topography in Late Antiquity*. Leiden: Brill, 299–334.

Hansen, W. (ed.) 1998. *Anthology of Ancient Greek Popular Literature*. Bloomington: Indiana University Press.

Husselman, E. M. 1975. *Karanis Excavations of the University of Michigan in Egypt, 1928–1935: Topography and Architecture*. Ann Arbor: University of Michigan Press.

Judge, E. A. 1987. 'The Magical Use of Scripture in the Papyri', in E. W. Contrad and E. G. Newing (eds), *Perspectives on Language and Text*. Winona Lake, Ind.: Eisenbrauns, 339–49.

Kaper, O. E. 2003. *The Egyptian God Tutu: A Study of the Sphinx-God and Master of Demons, with a Corpus of Monuments*. Leuven: Peeters.

Malinowski, B. 1948. *Magic, Science and Religion, and Other Essays*. Boston: Beacon Press.

Mathews, T. F. 2001. 'The Emperor and the Icon', *Acta ad Archaeologiam et Artium Historiam Pertinentia* 15: 163–77.

Meyer, M., and R. Smith (eds) 1994. *Ancient Christian Magic: Coptic Texts of Ritual Power*. San Francisco: Harper.

Papaconstantinou, A. 2001. *Le culte des saints en Egypte: Des Byzantins aux Abbassides: L'apport des inscriptions et des papyrus grecs et coptes*. Paris: CNRS.

Perpillou-Thomas, F. 1993. *Fêtes d'Égypte ptolémaïque et romaine d'après la documentation papyrologique grecque*. Leuven: Peeters.

Quack, J. F. 2006. 'The So-Called Pantheos: On Polymorphic Deities in Late Egyptian Religion', in H. György (ed.), *Aegyptus et Pannonia III: Acta Symposii anno 2004*. Budapest: Comité de l'Égypte Ancienne de l'Association Amicable Hongroise-Égyptienne, 175–90.

Quaegebeur, J. 1983. 'Cultes égyptiens et grecs en Égypte hellénistique: L'exploitation des sources', in E. van't Dack, P. van Dessel, and W. van Gucht (eds), *Egypt and the Hellenistic World*. Leuven: Studia Hellenistica, 303–24.

Reddé, M. 1992. *Le trésor de Douch*. Cairo: Institut Français d'Archéologie Orientale.

Ritner, R. K. 1989. 'Horus on the Crocodiles: A Juncture of Religion and Magic in Late Dynastic Egypt', in W. K. Simpson (ed.), *Religion and Philosophy in Ancient Egypt*. New Haven: Yale University Press, 103–16.

—— 1995. 'Egyptian Magical Practice under the Roman Empire: The Demotic Spells and their Religious Context', in W. Haase and H. Temporini (eds), *Aufstieg und Niedergang der römischen Welt* II 18.5. Berlin: de Gruyter, 3333–79.

Sansterre, J.-M. 1991. 'Apparitions et miracles à Menouthis: De l'incubation païenne à l'incubation chrétienne', in A. Dierkens (ed.), *Apparitions et miracles*. Brussels: Université Libre, 69–83.

Satzinger, H. 1975. 'The Old Coptic Schmidt Papyrus', *Journal of the American Research Center in Egypt* 12: 37–50.

Sauneron, S. 1960. 'Le nouveau Sphinx composite du Brooklyn Museum et le rôle du dieu Toutou-Tithoès', *Journal of Near Eastern Studies* 19: 269–87.

—— 1970. *Le Papyrus magique illustré de Brooklyn*. Brooklyn: Brooklyn Museum.

Smith, J. Z. 1995. 'Trading Places', in M. Meyer and P. Mirecki (eds), *Ancient Magic and Ritual Power*. Leiden: Brill, 13–27.

—— 2004. 'Here, There, and Everywhere', in Smith (ed.), *Relating Religion: Essays in the Study of Religion*. Chicago: University of Chicago Press, 323–39.

Timbie, J. A., and J. R. Zaborowski. 2006. 'Shenoute's Sermon *The Lord Thundered*: An Introduction and Translation', *Orients Christianus* 90: 91–123.

Watts, E. 2010. *Riot in Alexandria: Tradition and Group Dynamics in Late Antique Pagan and Christian Communities*. Berkeley: University of California Press.

Winkler, J. J. 1990. 'The Constraints of Desire: Erotic Magical Spells', in Winkler, *The Constraints of Desire: The Anthropology of Sex and Gender in Ancient Greece*. New York: Routledge, 71–98.

CHAPTER 21

COPING WITH A DIFFICULT LIFE
Magic, Healing, and Sacred Knowledge

JACCO DIELEMAN

LIFE was hard, unfair, and often short in Roman Egypt. Everyone lived with a keen sense of physical, social, and economic vulnerability, irrespective of gender, age, wealth, or social position (Tacoma 2006: 163–204). Life expectancy at birth averaged not more than twenty-two to twenty-five years for both males and females (Bagnall and Frier 1994: 109; but cf. Scheidel 2001: 178). Those lucky enough to survive childhood remained subject to high mortality. Every ten years, an age cohort was reduced in size by more than a quarter. The heavy taxation and liturgy regime posed a constant burden on the livelihood and property of most members of the population. Among the urban elites, social status and personal success were defined in terms of honour and shame and thus had to be constantly reconfirmed and renegotiated in competition with other individuals and families. In other words, good fortune was precious and, as it was easily lost, had to be guarded carefully.

How to cope with such circumstances in a time and place without proper health care or social security and little consideration for human rights? How to find meaning and purpose in misfortune? One approach was to locate causation in the domain of the supernatural. The supernatural was viewed as an integral part of the physical and social world. Misfortune could accordingly be explained in terms of divine will, demonic behaviour, sorcery, and the Evil Eye (i.e. envy). Hence, people employed various methods to identify and influence such intangible forces. Fate was considered erratic, for sure, but the entities responsible were not fully outside of human control and could be manipulated—provided one knew the right procedures, persons, and places to go to.

This chapter reviews the manifold ways in which people sought protection and assistance from supernatural agents for the purpose of acquiring a measure of control over one's good fortune. The strategies and methods were applied to protect the body against disease, shield the self from public dishonour, and acquire control over competitors in various agonistic contexts, both public and private. In short, people resorted to such methods in situations of personal crisis and interpersonal conflict. Today we recognize that the methods had no true effect on the course of events. Yet we can easily acknowledge that they were vital forms of stress management in channelling feelings of vulnerability, insecurity, inequity, and impotence, while bolstering self-confidence. They instilled a feeling that everything had been done that could be done to avert disaster or defeat. Over and above this psychological function, these practices constructed and structured social relationships, with both supernatural and human agents, and thus made misfortune socially meaningful (Trzcionka 2007). For this reason, they ought to be studied as social as much as religious behaviour.

A Protocol for Survival

One way of making sense of the various methods employed to contact and manipulate supernatural agents in daily life is to view them as elements or steps in a protocol for survival. This is admittedly a modern construct, but it serves the purpose of bringing out how the practices were interrelated in a meaningful system of action. The first concern was to discover what the future would bring or to understand what had happened in the past. Once one knew what the outcome of a certain choice or action might be or realized how the current situation had come about, one could decide to take proper action and thus avoid or overcome misfortune. As intelligence is critical to the success of any operation, divination was a well-developed institution in Roman Egypt, and multiple methods were available to acquire such insights, both temple-based and private. The second step was to protect oneself against any misfortune. Protection came in the form of amulets of various kinds and rites to subdue aggression, competition, or obstinacy in other people. But amulets were primarily used to prevent disease, whereas these rites were concerned with maintaining social status and repute through subjugating others to one's will or obstructing their success. Such aggressive rites were also employed to exact retribution or secure sexual favours. Large numbers of recovered apotropaic spells, engraved gemstones, and curse tablets and figurines testify to the popular use of these methods. In case foreknowledge and protection were of no avail and one fell victim to disease or injuries nonetheless, the third step came into effect: healing. Besides public physicians working in the traditions of Hippocrates and Galen, people visited healing shrines and ritual specialists to be cured by supernatural means. Finally, for those who wished to acquire advice or insight above and beyond the practical concerns of mundane life, there were multiple places and methods to contact and consult the divine on the secrets of life and the universe. Several temples were famous as incubation centres and attracted pilgrims from far afield in search of healing and dream visions. But one could also try to make a god appear in more private settings with the help of direct vision spells.

Continuity and Innovation

Most of these survival strategies continue long-established methods, media, and locations that had been available since Pharaonic times (Frankfurter 1998). However, with the establishment of Greek hegemony in the late fourth century BCE and the subsequent settlement of immigrants from the Greek world at large under Ptolemaic patronage, Egypt had become a multicultural and bilingual society. The tools, techniques, facilities, and ritual specialists were affected accordingly and adapted in a number of respects.

The most significant change concerns the relationship between temple and private ritual. In Pharaonic Egypt, a certain degree of symbiosis had always existed between the two. As houses of the gods, temples were centres of divine presence in the landscape. Hidden from the layman's view, priests performed rituals to safeguard the cycles of nature and protect the king and state. Temple sites also incorporated facilities for popular worship, healing, and oracles (see Chapters 20 and 24). They were usually located in gateways and outer areas of the sanctuary and along processional roads, spaces that were contiguous to the sacred power of the sanctuary and yet accessible to private individuals. Outside the sanctity of the temple, priests put their knowledge, skills, and ritual authority to further use in providing the local population with various rites and media for protection, healing, and fertility. A large corpus of formularies, amulets, moulded figurines, and healing statues attest to these activities (Koenig 1994; Pinch 1994). Unlike temple rites, these methods were not tied to a particular place, but could be executed wherever the need arose, be it a patient's house or a work site in the desert. Owing to their small-scale nature, they were portable and economical in expense, time, and effort. As freelance ritualist and cult officiant were but two roles of the same person, there existed a high degree of coherence—functionally, textually, and visually—between cult rituals and those addressing private concerns.

For Roman Egypt, the nature of this relationship appears to be more complicated. Whereas the official cult continued unchanged in the sanctuaries, popular methods of contacting and manipulating the supernatural show a marked degree of innovation in content and format. They participated in pan-Mediterranean developments and were thus not Egyptian per se. Some may well have developed out of indigenous practices, but, in the process, had shed their uniquely Egyptian character and acquired a Hellenized, more universal quality. The most obvious shifts concern language, iconography, and the identity of ritual power. Greek was now used alongside Egyptian for composing handbooks, inscribing amulets, submitting oracle tickets, and computing horoscopes. Eventually Greek replaced Demotic Egyptian altogether (Ripat 2006; Stadler 2008). As regards iconography, Egyptian deities retained their traditional appearance in the domains of temple cult and funerary practice, but in public and domestic contexts were often rendered in a hybrid Graeco-Egyptian style. The terracotta figurines of Harpocrates and Isis display this shift all too well. Newly devised supernatural agents, such as Abrasax and Chnoubis (Figs 21.1, 21.2), known only from magical gems and papyri, were depicted in a similarly innovative style. The cultural and religious horizons of the freelance ritualists had expanded likewise. The deities and demons addressed, the mythological precedents invoked, and the alleged sources of ritual authority were drawn from Egyptian, Greek, Jewish, and Near Eastern traditions and combined in creative ways. Moreover, the idiom, methods, and media that they employed were not particular to Egypt. Similar curse tablets and protective *lamellae* have been found all over the Roman empire. Astrology and divination by lots and dies were also pan-Mediterranean phenomena.

In the light of these shifts, it can be assumed that the marketplace of freelance diviners, healers, and magicians had diversified—and as a result become more competitive than in the Pharaonic period. The high degree of innovation may then well be a product of this heightened competition and not just a reflection of linguistic, social, and cultural transfor-

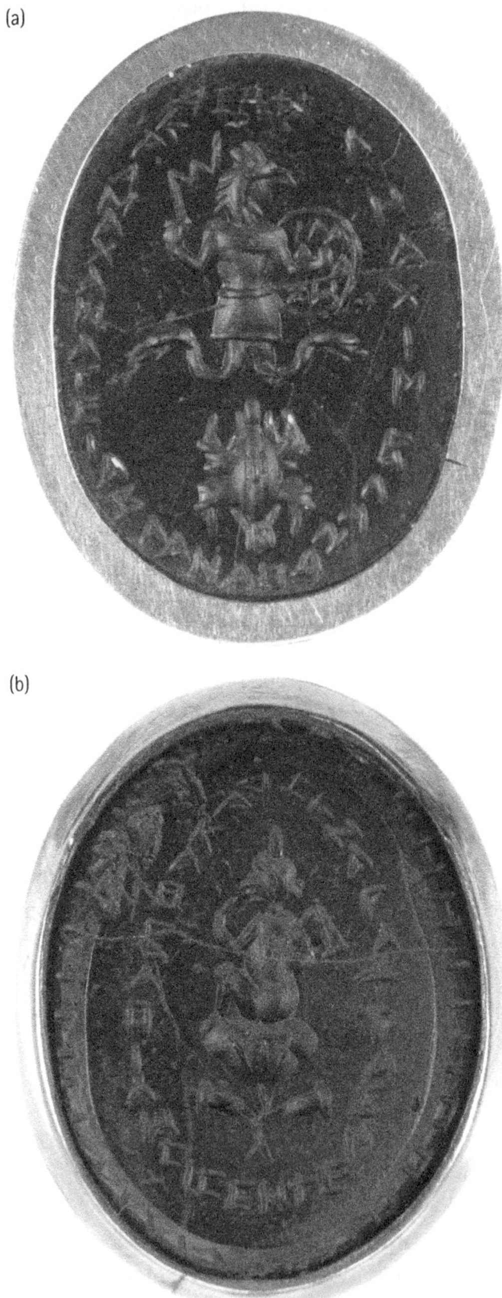

FIG. 21.1 Gem of heliotrope (bloodstone) showing, on one side, the rooster-headed anguipede in Roman armour holding whip and shield above a scarab beetle, and, on the other side, the sun child with finger to its mouth and royal flagellum in its hand sitting on a lotus flower. IAŌ is written above the anguipede's head; around the figure are written further divine names including Michael. On the reverse side, the seven vowels are written in ascending order along the rim. Date: second century CE. 2.19 × 1.75 × 0.33 cm (with modern bezel)

Institut für Altertumskunde, University of Cologne; Zwierlein-Diehl (1992, no. 9).

(a)

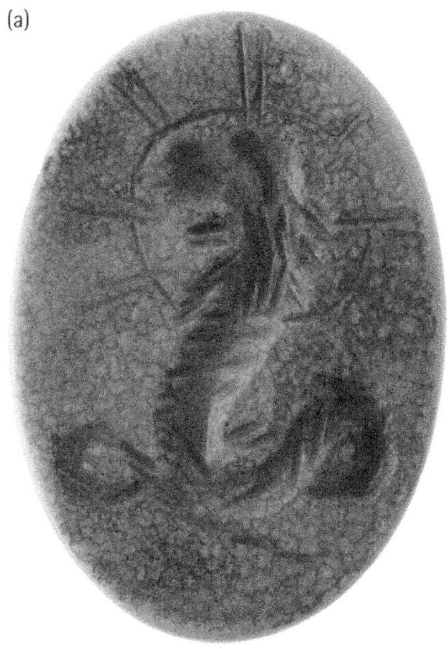

(b)

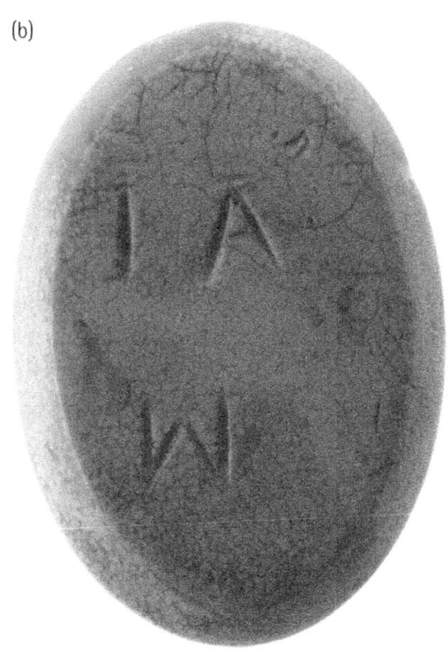

FIG. 21.2 Gem of quartz showing Chnoubis as a lion-headed snake with seven solar rays radiating from its head. On the reverse side, the Jewish name IAŌ is written. Date: second century CE. 1.82 × 1.29 × 0.33 cm

Institut für Altertumskunde, University of Cologne; Zwierlein-Diehl (1992, no. 15).

mations in contemporary society. In Egypt these activities are often found in association with indigenous priests and temples, both archaeologically and conceptually. For example, the astrological ostraca from Narmouthis in the Fayum were excavated at the temple of the goddess Renenutet (Thermouthis) (Menchetti 2009), while many recipes for private rites are marketed as having been discovered in an Egyptian temple (Dieleman 2005: 254–80). Whether or not the latter claims hold any truth, it is clear that the areas in and around indigenous temples were sites where the novel techniques were practised and, moreover, that Egyptian priests were instrumental in their development, dissemination, and administration.

Another important shift concerns the nature of private ritual. In the formularies from Pharaonic Egypt, healing is the most important category together with rites of protection and the production of amulets. In the Graeco-Egyptian formularies, attention has shifted to rites to conjure up a deity for private oracular consultation and rites to influence other people's behaviour or even to harm them. Recipes for healing and protection occur in small numbers only. The Graeco-Egyptian manuals are thus more concerned with social and spiritual than with physical well-being. This reflects changes in social structure and religious sensibilities in contemporary society.

With the shift to Roman rule, the status of private ritual and its practitioners also changed (Ritner 1993: 217–20; 1995: 3355–8). Whereas these practices had always been an intrinsic part of Egyptian culture, from a Roman perspective they were foreign and not integrated in civic religion and society. As deviant behaviour, they were even considered potentially disruptive to social and political order. Furthermore, Roman law recognized illicit forms of sorcery and divination, punishable by expulsion, confiscation of property, and even death. The Cornelian Law on Murderers and Poisoners, passed under the dictatorship of Sulla in 81 BCE, was initially a law about homicide only, but in the Imperial period came to outlaw more generally the selling, buying, possession, and administering of harmful drugs, including materials for cursing (Paulus, *Sent.* 5.23.14–19; *Dig.* 48.8.2). Private divination was suspect for offering the possibility of inquiring after the emperor's date of death, an offence that amounted to *maiestas*, or treason. In 198 CE the prefect of Egypt issued a ban on any oracular activities on penalty of death (*P Coll. Youtie* I 30), and in 359 Emperor Constantius II ordered an investigation into the Bes oracle in Abydos, which led to a series of sorcery trials and purges among courtiers (Amm. Marc. 19.12; Naether 2010: 411–26). To what extent these measures affected daily life is difficult to say. They appear to have been enforced in times of social and political crisis only. Nonetheless, freelance practitioners were criminalized and their activities were thus likely driven underground.

In the fourth century CE, Christianity was adopted as the official religion of the Roman empire and, accordingly, the practices, places, and ritual specialists became Christian in conception and outer form. However, from a more pragmatic perspective, there was little that truly changed. Instead of local deities, people implored local saints and Jesus Christ for assistance. Amulets were still being produced, oracle tickets could still be submitted, and incubation centres were still functioning. Now churches, monastic centres, and martyr shrines offered these services, while desert hermits and monks administered them (Hahn, Emmel, and Gotter 2008). This also led to the reintroduction of Egyptian in the form of amulets and oracle tickets in the Coptic language and script.

Sources and Classifications

There is a vast corpus of texts and artefacts that attest to these activities. Unfortunately, most of the materials are without provenance or proper archaeological record. As a result, the physical and institutional contexts of the activities can rarely be identified. Likewise, the social and cultural backgrounds of the practitioners and beneficiaries remain generally obscure.

Several temple sites preserve remains or traces of facilities for popular worship, healing, and oracles. The majority of preserved amulets, curse tablets, and figurines were undoubtedly found in cemeteries. Amulets were usually buried with the person who wore them during life, and curse materials were deposited in tombs to solicit the help of the spirits of the dead. Unfortunately, few of these materials were unearthed in controlled excavations. Public spaces such as agoras and hippodromes, sites that proved to be rich in curse tablets in Carthage, Caesarea, and Athens, have been poorly excavated in Egypt and have produced little evidence. For domestic contexts, ritual activities remain poorly attested and difficult to identify archaeologically (Wilburn 2012). In Kellis, in the Dakhla Oasis, divinatory, astrological, and magical texts were found together within a residential building of the fourth century (House 3, area A; *P Kellis* 1.82–9). The pictorial record is also sparse. Besides a few mummy portraits showing children wearing amulets, no depictions of rituals, ritualists, or objects in use are extant other than the standardized scenes of official cult on temple walls. The iconography of the divine can be studied, though, from the engraved gems and drawings in the magical papyri.

Textual evidence is abundant and highly diverse in terms of content, language, and writing media. Given the ambiguous status of magical practices in the Graeco-Roman world, it is important to distinguish between outsider and insider evidence, as they provide different types of information (Bohak 2008: 70). The former concerns accounts written about these practices by people not themselves involved in them, whereas the latter comprises the texts and artefacts produced by the actual ritualists. Outsider evidence such as imperial edicts, legal codes, and ancient historiography reveals that the Roman authorities were much concerned with policing such activities (Ogden 2002: 275–99). Literary representations of sorcerers and witches attest further to the fear, but also the fascination, that such figures elicited in elite audiences (Dieleman 2005: 221–54). Private letters express a genuine concern about people's health and well-being. In one exceptional case, a letter includes a copy of a magical spell sent from one friend to another (Kellis, fourth century; Mirecki, Gardner, and Alcock 1997). Of a very different kind are visitors' graffiti on temple walls. They inform us about the concerns and expectations of pilgrims and the areas they were allowed to access in the temple.

Insider evidence can be further subdivided into, on the one hand, formularies with instructions for private rituals, divinatory handbooks, and calendrical and astronomical tables, and, on the other hand, materials produced and activated during such rituals, consultation sessions, and horoscopic computations. As regards handbooks for private divination, the *Sortes Astrampsychi* and Homer Oracle are preserved in several witnesses (Naether 2010). A large collection of Greek astronomical tables comes from Oxyrhynchus (Jones 1999), while the temple library of Tebtunis kept Demotic handbooks with astrological interpretations among its holdings (Winkler 2009). The bulk of the magical texts are in Greek, about 350 manuscripts. Four formularies are partly or fully in Demotic and a few others include sections in Coptic. They are collectively known as the Greek (and Demotic) Magical Papyri after the standard edition by Preisendanz (1928–3; Betz 1986). Most materials date to the fourth and fifth centuries, but the earliest documents, all in Greek and mostly fragmentary, date to the first century BCE. The Demotic formularies date to the third, possibly even late second, century CE.

The formularies are eclectic collections of recipes for private ritual, ranging from divination to binding spells and healing. The most extensive and best-preserved exemplars were allegedly found together in Luxor around 1828 and are now collectively known as the Theban Magical Library. The hoard comprises scrolls and codices in Greek and Demotic Egyptian, including a few sections in Coptic, dated by palaeography to the third and fourth centuries CE. Similar formularies have been found at other sites in Egypt, suggesting that the format was to a large degree standardized. Whether their content is representative of formularies used in other areas of the Roman empire remains a question, as no such formularies have been preserved outside Egypt.

Whereas recipes give template texts, activated materials were produced for a particular situation and thus include the name of the beneficiary or victim, such as 'Ptolemais to whom Aias gave birth' (*Suppl. Mag.* I 47 *passim*), and occasionally further critical information. Most are amulets and curse tablets inscribed on small sheets of metal or papyrus. The large corpus of engraved gems, of which about 2,600 have now been systematically studied (Michel 2004), also belongs to this category. Their efficacy and application was thought to depend on stone type, colour, shape, design, and inscription. A small number of recovered gems were produced following instructions very similar to those found in the preserved formularies (Smith 1979; cf. *PGM* XII 202–10, 273–7). This shows that ritualists relied on formularies, but also reveals that they felt at liberty to make changes (Wilburn 2012). To date, more than 200 horoscopes, written in Greek and Demotic on papyrus and ostraca, have been published; many come from Oxyrhynchus and Narmouthis.

For a long time, there has been a tendency to organize these materials by language and to privilege textual content over material form. A classification by language such as the Greek Magical Papyri is convenient, but runs the risk of imposing a socio-linguistic division on the materials that is informed by modern academic divisions (i.e. classicists versus Egyptologists) rather than by the socio-linguistic realities of Roman Egypt. Recently, however, scholars have become more sensitive to the bilingual nature of society in Roman Egypt and have started to integrate sources in Greek, Demotic, and Coptic to study the dynamics of language use in these practices (e.g. Frankfurter 1998; Dieleman 2005; Naether 2010). The general disregard for the materiality and physical context of the texts is well illustrated by the fact that they are often studied as disembodied texts and intellectual discourse, rather than actual scribal artefacts, and with little or no regard for their local, i.e. Egyptian, context. The majority of the texts are admittedly in Greek, but the fact remains that they were found, and thus produced, in Egypt (Ritner 1993). Similarly, the formularies of the Theban Magical Library have never been published integrally in photo or facsimile like the more famous Nag Hammadi codices or the Dead Sea Scrolls. This has so far impeded a study of the scribal culture in which these manuscripts were produced.

Divination: Anticipating Misfortune

When faced with a critical life decision, many consulted the gods for clarification and advice on how to proceed in one's best interests. Questions ranged from practical concerns about family, health, and property to advice on career planning, safe travel, and judicial disputes; on the whole, the topics addressed amount to fifteen categories, as Naether (2010: 195–204) recently established.

To ascertain the will of the gods, private individuals had a range of options (see Chapter 24). Certain methods of divination continued Pharaonic practices, whereas others were products of the Hellenistic and Roman periods. The former were home-grown, localized, and institutionalized services that indigenous temples had provided for centuries. Oracular shrines existed throughout the country. They were firmly embedded in Egypt's sacred landscape, cult, and society. Most were merely of local significance, but some had a transregional appeal, attracting pilgrims and tourists from far afield. In general, Egyptian temples had always been centres of divination, both as repositories of omen literature and as providers of oracular services. In the former capacity, priestly scholars working in the scriptorium, or House of Life, assembled, organized, and archived omens of various sorts (dreams, animals, heavenly bodies) together with their interpretation (Ryholt 2005; Quack 2006; Winkler 2009). These extensive collections had a cultic function first and foremost, allowing the detection of deviations in the cosmic balance, and were accordingly used to determine proper ritual action in protecting state and society from collapse. How such texts might have played a role in daily life remains a topic of investigation. To accommodate private individuals, temples offered oracular services in the form of the processional oracle, the ticket oracle, and, for more involved questions and personal contact, incubation shrines. The existence of voice oracles, which some scholars consider an innovation of the Roman period, remains a matter of contention owing to the ambiguous nature of the alleged remains of contrivances to make statues 'speak' (Traunecker 1992: 379–84; Frankfurter 1998: 150–2; but cf. Naether 2010: 52–4).

Freelance diviners offered alternatives to these temple-based methods in the form of cleromancy and horoscopic astrology (Evans 2004; Naether 2010). These techniques are unconcerned with the cult statue; instead, they site divine agency and authority in the method of sortition and the sky respectively. The practitioners relied on manuals and tables, which were marketed as being of venerable age and being authored by culture heroes such as Imhotep (Imouthes), Petosiris, and Pythagoras, or even the god Hermes Trismegistos himself. By rolling a dice, drawing lots, or computing number combinations, the diviner generated a key to finding the answer applicable to the client's question in a table or manual with answers. The so-called *Sortes Astrampsychi* required an intricate computation, surely to leave the client mystified and accepting of the revealed answer (Stewart and Morrell 1998; Naether 2010). In contrast, Demokritos' Sphere (*PGM* XII 351–64), a prognostic to determine whether the patient will live or die, works with a straightforward calculation. Whereas these two methods generated unambiguous answers, the Homer Oracle led the client by dice throw to a Homeric verse, whose pertinence was only elucidated in the interaction between client and diviner. Horoscopes record the relative position of heavenly bodies at the native's day and hour of birth. These data, cast with the help of birth notes and astronomical tables, allowed for predictions concerning the client's well-being (Evans 2004; Jones 1994). Unfortunately, these predictions are only rarely included (Neugebauer and van Hoesen 1959: 162).

In the third century we can observe the rise of charismatic individuals, sometimes affiliated with a local shrine, with the ability to interpret omens and pronounce oracles through ecstatic seizure and an ascetic lifestyle (Frankfurter 1998: 184–93). Eventually this new social role of the holy man was taken on by Christian desert hermits in the fourth and fifth centuries (Brown 1982), at a time when the oracular techniques and facilities of pagan temples were being adopted and adapted by Christian martyr shrines throughout Egypt.

Private Ritual

Divination was a tool to acquire information about the past, present, and future, but did not offer the means to respond to predictions and forestall undesirable events. This required the manipulation of supernatural forces, something that could only be achieved through ritual. The various methods employed to do so add up to a relatively coherent system of thought and practice, often named 'Graeco-Egyptian magic' for lack of a better term. Its most striking feature is its inclusive and eclectic character. Mirroring the ethnic, linguistic, and social complexities of society in Egypt and the eastern Mediterranean, it adopted and adapted Egyptian, Greek, and Jewish methods, idioms, and names to establish contact with the preternatural world. Likely originating in late Hellenistic Alexandria, it spread eventually all over the Roman empire. Its associated material culture included engraved gems, inscribed metal sheets, papyrus amulets, figurines of wax and clay, and formularies. Its primary—and likely original—language of expression was *koine* Greek, but spells were also written in Demotic and Coptic (and outside Egypt, in Latin and Aramaic). Several formularies in fact combine spells in Greek and Egyptian and betray several layers of transcription and translation to and fro (Dieleman 2005; see Fig. 21.3).

Another distinctive characteristic is the reliance on writing. The relative homogeneity in techniques, divine names, and iconography among these materials can only be explained by wide dissemination of formularies and general compliance with their instructions (but cf. Wilburn 2012). Secondly, the act of writing itself was essential to the rituals (Frankfurter 1994). Again and again, recipes call for inscribing spells and names onto amulets and curse tablets as a means of activation, and indeed the recovered amulets and curse tablets are all covered with text. Most inscriptions were written in Greek letters, including foreign words and names, but local scripts such as Demotic, Coptic, Aramaic, and Latin were also used. Next to these ordinary scripts, a mystical alphabet was in use, a fluid set of invented graphemes called *kharakteres*, to establish unmediated written communication with supernatural agents (Fig. 21.4, see also Fig. 21.7). Finally, writing's function of making sounds visible and thus lending them a material quality was skilfully exploited. The use of the Greek alphabet allowed for manipulating the spellings of names and sounds of power so as to produce geometrical patterns or palindromes and thus imbue these names with enhanced ritual efficacy.

The rites envisage the supernatural world as populated by spirits of the dead, demons, and deities, entities that are ultimately governed by a supreme, transcendent, and self-begotten demiurge of a solar nature. This deity is most often invoked with the Jewish name Iaō (the

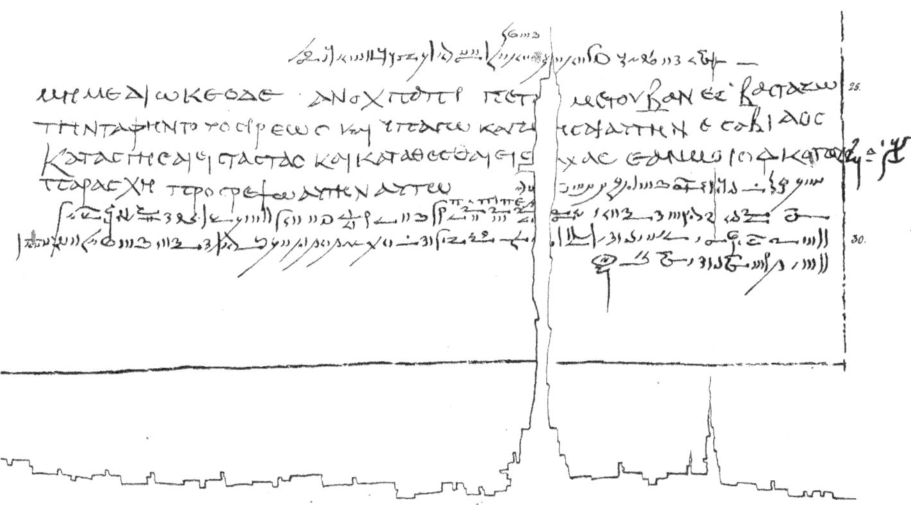

FIG. 21.3 Recipe to mollify an angry overseer. The incantation is given in Greek first and then in Demotic Egyptian. Judging from the glosses, the Demotic was translated from the Greek version. From Thebes, late second to third century CE.

Papyrus London-Leiden, col. 15/24–31 = *PDM* XIV 451–8 (*PGM* XIVb 12–15); after Leemans (1839).

standard Greek transliteration of the Tetragrammaton YHWH), usually in combination as Iaō Sabaōth Adōnai, but likewise as Helios, Pre, Serapis, and Mithras. Besides the names of conventional gods of Egyptian, Greek, Jewish, and Near Eastern origin, the rites also call upon deities and spirits with idiosyncratic names. Abrasax and Chnoubis (see Figs 21.1, 21.2) occur frequently, the former depicted as a rooster-headed anguipede in Roman armour and the latter as a snake with a radiant lion head. Most frequent are artificial name formations, the so-called *voces magicae*, which were considered the secret and true names of the gods. They lack any literal meaning, but many betray Egyptian, Greek, and Semitic roots and endings. Some may well be garbled versions of ancient epithets. They were often combined into a standard sequence, such as the Maskelli-Maskellō formula: Maskelli Maskellō Phnoukentabaō Oreobazagra Rhēxichthōn Hippochthōn Pyripēganyx.

As regards cosmology, old and new coexist. The notion of a geocentric, layered, and spherical cosmos governed by the movements of the stars and planets appears alongside the ancient view of a three-tier cosmos of sky, earth, and underworld, through which the sun-god travels in his barque in the course of one day (Gundel 1968). The significance of the planets is further borne out by the frequent use of the seven Greek vowels, in varying combinations (see Fig. 21.4). Being the sounds of the seven planets, their intonation was believed to affect the harmony of the spheres.

Protecting against Misfortune

Disease and misery were generally attributed to the malefic influences of demons, the angry dead, or malevolent sorcerers. To avert their hostile powers, people relied on amulets worn on the body. Amulets were commissioned to protect one's physical body from illness and

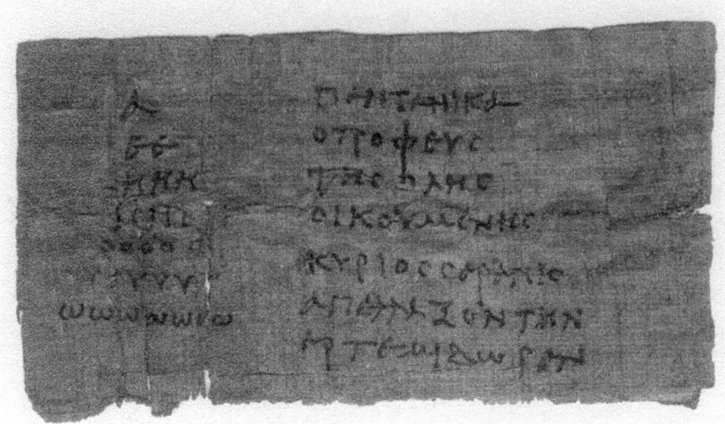

FIG. 21.4 Greek papyrus amulet inscribed for a certain Artemidora. To the right, an address to the god Serapis: 'The nourisher of the whole inhabited world is victorious over everything. Lord Serapis, deliver Artemidora.' To the left, the seven Greek vowels arranged in a pyramidal shape (*klima*). From Oxyrhynchus, third century CE. Height 6.5 cm, width 12.5 cm

Papyrus Köln inv. 1982 = *Suppl. Mag.* I 7 = *PGM* XCVIII. Courtesy of the University of Cologne.

injury, but could also shield one's social self from dishonour resulting from hostile magic. They came in two basic types: written charms and object amulets. The former were inscribed on thin sheets of silver and gold, so-called *lamellae*, folded and worn inside a tubular container around the neck (Kotansky 1994). Less expensive and thus more numerous were charms written on small pieces of papyrus, often in combination with *kharakteres* and drawings of supernatural agents (see Fig. 21.5). The second type is engraved gemstones, worn on a finger ring, around the neck, or sewn into clothing (Bonner 1950; Michel 2004). They were incised with images, words, and symbols of power.

Both types have obvious precedents in Pharaonic Egypt (Edwards 1960; Andrews 1994; Eschweiler 1994), while also exhibiting significant innovation. For the language of inscription, Greek appears to have fully replaced Egyptian; no amulets in Demotic or hieratic are extant for the Roman period. Foreign words and names are consistently transcribed in Greek letters. Likewise, the rich repertoire of Egyptian object amulets, such as scarabs, *djed* pillars, Isis knots, etc., was replaced by that of the engraved gems. The use of metal *lamellae* for inscribing apotropaic spells is also an innovation. In the Pharaonic period, papyrus was the sole medium for written charms.

The following Greek recipe from a third-century formulary describes how to produce such a written charm.

> A phylactery, a bodyguard against daimons, against phantasms, against every sickness and suffering, to be written on a leaf of gold or silver or tin or on hieratic papyrus. When worn it works mightily, for it is the name of power of the great god and [his] seal, and it is as follows: 'KMĒPHIS CHPHURIS IAEŌ IAŌ AEĒ IAŌ OŌ AIŌNIAE ŌBAPHRENEMOUNOTHILARIKRIPHIA–EU–AIPHIRKIRALITHANUOMENERPHABŌEAI.'

> These [are] the names; the figure is like this: let the snake be biting its tail, the names being written inside [the circle made by] the snake, and the *kharakteres* thus, as follows: [seven magical signs]. The whole figure is [drawn] thus as given below, with [the spell], 'Protect my body, and the entire soul of me, NN.' And when you have consecrated [it], wear [it]. (*PGM* VII 579–90; trans. Morton Smith)

Below the recipe is a drawing of the snake with the names written inside and around its coiled body (see Fig. 21.5). Below the *kharakteres* is added: 'Pro[tect my] body and the [entire] soul of me, NN (add the usual).' Of the recovered amulets, none has this particular design, but many have similar names, *kharakteres*, and drawings. Most are short, formulaic incantations to grant protection against disease and other ailments, such as this silver tablet from third-century Oxyrhynchus: 'I call upon you, who are over the air of the ocean, OBACH, and by BABARATHAN BAROCH ABRAHAM SABARAAM; protect him who wears you from fever and everything. If fever seizes him, extinguish it once and for all' (*Suppl. Mag.* I 2; trans. R. W. Daniel and F. Maltomini).

Of a different type is the use of individual verses from Homer, a practice allegedly already advocated by Pythagoras and Empedocles and often prescribed in the magic formularies and medical writers of the Roman period (Collins 2008a: 104–31; 2008b). They were used for a variety of purposes, including protection against illness, noxious animals, sorcery, potions, and poison (see *PGM* IV 2145–2240). With the shift to Christianity, Bible verses were used similarly (de Bruyn 2010).

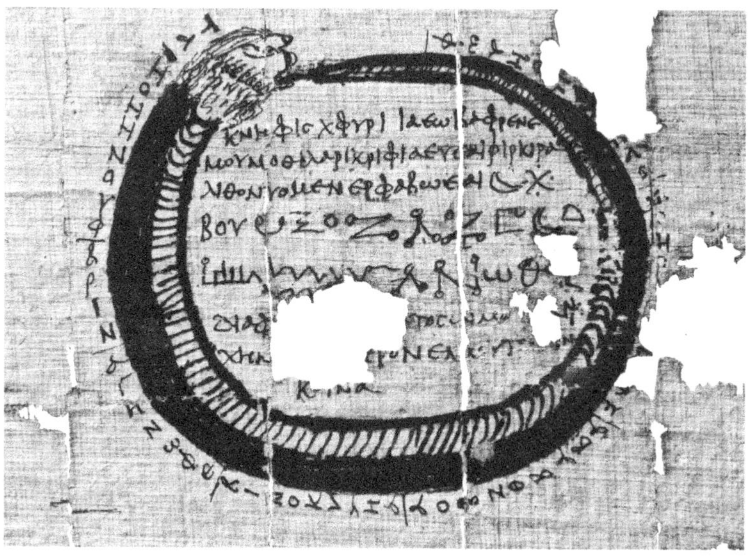

FIG. 21.5 Protective design to be inscribed on amulet. The design shows the *ouroboros* snake (which eats its own tail) encircling an incantation consisting of a series of *voces magicae*, *kharakteres*, and the request 'Protect my body and the entire life of me, NN' as prescribed in the accompanying recipe *PGM* VII 579–90. From Thebes, third century CE

Papyrus London 121, col. 17 = *PGM* VII; after Kenyon (1893, pl. 59).

Acquiring Control

Certain situations called for more than just protection. To maintain autonomy and control in agonistic contexts such as business, politics, litigation, athletic contests, chariot races, and love, a more assertive approach was required. One way of acquiring a competitive advantage over adversaries, or exacting retribution, was to seek control over their will, emotions, and actions through ritual. Such rites aimed at inhibiting competitors or attracting lovers through binding spells, at terrorizing adversaries at night with insomnia-inducing rites, at manipulating their dreams with dream-sending spells, or at influencing people's faculties of perception through favour charms and wrath-restraining spells. In all cases, the ultimate goal was to secure a successful livelihood and honourable reputation by breaking competition, subduing obstinacy, and deflecting hostility in others. To prevent falling victim to such aggression, amulets to dissolve spells acted as a counter-measure (e.g. *PGM* XXXVI 178–87, 256–64; Gager 1992: 218–42).

A binding spell (Greek: *katadesmos*; Latin: *defixio*) had the function of binding the thoughts and actions of adversaries or, in the case of attraction spells (*philtrokatadesmos*, or *agoge*), of arousing a frenzied lust in a desired person and leading her or him to one's house and bed (Winkler 1991; Gager 1992; Faraone 1999; Dickie 2000). The mechanics of such rites show a subtle interaction between invocation, object manipulation, and location of deposit. Although papyrus and ostraca were also used, lead tablets were the preferred material for inscribing a curse formula, such as 'I bind So-and-so with regard to such-and-such matter. Let him not speak, not be contrary, not oppose; let him not be able to look me in the face nor speak against me; let him be subjected to me, so long as this ring is buried. I bind his mind and his brain, his desire, his actions, so that he may be slow (in his dealings) with all men' (*PGM* V 321–9; trans. Morton Smith). The tablet was then folded, occasionally also bound, and pierced with pins, so as to transfer these properties of confinement to the victim. To solicit the assistance of chthonic deities and demons, it was then deposited in the grave of a 'restless dead' (someone who had died violently or before his or her time), or in a bath house. Alternatively, the tablet was hidden where the victim lived or did business. Attraction rites could include fashioning one or more figurines of wax or clay, whose limbs were twisted and bound or its body pierced with needles (e.g. *PGM* IV 296–466). To establish a tangible connection between the rite and the victim, a lock of hair or piece of clothing (simply called *ousia*, 'substance', in the formularies) could be added. The cultural origin of these techniques remains controversial, as they are well attested for both Pharaonic Egypt and classical Greece (Ritner 1993: 111–90; Faraone 2002).

In two rare cases, it is possible to connect multiple assemblages of activated materials to the same attraction rite. The first case represents two similar assemblages, each consisting of two wax figurines modelled in an embrace which were wrapped inside an inscribed papyrus and placed inside a clay vessel. The invocations are essentially identical (*Suppl. Mag.* I 45; *SB* XX 14664). The assemblages clearly represent two instances of the same rite. The other case comprises five variations on a ritual described in a fourth-century formulary (*PGM* IV 296–466; *Suppl. Mag.* I 46–51; Martinez 1991: 7; Faraone 2002). One of the assemblages even includes a nude female figurine of clay, bound and pierced with thirteen needles as prescribed in the formulary (du Bourguet 1975; Fig. 21.6). Both cases provide evidence that such rites were not improvised, but performed by trained individuals, likely hired for a fee, who relied on similar formularies in exercising their trade.

FIG. 21.6 Assemblage of a female figurine of clay pierced with thirteen needles, lead tablet inscribed with Greek curse, and clay vessel in which the former two were found. The figurine and tablet were prepared following instructions similar to recipe *PGM* IV 296–466. From Middle Egypt, second to third century CE

Musée du Louvre, Paris, E 27145.

A formal complaint sent to the *strategos* of the Arsinoite nome in 197 CE (*P Mich.* VI 423–4) reminds us that there were alternatives to hiring the services of such ritual experts (Frankfurter 2006). Gemellus Horion of the village of Karanis accuses his neighbours of having stolen his harvest with the use of binding magic. They had thrown an aborted or miscarried foetus (*brephos*) at the harvesters in order to 'surround [the victims] with malice' (*phthonoi…periklisai*) and thus prevented anybody from interfering. They performed the act a second time with similar success when confronted by two village elders for their robbery. Whatever the significance of the foetus, it is obvious that the victims perceived the conduct as hostile and felt inhibited to act—hence the foetus achieved what a *katadesmos* was supposed to accomplish. No recipe book, however, prescribes anything like this. As Frankfurter (2006: 42) writes: 'This absence immediately teaches us that the magical papyri, while immensely rich documentation for ritual practices in Roman Egypt, should not be taken as in any way exhaustive. Indeed, as documents for a fairly élite rank of priestly ritual expert, they may offer little information about local practices, which might never be written down or collected.'

Favour charms take an altogether different approach. They induce charm, affection, and loveliness and thus make the client appear desirable and successful in the eyes of others—or, as one recipe puts it: 'It makes men famous and great and admired and rich as can be, or it makes possible friendships with suchlike men' (*PGM* XII 271–2; trans. Morton Smith). Similarly, wrath-restraining spells mollify angry adversaries (e.g. *PGM* X 24–35; Fig. 21.7). The power resides in an inscribed metal tablet or engraved gem worn on the body like a talisman. Workshops could also be the object of such rites so as to attract customers and make them flourish (e.g. *PGM* IV 3125–71).

FIG. 21.7 Design to be inscribed on a gold or silver *lamella* and worn as a wrath-restraining amulet, as explained in its recipe, *PGM* X 24–35. The borders of the rectangle are inscribed with *voces magicae*. Its inside is filled with *kharakteres*. Provenance unknown, fourth century CE

Papyrus London 124, col. 1 = *PGM* X; after Kenyon (1893, pl. 69).

Aphrodisiacs, for which many recipes are found in the formularies, form a special category. They aim at overcoming either impotence in a man or reluctance to have sex in a woman. The former is most often treated with smearing a salve on the penis, the latter with making the woman drink a glass of wine mixed with a drug. The recipes, usually very short, are written for a male clientele and presume that the woman is unaware of her suitor's intentions. The recipes also presume that the man and woman are already in contact; in this respect, the aphrodisiacs are fundamentally different from the attraction spells.

Curing Illnesses and Ailments

Internal, mental, and chronic diseases were often attributed to divine will or demonic assault. Although public and private physicians were available in cities and towns (Hirt Raj 2006), many sought healing through supernatural means. Temple sites offered facilities in the form of healing chapels and incubation shrines (Dunand 2006). The former were small chapels that housed healing statues and Horus *cippi*, located in the temple precinct outside the sanctuary proper. Covered with magical spells in hieroglyphs and prophylactic imagery, these objects provided relief against scorpion stings and snakebites. The user first poured water over them and then drank the magically charged liquid. Incubation, i.e. sleeping in the temple to receive healing or therapeutic advice from a deity, is well attested textually, but remains difficult to identify archaeologically. Important centres were the Isis temple in Menouthis, the Memnonion (or Osireion) in Abydos, and the shrine dedicated to Amenhotep son of Hapu (Amenothes) and Imhotep (Imouthes; identified with Asklepios) in Deir el-Bahri. Whereas the former is only known from literary sources, the latter two structures have been preserved. The graffiti left by visitors, mostly in Greek, indicate that people visited these places in search of healing and oracles, occasionally staying for several nights (Rutherford 2003; Łajtar 2006). How these centres operated remains little understood, however. A large mud-brick building inside the temple precinct of Hathor in Dendara has been interpreted as a sanatorium for curative baths and incubation (Daumas 1957), but the identification is highly problematic. It may well have been a workshop for dyeing cloth used in the temple cult, as recently suggested (Cauville 2004).

The corpus of magical papyri and gems offers numerous examples of curative charms (Hirt Raj 2006: 268–78, 347–51). The most common ailments addressed are fever, shivering fits, migraine, eye inflammation, and scorpion stings. Most therapies consist of wearing on the afflicted body part a small metal foil, a sheet of papyrus, or a gem inscribed with a short charm, names of power, and prophylactic designs, as, for example, 'PHĒG GĒ... BALOCHRA THAMRA ZARACHTHHŌ, I conjure you all by the bitter compulsion: MASKELI MASKELŌ PHNOUKENTABAŌTH OREOBAZAGAR RHĒZICHTHŌN HIPPOCHTHŌN PYRIPĒGANYX. Deliver Ammon from the fever and shivering fit that restrain him, immediately, immediately, quickly, quickly, today!' (*Suppl. Mag.* I 12 = *PGM* CXV; trans. Roy Kotansky). Homeric verses were also used for such purposes (*PGM* XXIIa; Collins 2008a: 109–22), as were Bible verses with the shift to Christianity (de Bruyn 2010).

Their terse inscriptions and often obscure designs make it difficult to associate classes of gemstones with particular diseases (Bonner 1950: 51–94; Michel 2004: 146–202). Gems incised with the image of Chnoubis appear to have been used as a remedy for ailments related to the stomach (see Fig. 21.2). They often carry on the reverse side a symbol of three s-shaped signs struck through with a horizontal bar, which design goes back to that of the Egyptian decan Knum (*knmt*). Uterine gems show a schematic design of a uterus atop a door key, occasionally beneath several deities, including Chnoubis, a mummiform Anubis, Osiris, Isis, Bes, and Thoeris. One has an inscription in Greek that reads: 'Put the womb of So-and-so in its proper place, O you who [lifts up] the sun's disk' (Bonner 1950: 81). Such gems thus had the function of preventing the womb from wandering in the body, a common fear in antiquity (see also *PGM* VII 260–71). The key is likely connected with the promotion or prevention of conception (*PGM* XXXVI 320–2), but possibly also with exerting male control over female sexuality (see the pudenda-key spell, *PGM* XXXVI 283–94).

The number of recipes dealing with healing is relatively low in the formularies. Most give short and straightforward instructions for preparing amulets (e.g. *PGM* VII 193–221). The London–Leiden Demotic Papyrus does, however, contain a series of spells against animal bites and stings, poison, and a bone stuck in the throat (cols 19–20; *PDM* XIV 554–626) which, like Egyptian formularies of Pharaonic date, include incantations that invoke mythological precedents, all of which are purely Egyptian. The Parisian Codex includes two spells that aim at exorcising demons from the patient's body and betray engagement with Christian and Jewish ideas (*PGM* IV 1227–64, 3007–86; Kotansky 1994). In one case, the elements clearly stand out as secondary additions, for they are in Coptic, whereas the spell is otherwise in Greek:

> *Hail, God of Abraham; hail, God of Isaac; hail, God of Jacob; Jesus Chrestos, the Holy Spirit, the Son of the Father, who is above the Seven, who is within the Seven. Bring Iao Sabaoth; may your power issue forth* from him, NN, *until you drive away this unclean daimon Satan, who is upon him.* I conjure you, daimon, whoever you are, by this god, SABARBARBATHIŌTH SABARBARBATHIOUTH SABARBARBATHIŌNĒTH SABARBARBAPHAI. Come out, daimon, whoever you are, and stay away from him NN, now, now; immediately, immediately. Come out, daimon, since I bind you with unbreakable adamantine fetters, and I deliver you into the black chaos in perdition. (*PGM* IV 1231–48; trans. M. W. Meyer; the Coptic appears as italics)

On the reverse side of the London–Leiden papyrus, a selection of bilingual notes on mineralogy and botany is included, displaying traces of translation from the Greek into Egyptian (*PDM* XIV 886–952; Dieleman 2005: 111–20). The bilingual *P Leiden* I 384 verso contains a list of code names for minerals and plants (*PGM* XII 401–44); 'crocodile dung' stands for Ethiopian soil and 'semen of Hermes' for dill (LiDonnici 2002; Dieleman 2005: 189–203). The Parisian Codex also includes instructions on how to pick plants so as to preserve their efficacious qualities (*PGM* IV 286–95, 2967–3006).

Contacting the Divine

The oracular practices discussed above offered straightforward answers to circumscribed questions about matter-of-fact problems. As mediated procedures they did not offer the solicitant any experience of the divine presence. There was no opportunity to enter into personal contact with the deity. Anyone who desired immediate and unrestrained interaction with the divine, for example to obtain divine revelations first-hand, had to turn to methods that provoked a theophany, that is, the apparition of a deity.

It was a common belief that deities manifested themselves to humans and spoke to them in dreams (*P Oxy.* XI 1381; Harris 2009). The incubation shrines were places where such dreams could be provoked, merely by sleeping in the vicinity of the deity's presence. Judging from the numerous votive inscriptions, most visitors hoped to receive advice about healing, but some came in search of spiritual enlightenment (see the Mandulis-Aion inscription at Kalabsha; Nock 1972).

The formularies preserve multiple recipes to produce a theophany in a private setting, with great diversity and various levels of complexity in the procedures prescribed (Johnston 2008: 144–75). Most rites make a god appear in a dream, in the light of a lamp (*lychnomanteia*), or in the reflections of an oil slick in a bowl of water (*lekanomanteia*). These methods operate on the principle that the divine manifests itself as light. The rite is thus a means of channelling and focusing the light: 'Be great, be great, O light! Come forth, come forth, O light! Rise up, rise up, O light! Be high, be high, O light! He who is outside, come in!' (*P London–Leiden* 2/2–3 = *PDM* XIV 30–1; trans. Janet H. Johnson). In their format, most of these are modelled after the statue cult in Egyptian temples. In a dark, secluded, and purified room (like the sanctuary in an Egyptian temple), the ritualist, often attired in priestly garb, offers up incense and utters hymns and invocations to a lighted oil lamp. The lamp should not be red, owing to the colour's associations with Seth-Typhon, god of cosmic disorder. The wick of the lamp should be of linen, inscribed in a special myrrh ink with magical spells and designs. The ritualist then goes to sleep without speaking with anyone, and the god comes to him in a dream. Alternatively, the god appears in the flickering flame of the lamp or the reflections on the lamp oil. Some recipes even prescribe preparing a throne so that the deity can take a seat during the interview. In those cases, the invocations, with their long strings of *voces magicae* and vowel combinations, uttered while gazing intently at the flame or the oil film, likely helped induce the ritualist into a trance:

> I call upon you, the living god, fiery, invisible begetter of light, IAĒL PEIPTA PHŌS ZA PAI PHTHENTHA PHŌSZA PYRI BELIA IAŌ IAO EYŌ OEĒ A ŌY EOI A E Ē I O Y Ō give your strength, rouse your daimon, enter into this fire, fill it with a divine spirit, and show me your might. Let there be opened for me the house of the all-powerful god ALBALAL, who is in this light. Let there be light, breadth, depth, length, height, brightness, and let him who is inside shine through, the lord BOUĒL PHTHA PHTHA PHTHAĒL PHTHA ABAI BAINCHŌŌŌCH, now, now; immediately, immediately; quickly, quickly. (*PGM* IV 959–73; trans. W. C. Grese)

Several recipes also call for putting a special ointment in the eyes to bring the hazy shapes into focus: 'a tested [spell] for the security of shadows: hawk's egg and myrrh; rub, put some of it on your eyes. You secure shadows' (*P London-Leiden* 4/23 = *PDM* XIV 115; trans. Janet H. Johnson). The ritualist could perform these rites by himself, but multiple recipes prescribe the use of a child medium (Johnston 2001).

The goal of these rites was to produce a face-to-face encounter (*sustasis*, or, in Egyptian, (*peh-netjer*) with a divinity or, depending on the procedures, the spirit of a dead person. This would enable the ritualist to receive information about whatever he desired: 'Tell me an answer to everything about which I am asking here today, truly, without telling me falsehood' (*P London-Leiden* 8/11 = *PDM* XIV 231; trans. Janet H. Johnson). In the story of Thessalos of Tralles, such a rite is performed to receive clarification from Imouthes-Asklepios about King Nechepso's book on botany (Festugière 1939; Friedrich 1968; Moyer 2003). One elaborate ritual, described in the Eighth Book of Moses, is for acquiring from the supreme deity 'the Holy Name', possession of which would give the ritualist great magical powers (*PGM* XIII). The same recipe also offers an opportunity to inquire after one's fate, which could then be altered if desired:

> You, then, ask, 'Master, what is fated for me?' And he will tell you even about your star and what kind of daimon you have, and your horoscope and where you may live and where you will die. And if you hear something bad, do not cry out or weep, but ask that he may wash it off or circumvent it, for this god can do everything. (*PGM* XIII 709–14; trans. Morton Smith)

Though conceptually related and making use of similar techniques, the divine-encounter rites in the magical papyri differ fundamentally from Neoplatonic theurgy in their practical concerns and applications. Theurgy, popular between the second and fifth centuries, was in essence a revelatory religion that promised personal spiritual benefits to the individual initiate (Johnston 1997). Personal contact with the divine was achieved through a ritualized ascent to the heavens brought about by procedures very similar to the encounter rites described in the magical papyri. In fact, the Parisian Codex includes just such an ascent text, the so-called Mithras Liturgy (*PGM* IV 475–829; Betz 2003). The rite promises 'immortalization' (*apathanatismos*; *PGM* IV 476, 747), likely a temporary state of spiritual completion, resulting from an ascent through the heavenly layers to the supreme deity Helios-Mithras. Here we are far removed from the daily concerns about physical and social survival that inform most recipes in the formularies. Instead we touch upon the religious sensibilities of the day, a desire for revelatory knowledge and personal control over access to divine presence.

Conclusion

This chapter has reviewed the various methods that private individuals employed in Roman Egypt to secure protection and assistance from supernatural entities in their daily lives. Only when studied in combination, for example as a protocol for survival, does a meaningful system of thought and action become apparent. Taken together, they present a fascinating mixture of old and new practices, of temple-based facilities and portable methods, of local and international trends. To further our understanding, it is imperative to study the phenomena and corpora across languages and, if at all possible, in their archaeological context. Future research will, it is hoped, throw more light on the social, cultural, and institutional backgrounds of the practitioners and their clients. It also remains to be determined in more detail which innovations were home-grown and which came about under the impact of the Roman empire.

Suggested Reading

To explore this topic in more detail, I suggest starting with Frankfurter (1998), an insightful and thought-provoking analysis of popular religion in Roman Egypt. I also recommend reading Trzcionka (2007), which deals with magic and the supernatural in late Roman Syria and Palestine, for a comparative perspective. It provides a framework for understanding the magical practices discussed in this chapter as social behaviour. A good introduction to magic in the Graeco-Roman world is Graf (1997).

The source materials have been classified and collected in various corpora. The Greek Magical Papyri, including sections in Coptic found on the same manuscripts, are conveniently collected in the *Papyri Graecae Magicae* (Preisendanz 1928–31) and *Supplementum Magicum* (Daniel and Maltomini 1990–2). They are also available for full-text search in the *Thesaurus Linguae Graecae*, <http://stephanus.tlg.uci.edu/>. Spells published since 1992 can be found through the web portal Trismegistos Magic, <http://www.trismegistos.org/magic/index.php>. English translations are in Betz (1986), which includes translations of the Demotic spells. Quack (2008) offers a representative selection of Demotic spells in German translation. Several are already available for full-text search in the online *Thesaurus Linguae Aegyptiae*, <http://aaew.bbaw.de/tla>. Greek and Coptic spells of a Christian nature are available in English translation in Meyer and Smith (1999). Gager (1992) is a convenient collection of translated curse tablets and binding spells. The protective *lamellae* are collected, translated, and annotated in Kotansky (1994). The corpus of magical gems is studied systematically in Michel (2004) and Bonner (1950); important catalogues of individual collections are Michel (2001), Zwierlein-Diehl (1992), Philipp (1986), and Delatte and Derchain (1964). Greek horoscopes are collected in Neugebauer and van Hoesen (1959), Baccani (1992), and Jones (1999). No corpus of Demotic horoscopes exists as yet, but see Neugebauer (1943), Ross (2006, 2007), and Menchetti (2009). Ogden (2002) is recommended as a general source book on Greek and Roman magic.

Brashear (1995) offers a comprehensive survey of the Greek Magical Papyri. For the Demotic spells, I refer to Ritner (1995) and Quack (1998). The various divination methods available in Roman Egypt are surveyed in von Lieven (1999). Naether (2010) offers a thorough study of oracle books and oracle tickets. Hopfner (1921–4) remains a classic study on divination in the magical papyri; the topic is now also well described in Johnston (2008: 144–79). For the archaeological context of the magical materials, see Wilburn (2012).

Bibliography

Andrews, C. 1994. *Amulets of Ancient Egypt*. London: British Museum Press; Austin: University of Texas Press.

Baccani, D. 1992. *Oroscopi greci: Documentazione papirologica*. Messina: Sicania.

Bagnall, R. S., and B. W. Frier. 1994. *The Demography of Roman Egypt*. Cambridge: Cambridge University Press.

Betz, H. D. (ed.) 1986. *The Greek Magical Papyri in Translation, including the Demotic Spells*. Chicago: University of Chicago Press.

—— 2003. *The Mithras Liturgy: Text, Translation, and Commentary*. Tübingen: Mohr Siebeck.

Bohak, G. 2008. *Ancient Jewish Magic: A History*. Cambridge: Cambridge University Press.

Bonner, C. 1950. *Studies in Magical Amulets, Chiefly Graeco-Egyptian*. Ann Arbor: University of Michigan Press.

Brashear, W. M. 1995. 'The Greek Magical Papyri: An Introduction and Survey: Annotated Bibliography (1928–1994)', in W. Haase and H. Temporini (eds), *Aufstieg und Niedergang der römischen Welt* II 18.5. Berlin: de Gruyter, 3380–684.

Brown, P. 1982. 'The Rise and Function of the Holy Man in Late Antiquity', repr. with additional notes in Brown, *Society and the Holy in Late Antiquity*. Berkeley: University of California Press, 103–52; first pub. in *Journal of Roman Studies* 61: 80–101.

Cauville, C. 2004. 'Dendara: Du sanatorium au tinctorium', *Bulletin de la Société Française d'Égyptologie* 161: 28–40.

Černý, J. 1962. 'Egyptian Oracles', in R. A. Parker (ed.), *A Saite Oracle Papyrus from Thebes in the Brooklyn Museum (Papyrus Brooklyn 47.218.3)*. Providence, RI: Brown University Press, 35–48.

Collins, D. 2008a. *Magic in the Ancient Greek World*. Malden, Mass.: Blackwell.

—— 2008b. 'The Magic of Homeric Verses', *Classical Philology* 103: 211–36.

Daniel, R. W., and F. Maltomini. 1990–2. *Supplementum Magicum*, I: nos 1–51; II: nos 52–100. Opladen: Westdeutscher.

Daumas, F. 1957. 'Le sanatorium de Dendara', *Bulletin de l'Institut Français d'Archéologie Orientale* 56: 35–57.

de Bruyn, T. 2010. 'Papyri, Parchments, Ostraca, and Tablets Written with Biblical Texts in Greek and Used as Amulets: A Preliminary List', in T. J. Kraus and T. Nicklas (eds), *Early Christian Manuscripts: Examples of Applied Method and Approach*. Leiden: Brill, 145–90.

Delatte, A., and P. Derchain. 1964. *Les intailles magiques gréco-égyptiennes de la Bibliothèque Nationale*. Paris: Bibliothèque Nationale.

Dickie, M. W. 2000. 'Who Practised Love-Magic in Classical Antiquity and in the Late Roman World?', *Classical Quarterly*, new ser. 50/2: 563–83.

Dieleman, J. 2005. *Priests, Tongues, and Rites: The London–Leiden Magical Manuscripts and Translation in Egyptian Ritual (100–300 CE)*. Leiden: Brill.

du Bourguet, P. 1975. 'Ensemble magique du période romaine en Égypte', *Revue du Louvre* 25: 255–7.

Dunand, F. 2006. 'La guérison dans les temples (Égypte, époque tardive)', *Archiv für Religionsgeschichte* 8: 4–24.

Edwards, I. E. S. 1960. *Hieratic Papyri in the British Museum, Fourth Series: Oracular Amuletic Decrees of the Late New Kingdom*. London: Trustees of the British Museum.

Eschweiler, P. 1994. *Bildzauber im alten Ägypten: Die Verwendung von Bildern und Gegenständen in magischen Handlungen nach den Texten des Mittleren und Neuen Reiches*. Freiburg: Universitätsverlag; Göttingen: Vandenhoeck & Ruprecht.

Evans, J. 2004. 'The Astrologer's Apparatus: A Picture of Professional Practice in Greco-Roman Egypt', *Journal for the History of Astronomy* 35/1: 1–44.

Faraone, C. A. 1999. *Ancient Greek Love Magic*. Cambridge, Mass.: Harvard University Press.

—— 2002. 'The Ethnic Origins of a Roman-Era Philtrokatadesmos (*PGM* IV.296–466)', in P. Mirecki and M. Meyer (eds), *Magic and Ritual in the Ancient World*. Leiden: Brill, 319–43.

Festugière, A.-J. 1939. 'L'expérience religieuse du médecin Thessalos', *Revue Biblique* 48: 45–77.

Frankfurter, D. 1994. 'The Magic of Writing and the Writing of Magic: The Power of the Word in Egyptian and Greek Traditions', *Helios* 21: 189–221.

—— 1998. *Religion in Roman Egypt: Assimilation and Resistance*. Princeton: Princeton University Press.

—— 2006. 'Fetus Magic and Sorcery Fears in Roman Egypt', *Greek, Roman and Byzantine Studies* 46: 37–62.

Friedrich, H.-V. 1968. *Thessalos von Tralles: Griechisch und lateinisch: Thessali philosophi De Virtutibus Herbarum*. Meisenheim am Glan: Anton Hain.

Gager, J. G. 1992. *Curse Tablets and Binding Spells from the Ancient World*. New York: Oxford University Press.

Gordon, R. 2002. 'Shaping the Text: Innovation and Authority in Graeco-Egyptian Malign Magic', in H. F. J. Horstmanshoff (ed.), *Kykeon: Studies in Honour of H. S. Versnel*. Leiden: Brill, 69–111.

Graf, F. 1997. *Magic in the Ancient World*. Cambridge, Mass.: Harvard University Press.

Gundel, H. G. 1968. *Weltbild und Astrologie in den griechischen Zauberpapyri*. Munich: Beck.

Hahn, J., S. Emmel, and U. Gotter (eds) 2008. *From Temple to Church: Destruction and Renewal of Local Cultic Topography in Late Antiquity*. Leiden: Brill.

Harris, W. V. 2009. *Dreams and Experience in Classical Antiquity*. Cambridge, Mass.: Harvard University Press.

Hirt Raj, M. 2006. *Médecins et malades de l'Égypte romaine: Étude socio-légale de la profession médicale et de ses praticiens du Ier au IVe siècle ap. J.-C.* Leiden: Brill.

Hopfner, T. 1921–4. *Griechisch-ägyptischer Offenbarungszauber*. Leipzig: Haessel.

Johnston, S. I. 1997. 'Rising to the Occasion: Theurgic Ascent and its Cultural Milieu', in P. Schäfer and H. G. Kippenberg (eds), *Envisioning Magic: A Princeton Seminar and Symposium*. Leiden: Brill, 165–94.

—— 2001. 'Charming Children: The Use of the Child in Ancient Divination', *Arethusa* 34/1: 97–117.

—— 2008. *Ancient Greek Divination*. Malden, Mass.: Wiley-Blackwell.

Jones, A. 1994. 'The Place of Astronomy in Roman Egypt', *Apeiron: A Journal for Ancient Philosophy and Science* 27/4, special issue: *The Sciences in Greco-Roman Society*, ed. T. D. Barnes, 25–52.

—— 1999. *Astronomical Papyri from Oxyrhynchus (P. Oxy. 4133–4300a)*. Philadelphia: American Philosophical Society.

Kenyon, F. G. 1893. *Greek Papyri in the British Museum: Catalogue with Texts*, vol. 1. London: British Museum.

Koenig, Y. 1994. *Magie et magiciens dans l'Égypte ancienne*. Paris: Pygmalion.

Kotansky, R. 1994. *Greek Magical Amulets: The Inscribed Gold, Silver, Copper, and Bronze Lamellae*. Opladen: Westdeutscher Verlag.

Łajtar, A. 2006. *Deir el-Bahari in the Hellenistic and Roman Periods: A Study of an Egyptian Temple Based on Greek Sources*. Warsaw: Warsaw University, Institute of Archaeology, and Raphael Taubenschlag Foundation.

Leemans, C. 1839. *Papyrus égyptien à transcriptions grecques du Musée d'Antiquités des Pays-Bas à Leide: Description raisonnée I 383*. Leiden: Brill.

LiDonnici, L. R. 2002. 'Beans, Fleawort, and the Blood of a Hamadryas Baboon: Recipe Ingredients in Greco-Roman Magical Materials', in P. Mirecki and M. Meyer (eds), *Magic and Ritual in the Ancient World*. Leiden: Brill, 359–77.

Martinez, D. 1991. *P. Michigan XVI: A Greek Love Charm from Egypt*. Atlanta: Scholars Press.

Menchetti, A. 2009. 'Un aperçu des textes astrologiques de Médinet Madi', in G. Widmer and D. Devauchelle (eds), *Actes du IXe Congrès International des Études Démotiques*. Cairo: Institut Français d'Archéologie Orientale, 223–41.

Meyer, M., and R. Smith (eds) 1999. *Ancient Christian Magic: Coptic Texts of Ritual Power*. Princeton: Princeton University Press.

Michel, S. 2001. *Die magischen Gemmen im Britischen Museum*. London: British Museum Press.

—— 2004. *Die magischen Gemmen: Zu Bildern und Zauberformeln auf geschnittenen Steinen der Antike und Neuzeit*. Berlin: Akademie.

Mirecki, P., I. Gardner, and A. Alcock. 1997. 'Magical Spell, Manichaean Letter', in P. Mirecki and J. BeDuhn (eds), *Emerging from Darkness: Studies in the Recovery of Manichaean Sources*. Leiden: Brill, 1–32.

Moyer, I. 2003. 'Thessalos of Tralles and Cultural Exchange', in S. B. Noegel, J. T. Walker, and B. M. Wheeler (eds), *Prayer, Magic, and the Stars in the Ancient and Late Antique World*. University Park: Pennsylvania State University Press, 39–56.

Naether, F. 2010. *Die Sortes Astrampsychi: Problemlosungsstrategien durch Orakel im römischen Ägypten*. Tübingen: Mohr Siebeck.

Neugebauer, O. 1943. 'Demotic Horoscopes', *Journal of the American Oriental Society* 63: 115–26.

—— and H. B. van Hoesen. 1959. *Greek Horoscopes*. Philadelphia: American Philosophical Society.

Nock, A. D. 1972. 'A Vision of Mandulis Aion', repr. in Nock, *Essays on Religion and the Ancient World*, vol. 1. Oxford: Clarendon Press, 356–400; first pub. in *Harvard Theological Review* 27/1: 53–104.

Ogden, D. 2002. *Magic, Witchcraft, and Ghosts in the Greek and Roman Worlds: A Sourcebook.* Oxford: Oxford University Press.

Philipp, H. 1986. *Mira et Magica: Gemmen im Ägyptischen Museum der Staatlichen Museen Preussischer Kulturbesitz, Berlin Charlottenburg.* Mainz: von Zabern.

Pinch, G. 1994. *Magic in Ancient Egypt.* London: British Museum Press.

Preisendanz, K. (ed.) 1928–31. *Papyri Graecae Magicae: Die griechischen Zauberpapyri*, 2 vols. Leipzig: Teubner; 2nd edn (ed. A. Henrichs), Stuttgart: Teubner, 1973–4.

Quack, J. F. 1998. 'Kontinuität und Wandel in der spätägyptischen Magie', *Studi epigrafici e linguistici sul Vicino Oriente antico* 15: 77–94.

—— 2006. 'A Black Cat from the Right, and a Scarab on your Head: New Sources for Ancient Egyptian Divination', in K. Szpakowska (ed.), *Through a Glass Darkly: Magic, Dreams and Prophesy in Ancient Egypt.* Swansea: Classical Press of Wales, 175–87.

—— 2008. 'Demotische magische und divinatorische Texte', in B. Janowski and G. Wilhelm (eds), *Omina, Orakel, Rituale und Beschwörungen.* Gütersloh: Gütersloher Verlagshaus, 331–85.

Ripat, P. 2006. 'The Language of Oracular Inquiry in Roman Egypt', *Phoenix* 60: 304–28.

Ritner, R. K. 1993. *The Mechanics of Ancient Egyptian Magical Practice.* Chicago: Oriental Institute.

—— 1995. 'Egyptian Magical Practice under the Roman Empire: The Demotic Spells and their Religious Context', in W. Haase and H. Temporini (eds), *Aufstieg und Niedergang der römischen Welt* II 18.5. Berlin: de Gruyter, 3333–79.

Ross, M. 2006. 'An Introduction to the Horoscopic Ostraca of Medînet Mâdi', *Egitto e Vicino Oriente* 29: 147–80.

—— 2007. 'A Continuation of the Horoscopic Ostraca of Medînet Mâdi', *Egitto e Vicino Oriente* 30: 153–71.

Rutherford, I. 2003. 'Pilgrimage in Greco-Roman Egypt: New Perspectives on Graffiti from the Memnonion at Abydos', in R. Matthews and C. Roemer (eds), *Ancient Perspectives on Egypt.* London: UCL Press, 171–89.

Ryholt, K. 2005. 'On the Contents and Nature of the Tebtunis Temple Library: A Status Report', in S. Lippert and M. Schentuleit (eds), *Tebtynis und Soknopaiu Nesos: Leben im römerzeitlichen Fajum.* Wiesbaden: Harrassowitz, 141–60.

Scheidel, W. 2001. *Death on the Nile: Disease and the Demography of Roman Egypt.* Leiden: Brill.

Smith, M. 1979. 'Relations between Magical Papyri and Magical Gems', in J. Bingen and G. Nachtergael (eds), *Actes du XVe Congrès International de Papyrologie*, vol. 3. Brussels: Fondation Égyptologique Reine Élisabeth, 129–36.

Stadler, M. A. 2008. 'On the Demise of Egyptian Writing: Working with a Problematic Source Basis', in J. Baines, J. Bennet, and S. Houston (eds), *The Disappearance of Writing Systems: Perspectives on Literacy and Communication.* London: Equinox, 157–81.

Stewart, R., and K. Morrell. 1998. 'The Oracles of Astrampsychus', in W. Hansen (ed), *Anthology of Ancient Greek Popular Literature.* Bloomington: Indiana University Press, 285–324.

Tacoma, L. E. 2006. *Fragile Hierarchies: The Urban Elites of Third Century Roman Egypt.* Leiden: Brill.

Traunecker, C. 1992. *Coptos, hommes et dieux sur le parvis de Geb.* Leuven: Peeters.

Trzcionka, S. 2007. *Magic and the Supernatural in Fourth-Century Syria.* London and New York: Routledge.

von Lieven, A. 1999. 'Divination in Ägypten', *Archiv für Orientforschung* 26: 77–126.

Wilburn, A. 2012. *Materia Magica: The Archaeology of Magic in Roman Egypt, Cyprus and Spain*. Ann Arbor: University of Michigan Press.
Winkler, A. 2009, 'On the Astrological Papyri from the Tebtunis Temple Library', in G. Widmer and D. Devauchelle (eds), *Actes du IX*[e] *Congrès International des Études Démotiques*. Cairo: Institut Français d'Archéologie Orientale, 361–75.
Winkler, J. J. 1991. 'The Constraints of Eros', in C. A. Faraone and D. Obbink (eds), *Magika Hiera: Ancient Greek Magic and Religion*. New York: Oxford University Press, 214–43.
Zwierlein-Diehl, E. 1992. *Magische Amulette und andere Gemmen des Instituts für Altertumskunde der Universität zu Köln*. Opladen: Westdeutscher Verlag.

CHAPTER 22

EGYPTIAN TEMPLES

MARTINA MINAS-NERPEL

FROM the beginning of their rule in Egypt, the Ptolemies initiated a gigantic temple construction and decoration programme, which the Roman emperors continued well into the second century CE. Temples were still decorated on a much smaller scale into the third and the beginning of the fourth centuries. The last known cartouche of a Roman emperor in a temple was inscribed under Maximinus Daia (305–13 CE) on blocks belonging to the temple of Horus at Tahta (Hölbl 2000: 45 n. 177; 114, fig. 157). Otherwise, the latest evidence comes from Esna (Sauneron 1975: 65–6, no. 495; 84–7, no. 503), where the temple of Khnum was still being decorated under Decius (249–51 CE). Stelae inscribed in hieroglyphs continued to be set up in Egyptian temples, for example in the Bucheum at Armant, of which the latest is dated to 340, the fifty-seventh year of the era of Diocletian (Hölbl 2000: 45 n. 178; Goldbrunner 2004: 78–9, 302). The temple of Isis at Philae, where hieroglyphs were carved in the temple of Harendotes as late as 394 (Winter 1982: 1023), was the last to be kept open, being closed down under Justinian between 535 and 537 (Winter 1982: 1026), when it was converted to a church (Dijkstra 2008).

The Hellenistic and Roman periods of Egypt are often subsumed under the term 'Graeco-Roman Egypt'. In his examination of Egyptian society under Ptolemaic and Roman rule, Naphtali Lewis (1970) correctly pointed out that this phrase should not be used to imply continuity between the two eras, since the changes in the governmental structure, social patterns and politics, administration, and the economy were so fundamental in Roman times as to render the term misleading. Nonetheless, for the indigenous temples, the term 'Graeco-Roman' is appropriate as it emphasizes the continuity of temple construction and decoration throughout the longer period.

In view of the massive amount of evidence, this chapter concentrates on architecture, decoration, and certain questions of cult topography. The relations of temple and king and the interaction of Egyptian deities and humanity's protagonist, the Roman emperor as the Egyptian pharaoh, were central to the development of the Roman province, at least in the understanding of the Egyptian priests. The temples' socio-cultural context (Finnestad 1997: 198, 227–32), their function as centres of learning that produced vast numbers of hieroglyphic and literary texts, and their artistic aspects are mentioned, but not discussed in detail.

The Egyptian Temples and their Texts and Writing System(s)

Egyptian scholar priests of the Graeco-Roman period developed for the indigenous temples a highly intellectual, very artificial language and a vastly expanded writing system. The temple walls were decorated on an unprecedented scale with scenes and inscriptions that provide manifold insights into the religious thinking of the priests, cult topography, mythology, religious festivals, daily cults, the ruler cult, and building history, as well as the function of various rooms.

Patterns in the inscription of texts show that those of both Ptolemaic and Roman periods should be studied together. Since the temple of Horus at Edfu is almost complete and is rich in inscriptions that are published and accessible, it has become a focal point for studies on hieroglyphic texts of these periods, cult topography, and temple ritual—despite its provincial location. The cultural centre was in the north and the most creative regions were probably in the Delta and the Memphis area. Therefore, one could assume that Roman temples there were probably even larger and more richly decorated than those in the south, but almost all surviving buildings of the Roman period are in Upper Egypt, and this bias causes well-known problems of interpretation. According to Penelope Wilson (1997, p. x), the temple of Edfu, founded in 237 and completed in 57 BCE, is regarded in many ways as 'the leader of this series of Upper Egyptian temples whose texts provided the standards for the temples which followed', at least in the south. For example, under Ptolemy XII, texts from Edfu were copied with some variant writings in the Second East Colonnade leading to the temple of Isis at Philae. From the differences in script, Erich Winter (1995: 310–19) presumes that the inscriptions were not copied from papyri, but that the priests from Edfu travelled to Philae, taking with them their knowledge. Another text in the Second East Colonnade at Philae, also of the reign of Ptolemy XII, was copied under Augustus at Kalabsha (Winter 1995: 306–10, 319). In this case graphic similarities suggest that a papyrus template was used. These two cases show a rather smooth transition from Ptolemaic to Roman period practices. Obvious variations in script and texts occur in different temples (Junker 1906, p. v), since mythological and ritual requirements would produce specific interpretations. The variety of texts and orthography is one index of energetic creativity in the Graeco-Roman temples.

The temple texts of the Graeco-Roman period have attracted much philological attention, from analyses of individual hieroglyphic signs (Fairman 1943, 1945) and wordplay (e.g. Preys 2009) to complete text publications of entire temples such as Edfu. Work on Graeco-Roman temple inscriptions is very active and no longer considered as an arcane specialization, nor are the texts regarded as faint imitations of earlier periods. On the contrary, the texts display the maintenance of textual tradition (Quack 2010) and show a new level of integration of mythical motifs. Phrases in texts as early as the Pyramid Texts are incorporated in Ptolemaic and Roman compositions (Graefe 1991), exemplifying that Graeco-Roman temples should be studied not in isolation, but in the broader context of ancient Egypt. The origin of many features can be traced back to the Dynastic period; these were developed dynamically in Graeco-Roman temples. This is true for architecture (discussed below) as well as texts. An example is the highly developed schematic framing columns of inscriptions in scenes and their formulas, whose organization was discovered by Erich Winter (1968) in his pioneering work on the organization of Graeco-Roman period temple reliefs and of their distribution in registers. Almost thirty years later, John Baines (1994) discussed the New Kingdom forerunners to these formulas that express the idea of the temple as the cosmos and its eternal duration.

Since Philippe Derchain (1962a) proposed the existence of a 'temple grammar', an idea taken up and developed by Erich Winter (1987), texts and architecture are no longer viewed separately. In order to understand the underlying 'grammar' of a specific temple, one should take into account that temples were built and decorated according to specific rules that included the inscriptions as well as architectural and iconographic characteristics. This has been discussed in detail, for example, for the outer wall of the sanctuary at Dendara (Leitz 2001). Graeco-Roman temples were highly and comprehensively systematized. Baines (1994: 31) concludes, 'Their inventiveness lies partly in the creation of complex and rigid structures,' which is a 'salient distinction between the designs of the New Kingdom and the Greco-Roman period'.

Although many of the hieroglyphic inscriptions are accessible in extensive publications and, to a much lesser extent, in translation (see Grenier 1980; Leitz 2002), a vast number of texts remain to be copied, translated, and especially analysed. Each temple was a world of its own, with the logical consequence that each temple complex needs to be published completely. Besides the temple of Edfu, whose texts are pretty much all published, long-standing projects have been initiated for the large temples at Dendara, Esna, Kom Ombo, and Philae (for an overview and bibliography, see Kurth 1997: 154) and now Athribis (Leitz, Mendel, and el-Masry 2010), as well as smaller ones such as el-Qal'a (Pantalacci and Traunecker 1990–8) and Shanhur (Willems et al. 2003; Minas-Nerpel et al. forthcoming). Penelope Wilson's dictionary (1997) and the grammars of Hermann Junker (1906) and Dieter Kurth (2007–8) are important results of these publications. Owing to the enormous amount of evidence, no overview of all the Egyptian temples of the Graeco-Roman period has ever been attempted. A major goal should be to classify the temple texts properly. Christian Leitz has initiated a research project at the University of Tübingen, 'The Temple as Canon of Egypt's Religious Literature', which aims at a classification, analysis, and comprehensive interpretation of the hieroglyphic texts of all temples.

Dendara: An Egyptian Temple of the Graeco-Roman Period

Besides the temple of Horus at Edfu, the temple of Hathor at Dendara is one of the best-preserved temples in Egypt (Daumas 1974). The question of how typical it was cannot be evaluated easily because roughly 90 per cent of the temples north of Athribis are lost. However, the Book of the Temple, a manual that describes how the ideal Egyptian temple should be built and operated, might shed light on this question. This handbook is attested in over forty fragmentary manuscripts, demonstrating its wide and supra-regional use in antiquity. The mostly unpublished papyri all date to the Roman period, but the manual's origin predates the foundation of Edfu in 237 BCE (Quack 2009).

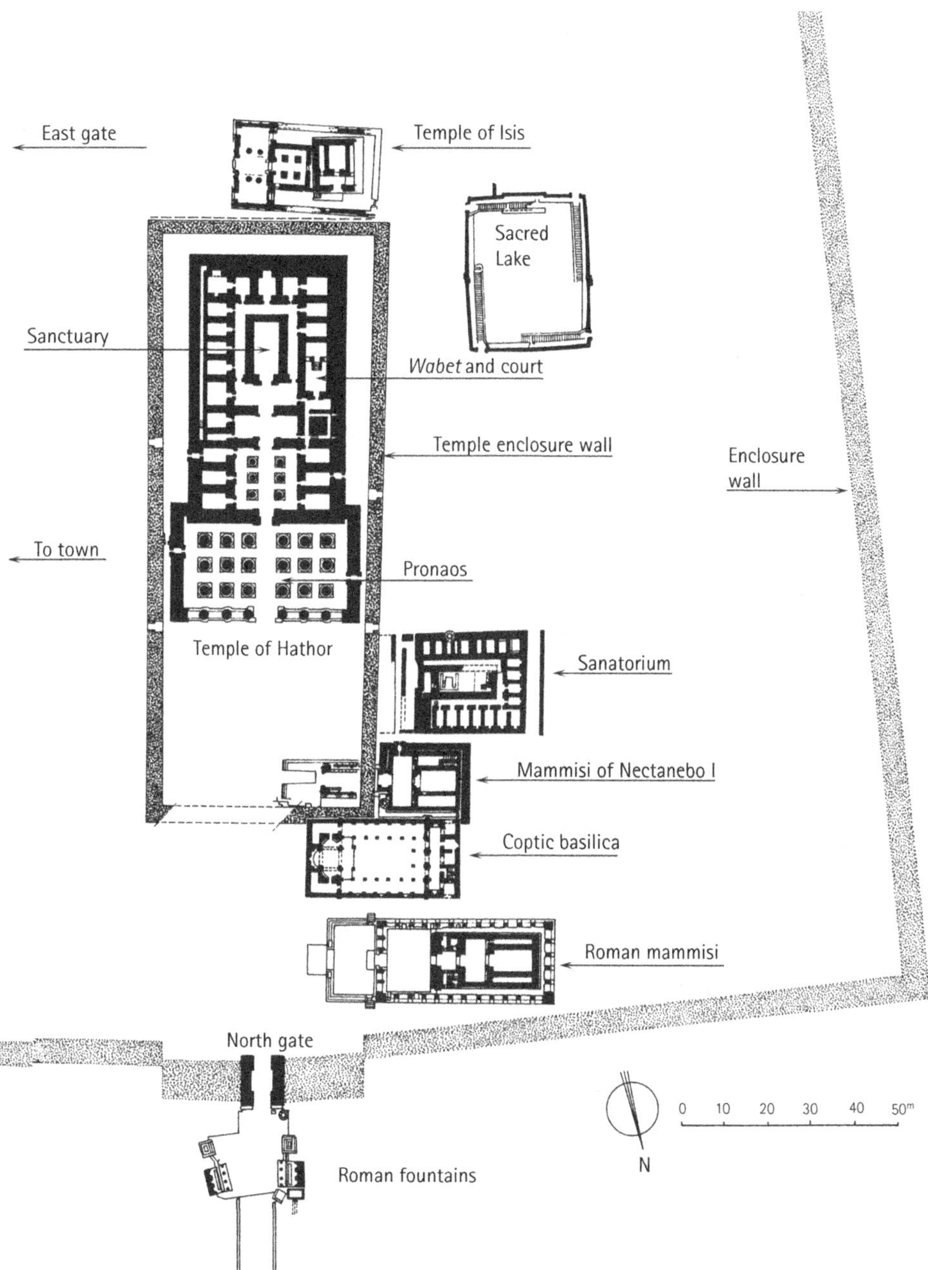

FIG. 22.1 Plan of the temple complex at Dendara

Based on Cauville (1990*b*: 27).

The Dendara temple complex, which is the result of a radical architectural renewal in late Ptolemaic and Roman periods, exemplifies the characteristics of temples of its period and demonstrates the smooth transition in temple construction and decoration from Hellenistic to Roman times. Decoration at Dendara was beginning as it ended at Edfu in the mid-50s BCE. Thus, the construction teams were probably transferred from Edfu to Dendara so that work could begin there without any disruption (Hölbl 2000: 75). This might also explain the obvious similarities in the layout of the Edfu and Dendara temples, whose ground-plans are distributed around a central axis with almost perfect axial symmetry (Fig. 22.1), only broken by specific elements such as the *wabet* (see below) and the stairs. However, the plan of Edfu went back around 175 years, and the plans of Edfu and Dendara could have been devised elsewhere, for example in Memphis. The two temples were connected cultically by the union of Hathor of Dendara and Horus of Edfu and the birth of their child Ihi, or Harsomtus, celebrated in their birth houses, or mammisis. Although the temple of Edfu was built and decorated entirely in the Ptolemaic period—Tiberius is the only Roman pharaoh whose cartouches are attested there, on the pylon (Porter and Moss 1939: 121, nos 1–2, with bibliography)—it served as a major religious centre in Roman Egypt, participating in one of the main Upper Egyptian festivals, when Hathor travelled annually about 180 km in order to visit Horus at Edfu. A long building inscription (Amer and Morardet 1983; Winter 1989; Cauville 1990a) describes the temple of Dendara and its mythological background, as well as measurements of the different halls and rooms, although it is not as elaborate as the corresponding Edfu text (Kurth 2004b; see also Quack 2009).

The temple of Dendara is oriented, as usual, towards the Nile, which here flows east–west. Although the temple faces north, it was symbolically 'east' for the Egyptians. Both modern and ancient visitors enter the temple complex of Hathor along its main north–south cult axis, through the north gateway in the complex's enclosure wall (Fig. 22.2). This wall, roughly 280 × 290 metres, was completed under Tiberius in 23 CE (Hölbl 2000: 74). The monumental

FIG. 22.2 Temple of Hathor and north gateway, Dendara

Author's photograph.

stone gateway was decorated under Domitian (81–96) and Trajan (98–117) and was once integrated into a mud-brick pylon.

A second gateway in the enclosure wall, the east gateway, had been built earlier under Augustus and was decorated from then to the time of Nero (Cauville 1999). It leads to the secondary east–west cult axis, which related to an earlier building from the Ramesside period, to the (birth) temple of Isis (Cauville 2007). The east gateway also led across the town to a second temple complex to the east. The temple of Isis is located at the back of the Hathor temple (Fig. 22.3). It was originally built under Nectanebo I in the 30th dynasty as a birth house, in which the birth of Harsiese, the youthful Horus, son of Isis and Osiris, as the legal successor and royal heir, was celebrated. It had been extended in the Ptolemaic period, before it was entirely rebuilt and further decorated under Augustus, demonstrating once again the continuity of temple construction and decoration in the Graeco-Roman period.

For the temple of Hathor itself, construction began with the main temple, the naos, 36 × 60 metres and 12.5 metres high (Cauville 1990b: 28). The building inscription on its exterior, from the time of Augustus (Amer and Morardet 1983; Winter 1989), dates the first foundation rituals to 16 July 54 BCE, in year 27 of Ptolemy XII. The naos and its surrounding chapels were completed thirty-four years later, in 22/21 BCE, year 9 of Augustus. Hathor had already taken possession of her temple by ceremonial entry in August 30 BCE, the very first month of the first year of Roman rule, thus demonstrating that the new regime probably took the opportunity to make the inauguration coincide with its installation in Alexandria.

FIG. 22.3 Temples of Hathor and Isis at Dendara, from the south-east

Author's photograph.

The subterranean crypts (Waitkus 1997), which were decorated under Ptolemy XII and his co-regent Cleopatra VII until 51 BCE, had been completed before the walls of the naos were erected. They were regarded as the underworld and used as storerooms for the statues, which would be taken out and revived at various religious festivals (Coppens 2009).

All outer walls of the naos were decorated under Roman rule, except for the rear wall, which had been executed first, probably because of the important locus of the contra-chapel around the large Hathor head, carved in the middle of the wall, which was originally gilded and surrounded by a wooden canopy (Hölbl 2000: 74, fig. 83). On the rear wall, Cleopatra VII is depicted in the famous offering scenes together with her son King Ptolemy XV Caesarion (Figs 22.3 and 22.4), called Philometor Philopator, who combined in his name and person the legacy of the Ptolemaic dynasty and his Roman heritage. Thus, the foundation was laid for a Hellenistic–Roman dynasty (Heinen 2007: 186–7), but with the death of Julius Caesar in 44 and that of his son Ptolemy in 30 BCE, this idea was abandoned. Instead, Egypt became a Roman province.

The sanctuary at Dendara, the innermost part of the temple, was a separate structure completely enclosed within the naos. Here, sheltered from everything outside, the principal cult image of the main deity, Hathor, stood within a shrine, accompanied by the cult barques of

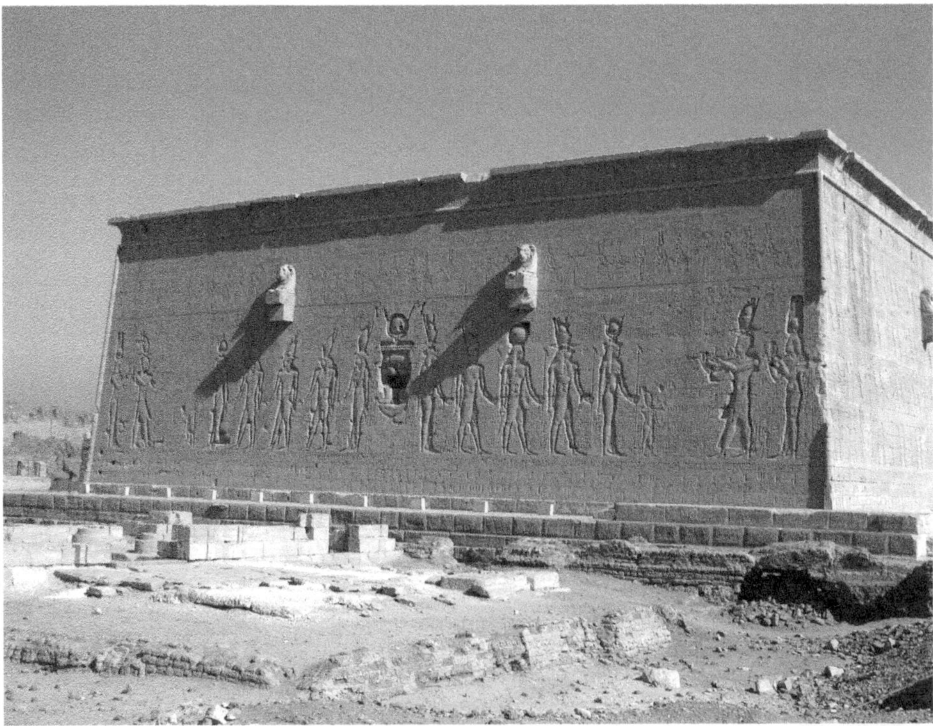

FIG. 22.4 Naos on the rear wall of the temple of Hathor at Dendara: Cleopatra VII and Ptolemy XV Caesarion offer to the deities of Dendara at both ends of the wall. The large Hathor head carved in the middle of the wall marks the location of the contra-chapel

Author's photograph.

Horus of Edfu, Harsomtus, and Isis. The sanctuary is surrounded by a corridor, from which the surrounding chapels can be reached. They are dedicated to Hathor, Isis, Sokar-Osiris, Harsomtus, and Horus of Edfu. Directly in front of the sanctuary are two transverse halls, first the Hall of the Ennead, where the deities' statues were assembled for processions during festivals, and secondly the Offering Hall, where the offering tables were placed. The deities' statues appeared in the Hall of Appearance, which was supported by six composite columns with plant motifs and the sistrum capitals, comprising four Hathor masks, one facing in each direction. Around the Hall of Appearance six further chambers are located, such as the treasury, in which precious cult objects were kept.

The Hall of the Ennead gives access to a small open court leading to the *wabet*, the 'pure chapel' (Fig. 22.5), where all the cult images of the temple were assembled in order to be purified, clothed, and adorned for the festival of the 'unification with the solar disk' at the New Year. From the open court priests would carry the images up the western staircase to the temple roof, where the procession went to the kiosk at the back. Here, the main ceremony of the festival was celebrated (Cauville 2002: 35–49), when the statues of the deities were exposed to

FIG. 22.5 *Wabet* and open court at the temple of Hathor, Dendara

Author's photograph.

the rejuvenating rays of the sun, being finally carried back into the temple down the eastern stairway, as depicted on the walls. The open court and the *wabet* are specific Graeco-Roman transformations of features that had existed at least since the New Kingdom, the 'sunshades' (*šw.t Rꜥ*) of the New Kingdom Theban temples, the open solar court in Taharqa's edifice in Karnak, or the Ra-Horakhty chapels of the Nubian temples (Coppens 2007: 209–19).

In the temple of Hathor, there were two further rooftop chapels, consisting of several adjoining rooms, dedicated to the cult of Osiris, especially for the mysteries performed in the month of Khoiak, the fourth month of the inundation. This ritual included the annual production of two types of Osiris figurine, 'corn mummies' made from earth and grain, which would sprout and symbolize the resurrection of Osiris (Raven 1982), and the recently identified Sokar-Osiris figurines. Both types of figurine are described in the Khoiak texts (Chassinat 1966–8; Cauville 1997a,b), and archaeologically attested (Minas-Nerpel 2006). This example illustrates how temples need to be interpreted in their archaeological, architectural, and textual context, using all categories of evidence. Only then can the cult be analysed in full in its topographical setting.

The ceiling of the great pronaos, or outer hypostyle hall, rests on twenty-four Hathor columns, of which six are linked by intercolumnar screen walls to form the façade of the building, another feature typical of the Graeco-Roman period that can be traced back to the New Kingdom (Elgawady 2010). The Dendara pronaos is the largest completely preserved structure of Roman Egypt, 43 metres wide, 26 metres long, and 17.2 metres high (Cauville 1990b: 28). In comparison, only eighteen columns support the Edfu pronaos. The Dendara hall was added to the naos in a second building phase, of which the completion is commemorated in a Greek dedication inscription on the façade, dating to 32–7 CE, the last years of Tiberius (Bernand 1984, no. 28; Winter 1989: 76 n. 2; Hölbl 2000: 78–9). Most parts of the pronaos were decorated later, under Claudius and Nero. The dedication inscription emphasizes that the inhabitants of the *metropolis* and the nome have dedicated this pronaos to Aphrodite-Hathor. This corresponds to the Greek building inscription on the east gate in the enclosure wall (Hölbl 2000: 74 n. 233), which had also been paid for by the inhabitants, who thus initiated the construction of important temple parts. This leads to the central question of who initiated and financed Egyptian temple buildings in the Roman period and how much land and therefore resources the temples and the Egyptian priests still possessed. Most of the land belonging to temples had been appropriated by the state in the early Roman period, and the privileges the Egyptian priests enjoyed had been curtailed, but the Egyptian temples as institutions obviously still possessed the means to continue to build and decorate temples during the principate (Monson 2005; Herklotz 2007: 114–16; for the Ptolemaic period, see Manning 2003). It seems unlikely, however, that the monumental temple complexes resulted from initiatives other than of the rulers (or the state). With the aid of royal and also private donations from non-Egyptian officials, private citizens, and Roman soldiers (Kockelmann and Pfeiffer 2009), the Egyptians were able to build new temples or to extend those already existing. The wealthy elite thus funded not only classical-style city construction (McKenzie 2007: 154, 162, 170) but also to a certain extent some Egyptian temples. Arthur F. Shore (1979) discussed votive objects from Dendara with Greek, hieroglyphic, and Demotic inscriptions, which provide information concerning high officials of the Tentyrite nome and their contributions to the building and decoration of its principal temples in the late Ptolemaic and the early Roman period.

In the reign of Nero (54–68), after the pronaos had been completed, a stone enclosure wall was planned and had been partly erected around the entire temple, but it was never completed. The north-west corner of this wall cuts through the 30th dynasty birth house, the oldest archaeologically surviving example, which was replaced by one of the Roman period, dedicated to Ihi, the son of Hathor. In a birth house (Daumas 1958), which was usually a separate building facing the axis of a main temple, the birth and enthronement of an infant god as part of the local divine triad was celebrated in the form of a mystery drama that identified the young deity with the rising sun, and so took on cosmic dimensions (Louant 2003). The concept of the child-god and the daily rebirth of the sun supported the equation between the king and the eternal regeneration of kingship, already attested in New Kingdom Theban temples, for example for Hatshepsut in her temple at Deir el-Bahri on the west bank and for Amenhotep III in the temple of Luxor.

Architectural and Theological Variation

Although Dendara and Edfu are closely linked and the design of their two main temples is rather similar, there are clear differences in their architecture, for example the number of columns in the Halls of Appearance (six in Dendara, twelve in Edfu) and the pronaoi (twenty-four in Dendara, eighteen in Edfu). Graeco-Roman temples could vary greatly in their function, design, and size. Already in Ptolemaic times, Egyptian temples were classified into first, second, and third rank, as known from the sacerdotal decrees (Pfeiffer 2004: 194–6). From the Mediterranean coast to Nubia and from the oases in the Western Desert to the Red Sea, more than a hundred Egyptian temples of the Graeco-Roman period are known (Kurth 1997: 152). It is beyond the scope of this chapter to list or discuss all Egyptian temples built, extended, and/or decorated in the Roman period. The presentation of Dieter Arnold (1999) needs to be updated, especially for decoration executed after Antoninus Pius (Hölbl 2000, 2004b, 2005; Hallof 2010), and further analysed (Minas forthcoming). Here, I concentrate on two further examples, Kom Ombo and el-Qal'a.

At Kom Ombo (Fig. 22.6), temple construction and decoration started under Ptolemy VI Philometor and continued through to the early third century CE. This large building, which replaced an earlier one, was conceived as a unique double temple with two main east–west temple axes, the southern one leading to the sanctuary of Sobek, the northern one to the sanctuary of Haroeris, Horus the Elder. The temple thus exhibits an architectural doubling of many features, except for such elements as the *wabet* complex, which occurs only on the north (Haroeris) side. Both principal deities formed the centre of a triad: Haroeris was linked to Hathor and Khonsu, Sobek to rather abstract deities with almost no individual characteristics, Tasenetnofret ('the Good Sister/Spouse') and the child-god Panebtawy ('the Lord of the Two Lands'), whose name alludes to the king's role. Sobek's family is exceptional, and the names look Late Egyptian rather than belonging to a subsequent linguistic phase, so that the deities might have existed long before the temple was built (Baines 1997: 231). Kom Ombo thus perfectly demonstrates the continuation and elaboration of theological traditions and the ongoing creative thought processes of the priests, which can be detected in the architecture as well as in the iconography and the texts.

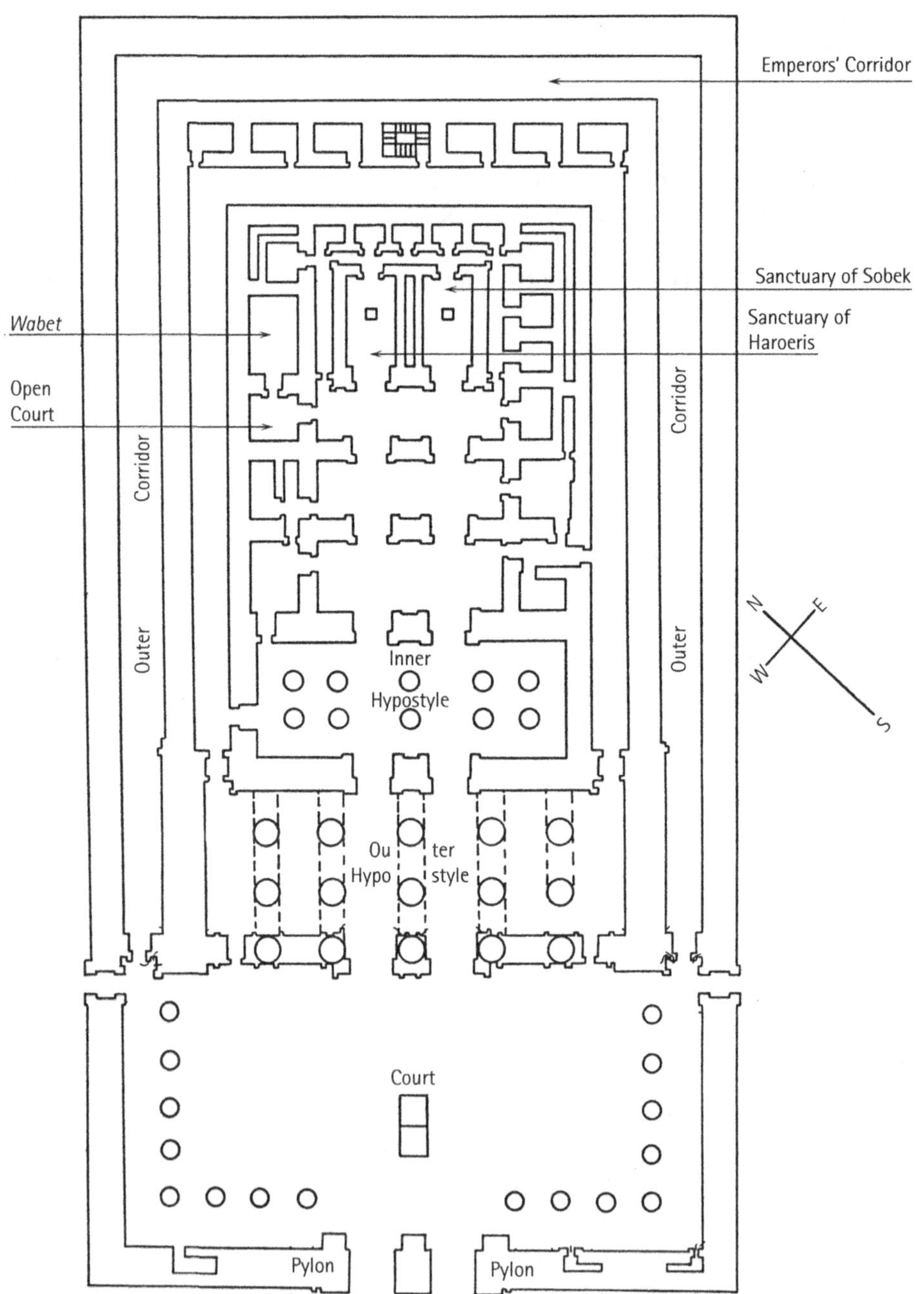

FIG. 22.6 Plan of the temple of Sobek and Haroeris at Kom Ombo

Based on Porter and Moss (1939: 180).

A dual temple, but of a different form, again with abstract concepts of deities, is also found at el-Qal'a, a small, rather well-preserved and richly decorated structure located 600 metres north of the temenos of Min and Isis at Koptos, at the edge of the local region where these gods were worshipped (Pantalacci and Traunecker 1990–8). It has a main east–west axis and was built in limestone, unlike most temples of the period; it was begun during the reign of Augustus and decorated until the time of Claudius. As a small temple (26 × 16 metres), it is 'a kind of an abstract for the architecture of the large temples like Dendera and Edfu' (Traunecker 1997: 170). The main sanctuary is on the west side, surrounded by a corridor that gives access to two chapels and the *wabet* complex. The sanctuary is reached from the east through three halls, an entrance hall, an intermediary room, and the Offering Hall. The temple has a secondary north–south axis, with a small entrance hall to the south of the Offering Hall and a secondary sanctuary to its north, perhaps a birth house for the divine child. The Offering Hall thus served both sanctuaries. As at Kom Ombo, the temple had two axes, but this time not two parallel ones but two perpendicular ones, like the temple of Isis at Dendara. The main goddess of the temple at el-Qal'a, 'Isis, the Great, the Mother of Horus', was also named 'the Great Goddess' during the reign of Augustus, whereas under Claudius this epithet became a deity, so that Isis and 'the Great Goddess' figure separately on the temple walls. A similar process can be observed for the local child-god Harpocrates, who splits into 'the eldest (son) of Amun' and the son of Osiris (Traunecker 1997: 171–6). Neither at el-Qal'a nor at Kom Ombo should this abstraction be taken as a sign of decline in the vitality of the ideas propounded in the temple.

Even if el-Qal'a was a relatively minor sanctuary on the periphery of a city, its theological and cultic system is connected to the small contemporaneous temple at Shanhur, located between Koptos and Thebes, which was influenced by both theological systems, but mainly by the Koptite one. The main goddess of Shanhur is 'the Great Goddess Isis', sometimes abbreviated to 'the Great Goddess'; even the Theban triad is represented in its Koptite variant (Willems et al. 2003). Although Thebes had been a dominant religious centre in earlier times, in the Roman period construction and decoration in the Theban area were confined to smaller temples such as that of Isis at Deir el-Shelwit at the south end of the religious territory of the Theban west bank or relatively modest additions to existing temples. The enormous ancient temples at Thebes were kept in use and extended selectively, but not replaced. The Koptite region, on the other hand, enjoyed particular interest in the Roman period. The quarries of the Eastern Desert were heavily exploited under Roman rule and were supported by a major road system, with Koptos being the principal emporium for the caravan routes to the Red Sea ports, including the route through the Wadi Hammamat. In the remote regions of the Western Desert, especially Kharga and Dakhla (Kaper 1998; Chapter 43), the Roman period is also characterized by the new construction or extension of temples on a large scale. These areas reached a peak of importance and prosperity in the Roman period (Hölbl 2005: 9–101).

Under Augustus the state reconquered part of Lower Nubia and undertook a copious construction programme. Because of its military importance the Dodekaschoinos (the northern part of Lower Nubia) received substantial political and ideological attention. In particular after the peace treaty of Samos (21/20 BCE), when the southern frontier of the Imperium Romanum was established at Hierasykaminos (Maharraqa) and the conflict between Rome and Meroe was brought to an end, an explicit manifestation of the new ruler as pharaoh was required to mark the reincorporation of the region. At Philae, Biga, Debod, Kertassi, Tafa,

Kalabsha, Ajuala, Dendur, Dakka, and Maharraqa, Egyptian temples were built or extended, and in these Augustus appears venerating Egyptian and local Nubian gods (Hölbl 2004b; Verhoeven 2008; Minas-Nerpel 2011). The reign of Augustus exemplifies the pattern of royal involvement in construction to a high degree along the Nile. Under his rule, more temples were initiated and decorated than under any other Roman pharaoh.

A final peak of construction and decoration of Egyptian temples was reached in the reigns of Trajan (98–117), Hadrian (117–38), and Antoninus Pius (138–61), but this was not on the same level as that of Augustus. According to Arnold (1999: 265), the reign of Antoninus Pius was the last productive phase of Egyptian temples of the Roman period. However, under Marcus Aurelius (161–80), Lucius Verus (161–9), and Commodus (180–92), the indigenous temples continued to be extended and decorated far more than Arnold (1999) notes (see Minas-Nerpel forthcoming). Even in the time of Septimius Severus (193–211) and his sons Caracalla (198–217) and Geta (198–211), the temple of Khnum at Esna was further decorated, for example with the significant scene of the Severan family inside the pronaos (Sauneron 1975: 68–70, no. 496; Hölbl 2000: 108–9, fig. 49a–b), which was carved, including the names, when the imperial family visited Egypt (Sauneron 1952). Geta was later erased, demonstrating that the Egyptian priests were informed about his *damnatio memoriae*. Judith McKenzie (2007: 170) notes that, after Antoninus Pius' reign, construction in the Egyptian style in Egyptian temple complexes ceased, while new classical buildings continued to be erected. There may have been a shift in use of resources from Egyptian temples to classical civic buildings and temples, but the Egyptian temples still received enough attention to be extended and further decorated, although on a much smaller scale, until the early third century.

The Roman Emperor as Pharaoh and the Principles of Decoration

The Egyptian temples of the Graeco-Roman period are the principal surviving monuments of the Ptolemies and the Roman emperors in the country, so it seems obvious that these rulers attached great importance to these enormous buildings. The big temples such as Dendara, Edfu, and Kom Ombo are also much larger than anything that went before. Yet these foreign rulers, especially the Romans, knew little of the meaning of these buildings, and they could not read their inscriptions. The building and decoration policy must have been stimulated by the priests and native elite, whose lives focused around the temples, which were fundamental repositories of native Egyptian culture—under Roman rule almost its sole carriers (Baines 1997: 216, 231). At the same time, two different worlds could be joined in a temple complex, the Egyptian and the Hellenic–Roman one, as exemplified by the Greek building inscriptions in Dendara. In addition, outside the main entrance are classical structures, while within the temple of Hathor, the traditionally styled Egyptian decoration dominated. Very few hellenistic features are present in the Egyptian temples proper, for example in the zodiac on the ceiling of one of the Osiris rooftop chapels at Dendara (Cauville 1997a,b). The zodiac is a rather unique planisphere, a map of the stars or the sky on a plane projection in circular form, reflecting Greek and Babylonian influences in astronomy. In the temple, however, the zodiac signs themselves take Egyptian representational form whereas in tombs and on the Soter coffins, some signs are in classical artistic form (Riggs 2005: 201–3).

The Egyptian temples of the Graeco-Roman period were not only architecturally and textually sophisticated, but also decorated and originally painted in very complex ways (for principles of decoration, see Kurth 1994, with bibliography). Despite their provincial locations, many of these temples display a high standard of execution, but they have hardly been studied from an art-historical perspective, with few exceptions, such as Eleni Vassilika's *Ptolemaic Philae* (1989) or Judith McKenzie's *The Architecture of Alexandria and Egypt* (2007: 119–46). New insight into the temple decoration of this period might be gained from an as yet unpublished papyrus from Tanis (Papyrus Bodleian Library Egyptian p. A5–8), which Joachim F. Quack (2010) has recently identified as a handbook for temple decoration, including drawings, written in hieroglyphic script but mainly in Demotic grammar.

Cosmological associations vouchsafed the integrity of the temple, which served as an image of the world (Hornung 1992: 115–29). Every single temple mirrored the entire cosmos and was a microcosmos as well as the earthly residence of the main deity. The Egyptians re-enacted creation by ceremonially founding and constructing a temple, in the process re-establishing *maat*, universal order. The inner sanctuary symbolizes the primeval mound of earth that emerged from the marshy waters at creation. The cosmic dimension of the temple is reflected in the depiction of the ceiling as sky, the plant decoration on the base of the wall, or the columns of the pillared halls, which have the forms of aquatic plants. In the Graeco-Roman period they often have composite capitals, which bring together different vegetal elements (McKenzie 2007: 122–32) and also form a point of contact with the column capitals of classical architecture.

The ritual scenes show two categories of protagonists involved, the Roman emperor as pharaoh in traditional Egyptian regalia and one or several deities. The offerings the king presents are diverse, ranging from real objects, such as food, flowers, or amulets, to symbolic acts like smiting the enemies or presenting *maat*. Further topics of the temple decoration included the festivals, foundation, and protection of the temple and its gods. In their database SERaT, Horst Beinlich and Jochen Hallof (2007) offer an overview of all ritual scenes of the Graeco-Roman period. It was a cultic requirement to show the pharaoh performing the rituals that would guarantee the existence of Egypt. The necessity of this is explained, for example, in the Ptolemaic period Papyrus Jumilhac, a cult handbook from the eighteenth Upper Egyptian nome, which includes a discourse on the importance of maintaining the cults of the deities. If the king and the priests were to fail to do so, Egypt would be obliterated (Vandier 1961: 129–31, col. xvii, line 14–col. xviii, line 21; Derchain 1990).

From the very beginning of Roman rule Octavian was depicted as a pharaoh, as exemplified by the Kalabsha gateway, now reconstructed in Berlin. When the temple of Kalabsha was moved because of the construction of the Aswan High Dam, the gate was discovered reused as building material in the late Augustan temple. The gate had been constructed and decorated before Octavian was even named Augustus in 27 BCE (Winter 2003), which means that this is one of the first buildings to be decorated under Roman rule. In several of the ritual scenes, Octavian offers a field that symbolizes the Dodekaschoinos (Winter 2003: 200, pls 46, 50, scenes 18, 24, 33), reaffirming an ancient donation, a fact that was important for the priests. In reality, Octavian did not present the offerings to the Egyptian gods, especially not the deities in animal form such as the Apis, whom he detested (Minas-Nerpel 2011). As a Roman magistrate whose nominal desire was to serve the Roman republic in theory, he could not assume royal power in a

Roman province. The priests, on the other hand, needed to sustain their religious claims and probably saw through the Roman propaganda: for them, Octavian was simply a ruler. The fictitious role of a cultic pharaoh in the temple decoration was sufficient for them and did not threaten Octavian's republican claims. He and the following Roman emperors officially played a cosmic role in the temple, but it was a theoretical or abstract one (Derchain 1962b).

For the Egyptians, the Roman emperor as the pharaoh still represented the entire world of Egypt in dealings with the divine realm (Otto 1964: 69–74). Although a non-Egyptian, he was in theory the high priest who approached the divine power in order to sustain *maat* and thus the well-being of the world. In everyday rituals the priests fulfilled assigned duties, officially in the name of the king. The pharaoh was the essential element of the iconographic system, but outside the pictorial context he seems to have been conceptually dispensable (Baines 1997: 230–1). The Ptolemies might have regarded it as beneficial to be provided with this religious legitimacy, but Roman emperors do not seem to have been concerned about this, even if they might have minded about being seen to do the proper thing in the temple context. Few emperors visited Egypt, which means that Egypt was not high on their list of priorities. Hölbl (2000: 18, 117; 2004b: 102–5) hence concludes that the Roman emperor should be seen as a 'cultic pharaoh' who had lost his historical significance. The Roman pharaohs were therefore rather timeless, especially since they were rarely present in the country. This seems to be valid for most relief scenes, but a political or historical meaning can be detected in several instances, for example the above-mentioned offering scene at Esna which resulted from a royal visit and exhibits Geta's *damnatio memoriae*.

The fact that those priests responsible for the temple decoration took note of the identity and the standing of the emperor is further demonstrated by Galba's cartouches at Ain Birbiya in Dakhla Oasis. The change of his name from Lucius Galba Caesar to Servius Galba Imperator Caesar Augustus, resulting from the events in Rome in September 68, and the names' unusual phonetic features on the western, or rear, wall of the sanctuary remarkably demonstrate the priests' alert allegiance. In the name of Galba, the letter *l* is consistently rendered as *m*, which is unparalleled, since *l* would usually be rendered with an Egyptian *r*, as for example in the names of Ptolemy and Cleopatra when written in hieroglyphs. According to Olaf Kaper (2010: 195), these details suggest that the secular authorities were closely involved in the execution of the temple decoration, as they were roughly 150 years later at Esna. Kaper has further established that the depiction of the Roman pharaoh with his full name in hieroglyphs was still of vital importance, but the spelling of the name could be adapted according to local preferences (Kaper 2010: 199).

Some of the most interesting 'historical–political' ritual scenes were carved between the second half of the second century to the second decade of the third century CE in the temple of Kom Ombo, on the inner east face of the outer corridor at the back of the temple (de Morgan 1902, nos 946–56; Porter and Moss 1939: 197, nos 228–31; Hölbl 2000: 94–9, figs 119, 121–5), now called the 'Emperors' Corridor' (Figs 22.6 and 22.7). On the northern half of the wall (Porter and Moss 1939, nos 228–9), seven ritual scenes depict Marcus Aurelius (161–80) either as the sole ruler or accompanied by his co-regent Lucius Verus (161–9). The southern half (Porter and Moss 1939, nos 230–1) has only three scenes, of which the earliest are the two northern ones, bearing the cartouches of Commodus (180–92). In each case, parts of his name were erased, exhibiting his *damnatio memoriae* and reflecting developments that affected the Roman world as far as the indigenous temples in Egypt. The latest relief scene on this wall was decorated under Macrinus Augustus and his son Diadumenianus (217–18), who is otherwise not attested in Egyptian temples. The southern half of the Emperors' Corridor follows a pattern known from elsewhere, that the ambulatory would be decorated from the middle to the outer edges: since the first scene shows Marcus Aurelius with his co-regent, we can assume that the last one on the northern half was carved after the death of Lucius Verus, that is, between 169 and 180. The empty panels on the southern half show that the decoration of the corridor (and the temple) was abandoned after the death of Diadumenianus. Even if Egyptian temples received less attention than before, the degree of historical and political reflection in such an atmosphere, as exemplified in the Emperors' Corridor, is still quite impressive, but the style is arguably less accomplished and more 'provincial' than earlier in the empire, thus reflecting the general decline in funding and requisite artistic skills in the Egyptian temples.

The amount of temple decoration that was executed decreased rapidly in the third century CE. Frankfurter (1998: 27) states that 'the Egyptian temples were doomed to follow the empire's downward spiral in the various economic catastrophes of the third century'. This does not take into account the fact that construction work on classical buildings continued in Egypt during the third century, with a considerable amount being spent during the middle and later third century (McKenzie 2007: 170, 399 n. 96). The shift to classical forms in the

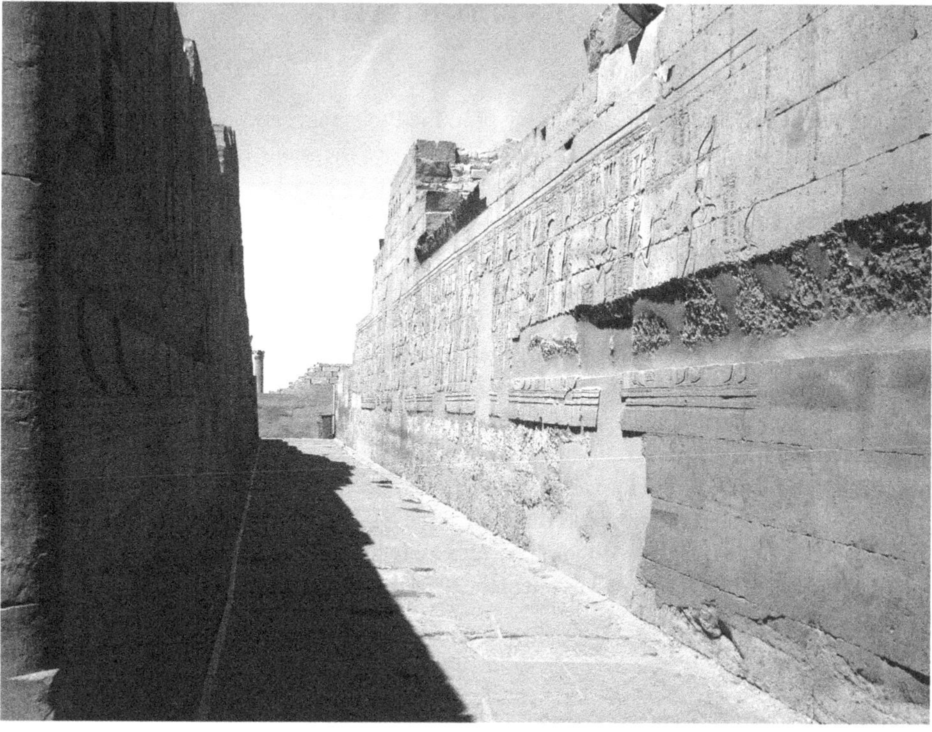

FIG. 22.7 The Emperors' Corridor at the temple of Sobek and Haroeris, Kom Ombo, viewed from the south

Author's photograph.

third century reflects a shift in the focus of attention, and paved the way for the decline of religious centres in the fourth century.

Conclusion

In a rather smooth transition from the Ptolemaic to the Roman period, Egyptian temples continued to be built and decorated well into the second century CE and, on a much smaller scale, into the beginning of the fourth century. The Egyptian temples of the Graeco-Roman period mostly survive from Athribis in Middle Egypt up the Nile, including the Dodekaschoinos, and also in the deserts, mainly in the Kharga and Dakhla oases. The temples and their decoration were highly systematized, but theological and architectural variations were prevalent. The Roman pharaoh was the essential element of their iconographic system, but outside the pictorial context of the Egyptian temples he seems to have been conceptually dispensable. The Roman emperors therefore primarily played a rather fictitious role as 'cultic' pharaohs, though historical–political facts were reflected in the cult reliefs and inscriptions as late as the beginning of the fourth century.

Suggested Reading

In their archaeological introduction to Egypt in the Ptolemaic and Roman periods, Bagnall and Rathbone (2004) provide a cursory description of the main Egyptian temples. Hölbl (2000, 2004b, 2005) presents a detailed overview of the Egyptian temples of the Roman period with excellent photographs in three volumes and also discusses the perception of the Roman emperors as 'cultic' pharaohs. Minas-Nerpel (2011) examines Octavian-Augustus as pharaoh in detail and is preparing a thorough study on all Roman pharaohs as reflected in the Egyptian temples. Finnestad (1997) supplies a valuable introduction to the social and cultural context of the Graeco-Roman period temples. For general architectural studies, see Arnold (1999) and also McKenzie (2007), who looks at both the classical and the Egyptian temples, while Coppens (2007) illuminates the *wabet*, a specific architectural feature of Egyptian temples in the Graeco-Roman period, and its cultic significance. Kurth's (2004b) short book on the building inscription of the temple of Horus at Edfu offers easy access to the long hieroglyphic text in translation and its interpretation. It is thus a valuable insight into how Egyptians of the Ptolemaic period thought. Cauville (1990a) provides a French translation and rather specialized interpretation of the building inscription of the temple of Hathor at Dendara.

Bibliography

Amer, H. I., and B. Morardet. 1983. 'Les dates de la construction du temple majeur d'Hathor à Dendara à l'époque gréco-romaine', *Annales du Service des Antiquités de l'Égypte* 69: 255–8.

Arnold, D. 1999. *Temples of the Last Pharaohs*. New York: Oxford University Press.

Bagnall, R. S., and D. W. Rathbone. 2004. *Egypt from Alexander to the Copts: An Archaeological and Historical Guide*. London: British Museum Press.

Baines, J. 1994. 'King, Temple, and Cosmos: An Earlier Model for Framing Columns in the Temple Scenes of the Greco-Roman Period', in M. Minas and J. Zeidler (eds), *Aspekte spätägyptischer Kultur: Festschrift für Erich Winter zum 65. Geburtstag*. Mainz: von Zabern, 23–33.

——1997. 'Temples as Symbols, Guarantors, and Participants in Egyptian Civilization', in S. Quirke (ed.), *The Temple in Ancient Egypt: New Discoveries and Recent Research*. London: British Museum Press, 216–41.

Beinlich, H., and J. Hallof. 2007. *Einführung in das Würzburger Datenbanksystem SERaT*. Dettelbach: Röll.

Bernand, A. 1984. *Les portes du désert: Recueil des inscriptions grecques d'Antinooupolis, Tentyris, Koptos, Apollonopolis Parva et Apollonopolis Magna*. Paris: Centre National de la Recherche Scientifique.

Cauville, S. 1990a. 'Les inscriptions dédicatoires du temple d'Hathor à Dendera', *Bulletin de l'Institut Français d'Archéologie Orientale* 90: 83–114.

——1990b. *Le Temple de Dendera: Guide archéologique*. Cairo: Institut Français d'Archéologie Orientale du Caire.

——1997a. *Le Temple de Dendara: Les chapelles osiriennes*, Dendara X/1. Cairo: Institut Français d'Archéologie Orientale.

——1997b. *Le Temple de Dendara: Les chapelles osiriennes: Transcription et traduction*, 3 vols. Cairo: Institut Français d'Archéologie Orientale.

——1997c. *Le Zodiaque d'Osiris*. Leuven: Peeters.

——1999. *Le Temple de Dendara: La porte d'Isis*. Cairo: Institut Français d'Archéologie Orientale.

——2002. *Dendara: Les fêtes d'Hathor*. Leuven: Peeters.

——2007. *Dendara: Le temple d'Isis* I–II. Cairo: Institut Français d'Archéologie Orientale.

Chassinat, É. 1966–8. *Le mystère d'Osiris au mois de Khoiak*. Cairo: Institut Français d'Archéologie Orientale.

Coppens, F. 2007. *The Wabet: Tradition and Innovation in the Temples of the Ptolemaic and Roman Period*. Prague: Czech Institute of Egyptology, Charles University.

——2009. 'Temple Festivals of the Ptolemaic and Roman Periods', in J. Dieleman and W. Wendrich (eds), *UCLA Encyclopedia of Egyptology*. Los Angeles. <http://escholarship.org/uc/item/4cd7q9mn>.

Daumas, F. 1958. *Les mammisis des temples égyptiens*. Paris: Belles Lettres.

——1974. 'Le temple de Dendera', in *Textes et langages de l'Égypte pharaonique*, vol. 3. Cairo: Institut Français d'Archéologie Orientale, 267–73.

de Morgan, Jacques. 1902. *Catalogue des monuments et inscriptions de l'Égypte antique: Première série: Haute Égypte III, Kom Ombos* 2. Vienna: Holzhausen.

Derchain, P. 1962a. 'Un manuel de géographie liturgique à Edfou', *Chronique d'Égypte* 37: 31–65.

——1962b. 'Le rôle du roi d'Égypte dans le maintien de l'ordre cosmique', in L. de Heusch et al. (eds), *Le pouvoir et le sacré*. Brussels: Université Libre de Bruxelles, Institut de Sociologie, 61–73.

——1990. 'L'auteur du Papyrus Jumilhac', *Revue d'Égyptologie* 41: 9–30.

Dijkstra, J. H. F. 2008. *Philae and the End of Ancient Egyptian Religion: A Regional Study of Religious Transformation (298–642 CE)*. Leuven: Peeters.

Elgawady, K. M. 2010. *Die Schranken in den ägyptischen Tempeln der griechisch-römischen Zeit*, doctoral dissertation, University of Trier.

Fairman, H. W. 1943. 'Notes on the Alphabetic Signs Employed in the Hieroglyphic Inscriptions of the Temple of Edfu', *Annales du Service des Antiquités de l'Égypte* 43: 193–310.

Fairman, H. W. 1945. 'An Introduction to the Study of Ptolemaic Signs and their Value', *Bulletin de l'Institut Français d'Archéologie Orientale* 43: 51–138.

Finnestad, R. B. 1985. *Image of the World and Symbol of the Creator: On the Cosmological and Iconological Values of the Temple of Edfu*. Wiesbaden: Harrassowitz.

——1997. 'Temples of the Ptolemaic and Roman Periods: Ancient Traditions in New Context', in B. E. Shafer (ed.), *Temples of Ancient Egypt*. Ithaca, NY: Cornell University Press, 185–237 (text), 302–17 (notes).

Frankfurter, D. 1998. *Religion in Roman Egypt: Assimilation and Resistance*. Princeton: Princeton University Press.

Goldbrunner, L. 2004. *Buchis: Eine Untersuchung zur Theologie des heiligen Stieres in Theben zur griechisch-römischen Zeit*. Turnhout: Brepols.

Graefe, E. 1991. 'Über die Verarbeitung von Pyramidentexten in den späten Tempeln', in U. Verhoeven and E. Graefe (eds), *Religion und Philosophie im alten Ägypten: Festgabe für Philippe Derchain zu seinem 65. Geburtstag am 24. Juli 1991*. Leuven: Peeters, 129–48.

Grenier, J.-C. 1980. *Temples ptolémaïques et romains: Répertoire bibliographique: Index des citations 1955–1974, incluant l'index des citations de 1939 à 1954 réunies par N. Sauneron*. Cairo: Institut Français d'Archéologie Orientale.

Hallof, J. 2010. *Schreibungen der Pharaonennamen in den Ritualszenen der Tempel der griechisch-römischen Zeit Ägyptens*, vol. 1: *Die griechischen Könige*, vol. 2: *Die römischen Kaiser*. Dettelbach: Röll.

Heinen, H. 2007. 'Ägypten im römischen Reich: Beobachtungen zum Thema Akkulturation und Identität', in S. Pfeiffer (ed.), *Ägypten unter fremden Herrschern zwischen persischer Satrapie und römischer Provinz*. Frankfurt: Antike, 186–207.

Herklotz, F. 2007. *Prinzeps und Pharao: Der Kult des Augustus in Ägypten*. Frankfurt: Antike.

Hölbl, G. 2000. *Altägypten im Römischen Reich: Der römische Pharao und sein Tempel*, vol. 1. Mainz: von Zabern.

——2004a. 'Die römischen Kaiser und das ägyptische Königtum', in P. C. Bol, G. Kaminski, and C. Maderna (eds), *Fremdheit—Eigenheit: Ägypten, Griechenland und Rom: Austausch und Verständnis*. Stuttgart: Scheufele, 525–35.

——2004b. *Altägypten im Römischen Reich: Der römische Pharao und sein Tempel*, vol. 2: *Tempel des römischen Nubien*. Mainz: von Zabern.

——2005. *Altägypten im Römischen Reich: Der römische Pharao und sein Tempel*, vol. 3: *Heiligtümer und religiöses Leben in den ägyptischen Wüsten und Oasen*. Mainz: von Zabern.

Hornung, E. 1992. *Idea into Image: Essays on Ancient Egyptian Thought*. New York: Timken.

Junker, H. 1906. *Grammatik der Denderatexte*. Leipzig: Hinrichs.

Kaper, O. 1998. 'Temple Building in the Egyptian Deserts during the Roman Period', in O. Kaper (ed.), *Life on the Fringe: Living in the Southern Egyptian Deserts during the Roman and Early-Byzantine Periods*. Leiden: Research School CNWS, 139–58.

——2010. 'Galba's Cartouches at Ain Birbiyeh', in K. Lembke, M. Minas-Nerpel, and S. Pfeiffer (eds), *Tradition and Transformation: Egypt under Roman Rule*. Leiden: Brill, 181–201.

Kockelmann, H., and S. Pfeiffer. 2009. 'Betrachtungen zur Dedikation von Tempeln und Tempelteilen in ptolemäischer und römischer Zeit', in R. Eberhard et al. (eds), '*... vor dem Papyrus sind alle gleich!*': *Papyrologische Beiträge zu Ehren von Bärbel Kramer (P. Kramer)*. Berlin: de Gruyter, 93–104.

Kurth, D. 1994. 'Die Friese innerhalb der Tempeldekoration griechisch-römischer Zeit', in M. Minas and J. Zeidler (eds), *Aspekte spätägyptischer Kultur: Festschrift für Erich Winter zum 65. Geburtstag*. Mainz: von Zabern, 191–201.

——1997. 'The Present State of Research into Greco-Roman Temples', in S. Quirke (ed.), *The Temple in Ancient Egypt: New Discoveries and Recent Research*. London: British Museum Press, 152–8.

——2004a. 'A World Order in Stone: The Late Temple', in R. Schulz and M. Seidel (eds), *Egypt: The World of the Pharaohs*. Königswinter: Könemann, 296–311.

——2004b. *The Temple of Edfu: A Guide by an Egyptian Priest*. Cairo: American University in Cairo Press.

——2007–8. *Einführung ins Ptolemäische: Eine Grammatik mit Zeichenliste und Übungsstücken*, 2 vols. Hützel: Backe.

Leitz, C. 2001. *Die Aussenwand des Sanktuars in Dendera: Untersuchungen zur Dekorationssystematik*. Mainz: von Zabern.

——2002. *Kurzbibliographie zu den übersetzten Tempeltexten der griechisch-römischen Zeit*. Cairo: Institut Français d'Archéologie Orientale.

——2004. *Die Tempelinschriften der griechisch-römischen Zeit*. Münster: Lit.

——D. Mendel, and Y. el-Masry. 2010. *Der Tempel Ptolemaios XII: Die Inschriften und Reliefs der Opfersäle, des Umgangs und der Sanktuarräume*, 3 vols. Cairo: Institut Français d'Archéologie Orientale.

Lewis, N. 1970. '"Greco-Roman Egypt": Fact or Fiction?', in D. H. Samuel (ed.), *Proceedings of the Twelfth International Congress of Papyrology*. Toronto: Hakkert, 3–14.

Louant, E. 2003. 'Les fêtes au mammisi', *Égypte, Afrique & Orient* 32: *Les Fêtes égyptiennes d'après les temples d' époque tardive*, 31–48.

McKenzie, J. 2007. *The Architecture of Alexandria and Egypt, c.300 BCE to CE 700*. New Haven: Yale University Press.

Manning, J. G. 2003. *Land and Power in Ptolemaic Egypt: The Structure of Land Tenure*. Cambridge: Cambridge University Press.

Minas-Nerpel, M. 2006. 'Die ptolemäischen Sokar-Osiris-Mumien: Neue Erkenntnisse zum ägyptischen Dynastiekult der Ptolemäer', *Mitteilungen des Deutschen Archäologischen Instituts, Abteilung Kairo* 62: 197–215.

——2011. 'Augustus, Prinzeps und Pharao zwischen politischer Realität und ideologischem Anspruch', in G. Moosbauer and R. Wiegels (eds), *Fines Imperii, Imperium Sine Fine? Roman Frontier and Occupation Policies in the Early Principate*. Rahden: Marie Leidorf GmbH, 131–42.

——Forthcoming. *Politics and Propaganda: The Roman Emperor and the Egyptian Temples*.

——et al. Forthcoming. *The Temple of Shanhûr* II. Leuven: Peeters.

Monson, A. 2005. 'Sacred Land in Ptolemaic and Roman Tebtunis', in S. Lippert and M. Schentuleit (eds), *Tebtynis und Soknopaiu Nesos: Leben im römerzeitlichen Fajum*. Wiesbaden: Harrassowitz, 79–91.

Otto, E. 1964. *Gott und Mensch nach den ägyptischen Tempelinschriften der griechisch-römischen Zeit*. Heidelberg: Carl Wintzer Universitätsverlag.

Pantalacci, L., and C. Traunecker. 1990–8. *Le temple d'El-Qal'a* I–II. Cairo: Institut Français d'Archéologie Orientale.

Pfeiffer, S. 2004. *Das Dekret von Kanopos (238 v. Chr.): Kommentar und historische Auswertung eines dreisprachigen Synodaldekretes der ägyptischen Priester zu Ehren Ptolemaios' III. und seiner Familie*. Munich: Saur.

Porter, B., and R. L. B. Moss. 1939. *Topographical Bibliography of Ancient Egyptian Hieroglyphic Texts, Reliefs, and Paintings*, vol. 6: *Upper Egypt: Chief Temples*. Oxford: Clarendon Press.

Preys, R. 2009. 'Le vautour, le cobra et l'œil: Jeu de mots et jeu des signes autour d'une déesse', in W. Claes et al. (eds), *Elkab and Beyond: Studies in Honour of Luc Limme*. Leuven: Peeters, 477–84.

Quack, J. F. 2009. 'Die Theologisierung der bürokratischen Norm: Zur Baubeschreibung in Edfu im Vergleich zum Buch vom Tempel', in R. Preys (ed.), *7. Ägyptologische Tempeltagung: Structuring Religion*. Wiesbaden: Harrassowitz, 221–9.

——2010. 'Was ist das "Ptolemäische"?', *Welt des Orients* 40/1: 70–92.

Raven, M. J. 1982. 'Corn-Mummies', *Oudheidkundige Mededelingen uit het Rijksmuseum van Oudheden te Leiden* 63: 7–38.

Riggs, C. 2005. *The Beautiful Burial in Roman Egypt: Art, Identity, and Funerary Religion*. Oxford: Oxford University Press.

Sauneron, S. 1952. 'Les querelles impériales vues à travers les scènes du temple d'Esné', *Bulletin de l'Institut Français d'Archéologie Orientale* 51: 111–21.

——1975. *Le temple d'Esna* VI/1: *Nos. 473–546*. Cairo: Institut Français d'Archéologie Orientale.

Shore, A. F. 1979. 'Votive Objects from Dendera of the Greco-Roman Period', in G. A. Gaballa, K. A. Kitchen, and J. Ruffle (eds), *Glimpses of Ancient Egypt: Studies in Honour of H. W. Fairman*. Warminster: Aris and Phillips, 138–60.

Traunecker, C. 1997. 'Lessons from the Upper Egyptian Temple of el-Qal'a', in S. Quirke (ed.), *The Temple in Ancient Egypt: New Discoveries and Recent Research*. London: British Museum Press, 168–78.

Vandier, J. 1961. *Le papyrus Jumilhac*. Paris: Centre National de la Recherche Scientifique.

Vassilika, E. 1989. *Ptolemaic Philae*. Leuven: Peeters.

Verhoeven, U. 2008. 'Neue Tempel für Ägypten: Spuren des Augustus von Dendera bis Dendur', in D. Kreikenbom (ed.), *Augustus—Der Blick von aussen: Die Wahrnehmung des Kaisers in den Provinzen des Reiches und in den Nachbarstaaten*. Wiesbaden: Harrassowitz, 229–48.

Waitkus, W. 1997. *Die Texte in den unteren Krypten des Hathortemples von Dendera: Ihre Aussagen zur Funktion und Bedeutung dieser Räume*. Mainz: von Zabern.

Willems, H., et al. 2003. *The Temple of Shanhûr* I. Leuven: Peeters.

Wilson, P. 1997. *A Ptolemaic Lexicon: A Lexicographical Study of the Texts in the Temple of Edfu*. Leuven: Peeters.

Winter, E. 1968. *Untersuchungen zu den ägyptischen Tempelreliefs der griechisch-römischen Zeit*. Vienna: Böhlhaus.

——1982. 'Philae', in W. Helck and E. Otto (eds), *Lexikon der Ägyptologie*, vol. 4. Wiesbaden: Harrassowitz, 1022–7.

——1987. 'Weitere Beobachtungen zur "grammaire du temple" in der griechisch-römischen Zeit', in W. Helck (ed.), *Tempel und Kult*. Wiesbaden: Harrassowitz, 61–76.

——1989. 'A Reconsideration of the Newly Discovered Building Inscription of the Temple of Denderah', *Göttinger Miszellen* 108: 75–85.

——1995. 'Zeitgleiche Textparallelen in verschiedenen Tempeln', in D. Kurth (ed.), *Systeme und Programme der ägyptischen Tempeldekoration: 3. Ägyptologische Tempeltagung, Hamburg, 1.–5. Juni 1994*. Wiesbaden: Harrassowitz, 305–19.

——2003. 'Octavian/Augustus als Soter, Euergetes und Epiphanes: Die Datierung des Kalabscha-Tores', *Zeitschrift für Ägyptische Sprache und Altertumskunde* 130: 197–212.

CHAPTER 23

FUNERARY RELIGION

The Final Phase of an Egyptian Tradition

MARTIN ANDREAS STADLER

Egyptian funerary religion overwhelmingly dominates our view of ancient Egypt throughout all periods of its history, because major parts of the material culture stem from burials and commemorative contexts. Bearing this bias in mind, the starting point of this chapter is a mummy breastplate made of linen stiffened with plaster (cartonnage), which probably dates to the early Roman period (Fig. 23.1; see Zauzich 2002: 57–8; Stadler 2005: 144–5). It epitomizes the key issues in studying funerary religion during the Roman period. It once formed part of an ensemble consisting of a mask, this shield over the breast, a further overlay for the legs, and a foot case. Such ensembles replaced a complete mummiform coffin in some regions of Egypt (Grimm 1974: 45), but in this case it is more likely that the mummy and the ensemble were placed in a coffin, because the mummy shield is too well preserved to have lain unprotected in a burial. The breastplate under consideration here is a very finely painted specimen which shows several stages of the deceased's journey to the hereafter (from bottom to top): the transport of the mummy in a boat, the embalming, and the judgement of the dead. Above these vignettes is a winged scarab alluding to the newborn sun and the scarab on the corpse of Osiris (Stadler 2001a: 82–3), and two assemblies combining Heliopolitan (solar) and Osirian deities. The upper part comprises a painting of a so-called *wesekh* collar—made out of multiple rows of beads of various forms and materials (Riggs 2001)—and finally a falcon whose head is lost. That central part is framed by two columns. The column on the viewer's left (the right side, from the perspective of the mummy beneath) shows twenty-one mummiform figures armed with knives, which stress their apotropaic nature. On the opposite side a hieroglyphic column reads as follows: 'Greetings to (you), Atum, greetings to (you) Khepri. You have been exalted after having appeared (on top of) the *benben* stone in the House of the *Benu* bird in Heliopolis, Osiris Hor, son of Paiun, borne by Tjeset, justified.'

The text's brevity belies its meaningfulness as it is an abridged version of a spell that is found as spell 600 in the Pyramid Texts (PT), first attested some 2,300 years earlier. The Pyramid Texts are the oldest large corpus of religious texts in human history; they comprise recitation texts for both the king's burial rites and his (in theory) eternal mortuary cult, as well

FIG. 23.1 Mummy breastplate inscribed for a man named Hor, late Ptolemaic to early Roman period. The Egyptian design depicts the stages of the deceased's transformation in the afterlife, including his mummification and judgement. The hieroglyphic inscription (viewer's right) derives from religious texts dating to the third millennium BCE. Painted openwork cartonnage. Height 43 cm, width 30 cm

Martin von Wagner Museum der Julius-Maximilians University, Würzburg, A 201. Copyright the Martin von Wagner Museum der Julius-Maximilians University, Würzburg.

as texts for use during his afterlife. PT 600 tells us how the creator god transferred the vital forces to his two children, Shu and Tefnut, by embracing them (Allen 2005: 269), and captions to the ritual scenes in Ptolemaic and Roman temples adapted this spell to combine it with the offering of a *wesekh* collar, which embraces and vitalizes its wearer (Graefe 1991). The hieroglyphic column on the mummy breastplate thus explains the funerary significance of the depicted *wesekh* collar. Textual sources also help us to understand the significance of the other images. The judgement scene refers to chapter 125 of the Book of the Dead (BD) (Stadler 2008a), and the twenty-one apotropaic demons, guards to the twenty-one gates to the netherworld, stem from BD 145 and 146, which provide the necessary knowledge to pass by those gates (Stadler 2009b: 264–314). Whereas BD 125 is first attested in the New Kingdom (1550–1070/69 BCE), the idea of gates to the netherworld goes back as far as the Middle Kingdom (2119–1794 BCE) if not further (Stadler 2009b: 252–63, 274–8). With its references to ancient texts, the presence of the solar as well as the Osirian dimension, and the mobilization of the creation myths, the cartonnage breastplate demonstrates the longevity of Egyptian funerary religion. It also exemplifies the two types of evidence—textual and visual—to be taken into account for understanding Egyptian funerary religion.

As the breastplate's iconography and inscription demonstrate, continuity seems to be an essential feature of Egyptian funerary religion. Consequently, funerary religion in the Roman period cannot be understood without a profound familiarity with the long-standing history of Egyptian religion in general going back as far as the twenty-fourth century BCE, when the Pyramid Texts were carved onto the walls of the inner chambers of King Unas' pyramid at Saqqara. Although this corpus might seem to be quite remote from the period studied in this volume, there are more texts, other than the breastplate, which date to Ptolemaic and Roman times and cite from the Pyramid Texts (Szczudłowska 1973; Assmann, Bommas, and Kucharek 2008: 227–498; Smith 2009a: 16–17, 650–62). The textual tradition concords with an artistic archaism that is a recurrent feature of the funerary art of Roman Egypt (Riggs 2005, 2006) and which also characterizes the aforementioned breastplate, as any trace of Greek or Roman art is absent in its design. Tradition and continuity, however, should not be understood as a lack of change, nor as any less self-conscious than innovation. Despite this, scholarly debate has tended to focus on the *degree* of continuity or change in Egyptian funerary religion from the Pharaonic to the Roman periods. One aim of this chapter is to review this discussion critically, and argue that any attempt to measure a degree of change brings with it an element of subjectivity.

The Sources: Language, Dates, and Provenance

The source basis of this chapter is chiefly textual, and its main focus lies in material that is written in Egyptian. From this follows the basic assumption that those who chose Egyptian texts and Egyptian-style objects for their tomb equipment, or opted for the specific Egyptian way of mummification, wanted to be considered as Egyptians or to be part of the Egyptian culture for their afterlife. This is one of many examples of the ways in which identity is situational and negotiable, but the complex question of ethnicity and its influence on the sources will not be discussed further here (see Chapter 16; Collombert 2000; Riggs 2005: 18–23). Furthermore, although works of art and modes of mummification and burial are essential for the study of Egyptian funerary religion, these topics are considered elsewhere in this volume.

Despite the various scripts in which the texts are notated (hieroglyphic, hieratic, and Demotic; see Chapter 33), these sources are taken as one corpus (see Smith 2009a). Most manuscripts are written in hieratic, and some are in Demotic; the two Rhind papyri (*P Rhind* I and II) contain the same text in two versions, one hieratic, the other Demotic (Möller 1913; Smith 2009a: 302–48). The language, as opposed to the script, of all the texts can be either

Middle Egyptian, Demotic with archaisms taken from Middle Egyptian, or a 'pure' Demotic. Although the majority of hieratic texts were authored in Middle Egyptian, Demoticisms, i.e. features of the current language, may intrude. Graphically Demotic texts may be linguistically Demotic (among them translations from Middle Egyptian) or in rare cases Middle Egyptian.

The careful identification of these features may give a clue to the age of a particular text, using a methodology described by Hoffmann (Chapter 33). Bearing this in mind, the textual sources concerning Egyptian funerary religion can be divided into two groups: (A) Roman manuscripts of older texts, which are valuable evidence for which ideas were still current in Roman Egypt, and (B) texts whose date of composition is more recent, potentially contemporary to the act of writing. For group A, palaeography (albeit notoriously unreliable in terms of an absolute dating; see Coenen 2001 for examples) can be used as a chronological criterion, if internal evidence, such as an introductory section or a colophon telling us when the papyrus was inscribed, is lacking. Papyri chiefly qualify for group B, if the language of the text with which they are inscribed is Demotic. Significant Demotic influence on the language of a given text which is otherwise written in Middle Egyptian is not necessarily a symptom of a late composition, as texts are not transmitted exactly over the centuries, but may undergo a substantial change through the scribe's adaptation of the actual language (Smith 2009a: 20–2; Stadler 2009a; 2009b: 47–50). Even purely Demotic texts might be translations from Middle Egyptian whose original is lost or not yet known. Dating texts based on linguistic criteria must therefore regard this caveat.

Those sources that are likely to have been authored in the Roman period have a particular significance, for they offer insights into the ongoing productivity of the indigenous scribes. Arranging in a table the corpus that Smith (2009a) has collected, which is representative but not comprehensive, and looking at the range of dates assigned to the manuscripts, there appear to be no elaborate manuscripts with funerary compositions attested after 150 CE (Stadler forthcoming). Therefore, it is difficult to judge the extent to which the intellectual conceptualization of Egyptian funerary religion persisted after 150 CE. Later texts are significantly shorter than those of the first centuries BCE and CE, at which point the short so-called Letters, or rather Documents, for Breathing appear, characterized by the formula 'May his/her *ba* live for ever' (Stadler 2004, forthcoming; Smith 2009a: 557–68). The same formula appears on mummy labels, the latest dated example of which was written around 275 CE in Akhmim, making it one of the last textual witnesses for Egyptian funerary religion (Arlt 2011). But such conclusions are to be drawn cautiously, because the relative chronology of the individual texts is unknown in most cases. At the moment, however, it seems as if funerary texts in Egyptian ceased to exist well before the demise of vernacular writing systems in Egypt in the mid-fifth century CE (Stadler 2008b).

As to the provenances of the relevant compositions, there is a noteworthy focus on the Thebaid. Reckoning on the basis of pages that Smith in his anthology (2009a) devotes to the individual texts, 65 per cent of the corpus is attested in that region, many texts even exclusively. The only other area of some importance is Akhmim and Antaeopolis: approximately 23 per cent stem from both places taken together. What is remarkable is the absence of sites such as Soknopaiou Nesos, which is one of the most important find spots for Demotic papyri in the Roman period. This might be due to the lack of scientific exploration in the necropolis there. Only one text, the 'Recitations of the Glorifications, which the Two Sisters Performed'—a funerary liturgy which is considered to be an adaptation from an Osiris ritual—is also attested in a parallel manuscript from Tebtunis, the other important site in terms of Egyptian papyri from the Roman period. But, as a temple manuscript, this might be evidence for the composition's original context (*P Carlsb.* 589 = *PSI* I 104 = *P Berlin* 29022; von Lieven 2006b; Hoffmann 2008; Smith 2009a: 124–34; Vittmann 2009: 186–8).

When using texts to study Egyptian funerary religion in the Roman period, some sources from the Ptolemaic period should not be ruled out. For example, the papyrus of Imhotep son of Pasherentaihet (Metropolitan Museum of Art *P MMA* 35.9.21; Goyon 1999; Smith 2009a: 67–95, 135–66) dates to the late fourth century BCE. Its first section, the 'Decree to the Nome of the Silent Land' (see Beinlich 2009 for a further Ptolemaic parallel), which establishes Osiris as ruler of the underworld, also appears in part, naming the deceased, rather than Osiris, on contemporaneous funerary stelae, but also in an abridged Demotic version inscribed on an ostracon from the first century BCE (*O Stras.* D 132 + 133 + 134; Smith 2009a: 599–609; 2010). The early Roman date of the ostracon justifies including the 'Decree to the Nome of the Silent Land' among the relevant sources. Furthermore, the 'Decree' confirms certain information reported in Plutarch's *De Iside et Osiride* (Quack 2004; Smith 2009a: 74–5). Plutarch's familiarity with the text shows that these ideas persisted into at least the second century CE. Hence—just as for earlier epochs (Smith 2009b)—it would not be prudent to draw a sharp borderline between the Ptolemaic and the Roman periods in studying funerary religion. It seems to be more appropriate to perceive it as a developing continuum. Such an approach is supported by further Ptolemaic textual sources that are also attested after 30 BCE (Stadler forthcoming).

Returning to Thebes as the primary find spot of funerary texts in Roman Egypt, Egyptologists may see a parallel with the Theban role in the formation process of the Book of the Dead, which was the most popular collection of funerary spells for almost 1,500 years (Gestermann 2004, 2006; Stadler 2009b: 98–9, 103–4; trans. Allen 1974). The Theban region was also marked by conservatism and a strong local identity, which resulted in a certain resistance against the Alexandrian government during the Ptolemaic period and an ongoing insistence on Egyptian traditions (Blasius 2002; von Recklinghausen 2007). The textual evidence corroborates the same intellectual atmosphere in the sphere of funerary beliefs, parallel to the archaizing trend of funerary art in Roman Thebes (Riggs 2005, 2006). Even in Thebes, however, the Book of the Dead as the most prominent Egyptian corpus of funerary spells was superseded and finally replaced by other compositions in the Ptolemaic period, from around 200 BCE onward (Coenen 2001). Among those the Documents for Breathing (Herbin 2008; Smith 2009a: 462–525), the Books of Transformation (Smith 2009a: 610–49), and the Book of Traversing Eternity (Herbin 1994; Smith 2009a: 395–436) were the most prominent and widespread texts. The situation concerning the Book of the Dead in other Egyptian areas, especially in Memphis, is difficult to ascertain; the limited documentation may be significant, or an accident of preservation (see Mosher 1992). Nevertheless, the spells from the Book of the Dead were not completely forgotten about in Thebes; for instance, a first- to second-century CE papyrus in Berlin (*P Berlin* 3030) combines younger funerary compositions with BD 162 and 72, as does the contemporary *P Louvre* N 3148 (Herbin 1984; Smith 2009a: 592–3). Furthermore, BD 125, the 'negative confession' in the hall of judgement, not only was adapted in the Document for Breathing which Isis Made for her Brother Osiris (Herbin 1994: 25–7, pl. 30; Smith 2009a: 474–5), but also survived in a Demotic translation that was written down in Thebes in 63 CE, as stated in its colophon (*P Paris* BN 149; Stadler 2003; Smith 2009a: 437–54).

Yet extensive manuscripts of the Book of the Dead are not attested in Roman Thebes, and the isolated spells that are also occasionally found in other manuscripts do not suggest an ongoing and general circulation of the Book of the Dead (see Quack 2009: 617–21). Therefore, it would be misleading to speak of Book of the Dead papyri being written in the Theban area during the Roman period. The latest Book of the Dead papyri come from Akhmim; they have been dated to the first century BCE on stylistic grounds and because, judging from the degree of the text's corruption, some scholars think that the scribes referred to damaged and fragmented source documents, which they would not have done if better ones had been available (thus Mosher 2001, esp. 31–6). A later date in the first century CE is also possible, if one accepts Derchain-Urtel's argument (2000: 44–5) based on a palaeographical analysis comparing the Akhmim Book of the Dead hieroglyphs with hieroglyphs in Roman period temple inscriptions (disputed by von Lieven 2002: 480–1).

Two of the Akhmim Book of the Dead papyri include another text, which seems to be a distinct composition; so far, it is only known in these two manuscripts. The text is chiefly concerned with the soul-like constituent of a human being, the *ba*, and the *ba*'s admission to and acceptance in the hereafter—hence its modern name, the Book of Ba (Beinlich 2000; Mosher 2001, pls 16–17). The age of the Book of Ba is uncertain; its corruptions and inclusion of parts of BD 17 could suggest that it stems from a long-standing tradition, but the presence of some Demoticisms could also indicate that more recent layers accumulated during the text's transmission and its editorial process over time (Beinlich 2000; Quack 2001; von Lieven 2006a).

Egyptian Religion and Egyptian Funerary Religion

The transmission and adaptation of such texts probably took place within and around the temples' scriptoria and libraries. Much as Theban funerary art draws on temple decoration as a model (Riggs 2006), some members of the priestly elite adapted temple ritual texts for funerary purposes, among them Osiris liturgies and the collection of compositions handed down in the aforementioned papyrus of Imhotep. As Osiris is the central figure of belief around an afterlife, the ritual texts that served as models were particularly those of the Osiris and Sokar cult. The other important focus of funerary belief in Egypt was the deceased's participation in the solar cycle, yet texts that were clearly adapted from the cult of the sun-god are unattested, although the solar aspect is not absent from the sources as, for instance, the 'Intercessory Hymn to the Solar Deity' (*P Berlin* 3030 VI 17–IX 6) proves. Its phraseology is very akin to cultic solar hymns (Herbin 1984; Smith 2009a: 590–8).

While there is no doubt about the fact of borrowings from the temple sphere, it is hard to classify the texts exclusively in this way, since some manuscripts combine works that were copied from temple liturgies with original funerary texts in different sections (Stadler forthcoming). It is certainly not a new phenomenon, but intrinsic to the corpus of funerary texts from the very beginning; the oldest religious corpus, the Pyramid Texts, has survived in a funerary context, and nothing is known about temple ritual at the time. Thus, there is no way of identifying how much the Pyramid Texts might owe to the latter, and vice versa. The texts of the daily temple ritual cite from the Pyramid Texts, and may indicate their original use (Allen 1950). But the other way round, from the tomb to the temple, is possible, too, as spells from the Book of the Dead were inscribed on the walls of temples, in particular of those with an Osirian connection (von Lieven 2007, forthcoming), if, again, the temple sphere was not already their source (see Gee 2006). In some cases the contents or passages in a funerary text recommend its use during festivals, which suggests a transposition from the temple to the tomb, e.g. BD 137 (Luft 2009) or BD 144 (Stadler 2009b: 252–63). The chronology of the surviving texts is not decisive, because it can be inverted owing to accidents of preservation. For example, BD 125 is first attested in funerary papyri, but with good reason it is assumed that it actually derives from the priestly oaths of purity that are exclusively known from manuscripts dating to the Roman period (Stadler 2008a). Another example is the aforementioned 'Recitations of the Glorifications, which the Two Sisters Performed'.

Language does not always help in determining a text's age, either. Therefore, it is difficult to establish an accurate chronology and thus better understand the interdependences and derivations of funerary and temple texts. A good example is the 'Decree to the Nome of the Silent Land', which is best preserved in the early Ptolemaic papyrus of Imhotep (*P MMA* 35.9.21), and considered here for reasons explained above. The redaction left clear signs of Demotic in the present manuscript (Smith 2006), but it draws from much older sources, e.g. BD 145 (first attested in the New Kingdom) and BD 144, whose roots go back to the Middle Kingdom Coffin Texts (Stadler 2009b: 256–8, 275–6). However, certain passages are reminiscent of the Djoser precinct at Saqqara: could this late first-century funerary text go back in part to a royal ritual of the Old Kingdom that has been transposed to Osiris and then to an ordinary deceased? This is highly speculative, but nonetheless a possibility (Quack 2011: 141; Stadler forthcoming).

Much as the classification of the texts as either mortuary (performative) or funerary (for deposit in the burial) is unproductive (Smith 2009a: 209–14; Stadler 2009b: 42–3), it can be concluded on the basis of these examples that there are no further insights to be gained from the question of whether a given text is primarily or secondarily designed for funerary use, because there was an active exchange between both spheres—temple and tomb—throughout Egyptian history. Apparently these were not categories recognized by the Egyptians, but have been imposed on the material in Egyptological scholarship.

Change or Continuity?

The chapter started with an example illustrating the stability, continuity, and long-standing tradition of Egyptian funerary religion. In contrast, the survey of the sources has demonstrated phenomena of change—the end of the time-honoured Book of the Dead in Thebes and the rise of new compositions, which Sethe (1931: 537) called 'inconsistent compilations, unpleasant products of an epigonical period'. Sethe's verdict is symptomatic of an old-fashioned, albeit rather influential, approach to late sources. Research on Ptolemaic and Roman funerary texts remained somewhat marginal for a long time. However, during the past thirty years or so scholars have increasingly appreciated the sources' relevance for understanding Egyptian religion. By stressing the continuities, some scholars may seek to underline the texts' (and their own) connection to the subject matter of classical Egyptology, but continuities can be perceived as an unproductive torpidity as well. Likewise, 'change' could be used to emphasize the ongoing vitality of Egyptian funerary religion, but it also contributes to a problematic trope in Egyptological scholarship whereby 'change' implies a (negative) process of something becoming allegedly 'un-Egyptian'. In fact, of course, changes in religious beliefs and practices characterized all periods of Egyptian history (see Smith 2009b), but in the Roman period, in particular, the question of change, or the lack thereof, has been especially charged through its implicit connection with the question of 'decline'.

Nowadays the approach to epochs that previous generations of scholars would have called times of 'decay' or 'decline' has significantly changed. Modern research acknowledges the value of those periods as periods of transition and of particular historical interest. Therefore, no Egyptologist would any longer commit to writing such a bold and subjective statement as Sethe did. Yet there is some controversy over how persistent or how mutable funerary religion was in the last centuries of its existence. Assmann (2001: xi–xiii, not included in the English version, Assmann 2005), who advocated for a significant historical development in Egyptian religion in the aftermath of the Amarna period, surprisingly states that he cannot detect any change in funerary religion over the centuries. On the opposite side Quack (2006, 2009), who otherwise tends to date religious texts as early as possible and who thus indirectly argues for a greater stability in Egyptian thinking, advocates in explicit contradiction to Assmann for a significant change from the Third Intermediate period (1070–712 BCE) onward. Likewise, Frankfurter (1998: 10–11) accentuates the 'vivid continuity throughout the Roman and Coptic periods' of mortuary practices and calls the beliefs 'so historically resilient, so impervious to the vicissitudes of ideology' that he feels justified in excluding them from his study, although his book's overall aim is to demonstrate a longer persistence of Egyptian religion than other scholars (especially Bagnall 1993: 261–309; 2008) would accept. Others have suggested a dramatic alteration in Egyptian funerary beliefs and practices (e.g. Kaper 2000: 124, 126; 2001: 131–2). The interpretation of the evidence is unquestionably difficult, because ideally one would wish to be able to identify material from different regions, date it securely, and examine the socio-economic situation in that locality as well; the sources rarely permit such a tidy study. And how can scholars quantify change by comparing evidence from different periods? To put it polemically: how many funerary papyri does one need to counterbalance a mummy mask with supposedly Greek hair, or vice versa? It can also be asked whether the new funerary texts, or ritual texts newly adapted for funerary purposes, communicate old beliefs rather than newly developed ones (Kaper 2000, 2001; Quack 2009). The following paragraphs cannot claim to overcome this, but their aim is to highlight some of the problems.

The historical and economic circumstances may have a stronger influence on the specific forms of burial equipment comprising both the textual and the material aspect. It makes a difference whether the majority of the elite served as officials in an Egypt that was an independent great power in the ancient Near East or in an Egypt that was a province whose resources served interests other than primarily the country's own. This, one should think, is also reflected in a person's funerary representation and expenditure for a burial. Nevertheless, elaborate and monumental funerary architecture was still built. Kaper (2000) mentions some sites with painted tombs in the Roman period and interprets the decline in quantity as an indicator of a considerable change in funerary religion between 100 BCE and 100 CE. It is true that burial equipment is reduced compared with earlier phases of Egyptian history, but there seems to be a regional shift rather than a general decline. For instance, in the Dakhla Oasis in the first century CE, Petosiris commissioned a rock-cut decorated tomb, which is not as large as the tombs of high officials in Saite era Thebes (Fakhry et al. 1982, *passim*, pls 25–30; Riggs 2005: 161–4, with further references). However, in Roman Thebes, New Kingdom tombs were reused in most cases. In the necropolis of contemporary Hermopolis the so-called House 21 is a large, painted, five-room tomb chapel (Gabra 1941: 39–50, pls 8–18; Riggs 2005: 129–39) and in 2007 another one was discovered that even had a small pyramid on top (Kessler and Brose 2008; see Chapter 13). For a full appreciation of continuity versus change, such an archaizing sepulchral architecture must be seen in conjunction with the broad range of its grave goods: next to an Egyptian-style coffin were found amulets and figurines in a purely Greek artistic language, as well as Egyptian *shabti* figures. It had been thought that *shabtis* were no longer part of burial equipment in the Roman period, but this case adds another layer to the issue: the *shabtis* were already antiquities when they were deposited in this tomb, which suggests that the tomb owner was aware of older traditions, and cherished them.

Thus, structures that are familiar from former times, but which were stylistically interpreted in a contemporary way, do exist in the Roman period. The catacomb of Kom el-Shuqafa (Schreiber 1908) is a very particular case which may not be representative for the whole of Egypt, as its Alexandrian environment calls for a sensitive analysis of the various layers of meaning. In another area, the burial equipment of Tanaweruow shows how in 61 CE her father, Hartophnakhtes, tried to provide a proper, albeit by New Kingdom standards relatively poor, Egyptian burial (Smith 2005: 16–21). However, in writing down the texts now known as *P Harkness*, Hartophnakhtes allows us to reconstruct the sequence of the funerary rites that occurred from the last night of the mummification and the hourly vigils (*Stundenwachen*), through the festive decoration of the tomb, to the interment of Tanaweruow and the concluding rites. All is deeply rooted in Egyptian tradition (Smith 2005; 2009a: 264–301). The evidence suggests a persistence of traditional beliefs concerning the afterlife rather than their alteration. Therefore, from a methodological point of view the concrete, material manifestations of funerary religion and the underlying mythology of its contents must be kept apart in order to identify a true change. Thus, new forms of equipment, tomb decoration, and types of text accompanying the dead cannot be denied, but the conceptual foundations might be the same.

In pointing to the Third Intermediate period, which Quack (2009) convincingly sees as a turning point in the history of Egyptian funerary religion, a further contradiction among students of Egyptian religion is encountered, because Kaper (2000) thinks that the major changes took place during the Hellenistic period. Although Kaper also acknowledges the far-reaching roots of Egyptian tradition, he sees an engagement with contemporary hellenistic religion and philosophy at work. This may have led, for instance, to seeing the nocturnal passage of the sun-god as awkward, which would not leave any room for the Books of the Underworld, formerly so prominent. While this may be true, it is questionable whether the astral life of the *ba* is so central to mortuary belief in this period; moreover, the *ba*'s astrality is a recurrent theme in Egyptian religious texts from the Pyramid Texts onward, and thus has an affinity with Greek thought, without necessarily being a consequence of it. Despite a popular increase in astronomy and astrology (Dieleman 2003a, b), it is also possible to see the zodiacs on coffin lids (e.g. the coffin of Soter, British Museum EA 6705, in Riggs 2005: 201–3) as a supplementation of older models depicting the sky goddess Nut as early as the New Kingdom, rather than perceiving it as an intrusion of something new. Already in Middle Kingdom Asyut, some officials commissioned coffins with an astronomical calendar on their lids (Brunner-Traut and Brunner 1981: 216–19; Schramm 1981: 219–27). Although the purpose might be different, the repeated use of astronomical representations on coffin lids characterizes the practice as Egyptian. This feature may also be inspired by the astrological ceilings in the Ramesside royal tombs. The same can be said about the representation of the four winds at the cardinal points, namely the four corners of a coffin, which are thought to help the deceased rise (as on Soter's coffin: Riggs 2006). They are not new, because already 18th dynasty coffins as well as sarcophagi and Ramesside tombs have BD 161 painted or carved at the four corners, and the spell is to safeguard the entrance of the life-bringing winds (Stadler 2009b: 236–9). To derive the use of mummy portraits from the impact of the Roman and Greek ancestor cult is based largely on Diodorus' report of having kept mummies in the living area of homes, a report that was influential among classical authors but seems to be untrue (Römer 2000; Stadler 2001b; compare Borg 1996: 196–203; Kaper 2000). New forms of commemoration may have been one facet of mummy portraits, but there were Egyptian precedents for ancestor worship in a domestic context (Exell 2008) or during various feasts in the necropolis, like the Theban Beautiful Feast of the Valley (Schott 1953; Graefe 1986; Cabrol 2001, esp. 711–76). In other words, fitting Greek forms may have been integrated into Egyptian concepts, rather than being introduced as a radical innovation.

Conclusion

Changes in Egyptian funerary religion during the Roman period were part of an organic development marked by reinterpreting, and perpetuating, a number of earlier features. For much of the evidence, the lack of accurate dating and other information hampers a methodological approach (Smith 2009b), but some general observations can still be made. During the Roman period, there was a greater diversity of modes in which individuals could be commemorated and at the same time envisage the afterlife—as Egyptian, Hellenized Egyptian, Egyptianized Greek, and so on, depending on personal and local circumstances. The textual sources superficially show a similar variety: some compositions survive in numerous copies, while other, quite extensive texts are unique and may represent an individual creation, for instance the aforementioned *P Harkness* or the two Rhind papyri. The texts themselves are not entirely new, and their 'new' elements may be inadvertent, owing to the scribe not fully understanding the earlier language of his source. The ideas and concepts, however, are deeply rooted in an Egyptian tradition reaching back as far as the Pyramid Texts. The end of the once dominant Book of the Dead tradition is a marked difference from the New Kingdom, or even the Late period revival and revision of Book of the Dead texts, which 'canonized' them. By the start of the Ptolemaic period, funerary compositions adapted from temple ritual texts began to appear, highlighting a connection between tomb and temple functions that became increasingly evident in the Roman period but no doubt reflects long-standing practices as well. Thus, the period between 100 BCE and around 250 CE, the point when Egyptian funerary texts are no longer found on mummy labels, coffins, or papyri, was not so different from previous phases of Egyptian history in terms of religious developments in the funerary sphere. In keeping with the expanded modes of cultural expression at the time, the Roman period in Egypt offered a broader and more varied range of approaches to the universal concern of life after death.

Suggested Reading

For a long time Goyon's anthology (1972) of late funerary rituals was the standard reference work. However, it has been superseded by Smith (2009a), which gives new, improved, and reliable translations of virtually all textual sources relevant to Egyptian funerary religion in the Ptolemaic and Roman periods. Its importance is reflected in the number of references made to this publication in the preceding paragraphs. An up-to-date study of the material and artistic aspects of funerary belief is Riggs (2005). For contextualizing the subject of funerary religion in the Egyptian tradition, Assmann (2001) is helpful; the English version (Assmann 2005) is abbreviated compared with the German original. Finally, there is a valuable research tool online, Trismegistos, through which current publications and studies of the texts can be found: <http://www.trismegistos.org>.

Bibliography

Allen, J. P. 2005. *The Ancient Egyptian Pyramid Texts: Edited by P. Der Manuelian*. Leiden: Brill.

Allen, T. G. 1950. *Occurrences of Pyramid Texts with Cross Indexes of These and Other Egyptian Mortuary Texts*. Chicago: University of Chicago Press.

——1974. *The Book of the Dead, or, Going Forth by Day: Ideas of the Ancient Egyptians concerning the Hereafter as Expressed in their Own Terms*. Chicago: University of Chicago Press.

Arlt, C. 2011. *Deine Seele möge leben für immer und ewig: Die Mumienschilder im British Museum*. Leuven: Peeters.

Assmann, J. 2001. *Tod und Jenseits im Alten Ägypten*. Munich: Beck.

——2005. *Death and Salvation in Ancient Egypt*. Ithaca, NY: Cornell University Press.

——M. Bommas, and A. Kucharek. 2008. *Altägyptische Totenliturgien*, vol. 3: *Osirisliturgien in Papyri der Spätzeit*. Heidelberg: Winter.

Bagnall, R. S. 1993. *Egypt in Late Antiquity*. Princeton: Princeton University Press.

——2008. 'Models and Evidence in the Study of Religion in Late Roman Egypt', in J. Hahn, S. Emmel, and U. Gotter (eds), *From Temple to Church: Destruction and Renewal of Local Cultic Topography in Late Antiquity*. Leiden: Brill, 23–41.

Beinlich, H. 2000. *Das Buch vom Ba*. Wiesbaden: Harrassowitz.

——2009. *Papyrus Tamerit 1: Ein Ritualpapyrus der ägyptischen Spätzeit*. Dettelbach: Röll.

Blasius, A. 2002. 'Zur Frage des geistigen Widerstandes im griechisch-römischen Ägypten: Die historische Situation', in A. Blasius and B. U. Schipper (eds), *Apokalyptik und Ägypten: Eine kritische Analyse der relevanten Texte aus dem griechisch-römischen Ägypten*. Leuven: Peeters, 41–62.

Borg, B. 1996. *Mumienporträts: Chronologie und kultureller Kontext.* Mainz: von Zabern.
Brunner-Traut, E., and H. Brunner. 1981. *Die ägyptische Sammlung der Universität Tübingen.* Mainz: von Zabern.
Cabrol, C. 2001. *Les voies processionnelles de Thèbes.* Leuven: Peeters.
Coenen, M. 2001. 'On the Demise of the Book of the Dead in Ptolemaic Thebes', *Revue d'Égyptologie* 52: 69–84.
Collombert, P. 2000. 'Religion égyptienne et culture grecque: L'exemple de *Διοσκουρίδης*', *Chronique d'Égypte* 75: 47–63.
Derchain-Urtel, M.-T. 2000. 'Datierung', in B. Lüscher (ed.), *Das Totenbuch pBerlin P. 10477 aus Achmim (mit Photographien des verwandten pHildesheim 5248).* Wiesbaden: Harrassowitz, 44–5.
Dieleman, J. 2003a. 'Claiming the Stars: Egyptian Priests Facing the Sky', in S. Bickel and A. Loprieno (eds), *Basel Egyptology Prize 1: Junior Research in Egyptian History, Archaeology, and Philology.* Basel: Schwabe, 277–89.
——2003b. 'Stars and the Egyptian Priesthood in the Greco-Roman Period', in S. B. Noegel, J. T. Walker, and B. M. Wheeler (eds), *Prayer, Magic, and the Stars in the Ancient and Late Antique World.* University Park: Pennsylvania State University Press, 137–53.
Exell, K. 2008. 'Ancestor Bust', in W. Wendrich (ed.), *UCLA Encyclopedia of Egyptology.* Los Angeles. <http://escholarship.org/uc/item/59k7832w>.
Fakhry, A., et al. 1982. *Denkmäler der Oase Dachle, aus dem Nachlass bearbeitet von Jürgen Osing.* Mainz: von Zabern.
Frankfurter, D. 1998. *Religion in Roman Egypt: Assimilation and Resistance.* Princeton: Princeton University Press.
Gabra, S. 1941. *Rapport sur les fouilles d'Hermoupolis ouest (Touna el-Gebel).* Cairo: Institut Français d'Archéologie Orientale.
Gee, J. 2006. 'The Use of the Daily Temple Liturgy in the Book of the Dead', in B. Backes, I. Munro, and S. Stöhr (eds), *Totenbuch-Forschungen: Gesammelte Beiträge des 2. Internationalen Totenbuch-Symposiums Bonn, 25. bis 29. September 2005.* Wiesbaden: Harrassowitz, 73–86.
Gestermann, L. 2004. 'Sargtexte aus Dair al-Biršā: Zeugnisse eines historischen Wendepunktes?', in S. Bickel (ed.), *Textes des pyramides et textes des sarcophages: D'un monde à l'autre.* Cairo: Institut Français d'Archéologie Orientale, 201–17.
——2006. 'Aufgelesen: Die Anfänge des altägyptischen Totenbuchs', in B. Backes, I. Munro, and S. Stöhr (eds), *Totenbuch-Forschungen: Gesammelte Beiträge des 2. Internationalen Totenbuch-Symposiums Bonn, 25. bis 29. September 2005.* Wiesbaden: Harrassowitz, 101–13.
Goyon, J.-C. 1972. *Rituels funéraires de l'ancienne Égypte.* Paris: Cerf.
——1999. *Le papyrus d'Imouthès, fils de Psintaês au Metropolitan Museum of Art de New York (Papyrus MMA 35.9.21).* New York: Metropolitan Museum of Art.
Graefe, E. 1986. 'Talfest', in W. Helck and W. Westendorf (eds), *Lexikon der Ägyptologie*, vol. 6. Wiesbaden: Harrassowitz, 187–9.
——1991. 'Über die Verarbeitung von Pyramidentexten in den späten Tempeln', in U. Verhoeven and E. Graefe (eds), *Religion und Philosophie im alten Ägypten: Festgabe für Philippe Derchain zu seinem 65. Geburtstag am 24. Juli 1991.* Leuven: Peeters, 129–48.
Grimm, G. 1974. *Die römischen Mumienmasken aus Ägypten.* Wiesbaden: Steiner.
Herbin, F.-R. 1984. 'Une nouvelle page du Livre des respirations', *Bulletin de l'Institut Français d'Archéologie Orientale* 84: 249–302.
——1994. *Le livre de parcourir l'éternité.* Leuven: Peeters.

——2008. *Books of Breathing and Related Texts*. London: British Museum Press.

Hoffmann, F. 2008. 'Zur angeblichen musikalischen Notation in einer ägyptischen Osirisliturgie', in B. Rothöhler and A. Manisali (eds), *Mythos und Ritual: Festschrift für Jan Assmann zum 70. Geburtstag*. Berlin: Lit, 71–6.

Kaper, O. E. 2000. 'Des dieux nouveaux et des conceptions nouvelles', in W. Clarysse and H. Willems (eds), *Les Empereurs du Nil*. Louvain: Peeters, 123–6.

——2001. Review of D. Frankfurter, *Religion in Roman Egypt: Assimilation and Resistance*, *Bibliotheca Orientalis* 58: 126–32.

Kessler, D., and P. Brose. 2008. *Ägyptens letzte Pyramide: Das Grab des Seuta(s) in Tuna el-Gebel*. Haar: Brose.

Kucharek, A. 2010. *Die Klagelieder von Isis und Nepthys in Texten der Griechisch-Römischen Zeit*. Heidelberg: Winter.

Luft, D. 2009. *Anzünden der Fackel: Untersuchungen zu Spruch 137 des Totenbuches*. Wiesbaden: Harrassowitz.

Lüscher, B. 2000. *Das Totenbuch pBerlin P. 10477 aus Achmim (mit Photographien des verwandten pHildesheim 5248)*. Wiesbaden: Harrassowitz.

Möller, G. 1913. *Die beiden Totenpapyrus Rhind des Museums zu Edinburg*. Leipzig: Hinrichs.

Mosher, M. 1992. 'Theban and Memphite Book of the Dead Traditions in the Late Period', *Journal of the American Research Center in Egypt* 29: 143–72.

——2001. *The Papyrus of Hor (BM EA 10479) with Papyrus MacGregor: The Late Period Tradition at Akhmim*. London: British Museum Press.

Quack, J. F. 2001. Review of H. Beinlich, *Das Buch vom Ba*, *Enchoria* 27: 209–11.

——2004. 'Der pränatale Geschlechtsverkehr von Isis und Osiris sowie eine Notiz zum Alter des Osiris', *Studien zur Altägyptischen Kultur* 32: 327–32.

——2006. 'Das Grab am Tempeldromos: Neue Deutungen zu einem spätzeitlichen Grabtyp', in H.-W. Fischer-Elfert and K. Zibelius-Chen (eds), *'Von reichlich ägyptischem Verstande': Festschrift für Waltraud Guglielmi zum 65. Geburtstag*. Wiesbaden: Harrassowitz, 113–32.

——2009. 'Grab und Grabausstattung im späten Ägypten', in A. Berlejung and B. Janowski (eds), *Tod und Jenseits im alten Israel und in seiner Umwelt: Theologische, religionsgeschichtliche, archäologische und ikonographische Aspekte*. Tübingen: Mohr Siebeck, 597–629.

——2011. Review of H. Beinlich, *Papyrus Tamerit 1: Ein Ritualpapyrus der ägyptischen Spätzeit*, *Welt des Orients* 41/1: 131–43.

Riggs, C. 2001. 'Forms of the *Wesekh* Collar in Funerary Art of the Graeco-Roman Period', *Chronique d'Égypte* 76: 57–68.

——2005. *The Beautiful Burial in Roman Egypt: Art, Identity, and Funerary Religion*. Oxford: Oxford University Press.

——2006. 'Archaism and Artistic Sources in Roman Egypt: The Coffins of the Soter Family and the Temple of Deir el-Medina', *Bulletin de l'Institut Français d'Archéologie Orientale* 106: 315–32.

Römer, C. 2000. 'Das Werden zu Osiris im römischen Ägypten', *Archiv für Religionsgeschichte* 2/2: 141–61.

Ryholt, K. (ed.) 2006. *The Carlsberg Payri 7: Hieratic Texts from the Collection*. Copenhagen: Museum Tusculanum Press.

Schott, S. 1953. *Das schöne Fest vom Wüstentale: Festbräuche einer Totenstadt*. Wiesbaden: Akademie der Wissenschaften und der Literatur in Mainz.

Schramm, M. 1981. 'Astronomische Interpretation der Diagonalsternuhr', in E. Brunner-Traut and H. Brunner, *Die ägyptische Sammlung der Universität Tübingen*. Mainz: von Zabern, 219–27.

Schreiber, T. 1908. *Die Nekropole von Kom-Esch-Schukafa*. Leipzig: Giesecke & Devrient.

Sethe, K. 1931. 'Die Totenliteratur der alten Ägypter: Die Geschichte einer Sitte', *Sitzungsberichte der Preußischen Akademie der Wissenschaften, Philosophisch-historische Klasse* 18: 412–33.

Smith, M. 2005. *Papyrus Harkness (MMA 31.9.7)*. Oxford: Oxbow.

Smith, M. 2006. 'The Great Decree Issued to the Nome of the Silent Land', *Revue d'Égyptologie* 57: 217–32.

——2009a. *Traversing Eternity: Texts for the Afterlife from Ptolemaic and Roman Egypt*. Oxford: Oxford University Press.

——2009b. 'Democratization of the Afterlife', in J. Dieleman and W. Wendrich (eds), *UCLA Encyclopedia of Egyptology*. Los Angeles. <http://escholarship.org/uc/item/70g428wj>.

——2010. 'A Divine Decree for the Deceased (O. Strasbourg D. 132 + 133 + 134)', in H. Knuf, C. Leitz, and D. von Recklinghausen (eds), *Honi soit qui mal y pense: Studien zum pharaonischen, griechisch-römischen und spätantiken Ägypten zu Ehren von Heinz-Josef Thissen*. Leuven: Peeters, 439–45.

Stadler, M. A. 2001a. 'Der Skarabäus als osirianisches Symbol vornehmlich nach spätzeitlichen Quellen', *Zeitschrift für ägyptische Sprache und Altertumskunde* 128: 71–83.

——2001b. 'War eine dramatische Aufführung eines Totengerichtes Teil der ägyptischen Totenriten?', *Studien zur Altägyptischen Kultur* 29: 331–48.

——2003. *Der Totenpapyrus des Pa-Month (P. Bibl. nat. 149)*. Wiesbaden: Harrassowitz.

——2004. 'Fünf neue funeräre Kurztexte (Papyri Britisches Museum EA 10121, 10198, 10415, 10421a, b, 10426a) und eine Zwischenbilanz zu dieser Textgruppe', in F. Hoffmann and H.-J. Thissen (eds), *Res Severa Verum Gaudium: Festschrift für Karl-Theodor Zauzich zum 65. Geburtstag am 8. Juni 2004*. Leuven: Peeters, 551–72.

——2005. *Wege ins Jenseits: Zeugnisse ägyptischer Totenreligion im Martin von Wagner Museum der Universität Würzburg*. Würzburg: Ergon.

——2008a. 'Judgment after Death (Negative Confession)', in J. Dieleman and W. Wendrich (eds), *UCLA Encyclopedia of Egyptology*. Los Angeles. <http://escholarship.org/uc/item/07s1t6kj>.

——2008b. 'On the Demise of Egyptian Writing: Working on a Problematic Source Basis', in J. Baines, J. Bennet, and S. Houston (eds), *The Disappearance of Writing Systems: Perspectives on Literacy and Communication*. London: Equinox, 157–81.

——2009a. 'Spätägyptische Hymnen als Quellen für den interkulturellen Austausch und den Umgang mit dem eigenen Erbe: Drei Fallstudien', in M. Witte and J. F. Diehl (eds), *Orakel und Gebete: Interdisziplinäre Studien zur Sprache der Religion in Ägypten, Vorderasien und Griechenland in hellenistischer Zeit*. Tübingen: Mohr Siebeck, 141–63.

——2009b. *Weiser und Wesir: Studien zu Vorkommen, Rolle und Wesen des Gottes Thot im ägyptischen Totenbuch*. Tübingen: Mohr Siebeck.

——Forthcoming. Review of M. Smith, *Traversing Eternity: Texts for the Afterlife from Ptolemaic and Roman Egypt*, *Enchoria* 31.

Szczudłowska, A. 1973. 'Pyramid Texts Preserved on Sękowski Papyrus', *Zeitschrift für ägyptische Sprache und Altertumskunde* 99: 25–9.

Taylor, J. 2000. 'The Third Intermediate Period', in I. Shaw (ed.), *The Oxford History of Ancient Egypt*. Oxford: Oxford University Press, 330–68.

Töpfer, S., and M. Müller-Roth. 2011. *Das Ende der Totenbuchtradition und der Übergang zum Buch vom Atmen: Die Totenbücher des Monthemhat (pTübingen 2012) und der Tanedjmet (pLouvre N 3085)*. Wiesbaden: Harrassowitz.

Vittmann, G. 2003. *Ägypten und die Fremden im ersten vorchristlichen Jahrtausend*. Mainz: von Zabern.

——2009. Review of K. Ryholt (ed.), *The Carlsberg Payri 7: Hieratic Texts from the Collection*, *Enchoria* 30: 186–91.

von Lieven, A. 2002. Review of B. Lüscher, *Das Totenbuch pBerlin P. 10477 aus Achmim (mit Photographien des verwandten pHildesheim 5248)*, *Orientalistische Literaturzeitung* 97: 477–82.

——2006a. Review of H. Beinlich, *Das Buch vom Ba*, *Orientalistische Literaturzeitung* 101: 133–37.

——2006b. 'Eine punktierte Osirisliturgie (P. Carlsberg 589 + PSI Inv. I 104 + P. Berlin 29022)', in K. Ryholt (ed.), *The Carlsberg Payri 7: Hieratic Texts from the Collection*. Copenhagen: Museum Tusculanum Press, 9–38.

——2007. 'Bemerkungen zum Dekorationsprogramm des Osireion in Abydos', in B. Haring and A. Klug (eds), *6. Ägyptologische Tempeltagung: Funktion und Gebrauch altägyptischer Tempelräume*. Wiesbaden: Harrassowitz, 167–86.

——Forthcoming. 'Book of the Dead, Book of the Living: BD Spells as Temple Texts', *Journal of Egyptian Archaeology*.

von Recklinghausen, D. 2007. 'Anspruch und Wirklichkeit: Ptolemäische Beschreibungen der Stadt Theben', in S. Pfeiffer (ed.), *Ägypten unter fremden Herrschern zwischen persischer Satrapie und römischer Provinz*. Frankfurt: Antike, 140–64.

Zauzich, K.-T. 2002. 'Mumienbelag für einen Mann namens Hor', in I. Wehgartner and J. Wich (eds), *Schrift, Sprache, Bild und Klang: Entwicklungsstufen der Schrift von der Antike bis in die Neuzeit*. Würzburg: Ergon, 57–8.

CHAPTER 24

ORACLES*

GAËLLE TALLET

In 'Religion as a Cultural System', an essay he published in 1966, Clifford Geertz defined religion as a framework shared by a group of people that allows them to make sense out of life and guides their behaviour. According to Geertz, religious symbols perform a specific function: they aim to persuade us that there is a direct connection between our world-view and our ethos, our way of life—they provide us with both a model *of* how the world is and a model *for* how to live in this world (Geertz 1973: 94). When people or societies encounter times of crisis, 'a tumult of events which lack not just interpretations but *interpretability*' (Geertz 1973: 98), religious symbols help reassure people that their lives make sense, and that there is some meaningful order. The context in which such religious symbols are displayed is that of the ritual:

> it is in some sort of ceremonial form—even if that form be hardly more than the recitation of a myth, the consultation of an oracle, or the decoration of a grave—that the moods and motivations which sacred symbols induce in men and the general conceptions of the order of existence which they formulate for men meet and reinforce each other. (Geertz 1973: 112)

It is in this conceptual frame that I should like to set up this chapter on oracles in Roman Egypt, first because it provides us with an effective model for understanding oracles and divination in general, and secondly because it fits particularly well the Egyptian oracular context, which is attested from the New Kingdom on. My claim is that attending a procession and consulting an oracle offered a key opportunity for worshippers to take part in the ritual system. In Egypt, unlike in the Greek world, the ritual system was rather segregated: worshippers were not allowed to enter the temple precinct, apart from open spaces such as courtyards, and the god's statue was confined in the innermost sanctuary, accessible only to priests for cult activities that were kept secret. Therefore, religious festivals were a major social context for interaction between the sacred and profane worlds, between priestly monitoring of the sacred and popular needs. During festivals, the divine statues—the gods' bodies—went out in procession, allowing the crowd attending the procession more personal access to

* I should like to thank Hélène Cuvigny for providing me with an advance copy of her publication on the Dios shrine, and my research team, the EA 4270 CRIHAM, for its financial support for the images.

deities. Festivals thus allowed local people to participate in the ritual life of the temple, and this is the context in which most oracular consultations took place in Pharaonic times.

The Egyptian oracle was a point of contact between the two different 'worlds' described by Geertz, which the priestly institution tended to set apart: that of the sanctuary, home of the gods, bearing an idealized vision of the cosmos, and that of humans in their daily lives, involving labour and family concerns. Consequently, oracular consultations took place in in-between areas, either during processions or in peripheral areas of the temple precinct, where worshippers were allowed to behold images of the gods: chapels at the rear of the temple, and gateways or front courtyards where reliefs, sphinxes, and royal or private statues functioned as intercessors (Vernus 1975, 1977; Quaegebeur 1997; Frankfurter 1998). Personal piety and oracular consultation were always closely connected (Vernus 1977).

Divination and Dramatization

The oracle mediated between the human and the non-human realms, both articulating the separation between them and attempting to bridge it (Johnston 2005: 297). In this respect, oracular consultation played the same role as sacrifice did in other religions, and both acts were inextricably bound with divination in antiquity (Park 1963: 200–1; Burkert 2005). Specialists were needed to handle the powerful interaction between an absolute order, which ruled individual destinies, and the matter-of-fact reality of human lives, reflected in oracular questions addressed to the gods. This interaction was both complex and necessary, since fate was clearly not thought of as unalterable: if properly beseeched, deities could alter destiny (Quack 2006: 177).

Discussing divination in cross-cultural contexts, such as Ifa divination as practised by the Yoruba in the 1930s, George K. Park demonstrated that divination produces 'rather definite and useful results' because of the controlled way in which it intervenes in social processes (Park 1963: 195). In the Pharaonic period, Egyptian oracles played an important part in political decisions, the appointment of the high priests of Amun (see Černý 1962: 36; Kruchten 1985, 1986), and judicial trials (Parker 1962: 49–52; McDowell 1990: 107–41; Traunecker 1997). In a Ramesside papyrus, for instance (*P Brit. Mus.* EA 10335), a man named Amunemuia appealed to Amun of Pe-Khenty to reveal who stole five sacred garments from the storehouse he managed. The names of suspects were read before the god, who indicated a local farmer, Pethauemdiamun, as the guilty party. The farmer demanded a new 'trial' in front of two other gods, first Amun of Te-Shenyt and then Amun of Bukenen. When they confirmed the guilty verdict, Pethauemdiamun confessed his crime (Blackman 1925). As a legal forum, use of an oracle might seem to be lacking logic, justice, and efficiency, but, as Park points out, such cumulative trials, any of which might contradict the previous decision, have 'no lack of drama', and that is precisely the point (Park 1963: 203).

For oracular consultation *is* a social drama: it works as much by *performing* an answer through the dramatization of ritual as it does by *providing* the answer itself. In the Egyptian context, oracular consultation involved a direct contact with the deity, which was by its essence a rare and heightened occurrence. Special settings designed to impress the audience, for instance in the procession of the divine boat or in the staged opening and closing of chapel doors, displayed the oracle in a dramatized fashion. Mechanical devices helped establish the apparent presence of otherwise invisible beings, and it must be remembered that the Egyptian word for 'festival', *kha*, also meant 'apparition' or 'epiphany' (Assmann 1994). Questioning the oracle ultimately culminated in a meaningful resolution, and each stage in the process led to 'the dramatic establishment of an ostensibly irrevocable judgment' (Park 1963: 202). As such, divination played an important part in the regulation of social order: the oracle was a way to secure *maat*, that is, truth and cosmic order. It allowed humans to live according to the will of the gods and with the approval of society: 'I did what men loved and what gods praised,' claimed honest men in their autobiographies (Černý 1962: 35).

But because oracles were solicited in times of personal or social crisis, divination also revealed points of stress (Johnston and Struck 2005: 23). As Favret-Saada showed in her study of sorcery in contemporary Normandy (Favret-Saada 1977), when someone consults a fortune-teller, the fortune-teller is not expected to reveal an absolute truth about the future; instead, she is supposed to bring to light a person's deep desires and concerns, and connect them with the hidden order of things. Divination does not reveal the future: it helps solve problems first by putting them in the hands of gods and then by redirecting them from the world of the gods or the dead to the everyday world, where the problems can be dealt with by human means, as in the famous oracle uttered in Delphi before the battle of Salamine and debated in the Athenian assembly (Parker 1985; Johnston and Struck 2005: 297). But it is striking that, while Greek oracles are most often ambiguous and rely upon the consultant's freedom of interpretation, Egyptian oracles provide a clear yes or no answer.

Sources and Method

Any discussion of oracles in Roman Egypt must consider a variety of sources and approaches, and as a system of signs belonging to a given culture, oracles were enmeshed with other systems of signs, such as literature, mythology, and representations. Important sources include oracular material such as sundials, *astragaloi*, or dice for oracles by sortition (though very scarce); oracular questions written in hieratic, Demotic, Greek, or Coptic on chits of papyrus or ostraca; books of *sortes* written on papyrus, to be consulted by the diviner; and oracular answers written in Greek on papyrus, which are quite rare. Archaeological evidence includes the remains of oracular rear-chapels or similar facilities, 'speaking statues', and statues of saints or gods located at temple gateways or courtyards, which bear graffiti indicating that they were approached for oracles.

Another group of sources are the records of oracular consultations: official accounts from temples, with witness signatures, and memoranda of judicial oracles in Pharaonic times; private inscriptions on the walls of a temple, like the graffiti and proskynemata at Deir el-Bahri and Kalabsha; votive monuments; and papyri that mention consultations. There are also pictorial representations of consultations during festivals, and a wide range of depictions of oracular gods.

A third group of sources are literary or mythological references to oracles, in both Egyptian and classical texts. Thanks to the work of Quaegebeur (1975 and *passim*), we also know that naming practices (for humans, gods, and places) can help identify oracular practices connected to a specific form of a divinity or a specific shrine.

In terms of method, I believe it is important to evaluate these sources in conjunction with heuristic models elaborated in other fields, such as anthropology and the history of religions. Judicious comparison with societies that were remote from Roman Egypt, on geographical and chronological grounds, nonetheless can offer insights into the material evidence for oracular practice (Dunand and Boespflug 1997: 7–20). At the same time, divination was idiosyncratic to its culture, and mirrors developments within that culture. Consequently, oracular cults in Roman Egypt reflect wider innovations in religious practice, and had to address issues in keeping with dramatic social, economic, and cultural changes in the wake of Alexander's conquest and Rome's later takeover.

Defining the Traditional Egyptian Oracle

Oracles are often considered to be a late development in Egyptian religion as they are not clearly attested before the New Kingdom and the 18th dynasty, but previous attestations, though scarce, should not be discarded (Assmann 1996: 233–4; see also Baines and Parkinson 1997; von Lieven 1999; Quack 2006: 175). As Graf puts it (2005: 52), 'an oracle is a divine answer to a specific question; the question in turn results from an event that often is perceived as a crisis'. In most cases, an oracle is a direct answer (spoken, written, or given through another set of signs) from a divinity who has been sought by a consultant (Quaegebeur 1997: 17). It should be distinguished from a prophecy, which is initiated by the deity itself (Blumenthal 1982; Devauchelle 1994; Szpakowska 2006). Therefore, this chapter does not consider dream manuals and lists of omens, which were not specifically requested by individuals (Jasnow 1997; Quack 2006).

The range of questions an oracle could answer was as wide as the range of human concerns (Valbelle and Husson 1998). Marriage, health, and women's fecundity were three of the main subjects of questions. Fertility of the fields and abundance of crops were also a major concern in a rural society, and plenty of oracular demands deal with agricultural matters. Every important decision in a person's life could lead to an oracular consultation. Centuries after the oracular questions attested in Deir el-Medina in the New Kingdom (Černý 1962), the *Sortes Astrampsychi* includes similar questions such as 'Am I to be a sophist? Shall I open a factory? Am I to be reconciled with my masters? Am I to be restored to my position? Shall I be a fugitive? Have I been poisoned?' (Browne 1974: 22–3; see also Browne 1987). Oracles dealt with a multitude of anxious situations, bringing comfort and confidence to the inquirers.

Though the nature of oracular questions did not vary much over time, techniques for detecting the god's answer multiplied, especially in Roman times. From the New Kingdom on, the primary way to consult the gods was to appeal to them during their public appearances outside the temple, either personally or through the mediation of a priest. The procession of divine statues gave inquirers the opportunity to seek an oracle, and once the god had 'approved' the request, the procession stopped and the consultation could start. This kind of consultation could work through spoken address or through the medium of writing, whereby written questions and names were placed before the god. Written, or 'ticket', oracles were used in the case of Amunemuia's missing garments, where individual names were inscribed on ostraca and placed before the shrine in procession (Blackman 1926; McDowell 1990: 107–14; Černý 1935, 1941, 1942, 1972), and they appear in the accounts of Strabo and Diodorus, describing how the oracle of Zeus-Ammon in Siwa Oasis worked in the sixth century BCE (Strabo 17.2.43; Diod. Sic. 17.50.6–7; see Černý 1962). In ticket oracles, the god is often said to nod his head or 'say no', though it is doubtful that the god actually uttered an answer. Instead, some movement on the part of the priests carrying the shrine would have been required to choose the appropriate ostracon, or to indicate yes or no by moving forwards or backwards (Černý 1935: 56–7; 1962: 44–5; McDowell 1990: 108–11). This complex type of collectively inspired divination could require further interpretation by specialists.

Apart from processions, the oracle could be consulted in the temple or its precinct, a practice that also seems to have existed since the New Kingdom. An example of such oracular consultation is the rear wall of the temple of Ptah in Karnak, decorated with a Ptolemaic relief. The relief depicts Ptah and Hathor together with Imhotep and Amenhotep, and there are traces of an associated structure, probably made of wood (Wildung 1977: 201–6; Quaegebeur 1997: 21). Answers to site-based consultations relied on priests to transmit the words of the god to the client. The answer could be spoken, as seems to have happened at Deir el-Bahri for the soldier Athenodoros, who wanted to know where the voice he heard was coming from (Wildung 1977: 230; Dunand 1991; Łajtar 2006, no. 208; see also Bataille 1951). But most often the answer was apparently written, and probably obtained by sortition: papyrus or sherds with alternative answers were enclosed in a vessel and sorted out, by spilling them or using dice or *astragaloi*. By this process of randomization, participants were assured that the lots or the dice moved according to divine will and were not circumvented by men (Graf 2005).

The use of dice is scarce in Pharaonic Egyptian sources, and appears no earlier than the Late period. For instance, some papyrus strips (*P Berlin* 23701) bear inscriptions such as 'number eight: it stands for Horus'. According to Quack (2006), the strips might have been used to draw lots, with the outcome interpreted according to the number and the god involved. An icosahedron in the Kharga Museum, probably dating to the first century CE, has the name of a god written in ink in Demotic on each side, and could also be used in divination (Minas-Nerpel 2007). A similar object in the Petrie Museum is a die with six faces, each engraved with the names of gods (Fig. 24.1; Tait 1998: 263). The use of Greek, on this and

FIG. 24.1 Icosahedron (twenty-sided die) used in oracular practice

University College London, UC 44999. Copyright the Petrie Museum of Egyptian Archaeology, University College London.

similar objects, has raised the question of whether such techniques were imported, or whether they were an internal development of Egyptian practice in the Ptolemaic and Roman periods.

Consulting the Oracle in Roman Egypt

Consultation by ticket oracles was more and more privileged in Graeco-Roman Egypt, but by the Roman period the formula for oracle requests had changed. After an invocation to the local god, and sometimes a self-introduction by the petitioner, the request formula became: 'If (this is the answer), deliver this (ticket) to me', written on two tickets to provide for both alternatives (Frankfurter 1998: 153–6). This formula is attested by oracular demands in Demotic dating back to 150 CE in which a villager from the Fayum addresses the crocodile-god Soknopaios and his companion Isis-Nepherses, and consults them about his project to plough a new field on the site opposite Lake Moeris (*P Oxy*. Griffith D recto and B recto; Bresciani 1975: 2–3).

Important evidence for the use of ostraca in oracular consultation comes from the *praesidium* of Dios, a military fort built in 114/15 CE on the Berenike road in the Eastern Desert. Inside the fort, the *aedes*, or shrine, was probably in use between 160 and 250 CE; a podium was set against its rear wall to display the divine statues, three of which were found *in situ*, including a seated statue of Zeus Helios Megas Sarapis associated with a Cerberus head (Cuvigny 2010). The filling of the podium yielded eight contemporaneous oracular ostraca and a steatite tablet, together with a steatite sun-dial that may have been used in the mantic procedure. These ostraca contain several oracular answers, all mentioning a number and an indication concerning the auspicious time to consult the oracle. They apparently belong to a collection of oracles, classified according to numerals. The names of the gods giving the oracles are all Greek—Apollo, Leto, Typhon, and Kronos—but the *interpretatio Graeca* could possibly mask indigenous deities. Some of the consultants, such as the Alexandrian *naukleros* (ship-owner) Aurelius Sarapion, left a proskynema and made a small votive gift. Cuvigny notes the strong similarity between these ostraca and the *astragaloi* oracles from Asia Minor (recently published by Nollé 2007); the *astragaloi* involved different combinations of numbers obtained by throwing five knucklebones, and were most fashionable in the second and early third century CE. The process is described by Pausanias (7.25.10), in a passage devoted to Herakles at Bura in Achaia:

> There is a smallish Herakles in a cave. The person who consults the god makes a prayer before the statue, and, after praying, he picks four knucklebones (there are plenty of them on the ground near the Herakles) and throws them on the table. For each combination of the knucklebones, the board conveniently provides a written interpretation.

As Cuvigny points out, however, despite formal similarities, the numerals in the Dios oracles cannot represent a cast of dice, since the range of numbers preserved (between 2 and 26) is too wide. Instead, the inquirer would have drawn numbers on papyrus chits or ostraca, perhaps contained in the podium, or else would be asked to choose a number at random between

FIG. 24.2 The Book of the *Sortes Astrampsychi*, third century CE

Papyrus Leiden, 573 verso. Copyright the Papyrologisch Instituut, Leiden.

1 and 30, which might also refer to the number of days in the month and whether or not the day was auspicious.

Such a collection of oracular answers is to be found in the *Sortes Astrampsychi*, an oracular handbook dating probably to the third century CE, which relied on the Greek tradition of bibliomancy (Fig. 24.2; Stewart 1998, 2001). It was published under the aegis of an Egyptian sage named Astrampsychos, and addressed ninety-two numbered questions, among which the inquirer would find his concern and then, by an intricate procedure involving sortition, or the selection of a number in his mind, be directed to one particular answer among the columns (Naether 2010). Each question led to ten possible answers. The *sors* itself speaks in the present tense and in the first person, addressing the client with the second-person 'you'. It was the diviner's job to provide inquirers with access to the knowledge encoded in the *sors* along with an interpretation of it (Klingshirn 2005: 106–7).

In his study of a Demotic papyrus from Soknopaiou Nesos, dating to the first century CE, Stadler (2004) recently raised the possibility of a child intervening in the randomization process. Such a process would be reminiscent of Roman divination practices at the shrine of Fortuna Primigenia at Praeneste (Cic. *Div.* 2.46; Grotanelli 1993). The Soknopaiou papyrus (*P Vienna* D 12006) is organized in sections ordered by a sequence of three numbers adding up to 4, 14, or 24. They represent questions asked by Isis and a sun-god, and addressed to an *ʾl*. According to Stadler, the word *ʾl* might mean 'child' and refer to a child-god consulted for divination, probably Harpocrates. The word could also mean 'stone' (Stadler 2004: 88–9), a reading that is favoured by Quack (2006: 184); the 'stone' in this case would be a die. Plutarch (*De Is. et Os.* 43) and Aelian (*NA* 11.10) provide literary evidence for children giving omens, while Greek and Demotic papyri mention youths in a trance acting as intermediaries between the magician and the gods: in the London–Leiden Demotic Magical Papyrus (third century CE; Griffith and Thompson 1904–9, §§27–35), a youth is supposed to stand before a lamp, 'he being pure, he not having gone with a woman', and the magician must recite formulas to the youth and ask, 'What are the things which you have seen?' (see also Martin 1994).

The written medium played an important part in oracular consultation, and afterwards, the worshipper could keep with him the ostracon or papyrus chit bearing the god's answer. In a culture where writing was a prerogative of the priestly and administrative elite, and viewed as sacred, such written records inevitably conveyed a numinosity that gave the decision a kind of amuletic character (Frankfurter 2005: 237). Presented to the client as the local god's own oral decree, the inscribed item could be carried outside the temple or chapel and be worn as an apotropaic device and a bond of security between the client and the god (Edwards 1960; Klasens 1975; Brashear 1995: 3448–56; Frankfurter 1998: 148–9). For example, a third-century CE papyrus recording oracular predictions of a political and agricultural nature calls itself an 'amulet', *alexeterion* (*P Oxy*. XXXI 2554; Ritner 1993: 36, 214–17).

Although quite difficult to prove and not clearly attested in the sources, the possibility of spoken, or voice, oracles should not be discarded and, again, seems to be a later development of the Egyptian traditional oracle. The testimony of the soldier Athenodoros, who heard a voice coming from a chapel in Deir el-Bahri (the so-called sanatorium), is a case in point (Dunand 1997: 67–8; Frankfurter 1998: 173–4; 2005: 238–43; Łajtar 2006: 37–46). Dunand observes that a hole was dug in the rear wall of the outer part of the oracular shrine, above the gateway leading to the inner room where the divine statues were stored. The cella was not open to worshippers, and Dunand suggests that priests could have hidden and used the hole to communicate with the consultants gathered outside, who would hear the alleged divine words, uttered from inside. Dunand notes a similar arrangement in the temple of Osiris-Serapis and Isis at Kysis (Dush) in the Kharga Oasis, dating to the second century CE. Again, an opening was dug in the rear wall of the cella, no doubt after the temple was partly abandoned. An oracular shrine was probably available at the rear of the cella, where a mud-brick chapel was built and decorated with painted stucco and columns. This chapel might have been a meeting room for inquirers, while priests let the gods 'speak' from inside the cella. The local god Serapis was deemed to have oracular powers. Quaegebeur (1997) raised similar questions concerning the rear chapel of the temple of Shenhur, which depicts the oracular god Tutu, and Traunecker (1997: 38–41) offered the same analysis for a chapel in the shape of a processional barque pedestal, built into a brick wall at the temple of Koptos. All these structures date to the Roman period.

Some oracular objects also attest the existence of voice oracles. The pedestal of a hollow bronze statue of a bull from Kom el-Wist in the Delta was equipped with an acoustic pipe, 2.5 metres long, which would allow a hidden priest to utter spoken oracles (Brunton 1947; Habachi 1947). Other examples include an image of Re-Harmakhis (Loukianoff 1936) and a limestone statue exhibited in Cairo that depicts the hawk-headed god Horus with a radiated nimbus and a Roman uniform; it is also equipped with an acoustic pipe (Fig. 24.3; Cairo, Egyptian Museum JE 66143). These 'speaking statues' all derive from the Roman period. Traunecker (1997) considers this to have been a late phenomenon, and probably imported. But a Ptolemaic papyrus (*P Dodgson*) offers earlier evidence for the practice: it records a series of messages that were apparently delivered in the first person singular by the oracular gods of Elephantine (de Cenival 1987; Martin 1994).

The issuing of voice oracles within temples allowed them to assume a more discursive form, and the development of oracles as texts, such as in *P Dodgson*, presents the problem of oracle recordings and their purposes; for, as Dillery (2005) observes, there is a powerful tension lurking behind the textualization of oral divination. Although written texts preserve a

FIG. 24.3 Oracular statue of Horus, second to third century CE

Egyptian Museum, Cairo, JE 66143. Author's photograph, courtesy of the Egyptian Museum, Cairo.

message more accurately over the long term, it is during the transition from oral to written that human intervention, and thus the corruption of divinatory messages, is most likely to occur. While the *manteis* (diviners) communicated the divine will instantly, the *chresmologoi* (interpreters) collected and subsequently reinterpreted old oracles and might intentionally or unintentionally alter this material. The role played by oracles in apocalyptic literature (Ray 1981: 182–3) or temple propaganda is an issue I return to below.

The Innovations of the Egyptian Oracle in Roman Times

Roman Egypt was a bustling marketplace for oracular techniques, a 'chaos of divination systems' that could suggest that the period was 'an age of decadence, individualism, and spiritual marketing—an "age of anxiety"' (Frankfurter 2005: 234). But, as Frankfurter forcefully demonstrates, the specificity of Roman oracles does not lie in the wide range of personal, 'anxious' concerns displayed through oracular questions, which were long-standing and almost universal, but in characteristics such as the diversification of divination media, the development of new types of expectation from inquirers, and the shift of contexts and status of the actors involved in oracular consultations.

Interpreting an oracle was a skill that, in Pharaonic times, was conferred through priestly status and regulated by the institutional religion. While the restrictions and impoverishment imposed on temples during the Roman period were partly responsible for the dwindling of Egyptian religion from the third or fourth century onwards (Bagnall 1988, 2008), temples remained centres for religious and cultural traditions and contributed to collective self-definition in local communities (Frankfurter 1998: 27–30, 37–97). Throughout the

Roman period, and probably starting earlier, the oracular process shifted, probably relying less and less upon the context of statue processions (though still existing; see Bianchi 1998), and more and more upon personal contact with oracular deities in the temple periphery or domestic contexts. This development may be connected with a shift in the religious mentality and expectations of Roman Egypt, but we should not underestimate the financial aspects of these changes. In my view, oracles saw the most dramatic changes of any religious practice under Roman domination, as the status and role of priests were completely re-evaluated. Hence it is the identity of the mediator and the nature of the medium that require closer scrutiny.

The Diversification of Divination Media

Although some may have already existed in the Late and Ptolemaic periods, oracular techniques developed dramatically in Roman Egypt (Frankfurter 1998: 11–15, 174–9; 2005). The use of oracular handbooks, the *sortes* manuals, is not attested before the second century CE and thus seems to be a Roman period innovation. Another new technique is incubation, which gradually took centre-stage in Hellenistic and Roman times throughout the Greek world (Graf 1999: 295–6). The petitioner could spend the night in a shrine or holy site in order to have a premonitory dream, or receive directions for a cure, either for himself or for the sake of someone else (see Sauneron 1959: 40–53, for the two types of incubation). The sanctuary of Serapis in Canopus was famous for healing people through incubation, as attested by Strabo (17.17), who mentions archives of *therapeiai* (records of healings). Though there are Egyptian records of people sleeping in the temple forecourts since at least the First Intermediate period, and especially in the late New Kingdom, evidence for dreams being sought in connection with oracular consultations is very scarce prior to the Late period (Sauneron 1959: 40–53; Szpakowska 2003: 142–7). Documents mention devout people spending the night in the vicinity of a temple, such as Qenherqepeshef, who records that his 'body spent the night in the shadow of [Hathor's] face; [that he] slept in [her] temenos' in the shrine of Hathor of Deir el-Medina, but they do not report any subsequent divine dreams or visits (contra Bruyère 1930; Marciniak 1981). The number of texts referring to both spontaneous and sought dreams from a divine source significantly increased in the Late period (Szpakowska 2003: 147 n. 109).

Incubation is attested in Saqqara in the Hellenistic period, where the god Thoth appears as a 'young officer' to the priestly incubant Hor, together with Isis or Harpocrates; the incubation shrine was likely staffed with professional dream interpreters (second century BCE; Ray 1976: 38–73). Incubation was probably also possible in the temple of Imhotep-Asklepios in Saqqara, and in the Serapeum of Memphis (Dunand 2006: 11). In Roman Abydos, Serapis, deemed to be an alter ego of the Egyptian Osiris (both are indifferently addressed in graffiti), was associated with Bes in the Memnonion. The Memnonion of Abydos thus extended its activities to, first, an incubation oracle of Serapis from some point in the Hellenistic period, and then to the communications of Bes in the first centuries CE. The site had a high concentration of votive graffiti to Bes, including that of Harpocras, who claims to have 'slept often' in this place and received 'veridical dreams'; elsewhere Bes is hailed as 'lord, greatest god, truthful in oracles' and 'dream giver' (Perdrizet and Lefebvre 1919, nos 481, 488, 492–3, 500, 503, 505, 524, 528). Bes may also have spoken to consultants from the cella (Dunand 1997).

Does this mean that at Abydos or Deir el-Bahri, as in the famous oracular shrine of Asklepios at Epidaurus, the god's words, uttered in a consecrated place, required specific buildings or other arrangements? Such buildings are not clearly documented in Egypt, and it seems more likely that rooms not specifically designed for the purpose were later converted to host incubation; priestly staff were most probably involved in running the incubation activities. Proskynemata from the temple of Mandulis in Talmis (Kalabsha) describe rituals preceding incubation, involving purification, fasting, sexual abstinence, and sacrifice, just as it was organized in Epidaurus: 'I made myself a stranger to all vice and all godlessness, was chaste for a considerable period, and offered the due incense offering in holy piety. I had a vision and found rest for my soul,' a *dipinto* says (Nock 1934: 64; see also Lewy 1944).

It is likely that these innovations—*sortes* and incubation—are connected to the transformations undergone by Egyptian society since the Graeco-Macedonian conquest and to the massive immigration to Egypt from all over the Greek world. The question of whether incubation was a natural development within Egypt or a Hellenistic influence is still debated. Under Roman rule, the settlement of soldiers, who came from abroad at least until the time of Trajan, brought different oracular traditions into the province and further contributed to the diffusion of such innovations. The Mandulis shrine in Kalabsha was frequented by an important clientele of Roman soldiers from the neighbouring garrison of Talmis until the third century CE, and it is no surprise that the god manifested himself in the guise of Apollo, most familiar to such soldiers. They left inscriptions that are, for the most part, the usual proskynemata, inscribed after either a simple visit to the temple or a full consultation with the local oracle. Among these, some are very elaborate and reflect upon the nature of Mandulis. The use of Greek metrical sections and the presence of an acrostic providing us with the name of its dedicator, the Roman centurion Paccius Maximus (*IMEGR* 168; Bernand 1969; Burstein 1998), may be related to the alphabetical oracles known in Asia Minor (Nollé 2007), while the phrasing of the oracular inquiries clearly echoes that of the inscriptions from Apollo's shrine in Claros in the second and third centuries (Tallet 2011). In the Eastern Desert, soldiers adored a god that was probably connected to the oracular shrine of Canopus: Zeus Helios Megas Sarapis. The set of oracular ostraca discovered *in situ* in Dios attest the presence of a team of *chresmologoi*, who were allowed to officiate in the god's chapel and who used an oracular handbook probably designed for travellers. In such a remote location on the Eastern Desert trade routes, all inquirers were either soldiers or travellers, and it is no surprise that the metaphor of a road is the most frequent among the oracular answers (Cuvigny 2010). At the small fort of Didymoi, also in the desert, two versions of an identical inscription thanking Serapis for sending dreams were displayed in the *aedes* (Cuvigny 2001), and in Mons Claudianus a quarry was called Chresmosarapis, that is, 'Serapis' oracle'.

Astrological forecasts also became increasingly practised in Egypt, beginning in the Hellenistic period. Often affiliated to temples, and documented in several Roman era papyri, astrologers worked to assimilate astrology's innovations to Egyptian traditions (Jones 1994). Astrological ceilings in Egyptian temples of the Roman period (e.g. Dendara, Deir el-Hagar) seem to be related to this trend, as is the presence of a sundial among the numbered oracular ostraca of Dios, with their concern for auspicious days (Cuvigny 2010). A papyrological parallel among the Greek magical papyri (*PGM* VII 155–67) also lists auspicious and inauspicious moments for consultation, on twenty days of an unknown month. This rendered possible 'magical' interventions in the political order, and might explain a series of interdictions promulgated by the imperial powers (Frankfurter 1998: 25–6): Quintus Aemilius Saturninus, prefect of Egypt, promulgated a law in 199 CE, apparently within Egypt only, that made it a capital offence to use oracles or to practise divination, although this was to no avail (Ritner 1995: 3355–6). At Abydos, where Romans of high station apparently submitted inquiries of a political nature, an envoy was sent by the emperor Constantius II in 359 to shut down the cult and set a trial for the numerous consultants (Amm. Marc. 19.12.14; Frankfurter 2000).

The Privatization of the Oracle

The use of practical handbooks such as the *Sortes Astrampsychi* located communication with the divine within a text, allowing divination to be carried out inside a private, domestic context. This type of oracular consultation evolved in about the third century CE as a hybrid of the ticket oracle: it is not a new type of divination medium, rather a late development of a traditional one (Browne 1987; Frankfurter 2005: 247).

A general feature of the Egyptian oracle in the Roman period is the use of new spaces, outside the temple and its immediate surroundings, and far from the immediate control of the priestly institutions. The god could then utter his words in any place, and especially within the domestic sphere, as is the case with magical oracles. The consultation still required a certain frame: the inquirer had to write a spell on a specific medium, using a special ink. After offering various products and burning of incense, the inquirer uttered the appropriate spell above a lamp and repeated it seven times. This procedure opened the way for freelance magicians and professional diviners, though most of them were also priests. The process became known by the Egyptian phrase *peh-netjer*, 'reaching the god', an expression first attested in the 21st dynasty in a priestly oracular context (Kruchten 1986: 328–31). In the London–Leiden Demotic Magical Papyrus (§§27–35), a private incubation that takes place in a pure and dark room, without any priestly intervention, is described as a *peh-netjer* (Ritner 1993: 214–20). In this case, a traditional ritual with a temple context became a quasi-mystical experience in a domestic context, allowing the client to meet the god directly through a dream or a vision.

In this new frame, the range of potential oracular gods exploded, bringing together various pantheons: in the Greek and Demotic Magical Papyri, Greek gods, such as Kronos, Zeus, Hermes, and Helios, were called on alongside Egyptian (Osiris, Isis, Seth, Serapis, Nut, Ptah, Thoth, Sekhmet), or even Persian (Mithras), Assyrian (Shamash), and Judaeo-Christian (Iaō, Jesus, the archangel Michael). The more gods, the more efficient the oracle.

The Quest for Personal Contact with the Divine

The privatization of the Egyptian oracle is a corollary to new expectations from the inquirers. Since the New Kingdom, the Egyptian oracle was connected to personal piety, because it was a privileged mode of direct contact with gods (Vernus 1975: 109–10; 1977: 146; Quaegebeur 1997: 17–18). Most oracular gods, such as Ptah, Amun, Imhotep, Sobek, or Tutu, were also 'gods who listen' to the prayers of their worshippers, or 'who come to the

FIG. 24.4 Stela of the oracular god Tutu with the griffin of Petbe-Nemesis, from the Fayum, Roman period

Musées Royaux d'Art et d'Histoire, Brussels, A.1505. Copyright the Musées Royaux d'Art et d'Histoire, Brussels.

one calling (them)' (Otto 1964: 28–9; Quaegebeur 1997: 23–34), a formula that was most popular at the end of the Ptolemaic period and during Roman times. One feature that developed in divine iconography might be connected to an oracular character, namely the frontal depiction of gods, sometimes underlined by a radiating nimbus that enhanced the intensity of the divine epiphany (Meeks 1986: 179; Volokhine 2000). The oracular god Tutu is an example of this frontality (Fig. 24.4; Brussels, Musées Royaux d'Art et d'Histoire A.1505). In anthroponyms, he is often designed as Tithoentos, 'Tutu is the speaking face', or Pneferontithoes, 'the beautiful of face is Tutu', and such descriptions insist on the god's ability to answer the worshippers who addressed their questions and requests to him, sometimes through the medium of the oracle (Quaegebeur 1977; Kaper 2003: 151–2). In the Roman temple of Qasr el-Aguz, Thotsytmis, 'Thoth who listens', who could be depicted as a god with the head of an ibis with human ears, is paralleled with Teephibis, 'the face of the speaking Ibis' (Quaegebeur 1975; 1997: 19–31; Volokhine 2002). The oracular character of Teephibis is attested by questions in Demotic addressed to him (Zauzich 1974). Coroplastic workshops and tempera painters, responsible for wooden 'icons' and frescos, probably played an important role in the diffusion of new iconographies, in connection with new modes of relationship with the gods.

The Transformation of the Status of the Diviner

In this quest for direct contact with the gods, freelance diviners and magicians seem to have been increasingly important, but private oracles were not necessarily segregated from priestly traditions. Three private Bes oracles preserved among the Greek and Demotic spell manuals suggest that some priests took the Bes oracle 'on the road' (Frankfurter 1997: 123; 2005: 241). The texts invoke Bes as 'oracle-giving' and describe rites in preparation for incubatory sleep. They clearly manifest a deliberate adherence to Egyptian gods and to priestly tradition, and it should be assumed that the Greek examples stem from an original (Demotic or Greek) maintained in the scriptorium of Abydos. As this case shows, the diversification in the media of divination still depended on a tradition, and many forms of divination derived authority from their association with well-established centres of power, most notably temples, where priests might offer divinatory practices in addition to the role they played within the temple cult itself.

The Oracle: An Issue for Priests in Roman Egypt

Priests did not abandon their status as mediators in the oracular process. The social dialogue between diviners and clients (Zeitlyn 1995), and their collaboration in making decisions and formulating 'plans of action' (Peek 1991), was central to the Roman Egyptian oracle, even in *sortes* divination, where the answers were already written before the consultation (Klingshirn 2005: 108–10). Whatever the kind of consultation, the diviner needed to interview his client in order to determine the exact nature of the problem and how the question should be formulated. Then the divine answer had to be interpreted and to lead to a concrete plan.

These considerations relate to the historical context of Roman Egypt and the balance created between the temples and the imperial powers, beginning with Augustus and especially marked from the third century CE on. The drop in economic and political status that the temple institution had to cope with was certainly not accompanied by any loss of charismatic authority for the priests (Frankfurter 1998). The spaces and media through which they expressed their authority simply shifted from one context to another, and oracular consultation was one of the most important contexts in which this shift in the locus of the holy occurred.

Deprived of previous revenues and privileges, the clergy was highly dependent on private income. The priests sought local patronage and thus had no choice but to adapt themselves to the expectations of their prospective clients and meet their need for personal contact with the divine. Maintaining their authority within society involved continued control of the relationships between humans and gods; as a result, the oracle became a major issue for the priesthood.

Experts almost certainly received monetary rewards (or offerings) in exchange for their prestation, whether as magicians, physicians, or as professional interpreters or scribes in incubation shrines and around rear-chapels (see Migne, *PG* 77.105, for a Christian denunciation). Gaining a local, regional, or even international reputation was valuable, like the mid-fourth-century oracle of Bes at Abydos, remarked on by Ammianus Marcellinus (19.3–4). This oracle held long-distance consultations by letter or intermediary, bringing wealth and renown to the sanctuary. But most of the time, the clientele was merely local, as was the case even with international shrines such as Epidaurus. At Deir el-Bahri the onomastics of the proskynemata show that the clientele mainly came from the Theban area, with some travellers like the soldiers stationed at Koptos, or visiting Roman officials such as the *strategos* Celer.

Oracular shrines used a form of marketing to reach their prospective clientele. In Epidaurus, while some priests were devoted to healing the consultants, others were dedicated to recording the miracles, the *iamata*. Such practices to secure and publicize the sanctuary are also attested in the literary tradition for the temple of Serapis and Isis in Canopus, and can be deduced from the proskynemata in the shrine of Mandulis at Kalabsha. These proskynemata date to between the first and third centuries CE, and are mostly made by Roman soldiers stationed there, at Talmis. Strategically important, Talmis was quite remote, and mainly consisted of the temple and garrison. Most of the Kalabsha inscriptions were dedicated by men from the *legio III Cyrenaica* and auxiliary troops protecting the southern border. Scribes in the temple probably inscribed the proskynemata for visitors with the clergy's permission, which, in my view, implies that although they were not pilgrimages in the modern sense, the visits were organized and overseen by the priests (Tallet 2011).

Furthermore, the Greek hymns inscribed at Kalabsha were probably composed in Egyptian priestly circles. They show how involved in Hellenism the Egyptian priests were, as early as the second or third century CE. They were familiar not only with the literary images, poetical forms, philosophical traditions, and classical references of Greek culture, but also with its rituals and practices. The ratio of oracular questions in Greek and in Demotic changed from the Hellenistic to the Roman period, when Demotic questions almost disappear (Valbelle and Husson 1998: 1069). The priests of Kalabsha might have seized the opportunity to attract visitors eager to have an 'esoteric' experience, and the proskynemata themselves helped attract new clients by stressing the oracular features of Mandulis. The temple inscriptions call him a god 'who comes to the one calling him', in the Egyptian fashion, but in the Greek hymns he is also assimilated with Apollo Pythios or with Aion, the master of time and destiny, who often holds a zodiac for his emblem (Nock 1934). Promoting the oracular powers of Mandulis seems to have been the best way to gain local patronage—otherwise, why would some inscriptions have displayed the revelation of an epiphany that was usually kept secret? The proskynemata were painted in an open part of a temple, on the walls of the courtyard. Promoting 'holy Talmis' and its sanctuary seems to have been the goal (see the hymn in Bernand 1969: 576–83; Dunand 2002: 38 n. 68).

The oracular consultations recorded and displayed at Talmis reveal soldiers worrying about their health, their welcome back home, or their relatives. They take the standard form of a narrator–inquirer who comes from the outside, puts his question to the god, and receives an answer. In a sense, the inscriptions are addressed to a Greek-speaking reader who was also a potential client, and resemble the so-called 'dice oracles' from south-western Anatolia, which were recorded on the marketplace, where potential consultants (merchant travellers) would see them (Graf 2005: 71–8; on religious propaganda, see Łajtar 2006: 23–4). As Frankfurter (2005: 238) points out, this was not 'shameless marketing by decrepit temple staff', but a reasoned response to exigencies, which in the case of Talmis may have involved an appeal to Roman ideas of Egyptian esoterica.

Conclusion

In contrast to the public testimonies at Kalabsha, the ostraca of Dios were found *inside* a shrine, where an oracular handbook might have been used for divination. The same is true for fragments of the *Sortes Sanctorum* later found in the Church of St Colluthus at Antinoopolis (Papini 1998; Frankfurter 2005). Innovations of the Roman period, oracular manuals were not only for use outside the sanctuaries, nor did the development of the oracle in the Roman period occur in opposition to Egyptian priests, but with their cooperation and participation. Oracles thus offer key evidence for religious changes during the Roman period. Further transformation of divinatory practice eventually took place with the demission of sacerdotal control in the face of Christianization, and it is no surprise to find ticket oracles in St Colluthus' church or to read, in a Christian papyrus from seventh- or eighth-century Oxyrhynchus, the request, 'O God almighty, if thou dost instruct me, thy servant Paulos, to go to Antinoo[polis], give me order through this label!' (Černý 1962: 47).

Suggested Reading

An excellent introduction to the various questions raised by oracles in Roman Egypt is found in Frankfurter (1998: 145–97) and his further publications, while Černý (1962) provides a good overview of the traditional Egyptian oracle. For a methodological frame, see Vernant (1991) and Johnston and Struck (2005).

Bibliography

Assmann, J. 1994. 'Ocular Desire in a Time of Darkness: Urban Festivals and Divine Visibility in Ancient Egypt', in A. E. E. Agus and J. Assmann (eds), *Ocular Desire*. Berlin: Akademie, 13–29.

—— 1996. *Ägypten: Eine Sinngeschichte*. Munich: Hanser.

Bagnall, R. S. 1988. 'Combat ou vide: Christianisme et paganisme dans l'Égypte romaine tardive', *Ktêma* 13: 285–96.

—— 2008. 'Models and Evidence in the Study of Religion in Late Roman Egypt', in J. Hahn, S. Emmel, and U. Gotter (eds), *From Temple to Church: Destruction and Renewal of Local Cultic Topography in Late Antiquity*. Leiden: Brill, 23–41.

Baines, J., and R. B. Parkinson 1997. 'An Old Kingdom Record of an Oracle? Sinai Inscription 13', in J. van Dijk (ed.), *Essays on Ancient Egypt in Honour of Herman te Velde*. Groningen: Styx, 9–27.

Bataille, A. 1951. *Les inscriptions grecques du temple de Hatshepsout à Deir el-Bahari*. Cairo: Institut Français d'Archéologie Orientale.

Bernand, É. 1969. *Inscriptions métriques de l'Égypte gréco-romaine: Recherches sur la poésie épigrammatique des Grecs et Égypte*. Paris: Belles Lettres.

Bianchi, R. S. 1998. 'The Oracle at the Temple of Dendur', in W. Clarysse, A. Schoors, and H. Willems (eds), *Egyptian Religion: The Last Thousand Years: Studies Dedicated to the Memory of Jan Quaegebeur*, vol. 2. Leuven: Peeters, 773–80.

Blackman, A. M. 1925. 'Oracles in Ancient Egypt', *Journal of Egyptian Archaeology* 11: 249–55.
——1926. 'Oracles in Ancient Egypt', *Journal of Egyptian Archaeology* 12: 176–85.
Blumenthal, E. 1982. 'Prophétie', in W. Helck and W. Westendorf (eds), *Lexikon der Ägyptologie*, vol. 4. Wiesbaden: Harrassowitz, 380–1.
Brashear, W. 1995. 'The Greek Magical Papyri: An Introduction and Survey', in W. Haase and H. Temporini (eds), *Aufstieg und Niedergang der römischen Welt* II 18.5. Berlin: de Gruyter, 3380–3684.
Bresciani, E. 1975. *L'archivio demotico del tempio di Soknopaiu Nesos nel Griffith Institute di Oxford*. Milan: Cisalpino—La Goliardica.
Browne, G. M. 1974. *The Papyri of the Sortes Astrampsychi*. Meisenheim: Hain.
——1987. 'The *Sortes Astrampsychi* and the Egyptian Oracle', in J. Dummer (ed.), *Texte und Textkritik: Eine Aufsatzsammlung*. Berlin: Akademie, 67–71.
Brunton, G. 1947. 'The Oracle of Kôm el-Wist', *Annales du Service des Antiquités de l'Égypte* 47: 293–5.
Bruyère, B. 1930. *Mert-Seger à Deir el Médineh*. Cairo: Institut Français d'Archéologie Orientale.
Burkert, W. 2005. 'Signs, Commands and Knowledge: Ancient Divination between Enigma and Epiphany', in S. I. Johnston and P. Struck (eds), *Mantikê: Studies in Ancient Divination*. Leiden: Brill, 29–49.
Burstein, S. M. 1998. 'Paccius Maximus: A Greek Poet in Nubia or a Nubian Greek Poet?', *Cahiers de Recherches de l'Institut de Papyrologie et d'Égyptologie de Lille* 17/3: 47–52.
Černý, J. 1935. 'Questions adressées au oracles', *Bulletin de l'Institut Français d'Archéologie Orientale* 35: 41–58.
——1941. 'Le tirage au sort', *Bulletin de l'Institut Français d'Archéologie Orientale* 40: 135–41.
——1942. 'Nouvelle série de questions adressées aux oracles', *Bulletin de l'Institut Français d'Archéologie Orientale* 41: 13–24.
——1962. 'Egyptian Oracles', in R. A. Parker (ed.), *A Saite Oracle Papyrus from Thebes in the Brooklyn Museum (Papyrus Brooklyn 47.218.3)*. Providence, RI: Brown University Press, 35–48.
——1972. 'Troisième série de questions adressées aux oracles', *Bulletin de l'Institut Français d'Archéologie Orientale* 72: 49–69.
Cuvigny, H. 2001. 'Un soldat de la *cohors I Lusitanorum* à Didymoi: Du nouveau sur l'inscription I. Kanais 59 *bis*', *Bulletin de l'Institut Français d'Archéologie Orientale* 101: 153–7.
——2010. 'The Shrine in the *Praesidium* of Dios (Eastern Desert of Egypt): Graffiti and Oracles in Context', *Chiron* 40: 245–99.
de Cenival, F. 1987. 'Le papyrus Dodgson (P. Ashmolean Museum Oxford 1932-1159): Une interrogation aux portes des dieux?', *Revue d'Égyptologie* 38: 3–11.
Devauchelle, D. 1994. 'Les prophéties en Égypte ancienne', *Prophéties et Oracles II: En Égypte et en Grèce, Cahiers Évangiles* 89, suppl., 6–31.
Dieleman, J. 2005. *Priests, Tongues, and Rites: The London-Leiden Magical Manuscripts and Translation in Egyptian Ritual (100–300 CE)*. Leiden: Brill.
Dillery, J. 2005. 'Chresmologues and *Manteis*: Independent Diviners and the Problem of Authority', in S. I. Johnston and P. Struck (eds), *Mantikê: Studies in Ancient Divination*. Leiden: Brill, 167–231.
Dunand, F. 1991. 'Miracles et guérisons en Égypte tardive', in N. Fick and J.-C. Carrière (eds), *Mélanges Étienne Bernand*. Paris: Belles Lettres, 235–50.
——1997. 'La consultation oraculaire en Égypte tardive: L'oracle de Bès à Abydos', in J.- G. Heintz (ed.), *Oracles et prophéties dans l'antiquité: Actes du Colloque de Strasbourg*. Paris: de Boccard, 65–84.

—— 2002. 'Le désir de connaître Dieu: Une vision de Mandoulis au temple de Kalabscha', in F. Boespflug and F. Dunand (eds), *Voir les dieux, voir Dieu*. Strasbourg: Presses Universitaires de Strasbourg, 23–38.

—— 2006. 'La guérison dans les temples (Égypte, époque tardive)', *Archiv für Religionsgeschichte* 8: 4–24.

—— and F. Boespflug (eds) 1997. *Le comparatisme en histoire des religions*. Paris: Cerf.

Edwards, I. E. S. 1960. *Oracular Amuletic Decrees of the Late New Kingdom*. London: British Museum Press.

Favret-Saada, J. 1977. *Les mots, la mort, les sorts*. Paris: Gallimard.

Frankfurter, D. 1997. 'Ritual Expertise in Roman Egypt and the Problem of the Category "Magician"', in P. Schäfer and H. G. Kippenberg (eds), *Envisioning Magic: A Princeton Seminar and Symposium*. Leiden: Brill, 115–35.

—— 1998. *Religion in Roman Egypt: Assimilation and Resistance*. Princeton: Princeton University Press.

—— 2000. 'The Consequences of Hellenism in Late Antique Egypt: Religious Worlds and Actors', *Archiv für Religionsgeschichte* 2: 162–94.

—— 2005. 'Voices, Books and Dreams: The Diversification of Divination Media in Late Antique Egypt', in S. I. Johnston and P. Struck (eds), *Mantikē: Studies in Ancient Divination*. Leiden: Brill, 233–54.

Geertz, C. 1973. 'Religion as a Cultural System', in Geertz, *The Interpretation of Culture*. New York: Basic Books, 87–125; first pub. 1966.

Graf, F. 1999. 'Magic and Divination', in D. R. Jordan, H. Montgomery, and E. Thomassen (eds), *The World of Ancient Magic: Papers from the First International Samson Eitrem Seminar at the Norwegian Institute at Athens, 4–8 May 1997*. Bergen: Astrom, 283–98.

—— 2005. 'Rolling the Dice for an Answer', in S. I. Johnston and P. Struck (eds), *Mantikê: Studies in Ancient Divination*. Leiden: Brill, 51–97.

Griffith, F. L., and H. Thompson. 1904–9. *The Demotic Magical Papyrus of London and Leiden*, 3 vols. London: Grevel.

Grotanelli, C. 1993. 'Bambini e divinazione', in O. Niccoli (ed.), *Infanzie: Funzioni di un gruppo liminale dal mondo classico all'eta moderna*. Florence: Ponte Alle Grazie, 23–72.

Habachi, L. 1947. 'Finds at Kôm el-Wist', *Annales du Service des Antiquités de l'Égypte* 47: 285–7.

Heintz, J.-G. (ed.) 1997. *Oracles et prophéties dans l'antiquité: Actes du Colloque de Strasbourg, 15–17 juin 1995*. Paris: de Boccard.

Jasnow, R. 1997. 'A Demotic Omen Text? (P. BM 10238)', in J. van Dijk (ed.), *Essays on Ancient Egypt in Honour of Herman te Velde*. Groningen: Styx, 207–18.

Johnston, S. I., and P. Struck (eds) 2005. *Mantikê: Studies in Ancient Divination*. Leiden: Brill.

Jones, A. 1994. 'The Place of Astronomy in Roman Egypt', in T. D. Barnes (ed.), *The Sciences in Greco-Roman Society*. Edmonton: Academic Printing, 25–51.

Kaper, O. E. 2003. *The Egyptian God Tutu: A Study of the Sphinx-God and Master of Demons with a Corpus of Monuments*. Leuven: Peeters.

Klasens, A. 1975. 'An Amuletic Papyrus of the 25th Dynasty', *Oudheidkundige Mededelingen vit het Rijksmuseum van Oudheden* 56: 20–8.

Klingshirn, W. E. 2005. 'Christian Divination in Late Roman Gaul: The *Sortes Sangallenses*', in S. I. Johnston and P. Struck (eds), *Mantikê: Studies in Ancient Divination*. Leiden: Brill, 99–128.

Kruchten, J.-M. 1985. 'Un instrument politique original: La "belle fête de *peh-netjer*" des rois-prêtres de la XXIe dynastie', *Bulletin de la Société Française d'Égyptologie* 103: 6–26.

Kruchten, J.-M. 1986. *Le grand texte oraculaire de Djéhoutymose*. Brussels: Fondation Égyptologique Reine Élisabeth.

Łajtar, A. 2006. *Deir el-Bahari in the Hellenistic and Roman Periods: A Study of an Egyptian Temple Based on Greek Sources*. Warsaw: Institute of Archaeology, Warsaw University, and Raphael Taubenschlag Foundation.

Lewy, H. 1944. 'A Dream of Mandulis', *Annales du Service des Antiquités de l'Égypte* 44: 227–34.

Loukianoff, G. 1936. 'Une statue parlante ou oracle du dieu Ré-Harmakhis', *Annales du Service des Antiquités de l'Égypte* 36: 187–93.

McDowell, A. G. 1990. *Jurisdiction in the Workmen's Community of Deir el-Medina*. Leiden: Nederlands Instituut voor het Nabije Oosten.

Marciniak, M. 1981. 'Un texte inédit de Deir el-Bahari', *Bulletin de l'Institut Français d'Archéologie Orientale* 81, suppl., 283–91.

Martin, C. G. 1994. 'The Child Born in Elephantine: Papyrus Dodgson Revisited', *Acta Demotica: Acts of the Fifth International Conference for Demotists, Pisa, 4th–8th September 1993*. Pisa: Giardini, 199–212.

Meeks, D. 1986. 'Zoomorphie et image des dieux dans l'Égypte ancienne', in C. Malamoud and J.-P. Vernant (eds), *Le Corps des dieux*. Paris: Gallimard, 171–91.

Minas-Nerpel, M. 2007. 'A Demotic Inscribed Icosahedron from Dakhleh Oasis', *Journal of Egyptian Archaeology* 93: 137–48.

Naether, F. 2010. *Die Sortes Astrampsychi: Problemlosungsstrategien durch Orakel im römischen Ägypten*. Tübingen: Mohr Siebeck.

Nock, A. D. 1934. 'A Vision of Mandulis Aion', *Harvard Theological Review* 27: 53–104.

Nollé, J. 2007. *Kleinasiatische Losorakel: Astragal- und Alphabetchresmologien der hochkaiserzeitlichen Orakelrenaissance*. Munich: Beck.

Otto, E. 1964. *Gott und Mensch nach den ägyptischen Tempelinschriften der griechisch-römischen Zeit*. Heidelberg: Winter.

Papini, L. 1998. 'Fragments of the *Sortes Sanctorum* from the Shrine of St. Colluthus', in D. Frankfurter (ed.), *Pilgrimage and Holy Space in Late Antique Egypt*. Leiden: Brill, 393–401.

Park, G. K. 1963. 'Divination and its Social Contexts', *Journal of the Royal Anthropological Institute of Great Britain and Ireland* 93: 195–209.

Parker, R. 1985. 'Greek States and Greek Oracles', in P. Cartledge and F. D. Harvey (eds), *Crux: Essays Presented to G. E. M. de Ste Croix on his 75th Birthday*. Exeter: Exeter University Press, 298–326.

Parker, R. A. 1962. *A Saite Oracle Papyrus from Thebes in the Brooklyn Museum (Papyrus Brooklyn 47.218.3)*. Providence, RI: Brown University Press.

Peek, P. M. 1991. 'The Study of Divination, Present and Past', in Peek (ed.), *African Divination Systems: Ways of Knowing*. Bloomington: Indiana University Press, 1–22.

Perdrizet, P., and G. Lefebvre. 1919. *Les graffites grecs du Memnonion d'Abydos*. Nancy: Berger-Levrault.

Quack, J. F. 2006. 'A Black Cat from the Right, and a Scarab on your Head: New Sources for Ancient Egyptian Divination', in K. Szpakowska (ed.), *Through a Glass Darkly: Magic, Dreams and Prophesy in Ancient Egypt*. Swansea: Classical Press of Wales, 175–87.

Quaegebeur, J. 1975. 'Teëphibis, dieu oraculaire?', *Enchoria* 5: 19–24.

—— 1977. 'Tithoes, dieu oraculaire?', *Enchoria* 7: 103–8.

—— 1997. 'L' appel au divin: Le bonheur des hommes mis dans la main des dieux', in J.- G. Heintz (ed.), *Oracles et prophéties dans l'antiquité: Actes du Colloque de Strasbourg, 15–17 juin 1995*. Paris: de Boccard, 15–34.

Ray, J. 1976. *The Archive of Hor*. London: Egypt Exploration Society.
—— 1981. 'Ancient Egypt', in M. Loewe and C. Blacker (eds), *Divinations and Oracles*. London: Shambhala, 174–90.
Ritner, R. K. 1993. *The Mechanics of Ancient Egyptian Magical Practice*. Chicago: Oriental Institute.
—— 1995. 'Egyptian Magical Practice under the Roman Empire: The Demotic Spells and their Religious Context', in W. Haase and H. Temporini (eds), *Aufstieg und Niedergang der römischen Welt* II 18.5. Berlin: de Gruyter, 3333–79.
Sauneron, S. 1959. 'Les songes et leur interprétation dans l'Égypte ancienne', in Sauneron et al., *Les Songes et leur interprétation*. Paris: Seuil, 17–61.
Stadler, M. A. 2004. *Isis, das göttliche Kind und die Weltordnung: Neue religiöse Texte aus dem Fayum nach dem Papyrus Wien D. 12006 recto*. Vienna: Hollinek.
Stewart, R. 1998. 'The Oracles of Astrampsychus', in W. Hansen (ed.), *Anthology of Ancient Greek Popular Literature*. Bloomington: Indiana University Press, 285–324.
—— 2001. *Sortes Astrampsychi*. Munich: Saur.
Szpakowska, K. (ed.) 2003. *Behind Closed Eyes: Dreams and Nightmares in Ancient Egypt*. Swansea: Classical Press of Wales.
—— (ed.) 2006. *Through a Glass Darkly: Magic, Dreams and Prophesy in Ancient Egypt*. Swansea: Classical Press of Wales.
Tait, J. 1998. 'Dicing with the Gods', in W. Clarysse, A. Schoors, and H. Willems (eds), *Egyptian Religion: The Last Thousand Years: Studies Dedicated to the Memory of Jan Quaegebeur*, vol. 1. Leuven: Peeters, 257–64.
Tallet, G. 2011. 'Voir et interpréter les signes du dieu: Une apparition de Mandoulis au temple de Kalabchah (Nubie)', in S. Georgoudi, R. Koch-Piettre, and F. Schmidt (eds), *La Raison des signes: Langages divinatoires, rites et destines dans les sociétés de la Méditerranée ancienne. Actes du Colloque International organisé par le Centre G. Glotz et l'École Pratique des Hautes Études (16–18 octobre 2005)*. Leiden: Brill, 343–83.
Traunecker, C. 1997. 'L'appel au divin: La crainte des dieux et les serments du temple', in J.-G. Heintz (ed.), *Oracles et prophéties dans l'antiquité: Actes du Colloque de Strasbourg, 15–17 juin 1995*. Paris: de Boccard, 35–54.
Valbelle, D., and G. Husson. 1998. 'Les questions oraculaires d'Égypte: Histoire de la recherche, nouveautés et perspectives', in W. Clarysse, A. Schoors, and H. Willems (eds), *Egyptian Religion: The Last Thousand Years: Studies Dedicated to the Memory of Jan Quaegebeur*, vol. 2. Leuven: Peeters, 1055–71.
Vernant, J.-P. 1991. 'Speech and Mute Signs', in F. M. Zeitlin (ed.), *Mortals and Immortals*. Princeton: Princeton University Press, 303–17; trans. of 'Paroles et signes muets', in Vernant (ed.), *Divination et rationalité*. Paris: Seuil, 1974.
—— (ed.) 1974. *Divination et rationalité*. Paris: Seuil.
Vernus, P. 1975. 'Un texte oraculaire de Ramsès VI', *Bulletin de l'Institut Français d'Archéologie Orientale* 75: 103–10.
—— 1977. 'Le dieu personnel dans l'Égypte pharaonique', in *Colloques d'Histoire des Religions organisés par la Société Ernest-Renan, Société Française d'Histoire des Religions 1976 et 1977*. Orsay: CIEEIST, 143–57.
Volokhine, Y. 2000. *La frontalité dans l'iconographie de l'Égypte ancienne*. Geneva: Société d'Égyptologie.
—— 2002. 'Le dieu Thot au Qasr el-Agoûz', *Bulletin de l'Institut Français d'Archéologie Orientale* 102: 405–23.

von Lieven, A. 1999. 'Divination in Ägypten', *Archiv für Orientforschung* 26: 77–126.
Wildung, D. 1977. *Imhotep und Amenhotep: Gottverdung im alten Ägypten*. Munich: Deutscher Kunstverlag.
Zauzich, K.-T. 1974. 'Teëphibis als Orakelgott', *Enchoria* 3: 163.
Zeitlyn, D. 1995. 'Divination as Dialogue: Negotiation of Meaning with Random Responses', in E. Goody (ed.), *Social Intelligence and Interaction*. Cambridge: Cambridge University Press, 189–205.

CHAPTER 25

ISIS, OSIRIS, AND SERAPIS

MARTIN BOMMAS

It was not until Greek settlers appeared in Egypt that certain aspects of Egyptian religion were gradually and selectively transformed into foreign thinking. Newly shaped and customized as an all-embracing universal religion, the cult of Isis, accompanied by Serapis and Harpocrates, appeared on Greek shores after Alexander the Great had conquered Egypt. By the second century CE and especially under Roman influence, Egyptian cults were carried out even in remote places of the known world.

The Worship of Isis, Osiris, and Serapis

According to Egyptian myth, Isis plays the role of devoted sister and wife of Osiris and mother of their child Horus. As Isis *lactans*, she is mostly depicted sitting on a throne, suckling her son, who sits on her lap (Fig. 25.1). In Pharaonic times, Isis is usually either shown wearing the horns of a cow with a sun-disc as her headdress or with the emblem of a throne on her head, a reference to the hieroglyphic writing of her name, which originally might have meant 'throne' (Egyptian: *set*, or *aset*). According to the myth, Isis gave birth to her son in the Delta marshes, hiding him from the threats of Seth, who wanted to rule Egypt and aimed at neutralizing Osiris' rightful heir. Linking to her qualities as a mother goddess, Isis is also addressed as 'Great of Magic', protecting young people and pregnant women from injuries and illnesses. Owing to her many syncretistic assimilations with other female divinities, such as Hathor Renenutet and Neith, sanctuaries for Isis spread throughout the whole of Egypt, while the temples of Philae and Behbeit el-Hagar stand out as her most important places of worship, especially in Roman times. In post-Pharaonic times, Isis was increasingly regarded as a universal goddess owing to her ability to adapt functions of other Egyptian and Greek goddesses.

Osiris is associated with death, resurrection, and fertility. He is mostly depicted as a wrapped (or mummiform) figure standing upright (Fig. 25.2) or seated on a throne with his

FIG. 25.1 Faience figure of Isis and the infant Horus, dated to the Late or Ptolemaic period. Height *c.*10 cm

Eton College, Myers Collection, 1717. Photograph copyright Graham Norrie.

hands projecting through the shroud in order to hold the crook and the flail, both royal insignia. He usually wears the so-called *atef* crown, which is composed of the (Upper Egyptian) White Crown, flanked by two plumes and sometimes the horns of a ram. The colour of his body usually refers to the context in which Osiris appears: white stands for the colour of mummy bindings (death), green for his netherworldly existence (resurrection), and black for Egypt as the 'black land' (fertility). The origins of Osiris as a god of the inundation and the fertile alluvium are not fully understood but remain important until the end of Roman rule. He is associated both with Buto in the Delta and with Abydos in southern Egypt, and there are arguments for his origin in either of those places. Osiris' royal insignia may reflect Buto's status as one of the earliest centres of political power in Egypt, and Busiris and Buto both claimed to house his backbone (*djed* pillar). One argument for his southern origins is that later versions of the myth suggest that he was killed there, and that parts of his dismembered body were swept down the Nile to the Delta. The nature of the sources, especially from early periods, makes it unlikely that the question of origins can be resolved, but in any case, his association with both a northern and a southern cult centre emphasized the idea that Osiris was a true ruler over the whole of Egypt. This concept was still viable in Roman Egypt, when Osiris was regarded as a god throughout the country.

Whatever preference for his place of origin is given depends on whether one is prepared to give priority either to his link with the inundation of the Nile or to the Delta kingship as being key to the understanding of Osiris. Closely linked with this question is the fact that Abydos was regarded as his main southern cult centre and was thought to be the burial place

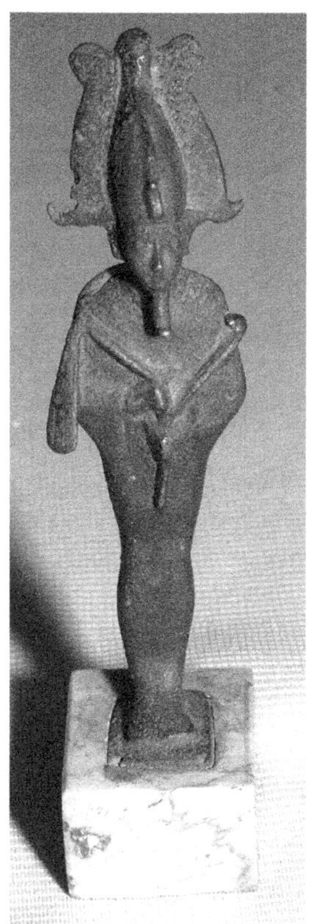

FIG. 25.2 Bronze figure of Osiris, dated to the Late or Ptolemaic period. Height *c.*10 cm

Eton College, Myers Collection, 720. Photograph copyright Graham Norrie.

of Osiris' head. Already during the Middle Kingdom (2055–1650 BCE), the tomb of the 1st dynasty ruler Djer (*c.*3000 BCE) was converted into a cenotaph for Osiris and achieved cultic significance. Especially during the Middle Kingdom, Abydos became an important pilgrimage site, where the great festival of Osiris was celebrated along the route from the main temple to the 1st dynasty tombs, and it remained a sacred site throughout Roman times (see Chapters 24 and 42).

His aspect of fertility, as well as his fate as a god who could be 'healed' from death, made Osiris a focus of funerary culture from the early Old Kingdom onwards. The so-called Bent pyramid of Pharaoh Seneferu at Dahshur, dating to the beginning of the 4th dynasty, is the first funerary monument that contains a valley temple and causeway leading to the pyramid. The construction of the causeway was indebted to a linear funerary procession, obviously linked with the Osirian funerary procession. This concept remained largely unchanged until the end of the Roman period. Minor changes such as the introduction of the solar concept during the New Kingdom, and Amun as an advocate of the worries and fears of the dead during the Third Intermediate period, helped Osiris shape his future profile in Roman times.

The myth that equated parts of his body with different nomes meant that all the provinces of Egypt contributed to his resurrection (Beinlich 1984). By the Ptolemaic and Roman periods, nome capitals that were graced with the washed-up body parts of Osiris consequently worshipped them as relics. The worship of Osiris as a national god was incorporated in all the major temples of the Graeco-Roman period (Burkard 1995), which suggests that the significance of his resurrection extended beyond the mortuary realm. Deeply rooted in his functions as a god of fertility, the ancient festival of Khoiak became an important point of reference: here, moulds in the form of Osiris were filled with growing grain at temples in the whole of Egypt, during the month of Khoiak. His role in funerary practices continued to be important, and in the Roman era, a tendency to intensify the deceased's identification with Osiris is attested by representations of the dead as the god.

When military settlers of Greek origin came into contact with Egyptian cults during the seventh century BCE, they were especially interested in rituals that could easily be linked with Greek religious practice. The ancient god Apis was worshipped all over Egypt but had a cult centre at Memphis, the ancient capital. Associated with kingship and ruling power, the Apis was represented as a bull, and a living, sacred bull was the focus of the Memphite cult. Bull burials are attested as early as the reign of Amenhotep III, and subterranean galleries for burials of Apis bulls were begun during the reign of Ramesses II at Saqqara. The Serapeum at Memphis was built during the 26th dynasty, and by the 30th dynasty there were 134 sphinxes in place along the Serapeum's processional way. Here and elsewhere, Greek settlers had ample chance to have their dreams interpreted and their future foretold inside the temples of the joint deity Apis-Osiris, by either children, priests, or professional interpreters (Kessler 2000: 170–2 and 225, fig. 1). This practice made room for a new god: the Egyptian word for 'to foretell' is *ser*; thus, Ser-Apis is a 'foretelling Apis', despite later Greek interpretations such as Osirapis or Osiris-Apis. The further development of Serapis beyond these Late period oracles remains unclear, but it seems at least likely that the early Ptolemies regarded Serapis as the ideal source to create a dynastic god with genuine Greek roots. Given the strong presence of Isis at Alexandria, especially in the harbour regions and Rhakotis, which was largely inhabited by Egyptians, one of the important theological achievements of the time was making Serapis the consort of Isis, thus creating a dyad with Egyptian and Greek origins. Being a god without myth, Serapis was indeed the ideal consort for Isis, amplifying her transformation from an Egyptian into a Greek deity. Both were worshipped at the Serapeum at Alexandria, and it is from this city that the cult of Isis and Serapis spread into the Aegean during the fourth century BCE.

It is impossible to establish precisely the date when Isis was transformed into a hellenistic goddess. However, two aspects of this change have to be taken into account. First, it took place in Egypt without indigenous Egyptians being involved. Secondly, the concept that intellectually supported this development was the Greek translation of ancient Egyptian cultural elements, the so-called *interpretatio Graeca*. *Interpretatio Graeca* is the identification of a foreign divinity with a member of the Greek pantheon. In Herodotus, for instance, Greek names are used for non-Greek divinities (Burkert 1985), be it on the basis of similar phonetic sound values or on the grounds of similar characters and parallel functions. The first approach is highlighted by the nearly constant use of the names Isis and Osiris rather than the Egyptian Aset or Wesir, which probably sounded less familiar to Greek ears. The second approach can be found fully laid out in Herodotus' *Histories*, namely when he occasionally refers to Demeter and Dionysos (2.59.2 and 42.2) instead of Isis and Osiris. In addition to the *interpretatio*, this almost certainly has to do with a process of acculturation, which translated new (religious) concepts into unfamiliar cultural environments by the use of familiar languages and semiotics. It therefore comes as no surprise that in the exclusively Greek Isis Aretalogies (such as the one of Kyme in modern Turkey), Isis claims to be an Egyptian goddess but speaks Greek to her Greek audience (Merkelbach 2001: 115–18), rather than Demotic (contra Quack 2003). By the third century BCE Isis already appears following the hellenistic dress code when depicted in statues and figurines (Albersmeier 2005: 311). This interpretation certainly helped Isis to become a universal goddess, referred to as the 'One with Ten Thousand Names' or simply 'The One' (Bricault 1994; Merkelbach 2001: 94–5). If divinities can be amalgamated on the basis of their names, it becomes evident that they share one divine entity. This henotheistic development is laid out in the second century CE by Apuleius (*Met.* 11.4), who equated Isis with countless other female divinities. Not only names underwent an *interpretatio Graeca*: rituals were also translated into forms familiar to Greek practice, most prominently the so-called Daily Ritual performed for the cult statue (Bommas 2005b: 243–5).

Similarly, an *interpretatio Romana* equated Egyptian divinities with Roman gods, and one can also speak of the reverse, an *interpretatio Aegyptiaca*, which interpreted Greek mythology as originating from Egyptian traditions (Merkelbach 2001: 231; Bommas 2006: 234–8). Prominent protagonists of the *interpretatio Aegyptiaca* were Diodorus Siculus (1.96–7) and Plutarch (*De Is. et Os.* 10). By the second century BCE, the cults of Egyptian gods had spread all over the Mediterranean and neighbouring regions, which explains the need for regional translations of foreign religious concepts. This, however, came at the price of a fading knowledge of the origins of these religions. Where detailed information is available, it points in the direction of national, if not local, interpretations of cult practices, with little interest in original Egyptian thinking (e.g. Pausanias' account of the Isis festival at Thitorea; Paus. 10.32.13–17). Plutarch was the first who sought to remedy this unbalanced situation by researching what he believed were Egyptian sources. With his work *De Iside et Osiride*, from *c.*120 CE, he published the first book about ancient Egyptian myth and religion with the aim of providing a basis for cult practices. Consequently, Plutarch investigated Osiris and not Serapis.

The Myth of Osiris

In Egyptian sources, the myth of Osiris underwent various modifications until the New Kingdom before it was increasingly canonized in later periods. Already during the Old Kingdom, isolated spells or utterances were arranged according to their contents in groups of texts, the majority of which can be identified as mortuary liturgies that aim at the glorification and transformation of the deceased as the Osiris, or Osiris form of, such-and-such a person. Written on papyri, these liturgies were still known, copied, and recited in Roman times (Assmann 2008), sometimes in new arrangements, thus pointing at the long tradition and the high degree of canonization of funerary belief over a period of nearly 3,000 years.

Mortuary liturgies of the Graeco-Roman period, largely based on and inspired by the Old Kingdom Pyramid Texts, had more than one *Sitz im Leben*. On the one hand, they were used in funerary contexts, thus marking the continuation of funerary rituals; on the other hand, they were transformed into Osiris liturgies, exclusively recited and performed in the Osiris chapels of Graeco-Roman temples. Instances are known where priests, obviously responsible for carrying out these Osiris rituals, relabelled the papyri manuscripts used in the temple cult in order to have them incorporated into their own tomb archives after death (Caminos 1972). The view taken by previous scholars, namely that scribes invaded Old Kingdom pyramids in order to copy recovered ancient texts for use in funerary and temple cults, can be rejected on the grounds of new evidence: Pyramid Texts never went out of fashion during the New Kingdom and later periods. A papyrus in the British Museum (EA 10819) clearly shows that long liturgies belonging to the offering cult were always recited during burials (Assmann 2005), and it has to be assumed that similar manuscripts were always to hand before Pyramid Texts and liturgies reappear in high numbers in Graeco-Roman times.

Unlike other religious texts of the time, mortuary liturgies, as well as the Pyramid Texts they are largely based on, do not give a consecutive account of the Osiris myth, as would be the case, for example, with ancient Greek mythology. Nowhere in the Pyramid Texts is the myth of Osiris explained or narrated, and the mortuary liturgies also use only brief allusions. In ancient Egypt, myth was mainly hidden (Assmann 1977; Bommas 2004b) and where a narrative approach is chosen, this can be seen as a later development. There are two answers to why the myth of Osiris was kept secret: some scholars believe that funerary texts do not contain the secrets of the myth of Osiris because anyone would have known the details anyway. Others, like Jan Assmann, believe that in ancient Egypt, myth was hidden in order to keep it from the attention of outsiders (Assmann 1977), such as non-specialists or the illiterate, who might have made their own use of what they had overheard from professional priests. Only the correct performance of funerary rites would guarantee a safe journey to the afterworld.

Based on the Egyptian sources, reticent as they are, the myth of Osiris can partly be reconstructed. What is left untold is who the mythical figure Osiris was and what exactly led to his untimely death at the hand of his brother Seth. One version runs as follows. Smitten by his brother Seth at a place called Nedit (the Egyptian word means '[the place] to lie down'), possibly over a row about the rule of Egypt, Osiris rested close to a desert dune, where the burning sun caused his body to decompose. Osiris' bodily liquids seeped out to the north and quickly formed a river, which was regarded as the source of the Nile, and had healing properties. As decomposition progressed, parts of Osiris' body fell away and floated to the north. Another version, based on other sources, suggests that Seth killed Osiris by dismembering him before the Nile dispersed the body parts all over Egypt. In any event, Isis and her sister Nephthys gathered the parts and restored Osiris' body, and Isis magically conceived her child Horus.

Plutarch's *De Iside et Osiride*

The lack of a genuine Egyptian account of the myth of Osiris is regarded as uncomfortable by modern Egyptologists, who have painstakingly reconstructed the myth by assessing allusions and isolated citations from religious texts. The accounts of ancient Greek authors, however, suggest that an Egyptian narrative probably existed in the form of an oral tradition, alongside the texts that lector priests used. These sources might have been known to Plutarch (before 50–after 120 CE), a Delphic priest, writer, philosopher, and historian who travelled to Egypt, where he most likely gained access to relevant written (Greek) sources. Widely recognized in Rome during the reign of Trajan, Plutarch's work did not become accessible to Western scholars until the fifteenth century, when it was translated into Latin. In many respects his work *De Iside et Osiride* ('On Isis and Osiris') is the major source for Egyptian Isis religion and can count as a formative influence on the Roman approach to 'Egyptian' religion. Interestingly, his exaltation of Osiris over Isis disregards the contemporary scene. From the end of the fourth century BCE, when Egyptian religion spread into the Mediterranean world, Osiris had not played a major role in Greek versions of the Egyptian cults. He did receive some sort of cult at the island of Delos from the third century BCE, which apparently continued into the second century CE (Fig. 25.3). The Egyptian cults in the Aegean and Rome were not as formally structured as the cults in Egypt, which led to a variety of cult practices, especially in Roman times.

According to Plutarch's foreword to *De Iside et Osiride*, a Delphic priest named Klea, who was consecrated in both Egyptian and Dionysiac rites, asked Plutarch to investigate the origins of these gods in ancient Egypt. Plutarch was largely familiar with the religions of his time when he wrote this book towards the end of his life, around 120 CE. He had been educated by Ammonius, a Platonist who came from Egypt to Athens; Ammonius is thought to have spent time in Alexandria and probably helped nourish Plutarch's interest in Egyptian religion. Although it is not known which sources Plutarch used in order to write his treatise (apart from the ones he refers to himself), and in all likelihood he was unable to read hieroglyphic, hieratic, or Demotic texts, he arrived at a picture of Isis and Osiris that is largely supported by the ancient Egyptian evidence. Lost works by Hermaeus (*On the Egyptians*, *On the Festivals of the Egyptians*), together with Manetho's *Aigyptiaca* and Hecataeus of Abdera's *Aigyptiaca* from the earlier Ptolemaic period, must have been of influence (Griffiths 1970: 75–101). Plutarch added a Greek eschatology to Osiris, which helped regularize and popularize the Egyptian cult for a Greek and Roman audience; this is reflected in the final passages of

FIG. 25.3 Dedication mentioning a priest of Osiris, island of Delos, Greece

Author's photograph.

Apuleius' *Metamorphoses* book 11, an account of initiation into the Isis cult composed in the late second century CE. Plutarch treated the death and resurrection of Osiris in great detail, but he refers to Osiris not as a god but as a *daimon* (*De Is. et Os.* 360E–361F): first, Osiris does not become king of the dead but ruler within ethereal regions, and secondly he is identified with the Platonic sun, the visible image of the Good (Brenk 2001: 94).

Plutarch's personal and positive attitude towards mythology (Burkert 1996) offers a fascinating addition to the myth of Osiris, although it must be stated that Plutarch was a Greek author, writing an essentially Greek account for a Greek audience. Two areas in which he goes considerably beyond any Egyptian sources are the biography of King Osiris (chapter 13) and Osiris' return from the underworld to teach fighting techniques to Horus (chapter 19). But where comparable ancient Egyptian sources are available, Plutarch is remarkably close to them, even though his interpretations are widely influenced by Pythagorean, Platonic, Stoic, and Gnostic thought (Griffiths 2001: 54–5). Before ancient Egyptian funerary texts were made accessible by modern Egyptology, Plutarch's *De Iside et Osiride* was regarded as the main source of information for the myth of Isis and Osiris.

Hellenistic Isis in Roman Egypt

Compared with the abundance of studies on the hellenistic (that is, the Greek-inflected) form of Isis in Greece and Rome, her worship in Roman Egypt is still under-investigated. To date, no collection of epigraphic data is to hand, surviving sanctuaries have hardly ever been discussed in comprehensive studies, and no attempt has been made to collect the *res sacrae* linked with the cult of Isis, Osiris, and Serapis in Egypt. This situation is partly self-made. Egyptologists in the past have shown little to no interest in the transformation of aspects of ancient Egyptian religion into the hellenistic Isis cult, despite the fact that the development was initiated in Egypt. This process was by no means a short-lived phenomenon: from the reign of Amasis in the 26th dynasty to the worship of Isis by the Blemmyes and Nobadae at the temple of Philae in the sixth century CE, the history of Isis as a universal goddess extended over more than 1,100 years in Egypt. With the relevant material spread among museums and excavation store-rooms, making it difficult to collect, there is little hope that this task will ever be achieved in a way that could compare to the study of pharaonic religion.

In Roman Egypt both the traditional as well as the hellenistic Isis enjoyed worship in several temples, some of which still stand today (Haase 2005). The most prominent of these was certainly the temple of Philae at the southernmost border of Egypt, where a substantial amount of decoration and also new buildings were added in Roman times. Philae is regarded as a major late cult centre in Egypt, and it is here that the latest datable hieroglyphic and Demotic inscriptions are found, the former celebrating the 'birthday' of Osiris (24 August 394) and the latter a dedication from 2 December 452, written by two priests of Isis (Dijkstra 2008: 208, 214). In Roman times, the birth house (mammisi) was added during the reigns of Augusts and Tiberius. In the north of the main temple, a sanctuary was dedicated to Harendotes, the son of Osiris as champion and protector of his father. A little further to the north, at Aswan, Isis was worshipped as 'Isis at the head of the army': although built under the Ptolemies, her temple in the centre of the nome capital Syene (modern Aswan) continued to operate under Roman rule.

The 'temple of Isis at the south-western end of the lake' is the name of a sanctuary of Isis in modern Deir el-Shelwit on the west bank of Thebes. Although Isis was regarded as being the main goddess here, hymns in the temple also address Osiris, and the Theban god Montu seems to have received a cult, too. Isis, as well as Mut, enjoyed a cult at Shanhur, on the east bank of the Nile between Koptos and Thebes, while in el-Qal'a, 15 miles north of Shanhur, Isis was accompanied by Nephthys. Both temples received additions or new buildings during the reign of Augustus. At Koptos, Isis was part of the local pantheon including Min and Geb. A trilingual inscription from the first century CE testifies to the involvement of a priest of Isis, a certain Parthenios, in the building of new temples at the site. At Luxor a small peripteral temple built of sun-dried mud-bricks, with architectural elements made of sandstone, was dedicated to 'Zeus Helios Megas Serapis' on Hadrian's birthday, 24 January 126, but the limestone statue that survives in the sanctuary shows Isis in hellenistic form, suggesting that the temple accommodated her cult as well.

The small temple of Isis at Dendara was a separate building from the main temple of Hathor and had its own temenos wall and access; the site was one of several that claimed to be the birthplace of the goddess. A Greek dedication dating to the year 1 CE sheds some light on the multilingual approach to sanctuaries for Isis, which is further confirmed by a depiction of Isis Thermouthis in the main temple. Thermouthis (Renenutet) was an agricultural goddess, pointing to Isis' role in agricultural fertility, a trait she shared with Osiris. Beyond the Nile Valley, temples for Isis were also erected in the Eastern Desert at Mons Porphyrites (113 CE) as well as at Dush in southern Kharga Oasis in the Libyan Desert, where Serapis received a cult, too.

At Alexandria there is some evidence for sanctuaries dedicated to Isis *pharia* and Isis *lochias* in the harbour area, but no building has been identified with certainty so far. However, at Ras el-Soda, Isis is attested through a statue in hellenistic form together with statues of Hermanubis, two statues of Osiris-Canopus, and two sphinxes (Bommas 2010). Her sanctuary here, which is partly reconstructed, was made possible through private dedication. Not all sanctuaries of Isis received the same attention: Behbeit el-Hagar in the central Delta (Latin: Iseum; Greek: Isidospolis) was regarded as the birthplace of Isis and, together with Philae, was probably the most important sanctuary for Isis in Egypt. However, instead of allowing worship at the site to continue, the Romans dismantled the temple and shipped parts of it to Rome, where they were displayed, for instance in the Iseum Campense.

The worship of Osiris was less easily incorporated into the Greek approach, simply because the ancient Greeks did not fancy dead gods. Accordingly, reference to his worship is rare but not unknown in the Hellenistic period (Bommas 2005a: 96, fig. 116). Animal worship presented a similar problem, which ancient Greek settlers in Egypt solved by turning to Apis-Osiris or Serapis, in the process making the Serapeum at Saqqara one of the most important temples for this god (Lauer and Picard 1955; Thompson 1988: 212–66; Kessler 2000).

Isis Cults in the Mediterranean

Although figurines of Isis are attested in the Aegean as early as the seventh century BCE, such as the ones found at the temple of Athena at Kameiros on Rhodes (Hölbl 1994), the spread of Egyptian cults into the Mediterranean world stems primarily from the Hellenistic era. The dedication of a sanctuary for Isis at Piraeus coincides with Alexander the Great's conquest of Egypt, and the worship of Isis abroad can be linked to Egyptian and Greek sailors and businessmen who travelled between Alexandria and Greek harbour cities from the fourth century BCE onwards. The interest in Isis, however, dates back to even earlier times: Greek settlers came into contact with Egyptian religion during the seventh century BCE, and the spread of Egyptian cults to the Aegean, making Isis a universal goddess, was an entirely Greek enterprise. The 'mysteries of Isis' (Burkert 1987: 38–41; Bowden 2010: 156–80) were essentially a Greek version of the cult, perhaps with some basis in the fact that certain religious knowledge in Egypt was restricted. Ancient Greek visitors, such as Herodotus (2.59–60), did witness religious customs such as the festival of Isis at Bubastis. In some sense, this must have seemed comparable to panhellenic religious festivals, or the Eleusinian mysteries of Artemis at Eleusis, which is probably why Herodotus speaks of 'mysteries' in his account of the temple of Neith (Athena) at Sais.

The earliest attestation of Serapis outside Egypt was found on a private inscription from Halikarnassos on the west coast of Turkey, which can be dated to the reign of Alexander IV or Ptolemy I Soter, roughly at the beginning of the third century BCE (Bommas 2005a: 34, fig. 42). This is enough to suggest that the earliest development of the cult of Egyptian gods in the Aegean was of a private nature and was promoted by sailors and traders who travelled the route between Greek harbour cities and Egypt. The spread of Egyptian cults into the Mediterranean was not politically motivated, as suggested by some scholars, the most influential of whom is R. E. Witt (1971: 48, 53, 55). Soldiers serving in the armies of the Ptolemies also exported the worship of Egyptian gods: the sanctuary for Egyptian gods at Thera on the island of Santorini—the most ancient within the Cyclades—was probably hewn from the living rock by sailors serving at the naval base (Bommas 2005a: 42–4, figs 53 to 55a–b). At the same time, places under the influence of the Antigonide rulers of Macedonia, such as Eritrea on Euboea, also had sanctuaries for Egyptian gods available since the beginning of the third century BCE (Bommas 2005a: 39–42, figs 48–50).

To summarize the earliest expansion of Egyptian gods into the Mediterranean, it appears that this process began during the late fourth century BCE and had its first peak during the third century BCE, through harbour cities (Bommas 2005a: 35–63) (Fig. 25.4). During the second century BCE the cults of Isis, Serapis, and Harpocrates reached remote Aegean islands and the hinterland of mainland Greece and modern Turkey (Bommas 2005a: 64–78). As a rule, all new sanctuaries were first established in city centres, sometimes sharing cult places with local deities such as Aphrodite at Kyme (Turkey). Secondly, all temples were built close to natural water sources such as rivers (Wild 1981, fig. 4), but never lakes. Where water as a natural source was not available, vicinity to large wells (e.g. Eritrea) or water basins (e.g. Priene) was regarded as essential in order to perform rites that could be linked with a re-created Egyptian landscape. Thus, on the island of Delos it was believed that the River Inopus was actually the River Nile, passing under the Mediterranean from the Nile Delta and reappearing close to Mount Kynthos on Delos (Roussel 1916: 20, fig. 2), as described in the hymn to Delos by Callimachus (lines 206–8; trans. Mair and Mair 1921: 102–3).

Closely linked with the island of Delos, the second expansion of Egyptian cults took place in the second century BCE, this time spreading to Italian harbour cities like Puteoli and later Miseno and Ostia (Malaise 1972; Tran Tam Tinh 1972). After the Third Macedonian War (171–168 BCE), Rhodes lost its role as the main Roman free port in favour of Delos, which made the island the most important trading place after Alexandria. For eighty years, before

FIG. 25.4 Sanctuary for Egyptian gods at Dion, Greece, viewed from the north; dated to the early third century CE

Author's photograph.

Delos was destroyed by Mithridates IV in 88 BCE, Delos was the launch pad for Mediterranean trade and with it the expansion of Greek religious concepts to Italy. As with the first expansion, the second wave of Egyptian cult expansion was again promoted by sailors and traders. As early as 105 BCE, a sanctuary was dedicated to Serapis in Puteoli, which is unfortunately lost today (a *macellum* in the city was misidentified as a Serapeum; on which, see Bommas 2005a: 76–8). Simultaneously, a temple for Isis was built in Pompeii (105–88 BCE; Hofmann 1993) and at the Capitoline Hill in Rome (100 BCE), both being private dedications. Evidence for the presence of Egyptian gods in Rome has been made accessible (e.g. Malaise 1972) and frequently discussed (Turcan 1996), including fresh and stimulating approaches to the interpretation of the material collected (Lembke 1994; Takács 1995). Studies on the spread of Egyptian gods into the Mediterranean have been structured in various ways: stress was laid on topography (Malaise 1972; Dunand 1973; Bricault 2001) and religious phenomena (Witt 1971; Merkelbach 2001), as well as chronology and the political and economic implications, and how these either supported or slowed down the process (Bommas 2004a; 2005a, esp. 80–1). The majority of studies have focused on the importance of textual evidence, but it has proven to be vital to focus also on the archaeological evidence, including artefacts (Arslan 1997) and architectural remains (Bommas 2005a); this combination of evidence allows better conclusions to be drawn about cult practice at Mediterranean sites.

Isis and Osiris in Rome

According to Apuleius, Rome was the *sacrosancta civitas* for devotees to Isis (Apul. *Met.* 11.26.2). Among the six major sanctuaries for Egyptian gods in Rome prior to the reign of Constantine (293–337), the Iseum at the Field of Mars (Iseum Campense) stands out and deserves a detailed description. According to the *forma urbis Romae*, the Severan era marble plan, the Serapeum was located in the centre of the northern main part of the Campus Martius, strictly oriented to the north and alongside the street Porticus Meleagri (today the Via del Gesú). The area between the later Iseum and the Pantheon was occupied by the *saepta Iulia*, the Roman polling station, before being changed into a monumental square in Augustan times. This temple is referred to by Apuleius as being 'called Campensis, and continually adored of the people of Rome: her minister and worshipper was I, a stranger to her church, but not unknown to her religion' (*Met.* 11.26). The Iseum Campense was supposedly the third place where Lucius, the protagonist of the *Metamorphoses*, was initiated into the mysteries of Isis, after he met the goddess for the first time during her procession at the harbour of Corinth in Greece, where a sanctuary for Isis can be identified archaeologically (Bommas 2005a: 109–12).

Temples for Egyptian gods offered housing to devotees of Egyptian gods. This becomes apparent from Apuleius' reference to his move into rented property within the temple walls (*Met.* 11.19). Almost every Isis temple with extant architectural remains contains areas that can be identified as living space for pilgrims, especially since the process of initiation into the mysteries of Isis sometimes took several weeks (Bommas 2005b: 234). Clear examples of 'pilgrim quarters' have been found at Memphis (Lauer and Picard 1955, pls 25–8), the Iseum Campense (Lembke 1994: 52–3), Philippi (Bommas 2005a: 100–2), and probably at the basement of the southern part of the Ptolemaic Serapeum at Alexandria, as suggested by the architectural remains (Sabottka 2008: 139 and figs 25–8). Some temples had advantages over others, owing to their size. Among the largest temples ever dedicated to Egyptian gods outside Egypt are the Iseum Campense and the so-called Red Hall at Pergamon, both characterized by large open courts (Hoffmann 2005: 14–15 and fig. 11; Bommas 2005a: 113). The court at the Red Hall is around 280 metres in length, while the Iseum Campense measured around 275 metres. This gave enough room for pilgrim quarters but also to re-create an Egyptian landscape, which seems to have taken place at both Pergamon and Rome. The decoration of a column found within the former area of the Iseum Campense shows the feeding of crocodiles that supposedly lived within the precinct. Frescos from Herculaneum and Pompeii show ibises swaggering around during Isiac ceremonies, and although this is a pictorial device, it may suggest that Egyptian animals were kept in some temples. In the Red Hall several basins are still visible today that seem to support the view that the sanctuaries for Egyptian gods were not only sacred places but also multifunctional buildings, evoking the splendours of Egypt. In addition, finds from the Iseum Campense and the Iseum at Benevento include a remarkable amount of Egyptian antiquities (known as 'aegyptiaca') that were transported from Egypt to Italy for the enjoyment of visitors and initiated devotees alike (Lembke 1994: 25–50; Bommas forthcoming).

As stated above, the Greeks found Osiris to be a problematic addition to their pantheon, which otherwise lacked 'dead' divinities. The Roman approach to Osiris was less strict.

Although comprehensive studies are lacking, it is evident that Osiris was known to the Romans in various appearances, one of which was Osiris Chronocrator (Manera and Mazza 2001: 49, 56). On closer examination it seems to be the case that the Isis religion became increasingly Osirian in nature during the Roman empire. This development, different from the earlier process attested for the Aegean, is backed by the works of Plutarch and Apuleius. The exaltation of Osiris over Isis is further supported by literary references to Osiris (see below), the building of pyramid tombs in Rome (Bommas 2011), and the spread of Osiris to the rather remote area of the Marche (Capriotti Vitozzi 1999).

The battle of Actium in 31 BCE whetted Roman interest in Egypt. The Roman reception of Osiris identified him with Dionysos, another eastern god; this association evoked exuberant joy and an everlasting easy life, perhaps more appealing to the Roman upper classes than the grief personified by Osiris. This new approach is evident in a birthday poem dedicated to M. Valerius Messalla Corvinus, who took part in the battle of Actium as a battleship commander and later became governor of the province of Syria, from where he visited Egypt (Lyne 2001: 188–9). The poem contains a hymn to Osiris that describes him as a benefactor, the inventor of wine, and a dispenser of solicitudes (Tib. 1.7.21–48; trans. Postgate 1988: 228–31). The fact that this hymn was given as a birthday present suggests that the transformation of Osiris into a god of celebration must have been widely accepted. Several pyramids in ancient Rome, of which only that erected by Gaius Cestius between 18 and 12 BCE is still standing, refer to rejuvenation rather than an unending death, fitting their use as tombs. Again, festivals linked with Egyptian gods were generally regarded as moments of joy, abundance, and ecstasy.

In Roman times, festivals for Isis were arranged according to the civic calendar and were therefore attended by large communities (Lembke 1994: 96–8, 129; Egelhaaf-Gaiser 2005: 268). The *navigium Isidis* (*ploiapharia*) was a spring festival that took place during the full moon in March or April, and marked the annual redeployment of the navy after the winter storms had passed. The autumn festival (29 October–2 November) is known under the name *inventio Osiridis* (*heuresis*). Like the cults of Egyptian gods, Isis festivals also enjoyed international diffusion (Malaise 1972: 217–28; Dunand 1973: 3.223–38; Merkelbach 2001: 147–60), making them the most visible aspect of the religious practice of Isis worshippers.

Conclusion

The spread of the cults of Egyptian gods from Alexandria to the rest of the known world—from Maharraqa in modern Sudan to York in Britain, and from modern Iraq to Empúries in Spain—is one of the most remarkable religious developments throughout antiquity. The initial move of Isis into the Aegean in the second half of the fourth century BCE is even more astonishing since she left as a Hellenized goddess who had little in common with ancient Egyptian wisdom or knowledge, which was not accessible to the sailors and soldiers who exported Isis to Greek harbour cities. The mysteries of Isis are an entirely Greek development, which is also responsible for the fact that Osiris, as a dead god, was never really accepted among Greek cult communities. This reservation changed with Rome's interest in Egyptian religious practice: Osiris was integrated in the Roman pantheon through his Dionysiac aspects, transforming him into a god of joy and abundance rather than a ruler of the underworld. Although the cult of Isis and Serapis was, first and foremost, the most prominent face of personal religion over a period of around 650 years, Ptolemaic rulers as well as Roman emperors had a keen interest in these gods, first transforming Serapis into a dynastic god and then themselves into divinities of Egyptian design. The cult of Egyptian gods not only embraced all levels of society but also caught the interest of philosophers and writers, which underscores the point that the acceptance of Egyptian gods outside Egypt was an intellectual challenge that could only flourish after it had gradually abandoned its Egyptian roots.

Suggested Reading

Hugh Bowden's recent book on mystery cults is an up-to-date and original approach to the subject, with a chapter on Egyptian cults (Bowden 2010: 156–80). Burkert (1987) is a classic introduction to mystery cults, and several specialists in the field have written essays in conjunction with the recent exhibition 'Il rito segreto' (Bottini 2005). The proceedings of a 2005 conference on Isis studies are useful (Bricault, Versluys, and Meyboom 2007), as are the essays in the exhibition catalogue *Iside* (Arslan 1997), focusing on the Isis cult outside Egypt. Merkelbach (2001) is a richly detailed study, indispensable for the Isis and Serapis cults. See also Takács (1995), which observes several misconceptions about the cults, and Wild (1981), which is the most comprehensive study of the role of water in the cult rites. A valuable earlier work, Malaise (1972) is still relevant for its global way of looking at the development of Egyptian cults in Italy, but for the most part it has been superseded by more recent and detailed studies.

For the cult of Serapis, Hornbostel (1973) presents relevant evidence, but its conclusions are now superseded. For Isis in the Greek and Roman world, Witt (1971) is also outdated, though influential. Dunand (1973) is a detailed work presenting developments in the Isis cult in geographical order, while Bommas (2005a) discusses developments in chronological order, with a focus on architecture, ritual, and meaning. Despite its recent date, Donalson (2003) discounts key recent literature in languages other than English. Eingartner (1991) is an indispensable study of the iconography of Isis and her priestesses in the Roman empire. Finally, for the Osiris cult, Assmann (2008) is the first comprehensive edition of Late Egyptian texts concerned with transforming the dead into Osiris, with allusions to the god's mythology in its Egyptian context.

Bibliography

Albersmeier, S. 2005. 'Griechisch-römische Bildnisse der Isis', in H. Beck, P. C. Bol, and M. Bückling (eds), *Ägypten, Griechenland, Rom: Abwehr und Berührung*. Tübingen: Wasmuth; Frankfurt: Liebighaus, 310–14.

Arslan, E. A. (ed.) 1997. *Iside: Il mito, il mistero, la magia*. Milan: Electa.

Assmann, J. 1977. 'Die Verborgenheit des Mythos in Ägypten', *Göttinger Miszellen* 25: 7–43.

——1999. *Ägyptische Hymnen und Gebete*, 2nd edn. Freiburg: Universitätsverlag.

——2000. *Weisheit und Mysterium: Das Bild der Griechen von Ägypten*. Munich: Beck.

——2002. *The Mind of Egypt: History and Meaning in the Time of the Pharaohs*. New York: Metropolitan Books.

——2005. *Altägyptische Totenliturgien*, vol. 2: *Totenliturgien und Totensprüche in Grabinschriften des Neuen Reiches*. Heidelberg: Winter.

——2008. *Altägyptische Totenliturgien*, vol. 3: *Osirisliturgien in Papyri der Spätzeit*. Heidelberg: Winter.

Bommas, M. 2004a. '"Du, der du eintrittst, wirst das Seiende erkennen": Zur Verbreitung der Isisreligion in der Ägäis von den Anfängen bis zu ihrem Niedergang', in P. C. Bol, G. Kaminski, and C. Maderna (eds), *Fremdheit—Eigenheit: Ägypten, Griechenland und Rom: Austausch und Verständnis*. Munich: Prestel, 141–54.

——2004b. 'Zwei magische Sprüche in einem spätägyptischen Ritualhandbuch (pBM EA 10081): Ein weiterer Fall für die "Verborgenheit des Mythos"', *Zeitschrift für Ägyptische Sprache* 131: 95–113.

——2005a. *Heiligtum und Mysterium: Griechenland und seine griechischen Gottheiten*. Mainz: von Zabern.

——2005b. 'Das Isisbuch des Apuleius und die Rote Halle von Pergamon: Überlegungen zum Kultverlauf in den Heiliugtümern für ägyptische Gottheiten und seinen Ursprüngen', in A. Hoffmann (ed.), *Ägyptische Kulte und ihre Heiligtümer im Osten des Römischen Reiches*. Istanbul: Ege Yayınları, 227–45.

——2006. 'Die Genese der Isis Thermouthis im kaiserzeitlichen Ägypten sowie im Mittelmeerraum zwischen Aufnahme und Abgrenzung', *Mediterraneo Antico* 9: 221–39.

——2010. 'Isis in Alexandria', *Biblische Notizen* 147: 25–47.

——2011. 'Pyramids in Ancient Rome: Images without Cult?', in M. M. Luiselli, S. Griepentrog, and J. Mohn (eds), *Bild und Kult: Die bildliche Dimension des Kultes in der Antike*. Würzburg: Ergon.

——Forthcoming. 'The Iseum Campense as a *lieu de mémoire*', in Bommas et al. (eds), *Cultural Memory, Religion and the Ancient City*. London: Continuum.

Bottini, A. 2005. *Il rito segreto: Misteri in Grecia e a Roma: Exhibition Catalogue, Rome 22 July 2005–8 January 2006*. Milan: Electa.

Bowden, H. 2010. *Mystery Cults in the Ancient World*. London: Thames and Hudson.

Brenk, F. E. 2001. 'In the Image, Reflection and Reason of Osiris: Plutarch and the Egyptian Cults', in A. P. Jiménez and F. C. Bordoy (eds), *Estudios sobre Plutarco: Misticismo y religions mistericas en la orba Plutarco: Actas del VII Simposio Español sobre Plutarco*. Madrid: Clásicas, 83–98.

Bricault, L. 1994. 'Isis Myrionyme', in C. Berger, G. Clerc, and N. Grimal (eds), *Hommages à Jean Leclant: Études isiaques*, vol. 3. Cairo: Institut Français d'Archéologie Orientale, 67–86.

——2001. *Atlas de la diffusion des cultes isiaques (IVe s. av. J.-C.–IVe s. apr. J.-C.)*. Paris: de Boccard.

——M. J. Versluys, and P. G. P. Meyboom. 2007. *Nile into Tiber: Egypt in the Roman World*. Leiden: Brill.

Burkard, G. 1995. *Spätzeitliche Osirisliturgien im Corpus der Asasif-Papyri*. Wiesbaden: Harrassowitz.

Burkert, W. 1985. 'Herodot über die Namen der Götter: Polytheismus als historisches Problem', *Museum Helveticum* 42: 121–32.

——1987. *Ancient Mystery Cults*. Cambridge, Mass.: Harvard University Press.

——1996. 'Plutarcho: Religiosità personale e teologica filosofica', in I. Gallo (ed.), *Plutarco e la religione: Atti del VI Convegno Plutarcheo*. Naples: d'Auria, 11–29.

Caminos, R. A. 1972. 'Another Hieratic Manuscript from the Library of Pwerem Son of Kiki', *Journal of Egyptian Archaeology* 58: 205–24.

Capriotti Vitozzi, G. 1999. *Oggetti, idee, culte egizi nelle Marche: Dalle tomb epicene al tempio di Treia*. Tivoli: Tipigraf.

Dijkstra, J. H. F. 2008. *Philae and the End of Ancient Egyptian Religion: A Regional Study of Religious Transformation (298–642 CE)*. Leuven: Peeters.

Donalson, M. D. 2003. *The Cult of Isis in the Roman Empire*. New York: Edwin Mellen.

Dunand, F. 1973. *Le culte d'Isis dans le basin oriental de la Méditerranée*, 3 vols. Leiden: Brill.

Egelhaaf-Gaiser, U. 2005. 'Exklusives Mysterium oder inszeniertes Wissen? Die ägyptischen Kulte in der Darstellung des Pausanias', in A. Hoffmann (ed.), *Ägyptische Kulte und ihre Heiligtümer im Osten des Römischen Reiches*. Istanbul: Ege Yayınları, 259–80.

Eingartner, J. 1991. *Isis und ihre Dienerinnen in der Kunst der römischen Kaiserzeit*. Leiden: Brill.

Griffiths, J. G. 1970. *Plutarch's De Iside et Osiride*. Cardiff: University of Wales Press.

——2001. 'Plutarch', in D. B. Redford (ed.), *The Oxford Encyclopedia of Ancient Egypt*, vol. 2. Oxford: Oxford University Press, 53–6.

Haase, M. 2005. 'Zu einem Repertoire der Isis-Heiligtümer im kaiserzeitlichen Ägypten', in A. Hoffmann (ed.), *Ägyptische Kulte und ihre Heiligtümer im Osten des Römischen Reiches*. Istanbul: Ege Yayınları, 197–208.

Hoffmann, A. 2005. 'Die Rote Halle in Pergamon: Eine komplizierte Forschungsgeschichte mit Zukunfstperspektiven', in A. Hoffmann (ed.), *Ägyptische Kulte und ihre Heiligtümer im Osten des Römischen Reiches*. Istanbul: Ege Yayınları, 3–20.

Hofmann, P. 1993. *Der Isis-Tempel in Pompeji*. Münster: Lit.

Hölbl, G. 1994. 'Vorhellenistische Isisfigürchen des ägäischen Raumes, insbesondere von der Insel Rhodos', in C. Berger, G. Clerc, and N. Grimal (eds), *Hommages à Jean Leclant: Études isiaques*, vol. 3. Cairo: Institut Français d'Archéologie Orientale, 271–85.

Hornbostel, W. 1973. *Sarapis: Studien zur Überlieferungsgeschichte, den Erscheinungsformen und Wandlungen der Gestalt eines Gottes*. Leiden: Brill.

Kessler, D. 2000. 'Das hellenistische Serapeum in Alexandria und Ägypten in ägyptologischer Sicht', in M. Görg and G. Hölbl (eds), *Ägypten und der östliche Mittelmeerraum im 1. Jahrtausend v. Chr*. Wiesbaden: Harrassowitz, 163–230.

Lauer, J.-P., and C. Picard. 1955. *Les statues ptolémaïques de Serapieion de Memphis*. Paris: Presses Universitaires de France.

Lembke, K. 1994. *Das Iseum Campense in Rom: Studie über den Isiskult unter Domitian*. Heidelberg: Archäologie und Geschichte.

Lyne, R. O. A. M. 2001. 'Augustan Poetry and Society', in J. Boardman, J. Griffin, and O. Murray (eds), *The Oxford Illustrated History of the Roman World*. Oxford: Oxford University Press.

Mair, A. W., and G. R. Mair. 1921. *Callimachus, Hymns and Epigrams: Lycophron*. London: Heinemann.

Malaise, M. 1972. *Les conditions de pénétration et de diffusion de cultes égyptiens en Italie*. Leiden: Brill.

Manera, F., and C. Mazza. 2001. *Le collezioni Egizie del Museo Nazionale Romano*. Milan: Electa.

Merkelbach, R. 1973. 'Zwei Texte aus dem Serapeum zu Thessalonike', *Zeitschrift für Papyrologie und Epigraphik* 10: 45–54.

——2001. *Isis regina—Zeus Sarapis*, 2nd edn. Munich: Saur.

Moret, A. 1930. 'Légende de Osiris à l'époque thébaine d'après l'hymne à Osiris du Louvre', *Bulletin de l'Institut Français d'Archéologie Orientale* 30: 725–50.
Postgate, J. P. 1988. 'Tibullus', in G. P. Goold (ed.), *Catullus, Tibullus and Pervigilium Veneris*. Cambridge, Mass.: Harvard University Press.
Quack, J. F. 2003. '"Ich bin Isis, die Herrin der beiden Länder": Versuch zum demotischen Hintergrund der memphitischen Isisaretalogie', in S. Meyer (ed.), *Egypt, Temple of the Whole World: Studies in Honour of Jan Assmann*. Leiden: Brill, 319–65.
Roussel, P. 1916. *Les cultes égyptiens à Delos du IIIe au Ier siècle av. J.-C.* Paris: Berger-Levrault.
Sabottka, M. 2008. *Das Serapeum in Alexandria: Untersuchungen zur Architektur und Baugeschichte des Heiligtums von der frühen ptolemäischen Zeit bis zur Zerstörung 391 n. Chr.* Cairo: Institut Français d'Archéologie Orientale.
Smith, M. 2009. *Traversing Eternity: Texts for the Afterlife from Ptolemaic and Roman Egypt*. Oxford: Oxford University Press.
Takács, S. 1995. *Isis and Sarapis in the Roman World*. Leiden: Brill.
Thompson, D. J. 1988. *Memphis under the Ptolemies*. Princeton: Princeton University Press.
Tran Tam Tinh, V. 1972. *Le culte des divinités orientales en campanie en dehors de Pompéi, de Stabies et d'Herculaneum*. Leiden: Brill.
Turcan, R. 1996. *The Cults of the Roman Empire*. Oxford: Oxford University Press.
Wild, R. A. 1981. *Water in the Cultic Worship of Isis and Sarapis*. Leiden: Brill.
Witt, R. E. 1971. *Isis in the Graeco-Roman World*. London: Thames and Hudson.

CHAPTER 26

IMPORTED CULTS

GAËLLE TALLET AND
CHRISTIANE ZIVIE-COCHE

IMPORTED cults in Roman Egypt are rooted in the oldest history of the Egyptian pantheon. Non-native gods were already attested in the oldest funerary texts, the Pyramid Texts, with mentions of the god Dedun, of Nubian origin. Divinities from the fringes of the Delta (Ha in the west and Sopdu in the east) were also ancient imports, connected with the Libyan desert and the Near East, whereas some traditional divinities, of which one cannot doubt the Egyptian origin, had functions going far beyond the frontiers of Egyptian territory: Min watched over the Eastern Desert, while Hathor played a leading role in Sinai and Byblos.

The prevailing polytheistic system, in Egypt and the neighbouring area, allowed the introduction and naturalization of foreign deities. As a matter of fact, as no god was deemed to be more authentic than another, and none was considered to be exclusive of the others, the very concept of a false god was alien to the polytheistic mind. The system was based on acknowledgement of an unlimited plurality of gods. Moreover, Egyptian gods were characterized by their polymorphy and by the plasticity of their representations. Theological texts claim that their true essence lies beyond human knowledge and understanding: one can only attempt to seize their individual essence by multiplying their denominations, epithets, and representations (Hornung 1990). Each god had specific powers that might be useful for his worshippers. That is the reason why magical texts call for divine powers far beyond the native pantheon and thus provide us with manifold occurrences of foreign deities.

Historical Frame: Imported Cults in Pharaonic Egypt

During the New Kingdom, in a context of intensive contacts with neighbouring cultures, major importations of foreign cults took place as early as the 18th dynasty and lasted until the Ptolemaic and Roman periods, as is clearly attested in temple texts and decoration. One can draw a clear picture of the historical context of these mutations from analysis of the various sources—royal and private stelae and literary and magical texts. The introduction of foreign cults, all coming from Syria–Palestine, was a consequence of a deliberate royal policy and not, as has often been assumed, of the settlement of Near Eastern people, either willingly or as war captives and slaves.

The first occurrences of this constellation of oriental gods, Reshep, Astarte, Baal, Houroun, and Qadesh, 'the Holy One'—an Egyptian creation based on pre-existing eastern features—were to be found under the reign of Amenhotep II, while Anat did not appear in the sources before the Ramesside period, despite her strong connections with Astarte. Once imported to Egypt, these foreign gods were granted full divine status: they were addressed as *netjer*, 'god' in Egyptian, just as the native gods were. As their original iconography was either poor or non-existent, they were dressed with the ornaments and trappings of the Egyptian gods, according to the current Egyptian iconographic code. Their names have been preserved in Egyptian and transcribed in hieroglyphs, sometimes with a syllabic spelling, which is frequent with foreign terms adopted in Egyptian. Thus, there was no *interpretatio Aegyptiaca* of the new gods, even though they were sometimes matched with one Egyptian god or another: for instance, Baal and Seth, or Houroun and Harmachis, were associated, while others found their place in divine genealogies, such as Astarte, who was deemed to be the daughter of Ptah (see Gardiner 1932). The foreign origin of these deities is hardly mentioned in the sources; they received cult worship of the Egyptian type, with offerings and prayers similar to those dedicated to the native gods, either in the royal cult or in private devotions. Their epithets show that people attached beneficial powers of protection and healing to them, as attested in magical formulas.

It seems that a Greek visitor such as Herodotus in the fifth century BCE perceived no strong difference between Astarte and her Egyptian counterpart, the goddess Hathor: for instance, the temple located in the southern quarter of Memphis, which Herodotus calls that 'of the foreign Aphrodite' (2.112), was likely to be a temple of Astarte; but he clearly considers Astarte as the counterpart of Hathor, that is to say Aphrodite according to the *interpretatio Graeca*. She also had a shrine in the necropolis, within the complex of the Serapeum of Memphis (Kiessling 1953; Thompson 1988). As Herodotus was aware, Greek communities had lived in Egypt since the seventh century BCE: Milesians had founded an *emporion* at Naukratis in the Delta, and the city of Memphis included Greek quarters that were home to so-called Helleno-Memphites, the descendants of Carian and Ionian mercenaries who had settled in Egypt at the end of the sixth century BCE. In both places they brought their own gods and cults, and Herodotus (2.178) describes the numerous Greek sanctuaries at Naukratis, all enabled by the 26th dynasty king Amasis. Excavators at the site discovered a temple of Aphrodite, located in the southern part of the town, while sanctuaries of Hera, Apollo, the Dioscuri (two young twins), and the Hellenion were to the north. In Memphis a Carian temple is mentioned in a letter from the priests of Astarte (*PSI* V 531), which must have been the temple of the Carian Zeus, Zeus of Labraunda, for whom 120 arouras of land are recorded in the neighbourhood close to the land of Imhotep (Asklepios) and Serapis (*P Mich. Zenon* 31.5 (256/5 BCE)). As in Naukratis, the Helleno-Memphites had their central temple in Memphis, which is known as the Hellenion: in the third century BCE Zenon of Caunos visited the place and performed sacrifices (*P Cair. Zen.* 59593.7–8). Zeus Basileus, to whom Alexander sacrificed in the city, was perhaps the main deity of the shrine (Thompson 1988).

Thus, long before the developments that occurred in the Hellenistic period, the Egyptians had adopted a number of eastern gods and granted them the same status as the native ones. By this time, they were considered as foreign gods no more, but were fully part of the Egyptian pantheon. This was probably not a major phenomenon, but it shows the plasticity of a religious system that was always predisposed to welcome new deities. Foreign gods were tolerated in Egypt, sometimes even encouraged, as they remained a minority that could be fully integrated in the Egyptian pantheon.

A New Situation: The Graeco-Macedonian Conquest

Strikingly enough, the Greek, and later Roman, gods were never integrated in the native pantheon; but the political situation was totally different. After the Graeco-Macedonian conquest in 332 BCE, Egyptian culture underwent major social, economic, and political changes under Greek influence. A new population settled in Egypt: Graeco-Macedonian soldiers and mercenaries, but also civilians—merchants trading overseas, adventurers, artists, all of them looking for a new 'Eldorado on the Nile' (Lewis 1986)—emigrated en masse to Egypt from the fourth century to the end of the third century BCE, joining the older Greek communities. This immigration was different in scale and in kind, and resulted in a major change in the balance of the population. For the first time in Egyptian history, the newcomers did not blend with the native population: they clearly outnumbered previous influxes and held stronger positions in the new Egyptian society, where they now formed the ruling classes. Moreover, these settlers, coming from central Greece, the Aegean islands, and Asia Minor, drawn from all over the Greek-speaking world, were encouraged to stay in Egypt through the Ptolemaic policy of giving land estates (*doreai*) to high-ranking officials, or plots (*kleroi*) to Greek soldiers. In the fourth and third centuries BCE these men were in command of all the main military and political positions in Egypt and controlled the levers of the new economic system: the bank, money, and farming of taxes were all Greek imports. In this switching of roles, Egyptian people were highly exposed to a brutal social and cultural drop in status and had no choice but to acculturate (Dunand 1983). Nevertheless, the religious field proved to be exceptionally resilient as far as acculturation was concerned.

Former imported cults benefited, as did the native cults, from the rulers' policy of support towards local cults and their priests. In any case, they were already tightly connected to native cults: in Memphis, Astarte was associated with Isis, as attested by a dedication in Phoenician to Isis-Astarte, set up by one Feʾlʾaštort son of ʿAbdmilkot, a military man from the garrison of Thebes visiting the city, probably in the second century BCE. He asks the Egyptian god Horus for protection and blessing, and the inscription is surmounted by a stela depicting Horus standing on crocodiles in a traditional way, with spells against snakes and scorpions (Milik 1967: 564–5; Thompson 1988: 88–9). Similarly, by the fourth century, among the Carian and Ionian communities settled in Memphis (Thompson 1988: 93–7), the Carian Zeus of Labraunda may have been identified with 'Amun-Ra of the strong arm' (Wildung 1977: 49–50).

Highly problematic is the question of the importation of the cult of Mithras in the Ptolemaic period. Harris's (1996) study of the Mithraic cult takes into account the specifically Roman cult established at the turn of the first to second century CE. However, Kaper (2004) has recently drawn attention to an unpublished papyrus fragment (*P Tebt.* fr. 13385) from Tebtunis (Fayum), dating back to the second century BCE, and he draws a rather different picture. Though documents such as the zodiac depicted in the tomb of Petosiris in el-Muzawwaqa (Dakhla Oasis) or the so-called Mithras liturgy are no longer interpreted as Mithraic, Kaper assumes from this early document that a Persian origin is likely for the introduction of the cult of Mithras to Egypt; it spread all over the Hellenistic world after Alexander took over the Achaemenid empire and was Romanized only afterwards, in a second phase. Memphis, where an important Persian settlement is attested from the Persian domination on, was one of the main centres for this cult, together with the Fayum: a temple seems to have been established in Gurob by Iranian settlers and their descendants. As Beck (1984: 2086–9) points out, the reference occurs in connection with shrines of several gods: Nachbanis (Nectanebo?), Aphrodite, Hermes, Sekhmet, Nefertem, and Pan. This connection with cults performed publicly leads Beck to think that this Mithraeum was not a place for mystery cults, as was common in Roman times. The Tebtunis papyrus also indicates that the god was well integrated in the Egyptian pantheon and depicted according to Egyptian convention, through a kind of *interpretatio Aegyptiaca*, for the fragment represents a man with long hair, holding a bull, together with a depiction of Bes and the sphinx-god Tutu.

The new Greek immigrants certainly brought their own cults with them, and Demeter, Dionysus, Aphrodite, etc. are attested in Egypt in Greek settlements, as they were in the past in Naukratis and Memphis. Popular deities such as the Agathos Daimon (the Good Genius), well known in Alexandria, and connected with Zeus Ktesios and the Egyptian snake Shai (Dunand 1969, 1981; Quaegebeur 1975), were adopted together with more official deities, such as Dionysus, patron of the Ptolemaic dynasty, who was interpreted as Osiris in Memphis. The dynastic god was celebrated close to the temple of Osirapis, dedicated by Nectanebo II, with a set of Dionysiac statues put on mastabas along the dromos, associated with traditional representations of the Apis bull (Lauer and Picard 1955; Thompson 1988: 27–9). Greek festivals also cohabited with Egyptian ones; for instance, the Eleusinian Thesmophoria are attested as early as the third century BCE in Alexandria, in connection with Isis (Perpillou-Thomas 1993: 78–81).

This imported pantheon was far wider and more diverse than in earlier periods. The new gods reflected the manifold backgrounds of their promoters: they came from all over the Hellenistic world and were sometimes very specific to a city or a region. Many of them were imported by the mercenaries hired by the Ptolemies, such as the Thracian god Heron, with his companion the god with a double axe. Most of the occurrences of Heron come from the Fayum and are to be connected with the cleruchic settlement of Thracian mercenaries from the second part of the fourth century BCE onwards. This Thracian immigration was mostly military, as Thrace was traditionally a breeding ground for Greek armies; under Ptolemy II and Ptolemy III, Thracian mercenaries and soldiers were systematically encouraged to enrol in the army, and then to settle in specific regions of Egypt such as the Herakleopolite, Oxyrhynchite, and Arsinoite nomes (Launey 1949–50: 2.959–74).

Thus, the sociological background of these new importations was strikingly different from previous periods. Even if one leaves apart dynastic gods such as Dionysus, it is striking that foreign gods in Ptolemaic Egypt were now gods of the ruling classes: they were brought to

Egypt by people who held high positions in the new Graeco-Egyptian society and in the Greek army. The diffusion of a god like Heron was clearly connected with cleruchic areas such as the Fayum, and its first promoters, Thracian mercenaries, were not low-ranking soldiers but an important military society (Bingen 1983). The upkeep of the cult of Heron remained mostly in military hands: in Magdola, for instance, a *hipparchus* at the head of the cavalry settlers dedicates a gateway to Heron (*I Fay*. III 151 (118 BCE)) and a decree of Ptolemy X granted immunity and the right of asylum to the temple of Heron, requested by two military men who took care of the place (*I Fay*. III 152 (95 BCE)).

Like its Graeco-Macedonian promoters, the imported pantheon was characterized by a double and somewhat contradictory tendency in its interaction with the Egyptian context: on the one hand, immigrants tended to be self-sufficient and to abide by Greek customs, organizing Greek cults with Greek priests and cultic activities in Greek-like sanctuaries; on the other hand, they entered into a process of contact and interaction with the Egyptian environment. Their gods and cults became involved in an *interpretatio Graeca*, and the process sometimes resulted in an *interpretatio Aegyptiaca*. A god like Hermes is characteristic of the two tendencies: in Hermopolis and elsewhere in the *chora*, he was closely identified with the Egyptian god Thoth and celebrated as 'thrice greatest god', *theos tris megistos* (Fowden 1986). But in Alexandria he retained a very specific Greek character and his name was given to one of the Alexandrian demes. Both there and in *metropoleis*, in Roman times, he appeared along with Herakles as the patron deity of the gymnasium, the core of Hellenized society, and from throughout Egypt there are numerous dedications made to the two of them by ephebes or ex-ephebes. There are also traces of both aspects in Roman Oxyrhynchus, as Whitehorne points out (1995: 3069–70): a fragmentary religious text of the early second century CE (*P Oxy*. XXXI 2552), written in Greek but with Egyptian illustrations, seems to record knowledge of Hermes-Thoth, while a third-century CE encomium (*P Oxy*. VII 1015), written in hexameters, celebrates him as 'ruler of the games' and 'warden of the gymnasia'.

Imported Cults in Roman Egypt: What's New?

The Roman conquest did not lead to major changes in the local pantheon, since few Roman people emigrated to Egypt; therefore, the situation is concerned with formerly imported gods, drawn from the east in Pharaonic times and from the Greek world in the Ptolemaic period. While the former were fully integrated in the Egyptian native pantheon, the latter were still considered to be foreign gods from the Egyptian point of view.

In Roman Oxyrhynchus one could find, along with Egyptian temples, the Syrian cult of Atargatis, Greek temples of Demeter, the Dioscuri, Hermes, Tyche, and many others, and a few Roman cults (Whitehorne 1995). The cult of Atargatis is attested by *P Oxy*. XII 1449 (213–17 CE), a return of temple property made by priests of 'Zeus, Hera, Atargatis, Kore, Dionysus, Apollo, Neotera, and the associated gods', which lists three temples in which the goddess was worshipped in association with Zeus, Hera, and Kore (see also *P Oslo* III 94 (second–third century CE)). The declarants are also 'celebrants of the bust of the August Lord (i.e. Caracalla) and his approaching Victory, and Julia Domna, and his divine father Severus', but no Roman gods are mentioned. The Syrian goddess, whose cult is attested elsewhere in Egypt from the third century BCE, seems to have resulted from an association of Astarte and Anat. She was identified by the Greeks as Aphrodite and Hera, and by the Egyptians as a counterpart of Isis and Hathor. As for her Greek associates, they are frequently attested in Oxyrhynchus. Former Greek cults were adopted by Roman immigrants, as, for instance, that of Demeter, mentioned in several documents: a letter from one M. Aurelius Ammonius, *hierophantes*, to the *calathephorus* (basket carrier) of the nearby village of Nesmeimis instructs her to go to the temple of Demeter at Sinkepha 'to perform the accustomed sacrifices on behalf of our lords the *Imperatores* and their Victory and the rise of the Nile, the increase of the fruits and the healthy climate' (*P Oxy*. XXXVI 2782 (second or third century CE)). Festivals of Demeter are also attested: an Oxyrhynchite lease, *P Giss*. 49 (third century CE), includes 'each year for the Demetria a suckling pig worth thirty drachmas' as part of the rent (see Perpillou-Thomas 1993: 78–81).

As discussed above, the cult of Mithras underwent 'Romanization' during the Roman period, and a specific Roman Mithraism was established and developed by the end of the second century CE, mainly in Hermopolis and Memphis (Harris 1996). These sites yielded several reliefs depicting the Mithraic bull sacrifice, with material dating to the late second and third centuries, while a codex recently published as a Mithraic catechism suggests that Mithraism was still flourishing in the fourth century CE (Brashear 1992). A limestone relief depicting the lion-headed god Aion has been taken as evidence for a Mithraeum in Oxyrhynchus (Breccia 1934; Pettazzoni 1949).

Aside from the imperial cult, Roman cults seem to have been very scarce: in Oxyrhynchus they were limited to Jupiter Capitolinus and Mars. Saturnalia may also be attested in *P Oxy*. I 122.4 (late third or early fourth century CE), a letter from one Gaius to a legionary prefect mentioning 'the day of the Kronia', so that the festival may have been celebrated in a military context. The cult of Antinoos, Hadrian's favourite, who was drowned in the Nile in 130 CE and then divinized, became popular in Egypt and throughout the empire, but it was not an imported cult per se.

As Frankfurter points out, 'one of the singular developments in Egyptian religion under Roman administration was the addition of new priestly or quasi-priestly offices' (1998: 42–6). For both Roman and Greek cults, there was a strong contrast with Egyptian cults in terms of the nature of the clergy. The offices of Greek and Roman priests were of the same status and character as a civic magistracy: they were often appointed for a fixed term and tended to be members of the wealthy elite. For instance, supervision of the revenues and property of the temple of Jupiter Capitolinus at Arsinoe in the third century CE was in the hands of a high priest who was also a metropolitan counsellor (Glare 1992). A section of an account from the temple (*BGU* II 362 (215 CE)) records its income and expenditure for about eight months in 214–15 CE and shows that it was administered by the *boule* (town council) of Arsinoe. This institution was responsible for the appointment of the *epimeletes* (overseer), a liturgical official who served for a limited length of time and seems to have had a very administrative role. Moreover, the festivals celebrated at the temple were connected with Rome or members of the imperial family: the birthdays of the reigning emperor Caracalla and of his deceased father, the god Severus, were celebrated in the temple, along with the visit of the prefect, and it was most probably the statue of Jupiter Capitolinus that was then carried in procession. As Glare (1992) points out, while gods with Roman names are few and far between in Egypt, it is striking that one of them, Jupiter Capitolinus, appears with particular frequency in connection with the emperors in other provinces, for instance in North Africa. What is not clear is at what time the imperial cult and the temple of Jupiter Capitolinus were integrated; but certainly, most of the time, the imperial cult joined existing temples. For instance, in 163–4 CE the priests of the temple of Athena-Thoeris (Thoeris being the Egyptian Taweret) in Oxyrhynchus elected a sacred virgin to take part in a procession for the Tyche of the emperors (the deified personification of their good fortune) (*P Mert.* II).

Thus, most of the cults that were imported or that developed under Roman rule were connected with imperial power or with the monitoring of Egypt's fertility. For instance, the Roman administration became closely involved in the cult of the Nile-god, strongly connected to Rome's supply of wheat. In the reign of Augustus, Euthenia, the divine personification of abundance and newly created companion of the Nile-god, appeared on Alexandrian coins as a sort of Alexandrian counterpart of the Roman *annona*, the Roman goddess who personified the grain supply. She embodied the religious aspect of the new economic policy set by Augustus, relying on the products of a good flood (Bonneau 1964: 330–1). In a culture dependent economically on the annual swell of the river and in a system highly dependent on Egypt's fertility, the rites of celebration and anticipation of the flood, worshipped as Hapy or Neilos, proved enduring, and the various festivals dedicated to the Nile flood retained their importance. For example, the *semasia* (when the river attained a certain height, or gave its 'sign'), attested by papyrological, epigraphic, and numismatic documents from the second to the sixth centuries CE, from Akoris to the Fayum, were in a way secularized and presided over by Roman officials rather than priests (Bonneau 1964: 390–3; 1971: 56–9). The prefect now held the title of 'high priest of the most holy Nile' (*P Wisc.* 9.4 (Oxyrhynchus 183 CE); see Bonneau 1995: 3207–15; Cribiore 1995) and the Nile-god was regarded as a Roman god. The river-god Neilos was associated with nymphs and Euthenia, which makes the cult quite distinct from the Egyptian worship of Hapy.

Sources, Scope, and Method

The problem of identifying foreign gods in our sources is particularly complex in the Graeco-Roman period as one is confronted by a dichotomy between Egyptian sources, in which foreign gods are hardly mentioned (this is noteworthy as it was not previously the case), and papyrological and epigraphic Greek sources, which are bursting with occurrences: theonyms, theophoric anthroponyms, and toponyms, attestations of cults and sanctuaries, and mentions of priests, festivals, and associations (*synodoi*) (see Ronchi 1974–7). But of all these temples and cults the Egyptian scribes, *hierogrammateis*, hardly gave any account. This is quite similar to the case of the city of Alexandria, which is almost never given her usual name in Egyptian sources, but rather is called 'Rakote' (Greek: Rhakotis), in Egyptian, a temporary 'building site' (Depauw 2000; Chauveau 2001). Geographical lists from Egyptian temples deliberately ignore Rhakotis-Alexandria, as if the Egyptian priests had denied the city its place in the sacred space of the Nile Valley. Probably as a form of symbolic resistance to acculturation, a Greek-looking god such as Serapis was denied any legitimacy in Egyptian sacerdotal and theological texts. In the Oracle of the Potter, a seer predicts future calamities to a native king named Amenophis: foreign people will settle in a city 'by the sea' (Alexandria) and the images of the gods will be transformed. Fortunately, a rescuer will come and the Agathos Daimon (Serapis) will abandon the 'city under construction' in order to come back to Memphis (Dunand 1977; Blasius and Schipper 2002). Thus, there are almost no occurrences of foreign gods in the Egyptian temples, and they are always restricted to peripheral areas.

Another difficulty is that, as far as Greek sources are concerned, one must be very cautious when dealing with occurrences of Greek gods and their temples. The identity of a god may be difficult to grasp since a complex system of aliases developed, not dissimilar to personal names. Just as individuals could bear double Graeco-Egyptian names, gods could be designated in papyri under different names, either Greek or Egyptian, according to the principles of *interpretatio Graeca*: the Hephaesteion of Memphis was none other than the great temple of Ptah. While the worship of Aphrodite under her own name is frequently attested at Naukratis by dedicatory offerings in the early period, in Ptolemaic and Roman Egypt her cult is more likely to be absorbed into her Egyptian counterparts such as Hathor or Isis. In a similar way, in Greek papyri Athena quite often stands for the goddess Neith of Sais (el-Sayed 1982: 2.665–74; Quaegebeur 1985: 218), hardly ever called by her Egyptian name. The equivalence also appears in figurative representations (Dunand 1976: 80–2). But Athena could also stand for the goddess Thoeris (Taweret), for instance in documents from Oxyrhynchus, where she was never worshipped under a Greek guise (Whitehorne 1995: 3063), and for Isis (Quaegebeur 1985: 219). A declaration of property belonging to the temple of Apollo in Pela, in the western Oxyrhynchite nome, makes it clear that the god who is being invoked under that name is Horus, since he receives votive objects listed as '3 bronze statues of the hawk-shaped Apollo in 3 wooden shrines; 3 bronze hawks of which 2 are inlaid (?) with faience' (*P Oxy.* XLIX 3473 (161–9 CE)); in addition, a *pastophoros* is among the temple priests—an unmistakably Egyptian office (Whitehorne 1995: 3061–2).

But a reverse tendency was also possible: in Oxyrhynchus, Aphrodite and Dionysus had been absorbed almost totally into Isis and Osiris-Serapis, their Egyptian counterparts, but when the metropolitan cities founded sacred games in the early third century, a local association of Dionysiac artists emerged, with a distinctively Hellenic character to their meeting and ritual (Whitehorne 1995: 3056). Whitehorne's study also shows a difference between the *metropoleis* and their *chora*. For instance, Oxyrhynchus was an important cult centre for Amun from the New Kingdom, but in Roman times the papyrological sources mostly shed light on the sanctuary of Serapis, attested from the third century BCE (*BGU* VI 1245) to the sixth century CE (*PSI* V 466 (518 CE); Whitehorne 1995: 3078–80). It played a vital role in local economic life as it housed banking activities. The cult of Serapis was also very important in religious and civic life and the god was a *synnaos theos* (shared god) with the main deity of the town, Thoeris, and with Isis. He was apparently a Greek guise for Amun. Oddly enough, though, no mention of his cult is found in the nome villages: unlike Thoeris and Isis, Serapis was apparently limited to the metropole. Furthermore, although Amun does not seem to have received a proper cult in Oxyrhynchus, where he was absorbed by Zeus and Serapis, theophoric names such as Ammonas or Ammonios were very common in Oxyrhynchus and, in the nome, many sanctuaries and priests of Amun are attested during the Roman period. It is striking that Amun was enduringly implanted in the *chora* of Oxyrhynchus and almost absent in the capital. In fact, Whitehorne suggests that the Serapis cult in Oxyrhynchus could have included Egyptian features: thus, a list of payments made by people who attended the Serapeia at the end of the third century CE includes 'offerings for the one with a dog head', referring to Anubis (*SB* V 7336.24).

Lastly, iconographic sources prove extremely useful. The iconography of foreign gods is well attested outside the traditional temple precincts, and especially in domestic contexts. Techniques imported from Greece such as mass-moulded terracotta figurines, wooden painted panels or frescos, and numismatic iconography facilitated the diffusion of new gods. As far as iconography is concerned, one of the major issues remains the accurate identification of the gods: most often, no name is associated with the representation. With gods such as the Thracian horseman Heron, we are quite lucky to find manifold representations, sometimes clearly identified by an inscription, and often in connection with archaeological remains and cultic places. The god had two main cult centres in the Fayum, including a temple in Theadelphia, founded under Ptolemy VIII at the latest (*I Fay.* II 105). The oldest representation of Heron in Egypt is sculpted on a dedicatory stela dating to the reign of Ptolemy XII, when a second gateway at the site was dedicated by a certain Petosiris, son of Herakles. The stela was embedded in a temple wall and depicts Heron as a horseman riding to the viewer's right, wearing the full hellenistic military uniform and a diadem (*I Fay.* II 115 (67 BCE)). The cult retained its importance in the Roman period in Theadelphia, with the temple still attested in 107–8 CE (*P Tebt.* II 298.60). The god was also depicted on frescos of the second or third century CE, at the entrance of the temple of the main deity of Theadelphia, a crocodile god named Pnepheros (Breccia 1926: 111–12; Bernand 1981: 2.126–7): he is identified by *dipinti* as Heron or Heron Soubattos. A second cult centre was in the village of Magdola (Fayum), and a 'place (*topos*) of Heron' is also attested in Narmouthis, where the god appears as a secondary deity. These Fayum sites have yielded many objects, mainly painted wooden panels and frescos dating back to the second or third century CE, depicting Heron and sometimes his companion the god with a double axe .

But the quality of the Heron dossier is rather exceptional. Most foreign gods in Roman Egypt are attested through very scattered evidence and are difficult to connect with any precise cult place. Thus, the major difficulty is to bring together scattered material and combine these different kinds of evidence, ranging from textual sources to archaeological remains (sanctuaries, private chapels, places for *synodoi*) and iconographical corpora (frescos, stelae, coins, wooden panels, statues, figurines), in order to assess the identity and theology of these foreign gods and grasp their cultic roles. One means of approach is to look in detail at the spaces and contexts in which new images and theological features were elaborated and displayed: public and domestic contexts, temple spaces, and temple surroundings.

Interactions between Imported Cults and the Native Pantheon

Iconographic and theological features of foreign gods were subject to the double tendency described above: on the one hand, one notices internal mutations in connection with the Graeco-Roman world and its religious trends; on the other hand, contacts with the Egyptian environment were bound to occur.

For instance, Heron was identified from the start as a non-Egyptian god: neither his military costume nor his horse are Egyptian features. The Thracian Heros shared with the Egyptian Heron a homonymy, some of his epithets, and his iconography (Will 1955). Both rode a horse, which is very rare in Egyptian iconography, only found with the Syrian goddess Anat. While horse breeders were important in elite Thracian society, in Ptolemaic Egypt horses were connected with the cavalry and thus with military status. Heron appeared in Egypt as a protector first worshipped by soldiers, whereas in Thrace he was linked with peasants and hunters. Another shared feature is the depiction of a tree with a snake, standing next to the god; the snake was connected to domestic cults in Thrace and Phrygia, as the snake god Shai was in Egypt. In the hellenistic Egyptian representations, the snake lies on or coils up the tree and drinks from a patera that Heron offers. In Roman times, the snake was still depicted, together with the tree, but Heron did not handle the patera, instead performing a libation on an altar. Also, a small masculine character was often depicted next to him.

Thus, Heron appeared in Egypt as a Hellenized version of the Thracian god, and this Hellenization was strongly influenced by the military circles in which he was first popular; his military uniform is specific to his Egyptian cult. On Ptolemaic stelae, Heron was often depicted as an idealized, victorious Hellenistic king and borrowed, by *imitatio*, the royal uniform and solar rays. In Roman times, Heron's equipment was brought up to date and adapted to the uniform of the Roman army. In most Roman depictions, Heron was dressed like the victorious *Imperator*: on a wooden tablet from the Fayum (Fig. 26.1;

FIG. 26.1 Framed wooden panel depicting Heron (viewer's right) and the god with the double axe

Musées Royaux d'Art et d'Histoire, Brussels, E 7409.

Rassart-Debergh 1991) he wears a tunic, a *lorica squamata*, and a purple paludamentum attached at his chest with a gorgoneion; he is also wearing boots and a laurel crown with a nimbus. The very uniform of Heron was the subject of an *interpretatio Graeca* then *Romana*.

But these internal mutations of his iconography should not lead us to think that the cult of Heron was impervious to the Egyptian context. As we have already mentioned, representations of the god were found at the entrance of the temple of the crocodile god Pnepheros at Theadelphia: these frescos were not painted by Roman pilgrims or worshippers, but were probably integrated in the iconography of the temple within the remit of sacerdotal control, on behalf of a religious association devoted to Heron. Significantly, these frescos were not in the core of the temple, within the cella that was accessible only to priests; such paintings were only allowed in peripheral areas, such as entrance gates or open-air courtyards. It is nevertheless proof that in the second and third centuries CE, when the temple was still active, a Hellenized god could be integrated within delimited areas. Moreover, Heron here fulfils a very traditional function from Thrace, that of *propylaios*, guardian of the doors, an epithet that he also has in Theadelphia and Magdola (Bingen 1983).

No doubt the trappings of imperial authority and power were perceived as guarantees of effective protection. They were soon adopted by various indigenous gods as well, such as Horus (Kantorowicz 1961), Harpocrates, Apis (von Bissing 1926), Bes (Tran Tam Tinh 1986), Tutu (Kaper 2003: 46), and Anubis (Grenier 1977, 1978), and became very popular in the context of private and domestic worship. This integration within an Egyptian context also paved the way for interactions between Heron and native traditional gods. On the Theadelphia frescos (Fig. 26.2; Breccia 1926: 111–12, pls 57–9), Heron and the god with the double axe are depicted above representations of the local pair of crocodile gods. Heron (Fig. 26.2b) is identified by a *graffito* as Heron Soubattos, a form of the god Horus. This epitomizes the religious bilingualism at work in Roman Egypt, with manifold exchanges between the two pantheons. Analysing the composition of the two scenes on each side of the gate, what seems to be a double representation of Heron is in fact a subtle game, very typical of Egyptian iconography. The similarity of the two gods has led many scholars to identify both as Heron, and it is not surprising that many depictions of Heron have been mistaken for the Dioscuri, and vice versa. Heron and his double are not completely symmetrical, however, and the depiction of the god with the double axe at the upper corner of Fig. 26.2a suggests that it is he who is depicted mounted on a horse as well, not Heron. Another indication is that both are associated with the local crocodile god, Pnepheros, whose temple at Theadelphia housed two crocodiles, a young one assimilated to Horus, the heir of the Osirian throne, and an old one associated with Osiris, the dead king. On the frescos, the Osirian crocodile (at the bottom of Fig. 26.2a) wears the *atef* crown and *wesekh* collar, while the young crocodile (at the bottom of Fig. 26.2b) wears the solar disc of a young regenerated god. Hence the frescos associate Heron and his companion with both the Egyptian crocodile gods and the Greek Dioscuri.

The link between the Dioscuri and the crocodile gods was forcefully demonstrated by Quaegebeur (1983), using a census return that refers to priests of Isis in a temple of the 'Two Brothers' in Oxyrhynchus (*P Oxy*. II 254 (*c*.19/20 CE)), and another reference to such a temple in the isolated countryside (*P Oxy*. XLIX 3467 (98 CE)). These Two Brothers, formerly interpreted as the Dioscuri, were in fact a pair of crocodile gods that the Egyptians called

a

b

FIG. 26.2 Wall paintings of the god with the double axe (a) and the god Heron (b), from Theadelphia

Graeco-Roman Museum, Alexandria, 20223–4 and 20225; after Breccia (1926, pls. 57–9).

Senouy (Psosnaus in Greek), literally 'the Two Brothers'. They are also known from stelae depicting a pair of protective crocodiles, for instance in Theadelphia (*I Fay.* II 116–17 (57 BCE)), and by double cultic sets in most of the Fayum temples of crocodile gods.

The same is true at Akoris, where a relief sculpted on the rock overhanging the city depicts the Dioscuri with their sister Helena (Chapouthier 1935, no. 62; Bernand 1988; Drew-Bear 1991). The Dioscuri both wear a Roman uniform, curb a horse, and have a star surmounting their heads. Usually Helena was depicted with a nimbus or solar crescent, but here she too has a star, seemingly borrowed from Isis-Sothis, a goddess associated with the Dioscuri in Alexandria and connected to the Nile flood (Chapouthier 1935: 258–9; Bernand 1988, no. 10, pls 12–13; Tallet 2012). At Akoris the goddess was associated with a pair of local crocodile gods, and the city was also known as Krokodilopolis. The Greek toponym reflects the importance of a native crocodile cult, while personal names such as Castor, Polydeukes, and Helena, well attested in the Roman period, are evidence of the popularity of the Dioscuri among the Hellenized part of the population. The relief shows that the two cults were regarded as similar, the Dioscuri being an *interpretatio Graeca* of the Egyptian crocodile gods, and Helena of Isis-Sothis. The scene could be read in two different ways, according to the cultural background of the spectator. The Akoris relief and the Theadelphia frescos illustrate what Dunand (2000) calls the 'coexistence of images', a more accurate description of religious interactions in Roman Egypt than terms like 'syncretism' or even 'Hellenization' or 'Romanization'.

Imported gods thus lend their iconography to traditional gods, as well as the other way round, and they also provided a network for diffusion within Graeco-Roman society. This is strikingly the case with a Roman creation, Zeus Helios Megas Serapis. This form of the 'great god' of Alexandria appears to have been elaborated to please the soldiers of the Roman garrison in Nikopolis during the reign of Trajan, integrating key features of the Alexandrian iconography of the Great Serapis (Megas Serapis) and Jovian attributes of the Roman Zeus (Fig. 26.3). The cult is well attested in Alexandria and Canopus, and quickly spread to the Eastern Desert military settlements, where it soon replaced the god Pan-Min

FIG. 26.3 Bronze figure of Zeus Helios Megas Serapis. Height 6.3 cm

British Museum GRA 1772, 0302.172 (Walters 939). Courtesy of the Trustees of the British Museum.

(Bricault 2005; Cuvigny 2010; Tallet 2011). It is also attested at the Nile Valley end of the Eastern Desert routes, for instance in Luxor, Antinoopolis, and Akoris, where important garrisons were settled. In Akoris, for instance, the native god Amun-Re, who had a temple on the acropolis, was interpreted as Zeus Megistos and called by either name. When the *legio III Cyrenaica* settled in Akoris, in connection with the development of local quarries, the centurion Titus Egnatius Tiberianus dedicated an altar for Zeus Megistos in year 2 of Domitian (82/3 CE; Bernand 1988, no. 3). As the new form Zeus Helios Megas Serapis spread under Trajan and Hadrian, soldiers widely adopted him and he replaced Zeus in dedications.

But, even among soldiers and sailors, references to the new deity remain scarce in comparison with Amun. Amun tended to absorb Zeus Helios Megas Serapis and benefited from the new cult's infrastructures and network of worshippers. Adopted by Roman officers, soldiers, and officials, Amun borrowed from Zeus the epithets 'wealth provider' and *epiphanes* (e.g. Bernand 1988, no. 18), and the epithet Megas from Zeus Helios Megas Serapis, which appears on a statue dedicated to Amun Megas by the Roman official Dioscoros (Bernand 1988, no. 17). Another inscription confirms that Amun was involved in epiphanies with healing virtues, like Serapis and Zeus Helios Megas Serapis in Canopus (Bernand 1988, no. 22); like the Alexandrian god, he was also associated with the Dioscuri. Other Egyptian gods absorbed epithets and features of Greek or Roman gods as well. In the Saite nome, Isis was worshipped as 'victorious, Athena, nymph' (*P Oxy*. XI 1380.30 (early second century CE)), and in a metrical inscription Neith is given the epithet *treitogenes*, an allusion to the birth myth of the Greek Athena (see Quaegebeur 1985: 220).

The difficulty is to judge the 'theological' impact of such mutations. For instance, what did an imported cult such as that of Helios, the Greek solar god, bring to traditional Egyptian religion? He had many cultic centres in the Greek world, most famously on Rhodes, where his colossal statue guarded the harbour entrance. This image of the god was known in Ptolemaic Alexandria, as it appears on amphora stamps from Rhodes, now in the Graeco-Roman Museum of Alexandria. Representations of Helios, influenced by the Rhodian iconography, were probably imported by the Graeco-Macedonian conquerors and their followers, especially merchants trading overseas. In the Delta town of Athribis, Polish excavators unearthed a clay stamped relief from a rhyton, with Helios standing, sceptre in hand, framed by two eagles (Myśliwiec 2000: 257, pl. 127), and a small head from a terracotta depicting a radiated Helios (Szymańska 2005, no. 156). Helios was closely involved in Hellenistic royal ideology, with radiated Ptolemaic kings depicted on Alexandrian coins (Bergmann 1998). The cult of Helios, if there was one, was probably limited to restricted circles (contra Hoffmann 1963); the splendid fourth-century CE frescos in Amheida (Trimithis), in Dakhla Oasis, which depict Helios revealing the classical scene of Aphrodite's and Ares' adultery, are certainly not connected with a proper cult (Giddy 1980). But the iconography of the god, used by the Ptolemies after representations of Alexander the Great as Alexander-Helios, came to symbolize power and epiphany, and was borrowed by several Egyptian deities in the Roman period. Not only Apollo and Heron, but also Amun, Horus, Harpocrates, Tutu, and Mandulis, became radiated gods.

Did the introduction of solar rays 'translate' the solar nature of the Egyptian gods? This hypothesis has been used to explain the 'bilingual' iconography that developed in objects of private piety, such as terracotta figurines: the coroplasts may have been intended to redesign the Egyptian gods, with a kind of iconographic *interpretatio Graeca* that allowed them to sell figurines to mixed audiences at traditional festivals. Figurines depicting the so-called Hermopolitan solar child sitting on a lotus had solar rays added, as if to explain his solar nature, which the presence of the lotus already conveyed to an Egyptian audience (Fig. 26.4). However, Greeks or Romans living in the Egyptian *chora* probably did not need any guidelines for understanding the iconography of native gods.

In the temple of Tebtunis (Fayum), where two crocodile gods, Soknebtunis and an anonymous companion, were adored, wooden panels or terracottas (Fig. 26.5) depict an anthropomorphic deity facing the spectator and dressed according to Greek trends; in his hands he holds a small crocodile, which allows us to identify him as a Hellenized Sobek. These objects were probably manufactured as souvenirs from local festivals, where a mixed audience could attend the procession of statues or mummies of the gods; *deipneteria* (dining rooms) for religious associations are attested along the temple dromos (Rondot 2004: 37–46). Wooden panels were unearthed within the sanctuary precinct and in private houses, while terracotta imitations likely come from a domestic context (Dunand 1979: 274, pl. 126, no. 366). It is noteworthy that these objects were products of imported Greek techniques (tempera-painting, mass-moulded terracotta), and conveyed new iconographic codes, as

FIG. 26.4 Terracotta figure of the solar child

Musée du Louvre, E 30249. Photo courtesy of Françoise Dunand; after Dunand (1990).

FIG. 26.5 Stone relief representing the god Sobek in human form, with solar rays

Cairo, Egyptian Museum CG 26902. Courtesy of the Egyptian Museum, Cairo.

well as new ways of approaching the gods. The relationship with the deity was now face to face, an attitude in the past restricted to a specific priest, the *stolistes*, in ancient Egypt. Solar rays, combined with the frontal attitude of the deity, not only indicate the solar nature of the deity, but also mark the epiphany of the god, experienced during the procession of his statue. Thus, terracotta souvenirs extended the festival appearance to the domestic context.

Conclusion

Imported cults in Roman Egypt, though never fully integrated into the native pantheon, became part of religious constellations whereby Greek, Roman, and Egyptian gods cohabited with and influenced each other. These shifting frontiers between Egyptian culture and Hellenism are to be understood in the context of a multicultural society: the former Graeco-Macedonian immigrants had long been integrated into Egyptian society, while newcomers, such as Roman soldiers and officials, were far less impervious to the local society and culture than has often been assumed. Alston (1995: 41–2) demonstrates that veterans who settled in Egypt after their service never behaved as a military caste, even though recruitment took place among the community of veterans and was not local until the end of the second century CE. As the papyrological documentation shows, veterans were often given land plots and became involved in social interaction with the indigenous society. In Karanis in the Fayum, veterans and their families settled under Domitian and appear to have been well integrated in local civilian life, forming an important part of the population until the end of the third century CE (Alston 1995: 117–42). Matrimonial and economic strategies speak volumes: Roman veterans were more inclined to marry within the local society of their village than to look for a wife in neighbouring veteran communities of the Fayum. These people adopted the native cults, and the process of *interpretatio Aegyptiaca* of imported gods was probably as important as, if not more important than, that of *interpretatio Graeca*. But these imported cults also conveyed new ways of representing and addressing the gods that met the new expectations of Egyptian worshippers. In particular, in the second and third centuries CE, they fulfilled a need for a more direct relationship with gods, face to face, without an intermediary.

Thus, though the impacts of imported cults were not to be observed within the core of the Egyptian temple precincts or in the Egyptian theological texts, and though they were strictly limited to the periphery of temples and to the domestic cult, one is entitled to qualify the imperviousness of the Egyptian traditional religion to Hellenism and to innovations. These mutations of divine iconography and of the worshippers' relationships to Egyptian gods possibly had theological consequences, but did not develop in opposition to the sacerdotal vision of gods: as in a marketplace of religions and creeds (North 1992; Whitehorne 1995), private piety made choices and adapted traditional gods to new religious needs. In a way, it is likely that the Egyptian priests collaborated in these developments and elaborated a strategy for the adaptation of the native pantheon. In a world subject to profound changes, economic as well as socio-political, the Egyptian temples and clergies were compelled to seek local patronage and private stipends, and to adapt the native pantheon to the expectations of their benefactors.

Suggested Reading

The topic of imported cults in Roman Egypt has been masterfully dealt with in case studies by Fowden (1986) and Quaegebeur (1983, 1985, and *passim*). Readers will find a good introduction to the Roman-specific context and problematics in Frankfurter (1998) and an excellent presentation of the situation in Roman Oxyrhynchus in Whitehorne (1995). Dunand (2000) provides a very helpful methodological and conceptual frame, while her catalogue of terracotta figurines exhibited in the Louvre (Dunand 1990) and Kaper (2005) show the wide range of iconographic developments connected to imported cults.

Bibliography

Aimé-Giron, N. 1925. 'Un ex-voto à Astarté', *Bulletin de l'Institut Français d'Archéologie Orientale* 25: 191–211.

Alston, R. 1995. *Soldier and Society in Roman Egypt: A Social History*. London: Routledge.

Beck, R. L. 1984. 'Mithraism since Franz Cumont', in W. Haase and H. Temporini (eds), *Aufstieg und Niedergang der römischen Welt* II 17.4. Berlin: de Gruyter, 2002–115.

Bergmann, M. 1998. *Die Strahlen der Herrscher: Theomorphes Herrscherbild und politische Symbolik im Hellenismus und in der römischen Kaiserzeit*. Mainz: von Zabern.

Bernand, É. 1981. *Recueil des inscriptions grecques du Fayoum*, vols 2 and 3. Cairo: Institut Français d'Archéologie Orientale.

—— 1988. *Inscriptions grecques et latines d'Akôris*. Cairo: Institut Français d'Archéologie Orientale.

Bingen, J. 1983. 'Les Thraces en Égypte ptolémaïque', *Pulpudeva: Semaines Philippolitaines de l'Histoire et de la Culture Thrace* 4: 72–9; trans. as 'Thracians in Ptolemaic Egypt', in Bingen, *Hellenistic Egypt: Monarchy, Society, Economy, Culture*. Berkeley and Los Angeles: University of California Press, 2007, 83–93.

Blasius, A., and B. U. Schipper. 2002. 'Die "Apokalyptischen Texte" aus Ägypten: Ein Forschungsüberblick', in Blasius and Schipper (eds), *Apokalyptik und Ägypten: Eine kritische Analyse der relevanten Texte aus dem griechisch-römischen Ägypten*. Leuven: Peeters, 7–20.

Bonneau, D. 1964. *La crue du Nil: Divinité égyptienne, à travers mille ans d'histoire*. Paris: Klincksieck.

—— 1971. 'Les fêtes de la crue du Nil: Problèmes de lieux, de dates et d'organisation', *Revue d'Égyptologie* 23: 49–65.

—— 1995. 'La divinité du Nil sous le principat en Égypte', in W. Haase and H. Temporini (eds), *Aufstieg und Niedergang der römischen Welt* II 18.5. Berlin: de Gruyter, 3195–215.

Brashear, W. M. 1992. *A Mithraic Catechism from Egypt*. Vienna: Holzhausen.

Breccia, E. 1926. *Monuments de l'Égypte gréco-romaine*, vol. 1. Bergamo: Officine dell'Istituto Italiano d'Arte Grafiche.

—— 1932. 'Un "Cronos mitriaco" ad Oxyrhynchos', in *Mélanges Maspero*, vol. 2. Cairo: Institut Français d'Archéologie Orientale, 257–64.

—— 1934. *Terrecotte figurate greche e Greco-egizie del Museo di Alessandria, Monuments de l'égypte gréco-romaine*, vol. 2. Bergamo: Officine dell-Istituto italiano d'arti grafiche.

Bricault, L. 2005. 'Zeus Hélios Mégas Sarapis', in C. Cannuyer et al. (eds), *La Langue dans tous ses états*. Liège: Acta Orientalia Belgica, 243–54.

Chapouthier, F. 1935. *Les Dioscures au service d'une déesse: Étude d'iconographie religieuse*. Paris: de Boccard.

Chauveau, M. 2001. 'Rhakôtis et la fondation d'Alexandrie', *Égypte, Afrique et Orient* 24: 13–16.

Cribiore, R. 1995. 'A Hymn to the Nile', *Zeitschrift für Papyrologie und Epigraphik* 106: 97–106.

Cuvigny, H. 2010. 'The Shrine in the *Praesidium* of Dios (Eastern Desert of Egypt): Graffiti and Oracles in Context', *Chiron* 40: 245–99.

Depauw, M. 2000. 'Alexandria, the Building Yard', *Chronique d'Égypte* 75: 64–5.

Drew-Bear, M. 1991. 'La triade du rocher d'Akôris', in N. Fick and J.-C. Carrière (eds), *Mélanges Étienne Bernand*. Paris: Belles Lettres, 227–34.

Dunand, F. 1969. 'Les représentations de l'Agathodémon: à propos de quelques bas-reliefs du Musée d'Alexandrie', *Bulletin de l'Institut Français d'Archéologie Orientale* 67: 9–48.

——1976. 'Lanternes gréco-romaines d'Égypte', *Dialogues d'Histoire Ancienne* 2: 71–95.

——1977. 'L'Oracle du potier et la formation de l'apocalyptique en Égypte', in F. Raphaël et al. (eds), *L'Apocalyptique*. Paris: Geuthner, 39–67.

——1979. *Religion populaire en Égypte romaine: Les terres cuites isiaques du Musée du Caire*. Leiden: Brill.

——1981. 'Agathodaimon', in H. C. Ackermann, J.-R. Gisler, and L. Kahil (eds), *Lexicon Iconographicum Mythologiae Classicae*. Zurich: Artemis, 1/1. 277–82; 2.203–7.

——1983. 'Grecs et Égyptiens en Égypte Lagide: Le problème de l'acculturation', in *Modes de contact et processus de transformation dans les sociétés anciennes*. Rome: École Française de Rome, 45–87.

——1990. *Catalogue des terres cuites gréco-romaines d'Égypte, Musée du Louvre, Département des Antiquités Égyptiennes*. Paris: Réunion des Musées Nationaux.

——2000. 'Syncrétisme ou coexistence: Images du religieux dans l'Égypte tardive', in C. Bonnet and A. Motte (eds), *Les syncrétismes religieux dans le monde méditerranéen antique: Colloque de Besançon, 22–23 octobre 1973*. Brussels: Institut Historique Belge de Rome, 97–116.

el-Sayed, R. 1982. *La déesse Neith de Saïs*, 2 vols. Cairo: Institut Français d'Archéologie Orientale.

Fowden, G. 1986. *The Egyptian Hermes: An Historical Approach to the Late Pagan Mind*. Cambridge: Cambridge University Press.

Frankfurter, D. 1998. *Religion in Roman Egypt: Assimilation and Resistance*. Princeton: Princeton University Press.

Gardiner, A. H. 1932. 'The Astarte Papyrus', in *Studies Presented to F. Ll. Griffith*. London: Egypt Exploration Society, 74–85.

Giddy, L. M. 1980. 'The Roman Wall-Paintings from Amheida', *Journal of the Society for the Study of Egyptian Antiquities* 10: 331–78.

Glare, P. 1992. 'The Temple of Jupiter Capitolinus at Arsinoe and the Imperial Cult', in A. Bülow-Jacobsen (ed.), *Proceedings of the 20th International Congress of Papyrologists, Copenhagen, 23–29 August 1992*. Copenhagen: Museum Tusculanum Press, 550–4.

Grenier, J.-C. 1977. *Anubis alexandrin et romain*. Leiden: Brill.

——1978. 'L'Anubis cavalier du Musée du Louvre', in M. de Boer and T. A. Edridge (eds), *Hommages à Maarten J. Vermaseren*, vol. 1. Leiden: Brill, 405–8.

Harris, J. R. 1996. 'Mithras at Hermopolis and Memphis', in D. M. Bailey (ed.), *Archaeological Research in Roman Egypt*. Ann Arbor: Journal of Roman Archaeology, 169–76.

Hoffmann, H. 1963. 'Helios', *Journal of the American Research Center in Egypt* 2: 117–24.

Hornung, E. 1990. *Conceptions of God in Ancient Egypt: The One and the Many*. Ithaca, NY: Cornell University Press.

Kantorowicz, E. 1961. 'Gods in Uniform', *Proceedings of the American Philosophical Society* 105: 368–93.

Kaper, O. E. 2003. *The Egyptian God Tutu: A Study of the Sphinx-God and Master of Demons with a Corpus of Monuments*. Leuven: Peeters.

——2004. 'Mithras im ptolemäischen Ägypten', in P. C. Bol, G. Kaminski, and C. Maderna (eds), *Fremdheit—Eigenheit: Ägypten, Griechenland und Rom, Austausch und Verständnis*. Stuttgart: Scheufele, 557–64.

——2005. 'Synkretistische Götterbilder in hellenistischer und römischer Zeit', in H. Beck, P. C. Bol, and M. Bückling (eds), *Ägypten, Griechenland, Rom: Abwehr und Berührung*. Tübingen: Wasmuth; Frankfurt: Liebighaus, 611–19.

Kiessling, E. 1953. 'Die Götter von Memphis in griechisch-römischer Zeit', *Archiv für Papyrusforschung und verwandte Gebiete* 15: 7–45.

Lauer, J.-P., and C. Picard. 1955. *Les statues ptolémaïques du Sarapieion de Memphis*. Paris: Presses Universitaires de France.

Launey, M. 1949–50. *Recherches sur les armées hellénistiques*, 2 vols. Paris: de Boccard.

Lewis, N. 1986. *Greeks in Ptolemaic Egypt*. Oxford: Oxford University Press.

Milik, J. 1967. 'Les papyrus araméens d'Hermoupolis et les cultes syro-phéniciens en Égypte perse', *Biblica* 48: 546–622.

Myśliwiec, K. 2000. 'Researches on Hellenistic Pottery from Athribis (Lower Egypt)', in E. Kypraiou (ed.), *Η επιστημονική συναντήση γιά την Ελληνιστική κεραμικήν, Χανιά, 1997* [Scientific Meeting on Hellenistic Pottery, Chania, 1997]. Athens: Archaeological Resources Fund Receipts, 253–8.

North, J. 1992. 'The Development of Religious Pluralism', in J. Lieu, J. North, and T. Rajak (eds), *The Jews among Pagans and Christians in the Roman Empire*. London: Routledge, 174–93.

Perpillou-Thomas, F. 1993. *Fêtes d'Égypte ptolémaïque et romaine d'après la documentation papyrologique grecque*. Leuven: Peeters.

Pettazzoni, R. 1949. 'Kronos-Chronos in Egitto', in *Hommages à Joseph Bidez et à Franz Cumont*, vol. 2. Brussels: Latomus, 245–56.

Quaegebeur, J. 1975. *Le dieu égyptien Shaï dans la religion et l'onomastique*. Leuven: Peeters.

—— 1983. 'Cultes égyptiens et grecs en Égypte', in E. van't Dack, P. van Dessel, and W. van Gucht (eds), *Egypt and the Hellenistic World: Proceedings of the International Colloquium, Leuven, 24-26 May 1982*. Leuven: Peeters, 314–16.

—— 1985. 'Athena, Neith and Toeris in Greek Documents', *Zeitschrift für Papyrologie und Epigraphik* 60: 217–32.

Rassart-Debergh, M. 1991. 'Trois icônes romaines du Fayoum', *Chronique d'Égypte* 66: 349–55.

Ronchi, G. 1974–7. *Lexikon Theonymon rerum sacrarum et divinarum ad Aegyptum pertinentium quae in papyris ostracis titulis graecis latinisque in Aegypto repertis laudantur*. Milan: Istituto Editoriale Cisalpino.

Rondot, V. 2004. *Le temple de Soknebtynis et son dromos*. Cairo: Institut Français d'Archéologie Orientale.

Szymańska, H. 2005. *Terres cuites d'Athribis*. Turnhout: Brepols.

Tallet, G. 2011. 'Zeus Hélios Megas Sarapis, un dieu égyptien "pour les Romains"?', in N. Belayche and J.-D. Dubois (eds), *'L'oiseau et le poisson: Cohabitations religieuses dans les mondes grec et romain*. Paris: Presses Universitaires de la Sorbonne, 227–61.

—— 2012. 'Isis, the crocodiles and the mysteries of the Nile flood: Interpreting a scene from Roman Egypt exhibited in the Egyptian museum in Cairo (SE 30001)', in C. Giuffrè Scibona and A. Mastrocinque' (eds), *Demeter, Aphrodite, Isis, and Cybele: Studies in the Greek and Roman Religion in Honour of Giulia Sfameni Gasparro*. Stuttgart: Steiner, 137–60.

Thompson, D. J. 1988. *Memphis under the Ptolemies*. Princeton: Princeton University Press.

Tran Tam Tinh, V. 1986. 'Bès', in H. C. Ackermann, J.-R. Gisler, and L. Kahil (eds), *Lexicon Iconographicum Mythologiae Classicae*. Zurich: Artemis, 3/1.98–108; 2.74–86.

von Bissing, F. W. 1926. 'Eine Apisfigur in der Haltung der *Adlocutio*', in C. Adler and A. Ember (eds), *Oriental Studies Dedicated to Paul Haupt*. Baltimore: Johns Hopkins University Press, 295–9.

Whitehorne, J. 1995. 'The Pagan Cults of Roman Oxyrhynchus', in W. Haase and H. Temporini (eds), *Aufstieg und Niedergang der römischen Welt* II 18.5. Berlin: de Gruyter, 3050–91.

Wildung, D. 1977. *Imhotep und Amenhotep: Gottwerdung im alten Ägypten*. Munich: Deutscher Kunstverlag.

Will, E. 1955. *Le relief culturel gréco-romain*. Paris: de Boccard.

CHAPTER 27

EGYPTIAN CULT
Evidence from Temple Scriptoria and Christian Hagiographies

MARTIN ANDREAS STADLER

Egyptian Cult and Roman Rule

Everything could have turned out so well! The Persian kings and the Ptolemies had placed themselves in the tradition of the Egyptian kings and with varying success had taken over, at least formally, their very central role in Egyptian religion. Could one not have expected this of the Roman Octavian? When, however, his rule over Egypt began in 30 BCE and he viewed the conquered land, though paying his respects to Alexander the Great at his monument, he would not go on to visit the tombs of the Ptolemies (Cass. Dio 51.16.5; Cary 1960: 44–7). From the perspective of the Egyptian priesthood this would have been tolerable, but his refusal to present offerings at the altar of the Apis bull was not: the Apis was a living bull, selected on particular criteria by the priests, and worshipped as a god. Acting in this way, Octavian refused to carry out one of the most intrinsic duties of an Egyptian king (Suet. *Aug.* 93; Rolfe 1998: 284–5) and thus removed a foundation stone from the Egyptian world-view. According to Cassius Dio (51.16.5; Cary 1960: 46–7), he is even supposed to have said, when he declined to present offerings to the Apis, that he was accustomed to make offerings to gods and not cattle. In theory, however, a king who performed religious functions was indispensable to the Egyptian cult, as the priests acted only as his representatives. Octavian's affront posed difficult theological problems for the Egyptian priests, which carried over to the economic and administrative level (cf. Kockelmann 2010: 204–14 for the Fayum). Temple land was nationalized, at least in part, and the former owners received payments in lieu from the state in the form of grain and money, or they were allowed to lease back the land on favourable terms (Evans 1961; cf., however, Monson 2005). Thus, the temples, the centres of the Egyptian cult, lost a considerable part of their economic power.

A further change made by the Roman administration, which, though less serious, might nevertheless endanger the continuance of the Egyptian cult, was in the stipulations listed in the Gnomon of the *Idios Logos*, which were to be fulfilled if one was to serve as a priest (Moyer 2003: 53). It emerges from the edict of the *praefectus Aegypti* C. Turranius (7–4 BCE) that membership of the priestly class was indeed strictly controlled (*BGU* IV 1199; Geraci 1983: 185–7; Jördens 2009: 339–40 with n. 38). Admittedly this was probably a measure to prevent too many people from enjoying the priestly privilege of reduced taxation (Jördens 2009: 338–43). However, the number of those belonging to the class that performed the cult was thereby restricted.

Despite these initial stresses, the Egyptian cult was not destroyed. A circular of Q. Aemilius Saturninus of 199 CE, which forbade divination and typically Egyptian practices, such as obtaining oracular pronouncements by means of processions or via written notes, shows the continuance of certain forms of the practice of the Egyptian cult until at least the end of the second century (Ritner 1995: 3355–6; Jördens 2008: 445). The circular was not even particularly effective under some circumstances, and was obviously circumvented (Frankfurter 1998: 153–6). In this chapter I will also discuss several references to a continuation of the temple cult into the fifth century.

The rest of the imperial family, and subsequent rulers, did not take the negative attitude towards the Egyptian temples that Octavian had initially been forced to do in 30 BCE, against the background of his struggle against M. Antonius, which was presented as the defence of traditional Roman values against oriental decadence. A little less than fifty years later, in 19 CE, Germanicus, a high-ranking member of the imperial family, travelled to Egypt—though without Tiberius' permission—and, unlike Octavian, made offerings to the Apis. Germanicus was, however, not a ruler, and so his actions may have been presumptuous. The animal, as stated by Pliny (*HN* 185; Ernout 1952: 87–8) and Ammianus Marcellinus (22.14.8; Rolfe 1950: 278–9), did not eat. The refusal of the bull to accept the offering was seen as a premonition (*prodigium*) of the death of Germanicus, which was to occur in the same year. Meanwhile, a modus vivendi had evolved, and Tiberius could be represented without any difficulty in the ritual scenes of the temples.

This had not always been the case. At first the Egyptian priests needed to deal with the problem of how the king was to be named if the person first in question, Octavian, was so dismissive of the cult. In parallel with the establishment of the principate in Rome, the evolution of a Roman or cultic pharaoh progressed in several stages, in order to fill the gap left by the king, so keenly felt in the temple world (Hölbl 1996, 2000, 2004; also Chapter 22). Octavian-Augustus and his successors thus continued temple building, though on a smaller scale than the Ptolemies, and as a consequence took over the role of the pharaoh who performed the cult.

Practitioners of Religion and Cult

For Egyptian religion these problems are not mere matters of detail in the daily business of worship, or in theological discourses by a few priests, but have fundamental significance because the Egyptian religion was a cult religion (Assmann 1984). It was based not on revelation by a founder or a canonical sacred text, but lived through constant renewal in the exercise of the cult. If the rituals ceased, then the Egyptian religion would also come to an end. The Egyptian cult as it was performed in temples has a holistic character in its focus on cosmic connections, and claims to be effective in saving the world from destruction (Assmann 1990: 160–236). One of the most essential royal tasks is to nurture this through the building and maintenance of the temples. The building and maintenance of the temples is thus a divine offering in itself and part of the cult (see Chapter 22). The opportunities for private individuals to participate actively in these cult forms were, of course, restricted by their economic power. Yet there was always private participation in the cult, of the most diverse kinds, with contributions made according to the individual's means (Baines 1987, 1991). From the time of the Ptolemies and the Romans there are increased surviving sources evidencing private financial involvement in the temple cult, underestimated until now, or in the erection of temple buildings (Kockelmann and Pfeiffer 2009). The motivation for this could be the wish to prove one was a loyal functionary of the king, i.e. a public official who supports privately a cult fostered by the king, or it could be a real, personal religious relationship to an Egyptian deity (Heinen 1994; Kockelmann and Pfeiffer 2009).

Besides individuals, groups could also form in support of the cult, like the sheep-breeders of Neiloupolis in 24 BCE, for instance. Through their stela they informed posterity that they had financed the enclosing wall of the temple of Dime (Soknopaiou Nesos) (Bernand 1975: 142–4, no. 74). Mentions of such private endowments are significantly rarer in Roman than in Ptolemaic times in the Fayum, and even the more substantial endowments date from before 79 CE (Kockelmann 2010: 214–20). More common were the religious associations in which usually wealthier individuals from one place joined together (Lüddeckens 1968; de Cenival 1972; San Nicolò 1972: 11–29; Muszynski 1977). Such religious associations existed from at least the 26th dynasty, and though they are best documented and researched for the Ptolemaic period, were active even in Roman Imperial times (Monson 2006; Lippert 2008: 119). In their constitutions, adopted afresh every year, which are known from Demotic and Greek papyri, the members were obliged to pay a membership fee and participate in the cult of the temple concerned. Thus, they contributed offertory gifts like loaves of bread, salves, oil, and incense, took part in the burial of the sacred animal of their temple, and joined in the feasts and processions with burnt offerings and libations. They could also pay the costs of building works in the temenos (e.g. in Dendara (?), 19 CE; Vleeming 2001: 145–6, no. 159). A great deal of space in their constitutions is taken up by the social aspects, i.e. mutual support of the members in different situations in life (legal proceedings, mourning, death, and burial). This bonding into a group could count as reciprocation for their involvement in the cult. Cult communities, like church parishes, thus created a social network and the opportunity for lay people to take part in the temple cult.

The actual performance, of course, was in the hands of specialists, the priests, who were not necessarily members of the religious associations, though holders of the highest priestly offices do feature as contributors among the members. I highlighted earlier in this chapter the regulation of membership of the priestly class by the Roman provincial administration. Nevertheless, in the temple of Dime, for instance, one might count up to 130 priests who appeared daily (Lippert and Schentuleit 2006: 21–3). In Tebtunis there were still fifty priests early in the second century, but in other temples after 150 CE the temple staff was reduced (Kockelmann 2010: 212–14). The sanctuary of Dime was, as a building, only of moderate size, and for this reason the number 130 might be surprising. However, as far as taxation was concerned, Dime was in the first rank of temples, and thus among the more significant institutions of its kind in Imperial Egypt. Thanks to the Demotic documents from the site, produced by the temple administration, we are particularly well informed about Dime. They include the description of the priests' duties (*hn.w*), only a few of which have so far been published, which list the conditions for numerous vocations within the temple administration, including that of the priests (Lippert 2007). Breaches were punished with fines, and for this reason the agreements are similar in a certain way to the constitutions of the religious associations.

In addition, we are informed about the rules for priestly purity by the relevant vows, which are preserved in the Book of the Temple. The Book of the Temple is a substantial, comprehensive treatise, attested in many manuscripts, which describes the architecture, the organization, and the cult of an ideal Egyptian temple. It has not been published in its entirety, but it has been made known by its editor through more than a dozen preliminary reports (most recently Quack 2009b). In its completeness of content it must be a unique source for the Egyptian temple, and of course it also deals with the tasks of the priests. Among them are the vows of priestly purity, which are also known in a Greek translation (Quack 1997, 2005) and are connected with the Negative Confession of chapter 125 of the Book of the Dead (Stadler 2008). The Book of the Temple seems to have been particularly popular among Egyptian priests of the Imperial period, for we know of around thirty exemplars from Tebtunis alone and fifteen from Dime. In addition, there are other places in Egypt that are proven to have possessed this handbook. The great number of priests active in a temple of medium size, together with the high incidence of a treatise about the Egyptian temple, indicates in the first two centuries CE at least a very lively and active priestly milieu with functioning scriptoria (Egyptian: *prꜥnḫ*, 'House of Life') in which priestly training was carried out and priestly knowledge was cultivated. Numerous other sources, which cannot be treated here, enrich our knowledge of the creativity of the Houses of Life in Roman Egypt, like the Book of Thoth, itself a text for an initiation rite (Jasnow and Zauzich 2005; cf. Quack 2007) or the handbooks of priestly knowledge (Osing 1998; Osing and Rosati 1998), which summarize cult knowledge.

Cult and Magic

Rituals were not performed only in an official temple context, primarily by priests: rituals also have their place in the private sphere. They are made immediate and concrete by coroplastic figures of a whole bevy of deities and bear witness to the piety of the population (see Chapters 20 and 38). In the case of home cults there is, however, a fluid boundary with magic (see Chapter 21). A differentiation between religion and magic, or cult and magic practices, is problematic in the case of Egypt, for here magic, or more accurately the power of incantation (*ḥkꜣ*), is an integral component of the official temple cult, as an instrument of cult activity and religious practice (Baines 1987; Fitzenreiter 2004). Thus, there is hardly any recognizable distinction between religion and magic. For this reason a distinction of this kind in present-day Egyptological research is rejected out of a kind of political correctness (cf. Quack 2002, esp. 43), as the distinction between religion and magic would devalue the magic texts as compared with the religious texts. In doing so, however, scholarship adopts a particularly Christian, disparaging concept of magic, which at that time was applied without distinction to anything that was non-Christian. In a sermon, Shenoute of Atripe (died 465), for instance, gives a list of objects that he removed from a sanctuary or shrine. Among them was also 'the book which was filled with every kind of magic' (ⲡϫⲱⲱⲙⲉ ⲉⲧⲙⲉϩ ⲙⲙⲁⲅⲓⲁ ⲛⲓⲙ); Leipoldt 1908: 89, lines 15–16; the translation 'sorcery books' in Frankfurter 2008: 142 is misleading). As I shall argue below, it is very probable that this was a book of rituals that, on account of its heathen origins, was in Abbot Shenoute's eyes full of magic, and not religion, which for him could only be Christianity.

The eyes of magic are fixed not on the transcendent, but on everyday human life and the problems associated with it, while the aim of the temple ritual is directed at a much wider context, especially maintaining the journey of the sun. The temple ritual is directed towards gods, from earth to heaven, to make the gods benevolent to mankind, while the act of magic is essentially tied to the earth and seeks to bring the gods here by force. In all the acts of incantation that took place within the temple cult (Quack 2002), there are thus two different fundamental attitudes towards God: the one is that of the priest, which is exemplified in hymns praising God, his magnificence, his might, and his qualities as the primeval creator, on whose actions the welfare of the earth essentially depends; the other is that of a magician who puts pressure on a god, threatens the cessation of offering, and thus seeks to blackmail him into helping (Ritner 1992). The Egyptian magician thus places himself above the entity where power resides, and operates in a secular sphere, no longer serving the deity but attempting to make the perfection of divine power subservient to his own will. Magic thus takes a different position vis-à-vis the divine from that taken by the temple cult. The borderline is fluid, however, and depends on the cultural background or the point of view of the participants: if a Greek in Roman Imperial times receives in exchange for payment a vessel divination from an Egyptian priest, then the priest is performing a ritual. For the buyer, however, it is magic, not least because it is a bought product (Moyer 2003). The example of Shenoute and his attitude to temple books given above also shows that it is the observer who makes the distinction.

Despite all the commonality, namely the same processes and the uniform Egyptian terminology of (*ḥkꜣ*), 'incantation', the differences are retained, for incantatory power and magic are not the same thing. Incantatory power (*ḥkꜣ*), which the Egyptians considered really to exist, is an instrument that was used in the temple cult just as it was by private people in similar or related practices. Thus, (*ḥkꜣ*) is a connecting link between religion and magic, and it is tempting to confuse these two areas. Separating them does not, however, imply a value judgement, for magic in Egypt is not a degraded form of religion, but its twin sibling. An additional factor to this close relationship of cult and magic practice is that temples, of course, did not exist removed and isolated from the cares of mankind, but had to deal with human needs. This was the purpose of the oracle cults attached to the sanctuaries, or the cult at the contra temple, which enjoyed some popularity even in Imperial times (see Chapter 20; Stadler forthcoming). With other texts we can no longer distinguish with certainty whether they were used in the temple cult or in the domestic sphere and thus might be akin to the Greek, Latin, or Coptic *sortes* books (Stadler 2004, esp. 269–75; 2006; Dieleman 2009; Naether 2010).

The Reality of the Temple Cult in Roman Imperial Times

The magic texts that survive from Egypt from the third century CE and later, in Greek and in Demotic, fill a gap in the documentation of Egyptian rituals after *c.*200 CE. They continue into the fifth century and may be compared with texts from Pharaonic Egypt, to which they are related (Quack 2009c; Chapter 20). In the third century, however, the direct Egyptian sources for the cult diminish dramatically, and for this reason the magical papyri, despite the distinction just drawn, are still undeniably important in gaining an adequate understanding of the continuance of the Egyptian cult.

But what is the range of documentation of temple ritual texts in the Egyptian language for the period up to the rule of Septimius Severus? It includes the inscriptions and ritual scenes of the temples, papyrus manuscripts, and also isolated texts on other portable writing surfaces such as wooden panels (Widmer 2004). The documentation is so extensive that a description of Egyptian cult practice in Roman Imperial times must be restricted, given the space of this chapter, to Egyptian texts, and may create the erroneous impression that the temples were barely touched by close contact with foreign cultures and religions or by the changing historical conditions sketched briefly above, and that almost nothing had changed since the New Kingdom. The reality of the cult is, of course, much more colourful—the reference to magic has already made that clear—but I will focus on a description according to the Egyptian sources, while Frankfurter (Chapter 20 in this volume) describes religious practice outside the temple and highlights the interaction of non-Egyptian and Egyptian religions. It is this existence side by side with the traditional Egyptian temple cult and its adaptations in daily life, using forms of worship associated with non-indigenous Egyptian divinities, that makes the study of religion in the considerably Hellenized Egypt of Roman Imperial times so appealing.

While little is known of Thebes, at one time so significant in terms of cult, and still dominant in the domain of funerary texts in early Imperial times (see Chapter 23), Latopolis (Esna) situated about 55 km south of Thebes, offers a large corpus of inscriptions from which there emerges a very good picture of the festive events in this temple, where Khnum was worshipped as the main god (Sauneron 1962). From the sanctuaries still decorated in Roman Imperial times there also survive major corpora of inscriptions, above all from Dendara, Kom Ombo, and Philae. On the basis of the documentation we cannot determine with certainty in every case what is new in these sources and what is founded on ancient Pharaonic traditions. Yet the Imperial inscriptions differ so little from earlier Egyptian religious sources that we must assume there was a high proportion of old ideas, old concepts of the divine and the way the divine was worshipped, rather than an extreme degree of innovation. In the case of several hieratic manuscripts, unfortunately very fragmented, the older models are easily demonstrated. The papyri we are concerned with contain recitation texts for the daily ritual in the temple of Tebtunis and are dated from the first and second centuries CE. I shall call these texts simply the Daily Ritual; in Egyptian they are entitled (*rꜣ.w n.w ḫ.t-nṯr ỉry m pr Sbk nb Bdnw*, 'Utterances of the things of God which are performed in the temple of Soknebtunis'). Although dating from Imperial times, the papyri are clearly written, both graphically and linguistically, and are evidence of the competence of the priesthood there in dealing with religious texts. A few of the manuscripts have been published (Rosati 1998), others have not (Osing, personal communication), and still others have been dug up in recent years in Tebtunis (Guermeur 2008, forthcoming).

There is a surviving Demotic version of the Daily Ritual from Dime; eleven manuscripts of it are known, all of which date from the first two centuries CE, to judge by their palaeography (Stadler 2007). To perform the daily ritual of offerings, the priest had to enter the temple and head towards the innermost sanctuary with the cult image. Before he could go into the temple itself, he had to purify himself, and then in the case of the Dime temple walk through five gates. He then reached the hall (*wsḫ.t*, in Edfu the *wsḫ.t wr.t*, 'Great Hall'), and through the altar hall (*wsḫ.t ḥtp* in Edfu) and the central hall (*wsḫ.t ḥr.t-ỉb* in Edfu) he reached the sanctuary. The Daily Ritual as it can be reconstructed from the individual manuscripts is a collection of the words that the priest had to recite at each station. An extract is given by way of example, quoted from the Tebtunis version and supplemented according to the Dime version:

> *Utterance* on entering the hall. *Words to be spoken*:
> [Greeting to you, <Hall, as> the Hall, your name being Nut.]...pure.
> [I cense, I...so that] you [avert] away every evil harm,
> [driving back slaughter ...]
> I am pure. [My purity is the purity of the gods.
> Hail,] Nut, Geb, Osiris, Isis, Nephthys, Horus, son of Isis,
> May [you] drive away [every evil.
> Take action against evil.
> May you drive outside every evil enemy away from me,
> when t]hey enter the temple behind me,
> for I am [Thoth, who created the Horus eye] after his exhaustion.
> An offering that the king may give. I am pure.
> (*P Flor.* = *PSI* I 70 fr. A I, Z 1–3; Rosati 1998: 106)

The Demotic version from Dime is almost completely identical, and marks only the part from 'Hail, Nut, Geb, Osiris, Isis ...' as a variant (*ky rꜣ*) of what precedes it. The character and structure of the utterances can easily be illustrated with this quotation. After a title partly written in red ink (here given in italics), which announces a context of action, there follow short hymns or invocations to deities or the self-identification with the gods by the priest performing the ritual; here it is Thoth, in other places Horus or Anubis. The titles make it possible to follow the path the priest took.

The text itself is not a new creation of Ptolemaic and Roman times, but has, in parts, parallels in the description of the Daily Ritual and the associated subsidiary writings of the New Kingdom (Moret 1902; Kausen 1988; Osing 1999; Tacke 2003; Cooney and McClain 2005). Further parallels are preserved in the rituals for Amun and for Mut, among others, the manuscripts of which come from Thebes and were written in the Third Intermediate period (Generalverwaltung der königlichen Museen zu Berlin 1901; Guglielmi and Buroh 1997) and also in inscriptions from the temples of the Graeco-Roman period. This is the case with the ritual of the hourly vigil (Pries 2011), which in turn is based on a long tradition reaching back to the Old Kingdom. The versions of Tebtunis and Dime supplement this stock of texts with utterances coincidentally not attested until now. Though some parts are not paralleled in earlier sources, they are old, as is shown by their connection with demonstrably old language corpora and the Middle Egyptian language, i.e. the form of Egyptian as it was spoken roughly between the twentieth and the fifteenth centuries BCE. The texts are composed in a liturgical language, even if they are recorded in Demotic writing.

The significance of the Daily Ritual of Dime lies in the enrichment of the corpus of utterances, the transfer of a hieratic–hieroglyphic text into another written form, Demotic, and also the link with the architecture of the temple of Dime, which was dedicated to the local figure of the crocodile god Sobek, called Soknopaios in its Hellenized form (Egyptian: *Sbk nb Pay*, 'Sobek, the lord of Pai'). The ritual text corresponded exactly to the architecture of the sanctuary in its last building phase, when it was enlarged: a priest did indeed have to walk through five gates, as the anthology of utterances suggests, before he reached the *wsḫ.t* hall and then continued further (Stadler 2007; Davoli forthcoming). This yields a relative dating for the compilation and writing of the Daily Ritual of Dime, which must have occurred about the same time as the extension of the temple. In Tebtunis there is a less obvious parallel between architecture and ritual, owing to the poor state of preservation of the temple there (Stadler 2007).

The transfer of the Middle Egyptian text into Demotic writing was done using eccentric orthography (Widmer 2004: 669–83). These 'non-etymological' or 'phonetic' spellings are typical of a series of Demotic papyri with religious texts that extend into Imperial times, as well as liturgical texts that are transmitted on various papyri, the most complete example being *P Berlin* 6750—for the sake of brevity, I will use the name of the papyrus for the text (Spiegelberg 1902, table 71, 75–83). Like others discussed above, the papyrus originates from Dime and contains two liturgical compositions, the first of which is concerned above all with Osiris and his resurrection; the second, however, takes Horus, his birth, and his path to kingship as its theme (Widmer 1998; 2003: esp. 15–18). *P Berlin* 6750 shows, in the same way as the Daily Ritual, how the Imperial era exemplars of Egyptian ritual texts were based on earlier ones: short sections are quotations from older hieratic funerary papyri, or the well-known text of the ritual of the hourly vigil, which was part of the Osiris cult (Widmer forthcoming). The events surrounding the birth of Horus and his enthronement are praised in the form of a festive hymn that has some very similar counterparts from the mammisi (birth house) of Edfu, constructed around 100 BCE (Chassinat 1939: 196.6–10; 197.8–12; 205.11–16; see Quack 2001: 109 with n. 53).

As all the text exemplars originate in Dime, we must ask to what extent the content of *P Berlin* 6750 may be placed within the mythology and cult of Dime, since Sobek, the lord of Pai (Soknopaios), i.e. a crocodile god, was the main object of worship there. The naming of Soknapaios and Soknopiais in Greek sources from Dime gave rise to the assumption that a Horus deity was to be seen in Soknopaios and an Osiris deity in Soknopiais (Widmer 2005). Both might have been incarnated as crocodiles: when one sacred crocodile died, it became the Osiris crocodile, and a young crocodile was enthroned as the sacred animal of Dime, who would take over the function of Horus. For the associated cult, which accompanied, re-enacted, and supported the burial of the old crocodile, and the ensuing installation of the young one on the temple's roof, *P Berlin* 6750 is probably a compilation of relevant texts for recitation (Stadler forthcoming). This would correspond to what is known from other temples. In Edfu, for instance, a falcon was enthroned as a divine king and incarnation of the divine on earth, so to speak (Alliot 1954: 303–433; Fairman 1954–5). There are similarities in the Osiris part of *P Berlin* 6750 to the Khoiak festival rites, which are known mainly through inscriptions from the temple of Dendara. In Dime these rites, which perhaps were performed with crocodiles, might have taken place during the festival of Genesia, which was celebrated in Dime from 7 to 25 Hathyr (in Imperial times from 3 to 21 November), since a few days from this period are mentioned in *P Berlin* 6750. In this interpretation of cult practice in the Fayum, the solar and cosmic aspect of Sobek, which required a regular death and an equally regular rejuvenation and rebirth, was expressed through the Osiris-Horus constellation, projected onto Sobek, and ritually represented with real crocodiles.

Merely the fact that we are able to compare various temples with each other, independently of the chief deity of a sanctuary, shows how very transferable cult texts are. The exemplars of the Daily Ritual from Imperial times follow models that were originally meant for Osiris and place them, in part, alongside spells that were recited in Karnak for Amun-Re as the cosmic supreme god and his consort, Mut. *P Berlin* 6750 also contains essentially Osirian texts and some in honour of Horus, and yet despite this obvious connection to the Osiris-Horus myth complex, the contents may also be related to Sobek, if only hypothetically. Osiris, Isis, Horus, and the particular chief god are thus 'words' of a mythical ritual language and denote certain phenomena: the chief deity denotes the cosmic-solar supreme god, Osiris the dead and revived incarnation, Horus the successor or new incarnation of the divine on earth, all of which were made flesh and blood in the sacred animals: the species was again determined by the local environment and the particular mythology. Horus himself is a deity with manifold meanings within this language, for in him are united qualities of the child-god in the figure of Harpocrates, and also sun-god qualities, because Horus is also a god of heaven. Thus, the worship of Harpocrates is equally the worship of the young sun-god (Budde 2003; Sandri 2006; Stadler 2006). Of course, at many cult sites there were also original Osirian and Horus cults, and *P Berlin* 6750 may also have been part of this context, whereas within Dime such cults have not yet been located. The fundamental Egyptian myths could therefore be adapted for regional use and thus enacted in rites at different places.

Myth narratives themselves must also be counted as recitation texts for rituals, and thus as cult texts (Quack 2009a). For example, the Demotic version of the Myth of the Sun's Eye, whose surviving manuscripts date from Roman times, was probably intended for recitation at a festival. This is not an innovation of the Graeco-Roman period, but established Egyptian tradition (von Lieven 2007: 274–83). Likewise, a report of creation in narrative form, the Neith cosmogony of Esna, was clearly used ritually as a text for recitation. It is designated in the Egyptian itself as a ritual (*nt*ᶜ), and is related to the festival of 13 Epiphi (7 July) (Sauneron 1968: 28–34, no. 206; Sauneron 1962: 253–76; Sternberg-el Hotabi 1995: 1078–86; Broze 1999). Creation through the word, as described here, may be thought of as the fundamental model for all the texts that accompany ritual acts and which realize the acts through their performative power; that is to say, create them anew (Finnestad 1985: 68–78; Smith 2002b: 199–200; Quack 2009a).

The End of the Written Tradition of the Egyptian Cult

Philological competence seems to have varied greatly in different places. While the priests of Tebtunis maintained the hieratic script, those of Dime preferred the Demotic and even further developed non-etymological spelling, as mentioned above, into a complex system.

Meanwhile, at Esna the mythological play of visual and phonetic values of hieroglyphic writing was still understood in the second century. The inscriptions extend into the reign of Decius (249–52), yet their quality diminishes under Septimius Severus, until the hieroglyphs carved under Decius are barely comprehensible (Sauneron 1959: 43–4). Apparently the wooden panel Louvre E 10382, which is dated to the end of the Ptolemaic or the beginning of the Roman Imperial period, was used for direct recitation (Widmer 2004). In order to recite this hymn to an unnamed goddess, described as a daughter of the sun-god, it seemed appropriate to the writer to resort to phonetic Demotic spellings, i.e. to use above all spellings with Demotic single-consonant signs. Clearly this was easier for the performer to read than a hieratic or hieroglyphic text. It is not known which temple the wooden panel comes from, but on the basis of the dating we may say that it is not correct to claim that the newer a text, the less knowledge of hieroglyphic or hieratic script could be assumed. And yet we know of no Egyptian recitation texts associated with the temple cult that were written down after the second century CE. The lack of relevant evidence may not be explained only through the slow dying out of indigenous Egyptian script, as the rituals could have been noted down in Greek script supplemented with special Demotic signs, such as the magical-ritual papyrus *P Brit. Mus.* EA 10808 (Sederholm 2006; cf. on this point Quack 2009d).

Was there therefore no cult being practised in the temples from the third century? The continuance of an Egyptian cult is shown by objective sources, objective because they are documentary, like the ostraca from Narmouthis, from which it appears that in the late second and early third centuries CE a cult of offerings was still being practised in the temple of Narmouthis (Gallo 1997; Menchetti 2005). Scholars like to quote Philae as the latest example, where Nubian Blemmyans and Nobadians (but not Egyptians!) worshipped Isis until 535–7, and where there was a brief restoration of the cult in 567 (Dijkstra 2008; Hahn 2008). From as early as the 340s there was only one remaining temple priest in Philae (not more than one, as Frankfurter 2008: 142 suggests): this is the way it is formulated by the author of the episode in the Coptic life of Aaron (Dijkstra 2008: 235–7). According to this source, the priest's sons acted for him from time to time. On the other hand, the Demotic and Greek graffiti in Philae are evidence of a whole series of individuals acting as temple staff in Philae, though in a somewhat isolated way (Dijkstra 2008: 193–218). Among these were some who, judging by their titles, ought to have been in a position at least to read Egyptian texts. Apart from the high priests (*ḥm-nṯr*), these are, in the years 372/3 and 435 particularly, the writers of divine words (*sẖ mt.t-nṯr*, *hierogrammateus*) (Griffith 1935–7: 103, table 55; Eide et al. 1998: 1110–12) and in 407/8 the writer of the divine words together with a master of ceremonies (*<ḥry> sštꜣ*) (Griffith 1935–7: 102, table 54). To what extent the titles were actually held by living incumbents and were not merely handed down for reasons of tradition will probably never be completely certain.

In Lower Egypt, too, the activity of the priests seems to have continued in the temple of Isis in Menouthis. As late as the end of the fourth century the sanctuary was said to be full of young men who had worked as priests (Eunap. *VS* 471 = 6.9, 16; Wright 1952: 416–17). This community had gathered in quest of philosophy, around a certain Antoninus. We must assume from this that the circle was heavily Hellenized and cannot be considered Egyptian in the narrow sense. After the temple had been transformed into a church in 391, there had been attempts to link oracular practices with the relics of martyrs and thus put them into a Christian context; the Isis cult was simply moved to another building until the patriarch of Alexandria, Petros Mongos, intervened. He had this building and the images of gods found there destroyed (Zachariah of Mytilene, *Vita Severi* 27–9; Kugener 1907: 27–9; Herzog 1939).

The relevant description of this occurrence mentions a house whose walls were completely covered in heathen inscriptions, which makes one think of hieroglyphs (thus, Kugener 1907: 27, followed by Trombley 1994: 221–2). Was the building into which the cult of Isis had withdrawn not recognizable from the outside as a sanctuary, but set up on the inside as a new temple? These would have been the last hieroglyphic inscriptions to be carved or painted in Egypt. In addition, this would suggest that the form of the cult of Isis as practised there may have presented itself in a very Egyptian mode, while the people of the time were also enthusiastic about Greek philosophy.

The gap of about 300 years between the last cult texts and the violent ending of the worship of Isis in Menouthis or Philae may be bridged by other Coptic hagiographies, which, as in the case of Menouthis, describe the robust intervention by Coptic monks or bishops in the establishment of the Christian faith in Egypt during the fourth and fifth centuries. The historicity of those reports is in essence accepted, despite the fact that they possibly modelled themselves on biblical texts (Emmel 2008; Frankfurter 2008; el-Sayed 2010). A common factor in these episodes is that they speak of stamping out heathen ritual still practised in the temples. In a number of cases people like the abbot of the White Monastery, Shenoute of Atripe, had to justify their deeds in court or other state tribunals (Leipoldt 1908; Emmel 2008: 162–6). Pagan priests thus thought that they had been wronged and had some chance of getting the courts to impose punishment.

In one of his raids on pagan sanctuaries, Shenoute, as mentioned above, confiscated from a building 'the book which was filled with every kind of magic'. The definite article in **ⲡϫⲱⲱⲙⲉ**, '*the* book', may indicate that it must have been important to the sanctuary and may have been a book of ritual. From this we may understand the formulation 'which was filled with every kind of magic' (**ⲉⲧⲙⲉϩ ⲙⲙⲁⲅⲓⲁ ⲛⲓⲙ**), which has a different implication from 'sorcery incantation', even if this possibility cannot be completely excluded. As the cult, in its own words, used the power of incantation (*ḥkꜣ*), then even ritual papyri would be 'filled with magic', without being an actual sorcery book. Whether Shenoute could read the text may be in doubt, but for him all texts in an Egyptian script were the devil's work (Young 1981) and the 'book filled with every kind of magic' was a trophy with which he could demonstrate a victory in the struggle for the proper worship of God. It was thus to be presented as a document of false worship of God and with no application for Christians.

From Shenoute's note it could thus be concluded that, in the fifth century, ritual books or texts still existed and were subject to focused persecution, which might explain the gap in the written tradition of the fourth and fifth centuries: in the third century a decline in temples had begun (Grossmann 2008), and the most recent surviving Egyptian manuscripts, discussed above, come from sanctuaries that were abandoned together with their associated settlements in the third century, so that here the chances for preserving the papyri were good. However, the temples or shrines that were still used into the fourth or fifth centuries were subjected to destruction by Christians. Perhaps manuscripts that continued to be used here were also very old, for one cannot assume that ritual texts continued to be produced in any quantity. Presumably the decline in competence in writing Egyptian script greatly diminished the number of ritual manuscripts produced and thus the chances that any one exemplar was preserved. There are sometimes suggestions in the literature that fully functioning temples were closed (e.g. Trombley 1994: 5–6, 220–1; Frankfurter 1998; 2008: 142–5), but the sources hint, as shown above, that in the fifth century the Egyptian cult took refuge in houses and was therefore in retreat (cf. also Smith 2002a: 245–7).

Even if the temples became less numerous, they did not disappear completely. Only the conversion of the emperors to Christianity, and the imperial laws that turned a blind eye to Christian attacks against pagan religion, led to the complete extinction of the temple cult. Faced with the initial difficulties with the Roman emperor, then the reduction of temple land with the economic crisis of the empire in the third century, and then the ban on pagan cults, the priests had managed to continue the cult at a few places for more than 500 years from the time of Octavian—until the emperors went so far as to ban the cults they were once supposed to head.

Suggested Reading

The Egyptian temple cult during the Roman empire has not yet been treated in a coherent and concise manner. A number of individual studies are available, and the most important ones have been cited in this chapter. Of these, however, Sauneron (1962) is to be singled out and recommended for gaining an insight into the festivals of a temple in Imperial times, using the example of Esna temple; a similar study on Dendara (Cauville 2002) is also available. For the Daily Ritual in Roman times, however, there is no comparable study. As a case study for the existence of the cult at the Sobek temples in the Fayum, Kockelmann (2010) is recommended, as is Dijkstra (2008) for the end of the cult in Philae.

Bibliography

Alliot, M. 1954. *Le culte d'Horus à Edfou au temps des Ptolémées*. Cairo: Institut Français d'Archéologie Orientale.

Assmann, J. 1984. *Ägypten: Theologie und Frömmigkeit einer frühen Hochkultur*. Stuttgart: Kohlhammer. Trans. as *The Search for God in Ancient Egypt*. Ithaca, NY: Cornell University Press, 2001.

—— 1990. *Ma'at: Gerechtigkeit und Unsterblichkeit im Alten Ägypten*. Munich: Beck.

Baines, J. 1987. 'Practical Religion and Piety', *Journal of Egyptian Archaeology* 73: 79–98.

—— 1991. 'Society, Morality, and Religious Practice', in B. E. Shafer (ed.), *Religion in Ancient Egypt: Gods, Myths, and Personal Practice*. Ithaca, NY: Cornell University Press, 123–200.

Bernand, E. 1975. *Recueil des inscriptions grecques du Fayoum*, vol. 1. Leiden: Brill.

Broze, M. 1999. 'Les Sept Propos de Méthyer: Structure narrative et théorie du savoir dans la cosmogonie de Neith à Esna', *Bulletin de l'Institut Français d'Archéologie Orientale du Caire* 99: 63–72.

Budde, D. 2003. 'Harpare-pa-chered: Ein ägyptisches Götterkind im Theben der Spätzeit und griechisch-römischen Epoche', in D. Budde, S. Sandri, and U. Verhoeven (eds), *Kindgötter im Ägypten der griechisch-römischen Zeit: Zeugnisse aus Stadt und Tempel als Spiegel des interkulturellen Kontakts*. Leuven: Peeters, 16–110.

Cary, E. 1960. *Dio's Roman History* VI. London: Heinemann; Cambridge, Mass.: Harvard University Press.

Cauville, S. 2002. *Dendara: Les fêtes d'Hathor*. Leuven: Peeters.

Chassinat, É. 1939. *Le mammisi d'Edfou*. Cairo: Institut Français d'Archéologie Orientale.

Cooney, K. M., and J. B. McClain. 2005. 'The Daily Offering Meal in the Ritual of Amenhotep I: An Instance of the Local Adaptation of Cult Liturgy', *Journal of Ancient Near Eastern Religions* 5: 41–75.
Davoli, P. Forthcoming. 'Rapporto di scavo 2003–2009', in M. Capasso and P. Davoli (eds), *Soknopaiou Nesos Project I (2003–2009)*. Pisa: Fabrizio Serra.
de Cenival, F. 1972. *Les associations religieuses en Égypte d'après les documents démotiques*. Cairo: Institut Français d'Archéologie Orientale.
Dieleman, J. 2009. Review of M. A. Stadler, *Isis, das göttliche Kind und die Weltordnung: Neue religiöse Texte aus dem Fayum nach dem Papyrus Wien D. 12006 recto*, *Bibliotheca Orientalis* 66: 225–31.
Dijkstra, J. H. F. 2008. *Philae and the End of Ancient Egyptian Religion: A Regional Study of Religious Transformation (298–642 CE)*. Leuven: Peeters.
Eide, T., et al. (eds) 1998. *Fontes Historiae Nubiorum*, vol. 3: *Textual Sources for the History of the Middle Nile Region between the Eighth Century BC and the Sixth Century AD*. Bergen: Institutt for Klassisk Filologi, Russisk og Religionsvitenskap.
El-Sayed, R. 2010. 'Shenoute und die Tempel von Atripe: Zur Umnutzung des Triphisbezirks in der Spätantike', in H. Knuf, C. Leitz, and D. von Recklinghausen (eds), *Honi soit qui mal y pense: Studien zum pharaonischen, griechisch-römischen und spätantiken Ägypten zu Ehren von Heinz-Josef Thissen*. Leuven: Peeters, 519–38.
Emmel, S. 2008. 'Shenoute of Atripe and the Christian Destruction of Temples in Egypt: Rhetoric and Reality', in J. Hahn, S. Emmel, and U. Gotter (eds), *From Temple to Church: Destruction and Renewal of Local Cultic Topography in Late Antiquity*. Leiden: Brill, 161–99.
Ernout, A. 1952. *Pline l'Ancien: Histoire naturelle livre VIII*. Paris: Belles Lettres.
Evans, J. A. S. 1961. 'A Social and Economic History of an Egyptian Temple in the Greco-Roman Period', *Yale Classical Studies* 17: 149–283.
Fairman, H. W. 1954–5. 'Worship and Festivals in an Egyptian Temple', *Bulletin of the John Rylands Library* 37: 165–203.
Finnestad, R. B. 1985. *Image of the World and Symbol of the Creator: On the Cosmological and Iconological Values of the Temple of Edfu*. Wiesbaden: Harrassowitz.
Fitzenreiter, M. 2004. 'Bemerkungen zur Beschreibung altägyptischer Religion: Mit einer Definition und dem Versuch ihrer Anwendung', *Göttinger Miszellen* 202: 19–53.
Frankfurter, D. 1998. *Religion in Roman Egypt: Assimilation and Resistance*. Princeton: Princeton University Press.
—— 2008. 'Iconoclasm and Christianization in Late Antique Egypt: Christian Treatments of Space and Image', in J. Hahn, S. Emmel, and U. Gotter (eds), *From Temple to Church: Destruction and Renewal of Local Cultic Topography in Late Antiquity*. Leiden: Brill, 135–59.
Gallo, P. 1997. *Ostraca demotici e ieratici dall'archivio bilingue di Narmouthis* II. Pisa: ETS.
Generalverwaltung der königlichen Museen zu Berlin (ed.) 1901. *Hieratische Papyrus aus den königlichen Museen zu Berlin*, vol. 1: *Rituale für den Kultus des Amon und für den Kultus der Mut*. Leipzig: Hinrichs.
Geraci, G. 1983. *Genesi della provincia romana d'Egitto*. Bologna: CLUEB.
Griffith, F. L. 1935–7. *Catalogue of the Demotic Graffiti of the Dodecaschoenus*. Oxford: Oxford University Press for Service des Antiquités.
Grossmann, P. 2008. 'Modalitäten der Zerstörung und Christianisierung pharaonischer Tempelanlagen', in J. Hahn, S. Emmel, and U. Gotter (eds), *From Temple to Church: Destruction and Renewal of Local Cultic Topography in Late Antiquity*. Leiden: Brill, 299–334.

Guermeur, I. 2008. 'Les nouveaux papyrus hiératiques exhumés sur le site de Tebtynis: Un aperçu', in S. L. Lippert and M. Schentuleit (eds), *Graeco-Roman Fayum: Texts and Archaeology*. Wiesbaden: Harrassowitz, 113–22.

—— Forthcoming. 'À propos d'un nouvel exemplaire du rituel journalier pour Soknebtynis (pTebhéra 5 et autres Variantes)', in J. F. Quack (ed.), *Ägyptische Rituale der griechisch-römischen Zeit*. Tübingen: Mohr Siebeck.

Guglielmi, W., and K. Buroh. 1997. 'Die Eingangssprüche des Täglichen Tempelrituals nach Papyrus Berlin 3055 (I, 1–VI, 3)', in J. van Dijk (ed.), *Essays on Ancient Egypt in Honour of Herman te Velde*. Groningen: Styx, 101–66.

Hahn, J. 2008. 'Die Zerstörung der Kulte von Philae: Geschichte und Legende am Ersten Nilkatarakt', in J. Hahn, S. Emmel, and U. Gotter (eds), *From Temple to Church: Destruction and Renewal of Local Cultic Topography in Late Antiquity*. Leiden: Brill, 203–42.

Heinen, H. 1994. 'Ägyptische Tierkulte und ihre hellenischen Protektoren', in M. Minas and J. Zeidler (eds), *Aspekte spätägyptischer Kultur: Festschrift für Erich Winter zum 65. Geburtstag*. Mainz: von Zabern, 157–68.

Herzog, R. 1939. 'Der Kampf um den Kult von Menuthis', in T. Klauser (ed.), *Pisciculi: Studien zur Religion und Kultur des Altertums: Franz Joseph Dölger zum sechzigsten Geburtstage dargeboten von Freunden, Verehrern und Schülern*. Münster: Aschendorff, 117–24.

Hölbl, G. 1996. 'Ideologische Fragen bei der Ausbildung des römischen Pharaos', in M. Schade-Busch (ed.), *Wege öffnen: Festschrift für Rolf Gundlach zum 65. Geburstag*. Wiesbaden: Harrassowitz, 98–109.

—— 2000. *Altägypten im römischen Reich: Der römische Pharao und seine Tempel* I. Mainz: von Zabern.

—— 2004. 'Die römischen Kaiser und das ägyptische Königtum', in P. C. Bol, G. Kaminski, and C. Maderna (eds), *Fremdheit—Eigenheit: Ägypten, Griechenland und Rom, Austausch und Verständnis*. Stuttgart: Scheufele, 525–37.

Jasnow, R., and K.-T. Zauzich. 2005. *The Ancient Egyptian Book of Thoth: A Demotic*. Wiesbaden: Harrassowitz.

Jördens, A. 2008. 'Griechische Texte aus Ägypten', in B. Janowski and G. Wilhelm (eds), *Omnia, Orakel, Rituale und Beschwörungen*. Gütersloh: Gütersloher Verlaghaus, 417–45.

—— 2009. *Statthalterliche Verwaltung in der römischen Kaiserzeit: Studien zum praefectus Aegypti*. Stuttgart: Steiner.

Kausen, E. 1988. 'Das tägliche Tempelritual', in O. Kaiser et al. (eds), *Religiöse Texte: Rituale und Beschwörungen* II. Gütersloh: Gütersloher Verlagshaus, 391–405.

Kockelmann, H. 2010. 'Sobek und die Caesaren: Einige Bemerkungen zur Situation der Krokodilgötterkulte des Fayum unter römischer Herrschaft', in K. Lembke, M. Minas-Nerpel, and S. Pfeiffer (eds), *Tradition and Transformation: Egypt under Roman Rule*. Leiden: Brill, 203–30.

—— and S. Pfeiffer. 2009. 'Betrachtungen zur Dedikation von Tempeln und Tempelteilen in ptolemäischer und römischer Zeit', in R. Eberhard et al. (eds), '*... vor dem Papyrus sind alle gleich!': Papyrologische Beiträge zu Ehren von Bärbel Kramer (P. Kramer)*. Berlin: de Gruyter, 93–104.

Kugener, M. A. 1907. *Vie de Sévère, patriarche d'Antioche 512–518, par Zacharie le scholastique: Textes syriaques publiés, traduits et annotés*. Paris: Firmin-Didot.

Leipoldt, J. 1908. *Sinuthii archimandritae vita et opera omnia*, vol. 3. Paris: Poussielgue.

Lippert, S. L. 2007. 'Die Abmachungen der Priester: Einblicke in das Leben und Arbeiten in Soknopaiou Nesos', in M. Capasso and P. Davoli (eds), *New Archaeological and Papyrological Researches on the Fayyum*. Lecce: Congedo, 145–55.

—— 2008. *Einführung in die altägyptische Rechtsgeschichte*. Berlin: Lit Verlag Dr W. Hopf.

—— and M. Schentuleit. 2006. *Ostraka*. Wiesbaden: Harrassowitz.

Lüddeckens, E. 1968. 'Gottesdienstliche Gemeinschaften im pharonischen, hellenistischen und christlichen Ägypten', *Zeitschrift für Religions- und Geistesgeschichte* 20: 93–211.

Menchetti, A. 2005. *Ostraka demotici e bilingui da Narmuthis (ODN 100–188)*. Pisa: ETS.

Monson, A. 2005. 'Sacred Land in Ptolemaic and Roman Tebtunis', in S. Lippert and M. Schentuleit (eds), *Tebtunis und Soknopaiu Nesos: Leben im römerzeitlichen Fajum*. Wiesbaden: Harrassowitz, 79–91.

—— 2006. 'The Ethics and Economics of Ptolemaic Religious Associations', *Ancient Society* 36: 221–38.

Moret, A. 1902. *Le rituel du culte divin journalier en Égypte: D'après les papyrus de Berlin et les textes du temple de Séti Ier à Abydos*. Paris: Leroux.

Moyer, I. 2003. 'Thessalos of Tralles and Cultural Exchange', in S. B. Noegel, J. T. Walker, and B. M. Wheeler (eds), *Prayer, Magic, and the Stars in the Ancient and Late Antique World*. University Park: Pennsylvania State University Press, 39–56.

Muszynski, M. 1977. 'Les "associations religieuses" en Égypte d'après les sources hiéroglyphiques, démotiques et grecques', *Orientalia Lovaniensia Periodica* 8: 145–74.

Naether, F. 2010. *Die Sortes Astrampsychi: Problemlösungsstrategien durch Orakel im römischen Ägypten*. Tübingen: Mohr Siebeck.

Osing, J. 1998. *Hieratische Papyri aus Tebtunis* I. Copenhagen: Museum Tusculanum Press.

—— 1999. 'Zum Kultbildritual in Abydos', in E. Teeter and J. Larson (eds), *Gold of Praise: Studies on Ancient Egypt in Honor of Edward F. Wente*. Chicago: Chicago University Press, 317–34.

—— and G. Rosati. 1998. *Papiri geroglifici e ieratici da Tebtunis*. Florence: Istituto Papirologico G. Vitelli.

Pries, A. H. 2011. *Die Stundenwachen im Osiriskult: Eine Studie zur Tradition und Späten Rezeption von Ritualen im Alten Ägypten*: 2 vols. Wiesbaden: Harrassowitz.

Quack, J. F. 1997. 'Ein ägyptisches Handbuch des Tempels und seine griechische Übersetzung', *Zeitschrift für Papyrologie und Epigraphik* 119: 297–300.

—— 2001. 'Ein Standardhymnus zum Sistrumspiel auf einem demotischen Ostrakon (Ostrakon Corteggiani D 1)', *Enchoria* 27: 101–19.

—— 2002. 'La magie au temple', in Y. Koenig (ed.), *La magie en Égypte: à la recherche d'une définition*. Paris: Documentation Française, Musée du Louvre, 41–68.

—— 2005. 'Die Überlieferungsstruktur Buches vom Tempel', in S. L. Lippert and M. Schentuleit (eds), *Tebtunis und Soknopaiu Nesos: Leben im römerzeitlichen Fajum*. Wiesbaden: Harrassowitz, 105–15.

—— 2007. 'Ein ägyptischer Dialog über die Schreibkunst und das arkane Wissen', *Archiv für Religionsgeschichte* 9: 259–94.

—— 2009a. 'Erzählen als Preisen: Vom Astartepapyrus zu den koptischen Märtyrerakten', in H. Roeder (ed.), *Das Erzählen in frühen Hochkulturen*, vol. 1: *Der Fall Ägypten*. Munich: Fink, 291–312.

—— 2009b. 'Die Theologisierung der bürokratischen Norm: Zur Baubeschreibung in Edfu im Vergleich zum Buch vom Tempel', in R. Preys (ed.), *7. Ägyptologische Tempeltagung: Structuring Religion*. Wiesbaden: Harrassowitz, 221–9.

—— 2009c. 'Miniaturisierung als Schlüssel zum Verständnis römerzeitlicher ägyptischer Rituale?', in O. Hekster, S. Schmidt-Hofner, and C. Witschel (eds), *Ritual Dynamics and Religious Change in the Roman Empire*. Leiden: Brill, 349–66.

Quack, J. F. 2009d. 'Review of Sederholm, Papyrus British Museum 10808', *Orientalistische Literaturzeitung* 104: 27–33.

Ritner, R. K. 1992. 'Religion vs. Magic: The Evidence of the Magical Statue Bases', in U. Luft (ed.), *The Intellectual Heritage of Egypt: Studies Presented to L. Kákosy*. Budapest: Université Loránd Eötvös, 495–501.

—— 1995. 'Egyptian Magical Practice under the Roman Empire: The Demotic Spells and their Religious Context', in W. Haase and H. Temporini (eds), *Aufstieg und Niedergang der römischen Welt* II 18.5. Berlin: de Gruyter, 3333–79.

Rolfe, J. C. 1950. *Ammianus Marcellinus*, vol. 2. Cambridge, Mass.: Harvard University Press.

—— 1998. *Suetonius*, vol. 1. Cambridge, Mass.: Harvard University Press.

Rosati, G. 1998. 'PSI inv. I 70 e pCarlsberg 307 + PSI inv. I 79 + pBerlino 14473a + pTebt. Tait 25: Rituale giornaliere di Soknebtynis', in J. Osing and G. Rosati (eds), *Papiri Geroglifici e ieratici da Tebtunis*. Florence: Istituto Papirologico G. Vitelli, 101–28.

Sandri, S. 2006. *Har-pa-chered (Harpokrates): Die Genese eines ägyptischen Götterkindes*. Leuven: Peeters.

San Nicolò, M. 1972. *Ägyptisches Vereinswesen zur Zeit der Ptolemäer und Römer*. Munich: Beck.

Sauneron, S. 1959. *Quatre campagnes à Esna*. Cairo: Institut Français d'Archéologie Orientale.

—— 1962. *Les fêtes religieuses d'Esna aux derniers siècles du paganisme*. Cairo: Institut Français d'Archéologie Orientale.

—— 1968. *Le temple d'Esna*. Cairo: Institut Français d'Archéologie Orientale.

Sederholm, V. H. 2006. *Papyrus British Museum 10808 and its Cultural and Religious Setting*. Leiden: Brill.

Smith, M. 2002a. 'Aspects of the Preservation and Transmission of Indigenous Religious Traditions in Akhmim and its Environs during the Graeco-Roman Period', in A. Egberts, B. P. Muhs, and J. van der Vliet (eds), *Perspectives on Panopolis: An Egyptian Town from Alexander the Great to the Arab Conquest*. Leiden: Brill, 233–47.

—— 2002b. *On the Primaeval Ocean*. Copenhagen: Museum Tusculanum Press.

—— 2005. *Papyrus Harkness (MMA 31.9.7)*. Oxford: Griffith Institute.

Spiegelberg, W. 1902. *Demotische Papyrus aus den Königlichen Museen zu Berlin*. Leipzig: Hinrichs.

Stadler, M. A. 2004. *Isis, das göttliche Kind und die Weltordnung: Neue religiöse Texte aus dem Fayum nach dem Papyrus Wien D. 12006 recto*. Vienna: Hollinek.

—— 2006. 'Isis würfelt nicht', *Studi di Egittologia e di Papirologia* 3: 187–203.

—— 2007. 'Zwischen Philologie und Archäologie: Das Tägliche Ritual des Tempels in Soknopaiou Nesos', in M. Capasso and P. Davoli (eds), *New Archaeological and Papyrological Researches on the Fayyum*. Lecce: Congedo, 284–302.

—— 2008. 'Judgment after Death (Negative Confession)', in J. Dieleman and W. Wendrich (eds), *UCLA Encyclopedia of Egyptology*. Los Angeles. <http://escholarship.org/uc/item/07s1t6kj>.

—— Forthcoming. 'Interpreting the Architecture of the Temenos: Demotic Papyri and the Cult in Dime', in M. Capasso and P. Davoli (eds), *Soknopaiou Nesos Project I (2003–2009)*. Pisa: Fabrizio Serra.

Sternberg-el Hotabi, H. 1995. 'Der Mythos von der Vernichtung des Menschengeschlechts', in E. Blumenthal et al. (eds), *Mythen und Epen* III: *Texte aus der Umwelt des Alten Testaments* III. 5. Gütersloh: Gütersloher Verlagshaus, 1078–86.

Tacke, N. 2003. 'Das Opferritual des ägyptischen Neuen Reiches', in C. Metzner-Nebelsick et al. (eds), *Rituale in der Vorgeschichte, Antike und Gegenwart: Studien zur Vorderasiatischen, Prähistorischen und Klassischen Archäologie, Ägyptologie, Alten Geschichte, Theologie und Religionswissenschaft*. Berlin: Leidorf, 27–36.

Trombley, F. R. 1994. *Hellenic Religion and Christianization c.370–529*, vol. 2. Leiden: Brill.

Vleeming, S. P. 2001. *Some Coins of Artaxerxes and Other Short Texts in the Demotic Script Found on Various Objects Gathered from Many Publications*. Leuven: Peeters.

von Lieven, A. 2007. *Grundriß des Laufes der Sterne: Das sogenannte Nutbuch*. Copenhagen: Museum Tusculanum Press.

Widmer, G. 1998. 'Un papyrus démotique religieux du Fayoum: P. Berlin 6750', *Bulletin de la Société d'Égyptologie, Genève* 22: 83–91.

—— 2003. 'Les fêtes en l'honneur de Sobek dans le Fayoum à l'époque gréco-romaine', *Égypte, Afrique et Orient* 32: 3–22.

—— 2004. 'Une invocation à la déesse (tablette démotique Louvre E 10382)', in F. Hoffmann and H.-J. Thissen (eds), *Res Severa Verum Gaudium: Festschrift für Karl-Theodor Zauzich zum 65. Geburtstag am 8. Juni 2004*. Leuven: Peeters, 651–86.

—— 2005. 'On Egyptian Religion at Soknopaiu Nesos in the Roman Period', in S. L. Lippert and M. Schentuleit (eds), *Tebtunis und Soknopaiu Nesos: Leben im römerzeitlichen Fajum*. Wiesbaden: Harrassowitz, 171–84.

—— Forthcoming. 'Words and Writing in Demotic Ritual Texts from Soknopaiu Nesos', in J. F. Quack (ed.), *Ägyptische Rituale der griechisch-römischen Zeit*. Tübingen: Mohr Siebeck.

Wright, W. C. 1952. *Philostratus and Eunapius*. London: Heinemann; Cambridge, Mass.: Harvard University Press.

Young, D. W. 1981. 'A Monastic Invective against Egyptian Hieroglyphs', in Young (ed.), *Studies Presented to Hans Jakob Polotsky*. East Gloucester, Mass.: Pirtle and Polson, 348–60.

CHAPTER 28

CHRISTIANITY

MALCOLM CHOAT

According to tradition, Egypt's Coptic population descends from one of the oldest Christian communities in the world. Yet early sources are frustratingly silent about its origin and development in the first two centuries CE. The fragmentary, unprovenanced, or tendentious nature of much of the evidence—early copies of Christian texts, documentary references to Christians, church histories, and lives of prominent Christians such as Origen—means that the field is constantly developing as new sources come to light or scholars reinterpret earlier work. This chapter addresses Christianity in Egypt from its origins down to the martyrdoms under Diocletian in the early fourth century, looking at three key areas: the establishment of the church community and hierarchy in Alexandria, the manifestation of Christianity in the *chora*, and the Roman government's response to Christianity. The period closes with the development of the monastic tradition, one of Egypt's major contributions to Christianity and to Western culture.

Sources and Debates

The literary record produced by Christians in Roman Egypt is dominated by the works of Clement and Origen, although we gain from them more insight into their theology than into the communities in which they lived. Something of the character of early Egyptian Christianity can also be reconstructed from other works that are likely to have been composed in second-century Egypt, including extra-canonical texts such as the *Kerygma Petri* ('Preaching of Peter') and those from Gnostic circles (Jakab 2001: 65–58; Pearson 2006: 331–4, 336–7). For narrative history of early Christianity in Egypt we are heavily reliant on Eusebius, bishop of Caesarea Maritima (in Palestine), who wrote his monumental *Historia Ecclesiastica* in the early fourth century. In addition, there is a wealth of papyrological evidence, ranging from documents written by and about Christians, to the remains of their scriptures and other texts. This source body allows ample scope for continuing debate, including how Christianity reached Alexandria, the character of the Christian community there in the second century, the manner in which and pace at which it expanded through the *chora*, how papyri should be dated, and how we should read the papyrological record for early Christianity in Egypt.

The Origins of Christianity in Egypt

The New Testament records no apostolic journeys or letters to Alexandria, unlike the other major population centres in the first-century CE Mediterranean. Rather, a traveller *from* Alexandria provides the first evidence of Christianity in Egypt:

> Now there came to Ephesus a Jew named Apollos, a native of Alexandria. He was an eloquent man, well versed in the scriptures. He had been instructed in the way of the Lord; and he spoke with burning enthusiasm and taught accurately the things concerning Jesus, though he knew only the baptism of John. He began to speak boldly in the synagogue; but when Priscilla and Aquila heard him, they took him aside and explained the Way of God to him more accurately. (Acts 18: 24–6; trans. NRSV)

Since the fifth century people have speculated that Apollos 'had been instructed in the way of the Lord *in his homeland*' (ἐν τῃ πατρίδι, an addition to the text in Codex Bezae; cf. Metzger 1994: 413; Lang 2008: 11–14). Yet nothing confirms this, and he may have learnt the 'way of the Lord' elsewhere (e.g. in Judaea; Hvalvik 2007: 158). This passage may still, however, provide a guide to the form that earliest Christianity in Egypt took. No other first-century witnesses reliably suggest a Christian presence in Egypt. In their place are mere conjectures (on 1 Peter, see Davis 2004: 4–5; on *P Lond.* VI 1912, Jakab 2001: 43–5).

The origins of Christianity in Alexandria are not narrated until early in the fourth century, when Eusebius of Caesarea records the tradition that the evangelist Mark brought Christianity to Egypt (*Hist. Eccl.* 2.16.1): 'Now they say (φασίν) this Mark was the first sent to Egypt, to preach the Gospel which he had written, and the first to establish churches in Alexandria itself.' Prior to Eusebius, Mark's evangelization of Alexandria is mentioned only in the enduringly controversial Secret Gospel of Mark letter attributed to Clement (1.18–2.2); even if genuine, this account conflicts at many points with that reported by Eusebius, and cannot be his source (Davis 2004: 8–9; cf. Brown 2005: 59–60).

Along with the Mark tradition, Eusebius also knew the names and dates (though nothing more) of the next ten leaders of the Alexandrian Christian community (down to Julian, d. 189), 'a mere echo and a puff of smoke' according to Bauer (1971: 45), though their names at least may be correct (Wipszycka 2006: 81). They probably all derive from the same source; despite Eusebius' use of the word φασίν ('they say'), this probably is not oral, but more likely the third-century Christian chronographer Julius Africanus (Wallraff 2006: 53–6). The redaction of this history of the early Alexandrian Church probably took place in the late second or early third century (although Jakab 2001: 45–9 would put it in the late third), and should be contextualized in an effort to establish the authority and apostolic (in particular Petrine) heritage of the Alexandrian Church (Camplani 2004: 157–8; Davis 2004: 19).

While the Mark tradition has been argued to represent a reminiscence of a Hellenistic origin for the Church in Alexandria (e.g. Fernández Sangrador 1994: 167–81), that Christianity was first brought from Palestine to Alexandria's vibrant Jewish community should be strongly considered. Cultural memories of this might be reflected in the Pseudo-Clementine *Homilies* (1.8–11, 13–14; see Quispel 2008: 541–2), and the early Christian topography of the city as described in later texts such as the Acts of Mark and of Peter (bishop of Alexandria, 300–11 CE) (Pearson 1986: 145–54; Fernández Sangrador 1994: 115–24; Davis 2004: 9–14); early Christian scribal practice has also been adduced to support such an origin (Roberts 1979: 42–8). Even if some of the later details are fictitious, the proximity of Alexandria to Jerusalem, and the New Testament record of Jews from Alexandria and Egypt hearing the apostles in Jerusalem (Acts 2: 10, 6: 9), suggest that this was indeed the source by which Christianity reached Egypt (Jakab 2001: 49–52; Lang 2008: 21). The account of Apollos in Acts 18 thus points correctly towards Alexandria's large and already pluralistic Jewish community (see Chapter 17).

Pluralism and Philosophy: The Early Church in Alexandria

Basilides and Valentinus

The theological 'inaccuracy' of Apollos should be contextualized in an Alexandria in which Jewish and hellenistic Platonic traditions had already intermingled in the circle of Philo (Runia 1990), where they also came into contact with native Egyptian traditions. This provides a natural backdrop to Christian thought in the city as it developed over the next century. Notable among the Christian teachers associated with Alexandria in the early to mid-second century are the Gnostics Basilides and Valentinus. It is highly likely that both these influential Christian teachers came from Egypt, and certain that their doctrines, which emphasized among other things a dualist conception of a universe whose creation was attributed to various figures other than the Supreme God, were circulating in Alexandria by the mid-second century. Yet this does not mean that Alexandrian Christianity before the late second century was antithetical to 'ecclesiastically structured Christendom' and later 'orthodoxy' (Bauer 1971: 48), as continuities with the latter can be detected in the second-century papyri (Roberts 1979: 49–73) and early Christian literature of probable Alexandrian provenance (Pearson 2006: 332–7). Rather than dominating early Alexandrian Christianity, Gnostic thought, in its various strands, represents only one facet of a pluralistic, locally centred set of communities within the city, which came only in the late second century under the control of a monarchic episcopate (Jakab 2001: 63–89; Wipszycka 2006).

Clement, Origen, and the 'Catechetical School'

An important aspect of early Christian pluralism in Alexandria was engagement with the city's intellectual philosophical tradition. The impact of Stoic and Platonic thought can be seen in the systems of Basilides and Valentinus, and comes more clearly into view with Pantaenus, a Christian Stoic philosopher active in Alexandria under Commodus (r. 180–92). The nature of the 'school of sacred learning' Pantaenus led (Euseb. *Hist. Eccl.* 5.10.1, 4) has been the subject of much debate: rather than a catechetical school that operated under the official aegis of the Church, it was an establishment where Christian theology and philosophy was taught and expounded. It was neither outside the Christian community, nor an official organ of the Church; only in the third century did episcopal control over Christian teaching tighten.

Among Pantaenus' students was Titus Flavius Clemens, better known as Clement of Alexandria (*c*.150–*c*.215), who was active in Alexandria from the 180s to the early third century. Influenced by Platonic philosophy as he was by hellenistic Judaism through his reading of Philo (van den Hoek 1988; Runia 1993), Clement's works both illustrate Christian engagement with Hellenism and reflect Alexandrian Christianity in the late second century.

The engagement with Hellenic culture is visible in the range of Clement's reading and indebtedness to philosophical systems, as well as in the addressing of his works in part to educated non-Christians. We learn little from them, however, about the institutions of Christianity in Clement's Alexandria (Jakab 2001: 179–88). While forthright in his defence of his 'true Church' from its rivals, he is fundamentally concerned with his own teaching role (van den Hoek 1997: 64) and does not dwell on the ecclesiastical hierarchy or institutional Church. His testimony on Christian thought and life in second-century Alexandria, however, is profound: his many quotations and allusions are testimony to the range of texts and thought systems that circulated and flourished in the capital, and in his works we see the spread of the Christian message, in particular among the educated elites.

Rather than Clement's successor as head of the catechetical school (Euseb. *Hist. Eccl.* 6.3.3), Origen should be understood as an independent Christian philosophical teacher in the tradition of Clement (who probably did not formally teach him; see Davis 2004: 23). His life is well known, thanks both to the admiration of Eusebius and Gregory Thaumaturgus, and to later criticism (e.g. by Epiphanius; see McGuckin 2004: 1–2). Many of Origen's own works also survive, in spite of his later condemnation. Born *c*.185 in Alexandria, Origen progressed from training in the scriptures to studies in philology and instruction in Neoplatonic philosophy under Ammonius Saccas (Porphyry, in Euseb. *Hist. Eccl.* 6.19.4–8). He began in his late teens to offer both catechetical and grammatical instruction, but abandoned the latter when he considered it incompatible with sacred education. He continued to teach catechumens, an activity that in time acquired the official sanction of the bishop of Alexandria, Demetrius (189–233 CE), even if it was not yet under episcopal control (Grafton and Williams 2006: 76–7). In time he handed some of the teaching to his student Heraclas and reserved himself for more advanced instruction (van den Broek 1996: 204).

While steadily attracting students, Origen maintained a celibate and ascetic lifestyle (though his self-castration may be a historiographical fiction; see McGuckin 2004: 6–7). He developed his international profile by visits abroad, and embarked upon his extensive literary production (for works written in Alexandria, see Euseb. *Hist. Eccl.* 6.24). In 231 conflict with Demetrius led to his departure for Caesarea: among the causes were the bishop's concern for ecclesiastical authority and procedures; tensions between Origen's *didaskalos* (teacher) centred on Christian tradition and the monarchic episcopate, and theological issues (Jakab 2001: 141–73; McGuckin 2004: 13–16). Despite Origen's exile, his works continued to circulate within Egypt (McNamee 1973), and his intellectual heritage remained strong, both within Alexandria and in the early monastic movement (Rubenson 1999). The catechetical school maintained its place in Alexandria, and Demetrius' successors as bishop of Alexandria, Heraclas and Dionysius, both led it before their ordination (Euseb. *Hist. Eccl.* 6.29.5). However, it never regained its former independence from the ecclesiastical establishment.

Christianity in the *Chora*

Despite the energetic Alexandrian Christian community visible in Clement's works, neither there nor in other sources do we find any reliable indication that Christianity had spread beyond the capital in his day. This absence is mirrored in the documentary papyri (Judge and Pickering 1977) and inscriptions. A number of second-century papyrus letters have been suggested to reflect Christianity, but in no cases can this be proven, and some are unlikely (see Naldini 1998, nos 1–3; *C Epist. Lat.* 169; on *P Oxy.* XLII 3057, see Blumell 2010, with earlier bibliography).

With no secure documentary or narrative evidence for Christianity in the second-century *chora*, scholars have turned to the literary papyri (i.e. those copied for their inherent value, including scripture, apocrypha, and other literary texts such as homilies and commentaries). The papyri associated with Christianity that have been dated (solely on the basis of their handwriting) to the second century are listed in Table 28.1. Only fragments of each survive, and various dates within the century (and in some cases later) have been proposed for them.

The preference among the texts in Table 28.1 for the codex form is noticeable. Although Christians did not pioneer the use of the codex (a Roman invention that first appears in the first century CE), it is demonstrable that they overwhelmingly preferred this book form. Why is still not clear (for a recent survey, see Hurtado 2006: 43–93; compare Turner 1977), but the explanation may be as simple as increased Roman influence in Egypt (Bagnall 2009: 70–90). For several more centuries, the papyrus roll continued to be used for classical (and some few Christian) texts, as well as by Jews (though occasional Jewish use of the codex is known; Treu 1973: 138–44; Roberts 1979: 74–8). Thus, the Bodleian Library fragment of the Psalms may be

Table 28.1 Christian literary papyri dated to the second century CE

Papyrus	Format	Provenance	Contents
P Bad. IV 56 (LDAB 3086)	Papyrus codex	Hipponon (Herakleopolite nome)	Exodus, Deuteronomy
Oxford, Bodleian MS Gr. bibl.g.5 (P) (LDAB 3083)	Papyrus codex	Antinoopolis	Psalms
PSI Congr. XX 1 (LDAB 3085)	Papyrus sheet	Unknown	Psalms
P Ant. I 7 (LDAB 3087)	Papyrus codex	Antinoopolis	Psalms
P Oxy. LXIV 4404 (LDAB 2935)	Papyrus codex	Oxyrhynchus	Gospel of Matthew
P Oxy. L 3523 (LDAB 2775)	Papyrus codex	Oxyrhynchus	Gospel of John
P Ryl. III 457 (LDAB 2774)	Papyrus codex	Unknown	Gospel of John
P Oxy. LX 4009 (LDAB 4872)	Papyrus codex	Oxyrhynchus	Gospel of Peter (?)
PSI XI 1200bis (LDAB 4669)	Papyrus roll	Oxyrhynchus (?)	Discourse on eschatological matters (?)
P Monts. Roca II 2 (LDAB 3082)	Parchment roll	Unknown	Psalms

Note: The texts are placed in canon order merely out of convenience; full details on each may be found in the Leuven Database of Ancient Books, <http://www.trismegistos.org/ldab>.

tentatively associated with Christianity by its use of the codex form (Barns and Kilpatrick 1957: 230). The other four Septuagint papyri on the list (LDAB 3086, 3083, 3085, 3087), as well as the very fragmentary *PSI* XI 1200 *bis*, feature the so-called *nomina sacra*, the contracted forms of the sacred names that seem to be unique to Christianity and related scribal systems such as that of the Manichaeans (Roberts 1979: 26–48; Choat 2006: 119–25; Luijendijk 2008: 57–78), and may thus be accepted as Christian productions; with the Gospels there is, of course, no doubt.

In the absence of narrative or documentary evidence, scholars have often used the Christian literary papyri to show the spread of Christianity in the *chora* in the second century, following the work of C. H. Roberts (1979, esp. 1–25). Yet two problems attend such an analysis. First, it is not always possible to be sure if books were being read where they were found in the second century or were taken there later (though see Roberts 1979: 4, 9). A more systemic problem arises from the imprecision and subjectivity inherent in palaeographical dating, and the enthusiastic search for early Christian texts (Bagnall 2009: 9–24). Some of the texts listed in Table 28.1 have been argued to date from the turn of the third century or even later (Nongbri 2005; see also Turner 1977). Even if only a few are misdated, our ability to read the corpus as evidence for the dispersion of Christianity in the Nile Valley would diminish remarkably.

Given the imprecision of palaeographical dating, the haphazard preservation of the papyri, and the relatively small range of provenances, we cannot use the second-century Christian literary papyri either to map the spread of Christianity or to quantify it. At most, we can say that there were some Christians in the *chora*. Before the time of Demetrius, however, we should perhaps not see the few literary papyri as representatives of a much wider dispersion whose many other witnesses are lost in the sands, but as a representative sample of the relatively small Christian presence in the Nile Valley. The turn of the third century brings increasing papyrological evidence of Christian activity (Table 28.2).

It is possible that some of these papyri might also be dated too early (Bagnall 2009: 20–1), but even so we see the outlines of a much wider circulation of Christian literature in the

Table 28.2 Numbers of Christian literary papyri dated to the turn of the second–third or early third centuries CE

Text	Second/third century[a]		Early third century	
	Roll	Codex	Roll	Codex
New Testament	1	6	–	1
Septuagint	1	7	–	4
Apocrypha	1	2	1	1
Patristic texts	1	–	–	–
The Shepherd of Hermas	1	2	1	–
Unidentified homilies, commentaries, etc.	2	2	1	–

[a] The date 'second/third century' is conventionally used to indicate the late second or early third century, though at times it has been used to refer to texts dated to the second *or* third century; this table may thus overstate the figures somewhat.

chora, precisely when the narrative tradition tells us we should, during the long reign of Bishop Demetrius (see below). Alongside the Septuagint and the New Testament (with Gospels, Acts, Epistles, and Revelation all represented), we find a small amount of apocryphal Christian literature, including two copies of the Gospel of Thomas (LDAB 4028, 4029) and an otherwise unknown non-canonical gospel (LDAB 4736). Four copies of the Shepherd of Hermas testify to its popularity in pre-Constantinian Egypt, and a copy of Irenaeus' *Adversus Haereses* (LDAB 2459) fits neatly with contemporary concerns about apostolic succession in the Alexandrian Church. It is also notable that the roll format is mainly (though not uniformly) used for non-scriptural texts.

The Earliest Documentary Evidence

In the first half of the third century, Christianity makes its first appearance in the documentary papyri. A private letter (*P Bas.* 1.16), perhaps from the early third century (so Naldini 1998, no. 4), is the first to use the characteristic Pauline formula 'in the Lord' (ἐν κυρίῳ) and the *nomina sacra*. The discussion of the office of the gymnasiarch and the town council locates the correspondents in the landowning classes from which such officials were drawn.

A Christian from the same social class appears in *SB* XVI 12497 (Sijpesteijn 1980), a document from the first half of the third century that lists those nominated to serve various liturgies in the Fayum. Among the nominees for the position of 'supervision of the water-tower and fountains of the metropolis', who are probably all from the nome metropolis Arsinoe, is the first person labelled 'Christian' in the papyri: 'Antonios Dioscoros son of Origen, Alexandrian'. A second hand, which provides brief notations of the occupations, abodes, or distinguishing characteristics of those listed, notes under Dioscoros, 'he is the Dioscoros (who is a) Christian' (ἔστ(ι) Διόσκορος χρηστιανός). Dioscoros bears a Roman nomen (Antonios) and possessed (or his father did) Alexandrian citizenship, and is thus of a higher social rank than most of the others listed. Neither the supplementary notations nor the numbers to the left of five of the men ('2', in the case of Dioscoros) indicate that 'christianos' was used pejoratively. Whatever the significance of the numbers, the descriptions are more likely simply to provide information that would help locate the individual concerned, and thus indicate in Dioscoros' case a new level of public visibility for Christianity.

The Development of the Organized Church in Egypt

Under Demetrius the later narrative tradition at last begins to suggest the spread of Christianity outside Alexandria. Eusebius quotes a 'private letter' from the bishop of Jerusalem to the Christian community of Antinoopolis from around 200 CE (*Hist. Eccl.* 6.11.3; see Wipszycka 2006: 87–8), and the *Annals* of Eutychius (Saʿīd ibn Batrīq, Melchite patriarch of Alexandria 933–939/40), records that Demetrius ordained three bishops, the first in the province outside Alexandria (Migne, *PG* 111.982, at 332; on this work, see Wipszycka 2006: 74–6). These ordinations were probably a response to the existence of Christian communities in some towns, over which the bishop of Alexandria was now assuming more direct control, though some have portrayed it as more direct evangelization (Jakab 2001: 222–7).

Demetrius' successor Heraclas, the first bishop of Alexandria (232–48 CE) to be given the title *papas*, 'pope' (Euseb. *Hist. Eccl.* 6.7.4), continued his predecessor's development by ordaining twenty bishops (Migne, *PG* 111.982, at 332). The results of this more energetic evangelization of the *chora* (Jakab 2001: 222–7) can be seen in the episcopate of Dionysius (248–64 CE; see Bienert 1978; Clarke 1998; Jakab 2001: 227–55). This period offers evidence for a much deeper diffusion of Christianity in the *chora*, notably from Dionysius' own letters as preserved by Eusebius (Bienert 1978; Andresen 1979). Dionysius mentions bishops in Nilos in the Herakleopolite nome, Hermopolis, and two in the Libyan Pentapolis (Euseb. *Hist. Eccl.* 6.42.2–3; 7.26.1, 3). The title ἐπίσκοπος τῶν κατ' Αἴγυπτον, which might mean either 'bishop of (i.e. over) those in Egypt' or 'bishop, one of those in Egypt', also occurs twice (Euseb. *Hist. Eccl.* 7.21.2, 7.24.1; see Wipszycka 2006: 87). Further narrative and documentary evidence for the expansion of Christianity and its increasing social prominence comes early in Dionysius' episcopate.

The Persecution of Christians in Third-Century Egypt

Not long after Dionysius' accession, Christians in Alexandria were the subject of local attacks (Euseb. *Hist. Eccl.* 6.41.1–9; cf. Origen, *C Cels.* 3.15). Despite Dionysius' explicit statement, these were unconnected with the action begun by Decius soon after his rise to imperial power in 249. Perhaps as a way of initiating Rome's new millennium (celebrated in 248), Decius required every Roman citizen to affirm allegiance to Rome by sacrificing to 'the gods'. Dionysius' accounts, transmitted by Eusebius, are complemented by forty-six signed certifications of participation on papyrus; commonly called *libelli*, they were officially called 'declarations', *apographai*. In the absence of the edict itself, the *libelli* allow its provisions to be reconstructed. Locally recruited commissioners called citizens from specially prepared rolls. The performance of the sacrifice and the tasting of it were witnessed by multiple parties, and copies were made for official files and the participant.

None of those who sacrifice in the *libelli* have a Christian name (Thecla cannot be read in *P Oxy.* XII 1464; see Davis 1999), and one is a priestess of the crocodile-god Petesouchos (*W Chr.* 125). This indicates that the action was not directed solely against Christians, but was part of a wider campaign (Clarke 1984–9: 1.26–7; Luijendijk 2008: 168–74; compare e.g. Lane Fox 1986: 456). However, that Dionysius was an immediate target (Euseb. *Hist. Eccl.* 6.40.2) confirms that the imperial authorities recognized full well the particular applicability of the edict to Christians, and many believers suffered, both in the capital and in the *chora*. Dionysius was taken to Taposiris, but escaped and made his way to the Libyan Desert, where he remained isolated but safe. Several presbyters remained in Alexandria to minister to the community; others fled elsewhere.

By June 251 Decius was dead and the danger to Christians passed. Valerian, who came to power with his son Gallienus in 253, at first presented no threat to Christians (Euseb. *Hist. Eccl.* 7.10.3). Down the Nile, the social visibility of Christians increased. On 28 February 256 the *prytanis* (the chief officer of the *boule*) of Oxyrhynchus requested that the comarchs and 'superintendents of peace' of the nearby village of Mermertha send 'Petosorapis son of Horus, Christian' to the nome capital (*P Oxy*. XLII 3035; Luijendijk 2008: 177–84). That Petosorapis was identified explicitly as a Christian invites speculation that his religion itself was his crime. Yet if this were case, the village officials should not have been required to come up to Oxyrhynchus themselves if he could not be found (*P Oxy*. XLII 3035, line 6). The term 'Christian' here more likely functions as an additional means to identify Petosorapis, and may indicate that he was a member of the clergy (Luijendijk 2008: 180–1).

This document is too early to be connected with the well-organized campaign against the Christians that Valerian launched in 257. Unlike Decius' mass demonstration of adherence to the gods, Valerian's action was aimed squarely at Christian leaders (Musurillo 1972: 1.4–5; Euseb. *Hist. Eccl.* 7.11.3, 10, 11). Dionysius was summoned to the prefect Aemelianus, and was sent first to Cephro, in the west of the Delta, then on to the district of Colluthion, which was in fact closer to Alexandria. Most of his clergy were sent into exile in villages down the Nile, which may have strengthened those communities as Dionysius had gained new converts in Cephro. While Bishop Cyprian of Carthage perished, Dionysius outlived Valerian, whose death in Persia brought an end to both his control of the empire and the persecution. Gallienus confirmed the return of the 'places of religious worship'—*topoi threskeusimoi*, a formulation presumably fed to him by the Christians themselves—in a letter to Dionysius and other bishops, perhaps in late 261 or 262 (Euseb. *Hist. Eccl.* 7.13.2–3; cf. 7.23.4).

Owing to its nature, Valerian's persecution is not documented in the papyri as is that of Decius. Only one document may refer to it, an official letter from the Saite nome, which refers to an order of the prefect involving an 'assessment', possibly of the 'assets' (*poros*) and 'buildings' (*oikopedoi*) of Christians, though both words are restored (*P Oxy*. XLIII 3119; cf. Whitehorne 1977; Luijendijk 2008: 184–8). The order is dated to a year 7, which invites a connection with Valerian and Gallienus' seventh year in 259/60 and the confiscation of Christian property his edict of 258 commanded (Cyprian, *Epistulae* 80). Yet the heavily restored nature of crucial words and the insecurity of the date mean other interpretations remain possible. It may, for instance, document an investigation to ascertain who was responsible for the taxes owing on Christian property.

Further Expansion in the *Chora*

Maximus succeeded Dionysius as bishop of Alexandria in 264, followed by Theonas from 282 to 300. The expansion of the Church during the 'little peace' between Valerian and Diocletian has left little trace in the narrative record, though the papyri provide some illumination. A letter sent from Rome illustrates the economic links between Christian communities in Rome, Alexandria, and the Fayum (*P Amh.* I 3a; see Naldini 1998, no. 6). 'Maximus the *papas*' himself, Theonas (probably his successor), and a Christian lector (*anagnostes*) are all mentioned. The Christian context is further made clear by the later use of the papyrus for copying excerpts from the New and Old Testaments.

Another *papas* is the centre of a small dossier of letters on papyrus and parchment, probably to be dated in the episcopate of Maximus or Theonas (Luijendijk 2008: 81–151, with discussion of all relevant texts). This man, Sotas, was the bishop not of Alexandria but—most plausibly—of Oxyrhynchus; the title *papas* was used into the fourth century of bishops apart from that of Alexandria, and even of priests (Luijendijk 2008: 95–100). Three letters show him recommending Christian travellers, including catechumens, to other communities (*P Oxy.* IX 1041; *PSI* III 208; and probably *P Alex.* 29); in another he is asked by the priests (*presbyteroi*) of Herakleopolis Magna to receive a 'catechumen in Genesis... for edification' (*P Oxy.* XXXVI 2785). In a letter to his 'holy son' Demetrianus, Sotas attempts to solicit a donation of land for the local church (*P Oxy.* XII 1492). A letter sent from Antioch by an 'Olympic victor' informs his mother that he has sent two talents with 'Sotas the Christian' (*SB* XII 10772), perhaps, as with Petosorapis (see above), designating Sotas thus as a member of the clergy.

The 'letters of recommendation' written by Sotas are part of a group of such letters, mostly dated to the late third and early fourth centuries, that demonstrate the expanding networks of hospitality and education among Christian communities in Egypt (on the genre, see Teeter 1997; for a list, see the introduction to *P Oxy.* LVI 3857). A small number of other letters from the second half of the century can be associated with Christianity by their use of *nomina sacra*, phraseology that echoes the New Testament (*P Vind. Sijp.* 26; *P Oxy.* XX 2276; *PSI* III 209) or onomastics (*P Iand.* II 11). At least twelve more such letters (see Naldini 1998: 131–68, adding *P Congr.* XV 20; *P Prag.* II 191; *P PalauRib.* 37) have been dated to the late third or early fourth century.

Alongside these documents may be positioned the Christian literary papyri of the third century, both numerous and varied in their genre, of which Table 28.3 provides an overview. These show an expansion in production and use of Christian texts throughout the *chora* in the third century, confirming the impression gained from the narrative and documentary sources. Non-canonical texts (Gospels of Thomas and Mary; Acts of Paul and Thecla) retain a relatively low representation. Hermas continues to be more popular than some canonical works (e.g. the Gospel of Mark), and has as many copies as all the patristic authors combined (Melito of Sardis' *On the Passion*, Origen, and two codices of Philo made by Christians). The high number of otherwise unidentified homilies, commentaries, or treatises, some of which may be local productions, is also notable. The first Christian Coptic texts also appear in the second half of the third century (see Chapter 35), testifying to the advance of Christianity among the Egyptian-speaking population.

Asceticism, Millenarianism, and Dualism in the *Chora*

The low rate of survival for non-canonical texts does not mean that orthodoxy prevailed everywhere. Millenarian impulses may have been heightened by the seeming cataclysm of the mid-third-century persecutions. In Upper Egypt an ascetic group reworked Jewish

Table 28.3 Christian literary papyri from the third and turn of the third–fourth century CE

Text	Third century		Third/fourth century	
	Roll	Codex	Roll	Codex
New Testament	2	33	3	14
Septuagint	7	21	6	18
Apocrypha	4	1	–	2
Patristic texts	1	3	1	3
Hermas	2	4	1	1
Prayers	4	–	4	1
Unidentified homilies, commentaries, etc.	8	12	7	2

and Egyptian traditions into an anti-establishment and eschatological Apocalypse of Elijah (Frankfurter 1993), and in the Fayum, Dionysius had to confront the leaders of well-established millenarian communities in person early in the 260s (Euseb. *Hist. Eccl.* 7.24–5). This important episode shows not only the strong literalist understanding of scripture that was still prominent in many parts of Egypt, notwithstanding the allegorical exegesis of Alexandrian theologians such as Origen, but also the presbyter and teacher-centred nature of Christian authority in local communities even in the 260s (Wipszycka 2006: 85–6).

It may be presumed that behind the fourth-century translations into Coptic of the many Gnostic texts in the Nag Hammadi Library stand third-century communities sympathetic to their theology, although they are largely hidden from us (Williams 1996: 235–41; Brakke 2008). Manichaeans, who arrived in Egypt in the 270s (Lieu 1994: 61–105), are better documented. Already in the late third century a high-ranking Christian, perhaps the bishop of Alexandria Theonas, sent a letter warning against them (*P Ryl.* III 469; Gardner and Lieu 2004: 114–15), and a Platonic philosopher in Lykopolis wrote a treatise attacking their theology (van der Horst and Mansfeld 1974; Gardner and Lieu 2004: 115–16, 179–82).

The ascetic traditions traceable in Jewish and Gnostic texts, and in the theology of Origen, surface in various ways in the second half of the third century. The Manichaeans, whose elect lived a rigorously ascetic lifestyle, are followed in Epiphanius' *Panarion* by Hieracas (*Panarion* 67; Goehring 1999), who led an extreme ascetic sect in Leontopolis in the reign of Diocletian (284–305 CE). Far more influential in the long term was the decision by Antony (*c.*251–356) to abandon his inheritance and withdraw to the edge of his village to practice *ascesis* in solitude (*Life of Antony* 1–3). While this took place *c.*270, that the aged ascetic Antony had allegedly practised such a life 'since his youth' (*Life of Antony* 3) is testimony to the growth of ascetic traditions in Egypt during the third century, leading in the next century to the flowering of monasticism.

Conclusion

The third century closed with Christianity becoming increasingly more publicly visible, though not yet a dominant social force. Onomastic analysis, though by its nature imprecise, suggests that in the last decades of the third century little more than 10 per cent of the Egyptian population may have been Christian (Bagnall 2003a: 119–20; 2003b: 249). Theonas died in 300, and Peter was appointed bishop of Alexandria. He oversaw a Church with communities in most of the cities down the Nile, and even out into the villages (see e.g. *P Oxy.* XXXIII 2673 (304 CE)), beyond which stretched a desert soon to be made a city by monks. Yet conflict threatened: within a decade Melitius, bishop of Lykopolis, was to dispute with Peter over church order and authority and start a schismatic Church that would last for centuries. After Peter's death, the presbyter Arius, whose power base in Alexandria was the legacy of the 'academic' model of Christianity in the city, would begin teaching doctrines that split Christianity in the Roman world for the best part of a century. Peter would have been well aware of the traditional power of the presbyters and teachers in Alexandria, and of potential problems with keeping ecclesiastical order in a province the size of Egypt. Yet he can little have expected the terror that Diocletian would set loose on the Church in 303, and the many consequent martyrdoms, which would eventually lead the Coptic Church to begin its own calendar, the Era of the Martyrs, with the accession of Diocletian in 284.

Suggested Reading

Surveys of early Christianity in Egypt may be found in Davis (2004), Jakab (2001), Fernández Sangrador (1994), Griggs (2000), and Pearson (2006). On the Secret Gospel of Mark, compare Watson (2010) with Brown and Pantuck (2008). The literature on Gnosticism is vast: see Marjanan and Luomanen (2005), Markschies (1992), Brakke (2010), Pearson (2007), and Williams (1996). For the millenarian disputes, see Frankfurter (1993: 270–8) and Davis (2005). On Manichaeans in Egypt, see Gardner and Lieu (1996, 2004). On the catechetical school, see Jakab (2001: 91–115), Scholten (1995), van den Broek (1996), and van den Hoek (1997). On Clement, see Osborn (2005) and Jakab (2001: 117–39). On Origen, see McGuckin (2004) for his own writings, and the ancient accounts of Eusebius, *Hist. Eccl.* 6.1–39, Gregory Thaumaturgus' *Panegyric to Origin*, and Epiphanius, *Panarion* 64.1–72.9.

For the mid-third-century persecutions of Decius and Valerian, Eusebius (*Hist. Eccl.* 6.40.1–42.6, 44.1–6; 7.11.2–25) and the *libelli* on papyrus (Scholl 2002) may be compared with the works and Acts of Cyprian of Carthage (Clarke 1984–9: 1.21–39; 4.8–14; Musurillo 1972: 168–75); see also Clarke (2005: 625–47), Selinger (2002), and Rives (1999).On Christian papyri, see Martinez (2009), Turner (1977), Roberts (1979), Hurtado (2006), and Bagnall (2009), along with the Leuven Database of Ancient Books, <http://www.trismegistos.org/ldab>. On documents, see Judge and Pickering (1977), Naldini (1998), van Minnen (1994), Luijendijk (2008), and Choat (2006).

Bibliography

Andresen, C. 1979. '"Siegreiche Kirche" im Aufstieg des Christentums: Untersuchungen zu Eusebius von Caesarea und Dionysios von Alexandrien', in W. Haase and H. Temporini (eds), *Aufstieg und Niedergang der römischen Welt* II 23.1. Berlin: de Gruyter, 387–459.

Bagnall, R. S. 2003a. 'Religious Conversion and Onomastic Change in Early Byzantine Egypt', in Bagnall, *Later Roman Egypt: Society, Religion, Economy and Administration*. Aldershot: Ashgate Variorum, Article VIII.

—— 2003b. 'Conversion and Onomastics: A Reply', in Bagnall, *Later Roman Egypt: Society, Religion, Economy and Administration*. Aldershot: Ashgate Variorum, Article IX.

—— 2009. *Early Christian Books in Egypt*. Princeton: Princeton University Press.

Barns, J. W. B., and G. D. Kilpatrick. 1957. 'A New Psalms Fragment', *Proceedings of the British Academy* 43: 229–32.

Bauer, W. 1971. *Orthodoxy and Heresy in Earliest Christianity*, ed. R. A. Kraft and G. Krodel. Philadelphia: Fortress Press.

Bienert, W. A. 1978. *Dionysius von Alexandrien: Zur Frage des Origenismus im dritten Jahrhundert*. Berlin: de Gruyter.

Blumell, L. H. 2010. 'Is P. Oxy. XLII 3057 the Earliest Christian Letter?', in T. J. Kraus and T. Nicklas (eds), *Early Christian Manuscripts: Examples of Applied Method and Approach*. Leiden: Brill, 97–114.

Brakke, D. 2008. 'Self-Differentiation among Christian Groups: The Gnostics and the Opponents', in M. M. Mitchell and F. M. Young (eds), *The Cambridge History of Christianity*, vol. 1: *Origins to Constantine*. Cambridge: Cambridge University Press, 245–60.

—— 2010. *The Gnostics: Myth, Ritual, and Diversity in Early Christianity*. Cambridge, Mass.: Harvard University Press.

Brown, S. G. 2005. *Mark's Other Gospel: Rethinking Morton Smith's Controversial Discovery*. Waterloo, Ont.: Wilfrid Laurier University Press.

—— and A. J. Pantuck. 2008. 'Morton Smith as M. Madiotes: Stephen Carlson's Attribution of Secret Mark to a Bald Swindler', *Journal for the Study of the Historical Jesus* 6: 106–25.

Camplani, A. 2004. 'L'autorappresentazione dell'episcopato di Alessandria tra IV e V secolo: Questioni di metodo', *Annali di Storia dell'Esegesi* 21: 147–85.

Choat, M. 2006. *Belief and Cult in Fourth-Century Papyri*. Turnhout: Brepols.

Clarke, G. W. 1984–9. *The Letters of St. Cyprian of Carthage*, 4 vols. New York: Newman Press.

—— 1998. 'Two Mid-Third Century Bishops: Cyprian of Carthage and Dionysius of Alexandria: Congruences and Divergences', in T. W. Hillard et al. (eds), *Ancient History in a Modern University*, vol. 2. Grand Rapids, Mich.: Eerdmans, 317–28.

—— 2005. 'Third Century Christianity', in A. K. Bowman, A. Cameron, and P. Garnsey (eds), *The Cambridge Ancient History*, vol. 12, 2nd edn. Cambridge: Cambridge University Press, 589–671.

Davis, S. J. 1999. 'Namesakes of Saint Thekla in Late Antique Egypt', *Bulletin of the American Society of Papyrologists* 36: 71–81.

—— 2004. *The Early Coptic Papacy: The Egyptian Church and its Leadership in Late Antiquity*. Cairo: American University in Cairo Press.

—— 2005. 'Biblical Interpretation and Alexandria Episcopal Authority in the Early Christian Fayum', in G. Gabra (ed.), *Christianity and Monasticism in the Fayoum Oasis*. Cairo: American University in Cairo Press, 45–61.

Fernández Sangrador, J. J. 1994. *Los orígenes de la communidad cristiana de Alejandría*. Salamanca: Universidad Pontificia.

Frankfurter, D. 1993. *Elijah in Upper Egypt: The Apocalypse of Elijah and Early Egyptian Christianity*. Minneapolis: Fortress Press.

Gardner, I., and S. N. C. Lieu. 1996. 'From Narmouthis (Medinet Madi) to Kellis (Ismant El-Kharab): Manichaean Documents from Roman Egypt', *Journal of Roman Studies* 86: 146–69.

—— —— 2004. *Manichaean Texts from the Roman Empire*. Cambridge: Cambridge University Press.

Goehring, J. E. 1999. 'Hieracas of Leontopolis: The Making of a Desert Ascetic', in Goehring, *Ascetics, Society, and the Desert: Studies in Early Egyptian Monasticism*. Harrisburg, Pa.: Trinity Press, 110–33.

Grafton, A., and M. Williams. 2006. *Christianity and the Transformation of the Book: Origen, Eusebius, and the Library of Caesarea*. Cambridge, Mass.: Belknap Press.

Griggs, C. W. 2000. *Early Egyptian Christianity: From its Origins to 451* C.E. Leiden: Brill.

Hurtado, L. W. 2006. *The Earliest Christian Artifacts: Manuscripts and Christian Origins*. Grand Rapids, Mich.: Eerdmans.

Hvalvik, R. 2007. 'Named Jewish Believers Connected with the Pauline Mission', in O. Skarsaune and R. Hvalvik (eds), *Jewish Believers in Jesus: The Early Centuries*. Peabody, Mass.: Hendrickson, 154–78.

Jakab, A. 2001. *Ecclesia Alexandrina: Évolution sociale et institutionnelle du christianisme alexandrin (IIe et IIIe siècles)*. Bern: Peter Lang.

Judge, E. A., and S. R. Pickering. 1977. 'Papyrus Documentation of Church and Community in Egypt to the Mid-Fourth Century', *Jahrbuch für Antike und Christentum* 20: 47–71.

Lane Fox, R. 1986. *Pagans and Christians in the Mediterranean World from the Second Century* AD *to the Conversion of Constantine*. Harmondsworth: Penguin.

Lang, M. 2008. 'Das frühe ägyptische Christentum: Quellenlage, Forschungslage und -perspektiven', in W. Pratscher, M. Öhler, and M. Lang (eds), *Das ägyptische Christentum im 2. Jahrhundert*. Vienna: Lit, 9–43.

Lieu, S. N. C. 1994. *Manichaeism in Mesopotamia and the Roman East*. Leiden: Brill.

Luijendijk, A. 2008. *Greetings in the Lord: Early Christians in the Oxyrhynchus Papyri*. Cambridge, Mass.: Harvard University Press.

McGuckin, J. A. 2004. 'The Life of Origen', in McGuckin (ed.), *The Westminster Handbook to Origen*. Louisville, Ky: Westminster John Knox Press, 1–23.

McNamee, K. 1973. 'Origen in the Papyri', *Chronique d'Égypte* 27: 28–51.

Marjanan, A., and P. Luomanen (eds) 2005. *A Companion to Second-Century Christian 'Heretics'*. Leiden: Brill.

Markschies, C. 1992. *Valentinus Gnosticus? Untersuchungen zur valentinianischen Gnosis mit einem Kommentar zu den Fragmenten Valentins*. Tübingen: Mohr.

Martinez, D. 2009. 'The Papyri and Early Christianity', in R. S. Bagnall (ed.), *The Oxford Handbook of Papyrology*. Oxford: Oxford University Press, 590–622.

Metzger, B. M. 1994. *A Textual Commentary on the Greek New Testament*, 4th rev. edn. Stuttgart: Deutsche Bibelgesellschaft.

Musurillo, H. (ed.) 1972. 'Acta Proconsularia Sancti Cypriani', in *The Acts of the Christian Martyrs*. Oxford: Clarendon Press.

Naldini, M. 1998. *Il cristianesimo in Egitto: Lettere private nei papiri dei secoli II–IV*, 2nd edn. Florence: Nardini.

Nongbri, B. 2005. 'The Use and Abuse of P52: Papyrological Pitfalls in the Dating of the Fourth Gospel', *Harvard Theological Review* 98: 23–48.

Osborn, E. 2005. *Clement of Alexandria*. Cambridge: Cambridge University Press.

Pearson, B. A. 1986. 'Earliest Christianity in Egypt: Some Observations', in B. A. Pearson and J. E. Goehring (eds), *The Roots of Egyptian Christianity*. Philadelphia: Fortress, 132–57.

—— 2006. 'Egypt', in M. M. Mitchell and F. M. Young (eds), *The Cambridge History of Christianity*, vol. 1: *Origins to Constantine*. Cambridge: Cambridge University Press, 331–50.

—— 2007. *Ancient Gnosticism: Traditions and Literature*. Minneapolis: Fortress Press.

Quispel, G. 2008. *Gnostica, Judaica, Catholica: Collected Essays of Gilles Quispel*, ed. J. van Oort. Leiden: Brill.

Rives, J. B. 1999. 'The Decree of Decius and the Religion of Empire', *Journal of Roman Studies* 89: 135–54.

Roberts, C. H. 1979. *Manuscript, Society and Belief in Early Christian Egypt*. London: Oxford University Press.

Rubenson, S. 1999. 'Origen in the Egyptian Monastic Tradition of the Fourth Century', in W. A. Beinert and U. Kühneweg (eds), *Origeniana Septima: Origenes in den Auseinandersetzungen des 4. Jahrhunderts*. Leuven: Leuven University Press, 319–37.

Runia, D. T. 1990. 'Philo, Alexandrian and Jew', in Runia, *Exegesis and Philosophy: Studies on Philo of Alexandria*. Aldershot: Ashgate Variorum, 1–18.

—— 1993. *Philo in Early Christian Literature: A Survey*. Assen: van Gorcum; Minneapolis: Fortress Press.

Scholl, R. 2002. 'Libellus aus der Christenverfolgung des Kaisers Decius', in R. Duttenhöfer (ed.), *Griechische Urkunden der Papyrussammlung zu Leipzig (P. Lips. II)*. Munich: Saur, 218–41.

Scholten, C. 1995. 'Die alexandrinische Katechetenschule', *Jahrbuch für Antike und Christentum* 38: 16–37.

Selinger, R. 2002. *The Mid-Third Century Persecutions of Decius and Valerian*. Frankfurt: Peter Lang.

Sijpesteijn, P. J. 1980. 'List of Nominations to Liturgies', in R. Pintaudi (ed.), *Miscellanea Papyrologica*. Florence: Gonnelli, 341–47.

Teeter, T. M. 1997. 'Letters of Recommendation or Letters of Peace?', in B. Kramer et al. (eds), *Akten des 21. Internationalen Papyrologenkongresses, Berlin 13.–19.8 1995*, vol. 2. Stuttgart: Teubner, 954–60.

Treu, K. 1973. 'Die Bedeutung des Griechischen für die Juden im römischen Reich', *Kairos*, new ser. 15: 123–44.

Turner, E. G. 1977. *The Typology of the Early Codex*. Philadelphia: University of Pennsylvania Press.

van den Broek, R. 1996. 'The Christian "School" of Alexandria in the Second and Third Centuries', in R. van den Broek, *Studies in Gnosticism and Alexandrian Christianity*. Leiden: Brill, 197–205.

van den Hoek, A. 1988. *Clement of Alexandria and his Use of Philo in the Stromateis: An Early Christian Reshaping of a Jewish Model*. Leiden: Brill.

—— 1997. 'The "Catechetical" School of Early Christian Alexandria and its Philonic Heritage', *Harvard Theological Review* 90: 59–87.

van der Horst, P. W., and J. Mansfeld. 1974. *An Alexandrian Platonist against Dualism: Alexander of Lycopolis' Treatise 'Critique of the Doctrines of Manichaeus'*. Leiden: Brill.

van Minnen, P. 1994. 'The Roots of Egyptian Christianity', *Archiv für Papyrusforschung und verwandte Gebiete* 40: 71–85.

Wallraff, M. 2006. 'Die neue Fragmentensammlung der Chronographie des Julius Africanus: Bemerkungen zur Methodik anhand einiger Dubia vel Spuria', in Wallraff (ed.), *Julius Africanus und die christliche Weltchronistik*. Berlin: de Gruyter, 45–59.

Watson, F. 2010. 'Beyond Suspicion: On the Authorship of the Mar Saba Letter and the Secret Gospel of Mark', *Journal of Theological Studies*, new ser. 61: 128–70.

Whitehorne, J. E. G. 1977. 'P. Oxy. XLII 3119: A Document of Valerian's Persecution?', *Zeitschrift für Papyrologie und Epigraphik* 24: 187–96.

Williams, M. A. 1996. *Rethinking 'Gnosticism': An Argument for Dismantling a Dubious Category*. Princeton: Princeton University Press.

Wipszycka, E. 2006. 'The Origins of the Monarchic Episcopate in Egypt', *Adamantius* 12: 71–89.

PART V

TEXTS AND LANGUAGE

CHAPTER 29

LANGUAGE USE, LITERACY, AND BILINGUALISM

MARK DEPAUW

WHEN Cornelius Gallus, the first prefect of Egypt, decided to commemorate the Roman victory in the south of Egypt, he had a stela erected in 30/29 BCE with inscriptions in hieroglyphic, Latin, and Greek (Hoffmann, Minas-Nerpel, and Pfeiffer 2009). This may seem a logical selection: exotic and mysterious in Roman eyes, hieroglyphs represented the indigenous Egyptian language; Latin marked the arrival of the new Roman rulers; and Greek was the omnipresent language of the Ptolemaic administration. For the local population, however, there will have been an important absentee: Demotic.

For although hieroglyphic may have been emblematic, it was not the only type of indigenous script used to write down ancient Egyptian. Almost simultaneously with the creation of the figurative script at the end of the fourth millennium BCE, a cursive form more suitable for everyday use arose. This hieratic script, equally based on the same mixed phonetic–ideographic system, gradually grew more cursive and developed regional variants in the first millennium BCE. In the seventh century BCE the new Demotic script developed out of the Lower Egyptian stem. About a century later it had ousted the Upper Egyptian variant, unflatteringly called 'abnormal hieratic'.

The death of this last script is atypical, since despite the development of new forms of the Egyptian script, the pre-existing ones normally did not disappear. At the time of the Roman conquest, all others were still in use, in the way suggested by their Greek names. Hieroglyphs were adopted for official and 'sacred' inscriptions, on temple walls or in funerary monuments. Hieratic had become the 'priestly' script, used for literary texts and scholarly or scientific literature. At least since the fourth century BCE, however, it was increasingly replaced by Demotic, the 'popular' script initially only used for legal transactions and administrative purposes. As such it traditionally appeared next to Greek and hieroglyphs in the multilingual stelae used by the Ptolemies to publicize sacerdotal decrees, as on the Rosetta Stone. Since Gallus' stele apparently aimed at connecting to this tradition, the absence of Demotic in his monument is remarkable.

Language Use

As the language and script of administration, Demotic had, of course, been facing competition from Greek ever since the conquest of Egypt by Alexander in 332 BCE. Initially Greek had been a marginal language spoken by the mercenaries, who came to Egypt from the 26th dynasty onwards (Vittmann 2003). After 332 BCE it did not become omnipresent immediately: there are only a few Greek sources before about 260 BCE, perhaps because it may have taken the Ptolemies some time to set up their administration. From the middle of the third century BCE, however, a multitude of papyri illustrate how at the top level Greek was almost the only language. But even further down, the language of the new rulers became increasingly important, both through Greek imposition and through the collaboration of the Egyptian elite (Thompson 1994). The interdisciplinary online platform Trismegistos now permits one to evaluate the number of Demotic and Greek papyri statistically (Depauw forthcoming a). Although the rough figures have to be adjusted to allow for chance finds, such as the almost 2,000 papyri in the Zenon archive, and although the less precise dating of Demotic documents needs to be taken into account, the preponderance of Greek remains overwhelming. Demotic seems to be declining further in the first century BCE, with more and more papyri becoming bilingual as a result of the spread of Greek. Since the evidence is very scarce for this period, however, the figures should be treated with caution.

At the beginning of the first century CE some important developments took place. Demotic legal papyri, which for this period are almost exclusively attested from the Fayum Oasis, nearly always have long subscriptions. In these at least the first party to the contract was expected to express his agreement in Greek, in principle in his own hand. These lengthy additions repeating much of the content of the contract eventually led the scribes to omit the now irrelevant Demotic main text completely. Towards the end of the first century, Demotic was no longer used for sales or marriage settlements, for example (Depauw 2003; Muhs 2005; Schentuleit 2010). A similar evolution can be observed for ostraca. Although in the late first century BCE and the early first century CE there is still a very large body of evidence for Demotic tax receipts, this changes dramatically around the middle of the first century CE, and by the end Greek had taken over almost completely (Vandorpe and Clarysse 2008). In inscriptions the changes were sometimes even more abrupt. Whereas the earlier of two dedications in the precinct of the temple of Hathor in Dendara was still trilingual (12 BCE), the later one, dated to 1 CE, was exclusively in Greek (Bowman and Rathbone 1992). Rather than a spontaneous evolution, this obsolescence of Egyptian as an administrative and legal language was probably the result of a deliberate Roman policy favouring Greek (Lewis 1993). This preference also had its repercussions in more private contexts, as is illustrated by both papyrological and epigraphic sources. Even in the remote village of Soknopaiou Nesos early Roman statues in Egyptian style were inscribed in Greek (Bingen 1998). Private letters in Demotic virtually disappeared from the first century CE onwards and the switch to Greek was also made in texts addressing the gods such as oracle questions (Depauw 2006: 91–2; Naether 2010: 370–4). During most of the Roman period, the Egyptians thus indeed had no access to writing in their own language, at least for everyday purposes (Bagnall 1993: 237).

A niche where the Egyptian language did remain in use longer was literature, in the broadest sense of the word, including belles-lettres, scientific treatises, and religious or funerary compositions. All available indigenous scripts were employed, and sometimes appeared in conjunction. Demotic and hieratic could occasionally be 'mixed' in a single text in a script sometimes called semi-Demotic, and increasingly the traditional link between the stage of the language and the form of the script loosened: the classical form of the ancient Egyptian language typical for hieroglyphic and hieratic could also be written down in Demotic, while some hieratic texts clearly used the semi-Demotic language rather than the expected classical Egyptian (Quack 2010). Funerary texts illustrate this incongruence. Some new compositions that were created in the Roman period as successors to the Book of the Dead, and which illustrate the vitality of the Egyptian language in this area, still hung onto the more traditional hieratic script although the language was Demotic (e.g. Herbin 2008); others were written in Demotic script even if they preserved compositions written in a much older language stage (Smith 2009). For inscriptions on tomb equipment, from modest mummy cartonnage to impressive sarcophagi, hieroglyphs occasionally had their place complementing Demotic. Gradually, however, here also Greek pushed forward, perhaps initially for identification purposes only, but gradually replacing the Egyptian altogether.

The last strongholds for the Egyptian scripts were the temples, as is illustrated by the archives found in some small Fayum settlements such as Narmouthis (Medinet Madi), Soknopaiou Nesos (Dime), and Tebtunis. In these last two villages important priestly libraries were discovered containing a great variety of Demotic, hieratic, and even hieroglyphic papyri from the first and second centuries CE. At Tebtunis, for instance, about half of these were cultic texts, such as the Book of the Temple and the Book of Thoth, with the other half divided between narratives and scientific literature, from divination texts to legal manuals (Ryholt 2005). The libraries wanted to preserve sacerdotal knowledge, but in a very dynamic way. Rather than salvaging stale traditions, the priests conducted highly sophisticated intellectual and theological experiments. In hieratic letters they resuscitated archaic epistolary formulas that had become obsolete for a thousand years or more (Quack 2002). Ritual and other texts, often in classical Egyptian, were rendered in Demotic by means of 'unetymological writings'. In this procedure, especially common in Soknopaiou Nesos, the scribe replaced the standard spelling of a word by that of one or more etymologically unrelated groups that were phonetically identical: thus, 'Osiris' (*Wsỉr*) can be written as the similarly pronounced (*ws(r)-ỉr(y)*) ('powerful companion') in a list of epithets stressing the power of the god. To what extent the addition of extra layers of meaning (Widmer 2004: 672–83; Stadler 2008: 170–2) or the phonetically precise rendering (Quack 2010: 333–5) was the primary purpose of this procedure is debated.

The religious wisdom of the priests was also exhibited in the sacred texts written in hieroglyphs on the walls of Egyptian temples, especially concentrated in the south. In this typically Egyptian genre the Romans seem to have made an exception to their language policy because of the natural appeal of hieroglyphs and as a gesture to local sensitivities. Augustus and his successors sponsored the construction of several new temples such as Kalabsha, el-Qal'a, and Shenhur; the enlargement of some others, e.g. Esna (pronaos) and Philae (kiosk of Trajan); and the restoration of dilapidated sanctuaries such as that of the Thoth temple of Ramesses II in Hermopolis under Nero (Hölbl 2000; for the temples, see Chapter 22 in this volume). Hieroglyphic inscriptions remained essential, as in earlier periods, and here as well the Egyptian priests demonstrated their creativity. A last tour de force was the elaboration of a new theology on the occasion of the deification of Hadrian's deceased lover, Antinoos. This is preserved in the obelisk that originally stood in the new Greek *polis* Antinoopolis, but is now in Rome (Meyer 1994). When its text was composed in 130 CE, hieroglyphs were probably already the playground of a very small minority (Derchain 1987; Sternberg-el Hotabi 1994). This intellectual priestly elite occasionally developed the iconic reference of the signs, enhancing the theological value to the detriment of public interpretability (Thissen 1998; Stadler 2008). Extreme examples are two cryptographic hymns in Esna (late first century CE?) using almost exclusively signs depicting sacred animals of the god Khnum, one crocodiles, the other rams (Leitz 2001; Morenz 2002). It is this procedure that probably led to the myth that hieroglyphs depicted abstruse wisdom by complex allegorical hints, a tradition that would become canonized by Horapollon in the fifth century CE and would be so detrimental to the decipherment of the script in modern times (Thissen 2001).

In the end, however, the priestly class became increasingly Hellenized (Hickey 2009: 503–7) and the efforts of the few traditionalists that remained could not prevent the decline of the indigenous languages and scripts. The involvement of Roman authorities in temple construction and local religion had slackened quite substantially in the political tumult after Caracalla (211–17 CE), and the latest inscribed fragments of Egyptian temple decoration date to Maximinus Daia (305–13 CE). Signs of decay had already appeared earlier, however. From the reign of Marcus Aurelius (161–80 CE) onwards the quality of the hieroglyphic inscriptions in the temple of Esna deteriorated rapidly, and those of the third century are hardly legible (Sauneron 1959: 43–4). Equally, from the third century onwards very few papyrological texts were exclusively Demotic: the magical papyri from Thebes were thoroughly interspersed with Greek sections (Dieleman 2005), and Demotic mummy labels identifying the deceased as a rule had a Greek counterpart on the reverse (Arlt forthcoming). The few hieroglyphic inscriptions of the fourth century were mainly formulaic Buchis stelae, up to the last one of 340 CE (Goldbrunner 2004). The youngest inscriptions in the indigenous scripts were written by bilingual families of priests in the temple of Philae in the far south of the country (Dijkstra 2008: 176–201): a bilingual hieroglyphic–Demotic graffito dated to 394 CE and an exclusively Demotic one of 452 CE (Griffith 1935–7, nos 436 and 365 respectively).

Language Contact and Bilingualism

The language shift and the obsolescence of indigenous scripts were the result of more than a thousand years of contact between Greek and Egyptian. As a result of the increasing prominence of Greek culture and the creation of a new immigrant elite, there were, of course, intense dealings between Greeks and Egyptians on several levels. When learning Greek, the Egyptians became acquainted with the classics of Hellenic literature, particularly Homer, of which thousands of fragments have been preserved on papyrus (van Minnen 1998; Cribiore 2001, esp. 194–205). In the Ptolemaic period the Egyptian and Greek worlds as such remained largely separated, but certain individuals moved between them with great freedom, playing whatever role suited them best. Sometimes only the name allows one to recognize an intercultural switch: despite his Greek name and high office the *dioiketes* Dioskourides was buried in an impressive Egyptian sarcophagus (Collombert 2000; compare Coulon 2001). The members of a single family in Edfu even each owned two funerary stelae, one with a hellenistic poem in Greek and another with a perfect hieroglyphic inscription in the Egyptian tradition. Only thorough scholarly research identified the woman named Hathor-iy of the latter with the Aphrodisia of the former (Yoyotte 1969).

Already in the later Ptolemaic period the two cultures between which individuals could switch had occasionally coalesced into something new, with elements from both. In the Roman period this intercultural exchange intensified. Artistically the traditional Egyptian representational scheme was increasingly combined with Greek figurative style, including the famous 'mummy portraits', which often closely follow Roman fashion (Riggs 2005, 2010; Bergmann 2010). Greek and Egyptian legal traditions were integrated in the 'law of the Egyptians', probably the first code of law applicable to all Egyptians, Roman citizens excluded (Yiftach-Firanko 2009). The use of 'mixed' names combining an Egyptian root with a Greek derivational morpheme, or vice versa, explodes. In letters, short references to prayers to the local gods (the so-called proskynemata) appear, probably as the result of Egyptian influence (Depauw 2006: 180, 298). Egyptian literature may have undergone Greek influence and vice versa, although both directions are highly controversial (compare Thissen 1999 with Chauveau 2003; Jay 2008). Mothers' names were increasingly used in Greek identification from the second half of the first century CE onwards, sparked off by new Roman regulations on privileged groups, but probably also influenced by Egyptian traditions (Depauw 2009b).

Since language obviously played an important role in cultural identity, similar linguistic developments may be observed. The omnipresence of Greek soon after Egypt became a Hellenistic monarchy was reflected in diglossia (used here to designate the coexistence of two languages) as well as bilingualism (referring to individuals having at least some knowledge of the two languages). Private archives often contained texts in several languages (Clarysse 2010); Greek papyri were reused as old paper for Demotic literary texts and vice versa; and bilingual documents combined the two languages in varying degrees of intimacy (Depauw 2009a). In the Ptolemaic period, however, there is little evidence for the typical phenomena of bilingualism. Code switching, defined here as a full-blown (conscious) alternation between two languages in the same text or even sentence or phrase, was exceedingly rare. Interference, or the (non-conscious) influence of another language, generally the mother tongue, was equally uncommon. Those who had Greek as their second language seem to have been very proficient, with only few exceptions (Vierras 2003). In the third century BCE sometimes only the use of the Egyptian brush rather than the Greek pen betrays the scribe's ethnicity (Clarysse 1993). Borrowing, the integration of a word from another language to such an extent that eventually it may no longer be recognized as 'foreign', was limited. There are few Greek loan-words in Demotic, and most of them are honorific epithets of kings, official titles, or technical terms from the administration, the army, or the financial sphere. Generally scribes seem to prefer Egyptian alternatives, some of which are certainly calques, that is, translation loan-words (Clarysse 1987).

Again Roman rule seems to bring important changes. Greek vocabulary, especially designating ingredients, abounds in Demotic medical and magical books of the second and third centuries. More important, perhaps, is that quite a few of the non-technical loan-words are only attested in Roman texts. For code switching there is the evidence from Medinet Madi, where a very large temple archive of ostraca dated to the second century testifies to the progressive integration of Greek elements, including verbs, into Egyptian (Menchetti 2005; Rutherford 2009). These loan-words were written in the Greek alphabet and from left to right, despite all the difficulties this entails in a script written right to left such as Demotic. This illustrates the bilingual proficiency of these priestly scribes. Many different 'profiles' of bilingualism can be discerned, however, and not every new user of Greek was equally versed in the language. For many, Greek will have been an exclusively professional language, Egyptian still being preferred at home, perhaps even among the elite (Bingen 1991). Although a systematic survey of the subject is still lacking and much is obscured by the corrective practices of the editors, there is a growing body of evidence for anomalies in the Greek written by, for example, tax collectors. This ranges from unorthodox orthographies to confusion over the gender of nouns or problems with case endings, especially in variations of set phrases (Fewster 2002, esp. 228–45). Many of these phenomena were probably indeed caused by interference of the Egyptian mother tongue. To some extent, however, changes in phonetics, vocabulary, morphology, and syntax could also be the result of the language's internal natural development (Dickey 2009a).

That phenomena of bilingualism were more prominent in Roman Egypt when the indigenous scripts were rapidly losing ground may at first sight seem paradoxical. In fact, it may well have been precisely this obsolescence that led to an influx of non-native speakers into Greek and a greater spread of bilingualism. No doubt code switching, interference, and borrowing were even more pronounced in spoken language.

This raises an important point. The progressive disappearance of the indigenous scripts from the written record could have led to the assumption that the ancient Egyptian language was disappearing quickly, like so many local languages in the Roman provinces. Linguistic interference in Greek is only one of the arguments to suggest that the indigenous language was spoken by a large majority of the population, even under Roman rule. Egyptian names, for example, continued to be popular in Greek documents, not only for the lower classes but even for women belonging to the privileged groups such as the metropolitans or 'those of the gymnasion' (compare van Minnen 2002 with Rowlandson 2004). But no doubt the crucial evidence is the emergence of Coptic in the third and fourth centuries. This form of ancient Egyptian was not only written with the Greek alphabet complemented with a handful of Demotic phonetic signs. Greek is also very prominent in the vocabulary: not only nouns or verbs, but even prepositions and conjunctions have been borrowed. Syntactic influence is debated, however, and although some have called Coptic a mixed language (Reintges 2004), it still rather seems a form of ancient Egyptian.

The prominence of Greek elements in Coptic in comparison with earlier stages of the ancient Egyptian language and script is striking. In a frequently cited paper, Ray (1994a) has explained this by the fallacy of the written record, arguing that Demotic as a language stage does not adequately reflect the spoken vernacular. In his opinion the professional scribes filtered out everything they considered 'incorrect' or 'improper', from innovative grammatical constructions to colloquial vocabulary. Everything Greek surely belonged in this category, so that the scribal corps effectively formed some kind of 'Académie Égyptienne' barring the progressive Graecization of Egypt and Egyptian—or at least attempting this. The main problem is the chronology of this evolution. According to Ray, the 'upward substitution', replacing the spoken forms with others thought to be more suitable to writing, took place from the beginning of the second century BCE and probably even earlier. Already then there would have been a situation of diglossia similar to that of modern Egypt, with the official Modern Standard Arabic on the one hand and the everyday Egyptian Arabic on the other. The code switches of Medinet Madi would thus actually be no more than a breach in the code of conduct of Egyptian scribes, anticipating the situation in Coptic.

While this scenario seems plausible to explain the almost complete absence of Greek in Egyptian literary texts from the Roman period, it seems decidedly less acceptable for documents from the Ptolemaic period. To begin with, the emergence of Coptic did not take place overnight, but fits quite well into general linguistic evolutions. Its 'prehistory' consists of renderings of Egyptian proper names of places and people in Greek, attested from the earliest Greek texts in Egypt onwards. In the Ptolemaic period, however, there is little more than that, a few exceptional transliterations of royal or divine epithets and the occasional wordlist notwithstanding (Richter 2009). Things changed in the Roman period, when some scribes first attempted to write texts of varying length in Egyptian language using the Greek script. In this non-standardized 'Old Coptic' various Demotic signs are added for phonemes that are difficult to represent by Greek letters. This procedure may initially have been inspired by the alienation it creates, since most texts have to do with magic. The earliest example may be *P Schmidt*, a letter to the god Osiris of the first century CE, but its date is debated (Satzinger 1975). Much longer is *P British Museum* 10808, a papyrus with spells against fever that dates to the second century (Sederholm 2006 with Quack 2009).

In my opinion it is no coincidence that (Old) Coptic is not attested earlier than it is. It is a typical phenomenon illustrating the mix of cultures in Roman times rather than the 'living apart together' in Ptolemaic times. Since there are almost by definition few sources, it is, of course, theoretically possible to extrapolate the Greek influence in Coptic to the linguistic situation of half a millennium earlier and assume that spoken language must then have been heavily 'contaminated' already. This leads to the problem, however, that there would have been little or no evolution between 200 BCE and 300 CE, unless one assumes that Coptic was removed as far from the even more Graecized spoken language of the day as was Demotic. In that case it would have had little or no reason for existence, since it would have been practically indistinguishable from Greek.

Literacy

The scholarly debate on the incongruence of the written record with the spoken language is thus to a large extent based on assumptions that are not easy to falsify. This is even more true for the problem of literacy. While it is evident that only a minority of people could read and write, it is far more difficult to estimate what percentage of the population this minority made up. Traditional estimates for earlier periods of Egyptian history have oscillated around 1 per cent (Ray 1994b: 64–5), which is basically just a way of stating that the minority was very small. A lot will have depended on the community, since it seems that in the New Kingdom workmen's village of Deir el-Medina a much higher proportion of artisans could read and write (Janssen 1992). Demotic letters also seem to have been mostly written by the sender himself (Depauw 2006: 101–6), but here again the sacerdotal milieu may not be representative for the population at large. What is important, however, is that at least from the Ptolemaic period onwards the society was literate, even though many people may not have been. With the monetization of the economy (Manning 2010: 117–64) came a change in the taxing regimes and an increasing reliance on the paperwork of the administration. Tax receipts must have been omnipresent, and even those who could not read needed them.

In this world many people will have felt the urge to learn how to write, even if it was only their name. Perhaps apart from a few shaky signatures, there is little or no evidence for this type of limited literacy in Demotic, let alone the other Egyptian scripts. For Greek, however, there are school texts with 'evolving', 'alphabetic', or even 'zero-grade' hands (Cribiore 1996: 112), and *bradygraphontes*, or 'slow writers', are attested as signing documents in their clumsy hand. Some of these semi-illiterates were even village scribes, such as the famous Petaus (Youtie 1971). This raises the question whether there were any statistical differences in literacy according to the language or script. At least for the Roman period, however, for all practical purposes Greek literacy was almost the only relevant one. This is nicely illustrated by an elaborate Greek subscription under a mid-first-century Demotic contract stating that it had been written by a third party 'because the man cannot write—but he does write Egyptian', followed by his signature in Demotic (Youtie 1975a; Depauw 2003: 99–100). Perhaps, however, literacy increased because of the growing importance of autography as a legal principle since the later Ptolemaic period (Depauw forthcoming b). The required handwritten consent compelled those engaged in business transactions to search for a scribe who could replace them (Youtie 1975b). For women, this constituted another obstacle for their participation in public life, since they already needed a guardian unless they belonged to the happy few who were exempted because of the *ius trium liberorum* (Rowlandson 2004; Vandorpe and Waebens 2010). In Roman period letters, the much higher number of women appearing as sender or addressee is remarkable, but here again it remains very problematic whether these women have actually written these documents themselves (Bagnall and Cribiore 2006: 41–55).

The perhaps somewhat higher literacy in the Roman period may have inspired the traditional scholarly view that the difficulty of the Egyptian scripts was an important element in their disappearance. With their mixture of a great multitude of phonetic and ideographic signs they would have been much harder to learn than the Greek alphabet. This is no longer commonly accepted. Few scholars today would suggest that Coptic was created to get rid of the difficult Demotic script. The creation of Coptic may just have been an accidental offshoot of missionary propaganda: new religions based on texts expanded from the thoroughly Hellenized cities into the still predominantly Egyptian-speaking countryside. Since the Egyptian scripts were at that stage already marginalized, they needed a new vehicle to transfer their message in the local vernacular (Richter 2009). The Christianization of the fourth and fifth centuries will have spread the new Coptic script rapidly.

And Latin?

Based on the above discussions of language use, bilingualism, and literacy, the reader may have formed the impression that there were only two languages or scripts in Roman Egypt: Greek and ancient Egyptian in its various forms. There were, of course, other ones, and although only few attestations of Punic, Meroitic, Hebrew, or Syriac are dated to this period, they illustrate the international and multicultural character of Roman Egypt. Far more striking, however, is the absence of Latin in the above. This is a conscious choice, since in Egypt the language of the new Roman rulers led a life at the fringes. Numerically the Greek evidence is a multiple of the Latin counterparts with factor 25 for stone inscriptions, 60 for documentary papyri and ostraca, and 78 for literary texts. Almost a third of the Latin documentary papyri are bilingual, in striking contrast with a mere 5 per cent for Greek. With the exception of a few tax receipts in Latin and Demotic (Zauzich 1984) and the odd stela with hieroglyphs and Latin, there is no direct contact between Latin and the Egyptian languages or scripts. The relationship between Latin and Greek, in contrast, has been the subject of intensive research (Adams 2003: 527–641). The traditional *communis opinio* held that Latin was the language of the central administration when dealing with Roman citizens, and that it was common also among Roman magistrates and in the army. Recent research has shown that even in those contexts it functioned as an official imperial language of power. This explains its use in graffiti left by important administrators on the Colossus of Memnon, in petitions to the supreme authority of the emperor, and in the verdicts of judicial hearings. It was also compulsory for documents concerning Roman citizenship such as birth certificates or wills, but in that context it was often accompanied by a Greek translation. In all, the Romans accommodated to the local linguistic situation by their use of Greek in all but the most formal situations, even in an army context.

The high prestige of Latin is nonetheless also illustrated by its influence on Greek epistolary conventions: the insertion of vocatives to address people is a Roman period innovation coming from Latin, and specific formulaic expressions for greetings or requests were in all likelihood also calques (Dickey 2004, 2009b).

Conclusion

The Roman conquest brought about many changes in the political, social, and cultural life of Egypt, including the linguistic situation. At no stage, however, did the Romans impose their Latin language. On all but the most official and formal occasions Greek was the preferred idiom, as in the other eastern provinces of their empire. Nevertheless, in retrospect Gallus' stele did announce a Roman language policy of conscious elimination of the local Demotic in an administrative context. This accelerated the marginalization of ancient Egyptian to religious contexts. Eventually this resulted in its obsolescence as a written language and led to the almost complete extinction of indigenous scripts by the end of the third century CE. When the ancient Egyptian language was almost miraculously resuscitated in the transfigured form of Coptic, it was written in Greek letters with a few additions from Demotic. The alleged superiority of alphabetic scripts almost certainly played no role in this, nor did a perceived increase in literacy. The creation of the new script by what must undoubtedly have been perfectly bilingual individuals does, however, illustrate the growing cultural convergence in Roman times.

Suggested Reading

Although they do not offer a general survey of language use in Roman Egypt, recent handbooks (e.g. Bagnall 2009 for papyrology or Bagnall 2007 for Byzantine Egypt), as well as proceedings of large conferences (e.g. Cotton et al. 2009; Lembke, Minas-Nerpel, and Pfeiffer

2010), contain a wealth of introductory material about Egyptian society in this period, including language use, bilingualism, and literacy. The decline of Demotic has first been described in detail by Zauzich (1983), with Lewis (1993) providing a rationale for this evolution, further developed by Depauw (2003) and Muhs (2005). Stadler (2008) concentrates on internal changes in the indigenous scripts. For symptoms of contact with Egyptian visible in Greek, Fewster (2002) is a much-cited contribution opening up avenues for future research. The methodology proposed is similar to Adams (2003), which is the canonical work for Latin in Egypt, and remains an excellent starting point for all studies on bilingualism. For literacy, the articles by Youtie (e.g. 1971, 1975a, b) remain classic. Bilingual (and other) texts from Roman Egypt can be found via the interdisciplinary portal Trismegistos: <http://www.trismegistos.org>.

Bibliography

Adams, J. N. 2003. *Bilingualism and the Latin Language*. Cambridge: Cambridge University Press.

Arlt, C. Forthcoming. 'Zweisprachigkeit in Mumienschildern', in M. Depauw (ed.), *Multiplicity of Language and Script in Graeco-Roman Egypt: Studies on the Basis of the Interdisciplinary Platform 'Trismegistos'*. Leuven: Peeters.

Bagnall, R. S. 1993. *Egypt in Late Antiquity*. Princeton: Princeton University Press.

——(ed.) 2007. *Egypt in the Byzantine World, 300–700*. Cambridge: Cambridge University Press.

——(ed.) 2009. *The Oxford Handbook of Papyrology*. Oxford: Oxford University Press.

——and R. Cribiore. 2006. *Women's Letters from Ancient Egypt, 300 BCE–CE 800*. Ann Arbor: University of Michigan Press.

Bergmann, M. 2010. 'Stile und Ikonographien im Kaiserzeitlichen Ägypten', in K. Lembke, M. Minas-Nerpel, and S. Pfeiffer (eds), *Tradition and Transformation: Egypt under Roman Rule*. Leiden: Brill, 1–36.

Bingen, J. 1991. 'Notables hermopolitains et onomastique féminine', *Chronique d'Égypte* 66: 324–9.

——1998. 'Statuaire égyptienne et épigraphie grecque: Le cas de I. Fay. I 78', in W. Clarysse, A. Schoors, and H. Willems (eds), *Egyptian Religion: The Last Thousand Years: Studies Dedicated to the Memory of Jan Quaegebeur*, vol. 1. Leuven: Peeters, 311–19.

Bowman, A. K., and D. W. Rathbone. 1992. 'Cities and Administration in Roman Egypt', *Journal of Roman Studies* 82: 107–27.

Chauveau, M. 2003. 'Les richesses méconnues de la littérature démotique', *Bulletin de la Sociéte Française d'Égyptologie* 156: 20–36.

Clarysse, W. 1987. 'Greek Loanwords in Demotic', in S. P. Vleeming (ed.), *Aspects of Demotic Lexicography*. Leuven: Peeters, 9–33.

——1993. 'Egyptian Scribes Writing Greek', *Chronique d'Égypte* 68: 186–201.

——2010. 'Bilingual Papyrological Archives', in A. Papaconstantinou (ed.), *The Multilingual Experience in Egypt, from the Ptolemies to the Abbasids*. Farnham: Ashgate, 47–72.

Collombert, P. 2000. 'Religion égyptienne et culture grecque: L'exemple de *Διοσκουρίδης*', *Chronique d'Égypte* 75: 47–63.

Cotton, H. M., et al. (eds) 2009. *From Hellenism to Islam: Cultural and Linguistic Change in the Roman Near East*. Cambridge: Cambridge University Press.

Coulon, L. 2001. 'Quand Amon parle à Platon: La statue Caire JE 38033', *Revue d'Égyptologie* 52: 85–125.
Cribiore, R. 1996. *Writing, Teachers, and Students in Graeco-Roman Egypt*. Atlanta: Scholars Press.
——2001. *Gymnastics of the Mind: Greek Education in Hellenistic and Roman Egypt*. Princeton: Princeton University Press.
Depauw, M. 2003. 'Autograph Confirmation in Demotic Private Contracts', *Chronique d'Égypte* 78: 66–111.
——2006. *The Demotic Letter: A Study of Epistolographic Scribal Traditions against their Intra- and Intercultural Background*. Sommerhausen: Zauzich.
——2009a. 'Bilingual Greek: Demotic Documentary Papyri and Hellenization in Ptolemaic Egypt', in P. van Nuffelen (ed.), *Faces of Hellenism: Studies in the History of the Eastern Mediterranean (4th Century B.C.–5th Century A.D.)*. Leuven: Peeters, 113–46.
——2009b. 'Do Mothers Matter? The Emergence of Metronymics in Early Roman Egypt', in T. V. Evans and D. D. Obbink (eds), *The Language of the Papyri*. Oxford: Oxford University Press, 120–39.
——Forthcoming a. 'Quantifying Language Shifts in Egypt (800 BCE–CE 800) on the Basis of Trismegistos', in Depauw (ed.), *Multiplicity of Language and Script in Graeco-Roman Egypt: Studies on the Basis of the Interdisciplinary Platform 'Trismegistos'*. Leuven: Peeters.
——Forthcoming b. 'The Evolution and Use of Demotic Contracts in Epistolary Form', in U. Yiftach-Firanko (ed.), *The Letter: Epistolary Formats in the Ancient World, 3000 BCE—CE 533*. Wiesbaden: Harrassowitz.
Derchain, P. 1987. *Le dernier obélisque*. Brussels: Fondation Égyptologique Reine Élisabeth.
Dickey, E. 2004. 'The Greek Address System of the Roman Period and its Relationship to Latin', *Classical Quarterly* 54: 494–527.
——2009a. 'The Greek and Latin Languages in the Papyri', in R. S. Bagnall (ed.), *The Oxford Handbook of Papyrology*. Oxford: Oxford University Press, 149–69.
——2009b. 'Latin Influence and Greek Request Formulae', in T. V. Evans and D. D. Obbink (eds), *The Language of the Papyri*. Oxford: Oxford University Press, 208–20.
Dieleman, J. 2005. *Priests, Tongues, and Rites: The London–Leiden Magical Manuscripts and Translation in Egyptian Ritual (100–300 CE)*. Leiden: Brill.
Dijkstra, J. H. F. 2008. *Philae and the End of Ancient Egyptian Religion: A Regional Study of Religious Transformation (298–642 CE)*. Leuven: Peeters.
Fewster, P. 2002. 'Bilingualism in Roman Egypt', in J. N. Adams, M. Janse, and S. Swain (eds), *Bilingualism in Ancient Society: Language Contact and the Written Word*. Oxford: Oxford University Press, 220–45.
Goldbrunner, L. 2004. *Buchis: Eine Untersuchung zur Theologie des heiligen Stieres in Theben zur griechisch-römischen Zeit*. Turnhout: Brepols.
Griffith, F. L. 1935–7. *Catalogue of the Demotic Graffiti of the Dodecaschoenus*. Oxford: Oxford University Press for Service des Antiquités.
Herbin, F.-R. 2008. *Books of Breathing and Related Texts*. London: British Museum Press.
Hickey, T. M. 2009. 'Writing Histories from the Papyri', in R. S. Bagnall (ed.), *The Oxford Handbook of Papyrology*. Oxford: Oxford University Press, 495–520.
Hoffmann, F. 2010. 'Lost in Translation? Beobachtungen zum Verhältnis des lateinischen und griechischen Textes der Gallusstele', in K. Lembke, M. Minas-Nerpel, and S. Pfeiffer (eds), *Tradition and Transformation: Egypt under Roman Rule*. Leiden: Brill, 149–57.

Hoffmann, F. M. Minas-Nerpel, and S. Pfeiffer. 2009. *Die dreisprachige Stele des C. Cornelius Gallus: Übersetzung und Kommentar*. Berlin: de Gruyter.

Hölbl, G. 2000. *Altägypten im römischen Reich: Der römische Pharao und seine Tempel* I. Mainz: von Zabern.

Janssen, J. J. 1992. 'Literacy and Letters in Deir el-Medina', in R. Demarée and A. Egberts (eds), *Village Voices: Proceedings of the Symposium 'Texts from Deir el-Medîna and their Interpretation', Leiden, May 31–June 1, 1991*. Leiden: University of Leiden, Centre of Non-Western Studies, 81–94.

Jay, J. E. 2008. 'The Narrative Structure of Ancient Egyptian Tales: From "Sinuhe" to "Setna"', doctoral dissertation, University of Chicago.

Leitz, C. 2001. 'Die beiden kryptographischen Inschriften aus Esna mit den Widdern und Krokodilen', *Studien zur Altägyptischen Kultur* 29: 251–76.

Lembke, K., M. Minas-Nerpel, and S. Pfeiffer (eds) 2010. *Tradition and Transformation: Egypt under Roman Rule*. Leiden: Brill.

Lewis, N. 1993. 'The Demise of the Demotic Document: When and Why', *Journal of Egyptian Archaeology* 79: 276–81.

Manning, J. 2010. *The Last Pharaohs: Egypt under the Ptolemies, 305–30 BCE*. Princeton: Princeton University Press.

Menchetti, A. 2005. *Ostraka demotici e bilingui da Narmuthis (ODN 100–188)*. Pisa: ETS.

Meyer, H. (ed.) 1994. *Der Obelisk des Antinoos*. Munich: Fink.

Minas-Nerpel, M., and S. Pfeiffer. 2010. 'Establishing Roman Rule in Egypt: The Trilingual Stela of C. Cornelius Gallus from Philae', in K. Lembke, M. Minas-Nerpel, and S. Pfeiffer (eds), *Tradition and Transformation: Egypt under Roman Rule*. Leiden: Brill, 265–98.

Morenz, L. 2002. '"Schrift-Mysterium" Gottes-Schau in der visuelle Poesie von Esna: Insbesondere zu den omnipotenten Widder-Zeichen zwischen Symbolik und Lesbarkeit', in J. Assmann and M. Bommas (eds), *Ägyptische Mysterien?* Munich: Fink, 77–94.

Muhs, B. P. 2005. 'The *Grapheion* and the Disappearance of Demotic Contracts in Early Roman Tebtynis and Soknopaiou Nesos', in S. Lippert and M. Schentuleit (eds), *Tebtynis and Soknopaiu Nesos: Leben im römerzeitlichen Fajum*. Wiesbaden: Harrassowitz, 93–104.

Naether, F. 2010. *Die Sortes Astrampsychi: Problemlösungsstrategien durch Orakel im römischen Ägypten*. Tübingen: Mohr Siebeck.

Quack, J. F. 2002. 'Demotische Verwaltungstexte in hieratischer Schrift', Paper presented to the Eighth Demotic Congress, Würzburg.

——2009. Review of V. H. Sederholm, *Papyrus British Museum 10808 and its Cultural and Religious Setting*, *Orientalistische Literaturzeitung* 104: 27–33.

——2010. 'Inhomogenität von ägyptischer Sprache und Schrift in Texten aus dem späten Ägypten', in K. Lembke, M. Minas-Nerpel, and S. Pfeiffer (eds), *Tradition and Transformation: Egypt under Roman Rule*. Leiden: Brill, 313–41.

Ray, J. D. C. 1994a. 'How Demotic Is Demotic?', *Egitto e Vicino Oriente* 17: 251–64.

——1994b. 'Literacy and Language in Egypt in the Late and Persian Periods', in A. Bowman and G. Woolf (eds), *Literacy and Power in the Ancient World*. Cambridge: Cambridge University Press, 51–83.

Reintges, C. H. 2004. 'Coptic Egyptian as a Bilingual Language Variety', in P. Bádenas de la Peña et al. (eds), *Lenguas en contacto: El testimonio escritto*. Madrid: Consejo Superior de Investigaciones Cientificas, 69–86.

Richter, S. 2009. 'Greek, Coptic, and the "Language of the Hijra": Rise and Decline of the Coptic Language in Late Antique and Medieval Egypt', in H. M. Cotton et al. (eds), *From*

Hellenism to Islam: Cultural and Linguistic Change in the Roman Near East. Cambridge: Cambridge University Press, 401–46.
Riggs, C. 2005. *The Beautiful Burial in Roman Egypt: Art, Identity, and Funerary Religion*. Oxford: Oxford University Press.
——2010. 'Tradition and Innovation in the Burial Practices of Roman Egypt', in K. Lembke, M. Minas-Nerpel, and S. Pfeiffer (eds), *Tradition and Transformation: Egypt under Roman Rule*. Leiden: Brill, 343–56.
Rowlandson, J. 2004. 'Gender and Cultural Identity in Roman Egypt', in F. McHardy and E. Marshall (eds), *Women's Influence on Classical Civilization*. London: Routledge, 151–66.
Rutherford, I. C. 2009. 'Bilingualism in Roman Egypt? Exploring the Archive of Phatres of Narmuthis', in T. V. Evans and D. D. Obbink (eds), *The Language of the Papyri*. Oxford: Oxford University Press, 198–207.
Ryholt, K. 2005. 'On the Contents and Nature of the Tebtunis Temple Library: A Status Report', in S. Lippert and M. Schentuleit (eds), *Tebtynis und Soknopaiu Nesos: Leben im römerzeitlichen Fajum*. Wiesbaden: Harrassowitz, 141–70.
Satzinger, H. 1975. 'The Old Coptic Schmidt Papyrus', *Journal of the American Research Center in Egypt* 12: 37–50.
Sauneron, S. 1959. *Quatre campagnes à Esna*. Cairo: Institut Français d'Archéologie Orientale.
Schentuleit, M. 2010. 'Tradition und Transformation: Einblicke in die Verwaltung des römischen Ägypten nach den demotischen Urkunden', in K. Lembke, M. Minas-Nerpel, and S. Pfeiffer (eds), *Tradition and Transformation: Egypt under Roman Rule*. Leiden: Brill, 357–83.
Sederholm, V. H. 2006. *Papyrus British Museum 10808 and its Cultural and Religious Setting*. Leiden: Brill.
Smith, M. 2009. 'New Extracts from the Book of the Dead in Demotic', in G. Widmer and D. Devauchelle (eds), *Actes du IXe Congrès International des Études Démotiques, Paris, 31 août–3 septembre 2005*. Cairo: Institut Français d'Archéologie Orientale, 347–59.
Stadler, M. A. 2008. 'On the Demise of Egyptian Writing: Working on a Problematic Source Basis', in J. Baines, J. Bennet, and S. Houston (eds), *The Disappearance of Writing Systems: Perspectives on Literacy and Communication*. London: Equinox, 157–81.
Sternberg-el Hotabi, H. 1994. 'Der Untergang der Hieroglyphenschrift: Schriftverfall und Schrifttod im Ägypten der griechisch-römischen Zeit', *Chronique d'Égypte* 69: 218–45.
Thissen, H.-J. 1998. *Vom Bild zum Buchstaben—vom Buchstaben zum Bild: Von der Arbeit an Horapollons Hieroglyphika*. Stuttgart: Steiner.
——1999. 'Homerischer Einfluss im Inaros-Petubastis-Zyklus?', *Studien zur Altägyptischen Kultur* 27: 369–87.
——2001. *Des Niloten Horapollon Hieroglyphenbuch*, vol. 1: *Text und Übersetzung*. Munich: Saur.
Thompson, D. J. 1994. 'Literacy and Power in Ptolemaic Egypt', in A. Bowman and G. Woolf (eds), *Literacy and Power in the Ancient World*. Cambridge: Cambridge University Press, 67–83.
Vandorpe, K., and W. Clarysse. 2008. 'Egyptian Bankers and Bank Receipts in Hellenistic and Early Roman Egypt', in K. Verboven, K. Vandorpe, and V. Chankowski (eds), *Pistoi dia tèn technèn: Bankers, Loans and Archives in the Ancient World: Studies in Honour of Raymond Bogaert*. Leuven: Peeters, 153–68.
——and S. Waebens. 2010. 'Women and Gender in Roman Egypt: The Impact of Roman Rule', in K. Lembke, M. Minas-Nerpel, and S. Pfeiffer (eds), *Tradition and Transformation: Egypt under Roman Rule*. Leiden: Brill, 415–35.

van Minnen, P. 1998. 'Boorish or Bookish? Literature in Egyptian Villages in the Fayum in the Graeco-Roman Period', *Journal of Juristic Papyrology* 28: 99–184.
——2002. '*Αἱ ἀπὸ γυμνασίου*: "Greek" Women and the Greek "Elite" in the Metropoleis of Roman Egypt', in H. Melaerts and L. Mooren (eds), *Le rôle et le statut de la femme en Égypte hellénistique, romaine et byzantine*. Leuven: Peeters, 337–53.
Vierras, M. 2003. 'Everything Is Relative: The Relative Clause Constructions of an Egyptian Scribe Writing Greek', in L. Pietilä-Castrén and M. Vesterinen (eds), *Grapta Poikila* I. Helsinki: Finnish Institute at Athens, 13–23.
Vittmann, G. 2003. *Ägypten und die Fremden im ersten vorchristlichen Jahrtausend*. Mainz: von Zabern.
Widmer, G. 2004. 'Une invocation à la déesse (tablette démotique Louvre E 10382)', in F. Hoffmann and H.-J. Thissen (eds), *Res Severa Verum Gaudium: Festschrift für Karl-Theodor Zauzich zum 65. Geburtstag am 8. Juni 2004*. Leuven: Peeters, 651–86.
Yiftach-Firanko, U. 2009. 'Law in Graeco-Roman Egypt: Hellenization, Fusion, Romanization', in R. S. Bagnall (ed.), *The Oxford Handbook of Papyrology*. Oxford: Oxford University Press, 541–60.
Youtie, H. C. 1971. '*Βραδέως γράφων*: Between Literacy and Illiteracy', *Greek, Roman and Byzantine Studies* 12: 239–61.
——1975a. 'Because They Do Not Know Letters', *Zeitschrift für Papyrologie und Epigraphik* 19: 101–8.
——1975b. '*Ὑπογραφεύς*: The Social Impact of Illiteracy in Graeco-Roman Egypt', *Zeitschrift für Papyrologie und Epigraphik* 17: 201–21.
Yoyotte, J. 1969. 'Bakhthis: Religion égyptienne et culture grecque à Edfu', in P. Derchain (ed.), *Religions en Égypte hellénistique et romaine*. Paris: Presses Universitaires de France, 127–41.
Zauzich, K.-T. 1983. 'Demotische Texte römischer Zeit', in G. Grimm, H. Heinen, and E. Winter (eds), *Das römisch-byzantinische Ägypten: Akten des Internationalen Symposions 26.–30. September 1978 in Trier*. Mainz: von Zabern, 77–80.
——1984. 'Zwischenbilanz zu den demotischen Ostraka aus Edfu', *Enchoria* 12: 67–86.

CHAPTER 30

PAPYRI IN THE ARCHAEOLOGICAL RECORD

ARTHUR VERHOOGT

It is a general understanding in papyrological scholarship that texts in context are more informative historical sources than single texts: 'Where unrelated texts are like instant snapshots, archives present a coherent film of a person, a family, or a community' (Vandorpe 2009: 216). Various means can provide such context to individual texts. For example, one can look in more detail at the archaeological find circumstances if those are available, or one can collect and study other texts that illustrate and explain the people and/or issues at work in the text that is the focus of the research.

In one way or another all these different ways of providing contexts for papyri come together in recent debates about the reconstruction of (public and private) archives. There is much debate about what exactly an archive is, especially because papyrologists use the term in a different way from historians, but basically an archive is a group of texts that were selected and collected by someone in antiquity (in either a personal or a public capacity). Unfortunately, such groups of documents are almost never found in an undisturbed state, that is, in the same state as that person in antiquity meant it to be. More common are groups of documents that have come about in a different manner and need careful analysis to establish how they came to be together. More and more, papyrologists realize that what we have is not so much the archives as the wastepaper baskets of antiquity.

Beyond every identified archive lies a cache of documents that was discovered at some time in a specific location in Egypt (Cuvigny 2009). Sometimes this specific location and the precise circumstances of its discovery are known in more or less detail, but more often archaeological background is not available for such groups of documents because these papyri entered collections as purchases on the antiquities market. Here too, however, it has proven to be possible to make at least educated guesses about document groupings by looking at acquisition records (Vandorpe and Waebens 2009).

In this chapter, I shall discuss the relation between cache and archive in more detail in an attempt to treat such caches of papyri first of all as objects from an archaeological record. This is often lacking in many discussions about the archaeological context of papyri. In particular, it would be helpful for papyrologists to take into account recent debates in processual archaeology, especially of household activities (e.g. Allison 1999).

Grouping Texts in Roman Egypt

It is quite clear that in antiquity both private individuals and the state made a conscious effort to preserve documents in their possession. One obvious way to preserve documents is to collect them and to store them away in a special place. What is more difficult to discern, however, is which documents an individual or the state chose to preserve and for what reason. The main barrier to research here is that, as said above, we do not really have examples of undisturbed collections of such documents from antiquity. At the same time, the documents that do survive allow us to make some general statements.

The prevalent ideas in Roman Egypt about how and where to store documents have a modern ring about them. It is not surprising that no actual preservation guide survives from antiquity, but we can patch together some of the ideas about document storage from several texts. Chief among these is a small group of texts that survive in a so-called family archive from Tebtunis (*P Fam. Tebt.*), which all have to do with several hearings regarding the transfer of documents from one keeper of the archives (*bibliophylax*) to the next. What is interesting is that several descriptions of what went wrong with the documents allow us to reconstruct what was considered to be the right way to archive documents.

The first thing needed for good archival practice was a suitable place (*topos epitedeios*; *P Fam. Tebt.* 15.117–18). Such a place would be in good condition, preventing it from collapse, and would provide shelter against heat and animals. Within the building, one should take care not to heap many rolls on top of one another in confusion because this would surely damage the rolls (*P Fam. Tebt.* 15.65–70). It is quite clear that people knew that papyrus was very frail (*P Fam. Tebt.* 15.70) and would not survive intact unless care was taken. One way to do this was to paste documents and rolls together to form longer rolls, a process known as *diakollesis* or *sunkollesis* (Clarysse 2003), but it was known that not all papyrus documents allowed this procedure (*P Fam. Tebt.* 15.103–4). That these ideas about storage are not confined to the context of official state archives is clear not so much from references in documentary texts, but from archaeological find spots of such papyri. Documents were stored in jars in tombs, or under the threshold of doors in houses (Vandorpe 2009: 219–20 with figs 10.2a–c, 10.3).

For Roman Egypt there are several reconstructed groups of documents, known as archives. Some of these belong to private, or rather personal, archives, others to public archives. An up-to-date list of all archives from Egypt, often accompanied by explanatory narratives, can be found at the website of the Leuven-based project Papyrus Archives in Graeco-Roman Egypt, <http://www.trismegistos.org/arch/index.php>. At the time of writing this chapter the database lists 454 archives (accessed October 2011).

Of these 454 archives, about 150 date from the Roman period. Many archives are very small and comprise only a handful of texts, but there are about a dozen archives with more than one hundred texts. These, not surprisingly, consist of the well-known archives from Roman Egypt: the *strategos* Apollonios; the village scribe Petaus; the archive of Kronion son of Apion (otherwise known as the Tebtunis *grapheion* archive); and several family archives (the descendants of Patron, and the family of Eutychides son of Sarapion). Unfortunately, for almost none of these archives is there accurate information about the find circumstances as most were acquired on the antiquities market or no find circumstances were recorded. Most of these archives, then, are the result of reconstruction.

Even in a completely reconstructed state, it cannot be denied that many of these identified archives have made an important contribution to what we know (and are in the process of learning) about Roman Egypt. And indeed the 'film' presented by these archives has had more to contribute than the 'snapshots' of individual texts. The study of Roman metropolitan elites, for example, would not be possible without the various family archives from Egypt. The Heroninus archive provides detailed information about the working of a large estate in Roman Egypt.

Texts in the Archaeological Record

Recent years have seen ample discussion among papyrologists about what exactly a group of documents should be called (Pestman 1989; Martin 1994; Jördens 2001; van Beek 2007; Vandorpe 2009). What it comes down to is a distinction between a group of documents that was collected by someone in antiquity for a specific purpose and a group of documents that has been reconstructed by a modern scholar. Traditionally, the term used for the first grouping of texts is 'archive', and for the second, 'dossier', although it is quite apparent that this dichotomy does not do justice to the facts because in nearly all cases both archives and dossiers result from reconstruction. This is important to realize, because there is often the implied notion that an 'archive' is more interesting, perhaps even a more important historical source, than a 'dossier'. After all, when dealing with an archive it is the assumption that we are dealing with the actual archival choices of a person or entity in antiquity, not with the selective reconstruction of a modern scholar. This, however, is not necessarily true.

For one thing, not all groups of documents are created equal, or, as van Beek puts it, 'papyri found in the same house or temple or used for the same mummy cartonnage do not automatically constitute an archive' (van Beek 2007: 1034). This is especially true of documents collected for personal reasons. In nearly all the cases of a group of texts found in an archaeological context papyrologists will actively have to analyse the groups of documents and reconstruct the archive, or archives, that make up the archaeological find. The same applies to reconstructions of groups of texts that were purchased on the antiquities market. Archives do not fall into our laps; we have to work hard for them.

As an example it may suffice to refer to the so-called *cantina dei papyri* discovered during the Italian excavations in Tebtunis in 1934 (Gallazzi 1990). The *cantina dei papyri* refers to a cellar in a house where the excavators found hundreds of papyri, all dating to the Roman period. All these papyri, then, had the same archaeological find spot, and a find spot that we know the ancients themselves would consider a suitable place (see above). But does this cache form an archive? Is this group of texts the result of careful selection and collection of documents by somebody in antiquity? Or is this a dump of papyri to be used as fuel, as has been suggested by Gallazzi (1990)? Detailed analysis of the contents of the documents has shown that they belong to several different groups of documents in which different families are the main characters. So far, scholars have identified three archives in this group of documents: those of Kronion, of the descendants of Patron, and of the descendants of Pakekbis. All these are archives of the managers of landed property rather than family archives per se (Smolders 2005). At some point somebody decided to store (or dump?) all these archives, consisting of hundreds of documents, in a cellar. Were the documents deposited together as a group, or were they moved to the cellar on different occasions? Unfortunately, the precise find circumstances of the papyri were not recorded (for instance, were the different groups found in different parts of the cellar?), but analysis has shown that there could be a link between the family archives of the descendants of Patron and the descendants of Pakekbis, suggesting that those documents were all together and were perhaps moved as one group (Smolders 2004). Could a similar link be found for the other group as well? But at the same time, prosopographical analysis does not explain why the texts were in this cellar to begin with.

A second example is the cache of texts that was found in a cubbyhole under the stairs in a house in Karanis. Here, too, the find circumstances force us to consider the group of documents as a whole, but here, too, it readily becomes apparent that what we have is not an archive per se, but a collection of documents heaped together in this spot for an unknown reason (Stephan and Verhoogt 1995). About half of the cache consisted of personal letters, all related to a man called Claudius Tiberianus and his son (?) Claudius Terentianus (known as the archive of Tiberianus). The remainder of the texts, still unpublished, at first sight has nothing to do with these people, and may even date from about fifty years later than the period when Terentianus and Tiberianus were active (the early second century CE). These documents mention different people, and it would be unwarranted to consider all these texts to be part of the same archive only on the basis of their common find spot. Nonetheless, it cannot be excluded that here, too, as in the previous example, a link between the two groups of texts may be found, explaining why these texts were together in the cubbyhole.

The foregoing examples make clear that archival analysis of a group of documents can reconstruct connections between documents that were found in the same cache, but do not explain why these papyri were present in a specific archaeological location. In order to assess the precise nature of a cache of texts, it is first necessary to treat them as archaeological artefacts. Papyri form part of the archaeological assemblage, and they should first of all be interpreted as such.

Recent debates in archaeology have shown that in assessing an archaeological assemblage, one has to try to reconstruct the precise moment when this assemblage was deposited (Schiffer 1985; Allison 1999). By combining archaeological, ethno-archaeological, and ethnographic data, archaeologists have tried to provide a model of what exactly happens with objects when a domestic structure is inhabited, when it is abandoned, and when it finds a new use. This model helps in interpreting and understanding the objects found in a domestic structure, and hence reconstructing the life histories of ancient structures and their inhabitants. Although much of this archaeological theory is focused on prehistoric sites and therefore does not deal with texts, it cannot be denied that texts are sometimes part of the archaeological record. Here, perhaps, papyrology can contribute to the debate.

Archaeologists discern three stages in the life of a domestic structure: habitation, abandonment, and post-abandonment (LaMotta and Schiffer 1999). Habitation is the stage when the structure is in use, with people bringing in (a process called accretion), storing, and removing objects (a process called depletion). Accretion happens inside the structure and entails discarding and storing objects that are worn, broken, or otherwise not at that moment usable to the inhabitants of the structure. Of particular interest for papyrologists, as we shall see below, is what LaMotta and Schiffer term the 'provisional refuse deposition', the storing of objects to be used again later, or just for nostalgic reasons. In particular, 'provisionally discarded objects are frequently cached in out of the way places—not in the middle of activity areas' (1999: 22).

As a result, such objects will be clustered, providing a tool to distinguish discarded or provisionally discarded objects from those left behind when the structure was abandoned.

Abandonment is the phase when the people who were using the structure are preparing to leave and the structure is about to be left behind. At this moment the inhabitants will remove some of the still-usable objects and bring them to the new location (a process called curation), but at the same time leave other objects behind for varying reasons (because they are difficult to transport, easy to replace, and so on). Abandonment can either happen in a planned manner and at a slow pace, or it can happen in haste. In the first case, the refuse deposition will consist of objects that are really unusable, whereas in the second case, it will consist much more of a mix of objects, some of which are still usable and even valuable.

Post-abandonment is the final phase in the life of a domestic structure and is the moment when the original inhabitants have left but the structure's life history continues. In this phase, the structure may be reused as a dwelling (with other people moving in and a new cycle beginning), or used as a garbage dump, or it can simply collapse.

The three stages and their various formation processes are presented in Table 30.1. Careful analysis of several house assemblages has shown that most objects found on house floors result from the abandonment or post-abandonment phase (LaMotta and Schiffer 1999: 25). At the same time, as we have seen, clusters of objects in out-of-the-way places in a structure could point to refuse deposition in the habitation phase.

Processual archaeologists do not normally deal with textual material, and it is indeed quite difficult to fit texts into the neat schedule presented above except for texts explicitly found in a rubbish heap, such as the Oxyrhynchus papyri (Parsons 2007). In this case we are clearly dealing with secondary refuse deposition from various structures in the town itself during the habitation phase.

For texts actually found inside domestic structures the picture is less clear. At first sight, it is perhaps not very likely that people would throw away papyri and other documents when they are about to leave the house. Also not likely is that people who temporarily use a house as storage after it has been abandoned by others would store texts in that location. Does this mean that whenever documents are present in the archaeological record, we are dealing with the habitation phase and hence with primary or provisional refuse deposition?

In order to consider this question, perhaps we first have to step back and try to establish why people kept documents, and see whether that can help in establishing where papyri fit in this schedule. Following Pestman, Vandorpe distinguishes four categories of documents that people will keep (Vandorpe 2009: 238–40).

1. The first is the category of active legal documents that establish ownership of land and goods, payment of loans and other obligations, and so on. These documents are useful and need to be kept because they help establish claims and counterclaims should it ever come to a lawsuit. From the existing archives it is clear that such legal documents were kept over several generations.

2. A second category consists of documents that are kept for sentimental reasons. Among these are personal letters and, for example, the first writings of a younger brother or child. Here there is quite a direct connection between the person who is keeping the document and the text itself, and this connection can be lost once that person has died.

3. The third category that Vandorpe distinguishes are literary works. People keep books because they like them. Here too, as in the second category, the connection may not be preserved when the person dies.

Table 30.1 Deposition of objects in the lifecycle of domestic structures

Phase	Objects deposited in structure (accretion)	Objects removed from structure (depletion)
Habitation	Primary and loss refuse deposition: inhabitants discard items *inside* structure for later use, or accidentally lose them	Secondary refuse deposition: inhabitants remove objects from structure to another removed location
	Provisional refuse deposition: inhabitants store objects (broken and/or worn out) in structure to be used again later or for nostalgic reasons	
Abandonment	De facto refuse deposition: still-usable items left behind in structure	Curation: transfer of usable objects to new activity location
Post-abandonment	Reuse refuse deposition: reuse as domestic or other structure (introducing a new habitation phase)	Scavenging disturbance
	Secondary refuse deposition: structure used as dump	Decay
	Structural collapse	
	Disturbance	

Note: This table is based on LaMotta and Schiffer (1999: 20), but leaves out their discussion of ritual deposition and depletion in the abandonment phase as this does not really apply to documents that are left behind.

4. A fourth category is needed because we know that people also keep documents for reasons that do not include one of the previous three (even if those reasons are unclear to us). For example, it is quite clear that people sometimes keep texts because the back can be used as scrap paper. This category may explain the presence of long accounts in personal archives.

Of these four categories, two may—when present in the archaeological record—point to the habitation phase of a domestic structure. First, it is very unlikely that active legal documents (category 1) will be left inside the structure when inhabitants decide to abandon it. After all, the possible future claims and counterclaims are in most cases (unless the documents only concern the house itself) connected to the persons involved, not to the structure. At the same time, it is equally unlikely that others will store such important documents in an abandoned structure. So, indeed, the presence of such legal documents in a structure's archaeological record could point to its habitation phase. The same applies to literary texts (Vandorpe's third category) which again are not likely to be left behind in a structure when it is abandoned, or to be stored in an abandoned structure. The presence of literary works in the archaeological record of a domestic structure could point to the habitation phase of that structure. The Herculaneum library of literary works carbonized by the eruption of Mount Vesuvius in 79 CE is a case in point.

What both these categories have in common is that their replacement value is high and that therefore the owners of such documents will make sure to 'curate' these texts when they abandon a structure (and not leave them behind). Legal texts cannot be replaced at all, or only with great effort (copied from central archives), and literary texts present the owner with quite an investment, and difficulty of replacement.

The remaining two categories are less clear. Little can be said, of course, of the fourth category, other than that it may be relatively easy to find scrap paper, so that its replacement value is low, and people, when preparing to leave a structure, may decide to leave it behind. This could account for the presence of the papyri in the *cantina dei papyri*, if we are willing to accept them as fuel for ovens (Gallazzi 1990: 284). At the same time, the fact that we dealing not so much with personal archives (see above) but with professional archives may point in a different direction, and more research is needed here, outside the scope of the present cases. One thing to take into account with such documents is their archival value: how long do people consider it necessary to keep documents in the archive, and when will they remove them for a different use?

A similar low replacement value may apply to the documents of the second type (personal letters, and so on, with a high nostalgic character). These are likely to be stored in out-of-the-way places, because the owner of such documents does not consult them daily or need to have them available for easy consultation. The knowledge of having these documents is more important than knowing their precise location in the structure. What remains debatable, however, is the replacement value of such nostalgic documents. On the one hand, they are irreplaceable: the letter sent to you by your son is unique and cannot be sent anew; the first writings of your little brother are unique and cannot be replaced because he is now an adult. On the other hand, their value is very personal. They are important to the person who collects them, but will be less important to others: the letter sent by the son may become less nostalgic to the son himself, and even less to his own children, and the writing exercise is important to the older brother but will be of less importance to his children and grandchildren. The replacement value of nostalgic documents, then, is variable. It is high when there is a direct link between the collector and the documents, but it becomes lower when the collector is no longer there.

The presence of personal documents in the archaeological record of a domestic structure would suggest that their replacement value was low. The last inhabitants of the structure decided that it would be no use to 'curate' these documents to another structure, and left them behind. They become even more telling archaeological sources if such personal documents are found in an out-of-the-way place as they could be a clear sign of provisional refuse deposition and thus go back to the habitation phase of the structure.

This may be what happened in the case of the letters (and other documents) found in the cubbyhole under the stairs in a house in Karanis, discussed above. What we have here are personal documents that were provisionally discarded in a place in the house that was no longer in use (Stephan and Verhoogt 2005), together with other objects stored for later usage. When the inhabitants eventually abandoned the structure, the replacement value of these documents was low and the inhabitants decided to leave them behind.

Conclusion

Papyri are, first of all, objects of the archaeological record, and they need to be interpreted in that way. This can then pave the way for analysis of content and reconstruction of archives within caches of documents. Especially in the case of domestic structures, papyri can add a level of interpretation that is not available for archaeological sites without written records. It is important, however, to analyse carefully the papyri involved and try to establish why they would have been kept in a domestic structure because not all texts were kept for the same reason and for an equal amount of time. Texts found together do not automatically constitute an archive. The question why papyri are found where they are found may not be answered satisfactorily, but it has to be asked.

Suggested Reading

The best introduction to the world of archives from Egypt is Vandorpe (2009), which also provides a good summary of earlier literature. An up-to-date gazetteer of all identified archives from Greek and Roman Egypt can be found online, at the Leuven Archives project, <http://www.trismegistos.org/arch/index.php>. The classic discussion of archives in the whole of the ancient world is still Posener (1972), although Brosius (2003) provides more detailed analysis of a smaller number of archival traditions in the ancient world.

Bibliography

Allison, P. M. (ed.) 1999. *The Archaeology of Household Activities*. London: Routledge.

Brosius, M. (ed.) 2003. *Ancient Archives and Archival Traditions: Concepts of Record-Keeping in the Ancient World*. Oxford: Oxford University Press.

Burkhalter, F. 1990. 'Archives locales et archives centrales en Égypte romaine', *Chiron* 20: 191–216.
Clarysse, W. 2003. '*Tomoi synkollêsimoi*', in M. Brosius (ed.), *Ancient Archives and Archival Traditions: Concepts of Record-Keeping in the Ancient World*. Oxford: Oxford University Press, 344–59.
Cockle, W. E. H. 1994. 'State Archives in Graeco-Roman Egypt from 30 BC to the Reign of Septimius Severus', *Journal of Egyptian Archaeology* 70: 106–22.
Cuvigny, H. 2009. 'The Finds of Papyri: The Archaeology of Papyrology', in R. S. Bagnall (ed.), *The Oxford Handbook of Papyrology*. Oxford: Oxford University Press, 30–58.
Gallazzi, C. 1990. 'La "cantina dei papyri" di Tebtynis e ciò che essa conteneva', *Zeitschrift für Papyrologie und Epigraphik* 80: 283–8.
Jördens, A. 2001. 'Papyri und private Archive: Ein Diskussionsbeitrag zur papyrologischen Terminologie', in E. Cantarella and G. Thür (eds), *Symposion 1997: Vorträge zur griechischen und hellenistischen Rechtsgeschichte (Altafiumara, 8.–14. Sept. 1997)*. Cologne: Böhlau, 253–67.
LaMotta, V. M., and M. B. Schiffer. 1999. 'Formation Processes of House Floor Assemblages', in P. M. Allison (ed.), *The Archaeology of Household Activities*. London: Routledge, 19–29.
Martin, A. 1994. 'Archives privées et cachettes documentaires', in A. Bülow-Jacobsen (ed.), *Proceedings of the 20th International Congress of Papyrologists, Copenhagen, 23–29 August 1992*. Copenhagen: Museum Tusculanum Press, 569–77.
Messeri, G. 2001. 'Official and Private Archives in the Papyri', in B. G. Mandilaras (ed.), *First International Symposium of Archivists: Archival Perspectives in the New Millennium, Cyprus, 4–6 May 2000*. Athens: Hypargeio Paideias, 61–9.
Parsons, P. J. 2007. *City of the Sharp-Nosed Fish: Greek Lives in Roman Egypt*. London: Weidenfeld and Nicolson.
Pestman, P. W. 1989. *Familiearchieven uit het land van Pharao*. Zutphen: Uitgeverij Terra.
Posener, E. 1972. *Archives in the Ancient World*. Cambridge, Mass.: Harvard University Press.
Schiffer, M. B. 1985. 'Is There a "Pompeii Premise" in Archaeology?', *Journal of Anthropological Research* 41: 18–41.
Smolders, R. 2004. 'Two Archives from the Roman Arsinoites', *Chronique d'Égypte* 79: 233–40.
—— 2005. 'Patron's Descendants'. Papyrus Archives in Graeco-Roman Egypt, ArchID 66. <http://www.trismegistos.org/arch/archives/pdf/66.pdf>.
Stephan, R. P., and A. Verhoogt. 2005. 'Text and Context in the Archive of Tiberianus (Karanis, Egypt; 2nd century AD)', *Bulletin of the American Society of Papyrologists* 42: 189–201.
van Beek, B. 2007. 'Ancient Archives and Modern Collections: The Leuven Homepage of Papyrus Archives and Collections', in J. Frösén et al. (eds), *Proceedings of the 24th International Congress of Papyrology, Helsinki, 1–7 August, 2004*. Helsinki: Societas Scientiarum Fennica, 1033–44.
Vandorpe, K. 2009. 'Archives and Dossiers', in R. S. Bagnall (ed.), *The Oxford Handbook of Papyrology*. Oxford: Oxford University Press, 216–55.
—— and S. Waebens. 2009. *Reconstructing Pathyris' Archives: A Multicultural Community in Hellenistic Egypt*. Brussels: Koninklijke Vlaamse Academie van België voor Wetenschappen en Kunsten.

CHAPTER 31

LATIN IN EGYPT

T. V. EVANS

WITHIN the multilingual speech community of Roman Egypt the Latin language played a minor role. Greek, treated in the next chapter, was employed by the Romans as a spoken and written lingua franca. As far as we can judge from scattered and heterogeneous remains, the use of Latin was much more limited. Nevertheless, as a language of power and identity it had the potential to appear in many places. Its employment has considerable socio-linguistic significance. In addition, the Egyptian finds provide important information on bilingualism and non-standard varieties of the language.

THE EVIDENCE

Very little Latin material has in fact survived, viewed in relation to the mass of contemporary Greek texts. A search of the Trismegistos database turns up 794 Latin items from Egypt for the date range 30 BCE–300 CE (as at 5 October 2011). For the same range and region Trismegistos turns up 36,221 Greek items. Thus, the Latin material amounts to 2.19 per cent of the combined total. These figures, however raw, give a clear impression of the statistically marginal status of the language, and accord fairly closely with earlier estimates (Bagnall 1995: 22; Adams 2003: 527).

Written records can only give us a glimpse of the real picture. Latin presumably made greater inroads in Egypt as a medium of oral communication (Adams 1977: 4). It had a recorded, if rare, presence there from well before Augustus' annexation, the earliest inscription, *I Thèbes à Syène* 321 (= *CIL* I^2 2 2937a, from Philae), dating from 116 BCE (Beness and Hillard 2003). Latin did not arrive only with the conquest. Yet the written residue of its presence during the Roman period is suggestively slight.

The finds manifest considerable diversity. Bits and pieces of Latin occur in inscriptions, graffiti, papyri, ostraca, and tablets—often in bilingual texts—from all over Egypt. Different kinds of textual artefact have been recovered, according to the suitability of conditions for preservation, from Alexandria and the Delta, from the Fayum depression, from the valley of the Nile all the way up into Nubia in the south, from the desert stations and quarries, and from the Red Sea littoral.

The Latin texts are also scattered in the modern literature. There is no consolidated collection as such. For papyri and ostraca we do, however, have Cavenaile's *Corpus Papyrorum Latinarum* (1958) and Cugusi's *Corpus Epistularum Latinarum* (1992–2002), and the Trismegistos website offers increasingly comprehensive records and search capabilities for Latin. It may be used as a key to locate individual texts in the various corpora (for instance—to give an important example from the early Byzantine period—the two Latin papyri among eighty numbered Greek items in *P Abinn.*, the archive of Flavius Abinnaeus, *ala* commander at Dionysias in the Fayum in the 340s).

To describe the content of these Latin texts, generalizations are dangerous, and any categorization will be somewhat crude. For example, Katzoff (1996: 608) asserts that 'Latin documents from Egypt are almost all military,' yet while there are indeed many military communications of various sorts, a private letter from a soldier may not be at all 'military' in content. We also find numerous texts pertaining to the civil administration, legal documents, private letters, inscriptions and graffiti of the 'I was here' type or of a religious character, and epitaphs.

In addition, there are a number of literary and para-literary texts. A search of the Leuven Database of Ancient Books turns up fifty-one from Egypt for the date range 30 BCE–300 CE (as at 5 October 2011). Some of these are spectacular finds; for instance, the third-century copy of an epitome of Livy (*Per.* 37–40, 48–55) from Oxyrhynchus (*P Oxy.* IV 668 + *PSI* XII 1291) and the twelve-line fragment of Cornelius Gallus' poetry recovered in 1978 from Qasr Ibrim in Egyptian Nubia and dated before *c.*25 CE (Anderson, Parsons, and Nisbet 1979).

A sense of the diversity of the material can be gained quickly by a glance at the contents of *P Mich.* VII, which contains twenty-nine Latin and eight bilingual (Latin and Greek) items. This volume was published in 1947. Its thirty-six items (there are thirty-seven numbered ones, but two texts were later identified as parts of a single document) are more or less poorly preserved. Most of them have since been re-edited, and the original characterizations and editions of individual documents need to be checked carefully for accuracy (one may begin conveniently from Advanced Papyrological Information System entries). They include twenty-six papyri, nine wooden tablets (containing text either incised with a stylus on a film of wax or written with pen and ink directly on the wooden surface), and one text incised on bronze.

The *P Mich.* VII documents come from various places. Three or four are from Alexandria, twelve from Karanis in the northern Fayum, one from Philadelphia in the north-eastern Fayum, another two probably also from the Fayum region, two probably or perhaps from Oxyrhynchus, and one from Pselkis (Dakka) in Nubia, while fourteen are of unknown provenance. At least two texts date from the first century CE, one is from the first or second century, at least twenty-two are from the second, three are probably second or third, four are from the third century, and there are also four from the Byzantine period (three from the fourth century and one from the sixth).

They include three birth certificates, a certificate of the assumption of the *toga pura* by adolescent male citizens, two marriage contracts (one possibly an attestation of a marriage), a contract dealing with a dowry, a military diploma, a copy of the honourable discharge of a legionary soldier, a register of soldiers' receipts for legacy, two petitions, two reports of military units, a list of soldiers, two acknowledgements of debt, a freedman's certificate, three wills, another legal text of unidentified type, a report of some sort (perhaps of police action), a private letter (?), two writing exercises, a recipe (or recipes?), a treatise on Latin grammar, an Aesopic fable, a collection of brief sayings, and six other documents of uncertain nature.

This miscellany gives an instructive taste of the diverse, scattered, and fragmentary nature of our evidence. From such material we can only expect to piece together a partial understanding of the role of Latin in Egypt. It can easily mislead and needs to be interpreted with care.

Functions of Latin in Egypt

In Roman Egypt the Latin language tends to appear (in partial accordance with our random *P Mich.* VII sample) in documents of the higher administration (for example, correspondence between Roman magistrates, and edicts and decrees of the central government concerning Roman magistrates, Roman individuals, or the Roman army), in military communications, and in legal texts concerning Roman citizens (Kaimio 1979: 27; Fewster 2002: 224). Generalizing formulations like this cannot, however, capture the complexity or full range of the usage. The essential functions of Latin involve the expression of power and identity.

This is brought out especially in choices between Latin and Greek. Both were high-prestige languages in the Egyptian context. Greek was the usual language of administration for the Romans, as elsewhere in the eastern part of their empire (for the idea of increased use of Latin resulting from Diocletian-era reforms, see Rochette 1997: 116–26; for serious doubt over his interpretation of relevant evidence, Adams 2003: 635–7), and of high literary culture. Latin, when used in public environments, can be seen to possess a super-high political value (Adams 2003: 545–76, 637). Adams presents a series of illustrative case studies, for instance the sporadic injection of Latin into court hearings, which largely employ Greek, by Roman officials (Adams 2003: 383–90, 561), and the tendency of prefects and military officers to choose Latin instead of Greek for 'I was here' inscriptions at the Colossus of Memnon (on the left bank of the Nile opposite Thebes; see Chapters 11 and 42), a pilgrimage site of special significance for the Roman elite (Adams 2003: 546–7, 549–55). In such cases the occasional use of Latin is a symbolic expression of imperial power and authority. Its assertive use in political contexts can be traced back to the republic, and the Egyptian evidence aligns broadly with this general practice.

In certain contexts, however, we seem to find a different motivation for choosing between Greek and Latin. A remarkable example is found in papyrus letters from the archive of Claudius Tiberianus, which was discovered at Karanis and dates from the first quarter of the second century. This archive includes eleven published letters to Tiberianus from his son Claudius Terentianus (there are some additional unpublished fragments in the University of Michigan's collection). Five of these are in Greek, six in Latin (*P Mich.* VIII 467–71 and *Papyrus Michigan* 5395 (fr. A), on which, see the Advanced Papyrological Information System entry). The letters are in several hands, and were probably copied by scribes from Terentianus' dictation (see below).

We can do no more than speculate about the circumstances underlying the clear-cut bilingualism of father and son revealed in these documents. But Terentianus' usage indicates fluent control over a non-standard variety of Latin (see below), and the balance of probabilities suggests he may well be the son of a Latin-speaking immigrant (and a Greek-speaking mother?). He appears to have been a competent bilingual. There is no clear temporal motivation underpinning the language choice in the letters, and their content in part involves similar topics. It is possible, however, to link the Latin letters more closely to family affairs. For Terentianus this is perhaps the language more appropriate for mundane personal correspondence, opposed to the suitability of Greek for more formal topics, as the usual language of public administration (Adams 2003: 593–7; Clackson and Horrocks 2007: 249–50). If this interpretation is correct, Terentianus' choice of Latin is an expression of identity at a purely private level.

Terentianus happens to have been a soldier. As noted above, a good deal of our evidence for Latin in Egypt comes from military contexts, and it is often asserted that Latin was the 'official' language of the Roman army. Adams has, however, demonstrated the unreliability of this vague formulation, and has presented a much more nuanced view of the use of Latin and Greek in military documents (Adams 2003: 599–623). His analysis of the evidence reveals no rigid linguistic policy, but instead a willingness to exploit the language appropriate to the personnel of particular units, and an accompanying linguistic flexibility in prosecuting army business. Official military documents might be written in Greek both for a unit's internal record keeping and for external correspondence. In some circumstances the choice of Greek might have reflected the availability of scribes, but there are also indications of Greek use by individuals who could have employed Latin instead. A fair degree of discretion regarding language choice seems to have rested with commanding officers or supervising clerks. On the other hand, Latin seems to have been felt necessary, as the super-high prestige language, for some official correspondence, and there are certain types of text that foster its use as a mark of Roman identity, for instance *diplomata*, passwords, epitaphs, and honorific inscriptions for the emperor.

Character of the Latin

The finds may be meagre, but the Latin documents from Egypt offer rich linguistic evidence. Those emanating from sub-elite levels of the society tend to preserve non-standard features. In many cases these can be interpreted as ignorance or interference phenomena involving issues of Greek and Latin bilingualism, which have been analysed in detail by Adams (2003: 527–641) and are treated in this volume by Depauw (Chapter 29). Bilingualism is a key factor, from a linguistic as well as a functional perspective, in understanding the Latin material from Egypt. It by no means accounts, however, for all the non-standard elements. We also find many features that reflect natural varieties of Latin distinct from the classical standard. This evidence, of very great significance for the post-classical history of the language, involves the full gamut of orthography, morphology, syntax, and vocabulary.

The majority of the data have parallels in texts of the same period from other parts of the empire or are reflected in late Latin or Romance developments. There is no evidence for the development of any distinctively regional use, that is, for an 'Egyptian Latin'. Indeed, much of the material discovered in Egypt is likely to have been produced by visitors. Some Latin speakers certainly seem to have settled in Egypt, but we have only a few scraps of information indicating the language's employment within families over more than one generation; the letters of Claudius Terentianus and Claudius Tiberianus are a case in point (Adams 2003: 527–8).

Examples of non-standard Latin show up in different types of material, revealing various levels of competence. The text *P Vindob.* L 2, for instance, is a list of soldiers of the third Cyrenaic legion, written in the period 98–127 CE (Kramer 1993: 148–9). The author was presumably from a Greek-speaking background. It manifests clear signs of limited Latin competence in its nominal-case variations, as well as morphological interference from Greek, and an instance of alphabet switching to Greek (Adams 2003: 621–2). But it also contains 'a substantial number of misspellings determined by the sounds of colloquial Latin, and must therefore have been the work of someone familiar with ordinary Latin speech' (Adams 2003: 622). Note the forms *Cladius* = *Claudius* (reduction of *au* to *a* by dissimilation before a syllable containing *u*), *Flaus* = *Flauius* (*-aui-* > *-au-* where *i* is unnaccented), *Otaus* = *Octauus* (assimilation *Oct-* > *Ot(t)* and reduction *-auu-* > *-au-*; on the standard form of this name, see Kramer 1993: 156), and *Upis* = *Ulpius* (absorption of 'dark' *l* by the adjacent back vowel *u*).

Many additional features show up in more fluent and syntactically complex compositions from authors who are either native speakers or have acquired a fair level of competence. The five ostraca of the soldier Rustius Barbarus found at Wadi Fawakhir (*O Fawakhir* 1–5), of perhaps the mid-first century CE (Cugusi 1992–2002: 2.57), and some of the second-century ostraca from Mons Claudianus are important examples. But the letters of Terentianus (together with one from Tiberianus, *P Mich.* VIII 472) offer our most extensive sample and must be central to any discussion. Consider a short extract (*P Mich.* VIII 471 (= *CEL* 146) 29–35):

> ... non magis qurauit me pro xylesphongium
> sed sum negotium et circa res suas. attonitus
> exiendo dico illi da m[i] pauqum aes ut possim uenire
> con rebus meis Alexandrie im inpendia. negabit se
> abiturum. ueni dicet Alexandrie ed dabo t[i]bi. ego
> non abiui. mater ma nos assem uendedi lentiamina
> [u]t ueniam Alexandrie.

[He paid no more attention to me than to a sponge-stick, but (paid attention) to his own business and about his own affairs. Astonished, I say to him as he leaves, 'Give me a little money, that I may be able to go with my things to Alexandria, for expenses.' He said that he didn't have any. 'Come', he says, 'to Alexandria and I'll give it to you.' I did not go. My mother sold the linen for us for an *as*, in order that I might go to Alexandria.]

Terentianus was a 'fluent speaker of a non-standard variety of Latin' (Adams 2003: 750; cf. Adams 1977: 75, 86), which 'belongs some way down the social scale' (Adams 2003: 749; cf. 745). The language of the quoted passage in some places departs so far from the classical standard that it is very difficult to interpret his meaning, especially at *mater ma nos assem uendedi lentiamina*, which is perhaps equivalent to *mater mea nobis assem uendidit linteamina* (see Cugusi 1992–2002: 2.175). A cursory treatment of some of the non-standard material contained in these seven lines will amply illustrate their character. (The following observations are far from comprehensive. For detailed linguistic analysis of Terentianus' letters, see Adams 1977; 2003: 741–50; for complementary summaries, see Clackson and Horrocks 2007: 251–6; Dickey 2009: 162–4.)

There are a series of revealing misspellings here. For instance, the loss of phonemic quantitative distinctions in the vowel system in post-classical Latin causes widespread confusion of long *e* and short *i*. This is reflected in *dicet* = *dicit* and *lentiamina* = *linteamina*. Monophthongization of *ae* is reflected in *Alexandrie* = *Alexandriae*. Clear examples of contraction occur: *sum* = *suum* and *ma* = *mea*. Assimilation of final *-n*, frequent in Terentianus' letters, appears in *im inpendia* = *in impendia*, in this case followed by the recomposition *in-* (Adams 1977: 25). The form *uendedi* = *uendidit* manifests loss of final *-t*, while loss of aspiration is seen in *abiturum* = *habiturum* (initial position) and in *mi* = *mihi* (intervocalic; the example in our passage is damaged, but the form *mi* is frequent in the letters). The spelling *b* for *u*, which reflects qualitative merging of the original phonemes /b/ and /w/ to a bilabial fricative roughly similar to modern English *v*, appears in *negabit* = *negauit*. The confusion of final *-t* and *-d* seen in *ed dabo* is also frequent and extends beyond straightforward assimilation.

On the other hand, some characteristics of the orthography in Terentianus' letters are strikingly archaic; for instance, *q* for *c* before *u* in *qurauit* = *curauit* and *pauqum* = *paucum*, and probably also *o* for *u* in *con* = *cum*. Spelling tends to be conservative and here we see a retention of old conventions, even in a text where many phonetic spellings occur.

Turning to the sphere of morphology and syntax, the use of the locative *Alexandrie* = *Alexandriae* as a directional (as well as locative) complement is strikingly illustrated in the passage. It aligns with occurrence of other static complements with verbs of motion in these letters, such as *apud* with *uenio* in *spero me celerius aput te uenturum* at *P Mich.* VIII 472.10–11 (where, incidentally, *celerius* is comparative for positive; cf. Adams 1977: 58). Note also the generalization of the accusative as the prepositional case at the expense of the ablative. This is seen here in *pro xylesphongium*. In *con rebus meis* we see *con* = *cum* governing ablative according to standard use, but the accusative after *con* appears to be frequent, and occurs unambiguously in *con tirones* = *cum tironibus* earlier in this same letter (*P Mich.* VIII 471.22).

Meanwhile, the pronoun *ille* is seen in its extended function replacing the anaphoric *is* of the classical standard, here in the dative *illi*. An alternative dative form *illei* happens to occur five times elsewhere in Terentianus' letters, but with reference always to a woman, never to a man. It appears that this *illei* = *illaei* and reflects early innovation of a specifically feminine dative form of the pronoun, the ancestor of modern Italian *lei*. The phonetic change that produces the ending *-bit*, homophonous with *-uit*, in *negabit* seems to lead to confusion between perfect and future forms and thus the choice of future infinitive *abiturum* (*esse*), instead of the logical *habere*, in *negabit se abiturum* (Adams 1977: 48–9). We can also observe here the dearth of connective particles in Terentianus' Latin, which probably allows an insight into popular spoken practice (Adams 1977: 59), and changes from classical word order, in particular a tendency to place the verb before its object and any associated prepositional phrases.

The peculiar form *exiendo*, in sense equivalent to the dative of the present participle, *exeunti*, exhibits apparent morphological confusion with the gerund(ive) and presumably reflects a degree of functional overlap (see Adams 2003: 745, 748–9). This represents an extreme example of substandard usage, but analogical remodelling and regularization of verbal forms is well represented in Terentianus' letters and elsewhere. Remodelled forms are seen in *ualunt* = *ualent* (*P Mich.* VIII 468.40) and *collexi* = *collegi* (*P Mich.* VIII 471.12). Passage of a deponent into the active, a kind of regularization, is seen in *merca* = *mercare* at *P Mich.* VIII 469.17 (compare the centurion Januarius' use of active forms of *miror* in inscriptions from the Syringes of Thebes, interpreted as a solecism at Adams 2003: 584), and *posso* = *possum* at *P Mich.* VIII 469.15 represents a tendency to standardize irregular verbs that is also witnessed in other Egyptian documents. Note the infinitive of *refero* regularized to *referere* in *P Oxy.* I 32.15–16 (letter of recommendation, second century), the infinitive of *reddo* regularized to [*r*]*eddare* in *P Mich.* VII 438.5 (promissory note from Karanis, 140 CE), and its imperative *redda* in *O Fawakhir* 5a.13. This 'phenomenon was no doubt commonplace beneath a certain educational level all over the Empire' (Adams 2003: 613; cf. 745–6).

All these features give a mere taste of the non-standard Latin preserved in the Egyptian material. It is important to add finally some examples from the sphere of vocabulary, and again I draw on Terentianus' letters. There is evidence here and elsewhere for new senses of old words, for example *fortis*, 'healthy', and for replacement of higher-register vocabulary items in ordinary usage, as in *epistula* for *litterae* and *inuenio* for *reperio*, while a persistent colloquialism is seen in *adiuto* beside standard *adiuuo* (Adams 1977: 76–83).

There are, of course, other texts from Roman Egypt that are relatively polished compositions. It is worth concluding this section with an example, drawn from the archive of Successus (*O Claud.* I 124–36). Successus seems to have been a kind of quartermaster, dealing with the provision of supplies at Mons Claudianus in the early second century, and received letters in both Greek and Latin. The short letter from Agathon transcribed below displays essentially standard Latin, as far as it goes. There is a single case of syncope (common in Terentianus' letters; see Adams 1977: 21) in *benualere*, unless this is simply a graphic error.

Agathon Successó suó salutem.
accepi • a Melanippó tunicas duas et palliol(um)
et tunic(am) • albam • quam • mecum habeo.
tu curá id quod tibi mandaui
benual•ere te opto.

(*O Claud.* I 135 (*c.*107 CE))

[Agathon to his Successus greetings. I have received from Melanippus two tunics and a short cloak, and a white tunic which I have with me. You take care of what I entrusted to you. I hope that you are well.]

Some Directions for Future Study

The landmark study of Adams has established an excellent platform for future work on Latin in Egypt. There is, however, much more to be done. What has not yet been attempted is a systematic linguistic survey of all the sufficiently well-preserved Latin texts from the region. This is a central desideratum, which would powerfully develop our understanding of the data sample.

Any such treatment ought to include a focus on the language of individuals (and social groups). Adams has already demonstrated the possibilities in this area, observing differences of usage between Terentianus and his father. Tiberianus seems to have had greater stylistic pretensions (Adams 1977: 12). He uses the standard spelling of *Alexandriae* at *P Mich.* VIII

472.9, the one instance of the form in his letter, while Terentianus only has the non-standard *Alexandrie* (seven times). Tiberianus, also in contrast with his son, uses an ablative absolute construction (Adams 1977: 60–1), employs *reperio* whereas Terentianus always uses the 'everyday' *inuenio*, and has the archaic form *abs*. Because we have so few Latin texts from Egypt and they are so heterogeneous there is a limit to how many more data of this type we can expect to discover. But fresh documentary finds from other parts of the empire (e.g. the Vindolanda Tablets), together with new work on long-known data samples such as the Pompeian inscriptions (see Kruschwitz 2010), provide an increasing body of comparative material that can help build up personal linguistic profiles. Adams's experiment in contrasting the verbal morphology of Terentianus with that preserved in the archive of Cerialis from Vindolanda shows what is possible (Adams 2003: 741–9).

Ink-written documents possess unique value for interpreting the language of individual authors, and it will be crucial in future to combine palaeographic and linguistic analysis of such texts from Egypt. The process by which a named author's message reaches the writing surface may vary, and the different possibilities, including the linguistic input of scribes, need always to be borne in mind (Evans 2010). The letters of Rustius Barbarus are all written by a single hand (Cugusi 1992–2002: 2.57), perhaps his own, but Terentianus' are in various hands and were presumably, though not necessarily, written by professional scribes (see Cugusi 1992–2002: 2.131; Halla-aho 2003: 245). Adams has established the strong probability that his scribes copied verbatim from his dictation, on the basis of specific patterns of expression indicating linguistic unity (Adams 1977: 84; compare Halla-aho 2003: 246). He also entertains the possibility of a scribe copying Terentianus' own writing (Adams 1977: 48–9). On the other hand, it has been suggested on palaeographic grounds (the idea seems beyond proof) that Terentianus was the actual writer of one of his letters, *P Mich.* VIII 469 (Cugusi 1992–2002: 2.131; Clackson and Horrocks 2007: 249–50). These possibilities and their implications regarding the linguistic content could be teased out further and where possible applied to other corpora. Halla-aho (2003) has laid the groundwork for one way forward by examining the contrasting orthographic habits of Terentianus' scribes and isolating variations in their practice.

The identity of the scribes writing Latin in Egypt during the Imperial period also deserves general attention. An important by-product of Adams's work on bilingualism is his isolation of specific examples of scribal practice in military contexts that capture stages of Latin literacy among persons of Greek-speaking background (Adams 2003: 609–14, 617–23, 631–3). Non-native speakers were clearly used as scribes in the army for the writing of official Latin documents. There must have been a shortage in some units of native Latin speakers who could perform these tasks. He finds similar evidence in civil texts written in Greek-influenced Latin (Adams 2003: 623–30) and suggests 'that the imperial bureaucracy did not have at all times and in all places a ready stock of native speakers of Latin to draft quasi-official Latin texts when the need arose, and that in the time-honoured Roman way Greek clerks or scribes were sometimes used' (Adams 2003: 623). As well as this primary evidence we have morsels of less direct information indicating stages in the acquisition of Latin literary culture: writing exercises, grammatical works, and literary texts (Adams 2003: 623 n. 177). There is considerable scope for exploiting these data through the systematic linguistic analysis of the Latin texts called for above. That analysis would sharpen our awareness of the proportions of different varieties of Latin, including Greek-influenced Latin, within the data sample and help to refine understanding of the educational level and likely background of scribes.

SUGGESTED READING

The general topic of Latin in Egypt has been explored by several scholars, at length by Stein (1915: 132–86), and also by Cavenaile (1952), Kaimio (1979), Daris (1991), Ghiretti (1996), and Rochette (1996a, b, 1997). Without question the most significant contribution to date is Adams (2003: 527–641). This study provides a detailed examination of the surviving material with special reference to bilingualism, and is fundamental for future research. The present treatment owes a heavy debt to Adams's work, which it is a pleasure to acknowledge.

For linguistic analysis, the best starting point is Adams (1977) on the Latin letters of Terentianus and Cugusi (1981) on the ostraca of Rustius Barbarus. Cugusi (1992–2002: 1.27–45) provides a valuable linguistic survey of the documentary letters. Scattered comments on the language of Latin texts from Egypt also turn up in the modern editions and there are useful summary discussions in Clackson and Horrocks (2007) and Dickey (2009).

Allusion has been made above to the excellent electronic resources for accessing the material in modern collections. Trismegistos, together with its partner sites, <http://www.trismegistos.org>, and the Leuven Database of Ancient Books, <http://www.trismegistos.org/ldab>, are increasingly indispensable tools for locating texts, and the Advanced Papyrological Information System, <http://www.columbia.edu/cu/lweb/projects/digital/apis>, is another extremely valuable resource for checking editions. All include key bibliography on specific texts.

BIBLIOGRAPHY

Adams, J. N. 1977. *The Vulgar Latin of the Letters of Claudius Terentianus*. Manchester: Manchester University Press.

——2003. *Bilingualism and the Latin Language*. Cambridge: Cambridge University Press.

Anderson, R. D., P. J. Parsons, and R. G. M. Nisbet. 1979. 'Elegiacs by Gallus from Qasr Ibrim', *Journal of Roman Studies* 69: 125–55.

Bagnall, R. S. 1995. *Reading Papyri, Writing Ancient History*. London: Routledge.

Beness, J. L., and T. Hillard. 2003. 'The First Romans at Philae (*CIL* I^{2}.2.2937a)', *Zeitschrift für Papyrologie und Epigraphik* 144: 203–7.

Cavenaile, R. 1952. 'Quelques aspects de l'apport linguistique du grec au latin d'Égypte', *Aegyptus* 32: 191–203.

——1958. *Corpus Papyrorum Latinarum*. Wiesbaden: Harrassowitz.

Clackson, J., and G. Horrocks. 2007. *The Blackwell History of the Latin Language*. Oxford: Blackwell.

Cugusi, P. 1981. 'Gli ostraca latini dello Wâdi Fawâkhir: Per la storia del latino', in M. Simonetti and G. Simonetti (eds), *Letterature comparate, problemi e metodo: Studi in onore di Ettore Paratore*, vol. 2. Bologna: Pàtron, 719–53.

——(ed.) 1992–2002. *Corpus Epistularum Latinarum: Papyris Tabulis Ostracis Servatarum*, 3 vols. Florence: Gonnelli.

Daris, S. 1991. 'Latino ed Egitto romano', in *Il bilinguismo degli antichi*. Genoa: University of Genoa, 47–81.

Dickey, E. 2009. 'The Greek and Latin Languages in the Papyri', in R. S. Bagnall (ed.), *The Oxford Handbook of Papyrology*. Oxford: Oxford University Press, 149–69.

Evans, T. V. 2010. 'Identifying the Language of the Individual in the Zenon Archive', in T. V. Evans and D. D. Obbink (eds), *The Language of the Papyri*. Oxford: Oxford University Press, 51–70.

Fewster, P. 2002. 'Bilingualism in Roman Egypt', in J. N. Adams, M. Janse, and S. Swain (eds), *Bilingualism in Ancient Society: Language Contact and the Written Word*. Oxford: Oxford University Press, 220–45.

Ghiretti, E. 1996. 'Note sul bilinguismo greco-latino dell' Egitto romano', *Aevum Antiquum* 9: 275–98.

Halla-aho, H. 2003. 'Scribes and the Letters of Claudius Terentianus', in H. Solin, M. Leiwo, and H. Halla-aho (eds), *Latin vulgaire—latin tardif VI: Actes du VIe Colloque International sur le Latin Vulgaire et Tardif*. Hildesheim: Olms-Weidmann, 245–52.

Kaimio, J. 1979. 'Latin in Roman Egypt', in *Actes du XVe Congrès International de Papyrologie*, vol. 3. Brussels: Fondation Égyptologique Reine Élisabeth, 27–33.

Katzoff, R. 1996. 'The Latin Texts', in B. Porten et al. (eds), *The Elephantine Papyri in English: Three Millennia of Cross-Cultural Continuity and Change*. Leiden: Brill, 608–9.

Kramer, J. 1993. 'Die Wiener Liste von Soldaten der III. und XXII. Legion (P. Vindob. L 2)', *Zeitschrift für Papyrologie und Epigraphik* 97: 147–58.

Kruschwitz, P. 2010. '*Romanes eunt domus!* Linguistic Aspects of the Sub-Literary Latin in Pompeian Wall Inscriptions', in T. V. Evans and D. O. Obbink (eds), *The Language of the Papyri*. Oxford: Oxford University Press, 156–70.

Rochette, B. 1996a. 'Sur le bilinguisme dans l'Égypte gréco-romaine', *Chronique d'Égypte* 71: 153–68.

——1996b. 'Papyrologica bilinguia Graeco-latina', *Aegyptus* 76: 57–79.

——1997. *Le Latin dans le monde grec: Recherches sur la diffusion de la langue et de lettres latines dans les provinces hellénophones de l'empire romain*. Brussels: Latomus.

Stein, A. 1915. *Untersuchungen zur Geschichte und Verwaltung Aegyptens unter roemischer Herrschaft*. Stuttgart: Metzlersche Buchhandlung.

CHAPTER 32

GREEK LANGUAGE, EDUCATION, AND LITERARY CULTURE*

AMIN BENAISSA

WHEN Egypt came under the rule of Rome, all inhabitants of the province who were not citizens of Alexandria or the two Greek *poleis* of Naukratis and Ptolemais were, from the Roman juridical point of view, 'Egyptians'. For pragmatic and historical reasons, however, the Roman administration preserved Greek as the de facto official language of the province and continued to differentiate and favour a hereditary class of 'Greeks' among the landowning elite of the nome capitals, who enjoyed a lower rate of taxation, filled the towns' magistracies, and supplied a ready pool from which to select provincial administrators (Bowman and Rathbone 1992). For this redefined status group, it was ideologically and practically vital to continue affirming a distinct 'Greek' identity against the rest of the 'Egyptian' population.

Besides institutional determinants such as membership in the gymnasium (a hereditary privilege controlled through a rigorous examination), education and pride in the Greek language, its literary traditions, and the values embodied in them—in short, what Greeks called *paideia*—played a fundamental role in maintaining a stable Greek identity, a sense of continuity with the idealized classical past, and solidarity with other Greeks in the Roman east. Self-perceived cultural distinction reinforced and legitimized socio-economic privilege, especially since the acquisition of Greek culture presupposed some degree of wealth and leisure. Greek literature, nevertheless, was not restricted to consolidating the identity of a closed group of elites, for it could be co-opted by individuals of primarily Egyptian background to participate in the dominant culture, negotiate a supplementary Hellenic identity, and climb the social ladder.

It is partly against this complex socio-historical backdrop that the full-fledged Greek education and vigorous literary culture outlined in this chapter should be viewed. The important place of Greek literature in Roman Egypt is further underlined by the heritage of the Ptolemaic period, when Alexandria was a beacon of learning and culture in the Hellenistic world,

* I am grateful to Professor Peter Parsons for some helpful comments on a draft of this chapter.

a role it continued to play in the Imperial period, albeit in a significantly transformed Mediterranean context. After a brief characterization of the Greek spoken and written in Roman Egypt, this chapter examines the stages and social aspects of Greek education, the range of the period's literary papyri and what they reveal about the tastes and identities of their readers, and finally the literary and scholarly life of Roman Alexandria (the chronological framework is roughly the first three centuries CE).

Greek Language

The Greek language retained its prominence in Roman Egypt, as it did in other provinces of the Roman east with a former Greek presence. Greek continued to be the language of the administration, most legal documents, the urban elite, and the literature they read. The use of Egyptian Demotic for documents declined markedly in the Roman period, while Latin was restricted principally to the military and the minority of Roman citizens in the province. The Greek written and spoken in Egypt in this period was a version of the so-called *koine*, or 'common' dialect, that developed in the fourth century BCE and became widespread throughout the Near East after the diaspora of Greeks following Alexander the Great's conquests. This was a simplified and standardized form of Attic–Ionic Greek comparable to that encountered in the Gospels.

The reconstruction of the phonology, morphology, and syntax of this dialect as it was spoken in Roman Egypt relies primarily on the evidence of documentary papyri (Gignac 1976–81; summaries in Gignac 1985 and Dickey 2009). The irregularities exhibited by less proficient writers often furnish clues to the character of the spoken language, provided they are sufficiently frequent and consistent. The use of written evidence for the study of a once living and changing language, however, is not straightforward. On the one hand, variations could be insignificant, idiosyncratic, or due to scribal incompetence; on the other, the written language was naturally more uniform and conservative than speech. It is also difficult to date linguistic changes precisely on the basis of writing alone. Nevertheless, the sheer quantity and variety of documents and comparisons with modern Greek and other sources for *koine* Greek inspire sufficient confidence in the validity of the above method.

Orthographic variations, particularly the interchanges between some letters to represent the same phoneme, show that the pronunciation of Greek in Roman Egypt was closer to modern than to classical Greek. A pervasive feature was the merger of once distinct vowels, notably *αι* and *ε* (pronounced /ɛ/), *ι*, *ει*, and *η* (all approximating /i/), and *οι* and *υ* (representing /y/). Several phonetic phenomena, such as the equation of voiced and voiceless stops (e.g. *δ* and *τ*) and the liquids *λ* and *ρ*, suggest a significant level of 'bilingual interference' from Egyptian, although the extent to which monolingual speakers of Greek also acquired and exhibited these features in their daily speech is arguable. By the Roman period, Greek had also completely lost its pitch accent in favour of a stress accent, all distinction between long and short vowels, and probably all aspiration (initial *h* sound). In morphology, the declensional and conjugation systems were simplified considerably, irregular and complex forms becoming altered on the analogy of more regular forms. Apart from phonetic influences and some technical words inherited from the Ptolemaic period, Greek continued to be impervious to Egyptian loan-words, in marked contrast to Egyptian vis-à-vis Greek (as shown later by Coptic; see Chapter 35). Latin, on the other hand, the language of the new rulers of Egypt, does make gradual inroads into Greek vocabulary and syntax, reaching a peak of influence in the fourth century (Dickey 2003). Syntax remains a poorly studied aspect of the Greek language of the period, in which there is much scope for research (Porter 2007).

Greek Literary Education

The constantly evolving spoken *koine* was by the Roman period far removed from the language of the texts that had come to define the classical canon of Greek literature, such as Homer, the tragic and comic dramatists, Plato, and Demosthenes. The growing gap between everyday Greek and classical Greek made a rigorous education all the more imperative for the ability to read and understand literature and to write according to its models—in other words, for admittance to that narrow circle of 'cultured' Greeks, or *pepaideumenoi*. For Roman Egypt, we are particularly fortunate that the paper trail of the educational process survives. Various types of student exercises, teachers' models, and school texts have been preserved on papyrus, potsherds, and tablets, ranging from rudimentary first steps in writing to grammatical drills to advanced poetical and rhetorical compositions. In addition, private letters from parents to their children (or vice versa) and other documents occasionally illuminate the social context and organization of education, parental attitudes and levels of involvement, and students' concerns. Despite this wealth of primary materials, the subject received a solid and systematic grounding only in the relatively recent work of Raffaella Cribiore (1996a, 2001; cf. also Morgan 1998, problematic in places).

As in the rest of the contemporary Graeco-Roman world, education in Roman Egypt was a privately organized affair, unregulated by the state. Parents had to arrange, monitor, and determine the extent of their children's education, depending on their means, the local availability of teachers, and the expected future roles of their children in society. Only once in the mid-third century do we hear of a 'public grammarian' who received a stipend from the city council of Oxyrhynchus, but nothing is known about his specific remit (*P Oxy*. XLVII 3366). The physical setting of education could be rather informal and depended on the individual teacher. A schoolroom preserving a wall covered with poetic exhortations to students has been unearthed in Dakhla Oasis (Fig. 32.1; see Cribiore, Davoli, and Ratzan 2008). Despite its non-institutional character, education followed a broadly uniform cultural matrix throughout the Greek world, including Egypt. Cribiore and Morgan have shown that the evidence of the papyri largely agrees with literary sources on Graeco-Roman educational practices in the Imperial period such as Quintilian and Libanius, but helps to correct the idealistic and prescriptive tendencies of these writers by providing a more direct, variegated, and concrete perspective.

Greek education is traditionally divided into three stages, although actual practice may not have been so schematic (see below). The first stage, taught by the *grammatodidaskalos* ('teacher of letters'), attracted a greater number and wider variety of students, providing them with reading and writing skills and basic numeracy. In this and the succeeding stages, the main methodological principles governing education were those of imitation and

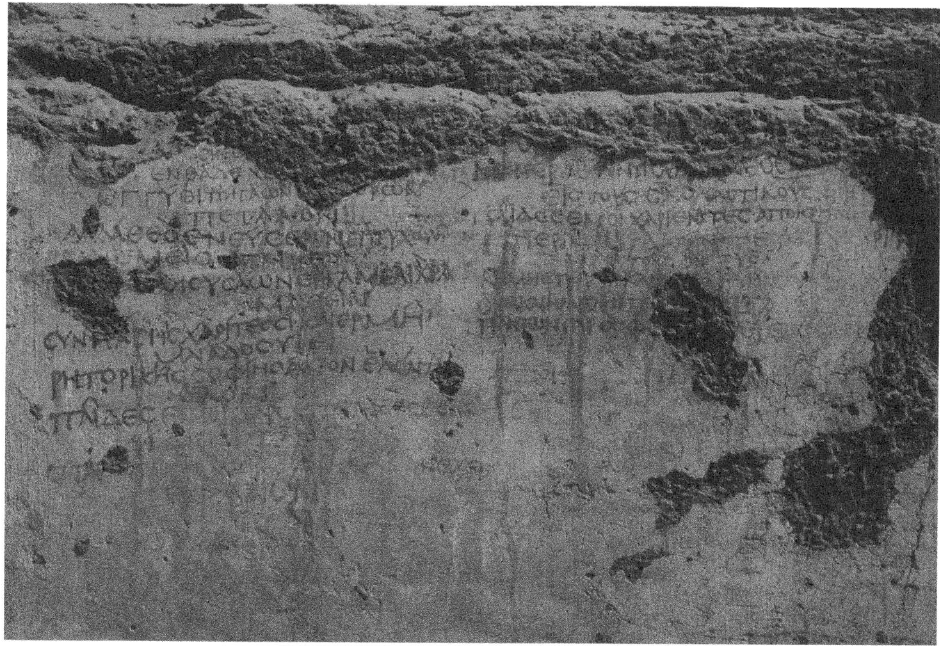

FIG. 32.1 The wall of a schoolroom painted by a teacher with short epigrams addressed to his students. This and other recent discoveries in the Great Oasis demonstrate that Greek education and literary culture were alive and well even in such remote parts of the province. Trimithis (Amheida), House B1, Room 15, east wall. First half of the fourth century CE

Photo courtesy of Amheida Excavations, New York University.

embryonic progression, each successive element building upon the previous one in a gradually ascending order of complexity. Thus, a pupil learning to read would usually begin with letters of the alphabet, proceed to all possible combinations of vowels and consonants in syllables, followed by words (themselves sometimes in an ascending number of syllables), sentences, and short passages. Students were confronted with a smattering of classical literature from this early stage. Although they may not have understood or even been able to read properly what they were copying, they were often given maxims and short passages from literature, especially Homer and Euripides, to copy for writing practice or to memorize. Wordlists employed in the learning of reading and writing were sometimes arranged in thematic groups (e.g. gods, mythological figures, birds) and thus served to build a cultural vocabulary.

After the acquisition of basic reading and writing skills, some children went on to learn grammar and study classical literature at the hands of a 'grammarian' (*grammatikos*). This was the essential formative stage of a 'liberal education', or 'culture' (*paideia*), and was focused on the reading and explication of poetry. Homer's *Iliad* was the staple element in the early educational diet. When a mother inquired from a teacher what her son was reading, the answer was 'the sixth book'—undoubtedly a reference to book 6 of the *Iliad* with its celebrated vignettes of life in besieged Troy (*P Oxy*. VI 930). The plays of Euripides, the most accessible of the classical tragedians, also figured prominently in the grammarian's classroom, with the moralistic orations of Isocrates, the comedies of Menander, and fables following closely behind in popularity. A common trait binding the selections of these authors (apart from Homer) is their sententious content, for they are typically interspersed with maxims (*gnomai*) and thus were perceived as effective vehicles for the moral instruction of children. In teaching literature, the grammarian's emphasis was on the elucidation of technical aspects (vocabulary, grammar, accentuation, tropes) and of content (paraphrases, explanation of places, persons, and events) rather than on holistic criticism. Students also learned declensions, conjugations, and grammatical concepts systematically, a Roman period innovation reflecting perhaps the growing distance of everyday speech from literary language. Composition does not appear to have been cultivated at this stage, except for the preparation of short paraphrases and elementary versification; but letters from children to their parents suggest that students were encouraged to develop epistolary skills as a means of displaying their education.

Finally, in the third stage, ambitious and gifted young men of the elite (from about the age of 15) learned the art of proper speech and rhetorical composition, prerequisite skills for eventual public careers, by attending the lectures of a *rhetor* or *sophistes*. Preliminary exercises, called *progymnasmata*, provided the student of rhetoric a transition from the predominantly poetic world of the grammarian by taking as subjects stock situations or characters from epic poetry or tragedy. The commonest types of exercise were *ethopoiiai*, in which the student was asked to impersonate a mythological figure responding to a particular situation, and *enkomia*, speeches of praise (e.g. the 'encomium of the fig' in *P Oxy*. XVII 2084). Strikingly, many such compositions found in Egypt are not in prose like the examples known from literary sources, but in verse. Whether this was an Egyptian peculiarity or the result of poorer evidence from elsewhere remains a debatable question. More advanced students engaged in the composition of declamations (*meletai*), usually on historical deliberative themes or fictitious forensic ones. One papyrus gives as an assignment for one such declamation a subject inspired by Thucydides' *Peloponnesian Wars*: 'For proposing to put to death the male population of Mytilene Cleon is accused of demagogy' (*P Oxy*. XXIV 2400; cf. *P Oxy*. LXXI 4810). This example implies that the study of rhetoric was accompanied by close scrutiny of the classical orators and historians, who were meant to serve as constant models.

It is important to stress that the three educational levels sketched here were not always discrete. A particular teacher could impart instruction at varying levels in one and the same classroom (as shown by tablets shared by different students, e.g. Cribiore 1996a, no. 388), and the contents of the different stages sometimes overlapped, borders being especially porous between advanced grammatical and early rhetorical education, where poetry and rhetoric freely intermingled. Progress through these three broad tracks was not simply meritocratic, but was heavily affected by socio-economic factors such as wealth, status, gender, and the resulting professional ambitions or expectations, not to mention the sometimes difficult availability of teachers for higher levels (compare *P Oxy*. VI 930; *SB* XXII 15708). Grammarians are not clearly attested in villages, for instance, so that only relatively well-off rural families could send their children to receive higher instruction in cities. Similarly, the best rhetorical education was to be obtained in Alexandria, where only the wealthy city elite could afford to send their children (together with 'pedagogues'—usually slaves—to look after them and supervise their studies). The economically privileged character of literary education emerges clearly from a speech in defence of an orphan's guardian, in which a distinction is made between the suitability of *paideia* for the better off and of a trade apprenticeship for the poorer lot (*P Mich.* IX 532 as corrected in *BL* IX 161). Although primary and grammatical education was not closed to women, and there is evidence for female teachers, women's education was even more tightly bound to socio-economic status: only girls from the upper classes could expect some instruction, which often did not proceed beyond the elementary stage (Fig. 32.2). Rhetorical training, a propaedeutic for public life, was a purely male affair. With its unwavering focus on the old authors and reverence for the classical past, Greek education mostly marginalized the Egyptian reality surrounding it. The few exceptions, such as a narrative about Amenophis written in an elementary hand that may be a student's (*P Oxy.* XLII 3011) and a couple of hymns to the Nile, do not significantly challenge this impression (Cribiore 1996b: 515–25).

That education was key to professional or social advancement in some circles was keenly felt. Upon his arrival in the port of Misenum in Italy, a young recruit in the Roman navy from the village of Philadelphia composed a fine letter to reassure his father and express thanks that 'you educated me well and I hope thereby to have quick advancement' (*Sel. Pap.* I 112). For those who, for various circumstances, could not progress beyond the elementary stage, the main benefit to their adult lives was functional literacy and a superficial familiarity with some important Hellenic cultural symbols. Those who were privileged enough to pursue a grammatical and rhetorical education acquired a decisive cultural capital that integrated them in a socio-political elite for which literary culture and monopoly of 'right' speech were closely associated with high status, authority, and power; they were thereby well placed for participating in civic life and pursuing careers in public administration and law. The more serious students had the potential to become amateur or even professional scholars, while a

FIG. 32.2 Portrait on the mummy of a woman from the Fayum, identifying her as Hermione *grammatike*, a word that may denote either a woman teacher of literature or an educated lady (see Montserrat 1997). She was about 25 at the time of her death. First century CE

Photo courtesy of the Mistress and Fellows, Girton College, Cambridge.

few gifted ones ended up as poets, orators, and writers in their own right (see below). Advanced students of literature and rhetoric already had opportunities to display their learning and talents in contests organized by cities. *P Oxy.* XXII 2338 (see Coles 1975) lists Oxyrhynchite participants in annual contests of trumpeters, heralds, and poets held in Naukratis, who as a result enjoyed exemption from taxation and honorary Naukratite citizenship; their ages range from 15 to 24, including a poet aged 19 who is 'learning letters', that is, still a student (some of the poets, it is worth remarking, have purely Egyptian names).

Beyond the public glare of spectators, educated adults could exhibit their Greek culture in everyday life. In a business letter to an estate manager (*P Flor.* II 259), the apparently exasperated sender added in the margin the first two lines of *Iliad* book 2, copying twice the phrase 'all night they slept'—a pointed accusation of the addressee's listlessness? (For other literary allusions or quotations in letters, see *P Oxy.* XXXIV 2728.9 with Pruneti 1996: 396–7; *W Chr.* 478; *SPP* XX 61.) A bilingual tax collector, the Socrates of Karanis mentioned below, even amused himself by translating Egyptian names of taxpayers into Greek, using in one instance an obscure word found only in the learned poet Callimachus (Youtie 1970). Others gave their private letters a literary flavour (e.g. *P Oxy.* LV 3812) or demonstrated their culture through the conspicuous consumption of luxury book-rolls.

Literary Papyri and their Readers

The works read by the educated stratum of the population are preserved in hundreds of fragments of papyrus book-rolls, the bulk of them from the Roman era. These literary papyri are celebrated chiefly for having resuscitated long-lost authors and works, thereby significantly expanding and sometimes revolutionizing our knowledge of ancient Greek literature. From a socio-historical perspective, they are also valuable for revealing the literary tastes and activities of the period as well as scribal practices and aspects of book production (the latter subject will not be broached here, but it should be mentioned that our period saw the beginning of the transition from roll to codex). Despite their chance survival, the sheer range, variety, and quantity of authors and works represented in the papyri of the first three centuries CE are remarkable, especially when compared with the period following the fourth century (Maehler 1998). They reflect a vibrant Hellenic cultural milieu in towns of the Nile Valley like Oxyrhynchus (Krüger 1990: 144–260; Bowman et al. 2007; Parsons 2007: 137–58) and Hermopolis (van Minnen and Worp 1993), and even in some villages of the Fayum (van Minnen 1998).

The frequency of papyri of various authors could serve as an impressionistic guide to literary tastes, but such 'statistics' should be used with caution given the papyri's random survival, their uneven chronological and geographical dispersal, editorial choice, and the continual publication of new texts (Willis 1968; Krüger 1990: 214–56). The most popular authors represent by and large an extension of the canonical authors read in school. Towering far above the rest was Homer, the focal point of Greek culture ('not a man but a god', according to a school exercise), especially his *Iliad*, whose Roman period papyri constitute about a quarter of published literary papyri, not counting the extensive apparatus of reading aids (commentaries, glosses, paraphrases, summaries) required for comprehending such an archaic author. Following behind 'the Poet' were many authors familiar to a modern audience, although the range of their works preserved in the papyri (especially the poets') is much wider than that which survived through medieval transmission: Hesiod (not only his two well-known didactic poems but also his mythological catalogue poetry), the odes of Pindar, the Attic dramatists (especially Euripides), Plato's dialogues, and the fifth- and fourth-century historians (Herodotus, Thucydides, Xenophon) and orators (Demosthenes and Isocrates taking pride of place).

This generally conservative taste and focus on canonical authors underscores the centrality of the classical past for Greek self-identity in the Imperial period (Swain 1996: 65–100). It is instructive to observe, however, that poets of the Hellenistic period, such as Callimachus, Apollonius Rhodius, and Euphorion, many of whose works did not make it through the early medieval bottleneck, were still avidly read. In contrast to Byzantine tastes, New Comedy and particularly Menander were more popular than the Old Comedy of Aristophanes. Contemporary literature, although more sparsely attested, was not altogether neglected, and papyri illustrate how Egypt participated in the new literary trends of the Imperial period (Reardon 1971). Chief among these was the 'novel' (Stephens and Winkler 1995), usually romances telling of the separation, adventures, and reunion of two noble adolescent lovers or more salacious narratives with scandalous heroes and satiric undertones like the *Iolaos*, in which a young man pretends to be a eunuch devotee of the goddess Cybele to gain access to his paramour (*P Oxy.* XLII 3010). Although a lighter type of literature, some of these works are written in a rhetorically accomplished style and polished language, suggesting that they were meant to be appreciated by a refined audience. Such rhetorical attainment was in keeping with the contemporary 'Second Sophistic' movement (see below), members of which, like Dio Chrysostom, Aelius Aristides, Lucian, and Favorinus, have left scattered witnesses in the papyri. Imperial period historians and geographers (Strabo, Josephus, possibly Arrian), philosophers (Philo, Cornutus, Plutarch), and poets (Oppian, Babrius, Ps.-Manetho, *Sibylline Oracles*) also make occasional appearances.

Among the papyri can also be detected more scholarly and learned readers who sought rare or difficult works, whether lyric poetry or specialist philosophy, and technical works like treatises, commentaries, and lexica. Besides their non-canonical content, the papyri they read are often recognizable from their marginal annotations, critical signs, and informed corrections of the text (Turner 1980: 92–4). The intellectuals who possessed them were probably those members of society who proudly bear the title of *philosophos* (not necessarily in the strict sense) in everyday documents (Pruneti 1996). Many will have had an educational background in Alexandria, maintained contact with the cultural capital, and even exercised didactic functions (*P Hamb.* I 37). The postscript of a letter from Oxyrhynchus vividly illustrates the world of the scholar, in which erudite books were eagerly sought among friendly circles, exchanged, and copied. The unknown but clearly learned sender requests from a friend who was probably in Alexandria: 'Make and send me copies of books 6 and 7 of Hypsicrates' *Characters in Comedy*; for Harpocration says they are among Pollio's books, but it is likely that others too have got them. He also has prose (?) epitomes of Thersagoras' *Myths of Tragedy*' (*P Oxy.* XVIII 2192, re-edited by Hatzilambrou 2007). This note reinforces the impression of strong cultural links binding Alexandria and provincial cities like Oxyrhynchus, for both Harpocration and (Valerius) Pollio are identifiable with known Alexandrian scholars (see below).

Not only were the province's inhabitants consumers of literature, but they were capable of producing their own. A number of original poems and rhetorical declamations have survived, sometimes in autograph form (Dorandi 2000: 51–75), most of which were composed either in an advanced educational context or for particular occasions such as festivals, contests, or official celebrations. The following examples give a flavour of the *pièces d'occasion* produced and appreciated in the towns of Roman Egypt: a hymn to Hermes leading to the praise of a young gymnasiarch, who is notably described as 'a man learned in the Muses' arts' (*P Oxy.* VII 1015); a speech in honour of some individual delivered by a professional rhetor in the gymnasium of Hermopolis (*P Brem.* 46); a dramatic performance in which the god Apollo announces the accession of Hadrian (*P Giss. Lit.* 4.4); a poem celebrating Diocletian and probably performed before dignitaries on the occasion of the Capitoline Games in Oxyrhynchus (*P Oxy.* LXIII 4352). Some poets, such as Anubion of Diospolis, author of an astrological didactic poem (see *P Oxy.* LXVI pp. 57–66), and Soterichus of Oasis (Livrea 2002), may have begun their careers in similar local contexts but found fame beyond Egypt, foreshadowing the empire-wide prominence of poets from the Nile Valley in late antiquity (Miguélez-Cavero 2008). Literary entertainment was also available in the towns in the form of performances by actors of Homeric scenes (*homeristai*; Husson 1993) and poetic competitions during festivals or games (*P Oxy.* III 519; VII 1025, 1050; *P Oslo* III 189; *SB* IV 7336) as well as theatrical shows ranging from popular mime to lofty tragedy (for actors' copies on papyrus, see Gammacurta 2006).

Although many papyri were recovered in uncontrolled excavations or were acquired on the antiquities market without any knowledge of their provenance and circumstances of discovery, one of the more exciting trends in recent scholarship has been the attempt to connect groups of literary papyri with the 'private library' of an individual or family, thanks to some knowledge of the archaeological context and the association of literary papyri with documentary archives (literary texts were not infrequently copied on the back of documents or vice versa; Lama 1991; cf. Clarysse 1983). These associations confirm the strong link between elevated socio-political status and literary culture. One find of literary texts from Oxyrhynchus comprising a varied collection of the classics is believed to relate to the well-known family of Sarapion alias Apollonianus, whose most illustrious member was governor of the Arsinoite and Hermopolite nomes and gymnasiarch and councillor of Oxyrhynchus in the early third century (Funghi and Messeri Savorelli 1992 with the correctives and caution of Houston 2007). A smaller group of papyri, including rare items like the *Charms* of Julius Africanus and an unknown history of Sikyon, was probably inherited by an Aurelia Ptolemais from her father, a wealthy man who served as president of the council of Oxyrhynchus (Bagnall 1992). Other anonymous private book collections can be glimpsed from lists of books and concentrations of papyri in particular finds (Houston 2009). Public libraries, incidentally, are not positively attested in Roman Egypt, though it has long been speculated that they existed in gymnasia.

Where their provenance is known, the great majority of literary papyri have been excavated from *metropoleis* rather than villages, reflecting the greater Hellenic character of the former over the latter. The villages of the Fayum (an area of heavy Greek settlement in the Ptolemaic period), however, have also yielded a significant number of literary texts, suggesting that their elites aspired to the same culture as their urban counterparts (van Minnen 1998). Some of these texts are associated with veterans and officials. The best known is the above-mentioned Socrates of Karanis, a tax collector and owner of a grand house in the village, in which was found a small collection of literary fragments including Menander, Callimachus, and two grammatical treatises (van Minnen 1998: 132–3). Interestingly, some of the

Greek literary texts from the villages of the Fayum were discovered in temple areas and belong to archives that include Egyptian literary and religious texts. Their readership apparently consisted of bicultural priestly families who appropriated and established points of contact with the Graeco-Roman culture of the urban elite. Similar milieus can be postulated to account for the continued circulation of Greek translations of Egyptian texts (e.g. 'The Myth of the Sun's Eye'; West 1969) and devotional literature inspired by Egyptian models (e.g. the aretalogies of Isis and Imouthes-Asklepios in *P Oxy*. XI 1380–1) (see Quack 2009). These works are a reminder that Greek literary expression, far from being the preserve of a parochial elite, could also serve the interests of the native tradition and help infiltrate or even challenge the politically dominant culture. The 'nationalistic' oracular literature translated from Demotic is another case in point (Koenen 2002).

Alexandria as Intellectual and Cultural Centre

As already noted, those parents of the provincial elite wishing to give their children the best grammatical and rhetorical education sent them to Alexandria, the traditional seat of Greek culture and learning, which radiated both inwards towards the Egyptian *chora* and outwards towards the wider Graeco-Roman world. Alexandria had certainly lost some of its pre-eminent status as a centre of literary culture and scholarship since Ptolemy VIII expelled many of its intellectuals upon ascending the throne in 145 BCE (*FGrH* 270 F 9 = Ath. 4.83). Even before the Imperial period, Rome had supplanted Alexandria as the prime magnet for poets, philosophers, and scholars seeking patronage and well-stocked libraries—including a great number of Alexandrians (Fraser 1972: 474–5; Turner 2007: 157). Writing in the reign of Augustus, Strabo (14.5.15) describes contemporary Rome as full of Tarsian and Alexandrian *philologoi*. The explosive popularity of the Second Sophistic in the late first and second centuries, an archaizing cultural movement promoting rhetorical display and a linguistic and literary revival of the classical past, which was enthusiastically fostered by philhellenic emperors like Hadrian and whose epicentre was in Asia Minor and Athens, also ensured a shift away from Alexandria and towards 'old Greece' among the educated Greek and Roman elite at large.

Despite these changes in the cultural geography of the Mediterranean, philological scholarship and literary production were by no means eclipsed in Roman Alexandria. In addition, the city continued to be a renowned centre for the study of medicine, mathematics, astronomy, and other sciences (witness only Ptolemy, author of the seminal *Almagest*), as well as philosophy and theology, areas that lie outside the scope of this chapter (for an overview, see Fraser 1972: 809–12; Bowman 1986: 227–30). Some of the greatest intellectuals of their time—Strabo, Plutarch, Dio Chrysostom, Aelius Aristides, Lucian, Galen—visited Alexandria and in some cases spent an extended period there. The Alexandrians themselves do not seem to have had doubts about their standing. Their cultural chauvinism manifests itself, for example, in a petition to an early Roman emperor in which they declare that they wish to guard the citizen body of Alexandria from corruption by 'the uncultured and uneducated' (*athreptoi kai anagogoi*), probably a reference to Egyptians and Jews (*C Pap. Iud.* II 150).

The museum of Alexandria, a 'shrine to the Muses' hosting a community of publicly maintained intellectuals and scientists, persisted under the patronage of the Roman emperors. Augustus directly appointed its head priest, a practice apparently maintained by his successors (Strabo 17.1.8). The bookish Claudius built a new wing, where he instituted annual public readings of his Greek histories of Etruria and Carthage (Suet. *Claud.* 42; Ath. 6.37). Caracalla, in contrast, appears to have abolished the benefits enjoyed by the museum's philosophers (Cass. Dio 78.7.3). An apparent novelty of the Roman period is that membership in the museum was now also conferred as an honour, sometimes by the emperor himself, to distinguished civic or military officials who were not necessarily scholars, littérateurs, or philosophers, although it is possible that some may have entertained literary ambitions (Lewis 1995). Like all members, they enjoyed the privileges of tax exemption (*ateleia*) and, if they resided in Alexandria, free maintenance (*sitesis*). Although often seen as a degeneration of the original function of the museum, such a practice demonstrates both imperial promotion and control of traditional Greek cultural institutions and the high prestige still associated with the museum.

The fate of the twin-sister institution of the museum, the famous library, is less clear. The topic has generated endless debate fed by contradictory ancient sources, uncertainty about the physical relationship between the museum and the library, and a fixation with identifying a single apocalyptic event marking the end of this semi-legendary establishment (Canfora 1989; el-Abbadi 1990; a brief but sober appraisal of the question in Bagnall 2002). The late first-century writer Plutarch (*Vit. Caes.* 49) says that the 'great library' was destroyed in the fire started by Caesar when he was besieged in the royal palace of Alexandria in 48 BCE, but some scholars have discredited this statement in confrontation with other ancient sources (particularly Cass. Dio 42.38.2); they suggest that only certain warehouses by the harbour in which books were stored caught fire and that the library, indivisible from the museum, met its real end in 272, when the whole Brucheion quarter in which the museum was situated was destroyed (Amm. Marc. 22.16.15). A confident solution is simply impossible on the basis of the available evidence. Whether the main library was destroyed or not, wholly or in part, some substantial collection of books must have underpinned the continuing scholarly activity and renown of Alexandria during the Roman period. Revealingly, Domitian, in his effort to rebuild the libraries of Rome that burned in the fire of 80 CE, sent scribes to Alexandria to copy lost works (Suet. *Dom.* 20; cf. Cass. Dio 66.24). The more shadowy 'daughter library' in the Serapeum would also have persisted until the destruction of the latter in 391.

The far from stagnant literary life of Roman Alexandria can be best illustrated by focusing on the age of Hadrian, an emperor who actively encouraged Greek literature and culture. During his visit to Egypt in 130, he is said to have 'put forth many questions to the professors in the museum' (SHA *Hadr.* 20). One of the heads of the museum under his reign was Julius Vestinus, an equestrian procurator and a scholar–sophist who eventually rose to become director of the imperial secretariat (Fein 1994: 267–70). Although apparently not an Alexandrian, he must have been at home in the city's intellectual climate, since he was responsible for epitomizing the enormous lexicon in ninety-five books by the first-century Alexandrian scholar Pamphilus (non-extant, but an ancestor of the partially surviving lexicon of Hesychius). At the same period and in a more technical vein, Nikanor was busy producing several works on punctuation, earning himself the sobriquet of 'Punctuator' (*stigmatias*), and even a treatise on Alexandria itself.

It was probably during Hadrian's stay in the city that the Alexandrian orator Aelius Sarapion wrote a panegyric on the emperor; he was also the author of a rhetorical treatise and various speeches, such as a declamation on the characteristically sophistic subject of 'whether Plato justly banned Homer from the Republic' (Suda, s.v. *Σαραπίων* 115). Before undertaking their fateful trip up the Nile, Hadrian and his young lover Antinoos participated in a lion hunt, which the Alexandrian Pancrates vividly related in an epic–encomiastic poem. In it he proposed that the colour of the red lotus derived from the blood spilled by the slain lion and renamed it accordingly 'the flower of Antinoos'. Gratified by the poem, Hadrian granted him membership in the museum (Garzya 1984; Fein 1994: 107–12). Antinoos was subsequently to become a popular literary theme in Egypt (see *P Oxy*. LXIII pp. 2–3). It is probably from among the entourage of Hadrian that another member of the museum, the self-styled 'Homeric poet' Areius, left an epigram inscribed on the Colossus of Memnon in Thebes (*IGLCM* 37; Fein 1994: 114–15). The best-known Alexandrian poet of this (and indeed the Imperial) period, however, is Dionysius Periegetes ('the Guide'), author of a popular didactic poem in hexameters describing the inhabited world (Amato 2005). His name, origin, and time are cleverly given away in two acrostics (lines 112–34, 513–32), where the initial letter of each verse spells out 'Dionysius of those within the Pharus (i.e. Alexandria)' and 'god Hermes (perhaps a reference to the deified Antinoos), in the time of Hadrian'.

Philological scholarship in Alexandria was not, of course, confined to the Hadrianic age, although it appears to have suffered a marked decline in the third century, and, in contrast to the early Ptolemaic period, the city was generally more an exporter than a magnet of scholarly talent and innovation. Standing at the threshold of the Roman period were some of the last representatives of the great period of Hellenistic scholarship, men like Tryphon, one of the key founders of normative grammar, and Didymus 'Brazen-Guts', who synthesized much of prior scholarship in an astonishing number of books. In the reigns of Augustus and Tiberius, the continuation of the Alexandrian critical and exegetical tradition is represented in the learned commentaries of Theon on the Classical and Hellenistic poets, the etymological Homeric dictionary of Apion (also notorious for his attacks on Jews in his *Aegyptiaca*), and the wide-ranging output of Seleucus 'Homericus'. One of the more original developments in scholarship was the systematic study of grammar and the codification of language. Among the greatest and most influential exponents of this trend must be counted Apollonius Dyscolus ('the Surly') of the second century, the first scholar to offer a systematic theory of syntax, and his son Herodian, who produced an exhaustive treatment of Greek accentuation. A contemporary Alexandrian, Hephaesteion, who is perhaps identical to the homonymous teacher of the emperor Lucius Verus (SHA *Verus* 2), wrote an extensive treatise on poetic metres. Lexicography and interest in things Athenian represent another popular strand of the scholarship of the time, which was partly motivated by the purist ambition of reviving the Attic dialect and the culture and values of classical Athens. Pamphilus' lexicon has already been mentioned. In the late second century, Valerius Harpocration composed an alphabetically ordered *Lexicon of the Ten Orators*, a work distinguished by a wealth of historical details on fifth- and fourth-century Athens. This same Harpocration may be attested in the above-quoted letter from Oxyrhynchus (*P Oxy*. 2192) in company with another known Atticist lexicographer, Valerius Pollio. While it is admittedly true that some of these scholars taught and lived in Rome, at least for parts of their careers, it must be remembered that their intellectual nourishment and rise to prominence occurred in Alexandria.

Naukratis, Alexandria's neighbour and the oldest Greek city in Egypt, boasted its own luminaries (Schubert 1995). Julius Pollux, who rose to obtain the prestigious imperial chair of rhetoric in Athens in 178, is known today chiefly for his *Onomasticon*, a thematically ordered lexicon covering the terminology of a wide range of learned and everyday spheres. His contemporary and compatriot Athenaeus lived mostly in Rome, but he may have developed much of the dazzling erudition displayed in his *Deipnosophistae* in Alexandria. This work in fifteen books purports to report a series of dinner party conversations among a group of learned banqueters, who discourse on a wide array of subjects, especially relating to food and drink, and string together extensive quotations of ancient poets, historians, and scholars to illustrate their points, making the *Deipnosophistae* a celebrated treasure-trove of citations of lost works (Olson 2006–12).

In contrast to Naukratis, famous orators are noticeably lacking from Alexandria. It has often been pointed out, for example, that no Alexandrian orators are mentioned in Philostratus' *Lives of the Sophists* as representatives of the Second Sophistic. A student's letter to his father complaining of a 'shortage of *sophistai* in this city' (understood to be Alexandria) would seem to reinforce this view (*SB* XXII 15708). However, that same letter testifies that it was possible to hear declamations by professional orators in the city, and although no illustrious ones are known, rhetorical education clearly flourished there (Schubert 1995: 184–8; Cribiore 2001: 58). In the first or second century, Aelius Theon of Alexandria wrote a handbook of rhetorical preliminary exercises as well as commentaries on the classical orators (Patillon 1997), while the above-mentioned Aelius Sarapion made a name for himself both as a practising sophist and as a theorist.

A distinctive literary genre that developed specifically in the Alexandrian context was that of the so-called *Acts of the Pagan Martyrs*, also known as the *Acta Alexandrinorum* (Musurillo 1954). This collective modern title refers to a series of works of unknown authorship straddling the documentary and literary spheres and preserved only through papyri. They present in the form of 'trial minutes' (*acta*) partly fictionalized and dramatized confrontations between distinguished Alexandrians and hostile Roman emperors, usually in the setting of an embassy to the imperial court or a trial before the emperor. The 'minutes' involve brazen addresses by Alexandrian noblemen to tyrannical, caricatured emperors, which often result in the pathetic execution of the Alexandrian 'heroes'. This literature is imbued with Alexandrian patriotism and glorification of Alexandria's superior Hellenic culture; it reflects in a distorted light the political tensions and civil disturbances of early Roman Alexandria, especially in relation to the large Jewish community of the city. Their survival through papyri in remote places like villages of the Fayum shows that these works were not merely pamphlets illicitly circulating among disaffected members of Alexandrian aristocratic clubs, but enjoyed a broad appeal among Hellenized elites throughout the province, probably more because of their affirmation of Hellenic identity, their entertainment value, and the provincials' fascination with Alexandria than for political or dissident reasons (so Harker 2008).

At the other end of the spectrum, Greek literary and philosophical traditions were also appropriated for the expression and interpretation of non-Greek ones. In the first century, the Hellenized Egyptian priest Chaeremon, tutor to Nero, offered a Stoic interpretation of Egyptian religion, while Philo developed a Platonic and allegorical exegesis of the Old Testament. About a century later, Clement and after him Origen similarly produced a profound synthesis of Greek philosophy and Christian scripture. These writers were thoroughly steeped in Greek literature and philosophy, even if at times polemical towards them, and were all products of the rich and multifaceted cultural milieu of Roman Alexandria.

Conclusion

When a boy in Roman Oxyrhynchus or Philadelphia began to trace painfully his first Greek letters under the supervision of a *grammatodidaskalos*, there was little prospect of his ending up as a member of the museum of Alexandria. Most of his peers would not attain more than literacy and a rudimentary knowledge of grammar and the 'classics'; but the competence in the normative language and the modicum of literary culture that such an education provided, together with certain institutional elements and other cultural habits, would serve to distinguish them as members of a relatively privileged 'Hellenic' stratum of the population, whose corporate identity as an elite was fostered by Roman rule. Whether middle-class scribes and administrators scribbling lines of Homer in the margins of letters, wealthy magistrates in possession of calligraphic book-rolls, or scholars exchanging obscure treatises, they shared in an empire-wide culture engrossed by the classical Greek past and in a tradition that was primarily literarily constructed. Because of its cultural prestige, Greek literature spread beyond this core group and penetrated even traditional Egyptian milieus such as temples in villages of the Arsinoite nome.

While our picture of education and literary culture in the *metropoleis* is informed by the randomly preserved papyri consumed by their inhabitants, for Alexandria we must rely on more selectively transmitted literary sources, which inevitably focus on 'high' literature and scholarship. They convey the impression of a city striving to live up to its Ptolemaic cultural heritage, regardless of the precise fate of its famous library and despite the undeniable shift to other cultural centres such as Rome and Athens. Although it may not have distinguished itself in Second Sophistic rhetoric then at the height of fashion, Roman Alexandria produced some poets of note and a series of high-profile scholars who made pivotal contributions in literary exegesis, grammar, and lexicography.

The intellectual splendour of Alexandria, however, should not obscure the fact that many *metropoleis* were capable of catering for the minority who proceeded to higher studies in poetry and rhetoric, whether institutionally through their public grammarians (in Oxyrhynchus at least), gymnasia, theatres, and poetry contests, or through the breadth of classical and contemporary literary works circulating in them. Moreover, both metropolite elites completing their higher education in Alexandria and the movement of books to and from the capital maintained a cultural bridge with the *metropoleis*, ensuring that the latest literary tastes and scholarly trends in Alexandria—and indirectly the wider empire—percolated to the rest of the province.

Suggested Reading

Swain (1996) and Whitmarsh (2001) provide theoretically informed discussions of the central role of literature in the construction of Greek cultural identity in the Imperial period (not in specific relation to Egypt, however). Cribiore (2001) is an excellent and accessible account of Greek education in Ptolemaic and Roman Egypt. The best general introduction to literary papyri remains Turner (1980), to be supplemented with the relevant chapters in Bagnall (2009). There are two indispensable electronic databases of literary papyri: the

Leuven Database of Ancient Books, <http://www.trismegistos.org/ldab>, and the Base de données M-P[3] at the Centre de Documentation de Papyrologie Littéraire, <http://www.ulg.ac.be/facphl/services/cedopal>. For short discussions of most of the above mentioned scholars, and further bibliography, see Dickey (2007), General Index. There is unfortunately no global account of the intellectual life of Roman Alexandria similar to that of Fraser (1972) for Ptolemaic Alexandria.

Bibliography

Amato, E. 2005. *Dionisio di Alessandria: Descrizione della terra abitata*. Milan: Bompiani.

Bagnall, R. S. 1992. 'An Owner of Literary Papyri', *Classical Philology* 87: 137–40.

—— 2002. 'Alexandria: Library of Dreams', *Proceedings of the American Philosophical Society* 146: 348–62.

—— (ed.) 2009. *The Oxford Handbook of Papyrology*. Oxford: Oxford University Press.

Bowman, A. K. 1986. *Egypt after the Pharaohs, 332 BC–AD 642: From Alexander to the Arab Conquest*. London: British Museum Press.

—— and D. W. Rathbone. 1992. 'Cities and Administration in Roman Egypt', *Journal of Roman Studies* 82: 107–27.

—— et al. (eds) 2007. *Oxyrhynchus: A City and its Texts*. London: Egypt Exploration Society.

Canfora, L. 1989. *The Vanished Library*. London: Hutchinson Radius.

Clarysse, W. 1983. 'Literary Papyri in Documentary "Archives"', in E. van't Dack et al. (eds), *Egypt and the Hellenistic World*. Leuven: Orientaliste, 43–61.

Coles, R. 1975. 'The Naucratites and their Ghost-Names: *P. Oxy*. 2338 Revised', *Zeitschrift für Papyrologie und Epigraphik* 18: 199–204.

Cribiore, R. 1996a. *Writing, Teachers, and Students in Graeco-Roman Egypt*. Atlanta: Scholars Press.

—— 1996b. 'Gli esercizi scolastici dell'Egitto greco-romano: Cultura letteraria e cultural popolare nella scuola', in O. Pecere and A. Stramaglia (eds), *La letteratura di consumo nel mondo greco-latino*. Cassino: Università degli Studi di Cassino, 505–28.

—— 2001. *Gymnastics of the Mind: Greek Education in Hellenistic and Roman Egypt*. Princeton: Princeton University Press.

—— P. Davoli, and D. M. Ratzan. 2008. 'A Teacher's Dipinto from Trimithis (Dakhleh Oasis)', *Journal of Roman Archaeology* 21: 170–91.

Dickey, E. 2003. 'Latin Influence on the Greek of Documentary Papyri: An Analysis of its Chronological Distribution', *Zeitschrift für Papyrologie und Epigraphik* 145: 249–57.

—— 2007. *Ancient Greek Scholarship*. Oxford: Oxford University Press.

—— 2009. 'The Greek and Latin Languages in the Papyri', in R. S. Bagnall (ed.), *The Oxford Handbook of Papyrology*. Oxford: Oxford University Press, 149–69.

Dorandi, T. 2000. *Le stylet et la tablette: Dans le secret des auteurs antiques*. Paris: Belles Lettres.

el-Abbadi, M. 1990. *The Life and Fate of the Ancient Library of Alexandria*. Paris: Unesco.

Fein, S. 1994. *Die Beziehungen der Kaiser Trajan und Hadrian zu den Litterati*. Stuttgart: Teubner.

Fraser, P. M. 1972. *Ptolemaic Alexandria*. Oxford: Clarendon Press.

Funghi, M. S., and G. Messeri Savorelli. 1992. 'Lo "scriba di Pindaro" e le biblioteche di Ossirinco', *Studi Classici e Orientali* 42: 43–62.

Gammacurta, T. 2006. *Papyrologica scaenica: I copioni teatrali nella tradizione papiracea*. Alexandria: Orso.

Garzya, A. 1984. 'Pankrates', in *Atti del XVII Congresso Internazionale di Papirologia*. Naples: Centro Internazionale per lo Studio dei Papiri Ercolanesi, 319–25.

Gignac, F. T. 1976–81. *A Grammar of the Greek Papyri of the Roman and Byzantine Periods*. Milan: Istituto Editoriale Cisalpino—La Goliardica.

—— 1985. 'The Papyri and the Greek Language', *Yale Classical Studies* 28: 155–65.

Harker, A. 2008. *Loyalty and Dissidence in Roman Egypt: The Case of the Acta Alexandrinorum*. Cambridge: Cambridge University Press.

Hatzilambrou, R. 2007. '*P. Oxy*. XVIII 2192 Revisited', in A. K. Bowman et al. (eds), *Oxyrhynchus: A City and its Texts*. London: Egypt Exploration Society, 282–6.

Houston, G. W. 2007. 'Grenfell, Hunt, Breccia, and the Book Collections of Oxyrhynchus', *Greek, Roman and Byzantine Studies* 47: 327–59.

—— 2009. 'Papyrological Evidence for Book Collections and Libraries in the Roman Empire', in W. A. Johnson and H. N. Parker (eds), *Ancient Literacies: The Culture of Reading in Greece and Rome*. Oxford: Oxford University Press, 233–67.

Husson, G. 1993. 'Les Homéristes', *Journal of Juristic Papyrology* 23: 93–9.

Koenen, L. 2002. 'Die Apologie des Töpfers an König Amenophis oder das Töpferorakel', in A. Blasius and B. U. Schipper (eds), *Apokalyptik und Ägypten: Eine kritische Analyse des relevanten Texte aus dem griechisch-römischen Ägypten*. Leuven: Peeters, 139–87.

Krüger, J. 1990. *Oxyrhynchos in der Kaiserzeit: Studien zur Topographie und Literaturrezeption*. Frankfurt: Peter Lang.

Lama, M. 1991. 'Aspetti di tecnica libraria ad Ossirinco: Copie letterarie su rotoli documentari', *Aegyptus* 71: 55–120.

Lewis, N. 1995. 'Literati in the Service of the Roman Emperors: Politics before Culture', in A. E. Hanson (ed.), *On Government and Law in Roman Egypt: Collected Papers of Naphthali Lewis*. Atlanta: Scholars Press, 257–74.

Livrea, E. 2002. 'Poema epico-storico attribuito a Soterico di Oasi', *Zeitschrift für Papyrologie und Epigraphik* 138: 17–30.

Maehler, H. 1998. 'Élites urbaines et production littéraire en Égypte romaine et byzantine', *Gaia* 3: 81–95.

Miguélez-Cavero, L. 2008. *Poems in Context: Greek Poetry in the Egyptian Thebaid 200-600 AD*. Berlin: de Gruyter.

Montserrat, D. 1997. 'Heron "Bearer of *Philosophia*" and Hermione *Grammatike*', *Journal of Egyptian Archaeology* 83: 223–6.

Morgan, T. 1998. *Literate Education in the Hellenistic and Roman Worlds*. Cambridge: Cambridge University Press.

Musurillo, H. 1954. *The Acts of the Pagan Martyrs: Acta Alexandrinorum*. Oxford: Clarendon Press.

Olson, S. D. 2006–12. *Athenaeus: The Learned Banqueters*, 8 vols. Cambridge, Mass.: Harvard University Press.

Parsons, P. J. 2007. *The City of the Sharp-Nosed Fish: Greek Lives in Roman Egypt*. London: Weidenfeld and Nicolson.

Patillon, M. 1997. *Aelius Théon: Progymnasmata*. Paris: Belles Lettres.

Porter, S. E. 2007. 'Prolegomena to a Syntax of the Greek Papyri', in J. Frösén et al. (eds), *Proceedings of the 24th International Congress of Papyrology, Helsinki, 1-7 August 2004*. Helsinki: Societas Scientiarum Fennica, 921–33.

Pruneti, P. 1996. 'Il termine ΦΙΛΟΣΟΦΟΣ nei papiri documentari', in M. S. Funghi (ed.), *Le vie della ricerca: Studi in onore di Francesco Adorno*. Florence: Olschki, 389–401.

Quack, J. F. 2009. *Einführung in die altägyptische Literaturgeschichte* III: *Die demotische und gräko-ägyptische Literatur*, 2nd edn. Berlin: Lit.

Reardon, B. P. 1971. *Courants littéraires grecs des IIe et IIIe siècles après J.-C.* Paris: Belles Lettres.

Schubert, P. 1995. 'Philostrate et les sophistes d'Alexandrie', *Mnemosyne* 48: 178–88.

Stephens, S. A., and J. Winkler. 1995. *Ancient Greek Novels: The Fragments*. Princeton: Princeton University Press.

Swain, S. 1996. *Hellenism and Empire: Language, Classicism, and Power in the Greek World* AD *50–250*. Oxford: Clarendon Press.

Turner, E. G. 1980. *Greek Papyri: An Introduction*, 2nd edn. Oxford: Clarendon Press.

—— 2007. 'Oxyrhynchus and Rome', in A. K. Bowman et al. (eds), *Oxyrhynchus: A City and its Texts*. London: Egypt Exploration Society, 155–70.

van Minnen, P. 1998. 'Boorish or Bookish? Literature in Egyptian Villages in the Fayum in the Graeco-Roman Period', *Journal of Juristic Papyrology* 28: 99–184.

—— and K. A. Worp 1993. 'The Greek and Latin Literary Texts from Hermopolis', *Greek, Roman and Byzantine Studies* 34: 151–86.

West, S. 1969. 'The Greek Version of the Legend of Tefnut', *Journal of Egyptian Archaeology* 55: 161–83.

Whitmarsh, T. 2001. *Greek Literature and the Roman Empire: The Politics of Imitation*. Oxford: Oxford University Press.

Willis, W. H. 1968. 'A Census of the Literary Papyri from Egypt', *Greek, Roman and Byzantine Studies* 9: 205–41.

Youtie, H. C. 1970. 'Callimachus in the Tax Rolls', in D. H. Samuel (ed.), *Proceedings of the Twelfth International Congress of Papyrology*. Toronto: Hakkert, 545–51.

CHAPTER 33

HIERATIC AND DEMOTIC LITERATURE

FRIEDHELM HOFFMANN

Scripts and Writing

In the third millennium BCE, hieratic script (Fig. 33.1) developed from hieroglyphic script. The signs became simplified so that they could be written more quickly. The two scripts are somewhat like our printing and handwriting. Hieratic was used for both documentary texts and literary works. Around the middle of the first millennium BCE, the use of hieratic writing became restricted. From that time onwards it was used only for literary texts in the broadest sense. For documentary texts, however, there was a new script: Demotic.

Around 650 BCE, probably in Lower Egypt, Demotic script came into existence (Vleeming 1981). It is written from right to left like hieratic (Fig. 33.2). Often several signs that were originally separate are connected to form a single ligature. Demotic script spread through the whole of Egypt in the sixth century BCE (Donker van Heel 1994). In the fifth century BCE, when the Greek historian Herodotus wrote about the land by the Nile, Demotic was the normal form of writing used in administration and in everyday life, while hieratic was used for literature and sacred works. The terms 'hieratic' and 'Demotic' that are used today go back to Herodotus' designation of the two Egyptian forms of writing as 'holy' and 'secular' (*Histories* 2.36.4).

The functional split between hieratic and Demotic, correctly observed by Herodotus, gradually disappeared, however. In the Hellenistic period at the latest, only the Egyptian priests could write hieratic and Demotic. Thus, hieratic script was occasionally also used for documentary texts while, more often, Demotic was used for religious texts.

The texts first recognized by researchers as being written in Demotic script show a form of speech that lies between Late Egyptian and Coptic, and so the phase of the Egyptian language written in Demotic script is also called Demotic. But the Demotic form of the language can also be written in other scripts while, conversely, not every text written in Demotic script is also in the Demotic form of the language.

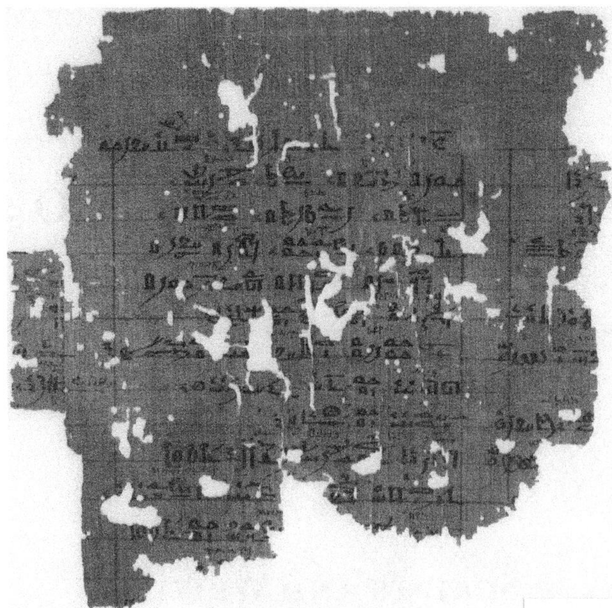

FIG. 33.1 List of quarries and mountains, written in hieratic with Demotic and Old Coptic supralinear glosses. Height 15 cm

Papyrus Carlsberg 180, fr. J 21. Courtesy of the Papyrus Carlsberg Collection, Egyptological Institute, University of Copenhagen.

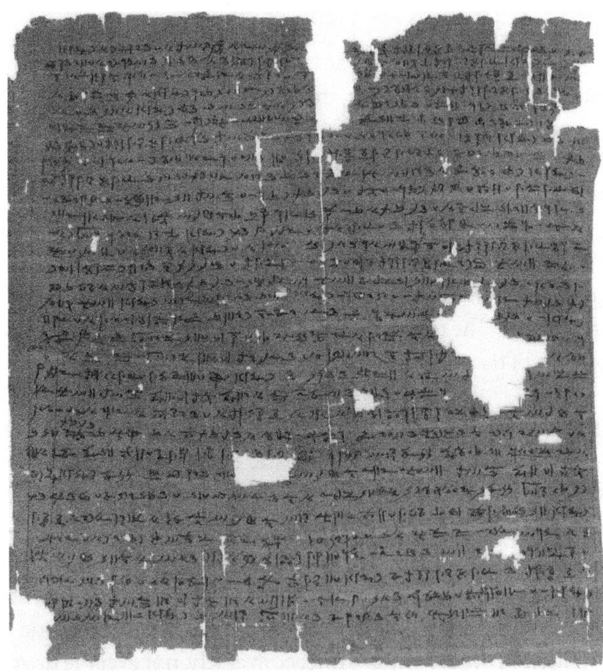

FIG. 33.2 A Demotic papyrus with one of the Inaros and Petubastis tales ('The Contest for the Armour of Inaros'). Height 29.5 cm

Papyrus Vienna D 6251, col. 9. Used with kind permission of the Österreichische Nationalbibliothek, Vienna.

Hieratic and Demotic in Roman Times

As in pre-Roman times, hieratic script was mainly used for works of almost exclusively priestly scholarship and for religious and magical texts. Demotic, however, was also used for these, as well as every other type of Egyptian text, including documentary texts. Occasionally both scripts were used side by side in the same text. There may be two reasons for this: an old text, written in hieratic, may have been partially transcribed into the more modern medium of Demotic. Or, to demonstrate his erudition, a scribe may have interspersed hieratic signs in a text that was otherwise written in Demotic.

The hieroglyphic script did not die out when hieratic and, later, Demotic emerged, but continued in use well into the Roman period as a monumental script (see Chapter 34). The last hieroglyphic inscription that can be precisely dated comes from 394 CE. Some hieroglyphs can occur in texts written otherwise in hieratic or Demotic.

For correspondence with government agencies in the Roman period, Greek was used. The use of a mixture of the Greek alphabet and some additional Demotic characters for writing Egyptian words is called Old Coptic (see Chapter 35).

Writing Materials

The rush, traditionally used by the Egyptians, fell out of use in the Roman period. In its place came the reed pen (*calamus*) that had been adopted from the Greeks. It is much harder than the rush, which was more like a brush, and resulted in a consistently thin line-width for writing signs.

The ink used was lamp-black ink, which had been standard for many centuries. In addition, iron gall ink was occasionally used too. For headings and emphasis, red ink, made from ochre or other dyes, was often used.

The writing materials, as in earlier times, were principally papyrus and pieces of stone or pottery vessels (ostraca). Papyrus was so expensive that Egyptian texts are often found written on the back of Greek documents that were no longer wanted. In addition, depending on their purpose or the situation, other materials could also be used, such as wooden tablets (especially for mummy labels, but also for the astronomical Stobart tablets and drafts of recitations of hymns; for which, see Widmer 2004), stones, walls, bones, palm ribs, textiles (especially for inscribed mummy wrappings), vessels (particularly for dockets), and other materials. Finally, hieratic and, particularly, Demotic script were also carved into stone (Farid 1995).

Scribes

In Roman times, only people who had completed scribal training at an Egyptian temple could write in Egyptian. They were all charged with various tasks in the temple, for example in temple administration, which one should envisage as a commercial enterprise rather like a medieval monastery; as a notary; as a scholar in the scriptorium of the temple (the 'house of life'); or as a reciter of texts in the cult. This does not mean that each scribe was equally competent in each script. Conversely, in Roman times it was only the Egyptian priests who maintained the use of all the Egyptian scripts (hieroglyphs, hieratic, and Demotic).

From surviving written documents it can be seen that the education of Egyptian scribes was organized very locally in the Graeco-Roman period. Apparently, each temple was left to its own preferences, which meant that the Demotic scribal tradition took a different course in different locations.

Scribes often identified themselves in the colophon at the end of a document. The author or editor of a text remains anonymous, apart from the wisdom literature and occasionally medical texts. However, some of these are probably pseudepigraphic attributions.

Egyptian Literature in the Roman Period

What literature actually is, indeed whether there ever was such a thing as literature for the Egyptians, is not absolutely clear from the sources. Although Egyptian assertions about the quality of texts appear repeatedly, they are not sufficient to enable us to reconstruct a fully fledged Egyptian theory about literature or a comprehensive set of genres to be established. Furthermore, it is not useful to approach Egyptian material using modern criteria. The result would be only to establish whether or not, according to this or that literary theory, an Egyptian text would be considered a work of literature today. It might make more sense to approach the question of literary merit and genres in Egypt on the basis of the widest possible material and taking account of its cultural situation. Since this essentially remains work yet to be done, I shall confine myself in the following overview to a selection structured on the basis of a more practical point of view, arranged arbitrarily. And, for the present, I am counting all non-documentary texts as literature.

The Outward Appearance of the Texts

For papyri, the custom of surrounding the columns with borders starts in Roman times (see Figs 33.1 and 33.2). A characteristic innovation of manuscripts of the late Roman period is the use of lines ruled for each row of text (Fig. 33.1; see Tait 1986). That does not mean, however, that every Roman papyrus text has borders or rulings.

Texts could also be illustrated, for example to demonstrate a geometric problem or to provide a religious text with representations of gods. Interestingly, the illustrations do not seem to have been regarded as essential, and at times editions of the same work exist both with and without pictures, for example the Book of the Fayum (Beinlich 1991).

Meta-information is optional. In this I include page numbers or information about where an image is placed (as in *P Boulaq*, *P Hearst*, *P Amherst*, and the Book of the Fayum; Beinlich 1991: 45–53). In the Second Tale of Setne, the use of catchwords (where the last words of the previous page are repeated at the beginning of the next one) is unusual but not without earlier parallels. Interlinear glosses may be placed above the appropriate word (as in Fig. 33.1).

Transmission of Texts

The most commonly preserved texts are in the form of original manuscripts. Of course, the delicate papyri or other writing materials have often suffered damage so that many texts are only preserved in fragmentary form. The preservation of funerary texts, which were put into the grave and then left undisturbed, is often very good, however. Other than this, the bulk of Roman period manuscripts containing Egyptian literary texts come from the refuse of settlements or Geniza-like hiding places within a temple complex. The quality of the surviving textual evidence is uneven. Some have been very carefully written by highly competent scribes, while others rather give the impression of hastily made copies for their own use. In yet other cases the only remaining versions of texts come from error-ridden copies made by students.

Where two or more copies of a text have survived, they can complement each other. However, in the case of literary tales the surviving versions differ from one another. These texts have no fixed wording, but were formulated afresh over and over again. A separate matter are textual deviations that have crept in over time in textual transmission. In scientific and religious texts, in which the exact wording was important, the scribes have sometimes merged two divergent originals so that a variant, labelled as such, or as 'another book', becomes inserted into the new copy.

Manuscript and Text

It is necessary to distinguish between a specific manuscript and the work written on it. This is important in two respects. First, there may be multiple copies of a text. Secondly, the surviving manuscripts represent textual evidence that has been randomly preserved. A common mistake is to equate the age of the earliest manuscript with the age of the text. The text itself, however, may actually have been composed centuries earlier and only been preserved in a more recent copy. For that reason each individual text has to be thoroughly studied to determine its age reliably. It is also important to note that many Egyptian texts were typically revised over and over again and formulated anew. There may be some justification, therefore, for understanding a manuscript as merely evidence about the version written on it, which would then be in fact exactly the same age as the text surviving on it.

Innovations in the Roman Period

Egyptian literature of the Roman period was the preserve of the priesthood of the Egyptian temples and formed part of the scholarly cultural tradition nurtured there. As a result, the new political situation did not spawn any new themes or genres. Innovations can mainly be observed in the more mechanical aspects of writing. In addition to the use of Greek letters for the purpose of glossing or the transcription of complete Egyptian texts into Greek script, the use of the *calamus* and the use of frames and interlinear rulings may be mentioned here. Because, in Roman times, both hieratic and Demotic literature were under the care of the same people, that is Egyptian priestly scholars, there was also a tendency to mix hieratic and Demotic script.

The Current State of Research

As is true of the entire period, Egyptian literary texts of the Roman period have been, and often continue to be, erroneously interpreted as a phenomenon demonstrating a late decline of Egyptian culture and not worthy of closer study—first, because they are so late and hence show only epigonic traits, and secondly, because this period was after all not really Egyptian, and moreover it was so heavily influenced by external forces that the contents of the texts are hardly relevant for the study of Egyptian culture. It seemed to be possible to make an exception for the temple texts since, as hieroglyphic texts, they clearly came from an older tradition.

It must be said that in the first instance every period of Egyptian history must be researched and evaluated against its own standards. The extent to which, for example, Demotic literature came to include Greek influences may well be disputed—and maybe it was exactly the opposite way round!—but the fact that we are dealing with late and, in some respects, different types of text from, for example, those of the Middle Kingdom does not simply mean that there were no more Egyptian texts to deal with in the Roman period. It also says more about the researchers than about the texts whether a work in which foreign influences are observed is simply regarded as un-Egyptian or as the product of a modified, and possibly enriched, Egyptian tradition. And the special role accorded to temple texts is unwarranted, the monumental versions being based precisely on the books in priestly libraries written in hieratic and Demotic script (Ryholt 2005).

The range of hieratic and Demotic literature is constantly being expanded through newly published or newly discovered texts. The number of entirely unpublished texts is extremely large, which means that the view presented here is very preliminary. Moreover, the available material is one-sided. In the first place the pertinent texts have mainly been found in Soknopaiou Nesos and Tebtunis (both in the Fayum) and less frequently in Upper Egypt. Secondly, the better-preserved and particularly interesting texts, or those that are most easily understood, are usually the ones to be published first so that a bias based on the history of research is added to the geographical bias of the basic material.

The meta-database Trismegistos (<http://www.trismegistos.org>) provides very useful access to texts and secondary literature, so that I can restrict my references in the discussion below.

Texts from the Belles-Lettres ('Beautiful Literature')

In Roman times, belles-lettres texts were written almost exclusively in Demotic script and language (Hoffmann and Quack 2007; Hoffmann 2009; Quack 2009; no further secondary literature is given here for the texts dealt with in these studies). Most texts are in prose, as far as one can tell. Versified works are rare. A characteristic feature is the occurrence of repeated narrative formulas, through which certain transactions are normally expressed, similar to the introductory formula 'Once upon a time…' in our own fairytales. That does not mean, however, that there was no striving for variation.

The structure of Demotic tales can be very complex owing to the inclusion of two or more narrative strands, or stories, being embedded in the main narrative. Surprising twists can make the plot very lively. Interestingly, some of the texts form clusters in which the same characters appear. And this also determines the nature of the text: the group known today as the Inaros and Petubastis Cycle, after two of its characters, includes tales of battles and adventures, while the texts about Setne are magical tales. Where stories are preserved in several manuscripts, it can be seen that the texts had no fixed form but were continuously changed. But there are exceptions: in the so-called Myth of the Sun's Eye, variations are recorded in a text-critical fashion, a phenomenon that is typical of religious and scientific texts. It may well be that the way a text was handled corresponds to the Egyptian concept of literary genres.

For many centuries, Egypt had an exchange with neighbouring cultures, and foreign conquests of Egypt—including those by Alexander the Great and later Octavian—made Egypt even more receptive to political as well as cultural influences. The multifaceted contacts of Egyptian literature with Greek culture will be repeatedly addressed in what follows; I do not need to rehearse them here, but it is particularly important to point out the still totally unexplored interactions between Egypt and India and the possible reception of Egyptian literature in Meroe, which for the time being admittedly remains unclear owing to the lack of comprehensible sources. The reception of Akkadian material is also remarkable.

The Inaros and Petubastis Cycle

This is a large group of mostly long, pseudo-historical narratives, which are characterized by a common cast of characters. Most of these figures date back to historical personalities from the second half of the seventh century BCE. There is some debate whether there was any Homeric influence on the Inaros and Petubastis Cycle and whether the literary genre of the novel developed within this group of texts. The earliest story belonging to the Inaros and Petubastis Cycle is an Aramaic version from the early fifth century BCE. From the Roman period the following tales are attested from manuscripts: 'The Inaros Epic', 'Inaros, Bes and the Talking Donkey', 'The Contest for the Armour of Inaros', 'The Contest for the Benefice of Amun', and 'Egyptians and Amazons' (Hoffmann 1996a, b).

The Tales of Setne

'Setne' is actually the late form of the priestly title 'Sem'. In the Demotic tales, however, 'Setne' seems instead to have been used as a name; in addition to stories about Setne Khaemwase, a historical personage who was the fourth son of Ramesses II, there are stories about Setne Ptahhotep and other 'Setne' heroes.

Setne is always a magician and the narratives are related in a highly imaginative and amazingly refined way. Thanks to an Aramaic papyrus, the origin of the Setne tales can be traced back to at least the fifth century BCE. The fragment of *P Carlsb.* 207 (Quack 2009: 40–1) and the so-called Second Setne tale, which is relatively well preserved apart from the beginning, are particularly noteworthy from the Roman period. *P Vienna* D 62 is also interesting, containing the beginning of what appears to be a magical story, while there is a mythological tale on the recto (Hoffmann 2004).

The Petese Stories

Petese is a priest, skilled in magic, who appears in Demotic narratives from the fourth century BCE onwards. It is prophesied to him that he has only forty days left to live. Consequently, he takes care of arranging his burial, and also entertainment for the rest of his life. This he does by having animals write down a total of seventy short stories about women, some of which at least are preserved in fragments. It is noteworthy that one of them already has a parallel in Herodotus 2.111 and that the whole composition has striking parallels with the Indian Śukasaptati, the 'Seventy Tales of the Parrot' (Vittmann 2006–7). Petese could also perhaps be related to the philosopher Petesis known from Greek sources and to the Petasios known from the alchemical literature.

Stories about Nectanebo

A set of stories developed around Nectanebo (360–342 BCE), the last native Egyptian king, which have survived in fragmentary form in a Greek translation from the second century BCE and in Demotic versions of the Roman period; they also found their way into the Greek Alexander Romance and from there into an almost global narrative tradition.

Other Stories

The manuscripts surviving from the Roman period include a story that is still unpublished about King Djoser, Imhotep, and an Asian magician; an also unpublished story about the campaigns of King Amenemhet and Prince Sesostris (see parallels in Herodotus and the Greek Sesonchosis Romance); and an unpublished tale of Nakhthorshena, which may go back to a local ruler called Nakhthornashena referred to in the annals of the Assyrian king Assurbanipal and on the victory stela of the Kushite king Pije.

Another tale, 'The Swallow and the Sea', has been known for a long time as a school exercise, and it has a close parallel in one of the embedded tales from the Indian Panchatantra. An 'aretalogical' tale of wonder about salvation through Isis, and several other stories, also exist in the form of school exercises.

Mythological Tales

Hieratic texts from this genre belong to the area of cult topographic literature. In addition, there are Demotic works that may clearly be regarded as part of the belles-lettres genre, because they are detached from a theological context. From ancient times onwards, the conflict between Horus and Seth played a major role, and its literary form was fleshed out in the Middle Kingdom. There are Demotic versions of the Horus and Seth tales from the Ptolemaic era and also one from the Roman period (Hoffmann 1996b). In another fragment of Roman date (*P Vienna* D 62) we learn about different gods who go to certain places and transform their shapes (Hoffmann 2004). Is there a link with the Greek tradition about the gods fleeing from Typhon, when they assume animal form?

The Myth of the Sun's Eye

To date, about eleven papyri from the second century CE are known that contain this extremely complex work, originally more than a hundred columns long; in addition, there is a Greek translation from the third century. Portions of the text are, however, much older and some may perhaps go back to the New Kingdom.

The myth is a religious text, whose mythological storyline is interpreted theologically: Tefnut, daughter of the sun-god, moves to Nubia, from where she is brought back by Shu and Thoth. As they travel, Tefnut and Thoth have profound discussions, and Thoth tells various animal stories to underpin his argument. Because of these fables, some of which have close parallels with the Akkadian Etana myth and the works of Archilochus and Aesop, this Demotic text has been regarded in traditional research as a work from the genre of belles-lettres. It should not be overlooked, however, that the text, with its commentary made up of various explanatory additions and learned exposition, may well have had its place in cultic festivals.

Wisdom Literature

So long as the formal principles of Demotic poetry, in terms of rhythm and versification, remain unknown, one can only occasionally guess that, in the case of texts written in a stichic form, with one sentence per line, there must be works written in verse among them. In the wisdom texts, however, one has the impression that, although many are written in stichs, they are not poetry, and that their graphic form results rather from the desire to emphasize a particular compositional principle, namely the series of individual sayings.

The literary tradition of teachings given by a father to his son dates back to the third millennium BCE in Egypt. Thematically separate from them is the extensive Egyptian text entitled 'The Way to Know Knowledge', which is well attested in the late Ptolemaic *P Insinger*, but of which there are also several manuscripts from Roman times, including an abridged version. The teaching of Ankhsheshonqy exists not only in Ptolemaic editions but also in a version from the second century CE. This later version is more detailed, but so far only pieces of the narrative framework are generally known. A smaller fragment containing rules for living in continuous writing is *P Ashm.* 1984.77. Finally, there are two important Demotic pieces with the remains of the story within a story from the teaching of Ahiqar, an Assyrian wise man of the seventh century BCE, of which the oldest attestation to date is in an Aramaic papyrus of the fifth century BCE found in Egypt.

The Book of Thoth

The text known today by this name is an extensive composition, of which one hieratic and many Demotic manuscripts, especially from the Roman period, have survived. Some are written stichically. The text may well have been composed in pre-Ptolemaic times.

The text sets out notions about the importance of priestly knowledge in the form of a conversation in which, among others, 'the One Who Loves Knowledge', Wepwawet, and Thoth (?) take part. The language is sometimes archaic and the orthography is interspersed with non-etymological spellings. Because of its allegorical nature and many allusions, the text is difficult to understand. How far one may draw links to Greek Hermetic literature still requires detailed research (Jasnow and Zauzich 2005; Quack 2007b, c).

Poetry for Cultic Revelry

A poem about a degenerate harper is preserved in a manuscript from the first century CE. Each verse is divided in two halves by red dots, a phenomenon so far unique in Demotic texts. The beginning and ending are lost, so that an overall interpretation of the text is difficult. The preserved part tells of a useless, gluttonous harper who neither plays his harp well nor knows how to behave. The text was probably recited during a religious festival, as suggested by an invocation addressed to the temple of the goddess Mut.

Of a similar character are the texts relating to the festival of Bastet (Hdt. 2.60), which are preserved in three manuscripts of the second century CE. The festival's goings-on, which are characterized by mockery and obscene jokes, deal with the following themes: individuals are reviled; twisted scholarship is used to explain the digestive processes and to urge further eating and drinking; the festival events are interpreted mythologically; and erotic activities are described.

Prophetic Literature

There is a long history of stylized texts being used as prophecies in Egypt. From the Roman period in particular, there are Demotic texts in which predictions are made about a partly distant future. Especially prominent are warnings of disasters, but these are followed by promises of salvation. In none of these texts will the salvation predicted only occur at the end of time; hence the Egyptian texts are prophetic, but not apocalyptic.

A Demotic manuscript of 4 CE contains the end of the Oracle of the Lamb of Bocchoris; the original Egyptian title is 'The Curse that Re Put on Egypt from Year 6 of King Bocchoris' (= 714 BCE). At that time, according to the text, a lamb predicted a long period of hardship during which, among other things, the 'Medes' would penetrate Egypt, which researchers have seen as the Persians but which could, perhaps, be an allusion to the Assyrians, who conquered Egypt in 671 BCE. This would be supported by the predicted revenge against Nineveh etc. during the period of salvation that was to follow, and a king 'of 55 years', mentioned earlier, would perhaps have been Pammetichus I (664–610 BCE), who was installed by the Assyrians.

It is interesting that it is not only the classical authors (including Manetho writing about Bocchoris) who record that a lamb spoke during the time of Bocchoris: it is also recorded in the Potter's Oracle, so far only known from Greek, but which may go back to an Egyptian original, which quotes from the Oracle of the Lamb of Bocchoris.

A poorly preserved prophetic text with the remains of prophecies of disaster and salvation comes from the second century CE. It is also written in Demotic (Quack 2002).

Scientific and Scholarly Texts

By 'scientific and scholarly', I am referring here to any type of reflection about phenomena relating to animate and inanimate nature and to human culture. This is a deliberately broad working definition by which I am seeking to avoid modern ideas that might cause a narrowing of perspective. However, I am adopting modern classifications in the following overview, because there are no Egyptian meta-statements about the boundaries and connections between the branches of science. There is also no Egyptian equivalent for the words 'science' or 'scholarship'. The closest term is probably *rḫ*, 'to know', or 'knowledge'.

Egyptian science was very much a form of practical theology: it sought to discover the divine in nature. Science in this sense meant, for the Egyptians, searching for divine action in nature and uncovering the order of creation that operated behind observable phenomena.

The list is one of the basic organizational forms for Egyptian texts concerned with knowledge; another is the fully expanded text. Both forms can be transformed into each other: thus, the terms set out in a list could be expanded into a text by explanations or, the other way around, a text could be reduced to its basic terms. At a higher level, individual expanded texts can be amalgamated into a collective work ('monograph') just as, conversely, individual passages could be extracted from a monograph and take on an independent form of their own in a new context. In addition to texts containing 'facts', there are instructional or procedural texts.

Unlike in literary works, scholarly texts deal with statements of fact and ideas. This means that the amalgamation of possible secondary examples, in order to achieve precision or completeness, can lead to confusing sentence structures or constructions that would be unusual in everyday language. Certain verb forms are also typical of these texts. In other words, there was a technical language. None of these features are a phenomenon found only in texts of the Roman period; it appears as early as the oldest scientific manuscripts from the early second millennium BCE. The focus on the transmission of information, however, together with the fact that in many texts the material has been passed down over a long period, means that the texts were repeatedly modified linguistically to conform with changes to the Egyptian language. At the same time, some old expressions were accepted as convenient abbreviations and perhaps played to the vanity of the educated; hence, scientific texts of the Roman period often show a wild mixture of antique elements from different orthographic and linguistic traditions.

As explained above, in Roman times the priests were the only keepers of the Egyptian scribal tradition. Consequently, the nurturing of science and scholarship was in the hands of the same people who were also responsible for the planning of Egyptian temples. That knowledge, written down in hieratic and Demotic texts and kept in the temple libraries, naturally formed, together with the religious texts, the basis for ensuring the learned formulation of the temple texts, the correct iconography, and the correct proportions of the representations as well as the layout of the scenes in accordance with the rules.

The traces left behind by the Persian period (525–404 BCE) and the Macedonian and Ptolemaic periods (332–30 BCE) are particularly visible (Hoffmann forthcoming). For example, Semitic and Greek words are found in medical texts, and concepts like the Babylonian sexagesimal numeral system and Mesopotamian planetary theory appear in Egyptian astronomical texts. The knowledge of the Egyptians was readily taken up by classical antiquity (Tait 2003).

This happened mainly through Greeks in Egypt, already during the Ptolemaic period; see, for example, the Greek letter *UPZ* I 148, which shows how the recipient learns Egyptian in order to be able to work with an Egyptian doctor. Through Latin authors, who in turn drew from Greek sources, some things found their way into the European Middle Ages (Morenz 1969). This cannot be pursued here, however.

Astronomy and Astrology

Although nowadays we usually distinguish between astronomy as a science and astrology as superstition, for the Egyptians astrology was simply the practical application of astronomical knowledge. We encounter this in what are often extremely dry texts, such as tables and lists of the positions of the planets (Neugebauer and Parker 1960–9), which were based, at least in part, on Mesopotamian theories. In general, the use of sexagesimal numbering shows clearly that Egyptian astronomy in the Roman period assimilated some quite crucial influences from Mesopotamia, which probably date back to the Persian period and even go back in part to the 26th dynasty (664–525 BCE). One such example is a Roman copy of an earlier text about solar and lunar eclipses and omens (*P Vienna* D 6278; Parker 1959). It is attributed to a King Nekhepsos, now identified as Necho II, who reigned 610–595 BCE (Ryholt 2011). In this text even the Babylonian calendar is used.

Among the astronomical papyri of the Roman period, *P Carlsb.* 1 and 1a are particularly significant. They incorporate a well-known New Kingdom hieroglyphic composition from the cenotaph of Seti I at Abydos about the course of the stars, the so-called Book of Nut (von Lieven 2007). In the papyrus versions, the traditional text is reproduced in hieratic script and supplemented with a Demotic commentary. The Demotic *P Carlsb.* 9 sets out the schema for a lunar calendar (Hoffmann 1997–8; Depuydt 1998). *P Carlsb.* 638 (in Demotic) provides the earliest evidence of the Standard Lunar Scheme (Hoffmann and Jones 2006–7; for further lunar texts, see Hoffmann and Jones 2010). Also worth mentioning are Demotic horoscopes (Neugebauer 1943), on ostraca; and notes on creating horoscopes written in Demotic (Hoffmann 1995); as well as a Demotic Table of Terms—the only ancient copy that survives at all (Depuydt 1994). In addition, there are Demotic astrological handbooks (Hughes 1986; Chauveau 1992).

Mathematics

Compared with Egyptian mathematics in the Middle and New Kingdoms, some fundamental changes can be seen with the restoration of Egyptian mathematical traditions in the second half of the first millennium BCE. These relate to the types of problem, measurements (e.g. an approximate value for pi), and occasionally the representation of numbers (including more extensive use of vulgar fractions in addition to unit fractions). Mesopotamian influence can be felt here (Friberg 2005). This does not mean that there was a complete break with distinctive Egyptian tradition. Rather, the Demotic mathematical texts sometimes articulate methods that were used, but never explained, in the older texts (Vogel 1975). *P British Museum* EA 10520 (dealing with progressions, multiplication, fractions, roots, and calculating areas) and *P Carlsb.* 30 (dealing with areas and proportions) date to the Roman period. These papyri also have drawings to illustrate the geometrical problems (Parker 1972).

Medicine

There is extensive Egyptian medical literature from the Roman period, but it has been insufficiently published or not at all. *O Berl.* P 5570 (late Ptolemaic or early Roman) is in hieratic; *P Vienna* D 6257, from Soknopaiou Nesos, is written in a mixture of hieratic and Demotic script (Reymond 1976; Hoffmann and Quack 2010); *O Medin. Madi* 155 combines Demotic and Greek script; while all the other texts are written in Demotic. These are all collections of recipes, not texts containing medical lore. Material relating to medicine is also found scattered in magical texts (Hoffmann and Quack 2010), which address illnesses and cures in another way (see Chapter 21).

In addition to a strong Egyptian tradition, a Mesopotamian influence (Semitic names of drugs, a Persian measure of capacity in the Vienna Papyrus) and Greek influence (Greek names of drugs) can be discerned in these texts. Owing to its linguistic and structural inconsistencies, *P Vienna* D 6257 is an almost classic example of an accumulative text that was handed down over many centuries and repeatedly changed, which probably ceased to be modified in the Ptolemaic period.

Biology

Egyptian texts on biology as applied theology (von Lieven 2004) are mainly found in compilations of priestly knowledge. Those that survive consist of, for example, descriptions of birds (in hieratic; Osing 1998) and medicinal plants (in Demotic; Tait 1977). In addition, there are also more philologically arranged collections of animal names (in hieratic; Osing 1998).

Philology

The material relating to Egyptian philology from the Roman period is quite remarkable. We have, for example, substantial portions of the so-called Tanis Sign Papyrus (Griffith and Petrie 1889), which explains what the hieroglyphs represent. The papyrus is also of interest because of the arrangement of the hieroglyphs according to the appearance of the signs (e.g. people, animals, plants, vessels, etc.); this is how Egyptologists still do it today. Inserted in the Sign Papyrus is an alphabetical list of uniliteral signs, which uses a Semitic alphabetical order (Quack 2003).

P Carlsb. 7 is also important, in which all the hieroglyphs are arranged alphabetically (Iversen 1958). In this hieratic text, they are interpreted not only in terms of what they represent externally, but also from a detailed theological or mythological perspective. The first sign listed is the ibis, thus confirming the information transmitted in classical antiquity that it was the first letter of the Egyptian alphabet (Plut. *Quaest. Conv.* 9.3 §11). Incidentally, the Egyptians used the names of birds to denote the letters of the alphabet even before the Roman period (Zauzich 2000: 29–30).

In wordlists, related words are grouped together, e.g. verbs to do with building, synonyms for 'battle', terms for buildings, and so forth (Osing 1998). These lists may also contain the lists of animal names mentioned under 'Biology' above. The texts are in part provided with glosses in Demotic and Old Coptic script. These indicate, most importantly of all, the contemporary pronunciation of traditionally written words. I would also draw attention to a

Demotic ostracon containing words for 'image' (Wångstedt 1976–7: 17–18) and an unpublished onomastic writing board in hieratic (Schøyen Collection MS 189).

Geography

The hieratic priestly handbooks (Osing 1998) also contain lists of places and countries. Collections of holy sites formed part of this group of texts for the Egyptians. The Demotic ostracon *Ashm.* DO 956, also in the form of a list, has the beginning of a geographical onomasticon naming a number of towns in each nome (Smith 1988: 78–84).

Dream Books

Just like the corresponding New Kingdom texts, Demotic dream books from the Roman period were used to learn something about a person's future from his or her dreams. Analogous dreams and interpretations can occasionally be found in earlier Egyptian or Greek dream books (Volten 1942).

Omen Texts

Predictions about the future of a person were also made based on animal omens. The relevant texts (papyri in Vienna and Berlin) remain essentially unpublished.

Other Texts

A surviving hieroglyphic papyrus from Tanis contains information about the layout of relief scenes (Griffith and Petrie 1889: 2 right–3 left (no. 118)). A Demotic papyrus from Soknopaiou Nesos deals with the decorative programme of complete temple walls (Vittmann 2002–3).

Religious Texts

In this Handbook, the chapters in Part IV examine religious practice in some depth, in conjunction with relevant texts. Here I briefly discuss some additional religious textual sources from the point of view of hieratic and Demotic evidence in the Roman period.

Cultic Topography and Mythological Handbooks

The Egyptians not only recorded the names of toponyms, but also compiled information about the religious and cultic aspects of towns or larger areas into individual handbooks. These could be lists of gods, sacred sites, sacred trees, festivals, priests and priestesses, taboos, and so on (e.g. Griffith and Petrie 1889; Osing 1998; Osing and Rosati 1998), as well as lavishly illustrated papyri, in which the area under consideration is illustrated schematically or religious and mythological ideas are discussed in even greater detail (e.g. Beinlich 1991; Osing and Rosati 1998). These texts are often in hieratic or even hieroglyphic script. There are also texts surviving in Demotic, for example on the subject of the Memphite theology (Erichsen and Schott 1954) and on the primeval ocean (Smith 2002).

The Book of the Temple

This is an extended composition dealing with constructing and equipping an ideal temple, and the work of the temple staff (most recently Quack 2007a). It is preceded by a historical section, set in the time of Khufu. The text, which has not yet been published in continuous form, has survived in numerous hieratic and Demotic manuscripts and a fragmentary Greek translation (Quack 1997).

The End of Pagan Egyptian Literature

The preceding overview of hieratic and Demotic literature clearly shows that the Egyptian priestly scholars of the Roman period were still very active. One can be certain that the copying of older texts that may have originated from a much older tradition was part of their work (Hoffmann 1996a: 124; von Lieven 2007: 272; Ryholt forthcoming). In the Roman period, texts also received some editing. An important example of this is the Magical Papyrus of London and Leiden, which has striking late Demotic linguistic features in places.

Egyptian literature increasingly disappears from the public sphere during the Roman period. At the same time, literary texts survived longer than legal and administrative texts, which no longer appear in post-Augustan times other than in the Fayum. Stories and religious texts that had a significance for the Egyptian priesthood survive even longer. Magical literature on papyrus lasts the longest—in other words, texts that had the least importance in public life and that were only of importance to a few individuals (Zauzich 1983).

In the third century CE there is a clear break. Soknopaiou Nesos and Tebtunis, which were so rich in finds of papyrus, were abandoned around or shortly after 250 CE, and the inhabitants who moved away do not seem to have continued their tradition elsewhere. This rapid decline in the third century is surely connected with the political and economic problems of the Roman empire at this time. When, in the course of the fourth century CE, Christianity became the state religion, it set the final seal on the demise of Egyptian culture linked to the temples.

In light of what has just been said, it seems to me to be no accident that a remarkable number of translations of Egyptian literary works exist from the period around 300 CE. Although such translations did already exist in the Ptolemaic period, the sheer number from around 300 CE is very striking (Quack 1997; Hoffmann 2009: 362). This seems to be another example of the intensified adoption—or perhaps adaptation—of Egyptian literature into the universal language of the day and thereby into Western tradition.

For the kingdom of Meroe to the south of Egypt, which was closely bound to Egyptian culture through centuries of contact with Egypt, the temple of Isis on Philae was an important place of pilgrimage. Many graffiti provide evidence of visits by the Meroites (Burkhardt 1985).

Among them we find still in the third century CE scholars who could write not only Meroitic, but also Egyptian and Greek, and used them in their inscriptions, and their titles indicate a familiarity with Egyptian priestly scholarship.

When Diocletian (284–305 CE) moved the southern border of the Roman empire back to Aswan, Philae was actually situated outside the Roman empire. In this 'exclave', the cult of Isis held out against the Christianization of Egypt (Dijkstra 2008). After the fall of the kingdom of Meroe, it was in the hands of the nomadic Blemmyes and finally in a single priestly family, who were perhaps not permanently resident on Philae. These people seem to have left no hieratic or Demotic literature behind, but an instance of the title 'scribe of the house of writing of Isis' (*Graffito Philae* 436) suggests that texts relating to the cult still existed in the late fourth century. Egyptian textual transmission ceases with the last dated Demotic text (*Graffito Philae* 365) in December 452 CE.

Directions for Future Research

I see it as a particularly urgent research priority to work on the large number of unpublished texts—which, thanks to the many excavation projects under way, are constantly growing in number. This cannot be achieved by an individual or a museum on their own. In view of the good results from the International Committee for the Publication of the Carlsberg Papyri in Copenhagen (Zauzich 1991), it would be beneficial and efficient if a compilation of all the findings already made in a particular museum or collection was kept within that institution's archive. The coordinated study of entire collections, by several appropriate specialists, is what is generally needed to advance research.

Analysis of the texts must seek to uncover the concepts that were peculiar to the Egyptians during the Roman period (emic approach). Only then can we understand what the authors were thinking or what functions their writings had if these texts were formulated in a particular way. Given the rich source material, I also see a good chance, for example, of distinguishing different levels of style in Egyptian narratives of the Roman period.

Although the Roman period was different in many ways from earlier periods, it continued ancient Egyptian traditions in its own way. This statement, trivial in itself, seems to me to be absolutely necessary to make, because until now Roman Egypt is often dismissed as a priori 'un-Egyptian'. Cognate disciplines should see Roman Egypt as more than the source of some interesting Greek papyri. The particular and quite different interests of the subjects of Egyptology, ancient history, epigraphy, classical archaeology, Meroitic studies, and papyrology must be overcome and united to create interdisciplinary cooperation.

Conclusion

For assessing the significance of late Egyptian literature to other cultures, especially Graeco-Roman antiquity, the study of Roman Egypt and the specific aspects that differentiate it from older traditions in Egypt is essential. It is too often forgotten that statements about Egypt made by authors from the Roman period, or late antique Greek or Latin authors, if they are not quoting an older Greek writer and thus bound to their own tradition, must be measured against circumstances in *Roman* Egypt. It does not matter that, in reality, in the Middle Kingdom things were different from what, for example, a later Greek author writes. This does not mean he is saying something false. The information he provides has to be measured against what the Egyptians knew or thought about the Middle Kingdom during the Roman period. And that sort of information can only be obtained from Egyptian literary texts of the Roman period, which survive in vast but undervalued numbers in the hieratic and Demotic scripts of the indigenous language.

Suggested Reading

On writing in ancient Egypt generally, Schlott (1989) is well worth reading. For the hieratic texts of the Roman period, there is, as yet, no overview available. Late period Egyptian literature, including Demotic material, is collected in Ryholt (2010). Online, the Trismegistos database, <http://www.trismegistos.org>, provides a search tool. The Demotic material has been compiled, with annotated bibliography, in Depauw (1997), while Hoffmann (2000) offers a more cultural-historical interpretation. Depauw et al. (2007) brings together texts with exact dates (mostly documentary). Houston, Baines, and Cooper (2003) presents an account of the disappearance of pagan Egyptian scripts.

Bibliography

Beinlich, H. 1991. *Das Buch vom Fayum: Zum religiösen Eigenverständnis einer ägyptischen Landschaft*, 2 vols. Wiesbaden: Harrassowitz.

Burkhardt, A. 1985. *Ägypter und Meroiten im Dodekaschoinos: Untersuchungen zur Typologie und Bedeutung der demotischen Graffiti*. Berlin: Akademie.

Chauveau, M. 1992. 'Un traité d'astrologie en écriture démotique', *Cahiers de Recherches de l'Institut de Papyrologie et d'Égyptologie de Lille* 14: 101–5.

Depauw, M. 1997. *A Companion to Demotic Studies*. Brussels: Fondation Égyptologique Reine Élisabeth.

——et al. 2007. *A Chronological Survey of Precisely Dated Demotic and Abnormal Hieratic Sources*. Cologne: Trismegistos Publications. <http://www.trismegistos.org/top.php>.

Depuydt, L. 1994. 'A Demotic Table of Terms', *Enchoria* 21: 1–9.

——1998. 'The Demotic Mathematical Astronomical Papyrus Carlsberg 9 Reinterpreted', in W. Clarysse, A. Schoors, and H. Willems (eds), *Egyptian Religion: The Last Thousand Years: Studies Dedicated to the Memory of Jan Quaegebeur*, vol. 2. Leuven: Peeters, 1277–97.

Dijkstra, J. H. F. 2008. *Philae and the End of Ancient Egyptian Religion: A Regional Study of Religious Transformation (298–642 CE)*. Leuven: Peeters.

Donker van Heel, K. 1994. 'The Lost Battle of Peteamonip Son of Petehorresne', in E. Bresciani (ed.), *Acta Demotica: Acts of the Fifth International Conference for Demotists, Pisa, 4th–8th September 1993*. Pisa: Giardini, 115–24.

Erichsen, W., and S. Schott. 1954. *Fragmente memphitischer Theologie in demotischer Schrift (Pap. demot. Berlin 13603)*. Wiesbaden: Akademie der Wissenschaften und der Literatur in Mainz.

Farid, A. 1995. *Fünf demotische Stelen aus Berlin, Chicago, Durham, London und Oxford mit zwei demotischen Türinschriftn aus Paris und einer Bibliographie der demotischen Inschriften*. Berlin: Achet.

Friberg, J. 2005. *Unexpected Links between Egyptian and Babylonian Mathematics*. Singapore: World Scientific.

Griffith, F. L., and W. M. F. Petrie. 1889. *Two Hieroglyphic Papyri from Tanis*. London: Trübner.

Hoffmann, F. 1995. 'Astronomische und astrologische Kleinigkeiten I: Pap. Wien D6005', *Enchoria* 22: 22–6.

——1996a. *Der Kampf um den Panzer des Inaros: Studien zum P. Krall und seiner Stellung innerhalb des Inaros-Petubastis-Zyklus*. Vienna: Hollinek.

——1996b. 'Der literarische demotische Papyrus Wien D6920-22', *Studien zur Altägyptischen Kultur* 23: 167–200.

——1997–8. 'Astronomische und astrologische Kleinigkeiten II: P. Heidelberg Inv. Dem. 40 und 41', *Enchoria* 24: 34–7.

——2000. *Ägypten: Kultur und Lebenswelt in griechisch-römischer Zeit: Eine Darstellung nach den demotischen Quellen*. Berlin: Akademie.

——2004. 'Zwei neue demotische Erzählungen (P. Wien D 62)', in F. Hoffmann and H.-J. Thissen (eds), *Res Severa Verum Gaudium: Festschrift für Karl-Theodor Zauzich zum 65. Geburtstag am 8. Juni 2004*. Leuven: Peeters, 249–59.

——2009. 'Die Entstehung der demotischen Erzählliteratur: Beobachtungen zum überlieferungsgeschichtlichen Kontext', in H. Roeder (ed.), *Das Erzählen in frühen Hochkulturen I: Der Fall Ägypten*. Munich: Fink, 351–84.

——Forthcoming. 'Internationale Wissenschaft im hellenistischen Ägypten', in W. Held et al. (eds), *Orient und Okzident: Antagonismus oder Konstrukt? Machtstrukturen, Ideologien und Kulturtransfer in hellenistischer Zeit. Akten des Würzburger Symposions, 10.–13. April 2008*. Marburg: Archäologisches Seminar.

——and A. Jones. 2006–7. 'Astronomische und astrologische Kleinigkeiten V: Die Mondephemeride des P. Carlsberg 638', *Enchoria* 30: 10–20.

————2010. 'Astronomische und astrologische Kleinigkeiten VI: Neumonddaten aus dem Jahre 184/185 n. Chr.', in H. Knuf, C. Leitz, and D. von Recklinghausen (eds), *Honi soit qui mal y pense: Studien zum pharaonischen, griechisch-römischen und spätantiken Ägypten zu Ehren von Heinz-Josef Thissen*. Leuven: Peeters, 233–6.

——and J. F. Quack. 2007. *Anthologie der demotischen Literatur*. Berlin: Lit.

————2010. 'Demotische Texte zur Heilkunde', in B. Janowski and G. Wilhelm (eds), *Texte aus der Umwelt des Alten Testaments*, new ser., vol. 5: *Medizinische Texte*. Gütersloh: Gütersloher Verlagshaus, 298–316.

Houston, St., J. Baines, and J. Cooper. 2003. 'Last Writing: Script Obsolescence in Egypt, Mesopotamia, and Mesoamerica', *Comparative Studies in Society and History* 45: 430–79.

Hughes, G. R. 1986. 'An Astrologer's Handbook in Demotic Egyptian', in L. H. Lesko (ed.), *Egyptological Studies in Honor of Richard A. Parker: Presented on the Occasion of his 78th Birthday, December 10, 1983*. Hanover: University Press of New England, 53–69.

Iversen, E. 1958. *Papyrus Carlsberg Nr. VII: Fragments of a Hieroglyphic Dictionary*. Copenhagen: Munksgaard.

Jasnow, R., and K.-T. Zauzich. 2005. *The Ancient Egyptian Book of Thoth*, 2 vols. Wiesbaden: Harrassowitz.

Morenz, S. 1969. *Die Begegnung Europas mit Ägypten*. Zurich: Artemis.

Neugebauer, O. 1943. 'Demotic Horoscopes', *Journal of the American Oriental Society* 63: 115–26.

——and R. A. Parker. 1960–9. *Egyptian Astronomical Texts*, 3 vols in 4 pts. Providence, RI: Brown University Press.

Osing, J. 1998. *Hieratische Papyri aus Tebtunis* I. Copenhagen: Museum Tusculanum Press.

——and Rosati, G. 1998. *Papiri geroglifici e ieratici da Tebtynis*. Florence: Istituto Papirologico G. Vitelli.

Parker, R. A. 1959. *A Vienna Demotic Papyrus on Eclipse- and Lunar-Omina*. Providence, RI: Brown University Press.

——1972. *Demotic Mathematical Papyri*. Providence, RI: Brown University Press.

Quack, J. F. 1997. 'Ein ägyptisches Handbuch des Tempels und seine griechische Übersetzung', *Zeitschrift für Papyrologie und Epigraphik* 119: 297–300.

——2002. 'Ein neuer prophetischer Text aus Tebtynis', in A. Blasius and B. U. Schipper (eds), *Apokalyptik und Ägypten: Eine kritische Analyse der relevanten Texte aus dem griechisch-römischen Ägypten*. Leuven: Peeters, 253–74.

——2003. 'Die spätägyptische Alphabetreihenfolge und das "südsemitische" Alphabet', *Lingua Aegyptia* 11: 163–84.

——2007a. 'Die Götterliste des Buches vom Tempel und die überregionalen Dekorationsprogramme', in B. Harig and A. Klug (eds), *6. Ägyptologische Tempeltagung: Funktion und Gebrauch altägyptischer Tempelräume*. Wiesbaden: Harrassowitz, 213–35.

——2007b. 'Die Initiation zum Schreiberberuf im Alten Ägypten', *Studien zur Altägyptischen Kultur* 36: 249–95.

——2007c. 'Ein ägyptischer Dialog über die Schreibkunst und das arkane Wissen', *Archiv für Religionsgeschichte* 9: 259–94.

——2009. *Einführung in die altägyptische Literaturgeschichte* III: *Die demotische und gräko-ägyptische Literatur*, 2nd edn. Münster: Lit.

Reymond, E. A. E. 1976. *From the Contents of the Libraries of the Suchos Temples in the Fayyum*, vol. 1: *A Medical Book from Crocodilopolis. P. Vindob. D. 6257*. Vienna: Hollinek.

Ryholt, K. 2005. 'On the Contents and Nature of the Tebtunis Temple Library: A Status Report', in S. Lippert and M. Schentuleit (eds), *Tebtynis und Soknopaiu Nesos: Leben im römerzeitichen Fajum*. Wiesbaden: Harrassowitz, 141–70.

——2010. 'Late Period Literature', in A. B. Lloyd (ed.), *A Companion to Ancient Egypt*, vol. 2. Oxford: Wiley-Blackwell, 709–31.

——2011. 'New Light on the Legendary King Nechepsos of Egypt', *Journal of Egyptian Archaeology* 97: 61–72.

Schlott, A. 1989. *Schrift und Schreiber im Alten Ägypten*. Munich: Beck.

Smith, M. 1988. 'Four Demotic Ostraca in the Collection of the Ashmolean Museum', *Enchoria* 16: 77–88.

——2002. *On the Primaeval Ocean*. Copenhagen: Museum Tusculanum Press.

Tait, J. 2003. 'The Wisdom of Egypt: Classical Views', in P. Ucko and T. Champion (eds), *The Wisdom of Egypt: Changing Visions through the Ages*. London: University College London, 23–37.

Tait, W. J. 1977. *Papyri from Tebtunis in Egyptian and in Greek (P. Tebt. Tait)*. London: Egypt Exploration Society.

——1986. 'Guidelines and Borders in Demotic Papyri', in M. L. Bierbrier (ed.), *Papyrus: Structure and Usage*. London: British Museum Press, 63–89.

Vittmann, G. 2002–3. 'Ein Entwurf zur Dekoration eines Heiligtums in Soknopaiu Nesos (pWien D 10100)', *Enchoria* 28: 106–36.

——2006–7. Review of K. Ryholt (ed.), *The Petese Stories II*, *Enchoria* 30: 182–85.

Vleeming, S. P. 1981. 'La phase initiale du démotique ancien', *Chronique d'Égypte* 56: 31–48.

Vogel, K. 1975. 'Ein arithmetisches Problem aus dem Mittleren Reich in einem demotischen Papyrus', *Enchoria* 4: 67–70.

Volten, A. 1942. *Demotische Traumdeutung (Pap. Carlsberg XIII und XIV Verso)*. Copenhagen: Munksgaard.

von Lieven, A. 2004. 'Das Göttliche in der Natur erkennen: Tiere, Pflanzen und Phänomene der unbelebten Natur als Manifestationen des Göttlichen: Mit einer Edition der Baumliste P. Berlin 29027', *Zeitschrift für Ägyptische Sprache und Altertumskunde* 131: 156–72.

——2007. *Grundriss des Laufes der Sterne: Das sogenannte Nutbuch*, 2 vols. Copenhagen: Museum Tusculanum Press.

Wångstedt, S. V. 1976–7. 'Demotische Ostraka: Varia I', *Orientalia Suecana* 25: 5–41.

Widmer, G. 2004. 'Une invocation à la déesse (tablette démotique Louvre E 10382)', in F. Hoffmann and H.-J. Thissen (eds), *Res Severa Verum Gaudium: Festschrift für Karl-Theodor Zauzich zum 65. Geburtstag am 8. Juni 2004*. Leuven: Peeters, 651–86.

Zauzich, K.-T. 1983. 'Demotische Texte römischer Zeit', in G. Grimm, H. Heinen, and E. Winter (eds), *Das römisch-byzantinische Ägypten: Akten des Internationalen Symposions 26.–30. September 1978 in Trier*. Mainz: von Zabern, 77–80.

——1991. 'Einleitung', in P. J. Frandsen (ed.), *Demotic Texts from the Collection*. Copenhagen: Museum Tusculanum Press, 1–11.

——2000. 'Ein antikes demotisches Namenbuch', in P. J. Frandsen and K. Ryholt (eds), *A Miscellany of Demotic Texts and Studies*. Copenhagen: Museum Tusculanum Press, 27–52.

CHAPTER 34

EGYPTIAN HIEROGLYPHS

DAVID KLOTZ

Despite the ever-increasing dominance of Greek in administrative documents and Demotic for literary and funerary papyri, the traditional hieroglyphic script of the Pharaonic period remained a vibrant medium for Egyptian religious and historical compositions in a variety of contexts. Although the lengthy texts of this era fascinated early Egyptologists, they have since gained a reputation among scholars for being exceptionally difficult, either because they are filled with orthographic and grammatical errors, or because they are deemed to be enigmatic and obscure. This common perception is rooted in two simplistic assumptions about scribes of the Roman period. The first maintains that literacy in hieroglyphs declined rapidly in the final years of paganism, so that the ever-narrowing circle of scribes could only hope to produce degenerate imitations of earlier inscriptions. An opposite view posits that while the scribes were perfectly competent in the hieroglyphic script, they employed increasingly complex orthographies and cryptograms to obscure the theological content, attempting to magnify their prestige among Egyptians and Romans alike in the domain of restricted, arcane knowledge at a time when their political and social authority was in sharp decline (e.g. Iversen 1993: 24–6; Assmann 2002a: 414–20).

Hieroglyphs of the Roman period developed organically from the system used in the Ptolemaic period, and scribes continued to produce volumes of fascinating compositions employing complex graphic and phonetic wordplay. Since temple scribes became steadily more prolix over time, texts from this era provide valuable new details on religious beliefs and cult practices, making the extensive corpus of Roman period hieroglyphic texts—many of which have only been recently published—valuable sources for the study of Egyptian religion in all periods.

Owing in part to Roman 'Egyptomania', the hieroglyphic script itself became a popular subject of study across the empire. Egyptians produced annotated sign-lists and copies of classical Pharaonic texts, international scholars described the principles of hieroglyphic writing, and new inscriptions were commissioned for obelisks in Rome. The efforts of the indigenous clergy to preserve their religious heritage, combined with the insatiable academic curiosity of Roman scholars seeking ancient wisdom across the world, helped sustain the hieroglyphic script long after it might have otherwise become obsolete.

Sources for Egyptian Hieroglyphs: The Varieties of Hieroglyphic Texts

Temples

The vast majority of hieroglyphic inscriptions from this period appear on temple walls. Given the relative lack of interest in this material among Egyptologists, the sheer quantity might come as a surprise. The best-preserved corpus of texts belongs to the temple of Hathor at Dendara, where Roman period inscriptions cover the entire pronaos, most of the exterior wall, the larger mammisi, the temple of Isis, and three monumental gates, totalling almost 2,000 pages of published hieroglyphs. The temple of Esna, of which only the pronaos survives, consists of roughly 1,100 pages of texts dating to the Roman period.

Additional inscriptions occur at practically every surviving temple from Egypt, most notably at Philae, Elephantine, Kom Ombo, Tod, Medinet Habu, Opet, Deir el-Shelwit, Koptos, el-Qal'a, Shanhur, Dush, and Deir el-Hagar. For smaller temples like Deir el-Shelwit, all decoration dates to the Roman period. At most temples, however, the inscriptions fit on spaces left undecorated in the Ptolemaic period, namely exterior walls, newly constructed propylons, pronaoi, or processional gates. Occasionally, one finds inscriptions within the temple proper, as at Karnak, where Domitian renovated the New Kingdom contra-temple of Thutmose III adjoining the sanctuary of Amun (Klotz 2008a).

Temple inscriptions can be divided into several genres (see Leitz 2004). The most frequent texts are the ubiquitous offering scenes in which the king presents various gifts to divinities, while captions reproduce the ritual incantations and explain the theological significance of each sacrifice. While these scenes often feature traditional liturgical formulas originating in the Pyramid Texts of the Old Kingdom, scribes frequently sought to employ novel expressions and adapt the vocabulary to the local context.

More substantial inscriptions include lengthy hymns recited at specific occasions. Some of these were standardized and occur in many different temples (e.g. Sternberg el-Hotabi and Kammerzell 1992; Cauville 2002: 82–95). Others incorporate passages from earlier hymns into newer religious compositions, updated to include contemporaneous scientific theories or philosophical trends (see Derchain 1998). Liturgical texts at Esna incorporate many excerpts of earlier hymns (e.g. Klotz 2006: 224), and one particular hymn from the temple elaborates on traditional creation accounts and details how the god Khnum fashions humans, including the intertwining of bones, veins, arteries, and internal organs (Derchain 2004). At Kom Ombo a lengthy ode to Sobek develops into a naturalistic treatise on the behaviour of crocodiles (Derchain 2002; Leitz 2010), and a hymn from Medamud celebrates the return of the Wandering Goddess, Rattawy, depicting a ceremony in which even desert people, animals, and fantastic creatures participate (Darnell 1995). In addition to numerous songs praising Khnum and Neith from Esna (Sauneron 1962a), the Roman period provides some of the most informative hymns in honour of Imhotep (Sauneron 1965; Cauville 2010), Isis (von Lieven 2006), and Amun (Jambon and Fortier 2009), among other divinities (e.g. Junker 1931; es-Saghir and Valbelle 1983).

Other hieroglyphic inscriptions outline the protocol for religious festivals, monumentalizing information usually kept on papyri or ritual tablets (Sauneron 1962a; Grimm 1994; Cauville 2002). These sources provide valuable information on the course of divine processions and the various duties of certain priesthoods. Roman period texts provide the most information on the birthday celebrations of Osiris and Isis at the Opet temple in Karnak and Dendara during the epagomenal days (Bergman 1970: 73–98; Herbin 2003; Cauville 2009), and the mammisi festivals for local child-gods during the harvest festival of Pachons (Daumas 1958; Klotz 2009b). These sources also specify the degrees of ritual purity required for different sacerdotal jobs, even banning certain groups (e.g. foreigners, women, lepers) from the temple (Sauneron 1960; Derchain-Urtel 1998; Quack 2005), and proscribing profane activities such as fishing and loud music during the Osiris mysteries (Junker 1913; Sauneron 1958; Emerit 2002).

Another major genre of temple inscriptions are cult-topographical 'monographies' (Gutbub 1973; Leitz 2004: 63–7; Klotz 2009a), longer texts that summarize the fundamental theological information about a temple, city, or entire district, presenting the chief divinities, festivals, priesthoods, and local myths in an abbreviated narrative. Related in content are cosmogonic inscriptions recounting the creation of the universe according to local traditions; the most extensive Roman period example comes from Esna (Sauneron 1962a: 253–70; Broze 1993, 1999), but similar themes occur at Dendara (Cauville 2009: 18) and Kom Ombo (Leitz 2010). Finally, the ceilings and architraves of Esna and Dendara preserve lengthy astronomical hymns accompanied by representations of the zodiac, decan stars, and other celestial entities (Neugebauer and Parker 1969; von Lieven 2000; Cauville 2008).

Stelae

In contrast to the multiple sacerdotal and royal decrees of the Ptolemaic period (Rosetta Stone, Canopus Decree, Raphia Decree), official, imperial hieroglyphic stelae are rare in the Roman period. The most extensive such text is the trilingual decree of Cornelius Gallus from Philae, although the hieroglyphic portion varies considerably from the Greek and Latin versions (Hoffmann, Minas-Nerpel, and Pfeiffer 2009). The only other royal decree, granting certain privileges to agricultural properties sacred to the Isis temple at Philae, was carved on a temple wall under Marcus Aurelius, not on a stela (Junker 1924).

A nearly continuous series of hieroglyphic epitaphs for the sacred Buchis bulls of Armant are preserved from the reigns of Augustus to Constantius II (340 CE) (Grenier 1983; Goldbrunner 2003). However, the corpus of over 1,200 hieroglyphic and Demotic stelae from the Serapeum, going back to the New Kingdom and recording burials of the Apis bull and genealogies of the high priests of Memphis, ends abruptly with the arrival of Augustus (Quaegebeur 1980: 74). Finally, a considerable number of smaller royal stelae from Thebes commemorate temple construction or renovation projects sponsored by Augustus (Revez 2004) and Tiberius (de Meulenaere 1978).

Private individuals also commissioned hieroglyphic stelae to record their benefactions to temples. Both a priest from Dendara (Vleeming 2001: 151–4) and the industrious *prostates* (supervisor) Parthenios from Koptos (Vleeming 2001: 170–97; Pasquali 2007) left monuments in hieroglyphs, Demotic, and Greek. Hieroglyphic funerary stelae appear to have fallen out of fashion in the Roman period, but two notable exceptions are the eloquent monument of a priest from Akhmim active under the reign of Hadrian (Scharff 1926) and the trilingual stela of the hieroglyph carver Besas of uncertain date (Riggs 2005: 249–51).

Statues

While a fair number of archaizing statues of Roman emperors survive, very few bear hieroglyphic inscriptions. Exceptions include two striding statues, one bearing cartouches of Commodus (Minneapolis Institute of Arts 58.14, unpublished), the other attributed to Caracalla, although only the beginning of the royal titulary remains (Hawass 1997).

One inscribed statue of a priest from Mendes explicitly mentions Augustus (Grenier 1986). Otherwise, it is difficult to ascertain whether other late private statues belong to the late Ptolemaic or early Roman periods (e.g. Abdalla 1994), since such monuments rarely include royal names. The problem of dating is further complicated by the Roman predilection for adapting or creating Egyptian works of art, as the heads of several inscribed statues of the Ptolemaic period appear to have been reworked in the first century CE (Jansen-Winkeln 1998; Lembke and Vittmann 1999). It is perhaps significant that none of the several hundred statues from the Karnak Cachette can be dated to the Roman period (Coulon and Jambon 2010).

Papyri

In the Pharaonic period, scribes preferred the hieratic script for writing on papyri and ostraca, reserving hieroglyphs almost exclusively for lapidary inscriptions. Nonetheless, several archaizing funeral papyri of the Roman period contain variants of the Books of Breathing composed in ornate hieroglyphs employing the same enigmatic script popular in temple inscriptions of the era (Herbin 1984, 2008).

In addition, several cult-topographical priestly manuals—reference papyri compiling religious and mythological information from different geographical regions—also used fanciful hieroglyphs instead of hieratic or Demotic. These papyri include the Book of the Fayum (Beinlich 1991; Tait 2003); *P Jumilhac*, dealing exclusively with the seventeenth and eighteenth Upper Egyptian nomes (Vandier 1961; Quack 2008); and the more comprehensive geographic manuals covering all of Egypt (Griffith and Petrie 1889: 20–5, pls 9–15; Osing and Rosati 1998: 19–54, pls 1–5). The use of fanciful hieroglyphs, primarily arranged in columns rather than lines, gives the impression that these texts were copied directly from the walls of temples, tombs, or other monuments, even if the redaction process was actually more complicated (Quack 2008). The Book of the Fayum has direct parallels in the temple of Kom Ombo, while the Tanis papyrus links the cult-topographical charts to a copy of a private autobiographic inscription, suggesting that all the texts were copied from a now lost funerary monument (Griffith and Petrie 1889: 24–5, pl. 14). Earlier compilations of theological knowledge were occasionally recorded on large granite naoi (free-standing shrines) or stelae, such as the well-known Shabaka Stone from Memphis, and similar hieroglyphic inscriptions may have served as models for the later priestly manuals (e.g. Goyon 1937; Rondot 1989; von Bomhard 2008).

Tombs and Mortuary Equipment

Hieroglyphs also feature on both traditional and Hellenizing funerary art from the Roman period. Such decoration occasionally accompanies painted decoration on the walls of private tombs, most notably at Tuna el-Gebel, Atripe, and el-Muzawwaqa (Kaplan 1999), as well as on coffins, shrouds, mummy-beds, and other burial objects (Kurth 1990, 2010a). While the hieroglyphic texts on these objects consist largely of short captions to divinities and individuals, more complex mortuary formulas are also attested (e.g. Petrie 1908, pl. 42; Beinlich-Seeber 1998).

Graffiti

While the majority of graffiti on temples and statues were composed in Demotic or Greek, several votive inscriptions employed the hieroglyphic script. These include a small relief on the seventh pylon of Karnak temple from the reign of Nero (Barguet 2008: 254, 287), and the well-known graffito of Esmet-Akhom from Philae, the last datable hieroglyphic inscription in Egypt (396 CE) (Hölbl 2000: 46).

Obelisks

Ever since Augustus transported two New Kingdom specimens to Rome, the obelisk became one of the most enduring symbols of Egypt in the Roman imagination. Although most inscribed obelisks in Rome or Istanbul were originally carved and erected in the Pharaonic period (Iversen 1968–72; Ciampini 2004), several new obelisks with original hieroglyphic texts were commissioned in Rome. These include two obelisks of Domitian in the Piazza Navona (Grenier 1987b) and Benevento (Iversen 1973; Colin 1993), and the obelisk of Antinoos, apparently meant to adorn his funeral complex near the Palatine during the reign of Hadrian (Grenier 2008). The inscriptions on the latter obelisk have fascinated and perplexed Egyptologists over the years, but the palaeography and spellings are comparable to contemporaneous texts from Upper Egypt, and it is almost certain that a highly educated Egyptian scribe was responsible for its composition (Derchain 1987).

Language and Epigraphy

In previous discussions, scholars have overemphasized the presence of grammatical errors and confusion between signs in Roman period inscriptions, interpreting these scribal mistakes within the narratives of the decline of paganism, language death, illiterate scribes, and an increasingly irrelevant priesthood (Houston, Baines, and Cooper 2003: 445–7). Certainly these types of error exist (Sauneron 1959: 43–52), mainly resulting from confusion between similar hieroglyphic or hieratic signs, but such scribal error is extant in hieroglyphic texts of all eras (e.g. Kurth 1999). The inscriptions on the exterior wall, pronaos, and mammisi of Dendara (all from the first century CE) represent some of the finest inscriptions in Egyptian history (Fig. 34.1), with meticulously carved, evenly proportioned signs, and only rare mistakes (Cauville 2008: 6–7).

Inscriptions dating to Antoninus Pius from Medinet Habu, Tod, Esna, Deir el-Shelwit, and Nadura likewise remain excellent, and the quality of workmanship only begins to deteriorate in the reign of Marcus Aurelius at Esna (Sauneron 1959: 44). Magical stelae and *cippi* have been cited as examples of the rapid decline of scribal competence outside the temples and the rise of pseudo-hieroglyphic inscriptions (Sternberg-el Hotabi 1994). However, the evidence in question is of uncertain provenance and dated only by vague stylistic criteria, so it provides no definite information about Egyptian literacy in the Roman period.

Detailed palaeographic study of Roman inscriptions is a relatively new field of research (e.g. Dils 2000, pls 83–96; Meeks 2004; Guermeur 2007), since earlier text editions primarily employed typeset or normalized hand-drawn hieroglyphs. Nonetheless, facsimile editions are gradually becoming the accepted standard for publication of later material (Cauville 1990; Dils 2000; Willems, Coppens, and de Meyer 2003). In general, hieroglyphs are slightly rounder and taller than in the Pharaonic period (Fig. 34.2), and each sign can contain a large amount of internal details.

The language of Roman period hieroglyphic texts is what Egyptologists have termed *Spätmittelägyptisch* or *l'Égyptien de tradition*, an archaizing form of Middle Egyptian (the classical language of the Middle and New Kingdoms) with simplified verbal forms (i.e. superficial

FIG. 34.1 Relief of Trajan, from the birth house at Dendara

Author's photograph.

FIG. 34.2 Detail of a hymn to Amun from Karnak, from the reign of Domitian

Author's photograph.

opposition between *sḏm=f* and *sḏm.n=f*; no morphological distinction between circumstantial and nominal forms) and minor changes in syntax and vocabulary (see primarily Broze 1993; Engsheden 2003; Paulet 2006; Kurth 2007–8). While the more colloquial Late Egyptian frequently appears in monumental inscriptions of the New Kingdom and Third Intermediate period, archaizing texts of the Roman period betray only minor traces of the spoken language of the era (late Demotic, early Coptic). This linguistic evolution is most apparent in the unconventional orthographies, frequently resulting from phonetic changes (as discussed above), but also in alternative forms of dependent pronouns and stative endings. One particular hymn from Esna exhibits strong traces of Late Egyptian and Demotic grammar (Quack 1995). Since this text belongs more to the realm of personal piety, invoking Khnum primarily as a protector and a healing god, the scribes likely chose the more colloquial register of speech in order to replicate a popular song recited by the masses during festival processions.

Cryptography

Enigmatic spellings pervade hieroglyphic texts of the Ptolemaic period, and this trend developed even further under the Romans as scribes continued to invent sportive and theologically allusive orthographies for ordinary words and divine names (e.g. Derchain-Urtel 1999; Cauville 2001: 4). One of the most obvious changes occurs with simple uniliteral signs, where

Table 34.1 Common unilateral (alphabetic) signs used in hieroglyphic texts of the Roman period, especially in renderings of imperial titularies

Consonant	Traditional	Roman
ꜥ	𓂝	[illegible]
b	𓃀	[illegible]
p	𓊪	[illegible]
f	𓆑	[illegible]
m	𓅓, 𓐝	[illegible]
r	𓂋, 𓃭	[illegible]
s	𓋴, 𓊃	[illegible]
š	𓈙	[illegible]
k, q, g	𓎡, 𓈎, 𓎼	[illegible]
t, d	𓏏, 𓂧	[illegible]

texts usually favour smaller variants of the traditional hieroglyphs, most likely in order to save time and conserve space when writing the increasingly elaborate imperial titularies (e.g. Autokrator Kaisaros Titus Aelius Hadrianus Antoninus Sebastos Eusebius Augustus; see Grenier 1987a, 1989; Hallof 2010). The alphabetic substitutions shown in Table 34.1 were particularly popular in inscriptions of this era (see also Sauneron 1959: 52–3; 1982: 192–4).

Other innovative spellings are more complex, exploiting phonetic changes (the collapse of dentals and plosives), near-homonyms, novel depictions of standard hieroglyphs, or subtle allusions to theological concepts (Fairman 1945; Darnell 2004; Kurth 2007, 2010b). The following group, which occurs several times in the Roman period (e.g. *Dendara* XIV 69.13), is an elegant illustration of this process:

This 'cryptogram' writes two ubiquitous epithets that normally precede the royal titulary: 'Son of Re, Lord of Diadems'. The seated child writes 'son', the sun-disc on his head stands for 'Re', the cow obtains the value 'lord' through a series of theological and phonetic puns (cow = Hathor = *nbw.t*, 'the Golden one' > *nb*, 'lord'), and the final sign represents 'diadems' (*ḫꜥ.w* > *ḫꜥj*, 'to appear in glory'). At the same time, this compact orthography represents the newborn sun rising in the morning, specifically in his iconic image of a solar-child riding upon the horns of his bovine mother (see Verhoeven 2007), while the whole scene is determined by the hieroglyph of a rising sun. To label this spelling cryptographic would be incorrect, since the proper translation of these banal epithets is obvious from the context. Rather, this innovative orthography represents a scribal flourish aimed to draw attention to a formulaic text that ancient readers might have otherwise passed by.

The same type of cryptography was developed even further at Esna, where several litanies present lists of divine names composed entirely in enigmatic trigrams, groups of three hieroglyphs with unconventional phonetic values (Sauneron 1982; Leitz 2008). Once again, these texts are hardly cryptographic, as the repetitive structure makes the divine names easy to recognize. Instead, each unusual spelling alludes to the specific epithets in its associated verse, so that even the orthography of a divinity's name reflects the various aspects of its multidimensional nature. The most extreme example of this process can also be found at Esna, where two hymns were composed almost exclusively with crocodiles and rams (Leitz 2001; Hallof 2007).

'Egyptomania' in Egypt and Rome

This period also marks the apogee of ancient philological interest in hieroglyphs, among both Egyptians and Romans (Assmann 2002b). It is within this archaizing, academic context that one finds the first Egyptian 'sign-list', a catalogue of hieroglyphs arranged in broad conceptual subsets (e.g. body parts, plants) accompanied by descriptions of the signs written in hieratic (Griffith and Petrie 1889: 1–19, pls 1–8), as well as a fragmentarily preserved introduction to hieroglyphs (Iversen 1958). Egyptians remained fascinated by the hieroglyphic inscriptions of the Pharaonic period, as evidenced by a remarkable papyrus from Tebtunis containing copies of autobiographies from First Intermediate period tombs in Asyut (Osing and Rosati 1998: 55–100, pls 6–13). Similarly, *P. Carlsb.* 1 features a hieratic transcription of a New Kingdom cosmographic text originally composed in hieroglyphs (the Book of Nut) with extensive astrological commentary in Demotic (von Lieven 2007). Several bilingual ostraca from Medinet Madi (Narmouthis) feature hieroglyphic copies of certain divine epithets—some written in less conventional, Graeco-Roman orthographies—followed by transliterations of these signs in the Greek script (Gallo 1997: 3–21), demonstrating that educated scribes still took pains to pronounce hieroglyphs correctly.

Another Demotic ostracon from Medinet Madi records the beginning of an exchange between Hadrian and the local Egyptian priests during his visit in 131 CE, in which the curious emperor asked, 'Now what about this skill of writing?' (Menchetti 2004). Although the priests' reply is not preserved, it is likely that Hadrian was specifically inquiring about hieroglyphs. In one of her inscriptions on the Colossus of Memnon, Hadrian's poet Julia Balbilla addresses the statue as 'Amenothis, king of Egypt, according to what the priests learned in ancient myths relate' (*IGLCM* 29.3; Quaegebeur 1986: 100), indicating that members of the clergy accompanied the imperial party and translated hieroglyphic inscriptions, just like the priest who served as guide for Germanicus during his tour of Thebes over a century earlier (Tac. *Ann.* 2.60; Montet 1947).

Interest in the ancient inscriptions was not limited to the emperor and his entourage. Plutarch studied Egyptian in both Athens and Alexandria, and the various etymologies in *De Iside et Osiride* demonstrate his familiarity with the spoken language (Thissen 2009); one passage even suggests he could read certain hieroglyphs (Thissen 1985). Chaeremon, an

Alexandrian priest, Stoic philosopher, and Nero's personal tutor, composed what may be the earliest précis of the hieroglyphic script (Thissen 2006). This earlier sign-list apparently influenced the more extensive *Hieroglyphica* of Horapollo, composed as late as the fifth century CE (Thissen 2001, pp. xii–xiv). The more symbolic or mystical readings in the latter book shaped perceptions of hieroglyphs in Western thought for centuries (Iversen 1993). Neoplatonist and Gnostic thinkers were fascinated by the deeper implications of the hieroglyphic script (Motte 1986), and Hermetic texts claimed to be translations of ancient hieroglyphic texts found on stelae or tablets (Copenhaver 1992: 29–30).

The large number of authentic Egyptian artefacts brought to Rome at this time, including obelisks, stelae, and statues with inscriptions (Roullet 1972; Baines and Whitehouse 2005), presented valuable objects of study for philologically inquisitive Romans. Ammianus Marcellinus reproduces a rough translation of the inscription on a Ramesside obelisk in the Circus Maximus (now in the Piazza del Popolo) into Greek, attributing this work to the otherwise unknown Hermapion, and copies of the same hieroglyphic text were carved on a new obelisk in the Gardens of Sallust (Lambrecht 2001). Other attempts to reproduce the script in Rome were less successful, resulting in pseudo-hieroglyphic inscriptions on Egyptianizing monuments (e.g. Baines and Whitehouse 2005: 728–30).

Current and Future Research

The most important priority for research on Roman period hieroglyphs is the publication of all remaining temple inscriptions. Major steps have been taken in recent years, notably with the appearance of the final volumes of Esna (Sauneron 2009) and Dendara (Cauville 1999, 2007a, b, 2011), and the publication of smaller temples (Pantalacci and Traunecker 1990–8; Traunecker 1992; Dils 2000; Willems, Coppens, and de Meyer 2003; Rondot 2004).

The important temples of Philae present the biggest gap in our documentation. Although a significant portion of the Roman texts are already available (Junker 1913, 1924; Daressy 1917; Junker and Winter 1965; Daumas 1968), final editions of the Isis temple, second pylon, colonnade halls, and various chapels are still in preparation (but see Beinlich 2010–11). Another important site is Kom Ombo, where all the inscriptions were copied in the early twentieth century, unfortunately rather hastily and with many errors (de Morgan 1895–1909). Although a new edition of some of the Ptolemaic texts has recently appeared, the extensive Roman period inscriptions from the forecourt and exterior walls are only available in the outdated edition, with the exception of a few specific texts (e.g. Junker 1931; Derchain 2002).

The Epigraphic Survey of the University of Chicago will eventually record the important Roman inscriptions concerning Kematef, the Ogdoad, and the Sokar Festival at Medinet Habu (reigns of Claudius, Domitian, and Antoninus Pius), and Marc Gabolde is preparing the associated temple of Deir el-Rumi (Lecuyot and Gabolde 1998). Various missions are studying the Roman period temples in the oases, particularly Nadura and Qasr el-Zayyan in Kharga Oasis (Klotz 2009a, 2010), as well as Deir el-Hagar and Ain Birbiya in Dakhla (Kaper 1997).

In addition to the extant temples, some inscriptions only survive as fragments spread across scattered blocks. The Roman period material from the Khnum temple at Elephantine has already been published (Laskowska-Kusztal 1996), and a large number of blocks from

Tod and Armant are currently being studied and reassembled (Thiers 2007, 2009a, b); similar work remains for a collapsed gate of Tiberius at Medamud (Valbelle 1979). The temple of Thoth at Amheida, in Dakhla Oasis, survives only in fragments, but enough pieces remain to reconstruct entire chapels from the Flavian era (Kaper and Davoli 2006). A large number of blocks from the reign of Augustus have been found at Luxor temple, most likely deriving from a substantial Graeco-Roman addition to the Mut Precinct (Kariya and Johnson 2003; Johnson and McClain 2008).

Conclusion

Egyptian scribes continued to compose lengthy and stylistically complex hieroglyphic texts on temple walls and other media well into the early third century CE. Contemporaneous religious manuals and other papyri, meanwhile, attest to a concentrated effort to codify and transmit this written knowledge within temple libraries. The system of Egyptian hieroglyphs fascinated most prominent Roman scholars of the Second Sophistic, and the mystical interpretations of Horapollo influenced European thinkers through the Renaissance. Largely overlooked in Egyptological scholarship until recently, this subject is an area where much work remains to be done. The vast quantity of unpublished and recently edited temple texts has the potential to reshape our understanding of language, culture, and religion in Roman Egypt.

Suggested Reading

The biggest obstacle to reading hieroglyphic texts of the Roman period is the semi-enigmatic script. A very good introduction to the principles underlying the Graeco-Roman orthographies is Fairman (1945), as well as the important analysis of Pharaonic cryptography by Darnell (2004). To cope with the vastly expanded repertory of signs, one should consult Cauville (2001), Meeks (2004), and Kurth (2007–8). While there is not yet a specialized dictionary for Roman inscriptions, the large dictionary of Ptolemaic texts from Edfu is quite helpful (Wilson 1997). For reading the primary texts, the best introductions are the Graeco-Roman chrestomathy by Leitz (2004) and the Ptolemaic grammar with exercises by Kurth (2007–8, 2010b). For translations, the best introduction to the hymns and festival texts remains Sauneron's volume on Esna (1962a), as well as more recent books discussing Roman Dendara by Cauville (2002, 2009, 2011). Scattered translations of individual texts or even small excerpts are conveniently registered in the concordance of Leitz (2011).

Bibliography

Abdalla, A. O. A. 1994. 'Graeco-Roman Statues Found in the Sebakh at Dendera', in C. J. Eyre et al. (eds), *The Unbroken Reed: Studies in the Culture and Heritage of Ancient Egypt in Honour of A. F. Shore*. London: Egypt Exploration Society, 1–24.

Assmann, J. 2002a. *The Mind of Egypt: History and Meaning in the Time of the Pharaoh*. New York: Metropolitan Books.
——2002b. 'Etymographie: Zeichen im Jenseits der Sprache', in A. Assmann and J. Assmann (eds), *Hieroglyphen: Stationen einer anderen abenländischen Grammatologie*. Munich: Fink, 37–63.
Baines, J., and H. Whitehouse. 2005. 'Ägyptische Hieroglyphen in der Kaiserstadt Rom', in H. Beck, P. C. Bol, and M. Bückling (eds), *Ägypten, Griechenland, Rom: Abwehr und Berührung*. Tübingen: Wasmuth; Frankfurt: Liebighaus, 404–15, 718–20, 728–30.
Barguet, P. 2008. *Le temple d'Amon-Rê à Karnak: Essai d'exégèse*, 3rd edn. Cairo: Institut Français d'Archéologie Orientale.
Beinlich, H. 1991. *Das Buch vom Fayum: Zum religiösen Eigenverständnis einer ägyptischen Landschaft*, 2 vols. Wiesbaden: Harrassowitz.
——2010–11. *Die Photos der Preußischen Expedition, 1908–1910 nach Nubien*, 2 vols. Dettelbach: J. H. Röll.
Beinlich-Seeber, C. 1998. 'Ein römerzeitliches Sargfragment in Marseille', in A. Brodbeck (ed.), *Ein ägyptisches Glasperlenspiel: Ägyptologische Beiträge für Erik Hornung aus seinem Schülerkreis*. Berlin: Mann.
Bergman, J. 1970. *Isis-Seele und Osiris-Ei: Zwei ägyptologische Studien zu Diodorus Siculus I 27, 4–5*. Stockholm: Almqvist and Wiksell.
Broze, M. 1993. 'La création du monde et l'opposition *sḏm.f–sḏm.n.f* dans le temple d'Esna', *Revue d'Égyptologie* 44: 3–10.
——1999. 'Les sept propos de Méthyer: Structure narrative et théorie du savoir dans la cosmogonie de Neith à Esna', *Bulletin de l'Institut Français d'Archéologie Orientale du Caire* 99: 63–72.
Cauville, S. 1990. 'Les inscriptions dédicatoires du temple d'Hathor à Dendera', *Bulletin de l'Institut Français d'Archéologie Orientale* 90: 83–114.
——1999. *Le temple de Dendara: La porte d'Isis*. Cairo: Institut Français d'Archéologie Orientale.
——2001. *Dendara: Le fonds hiéroglyphiques au temps de Cléopâtre*. Paris: Cybèle.
——2002. *Dendara: Les fêtes d'Hathor*. Leuven: Peeters.
——2007a. *Dendara: Le temple d'Isis*. Cairo: Institut Français d'Archéologie Orientale.
——2007b. *Le temple de Dendara* XII. Cairo: Institut Français d'Archéologie Orientale.
——2008. *Dendara*, vol. 15: *Texte*. <http://www.dendara.net/download/Dendara-XV.pdf>.
——2009. *Dendara: Le temple d'Isis*, vol. 2: *Analyse à la lumière du temple d'Hathor*. Leuven: Peeters.
——2010. 'Imhotep: Un avatar de Thoth', *Göttinger Miszellen* 224: 17–25.
——2011. *Dendara: Traduction*, vols. 13–15. Leuven: Peeters.
Ciampini, E. M. 2004. *Gli obelischi iscritti di Roma*. Rome: Libreria dello Stato.
Colin, F. 1993. 'Domitien, Julie et Isis au pays des Hirpins (*CIL* IX 1153 et l'obélisque de Bénévent)', *Chronique d'Égypte* 68: 247–60.
Copenhaver, B. P. 1992. *Hermetica: The Greek Corpus Hermeticum and the Latin Asclepius in a New English Translation*. Cambridge: Cambridge University Press.
Coulon, L., and Jambon, E. 2010. *Karnak Cachette*, online database, updated 25 May 2010. <http://www.ifao.egnet.net/bases/cachette>.
Daressy, G. 1917. 'Légende d'Ar-hems-nefer à Philæ', *Annales du Service des Antiquités de l'Égypte* 17: 76–80.
Darnell, J. C. 1995. 'Hathor Returns to Medamûd', *Studien zur Altägyptischen Kultur* 22: 47–94.

——2004. *The Enigmatic Netherworld Books of the Solar-Osirian Unity*. Fribourg: Academic Press; Göttingen: Vandenhoeck & Ruprecht.
Daumas, F. 1958. *Les mammisis des temples égyptiens*. Paris: Belles Lettres.
——1968. 'Les propylées du temple d'Hathor à Philae et la culte de la déesse', *Zeitschrift für Ägyptische Sprache und Altertumskunde* 95: 1–17.
de Meulenaere, H. 1978. 'L'œuvre architecturale de Tibère à Thèbes', *Orientalia Lovaniensia Periodica* 9: 69–73.
de Morgan, J. 1895–1909. *Kom Ombos* I–III. *Catalogue des monuments et inscriptions de l'Égypte antique*, vols 2–3. Vienna: Holzhausen.
Derchain, P. 1987. *Le dernier obélisque*. Brussels: Fondation Égyptologique Reine Élisabeth.
——1998. 'Le stoïcien de Kom Ombo', *Bulletin de la Société d'Égyptologie de Genève* 22: 17–20.
——2002. 'Portrait d'un divin crocodile ou l'originalité d'un écrivain du temps de Domitien', in F. Labrique (ed), *Religions méditerranéennes et orientales de l'antiquité*. Cairo: Institut Français d'Archéologie Orientale, 79–99.
——2004. 'À eux le bonheur! (La naissance d'un homme, *Esna* 250, 6–11)', *Göttinger Miszellen* 200: 37–44.
Derchain-Urtel, M.-T. 1998. 'Die Festbesucher in Esna', in R. Gundlach and M. Rochholz (eds), *4. Ägyptologische Tempeltagung: Feste im Tempel*. Wiesbaden: Harrassowitz, 3–15.
——1999. *Epigraphische Untersuchungen zur griechisch-römischen Zeit in Ägypten*. Wiesbaden: Harrassowitz.
Dils, P. 2000. *Der Tempel von Dusch: Publikation und Untersuchungen eines ägyptischen Provinztempels der römischen Zeit*, doctoral dissertation, University of Cologne. <http://kups.ub.uni-koeln.de/volltexte/2006/1614>.
Emerit, S. 2002. 'À propos de l'origine des interdits musicaux dans l'Égypte ancienne', *Bulletin de l'Institut Français d'Archéologie Orientale* 102: 189–210.
Engsheden, Å. 2003. *La reconstitution du verbe en égyptien de tradition 400–30 avant J.-C.* Uppsala: Uppsala University.
es-Saghir, M., and D. Valbelle. 1983. 'The Discovery of Komir Temple: Preliminary Report', *Bulletin de l'Institut Français d'Archéologie Orientale* 83: 149–70.
Fairman, H. W. 1945. 'An Introduction to the Study of Ptolemaic Signs and their Values', *Bulletin de l'Institut Français d'Archéologie Orientale* 43: 51–138.
Fowden, G. 1993. *The Egyptian Hermes: A Historical Approach to the Late Pagan Mind*, 2nd edn. Princeton: Princeton University Press.
Gallo, P. 1997. *Ostraca demotici e ieratici dall'archivio bilingue di Narmouthis* II. Pisa: ETS.
Goldbrunner, L. 2003. *Buchis: Eine Untersuchung zur Theologie des heiligen Stieres in Theben zur griechisch-römischen Zeit*. Turnhout: Brepols.
Goyon, G. 1937. 'Les travaux de Chou et les tribulations de Geb d'après le naos 2248 d'Ismaïlia', *Kêmi* 6: 1–42.
Grenier, J.-C. 1983. 'La stèle funéraire du dernier taureau Bouchis', *Bulletin de l'Institut Français d'Archéologie Orientale* 83: 197–208.
——1986. 'Le prophète et l'Autokratôr', *Revue d'Égyptologie* 37: 81–9.
——1987a. 'Le protocole pharaonique des empereurs romains: Analyse formelle et signification historique', *Revue d'Égyptologie* 38: 81–104.
——1987b. 'Les inscriptions hiéroglyphiques de l'obélisque Pamphili: Un témoignage méconnu sur l'avènement de Domitien', *Mémoire de l'École Française de Rome: Section Antiquité* 99: 937–61.
——1989. *Les titulatures des empereurs romains dans les documents en langue égyptienne*. Fondation Égyptologique Reine Élisabeth.

——2008. *L'Osiris Antinoos*. Montpellier: Université Paul Valéry.

Griffith, F. L., and W. M. F. Petrie. 1889. *Two Hieroglyphic Papyri from Tanis*. London: Trübner.

Grimm, A. 1994. *Die altägyptischen Festkalender in den Tempeln der griechisch-römischen Epoche*. Wiesbaden: Harrassowitz.

Guermeur, I. 2007. 'À propos de l'épigraphie ptolémaïque: L' exemple du mammisi de Philae', *Égypte, Afrique & Orient* 46: 15–22.

Gutbub, A. 1973. *Textes fondamentaux de la théologie de Kom Ombo*. Cairo: Institut Français d'Archéologie Orientale.

Hallof, J. 2007. 'Der Tempel von Esna: Ein Tempel für zwei Götter', in B. Haring and A. Klug (eds), *6. Ägyptologische Tempeltagung: Funktion und Gebrauch altägyptischer Tempelräume*. Wiesbaden: Harrassowitz, 119–30.

——2010. *Schreibungen der Pharaonennamen in den Ritualszenen der Tempel der griechisch-römischen Zeit Ägyptens*, vol. 2: *Die römischen Kaiser*. Dettelbach: Röll.

Hawass, Z. 1997. 'A Statue of Caracalla Found in the Nile by Fishermen', in J. Phillips (ed.), *Ancient Egypt, the Aegean, and the Near East: Studies in Honor of Martha Rhoads Bell*, vol. 1. San Antonio, Tex.: van Siclen, 227–33.

Herbin, F.-R. 1984. 'Une nouvelle page du Livre des respirations', *Bulletin de l'Institut Français d'Archéologie Orientale* 84: 249–302.

——2003. 'La renaissance d'Osiris au Temple d'Opet (*P. Vatican Inv. 38608*)', *Revue d'Égyptologie* 54: 67–127.

——2008. 'Trois papyrus hiéroglyphiques d'époque romaine', *Revue d'Égyptologie* 59: 125–54.

Hoffmann, F., M. Minas-Nerpel, and S. Pfeiffer. 2009. *Die dreisprächige Stele des C. Cornelius Gallus*. Berlin: de Gruyter.

Hölbl, G. 2000. *Altägypten im römischen Reich: Der römische Pharao und seine Tempel* I. Mainz: von Zabern.

Houston, S., J. Baines, and J. Cooper. 2003. 'Last Writing: Script Obsolescence in Egypt, Mesopotamia, and Mesoamerica', *Comparative Studies in Society and History* 45(3): 430–79.

Iversen, E. 1958. *Papyrus Carlsberg Nr. VII: Fragments of a Hieroglyphic Dictionary*. Copenhagen: Munksgaard.

——1968–72. *Obelisks in Exile*, 2 vols. Copenhagen: Gad.

——1973. 'The Inscriptions from the Obelisks of Benevento', *Acta Orientalia* 35: 15–28.

——1993. *The Myth of Egypt and its Hieroglyphs in European Tradition*. Princeton: Princeton University Press.

Jambon, E., and A. Fortier. 2009. '*Médamoud* no. 343', in C. Thiers (ed.), *Documents de Théologies Thébaines Tardives*. Montpellier: Université Paul Valéry, 49–94.

Jansen-Winkeln, K. 1998. 'Die Inschrift des Porträtstatue des Hor', *Mitteilungen des Deutschen Archäologischen Instituts, Abteilung Kairo* 54: 227–35.

Johnson, W. R., and J. B. McClain. 2008. 'A Fragmentary Scene of Ptolemy XII Worshipping the Goddess Mut and her Divine Entourage', in S. H. d'Auria (ed.), *Servant of Mut: Studies in Honor of Richard A. Fazzini*. Leiden: Brill, 134–40.

Junker, H. 1913. *Das Götterdekret über das Abaton*. Vienna: Holder.

——1924. 'Schenkung von Weingärten an die Isis von Philae unter Marc Aurel', *Wiener Zeitschrift für die Kunde des Morgenlandes* 31: 53–81.

——1931. 'Ein Doppelhymnus aus Kom Ombo', *Zeitschrift für Ägyptische Sprache und Altertumskunde* 67: 51–5.

——and E. Winter. 1965. *Das Geburtshaus des Tempels der Isis in Philä*. Vienna: Böhlaus.

Kaper, O. E. 1997. *Temples and Gods in Roman Dakhleh: Studies in the Indigenous Cults of an Egyptian Oasis*, doctoral dissertation, University of Groningen.

——and P. Davoli. 2006. 'A New Temple for Thoth in the Dakhleh Oasis', *Egyptian Archaeology* 29: 12–14.

Kaplan, I. 1999. *Grabmalerei und Grabreliefs der Römerzeit: Wechselwirkung zwischen der ägyptischen und griechisch-alexandrinischen Kunst*. Vienna: Afro-Pub.

Kariya, H., and W. R. Johnson. 2003. 'The Luxor Temple Wall Fragment Project', *Egyptian Archaeology* 22: 21–4.

Klotz, D. 2006. *Adoration of the Ram: Five Hymns to Amun-Re from Hibis Temple*. New Haven: Yale Egyptological Seminar.

——2008. 'Domitian at the Contra-Temple of Karnak', *Zeitschrift für Altägyptische Sprache und Altertumskunde* 135: 65–79.

——2009a. 'The Cult-Topographical Text of Qasr el-Zayyan', *Revue d'Égyptologie* 60: 17–40.

——2009b. 'The Theban Cult of Chonsu the Child in the Ptolemaic Period', in C. Thiers (ed.), *Documents de Théologies Thébaines Tardives*, vol. 1. Montpellier: Université Paul Valéry, 95–134.

——2010. 'Chonsu at Nadura Temple', *Göttinger Miszellen* 226: 25–34.

Kurth, D. 1990. *Der Sarg der Teüris: Eine Studie zum Totenglauben im römerzeitlichen Ägypten*. Mainz: von Zabern.

——1999. 'Der Einfluß der Kursive auf die Inschriften des Tempels von Edfu', in Kurth (ed.), *Edfu: Bericht über drei Surveys; Materialien und Studien*. Wiesbaden: Harrassowitz, 69–96.

——2007–8. *Einführung ins Ptolemäische: Eine Grammatik mit Zeichenliste und Übungsstücken*, 2 vols. Hützel: Backe.

——2010a. *Materialen zum Totenglauben im römerzeitlichen Ägypten*. Hützel: Backe.

——2010b. *A Ptolemaic Sign-List. Hieroglyphs used in the Temples of the Graeco-Roman Period of Egypt and their Meanings*. Hutzel: Backe.

Lambrecht, B. 2001. 'L'Obélisque d'Hermapion (Ammien Marcellin, *Res Gestae*, XVII, 4, 17–23)', *Le Muséon* 14: 51–95.

Laskowska-Kusztal, E. 1996. *Die Dekorfragmente der ptolemäisch-römischen Tempel von Elephantine*. Mainz: von Zabern.

Lecuyot, G., and M. Gabolde. 1998. 'A "Mysterious dwAt" Dating from the Roman Times at the Deir er-Rumi', in C. J. Eyre (ed.), *Proceedings of the Seventh International Congress of Egyptologists, Cambridge, 3–9 September 1995*. Leuven: Peeters, 661–7.

Leitz, C. 2001. 'Die beiden kryptographischen Inschriften aus Esna mit den Widdern und Krokodilen', *Studien zur Altägyptischen Kultur* 29: 251–76.

——2004. *Quellentexte zur ägyptischen Religion* I: *Die Tempelinschriften der griechisch-römischen Zeit*. Münster: Lit.

——2008. 'Les Trente Premiers Versets de la litanie d'Osiris à Esna (*Esna* 217)', *Revue d'Égyptologie* 59: 231–66.

——2011. *Kurzbibliographie zu den übersetzten Tempeltexten der griechisch-römischen Zeit*. (5th rev. edn) Cairo: Institut Français d'Archéologie Orientale.

——2010. 'Der Lobpreis des Krokodils: Drei Sobekhymnen aus Kom Ombo', in H. Knuf, C. Leitz, and D. von Recklinghausen (eds), *Honi soit qui mal y pense: Studien zum pharaonischen, griechisch-römischen und spätantiken Ägypten zu Ehren von Heinz-Josef Thissen*. Leuven: Peeters, 291–365.

Lembke, K., and G. Vittmann. 1999. 'Die Standfigur des Horos, Sohn des Thotoes (Berlin, Ägyptisches Museum SMPK 2271)', *Mitteilungen des Deutschen Archäologischen Instituts, Abteilung Kairo* 55: 299–313.

Meeks, D. 2004. *Les architraves du temple d'Esna: Paléographie*. Cairo: Institut Français d'Archéologie Orientale.

Menchetti, A. 2004. '*Quando Adriano venne in Egitto*: Un nuovo testo demotico sul viaggio dell'imperator', *Egitto e Vicino Orient* 27: 27–31.

Montet, P. 1947. 'Germanicus et le vieillard de Thèbes', in *Mélanges 1945* III: *Études historiques*. Publications de la Faculté des Lettres de l'Université de Strasbourg 106. Strasbourg, 47–79.

Motte, L. 1986. 'L'hiéroglyphe, d'Esna à l'Évangile de vérité', in *Deuxième Journée d'Études Coptes, Strasbourg, 25 Mai 1984*. Leuven: Peeters, 111–16.

Neugebauer, O., and R. A. Parker. 1969. *Egyptian Astronomical Texts* III: *Decans, Planets, Constellations and Zodiacs*. London: Humphries.

Osing, J. 1998. *Hieratische Papyri aus Tebtunis* I. Copenhagen: Museum Tusculanum Press.

——and G. Rosati. 1998. *Papiri geroglifici e ieratici da Tebtynis*. Florence: Istituto Papirologico G. Vitelli.

Pantalacci, L., and C. Traunecker. 1990–8. *Le temple d'el-Qal'a* I–II. Cairo: Institut Français d'Archéologie Orientale.

Pasquali, S. 2007. 'Une nouvelle stèle de Parthénios fils de Paminis de Coptos', *Revue d'Égyptologie* 58: 187–92.

Paulet, A. 2006. 'Morphologie et graphies des formes verbales *sḏm.n=f* et *sḏm=f* dans les inscriptions du temple d'Opet', *Chronique d'Égypte* 81: 77–93.

Petrie, W. M. F. 1908. *Athribis*. London: University College London.

Quack, J. F. 1995. 'Monumental-demotisch', in L. Gestermann and H. Sternberg-el Hotabi (eds), *Per Aspera ad Astra: Wolfgang Schenkel zum neunundfünfzigsten Geburtstag*. Kassel: Gestermann, 107–21.

——2005. 'Tabuisierte und ausgegrenzte Kranke nach dem "Buch vom Tempel"', in H.-W. Fischer-Elfert (ed.), *Papyrus Ebers und die antike Heilkunde*. Wiesbaden: Harrassowitz, 63–80.

——2008. 'Corpus oder membra disiecta? Zur Sprach- und Redaktionskritik des Papyrus Jumilhac', in W. Waitkus (ed.), *Diener des Horus: Festschrift für Dieter Kurth zum 65. Geburtstag*. Gladbeck: PeWe, 203–28.

Quaegebeur, J. 1980. 'The Genealogy of the Memphite High Priest Family in the Hellenistic Period', in D. J. Crawford, J. Quaegebeur, and W. Clarysse (eds), *Studies on Ptolemaic Memphis*. Leuven: Peeters, 43–82.

——1986. 'Aménophis, nom royal et nom divin: Questions méthodologiques', *Revue d'Égyptologie* 37: 97–106.

Revez, J. 2004. 'Une stèle commémorant la construction par l'empereur Auguste du mur d'enceinte du temple de Montou-Rê à Médamoud', *Bulletin de l'Institut Français d'Archéologie Orientale* 104: 495–510.

Riggs, C. 2005. *The Beautiful Burial in Roman Egypt: Art, Identity and Funerary Religion*. Oxford: Oxford University Press.

Rondot, V. 1989. 'Une monographie bubastite', *Bulletin de l'Institut Français d'Archéologie Orientale* 89: 249–70.

——1990. 'Le naos de Domitien, Toutou, et les sept flèches', *Bulletin de l'Institut Français d'Archéologie Orientale* 90: 303–37.

——2004. *Le temple de Soknebtynis et son dromos*. Cairo: Institut Français d'Archéologie Orientale.
Roullet, A. 1972. *The Egyptian and Egyptianizing Monuments of Imperial Rome*. Leiden: Brill.
Sauneron, S. 1958. 'L'Abaton de la campagne d'Esna', *Mitteilungen des Deutschen Archäologischen Instituts, Abteilung Kairo* 16: 271–9.
——1959. *Quatres campagnes à Esna*. Cairo: Institut Français d'Archéologie Orientale.
——1960. 'Les possédés', *Bulletin de l'Institut Français d'Archéologie Orientale* 60: 111–15.
——1962a. *Les fêtes religieuses d'Esna aux derniers siècles du paganisme*. Cairo: Institut Français d'Archéologie Orientale.
——1962b. 'Les conditions d'accès à la fonction sacerdotale à l'époque gréco-romaine', *Bulletin de l'Institut Français d'Archéologie Orientale* 61: 55–7.
——1965. 'Un hymne à Imouthès', *Bulletin de l'Institut Français d'Archéologie Orientale* 63: 73–87.
——1982. *L'écriture figurative dans les textes d'Esna*. Cairo: Institut Français d'Archéologie Orientale.
——2009. *Le temple d'Esna, Nos 547–646*. Cairo: Institut Français d'Archéologie Orientale.
Scharff, A. 1926. 'Ein Denkstein der römischen Kaiserzeit aus Achmim', *Zeitschrift für Altägyptische Sprache und Altertumskunde* 62: 86–107.
Sternberg-el Hotabi, H. 1994. 'Der Untergang der Hieroglyphenschrift: Schriftverfall und Schrifttod im Ägypten der griechisch-römischen Zeit', *Chronique d'Égypte* 69: 218–48.
——and F. Kammerzell. 1992. *Ein Hymnus an die Göttin Hathor und das Ritual 'Hathor das Trankopfer darbringen': Nach den Tempeltexten der griechisch-römischen Zeit*. Brussels: Fondation Égytopologique Reine Élisabeth.
Tait, J. 2003. 'The "Book of the Fayum": Mystery in a Known Landscape', in D. O'Connor and S. Quirke (eds), *Mysterious Lands*. London: University College London, 183–202.
Thiers, C. 2007. 'Mission épigraphiques de l'IFAO dans les villes méridionales du Palladium thébain', in J.-C. Goyon and C. Cardin (eds), *Proceedings of the Ninth International Congress of Egyptologists, Grenoble, 6–12 September 2004*, vol. 2. Leuven: Peeters, 1807–16.
——2009a. 'Les "Quatre Ka" du démiurge memphite (à Tôd)', in I. Régen and F. Servajean (eds), *Verba Manent: Recueil d'études dédiées à Dimitri Meeks*. Montpellier: Université Paul Valéry, 425–37.
——2009b. 'Fragments de lions-gargouilles d'Ermant', in C. Thiers (ed.), *Documents de Théologies Thébaines Tardives* I. Montpellier: Université Paul Valéry, 147–65.
Thissen, H.-J. 1985. 'Osiris der "Vieläugige" (zu Plut.Is.10)', *Göttinger Miszellen* 88: 55–61.
——2001. *Des Niloten Horapollon Hieroglyphenbuch*, vol. 1: *Text und Übersetzung*. Munich: Saur.
——2006. 'Zum Hieroglyphen-Buch des Chairemon', in G. Moers et al. (eds), *jn.t-Dr.w: Festchrift für Friedrich Junge*, vol. 2. Göttingen: Lingua Aegyptia, 625–34.
——2009. 'Plutarch und die ägyptische Sprache', *Zeitschrift für Papyrologie und Epigraphik* 168: 97–106.
Traunecker, C. 1992. *Coptos: Hommes et dieux sur le parvis de Geb*. Leuven: Peeters.
Valbelle, D. 1979. 'La porte de Tibère dans le complexe religieux de Médamoud', in *Hommages à Serge Sauneron (1927–1976)*, vol. 1: *Égypte pharaonique*. Cairo: Institut Français d'Archéologie Orientale, 82–94.
Vandier, J. 1961. *Le papyrus Jumilhac*. Paris: Centre National de la Recherche Scientifique.

Verhoeven, U. 2007. 'Das Kind im Gehörn der Himmelskuh und vergleichbare Rindermotive', in J.-C. Goyon and C. Cardin (eds), *Proceedings of the Ninth International Congress of Egyptologists, Grenoble, 6–12 September 2004*, vol. 2. Leuven: Peeters, 1899–1910.

Vleeming, S. P. 2001. *Some Coins of Artaxerxes and Other Short Texts in the Demotic Script Found on Various Objects and Gathered from Many Publications*. Leuven: Peeters.

von Bomhard, A. S. 2008. *The Naos of the Decades: The Underwater Archaeology of the Canopic Region in Egypt, from the Observation of the Sky to Mythology and Astrology*. Oxford: Oxford Centre for Maritime Archaeology.

von Lieven, A. 2000. *Der Himmel über Esna: Eine Fallstudie zur Religiosen Astronomie in Ägypten*. Wiesbaden: Harrassowitz.

——2006. 'Der Isishymnus Deir Chelouit 154, 1–10', *Acta Antiqua Academiae Scientiarum Hungaricae* 46: 165–71.

——2007. *Grundriss des Laufes der Sterne: Das sogenannte Nutbuch*, 2 vols. Copenhagen: Museum Tusculanum Press.

Willems, H., F. Coppens, and M. de Meyer. 2003. *The Temple of Shanhûr* I: *The Sanctuary, the Wabet, and the Gates of the Central Hall and the Great Vestibule (1-98)*. Leuven: Peeters.

Wilson, P. 1997. *A Ptolemaic Lexikon: A Lexicographical Study of the Texts in the Temple of Edfu*. Leuven: Peeters.

CHAPTER 35

COPTIC

MALCOLM CHOAT

As Demotic withdrew into the temples and then faded from use in the Roman period, a new written expression of the Egyptian language arose. While much of the history of Coptic lies outside the period covered by this volume, the development of the system lies in the Roman period. Discussion of the rise of Coptic must navigate over several centuries and through various religious milieus, beginning with native Egyptian religion and ending with Christianity and its competitors. While the totality of the evidence cannot always be placed in one interrelated historical continuum, it should be discussed together and not artificially separated.

Overview

Coptic denotes both a written and a spoken stage of the Egyptian language. In scribal terms, it refers to the last written stage of the ancient Egyptian language, when the Egyptians finally gave up their predominantly phonographic and logographic systems in favour of the Greek alphabet. In standardized Coptic, this was supplemented by between six and eight (depending on dialect, see below) characters derived from Demotic to denote sounds not represented in Greek (namely, ϣ (*sh*), ϥ (*f*), ϧ, ⳉ (*kh*), ϩ (*h*), ϫ (*dj*), and ϭ (*ky/tch*); another letter, ϯ (*ti*), may also be derived from Demotic). Aside from isolated experiments in the Ptolemaic period, such systems were first used in the early Roman period, but the orthography was not systematized and standardized until the fourth century. In linguistic terms, Coptic may also refer to the vernacular Egyptian language in the first millennium CE, which the Coptic script represents much more closely than the archaizing Demotic script. As we largely only access this form of the Egyptian language through texts written in Coptic, we may to some degree collapse the distinction and use Coptic to refer to the Egyptian language from the third century CE on.

Coptic Dialects

In the third and following centuries Coptic is found in a number of dialects: Sahidic, the dialect of Upper Egypt (the Sa'id), was used as a pan-Egyptian literary and vehicular dialect. It shares important phonological characteristics with Bohairic, the dialect of the Delta, which superseded it as the standard 'official' ecclesiastical dialect late in the first millennium CE and remains in liturgical use in the modern Coptic Church. The distinct preference for the use of Sahidic for literary purposes may have to do with its linguistic neutrality, or reflect some pre-Coptic preference which we cannot now deduce (for one speculation, see Satzinger 1985); that it was not only a literary dialect but also a pan-Egyptian vehicular dialect is shown by its overwhelming usage throughout Upper Egypt for documents. The Fayumic dialect was used both for literary and documentary purposes until the tenth century, in contrast to other local dialects which were largely only used for literary texts, and which were superseded by Sahidic in the fifth century. These include the Upper Egyptian dialects Akhmimic, centred on Panopolis (Akhmim), and Lykopolitan (or Subakhmimic), which despite its name has little real association with Lykopolis (Asyut). There existed also Mesokemic, or Middle Egyptian, a dialect associated with Oxyrhynchus, as well as a number of sub-dialects related to Fayumic and Mesokemic. There are a small number of personal letters in Mesokemic, but no documentary papyri in Akhmimic. By contrast, excavations at Kellis (Ismant el-Kharab) in the Dakhla Oasis have uncovered a large archive of private letters in a variety of Lykopolitan that appears to have been a vehicular dialect used throughout Upper Egypt in the fourth century (Gardner, Alcock, and Funk 1999).

It seems difficult to believe that speakers of these dialects were mutually unintelligible, as the differences between them are no greater than those between, for example, dialects of Arabic, speakers of which are overwhelmingly comprehensible to one another. It has, in any case, been argued (by Loprieno 1982; cf. Puest 1999: 33–6) that the variations between the dialects are largely orthographic, and represent not differing pronunciations, but different choices on how to represent the Egyptian language in Greek letters. At a lexical level, however, some variation is discernible between regions, suggestive of actual dialects in the linguistic sense (Puest 1999: 33–6, 327–8). However the dialects might be defined linguistically, their propagation both bears witness to linguistic variety within Roman period (and earlier) Egyptian, and suggests that the process by which the Egyptian language came to be reduced to Greek letters was not as homogeneous and directed as the later overwhelming preference for Sahidic might suggest. It strongly indicates that Coptic came into being in the Roman period not via a centralized process, but by various groups operating with similar agendas in different parts of the country: only in the fourth and following centuries did a central authority, which can only have been the Egyptian Church and the influential productions of Upper Egyptian monastic scriptoria, favour Sahidic to the extent that the local dialects in Middle and Upper Egypt (with the exception of Fayumic) eventually fell out of use.

The Development of Coptic

Coptic is usually described as beginning with the earliest translations of the Septuagint and New Testament, the first evidence for which we encounter in the second half of the third century. However, this plots a religious event explicitly as part of the scribal and linguistic continuum, which may prejudge the factors that led to the adoption of the Greek alphabet for Egyptian. 'Coptic' may, however—and indeed should—be taken to include all attempts at systematically transcribing Egyptian into Greek. In this case, its history is much older than the mid-third century. At a very basic level, the fact that many Egyptian names are in fact short phrases in Egyptian (e.g. Petosiris, 'Given by Osiris') means that the writing of such names constitutes a form of transcribing Egyptian into Greek (Quaegebeur 1982). More concretely, we find already in 202/201 BCE an inscription carved on the Osireion in Abydos in which Egyptian is transcribed into Greek (Pestman 1977, no. 11) and a bilingual wordlist from the third century BCE that lists Greek words with their Egyptian translations written in Greek characters (Quecke 1997); these and several other short Ptolemaic texts (see Quaegebeur 1991) cannot be said to constitute any sort of system, and respond to individual circumstances that we are not able to divine. In the Roman period, we find more frequent use of transcription into Greek in ritual texts generated within the Egyptian temples and by its priests, followed by the rise of Coptic for Christian use in the third century. These various witnesses to the rise of Coptic are customarily listed separately, and even classified as 'Pre-Old Coptic' (no use of Demotic letters, see Quaegebeur 1991), 'Old Coptic', and 'Coptic'. In the interests both of allowing possible continuities to be considered, and of avoiding conflating religious and linguistic classifications, all Egyptian texts transliterated into Greek characters that date before *c.*300 CE are listed in Table 35.1.

Pre-Christian Coptic

The group of ritual (or 'magical') texts that date from the first to the fourth centuries CE are commonly referred to as 'Old Coptic', a usage retained here. This denomination, intended to separate them from later 'Coptic proper', encodes both a difference in the cultural context of their production (i.e. the Egyptian religion versus a Christian setting), and differences in the orthography, language, and scribal practice of these texts that differentiate them from later Coptic. However, as different as they are from the standardized manner of writing Coptic that evolved in the course of the third and fourth centuries, there are points of contact between, for example, the forms chosen for the Demotic letters in some of the Old Coptic texts and some of the earliest Christian Coptic texts. This indicates that, even if there was no formal contact, there may be some lines of continuity between the Old Coptic texts and the earliest texts in Coptic proper.

The Old Coptic script is largely used for spells or invocations that are either embedded in Greek or Demotic ritual texts, or written on single sheets of papyrus (Table 35.1a). In some instances, such as the mummy labels (on which, see Quaegebeur 1978: 254–5), no Demotic characters are used. These continuous texts of various lengths should be contextualized within a wider practice of transliteration visible in Roman period Egyptian texts produced in temple or priestly contexts, such as the Demotic ritual texts or the hieratic onomasticon from Tebtunis (Table 35.1b; on the glosses of *voces magicae*, see Dielemann 2005: 69–80; 2006: 73). Writing exercises from the temple at Narmouthis show a system of transcription being learned within a corpus where scribes engage in code switching between Demotic and Greek (Gallo 1997; Bresciani, Pernigotti, and Betrò 1983; Rutherford 2010); here, scribes have incorporated Demotic letters into the system: a small fragment of another Demotic writing exercise (?) from the first-century Fayum uses no Demotic letters in its transcription of the Egyptian (Spiegelberg 1928: 44–9).

Table 35.1 Egyptian texts in Greek characters before c.300 CE

Siglum	Century CE	Provenance	Dialect	Content
(a) Spells, Invocations, and Horoscopes				
P Lond. 98 recto (Černý, Kahle, and Parker 1957)	I/II (13 Apr. 95)	Unknown		Horoscope in Greek and Old Coptic on papyrus roll
P Brit. Mus. EA 10808 (Osing 1976; *Dieleman 2004*; Sederholm 2006)	*II*	*Oxyrhynchus*		*Invocations and spell*, Late *Middle* Egyptian *in* Old Coptic script on papyrus roll
P Mich. inv. 6131 verso (Worrell 1941)	II/III	Soknopaiou Nesos		Horoscope in Old Coptic on papyrus roll
CEML 616, 632 (Baratte and Boyaval 1975)	II–III	Unknown		Egyptian invocation in Greek transliteration on mummy label
P Schmidt (Satzinger 1975; for the date, see Richter 2002)	III ?	Hermopolite?		Complaint to Osiris in Old Coptic on single sheet of papyrus
P Brit. Mus. EA 10588 (Bell, Nock, and Thompson 1931)	III (second half)	Thebes		Demotic and Greek invocation and spells (with short Old Coptic sections) on papyrus roll
PGM I (Preisendanz 1973–4)	IV	Thebes		Greek invocations and spells with short sections in Old Coptic on papyrus roll
PGM III (Preisendanz 1973–4)	IV	Thebes		Greek invocations and spells with short sections in Old Coptic on papyrus roll
PGM IV (Preisendanz 1973–4)	IV	Thebes		Greek invocations and spells with Old Coptic invocations in papyrus codex
(b) Glosses on Egyptian Texts				
P Carlsb. II 1 (Osing 1998: 25–218)	II	Tebtunis		Hieratic religious handbook (onomasticon) with Old Coptic glosses on papyrus roll
P London–Leiden (Griffith and Thompson 1904–9)	III	Thebes		Demotic invocations and spells with Old Coptic glosses on papyrus roll
P Leiden I 384 (Johnson 1975)	III	Thebes		Demotic invocations and spells with Old Coptic glosses on papyrus roll

P Louvre E 3229 (Johnson 1977)	III	Thebes		Demotic spells with Old Coptic glosses on papyrus roll
(c) Documents				
Kellis 'Old Coptic Ostracon' (Gardner 1999; cf. Kasser 2004)	III (second half)	Kellis, Great Oasis		Private letter on ostracon
(d) Christian Texts				
P Beatty VII (Kenyon 1937)	Mid-III	Fayum?	('Old') Fayumic	Papyrus codex with Coptic glosses on Greek Isaiah
P Brit. Mus. EA 10825 (Bell and Thompson 1925)	III (second half)	Oxyrhynchus?	Mesokemic	Papyrus roll with Coptic–Greek glossary to Hosea and Amos
Bodl. Gr. Inscr. 3019.2, 6 (Crum 1934)	III (second half)	Thebes (Great Oasis?)	Achmimic	Wooden codex containing Coptic Psalm 46: 3–10 along with Greek educational texts
Freer MS V (Sanders and Schmidt 1927)	Late III	Fayum	Sahidic	Papyrus codex with Coptic glosses on Greek minor prophets
Schøyen MS 193 (Goehring 1990)	III/IV	Dishna?	Sahidic	Papyrus codex containing Melito; 2 Maccabees; 1 Peter; Jonah; and a short homily?
P Hamb. Bil. 1 (Diebner and Kasser 1989)	III/IV	Fayum	Fayumic (F7)	Papyrus codex with Song of Songs, Lamentations, and Ecclesiastes in Coptic; Acts of Paul and Ecclesiastes in Greek
P Bodm. 6 (Kasser 1960)	III/IV	Dishna?	P ('Proto-Theban')	Proverbs in parchment codex
Chester Beatty Ac. 1390 (Brashear et al. 1990)	III/IV	Dishna?	Lycopolitan (L5)	Papyrus codex with Greek mathematical exercises + John 10: 18–11: 43; 11: 55–12: 39
P Würzb. K 1003 (Brashear and Satzinger 1990)	III/IV	Unknown	Fayumic	Acrostic hymn in Greek and Coptic versions on papyrus sheet

The Old Coptic texts are clearly to some degree independent of one another, and represent various attempts at creating a system via which Egyptian could be represented in the more widely used (and understood) Greek script. In some cases Demotic letters are not used as part of the transcriptions; other attempts share some forms of the letters derived from Demotic (Kasser 1991a); an avoidance of Greek vocabulary, the use of which characterizes later standardized Coptic, is also common to these texts. In addition to their content, the very fact that most of their scribes knew Demotic, which by the second century CE was restricted to a relatively small number of Egyptian priests, anchors their production within the native Egyptian priesthood.

From Temple to Church

Overlapping with the use of Old Coptic, found still in some manuscripts copied in the fourth century (no doubt copies of earlier texts), is the rise of Coptic for Christian purposes in the third century. Grammar and orthography, not to mention religion, divide these two expressions of the Coptic language. Two liminal texts, however, assist navigation between them. *P Bodm.* 6 (see Table 35.1d), a codex containing the book of Proverbs, is written in an early dialect (proto-Theban or proto-Sahidic?; Kasser 1991c), and uses ten graphemes derived from Demotic, some of which are not found in these forms in later Coptic texts; they do, however, resemble forms used in the ritual Old Coptic texts (Kasser 2003).

Another liminal early Coptic text stands further apart in its context and content both from the Old Coptic and from the earliest Christian Coptic texts. Among the material used in the late third-century construction of a storage chamber adjoining the temple of Tutu in Kellis was an ostracon (Table 35.1c) bearing a short text: 'I greet Pse… and his children, and Hout and his children. I greet Moni and his servants. Imouthes it is who writes to you that, have confidence in us (?).' The reading and interpretation of the last two lines of the text—and thus its ultimate message—are unclear (see Kasser 2004: 81–5, canvassing various possibilities; compare Gardner 1999), and more of the text may also be lost at the top of the ostracon (Bagnall 2005: 13). However, it is clearly a personal letter of some sort, written in the second half of the third century by someone (Imouthes, or a scribe writing for him) who knew a system of representing Egyptian in Greek letters that shares Demotic letter forms and dialectal tendencies with certain Old Coptic texts and *P Bodm.* 6. This enigmatic text cannot on its own tell a whole story, but it strongly indicates that a literary, urban, and temple narrative for the rise of Coptic may not represent the entire picture.

Christian Use of Coptic

The true rise of Coptic belongs in the fourth century, to which we are able with some confidence to assign over 150 literary texts and around the same number of documents. Before then, we have only scattered examples of Christian use of Coptic, listed in Table 35.1d. Attempts to isolate this corpus are hindered by a still-limited understanding of early Coptic palaeography, which lags well behind that of Greek, owing in large part to the non-existence of dated Coptic texts before the sixth century and an only partially understood diachronic relationship between the use of similar styles of script in Greek and Coptic. Those listed here represent the Coptic texts most likely to date to the second half of the third or early fourth century, whose dates are controlled to some extent by association with more readily datable Greek material, non-standardized usage of Demotic letters, and dialectal usage that seems to lie before the standardization of the literary dialects in the fourth century. It should thus be noted that some of these texts may in fact date to later in the fourth century, and that there may be other, hitherto unrecognized, candidates for inclusion in this list among the published papyri (other texts suggested at various times to date to the third or fourth century are LDAB 5566, 87192, 107779, 107888, 107910, 107962, 108146, 108541, 113512; see <http://www. trismegistos.org/ldab>).

Among this group we have glosses or glossaries, educational exercises, one hymn, and three codices containing either one or multiple texts. While these texts belong grammatically with the later Coptic texts, some have the character of individual attempts made without recourse to a wider programme, and clearly made before the standardization of practice visible in fourth-century texts. Against *P Bodm.* 6 (see above) we may contrast the Coptic glosses on the Greek text of Isaiah in *P Beatty* VII, which do not use Demotic letters at all; this may represent a lack of knowledge of Demotic (or of any system for using the Demotic characters) rather than an ideological rejection of the idea of using them. The scribes of the Coptic texts in *P Hamb. Bil.* 1 (ed. Diebner and Kasser 1989) used an Old Fayumic dialect, and, in contrast to all later Coptic texts (but similar to Old Coptic texts), largely avoid using Greek words.

Coptic clearly did not spring into being with continuous translations. The previous stage seems to be represented among the surviving manuscripts by glosses and glossaries such as those in *P Beatty* VII, Freer MS V (ed. Sanders and Schmidt 1927), and *P Brit. Mus.* EA 10825. Before that we must rely on conjecture for how Christians first came to use Coptic. Imaginings of the first steps (e.g. Wisse 1995; Metzger 1977: 99–132) must necessarily proceed on the basis of little or no evidence, and may sometimes project stages such as extemporary translation for the purposes of preaching (for which process the glosses in Freer MS V and *P Beatty* VII may provide evidence) too far back. Reports such as that of Antony hearing the Gospel of Matthew in a village around 270 CE (*Life of Antony* 3), do not necessarily prove that the Gospels had been translated into Coptic by that point. As there is little firm evidence for any proselytization outside Alexandria in the second century, and little beyond the largely Greek-speaking Nile *metropoleis* before the mid-third (see Chapter 28), we may not reasonably project the earliest attempts at Christian Coptic too far before the earliest manuscripts we have in the mid-third century. That is, the third-century Coptic texts we have may not represent the very earliest phase of Christian use of Coptic, but they are likely to be broadly representative of the time at which Christians began experimenting with translating the scriptures into Egyptian.

The obvious necessity for the use of Coptic for proselytizing outside the Hellenized *metropoleis*, and the rural (though largely monastic) contexts in which reports of Egyptian-speaking Christians are frequently encountered in later narrative texts, leads one to imagine a rural context for the rise of Coptic. Yet the creators of both the Old Coptic and first Christian Coptic texts must have been by necessity highly bilingual, who knew both the Greek script and, in the case of Christian Coptic, the many Greek words that came to be present in Coptic (as high as 25 per cent in some texts): these include not only nouns and verbs, but many conjunctions and particles. Some of these had no doubt found their way into the Egyptian vernacular in the Ptolemaic and early Roman periods, though very few are present in Demotic (Clarysse 1987), just as they are avoided in the Old Coptic texts. Other words, however, must certainly rely on knowledge of the Greek Bible or other literary texts. Thus, the progenitors of these various systems (as it is too imprecise to speak of the 'creators of Coptic') must be located in the same social group—Hellenized Egyptians who maintained their native language while acquiring Greek language and culture in the centuries since the conquest of Alexander. The most plausible locations for such activity are the urban centres of literary culture down the Nile. While the Kellis Old Coptic Ostracon must be allowed to nuance this picture, it does not invalidate it.

It is notable that there is very little New Testament material among the earliest Christian Coptic texts, which, as far as palaeography will allow us to judge, are dominated by commentary on, and translation of, the Septuagint (LXX). Largely on text-critical grounds, Lefort (1948) argued that the LXX was translated into Coptic before the New Testament, and by Jews rather than Christians. Yet, as attractive as this proposition may appear (it is supported by, for example, Depuydt 2010), it encounters several problems. In the first place, palaeography is not precise enough to guarantee that no New Testament manuscripts are as early as the witnesses to the Coptic LXX. A more recent and thorough treatment of the citations of the LXX in the Coptic New Testament has also reached the opposite conclusion to Lefort, demonstrating that the Coptic LXX depends on the Coptic New Testament, not vice versa (Lussier 1998, esp. 269–72). Furthermore, the Coptic Old Testament is plainly a translation of the LXX, which Hellenophone Jews increasingly ignored in the Roman period in favour of other translations, precisely because of its use by Christians. An attendant historical problem is that the Jewish population in Egypt seems largely to have been decimated in the revolt under Trajan (115–17; see Chapter 17 in this volume), and did not have the critical mass required to generate translations into Coptic. The pre-Trajanic period, when Jews were more in the open and synagogues more publicly prominent, seems too early to locate such activity; nor is Jewish proselytizing among the Egyptian-speaking population well attested. Finally, the earliest Coptic texts of the LXX overwhelmingly use both the codex format and the abbreviations of the sacred names (the so-called *nomina sacra*). The first is suggestive of Christian usage, as Jews continued to favour the roll format for their scriptures, and the use of the *nomina sacra* is, as can be currently observed, confined to Christian scribes, though the question of its origin remains open. For these reasons it seems best to assume that the traditional picture, whereby Coptic came to be used in the third century by Christians as a means to missionize among and preach to the native-speaking population, is largely correct.

The breadth of early 'Christian' uses of Coptic should be emphasized. A substantial amount of literature produced by Manichaeans and so-called Gnostics of various theological systems survives from the fourth century, with both sets of material evidencing a textual history in Coptic that is likely to push the first translations of such material back into the early fourth or late third century. The followers of Mani clearly realized the potential of the new script for spreading their message soon after they arrived in Egypt around 270 CE; adherents of Gnostic systems, some of whom drew also on native Egyptian and Hermetic traditions (just as Gnostic material is found in 'magical' texts), may have had closer contacts with the native priestly context of the Old Coptic ritual texts (for some possibilities, see McBride 1989). Taken together, the textual remains in Coptic from the first to the fourth centuries should be placed in a continuum that allows for some relationship between the various forms of expression, and in a broader tent than the Christianity represented and promoted by the bishops of Alexandria.

Owing both to the fact that (as in the medieval west) monasticism in late antique Egypt was the prime engine of literary transmission (especially in Coptic), and to the rough contemporaneity of the rise of Coptic and of monasticism at the end of the period covered by this volume, it is easy to look for a relationship between these two great cultural events. The link between Coptic textual production (for both literary and documentary purposes) and monasticism is indeed strong in the fourth and following centuries. Several fourth-century archives containing Coptic documents have a monastic provenance (e.g. Bell 1924; Kramer and Shelton 1987), as may the Dishna Papers, a collection of Greek and Coptic codices that may have been part of the library at the Pachomian monastery of Pbow (Robinson 1990); that the more famous so-called Coptic Gnostic library in the Nag Hammadi codices had the same source is less certain (Williams 1996: 235–62). However, if the Coptic script came to be used extensively throughout monasteries in Egypt, and many monasteries were predominantly Egyptian-speaking establishments, that does not mean that monasticism, which did not develop as an institution until the fourth century, played a leading role in the rise of Christian use of Coptic in the previous century: its role should be seen more as promoting the use of Coptic, and the standardization of the literary language, through its scriptoria, such as in the White Monastery at Sohag.

Conclusions

Christianity did not 'invent' Coptic; both the idea, and elements of the system, had long existed when Christians began to use Coptic in the third century. But it was Christianity that brought Coptic out of the cloistered environments in which it had been used by non-Christians, which eventually enabled native Egyptians in towns and villages across the province to write literary works, personal letters, and documents in their own language. Witnessing the use of Coptic by Manichaeans and Gnostics, one might propose that an important factor in the spread of Coptic was competition between these 'Religions of the Book' (Morenz 1970), augmented by the desire, perhaps witnessed in the Kellis ostracon, for a written vernacular (Richter 2009: 415).

Into the fourth century, Coptic becomes increasingly (and rapidly) orthographically standardized, at least when used for copying manuscripts: documentary Coptic continues to show variations from literary norms throughout the period in which Coptic was used (Kahle 1954: 1.48–192). It begins to be used more widely for personal letters and some few other documents, both within a monastic context and in villages such as Kellis, where it was used (notably by Manichaeans, but also by others in the village) for communication within the village and with the Nile Valley. Coptic literature expands in quantity and variety. Too often it is classified as universally Christian and religious, yet within this is great variety: in the diversity of Christianities represented (including those whom we might call Gnostics or Manichaeans, but who called themselves Christians); in the genres of texts, apocryphal, canonical, magical, and otherwise, copied in scriptoria and in less controlled contexts; and in the local dialects that continue into the fifth century (and later in the case of Fayumic). Much of Coptic literature is translation of Greek (and in the case of the Manichaeans, perhaps Syriac) texts.

But the works of Shenoute, stretching across nine volumes of canons (in reality long letters) and eight of discourses (mainly sermons), show that Egyptian literary creativity had not died with its native scripts.

The standard narrative of Egyptian scripts, largely written by Egyptologists for whom the cultural zenith of Pharaonic Egypt was never again reached, sees the Roman period as a time of decline, of the death of autochthonous Egyptian: it is anything but. The Roman period witnesses nothing less than the birth of a new written expression of Egyptian—a birth to which many parts of Egyptian society contributed, and which would carry the language forward for nearly a millennium more, beyond the final extinction of the native Egyptian scripts in the fifth century, and beyond the arrival of a new language, religion, and culture with the Arab conquest in the seventh century (Richter 2009). Only in the early second millennium did Coptic finally succumb to Arabic and pass out of daily use into ecclesiastical and liturgical usage.

Suggested Reading

For recent general overviews of the rise of Coptic, see Depuydt (2010) and Richter (2009). Surveys of Coptic literature can be found in Smith (1998) and Emmel (2007). *The Coptic Encyclopedia* (Atiya 1991) contains articles on a wide range of aspects of Coptic language, literature, and history. On Coptic dialects, see Kasser (1990) and Funk (1988), as well as many articles in Atiya (1991, vol. 8). Old Coptic is treated by Satzinger (1991), and compare Kasser (2004); on the cultural and linguistic milieu, see Dieleman (2005). On Coptic palaeography, Kasser (1991b) sets out the major issues, with reference to previous scholarship; documentary texts await modern palaeographical treatment, on which, see Gardner and Choat (2004).

Bibliography

Atiya, A. S. (ed.) 1991. *The Coptic Encyclopedia*, 8 vols. New York: Macmillan.

Bagnall, R. S. 2005. 'Linguistic Change and Religious Change: Thinking about the Temples of the Fayoum in the Roman Period', in G. Gabra (ed.), *Christianity and Monasticism in the Fayoum Oasis*. Cairo: American University in Cairo Press, 11–19.

Baratte, F., and B. Boyaval. 1975. 'Catalogue des étiquettes de momies du Musée du Louvre (C.E.M.L.): Textes grecs: 2ème partie', *Cahiers de Recherches de l'Institut de Papyrologie et d'Égyptologie de Lille* 3: 151–261.

Bell, H. I., with W. E. Crum. 1924. *Jews and Christians in Egypt: The Jewish Troubles in Alexandria and the Athanasian Controversy, Illustrated by Texts from Greek Papyri in the British Museum*. London: British Museum Press.

—— and H. Thompson. 1925. 'A Greek–Coptic Glossary to Hosea and Amos', *Journal of Egyptian Archaeology* 11: 241–6.

—— A. D. Nock, and H. Thompson. 1931. 'Magical Texts from a Bilingual Papyrus in the British Museum, Edited with Translations, Commentary and Facsimile', *Proceedings of the British Academy* 17: 235–86.

Brashear, W., and H. Satzinger. 1990. 'Ein Akrostichischer Griechischer Hymnus mit koptischer Übersetzung (Wagner-Museum K 1003)', *Journal of Coptic Studies* 1: 37–58.
—— et al. 1990. *The Chester Beatty Codex Ac. 1390: Mathematical School Exercises in Greek and John 10:7–13:38 in Subachmimic*. Leuven: Peeters.
Bresciani, E., S. Pernigotti, and M. C. Betrò. 1983. *Ostraka demotici da Narmuti* I. Pisa: Giardini.
Černý, J., P. E. Kahle, and R. Parker. 1957. 'The Old Coptic Horoscope', *Journal of Egyptian Archaeology* 43: 86–100.
Clarysse, W. 1987. 'Greek Loanwords in Demotic', in S. P. Vleeming (ed.), *Aspects of Demotic Lexicography*. Leuven: Peeters, 9–33.
Crum, W. E. 1934. 'Un psaume en dialect d'Akhmim', in *Mélanges Maspero*, vol. 2. Cairo: Institut Français d'Archéologie Orientale, 73–6.
Depuydt, L. 2010. 'Coptic and Coptic Literature', in A. Lloyd (ed.), *A Companion to Ancient Egypt*, vol. 2. Chichester: Wiley-Blackwell, 732–54.
Diebner, B., and R. Kasser. 1989. *Hamburger Papyrus bil. 1: Die alttestamentlichen Texte des Papyrus bilinguis 1 der Staats- und Universitätsbibliothek Hamburg*. Geneva: Cramer.
Dieleman, J. 2004. 'Ein spätägyptisches magisches handbuch: Eine neue PDM oder PGM?', in F. Hoffmann and H.-J. Thissen (eds), *Res Severa Verum Gaudium: Festschrift für Karl-Theodor Zauzich zum 65. Geburtstag am 8. Juni 2004*. Leuven: Peeters, 121–8.
—— 2005. *Priests, Tongues, and Rites: The London-Leiden Magical Manuscripts and Translation in Egyptian Ritual (100–300 CE)*. Leiden: Brill.
—— 2006. 'Abundance in the Margins: Multiplicity of Script in the Demotic Magical Papyri', in S. Sanders (ed.), *Margins of Writing, Origins of Culture: New Approaches to Writing and Reading in the Ancient Near East*. Chicago: Oriental Institute, 67–81.
Emmel, S. 2007. 'Coptic Literature in the Byzantine and Early Islamic World', in R. S. Bagnall (ed.), *Egypt in the Byzantine World 300–700*. Cambridge: Cambridge University Press, 83–102.
Funk, W.-P. 1988. 'Dialects Wanting Homes: A Numerical Approach to the Early Varieties of Coptic', in J. Fisiak (ed.), *Historical Dialectology, Regional and Social*. Berlin: de Gruyter, 149–92.
Gallo, P. 1997. *Ostraca demotici e ieratici dall'archivio bilingue di Narmouthis* II. Pisa: ETS.
Gardner, I. 1999. 'An Old Coptic Ostracon from Ismant el-Kharab?', *Zeitschrift für Papyrologie und Epigraphik* 125: 195–200.
—— and M. Choat. 2004. 'Towards a Palaeography of Fourth Century Documentary Coptic', in M. Immerzeel and J. van der Vliet (eds), *Coptic Studies on the Threshold of a New Millennium: Proceedings of the Seventh International Congress of Coptic Studies, Leiden, August 27–September 2, 2000*, vol. 1. Leuven: Peeters, 501–9.
—— A. Alcock, and W. P. Funk. 1999. *Coptic Documentary Texts from Kellis*. Oxford: Oxbow.
Goehring, J. E. 1990. *The Crosby-Schøyen Codex MS 193 in the Schøyen Collection*. Leuven: Peeters.
Griffith, F. L., and Thompson, H. 1904–9. *The Demotic Magical Papyrus of London and Leiden*, 3 vols. London: Grevel.
Johnson, J. H. 1975. 'The Demotic Magical Spells of Leiden I 384', *Oudheidkundige Mededelingen uit het Rijksmuseum van Oudheden te Leiden* 56: 29–64.
—— 1977. 'Louvre E 3229: A Demotic Magical Text', *Enchoria* 7: 55–102.
Kahle, P. E. 1954. *Bala'izah: Coptic Texts from Deir el-Bala'izah in Upper Egypt*, 2 vols. Oxford: Oxford University Press.

Kasser, R. 1960. *Papyrus Bodmer VI: Livre des proverbes*. Louvain: Secrétariat du Corpus SCO.

—— 1990. 'A Standard System of Sigla for Referring to the Dialects of Coptic', *Journal of Coptic Studies* 1: 141–51.

—— 1991a. 'Alphabets, Old Coptic', in A. S. Atiya (ed.), *The Coptic Encyclopedia*, vol. 8. New York: Macmillan, 41–5.

—— 1991b. 'Paleography', in A. S. Atiya (ed.), *The Coptic Encyclopedia*, vol. 8. New York: Macmillan, 175–84.

—— 1991c. 'Dialect P', in A. S. Atiya (ed.), *The Coptic Encyclopedia*, vol. 8. New York: Macmillan, 82–7.

—— 2003. 'Considérations de phonologie dialectale copte, II: L'alphabet de *P* et de *pP*', *Le Muséon* 116: 289–328.

——2004. 'Protodialectes coptes à systèmes alphabétiques de type vieux-copte', in M. Immerzeel and J. van der Vliet (eds), *Coptic Studies on the Threshold of a New Millennium: Proceedings of the Seventh International Congress of Coptic Studies, Leiden, August 27–September 2, 2000*. Leuven: Peeters, 75–123.

Kenyon, F. G. 1937. *Chester Beatty Biblical Papyri*, vol. 6: *Isaiah, Jeremiah, Ecclesiasticus*. London: Walker.

Kramer, B., and J. C. Shelton. 1987. *Das Archiv des Nepheros und verwandte Texte*. Mainz: von Zabern.

Lefort, L.-T. 1948. 'EIMHTI dans le NT sahidique', *Le Muséon* 61: 153–70.

Loprieno, A. 1982. 'Methodologische Anmerkungen zur Rolle der Dialekte in der Aegyptischen Sprachenwicklung', *Göttinger Miszellen* 53: 75–95.

Lussier, P. 1998. *Les citations vetero-testamentaires dans les versions coptes des evangiles: Recueil et analyse critique*. Geneva: Cramer.

McBride, D. R. 1989. 'The Development of Coptic: Late-Pagan Language of Synthesis in Egypt', *Journal of the Society for the Study of Egyptian Antiquities* 19: 89–111.

Metzger, B. M. 1977. *The Early Versions of the New Testament: Their Origins, Transmission, and Limitations*. Oxford: Clarendon Press.

Morenz, S. 1970. 'Die koptische Literatur', in B. Spuler (ed.), *Handbuch der Orientalistik*, pts 1–2, 2nd edn. Leiden: Brill, 239–50.

Osing, J. 1976. *Der spätägyptische Papyrus BM 10808*. Wiesbaden: Harrassowitz.

—— 1998. *Hieratische Papyri aus Tebtunis*, 2 vols. Copenhagen: Museum Tusculanum Press.

Pestman, P. W., with J. Quaegebeur and R. L. Vos. 1977. *Recueil de textes démotiques et bilingues*. Leiden: Brill.

Preisendanz, K. (ed.) 1973–4. *Papyri Graecae Magicae: Die griechischen Zauberpapyri*, 2nd edn, 2 vols. Stuttgart: Teubner.

Puest, C. 1999. *Egyptian Phonology: An Introduction to the Phonology of a Dead Language*. Göttingen: Peust & Gutschmidt.

Quaegebeur, J. 1978. 'Mummy Labels: An Orientation', in E. Boswinkel and P. W. Pestman (eds), *Textes grec, démotiques et bilingual*. Leiden: Brill, 232–59.

—— 1982. 'De la préhistoire de l'écriture copte', *Orientalia Lovaniensia Periodica* 131: 125–36.

—— 1991. 'Pre-Old Coptic', in A. S. Atiya (ed.), *The Coptic Encyclopedia*, vol. 8. New York: Macmillan, 190–1.

Quecke, H. 1997. 'Eine griechisch-ägyptische Wörterliste vermutlich des 3. Jh. v. Chr. (P. Heid. inv.-nr. G 414)', *Zeitschrift für Papyrologie und Epigraphik* 116: 67–80.

Richter, S. 2002. 'Miscellania Magica', *Journal of Egyptian Archaeology* 88: 247–52.

—— 2009. 'Greek, Coptic and the "Language of the Hijra": The Rise and Decline of the Coptic Language in Late Antique and Medieval Egypt', in H. M. Cotton et al. (eds), *From Hellenism to Islam: Cultural and Linguistic Change in the Roman Near East*. Cambridge: Cambridge University Press, 401–46.

Robinson, J. M. 1990. *The Pachomian Monastic Library at the Chester Beatty Library and the Bibliothèque Bodmer*. Claremont, Calif.: Institute for Antiquity and Christianity.

Rutherford, I. 2010. 'Bilingualism in Roman Egypt? Exploring the Archive of Phatres of Narmuthis', in T. V. Evans and D. D. Obbink (eds), *The Language of the Papyri*. Oxford: Oxford University Press, 198–207.

Sanders, H. A., and C. Schmidt. 1927. *The Minor Prophets in the Freer Collection and the Berlin Fragment of Genesis*. New York: Macmillan.

Satzinger, H. 1975. 'The Old Coptic Schmidt Papyrus', *Journal of the American Research Center in Egypt* 12: 37–50.

—— 1984. 'Die altkoptischen Texte als Zeugnisse der Beziehungen zwischen Ägyptern und Griechen', in P. Nagel (ed.), *Graeco-Coptica: Griechen und Kopten im byzantinischen Ägypten*. Halle: Martin-Luther-Universität, 137–46.

—— 1985. 'On the Spread of the Sahidic Dialect', in T. Orlandi and F. Wisse (eds), *Acts of the Second International Congress of Coptic Studies, Rome, 22–26 September 1980*. Rome: CIM, 307–12.

—— 1991. 'Old Coptic', in A. S. Atiya (ed.), *The Coptic Encyclopedia*, vol. 8. New York: Macmillan, 169–75.

Sederholm, V. H. 2006. *Papyrus British Museum 10808 and its Cultural and Religious Setting*. Leiden: Brill.

Smith, M. 1998. 'Coptic Literature, 311–425', in A. Cameron et al. (eds), *The Cambridge Ancient History*, vol. 13. Cambridge: Cambridge University Press, 720–35.

Spiegelberg, W. 1928. 'Demotica II (20–34)', *Sitzungsberichte der Bayerischen Akademie der Wissenschaften: Philosophisch-philologische und historische Klasse* 1928/2: 1–57.

Williams, M. A. 1996. *Rethinking 'Gnosticism': An Argument for Dismantling a Dubious Category*. Princeton: Princeton University Press.

Wisse, F. 1995. 'The Coptic Versions of the New Testament', in B. D. Ehrman and M. W. Holmes (eds), *The Text of the New Testament in Contemporary Research: Essays on the Status Quaestionis: A Volume in Honor of Bruce M. Metzger*. Grand Rapids, Mich.: Eerdmans, 131–41.

Worrell, W. H. 1941. 'Notice of a Second-Century Text in Coptic Letters', *American Journal of Semitic Languages and Literatures* 58: 84–90.

PART VI

IMAGES AND OBJECTS

CHAPTER 36

FUNERARY ARTISTS

*The Textual Evidence**

MARIA CANNATA

THE phrase 'funerary art of Roman Egypt' conjures up, for many, an image of the celebrated mummy portraits, which, with their immediacy and their purported individuality and life-likeness, appeal to Western aesthetic sensibilities, giving the illusion of coming face to face with long-dead individuals. Yet this was but one of a range of funerary accoutrements available; cartonnage masks, painted shrouds, wooden coffins, and cartonnage cases were in use at the same time (Riggs 2002). Many artists were involved, including the individuals who produced elaborate mummy wrappings, those who manufactured the mask or coffin, those who decorated them, and those who painted the panel portraits or shrouds. A variety of materials were also required: bandages, wood, paints, gold leaf, papyrus waste, resin, plaster, and glue.

There is evidence that the cost of wrapping and decorating a mummy was an expensive enterprise, and considering the wide range of people involved and the materials required, one would expect transactions concerning such costly items to have generated some paperwork. However, textual evidence for the production of mummies, burial assemblages, or tombs in Roman Egypt is almost non-existent, so much so that funerary art could almost be defined as art without artists, created by invisible hands. This chapter collects the available evidence and attempts to understand better the working life of the funerary artists and craftsmen of Roman Egypt.

THE ARTISTS INVOLVED

Makers of Coffins and Mummy Masks

A handful of workshop scenes on the walls of Pharaonic tombs help visualize the carpenters and painters who manufactured coffins and mummy masks. However, no pictorial evidence

* I am grateful to the following, who generously provided some of the references, as well as copies of a number of articles: Christina Adams, Cisco Bosch Puche, Alan Bowman, Willy Clarysse, Matt Gibbs, Brian McGing, Margaret Maitland, Christina Riggs, Gaëlle Tallet, Dorothy Thompson, and Helen Whitehouse.

survives for such craftsmen in the Roman period, nor is there any textual evidence for the purchase or cost of these funerary items, despite the many examples that survive.

Another group of craftsmen for whom there is virtually no evidence are the producers of plaster or clay mummy masks and cartonnage cases. A plaster worker (γυφικῆς) is mentioned in a list of tax payments made by the temple at Soknopaiou Nesos (*BGU* II 471.15 (Roman period)), who may have been employed in the manufacture of mummy masks (Johnson 1936: 643). In Diocletian's Price Edict (301 CE), plaster workers are listed separately from sculptors and other categories of artists, which suggests that they formed a separate class. This was true in the Ptolemaic period, when the relevant tax-farmers granted permission to two painters and goldsmiths named Phatre and Psenobastis to travel freely around the nome in order to carry out work in temples and decorate mummy masks (*P Vindob. Barbara* 58 (183–2 or 159–8 BCE); Clarysse 2001). The fact that permission is granted to *decorate* the mummy masks suggests that the actual manufacture fell under the competence of a different class of artisans.

The process employed in the manufacture and gilding of the masks can be tentatively reconstructed from a third-century papyrus concerning the decoration of the ceiling in the gymnasium at Antinoopolis (*P Köln* I 52 (263 CE)). On the basis of this document, the editors suggest that the plasterer would first apply a layer of plaster, which when dry would be painted with gold-coloured paint, to which the gold leaves were then applied with glue (Kramer and Hübner 1976: 130–1, 141–2, note to lines 11/12 = 59/60). The pigment used to produce the bright

FIG. 36.1 Framed portrait of a woman, found leaning against a mummy in a burial at Hawara. Height 15 cm

British Museum GRA 1889.10-18.1. Courtesy of the Trustees of the British Museum.

yellow found on cartonnage of the Ptolemaic and Roman periods appears to have been orpiment, which occurs naturally in the form of arsenic sulphate, and, according to Pliny, was imported from Persia; it can also be artificially produced (Horak 1998: 122–3; Mitthof 2004b: 291–2). Used in Egypt since at least the 12th dynasty, orpiment yields a citrus to orange-yellow colour that makes it suitable as a substitute for gold or a substrate for gilding.

Painters

Yet another group of artists involved in the funerary sphere are the painters who executed the portraits found on wooden panels and linen shrouds, and the decoration of coffins and masks. A number of documents give the names of individual painters, although their specific expertise is never explicit. Consequently, it is unclear whether this class of artists was responsible for all painted decoration or if they specialized in different media or styles. The encaustic mummy portraits and framed panel paintings, for instance, required a specific set of skills, and may be what documents refer to by the Greek word *eikon* (Fig. 36.1). No documents link this word with a painter, however, and the only document that mentions a mummy and an *eikon* together is a bilingual Greek and Demotic mummy label, which mentions the portrait only to identify the mummy for transport. The Greek opens with the statement 'it [i.e. the mummy] has a portrait on it' (*SB* I 3939 (Roman period)).

Individuals identified as painters are attested in epitaphs, such as that of Sabinus, inscribed in Greek on a small slab of red marble discovered at Hawara and dated to the Roman period: 'Sabinus, painter, aged 26 years, farewell' (*SB* I 682.2; Bernard 1975: 97). A proskynema graffito at Philae names a painter (*SB* V 8681.5 (191 CE); Bernand 1969: 167), and an inscription on a column in the small temple north of Latopolis mentions the artists 'who decorated the column with painted sunk-reliefs' (*SB* V 8374 (147 CE); Bernand 1975: 98). A petition from Hermopolis is in the name of the painter Aurelius Leontius, son of Leontius (*CPR* II 9 (339 CE); Rea and Sijpsteijn 1976: 19–20), and a painter by the name of Flavius Isidoros, son of Phoibammon, acted as witness in a house sale contract (*SPP* XX 122.25 (439 CE)). The element 'Flavius' in this man's name may suggest that he enjoyed a high status in the Hermopolitan community of the time (Keenan 1973: 63).

An expenditure account of uncertain date names the painter Eudaimon (*BGU* I 34 iii.27), and another painter is attested in a tax roll dated to 216–17 CE (*P Yale* III 137; Schubert 2001). A list that appears to name the members of various guilds also mentions a painter (*P Bodl.* I 65 (first century CE?); Salomons 1996), as do *P Brem.* 23 (116 CE; Wilcken 1937: 61–6) and *PSI* VII 784 (362 CE; Nowicka 1979: 24). An edict of Septimius Severus and Caracalla, probably concerning the taxes of painters, is preserved in a very fragmentary papyrus, and mentions the title *zographos*, 'painter', followed by the name Neiko[medes] (*P Aberd.* 15.1.7 (3rd century CE); Nowicka 1993: 156).

Gilders

Despite the fact that the gilding of funerary items, such as mummy masks or even the entire cartonnage case, contributed to and expressed the deceased's rejuvenation and eternal survival in the afterlife, textual evidence for the goldsmith's trade, and particularly for the practical aspects of gilding, is quite limited (Depauw 2004). The fact that in the second century BCE, Phatre and Psenobastis (mentioned above) exercised the trades of both painter and goldsmith raises the possibility that the same may have been true in the Roman period. Gold-workers often appear employed in public and religious buildings, gilding the *xoanon* of Athena-Thoeris at Oxyrhynchus (*P Oxy*. I 117), working in various parts of the temple of Heseph-Herakles at Herakleopolis (Geoffret 2002: 19 and n. 37), gilding the naos of the god Soknopaios at Dime (*BGU* I 149), or gilding the ceiling of the gymnasium at Antinoopolis (*P Köln* I 52 (263 CE)). These documents hint at the luxurious accoutrements of both religious and civic buildings in the urban centres of Roman Egypt, and the same workforce may have been employed in gilding objects like statues and funerary art as well.

Bandagers

A final, anonymous, group worth mentioning are the craftsmen responsible for the elaborate bandaging displayed by some of the mummies of this period, who were probably low-ranking priests trained in this particular skill. There is a unique reference from the Ptolemaic period to an individual identified as 'the man who wraps' (*P Brit. Mus.* EA 10561 (157 BCE); Shore and Smith 1960), which records an agreement drawn up between two groups of lector-priests concerning the provision of cloths, as well as other items, during the various stages of the mummification process. Both human and animal mummies of the Roman period display intricate layers of folded bandages, such as the rhomboidal, net-patterned bandaging of mummies at Hawara.

Location of Workshops and Artists' Place of Residence

Little information survives about the places where artists worked. Depending on the specific crafts, methods, and materials used, workshops must have been filled with dust, dirt, noise, and chaotic activity (Burford 1972: 70–1). Manufacture of objects like coffins or large-format shrouds also required plenty of space. In some cases a workshop would be located by necessity in a particular area, for example near the source of the required raw materials (Burford 1972: 80). This would certainly have been the case for the so-called embalmers' workshops, which consisted of temporary structures erected in the necropolis. Individuals performing the wrapping of the body, if different from those who performed the embalming, would also be located in the necropolis. Documents from Dush, the single largest dossier of texts relating to the funerary industry in the Roman period, indicate that, although they all operated within the necropolis of Kysis, some of the *necrotaphoi* were residents of the town, some lived in nearby settlements, such as Mothis (*P Brit. Mus.* EA 715 (308 CE)), while others resided within the necropolis (*P Brit. Mus.* EA 717 (late fifth century); Grenfell and Hunt 1897, nos 75, 77).

Artists probably carried out their work in a back room or courtyard of their house, although the relationship between the dwelling and the workshop is seldom made explicit in textual evidence. One exception is a topographical list of habitations in Panopolis which records, among others, a carpenter's workshop together with his house (Burford 1972: 78; Husson 1983: 84–6). Further evidence for some artists living, and probably also working, in urban centres is a list drawn up by a clerk for the chief of police Apollonios, to organize security in the town of Heptakomia (*P Brem.* 23 (116 CE)). One of the village inhabitants was a painter named Chairas, whose house was located near the Serapeum (Wilcken 1937: 61–6, line 39). Further evidence for artists living in urban centres comes from Oxyrhynchus (*P Oxy.* LV 3791 (117–18 CE)) and Hermopolis (*CPR* II 9 (339 CE)).

In a few cases, textual sources indicate that particular crafts were grouped within the same area, as with the textile industry at Tebtunis and Arsinoe; both towns had a district or road called 'of the linen makers' (ἀμφοδον λινυφείων) (*P Tebt.* II 321.5.11; Daris 1981: 151; Geoffret 2002: 18). Arsinoe also had a 'road of those who work gold' (*BGU* I 127 (Augustan)). In other towns, similar crafts were located in different parts of the settlement; for instance, a topographic survey of Panopolis records several crafts, including at least six linen workshops, scattered around the settlement (*P Geneva* II 108 (third century CE); Geoffret 2002: 18).

What might be the remains of a workshop were unearthed by the Italian mission at Tebtunis. The studio was described as a small 'laboratory of coloured enamels: work tools, weights, moulds, containers, and many samples of enamels' (Anti 1930–1: 391; my trans.). In the same workshop excavators also found fragments of a tempera painting on a wooden panel depicting two gods, still retaining its frame (Anti 1930–1: 391). Given that the excavation season focused on the temple and the buildings near its enclosure wall, it seems likely that this was also the location of the artist's workshop.

In some instances artisans could have been attached to temples, with the latter paying the tax due on specific trades, such as that of painters and plasterers. One papyrus from Soknopaiou Nesos records a temple's payment of 8 drachmas in tax for a plaster worker (*BGU* 471.15 (Roman period)). This supports the suggestion that some works of funerary art were produced in temple workshops (Johnson 1936: 643). However, many artists may have been forced to travel to find work, taking their tools with them, and setting up a temporary studio wherever they received a commission (Ling 2000: 101). This certainly appears to have been the case with the painter–gilders Phatre and Psenobastis, mentioned above, and the *necrotaphoi* of Kysis, who may have been in charge of smaller cemeteries in nearby settlements, too (Dunand 1985: 117).

Apprenticeship

In terms of how workshops were organized, much depended on the craft. The fact that the painters in *P Oxy.* 3791 (117–18 CE) and in *PSI* VII 784 (362 CE) were paid personally suggests that they worked alone, though they may have had apprentices with them. Clearly the only way to acquire a skill was through training in a workshop, even for someone with a natural aptitude for a particular craft; this would start at a very young age, and probably often at home, with the craft handed down from father to son (Burford 1972: 82, 87–8). Textual evidence from Ptolemaic and Roman Egypt indicates that a formal agreement would be drawn up between the parents or guardian of the young apprentice and the master. Several apprenticeship contracts are known from Roman Egypt (Westermann 1914; Bergamasco 1995), but none relate specifically to funerary art. Two different apprenticeship contracts were in use: one in which a master received a fee for training the pupil, and another in which the master had to provide for the pupil's upkeep as well. The difference rested on the nature of the craft being taught, as did the length of the apprenticeship. Students were usefully employed in the workshop, starting with the simplest tasks, such as mixing paints (Burford 1972: 91 and n. 230; Ling 2000: 93).

Working Practice

A sketch on a wooden panel, now in the Phoebe Hearst Museum of Anthropology (Fig. 36.2), offers an insight into how painters worked. The sketch on one side of the panel depicts a woman wearing a tunic with a mantle over her left shoulder. To either side of her face, and on the upper left corner, are annotations in Greek, which the artist made concerning the colour of the *clavus*, eyes, and hair, and the presence of necklaces (Parlasca 1977: 76–7; Walker and Bierbrier 1997: 122–3, no. 118; Fournet 2004: 95–9). This unfinished panel suggests either that the artist saw the person at least once, when he perhaps adapted a standard model to the subject he was to portray, and jotted down notes about the most salient characteristics of the dress and hairstyle; or that he made these notes when the portrait was commissioned, perhaps by a relative of the deceased, without actually meeting the subject at all. It is interesting to note that the eyes, nose, and mouth are more carefully drawn than other details, which is perhaps to be expected since those are the details that would render the individual uniquely recognizable. The other side of the panel has traces of primer, gesso, and paint, as well as residues of resin from embalming or

FIG. 36.2 A sketch on a wooden panel with annotations by the artist, from Tebtunis

Phoebe Hearst Museum of Anthropology 6/21378b. Copyright the Phoebe Hearst Museum of Anthropology and the Regents of the University of California.

FIG. 36.3 Set of paint pots found in a grave at Hawara

British Museum GRA 1888.9-20.59. Courtesy of the Trustees of the British Museum.

wrapping. One suggestion is that the original panel was rejected or replaced, and the other side then reused for sketching (Walker and Bierbrier 1997: 123); it is also possible that the portrait was damaged in the embalming workshop, hence the traces of resin, and had to be replaced with a new one. Some mummy labels also show traces of resin (Sherwood Fox 1913: 441, 443; Boswinkel and Sijpesteijn 1968: 54; Quaegebeur 1978: 160–1), indicating that they too lay somewhere in the embalming place before being attached to the wrapped body.

Petrie found a painter's set of pigments (Fig. 36.3), together with brushes made from bundles of vegetable fibres tied together by means of a cord, in a grave at Hawara. He described the find as 'a set of paint saucers, piled together at the side of the painter's head, and two pots, probably used for water...They were placed one on the other in the following order: pink, yellow, white, blue, dark red, by the head and the red by the feet' (Petrie 1889: 11, pl. 13; Walker and Bierbrier 1997: 201). The pigments resemble those used to decorate cartonnage masks, but there is no firm evidence that the person in the grave was a painter. Additional examples of painters' tools and pigments were discovered at Tebtunis, in what the excavators identified as an enamelling workshop (Anti 1930–1: 391).

Provision and Acquisition of Materials and their Cost

Painting Materials and Dyes

There were no strict rules concerning the provision of materials, which in some instances were provided by the patron, and in others by the artists, who would be reimbursed for the expense. For instance, an estimate produced by the painter Theophilos gives alternative prices depending on who supplied the materials (mid-third century BCE; Nowicka 1984: 256–9; Ling 1991: 217). A painter named Artemidorus received payment 'for the price of pigments and the painting of divine features' in early fourth-century Oxyrhynchus (*P Oxy.* LV 3791 (317–18 CE); Rea 1988: 53), and several other papyri of the second to fourth centuries deal with the acquisition of paint and other materials (*P Lond.* III 928; *BGU* I 10, 25, 277; *P Harr.* 97).

A note concerning the transport of a number of substances, possibly pigments, and their subsequent transferral into *besa* vessels is inscribed in a bilingual ostracon (*O Narmouthis* 118 + dem. II 54 (second–third century CE)). The first part of the text is written in Demotic and gives instructions concerning transport and transferral of the materials, while the second part is a list of substances written in Greek and arranged in three parallel columns (Gallo 1997: 41–4). From the Byzantine period, there is evidence for a specialized occupation, that of the *pigmentarius*, an individual who manufactured and sold pigments or ointments, and this occupation may have existed earlier (see Horak 1998: 127).

The dye used for some mummy bandages could also be provided by the family of the deceased, and in one instance, the dye alone cost 4 drachmas (*SPP* XXII 56; Montserrat 1997: 40).

Gilding Materials

The acquisition of gold for gilding may have been more carefully controlled, given the value of the raw material; evidence from the Ptolemaic period appears to point to this (Depauw 2004). In the Roman period, documents mentioning the cost of gilt decoration suggest that during the first and second centuries, 1 *meaiaion* (*c.*28 grams) of gold cost 300 silver drachmas, or 2,100 obols (Kramer and Hübner 1976: 132–3; documents include *CPR* 12 (93 CE); *BGU* IV 1065 (97 CE); *P Oxy.* III 496 (127 CE); and *P Oxy.* unedited (158 CE)).

Linen

The cost of linen was probably the largest single outlay in the entire funeral procedure, and relatives of the deceased were responsible for providing it (Montserrat 1997: 37). Some information on the cost of the linen employed can be gathered from documentary evidence, such as accounts and letters. In a letter from the second century, for example, a man writes to a friend to ask him to buy 80 drachmas, or more, worth of fine linen for a burial (*P Haun.* II 17; see Montserrat 1997: 37). In another papyrus, the linen cost the family 600 drachmas (*P Giss.* 68 (*c.*118 CE)). The provision of cloth also features in *P Oxy.* LIV 3756 (325 CE; Johnson 1936: 322–3; Montserrat 1997: 37 n. 41), and in *P Amh.* II 125 although the amount paid is not preserved (first century CE; Grenfell and Hunt 1901: 150).

Wood

A single document dating to the fifth century records payments to a painter named Julianos, and mentions a 'block of wood' (*κορμίου*) in connection with the artist (*P Horak* 21; Harrauer and Pintaudi 2004). The wording of the text suggests that the wood is a block not yet cut into panels, thus indicating that it would be the painter's responsibility either to cut it himself or to have a carpenter do it for him.

Artists' Economic and Fiscal Position

Wages

Some idea of wages and prices in Roman times can be gathered from Diocletian's Price Edict, which represents a government attempt to fix the maximum price of about a thousand of the most common goods and services, together with the maximum wage rate for various classes of workers and craftsmen. The document has many limitations, because it remains unknown to what extent it applied in various parts of the empire, how closely the prices correspond to reality, how effective it was, or whether its relative values can be extrapolated to other periods (Elsner 1998: 239–40; Ling 2000: 105). The wage laid down for a figure painter (*pictor imaginarius*), who probably specialized in painting both wooden panels and the central pictures on walls, was 150 denarii/sesterces a day, plus subsistence, which is six times that earned by the lowest-paid workers (sewer cleaners, farm workers, and water carriers) at 25 denarii daily, and three times higher than that of most other craftsmen, such as carpenters, on 50 denarii daily. Another document that gives an indication of a painter's wage is an order issued by a certain Zoilos to his steward to make a payment in kind to a painter called Herakleides for work on a portrait (*PSI* VII 784 (362 CE)). The latter was to receive one artaba of wheat (about a month's grain allowance) and two Knidian jars of wine, which is perhaps in keeping with the subsistence prescribed by Diocletian's Price Edict for this class of worker (Nowicka 1979: 24; Rea 1988: 51). The high cost of a painted panel is also indicated by *P Oxy.* LV 3791 (117–18 CE), which, although damaged, shows that the sum was in talents (Rea 1988: 51). Similarly, one of the entries in *P Harr.* 97.12 (fourth century), a private account recording payments to different individuals, includes a painter who received 124 talents and 600 denarii. Interestingly, a painter is listed among the landowners of Philadelphia in *P Yale* III 137 (216–17 CE), a land assessment roll drafted for the purpose of determining the tax to be levied on individual landowners in the village (Schubert 2001: 5). The entry reads 'Valerius, painter, grain land 91/2 [arouras]' (Schubert 2001: 44, 61, column V, line 162).

The daily wage laid down in the Price Edict for the plaster or clay modellers was 75 denarii/sesterces. Whether this rate would have applied to making mummy masks cannot be known, but an indication of the cost of a mask is given in *SPP* XXII 56, which lists one mask costing 64 drachmas and another priced at 14 drachmas (Montserrat 1997: 40). In a first-century papyrus from the Fayum, the mask and the shroud (*himation*) together cost 24 drachmas (*P Amh.* II 125 (first century CE); Grenfell and Hunt 1901: 150; Clarysse 2001: 69, note to lines 5–6).

Some evidence for the wages paid to a team of gold-workers is found in *BGU* I 149 (Roman period), an account from Dime concerning the gilding of the naos of the god Soknopaios. The team was to receive 4 artabae of wheat daily for nine days, which the text editor estimates would be enough to feed about twenty artisans for nine days (Schubart 1910: 202 n. 5; Depauw

2004: 234–5). Diocletian's Edict fixed the wage of gilders at 10 per cent of the price per *litrai* of the raw material. This may be how payment for gilding the ceiling of the gymnasium of Antinoopolis was calculated, since the price includes the cost of the raw material but not the estimated length of the work (Kramer and Hübner 1976; Depauw 2004: 235).

The Edict makes no mention of the *necrotaphoi*, or of any other group of funerary priests. References to payments to embalmers are found in lists of funerary expenses, such as that in *P Amh.* II 125, recording a payment of 11 drachmas to the embalmer (first century CE; Grenfell and Hunt 1901: 150). Another embalmer may be the individual listed in *SPP* XXII 56, where one of the entries mentions 'wages of Turbon 8 drachmas' (Montserrat 1997: 40), although his exact role is not stated. Some indirect information on the economic position of the *necrotaphoi* is provided by documents from the necropolis of Kysis, in the Dush Oasis. In one document, two brothers authorize another man to make public before the authorities in Alexandria the cession their father made in their favour, of both his immovable property and his activity as *necrotaphos* (*P Brit. Mus.* EA DCCXI (244–8 CE); Grenfell and Hunt 1897, nos 68, 70, 71). The latter shows that, at least in some instances, the *necrotaphoi* owned considerable wealth, suggesting that their activity could be quite lucrative.

Taxes

A form of governmental control on painting is suggested by the presence of a duty paid on the trade of painters; this is identified as either *phoros genon zographicon* or *telos*, and attested from several second-century sources (*BGU* I 10.11 (192 CE); I 25.16 (200 CE); I 199 verso 3 (194 CE); I 277.1.13 (second century CE); II 652.12 (207 CE); see Johnson 1936: 334, 555; Wallace 1938: 222; Nowicka 1993: 155 n. 184; Worp 2004: 44). Otto (1908: 59) thought this might have been a tax on painters, while according to Wilcken (1899: 373) it was a tax on their works. Johnson suggested instead that, in view of the fact that it is called a 'rental', this may be a lease of a government concession granted to individual towns (Johnson 1936: 555–6; Wallace 1938: 189). This fits with the evidence from the Ptolemaic period, where a document from the Arsinoite nome indicates that the decoration of mummy coverings was under the control of the state administration and as such subject to a tax (Clarysse 2001). Similarly, during the Roman period, governmental control of the goldsmith industry was exercised not through a monopoly on production, but through granting individuals the right to operate in certain areas on payment of a fee (Johnson 1936: 331). This is indicated, for example, by *P Lond.* III 906 (129–33 CE), in which an offer is made to farm the goldsmiths' work in Euhemeria for four years, for 264 silver drachmas per year, to be paid in weekly instalments of 71/3 drachmas (Johnson 1936: 385, no. 236; Depauw 2004: 245).

A customs tax was also levied on paints (*P Lond.* III 928 (third century CE); Kenyon and Bell 1907: 190–1). Olive-, narcissus-, rose-, purple-, laurel-rose-, and almond-coloured paints were taxed at 9 drachmas and 1 obol per measure, with topaz colour at 9 drachmas and 1 obol per *xestes*. Paint pigments (?) were taxed at 7 drachmas and 1 obol per *xestes* (Johnson 1936: 474). Some form of governmental control also applied to the dyeing and fulling industry, although, as in the case of goldsmiths, this may have been replaced by a tax in the third century (Johnson 1936: 334). Embalming was also subject to a tax, shown indirectly by tax payments attested from two temple accounts from Soknopaiou Nesos (*SPP* XXII 183 (138 CE); *BGU* I 1 + 337 (140 CE)). These indicate that some embalmers were part of the temple's personnel. One entry in the first document records a payment of 16 drachmas for 'embalmers (?)', while in the second, an entry includes a payment of 16 drachmas for the 'embalmers at the village' (Johnson 1936: 656, 659).

Exemptions

Exemption from liturgies in Roman Egypt could be granted on several grounds: as hereditary privilege to particular social groups, in recognition of services to the state (a group that included veterans, weavers, office-holders, priests, and physicians), or because of physical or financial incapacity (a group that included the poor, the aged, the ill, and women). However, entitlement to such a privilege did not necessarily imply its enjoyment, since there was a tendency for the emperors or the prefects of Egypt to annul them, particularly from the middle of the second century (Lewis 1964: 69–71). The documentary evidence from Bacchias, for example, indicates that the priesthood of the temple of Soknobraisis did not enjoy any special privileges and fiscal exemptions, and that, at least in 171 CE, they were subject to performing liturgies, dyke work, cultivating state land, and paying the poll tax (Gilliam 1947: 199–206).

Of the various artists and artisans employed in the funerary industry, only painters and gilders enjoyed special treatment and privileges. The edict of Valentinian I and his co-emperors in 337 prescribed that 'artisans who dwell in each city and who practise the skills included in the appended (list) shall be free from all compulsory public services, since their leisure should be spent in learning these skills thereby they may desire the more to become more proficient themselves and to instruct their children' (Theodosian Code XIII 4.2; Pharr, Sherrer Davidson, and Brown Pharr 2001: 390–1). The list included carpenters, physicians, stonecutters, stonemasons, painters, sculptors, engravers, joiners, gilders, dyers in purple, and goldsmiths. Similarly, a later edict of 374 granted teachers of painting exemptions from taxes, both for themselves and for their dependants, providing the only goods handled were those produced by their own art (Theodosian Code XIII 4.4; Ling 1991: 216; Pharr, Sherrer Davidson, and Brown Pharr 2001: 391). It is possible that artists and craftspeople enjoyed similar privileges in earlier times.

Guilds

It has been argued that guilds fulfilled an important social and economic role by filling a gap, providing craftsmen and merchants with security 'through ties of "fictive kinship" and membership in "fictive polities"', while 'low economic, social and political status', as well as 'familial instability' have often been adduced as motivations for the creation and/or joining of guilds. However, an examination of the guilds' charters with regard to the cost of membership clearly indicates that 'financial hardship' cannot have been the reason for joining (Venticinque 2010: 273–4). Monson's analysis of the contributions paid by the members of the Ptolemaic era 'religious' associations in the Fayum, for example, shows that office-holders made annual payments that were sometimes higher than the value of one year's supply of wheat, while the contribution of the ordinary members corresponded to about a quarter of the members' annual consumption (Monson 2006: 227–8). It is undeniable that membership in associations, guilds, and *collegia* provided the members with economic benefits, for example in case of financial uncertainties, or to contribute towards the cost of burial. However, understanding them simply as economic institutions lessens the importance of their social role. Rather, they appear to have served many functions, not least the fact that they allowed non-elite members of society a formal but more accessible social and civic forum (Muhs 2001), thus further enhancing their position within the community (Venticinque 2010: 274–5).

In fact, there seems to have been no fixed rule or custom as to whether craftspeople organized themselves into guilds, associations, and *collegia*. The most numerous appear to have been guilds of carpenters and builders, followed by goldsmiths, while there is no firm evidence for guilds of painters and sculptors (Burford 1972: 162). A possible mention of a painter in relation to guilds is found in a first-century (?) papyrus that seems to list members of various guilds and payments made. In line 11 the text reads 'Olimpos (son of) Aphrodito, painter', while line 14 is tentatively interpreted by the editor as mentioning the 'president of (the) club' (*P Bodl.* I 65; Salomons 1996: 178–9). Some light on the apparent lack of guilds for the latter two groups may be shed by epitaphs, one for a goldsmith and the other for a blacksmith, in which the individuals are identified by their profession but are said to have belonged to the *collegia* of carpenters and builders (Burford 1972: 181–2). It is therefore possible that sculptors and painters belonged to other guilds whose nomenclature does not directly indicate the profession of all of its members.

Embalmers may also have been part of an association, but the evidence is far from definite. A late Ptolemaic document, possibly from the town of Oxyrhynchus, offers the only clear evidence, and is also the first document in which the title of *necrotaphos* is attested. It records the judicial sentence of the *chrematistai* court, which heard cases regarding documents written in Greek, concerning an agreement made by 'all the *necrotaphoi* belonging to an association' (*P Ryl.* 65 (57 BCE); Johnson, Martin, and Hunt 1915: 7 n. 2; Derda 1991: 27–8).

Gender and Ethnicity

It is possible that the types of craft practised in the Roman period were, in part, influenced by the cultural identity of the artist, with professions belonging in the Egyptian tradition—mainly embalming—being in the hands of the indigenous population, while those of the classical tradition—mainly portrait painting—being carried out by Hellenized individuals. In fact, the available evidence shows that the *necrotaphoi* of the Roman period were descended from indigenous Egyptians, even though a few bear both Egyptian and Greek or Latin names, while the few painters known bear, in the main, Greek names. Wilcken (1937) and Nowicka (1993) understood this as indicating the presence of expert Greek painters working in Egypt. However, by the Roman period it is not possible to argue about the ethnic background of an individual on the basis of a name alone: some people with Greek names may have been recent immigrants, while others will have been Hellenized Egyptians or of Greek descent.

An exception is the craft of mummification itself, which throughout the Roman period remains remarkably free from Greek-styled naming practices. The names of individuals in a burial-tax farming agreement, possibly from Oxyrhynchus, dated to 71–2 CE (*P Ryl.* 95; Johnson 1936: 323), are all Egyptian, and even after the decree of universal citizenship, *necrotaphoi* with Egyptian names are attested, for example in papyri that record a donation by Aurelius *Pꜣ–ty–wsỉr* of one quarter of his activity as *necrotaphos* to Aurelius *Pꜣ–ty–ḫnsw* (*P Brit. Mus.* EA 708 (247 CE), and its copy *P Brit. Mus.* EA 710 (267 CE); Grenfell and Hunt 1897, nos 68, 70).

This, in turn, seems to have had a certain influence on the gender of the artists and craftspeople. On the basis of the few surviving names of painters, it appears that this sphere was exclusively a male occupation. In contrast, female embalmers are attested in the documents belonging to *necrotaphoi* working in the necropolis of Kysis, such as *P Brit. Mus.* EA 715 (308 CE), and *P Brit. Mus.* EA 716, a divorce document from 295 CE stipulated between Soulis and Senpsais, both of whom are identified as *necrotaphoi* (Grenfell and Hunt 1897, nos 75, 76).

Conclusion

Unfortunately for us, the vast majority of ancient craftsmen and artists will remain anonymous 'faces in a crowd', even though this may not have been the case in their own time (Burford 1972: 13). The impression one gets from the scant evidence available is that, with the exception of the *necrotaphoi*, and despite a certain level of craft specialization, a class of artists specializing solely in the production of funerary equipment probably did not exist. This should not be surprising since it would have been difficult for such specialists to be in continuous employment and thus make a living. Instead, the production of funerary art reflected specializations used elsewhere. Carpenters, for instance, would have made different kinds of furniture as well as coffins (as was, in fact, the case in Europe until perhaps half a century ago). The gilders of masks were also engaged in the decoration of temples, and it is reasonable to suppose that a funerary portrait painter would also have been involved with mural painting in homes, civic buildings, and tombs, and in commemorative and cultic panel painting to be hung in houses or public places such as temples. Already from the Ptolemaic period there is evidence for the commissioning of a portrait (*eikon*) of rulers, officials, and members of the gymnasium, which would be displayed in public buildings or temples (Nowicka 1979: 22; Łukaszewicz 1987; Whitehouse 2010: 1011), so that this class of artists would not find it too difficult to make a living outside the funerary industry. Possession of a painted portrait may also have been a fairly common occurrence: in the second century, a recruit in the Misenum fleet, Apion, wrote to his family at Philadelphia to say that he had sent them a small portrait of himself (*BGU* II 423; Nowicka 1979: 24). Widespread possession of painted portraits is also indicated by an inventory of household items that lists '2 chairs, 1 bedcover, 3 containers, 1 stool, 2 small armchairs and 4 panels (ἰχόνες)', which may have been painted portraits depicting either individuals or gods (*SB* 4292; Nowicka 1979: 24).

The funerary priests and practitioners responsible for mummification, the execution of elaborate bandaging, and perhaps other forms of mummy decoration, however, may have had to perform other, outside, activities, since their costly skills were not required for each person who died. At Kysis the *necrotaphos* Tapaous acknowledged receipt of payment for her services as nurse, for instance (*P Brit. Mus.* EA 715 (308 CE); Grenfell and Hunt 1897, no. 75). In addition, in some instances, the *necrotaphoi* worked as temple *pastophoroi* (shrine carriers, a low rank of priest), as shown by a mummy label where the *necrotaphos* Pseneveris is also identified as a *pastophoros* of the Buchis bull at Hermonthis (*SB* 5538; Spiegelberg 1901: 340). Ultimately, however, artistic production and craftsmanship are inseparable from the contexts for which they were produced, and thus deeply embedded in Roman Egyptian life.

Suggested Reading

At present, the only translations of the documents from the necropolis of Kysis are those by Grenfell and Hunt (1897) and Hunt and Edgar (1932), while a brief socio-economic analysis of these texts can be found in Dunand (1985). For a survey of the various titles borne by the funerary priests of the Roman period, see Derda (1991). For an in-depth analysis of the funerary art of the Roman period in its socio-religious and art-historical context, see Riggs (2005). Burford's (1972) study of artists in the classical world, including both painters and sculptors, is still one of the more comprehensive works available. On paintings specifically, see Ling (1991, 2000) and Nowicka (1979, 1984, 1993). On mosaics and paintings, both vernacular and funerary, see most recently Whitehouse (2010). The literature on funerary portraits from Egypt is exhaustive; for a survey, see Riggs (2002), as well as Chapter 37, by Barbara Borg, in this volume.

Bibliography

Anti, C. 1930–1. 'Gli scavi della Missione archeologica italiana a Umm el Breighat (Tebtunis)', *Aegyptus* 11: 389–91.

Bergamasco, M. 1995. 'Le didascali nella ricerca attuale', *Aegyptus* 75: 95–167.

Bernard, É. 1969. *Les inscriptions grecques et latines de Philae*, vol. 2. Paris: Centre National de la Recherche Scientifique.

—— 1975. *Recueil des inscriptions grecques du Fayoum*, vol. 1. Leiden: Brill.

Boswinkel, E., and P. J. Sijpesteijn. 1968. *Greek Papyri, Ostraca and Mummy Labels*. Amsterdam: Hakkert.

Burford, A. 1972. *Craftsmen in Greek and Roman Society*. London: Thames and Hudson.

Clarysse, W. 2001. 'Gilding and Painting Mummy Masks', in B. Palme (ed.), *Wiener Papyri: Als Festgabe zum 60. Geburtstag von Hermann Harrauer*. Vienna: Holzhausen, 67–70.

Daris, S. 1981. 'I quartieri di Arsinoe in età romana', *Aegyptus* 61: 143–54.

Depauw, M. 2004. 'New Light on Gilding in Hellenistic Egypt: P. dem. Vindob. Barbara 58', in H. Harrauer and R. Pintaudi (eds), *Gedenkschrift Ulrike Horak (P. Horak)*. Florence: Gonnelli, 234–46.

Derda, T. 1991. 'Necropolis Workers in Greco-Roman Egypt in the Light of the Greek Papyri', *Journal of Juristic Papyrology* 21: 13–36.

Dunand, F. 1985. 'Les nécrotaphes de Kysis', *Cahiers de Recherches de l'Institut de Papyrologie et Égyptologie de Lille* 7: 117–27.

Elsner, J. 1998. *Imperial Rome and Christian Triumph: The Art of the Roman Empire* AD *100–450*. Oxford: Oxford University Press.

Fournet, J.-L. 2004. 'Deux texts relatifs à des couleurs', in H. Harrauer and R. Pintaudi (eds), *Gedenkschrift Ulrike Horak (P. Horak)*. Florence: Gonnelli, 91–9.

Gallo, P. 1997. *Ostraca demotici e ieratici dall'archivio bilingue di Narmouthis* II. Pisa: ETS.
Gascou, J. 1993. *Un codex fiscal Hermopolite (P. Sorb. II 69).* Atlanta: Scholars Press.
Geoffret, P. 2002. 'Artisanat et space vécu dans la *chôra* de l'Égypte romaine', in J.-C. Béal and J.-C. Goyon (eds), *Les artisans dans la ville antique.* Lyon: Centre National de la Recherche Scientifique, 15–22.
Gilliam, E. H. 1947. 'The Archives of the Temple of Soknobraisis at Bacchias', *Yale Classical Studies* 10: 179–281.
Grenfell, B. P., and A. S. Hunt. 1897. *New Classical Fragments and Other Greek and Latin Papyri.* Oxford: Clarendon Press.
—— —— 1901. *The Amherst Papyri: Being an Account of the Greek Papyri in the Collection of the Right Hon. Lord Amherst*, vol. 2. London: Frowde.
Harrauer, H., and R. Pintaudi. 2004. 'Abrechnung für den Maler Julianos', in Harrauer and Pintaudi (eds), *Gedenkschrift Ulrike Horak (P. Horak).* Florence: Gonnelli, 109–12.
Horak, U. 1998. 'Antike Farbenpracht: Zwei Farblisten aus der Papyrussammlung der Österreichischen Nationalbibliothek', *Tyche* 13: 115–33.
Hunt, A. S., and C. C. Edgar. 1932. *Select Papyri*, vols. 1 and 2. London: Heinemann.
Husson, G. 1983. *Oikia: Le vocabulaire de la maison privée en Égypte d'après les papyrus grecs.* Paris: Sorbonne.
Johnson, A. C. 1936. *Roman Egypt to the Reign of Diocletian: An Economic Survey of Ancient Rome*, vol. 2. Baltimore: Johns Hopkins University Press.
Johnson, J. de M., V. Martin, and A. S. Hunt. 1915. *Catalogue of the Greek and Latin Papyri in the John Rylands Library, Manchester: Documents of the Ptolemaic and Roman Periods*, vol. 2. Manchester: Manchester University Press.
Keenan, J. G. 1973. 'The Names Flavius and Aurelius as Status Designations in Later Roman Egypt', *Zeitschrift für Papyrologie und Epigraphik* 11: 33–63.
Kenyon, F. G., and H. I. Bell. 1907. *Greek Papyri in the British Museum: Catalogue, with Texts*, vol. 3. London: British Museum Press.
Kramer, B., and R. Hübner. 1976. *Kölner Papyri (P. Köln)*, vol. 1. Cologne: Westdeutscher.
Lewis, N. 1964. 'Exemption from Liturgy in Roman Egypt', in *Actes du Xe Congrès International de Papyrologues, Varsovie-Cracovie, 3–9 septembre 1961.* Warsaw: Zakład Narodowy Imienia Ossolińskich Wydawnictwo Polskiej Akademii Nauk, 69–79.
Ling, R. 1991. *Roman Painting.* Cambridge: Cambridge University Press.
—— 2000. 'Working Practice', in Ling (ed.), *Making Classical Art: Process and Practice.* Stroud: Tempus, 91–107.
Łukaszewicz, A. 1987. '*ΑΣΠΙΔΕΙΟΝ*', *Zeitschrift für Papyrologie und Epigraphik* 67: 109–10.
Mitthof, F. 2004a. 'Liste von Pigmenten und Farbstoffen für Malfarben (P. Horak 63)', in H. Harrauer and R. Pintaudi (eds), *Gedenkschrift Ulrike Horak (P. Horak).* Florence: Gonnelli, 181–3.
—— 2004b. 'Pigmente und Farbstoffe für Malfarben im spätantiken Ägypten: Die papyrologische Evidenz', in H. Harrauer and R. Pintaudi (eds), *Gedenkschrift Ulrike Horak (P. Horak).* Florence: Gonnelli, 289–304.
Monson, A. 2006. 'The Ethics and Economics of Ptolemaic Religious Associations', *Ancient Society* 36: 221–38.
Montserrat, D. 1997. 'Death and Funerals in the Roman Fayum', in M. L. Bierbrier (ed.), *Portraits and Masks: Burial Customs in Roman Egypt.* London: British Museum Press, 33–44.
Muhs, B. P. 2001. 'Membership in Private Associations in Ptolemaic Tebtunis', *Journal of the Economic and Social History of the Orient* 44: 1–21.

Nowicka, M. 1979. 'La peinture dans les papyrus grecs', *Archeologia* 30: 21–8.
—— 1984. 'Théophilos, peintre alexandrin, et son activité', in N. Bonacasa and A. di Vita (eds), *Alessandria e il mondo ellenistico-romano*. Rome: 'L'Erma' di Bretschneider.
—— 1993. *Le portrait dans la peinture antique*. Warsaw: Académie Polonaise des Sciences.
Otto, E. 1908. *Priester und Tempel im hellenistischen Ägypten*, vol. 2. Leipzig: Teubner.
Palme, B., and H. Tegel. 1990. 'Drei byzantinische papyri', in M. Capasso, G. Messeri Savorelli, and R. Pintaudi (eds), *Miscellanea papyrologica in occasione del bicentenario dell'edizione della Charta Borgiana*. Florence: Gonnelli, 451–9.
Parlasca, K. 1966. *Mumienporträts und verwandte Denkmäler*. Wiesbaden: Steiner.
—— 1977. *Repertorio d'arte dell'Egitto Greco-romano*, ser. B: *Ritratti di mummie, II (nos. 246–496)*. Rome: 'L'Erma' di Bretschneider.
Petrie, W. M. F. 1889. *Hawara, Biahmu, and Arsinoe*. London: Field and Tuer.
Pharr, C., T. Sherrer Davidson, and M. Brown Pharr. 2001. *The Theodosian Code and Novels, and the Sirmondian Constitutions*. Union, NJ: Lawbook Exchange.
Quaegebeur, J. 1978. 'Mummy Labels: An Orientation', in E. Boswinkel and P. W. Pestman (eds), *Textes grecs, démotiques et bilingues (P. L. Bat. 19)*. Leiden: Brill.
Rea, J. R. 1988. *The Oxyrhynchus Papyri*, vol. 55. London: Egypt Exploration Society.
—— and P. J. Sijpsteijn. 1976. *Corpvs Papyrorvm Raineri: Griechische Texte* II. Vienna: Hollinek.
Riggs, C. 2002. 'Facing the Dead: Recent Research on the Funerary Art of Ptolemaic and Roman Egypt', *American Journal of Archaeology* 106: 85–101.
—— 2005. *The Beautiful Burial in Roman Egypt: Art, Identity, and Funerary Religion*. Oxford: Oxford University Press.
Salomons, R. P. 1996. *Papyri Bodleianae* I. Amsterdam: Gieben.
Schubart, W. 1910. 'Gold- und Silberarbeiten in griechischen Papyrusurkunden', in J. H. Schäfer (ed.), *Ägyptische Goldschmiedearbeiten*. Berlin: Curtius, 191–203.
Schubert, P. 2001. *A Yale Papyrus (P Yale III 137) in the Beinecke Rare Book and Manuscript Library* III. Oakville, Conn.: American Society of Papyrologists.
Sherwood Fox, W. 1913. 'Mummy Labels in the Royal Ontario Museum', *American Journal of Philology* 34: 437–50.
Shore, A. F., and H. S. Smith. 1960. 'A Demotic Embalmers' Agreement', *Acta Orientalia* 25: 277–94.
Spiegelberg, W. 1901. 'Über einen Titel des Apisstieres', *Recueil de Travaux Realtifs à la Philology et à l'Archéologie Égyptiennes et Assyriennes* 23: 197–8.
Venticinque, P. F. 2010. 'Family Affairs: Guild Regulations and Family Relationships in Roman Egypt', *Greek, Roman and Byzantine Studies* 50: 273–94.
Walker, S., and M. Bierbrier (eds) 1997. *Ancient Faces: Mummy Portraits from Roman Egypt*. London: British Museum Press.
Wallace, S. L. 1938. *Taxation in Egypt from Augustus to Diocletian*. Princeton: Princeton University Press.
Westermann, W. L. 1914. 'Apprentice Contracts and the Apprentice System in Roman Egypt', *Classical Philology* 9: 295–315.
Whitehouse, H. 2010. 'Mosaics and Painting in Graeco-Roman Egypt', in A. Lloyd (ed.), *A Companion to Ancient Egypt*, vol. 2. Oxford: Wiley-Blackwell, 1008–31.
Wilcken, U. 1899. *Griechische Ostraka aus Aegypten und Nubien*. Leipzig: Giesecke & Devrient.
—— 1937. *Die Bremer Papyri*. Berlin: Akademie der Wissenschaften.
Worp, K. A. 2004. 'Zu den ζωγράφοι in Ägypten', in H. Harrauer and R. Pintaudi (eds), *Gedenkschrift Ulrike Horak (P. Horak)*. Florence: Gonnelli, 43–6.

CHAPTER 37

PORTRAITS

BARBARA E. BORG

ARGUABLY, there is no province within the Roman empire that had such a long tradition in portrait representation as Egypt did. From the very beginning of visual representation during the 1st dynasty, images of particular historical individuals—which I shall take to mean 'portrait' here—were part of the artistic repertoire and a focus of interest. In the tombs of pharaohs and high officials, the deceased figured prominently in scenes depicting his or her life both on earth and in the world beyond. While most of these representations are generic (in spite of their intention to depict specific individuals), from the Middle Kingdom onwards portrait sculpture was, at times, remarkably individualized, with different shapes of heads and reference to age (Assmann 1996). It is for this reason that the degree of impact that Greek (and Roman) culture had on Egyptian portraiture has long been debated. According to some, the highly individualized sculptures in question, usually rendered in local greenish-black hardstone, were partly created prior to Alexander's conquest, possibly even from the sixth century BCE (26th dynasty) onwards, i.e. during a time when Greece still had no comparably naturalistic portraits at all (Anthes 1939; Charmoux 1955; Bothmer 1960, 1988; Josephson 1997a, b). Others, however, have pointed out the similarities of these sculptures with Greek Hellenistic portraits and argued for a low chronology, which by now appears to be the majority view (Küthmann 1962; Bianchi 1982; Vandersleyen 1985; Josephson 1997a; Kaiser 1999).

In any case, there can be no doubt that Greek conquest and rule changed the style of portraits remarkably. In order to bridge the gap between local traditions and expectations, and the culture of the new rulers, the latter not only continued Egyptian forms alongside the newly introduced Greek forms, but also promoted a hybrid style and iconography combining, to various degrees, both traditional Egyptian elements and new Greek ones. R. R. R. Smith (1988: 87) has proposed a useful distinction between different styles of portraiture during the Hellenistic period: (1) Purely pharaonic (pharaonic regalia and stylized facial and bodily features); (2–3) portraits with pharaonic regalia but various degrees of individualized facial features, 'softened' bodily styles, or locks of hair over the brow; and (4) purely Greek portraits with no pharaonic regalia and bare heads. It is obvious that there is no sharp borderline between these categories, which were all employed in portrait representation in temples and sanctuaries, as was customary in both

Egypt and the Greek world (Kunze 1996; Stanwick 2002). The same applies to portraits of the rest of the elite.

After the conquest of Egypt, Roman attitudes to portraiture therefore fell on rather fertile ground, similar, in many ways, to the rest of the Greek east. It may be disputed what exactly could be called Roman, and what exactly can be attributed to Roman influence. This is not the place to embark on the debate about the difference between Greek and Roman portraits, but it is generally accepted that Roman art, in merely stylistic terms, is basically an extension and creative development of Greek art. What differs is the intentions and attitudes towards art. For our purposes it thus suffices to note a couple of changes in Egyptian use of portraiture, which occur around the same time as the establishment of Roman dominion and are therefore likely to be a result of or reaction to it. The most obvious change is a sudden increase in numbers of naturalistic portraits as well as in media, and the use of such portraiture not just by the ruling families and the highest levels of administrative and religious dignitaries but also by local elites.

Imperial Portraits

One reason for the success of the Roman empire was the integration, as far as possible, of local traditions into the new administrative organization and social system. Roman emperors, similarly to their Ptolemaic forebears, were also Egyptian pharaohs. The latter role was not just one of military and administrative power but of religious status as well: the pharaoh was the son of Re, the incarnation of Horus on earth, who received cult in the traditional temples and gained much of his power from this religious legitimization. Egyptian temples, in possession of major parts of the land, used to be rich and powerful, and their priestly administrators had always played a key role in the establishment of rule over Egypt (see Chapter 22). While it is debated to what extent Augustus diminished the power of the temples, he clearly paid tribute to them and received the support of their priests and traditional deities in return (Bowman 1986: 179–83; Dundas 2002; Capponi 2005: 98–9).

From Augustus onwards, Roman emperors therefore dedicated new Egyptian temples and added to existing ones, had themselves depicted in traditional iconographic schemes on their walls, and erected statues in the (Hellenized) Egyptian style in the sanctuaries (Bowman 1986: 168–70). Augustus was depicted making offerings to various divinities on temples newly erected during his reign, and on others he joins some of his Ptolemaic forebears as well as his successors. For instance, Augustus, Tiberius, Claudius, and Nero appear in reliefs on the Hathor temple at Dendara, one of the oldest temples of Egypt, to which Tiberius added an imposing colonnaded hall and Nero an enclosure wall (Arnold 1999: 248, figs 209–10). Later emperors up to and including Caracalla followed Augustus' example and dedicated buildings in sanctuaries, on which they duly appeared in Egyptian-style reliefs (Arnold 1999: 230–73). As the inscriptions accompanying these images make clear, they communicated the legitimacy of the ruler to a wider public and rendered acceptable his rule.

Portraits of Augustus in the round and in 'classical' style were found at Alexandria, Damanhur, Athribis, and Arsinoe, and range from miniature glass busts to acrolithic, colossal statues, including the famous busts from Arsinoe now in Copenhagen.[1] Portraits of most of his successors up to and including Alexander Severus are also known, though none of the later emperors received as many portraits as Augustus did—a pattern that is consistent with the rest of the empire. However, the Roman emperors seem to have largely abandoned Egyptian-style hardstone portrait statues. Only one such statue—from the temple of Karnak—is still accepted by many to represent Augustus (e.g. Smith 1988: 92 n. 35; Stanwick 2002: 88–9, 128, no. G2, on Cairo, Egyptian Museum CG 701), but except for the emperor Caracalla, to whom five heads and statues are attributed, no further emperors can be securely identified (Stanwick 2002: 129–30, nos G10–G14; see also Kiss 1984). All imperial portraits with a known provenance were found in sanctuaries, but honorific statues in public spaces within the towns also existed. There is no systematic study of epigraphic evidence for these, but high columns that were originally topped by statues are attested at several places (Bailey 1990: 129–33). A wooden tondo in Berlin of unknown provenance is a unique painted representation of the Severan family, with the portrait of Geta erased after his *damnatio memoriae* (Parlasca 1969–80: III, no. 390, pls 95.1, 96.1.2.4).

Private Portraits

Sculpture in the Round

During the Late and Ptolemaic periods, hardstone portrait statues of private individuals, i.e. non-ruling elite like priests and high-ranking administrative officers, were erected in sanctuaries in large numbers, doubtless in order not only to honour the gods but also to promote the individuals represented (Assmann 1996). Their adoption of naturalistic features may indeed be a result of this attitude, as well as a visual sign of integration within the ruling class that adopted parts of the culture of the rulers (Kaiser 1999: 251–2). These portraits clearly continued through the first century BCE but appear to have largely ceased after the firm establishment of Roman rule and administration, for no obvious reason. However, a seated marble statue of the physician Pappos Theognostos was dedicated in the Alexandrian Serapeum by the *epimeletes tou topou* (overseer of the district) Bassus, son of Straton, for curing his daughter (Turin, Egyptian Museum 269; Adriani 1961: 61–2, no. 209, pls 98, 323, 325; Tkaczow 1993: 244–5, no. 158), and it is likely that further examples escaped scholarly attention or were reduced to lime by the locals.

Evidence for the erection of portrait statues in public spaces within towns is equally scarce. The clearest example is the over life-size marble statue of a woman from the first quarter of the second century from Oxyrhynchus. The statue was found next to its high round base on an open piazza, probably the agora (Alexandria, Graeco-Roman Museum 24008; Breccia 1978: 39–40, pl. 17, fig. 58; pl. 25, fig. 77; here Fig. 37.1). A second female

[1] Massner (1986); Boschung (1993: 212); miniature head: Alexandria, Musée Gréco-Romain 3536, Boschung (1993: 139, no. 64, pl. 202); acrolith (posthumous from Athribis): Boschung (1993: 139, no. 65, pls 144, 194.7); busts from Arsinoe: Copenhagen, NCG inv. 1443 (with Livia and Tiberius): Boschung (1993: 156–7, no. 112, pls 79, 82.2, 194.1, 227.2); Johansen (1994: 90–1, no. 33; 96–7, no. 36; 114–15, no. 45); other portraits of Augustus from Egypt are Boschung (1993, nos 75, 128, 136, 180).

marble statue, headless but equally over life-size and found in the vicinity, is likely to have been another honorific portrait monument (Alexandria, Graeco-Roman Museum 23350; Breccia 1978: 40, pl. 25, fig. 78). A headless female statue with an artist's inscription was found in the town centre of Lykopolis (Asyut) (Alexandria, Graeco-Roman Museum 3882; Daressy 1896; Graindor 1937: 122–4, no. 62, pl. 55). Marble statues attested by fragments from the centre of Alexandria may also have honoured private individuals (Tkaczow 1993: 248, no. 168; 250–1, nos 174–5; 253–4, nos 183–4), and we can probably assume that Roman-type buildings featured portraits in the same way as they did in the rest of the empire (Bailey 1990).

Most private portraits with a known provenance, however, come from tombs. A pair of statues flanked the entrance to the Main Tomb of the Kom el-Shuqafa catacomb, the most remarkable of the Alexandrian hypogea both for its architecture and for its merging of Egyptian and Graeco-Roman styles and motifs (Venit 2002: 124–45, with further references; Empereur 2003). The statues equally display this double legacy, with their bodies in the Egyptian stance and dress, and their heads in the naturalistic Roman style and fashion (Venit 2002: 129, figs 107–11). The dates of both the tomb and the statues are debated. As the statues stand in niches created by blocking up previous openings in the wall, they are a secondary feature. The woman with her

FIG. 37.1 Honorific marble statue of a woman, from Oxyrhynchus, first quarter of the second century CE

Graeco-Roman Museum, Alexandria, 24008; after Adriani (1936, pl. 2.3).

single row of curls around the forehead would, if first century as usually assumed, be Tiberian, suggesting an even earlier date for the catacomb. But the plastic rendering of irises and pupils would be unique in that period, and since both portraits have good Antonine parallels (Borg 1996: 51–61, for the woman's hairstyle; for beardless men in the second century, see Smith 1988: 83–7), they are more likely second century in date. Differently from these images, most statues from Alexandria are carved in marble and unambiguously Roman in dress and style. The head of a priest comes from the necropolis of Kom el-Shuqafa (Schreiber 1908: 62–4; Graindor 1937: 88–9, no. 37, pl. 31; Breccia 1970: 42, fig. 10). Several statues were found beyond the city walls and thus must have adorned tombs as well (Tkaczow 1993: 243–60, nos 154–6, 188–91, 193–9, 201–4). One of them is a rare togate statue from the cemetery of *legio II Germanica* (Alexandria, Graeco-Roman Museum 3907; Graindor 1937: 106–7, no. 50, pl. 42b).

A much less naturalistic second-century statue of a man from Hawara was made in the local limestone (Petrie 1911: 21, no. 47, pl. 20). Marble statues are further attested for the cemeteries of Hagar el-Nawatieh (Alexandria, Graeco-Roman Museum 20931; Graindor 1937: 96–7, no. 44, pl. 38) and Oxyrhynchus, some of them standing (Petrie 1925: 17, pl. 46.2; Breccia 1978, pl. 39, fig. 137; Schmidt 2003: 69), but at least two reclining on a couch, very much like the deceased on metropolitan Roman grave monuments as well as on Egyptian funerary reliefs. The more elaborate one depicts the deceased dressed in a rich chiton and mantle. She is leaning on a small shield with the head of Medusa, a serpent at her feet, and three crowns in and beneath her left hand, suggesting that she was a priestess, possibly of Athena, the patron goddess of the city (Alexandria, Graeco-Roman Museum 23349; Breccia 1978: 42–3, fig. 11). A similar, perfectly preserved marble statue of a reclining man was found at Abusir el-Meleq (Alexandria, Graeco-Roman Museum 3897; Graindor 1937: 97–100, pl. 39; Breccia 1978, pl. 24, fig. 76; here Fig. 37.2), and the kline of a woman with early Severan hairstyle from Alexandria

FIG. 37.2 Marble funerary monument of a reclining man, from Abusir el-Meleq, second century CE (?) Length: 139 cm, height 67 cm

Graeco-Roman Museum, Alexandria, 3897. Deutsche Archäologisches Institut, Rome, negative 60.1829.

suggests that this is where the inspiration came from (Schmidt 2003: 73; cf. Breccia 1970: 42–3, fig. 11; pl. 29, figs 75–6; Said Mahmoud 1995).

Portrait busts were equally used in funerary contexts. Some of the most remarkable pieces have been found at Terenouthis on the western edge of the Delta. They include the exquisitely worked and perfectly preserved white marble bust of an early Antonine lady, the equally superb bust of an Antonine young priest of Serapis, and a slightly lesser bust of another young man (Cairo, Egyptian Museum JE 44672, 39468, and 44671; Grimm and Johannes 1975: 20–1, nos 24–6, pls 43–53).

Relief Sculpture

A large number of grave reliefs with portraits come again from Alexandria (Schmidt 2003). Greek marble reliefs were imported into Egypt by the Greek settlers after the conquest and foundation of the city, but similar ones were soon produced on site, now made in the local limestone that was covered with stucco and painted. They were exhibited on pedestals of different shapes within crowded open-air cemeteries, and the general trend was towards an increasing integration of Egyptian elements, mostly referring to religious beliefs. The Imperial period cemeteries were characterized by an intimate amalgamation of Egyptian and Greek cultural elements (Schmidt 2003: 35–43). One characteristic group of tombstones with 'Roman' portraits comes from a cemetery of members of *legio II Germanica*, made predominantly of marble, inscribed in Latin, and all from the brief period between 213 and 235 (Fig. 37.3). Their largely uniform designs present the deceased in belted tunics with *sagum* (military cloak) and sometimes weapons or other military paraphernalia, or rarely also in the toga. Stelae for women and girls created in the same workshop(s) and originating partly from the same necropolis show the deceased lying on klinai. Egyptian elements are very rare on these items but not lacking altogether. A few grave reliefs depicted the deceased as life-size figures in a naturalistic manner, and possibly inspired the much larger group of similar monuments from Oxyrhynchus (Schmidt 2003: 73, 122–4, nos 95–9, pls 33–6). Whether a rare relief with five individuals in familiar Graeco-Roman statue types and Roman hairstyles from the Antonine period also comes from Alexandria is not clear (Cairo, Egyptian Museum CG 27568; Riggs 2005, fig. 36).

The limestone reliefs from Oxyrhynchus are up to 180 cm high and decorated with almost life-size figures of the deceased standing in narrow, niche-like frames, some of them elaborate aediculae with Corinthian columns and shell-decorated semi-domes (Petrie 1925: 12–19; el-Fakharani 1965; Schmidt 2003: 62–73). A group of similar stelae for children, sometimes sitting on the ground, must be attributed to the same site.[2] Almost nothing is known about their original contexts as they appear to have been reused in late antiquity, but their form suggests their set-up as independent monuments, perhaps in an architectural setting with niches. The deceased are depicted in iconographies well known from Greek statue types that were used all over the Roman empire. They are wearing tunics with clavi and mantles, and feature fashionable hairstyles equally common to the empire-wide elite. Their hairstyles also

[2] This group is often believed to come from Antinoopolis, but no such stelae were found in excavations there. The two found by Petrie in Oxyrhynchus suggest that the group is likely from there: Schneider (1975); Parlasca (1978: 118); Boyd and Vikan (1981: 8–9); Schmidt (2003: 61–3); sceptical Thomas (2000: 11). The matter is further complicated by forgeries and reworking of these reliefs: Severin (1995).

FIG. 37.3 Marble grave stela of Aurelius Sabius, a Roman soldier from *legio II Germanica*, found at a cemetery at Alexandria. The legion used the cemetery between 213 and 235 CE. Height 75 cm, width 35 cm

Graeco-Roman Museum, Alexandria, 252. Deutsche Archäologisches Institut, Cairo, negative F 6944. Photo: Dieter Johannes, courtesy of Stefan Schmidt.

allow for the dating of the reliefs as there are no inscriptions or other external dating criteria. The earliest, most 'classical' examples with subtle rendering of the facial features date to the Severan period, while the latest and more schematic examples are from the turn of the fourth century. All male portraits appear beardless and are thus termed 'youths' in scholarship, but their short stubble beards must have been added in painting, as was the hair on the seemingly bald heads (Schmidt 2003: 67–8).

By far the largest number of grave reliefs with portraits comes from Terenouthis (Pelsmaekers 1989, 1995; Schmidt 2003: 44–61). Again, the stelae are rather consistent in iconography and workmanship, and were inserted into niches in the façades of often half-barrel-shaped tombs. They are all made from local limestone and mostly depict the deceased of both sexes reclining on a couch with tables, amphoras in stands, and bunches of grain in front of them. A second type, apparently used for the prematurely deceased only, depicts standing figures with their arms raised, often with Egyptian animal divinities above or flanking them, especially the jackal (Anubis) and falcon (Horus) (Schmidt 2003: 49–55). Owing to the lack of any useful evidence from archaeological contexts, the standardization of the reliefs, and the lack of individualizing features in the portraits, dates are extremely difficult to establish. Many of the graves are thought to be late antique, which, together with the rather schematic style of depiction, gave rise to the assumption that the reliefs all date to the third to fourth centuries. But the original necropolis may indeed be high Imperial, and the reliefs' inscriptions suggest that they were produced throughout the entire Imperial period (Schmidt 2003: 45–6).

Limestone stelae from Upper Egypt adhere much more strongly to Egyptian tradition. Only those from Abydos occasionally depict the deceased in tunic and/or mantle and with natural hair within the traditional scenes, or, more rarely still, a couple or even an entire family with their children (Abdalla 1983). Dating is again difficult, but Abdalla rightly warns against the assumption that the crude style must necessarily indicate a late date, and a few examples are clearly from the first and second centuries according to their inscriptions and hairstyles (Abdalla 1983: 125–32).

Mummy Decoration

Naturalistic features were introduced not only into the decoration of tombs and monuments but also into that of the mummies themselves, and, as in the previously discussed genres, naturalism was attempted to different degrees. During the entire Pharaonic period, the faces of the deceased were covered by masks that adhered to a rather stereotypical design, not for lack of inspiration but because the mask depicted the deceased in their other-worldly existence as an Osiris or, for females, a Hathor (Borg 1996: 196–7; 1998: 75–6; Aubert and Cortopassi 2004: 13–15; Riggs 2005: 42–3). From the first century BCE onwards, however, a considerable number of people decided to maintain some contemporary features of their life in this world, and it is on these that I shall focus here.

Mummy Masks and Coffins

During the Late and Ptolemaic periods, mummy masks still had generic faces and the typical head-cloth, often decorated with Egyptian scenes and symbols on the lower borders and at the back. Towards the end of the Ptolemaic period, elements of contemporary dress and coiffure started to emerge on the mummy decoration. The head-cloth first exposed a narrow strip of hair around the forehead (Grimm 1974: 45–7; Stadler 2004: 35), and in the Roman period more hair was uncovered, suggesting a proper fashion hairstyle beneath the head-cloth. Soon many masks dispensed of the head-cloth altogether (Petrie 1889: 16; Grimm 1974; Riggs 2005). Although 'Roman' masks, i.e. masks with fashionable hairstyles, prevail from the turn of the second century (Grimm 1974: 103–6; Stadler 2004: 31–48; Riggs 2005: 113–19, 125–6), masks without such elements persisted into the Roman period. Some graves with both 'Roman-style' portraits and traditional masks have been excavated (Roberts 1997: 22;

Hawass 2000), and a mask without any indication of hair in Ipswich, UK, bears the name of Titus Flavius Demetrius. It must therefore be of Flavian date and the deceased a Roman citizen (Stadler 2004: 34, fig. 4; Riggs 2005: 21–2, fig. 4).

The technique of these masks varies from place to place. Their core consisted most frequently of stucco only, but many were made of stucco-covered linen or papyrus (known as cartonnage) or, rarely, wood (Grimm 1974: 14–21; Aubert and Cortopassi 2004: 15–20). They were normally created from moulds, with details like the upper head, the ears, inset eyes, and (prefabricated) hands added in a second step. The mask was then covered with finer stucco, and hair, beards, wreaths, and similar delicate detail added. Finally, the entire mask was painted and gilded. Obviously, their creation from moulds resulted in standardized facial features, but various degrees of individualization are achieved by the addition of jewellery, certain types of dress, or a fashionable hairstyle.

'Roman' masks have been found at many places throughout the country but were particularly common in Middle Egypt (Grimm 1974, esp. 23–45; Riggs 2005). Tomb types and modes of deposition varied widely from shallow sandpits at Hawara in the Fayum to rock-cut tombs of various kinds at other places, from simple deposition on the floor or on a primitive bench to burial in elaborate coffins. Apparently, these habits depended mainly on available funds and local tradition, and to a lesser degree on membership in social or religious groups. Chronologically, these masks range from the Augustan era through the fourth century, but again with noticeable local differences. At Hawara, for instance, they started in the Augustan era but were already substituted by painted portraits around 100 CE (Grimm 1974: 47–54), while at Deir el-Bahri the relatively rare examples belong to the third and early fourth centuries (Riggs 2000; 2005: 232–43). Tuna el-Gebel yielded the largest number of stucco masks produced from the early Imperial period through the later third century (Grimm 1974: 71–91, 135–7). Fourth-century dates of masks based on style, as suggested by Grimm (1974) and others, are often problematic, especially after his comparisons with the painted portraits can no longer serve to support his view (see below). The latest type of Roman female hairstyle attested, characterized by a wide braided plait on the top of the head, is from the second half of the third century (e.g. Hildesheim inv. 574; Grimm 1974: 88 with n. 268, pl. 97.1; here Fig. 37.4). Mummy masks from Thebes do continue into the fourth century according to Constantinian coins from their contexts, but they lack any reference to Roman-fashion hairstyles and are characterized by very stylized faces and extreme rendering of eyes (Grimm 1974: 95–6).

Throughout the period, Egyptian elements of these masks were continuously reduced, and from the turn of the second century 'Roman' masks predominate. Interestingly, from around the same time, the deceased are beginning to lift their heads. Grimm has interpreted this as a reference to resurrection, but as the change only affects the 'Roman' mummies, a desire to render the head more visible on the lying mummy must also have encouraged this change. It supports the view that the more thorough individualization of portraits is linked to a desire for self-representation. On the mummies, however, Egyptian scenes and symbols appear throughout the Roman period, and the extent to which quotidian elements are integrated into the designs varies. On most masks, only the bust with summarily rendered tunics with clavi is depicted. At Meir, women are also wearing mantles, which are draped in ways similar to those on Roman marble busts, and Abusir el-Meleq yielded even a few coffins with the full, statue-like figure of the deceased (Riggs 2005: 105–26 (Meir), 148–55 (Abusir el-Meleq)).

FIG. 37.4 Mummy mask from Tuna el-Gebel (?) with a hairstyle typical of the second half of the third century

Roemer- und Pelizaeus-Museum, Hildesheim, 574; after Grimm (1974, pl. 97.1).

Painted Mummy Portraits

The genre of naturalistic portraits that has attracted most attention among both scholars and the general public is painted portraits (Fig. 37.5). They substituted for masks as face covers at several places throughout Egypt from the early first century CE onwards. Like the mummies with Roman masks, portrait mummies were found in a wide range of different types of tomb, the shallow sandpits of Hawara, stone-clad shaft graves, rock-cut, often reused chambers, and built tombs including a spectacular one at Marina el-Alamein on the coast west of Alexandria with a colonnaded front and dining room inside (Parlasca 1966: 18–58; Doxiadis 1995: 122–58; Borg 1998: 1–31; Daszewski 1997; Picton, Quirke, and Roberts 2007).

The paintings were executed either on the outer layer of the linen shrouds wrapping the mummy or, more frequently, on thin panels of imported or local wood (Doxiadis 1995: 93–101; Borg 1996: 5–18; Freccero 2000). Wax- and water-based colours were applied on the bare wood or on a primer, and a wide range of pigments created from mostly mineral but also organic and artificial substances was used. The 'encaustic' (from Greek *enkauein*, 'to burn in'), wax-based paintings are characterized by a certain lustre and rich colours, which were applied by a brush and blended in techniques similar to those of modern oil paintings. Tempera paintings, in contrast, have a matt surface and are created by layering different shades of colour on top of each other as in aquarelles. A small group of paintings are created using very liquid wax-based paint diluted by oil or water. This allows for an almost graphic mode of painting with shading applied by cross-hatching.

Some mummy portraits are extraordinarily naturalistic and individualized, so that they encourage comparison with modern portraits. Moreover, like the masks, almost all portraits

FIG. 37.5 Painted mummy portrait from the Severan era; tempera on wood. Height 32.5 cm, width 19.5 cm

Martin von Wagner Museum, Würzburg, H 2196. Photo: Karl Öhrlein. Copyright Martin von Wagner Museum, University of Würzburg.

were detached from their mummies and displayed in museums like modern paintings. This has misled people to believe that the portraits were painted during the lifetime of their patrons, an assumption that is surely wrong at least for the vast majority of cases (Borg 1996: 191–5; 1998: 67–8). We should also not forget that most of the 1,100 or so preserved paintings are rather generic except for the Roman hairstyles and Graeco-Roman dress and jewellery worn by virtually all of them. The isolation of portraits from their mummies has distracted from the fact that they originally were part of an ensemble that was firmly based in Egyptian religious belief. While a few mummies depicted the entire body of the deceased in contemporary dress and thus resemble a painted version of the Abusir el-Meleq coffins, others showed the deceased (in tunic and mantle, or mummiform) in a traditional scene flanked by Osiris and Anubis or Isis and Nephthys, while still others were either decorated with an elaborate pattern of three-dimensional lozenges formed by the narrow linen bands wrapped around the body, or combined the naturalistic portrait with Egyptian scenes and symbols on the coffin-like mummy (Corcoran 1995; Borg 1996: 129–48; Riggs and Stadler 2003; Riggs 2005: 156–60, 168–73, 222–32).

Scholars are still divided about when the portrait mummies ceased to be created. Traditional dating was largely based on artistic style and the assumption of a linear development from 'good' naturalistic paintings to 'poor', abstract, and generic ones, the latest of which were dated to the late fourth century (Parlasca 1966: 195–202; 1969–80; Parlasca and Seemann

1999; Parlasca and Frenz 2003; Aubert et al. 2008). More recently, the majority of scholars have accepted that there was always a plurality of styles, and that dates can and must be based on external criteria like the hairstyles (Borg 1996: 19–84, 177–8; 1998; Walker and Bierbrier 1997; Seipel 1998; Walker 2000; Picton, Quirke, and Roberts 2007). As with other genres of portraits discussed here, the persistence of painted mummy portraits is different at different locations. At the majority of places, and especially in the Fayum Oasis, from where by far the largest number of portrait mummies originates, numbers decline towards the end of the Severan era and cease completely around the middle of the third century. Only at Antinoopolis is the habit potentially continued into the fourth century (Walker 1999; Aubert et al. 2008).

Conclusion

While Egyptian pharaohs and nobles had employed portraiture in cult and funerary contexts from the earliest times, during the Roman period the use of portraiture spread widely to include local elites throughout the country. There had been a trend towards naturalistic portraits already during the Late and Ptolemaic periods, but with the Roman conquest, naturalistic, individualized portraits with fashionable Roman hairstyles and contemporary dress and jewellery were introduced into all artistic genres that depicted individual humans. Werner Kaiser (1999) has suggested that the first noticeable step in this direction on the part of private individuals in the later second century BCE was related to the fact that, at this time, Egyptians first ascended into the highest positions in Ptolemaic government and may have felt a need to adapt their habits to this new status. A similar motivation is likely to have inspired the changes in the Roman period. Throughout the empire, the ambitious followed the Romans in promoting themselves through honorific portraits in public places or their equivalent in sanctuaries and the funerary sphere. The local Egyptian elite were no exception and included people of different ethnic backgrounds from cities all over Egypt who cared enough about the new social order with its own status symbols to have a need for such portraits, and were wealthy enough to be able to afford them (see Borg 1996: 150–76; 1998: 33–59; Riggs 2005).

As we have seen, this did not mean that everybody slavishly strove to copy Roman styles as closely as they could, since, in most cases, Egyptian traditions were equally and confidently observed to various degrees. A lot of ink has been spilled over the question whether the Graeco-Roman elements of portraiture were just an add-on to Egyptian practice and belief, or the other way round. But from the start, the entire debate was strongly determined by scholarly bias and competition between disciplines. A more realistic scenario, that is also more in accordance with the diversity of the evidence, would allow for a wide range of attitudes and loyalties. With the increase in numbers and social groups using portraiture, the range of styles and iconographic solutions also widened dramatically in an excitingly creative response to new challenges and stimuli. Paradoxically, these scholarly biases taken together are probably to some extent reflective of the biases that existed in Roman Egypt as well, where different individuals had backgrounds shaped by Egyptian or Graeco-Roman culture to various degrees, but where also different social practices were shaped by different cultural traditions. What is painfully lacking—not least owing to insufficiently documented archaeological contexts—is knowledge about this actual practice, the rituals and performances that surrounded the material remains, which would have contributed immensely to the way in which these portraits were perceived.

Suggested Reading

A comprehensive study of portraiture in Roman Egypt is a desideratum. Graindor (1937), Adriani (1961), and Breccia (1970, 1978) are still indispensable as sources of information and illustrations. For funerary stelae in the Graeco-Roman Museum of Alexandria, Schmidt (2003) is an excellent resource, offering not only details and images of the wide range of items in this collection but also a great step forward in the interpretation of stelae from different sites.

The Terenouthis stelae, for instance, are particularly numerous and well known as museum exhibits but have never been studied extensively. For a preliminary list of published items and extended bibliography, see Pelsmaekers (1989, 1995); the best discussion available is Schmidt (2003: 44–61). Parlasca (1966) had concluded from the large number of these stelae that they were typical of the entire Delta, but all items with a known provenance are from Terenouthis, and the quarry was found there as well. There are informative entries on the site in the *Real-Encyclopädie der klassischen Altertumswissenschaft*, vol. 5A (1934), 718–19 (under 'Terenuthis', written by Hermann Kees) and the *Lexikon der Ägyptologie*, vol. 6 (1986), 424 (under 'Terenouthis', written by J. Gwyn Griffiths). For a general introduction to funerary practices and art in Roman Egypt, see especially Corbelli (2006) and Riggs (2005), and the bibliographical review in Riggs (2002).

On mummy masks and coffins, see Grimm (1974), Bayer-Niemeier (1993), and Riggs (2000, 2005). On painted mummy portraits, see Parlasca (1966, 1969–80), Parlasca and Frenz (2003), Parlasca and Seemann (1999), Doxiadis (1995), Bierbrier (1997), and Borg (1996, 1998, 2000, 2010). Important catalogues with scholarly contributions to the subject and excellent images include: Walker and Bierbrier (1997), Seipel (1998), Walker (2000), Picton, Quirke, and Roberts (2007), Aubert and Cortopassi (2004), and Aubert et al. (2008). There is no reliable list of imperial portrait sculpture from the province. Many proposed identifications are highly speculative, but see Strocka (1980), Jucker (1981), and Kiss (1984, 1995) for a range of suggestions.

Bibliography

Abdalla, A. O. A. 1983. *Graeco-Roman Funerary Stelae from Upper Egypt*. Liverpool: Liverpool University Press.

Adriani, A. 1936. 'Sculture del Museo greco-romano di Alessandria', *Bulletin de la Societé Archéologique d'Alexandrie* 9/1: 3–25.

—— 1961. *Repertorio d'arte dell'Egitto greco-romano: Architettura e topografia*. Palermo: Fondazione 'Ignazio Mormino' del Banco di Sicilia.

—— 1970. 'Ritratti dell'Egitto greco-romano', *Mitteilungen des Deutschen Archäologischen Instituts, Römische Abteilung* 77: 72–109.

Anthes, R. 1939. 'Ägyptische Bildwerke rings um den Grünen Kopf', *Archäologischer Anzeiger* 54: 376–402.

Arnold, D. 1999. *Temples of the Last Pharaohs*. New York: Oxford University Press.

Assmann, J. 1996. 'Preservation and Presentation of Self in Ancient Egyptian Portraiture', in P. der Manuelian (ed.), *Studies in Honor of William Kelly Simpson*. Boston: Museum of Fine Arts, 55–81.

Aubert, M.-F., and R. Cortopassi. 2004. *Portraits funéraires de l'Égypte romaine*, vol. 1: *Masques en stuc*. Paris: Réunion des Musées Nationaux.

—— et al. 2008. *Portraits funéraires de l'Égypte romaine* II: *Cartonnages, linceuls et bois*. Paris: Réunion des Musées Nationaux and Institut Khéops.

Bailey, D. M. 1990. 'Classical Architecture in Roman Egypt', in M. Henig (ed.), *Architecture and Architectural Sculpture in the Roman Empire*. Oxford: Oxford University Committee for Archaeology, 121–37.

Bayer-Niemeier, E. 1993. *Ägyptische Bildwerke*, vol. 3: *Skulpturen, Malerei, Papyri und Särge*. Melsungen: Gutenberg, 414–63.

Bianchi, R. S. 1982. 'The Egg-Heads: One Type of Generic Portrait from the Egyptian Late Period', *Wissenschaftliche Zeitschrift der Humboldt-Universität zu Berlin: Reihe Gesellschaftswissenschaften* 31: 149–51.

Bierbrier, M. (ed.) 1997. *Portraits and Masks: Burial Customs in Roman Egypt*. London: British Museum Press.

Borg, B. E. 1996. *Mumienporträts: Chronologie und kultureller Kontext*. Mainz: von Zabern.

—— 1998. *'Der zierlichste Anblick der Welt..': Ägyptische Porträtmumien*. Mainz: von Zabern.

—— 2000. 'The Face of the Élite', *Arion* 8/1: 63–96.

—— 2010. 'Painted Funerary Portraits', in J. Dieleman and W. Wendrich (eds), *UCLA Encyclopedia of Egyptology*. Los Angeles. <http://escholarship.org/uc/item/7426178c>.

Boschung, D. 1993. *Die Bildnisse des Augustus*. Berlin: Mann.

Bothmer, B. v. (ed.) 1960. *Egyptian Sculpture of the Late Period 700 B.C. to A.D. 100*. Brooklyn: Arno Press.

—— 1988. 'Egyptian Antecedents of Roman Republican Verism', in N. Bonacasa (ed.), *Ritratto ufficiale e ritratto privato: Atti del II Conferenza Internazionale sul Ritratto Romano, Roma, 26–30 settembre 1984*. Rome: Consiglio Nazionale delle Ricerche, 47–65.

Bowman, A. K. 1986. *Egypt after the Pharaohs, 332 BC–AD 642: From Alexander to the Arab Conquest*. London: British Museum Press.

Boyd, S. A., and G. Vikan. 1981. *Questions of Authenticity among the Arts of Byzantium: Catalogue of an Exhibition Held at Dumbarton Oaks, January 7–May 11, 1981*. Washington: Dumbarton Oaks.

Breccia, E. 1970. *Le Musée Gréco-Romain d'Alexandrie 1925–1931*. Rome: 'L'Erma' di Bretschneider.

—— 1978. *Le Musée Gréco-Romain d'Alexandrie 1931–1932*. Rome: 'L'Erma' di Bretschneider.

Calament, F. 2005. *La Révélation d'Antinoé par Albert Gayet: Histoire, archéologie, muséographie*, 2 vols. Cairo: Institut Français d'Archéologie Orientale.

Capponi, L. 2005. *Augustan Egypt: The Creation of a Roman Province*. New York: Routledge.

Cauville, S. 1990. *Le temple de Dendera: Guide archéologique*. Cairo: Institut Français d'Archéologie Orientale.

—— 2007. *Dendara: Le temple d'Isis*. Cairo: Institut Français d'Archéologie Orientale.

—— and Y. H. Hanafi. 1984. *Edfou*. Cairo: Institut Français d'Archéologie Orientale.

Charmoux, F. 1955. Review of H. Drerup, *Ägyptische Bildnisköpfe griechischer und römischer Zeit*, *Revue Archéologique* 45: 237–8.

Chassinat, É., and S. Cauville (eds) 2008. *Le temple de Dendara*. Cairo: Institut Français d'Archéologie Orientale.

Corbelli, J. 2006. *The Art of Death in Graeco-Roman Egypt*. Princes Risborough: Shire.
Corcoran, L. H. 1995. *Portrait Mummies from Roman Egypt (I–IV Centuries A.D.)*. Chicago: Oriental Institute of the University of Chicago.
Daressy, G. 1896. 'Inscriptions d'Égypte', *Bulletin de Correspondance Hellénique* 20: 248–9.
Daszewski, W. A. 1997. 'Mummy Portraits from Northern Egypt: The Necropolis in Marina el-Alamein', in M. L. Bierbrier (ed.), *Portraits and Masks: Burial Customs in Roman Egypt*. London: British Museum Press, 59–65.
Doxiadis, E. (ed.) 1995. *The Mysterious Fayum Portraits: Faces from Ancient Egypt*. London: Thames and Hudson.
Drerup, H. 1950. *Ägyptische Bildnisköpfe griechischer und römischer Zeit*. Münster: Aschendorff.
Dundas, G. S. 2002. 'Augustus and the Kingship of Egypt', *Historia: Zeitschrift für Alte Geschichte* 51: 433–48.
el-Fakharani, F. 1965. 'Semi-Dome Decoration in Graeco-Roman Egypt', *American Journal of Archaeology* 69: 57–62.
Empereur, J.-Y. 2003. *A Short Guide to the Catacombs of Kom el Shoqafa, Alexandria*, 2nd edn. Alexandria: Harpocrates.
Freccero, A. (ed.) 2000. *Fayum Portraits: Documentation and Scientific Analyses of Mummy Portraits Belonging to Nationalmuseum in Stockholm*. Göteborg: Acta Universitatis Gothoburgensis.
Giammarusti, A., and A. Roccati (eds) 1979. *I templi di File: Museo Egizio Torino, settembre-ottobre 1979*. Turin.
Graindor, P. 1937. *Bustes et statues-portraits d'Égypte romaine*. Cairo: Grenier; Barbey.
Grimm, G. 1974. *Die römischen Mumienmasken aus Ägypten*. Wiesbaden: Steiner.
—— and D. Johannes (eds) 1975. *Kunst der Ptolemäer- und Römerzeit im Ägyptischen Museum Kairo*. Mainz: von Zabern.
Haeny, G. 1985. 'A Short Architectural History of Philae', *Bulletin de l'Institut Français d'Archéologie Orientale* 85: 197–233.
Hawass, Z. 2000. *Valley of the Golden Mummies*. London: Virgin; Cairo: American University in Cairo Press.
Johansen, F. 1994. *Roman Portraits: Catalogue*. Copenhagen: Ny Carlsberg Glyptotek.
Josephson, J. A. 1997a. *Egyptian Royal Sculpture of the Late Period, 400–246 B.C.* Mainz: von Zabern.
—— 1997b. 'Egyptian Sculpture of the Late Period Revisited', *Journal of the American Research Center in Egypt* 34: 1–20.
Jucker, H. 1981. 'Römische Herrscherbildnisse aus Ägypten', in H. Temporini (ed.), *Aufstieg und Niedergang der römischen Welt* II 12.2. Berlin: de Gruyter, 667–725.
Kaiser, W. 1999. 'Zur Datierung realistischer Rundbildnisse ptolemäisch-römischer Zeit', *Mitteilungen des Deutschen Archäologischen Instituts, Abteilung Kairo* 55: 237–63.
Kamal, A. B. 1914. 'Rapport sur les fouilles exécutées dans la zone comprise entre Déîout au nord et Déîr e-Ganadlah, au sud', *Annales du Service des Antiquités de l'Égypte* 14: 62–7.
Kiss, Z. 1984. *Études sur le portrait impérial romain en Égypte*. Warsaw: PWN.
—— 1995. 'Quelques portraits impériaux romains d'Égypte', *Études et Travaux* 17: 53–71.
Kunze, C. 1996. 'Die Skulpturenausstattung hellenistischer Paläste', in W. Hoepfner and G. Brands (eds), *Basileia: Die Paläste der hellenistischen Könige*. Mainz: von Zabern, 109–29.
Küthmann, C. 1962. 'Der grüne Kopf des Berliner Ägyptischen Museums', *Zeitschrift für Ägyptische Sprache und Altertumskunde* 88: 37–42.
Massner, A.-K. 1986. 'Ägyptisierende Bildnisse des Kaisers Claudius', *Antike Kunst* 29: 63–7.

Papini, M. 2004. *Antichi volti della Repubblica: La ritrattistica in Italia centrale tra IV e II secolo* AC. Rome: 'L'Erma' di Bretschneider.
Parlasca, K. 1966. *Mumienporträts und verwandte Denkmäler*. Wiesbaden: Steiner.
—— 1969–80. *Repertorio d'arte dell'Egitto greco-romano*, ser. B: *Ritratti di mummie* I–III. Rome: 'L'Erma' di Bretschneider.
—— 1970. 'Zur Stellung der Terenuthis-Stelen: Eine Gruppe römischer Gabreliefs aus Ägypten in Berlin', *Mitteilungen des Deutschen Archäologischen Instituts, Abteilung Kairo* 26: 173–98.
—— 1978. 'Der Übergang von der spätrömischen zur frühkoptischen Kunst im Lichte der Grabreliefs von Oxyrhynchos', *Enchoria* 8: 115–20.
—— and H. G. Frenz. 2003. *Repertorio d'arte dell'Egitto greco-romano*, ser. B: *Ritratti di mummie* IV. Rome: 'L'Erma' di Bretschneider.
—— and H. Seemann (eds) 1999. *Augenblicke: Mumienporträts und ägyptische Grabkunst aus römischer Zeit*. Munich: Klinkhardt & Biermann.
Pelsmaekers, J. 1989. 'Studies on the Funerary Stelae from Kom Abou Billou', *Bulletin de l'Institut Historique Belge de Rome* 59: 5–29.
—— 1995. 'Studies on the Funerary Stelae from Kom Abou Billou, 2', *Bulletin de l'Institut Historique Belge de Rome* 65: 5–12.
Petrie, W. M. F. 1889. *Hawara, Biahmu, and Arsinoe*. London: Field and Tuer.
—— 1911. *Roman Portraits and Memphis* IV. London: School of Archaeology in Egypt.
—— 1925. *Tombs of the Courtiers and Oxyrhynchus*. London: British School of Egyptian Archaeology.
Philipp, H. 2004. 'Der Grüne Kopf in Berlin', *Städel-Jahrbuch* 19: 277–308.
Picton, J., S. Quirke, and P. C. Roberts (eds) 2007. *Living Images: Egyptian Funerary Portraits in the Petrie Museum*. Walnut Creek, Calif.: Left Coast Press.
Riggs, C. 2000. 'Roman Period Mummy Masks from Deir el-Bahri', *Journal of Egyptian Archaeology* 86: 121–44.
—— 2005. *The Beautiful Burial in Roman Egypt: Art, Identity, and Funerary Religion*. Oxford: Oxford University Press.
—— and M. A. Stadler. 2003. 'A Roman Shroud and its Demotic Inscriptions in the Museum of Fine Arts, Boston', *Journal of the American Research Center in Egypt* 40: 69–87.
Roberts, P. C. 1997. '"One of Our Mummies Is Missing": Evaluating Petrie's Records from Hawara', in M. L. Bierbrier (ed.), *Portraits and Masks: Burial Customs in Roman Egypt*. London: British Museum Press, 19–25.
Said Mahmoud, A. 1995. 'Tre donne semisdraiate al Museo Greco-Romano di Alessandria', in N. Bonacasa (ed.), *Alessandria e il mondo ellenistico-romano*, vol. 1. Rome: 'L'Erma' di Bretschneider, 412–14.
Schmidt, S. 2003. *Grabreliefs im Griechisch-Römischen Museum von Alexandria*. Berlin: Achet.
Schneider, H. D. 1975. 'Four Romano-Egyptian Tomb-Reliefs from el Behnasa, Egypt', *Bulletin Antieke Beschaving: Annual Papers on Classical Archaeology* 50: 9–12.
Schreiber, T. 1908. *Expedition Ernst von Sieglin*. Leipzig: Giesecke & Devrient.
Seipel, W. (ed.) 1998. *Bilder aus dem Wüstensand: Mumienportraits aus dem Ägyptischen Museum Kairo*. Milan: Skira.
Severin, H.-G. 1995. 'Pseudoprotokoptika', in C. Fluck et al. (eds), *Divitiae Agypti: Koptologische und verwandte Studien zu Ehren von Martin Krause*. Wiesbaden: Reichert, 289–99.
Smith, R. R. R. 1988. *Hellenistic Royal Portraits*. Oxford: Clarendon Press.
—— 1998. 'Cultural Choice and Political Identity in Honorific Portrait Statues in the Greek East in the Second Century AD', *Journal of Roman Studies* 68: 56–93.

Stadler, M. A. 2004. *Ägyptische Mumienmasken in Würzburg (Schenkung Gütte)*. Wiesbaden: Reichert.

Stanwick, P. E. 2002. *Portraits of the Ptolemies: Greek Kings as Egyptian Pharaohs*. Austin: University of Texas Press.

Strocka, V. M. 1980. 'Augustus als Pharao', in R. A. Stucky (ed.), *Eikones: Studien zum griechischen und römischen Bildnis: Hans Jucker zum 60. Geb. gewidmet*. Bern: Francke, 177–80.

Tanner, J. 2000. 'Portraits, Power, and Patronage in the Late Roman Republic', *Journal of Roman Studies* 90: 18–50.

Thomas, T. K. 2000. *Late Antique Egyptian Funerary Sculpture: Images for this World and the Next*. Princeton: Princeton University Press.

Tkaczow, B. 1993. *The Topography of Ancient Alexandria*. Warsaw: Centre d'Archéologie Méditerranéenne de l'Académie Polonaise des Sciences.

Vandersleyen, C. 1985. 'De l'influence grecque sur l'art égyptien: Plis de vêtements et plis de peau', *Chronique d'Égypte* 60: 358–70.

Venit, M. S. 2002. *The Monumental Tombs of Ancient Alexandria: The Theater of the Dead*. Cambridge, Mass: Cambridge University Press.

Wagner, G. 1994. 'Les stèles funéraires de Kom Abu Bellou (BSAA 44, 1991, 169–200)', *Zeitschrift für Papyrologie und Epigraphik* 101: 113–19.

—— 1996. 'Nouvelles inscriptions funéraires grecques de Kom Abu Bellou', *Zeitschrift für Papyrologie und Epigraphik* 114: 115–40.

Walker, S. 1999. 'Porträts auf Leichentüchern aus Antinoopolis: Eine Anmerkung zu Kleidung und Datierung', in K. Parlasca and H. Seemann (eds), *Augenblicke: Mumienporträts und ägyptische Grabkunst aus römischer Zeit*. Munich: Klinkhardt & Biermann, 366–7.

—— (ed.) 2000. *Ancient Faces: Mummy Portraits from Roman Egypt*. New York: Metropolitan Museum of Art.

—— and M. L. Bierbrier (eds) 1997. *Ancient Faces: Mummy Portraits from Roman Egypt*. London: British Museum Press.

CHAPTER 38

TERRACOTTAS

SANDRA SANDRI

GRAECO-ROMAN terracottas (derived from the Italian *terra cotta*, 'baked earth') are small sculptural artefacts (statuettes, figurative lamps and vessels, terracotta plaques with figurative relief decoration) made of clay that were made from the third century BCE until the fourth century CE. They are distinguished in style and motif by a conspicuous mixture of Egyptian and Greek elements. Thousands of these figures are preserved in the museums of the world today (see Hornbostel and Laubscher 1986: 446 n. 21) and show how popular and significant they were in the ancient world.

TECHNIQUE

For the manufacture of most terracottas, a negative mould, known as the matrix, was made from a hand-shaped prototype, the patrix (e.g. Weber 1914, no. 243; Schürmann 1989, no. 1100; Ewigleben and von Grumbkow 1991, no. 120; Szymańska 2005, no. 89 (patrix); Bailey 2008, nos 3028, 3087, 3194, 3335, 3570). A peculiarity of many Egyptian terracottas is that only the front was formed in a mould, while the back consisted of a curved, smooth shell, partly shaped by hand, so that many clay figures had a flat, relief-like appearance. The front and back were joined before firing, and the edges were smeared with clay. The individual parts of complex figures could be made in several part-shapes (Nachtergael 1995: 261; Szymańska 2005: 49–50; Bailey 2008: 5). By using moulds it was possible to manufacture a great number of figures of the same kind. As the moulds consisted mostly of plaster, more rarely of clay, they wore out very quickly (see Fig. 38.3), and details of the modelling needed to be scored into the unfired statuettes with sharp objects (Ballet 1998: 229–30, figs 15–16). As the figures also differ in size, owing to the varying amounts of water in the clay, which evaporated during firing, no terracotta is exactly like any other. It is common to observe that a negative form was made from a statuette already moulded in a matrix (Hornbostel and Laubscher 1986: 429). Furthermore, the new prototype could be altered before firing, so that a new type could be designed with little effort (Sandri 2008: 94).

Many of the Graeco-Egyptian terracottas have a round opening at the back, which has often been described as a firing hole. It has been assumed that through this hole, evaporated water could escape from the damp clay. However, in the case of most statuettes with a firing hole the base is also open, so another opening would not have been necessary. Possibly the hole was used to fix the statuette in position (Hornbostel and Laubscher 1986: 426; Nachtergael 1995: 259; Szymańska 2005: 50 n. 24). Thus, the statuettes, rather like modern picture frames, would be suitable for standing on a surface or hanging on a wall. After firing, the figures were coated mostly only on the front with white ground and then painted. Both the colours and the slip are usually preserved only in small remnants (Hornbostel and Laubscher 1986: 429; Szymańska 2005: 52–4; Bailey 2008: 6).

Very few terracottas have an inscription (five per thousand, according to Nachtergael 1994: 413). Mostly these are proper names scored in Greek script before firing, found as a rule on the back of the figures, and are presumably to be seen as the signatures of the workshop foreman (Nachtergael 1994). Alongside these there are a few inscriptions, also in Greek, which name or describe the figure represented (Sandri 2010: 327–8 with nn. 64 and 66, referring to a proper name in Demotic; see also Fink 2009: 339). In addition, on a few terracottas hieroglyphic inscriptions were added, presumably in the nineteenth century, in order to raise their price on the art market. At that time there was a great interest in new hieroglyphic texts, which could be read again only after Champollion's decipherment (Sandri 2010).

Discovery Sites and Uses

Only from the Late period (seventh century BCE) are terracotta statuettes widely disseminated in Egypt in great numbers. In Alexandria terracottas were made in moulds, modelled on Greek examples from the end of the fourth century BCE (Himmelmann 1983: 27–30). There are Egyptian influences on the motifs from an early stage, however. In early terracotta research a distinction was made between the Alexandrian terracottas and the Fayum terracottas, which reflect Egyptian characteristics to a greater degree and were believed to have originated in the first century BCE in the Fayum region. This distinction could not be sustained, however, as new finds show that exemplars of the so-called Fayum terracottas were common from the third century BCE not only in the Fayum, but also in Alexandria and other places in Egypt (Hornbostel and Laubscher 1986: 426–7). The division of Graeco-Egyptian terracottas into two groups, and the exclusive assigning of one of the two groups to the Fayum, are both untenable concepts.

Only a fraction of the terracottas preserved today were found in carefully documented excavations. Most of the *in situ* finds come from residential houses in Canopus, Naukratis, and Tanis in the Delta; in Bacchias, Dionysias, Euhemeria, Herakleopolis Magna, Karanis, Narmouthis, Philadelphia, Soknopaiou Nesos, Tebtunis, and Theadelphia in the Fayum; in Mons Claudianus in the Eastern Desert; and in Edfu and Koptos in the Nile Valley (Nachtergael 1985: 228–32; Bailey 2008: 1–5). Presumably they were stored there in niches in walls or on wooden shelves that served as house shrines (Dunand 1979: 8 with nn. 18–19; Frankfurter 1998: 134–6). Much smaller numbers of terracottas came from graves in Alexandria, Hawara, Karanis, Dush, Qau el-Kebir, Shurafa, Terenouthis, and Theadelphia (Bailey 2008: 1–5; on

Dush, Aubert and Cortopassi 1998: 153; on Terenouthis, Allen 1985: 550–8). Equally rare are finds in temples as in Bacchias, Karanis, Herakleopolis Magna, Magdola, and Theadelphia in the Fayum; the animal cemetery precinct of Memphis; and at the Sacred Lake of Mendes (López 1974: 300–2, pl. 15; Nachtergael 1995: 251–63; Bailey 2008: 1).

These finds indicate that the Graeco-Egyptian terracottas were made mainly for home worship. Apart from statuettes that presumably had a funerary character like the 'naked goddesses' (see below), the clay figures could also have been used in a subsidiary way as grave goods or votive images for cult purposes (Hornbostel and Laubscher 1986: 443).

Dating

The dating of Graeco-Egyptian terracottas is problematic (see Nachtergael 1995: 268–71; Bailey 2008: 3–5). The majority of the figures preserved today originate in the art trade or from older excavations where the exact circumstances of the discovery of the terracottas were not recorded, or they are part of undocumented old museum holdings, so that dating on the basis of stratigraphy is not possible (Bailey 2008: 1). Even in modern excavations a stratigraphic context is not necessarily given, as these easily moved, small-scale objects are often found on the surface. Terracottas that were found during Polish excavations in the years 1985–91 in Athribis in the Delta (Szymańska 2005) are important for the question of dating. The 269 clay figures mostly came from a Ptolemaic city district with workshops and baths used for a cult, and only a few came from Roman era strata (Szymańska 2005: 21, 42, 125–30). On the basis of these relatively accurately dated finds, we now assume pre-Imperial datings for many terracotta types (Fischer 2005: 347–8; Bailey 2008: 3). For the many types that were developed only in the Imperial period (Fischer 2005: 351), there are almost no comparable exemplars in the mainly Ptolemaic material from Athribis, so that we continue to rely on stylistic and typological analysis.

Using these analyses it is only possible, as a rule, to establish when the prototype was made; a mould taken from this prototype might have been in use for decades. Only very few terracottas can be dated absolutely, as we lack a context for the find, so it is difficult to place objects that are of the same style in chronological order. Bailey therefore speaks of 'guesswork and probabilities' (Bailey 2008: 3) in connection with dating many of the British Museum terracottas that he studied. In addition, stylistic differences arise not only owing to different dates of manufacture, but also through the idiosyncrasies of individual workshops (on the production centres of terracottas in Egypt, see Fischer 1994: 23–7; Ballet 1998). An example of the way a dating based on stylistic criteria can vary is the type of a standing child-god with a pot (Fig. 38.1), which was fabricated in large quantities. Different scholars have suggested: first century BCE–first century CE (Bailey 2008: 33, no. 302); first century CE (Fischer 1994: 274, no. 606); late first century CE (Bayer-Niemeier 1988: 95, no. 102); and second half of the second century CE (Hornbostel 1977: 177–8, no. 156). An exemplar identical in form was found at Karanis in the context of the second half of the third century CE (Allen 1985: 369, no. 57). This means that for figures of the same kind, we have datings from the late Ptolemaic to the high Imperial period. Despite the difficulties described, there have been a few stylistic–typological studies in recent decades that do offer a framework for the

FIG. 38.1 Terracotta figure of a child-god with a pot. Height 20.2 cm

Martin von Wagner Museum, Würzburg, A 607. Photo: Karl Öhrlein.

chronological development of the terracottas (Philipp 1972: 12–15; Bayer-Niemeier 1988: 19–36; Fischer 1994: 74–102; 2005).

Themes and Motifs

The surviving Graeco-Egyptian terracottas from the Roman Imperial period not only are extremely numerous, but are also distinguished by a plethora of motifs. The high point of their production was in the second century CE and at the beginning of the third (Fischer 1994: 99–102; 2005: 349). Alongside the types from the Hellenistic period that continued to be produced, many others were developed, until the production of non-Christian objects came to a halt in the fourth century CE (Fischer 1994: 102).

Egyptian and Greek Gods

The largest group among the Graeco-Egyptian terracottas consists of representations of Egyptian and Greek gods. Of these, the most numerous are portrayals of an Egyptian child-god, attested from the second half of the third century BCE, who is mostly identified as Harpocrates (Figs 38.1 and 38.2). However, Harpocrates is only one of several child-gods of the Graeco-Roman period who are worshipped as the son of a local triad and have similar iconographies (Sandri 2006: 126–7). Therefore, it is conceivable that alongside Harpocrates other Egyptian child-gods, like Somtus-pa-khered, Harsomtus-pa-khered, Khonsu-pa-khered, were modelled in clay (Sandri 2004). No other figure of a god is attested in such a great number of different types. The boy may be depicted as a small child sitting on the ground, not yet able to walk (e.g. Fischer 1994, no. 573), or as a standing youth (e.g. Dunand 1990, no. 146). His most important attribute is a round or oval pot (e.g. Bayer-Niemeier 1988, nos 102–4, 113–16; Dunand 1990, nos 140–64), frequently in combination with an amphora and a round, flat loaf of bread (e.g. Attula 2001, no. 26). The function of the pot in real life was to prepare and store food, and identifies the child-god as a provider of nourishment and guarantor of fertility, exactly in the manner of the originally Greek cornucopia (e.g. Bayer-Niemeier 1988, nos 86–101, 117–22; Fischer 1994, nos 595–604).

The motif of riding on many different kinds of animal, or playing with them, which was taken over from Greek depictions of (divine) children (Török 1995: 77), may also be considered as belonging partly to this context. This is the case when the animals in question are edible, such as poultry (e.g. Besques 1992, no. E 369; Pingiatoglou 1993, no. 25; Fjeldhagen 1995, no. 1) or are beasts of burden used for transporting foodstuffs, like donkeys (e.g. Dunand 1979, no. 267), mules (e.g. Bayer-Niemeier 1988, no. 139), and camels (e.g. Dunand 1990, no. 385). In addition, the child-god was depicted with sacred Egyptian animals like the

FIG. 38.2 Terracotta figure of a child-god with goose, pot, and round loaf. Height 12.2 cm

Martin von Wagner Museum, Würzburg, A 605. Photo: Karl Öhrlein.

cobra (e.g. Besques 1992, no. E 367), the falcon (e.g. Bailey 2008, no. 3083), the ram (e.g. Breccia 1934, no. 125), the sphinx (e.g. Dunand 1979, no. 219), the Apis bull (e.g. Schrijvers-van Battum 1974: 5–6, fig. 2), and the baboon (e.g. Perdrizet 1921, no. 92). Numerous terracottas also show the divine child on a horse; this animal only came into military use for riding in the Ptolemaic period (on this group, see Bayer-Niemeier 1985). Apart from the types showing a child enthroned (e.g. Schmidt 1997, no. 128) or sitting on a lotus calyx (e.g. Schürmann 1989, no. 1092; Dunand 1990, no. 210), which hark back to traditional Egyptian representations of child-gods (Sandri 2006: 120), the double crown that about half the child-god terracottas are wearing, the childish gesture of sucking one finger, and the child's hairstyle of a lock at the right temple of the otherwise shaven head are in many cases the only elements that are based on Egyptian tradition. A further feature of many child-god terracottas is the voluminous headdress composed of several parts, consisting of an Egyptian crown and plant components, like two lotus buds and wreaths of blossoms and leaves (e.g. Breccia 1934, no. 64; Fischer 1994, no. 604), as well as an exaggeratedly large, flaccid phallus (e.g. Bayer-Niemeier 1988, no. 115; Dunand 1990, no. 184). The non-erect condition of the latter possibly symbolizes the potential power of generation of the child-god which he is not (yet) putting to use owing to his young age.

The goddess Isis is represented in Graeco-Egyptian coroplasty with fewer examples and less variation in type. She appears in her Hellenized version with the so-called Isis robe, a corkscrew hairstyle, and the crown of Egyptian goddesses, which consists of two feathers with a sun-disc in a set of cow horns, and typical attributes like the sistrum and situla (e.g. Weber 1914, nos 27–8; Dunand 1979, nos 32–3; Bayer-Niemeier 1988, nos 216–19). In addition, she is represented from the beginning of the Imperial period as Isis *lactans* (Fig. 38.3), as the snake-like Isis Thermouthis (e.g. Schürmann 1989, nos 1025–8; Fischer 1994, nos 871–84), or as Isis-Sothis riding on a dog (e.g. Weber 1914, nos 36–8; Perdrizet 1921, no. 76; Dunand 1979, no. 36). The husband of Isis in the Alexandrian triad, Serapis, is found less frequently and in fewer types, namely as a bust (e.g. Török 1995, no. 121), as either a standing (e.g. Bailey 2008, no. 3028) or enthroned deity (e.g. Dunand 1979, nos 342–5), or as the snake-like Serapis Agathodaimon (e.g. Perdrizet 1921, no. 179). Alongside the figures of an Egyptian child-god and those of Isis and Serapis, among the Egyptian deities only Bes and Beset are represented in substantial numbers (e.g. Bayer-Niemeier 1988, nos 427–43; Dunand 1990, nos 30–65; Fischer 1994, nos 536–42, 546–52, 558–9). Of all the remaining Egyptian gods there is rarely more than one type and only very few exemplars: Osiris (mostly as Osiris Canopus or Osiris *in hydria*; e.g. Dunand 1990, nos 426–32, 434–6); Horus (e.g. Weber 1914, no. 82; Perdrizet 1921, no. 110); Anubis (e.g. Perdrizet 1921, nos 158–9; Dunand 1990, no. 1); Amun-Min (e.g. Weber 1914, no. 151; Perdrizet 1921, no. 188; Dunand 1979, no. 367); Sobek (Suchos) (e.g. Weber 1914, no. 213; Dunand 1979, no. 366); Bastet (e.g. Weber 1914, nos 172–4; Bayer-Niemeier 1988, no. 243); and Tutu (e.g. Perdrizet 1921, no. 191).

Among the Greek gods, too, a child-god is the kind most frequently found: there are twice as many surviving clay figures of Eros as of Aphrodite, who is often associated with him. They show him as a chubby winged child, often with a torch as an attribute (e.g. Dunand 1990, nos 89–93; Schmidt 1997, nos 117–20), riding on animals (e.g. Dunand 1990, nos 99–100), or together with his companion Psyche (e.g. Bailey 2008, no. 3368). Aphrodite herself is often depicted as a standing nude, wringing out her hair (Aphrodite Anadyomene type, e.g. Bayer-Niemeier 1988, nos 354, 356–7; Schürmann 1989, nos 1039, 1042), or covering her breasts and her pudenda with her hands (Aphrodite Pudica type; e.g. Weber 1914, nos

FIG. 38.3 Terracotta figure of Isis nursing (Isis *lactans*). Height 6.6 cm

Landesmuseum, Mainz, PJG 648. Copyright Landesmuseum, Mainz.

177, 183). Two other Greek goddesses enjoyed considerable popularity in the Imperial period: Athena (e.g. Breccia 1934, nos 134–41; Fjeldhagen 1995, nos 69–79) and Demeter (e.g. Besques 1992: D 4494–D 4500; Török 1995, nos 29–31). Both often hold large torches as attributes, which possibly indicate a connection with various feasts, for instance on the night before the rising of Sothis at the beginning of the year, which precedes the flooding of the Nile (Aubert 2004: 314–19). A further theme in Graeco-Egyptian terracottas is Dionysos (e.g. Dunand 1990, nos 77–81; Fjeldhagen 1995, no. 88) and his thiasos, while the depictions of his companions such as Pan, satyrs, Silene (e.g. Dunand 1990, nos 82–5, 87–8; Fischer 1994, nos 716–19), and particularly Priapos (e.g. Bayer-Niemeier 1988, nos 444–9; Ewigleben and von Grumbkow 1991, nos 59–63), are more numerous than those of the god himself. Neither Dionysos nor Herakles (e.g. Fischer 1994, nos 732–46; Fjeldhagen 1995, no. 91), who in the Ptolemaic period had a prominent position in royal ideology as ancestors of the dynasty, feature to any great extent in the terracottas of the Imperial period.

Other Greek deities and mythical figures are extant only in small numbers and/or variations of types: Zeus (e.g. Ewigleben and von Grumbkow 1991, no. 56); Apollo (e.g. Dunand 1990, no. 9; Fischer 1994, nos 804–5); Artemis (e.g. Pingiatoglou 1993, no. 86; Bailey 2008, no. 3327); Ares (e.g. Dunand 1990, nos 10–11); Hermes (e.g. Bayer-Niemeier 1988, nos 411–12); Helios (Weber 1914, no. 283); the Dioscuri (e.g. Perdrizet 1921, nos 250–3; Schürmann 1989, nos 1117–18); Nike (e.g. Pingiatoglou 1993, no. 87; Fischer 1994, no. 953?); Phtonos (e.g. Bailey 2008, no. 3384); Telesphoros (e.g. Perdrizet 1921, nos 271–3); Ganymede (e.g. Perdrizet 1921, no. 247); Amazons (e.g. Perdrizet 1921, no. 280; Bayer-Niemeier 1988, no. 374); and Sirens (e.g. Fischer 1994, no. 951; Fjeldhagen 1995, no. 83). Other foreign gods, like Cybele (e.g. Weber 1914, no. 284; Fischer 1994, nos 909–10?) and Heron (e.g. Perdrizet 1921, no. 266), are also uncommon.

Apart from Serapis, discussed above, there are a few other deities represented who came into being only in the Graeco-Roman period: Neilos (e.g. Dunand 1990, nos 424–45); Hermanubis or Hermes-Thoth (e.g. Fischer 1994, nos 798–800; Török 1995, nos 102–3); and Antinoos (e.g. Graindor 1939, no. 45; Weber 1914, no. 214, designated as Premarres).

Anonymous, Non-Human Beings

A second group among the Graeco-Egyptian terracottas consists of female and male figures that are distinguished by their emphasized sexuality and/or physical features that deviate from the norm. Clay figures of a female nude with extended legs and arms close to the body, of the 'naked goddess' type (e.g. Bayer-Niemeier 1988, nos 246–53; Besques 1992, no. E 352), hark back to Pharaonic depictions and are attested from the Hellenistic period (Fink 2008, 2009). In the Imperial period they wear a distinctive headdress with an overloaded effect, consisting of a double feather crown with a sun-disc in a set of cow's horns, a kalathos, a wreath of leaves, and several wreaths of blossoms. According to Fink, they were probably stored lying down, some in wooden boxes similar to coffins, which is indicated by the fact that their state of preservation, including the paint, is quite good, that the figures cannot be stood upright owing to the narrow base, and that their shape resembles that of female mummies (Fink 2009: 336–40). In contrast to most other Graeco-Egyptian terracottas it is likely that they were primarily used for funerary purposes.

A similar function is to be assumed for figures of the Anasyrma type (e.g. Perdrizet 1921, no. 157; Fischer 1994, nos 815–17), which wear a comparable headdress but, unlike the 'naked goddesses', wear a long garment that they hold up with both hands to expose their pudenda. This 'Anasyrma' gesture comes originally from the Near East, and from there entered Greek culture before it spread to Egypt in Hellenistic times (Fischer 2005: 347). Goddesses exposing their pudenda appear not only in Greek myth (Baubo does it to cheer up Demeter, who is mourning her daughter Persephone), but also in Egyptian myth (Hathor lifts her garment to cheer up Re in the tale of the fight between Horus and Seth); in addition there are similar rituals in Graeco-Roman Egypt within individual cults of the Apis bull and Bastet (Fink 2008: 301–7). Another derivative of the 'naked goddess' type shows a completely or partly unclothed standing woman with an Egyptian goddess's crown and several wreaths, raising her arms and clutching her long corkscrew curls with her hands (e.g. Bayer-Niemeier 1988, no. 355; Dunand 1990, nos 365–8). This is the gesture taken over from the Aphrodite Anadyomene type (see above). In addition, there was a version of the goddess's pudica gesture in which both hands cover the breasts and the pudenda (e.g. Weber 1914, no. 176). The gesture seems to have lost its point here, as the clay figure is completely clothed.

Alongside these is a series of statuettes that show a woman with the headdress described above; she is clothed only in a cloak draped around her legs and holds in her hands various attributes like a small pot, a mirror, a little cornucopia, or a palm frond (e.g. Dunand 1979, nos 50–1; Fischer 1994, nos 818–19). The female statuettes mentioned, which are presumably to be regarded as goddesses owing to their Egyptian double feather and cow horn crown, have been interpreted by scholars as being syncretistic associations or equivalents of the Egyptian goddesses Isis or Hathor and the Greek goddess Aphrodite (Walker and Higgs 2001: 108–9, no. 133, and Fink 2009: 338–9, who characterize the statuettes of 'naked goddess' type as Hathor). As there are no sources concerning the manner in which the makers or the original owners designated their statuettes, there are no certain indications as to whether this assumption is correct. Fischer (2005: 351) suggests that these figurines do not depict any particular goddess but are 'superhuman images which have as their theme the transition from being a girl to a sexually active woman'.

The divine character of statuettes of other women is not clearly discernible in their iconography, as they wear no head adornment apart from various wreaths of blossoms and leaves, which are not restricted to depictions of gods. A pose also derived from the Aphrodite Anadyomene type (Fischer 1994: 367, no. 930) is adopted by almost completely naked women with both arms raised, who are holding on their heads, instead of their hair, a basket mostly filled with fruits (e.g. Breccia 1934, nos 43–5; Dunand 1979, nos 124–32; on this type, see Schmidt 1997: 82–3). Alongside these there exist statuettes of standing, fat, small, naked women with heavy, pendulous breasts (e.g. Graindor 1939, nos 37–8; van Wijngaarden 1958, nos 74–5). From the early Ptolemaic period to the Imperial period, there also survive numerous figures of a corpulent naked woman, frequently with two lotus buds and a blossom wreath on her head, who is sitting on the ground with her legs spread wide and, in some cases, is putting her hand to her genitalia (e.g. Skupinska-Løvset 1978, no. UT 133; Fischer 1994, nos 834–9). These figures were first interpreted as being Baubo, a Greek deity connected with the Eleusinian mysteries, who exposed her genitalia to Demeter (see above). As this interpretation has increasingly been rejected, the designation 'Pseudo-Baubo' has come into use (for this discussion, see Hornbostel and Laubscher 1986: 441 with n. 102; Schürmann 1989: 296, no. 1119; Nachtergael 1995: 274–5; Török 1995: 132–3, no. 190; Fischer 2005: 348 with n. 15). The figures have also been designated as depictions of a woman in childbirth (Bayer-Niemeier 1988: 149, no. 268). As Perdrizet observed, a depiction of a naked woman sitting on an eye with her legs spread indicates an apotropaic function, to ward off the 'evil eye' (Perdrizet 1921: 124–5, no. 345; see also Schmidt 1997: 86). Therefore, it is probable that the 'Pseudo-Baubo' statuettes not only are symbols of fertility, but are also protective.

From the numerous pre-Ptolemaic clay figures of 'phallus men', which are connected with a phallus cult in the Serapeum at Memphis (Fischer 1998: 343–9), a few Roman period exemplars are presumably derived (e.g. Fischer 1994, nos 359–62): the most striking attribute of these figures is their hugely enlarged phallus, in some cases slung around the shoulder. In addition to all the statuettes of women and men that are distinguished by their flaunted genitalia, there are some that represent a couple engaged in sex (*symplegma*) (e.g. Pingiatoglou 1993, no. 280; Fischer 1994, nos 519–21). The wreaths of blossoms that adorn some of these figures indicate a ritual context.

A series of women and boys for which there are no Ptolemaic models are distinguished by their arms raised next to the body, with the palms turned towards the observer; the boys wear the Egyptian child's hairstyle consisting of a lock on the otherwise shaven head. Variants of these include: seated nude women (e.g. Török 1995, nos 170–1, 173, 181); standing nude women (e.g. Weber 1914, nos 217–18); seated clothed women (e.g. Ewigleben and von Grumbkow 1991, nos 112, 114–15); seated nude boys (e.g. Skupinska-Løvset 1978, no. UT 143; Besques 1992, no. 393); and seated clothed boys (e.g. Perdrizet 1921, no. 332; Fjeldhagen 1995, no. 107). The position of the arms in these figures probably symbolizes divine protection and should not be seen as a gesture of prayer (Nachtergael 1995: 272–3; 2009: 76–8; Bailey 2008: 43–5); the figures presumably are apotropaic in character. An additional aspect, fertility, is indicated (in conjunction with the corpulence of the figures) by the fact that a few statuettes have the same seated position with legs spread wide like the 'Pseudo-Baubo' figures discussed above (e.g. Dunand 1990, no. 569; Bayer-Niemeier 2008, nos 3131–3).

A substantial number of clay figures depict female dancers, nude or clothed with a chiton (e.g. Ewigleben and von Grumbkow 1991, nos 66–9). Their chains crossing on the breast and their voluminous hairstyle, which resembles that of the female figures with raised arms, could be an indication that they are not human but divine beings (Bailey 2008: 58). Further evidence for a connection with the figures with raised arms is provided by a statuette of a female dancer who is carrying a naked boy executing the raised-arm gesture (Fig. 38.4).

There is no scholarly agreement about the significance of a large number of female clay heads that occur only in the Imperial period and have no opening on the underside (e.g. Bayer-Niemeier 1988, nos 336–52; Bailey 2008, nos 3121–9)—thus this is the way they were made, and they are not pieces broken off a body. The objects, which are distinguished by complicated hairstyles consisting of several parts, have variously been described as models for contemporary Roman hair fashions, heads of dolls whose bodies are supposed to have consisted of cloth or something similar, women with festive hairstyles, surrogate heads with a funerary function, votive gifts, or surrogates for hair sacrifices. Bailey alludes to the iconographical accordance with the female figures with raised arms mentioned above. Therefore, he considers the female heads as abbreviated exemplars of these statuettes (Bailey 2008: 45).

A category of terracottas that enjoyed great popularity, from early Hellenistic times to the Imperial period, depicts men of mostly small stature, with misshapen facial features and a number of attributes that also occur in the child-god terracottas: two lotus buds (e.g. Weber 1914, no. 142), a wreath of blossoms as a head adornment (e.g. Fischer 1994, no. 377), a shaven head with the lock on the right temple (Török 1995, no. 166), an exaggeratedly

FIG. 38.4 Terracotta figure of a dancer with a boy. Height 16.3 cm

Museum für Kunst und Gewerbe, Hamburg, 1989.398. Copyright Museum für Kunst und Gewerbe, Hamburg.

large phallus (e.g. Perdrizet 1921, nos 103, 119, 290–1, 313, 316), and a pot, an amphora, and a round loaf (e.g. Graindor 1939, nos 20–1; Fjeldhagen 1995, no. 16). They are most often depicted performing servants' duties, such as carrying child-gods (e.g. Dunand 1990, nos 513–14), baskets (e.g. Weber 1914, no. 143), amphoras (e.g. Bayer-Niemeier 1988, no. 209) and other food containers, or preparing sacrifices (Fig. 38.5). Their clothing is usually taken from members of a low social class (see Fischer 1998: 338 with n. 71): the *exomis* tunic (e.g. Bayer-Niemeier 1988, no. 208) or a loincloth (e.g. Fischer 1994, no. 390). The figures have frequently been designated *pataikoi*. This term, coined in modern times, is derived from a description by Herodotus, who compares a cult image in the temple of Ptah at Memphis with small Greek and Phoenician deities (*pataikoi*; Hdt. 3.37). The concept of *pataikos* originally denoted Late period amulets of a male figure with the body of an achondroplastic dwarf. Dasen (1993: 85, 89, 92–3, 98) has pointed out that there is no evidence that the amulet in question was necessarily connected exclusively or particularly with Ptah. Likewise, there is no particular connection we can establish between Ptah and the Graeco-Egyptian terracottas of dwarf-like men, also known as *pataikoi*. In her study on the so-called grotesques of Egypt, Fischer developed the idea that these terracottas are in the tradition of anonymous dwarf-like beings (Fischer 1998: 3489), which had the function of bringing fertility, being derived from Egyptian gods of creation, the sun, and fertility. In addition, according to Fischer, from Hellenistic times they took on the role of the dwarf-bodied god Bes as the protector of children (Fischer 1998: 350).

Various grotesques depict men, for the most part, with extremely exaggerated facial features such as very prominent eyebrow ridges, hook noses, large protruding ears, furrowed

FIG. 38.5 Terracotta figure of cult servant with features of dwarfism, with an altar for incense and a round loaf of bread. Height 14.1 cm

After Perdrizet (1921, no. 315, pl. 114, lower left).

brows, fleshy lips, and physical deformities like extremely enlarged genitalia (e.g. Bayer-Niemeier 1988, nos 484–91; Fischer 1994, nos 409–20). Examples date mainly to the Hellenistic period, but there are some extending into the Imperial period. It is well known that figures with unusual features, like deformities and exaggerated, caricatured body shapes, were thought in the ancient world to have apotropaic powers (Himmelmann 1996: 75–9). Exhibiting male and female genitalia can also be interpreted in this way (Nachtergael 1995: 265–6; compare Fink 2008: 306), and this should not be neglected by the modern observer, to whom the fertility aspect may seem more obvious.

Humans

The third large group in the terracottas of the Roman period consists of representations of humans performing various activities and functions. Among these are Egyptian priests, who are recognized by their shaven heads and long aprons. They are depicted carrying figures of deities or bringing sacrificial gifts (e.g. Dunand 1990, no. 507; Fischer 1994, nos 382–5). Priestesses are clothed in the so-called Isis robe with the typical fringed hem and a knot between the breasts (e.g. Török 1995, nos 148–9). Sometimes they can be distinguished from clay figures of the goddess Isis only by the fact that they are not wearing an Egyptian crown; in a few cases a clear identification is not possible. Many of these cult servants, who often wear two lotus buds and/or a wreath of blossoms as a head adornment, or a corkscrew-lock hairstyle, are holding a musical instrument, mostly a tambourine (e.g. Dunand 1979, nos 80–94), but there are examples with a harp (e.g. Fischer 1994, no. 977), a *trigonon* (triangular harp; e.g. Breccia 1934, no. 341), or castanets (e.g. Fjeldhagen 1995, no. 106). Different kinds of male musicians are also represented (Fig. 38.6; e.g. Perdrizet 1921, no. 325, with double flute; Fischer 1994, no. 988, with syrinx and bagpipes; Fjeldhagen 1995, no. 118, with kithara). The wreaths of blossoms adorning some of these exemplars are an indication that they are taking part in a sacred feast.

From the Ptolemaic period, Greek theatre was very popular in Egypt, too (Bailey 2008: 136). Evidence for this is provided by the many clay figures of actors and clay theatre masks (e.g. Dunand 1990, nos 598–607). Other entertainers represented in terracotta are dancers and acrobats (e.g. Schürmann 1989, no. 1170; Fischer 1994, no. 985). The Roman predilection for diversion at the circus is expressed in the depiction of gladiators, circus riders, and charioteers (e.g. Breccia 1934, nos 318–56). In addition, workmen, servants, and slaves are shown carrying out their activities: slaves wait for their masters with lanterns (e.g. Breccia 1934, nos 292–3), prepare meals (e.g. Bailey 2008, no. 3543 *bis*), or transport food, such as a man with a calf or a sheep on his shoulders (e.g. Fischer 1994, no. 987). The motif lived on in Christian iconography as the representation of Jesus as the Good Shepherd (Fjeldhagen 1995: 141). Workmen are also shown producing food, such as harvesting dates (e.g. Perdrizet 1921, nos 354–5), or as individuals trampling grapes to make wine (Dunand 1990: 223–4, no. 614). Figures wearing a lotus leaf as a head covering (e.g. Perdrizet 1921, no. 300; Breccia 1934, no. 226) depict people earning their living as fishermen and workmen on the Nile and its banks (Nachtergael 1995: 278). Other groups of people represented in coroplasty are soldiers and armed horsemen. In addition, there are depictions of mothers with babies (e.g. Bailey 2008, no. 3530), some of whom are occupied with cooking food (e.g. Török 1995, no. 159), and boys, some of them toddlers crawling on the ground (e.g. Fjeldhagen 1995, no. 166) or moving with the help of a training device (e.g. Bailey 2008, no. 3533).

FIG. 38.6 Terracotta figure of a musician with syrinx and bagpipes. Height 9 cm

Museum für Kunst und Gewerbe, Hamburg, 1989.717. Copyright Museum für Kunst und Gewerbe, Hamburg.

Animals

Among the animal terracottas (numerous examples in Hoffmann and Steinhart 2001) there are sacred animals (bullocks, cows, baboons, cats, dogs—mostly Maltese—rams, crocodiles, ibises), sacrificial animals, some of them adorned with garlands (pigs, poultry, goats), working animals (horses, donkeys, camels, elephants), wild animals (monkeys, lions, hedgehogs, mice, frogs, fish), and mythical creatures such as the Sphinx (e.g. Fjeldhagen 1995, nos 65–8), griffin (e.g. Bayer-Niemeier 1988, nos 564–5), and phoenix (e.g. Bailey 2008, no. 3721).

Frequently the terracottas of musicians, actors, acrobats, workers, and so on are described as the profane or everyday world of Graeco-Roman Egypt, whereas the animal terracottas are seen as toys. But Nachtergael (1995: 264–5) has pointed out that these figures had religious significance just like the statuettes of Egyptian and Greek gods. The clay figures of humans represent people who are connected with divine festivals, such as workmen bringing and preparing the food for sacrifice and banquets (for the feeding of participants in Egyptian feasts; see Assmann 1991: 108–9). Significant elements in Egyptian sacred feasts include music and dance, and plays and ceremonial combat (Hombert and Préaux 1940:

140–5; Assmann 1991: 107; Perpillou-Thomas 1993: 216–18; Török 1995: 113; Bailey 2008: 55), which are also expressed in the corresponding terracotta types. According to Nachtergael, the animal terracottas are to be seen as sacred animals and therefore phenotypes of Egyptian gods, as sacrificial animals, or as creatures with apotropaic power.

The Graeco-Egyptian terracottas do not reflect everyday situations; rather, they preserve for use in the domestic cult the occasion of the feast day with its processions of gods, sacrifices to the gods, banquets, amusements, and entertainments (Frankfurter 1998: 55). The figures kept in domestic cult niches—gods, supernatural beings, and people taking part in the feasts, who thus attained particular closeness to the gods—are responsible for the protection and the welfare of the house and its inhabitants.

Assessment of Graeco-Egyptian Terracottas in Scholarship

Since the time when scholarly work on Graeco-Egyptian terracottas began, the way they were interpreted was heavily influenced by the subjective assessment of their aesthetics: 'Anyone who evaluates these artefacts will reach a dead end rapidly, if he begins at all' (Weber 1914, p. viii); 'perhaps the ugliest products of ancient art' (Himmelmann 1981: 197); 'cheap products for the masses with little aesthetic charm' (Hornbostel and Laubscher 1986: 427); 'These colours say a lot about the taste of the buyers of most of the terracottas. They were indeed bought by the poorest in the population...' (Szymańska 2005: 52 n. 33).

Although nothing is known about the material value of the terracottas or whether in the ancient world aesthetic criteria were of any significance in determining their non-material value, the clay figures were rejected in scholarship as cheap objects, most of which reflected the 'primitive' religious sentiments of the lower strata of the population, and others of which had the function of trinkets or toys (Weber 1914: 15–16; Otto 1928: 261; Vogt 1924, p. xii; Hornbostel and Laubscher 1986: 444; Bayer-Niemeier 1988: 19).

As to the economic status of the owners of the terracottas, there are no sources that indicate that the clay figures were disseminated only in the one stratum of society, namely the poorest one. The fact that terracottas were found in multi-room residential houses, some of them luxurious (e.g. Petrie 1905: 26–7, pl. 35; Allen 1985: 300, 323, 458, 545; Nachtergael 1985: 232–3, a lawyer's house), and also in opulent graves (e.g. Grenfell, Hunt, and Hogarth 1900: 41b), or together with other substantial funerary objects (e.g. Petrie 1889, pls 19–21), disproves the thesis that their owners were among the poorest people of Egypt (see also Fink 2009: 346–7).

The terracottas appear to reflect the contemporary high theology of the Egyptian temples and their gods only to a limited extent. However, they are an important source for the religion of Graeco-Roman Egypt, as they are evidence of the religious ideas of a great proportion of the people, who celebrated the gods in their own houses. The congruence of many clay figures with similar representations of gods on Roman coins in Egypt (Nachtergael 1985: 224; Fischer 2005: 351) shows that the themes of the terracottas at this time corresponded at least partly to the religion promoted by the state, and should not be judged merely as the religious sentiment of the common people.

Conclusion

Owing to their almost industrial mass production, Graeco-Egyptian terracottas are among the most widespread genres of artefacts in Ptolemaic and Roman Egypt. The small clay figures, with their characteristic mixture of Egyptian and Greek elements, represent gods and divine beings, humans and animals. There is a focus on the gods associated with the Isis religion and the adepts of its cult. The motifs are often connected to all aspects of religious festivals, of which there are many attested kinds. The majority of the terracottas were presumably made for private worship in residential houses, but a secondary use as votive and funerary objects is also attested. As the find context of most of the figurines is unknown, because they come from the art market or from undocumented (illicit) excavations, exact dating is problematic. Contrary to the opinion of previous scholarship, the possession of terracottas was not restricted to the poorest part of the population but was also widespread in more affluent classes. Furthermore, they reflect not only 'popular' religion but the contemporary religion generally prevalent in multicultural Egypt.

Suggested Reading

Among the numerous previously released catalogues of Graeco-Roman terracottas, the British Museum catalogue by Donald M. Bailey is characterized by a great breadth of terracotta types and many new conclusions about their interpretation (Bailey 2008). The author also mentions numerous parallels of the described figurines in other collections and deals critically with the dating of the objects (Bailey 2008: 3–5). The catalogue of the terracottas in Budapest presents a detailed stylistic examination of the figures and contains much information about religion and culture in Graeco-Roman Egypt (Török 1995). The review by Georges Nachtergael (1995) not only analyses four more terracotta catalogues (Bayer-Niemeier 1988; Schürmann 1989; Dunand 1990; Besques 1992), but also contains fundamental knowledge about the function of the Graeco-Roman terracottas.

Bibliography

Allen, M. L. 1985. 'The Terracotta Figurines from Karanis: A Study of Technique, Style and Chronology in Fayoumic Coroplastics', doctoral dissertation, University of Michigan.

Assmann, J. 1991. 'Das ägyptische Prozessionsfest', in Assmann (ed.), *Das Fest und das Heilige: Religiöse Kontrapunkte zur Alltagswelt*. Gütersloh: Mohn, 105–22.

Attula, R. 2001. *Griechisch-römische Terrakotten aus Ägypten: Bestandskatalog der figürlichen Terrakotten*. Rostock: University of Rostock, Philosophy Faculty.

Aubert, M.-F. 2004. 'Torches et candélabres dans les terres cuites de l'Égypte gréco-romaine', *Chronique d'Égypte* 79: 305–19.

——and R. Cortopassi (eds) 1998. *Portraits de l'Égypte romaine*. Paris: Réunion des Musées Nationaux.

Bailey, D. M. 2008. *Ptolemaic and Roman Terracottas from Egypt*. London: British Museum Press.

Ballet, P. 1998. 'Terres cuites d'Alexandrie et de la chôra: Essai d'étude comparative de quelques ateliers: Thèmes et techniques', in J.-Y. Empereur (ed.), *Commerce et artisanat dans l'Alexandrie hellénistique et romaine*. Athens: École Française d'Athènes, 217–43.

—— 2000. 'Terres cuites isiaques de l'Égypte hellénistique et romaine: État de la recherche et des publications', in L. Bricault (ed.), *De Memphis à Rome: Actes du Ier Colloque International sur les Études Isiaques: Poitiers—Futuroscope, 8-10 avril 1999*. Leiden: Brill, 93–110.

Bayer-Niemeier, E. 1985. 'Harpokrates zu Pferde und andere Reiterdarstellungen des hellenistisch-römischen Ägypten', *Städel Jahrbuch*, new ser., 10: 27–44.

—— 1988. *Griechisch-römische Terrakotten*, Liebieghaus—Museum Alter Plastik, Wissenschaftliche Kataloge, Bildwerke der Sammlung Kaufmann I. Melsungen: Gutenberg.

Besques, S. 1992. *Époques hellénistique et romaine, cyrénaïque, Égypte ptolémaïque et romaine, Afrique du Nord et Proche-Orient*. Paris: Réunion des Musées Nationaux.

Breccia, E. 1934. *Terrecotte figurate greche e greco-egizie del Museo di Alessandria*. Bergamo: Officine dell'Istituto Italiano d'Arti Grafiche.

Dasen, V. 1993. *Dwarfs in Ancient Egypt and Greece*. Oxford: Clarendon Press.

Deonna, W. 1924. 'Terres cuites gréco-égyptiennes (Genève, Musée d'Art et d'Histoire)', *Revue Archéologique* 20: 80–158.

Dunand, F. 1979. *Religion populaire en Égypte romaine: Les terres cuites isiaques du Musée du Caire*. Leiden: Brill.

—— 1990. *Catalogue des terres cuites gréco-romaines d'Égypte, Musée du Louvre, Département des Antiquités égyptiennes*. Paris: Réunion des Musées Nationaux.

Ewigleben, C., and J. von Grumbkow (eds) 1991. *Götter, Gräber und Grotesken: Tonfiguren aus dem Alltagleben im römischen Ägypten*. Hamburg: Hans-Jürgen Böckel.

Fink, M. 2008. '"Nackte Göttin" und Anasyroméne: Zwei Motive—eine Deutung? (1. Teil)', *Chronique d'Égypte* 83: 289–317.

—— 2009. '"Nackte Göttin" und Anasyroméne: Zwei Motive—eine Deutung? (2. Teil)', *Chronique d'Égypte* 84: 335–47.

Fischer, J. 1994. *Griechisch-römische Terrakotten aus Ägypten: Die Sammlungen Sieglin und Schreiber, Dresden, Leipzig, Stuttgart, Tübingen*. Tübingen: Ernst Wasmuth.

—— 1998. 'Der Zwerg, der Phallos und der Buckel: Groteskfiguren aus dem ptolemäischen Ägypten', *Chronique d'Égypte* 73: 327–61.

—— 2005. 'Die Entwicklung der Götterfigur in der griechisch-römischen Koroplastik Ägyptens', in H. Beck, P. C. Bol, and M. Bückling (eds), *Ägypten, Griechenland, Rom: Abwehr und Berührung*. Tübingen: Wasmuth; Frankfurt: Liebighaus, 347–54.

Fjeldhagen, M. 1995. *Graeco-Roman Terracottas from Egypt*. Copenhagen: Ny Carlsberg Glyptotek.

Frankfurter, D. 1998. *Religion in Roman Egypt: Assimilation and Resistance*. Princeton: Princeton University Press.

Graindor, P. 1939. *Terres cuites de l'Égypte gréco-romaine*. Antwerp: de Sikkel.

Grenfell, B. P., A. S. Hunt, and D. G. Hogarth. 1900. *Fayûm Towns and their Papyri*. London: Kegan Paul; Egypt Exploration Fund.

Himmelmann, N. 1981. 'Realistic Art in Alexandria', *Proceedings of the British Academy London* 67: 193–207.

—— 1983. *Alexandria und der Realismus in der griechischen Kunst*. Tübingen: Wasmuth.

—— 1996. *Minima Archaeologica: Utopie und Wirklichkeit der Antike*. Mainz: von Zabern.

Hoffmann, F., and M. Steinhart. 2001. *Tiere vom Nil*. Wiesbaden: Reichert.

Hombert, M., and C. Préaux. 1940. 'Les papyrus de la Fondation Égyptologique Reine Élisabeth', *Chronique d'Égypte* 15: 134–49.

Hornbostel, W. 1977. *Kunst der Antike: Schätze aus norddeutschem Privatbesitz*. Mainz: von Zabern.

—— and H. P. Laubscher. 1986. 'Terrakotten', in W. Helck and E. Otto (eds), *Lexikon der Ägyptologie*, vol. 6. Wiesbaden: Harrassowitz, 425–56.

López, J. 1974. 'Rapport préliminaire sur les fouilles d'Hérakléopolis (1966)', *Oriens Antiquus* 13: 299–316.

Nachtergael, G. 1985. 'Les terres cuites "du Fayoum" dans les maisons de l'Égypte romaine', *Chronique d'Égypte* 60: 223–39.

—— 1989. 'Le chameau, l'âne et le mulet en Égypte gréco-romaine: Le témoignage des terres cuites', *Chronique d'Égypte* 64: 287–336.

—— 1994. 'Statuettes en terre cuite de l'Égypte gréco-romaine: Recueil des signatures de coroplathes', in M.-O. Jentel and G. Deschênes-Wagner (eds), *Tranquillitas: Mélanges en l'honneur de Tran tam Tinh*. Quebec: Université Laval, 413–33.

—— 1995. 'Terres cuites de l'Égypte gréco-romaine: à propos de quatre catalogues récents', *Chronique d'Égypte* 70: 254–94.

—— 2009. 'Une "orante" à Bacchias', *Ricerche di Egittologia e di Antichità Copte* 11: 75–8.

Otto, W. 1928. Review of J. Vogt, *Terrakotten*, *Gnomon* 4: 257–62.

Perdrizet, P. 1921. *Les terres cuites grecques d'Égypte de la collection Fouquet*. Nancy: Berger-Levrault.

Perpillou-Thomas, F. 1993. *Fêtes d'Égypte ptolemaïque et romaine d'après la documentation papyrologique grecque*. Leuven: Peeters.

Petrie, W. M. F. 1889. *Hawara, Biahmu, and Arsinoe*. London: Field and Tuer.

—— 1905. *Ehnasya 1904*. London: Egypt Exploration Fund and Kegan Paul.

Philipp, H. 1972. *Terrakotten aus Ägypten*. Berlin: Mann.

Pingiatoglou, S. 1993. *I koroplastiki tis Aigyptou kata tous ellinistikous kai romaikous chronous*. Athens: Museum Benaki.

Pons, E. 1997. 'Conjunto de terracotas egipcias de época greco-romana des Museo arqueológico nacional', *Bolétin des Museo Arqueologico Nacional* 15: 95–119.

Sandri, S. 2004. 'Harpokrates & Co.: Zur Identifikation gräko-ägyptischer Kindgott-Terrakotten', in P. C. Bol, G. Kaminski, and C. Maderna (eds), *Fremdheit—Eigenheit: Ägypten, Griechenland und Rom, Austausch und Verständnis*. Munich: Scheufele, 499–510.

—— 2006. *Har-pa-chered (Harpokrates): Die Genese eines ägyptischen Götterkindes*. Leuven: Brill.

—— 2008. 'Variationen in Ton: Zur Herstellungsweise gräko-ägyptischer Terrakotten', *Göttinger Miszellen* 217: 89–95.

—— 2010. 'Echt oder falsch? Hieroglyphische Inschriften auf gräko-ägyptischen Terrakotten', *Chronique d'Égypte* 85: 314–30.

Schmidt, S. 1997. *Katalog der ptolemäischen und kaiserzeitlichen Objekte aus Ägypten im Akademischen Kunstmuseum Bonn*. Munich: Biering & Brinkmann.

Schmidt, V. 1911. *De græsk-ægyptiske terrakotter i ny Carlsberg Glyptothek*. Copenhagen: Høst.

Schrijvers-van Battum, C. M. 1974. 'Harpocrates', *Mededelingenblad Vereniging van Vrienden van het Allard Pierson Museum* 9: 4–7.

Schürmann, W. 1989. *Katalog der antiken Terrakotten im Badischen Landesmuseum, Karlsruhe*. Göteborg: Åström.

Skupinska-Løvset, I. 1978. *The Ustinov Collection: Terracottas*. Oslo: Universitetsforlaget.
Szymańska, H. 2005. *Terres cuites d'Athribis*. Turnhout: Brepols.
Török, L. 1995. *Hellenistic and Roman Terracottas from Egypt*. Rome: 'L'Erma' di Bretschneider.
van Wijngaarden, W. D. 1958. *De grieks-egyptische terracotta's en het Rijksmusuem van Oudheden te Leiden*. Leiden: Rijksmuseum van Oudheden.
Vogt, J. 1924. *Ausgrabungen in Alexandria*, vol. 2/2: *Terrakotten*. Leipzig: Giesecke & Devrient.
Walker, S., and P. Higgs. 2001. *Cleopatra of Egypt: From History to Myth*. London: British Museum Press.
Weber, W. 1914. *Die ägyptisch-griechischen Terrakotten*. Berlin: Curtius.

CHAPTER 39

POTTERY

JENNIFER GATES-FOSTER

THE chapter on Roman and Coptic pottery in Janine Bourriau's foundational diachronic catalogue of Egyptian pottery (1981) begins with the sentiment uttered by Flinders Petrie that 'the most ugly, smug, commonplace forms belong to the Roman age' (Petrie 1909). While attitudes towards Roman pottery in Egypt have changed considerably since Petrie made his pronouncement, the pace of change has accelerated most notably in the last thirty years with no small thanks to Bourriau and her contemporaries. During this time, excavation of sites dating to the Roman era have multiplied significantly, increasing our understanding of the period's pottery profile in new and exciting ways (Bagnall 2001; Bagnall and Davoli 2011).

Indeed, it is ever more difficult to generalize about the 'pottery of the Roman period in Egypt' because of the considerable regional and chronological diversity articulated by these new studies. This marks a sea change from the many decades of study that conflated the pottery of the 'Graeco-Roman era' with the assumption that these periods shared broad material characteristics. Just as it is increasingly understood that the cultural, social, and political worlds of Ptolemaic and Roman Egypt were dissimilar, it is acknowledged that the material culture of these periods differed in profound ways.

In addition to regional variations, recent scholarship has also demonstrated substantial differences in the pottery corpus of the early Roman era—the late first century BCE until the third century CE—and the later Roman era, roughly the fourth to seventh centuries CE. This chapter will focus on the first period, in keeping with the overall scope of the volume, although many later developments have received considerable (and fundamental) attention in the last few years (Pollard 1998; Faiers 2005). Indeed, there is considerable inconsistency in the use of these period designations from author to author, making it difficult to understand how these terms are used from site to site.

Within the confines of the 'early Roman' pottery corpus much attention has understandably been paid to working out the range of shapes, decorative practices, and fabrics that characterize this period, and the kinds of economic and social practice that are suggested by the production, trade, and consumption of pottery in Egypt. This chapter will endeavour to offer an overview of the kinds of development that have characterized the study of early Roman pottery by focusing first on the context of Egypto-Roman pottery studies within Egyptian pottery studies more generally. It will then turn to an examination of the production of pottery in Roman Egypt and the wares, fabrics, and forms of the kinds that are characteristic of the period, as well as the evidence for imports. A short section on amphoras, both imported and domestic, is also included, along with a final section on directions for future work and suggested reading.

Pottery Studies in Egypt

The study of pottery is central to the modern practice of archaeology and continues to form the backbone of the material chronologies employed by archaeologists working in Egypt, but it was not always thus. Pottery was not considered a meaningful category of artefact beyond its aesthetic value as a work of art until after the rudimentary system of contextual seriation was developed by Petrie during his work at Diospolis Parva (Hu) in Upper Egypt in the late nineteenth century. Petrie's innovation was his recognition that the stylistic and technological features of the ceramic vessels recovered from the sites he excavated in Egypt could be used to create groups of vessel types (assemblages) that regularly occurred in association with one another. These groups could then be arranged in a series that developed over time in a predictable way, making it possible to postulate a date of production for a particular vessel on the basis of its physical characteristics, in combination with its find spot or stratigraphic context (Rice 1987; Renfrew and Bahn 2000).

This approach revolutionized the value of even the humblest potsherd recovered from archaeological sites and as a result has made the collection, documentation, and analysis of pottery a critical aspect of modern archaeological work. The methods applied to the analysis of Egyptian pottery have made enormous strides in the many years since Petrie's work, most notably in the considerable attention devoted to technological analysis of the composition of Egyptian ceramics and the context of their manufacture (Nordström and Bourriau 1993; Bourriau, Nicholson, and Rose 2000). Pottery studies in Egypt have focused in large part on working out chronological aspects of the ceramic record, and significant strides have been made in that direction; most pottery recovered from excavations in Egypt can now be dated relatively securely, and this is a direct result of the intensive work undertaken over the last thirty years.

Because of the complexity of Egypt's ceramic record the analysis of Egyptian pottery remains almost entirely the domain of the specialist. Publications, which are highly formulaic, reflect the expected knowledge of the intended audience of fellow experts. Egyptian pottery assemblages are usually presented as a special section, often separate from discussions of stratigraphy or other context, in a larger, detailed report that covers some period of excavation at a particular site and/or its hinterland (see Table 39.1 for important sites in Roman Egypt). Most accounts of new material are to be found in this type of publication. The reliance on the site report as the main venue for publication, however, belies the intensive, comparative inter-site work that is undertaken in order to identify a sherd and its probable date. The dating of much pottery, particularly that collected from surface survey, relies on comparative work with pottery from other sites in order to develop a chronological framework.

Table 39.1 Important sites for the study of early Roman pottery in Egypt, first to third centuries CE

Site	Source[a]	Publication
Delta		
Alexandria	E	Élaigne (1998); Empereur and Nenna (2001, 2003); Hayes and Harlaut (2002)
Sa el-Hagar (Sais)	E, S	Wilson (2006)
Kom el-Giza, Kom Hammam (Schedia)	E, S	Martin (2008)
Tell Atrib (Athribis)	E, S	Szetetyłło and Myśliwiec (2000)
Tell el-Farama (Pelusium)	E, S	Bourriau and Valbelle (1997)
Tell el-Farein (Buto)	E, S	Hartung et al. (2003); Ballet (2004); Ballet et al. (2007); Bourriau and French (2007)
Fayum		
Kom Aushim (Karanis)	E	Johnson (1981); Pollard (1998)
Umm el-Boreigat (Tebtunis)	E, S	Marangou and Marchand (2007)
Hawara	S	Marchand (2009)
Kom Umm el-Atl (Bacchias)	E, S	Morini (2007)
Medinet Madi (Narmouthis)	E	Bresciani et al. (2006); Silvano et al. (2007)
Middle Egypt		
El-Sheikh Ibada (Antinoopolis)	E	Guidotti (2007); Pintaudi (2008)
El-Ashmounein (Hermopolis Magna)	E	Bailey et al. (1982); Bailey (1998)
Upper Egypt		
Qift (Koptos)	E	Herbert and Berlin (2002, 2003)
Dendara (Tentyris)	E, S	Marchand and Laisney (2000); Marchand (2007)
Thebes, Valley of the Queens	E, S	Lecuyot (1996, 2007)
Armant (Hermonthis)	E	Mond and Myers (1940)
Tod (Touphium)	E	Pierrat-Bonnefois (1996, 2002)
Karnak (Diospolis)	E	Béout et al. (1993); Marchand (2007); Marouard (2007)
Aswan (Syene)	E	Jaritz and Rodziewicz (1994); von Pilgrim et al. (2006)
Elephantine	E	Gempeler (1992); Rodziewicz (1992, 2005); Aston (2007)
Western Desert		
Dakhla Oasis Project	E, S	Hope and Mills (1999); Hope and Bowen (2002); Bowen and Hope (2003)
Douch (Kysis)	E	Reddé et al. (2004)
Eastern Desert		
Quseir al-Qadim	E, S	Whitcomb and Johnson (1979, 1982); Peacock and Blue (2005)

Site	Source[a]	Publication
Roman stations along the Koptos–Quseir road	E, S	Cuvigny (2003); Brun (2007); Tomber (2007)
Mons Claudianus	E, S	Tomber (1992, 2006)
Mons Porphyrites	E, S	Tomber (2007a, 2007b)
Berenike	E, S	Hayes (1996); Sidebotham and Wendrich (1996, 1998, 1999, 2007); Sidebotham et al. (2000); Tomber (1999, 2007a, 2008)

Note: This table updates the useful compendium made by McNally and Schrunk (2000). There are, of course, many other sites in these regions where materials dating to the early Roman era have been recorded. This table includes selected sites where pottery has been a significant component of the published results of the excavation through 2010.

[a]E = excavation; S = survey.

This kind of intensive collaboration is reflected in major publication series which, aside from site-specific reports, continue to be another key venue for the dissemination of new information related to Egyptian pottery of all periods. The *Bulletin de Liaison du Groupe International d'Étude de la Céramique Égyptienne* (BCE) was first published in 1975 as a record of current ceramic research in the field and was designed to be a short primer of important ongoing work organized by site. The regular appearance of these slim volumes attests to the dynamism of the field as well as the blistering pace of research that was set in the mid-1970s as ceramic research became more formalized. The *Cahiers de la Céramique Égyptienne* (CCE) appeared in the late 1980s as a venue for more substantial contributions, but is also largely restricted in practice to site-specific or specialized vessel studies.

It is noteworthy that much less attention has been paid in these publications to the social and economic context of pottery production and consumption or the contribution that pottery studies can make to broader narratives (with Redmount and Keller 2003 and McNally and Schrunk 2000 as notable exceptions). When studies of these kinds do appear, they often do so in journals associated with the national schools in Egypt: *Journal of Egyptian Archaeology* (*JEA*, Britain), *Journal of the American Research Center in Egypt* (*JARCE*, United States), *Mitteilungen des Deutschen Archäologischen Instituts Abteilung Kairo* (*MDAIK*, Germany), and *Bulletin de l'Institut Français d'Archéologie Orientale* (*BIFAO*, France). In practice, these publications are largely unknown to the greater archaeological community, and as a result the work of ceramicists in Egypt remains somewhat (and undeservingly) obscure and the implications of their observations largely unexplored by scholars in other fields.

Pottery Production in the Roman Era

The pottery of the Roman era in Egypt is actually, in some respects, an exception to the general trend outlined above. Because of the nature of the Roman imperial enterprise and resulting economic and cultural changes, the ceramic *koine* of the Mediterranean was deeply influential in Egypt and there is much about the pottery of this era that makes it interesting to scholars working outside Egypt's borders (Blondé et al. 2002). As Bourriau has noted, however, the number of Egyptian-made forms that exhibited any kind of Roman influence is rather more limited than these studies might imply (Bourriau 1981; McNally and Schrunk 2000). Nevertheless, an important component of the study of Roman era pottery in Egypt is the increasing sophistication of Roman pottery studies *outside* Egypt, particularly a growing familiarity with the North African and Cilician finewares of the Roman period and amphoras more generally (Hayes 1972, 1980, 1985, 1997; Peacock and Williams 1986; Empereur and Picon 1989).

This well-developed chronological and morphological framework for foreign-made vessels makes it much easier to determine not only which objects were manufactured in Egypt but also the way that local production responded to innovations by foreign workshops. It is also critical in dating the assemblages of Roman Egypt since dates of manufacture are often established for the imported types which then offer a way to date, at least approximately, the layers in which they are recovered from Egypt or the Egyptian vessels that imitate imported forms. Although imports, especially those from the Aegean and Near East, are important tools, much of the ceramic corpus of the early Roman period develops along a trajectory related to local trends and practices, and the importance of local custom and traditions cannot be forgotten. Accordingly, this chapter will consider Egyptian-made pottery of the early Roman era alongside a discussion of the most common contemporary imported types, including amphoras as well as other forms.

Before turning to the range of vessel types common to the period, it is necessary first to consider the production of pottery in Egypt during this time. The diversity of vessel types and fabric variations indicates that pottery manufacture (whether in workshops or in more informal settings) was present in all regions of the country with the exception of the Eastern Desert, where no pottery works have as yet been recorded (Bourriau, Nicholson, and Rose 2000). Kilns and workshops have been documented in Aswan, Dakhla Oasis, the Fayum, outside Alexandria, and many other places (Ballet 1992; Hope 1993). Little is known about the organization of pottery production, but a group of third-century papyri from Oxyrhynchus indicates that specialized production at least in the Fayum could be on quite a large scale, reflecting the importance of the wine industry in that part of Egypt (Cockle 1981).

Fabric (or paste) is now noted as a standard part of pottery recording, and close attention is paid to the characteristics of the fabric, including its matrix and inclusions. Texture, colour, porosity, and other qualities are carefully observed in a fresh break, when possible, and close descriptions are kept in an attempt to define a standard set of fabric types which can then be used by archaeologists to describe and catalogue finds from other sites, thereby increasing knowledge about production centres and potting traditions in a given area. In recent years, advanced techniques to assist in the analysis of pottery composition have been used by scholars working to refine our knowledge of Egyptian clays, although this has not been a major focus of scholars working on Roman pottery (Nordström and Bourriau 1993; Bourriau, Nicholson, and Rose 2000; Wodzińska 2010).

The composition of Egyptian pottery, as mentioned above, is exceedingly diverse within a narrow range. The two primary categories of Egyptian clays are Nile clays, also known as Nile alluvium or silt, and marl clays, formed from the calcareous soils of the deserts. Most Egyptian vessels are made from a variation on one of these two clay types, although these fabrics can be broken down into many subgroups on the basis of their texture, inclusions, and other characteristics (Ballet and Vichy 1992). They were also apparently mixed in antiquity. Silt clays seem to have been used throughout Egypt but especially in the Delta and the Nile Valley, while Upper Egypt is best known for its marl clays (Ballet 2001). For example, marl-based fabrics made from Aswan clay come into prominence during the late Hellenistic and early Roman eras and are a distinctive feature of the Roman period.

Fabric is, however, just one of the variables used to classify and analyse pottery of the Roman period. *Ware* is a category linked to function and is used by ceramicists (especially in Britain) to categorize pottery by the way it was likely used in the past. Finewares, for example, are vessels for the table and drinking, while cooking wares are obviously related to heated food preparation, and so on. Confusingly, 'ware' is employed by other scholars to indicate something quite different, so the meaning of this term is not always straightforward. *Form* is another category related to ware, but is more specific. An example of a form classification might include a cup or bowl, which would also be categorized as a fineware because of its likely use in dining contexts. Ware, fabric, and form are all intrinsic to the dating and identification of a piece and are almost always included as part of pottery publication.

Imported and Domestic Pottery of the Early Roman Period

It is extremely difficult, of course, to characterize the great diversity of wares, fabrics, and forms that are encompassed under the rubric of this chapter. Nevertheless, it is useful to have a sense of the kinds of vessel that are most commonly found in deposits of the early Roman period, with the necessary caveat that this will without doubt leave out vessels or trends that are special to a particular region or site. The excellent published corpora of Upper Egypt and the Eastern Desert will in part form the scaffolding for this discussion (e.g. Maxfield and Peacock 2006; Peacock and Maxfield 2007).

Egyptian finewares show the most evidence of influence by foreign shapes and decoration during the early Roman era, which is hardly surprising given the rapidity with which these imports arrived in Egypt after the conquest (Fig. 39.1). For example, Italian sigillatas appear in quantity during the last years of the first century BCE and the early years of the first century CE and are documented in surprisingly large quantities in locations as remote as Berenike and Quseir al-Qadim shortly thereafter. Eastern Sigillata B (ESB), likely produced in western Asia Minor, is a slightly later arrival and appears in Egypt in the mid-first century CE (Whitcomb and Johnson 1979; Hayes 1985, 1996). Cypriot Sigillata is most commonly found along the coast and in Sinai, where it was widely imitated in local fabrics (Bourriau and Valbelle 1997; Ballet 2001). Not imitated, but certainly as interesting, are the Indian finewares documented at Berenike as part of the early Roman trade between Egypt and the Indian Ocean (Tomber 2000, 2008).

Egyptian bowls and other table vessels imitate the shapes and decoration derived from the ceramic traditions of the Italian varieties and, in particular, Eastern Sigillata A (ESA), which was likely produced in northern Syria (Slane 1997) and first appears in Egypt in the early first century BCE, during the late Hellenistic period. These trends suggest an early integration of

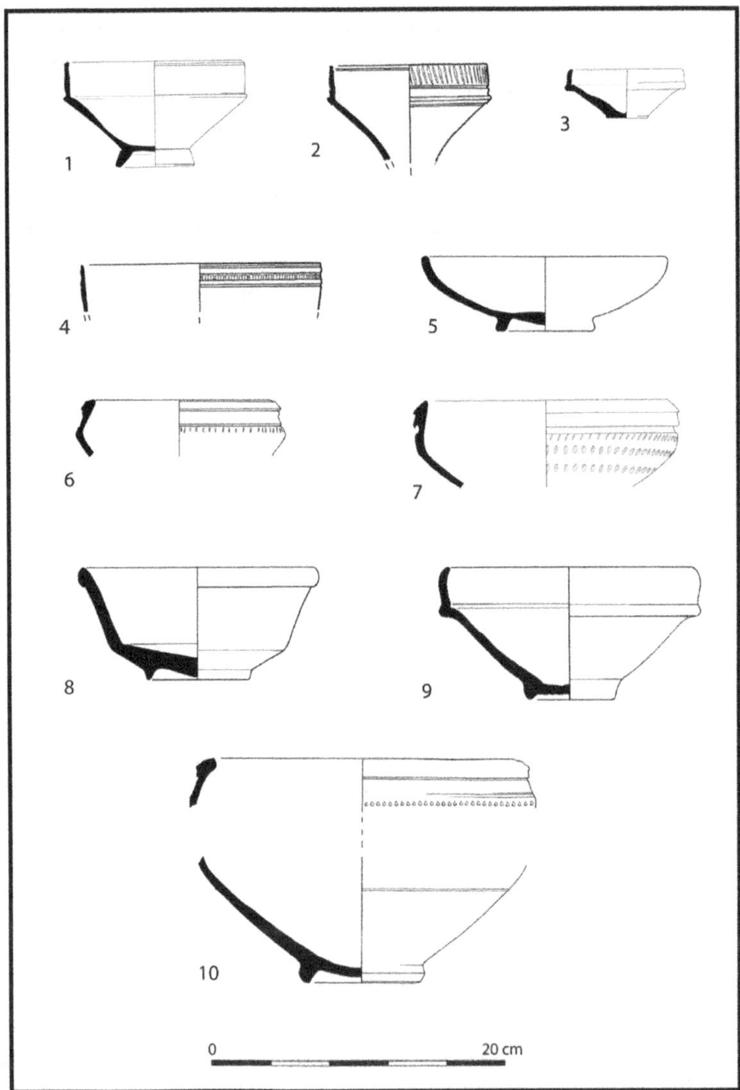

FIG. 39.1 Imported early Roman sigillatas and their Egyptian imitations
(1) Imported Eastern Sigillata A cup, Alexandria (after Hayes and Harlaut 2002, fig. 35). (2) Imported Arretine bowl, Koptos (after Herbert and Berlin 2003, fig. 80.R1.3). (3) Egyptian silt imitation of Eastern Sigillata A cup, Alexandria (after Hayes and Harlaut 2002, fig. 36). (4) Imported Italian Sigillata bowl, Koptos (after Herbert and Berlin 2003, fig. 80.R1.5). (5) Imported Cypriot Sigillata bowl, Mons Claudianus (after Tomber 2006, fig. 1.4-38). (6) Imported Cypriot Sigillata krater, Mons Claudianus (after Tomber 2006, fig. 1.4-40). (7) Egyptian silt imitation of Cypriot Sigillata krater, Alexandria (after Hayes and Harlaut 2002, fig. 43). (8) Early Egyptian Red Slip bowl in Aswan fabric, Mons Claudianus (after Tomber 2006, fig. 1.40-23.553). (9) Egyptian flanged bowl in Aswan fabric, Mons Claudianus (after Tomber 2006, fig. 1.40-30.572). (10) Imported Cypriot Sigillata krater, Alexandria (after Élaigne 1998, fig. 52).

Egypt into the Mediterranean trade networks that characterized the early Roman era and a quick absorption of these new items into the Egyptian market. This is particularly evident in Sinai and along the coast, especially Alexandria, where Cypriot sigillatas were heavily imitated in local fabrics beginning in the first century CE (Ballet and Harlaut 2001; Hayes and Harlaut 2002).

The early Roman red-slipped ware documented by Tomber at Mons Claudianus (Tomber 1992, 2006) is a particularly intriguing example of Egyptian imitation of these imported sigillatas. It is documented well before the appearance of the more familiar late Roman Egyptian Red Slip (ERS A/B) from Aswan, known to date to the fourth century and later, which is an imitation of the North African slipwares (ARS) that were produced in Tunisia (Hayes 1972, 1980). It appears in the form of bowls, dishes, beakers, and cups in shapes known to be part of the Aswan repertoire, and dates from the first to third century CE (Fig. 39.2).

Another distinctive local fineware associated with the Roman era is the so-called 'thin-walled' ware thought to have been produced at Aswan from the first to the third century. These delicate vessels are made of a well-levigated clay that fires to a distinctive pink, white, or orange hue. Many of these vessels are painted or carry barbotine decoration—another imitation of an Italian form. They date from the middle of the first to the third century.

Other early Roman forms, including cooking pots, storage jars, large bowls, and basins, saw considerable continuity with the pottery of the late Ptolemaic period, especially in the forms and fabrics of storage jars and cooking vessels (Ballet 2001; Ballet and Harlaut 2001; Herbert and Berlin 2003). The relative conservatism of these vessels and other more utilitarian shapes has been noted before, particularly with regard to the Elephantine pottery (McNally and Schrunk 2000) but also as a general trend in the pottery of this period (Bourriau 1981). The contrast with the finewares is strong and suggests a particular dynamic whereby new fashions in tableware were adopted at a relatively quick pace, while vessels devoted to food storage or preparation were slow to adapt to new fashions.

Amphoras: Imported and Domestic

Large transport amphoras were introduced to Egypt during the Late period and were common throughout the Hellenistic era both as imports from abroad and, later, as Egyptian products that imitated these imported forms (Peacock and Williams 1986; Marchand and Marangou 2007). The early Roman era is characterized by an explosion in the diversity of imported types, which is a testament to the wealth of new economic connections facilitated by the incorporation of Egypt into the Roman empire. The site of Tebtunis in the Fayum offers one snapshot of the range of imported amphoras recovered from the site in levels dating to the early Roman period. Points of origin include Cos, Crete, Brindisi, Tripolitania, Iberia, and North Africa (Marangou and Marchand 2007). The sites of Mons Claudianus and Mons Porphyrites in the Eastern Desert provide a supplementary catalogue for roughly the same period: Cilicia, Spain, Italy (including Campanian types), Gaul, Crete, Rhodes, Mauretania, North Africa, and Tripolitania (Tomber 1992, 2006, 2007b).

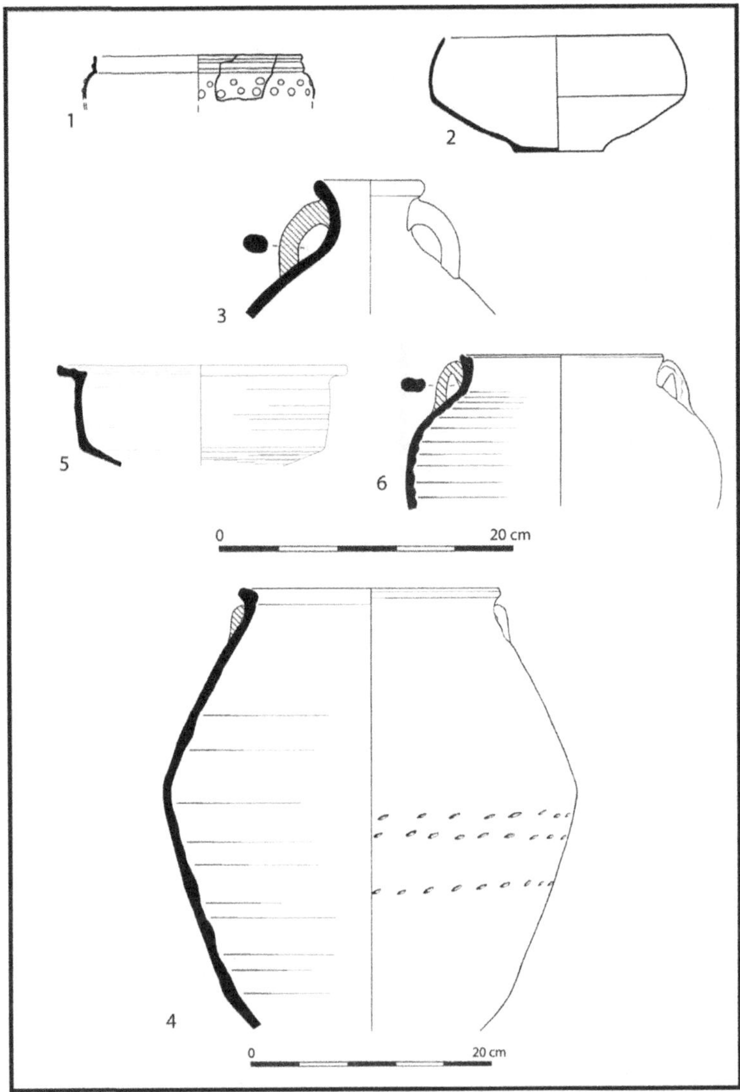

FIG. 39.2 Examples of Egyptian early Roman finewares, tablewares, and cooking and storage vessels (1) Barbotine cup, Koptos (after Herbert and Berlin 2003, fig. 87.R2.3). (2) Aswan thin-walled ware bowl, Koptos (after Herbert and Berlin 2003, fig. 80.R2.1). (3) Marl double-handled flagon, Mons Claudianus (after Tomber 2006, fig. 1.21-34.231). (4) Marl storage jar, Mons Claudianus (after Tomber 2006, fig. 1.34-78.452). (5) Silt casserole, Alexandria (after Hayes and Harlaut 2002, fig. 55). (6) Wide-mouth cooking pot in silt, Mons Claudianus (after Tomber 2006, fig. 1.30-37.380).

Alongside these imported forms are a wealth of Egyptian amphora types, the chronology for which is only now being worked out as scholars amass a critical amount of information on centres of production and regional variations (Marchand and Marangou 2007). Kilns that produced amphoras in the Roman period are increasingly well documented and include those at Mariout, Antinoopolis, Hermopolis Magna, Oxyrhynchus, and Akoris, among others. There are many more production centres than documented kilns, making it clear that other regions were also producing amphoras. Aswan is in this category (Gempeler 1992). Alluvial clays are the most common fabric for amphoras of the period but there are significant numbers of marl clays documented as well as some mixed examples. These amphoras were used to transport foodstuffs and liquids, and many of them are pitched in the interior to reduce porosity and protect the contents. Examples of amphora stoppers in clay or mud are also now published from several sites including Berenike, Mons Claudianus, and Bacchias (Davoli 2005; Thomas 2006; Mulder 2007).

Early Roman amphoras from Egypt are so diverse with regard to shape that it is virtually impossible to offer generalizations beyond some very basic observations (Fig. 39.3). Egyptian amphoras from this period are elongated and narrow and fall into three main types, as defined by Tomber and Williams (2000) and later tentatively revised by Tomber (2007a):

1. Dressel 2-4 amphora with a bead rim and handles divided into two segments and a short spike. These are imitations of an Italian form and have a documented range from the Hellenistic period through the mid-third century CE.
2. Amphora with an almond-shaped rim and two small looped handles, a spindle-shaped body, and a solid spike. Tomber and Williams date this type from the late first century BCE through, tentatively, the third century CE.
3. Biconical amphora with a grooved or beaded rim, two small handles, and a ribbed body with a solid spike. They date this type to the early Roman era with an indefinite end date. Tomber has recently proposed a refinement to this category based on her work in the Eastern Desert (2007a).

Within these very broad categories, there is immense morphological variation, making the secure identification of amphoras (often via quite small fragments) one of the most challenging aspects of ceramic analysis on Egyptian sites of this period. There is much to be gained, however, from a better understanding of both the chronological range and the distribution of these containers. On most archaeological sites, they constitute around half of the recovered pottery and represent an enormously important data set for the analysis of trade, distribution, and consumption of commodities, especially wine, in Roman Egypt.

Conclusion

As this chapter has made clear, the study of pottery in early Roman Egypt is, in certain respects, a field still in its infancy. While important strides have been taken in the collection, analysis, and publication of Egypto-Roman pottery, most studies are so narrowly focused on

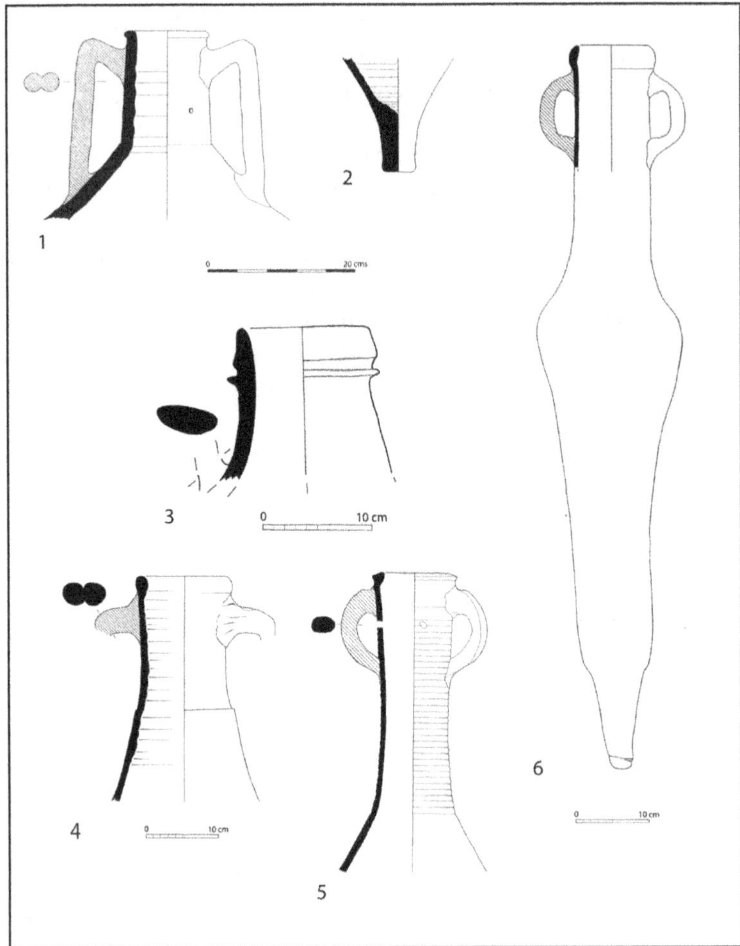

FIG. 39.3 Common imported and Egyptian amphora types of the early Roman period (1) Imported Dressel 2-4, Campanian, Berenike (after Tomber 1999, fig. 5-5.45). (2) Imported base of Dressel 2-4, Campanian, Berenike (after Tomber 1999, fig. 5-5.47). (3) Imported Aegean MR7 type, Koptos (after Lawall 2003, fig. 108.75). (4) Egyptian Mareotis imitation of Dressel 2-4, Mons Claudianus (after Tomber 2006, fig. 1.60-28.894). (5) Egyptian ribbed type, Mons Claudianus (after Tomber 2006, fig. 1.58-12.861). (6) Egyptian Type I Silt, Mons Claudianus (after Tomber 2006, fig. 1.60-1.826).

chronology that larger synthetic or even comparative statements are extremely rare. The technical demands of the field are such that this is entirely understandable. Yet to begin offering comprehensive analyses of the nature of Roman amphora production and its relationship to models of the Roman economy, for example, seems entirely within the realm of possibility given the state of knowledge. Likewise, an assessment of the value of stylistic influence as a marker of cultural exchange in Roman Egypt seems a topic that is also appropriate and accessible with the ceramic data sets currently available. Specialists who know this material best are ideally positioned to engage with these kinds of question and to deal directly with the broader narratives of the history of Roman Egypt.

Suggested Reading

Colin Hope's *Egyptian Pottery* (2001) is a slim introductory text that offers the absolute beginner an overview of pottery studies in Egypt in terms of the field's history, scope, and method. It is also quite well illustrated for such a small work. Arnold and Bourriau's foundational *An Introduction to Ancient Egyptian Pottery* (1993) is hardly introductory, being meant for the specialist who needs a primer, but is none the less valuable for that. In between these two is Anna Wodzińska's *A Manual of Egyptian Pottery*, vol. 4: *Ptolemaic Period–Modern* (2010). While of limited use to expert scholars of Egyptian pottery, it acts more as a comprehensive and organized introduction to methods of study and the materials of the period. It is hardly comprehensive as it draws most of its illustrated examples from Mons Claudianus, but it is nevertheless useful. For detailed study, the *BCE* and the *CCE* (both mentioned earlier in the text) are unparalleled collections of information that is otherwise scattered in obscure journals or specialized field reports. They are the best source for bibliography and ongoing work. Rice (1987) and Sinopoli (1991) are both excellent resources for the techniques and methods of pottery analysis, while Bourriau, Nicholson, and Rose (2000) offers the best overview of the technical aspects of Egyptian ceramic studies and Egyptian pottery production.

Bibliography

Arnold, D., and J. Bourriau (eds) 1993. *An Introduction to Ancient Egyptian Pottery*. Mainz: von Zabern.

Aston, D. A. 2007. 'Amphorae, Storage Jars and Kegs from Elephantine: A Brief Survey of Vessels from the Eighth–Seventh Centuries BC to the Seventh–Eighth Centuries AD', *Cahiers de la Céramique Égyptienne* 8, special issue: *Amphores d'Égypte de la Basse Époque à l'époque arabe*, ed. S. Marchand and A. Marangou, 419–45.

Bagnall, R. S. 2001. 'Archaeological Work on Hellenistic and Roman Egypt, 1995–2000', *American Journal of Archaeology* 105: 227–43.

—— and P. Davoli. 2011. 'Archaeological Work on Hellenistic and Roman Egypt, 2000–2009', *American Journal of Archaeology* 115: 103–57.

Bailey, D. M. 1998. *Excavations at el-Ashmunein V: Pottery, Lamps and Glass of the Late Roman and Early Arab Periods*. London: British Museum Press.

—— et al. 1982. *British Museum Expedition to Middle Egypt, Ashmunein (1980)*. London: British Museum Press.

Ballet, P. (ed.) 1992. *Ateliers de potiers et productions céramiques en Égypte, Cahiers de la Céramique Égyptienne* 3, special issue.

—— 2001. 'Céramiques hellénistiques et romaines d'Égypte', in P. Lévêque and J.-P. Morel (eds), *Céramiques hellénistiques et romaines* III. Paris: Belles Lettres, 105–44.

—— 2004. 'The Graeco-Roman Pottery Workshops of Buto', *Journal of Egyptian Archaeology* 21: 18–19.

—— and C. Harlaut. 2001. 'Introduction à la céramique de Gabbari', in J.-Y. Empereur and M.-D. Nenna (eds), *Necropolis I*. Cairo: Institut Français d'Archéologie Orientale, 295–364.

—— and M. Vichy. 1992. 'Artisanat de la céramique dans l'Égypte hellénistique et romaine', *Cahiers de la Céramique Égyptienne* 3, special issue: *Ateliers de potiers et productions céramiques en Égypte*, ed. P. Ballet, 109–19.

—— et al. 2007. 'Recherches sur les ateliers hellénistiques et romains de Buto (Delta)', in J.-C. Goyon and C. Cardin (eds), *Proceedings of the Ninth International Congress of Egyptologists, Grenoble, 6–12 September 2004*, vol. 1. Leuven: Peeters, 133–43.

Béout, P., et al. 1993. 'Fouilles dans le secteur nord-ouest du Temple d'Amon-Rê', *Cahiers de Karnak* 9: 161–203.

Blondé, F., et al. (eds) 2002. *Céramiques hellénistiques et romaines: Productions et diffusion en Méditerranée orientale (Chypre, Égypte et côte syro-palestinienne).* Lyon: Maison de l'Orient Méditerranéen—Jean Pouilloux.

Bourriau, J. 1981. *Umm el-Ga'ab: Pottery from the Nile Valley before the Arab Conquest.* Cambridge: Cambridge University Press.

—— and P. French. 2007. 'Imported Amphorae from Buto Dating from *c.*750 BC to the Early 6th Century AD', *Cahiers de la Céramique Égyptienne* 8, special issue: *Amphores d'Égypte de la Basse Époque à l'époque arabe*, ed. S. Marchand and A. Marangou, 115–34.

—— and D. Valbelle (eds) 1997. *An Introduction to the Pottery of Northern Sinai, Cahiers de la Céramique Égyptienne* 5, special issue.

—— P. Nicholson, and P. Rose. 2000. 'Pottery', in P. T. Nicholson and I. Shaw (eds), *Ancient Egyptian Materials and Technology.* Cambridge: Cambridge University Press, 121–47.

Bowen, G. E., and C. Hope. 2003. *The Oasis Papers 3: Proceedings of the Third International Conference of the Dakhleh Oasis Project.* Oxford: Oxbow.

Bresciani, E., et al. (eds) 2006. *Medinet Madi: Venti anni di esplorazione archeologica 1984–2005.* Pisa: University of Pisa.

Brun, J.-P. 2007. 'Amphores égyptiennes et importées dans les praesidia romains des routes de Myos Hormos et de Bérénice', *Cahiers de la Céramique Égyptienne* 8, special issue: *Amphores d'Égypte de la Basse Époque à l'époque arabe*, ed. S. Marchand and A. Marangou, 505–23.

Cockle, H. 1981. 'Pottery Manufacture in Roman Egypt: A New Papyrus', *Journal of Roman Studies* 71: 87–97.

Cuvigny, H. (ed.) 2003. *La route de Myos Hormos: L'armée romaine dans le désert oriental d'Égypte*, 2 vols. Cairo: Institut Français d'Archéologie Orientale.

Davoli, P. 2005. *Oggetti in argilla dall'area templare di Bakchias (el-Fayyum, Egitto).* Pisa: Giardini.

Élaigne, S. 1998. 'Alexandrie: Études préliminaire d'un contexte céramique du Haut-Empire', in J.-Y. Empereur (ed.), *Alexandrina 1.* Cairo: Institut Français d'Archéologie Orientale, 75–115.

Empereur, J.-Y., and M.-D. Nenna (eds) 2001. *Nécropolis 1.* Cairo: Institut Français d'Archéologie Orientale.

—— —— (eds) 2003. *Nécropolis 2.* Cairo: Institut Français d'Archéologie Orientale.

—— and M. Picon. 1989. 'Les Régions de production d'amphores impériales en Méditerranée orientale', *Amphores romaines et historique économique: Dix ans de recherche.* Rome: Collection de l'École Français de Rome, 223–48.

Faiers, J., with S. Clackson, B. Kemp, G. Pyke, and R. Reece. 2005. *Late Roman Pottery at Amarna and Related Studies.* London: Egypt Exploration Society.

Gempeler, R. D. 1992. *Elephantine X: Die Keramik römischer bis früharabischer Zeit.* Mainz: von Zabern.

Guidotti, M. C. 2007. 'La céramique d'Antinoopolis: Fouilles 2003 et 2004', in J.-C. Goyon and C. Cardin (eds), *Proceedings of the Ninth International Congress of Egyptologists, Grenoble, 6–12 September 2004*, vol. 1. Leuven: Peeters, 877–81.

Hartung, V. U., et al. 2003. 'Tell el-Fara'in—Buto', *Mitteilungen des Deutschen Archäologischen Instituts, Abteilung Kairo* 59: 220–63.

Hayes, J. 1972. *Late Roman Pottery.* London: British School at Rome.

—— 1980. *A Supplement to Late Roman Pottery*. London: British School at Rome.
—— 1985. 'Sigillate Orientali', *Enciclopedia dell'arte antica: Atlante delle forme ceramiche* II: *Ceramica fine romana nel bacino Mediterraneao (tardo ellenismo e primo impero)*. Rome: Istituto della Enciclopedia Italiana, 1–96.
—— 1996. 'The Pottery', in S. E. Sidebotham, W. Z. Wendrich, and F. Aldsworth (eds), *Berenike 1995: Preliminary Report of the 1995 Excavations at Berenike (Egyptian Red Sea Coast) and the Survey of the Eastern Desert*. Leiden: Research School CNWS, 147–78.
—— 1997. *Handbook of Mediterranean Roman Pottery*. London: British Museum Press.
—— and C. Harlaut. 2002. 'Ptolemaic and Roman Pottery Deposits from Alexandria', in J.-Y. Empereur (ed.), *Alexandrina*, vol. 2. Cairo: Institut Français d'Archéologie Orientale, 99–132.
Herbert, S. C., and A. Berlin. 2002. 'Coptos: Architecture and Assemblages in the Sacred Temenos from Nectanebo to Justinian', *Topoi*, suppl. 3: 73–115.
—— —— (eds) 2003. *Excavations at Coptos (Qift) in Upper Egypt, 1987–1992*. Portsmouth, RI: Journal of Roman Archaeology.
Hope, C. A. 1993. 'Pottery Kilns from the Oasis of el-Dakhla', in D. Arnold and J. Bourriau (eds), *An Introduction to Ancient Egyptian Pottery*. Mainz: von Zabern, 121–7.
—— 2001. *Egyptian Pottery*. Princes Risborough: Shire.
—— and G. E. Bowen (eds) 2002. *Dakhleh Oasis Project: Preliminary Reports on the 1994–1995 to 1998–1999 Field Seasons*. Oxford: Oxbow.
—— and A. J. Mills (eds) 1999. *Dakhleh Oasis Project: Preliminary Reports on the 1992–1993 to 1993–1994 Field Seasons*. Oxford: Oxbow.
Jaritz, H., and M. Rodziewicz. 1994. 'Syene: A Review of the Urban Remains and its Pottery', *Mitteilungen des Deutschen Archäologischen Instituts, Abteilung Kairo* 50: 115–41.
Johnson, B. 1981. *Pottery from Karanis: Excavations of the University of Michigan, Ann Arbor*. Ann Arbor: University of Michigan Press.
Lawall, M. 2003. 'Egyptian and Imported Transport Amphoras', in S. C. Herbert and A. Berlin (eds), *Excavations at Coptos (Qift) in Upper Egypt, 1987–1992*. Portsmouth, RI: Journal of Roman Archaeology, 157–91.
Lecuyot, G. 1996. 'La céramique de la Vallée des Reines: Bilan préliminaire', *Cahiers de la Céramique Égyptienne* 4: 145–69.
—— 2007. 'Amphores provenant de Thèbes-Ouest de la Basse Époque à l'époque copte', *Cahiers de la Céramique Égyptienne* 8, special issue: *Amphores d'Égypte de la Basse Époque à l'époque arabe*, ed. S. Marchand and A. Marangou, 377–87.
McNally, S., and I. Schrunk. 2000. 'The Impact of Rome on the Egyptian Pottery Industry', *Journal of the American Research Center in Egypt* 37: 91–114.
Marangou, A., and S. Marchand. 2007. 'Conteneurs importés et égyptiens de Tebtynis (Fayoum)', *Cahiers de la Céramique Égyptienne* 8, special issue: *Amphores d'Égypte de la Basse Époque à l'époque arabe*, ed. S. Marchand and A. Marangou, 239–94.
Marchand, S. 2007. 'Amphores de Karnak et de Dendera', *Cahiers de la Céramique Égyptienne* 8, special issue: *Amphores d'Égypte de la Basse Époque à l'époque arabe*, ed. S. Marchand and A. Marangou, 369–76.
—— 2009. 'Appendix 2: The Pottery from Hawara', in I. Uytterhoeven (ed.), *Hawara in the Graeco-Roman Period*. Leuven: Peeters, 685–813.
—— and D. Laisney. 2000. 'Le survey de Dendera (1996–1997)', *Cahiers de la Céramique Égyptienne* 6: 261–97.
—— and A. Marangou (eds) 2007. *Amphores d'Égypte de la Basse Époque à l'époque arabe*, *Cahiers de la Céramique Égyptienne* 8, special issue.

Marouard, G. 2007. 'Quelques amphores d'epoque hellénistique et romaine de Karnak', *Cahiers de la Céramique Égyptienne* 8, special issue: *Amphores d'Égypte de la Basse Époque à l'époque arabe*, ed. S. Marchand and A. Marangou, 345–59.

Martin, A. 2008. 'Pottery from Schedia near Alexandria (Egypt)', *Rei Cretariae Romanae Fautores Acta* 40: 263–9.

Maxfield, V. A., and D. P. S. Peacock (eds) 2006. *Mons Claudianus: Survey and Excavation 1987–1993*, vol. 3: *Ceramic Vessels and Related Objects*. Cairo: Institut Français d'Archéologie Orientale.

Mond, R., and O. H. Myers. 1940. *The Temples of Armant: A Preliminary Survey*. London: Egypt Exploration Society.

Morini, A. 2007. 'Bakchias XVI: I materiali della Campagna di scavo 2007', *Ricerce di Egittologia e di Antichità Copte* 9: 105–66.

Mulder, S. F. 2007. 'Jar Stoppers, Seals and Lids, 2000 Season', in S. E. Sidebotham and W. Z. Wendrich (eds), *Berenike 1999/2000: Report on the Excavations at Berenike, including Excavations at Wadi Kalalat and Siket, and the Survey of the Mons Smaragdus Region*. Los Angeles: Cotsen Institute of Archaeology, 270–84.

Nordström, H.-A., and J. Bourriau. 1993. 'Ceramic Technology: Clays and Fabrics', in D. Arnold and J. Bourriau (eds), *An Introduction to Ancient Egyptian Pottery*. Mainz: von Zabern, 149–86.

Peacock, D. P. S., and L. Blue. 2005. *Myos Hormos—Quseir al-Qadim, Roman and Islamic Ports on the Red Sea*, vol. 1: *The Survey and Report on the Excavations*. Oxford: Oxbow.

—— and V. A. Maxfield. 2007. *The Roman Imperial Quarries: Survey and Excavation at Mons Porphyrites 1994–1998*, vol. 2: *The Excavations*. London: Egypt Exploration Society.

—— and D. F. Williams. 1986. *Amphorae and the Roman Economy*. London: Longman.

Petrie, W. M. F. 1909. *The Arts and Crafts of Ancient Egypt*. London: Foulis.

Pierrat-Bonnefois, G. 1996. 'Evolution de la céramique de Tôd du IIe au VIIe s. apr. J.-C.', *Cahiers de la Céramique Égyptienne* 4: 189–214.

—— 2002. 'L'hellénisation des productions céramiques en Haute-Égypte: Le cas de Tôd', in F. Blondé, P. Ballet, and J.-F. Salles (eds), *Céramiques hellénistiques et romaines: Productions et diffusion en Méditerranée orientale (Chypre, Égypte et côte syro-palestinienne)*. Lyon: Maison de l'Orient Méditerranéen-Jean Pouilloux, 175–88.

Pintaudi, R. (ed.) 2008. *Antinoupolis: Scavi et materiali*, vol. 1. Florence: Istituto Papirologico G. Vitelli.

Pollard, N. 1998. 'The Chronology and Economic Condition of Late Roman Karanis: An Archaeological Reassessment', *Journal of the American Research Center in Egypt* 35: 147–62.

Reddé, M., et al. 2004. *Kysis: Fouilles de l'Ifao à Douch, oasis de Kharga (1985–1990)*. Cairo: Institut Français d'Archéologie Orientale.

Redmount, C., and C. Keller (eds) 2003. *Egyptian Pottery: Proceedings of the 1990 Pottery Symposium at the University of California, Berkeley*. Berkeley: University of California Publications in Egyptian Archaeology.

Renfrew, C., and P. Bahn (eds) 2000. *Archaeology: Theories, Methods and Practice*. New York: Thames and Hudson.

Rice, P. 1987. *Pottery Analysis: A Sourcebook*. Chicago: University of Chicago Press.

Rodziewicz, M. 1992. 'Field Notes from Elephantine on the Early Aswan Pink Clay Pottery', *Cahiers de la Céramique Égyptienne* 3, special issue: *Ateliers de potiers et productions céramiques en Égypte*, ed. P. Ballet, 103–17.

—— 2005. *Early Roman Industries on Elephantine*. Mainz: von Zabern.

Sidebotham, S. E., and W. Z. Wendrich. 1996. *Berenike 1995: Preliminary Report of the 1995 Excavations at Berenike (Egyptian Red Sea Coast) and the Survey of the Eastern Desert*. Leiden: Research School CNWS.

——— 1998. *Berenike 1996: Report of the 1996 Excavations at Berenike (Egyptian Red Sea Coast) and the Survey of the Eastern Desert*. Leiden: Research School CNWS.

——— 1999. *Berenike 1997: Report of the 1997 Excavations at Berenike (Egyptian Red Sea Coast) and the Survey of the Eastern Desert*. Leiden: Research School CNWS.

——— 2007. *Berenike 1999/2000: Report on the Excavations at Berenike, including Excavations at Wadi Kalalat and Siket, and the Survey of the Mons Smaragdus Region*. Los Angeles: Cotsen Institute of Archaeology.

—— et al. 2000. *Berenike 1998: Report of the 1998 Excavations at Berenike and the Survey of the Egyptian Eastern Desert, including Excavations in Wadi Kalalat*. Leiden: Research School CNWS.

Silvano, F., et al. 2007. 'Roman Amphorae from Fayoum Oasis (Medinet Madi)', in G. Goyon and C. Cardin (eds), *Proceedings of the Ninth International Congress of Egyptologists, Grenoble, 6–12 September 2004*, vol. 2. Leuven: Peeters, 1705–11.

Sinopoli, C. 1991. *Approaches to Archaeological Ceramics*. New York: Plenum Press.

Slane, K. 1997. 'The Fine Wares', in S. C. Herbert (ed.), *Tel Anafa II*, vol. 1: *The Hellenistic and Roman Pottery*. Ann Arbor: Kelsey Museum of the University of Michigan, 247–406.

Szetetyłło, Z., and K. Myśliwiec (eds) 2000. *Tell Atrib, 1985–1995*, vol. 1. Warsaw: Centre d'Archeólogie Méditerranéenne de l'Académie Polonaise des Sciences.

Thomas, R. 2006. 'Vessel Stoppers', in V. A. Maxfield and D. P. S. Peacock (eds), *Mons Claudianus: Survey and Excavation 1987–1993*, vol. 3: *Ceramic Vessels and Related Objects*. Cairo: Institut Français d'Archéologie Orientale, 239–58.

Tomber, R. 1992. 'Early Roman Pottery from Mons Claudianus', *Cahiers de la Céramique Égyptienne*, 3, special issue: *Ateliers de potiers et productions céramiques en Égypte*, ed. P. Ballet, 137–42.

—— 1999. 'The Pottery', in S. E. Sidebotham and W. Z. Wendrich (eds), *Berenike 1997: Report of the 1997 Excavations at Berenike (Egyptian Red Sea Coast) and the Survey of the Eastern Desert*. Leiden: Research School CNWS, 122–59.

—— 2000. 'Indo-Roman Trade: The Ceramic Evidence from Egypt', *Antiquity* 74/285: 624–31.

—— 2006. 'The Pottery', in V. A. Maxfield and D. P. S. Peacock (eds), *Mons Claudianus: Survey and Excavation 1987–1993*, vol. 3: *Ceramic Vessels and Related Objects*. Cairo: Institut Français d'Archéologie Orientale, 3–236.

—— 2007a. 'Early Roman Egyptian Amphorae from the Eastern Desert of Egypt: A Chronological Sequence', *Cahiers de la Céramique Égyptienne* 8, special issue: *Amphores d'Égypte de la Basse Époque à l'époque arabe*, ed. S. Marchand and A. Marangou, 525–36.

—— 2007b. 'Pottery from the Excavated Deposits', in D. P. S. Peacock and V. A. Maxfield (eds), *The Roman Imperial Quarries: Survey and Excavation at Mons Porphyrites 1994–1998*, vol. 2: *The Excavations*. London: Egypt Exploration Society, 177–208.

—— 2008. *Indo-Roman Trade: From Pots to Pepper*. London: Duckworth.

—— and D. Williams. 2000. 'Egyptian Amphorae in Britain and the Western Provinces', *Britannia* 31: 41–54.

von Pilgrim, C., et al. 2006. 'The Town of Syene: Report on the 3rd and 4th Season in Aswan', *Mitteilungen des Deutschen Archäologischen Instituts, Abteilung Kairo* 62: 215–77.

Whitcomb, D., and J. Johnson. 1979. *Quseir al-Qadim 1978*. Cairo: American Research Center in Egypt Press.

——— 1982. *Quseir al-Qadim 1980*. Malibu, Calif.: Undena.

Wilson, P. (ed.) 2006. *The Survey of Saïs (Sa el-Hagar) 1997–2002*. London: Egypt Exploration Society.

Wodzińska, A. 2010. *A Manual of Egyptian Pottery*, vol. 4: *Ptolemaic Period–Modern*. Boston: Ancient Egypt Research Associates.

CHAPTER 40

MUMMIES AND MUMMIFICATION*

BEATRIX GESSLER-LÖHR

SINCE the first discoveries in the Fayum Oasis in the 1880s, the investigation of Roman mummies wrapped up in a skilful geometrical system of bandages, and decorated with a painted wooden portrait or a gilded and painted stucco mask over the face of the deceased, has been guided by an art historical focus. Hence, the research, primarily from the perspectives of classical archaeology, has reached a very high and multilayered standard (see Chapter 37 in this volume). However, it took another century for scholars to become increasingly aware that the fascinating portraits and masks were taken from human burials or that they were still attached to a mummy (Fig. 40.1).

In fact, only members of the upper classes were provided with such elaborate funerary equipment: among about a hundred mummies just one or two were decorated in this precious manner, although the estimate is necessarily imprecise (Riggs 2002: 96 n. 69). With around a thousand wooden portraits and more than 1,200 masks known, the number of Roman mummies proves to be uncountable. In the nineteenth and early twentieth centuries, many vast cemeteries were ruthlessly pillaged by robbers, and hundreds of mummies were vandalized by pulling out their portraits or masks. Furthermore, during the treasure-hunt for amulets, jewellery, papyri, and colourful textiles among the wrappings, thousands of unmasked mummies and their archaeological contexts were destroyed, while the skeletal remains were left to decay naturally (for a drastic report on Akhmim, see Forrer 1895: 30–3).

In 1887 the Austrian merchant Theodor Graf instructed his agents to collect mummy portraits from the cemetery of er-Rubayat (near Philadelphia in the Fayum), which ended with the substantial yield of 330 samples and fragments. Only one intact portrait mummy was

* My thanks are due to many scholars for a wealth of information and advice, including R. S. Bagnall, Edward Bleiberg, Lorelei Corcoran, Renate Germer, Maria Cristina Guidotti, Stephanie Hardekopf, Ursula Höckmann, Andreas Hutterer, Adam Jaffer, Holger Kockelmann, Andrea Kucharek, Alexandra Küffer, Lesley-Anne Liddiard, Claudia Nauerth, Geneviève Pierrat-Bonnefois, J. F. Quack, Renate Siegmann, M. A. Stadler, Marie Svoboda, Susanne Töpfer, Marie-Paul Vanlathem, Alexandra von Lieven, Helen Whitehouse, and Orell Witthuhn. I am especially grateful to Wouter Claes and Isabel Stuenkel for furnishing references and article copies. Furthermore, I am much indebted to Susanne Binder (Sydney), Robert Avila (Heidelberg), and Christina Riggs for assistance with English.

FIG. 40.1 Mummy of a boy aged 4 to 6 years, in a six-layered rhomboid-patterned wrapping with a portrait painted on linen. An X-ray shows that the skull is flexed forward, and the skeleton is disordered, with many disarticulated bones. From Abusir el-Meleq, second half of the first century CE

Egyptological Institute, Heidelberg University, 1021. Photo: R. Ajtai, courtesy of the Trustees of the Egyptological Institute.

part of the lot that was later offered for sale in Europe and America, together with around ninety loose portraits. It was most probably this single mummy that made its way to Berlin (Parlasca and Seemann 1999, cat. 67; Germer, Kischkewitz, and Lüning 2009: 139–42). With the formidable quantity of portrait mummies found during early excavations, even the more scrupulous of the explorers were unable or unwilling to send many of the bulky lots to museums in Europe and America. For example, of the eighty-one portrait mummies excavated at Hawara in the winter of 1888–9, Petrie left a dozen intact; in 1911 about sixteen out of sixty-five left the site still complete (Roberts 1999: 54–5). In 1892 Heinrich Brugsch allegedly shipped another twenty-four out of 600 mummies from Hawara to Germany, but only four can be accounted for there (Germer, Kischkewitz, and Lüning 2009: 143–52 nn. 5 and 7). One of the most important Roman and Byzantine cemeteries was located at Antinoopolis, where from 1896 onwards Albert Gayet found around forty portrait mummies. The majority were allocated to museums throughout France (Calament 2005: 2.439–48).

To minimize transport risks, the fragile portraits were sometimes removed and posted separately, but with the intention of reinserting them after arrival. However, in some museums the detached portraits were not inserted back into their wrappings; others still on their mummies were removed. Subsequently, the portraits were exhibited as in a picture gallery and the wrapped remains were banished to the store-rooms, or disposed of. Meanwhile, the attitude of curators has changed, and some mummies have been reunited with their portraits (e.g. the mummy of Demetrios; see Vogel 2007; Bleiberg and Cooney 2008: 30–1). In the worst cases, the bodies have not survived owing to a variety of circumstances, such as improper storage conditions causing humidity and mould (sometimes because of the effects of war). Other reasons for destruction were the infestation by parasites ('museum beetle'), or examination by autopsy occasionally practised until the end of the twentieth century. Altogether the reduction in numbers is enormous: in a list of rhombic-wrapped portrait mummies only thirty-five out of sixty-two are marked as still extant (Corcoran 1995: 9–10, table 2). In sum, the database for studies on Roman mummies from museums looks sparse at first glance, especially by comparison with the number of preserved masks and portraits.

The Current State of Research

Since human remains belong to the research aims of biological and physical anthropology, archaeological studies have rightly concentrated their attention on the 'packaging' and equipment of mummies rather than on their 'contents', the body itself. Prior to the invention of non-invasive technologies (especially radiography), the investigation of the corpses could only be carried out by autopsy. Fortunately, the destruction of the mummies as the inevitable consequence has often prevented scholars from unwrapping them. Nevertheless, hundreds of mummies were unrolled by physicians and pharmacists from the Renaissance and the Baroque periods onwards and are lost for ever (Raven and Taconis 2005: 40–2).

At that time, additional information could only be obtained from the classical authors' intriguing reports on mummification and burial practices in Egypt, above all Herodotus (2.85–90), who visited Egypt around 450 BCE, and Diodorus Siculus (1.91–3), present around 60 BCE. These documents are still an essential source of information, but in detail their reliability has to be verified at times. For example, for Petrie, the statements made by several authors that the Egyptians kept the mummies of their relatives above ground and even at home as 'guests at the table' (e.g. Teles, third century BCE; Diodorus and Cicero, first century BCE; Lucian, second century CE) seemed to match closely his observations on some Roman mummies from Hawara (Borg 1997; Montserrat 1997: 38–40). The suggestion that the mummies were placed only temporarily in 'banquet halls' in the necropoleis before their final burial turns out to accord better with the course of events (Römer 2000). Furthermore, on occasion cemetery officials illegally used their houses for the interim storage of mummies, which might have been reported to Greek travellers who mistook this as an Egyptian custom (Stadler 2001: 346–8).

Once Egyptology established itself as a primarily philological discipline, the increasing number of Egyptian texts from the Graeco-Roman period attesting the funerary practices and the rituals of embalming became the focus of continually developing research (Riggs 2010). However, attempts to reach a more detailed view of mummification techniques by comparing the textual information with the observed mortuary practices have only occasionally been successful. The difficulties are due in part to the fragmentary nature of the ancient texts, which by no means comprise a systematic and exhaustive description of embalming procedures, and to various philological and lexical problems (e.g. Quack 1997–8; Smith 2009: 216–24). Furthermore, in these texts the facts and operations are intermingled with a complex network of ritual instructions and mythological associations, which makes a distinction between the various levels of meaning extremely difficult.

Therefore, the scientific examination of mummies as the authentic physical remnants of mummification and embalming practices appears to remain an inescapable mission. The thorough investigation of well-dated specimens might provide us with time-dependent criteria of embalming, thus helping to solve, for instance, the sometimes difficult distinction between late Ptolemaic and Roman mummies. A substantial, recently published overview points to many significant features of mummification in the Graeco-Roman period, based on the inscriptional, archaeological, and anthropological evidence (Smith 2009: 30–49).

Fieldwork in Egypt and in the Roman Empire

Over a decade ago the comment was made that Roman mummies await a fundamental study, and this is still the case today (Lichtenberg 1996: 2741). This target can only be met by consolidating research in the humanities on the one hand with the aims of the sciences on the other. Looking at the interdisciplinary investigation of human and animal mummies, research has been accomplished by teams of specialists representing both sides at many sites in Egypt (e.g. Ikram 2005 on animal mummies). Extremely fruitful work has been undertaken from the 1980s in three areas in the Kharga Oasis: Dush, Ain el-Labakha, and el-Deir. Outstanding results have also been achieved in the Dakhla Oasis and at Thebes, where numerous secondary Roman burials from the Valley of the Queens have been investigated (see below).

Despite our knowledge of Roman period mummification techniques from these sites, we are still in the early stages. A list of Graeco-Roman cemeteries shows the amount of material that has yet to be examined or has simply been set aside (Dunand and Lichtenberg 1995: 3219–41). Newly discovered locations—above all Bahariya Oasis, with at least 100 to 250, but probably up to some thousand, Roman mummies—could potentially provide us with a bulk of additional information (Hawass 2000; Bagnall 2006: 18).

At Alexandria mummified bodies are only sporadically preserved. In fact, besides the adverse circumstances in the wet ground, embalming practices in the various cemeteries there probably never became as important as inhumation or as the adopted Greek custom of cremation (Grévin and Bailet 2002; Schmidt 2003: 34–5). Nevertheless, Strabo's description of the necropolis in the western part of the city mentioning embalming institutions (*ταριχεία*) cannot be ignored (17.1, 10 (about 20 BCE)). The reference to the embalming of Antony and Cleopatra in Dio Cassius (51.11, 15 (second–third century CE)) also documents Egyptian funerary practices in Alexandria for the end of the Ptolemaic era (Counts 1996: 192 n. 15;

Grimm 1997: 248). The exceptional status of mummification there during Roman times became apparent when a mummified body was found at Gabbari (excerebrated, with a gilded face and wrapped up in many layers of linen fabric): it was placed among inhumations with only the bones preserved (pit burial 350; Boës, Georges, and Alix 2002: 68–71, figs 39, 41–3). However, Egyptian burial practices used in parallel with hellenistic ones (corpses wrapped in clothes or textiles, without a 'mummiform' shape) have also been observed at Antinoopolis (Calament 2005: 1.142, 268, figs 49b–50; 2.419–21).

The Egyptian practice of embalming made its way to Rome and to the Roman empire in conjunction with other 'exotic' Egyptianizing trends from the first century to the first half of the fourth century CE. This phenomenon is documented by both the inscriptional and the archaeological evidence (Counts 1996: 189–202; Ascenzi and Bianco 1998; Chioffi 1998; Budischovsky 2004: 180–1).

Research in Museums

The present state of fieldwork should not obscure the fact that some of the most important Graeco-Roman cemeteries, such as Hawara, Abusir el-Meleq, el-Hibeh, Hermopolis, Akhmim (Panopolis), and Antinoopolis, were pillaged and excavated from the nineteenth century onwards, and are in the main lost for ever. Hence, our knowledge of the mummification techniques at these places is based on early, not very detailed records. It can be upgraded only by investigating the mummies still extant in museums: roughly 150 corpses are now datable as Roman (plus an unknown number of unprovenanced or not yet precisely dated specimens). The majority are expensively decorated and in all likelihood made for wealthy people (e.g. Borg 1998: 56–9). Many of these mummies represent a predominantly urban class (especially in Antinoopolis) as opposed to people who lived in outlying areas as farmers, traders, and craftsmen. Consequently, painted mummy portraits were, for instance, not in use at Kharga or Dakhla. The observation that the various kinds of mummy and coffin decoration—as well as the manifold types of portrait and mask—reflect distinctive local workshops has long become the general consensus (e.g. Parlasca and Seemann 1999; Riggs 2005).

By striking contrast, embalming techniques are often described as 'typically Roman' without taking comparable variations into account. Even though similar features in mummification methods have been observed in a variety of locations, differences from one cemetery to the next, even within the same oasis, occur. In order to distinguish between local, inter-regional, social, and chronological changes, the results from the various sites need further comparative study with the inclusion of mummies in museums. For example, while the use of natron mixtures as the main dehydrating substance is still attested, whether among remnants of embalming material (e.g. Dunand and Lichtenberg 2008: 268, 273), or put in linen bags into the body cavities and occasionally left there by forgetful embalmers (Macke, Macke-Ribet, and Connan 2002: 117–27, pl. XIC–d), its complete absence in the Roman mummies from Dakhla remains exceptional (Aufderheide et al. 2004: 63). Hence, the absence of natron might be due to local availability (Roger Bagnall, personal communication), but this issue can only be revised on the basis of a much larger set of data.

Although interdisciplinary cooperation on excavations in Egypt is well established and highly effective, mummy research in museums has been conducted rather intermittently and according to different standards (Raven and Taconis 2005: 42–51). The pioneering studies from the 1960s onwards are still useful (e.g. Dawson and Gray 1968; Gray and Slow 1968;

David 1979; Cockburn and Cockburn 1980), but partially outdated because of the advances in radiology over the past twenty-five years, especially CT scanning, and because of changes in Egyptological knowledge and interpretation.

Meanwhile, some museums have updated the studies on their human and animal remains from Egypt, above all the Rijksmuseum van Oudheden in Leiden, in a path-breaking collaboration with the Academic Medical Centre of the University of Amsterdam (Raven and Taconis 2005). Other collections have published interdisciplinary mummy projects including Graeco-Roman mummies, either as monographs (e.g. Delorenzi and Grilletto 1989; Francot et al. 1999; Guidotti et al. 2001; Matouschek 2002; Wisseman 2003; Küffer et al. 2007; Germer, Kischkewitz, and Lüning 2009), in exhibition catalogues (e.g. Germer and Drenkhahn 1991; Germer 1997; Landesmuseum Württemberg 2007), or in the form of articles (e.g. Germer et al. 1995; Filer 1997). Selected results from elsewhere are scattered in scholarly journals and therefore difficult to locate, if available at all (e.g. Christensen 1969; Janssens and Duquenne 1973; Mininberg 2001), while work on other projects is referred to as being in progress. Nevertheless, mummy research is ongoing worldwide, backed by steadily advancing technologies.

General Knowledge and General Prejudice

The artificial mummification of corpses in order to protect them from destruction, and to provide the deceased's soul with a complete and functioning body for the afterlife, was practised in ancient Egypt for more than 4,000 years. From the earliest attempts around the middle of the fourth millenium BCE (at Hierakonpolis) until the last examples in the sixth to seventh centuries CE, embalming techniques, as well as funerary rituals and burial practices, underwent major changes (surveys include Dunand and Lichtenberg 1998; Ikram and Dodson 1998; Taylor 2001). It is well known that the methods of mummification developed from experimental stages to various types, which are characteristic of their respective eras. There has also been common consensus that, after a peak during the 21st dynasty, the techniques gradually declined throughout the Late period, mainly owing to increasing production and negligent workmanship. Especially for the Graeco-Roman era, when the emphasis seemed to be placed on the decoration and equipment of a mummy rather than on the body itself, embalmers and their workshops became discredited in the Egyptologist's eyes (e.g. Smith and Dawson 1924: 123–32; Bataille 1952: 216–17; Gray and Slow 1968: 6).

This view, based on previous research by autopsy and by X-ray examination of mummies, has remained a doctrine to the present day (e.g. Ikram and Dodson 1998: 51; Wisseman 2003: 9; Aufderheide 2005: 248–9), and is only gradually changing (Calament 2005: 1.293–9; and see below). However, with a figure of around fifty Roman samples then available, the results can by no means be considered representative in view of the thousands of bodies from the period, when a large part of the population underwent mummification procedures (Dunand and Lichtenberg 1995: 3260; Lichtenberg 1996: 2751–2). To do justice to the Roman embalmers, one has to judge the issue by including the numerous examples now known, and by considering the evidence in a wider context.

The reasons for careless workmanship appear to have remained the same at least from the New Kingdom onwards. As early as the 18th dynasty, mummies of non-royal individuals sometimes feature only rudimentary mummification techniques, without evisceration or brain removal (Taylor 2001: 85–7). In all periods, one frequent reason for the poor condition of mummies was to reduce expenses, and another was the advanced decomposition of the corpses before embalmers could begin their work (Taylor 1995: 82–4, 86–8, 90). The environment of a hot country like Egypt caused bodies to deteriorate rapidly. Beyond that, fatal accidents could effect massive damage, necessitating restoration efforts that were still employed in Roman times (e.g. Macke 2002: 88–9, pl. 55; Macke, Macke-Ribet, and Connan 2002: 100–3, fig. 30, pl. IXa–b; Aufderheide et al. 2004: 66, 85). Since mummies of private persons from earlier periods are rare, these features turn up especially in Graeco-Roman times. At worst, the estimated number of carelessly embalmed corpses during the Roman era rises to 50 per cent, which was probably an unvarying average (Dunand and Lichtenberg 1995: 3261). The radiological examination of seven Roman mummies from the British Museum showed two of the skeletons as being in excellent order, three in good order, one in some disorder, and only one in poor anatomical order (Filer 1997).

In fact, many of the significant post-mortem bone defects and fractures in corpses of this period were caused by the intense pressure applied by embalming priests during the process of arranging the close-fitting geometrical bandaging, or by putting the mummies into narrow coffins (e.g. Germer, Kischkewitz, and Lüning 2009: 65, 140–1, 155–7). In sum, one can conclude that embalming practices in the first three centuries CE were, as always, largely a question of cost rather than a matter of deteriorating standards (see below).

Mummification at Thebes in the Roman Period

Outside of the specific Graeco-Roman necropoleis, many of the most carefully prepared Roman mummies found in Egypt came to light at the cemeteries on the west bank of Thebes, where from the late first century BCE until the late third century CE deceased members of the elite were treated with both traditional and innovative mummification techniques. Besides the gilding of the skin, the extended arm position in contrast to the typical Ptolemaic 'Osiris position' (arms crossed over the chest) soon became general practice (Gray 1972; Raven and Taconis 2005: 157, 170; and see below). Furthermore, the reuse of earlier tombs made this area a centre of collective inhumations for the inhabitants of the local villages in Roman times until the mid-fourth century (Vandorpe 1995: 237–8; Strudwick 2003: 167–88). With the substantial number of more than 300 Roman specimens from the Valley of the Queens, a variety of generally good mummification methods employed could be investigated (Macke 2002; Macke, Macke-Ribet, and Connan 2002). This section considers one group of unprovenanced specimens in museums, for which a previously suggested Theban origin can now be confirmed, as well as several groups of mummies found in earlier excavations (Riggs 2003; 2005: 175–244).

Mummies with Individually Wrapped Limbs

To date, only one group of very well-mummified corpses has been considered as being of exceptional quality for Roman times. These mummies—males, females, and one child—were bandaged with the limbs extended and wrapped separately before the outer bandaging took place. Any outer wrappings are now lost, and the original methods of burial remain unknown, since the mummies were purchased around the 1840s from the Egyptian antiquities trade. The corpses received careful treatment, including excerebration and evisceration; occasionally some visceral packages were returned into the body cavities. This group, of a very similar, integral type, is represented by eight anonymous examples, some of them with a painted face-wrapping: one in the British Museum (Dawson and Gray 1968, no. 64); two in Liverpool (Gray and Slow 1968, nos 1–2); one in Rio de Janeiro (Kitchen and da Beltrão 1990: 227–8); one in Avignon (Foissy-Aufrère 1985: 101–2, 271 inv. A.84); and three in Leiden (Raven and Taconis 2005, cat. 29–31). Two of the male adults and the child in Avignon show a peculiar and artificial accentuation of the breasts.

To these examples, several skulls (e.g. Aubert and Cortopassi 1998, cat. 25; Raven and Taconis 2005, cat. 43) and a well-preserved female mummy, brought from Thebes to Berlin in 1826 together with its painted wooden coffin, can be added (Berlin, Ägyptisches Museum und Papyrussammlung ÄM 836–7, in Germer, Kischkewitz, and Lüning 2009: 87–91, figs 126–36). With the elaborate bandaging and modelling of the corpse (arms extended alongside the body; arms, legs, fingers, and toes wrapped separately; coloured linen straps imitating sandals; toenails covered with dyed linen; accentuation of the breasts), the 'Osiris Hathor' Ta-sherit-net-Osiris fits perfectly into the scheme of this mummy type (for the designation of deceased females as 'Hathor' or 'Osiris Hathor', see Riggs 2005: 45; for its further use in Roman times, see Smith 1987: 129–31). Since the (most probably associated) anthropoid coffin is also preserved, it is possible to assign the ensemble on iconographic and stylistic grounds to a date slightly earlier than the coffins belonging to the 'Soternalia' (see below; Riggs and Depauw 2002, pls 9–11), and a date in the late first or early second century CE seems probable.

Raven and Taconis (2005: 195, 199, 203) date the whole group to the third century CE, which seems too late in the light of this new evidence, and also considering the Ptolemaic forerunners. At that time, the practice of wrapping the (then crossed) arms and all other limbs separately was already in use, as well as the painted face-wrapping (e.g. Munich, Staatliches Museum Ägyptischer Kunst ÄS 73b; Ziegelmayer 1985, figs 1, 17–22, front and back cover). Certainly, the distinction between late Ptolemaic and Roman specimens of this group and their precise dating needs further investigation (Taylor 2001: 90–1, no. 53 ('Ptolemaic or Roman Period')). In any event, the costly embalming methods attest to a prosperous social status for people of this group and their relatives, even in the absence of names and titles.

Mummies from the Rhind Tomb (Not Preserved)

When Alexander Rhind explored a rock-cut New Kingdom tomb at Gurna in 1857 (not yet relocated; Riggs 2005: 179–82), he found several intrusive burials from the time of Augustus including the mummies of Montsuef and his wife, Tanuat, most famous because of their funerary papyri (*P Rhind* I and II; Smith 2009, texts 14–15). Montsuef himself died in 9 BCE, and the whole group can be dated to the late first century BCE or early first century CE. Since he and his male relatives had attained high military offices during the end of the Ptolemaic and the early Roman periods, their burials might well reflect the mummification methods used for members of the Theban elite during this period of transition. Although Rhind's description is not very detailed, the equipment of the mummies with numerous layers of resin-soaked textiles, exterior shrouds with a painted bead net pattern, and especially

Montsuef's gilded face mask and wreath of golden leaves are proof of the very elaborate practices employed (Rhind 1862: 103–11, pl. 6; Manley and Dodson 2010, nos 50–1).

The technique of embedding funerary amulets in a layer of heated black resins, which later hardened and thus held them in place within the wrappings, is recorded here for the last time, to the best of my knowledge (compare a Ptolemaic mummy in Liverpool; Gray and Slow 1968, no. 13). The position of the glass amulets of the four sons of Horus (the protective deities for the internal organs), over the left part of the abdomen, is quite significant and points indirectly to an incision beneath the inner wrappings (Rhind 1862: 110–11, pl. 7). The arms are described as first bound individually and then brought down by the sides, with the hands resting under the thighs. The gilding of the upper part of Montsuef's body with thick gold leaf, described also for other mummies from the tomb, shows the expensive and at least partially innovative standard of these burials.

Mummies of the Soter Family

The extant mummies of this family group are now in museums in Paris, Leiden, London, Berlin, and Turin, and all appear to come from TT 32, a 19th dynasty tomb at Sheikh abd el-Gurna (Karig 2008). The elaborate embalming techniques employed, comprising excerebration, evisceration, and the abundant use of costly resins, attest to a comparably high standard for the late first and early second centuries CE. The corpse of Petamenophis (Ammonios), who died in 116 CE, is still in excellent condition with his curly hair completely preserved (Aubert and Cortopassi 1998, cat. 2; Herbin 2002, figs 35–6). There is a prominent incision in the left side of the abdomen, and the whole corpse shows a very deep black colour. The analysis of the embalming substances, including beeswax and different vegetal and animal fats and oils, has revealed that the dark colour of the skin is caused by the colouring effects of pitch and bitumen, most probably originating from the Dead Sea region (Connan 2005: 179–80, fig. 7, table 4).

Besides some remnants of leaf gilding on the skin (Zimmer 1993, no. 7), two eye plates and a tongue plate of gold leaf were found (Herbin 2002, figs 36, 38). Finally, his mummy was wrapped in a bead-net-painted shroud and adorned with a gilded copper crown imitating myrtle (Herbin 2002, fig. 37; Aubert et al. 2008, cat. 19). The production of faience bead nets had ceased at the end of the Ptolemaic era, and the bead net ascribed (Herbin 2002, fig. 39) seems not to have belonged to this burial, according to early nineteenth century reports of the unwrapping in Paris (G. Pierrat-Bonnefois, personal communication).

Another characteristic feature of these mummies is the enormous amount of linen, which gives the impression of a bulky cocoon (Herbin 2002, figs 13, 19, 23, 34; Raven and Taconis 2005, figs I.4, 26.1). In combination with several layers of resins between the wrappings and large quantities of embalming liquids poured into the abdominal cavities, the mummies became very heavy: Petamenophis, whose corpse weighs around 40 kg, had a wrapped weight of 106 kg (Aubert et al. 2008: 130); his sisters Sensaos and Kleopatra were treated in a similar way (Dawson and Gray 1968, no. 63; Raven and Taconis 2005, cat. 26; Riggs 2005, nos 76, 78). The same method of bulky wrappings and an abundance of resins, partially soaking through the bandages, was used for the embalming of the children Phaminis (?), Sensaos, and Tkauthi (Germer, Kischkewitz, and Lüning 2009: 57–67, figs 78–90; Riggs 2005, nos 74, 75). In addition, the mummy of a boy also named Petamenophis shows an elaborate lozenge pattern for its outer bandages (Delorenzi and Grilletto 1989: 23, pl. VIa–b; Herbin 2002, fig. 23; Riggs 2005, no. 82).

He also wears a gilded myrtle wreath, a feature that points to Greek funerary customs (Blech 1982: 81–109). However, the manifest connection with the Egyptian concept of the 'crown of justification' presented to the deceased and symbolizing the positive outcome of the judgement of the dead (Beinlich-Seeber 2006: 30–1, 40, nn. 15–19, pl. 7a,c) is, from the perspective of classical archaeology, not beyond question (e.g. Borg 1998: 71–2).

Mummies with Similarities to the Soter Group

Several mummies with coffins whose decoration broadly resembles that of the Soter family's coffins have no specific link with the family ('Soternalia'; see Riggs and Depauw 2002; for the strange-looking headpieces of the anthropoid coffin lids, see Haslauer 2006). Instead, the similarities in decoration may be due to work carried out in the same workshops, perhaps by different artisans and over a longer period of time (probably all dating to the second century CE). The mummies are presented below, according to their present museum locations.

Edinburgh, National Museum of Scotland

Two mummies of infant boys named Petamun and Penhorpabik were buried in a unique double, anthropoid coffin (Dawson 1927: 290–1, figs 2–3; Riggs 2005, no. 89; Manley and Dodson 2010, no. 61). They were adorned with bead necklaces, some amulets, and a funerary papyrus (Coenen 2003: 112–18). Here again, a very elaborate treatment of body and skin could be observed on one of the mummies unwrapped before it entered the museum; it was eviscerated (small incision mentioned), and had had the brain removed via the left nostril. Dawson remarked that in contrast to the generally very summary treatment of children's mummies, extraordinarily careful embalming methods had been employed for this boy, and concluded a wealthy family background (Dawson 1927: 292–4). CT scanning of the unwrapped boy revealed that the arms are extended with the palms resting on the outer surface of the thighs (L.-A. Liddiard, personal communication).

Florence, Archaeological Museum

Three coffins brought from Thebes in 1828–9 contained the well-preserved mummies of a man, a woman, and a girl. The man's coffin is inscribed for Telesphoros (Guidotti et al. 2001, no. 11/11A; Riggs 2005, no. 90); the woman's coffin is anonymous (Guidotti et al. 2001, no. 9/9A); and the girl can be identified as Kuper (Guidotti 2001 et al., no. 10/10A, as 'Giupra'; Riggs 2005, no. 92). This name is attested on two papyri found in her coffin, which are a pair of texts called the Book of Breathing (M. C. Guidotti, personal communication). As the blossoms of the henna shrub are intensely fragrant, Kuper appears appropriate as a girl's name (*kwpr* = blossom of henna; reading and translation by J. F. Quack, personal communication).

Tübingen, Collection of the Institute of Egyptology

A decorated anthropoid coffin, formerly in the Lindenmuseum in Stuttgart, contained the mummy of an adult male of advanced age (Brunner-Traut and Brunner 1981: 207–8, 234–7,

251, 253, pls 156–7; Riggs 2005, no. 103; Haslauer 2006: 125–6, fig. 4c). The mummy is well preserved owing to the embalming methods (transnasal excerebration; evisceration via the abdominal incision in the left flank), and the arms are extended. Traces of gold on the face and chest point to the typical Roman leaf gilding of the skin (Zimmer 1993, no. 25).

Mummies in London, Turin, and Klagenfurt

Other well-mummified corpses of this group (excerebrated, eviscerated, and with the arms extended) include a male mummy in London, wrapped in a bead-net-painted shroud (British Museum; Dawson and Gray 1968, no. 61; Riggs 2005, no. 97); a similarly decorated boy's mummy in Turin (Egyptian Museum; Delorenzi and Grilletto 1989: 26, pl. IXa–b); and a masked female mummy in Klagenfurt (Landesmuseum; Horak, Hamernik, and Harrauer 1999, cat. 43). Although this mummy was perhaps not originally associated with the coffin, all certainly belong to the same workshop and date range (Riggs 2005, no. 93, pl. 10).

Mummies of the Pebos Family Group (Not Preserved)

Another group of Roman mummies was found undisturbed in a chamber beneath an abandoned house at Deir el-Medina. The mummies appear to date to the mid- to late second century CE, based on the style of mummy mask decoration and coffin inscriptions, and were unwrapped on site by the excavators (Riggs 2005: 205–17, figs 102–3, and nos 109–14 for the masks). The well-recorded observations made at the autopsy of these mummies clearly disprove the prejudice of negligent and hasty Roman embalming techniques (Bruyère and Bataille 1936–7, 1939). However, the careful treatment and the consistently high quality of the workmanship, which includes evisceration, partial gilding of the skin (Zimmer 1993: 15, 17–18, nos 1–4), and adornment with gilded wax amulets on certain parts of the body, have only exceptionally been noticed by scholars (Montserrat and Meskell 1997: 189–90; Riggs 2005: 211). Five of the six masked mummies, all with their arms extended and wrapped in many layers of linen, had a red shroud with a painted bead net (Bruyère and Bataille 1936–7: 152–3, pls 3–4, 7).

Mummies of the Deir el-Bahri Group

Similar observations on excellent mummification methods were made on a group of mummies at Deir el-Bahri, most of which were unwrapped on site in the 1920s by the expedition of the Metropolitan Museum of Art, New York (Riggs and Depauw 2002; Riggs 2005: 232–43, reference on p. 243): 'The skilful mummification…is significant; the corpses were eviscerated, embalmed, gilded, and carefully wrapped in layers of sheets and padding, attesting that this treatment was still valued and practised for the dead.' Along with the numerous mummy masks of this group, all datable to the late third century CE (Riggs 2005, nos 122–50), at least five complete mummies made their way into museums and are still extant (Riggs 2005, nos 125 and 142 (Egyptian Museum, Cairo); no. 132 (Peabody Museum of Natural History, Yale University); no. 133 (Metropolitan Museum of Art); and no. 141 (Brooklyn Museum of Art)).

The male mummy in Brooklyn, lying on its back with the arms extended and the hands resting on the thighs, was in excellent condition, with the soft tissue almost perfectly preserved except for the original leaf gilding of the skin (E. Bleiberg, personal communication). After radiological examination, this mummy has recently been rewrapped in its enormous amount of original linen, with the mask on top (Loos 2010).

Mummies from Cemeteries in the Kharga and Dakhla Oases

More recent excavations at various sites in Kharga and Dakhla have incorporated the anthropological study of a substantial number of Roman (and some Ptolemaic) mummies. This material has enabled scientific research on the physical remains of nearly the entire population of the respective settlements (Dunand and Lichtenberg 2002: 75–8, 91–107; Bowen and Hope 2003; Aufderheide et al. 2004). The formidable results offer significant proof that the observable differences in the quality of the embalming in Roman Egypt by no means attest to an all-time low, but are in fact an indication of social stratification. Even for a relatively poor population living in rural communities, the mummification methods employed from the first century CE onwards were of rather good quality and reflect various levels of body treatment (e.g. Dunand et al. 1992: 199–206, 266; Ibrahim et al. 2008).

Gilding the Skin: Gold, the 'Flesh' of the Gods

From ancient times, gold was considered the colour of the life-giving sun-god and of gods in general. As Egyptian funerary belief entailed the deceased's transition into the divine sphere, mummies could be equipped with gold-coloured (or, for kings, solid gold) face masks and coffins. The gilding of the skin itself, mainly on the face, chest, arms, and legs, or even a complete gilding of the body with very thin gold leaf, became common only in the Roman period; its earlier antecedents are unclear (Dunand and Lichtenberg 1995: 3266–8; 1998: 109). For Antinoopolis, gilding was reportedly done with thin plates around 4 cm long, the longest one up to 10 cm. The most spectacular mummy of this type is housed in the Museum of Dunkirk (Zimmer 1993, no. 11, pl. I; Calament 2005: 1.297–8, fig. 38b; 2.420 n. 555; and *passim*). Zimmer lists twenty-eight complete mummies with skin gilding, twenty-five heads, and several parts of bodies (which could be updated to include, for example, Aubert and Cortopassi 1998, cat. 9).

In addition to the distinctive feature of the extended arm position, gilding can thus be a dating criterion for Roman period mummies, used, for instance, to date three unwrapped children's mummies in the British Museum (Dawson and Gray 1968, nos 71–3; Zimmer 1993, nos 19–21). There are similarly ornamented mummies of children in Frankfurt (Schultz, Gessler-Löhr, and Kollath 1995: 317, one of two examples); Leipzig (Germer et al. 1995: 141–2, 144–5, figs 2–3); Cairo (Hawass 2004–5: 35); Aargau (Küffer et al. 2007: 189, fig. 3); and Berlin (Germer, Kischkewitz, and Lüning 2009: 207–8, fig. 323).

Besides, or as an alternative to, gilding the skin, mummies could be equipped with gold leaf in the form of small objects placed into the mouth or directly on the skin, in order to protect and to revive vital parts of the body, such as the eyes, lips, tongue, breasts, navel, genitals, and the nails of fingers and toes (Andrews 1994: 69–70, fig. 73b, d; Depauw 2004: 234). Many of these flimsy amulets, which often imitate the shape and the texture of the respective parts of the body (Fig. 40.2), were found during excavations, for instance at Hawara (Petrie 1912, pl. 36.1–16) and Marina el-Alamein (Daszewski 1997: 63–4, pl. 6.4). Others were found in mummies in museums by autopsy (e.g. Janssens and Duquenne 1973: 22–3, figs 24–5; Herbin 2002, fig. 38) or by radiographic examination (e.g. Gray and Slow 1968, no. 7; Macleod et al. 2000, figs 3–4; Raven and Taconis 2005: 180, fig. 2; 183).

Sometimes the round shape and the relative thickness of a tongue plate reveals the object to belong to another type of amulet (e.g. Janssens and Duquenne 1973: 3–4, fig. 2; 12–13, fig. 11 (from Bruxelles E. 4857, only the mummy portrait preserved)), or to represent an obol, a coin that attests to the Greek practice of providing the deceased with the fare for the ferryman Charon in the netherworld (Germer et al. 1995: 148, fig. 8; 150; Kákosy 1995: 3012–13; Nenna 2002, fig. 28). In fact, in Roman Egypt this custom was more often practised by putting the coin into the wrappings in or above the mummy's hand (e.g. Janssens and Duquenne 1973: 17–18, fig. 18; 20–1, fig. 22; Hawass 2000: 78–9).

FIG. 40.2 Gold foil eye and tongue plates were found in Roman mummies as protective amulets for the respective organs, and to guarantee the faculties of sight and speech

British Museum EA 15717 and 16519. Courtesy of the Trustees of the British Museum.

In the Valley of the Queens nineteen well-mummified bodies of people of a presumably privileged social status had been provided with small pastilles made of gilded, bitumen-covered beeswax in various forms (round, oval, oblong, rectangular, each around 1–1.5 cm). As a rule, between one and four items were put on different parts of a corpse and even inside the abdominal cavities, which has been explained as a local practice (Macke, Macke-Ribet, and Connan 2002: 107–11, fig. 33, pl. xc–d). Small gilded plates of bitumen or wood were found in the orbits and on the front of a mummy named Leukyone at Antinoopolis (Calament 2005: 1.298, fig. 38a; 2.389 n. 409; cf. Parlasca and Seemann 1999: 31, fig. 16). Eye prostheses of beeswax or gilded stucco, as well as gilded wax amulets on the front, mouth, chest, and feet, were identified on some of the mummies of the Pebos family group, discussed above.

Mummification as a Question of Cost

In sum, Roman embalming practices turn out to be in agreement with Herodotus' oft-quoted observation about three different classes of mummification, depending on the expenses that the relatives could afford (Taylor 2001: 50–1; Dunand and Lichtenberg 2002: 24–8). Similar information was given for the first century BCE by Diodorus (1.91), who records three price levels: high (1 talent = 60 minae = 6,000 drachmas), middle (20 minae = 2,000 drachmas, i.e. one-third of the best quality), and low (unspecified amount) (Counts 1996: 201 and n. 60). In a Ptolemaic papyrus, the price of a funeral is attested to be 2,000 silver drachmas, which thus corresponds to the middle price class of Diodorus (Depauw 2004: 241).

Since the estimated annual middle-class income in the second to third century CE was around 200 to 300 drachmas, and the expenditures for a mid-level funeral in an inscription from Soknopaiou Nesos amounted to over 440 drachmas (Parlasca and Seemann 1999, cat. 108), there was a great difference between most people's means and the costs of mummification and burial (Montserrat 1997; Borg 1998: 56–9).

The leaf gilding of the skin has been observed on Roman mummies at many cemeteries in Egypt (see above and Zimmer 1993: 35; for evidence in Rome, see Chioffi 1998, nos 11, 12), and was a typical feature of embalming methods for the upper classes. In Kharga Oasis investigation has revealed that this costly practice was apparently carried out only on the notables of a community: twelve out of 345 mummies at Douch, and twelve (or fourteen) out of seventy (or sixty-seven) specimens at Ain el Labakha had small pieces of gold foil applied to different parts of the body (Dunand and Lichtenberg 1998: 102; 2002, pls 15, 24; Ibrahim et al. 2008: 125–6, figs 39, 133, 171, 187, 207).

Conclusion

The question of whether mummies from Roman Egypt attest a decline or a late heyday of mummification techniques can be answered firmly in favour of the latter. The different but generally high standards of embalming, using traditional as well as innovative Egyptian craftsmanship including excerebration, evisceration, and large quantities of embalming resins and linen, were dependent on two factors: cost and local practices. The use of extensive linen wrappings, mummy decoration (masks, shrouds, portraits, etc.), amulets, jewellery, and other burial goods, and the gilding of the skin, often correspond to high-quality mummification. However, the extremely high expense of a first-class burial in Roman Egypt was beyond almost everyone's reach.

Suggested Reading

Several substantial publications by Dunand and Lichtenberg cited in the Bibliography provide an excellent and multifarious insight into mummification practices in Roman Egypt. They are in the main based on the authors' work in Kharga Oasis, but include studies on different sites in Egypt and from several museums as well. Considerable results have been accomplished by Bowen, Hope, and Aufderheide in Dakhla Oasis. Other collaborative studies, such as Macke, Macke-Ribet, and Connan (2002) (based on excavations in Thebes), offer a remarkable insight into mummification techniques in the Nile Valley during Roman times, and throw light on the unexpected possibilities of present-day radiological technologies (based on museum research; Raven and Taconis 2005; Küffer et al. 2007). For elaborately decorated mummies from Hawara, see the scientific study of a rhomboid-wrapped male portrait mummy in Edinburgh (Macleod et al. 2000; compare Walker and Bierbrier 1997, cat. 22). See further Germer et al. (1993) and Germer, Kischkewitz, and Lüning (2009: 153–60) on children's mummies from the so-called 'tomb of Aline', and Filer (1999), which discusses, among others, the well-known portrait mummies of Hermione and Artemidorus (Walker and Bierbrier 1997, cat. 11 and 32). A very special feature of mummification practices in Roman Egypt is provided in the publication of the red-shrouded portrait mummy of Herakleides in the Getty Museum, with a mummified ibis lying across the abdomen within the wrappings, detected by CT scanning (Corcoran and Svoboda 2011).

Bibliography

Andrews, C. 1994. *Amulets of Ancient Egypt*. London: British Museum Press; Austin: University of Texas Press.

Ascenzi, A., and P. Bianco. 1998. 'The Roman Mummy of Grottarossa', in A. Cockburn, E. Cockburn, and T. A. Reyman (eds), *Mummies, Disease and Ancient Cultures*, 2nd edn. Cambridge: Cambridge University Press, 263–6.

Aubert, M.-F., and R. Cortopassi (eds) 1998. *Portraits de l'Égypte romaine*. Paris: Réunion des Musées Nationaux.

—— et al. 2008. *Portraits funéraires de l'Égypte romaine* II: *Cartonnages, linceuls et bois*. Paris: Réunion des Musées Nationaux and Institut Khéops.

Aufderheide, A. C. 2005. *The Scientific Study of Mummies*. Cambridge: Cambridge University Press.

—— et al. 2004. 'Mummification Practices at Kellis Site in Egypt's Dakhleh Oasis', *Journal of the Society of the Studies of Egyptian Antiquities* 31: 63–86.

Bagnall, R. S. 2006. *Hellenistic and Roman Egypt: Sources and Approaches*. Aldershot: Ashgate Variorum.

Bataille, A. 1952. *Les Memnonia: Recherches de papyrologie et d'épigraphie grecque sur la nécropole de la Thèbes d'Égypte aux époques hellénistiques et romaine*. Cairo: Institut Français d'Archéologie Orientale.

Beinlich-Seeber, C. 2006. 'Painted Judgement Scene on Wood, R344', in K. N. Sowada and B. G. Ockinga (eds), *Egyptian Art in the Nicholson Museum, Sydney*. Sydney: Mediterranean Archaeology, 27–43.

Blech, M. 1982. *Studien zum Kranz bei den Griechen*. Berlin: de Gruyter.

Bleiberg, E., and K. M. Cooney. 2008. *To Live Forever: Egyptian Treasures from the Brooklyn Museum*. Brooklyn: Brooklyn Museum; London: Giles.

Boës, É., P. Georges, and G. Alix. 2002. 'Des momies dans les ossuaires de la Nécropolis d'Alexandrie: Quand l'éternité a une fin', in A. Charron (ed.), *La mort n'est pas une fin*. Arles: Musée de l'Arles Antique, 68–71.

Borg, B. E. 1997. 'The Dead as Guest at the Table?', in M. L. Bierbrier (ed.), *Portraits and Masks: Burial Customs in Roman Egypt*. London: British Museum Press, 26–32.

—— 1998. *Der zierlichste Anblick der Welt*. Mainz: von Zabern.

Bowen, G. E., and C. A. Hope (eds) 2003. *The Oasis Papers 3: Proceedings of the Third International Conference of the Dakhleh Oasis Project*. Oxford: Oxbow.

Brunner-Traut, E., and H. Brunner. 1981. *Die ägyptische Sammlung der Universität Tübingen*. Mainz: von Zabern.

Bruyère, B., and A. Bataille. 1936–7. 'Une tombe gréco-romaine de Deir el Médineh, I–II', *Bulletin de l'Institut Français d'Archéologie Orientale* 36: 145–63.

—— —— 1939. 'Une tombe gréco-romaine de Deir el Médineh, III–IV', *Bulletin de l'Institut Français d'Archéologie Orientale* 38: 73–107.

Budischovsky, M.-C. 2004. 'Témoignages de dévotion isiaque et traces culturelles le long du limes danubien', in L. Bricault (ed.), *Isis en Occident*. Leiden: Brill, 171–91.

Calament, F. 2005. *La révélation d'Antinoé par Albert Gayet: Histoire, archéologie, muséographie*, 2 vols. Cairo: Institut Français d'Archéologie Orientale.

Chioffi, L. 1998. *Mummificazione e imbalsamazione a Roma ed in altri luoghi del mondo romano*. Rome: Quasar.

Christensen, O. E. 1969. 'Un examen radiologique des momies égyptiennes des musées danois', *La Semaine des Hôpiteaux de Paris* 45/28 (14 juin), 1990–8.

Cockburn, A., and E. Cockburn (eds) 1980. *Mummies, Disease and Ancient Cultures*. Cambridge: Cambridge University Press.

Coenen, M. 2003. 'The *Documents of Breathing* in the Royal Museum of Edinburgh', *Studien zur Altägyptischen Kultur* 32: 105–18.

Connan, J. 2005. 'La momification dans l'Égypte ancienne: Le bitume et les autres ingrédients organiques des baumes de momies', in S. H. Aufrère (ed.), *Encyclopédie religieuse de l'Univers végétal*, vol. 3. Montpellier: Université Paul Valéry, 163–211.

Corcoran, L. H. 1995. *Portrait Mummies from Roman Egypt (I–IV Centuries A.D.)*. Chicago: Oriental Institute.

Corcoran, L. H. and M. Svoboda. 2011. *Herakleides: A Portrait Mummy from Roman Egypt*. Malibu, Calif.: Getty.

Counts, D. B. 1996. '*Regum Externorum Consuetudine*: The Nature and Function of Embalming in Rome', *Classical Antiquity* 15: 189–202.

Daszewski, W. A. 1997. 'Mummy Portraits from Northern Egypt: The Necropolis in Marina el-Alamein', in M. L. Bierbrier (ed.), *Portraits and Masks: Burial Customs in Roman Egypt*. London: British Museum Press, 59–65.

David, A. R. (ed.) 1979. *Manchester Museum Mummy Project: Multidisciplinary Research on Ancient Egyptian Mummified Remains*. Manchester: Manchester University Press.

Dawson, W. R. 1927. 'On Two Egyptian Mummies Preserved in the Museums of Edinburgh', *Proceedings of the Society of Antiquarians of Scotland* 61: 290–6.

——and P. H. K. Gray. 1968. *Catalogue of Egyptian Antiquities in the British Museum*, vol. 1: *Mummies and Human Remains*. London: British Museum Press.

Delorenzi, E., and R. Grilletto (eds) 1989. *Le mummie del Museo Egizio di Torino N. 13001–13026, indagine antropo-radiologica*. Milan: Istituto Editoriale Cisalpino—La Goliardica.

Depauw, M. 2004. 'New Light on Gilding in Hellenistic Egypt: P. dem. Vindob. Barbara 58', in H. Harrauer and R. Pintaudi (eds), *Gedenkschrift Ulrike Horak (P. Horak)*. Florence: Gonnelli, 233–46.

Dunand, F. 2004. 'Funerary Beliefs and Rituals', in F. Dunand and C. Zivie-Coche, *Gods and Men in Egypt: 3000 BCE to 395 CE*. Ithaca, NY: Cornell University Press, 319–38.

——and R. Lichtenberg. 1995. 'Pratiques et croyances funéraires en Égypte romaine', in W. Haase and H. Temporini (eds), *Aufstieg und Niedergang der römischen Welt* II 18.5. Berlin: de Gruyter, 3216–3315.

————1998. *Les momies et la mort en Égypte*. Paris: Errance.

————2002. *Momies d'Égypte et d'ailleurs*. Monaco: Rocher.

————2008. 'Dix ans d'exploration des nécropoles d'el-Deir (Oasis de Kharga): Un premier bilan', *Chronique d'Égypte* 83: 258–76.

——et al. 1992. *La nécropole: Exploration archéologique*. Cairo: Institut Français d'Archéologie Orientale.

——et al. 2005. *La nécropole de Douch: Exploration archéologique*, vol. 2. Cairo: Institut Français d'Archéologie Orientale.

Filer, J. 1997. 'If the Face Fits... A Comparison of Mummies and their Accompanying Portraits Using Computerised Axial Tomography', in M. L. Bierbrier (ed.), *Portraits and Masks: Burial Customs in Roman Egypt*. London: British Museum, 121–6.

——1999. 'Ein Blick auf die Menschen hinter den Porträts', in K. Parlasca and H. Seemann (eds), *Augenblicke: Mumienporträts und Ägyptische Grabkunst aus Römischer Zeit*. Munich: Klinkhardt & Biermann, 79–86.

Foissy-Aufrère, M.-P. (ed.) 1985. *Égypte et Provence*. Avignon: Musée Calvet.

Forrer, R. 1895. *Mein Besuch in el-Achmim: Reisebriefe aus Ägypten*. Strasbourg: Schlesier.

Francot, C., et al. 1999. *Les momies égyptiennes des Musées Royaux d'Art et d'Histoire à Bruxelles et leur étude radiographique*. Turnhout: Brepols.

Germer, R. 1997. *Das Geheimnis der Mumien: Ewiges Leben am Nil*. Munich: Prestel.

——and R. Drenkhahn (eds) 1991. *Mumie und Computer: Ein multidisziplinäres Forschungsprojekt in Hannover*. Hannover: Kestner Museum.

——H. Kischkewitz, and M. Lüning. 2009. *Berliner Mumiengeschichten: Ergebnisse eines multidisziplinären Forschungsprojektes*. Berlin: Staatliche Museen zu Berlin—Stiftung Preußischer Kulturbesitz.

——et al. 1993. 'Das Grab der Aline und die Untersuchung der darin gefundenen Kindermumien', *Antike Welt* 24/3: 186–96.

——et al. 1995. 'Untersuchung der altägyptischen Mumien des Ägyptischen Museums der Universität Leipzig und des Museums für Völkerkunde Leipzig', *Zeitschrift für Ägyptische Sprache und Altertumskunde* 122: 137–54.

Gray, P. H. K. 1972. 'Notes Concerning the Position of Arms and Hands of Mummies with a View to Possible Dating of the Specimen', *Journal of Egyptian Archaeology* 58: 200–4.

—— and D. Slow. 1968. *Egyptian Mummies in the City of Liverpool Museums*. Liverpool: Liverpool Corporation.

Grévin, G., and P. Bailet. 2002. 'La crémation en Égypte au temps des Ptolémées', in A. Charron (ed.), *La mort n'est pas une fin*. Arles: Musée de l'Arles Antique, 62–5.

Grimm, G. 1997. 'Verbrannte Pharaonen?', *Antike Welt* 28/3: 233–49.

Guidotti, M. C., et al. 2001. *Le mummie del Museo Egizio di Firenze*. Florence: Giunti.

Haslauer, E. 2006. 'Gesichter von Särgen aus dem Asasif: Eine Ergänzung zu den Särgen der Soter-Familie', in E. Czerny et al. (eds), *Timelines: Studies in Honour of Manfred Bietak*, vol. 1. Leuven: Peeters, 121–8.

Hawass, Z. 2000. *Valley of the Golden Mummies*. London: Virgin; Cairo: American University of Cairo Press.

—— 2004–5. 'The EMP: Egyptian Mummy Project', *KMT: A Modern Journal of Ancient Egypt* 15/4: 29–38.

Herbin, F.-R. 2002. *Padiimenipet fils de Sôter: Histoire d'une famille dans l'Égypte romaine*. Paris: Réunion des Musées Nationaux.

Horak, U., G. Hamernik, and H. Harrauer. 1999. *'Mumie-Schau'n': Totenkult im hellenistisch-römerzeitlichen Ägypten*. Linz: Magistrat der Landeshauptstadt Linz.

Ibrahim, B. A., et al. 2008. *Le matériel archéologique et les restes humains de la nécropole d'Aïn el-Labakha (Oasis de Kharga)*. Paris: Cybèle.

Ikram, S. (ed.) 2005. *Divine Creatures: Animal Mummies in Ancient Egypt*. Cairo: American University in Cairo.

—— and A. Dodson. 1998. *The Mummy in Ancient Egypt: Equipping the Dead for Eternity*. London: Thames and Hudson.

Janssens, P. A., and F. Duquenne. 1973. 'Radiografisch en autoptisch onderzoek van twee mummies uit de romeinse periode 1970–1971', *Hades: Periodisch tijdschrift van de Antwerpse vereniging voor Boden- en Grotonderzoek* 26/12: 1–27.

Kákosy, L. 1995. 'Probleme der Religion im römerzeitlichen Ägypten', in W. Haase and H. Temporini (eds), *Aufstieg und Niedergang der römischen Welt* II 18.5. Berlin: de Gruyter, 2895–3048.

Karig, J. S. 2008. 'Das Grab des Soter: Zur Geschichte eines Fundkomplexes', *Hildesheimer Ägyptologische Beiträge* 50: 141–52.

Kitchen, K. A., and M. da Beltrão (eds) 1990. *Catalogue of the Egyptian Collection in the National Museum, Rio de Janeiro*. Warminster: Aris and Phillips.

Küffer, A., et al. 2007. *Unter dem Schutz der Himmelsgöttin: Ägyptische Särge, Mumien und Masken in der Schweiz*. Zurich: Chronos.

Kurth, D. 1990. *Der Sarg der Teüris: Eine Studie zum Totenglauben im römerzeitlichen Ägypten*. Mainz: von Zabern.

—— 2010. *Materialien zum Totenglauben im römerzeitlichen Ägypten*. Hützel: Backe.

Landesmuseum Württemberg, Stuttgart (ed.) 2007. *Ägyptische Mumien: Unsterblichkeit im Land der Pharonen*. Mainz: von Zabern.

Lichtenberg, R. 1996. 'La momification en Egypte à l'époque tardive', in W. Haase and H. Temporini (eds), *Aufstieg und Niedergang der römischen Welt* II 37.3. Berlin: de Gruyter, 2741–60.

Loos, T. 2010. 'Melvin the Mummy's New Clothes', *New York Times*, 6 May. <http://www.nytimes.com/2010/05/09/arts/design/09mummies.html>.

Macke, A. 2002. 'Les momies de la Vallée des Reines', in F. Dunand and R. Lichtenberg (eds), *Momies d'Égypte et d'ailleurs*. Monaco: Rocher, 78–91.

—— C. Macke-Ribet, and J. Connan. 2002. *Ta Set Neferou, une nécropole de Thèbes-Ouest et son histoire: Momification, chimie des baumes, anthropologie, paléopathologie*. Cairo: Dar Namatallah Press.

Macleod, R. I., et al. 2000. 'Mummy 1911-210-1', *Journal of the Royal College of Surgeons of Edinburgh* 45/2: 85–92. <http://www.rcsed.ac.uk/journal/vol45_2/4520022.htm>.

Manley, B., and A. Dodson. 2010. *Life Everlasting: National Museums Scotland Collection of Ancient Egyptian Coffins*. Edinburgh: NMS Enterprises.

Matouschek, E. (ed.) 2002. *Sieben Münchner Mumien: Anmerkungen und Untersuchungsberichte*. Wessobrunn: Socio-Medico & Agentur für medizinische Informationen GmbH.

Mininberg, D. T. 2001. 'The Museum's Mummies: An Inside View', *Neurosurgery* 49/1: 192–9.

Montserrat, D. 1997. 'Death and Funerals in the Roman Fayum', in M. L. Bierbrier (ed.), *Portraits and Masks: Burial Customs in Roman Egypt*. London: British Museum Press, 33–44.

—— and L. Meskell. 1997. 'Mortuary Archaeology and Religious Landscape at Graeco-Roman Deir el-Medina', *Journal of Egyptian Archaeology* 83: 179–97.

Nenna, M.-D. 2002. 'Les inhumations', in A. Charron (ed.), *La mort n'est pas une fin*. Arles: Musée de l'Arles Antique, 50–5.

Parlasca, K., and H. Seemann (eds) 1999. *Augenblicke: Mumienporträts und Ägyptische Grabkunst aus Römischer Zeit*. Munich: Klinkhardt & Biermann.

Petrie, W. M. F. 1912. *The Labyrinth Gerzeh and Mazgunah*. London: School of Archaeology in Egypt.

Quack, J. F. 1997–8. 'Beiträge zum Verständnis des Apisrituals', *Enchoria* 24: 43–53.

Raven, M. J., and W. K. Taconis. 2005. *Egyptian Mummies: Radiological Atlas of the Collections in the National Museum of Antiquities in Leiden*. Turnhout: Brepols.

Rhind, A. H. 1862. *Thebes, its Tombs and their Tenants, Ancient and Present*. London: Longman.

Riggs, C. 2002. 'Facing the Dead: Recent Research on the Funerary Art of Ptolemaic and Roman Egypt', *American Journal of Archaeology* 106: 85–101.

—— 2003. 'The Egyptian Funerary Tradition at Thebes in the Roman Period', in N. Strudwick and J. H. Taylor (eds), *The Theban Necropolis: Past, Present, Future*. London: British Museum Press, 189–201.

—— 2005. *The Beautiful Burial in Roman Egypt: Art, Identity, and Funerary Religion*. Oxford: Oxford University Press.

—— 2010. 'Funerary Rituals (Ptolemaic and Roman Periods)', in J. Dieleman and W. Wendrich (eds), *UCLA Encyclopedia of Egyptology*. Los Angeles. <http://escholarship.org/uc/item/1n10x347>.

—— and M. Depauw. 2002. '"Soternalia" from Deir el-Bahri, including Two Coffins with Demotic Inscriptions', *Revue d'Égyptologie* 53: 75–90.

Roberts, P. C. 1999. 'Suche im Sand', in K. Parlasca and H. Seemann (eds), *Augenblicke: Mumienporträts und Ägyptische Grabkunst aus Römischer Zeit*. Munich: Klinkhardt & Biermann, 49–70.

Römer, C. 2000. 'Das Werden zu Osiris im römischen Ägypten', *Archiv für Religionsgeschichte* 2/2: 141–61.

Schmidt, S. 2003. *Grabreliefs im Griechisch-Römischen Museum von Alexandria*. Berlin: Achet.

Schultz, M., B. Gessler-Löhr, and J. Kollath. 1995. 'The First Evidence of Microfilariasis in an Old Egyptian Mummy', in *Actas del I Congreso Internacional de Estudios sobre Momias 1992/Proceedings of the I World Congress on Mummy Studies 1992*. Santa Cruz de Tenerife: Museo Arqueologico y Etnografico de Tenerife, 317–20.

Smith, G. E., and W. R. Dawson. 1924. *Egyptian Mummies*. London: Allen and Unwin.

Smith, M. 1987. *Catalogue of Demotic Papyri in the British Museum*, vol. 3: *The Mortuary Texts of Papyrus BM 10507*. London: British Museum Press.

—— 2009. *Traversing Eternity: Texts for the Afterlife from Ptolemaic and Roman Egypt*. Oxford: Oxford University Press.

Stadler, M. A. 2001. 'War eine dramatische Aufführung eines Totengerichts Teil der ägyptischen Totenriten?', *Studien zur Altägyptischen Kultur* 29: 331–48.

Strudwick, N. 2003. 'Some Aspects of the Archaeology of the Theban Necropolis in the Ptolemaic and Roman Periods', in N. Strudwick and J. H. Taylor (eds), *The Theban Necropolis: Past, Present, Future*. London: British Museum Press, 167–88.

Taylor, J. H. 1995. *Unwrapping a Mummy: The Life, Death and Embalming of Horemkenesi*. London: British Museum Press.

—— 2001. *Death and the Afterlife in Ancient Egypt*. London: British Museum Press.

Vandorpe, K. 1995. 'City of Many a Gate, Harbour for Many a Rebel', in S. P. Vleeming (ed.), *Hundred-Gated Thebes: Acts of a Colloquium on Thebes and the Theban Area in the Graeco-Roman Period*. Leiden: Brill, 203–39.

Vogel, C. 2007. 'Mummy's Log: Visited Scan God in Land of the Dead', *New York Times*, 6 Aug. <http://www.nytimes.com/2007/08/06/arts/06mumm.html>.

Walker, S., and M. Bierbrier (eds) 1997. *Ancient Faces: Mummy Portraits from Roman Egypt*. London: British Museum Press.

Wisseman, S. U. 2003. *The Virtual Mummy*. Urbana: University of Illinois Press.

Ziegelmayer, G. 1985. 'Münchner Mumien', *Schriften aus der Ägyptischen Sammlung* 2, unpaginated.

Zimmer, T. 1993. 'Momies dorées: Matériaux pour servir à l'établissement d'un corpus', *Acta Antiqua Academiae Scientiarum Hungaricae* 34: 1–38.

CHAPTER 41

NILOTICA AND THE IMAGE OF EGYPT

MOLLY SWETNAM-BURLAND

THIS chapter surveys Roman art known as 'nilotica'—artistic representations of Egypt and its residents. Though the word is ancient (derived from a Latin adjective meaning 'of or belonging to the Nile'), the underlying concept is best understood as a scholarly construct, used to describe material in a range of media (coins, sculptures, mosaics, and frescos) that portray the Nile or people living near it. Romans imported Egyptian antiquities—including scarabs, canopic jars, sculptures, and obelisks—but the majority of nilotic material was made for display in Roman homes, gardens, baths, and tombs. For this reason, these artworks reveal as much or more about what their producers and consumers in Italy *thought* about Egypt as they do about the social realities of Egypt. Of particular interest are two themes: what this material tells us about the cult of Isis in Italy, and what it tells us about how Roman attitudes to Egypt (and Egyptians) evolved after Egypt became a Roman province. I structure my discussion around two examples from Italy, each a *locus classicus* of the genre: the Nile Mosaic of Palestrina and the Vatican Nile. These artworks also represent the most commonly employed media—two-dimensional landscapes in painting or mosaic, and three-dimensional personifications sculpted in the round. As the Nile Mosaic pre-dates Roman conquest and the Vatican Nile post-dates it, these examples also illustrate the changing nature of the Roman conception of Egypt from foreign territory to imperial possession.

Before Conquest: Historical Context

Romans were in contact with Egypt long before it was annexed as a province. For centuries, beginning in 273 BCE (after Pyrrhus' expulsion from Italy and Rome's entrance into the political affairs of the Hellenistic east), Rome and the Ptolemies enjoyed a diplomatic relationship of *amicitia*, though it was dispassionate and somewhat sporadic; neither state meddled much in the affairs of the other, until the late Republic. By the second century BCE, there was consistent contact between Egypt and the wider Mediterranean world, based on trade. Luxury goods, possibly including ivory, lapis lazuli, spices, and fineware (and also people, both as merchants and sometimes chattels), moved through port cities like Rhodes, and later Delos. These goods were not necessarily bound for Italy; rather, Italy was part of a wider Mediterranean trading network.

A by-product of Egyptian trade was the spread of its cults into the western Mediterranean. On Delos there were three temples dedicated to Serapis, with numerous dedications made to both Isis and Serapis by people from throughout the Mediterranean world (see Chapter 25). The priests appear to have been locals, and dedications show that the cults had adherents among Italians who either resided or traded at Delos as well. Literary sources show that by the first century BCE, Egyptian cults had taken hold in Italy, to the discomfort of the senate. These sources appear to document official actions taken against the cult (e.g. Val. Max. 1.3.4), but current scholarship argues that Roman 'resistance' to Egyptian cults was political, motivated by fear of the opportunity that membership afforded members of the lower classes to mix and assemble, rather than by negative beliefs about the cult or its deities.

Long before conquest, then, Rome's contact with Egypt was not different in kind from her interactions with the rest of the Greek east. Contact with Egypt was part of an increasingly cosmopolitan Roman culture. Alexandria was known for the wisdom contained in its library and the quality of its art. Italian familiarity with the Egyptian pantheon and the great works of the Egyptians contributed to the appeal of artworks on Egyptian themes in Roman Italy.

The Nile Mosaic

The Nile Mosaic is the earliest and most famous example of nilotica (Fig. 41.1). It is an elaborate pavement, roughly 4 × 6 metres. It depicts the Nile from the Delta to its source in the mountains of Ethiopia, and includes vignettes of people, places, and animals, labelled throughout in Greek. It originally formed the floor of a man-made cave associated with a large columned hall (a basilica or a library) at the foot of the hillside sanctuary to Fortuna in ancient Praeneste. A second mosaic, called the Fish Mosaic and depicting Mediterranean marine life, was a pendant to the Nile Mosaic, located in a similar artificial cave on the opposite side of the hall.

The Nile Mosaic has a long post-antique history that continues to influence its interpretation today in a number of respects. Early antiquarians and scholars connected it with a passage in Pliny's *Natural History* that claimed that mosaics (called 'lithostrota', artwork inlaid with stones) were first seen in Italy in the age of Sulla, and noted that a particularly fine example of the type existed in Praeneste (Plin. *HN* 36.64.189). The association between Sulla and the sanctuary persists, though the great weight of the evidence suggests that the mosaic itself was not associated with the sanctuary proper, and, thus, it is unlikely that Pliny was describing the Nile Mosaic itself. Sometime between 1624 and 1626 the Nile Mosaic was removed from its original context and divided into sections, with the result that the structure and composition of the mosaic were lost. What viewers see today is heavily, if carefully, reconstructed on the basis of drawings and copies made for the antiquarian Cassiano dal Pozzo

FIG. 41.1 The Nile Mosaic (reconstructed), Palestrina, last quarter of the second century BCE to first quarter of the first century BCE

Museo Prenestino Barberino, Palestrina, Italy. Copyright Nimatallah/Art Resource, NY.

after its initial discovery. On one estimate, the reconstructed mosaic represents perhaps half the original composition (Ferrari 1999: 362; for discovery, condition, and reconstruction, see Whitehouse 1976; Meyboom 1995: 4–19; La Malfa 2003; Hinterhöller 2009).

The complicated history and reconstruction renders the Nile Mosaic something of an enigma, prompting debate over the date of its first construction and its interpretation. Any discussion must acknowledge that the date has not been settled, with suggestions ranging from the late second century BCE through the reign of Augustus to the reign of Hadrian (see Meyboom 1995: 16–19). Further, the various arguments for each of these dates rest on primarily subjective grounds. The majority of scholars date the Nile and Fish mosaics to the Republican period (120–80 BCE), based on their architectural setting and literary evidence associating the Praeneste sanctuary with renovations carried out by Sulla (Plin. *HN* 36.64.189). This argument also relies on stylistic criteria, such as details of dress and comparison with the handful of other early examples of nilotica from the large Hellenistic and Republican period houses and villas surrounding Pompeii. Yet none of these are directly comparable—in size, scope, or in many details of the iconography. Further, the emphasis on the mosaic's origins downplays other factors of its display. Whatever the date of its first construction, the Nile Mosaic remained on public view for centuries, through multiple renovations of the sanctuary and civic space, until the eventual abandonment of the site in late antiquity. The Fish Mosaic remains *in situ* today.

The significance of the Nile Mosaic has likewise largely been approached using iconographic methodology, with scholars treating its subject matter as related to the cult of Isis in Italy, and its imagery as reflective of the culture of the Ptolemaic court. Its subject is the land of Egypt, comprehensively understood. It presented the viewer with an extended panorama of the entire expanse of the Nile's course, unfurling in curves from its source in Ethiopia to the Delta. The mosaic is at once cartographic, a unified portrait of a place, and narrative, a journey of the mind. In navigating its curving and flooded waters, an ancient viewer toured the region and along the way was presented with vignettes illustrating Egyptian life and customs.

The organization divides into two distinct parts. The mountainous, less populous Upper Egypt is presented in the upper register as if at a far remove. The lower zone, in contrast, provides a closer focus on the people of Egypt and their day-to-day lives. Read from the top, the mosaic follows the Nile from its putative source, through lands populated by exotic animals and Ethiopian hunters. It traces the course of the Nile through Middle Egypt, past monumental architectural complexes, a religious procession, and a cluster of smaller towns. The river terminates in the marshy Delta, whose more cosmopolitan inhabitants congregate and dine in elegant settings.The Mosaic is rich with details that suggest its designers' familiarity with Ptolemaic Egypt: the residents depicted include native Egyptians in priestly dress, but also Greek or Roman soldiers in military kit. The architectural complexes include a traditional Egyptian temple, what appears to be a nilometer (to the far left of 'Middle Egypt'), and a Greek-style building, draped with a royal-purple *velum* (canopy). The world of the Nile Mosaic reflects the complex hybrid culture of Ptolemaic Egypt.

For this reason, many scholars associate this mosaic with the cultural production of ancient Alexandria, known for its innovative museum and community of scholars and artists, and as the locus of production of poetry on bucolic themes that celebrated landscape, geography, and topography. Much ink has been spilled exploring possible models for the mosaic, generally assumed to be paintings. Comparison with other contemporary mosaics from Campania—such as the Alexander Mosaic, from the House of the Faun in Pompeii—suggests that such a relationship is possible, even probable; the Alexander Mosaic, also a large-scale composition, appears to draw from a painted model (Cohen 1997: 51–82). Further, the technique employed in the Nile Mosaic—using outline to pick out figures, but leaving details hazy—is 'painterly', a method also used in mosaics excavated in Hellenistic Alexandria (for example, a mosaic of a dog from Alexandria, in Walker and Higgs 2001, cat. 95; on technique, see Dunbabin 1999: 49–52).

There are a small number of possible prototypes and comparanda for the iconography of the Nile Mosaic, in particular hunting scenes with exotic animals, coming from Egypt and the east. The most compelling is a tomb painting from a third-century BCE cemetery at the site of Marisa, in modern Israel, which appears to represent a hunt taking place in Ethiopia. Like the Nile Mosaic, it labels the animals, which include both riverine and desert animals associated with Egypt, many of which appear on the Nile Mosaic (Meyboom 1995: 44–50). The form of the tomb appears similar to those known from Hellenistic Alexandria, which might suggest a direct Alexandrian influence; but, even considered in the context of contemporary Alexandrian funerary art, the motif finds few direct comparisons and is not itself thought to emulate any model (Jacobsen 2007: 39–40). It must be stressed that the relationship between the Nile Mosaic and these comparanda does not offer proof of a lost original.

For even if the prototype for the Nile Mosaic was a frieze similar to that at Marisa or other unknown work, there was significant adaptation to the medium of the mosaic, especially the imposition of the bird's-eye perspective and the use of a curvilinear narrative structure suited to its context in Praeneste. Other examples illustrate that similar ideas and motifs were in currency in the ancient Mediterranean, but do not explain the complex and unparalleled landscape of the Nile Mosaic.

Interpretations of the mosaic's significance have similarly centred on its Alexandrian and Egyptian subject matter, and have identified its scenes as depictions of historical events or reflections of Egyptian rituals and festivals. One school of thought sees the mosaic as reflective of the culture of the Ptolemaic court of the third century BCE. Angela Steinmeyer-Schareika (1978) has suggested that the mosaic reflects an expedition sent by Ptolemy II (r. 283–246 BCE) into Ethiopia, intended to explore the limits of the known world. Coarelli (1990) has pointed out that many of the exotic animals are associated in literature with Ptolemy II's so-called Grand Procession, an elaborate ritual that perhaps celebrated his coronation and kingship. P. G. P. Meyboom's seminal work explores the way that the mosaic presents contemporary Ptolemaic Egyptian culture and religion (Meyboom 1995). He focuses on the representation of Egyptian ritual in the world of the mosaic, suggesting that many of its ritual scenes depict the Khoiak festival of Osiris, celebrated for the Nile flood.

All of these interpretations share what can be characterized as an 'internal' focus, seeking answers within the mosaic's own iconography. Recent approaches attempt to situate the mosaic within broader contexts, placing greater emphasis on the artwork's physical context and relationship to literary genres that explore geography (Schrijvers 2007). Ferrari (1999) suggests that the Nile and Fish mosaics are pendants within a 'Musarum' (shrine of the Muses) attached to a Greek and Latin library, the former representing 'Chorography' and the latter 'Geography'. Hinterhöller (2009) rejects one-to-one correlation with literary genres, but provides formal examination of the modes of perspective that shows how carefully the mosaicist manipulated putative physical space. On all of these views, the Nile Mosaic is a deliberate exploration of how landscape shapes history and culture.

What 'image of Egypt' did the Nile Mosaic present to Romans in the first century BCE? As Miguel John Versluys (2002: 285–94) has shown, pre-conquest nilotica reflect what might best be characterized as an ethnographic interest in Egypt. In the handful of examples that pre-date Roman conquest, attention is paid to minutiae of architecture and dress; both flora and fauna are presented so that they may be accurately classified, and are further identified on the Nile Mosaic in the textual legends. Attention to the legends and animals reveals that, while many correspond to the animals encountered in Ethiopia at that time, others are fantastical: enormous serpents, creatures with human faces, others with vibrantly coloured coats, and so forth. From the perspective of even an educated Roman viewer in the early first century BCE, however, all would have been exotic. The 'information' within the mosaic represented cutting-edge thought about Egypt, and was in a sense didactic, in the view of some drawing on the work of Hellenistic geographers; Ferrari has shown that two names of animals on the mosaic, the kepos and the onokentauros, appear in the work of the scholiast Claudius Aelinianus, said to have lived in Praeneste (Ferrari 1999: 363). The layout of the mosaic, considered in context, invited those who saw it to take an active part in the process of discovery. A Roman looking at the mosaic would first have seen the Nile's terminus, since the scenes of life at the Delta were flush against the opening of the artificial cave. From this point, the viewer could trace the Nile's course upriver to its source, which was a point of debate among ancient scholars and philosophers. Imaginary though some of the creatures near the source of the Nile are, the mosaic as a whole shows Egypt in a positive light, informing its viewer of 'known' fact rather than relying on vague stereotypes. After conquest, however, the mode of representing Egypt changed dramatically.

After Conquest: Historical Background

Octavian's victory at the battle of Actium and the subsequent siege of Alexandria ended Egypt's status as a sovereign state. In addition to effecting numerous changes within Egypt, the annexation of Egypt as a province coincided with sea-changes in the governance of the Roman state, now a de facto monarchy, and in the society and culture of Roman Italy. As a direct result, the cult of Isis, though long known, now flourished throughout the western Mediterranean. Though some sources suggest that in the early empire Augustus and his successors were reluctant to allow the cult purchase in Rome (Tac. *Ann.* 2.85; Suet. *Tib.* 36.1), archaeological and epigraphic evidence shows to the contrary that a number of cult sites were founded or improved in the early years of the first century. The sanctuary of Isis in Pompeii was built anew in the Augustan period (Blanc, Eristov, and Fincker 2000). Throughout the Imperial period, there is evidence of the cult to be found in major port cities, from the Bay of Naples to Ostia to Pisa and beyond. It is also clear that the cult played an important role in the religious landscape of Rome. Literary and epigraphic testimonia suggest there were seven or eight separate shrines to Isis in the capital, though the Iseum and Serapeum Campensis is the largest. This sanctuary was located in the heart of the Campus Martius, near the Saepta Julia (an open-air portico famed for its paintings), and inscriptions and artworks near the site show that it was imposing and impressively decorated. Under certain emperors, the temple and cult even enjoyed imperial patronage—particularly in the late first century, when Vespasian used his patronage to telegraph to the urban plebs his military control of Egypt and Alexandria. Apuleius mentions this temple in his *Metamorphoses* as the most important cult centre outside Egypt, where his narrator, Lucius, must go to complete his initiation in the cult's mysteries (Apul. *Met.* 11.26). Though Apuleius' characterization is not an entirely positive one (it strongly suggests that Lucius must pay so dearly for this ritual instruction that he becomes a pauper), his text is still a valuable resource, and shows how familiar Roman audiences were with its practices. Inscriptions from throughout the Roman world attest to the importance of these cults in their communities in the Imperial period, and members of the cult of Isis included men and women from all walks of life and social classes.

An additional result of the Roman conquest of Egypt was the proliferation of 'Egyptianizing' art and nilotica. Augustus imported the first monumental obelisks to Rome in the years just following conquest (Fig. 41.2). He placed one in the so-called Horologium, or 'Sun-dial', where it acted as the gnomon of the sun-dial, and formed part of a monumental complex including his own mausoleum and the Ara Pacis. These expressed his patronage visibly in the city, and celebrated the conclusions of Rome's civil wars as a victory over a foreign enemy,

Cleopatra (Swetnam-Burland 2010). The Julio-Claudian emperors followed suit, often re-erecting Egyptian obelisks in Roman circuses, where they came to symbolize the emperor's patronage of the people and position at the head of the Roman state. Nilotica became popular in the private sphere as well, likely inspired by these imperial monuments.

The range and breadth of nilotica and Roman 'Egptianizing' art are difficult to characterize, for these materials ranged widely in the visual styles employed and subjects depicted. Artworks that described the entire territory, either through landscape or through personification, were common. In the years just following conquest, Egypt held a special allure for Romans living outside Egypt, and Egyptian motifs were emulated in Roman homes in ways

FIG. 41.2 Montecitorio Obelisk, 26th dynasty, brought to Rome in 10 BCE

Author's photograph.

that sometimes celebrated and sometimes lampooned Egyptian culture. A number of early imperial homes include 'Egyptianizing' frescos that feature scenes of Egyptians, usually in the process of animal worship (De Vos 1980; Söldner 1999, 2004). These are surprisingly detailed, and reflect what seems to be a sincere interest in Egyptian culture. Yet it was also in this same period that Nilotic pygmy landscapes, discussed below, became most popular. These portrayed the residents of Egypt as dwarves or pygmies, and often showed them in compromising—and humorous—situations. The Vatican Nile exemplifies post-conquest nilotica, because it combines both modes of representation.

The Vatican Nile

The Vatican Nile is a large marble sculpture roughly 2 metres in total height, and 3 metres in length, dating to the early second century CE (Fig. 41.3). The sculpture represents the Nile in the form of a reclining man; sixteen children, also known as 'cubits' (child-like personifications of the measurement of the rise of the annual flood), surround him. The base was decorated with pygmies boating on the Nile (Fig. 41.4). The sculpture was found in 1513, and has long been associated with the Iseum and Serapeum Campense, though the manner of its original display remains unclear. Two years before its discovery, a personified Tiber had been found in roughly the same location, and the two were clearly a pair, symbolizing the two most famous rivers of the empire.

FIG. 41.3 The Vatican Nile, front view, second century CE

Photo: H. Schwanke. DAI Rome, negative 1981.2187. Copyright Deutsche Archäologisches Institut, Rome.

FIG. 41.4 The Vatican Nile, rear detail with pygmies

DAI Rome, negative H 1931.705. Copyright Deutsche Archäologisches Institut, Rome.

As with the Nile Mosaic, the Vatican Nile has an involved post-antique history, which has impacted its modern interpretation. After their discovery, both the Nile and the Tiber were acquired by the Vatican and displayed in the Belvedere gardens. In the eighteenth century, an artist named Gaspare Sibilla restored the Nile, reconstructing the 'cubits' from remains as minimal as a few preserved fingers and toes. At this time, both the Nile and the Tiber were the subject of artists' studies, and favourites with those making the Grand Tour. A biscuit porcelain copy of the Vatican Nile done by Giovanni Volpato, for example, was the most expensive of his offerings of trinkets on sale to elite tourists (Draper 2002).

In 1797 both artworks were seized by Napoleon, along with many others deemed 'masterpieces', after the Treaty of Tolentino. The artworks were marched through Paris in mock Roman triumph, with banners that read, 'Greece gave them up, Rome lost them, their fate has changed twice, it will not change again!' (Mainardi 1989: 158). The Tiber has remained in the Louvre ever since, but in 1815 the Nile was returned to the Vatican through the diplomatic intervention of Antonio Canova. A lunette fresco by Francesco Hayez from the Cortile della Pigna in the Vatican depicted the return of the Roman antiquities, accompanied by the celebratory legend 'Famous works of excellent skill, hauled away to strange lands, recovered for the city' in Latin, borrowing heavily from the language of Pliny the Elder describing Vespasian's Templum Pacis, in which he made public a number of artworks from Nero's Golden Palace (Plin. *HN* 34.84).

An understanding of the Nile's long history—as with the Palestrina mosaic—reminds modern students and scholars to be careful in relying heavily on individual details or stylistic features, the reconstruction of which may have deviated from the original in important ways. Sibilla's restorations of the 'cubits' without doubt were inspired by a description of an imaginary artwork depicting the Nile by the Roman period writer Philostratus, in his *Imagines* 1.5. As importantly, the Vatican Nile and others like it, when taken to Paris, were partially selected because they were thought to be Greek masterpieces, taken by the Romans—the act of plundering now a metaphor for the creation of an imperial capital (Mainardi 1989). This meaning was not lost on the contemporary Italians: the use of Pliny's description of the Templum

Pacis made it clear that the artworks' return was a metaphor for liberation from tyrannical government. Embedded in the work's history, then, is the notion that it was, or closely copied, a Greek masterpiece, an assumption that has guided academic treatment of the piece, which has focused on its type rather than its physical setting or historical context.

The Vatican Nile has long been understood as the epitome of a sculptural type known as the 'personified Nile'. The origin of the type is disputed: some believe this 'type' was created in Egypt, commissioned by the Ptolemaic court and typical of a distinctly Alexandrian style; others see it rather as reflecting a statue that Pliny says was put on display in Vespasian's Templum Pacis (Plin. *HN* 36.58; see Swetnam-Burland 2009: 440 n. 6). Stylistically, the Vatican Nile is comparable both to Hellenistic and to Roman artworks (such as the Laocoön or the Sperlonga group) that played to the same aesthetic. Arguments for dating, therefore, based solely on details internal to the work are not entirely persuasive either way.

Other approaches look at the type of the personified Nile as distributed throughout the Mediterranean, in a number of iterations, or put somewhat greater focus on contextual display. Over twenty examples are known from the ancient world, with differences in details of iconography—though always surrounded by animals evocative of Egypt and often accompanied by two or more 'cubits'. The vast majority of these belong to the post-conquest period (Klementa 1993; Swetnam-Burland 2009). When paired with the Tiber—as in the case of the Vatican Nile—sculptures of the two rivers came to stand for the extent of Rome's dominion, east to west, and for the trade routes and networks that bound the Roman empire together. Statues of personified rivers were well known to Roman audiences, often from triumphal processions that included spolia and artistic representations symbolic of the culture and geography of conquered lands. The Arch of Titus, for example, depicts soldiers carrying the Great Menorah, seized from Jerusalem, and in a small scene above shows other soldiers carrying what appears to be a monumental sculpture of a river. Sculptures described as 'Niles' were included in the triumphs of both Caesar and Augustus, thus linking this mode of representation to the celebration of the act of conquest (Caesar, e.g. Flor. 2.13.88; Augustus, e.g. Prop. 2.1.31–34). Yet, understood as an 'image of Egypt', personified Niles celebrated the province, emphasizing those attributes that benefited Rome—in this case, the Nile's fertility. This image of Egypt's place in the empire was embraced even within the province of Egypt: a number of personified Niles of Imperial date have been unearthed in Egypt, including a Neilos from the small town of Karanis (Ann Arbor, Kelsey Museum of Archaeology 2.5747) and one of greywacke found underwater at the temple site at Canopus (Alexandria, Maritime Museum SCA 842; Goddio and Clauss 2008: 80–3, cat. 29).

The base of the Vatican Nile uses a stock motif to describe the land of Egypt, but takes a different approach. The base is sculpted on all four sides and includes depictions of typical Egyptian flora and fauna, including crocodiles and hippopotami. Here, there is a marked change from the Nile Mosaic, with its fanciful animals, but relatively realistic portrayal of Egyptian culture. The processions, priests, and soldiers have been replaced with pygmies (small men displaying physical features associated with achondroplastic dwarfism, with long torsos but disproportionately short extremities). Often—as on the Vatican Nile, where the pygmies fight for their lives against Egypt's exotic animals—populated landscapes present these diminished figures in compromising situations, often with an element of sexual humour. One predominant theory sees this change in characterization of the residents of Egypt from the relatively 'ethnographic' to the overtly stereotyped as reflective of an imperialist discourse (Versluys 2002).

As an artistic motif, pygmy landscapes became popular in a variety of media in the post-conquest period, including gems, lamps, terracotta 'campana' plaques, marble reliefs, mosaics, and wall paintings. The motif is most commonly found in the frescos of Pompeii and Campania, though this almost certainly reflects an accident of preservation; nevertheless, the unparalleled record of the region around the Bay of Naples has allowed for a more statistical approach to understanding these motifs and their appeal. Miguel John Versluys's comprehensive work on the scenes has shown that the motif appears by far the most often in the private sphere in the first and second centuries CE—often in areas of homes suited to entertainment, including gardens, triclinia, or private baths. In Versluys's opinion, the appeal of these scenes was multivalent: they were amusing, intending to evoke a laugh; they presented the owner of the house as urbane and worldly; and they celebrated the riches brought to Rome from the conquered province (Versluys 2002). John Clarke has suggested that one key to their appeal lies not so much in the stereotyping of the residents of Egypt, but in the comical, even if compromising, situations in which they find themselves. Especially when in baths, these motifs are found in locations that Romans believed were dangerous or fraught, where ill humours might overtake the body (Clark 2007a; 2007b, 87–107). The appeal of pygmy scenes in these contexts might be explained through the apotropaic power of humour. Similarly, Versluys and Meyboom have explored the positive association of scenes of dwarves and pygmies in Egyptian tradition, showing a connection with the Nile understood to be at the height of its flood (Versluys and Meyboom 2007). In this view, too, there was a positive valence to these images in Italy, where they evoked a world so distant as to be almost imaginary, but which was also the source of the grain that fuelled the empire. In the case of the Vatican Nile, on prominent display with its Tiber counterpart in the Iseum and Serapeum Campense, it is fair to assume the Roman viewers of the artwork were intended to understand Egypt (and indeed the relationship between Egypt and Rome) in a largely positive light: Egypt was not just the source of tangible benefits, but also the homeland of Isis and Serapis.

Conclusion

The Palestrina mosaic and the Vatican Nile, as nilotica, present Egypt in different ways that reflect the changing relationship between Egypt and Rome in the pre- and post-conquest periods. In my view, this difference cannot be characterized in binary terms—the former as wholly positive, the latter pejorative. Though it is true that many Roman beliefs about Egypt and Egyptians did grow more negative over time, especially as reflected in literary sources (thus, for instance, Smelik and Hemelrijk 1984), that does not present the whole picture. The Nile Mosaic is a depiction of Egypt from a period in which the land was little known to the 'average' citizens of Roman Italy, and has an educative aim. Presented in cartographic form, and in a context that required not just access to the grotto but the ability to read its legends in Greek, the Nile Mosaic presented Egypt in a didactic manner aimed at an erudite elite. It relied on no presupposed knowledge on the part of its viewer, other than the ability to recognize certain exotic animals—the crocodile, hippopotamus, and so on—as fundamentally Egyptian. In this period, nilotica as a genre were rare, found only in the homes of the wealthy, and reflected to some extent the cutting edge of geographic and cultural knowledge.

The post-conquest Vatican Nile describes Egypt using an altogether different strategy to an altogether different purpose. The work employs (and blends) two visual tropes for characterizing the land and its people: first, the personification, which makes the landscape comprehensible by humanizing the Nile as a generous man, and the flooded waters as his children, themselves symbols of life-giving fertility; secondly, the pygmy landscape, which makes the Nile more readily comprehensible by reducing its features to the miniature, and by treating its people as stock figures that—through metonymy—come to stand for the entire region. Both these tropes work well in this time period in large part because they were, by the second century CE, widely recognizable, to be found throughout the empire and in the homes of elite and 'average' Romans alike. The goal, then, of the Vatican Nile—set in an Egyptian cultic context—was not to educate viewers about the foreign, but to encapsulate existing knowledge presumed to be shared by all who saw it.

In my focus on these two well-known examples of nilotica, I have stressed their post-antique histories. It is vital to be aware of the multiple 'lives' of these objects because the documentation that allows us to reconstruct their function and display in antiquity comes to us only as the product of Renaissance scholarship. Both artworks were discovered—and later prized—in historical periods in which Egypt's political relationship with the West had contemporary relevance, and in which the nascent discipline of Egyptology was emerging. The earliest studies of Egyptian culture were informed and shaped by Roman interest in Egypt, because the exemplary 'Egyptian' artworks studied were those that had been transported to Italy in antiquity; Athanasius Kircher, for example, based his early studies of hieroglyphs on the most readily available materials, which were those found in Italy. Because both the Vatican Nile and the Nile Mosaic were prized in the Renaissance, we have ample information about them, which aids our ability to reconstruct the ancient artworks and the settings in which each were put on display. But we do not have unmediated access to these works, or to their ancient contexts, a fact we must always bear in mind in viewing and studying them. Nevertheless, through the centuries, nilotica—whether monumental sculptures or minute gems—have exercised a wide-ranging appeal that tells much about our own fascination with Egypt.

Suggested Reading

Roman 'Egyptomania' encompasses a number of sub-specialities, and draws on a vast literature related to the cult of Isis in the Roman world (for which, see Chapter 25). The following works provide a good foundation on Egyptian culture in Italy, with an emphasis on those for the English-language reader. For pygmy and nilotic landscapes, see Meyboom (1995), Versluys (2002), and Whitehouse (1980). For discussion of artworks imported from Egypt or in Egyptian style, see Elsner (2006), Swetnam-Burland (2007), and Vout (2003); Roullet (1972) is a good and still-useful catalogue of works. Similarly, Iversen's two-volume study (1968–72) of obelisks in Rome remains an important reference, but see now Curran et al. (2009), Parker (2007), and Swetnam-Burland (2010). For antiquarianism and ancient Egypt, see Curran (2007), Rowland (2008), and Whitehouse (2001). Finally, several works in Italian, German, and French are indispensable for advanced study, including comprehensive catalogues of primary materials related to the Italian cults of Isis, such as Arslan et al. (1997), De Caro (2006b), Lembke (1994), Malaise (1972a,b), and Tran Tam Tinh (1964, 1971). De Vos (1980) deals with Egyptianizing frescos, and epigraphic material has been collected in Bricault (2005).

Bibliography

Arslan, E. A., et al. (eds) 1997. *Iside: Il mito, il mistero, la magia.* Milan: Electa.

Blanc, N., H. Eristov, and M. Fincker. 2000. '*A Fundamento Restituit*? Reflections dans le Temple d'Isis a Pompei', *Revue Archéologique* 2: 227–309.

Bricault, L. (ed.) 2005. *Recueil des inscriptions concernant les cultes isiaques.* Paris: Académie des Inscriptions et Belles-Lettres.

Clarke, J. 2007a. 'Three Uses of the Pygmy and the Aethiops at Pompeii: Decorating, "Othering", and Warding off Demons', in L. Bricault, M. J. Versluys and P. G. P. Meyboom (eds), *Nile into Tiber: Egypt in the Roman World: Proceedings of the IIIrd International Conference of Isis Studies.* Leiden: Brill, 155–69.

—— 2007b. *Looking at Laughter: Humor, Power, and Transgression in Roman Visual Culture.* Berkeley: University of California Press.

Coarelli, F. 1990. 'La Pompé di Tolomeo Filadelfo e il mosaico nilotico di Palestrina', *Ktema* 15: 225–51.

Cohen, A. 1997. *The Alexander Mosaic: Stories of Victory and Defeat.* Cambridge: Cambridge University Press.

Curran, B. 2007. *The Egyptian Renaissance: The Afterlife of Ancient Egypt in Early Modern Italy.* Chicago: University of Chicago Press.

——et al. 2009. *Obelisk: A History.* Cambridge, Mass.: MIT Press.

De Caro, S. 2006a. *Il santuario di Iside a Pompei e nel Museo archeologico nazionale.* Naples: Electa.

——(ed.) 2006b. *Egittomania: Iside e il mistero.* Milan: Electa.

De Vos, M. 1980. *L'egittomania in pitture e mosaici romano-campani della prima età imperial.* Leiden: Brill.

Draper, J. 2002. 'The River Nile, a Giovanni Volpato Masterwork', *Metropolitan Museum Journal* 37: 277–82.

Dunbabin, K. 1999. *Mosaics of the Greek and Roman World.* Cambridge: Cambridge University Press.

Elsner, J. 2006. 'Classicism in Roman Art', in J. Porter (ed.), *Classical Pasts: The Classical Traditions of Greece and Rome.* Princeton: Princeton University Press, 270–301.

Ferrari, G. 1999. 'The Geography of Time: The Nile Mosaic and the Library at Praeneste', *Ostraka* 8: 359–86.

Goddio, F., and M. Clauss (eds) 2008. *Egypt's Sunken Treasures.* Munich: Prestel.

Hinterhöller, M. 2009. 'Das Nilmosaik von Palestrina und die Bildstruktur eines geographischen Großraums', *Römische historische Mitteilungen* 51: 15–130.

Iversen, E. 1968–72. *Obelisks in Exile*, 2 vols. Copenhagen: Gad.

Jacobsen, D. 2007. *The Hellenistic Paintings of Marisa.* Leeds: Maney.

Klementa, S. 1993. *Gelagerte Flußgötter des Späthellenismus und der römischen Kaiserzeit.* Cologne: Böhlau.

La Malfa, C. 2003. 'Reassessing the Renaissance of the Palestrina Nile Mosaic', *Journal of the Warburg and Courtauld Institutes* 66: 267–71.

Lembke, K. 1994. *Das Iseum Campense in Rom: Studie über den Isiskult unter Domitian.* Heidelberg: Archäologie und Geschichte.

Mainardi, P. 1989. 'Assuring the Empire of the Future: The 1798 Fête de la Liberté', *Art Journal* 48/2: 155–63.

Malaise, M. 1972a. *Les conditions de pénétration et de diffusion des cultes égyptiens en Italie*. Leiden: Brill.

——1972b. *Inventaire préliminaire des documents égyptiens découverts en Italie*. Leiden: Brill.

Meyboom, P. G. P. 1995. *The Nile Mosaic of Palestrina: Early Evidence of Egyptian Religion in Italy*. Leiden: Brill.

Parker, G. 2007. 'Obelisks Still in Exile: Monuments Made to Measure', in L. Bricault, M. J. Versluys, and P. G. P. Meyboom (eds), *Nile into Tiber: Egypt in the Roman World: Proceedings of the IIIrd International Conference of Isis Studies*. Leiden: Brill, 209–22.

Roullet, A. 1972. *The Egyptian and Egyptianizing Monuments of Imperial Rome*. Leiden: Brill.

Rowland, I. 2008. 'Athanasius Kircher and Impressions of Egypt in the Seventeenth Century', in E. Lo Sardo (ed.), *The She-Wolf and the Sphinx: Rome and Egypt from History to Myth*. Milan: Electa, 180–9.

Schrijvers, P. 2007. 'A Literary View of the Nile Mosaic', in L. Bricault, M. J. Versluys, and P. G. P. Meyboom (eds), *Nile into Tiber: Egypt in the Roman World: Proceedings of the IIIrd International Conference of Isis Studies*. Leiden: Brill, 223–44.

Smelik, K., and E. Hemelrijk. 1984. '"Who Knows Not What Monsters Demented Egypt Worships?" Opinions on Egyptian Animal Worship in Antiquity as Part of the Ancient Conception of Egypt', in W. Haase and H. Temporini (eds), *Aufstieg und Niedergang der römische Welt* II 17.4. Berlin: de Gruyter, 1852–2000.

Söldner, M. 1999. 'Ägyptische Bildmotive im augusteischen Rom: Ein Phänomen im Spannungsfeld von Politik, Religion und Kunst', in H. Felber and S. Pfisterer-Hass (ed.), *Ägypter, Griechen, Römer: Begegnung der Kulturen*. Leipzig: Wodtke und Stegbauer, 95–113.

——2004. 'Zur Funktion ägyptischer Elemente in der römischen Wanddekoration', *Städel-Jahrbuch* 19: 201–12.

Steinmeyer-Schareika, A. 1978. *Das Nilmosaik von Palestrina und eine ptolemäische Expedition nach Äthiopien*. Bonn: Habelt.

Swetnam-Burland, M. 2007. 'Egyptian Objects, Roman Contexts: A Taste for *Aegyptiaca* in Italy', in L. Bricault, M. Versluys, and P. G. P. Meyboom (eds), *Nile into Tiber: Egypt in the Roman World: Proceedings of the IIIrd International Conference of Isis Studies*. Leiden: Brill, 113–36.

——2009. 'Egypt Embodied: The Vatican Nile', *American Journal of Archaeology* 113: 439–57.

——2010. '*Aegyptus Redacta*: The Egyptian Obelisk in the Augustan Campus Martius', *Art Bulletin* 92/3: 135–53.

Tran Tam Tinh, V. 1964. *Essai sur le culte d'Isis à Pompéi*. Paris: de Boccard.

——1971. *Le culte des divinités orientales à Herculanum*. Leiden: Brill.

Versluys, M. J. 2002. *Aegyptiaca Romana: Nilotic Scenes and the Roman Views of Egypt*. Leiden: Brill.

——and P. G. P. Meyboom. 2007. 'The Meaning of Dwarfs in Nilotic Scenes', in L. Bricault, M. J. Versluys, and P. G. P. Meyboom (eds), *Proceedings of the Third International Conference of Isis Studies*. Leiden: Brill, 170–208.

Vout, C. 2003. 'Embracing Egypt', in G. Woolf and C. Edwards (eds), *Rome the Cosmopolis*. Cambridge: Cambridge University Press, 177–203.

Walker, S., and P. Higgs (eds) 2001. *Cleopatra of Egypt: From History to Myth*. London: British Museum Press.

Whitehouse, H. 1976. *The Dal Pozzo Copies of the Palestrina Mosaic*. Oxford: Archaeopress/BAR.

——1980. 'A Catalogue of Nilotic Landscapes in Roman Art', doctoral dissertation, Oxford University.

——2001. *Ancient Mosaics and Wallpaintings*. London: Miller.

PART VII

BORDERS, TRADE, AND TOURISM

CHAPTER 42

TRAVEL AND PILGRIMAGE

IAN C. RUTHERFORD

For anyone intending to study patterns of travel in the Roman world, Egypt is unusual in several respects. First, the evidence for the travel is particularly good: not only do we have papyri and ostraca; we also have large numbers of graffiti or *dipinti* adorning important monuments. Secondly, motivation for travel is to some extent atypical: a major motivation is tourism or cultural pilgrimage to see the great wonders of Egypt—two of the canonical Seven Wonders, established in the late Hellenistic period, were in fact in Egypt, the Lighthouse at Pharos and the Pyramids (Brodersen 1992; Höcker 2010). Finally, the routes of travel are unusual: the Nile and the Nile Valley obviously dominate, at least south of Memphis. East of the Nile, land routes connect through the desert to the Red Sea, to the ports of Myos Hormos and Berenike, which gave access to India (see Chapter 44); and to the west there were more or less well-defined routes through the desert to the Oases (see Chapter 43). In all three respects, the situation seems largely to continue that of the Hellenistic period, though some sites seem to have been particularly popular in the Roman period, such as the royal tombs and the statues of Memnon at Thebes.

Primary Sources

Primary evidence for travel survives in the form of informal inscriptions—graffiti or *dipinti*—recording the presence of visitors. Most are in Greek, only a few in Latin. Demotic graffiti are found also, but they have not been systematically published for many sites (though for Philae and the Dodekaschoinos, see Griffith 1937; for the temple of Hibis, Cruz-Uribe 2008; for Wadi Hammamat, Cruz-Uribe 2001). Graffiti are sometimes found in other languages, e.g. Meroitic from Philae or South Arabic from Wadi Hammamat (Tokunaga 2003). The most comprehensive survey is the unpublished doctoral thesis of Victoria Foertmeyer (1989). The principal advances in recent years arise from discoveries of new material in the Western Oases and also on the routes from the Nile to the Red Sea, and from the publication of more Demotic graffiti.

The most common types of graffiti, besides simple names, are: records of an act of proskynema, or adoration before a deity (Geraci 1971); statements that someone 'remembered' someone else (*emnesthe*; Rehm 1939); and statements that someone has arrived (*hekei*). We also find more complex forms, such as short poems (see *IMEGR*), and occasional images of feet (see Guarducci 1942–3).

The most important sites are the following:

- *Abydos*, particularly the building known to the Greeks as the Memnonion, originally the mortuary temple of Seti I, which served as a temple of Serapis and later housed an oracle of Bes (Perdrizet and Lefebvre 1919; Rutherford 2003). The Osireion also had graffiti (Boyaval 1969).
- *Philae*, in particular the famous temple of Isis (*IGP*, with additions in Roccati 1981 and A. Bernand 1989: 282–318).
- *Thebes*, especially the statues of Memnon (*IGLCM*), the royal tombs (Baillet 1920–6; Speidel 1974; Martin 1991), and the sanctuary of Asklepios (Imhotep) at Deir el-Bahri (Bataille 1951; Łajtar 2006). The temple at Luxor also contains some Greek and Latin graffiti (Riad 1968).
- *Nubia*: the temple of Mandulis at Talmis (Kalabsha) (Gauthier 1911), where several longer verse examples were also found (see *IMEGR*; Nock 1934). Most of the writers were Roman soldiers stationed locally (see also Chapter 24).

Less important sites include:

- The Sphinx at *Giza*, with three remarkable poems (*RIGLE* 2.460–86; *IMEGR*, nos 127–8, 130; É. Bernard 1983).
- *Narmouthis* in the Fayum (É. Bernand 1981, nos 173–81).
- *Amarna* (*IMEGR* 126 = *RIGLE* 2.455–6, by Catulinus).
- *Pathyris* (A. Bernand 1989, nos 7–10).
- *Latopolis* (A. Bernand 1989, nos 14–18).
- *Kom Ombo* (A. Bernand 1989, nos 199–212).
- The sanctuary of Khnum, Satet, and Anuket at *Elephantine* (A. Bernand 1989; Jaritz, Maehler, and Zauzich 1979; Maehler 1992).
- The temples of the *Dodekaschoinos* (Ruppel 1930; Nachtergael 1999, for Pselkis (Dakka)).

Graffiti are also found on routes from the Nile to the Red Sea, especially in this period on the routes from Koptos heading east to Myos Hormos (Fournet 1995; Cuvigny 2003) or south-east to Berenike. Along the way, travellers could visit 'Paneia', honouring the god Min (Greek Pan) of Koptos, in the Wadi Hammamat (A. Bernand 1972a), at el-Buwayb (Cuvigny and Bülow-Jacobsen 2000), in Wadi Minayh (Cuvigny and Bülow-Jacobsen 1999, with de Romanis 1996), and at many other sites (see A. Bernand 1977). Further south was the route from Edfu, with a Paneion at el-Kanais (A. Bernand 1972b), where one of the few non-Ptolemaic graffiti (59 *bis*) records an announcement by a soldier, Crispinus, of the *cohors I Lusitanorum* that he would organize a banquet for Serapis. New material has more recently been published from the Oases in the Western Desert, for instance in the Kharga Oasis from Hibis (Cruz-Uribe 2008) and Ain Labakha (Wagner 1996; Hussein 2000), from Bahariya in the Bahariya Oasis (Colin 1997), and from Deir-el-Hagar in the Dakhla Oasis (Kaper and Worp 1999).

The surviving distribution is uneven. For example, we know that the polished limestone surfaces of the Pyramids were covered in graffiti, but almost all of these are lost. The sites of the Delta are equally lacking in recorded graffiti. Some places have comparatively few inscriptions where we might expect more evidence. These include the temple of Horus at Edfu (Apollonopolis Magna) and the great temple of Hathor at Dendara (Tentyris), where there is just one proskynema relating to the foundation of a well (A. Bernand 1984, with no. 33 for the well; Martin 1983).

Such graffiti do not always indicate that the writer has travelled a distance to the sanctuary. In some cases, writers were certainly local. The graffiti at Talmis, for example, seem to have been written by Roman soldiers stationed locally, and at Philae some graffiti on the roof of the temple of Isis were written by members of a family of local priests.

Motivations for Travel

Visits to monuments took place for all sorts of reasons. One major motivation in the Roman empire was to see the wonders of Egypt—a form of tourism. That is clear from the evidence of the Theban royal tombs (see below), and it is a large part of the draw of the Memnon statues as well.

Another motivation must have been religious observance, and to that extent it seems justifiable to talk about 'pilgrimage', even though some of the modern associations of that word were probably not present (cf. Yoyotte 1960; Malaise 1987; Elsner and Rutherford 2006). Evidence for festival attendance in Roman Egypt is mostly confined to pilgrimage within the nome (Perpillou-Thomas 1993: 271–6), although a document from Oxyrhynchus refers to a festival in Hermopolis (Perpillou-Thomas 1993: 124, 272 n. 25). Evidence for long-distance pilgrimage to the cult of Isis at Philae is significantly less from the Roman period than from the Hellenistic period, though we do have one proskynema attesting visitors from Alexandria in 191 CE (*IGP* 2.166–74, no. 168). The coastal sanctuary of Isis at Menouthis presumably drew more Alexandrians (Trombley 1993–4: 2.6–9, 220).

At Deir el-Bahri pilgrims came to the healing sanctuary of Imhotep to be cured but they were mostly local; only one from outside the immediate vicinity (Koptos) is known. A recent discovery is of inscriptions recording the journey there of a group of ironworkers from Hermonthis, 10 miles to the south (Łajtar 2006, nos 163–4, 168–9). Other centres of healing pilgrimage may have been at Dendara (Daumas 1956) and Kom Ombo (Gutbub 1973: 94–5; Frankfurter 1998: 48, 51). Some visitors would spend the night in the temple, in the hope that through incubation they would receive a dream-vision of the deity (see, for example, the long graffito from Deir el-Bahri by Amenothes, in Łajtar 2006, no. 208).

The best-attested transregional pilgrimage centre is probably the oracle of Bes housed in the Memnonion at Abydos (Dunand 1997; Rutherford 2003). Graffiti on the walls of the building amply demonstrate this, and we have independent testimony from the historian Ammianus Marcellinus (19.12), who narrates how in 359 CE the emperor intervened because he was concerned that the oracle was becoming a focus for anti-imperial sentiment (Frankfurter 1998: 169–74, 190–7).

By the Roman period, Egypt was regarded as a centre for mystical knowledge, and one might have expected people to visit Egypt for this reason. Plutarch, in *On the Cessation of Oracles*, set in the late first century, describes how two 'holy men' met at Delphi on the way to Tarsus from Britain. The men were Demetrius the grammarian and a certain Cleombrotus:

> Cleombrotus the Lacedemonian, after long wandering in Egypt, and up and down the region of the Troglodytes, and after voyaging beyond the Red Sea—not for the purpose of trading, but as being a person fond of seeing and fond of learning, having sufficient wealth, and not esteeming it a matter of importance to have more than sufficient—he employed his leisure for such purposes, and was collecting information as the materials for philosophy that had, as he himself expressed it, Theology for its end. Having lately been to the temple of Ammon, he evidently had not been greatly struck with the other things there, but with respect to the unextinguishable Lamp he relates a story well deserving of attention, told him by the priests; namely, that every year it consumes less oil, and that they took this for a proof of the inequality [diminution] of the years always making the last one shorter than that preceding it; for it was to be expected that with a shorter time the consumption of oil would be less also.

Another important source bearing on this motivation for travel is a narrative describing the experience of a certain Thessalos of Tralles, who first came to Alexandria in search of the book of the magician Nechepso, then went up the Nile to Thebes, where he had an audience with the deity Asklepios (Imhotep), who revealed mystic secrets to him (Totti 1985, no. 5; Moyer 2003, 2004). In one late source, the emperor Hadrian is said to have been motivated to visit Egypt by a desire to find a cure for an illness (Epiph. *De Mensuribus et Ponderibus* 14); another tradition about a charm revealed to Hadrian by the prophet Pachrates of Heliopolis (*PGM* IV 2447–50) may relate to this trip (Foertmeyer 1989: 117, 145).

Besides this, people must have made passing visits to these places in the course of longer journeys. Graffiti written at sites along the routes east of the Nile record the journeys of people in transit, such as one C. Numidius Eros at Wadi Minayh, inscribed during his return from India (Cuvigny and Bülow Jacobsen 1999, no. 5). Administrators, including Roman prefects, visited religious centres while on official trips, and several visited the royal tombs at Thebes, including Kladon, an envoy to Ethiopia (Baillet 1920–6, no. 1094; and see pp. xxxv–xliv in general).

Who Travelled?

Romans began travelling to Egypt in the second century BCE, after the start of diplomatic contact with the Ptolemies (see van't Dack 1980; Lampela 1998). A well-known early Roman visitor was L. Memmius, who visited the crocodiles in the Fayum in 112 BCE (Lampela 1998: 216, no. 92). Diodorus Siculus (1.83.8) claims to have seen a Roman being lynched in Egypt, probably around 60–57 BCE. The volume of Romans visiting Egypt is bound to have increased after 31 BCE, since Roman rule necessitated a major Roman presence: an administration headed by the prefect, who also travelled around Egypt as part of his professional duties; the military; and occasional visits by emperors or members of the imperial family.

However, we hear of few Roman citizens making unofficial trips to Egypt. One factor may have been Augustus' ban on visits there by senators and equites, for which the historian Tacitus is our only testimony (*Ann.* 2.59; Adams 2001: 157–8). Juvenal's description of a Roman woman who travelled all the way to Meroe to get sacred water for use in Isiac cult is probably no more than satirical fantasy (Juv. 6.526–30). For *CIL* III 83, which has erroneously been taken as evidence for a Roman pilgrim in Meroe, see Łajtar and van der Vliet (2006). The same pattern is borne out by the inscriptions: almost all the Roman visitors are either dignitaries or soldiers, who were in Egypt anyway. Among the 2,000 graffiti in the Theban tombs, almost none are in Latin, and few of the writers come from Italy. Apparent exceptions are the Italian writers of the poem in the Osireion of Abydos (see below).

In contrast, Greeks, and people who wrote in Greek, travelled as much as they had in the Hellenistic period. Greek visitors include famous intellectuals, such as Strabo (Yoyotte, Charvet, and Gompertz 1997); Pausanias the Periegete, who visited the Pyramids (9.36.5), Memnon (1.42.3), and the temple of Ammon in Siwa Oasis (9.16.1); and Aelius Aristides (second century CE), who claimed to have visited Egypt four times 'and left nothing unexamined, not the pyramids, the Labyrinth, no temple, no canals' (*Or.* 36.1). In the *Life of Apollonius* (early third century CE), Philostratus talks about large numbers of people both leaving and entering Egypt (*VA* 5.24).

The best-documented visits are those of emperors and the imperial family. The visit of Germanicus in 19 CE is described by Tacitus (*Ann.* 2.59–61), who says its purpose was ostensibly to bring economic relief but really 'to get to know antiquity' (*cognoscendae antiquitatis*). Sites he visited included Alexandria, Canopus, Thebes, Memnon, and Syene. Tacitus also says that Tiberius was offended because Germanicus had not asked his permission to enter the closed province (see Weingärtner 1969; Halfmann 1986: 169–70; Kelly 2010). Vespasian visited the Serapeum at Alexandria in 69–70, when several miracles presaging his elevation to emperor are supposed to have occurred (Derchain 1953; Henrichs 1968; Halfmann 1986: 178–9). His son Titus came to Memphis the following year (Halfmann 1986: 181). An especially well-documented visit is that of Hadrian, his wife, Sabina, and Julia Balbilla, who toured Egypt in 130; the visit was marred by the death of Antinoos on the Nile (Sijpestein 1969; Halfmann 1986: 207). Septimius Severus visited Egypt in 199–200 (Halfmann 1986: 217–18), and both Marcus Aurelius and Caracalla are known to have visited Alexandria, the former in 175/6 (Halfmann 1986: 213), the latter in 215–16 (Halfmann 1986: 225).

Sites

The Colossi of Memnon

In Thebes, one of the most visited sites was the colossi of Amenhotep III on the west bank, known to the Romans as statues of Memnon (see Fig. 11.4). As early as the visit of Strabo and Aelius Gallus in 27 BCE, one of the statues made a strident noise in the morning, which was

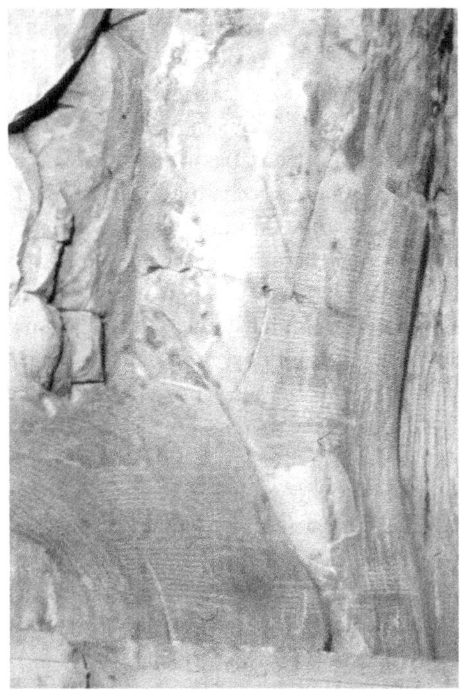

FIG. 42.1 Inscriptions on the foot and ankle of one of the Memnon colossi

Photo: Christina Riggs.

generally interpreted as Memnon hailing his mother, Dawn. The miracle is recorded in numerous inscriptions left on the statue, mostly in Greek, some in Latin, and one in Demotic (Zauzich 1973), almost all left by or on behalf of Roman dignitaries and soldiers (Fig. 42.1). There are numerous short poems, almost all in Greek, and many by women poets, writing in the Aeolic dialect in imitation of Sappho (Bowie 1990: 62–6; Brennan 1998). The peak of the 'singing' statue's popularity was the epoch of Hadrian, but by the fourth century CE the noise seems to have stopped. It used to be believed that the cause was hypothetical reconstruction carried out by Septimius Severus when he visited in 199 CE, but Bowersock (1984) pointed out that some of the inscriptions are later than that, and he suggested that if the statue was silenced by reconstruction work, it is better attributed to Queen Zenobia, who occupied Egypt for a period around 270 CE.

We do not know when the identification of the statues with Memnon began. Strabo mentions them, and says the sound was the result of an earthquake (17.1.46), but the identification with Memnon could easily pre-date Strabo, since the throne name of Amenhotep III—Neb-maat-re, pronounced 'Nimmuria' or 'Mimurria'—might have sounded like 'Memnon' to Greek ears (Gardiner 1961; Théodoridès 1989: 273). While there is no sign of the Memnon statues in Herodotus, it is likely that already in the Hellenistic period the Greeks associated western Thebes with Memnon (Bataille 1952: 1–4; Gardiner 1961; Agatharcides of Cnidus, in Burstein 1989: 67). The idea that an Ethiopian prince had been memorialized in Egypt may have seemed quite plausible to Greek writers, who knew that kings from Nubia (Ethiopia, to the Greeks) had ruled Egypt in the eighth century BCE. There were alternative identifications of the statues, too. Visiting in the second century CE, Pausanias the Perigete (1.42.3) was told by Egyptians that the statue was a king named Phamenoph or Sesostris; the name Phamenoph is also used in an epigram by Balbilla (*IGLCM* 31). Memnon also seems to have been regarded as buried in the Valley of the Kings (tomb KV 6), apparently because Ramesses IX had the same royal name (Bataille 1952: 1). Some visitors went to both sites.

No doubt far more people came to visit than are recorded on the monument. One verse inscription talks of Memnon prophesying to people who come 'from all the earth' (*IGLCM* 100, and cf. 88). Some visitors went more than once because they failed either to hear it the first time (Celer, in *IGLCM* 23) or to hear it again (*IGLCM* 4, 93); others record religious actions, e.g. Funisulanus Charisios in *IGLCM* 19. Some describe the voice as oracular (*IGLCM* 100).

Inscribed poems find novel angles to talk about Memnon: several say that he has survived an attempt by the Persian king Cambyses to damage the statues (Balbilla in *IGLCM* 29; also Paus. 1.101), while some late sources say that Cambyses was trying to discover the secret of the voice (Bataille 1952: 158). Others trace Memnon back to the Trojan War: he has survived when Achilles has not (*IGLCM* 62), and his cry is like the clash of his weapons at Troy (*IGLCM* 36). Another poem, this time in Latin and from Talmis in Nubia, sees the speaking of the statues as a sign of the return of a golden age (Courtney 1995: 51–2, no. 26). This 'discourse of Memnon' is found in Graeco-Roman literature of the period, e.g. in the *ekphrases* of Philostratus (*Imag*. 1.7) and Callistratus (*Descriptions* 1 and 9).

Tourism to the Nile Cataracts

A unique letter surviving on a papyrus from a certain Nearchus to a certain Heliodorus, apparently describing a tour round Egypt, singles out Syene, 'where the Nile flows from', and the oracle of Ammon at the Siwa Oasis (Totti 1985: 112–13). This First Cataract is also the destination of Charicles, priest of Apollo in Heliodorus of Emesa's novel the *Aethiopika* (2.29), where he encounters an Ethiopian ambassador. The border with Meroe was Maharraqa (Hierasykaminos), 70 miles to the south, at the southern end of the Dodekaschoinos.

The islands of Elephantine and Philae have left a rich epigraphic dossier (Fig. 42.2). Philae was on the route followed by Roman prefects, who at least sometimes made offerings to the Nile, as pharaohs had done before (Sen. *Q Nat*. 4A2.7; Bonneau 1964: 391). Graffiti record numerous visitors, particularly to the temple of Isis at Philae (Rutherford 1998; Dijkstra 2008: 186–92), but also to Elephantine, site of the temple of Khnum (Maehler 1992). Dignitaries from Meroe also visited Philae (Burkhardt 1985; Pope 2008–9), and the sight of their ships coming up the Nile may have been another attraction for visitors (*IGP* 158).

One of the main attractions was water rafting. Here is the account of Seneca the Elder (*Q Nat*. 4A2.7):

> Among other marvels of the river, I have heard about the incredible daring of the inhabitants. Two of them board a small boat. One rows, the other bails. Then they are violently buffeted among the raging rapids of the Nile and the back-swirling waves of water. At last they reach the narrowest channels, and through them they escape the rocky gorge. Then they are swept along by the entire force of the river, guiding the rushing boat by hand, plunging head down. The onlookers are filled with fright. You would lament and believe that they had been crushed by such a mass of water. They are shot out as from a catapult and float in their vessel far from

FIG. 42.2 Graffiti near the first pylon of the Temple of Isis at Philae

Photo: Christina Riggs.

> the place where they had fallen. The wave which deposits them does not submerge them, but carries them to smooth waters.

Strabo (17.1.49) describes the 'spectacle' that the boatmen put on for the prefects at the cataract: 'they are thrust along with the boat over the precipice, and escape unharmed, boat and all'. Aelius Aristides, in his *Egyptian Discourse* (36.47–51; Waddell 1935: 147 n. 57), narrates how on his trip to Egypt he actually took part in this event himself. The cataracts were given a fantastic literary spin by Philostratus in his *Life of Apollonius of Tyana* (6.26), which describes how Apollonius was warned to avoid the cataracts, but persisted and finally made his way to the Third Cataract, where the roar of the water was overwhelming. Seneca (*Q Nat.* 4A.2.5), Pliny (*HN* 6.181), Cicero (*Rep.* 6.19), and Ammianus Marcellinus (22.15.9) also comment on the deafening roar of the Nile cataracts.

The Royal Tombs

The royal tombs in the Valley of the Kings at Thebes are the best-documented tourist attraction in Roman Egypt, and most of the graffiti are from that period, although a few are Ptolemaic (Winnicki 1995). The tombs were known as the Syringes, after their narrow, rock-cut corridors and chambers, which resembled the syrinx, or panpipe. As elsewhere, the vast majority of the graffiti are in Greek. Tourists came from all over Egypt and all over the western Mediterranean (Baillet 1920–6, pp. xxviii–xxxii). There are, however, remarkably few from Italy. Visitors include soldiers, government officials, doctors, lawyers, and poets, and a few poems are found among the graffiti. There are just a handful of Latin graffiti, including one from a soldier, M. Ulpius Antichianus Pulcher, dated 168 CE (Baillet 1920–6, no. 1448). About half of all the inscriptions come from KV 6, the tomb of Ramesses IX, which was clearly believed to belong to Memnon.

The most common attitude expressed in the graffiti is one of wonder: the word *thauma* ('marvel', or 'wonder') and its derivates are common; one text reads *idion idion idion*, which must mean 'peculiar' or 'extraordinary' (Baillet 1920–6, no. 602; cf. 1268, *idion tris*). There is little sign of religious interest in the tombs, although there is one proskynema to Hermes Trismegistos (Baillet 1920–6, no. 1054b) and an appeal to the mountain nymphs (Baillet 1920–6, no. 319 = *IMEGR* 138). One visitor whose motives were partly religious may have been Nikagoras, son of Minoukianos, of Athens (Baillet 1920–6, nos 1265, 1293), who was a priest at Eleusis under Constantine and may have come to Egypt on a religious mission (Lane Fox 1986: 640–1; Fowden 1987).

There is a question about how Greeks and Romans interpreted the Syringes. In general, the graffiti do not make much reference to death, and it seems to be the craftsmanship they wonder at. An exception is 'Marinos says "Rejoice! No man is immortal"' (Baillet 1920–6, no. 1818 = *IMEGR* 156). Ammianus Marcellinus (22.15.30), in his survey of Egyptian matters, saw them as a defensive strategy against natural disaster:

> There are also subterranean syringes and winding passages which, it is said, those acquainted with the ancient rites, since they had foreknowledge that a deluge was coming, and feared that the memory of the ceremonies might be destroyed, dug in the earth in many places with great labour; and on the walls of these caverns they carved many kinds of birds and beasts, and these countless forms of animals which they called hieroglyphic writing.

Contrast this with the priest of Sais in Plato's *Timaeus* (22d–e), who explains to Solon that the durability of Egyptian culture over many millennia is due to Egyptian geography, which protects the country against the effects of natural calamities.

The Pyramids and Sphinx

The Pyramids at Giza were not only one of the Wonders of the World, but also a superb location for inscriptions and graffiti. Cornelius Gallus is said to have inscribed his achievements on them in 26 BCE (Cass. Dio 53.23). Almost all the graffiti that must have been on the Pyramids have been lost, however (but see *RIGLE* 2.487–518). Among the few exceptions is a short Latin poem copied by William of Boldensele in the fourteenth century:

> I have seen the Pyramids, without you, my dear brother, and in sorrow I have shed tears, all I could do, and inscribe this lament in record of my grief. So may the name of Decimus Gentianus, pontifex and participant in the triumph of Trajan, census-supervisor and consul before his thirtieth birthday, survive on the lofty pyramid. (Courtney 1995, no. 74; cf. van der Walle 1963)

The poem is a beautiful literary expansion of the *emnesthe* formula found in commemorative graffiti. In addition, one fragmentary verse inscription may come from one of the Pyramids (*IMEGR* 128), as may another epigram, cited by an ancient scholar: 'Seeing the monuments of Kaiphren, god-like Mukerenos and Kheops, I, Maximos, was amazed' (*IMEGR* 508). The author, Maximos, may be T. Statilius Maximus Severus, an *idiologos* also mentioned in the Syringes graffiti (*IGLCM* 54; Buecheler 1883: 132–39629:3329629:332; Baillet 1920–6, no. 76).

The nearby Sphinx at Giza seems to have attracted pilgrims and religious visitors from the New Kingdom on (Yoyotte 1960: 50–2), but is not mentioned in classical sources before Pliny the Elder (*HN* 36.77), perhaps because it had become covered in sand, from which it was apparently cleared in the reign of Nero (Adams 2007b: 169–70). A number of Greek graffiti survive, including three poems (*IMEGR* 127, 129–30), the third an acrostic (Carrez-Maratray 1993). The first two of these contrast the peaceful Egyptian Sphinx with the violence of the Greek Sphinx who haunted Oedipus' Thebes, and the first calls the Egyptian Sphinx 'Harmakhis', i.e. 'Hor-em-akhet', 'Horus in the Horizon'.

Seeing Egypt through Greek Culture

Most Greek and Roman visitors to Egypt in the Roman period saw Egypt through the prism of centuries of cultural shaping by Greek writers. Herodotus was particularly important in this ideological construction (Foertmeyer 1989: 109–10; Adams 2007b: 175–6), but so was Homeric epic. We have already seen how Homer and Herodotus conspire to authenticate the traditions about Memnon: Memnon himself comes from the epic tradition, although he is not connected with Egypt until the Hellenistic period, while Cambyses' attack on the statue seems to be an adaptation of Herodotus' Cambyses narrative.

The influence of Homer can be seen, for instance, in a poem that survives in part from the Osireion at Abydos (Boyaval 1969), in which two Italians, Dorotheos and Onesikrates, call on Hermes to save them, as he saved Odysseus on the island of Circe by giving him the drug *molu*. This text seems to represent a sort of fusion between Hermes Trismegistos, presumably identified as the god of the mysterious subterranean Osireion, and the Hermes of Homer's *Odyssey*.

Visitors' attitudes towards earlier Greek visitors are not always positive. A good example is Aelius Aristides, who claims to have got as far as Ethiopia in 141 CE. His whole engagement with Egypt is through Greek writers who have written on the sources of the Nile, and he is particularly keen to criticize Herodotus' account of the course of the Nile through Upper Egypt and of the 'springs of the Nile' at the two mountains between Syene and Elephantine. He doubts whether Herodotus ever got to Elephantine (36.51), and points out that there are no mountains between Syene and Elephantine. Although Aristides admits that there are springs at this point (36.54), the Nile does not originate from them. Unlike Herodotus, Aristides claims to have been briefed by an Ethiopian, who had reliable information about the upper reaches of the Nile. In the end, Aristides rejects the view of every Greek writer, including Homer, and concludes that the Nile is an ineffable mystery. At the same time, it is clear from every paragraph of his treatise that Aristides approaches Egypt through the intellectual framework that earlier Greek writers had constructed, and his attitude of 'inquiry' is, after all, essentially like that of Herodotus.

One feature of the graffiti in the Syringes that suggests the influence of Herodotus is the frequent use of the verb *historeo*, 'inquire, research', corresponding to *historia*, the term Herodotus uses for his historical researches. Although surprisingly not discussed in Baillet's survey of the 'psychology' of the visitors (1920–6, p. lxvi), the verb is used in over 200 texts, such as 'I, Philoxenos son of Philoxenos, researched all the syringes, year 11, Phaophi 20'

(Baillet 1920–6, no. 825), and 'Elpidios, the lawyer and historian from Alexandria, researching, I marveled' (Baillet 1920–6, no. 1861). The same word occurs in the letter of Nearchus, and in Philostratus' fictional account of Apollonius of Tyana's journey up the Nile, in which Apollonius crosses the river frequently 'for the sake of *historia*' (book 5, end). The fourth-century Church Father (Epiph. *De Mensuribus et Ponderibus* 14) attributes to illness Hadrian's desire to visit Egypt and calls the emperor *philohistor*, 'inquiry-loving'. Greeks, and some Romans, thus viewed Egypt in a manner that Greek intellectuals had done before them.

Conclusion

To sum up, the epigraphic habits of tourists, pilgrims, and other travellers in Roman Egypt allow us to trace their movements to a degree unparalleled elsewhere in the Roman empire. To judge from surviving evidence, the provenance of almost all the visitors was Egypt itself or the eastern half of the Mediterranean; visitors from Italy are more rare. Most wrote in Greek, though the volume of graffiti in Demotic remains difficult to quantify with precision when so many remain unpublished. As might be expected, most of the visitors tend to see Egypt through the lens of earlier Greek writers who had written about Egypt.

Suggested Reading

The best survey of the subject is Victoria Foertmeyer's doctoral dissertation, written at Princeton University (Foertmeyer 1989); although never published, it is available to order through ProQuest Dissertation Publishing. Also useful as general introductions are two recent articles by Colin Adams (2001, 2007b); on pilgrimage, see Volokhine (1998), É. Bernand (1988), and Malaise (1987) (all three in French). Adams (2007a) is an excellent survey of land transport in Roman Egypt.

The only overview of all Greek inscriptions then known in Egypt is Letronne (1842–8), which is obviously extremely out of date. Many relevant inscriptions can be found in Cagnat 1891. Metrical inscriptions, with the exception of Philae and Memnon, are collected in *IMEGR*. Totti (1985) provides a selection of relevant inscriptions in Greek. Latin inscriptions can be found in *CIL*. For Demotic inscriptions, the most important collection is Griffith (1937), for the Dodekaschoinos.

Bibliography

Adams, C. E. P. 2001. '"There and Back Again": Getting around in Roman Egypt', in C. E. P. Adams and R. Laurence (eds), *Travel and Geography in the Roman Empire*. London: Routledge, 138–66.

—— 2007a. *Land Transport in Roman Egypt: A Study of Economics and Administration in a Roman Province*. Oxford: Oxford University Press.

—— 2007b. '"Travel Narrows the Mind": Cultural Tourism in Graeco-Roman Egypt', in C. E. P. Adams and J. Roy (eds), *Travel, Geography and Culture in Ancient Greece, Egypt and the Near East*. Oxford: Oxbow, 161–84.

Baillet, J. 1920–6. *Inscriptions grecques et latines des Tombeaux des Rois ou syringes*, 3 vols. Cairo: Institut Français d'Archéologie Orientale.

Bataille, A. 1951. *Les inscriptions grecques du Temple de Hatshepsout à Deir el Bahari*. Cairo: Institut Français d'Archéologie Orientale.

—— 1952. *Les Memnonia: Recherches de papyrologie et d'épigraphie grecques sur la nécropole de la Thèbes d'Égypte aux époques hellénistique et romaine*. Cairo: Institut Français d'Archéologie Orientale.

Bernand, A. 1972a. *De Koptos à Kosseir*. Leiden: Brill.

—— 1972b. *Le Paneion d'el-Kanais: Les inscriptions grecques*. Leiden: Brill.

—— 1977. *Pan du désert*. Leiden: Brill.

—— 1984. *Les portes du désert: Recueil des inscriptions grecques d'Antinooupolis, Tentyris, Koptos, Apollonopolis Parva et Apollonopolis Magna*. Paris: Centre National de la Recherche Scientifique.

—— 1989. *De Thèbes à Syène*. Leiden: Brill.

—— and É. Bernand. 1960. *Les inscriptions grecques et latines du Colosse de Memnon*. Cairo: Institut Français d'Archéologie Orientale.

—— —— 1969. *Les inscriptions grecques de Philae*, 2 vols. Leiden: Brill.

Bernand, É. 1969. *Inscriptions métriques de l'Égypte gréco-romaine: Recherches sur la poésie épigrammatique des grecs et Égypte*. Paris: Belles Lettres.

—— 1981. *Recueil des inscriptions grecques du Fayoum*, vol. 3: *La 'Méris' de Polémon*. Cairo: Institut Français d'Archéologie Orientale.

—— 1983. 'Pélerinage au grand Sphinx de Gizah', *Zeitschrift für Papyrologie und Epigraphik* 51: 185–9.

—— 1988. 'Pélerins', in M.-M. Mactoux and E. Geny (eds), *Mélanges Pierre Lévêque*, vol. 1. Paris: Belles Lettres, 49–63.

Bonneau, D. 1964. *La crue du Nil, divinité égyptienne, à travers mille ans d'histoire (332 av.–641 ap. J.-C.): D'après les auteurs grecs et latins, et les documents des époques ptolémaique, romaine et byzantine*. Paris: Klincksieck.

Bowersock, G. 1984. 'The Miracle of Memnon', *Bulletin of the American Society of Papyrologists* 21: 21–32.

Bowie, E. L. 1990. 'Greek Poetry in the Antonine Age', in D. A. Russell (ed.), *Antonine Literature*. Oxford: Oxford University Press, 53–90.

Boyaval, B. 1969. 'Graffite grec de l'Osireion d'Abydos', *Chronique d'Égypte* 44: 353–9.

Brennan, T. C. 1998. 'The Poets Julia Balbilla and Damo at the Colossus of Memnon', *Classical World* 91: 215–34.

Brodersen, K. 1992. *Reiseführer zu den Sieben Weltwundern: Philo von Byzanz und andere antike Texte*. Frankfurt: Insel.

Buecheler, F. 1883. 'Coniectanea', *Rheinisches Museum für Philologie* 38: 132–3.

Burkhardt, A. 1985. *Ägypter und Meroiten im Dodekaschoinos: Untersuchungen zur Typologie und Bedeutung der demotischen Graffiti*. Berlin: Akademie.

Burstein, S. (ed.) 1989. *Agatharchides of Cnidus: On the Erythraean Sea*. London: Hakluyt Society.

Cagnat, R. (ed.) 1891. *Inscriptiones Graecae ad res Romanas Pertinentes*, I. Paris: Ernest Leroux.

Carrez-Maratray, J.-V. 1993. 'Une énigme du Sphinx: I. Metr. 130', *Zeitschrift für Papyrologie und Epigraphik* 95: 149–52.

Colin, F. 1997. 'Un ex-voto de pèlerinage auprès d'Ammon dans le temple dit "d'Alexandre" à Bahariya (désert Libyque)', *Bulletin de l'Institut Français d'Archéologie Orientale* 97: 91–6.

Courtney, E. 1995. *Musa Lapidaria: A Selection of Latin Verse Inscriptions*. Atlanta: Scholars Press.

Cruz-Uribe, E. 2001. 'Demotic Graffiti from the Wadi Hammamat', *Journal of the Society for the Studies of Egyptian Antiquities* 28: 26–54.

—— 2008. *Hibis Temple Project 3: The Graffiti from the Temple Precinct*. San Antonio, Tex.: van Siclen.

Cuvigny, H. 2003. 'Les documents écrits de la route de Myos Hormos à l'époque gréco-romaine', in Cuvigny (ed.), *La route de Myos Hormos*, vol. 2. Cairo: Institut Français d'Archéologie Orientale, 265–94.

—— and A. Bülow-Jacobsen. 1999. 'Inscriptions rupestres vues et revues dans le désert de Bérénice', *Bulletin de l'Institut Français d'Archéologie Orientale* 99: 133–93.

—— —— 2000. 'Le Paneion d'Al-Buwayb revisité', *Bulletin de l'Institut Français d'Archéologie Orientale* 100: 243–66.

Daumas, F. 1956. 'Le sanatorium de Dendara', *Bulletin de l'Institut Français d'Archéologie Orientale* 56: 35–57.

Derchain, P. 1953. 'La visite de Vespasien au Sérapeum d'Alexandre', *Chronique d'Égypte* 28: 261–79.

de Romanis, F. 1996. *Cassia, Cinnamono, Ossidiana: Uomini e merci tra Oceano Indiano e Mediterraneo*. Rome: 'L'Erma' di Bretschneider.

Dijkstra, J. H. F. 2008. *Philae and the End of Ancient Egyptian Religion: A Regional Study of Religious Transformation (298–642 CE)*. Leuven: Peeters.

Drioton, E. 1943. 'Les fêtes de Bouto', *Bulletin de l'Institut d'Égypt* 25: 1–19.

Dunand, F. 1997. 'La consultation oraculaire en Egypte tardive: L'oracle de Bès à Abydos', in J. G. Heintz (ed.), *Oracles et prophéties dans l'antiquité: Actes du Colloque de Strasbourg, 15–17 juin 1995*. Paris: de Boccard, 65–84.

Elsner, J., and I. Rutherford (eds) 2006. *Pilgrimage in Early Christian and Greco-Roman Antiquity: Seeing the Gods*. Oxford: Oxford University Press.

Festugière, A.-J. 1971. *Sainte Thècle, saints Come et Damien, saints Cyr et Jean (extraits), saints Georges: Traduits et annotés*. Paris: Picard.

Foertmeyer, V. A. 1989. 'Tourism in Graeco-Roman Egypt', doctoral dissertation, Princeton University.

Fournet, J.-L. 1995. 'Les inscriptions grecques d'Abu Kueh et de la route Quft-Qusayr', *Bulletin de l'Institut Français d'Archéologie Orientale* 95: 173–233.

Fowden, G. 1987. 'Nicagoras of Athens and the Lateran Obelisk', *Journal of Hellenic Studies* 107: 51–7.

Frankfurter, D. 1998. *Religion in Roman Egypt: Assimilation and Resistance*. Princeton: Princeton University Press.

Gardiner, A. 1961. 'The Egyptian Memnon', *Journal of Egyptian Archaeology* 47: 91–9.

Gauthier, H. 1911. *Le temple de Kalabchah*, vol. 1. Cairo: Institut Français d'Archéologie Orientale.

Geraci, G. 1971. 'Ricerche sul Proskynema', *Aegyptus* 51: 3–211.

Griffith, F. L. 1937. *Catalogue of the Demotic Graffiti of the Dodecaschoenus*, vol. 1 (Text). Oxford: Oxford University Press.

Guarducci, M. 1942–3. 'Le impronte del Quo Vadis e monumenti affini, figurati ed epigrafici', *Rendiconti della Pontificia Accademia di Archaeologia* 19: 305–44.

Gutbub, A. 1973. *Textes fondamentaux de la théologie de Kom Ombo*. Cairo: Institut Français d'Archéologie Orientale.

Halfmann, H. 1986. *Itinera Principum: Geschichte und Typologie der Kaiserreisen im römischen Reich*. Stuttgart: Steiner.

Henrichs, A. 1968. 'Vespasian's Visit to Alexandria', *Zeitschrift für Papyrologie und Epigraphik* 3: 51–80.

Höcker, C. 2010. 'Wonders of the World', in H. Cancik and H. Schneider (eds), *Brill's New Pauly: Encyclopaedia of the Ancient World*, pt I: *Antiquity*, vol. 15. Leiden: Brill, 724–5.

Hohlwein, N. 1940. 'Déplacements et tourisme dans l'Égypte romaine', *Chronique d'Égypte* 15: 253–78.

Hussein, A. 2000. *Le sanctuarie rupestre de Piyris à Ayn al-Labakha*. Cairo: Institut Français d'Archéologie Orientale.

Jaritz, J., H. G. Maehler, and K.-T. Zauzich. 1979. 'Inschriften und Graffiti von der Brüstung der Chnumtempel-Terrasse in Elephantine', *Mitteilungen des Deutschen Archäologischen Instituts, Abteilung Kairo* 35: 125–54.

Kaper, O. E., and K. A. Worp. 1999. 'Dipinti on the Temenos Wall at Deir-el-Haggar (Dakhla Oasis)', *Bulletin de l'Institut Français d'Archéologie Orientale* 99: 233–58.

Kelly, B. 2010. 'Tacitus, Germanicus and the Kings of Egypt (Tac. *An.* 2.59–61)', *Classical Quarterly* 60: 221–37.

Łajtar, A. 1991. 'Proskynema Inscriptions of a Corporation of Iron-Workers from Hermonthis in the Temple of Hatshepsut in Deir el-Bahari: New Evidence for Pagan Cults in Egypt in the 4th Cent. A.D.', *Journal of Juristic Papyrology* 21: 53–70.

—— 2006. *Deir el-Bahari in the Hellenistic and Roman Periods: A Study of an Egyptian Temple Based on Greek Sources*. Warsaw: Institute of Archaeology, Warsaw University, and Raphael Taubenschlag Foundation.

—— and J. van der Vliet. 2006. 'The Southernmost Latin Inscription Rediscovered (*CIL* III 83)', *Zeitschrift für Papyrologie und Epigraphik* 157: 193–8.

Lampela, A. 1998. *Rome and the Ptolemies of Egypt: The Development of their Political Relations, 273–80 B.C.* Helsinki: Societas Scientiarum Fennica.

Lane Fox, R. 1986. *Pagans and Christians*. Harmondsworth: Viking.

Letronne, A. J. 1842–8. *Recueil des inscriptions grecques et latines de l'Égypte, étudiées dans leur rapport avec l'histoire politique, l'administration intérieure, les institutions civiles et religieuses de ce pays depuis la conquête d'Alexandre jusqu'à celle des Arabes*. Paris: Imprimerie Royale.

Maehler, H. G. T. 1992. 'Visitors to Elephantine: Who Were They?', in J. H. Johnson (ed.), *Life in a Multi-Cultural Society Egypt from Cambyses to Constantine and Beyond*. Chicago: Oriental Institute of the University of Chicago, 209–13; repr. as H. G. T. Maehler, *Schrift, Text und Bild: Kleine Schriften von Herwig Maehler*. Munich: Saur, 2006, 230–37.

Malaise, M. 1987. 'Pèlerinages et pèlerins dans l'Égypte ancienne', in J. Chelini and H. Branthomme (eds), *Histoire des pèlerinages non Chrétiens: Entre magique et sacré: Le chemin des dieux*. Paris: Hachette, 55–82.

Martin, A. 1983. 'Un proscynème inédit d'Edfu', *Chronique d'Égypte* 58: 235–6.

—— 1991. 'De quelques inscriptions des Syringes', *Chronique d'Égypte* 66: 356–60.

Moyer, I. 2003. 'The Initiation of the Magician: Transition and Power in Graeco-Egyptian Ritual', in D. B. Dodd and C. A. Faraone (eds), *Initiation in Ancient Greek Rituals and Narratives: New Critical Perspectives*. London: Routledge, 219–38.

—— 2004. 'Thessalos of Tralles and Cultural Exchange', in S. B. Noegel, J. T. Walker, and B. M. Wheeler (eds), *Prayer, Magic, and the Stars in the Ancient and Late Antique World*. University Park: Pennsylvania State University Press, 39–56.
Murray, M. A., with J. Grafton Milne and W. E. Crum. 1904. *The Osireion at Abydos*. London: Quaritch.
Nachtergael, G. 1999. 'Retour aux inscriptions grecques du Temple de Pselkis', *Chronique d'Égypte* 74: 133–47.
Nock, A. D. 1934. 'A Vision of Mandulis Aion', *Harvard Theological Review* 27: 53–104; repr. as A. D. Nock, *Essays on Religion and the Ancient World*, vol. 1. Oxford: Oxford University Press, 1972, 357–400.
Perdrizet, P., and G. Lefebvre. 1919. *Les graffites grecs du Memnonion d'Abydos*. Nancy: Berger-Levrault.
Perpillou-Thomas, F. 1993. *Fêtes d'Égypte ptolémaïque et romaine d'après la documentation papyrologique grecque*. Leuven: Peeters.
—— 1995. 'Artistes et athlètes dans les papyrus grecs d'Égypte', *Zeitschrift für Papyrologie und Epigraphik* 108: 225–51.
Pope, J. 2008–9. 'The Demotic Proskynema of a Merotic Envoy to Roman Egypt (Philae 416)', *Enchoria* 31: 68–103.
Rehm, A. 1939. '*Μνήσθῃ*', *Philologus* 94: 1–30.
Riad, H. 1968. 'Quelques inscriptions grecques et latines du temple de Louxor', *Annales du Service des Antiquités de l'Égypte* 60: 281–95.
Roccati, A. 1981. 'Alcune iscrizioni greche da file di eta' imperiale', *Bulletin de l'Institut Français d'Archéologie Orientale* 81: 437–42.
Ruppel, W. 1930. *Die griechischen und lateinischen Inschriften von Dakke*. Cairo: Institut Français d'Archéologie Orientale.
Rutherford, I. C. 1998. 'The Island at the Edge: Space, Language and Power in the Pilgrimages Traditions of Philae', in D. Frankfurter (ed.), *Pilgrimage and Holy-Space in Late Antique Egypt*. Leiden: Brill, 229–56.
—— 2003. 'Abydos: A Pilgrimage-History', in R. Matthews and C. Roemer (eds), *Ancient Perspectives on Egypt*. London: UCL Press, 171–89.
Sijpestejn, P. J. 1969. 'A New Document concerning Hadrian's Visit to Egypt', *Historia* 18: 109–18.
Speidel, M.-P. 1974. 'Two Greek Graffiti in the Tomb of Ramses V', *Chronique d'Égypte* 49: 384–6.
Théodoridès, A. 1989. 'Pélerinage au Colosse de Memnon', *Chronique d'Égypte* 64: 267–82.
Tokunaga, R. 2003. 'South Arabic Graffiti in the Eastern Desert (Wadi Hammamat and Wadi Manih)', *Annales du Service des Antiquités de l'Égypte* 77: 181–6.
Totti, M. 1985. *Ausgewählte Texte der Isis- und Sarapis-Religion*. Hildesheim: Olms.
Trombley, F. R. 1993–4. *Hellenic Religion and Christianization, c.370–529*, 2 vols. Leiden: Brill.
van der Walle, B. 1963. 'À propos du graffite latin de la grande pyramide (*CIL* III, 1, no. 21)', *Chronique d'Égypte* 38: 156–60.
van't Dack, E. 1980. *Reizen, expedities en emigratie uit Italië naar ptolemaeïsch Egypte*. Brussels: AWLSK.
Volokhine, Y. 1998. 'Les déplacements pieux en Égypte pharaoniques: Sites et pratiques culturelles', in D. Frankfurter (ed.), *Pilgrimage and Holy-Space in Late Antique Egypt*. Leiden: Brill, 51–97.
Waddell, W. G. 1935. *On Egypt: A Discourse by P. Aelius Aristides of Smyrna*. Cairo: Barbey.

Wagner, G. 1976. 'Inscriptions et graffiti grecs inédits de la grande oasis (Rapport préliminaire: Khargeh et Dakhleh, mars et juin 1975)', *Bulletin de l'Institut Français d'Archéologie Orientale* 76: 283–8.

—— 1996. 'Les inscriptions grecques d'Ain Labakha (steles, graffites, depinti)', *Zeitschrift für Papyrologie und Epigraphik* 111: 97–114.

Weingärtner, D. G. 1969. *Die Ägyptenreise des Germanicus*. Bonn: Habelt.

Winnicki, J. K. 1987. 'Vier demotische Graffiti in den Königsgräbern in Theben', *Enchoria* 15: 163–7.

—— 1995. 'Der Besuch Drytons in den Königsgräbern von Theben', in M. Capasso (ed.), *Papiri documentari greci: Papyrologica Lupiensia* 2. Galatina: Congedo, 89–94.

Yoyotte, J. 1960. 'Les pèlerinages dans l'Égypte ancienne', in *Sources orientales*, vol. 3: *Pèlerinages: Égypte ancienne, Israël, Islam, Perse, Inde, Tibet, Indonésie, Madagascar, Chine, Japon*. Paris: Seuil, 19–74.

—— P. Charvet, and S. Gompertz. 1997. *Strabo: Le voyage en Égypte: Un regard romain*. Paris: Nil.

Zauzich, K.-T. 1973. 'Die unbekannte Schrift auf dem Memnonskoloß', *Enchoria* 3: 159–60.

CHAPTER 43

THE WESTERN OASES*

OLAF E. KAPER

THE Western Oases formed part of the Egyptian cultural realm from the time of the early Old Kingdom. The large oases of Bahariya, Dakhla, and Kharga are known to have had a continuous occupation and intensive contacts with the Nile Valley throughout their history. Only Siwa remained beyond Egyptian control until the Late period. Thanks to a well-organized system of trade and transportation, the oases were able to expand gradually but steadily from the 26th dynasty. The Roman period is of special significance in the history of the oases because it was the time of their greatest agricultural expansion and biggest population increase until modern times. Their economic importance was based on the production of olives, olive oil, wine, and dates, and on the exploitation of natural resources such as alum, salt, and ochre. The Fayum and the Wadi Natrun, although technically also oases within the Western Desert, will not be discussed in this chapter, because their cultural history was different owing to their proximity and easy access to the Nile Valley.

For the Ptolemaic and Roman periods, a first synthesis of the history and culture of the entire Western Desert was written by Guy Wagner (1987). He worked on the basis of Greek documents from and about the oases and also, to a limited degree, archaeological data. Since that publication, research in the oases has progressed rapidly. Scholars from many different disciplines have become involved in the study of the oases, bringing to light a considerable amount of new information. The study by Wagner still stands as the only synthesis of the entire Western Desert in the Graeco-Roman era, but a large amount of new information has become available, of which this chapter aims to present an overview and draw some conclusions.

GEOGRAPHY

Geographically, life in the Western Desert of Egypt is determined by only a small number of factors. The southern half of this desert, which is the eastern part of the Libyan Desert, counts among the driest regions on earth, with no rain of any significance. Only the northern coast

* Colin Hope and Roger Bagnall commented on a draft version of this chapter, for which I am most grateful.

has rain in winter. There is, however, a large amount of water present in subterranean aquifers throughout the Western Desert. This water is accessible only in depressions in the desert surface, which has led to the formation of corresponding oases, except for the Qattara Depression, where the subterranean water is too salty.

The oases are characterized by methods of water management and agriculture that are different from the Nile Valley. Until recently, the water was brought to the surface of the springs or wells by artesian pressure, and it would be led through channels to the fields. Recent research in southern Kharga (Bousquet 1996; Reddé et al. 2004: 187–96) has successfully combined a geological study with ethno-archaeology, archaeology, and the study of Greek and Demotic textual sources to describe this process in antiquity. From the Persian period onwards, the oases of Bahariya and Kharga had developed their agricultural potential through the carving of subterranean aqueducts known as *qanats*. This system persisted into Roman times, as can be seen at Ain Manawir, Umm el-Dabadib, and Ain el-Labakha in Kharga (Wuttmann et al. 1998; Schacht 2003; Rossi and Ikram 2006), and at el-Haiz in Bahariya (Verner and Benesovska 2008: 54–5).

In the Ptolemaic period the invention of the waterwheel (*saqiya*; Hairy 2009: 558–60) enabled the farmers to lift water efficiently to higher levels, and thus cultivate fields at greater distances from the wells without the need for carving *qanats*. In this way, the agricultural potential of the oases was enlarged considerably and it made possible the rapid population growth that is visible in the archaeological remains of the early Roman period.

Wind is another notable natural feature of life in the Western Desert, which has shaped its landscape. Its prevailing direction is north (El-Baz and Wolfe 1981), and it brings with it sand from the northern coast, amassed into dunes. The dunes are one of the particular afflictions of life in this desert, because they may in the course of time wander over fields and houses, and sometimes entire buildings are covered by them, as happened to the temples of Ain Manawir (Wuttmann et al. 1998: 431), Ain Birbiya, and perhaps also Deir el-Hagar.

The significant increase of the population in the oases during the first century CE lasted until the end of the fourth century. During the subsequent Byzantine and Islamic eras, the oases became more lightly populated, which partly explains why so many monuments from the Roman period have survived to this day. In comparison to the Nile Valley, the oases are remarkable for the large number of Roman period sites and monuments and their excellent state of preservation. This is also due to the shifting patterns of habitation sites in the oases, which periodically alter because of the depletion of the water wells on which they depend. Abandoned houses and villages were not always built over as they were in the Nile Valley.

In the Roman period, the five large oases of the Western Desert were administered under the following names:

- Siwa was known as the Oasis of Ammon, Hammon, or Ammoniake. Its Egyptian name was *Ṯꜣ(j)-n-ḏrw*, pronounced 'Santer' (Kuhlmann 1998: 160).
- Bahariya was known as the Northern Oasis or *Ḏsḏs* in Egyptian, and as the Small Oasis in Greek, which may well have included Farafra, although very little is yet known about that oasis in Roman times.
- Dakhla and Kharga were traditionally grouped together under the name Southern Oasis or *Knmt* in Egyptian, and as Oasis of the Thebaid or Great Oasis in Greek. The capital city of the two was at Hibis. It was subdivided into two nomes shortly before

301 CE (*P Kellis* IV 73), called the Hibite (Kharga) and Mothite (Dakhla) nomes. Olympiodorus of Thebes in the early fifth century CE was the first to refer to the two oases as 'outer' and 'inner' (Wagner 1987: 131), which corresponds to their modern names in Arabic. The evidence from textual and archaeological sources shows that Dakhla was always more populous and wealthy than Kharga, but the population of Kharga must also have been considerable in late antique times, when it developed an extensive military network.

Archaeology

Several archaeological missions have focused on sites from the Roman period in the oases. The first site to be explored was Dush in Kharga, chosen by Serge Sauneron to be the focus of investigations by the Institut Français d'Archéologie Orientale from 1976 onwards. This village was known in Egyptian as *Kšt* and in Greek as Kysis, and it was the capital of its own toparchy. Excavations have focused on the stone temple of Sarapis and Isis (Dils 2000; Reddé et al. 2004), on considerable parts of the cemeteries (Dunand et al. 1992, 2005), and on a selection of residences (Reddé et al. 2004). The finds include several hundred ostraca (*O Douch* I–V), but also a pot with gold jewellery belonging to the temple (Reddé 1992). Work was expanded in 2001 to include the entire region of southern Kharga.

In the northern part of Kharga, an archaeological and architectural survey is being carried out by Corinna Rossi and Salima Ikram (Ikram 2008), documenting many sites from the Roman and late Roman periods. Military sites in northern Kharga are at Umm el-Dabadib, el-Gib, Someira, el-Deir, and formerly also at Hibis, now gone. The interpretation of these sites as part of a Roman defence system aimed at protecting trade routes is due to Michel Reddé (1999). Excavations in this area have been carried out at the cemetery at Ain el-Labakha by Egypt's Supreme Council of Antiquities (SCA), which includes a rock-cut temple (Hussein 2000; Ibrahim et al. 2008), and at the cemeteries of el-Deir. At the latter site a multi-disciplinary research team is directed by Gaëlle Tallet of Limoges University. Previously, Françoise Dunand and her team excavated the cemeteries at this site and conducted an anthropological study (Dunand, Heim, and Lichtenberg 2010).

In Dakhla a full archaeological survey was conducted between 1977 and 1983 by the Dakhleh Oasis Project under the direction of Anthony J. Mills (Churcher and Mills 1999), which examined and described all settlements, cemeteries, and other ancient remains of the oasis. Since 1986 excavations have been conducted at the village of Kellis (Ismant el-Kharab) by Colin A. Hope of Monash University, Melbourne, for the Dakhleh Oasis Project. The excavations have aimed at obtaining a comprehensive view of the history and composition of this village, and it has become one of the most important sites yielding new information on Roman Egypt. The following buildings may be reported.

- The temple complex for the god Tutu was built in the first century CE and extended in 193 CE. It appears to have functioned into the 330s (Hope 2004: 11–13). Despite its subsequent destruction, much remained of the temple's plaster decoration, its furniture, and its votive gifts. Most notable is the large mud-brick mammisi (birth house) next to the temple, described below.

- At a distance of about 1 km east of the temple, an area of small houses and workshops from the second and third centuries was found (Hickson 2002; Hope 2002: 172–8).
- From the same time are a few large, rich villas decorated with painted plaster (Hope and Whitehouse 2006; Hope 2009).
- Cemeteries of the village are located to the north-east and south of the temple area, partly built as mausoleum tombs in plastered mud-brick with an outwardly classical appearance (Hope 2003: 247–86). Inside, remains of pharaonic burial equipment were found, and one tomb contained a stone offering chapel with pharaonic-style painted decoration (Kaper 2003b).
- Other tombs were cut into the rock of a ridge of low hills to the north-west of the village (Birrell 1999).

The excavations at Kellis have also shown how Christianity became the dominant religion during the fourth century. Three churches have been excavated, among which is the large east church. This is a three-aisled basilica with a raised apse and a row of side rooms built around the time of Constantine to serve a community of some 200 members (Bowen 2002). A contemporary church, albeit smaller, has since been excavated at the site of Ain el-Gedida, situated a few kilometres north-west of Kellis (Aravecchia forthcoming). A Christian cemetery to the north of Kellis has been investigated by a team of anthropologists who have used the approximately 700 bodies exhumed for a wide range of investigations (Molto 2002a). The important results of these studies include early attestations of TB and leprosy (Molto 2002b: 249–50).

The dry conditions at Kellis have been favourable for the preservation of human tissue and bones, but also for papyrus and a wide range of other organic materials. The numerous papyrus documents from the village are written in Greek (*P Kellis* I) and Coptic (*P Kellis* II, V, VI), but there are also a few in Demotic (Tait 2002), Latin (*P Kellis* I 26), and Syriac (Franzmann in *P Kellis* II and VI). Apart from papyri and ostraca, a remarkably large number of inscribed wooden boards and wooden codices have been found. One of the houses preserved a wooden codex inscribed with agricultural accounts, which has been of great value in reconstructing the ancient economy of the oasis (*P Kellis* IV). Another codex contained orations by Isocrates (*P Kellis* III), which were used in the teaching of poetry. The documents have also revealed the presence of a Manichaean community at Kellis, attested in several houses of the village from the fourth century.

One of the largest towns of Dakhla, called *Ỉmrt* in Egyptian and perhaps Mesobe in Greek (see *P Kellis* IV 74–5), lies in the eastern part of Dakhla at the site of Ain Birbiya. It has been investigated since 1985 by Anthony Mills for the Dakhleh Oasis Project (Mills 1999). The large temple of Ptolemaic date at this site was decorated and extended during the first and early second centuries CE (Kaper 2010). The remains of the temple and the town have been badly affected by the subsequent cultivation of the entire site, so that no organic materials survive.

Better conditions exist in the western end of Dakhla, where a team led by Roger S. Bagnall of New York University (previously of Columbia University) started excavations at Amheida in 2004 (Ruffini and Bagnall 2004) for the Dakhleh Oasis Project. This site is the best-preserved ancient city in the Western Desert. Its name was Trimithis, in Egyptian *St-wꜣḥ*, to which belonged the neighbouring military fort at el-Qasr (Dakhla), remains of which were discovered by Fred Leemhuis in 2008. The town itself has thus far yielded a pottery workshop with five kilns (Hope 1993: 126), a demolished temple (Davoli and Kaper 2006), a small house from the third century (Boozer 2007), and a larger house with wall paintings from the early fourth century (Leahy 1980). A vast cemetery borders Trimithis on its southern side, but the rock tombs of el-Muzawwaqa (Osing et al. 1982) further to the north also belonged to this town. The nearby temple of Deir el-Hagar, decorated in the second half of the first century CE, was probably dependent on this city as well.

The capital of the oasis, Mothis, seems to have largely disappeared beneath the modern town of Mut. The only visible remains are a large temple enclosure, which is being excavated by Colin A. Hope. Among its disturbed remains from the Graeco-Roman period are parts of a brick platform from the foundations of the temple of Seth (Hope et al. 2009: 65).

In Bahariya excavations by the SCA, directed by Zahi Hawass, have uncovered part of a vast cemetery of the Roman period at a few kilometres south-west of Bawiti (Hawass 2000). The settlement to which this cemetery belongs has not yet been identified. The area of el-Haiz in the south of Bahariya has been surveyed by the SCA and two small churches have been found, as well as a late Roman cemetery (Hawass and Grossmann 1993). A Czech mission directed by Miroslav Bárta has started excavating the late Roman settlement at Bir el-Showish (Verner and Benesovska 2008: 54). Elsewhere in el-Haiz, oil and wine presses of late Roman date have been found, as well as the remains of military architecture (Hawass 2000: 148–67).

As for Siwa, the SCA has carried out excavations at the cemetery of Bilad el-Rum, which has elaborate rock-cut tombs with entrance doorways and exterior chambers constructed in limestone. No settlement has yet been excavated in Siwa.

Cultural Idiosyncrasies

The recent projects working in the oases have uncovered settlements that were similar yet in some aspects distinct from contemporary settlements in the Nile Valley. In the following section, I shall list some of the most remarkable features that set them apart from the rest of Egypt. Egyptian provinces each had their own history and they could have unique local traits and traditions, but it seems that the oases may have surpassed the other provinces in the number of cultural idiosyncrasies. I shall select and describe those features that I consider to be significant within the religion, literature, architecture, and funerary customs of the oases. The features are considered significant when they are observable at several different archaeological sites or at different points of time spanning several generations.

Religion

In the domain of the indigenous religion, several remarkable features are observable in the Egyptian temples of the oases.

The deities worshipped in the oases in the Roman period mainly originated from cult centres along the Nile, notably from Thebes, Heliopolis, and Hermopolis. The cult of the Theban god Amun-Re had been firmly implanted in the entire Western Desert, probably since the New Kingdom. In the 26th dynasty, the same god also became adopted in Siwa, under the Greek name Ammon. The gods of Heliopolis are prominently present in the Persian period temple of Hibis, together with those of Memphis and Thebes (Osing 1990), and the same gods are still venerated in Dakhla in the Roman period (Kaper 1997: 41–54). The god Thoth of Hermopolis was venerated in Qasr Bahariya and in Trimithis in Dakhla, and sacred ibises were found buried at both locations. Seth was originally one of the Egyptian state gods that was venerated in Egypt and in the desert. He was redefined as the symbol of evil in the late New Kingdom (te Velde 1977: 138–51), but by contrast, his cult continued in Dakhla Oasis into the early second century CE at least (Kaper 2002a), centred on the principal and largest temple of the oasis at Mut el-Kharab (Hope et al. 2009).

In general, a remarkably large number of protective deities were venerated in the oases. The god Seth should be considered as such, as his principal title was always 'great of strength', but also the great god Amun-Re of Hibis, whose principal title, 'mighty of arm', distinguished him from Amun-Re of Karnak (Guermeur 2005: 565, 582). The apotropaic god Bes is not known to have received a temple cult in the Nile Valley, yet he had a temple at Bawiti (Fakhry 1950; Hawass 2000: 167–73). The protective god Tutu was venerated widely in temples in the Nile Valley, but always in subsidiary cults. Only in Kellis did the god become the principal god of a village temple (Kaper 2003a). The temple at Ain Birbiya was dedicated to a local syncretistic deity combining Amun-Re and Horus under the name Amunnakht (Kaper 1987, 1997). This was again a protective deity, depicted spearing his enemies (Fig. 43.1). In Bahrein Oasis, close to Siwa, a sanctuary from the 30th dynasty was dedicated to Amun-Ir-Nakht (Gallo 2006), which may be a related divinity. Probably Herakles (Khonsu) of Qasr Bahariya (Colin 1997) should also be classified as a protective god. In the temple of Nadura, which was dedicated to Khonsu, a relief depicting Herakles (Kurth 1991–2) seems to point to the identification of these two divine figures, which were known in Bahariya and also in Karnak (Quaegebeur 1975–6). On the identity of the cults in Roman Siwa not enough is known at present.

In Dakhla, Kharga, and Siwa the architecture of the temples of the Roman period is distinctive because of its relatively frequent use of vaulted ceilings. The temples built of mud-brick in Kharga had elliptical vaults (Naumann 1938; Hussein 2000), but the same shape is also encountered in the stone temples at Kysis and Qasr el-Ghueita in Kharga and at el-Zeitun in Siwa (Kuhlmann 1998: 168). In Dakhla several mud-brick temples, such as those at el-Qusur and Qasr el-Halaka and the mud-brick temple at el-Sheikh Mansur, between Bashendi and Ain Birbiya, had vaulted roofs throughout (Kaper 1997: 7–8; Mills 1983: 129–38), but none of the stone temples had vaulted roofs. The dating of the mud-brick temples has not been established with certainty in all cases as very few have been excavated, but many appear to be Roman in date. The building of vaulted sanctuaries in the oases certainly goes back to earlier models. At Amheida in Dakhla, the stone temple for Thoth built during the reign of Amasis had a vaulted roof, as did the temple built under Darius I at that location. The mud-brick temple at Ain Manawir, of the Persian period, also had a vaulted roof (Grimal 1995: 567–72), as did the mud-brick temple of Kysis, which may pre-date the Roman period (Reddé et al. 2004: 180, 184). The stone vaulted side rooms to the sanctuary of the Ghueita temple are

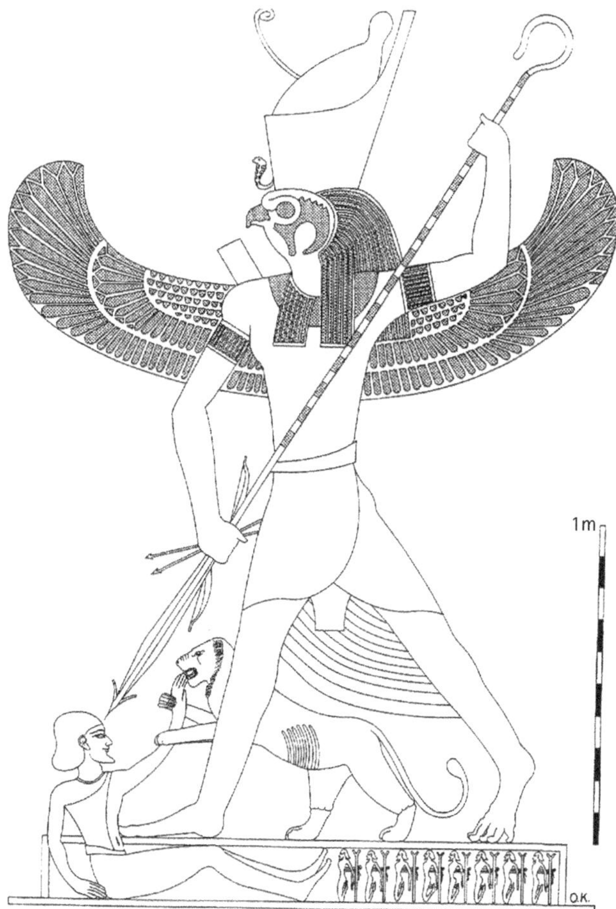

FIG. 43.1 Reconstruction drawing of a relief at Ain Birbiya from the time of Augustus, depicting the local god Amunnakht

Drawing by O. E. Kaper.

also likely to have been built in the Ptolemaic period (Darnell 2007). The occurrence of vaulted ceilings is remarkable because in the Nile Valley such ceilings had a specific mortuary association. They are found exclusively in royal mortuary temples and in tombs, perhaps in imitation of subterranean chambers (Goyon et al. 2004: 328). Even though vaults were also common in the mortuary architecture of the oases, the shape was not considered taboo in temples, perhaps because it was also prevalent in the domestic architecture of the oases. Alternatively, the gods of the oases were considered to reside in caverns or tombs, but there is little textual justification for that view (contra Klotz 2009).

One of the vaulted shrines in the oasis deserves special mention. It is the mammisi of the god Tutu in Kellis, which was erected in mud-brick next to the stone temple (Dobrowolski 2002). Apart from the impressive size of its inner room (4.8 × 12 × c.5 metres high), its decoration is without parallel (Fig. 43.2). First, it focuses on the divine world, depicting only a

FIG. 43.2 The mammisi of Kellis (Ismant el-Kharab), west wall, showing a decorative scheme with classical and Egyptian paintings

Photo: O. E. Kaper.

single anonymous pharaoh on its walls together with more than 400 divine figures (Kaper 2002b). This makes the Kellis mammisi the only temple in which the role of the pharaoh has been suppressed, as it was in Egyptian temples outside Egypt (Hölbl 2005: 93). Secondly, the painted plaster decoration of the mammisi was divided equally between ancient Egyptian paintings with religious content and Roman wall paintings of a kind that was also applied in private residences. This unconventional twofold scheme is to be dated to the early second century CE, and it reflects the greater freedom from decorum enjoyed in the oases (Kaper 2010). A similar case of a mixture of styles within a temple, though far less extreme, is presented by the temple of Khonsu at Nadura, Kharga, in which a relief depicting two forms of Herakles is included in the pronaos decoration (Kurth 1991–2). In two temples of Siwa, at Bilad el-Rum and Ain el-Qurayshat, a mixed architecture may be observed with both Egyptian and Greek elements (Kuhlmann 1998: 164–7; Hölbl 2005: 96), but this may have been more common in Siwa, because the Ammoneion also had Greek and Egyptian architectural traits (Kuhlmann 1988). No temple in the Nile Valley dedicated to Egyptian gods ever incorporated foreign cultural elements in its interior.

There are other indications that the temples in Kharga and Dakhla were less bound by tradition than the temples in the Nile Valley. An important insight into the priests' independent attitude appears from the writing of the Roman emperors' names in hieroglyphs on the temple walls of the Great Oasis. First, the order of the names was reversed. From the reign of

Claudius, the order of names in hieroglyphs was normally the title Autokrator Caesar within the first cartouche and the birth name of the emperor in the second (Hallof 2010). By contrast, the hieroglyphic writings in the oases placed the element Caesar within the second cartouche and the personal name in the first. Even when the names were combined within a single cartouche, this reversed order was maintained as in, for example, Hadrianus Caesar (Grenier 1989: 414 n. 12). This pattern was adopted officially for the name of Tiberius in Egypt (Grenier 1989: 419 n. 28), after which it was reversed for his successors, but the *hierogrammateis* in the oases adhered to this order. Apart from this, the common imperial titles of Autokrator and Sebastos (the Latin Imperator and Augustus) were omitted from the cartouches of the oases. The priests abbreviated the imperial names, which had the effect of making them appear visually more similar to the names of the Ptolemies, in particular to that of Ptolemy Caesar. Because the order of the names in the oases is also identical to that of the final Ptolemy, it is my contention that this represents a deliberate expression of archaism in the temple inscriptions of the Great Oasis. It is not yet known whether the same practice was also adopted in Bahariya or Siwa.

The archaizing writings never appear in Greek in the oases, which makes the cartouches of the emperors appear as an act of political subversion in the oasis temples. Yet, the priests were highly loyal to the imperial authorities. The temples in Dakhla even preserve names of two Roman emperors in hieroglyphs that have not been encountered in the Nile Valley, namely the early version of the name of Galba (Kaper 2010) and the name of Pertinax (Kaper 1997: 30). These instances show that the imperial succession remained of great concern to the priestly scribes, and that the reason for altering the names on the temple walls must be sought elsewhere.

A further demonstration of archaism in the oases is found in the Greek papyri. Under Augustus the length of the year was extended, with leap days that would make the year conform more closely to the solar year (Hagedorn 1994). The inhabitants of Dakhla adopted this calendar reform as elsewhere in Egypt, but they simultaneously continued to make use of the traditional Egyptian calendar (*annus vagus*, the 'wandering year') for secular purposes. This was discovered by Dieter Hagedorn and Klaas Worp (1994), who noted that in Dakhla, even as late as 373 CE, horoscopes and some other private documents continued to make reference to the old calendar, whereas this had become a marginal phenomenon in the Nile Valley, used only sporadically in specific religious contexts.

Literary Culture

In late antique Egypt, educated people often aspired to express themselves poetically. There is considerable evidence from Dakhla for the writing of verses as an outward sign of literary culture (*paideia*). In Amheida a teacher's *dipinto* in verse has been preserved (Cribiore, Davoli, and Ratzan 2008), as well as remains of poetic texts on plaster in another building (Wagner 1987: 79). In Kellis a wooden codex was found with Isocratean orations (*P Kellis* III), several papyri with Homeric texts (Hope and Worp 1998, 2006), and an ostracon with a mythological text about Kyknos (Worp 2003). At Ain Birbiya temple a literary text was inscribed as a graffito on the temple's outer gateway (unpublished). Because of this extensive evidence, it is clear there was a rhetor present in Dakhla, who instructed children in rhetoric and poetry (Cribiore, Davoli, and Ratzan 2008: 190). Indeed, the Great Oasis is known to have produced a famous poet, Soterichus the Oasite (Derda and Janiszewski 2002: 51–70; Miguélez Cavero 2008). This aspect of life in the Western Desert is worth commenting upon here, as it shows that the cultural aspirations of the oasis dwellers were focused on Greek literary culture.

Robert Salomons and Klaas Worp (2009) have compiled an index of all personal names occurring in Greek documents from the Great Oasis. The richness of this documentation appears from the number of names recorded: for Kharga some 1,800 names, mainly from Kysis, and from Dakhla some 1,900, mainly from Kellis. Among these names are a considerable number that had not been reported previously from the Nile Valley, and the most remarkable are those that may be termed classicizing. For instance, among the names given to boys in the Roman period are Isokrates, Ploutogenes, Aristonikos (Wagner 1987: 225), Faustianos (*P Kellis* IV 70), Pisistratos (*P Kellis* I 46 and 63), Memnon (Bagnall and Ruffini 2012), Ophellianos (Worp and Hope 2002), and Nestorios (*P Kellis* I 72). Such names refer to classical Greece, and they are intended to demonstrate, if not show off, the classical education of the parents. Wagner first remarked on this phenomenon in the Great Oasis, and he observed that it may be found among high officials but also among people of humble birth (Wagner 1987: 225–6).

Another surprise emerged from the excavations at Kellis in 1995, when the first of two clay tablets came to light written in Greek (Worp and Hope 2000; Hope et al. 2006: 26–7). Later, the excavations at Amheida also yielded two such tablets (Fig. 43.3). They are inscribed with

FIG. 43.3 A clay tablet from Trimithis (Amheida), inscribed in Greek

Photo: B. Bazzani. Copyright New York University.

texts that would normally appear on potsherds (ostraca). The use of clay for writing purposes is unknown in other parts of Egypt, but specifically in Dakhla a local tradition had existed previously in writing on clay tablets, attested at the Old Kingdom sites of Ain Asil (Posener-Kriéger 1992) and Ain el-Gazzareen. There is no evidence for this practice in the intervening periods, so we must assume that the writing material had been reintroduced in the Roman period.

Mortuary Culture

The final cultural domain I wish to address is that of the traditional mortuary practices in the oases in Roman times. A large number of cemeteries are preserved and some of these have been partially excavated. Again, I shall highlight the more unusual aspects of these finds.

The discovery of gilded cartonnages in Bahariya (Hawass 2000) has led to much publicity. But this is not the only location where mummies with elaborate cartonnage masks and foot-cases have been found. In Kharga, they are known from the cemeteries at Kysis, el-Deir, and Labakha (Dunand 2004; Dunand, Heim, and Lichtenberg 2010), and the cemetery of Kellis (Dakhla) has yielded cartonnage masks and footcases, but also complete body coverings (Schweitzer 2002). In Kysis and Labakha, the faces of mummies were sometimes gilded (Dunand and Lichtenberg 2006: 77), which is known from other cemeteries in the Nile Valley and Alexandria. A unique feature of the burials at Kysis seems to be the offering of human hair in the tombs, perhaps in imitation of the goddess Isis (Dunand, Heim, and Lichtenberg 1998: 130). A different feature that is known both in Dakhla and in Kharga is the use of small wooden sculptures that depict the soul of the deceased as a bird with a human head (*ba*), usually with outspread wings (Fig. 43.4). This custom is only rarely attested in the Nile Valley (d'Auria, Lacovara, and Roehrig 1988: 199–200), and never with outspread wings. Since the earliest examples of wooden *ba* bird statues are known from 18th dynasty burials in the Nile

FIG. 43.4 A wooden *ba* bird found at Kellis (Ismant el-Kharab), North Tomb 2

Photo: O. E. Kaper. Copyright C. A. Hope.

FIG. 43.5 Large pyramid superstructure over a tomb at Trimithis (Amheida)

Photo: O. E. Kaper.

Valley (Bongioanni, Sole Croce, and Accomazzo 2001: 495), such bird statuettes may represent an archaizing feature in the tomb equipment of the oases that had virtually disappeared elsewhere.

The cemetery of Trimithis (Amheida) contains several large mud-brick pyramid superstructures of mausoleum tombs. One of these survives largely intact and has recently been restored (Fig. 43.5). The SCA has in recent years excavated in a cemetery of ancient Mothis, at Bir Shaghala, where another series of elaborately decorated pyramid tombs has come to light. It is remarkable that this type of tomb has not been preserved elsewhere in the Nile Valley or in the Fayum. Smaller pyramid structures at Tuna el-Gebel (Kessler and Brose 2008) and the mention of a contemporary pyramid in a third-century CE papyrus from Oxyrhynchus (*P Lips.* 30) provide limited evidence that the architectural type had not disappeared altogether. Nonetheless, the introduction of large pyramid tombs at two of the major cemeteries of Dakhla is remarkable, pointing at a local tradition that did not exist anywhere else.

Another remarkable tomb type in Dakhla is that of a man named Katenos, which is located in the modern village of Bashendi (Osing et al. 1982: 58–69; on the name, see Bagnall and Worp forthcoming). In its architecture and relief decoration, the tomb imitates an Egyptian temple, which is without parallel in Roman Egypt (Traunecker 2009: 77). Since no trace was found of a subterranean burial chamber, the inhumations may have been placed in the various chambers of the tomb, as was done in the mausoleum tombs at Kellis (Hope 2002). The adjacent tombs in the same cemetery at Bashendi are built in a Hellenistic–Roman style of architecture (Yamani 2001).

Conclusion

At this moment, the culture of the Great Oasis is much better known than that of the Small Oasis or Siwa. Most of the material cited here derives from Dakhla and Kharga, where most of the archaeological work has been carried out. Yet, the phenomena described above seem to have a wider validity for the Western Desert as a whole. They share some common themes, which may be understood as expressions of the cultural identity of the oases dwellers. It is striking how in many aspects of their culture, the inhabitants of the oases asserted a fervent attachment to the past. In their cemeteries, some city dwellers of Dakhla constructed pyramids as an affirmation of their Egyptian roots. In the temples, the priests recorded the names of the Roman emperors in a fashion that referred to the Ptolemaic past rather than to the political reality. Outside the temples, the inhabitants of the Great Oasis used the reformed calendar of the emperor Augustus, but at the same time a few people kept recording dates according to the ancient Egyptian calendar.

Sometimes the writing of everyday matters would not be done on a potsherd, as was customary, but on a clay tablet. By reintroducing this curious practice, the inhabitants of Dakhla distinguished themselves from outsiders by handling a medium that had once been common in the distant past of the oasis. It appears to show that this custom had been consciously reintroduced as a result of historical interest in the local past, because there is no evidence for a living tradition between the Old Kingdom and the Roman period in this respect. The maintenance of specifically local traditions was also behind the construction of vaulted roofs inside the sanctuaries to the gods, which had been customary in the oases at least since the 26th dynasty. Despite these obvious attachments to Egyptian and local traditions, the oasis dwellers held Greek culture in high regard, and more demonstrably so than in the Nile Valley. There was a vivid tradition in writing Greek poetry and studying oration, and people from different strata of society could give their children an archaic Greek name. These aspects of life in the oases can only be described as invented traditions, in a manner that purposely constructs a collective identity for the community.

At the same time, we see signs of innovation, and even radical new forms appearing within the oasis culture. The mammisi of Kellis combines classical wall painting with Egyptian temple decoration in a new and radical fashion. Moreover, the Roman emperor has been omitted from its ritual scenes, going against the generally accepted decorum. A different, less radical breach of standards is visible in Bashendi, where the stone tomb of Katenos was built and decorated in the manner of an Egyptian temple. Both cases demonstrate a freedom to adopt new forms that was not available in the Nile Valley, yet both monuments were created within a largely traditional setting. The stone village temple of Kellis was decorated in the usual way with images of the emperor in Egyptian style (Hope et al. 1989: 13–15), and the tomb of Katenos lies amid a series of mausoleum tombs with a classical appearance.

We must assume that the oases were confronted with a large influx of people in the early Roman period from different parts of Egypt and perhaps also from abroad. As a result a new cultural memory of the oases came into being, which was largely artificial, as the invented tradition of the clay tablets demonstrates most clearly. In his study of cultural memory, Jan Assmann (1992: 18) has observed that 'societies create self-images and perpetuate an identity throughout the generations, while creating a culture of memory. This they do in widely different ways.' The examples listed above show that the local identity was created on the basis of three different sources: the traditions of the local past, Egyptian symbols, and Greek literary culture. The distance from the Nile Valley created a sense of isolation, in which the oasis inhabitants could form their own vision of themselves. New rules of decorum were created as part of a new self-image.

When should we assume that this process of identity building took place? The temple buildings of the oases seem to provide the best answer to this question. The building of new temples took place largely in the second half of the first century CE (Kaper 1998), which must correspond to the period of growth of the settlements to which they belong. Already in the Ptolemaic period there was much activity, as is visible in the abundant ceramics and ostraca from that period found at Mut el-Kharab, but I think that the temples may have been of mud-brick at this time, or reused older buildings as at Amheida. The temple at Amheida demonstrates that Saite and Persian period temples were replaced in the Roman period, but not earlier. Only Ain Birbiya has a newly built stone temple of Ptolemaic date, albeit without decoration. In Kharga the picture is comparable, with only Hibis and Ghueita preserving stone temples that had been extended in the Ptolemaic period and decorated with wall reliefs. The building activities then increased dramatically in Roman times.

In the case of the specific writing of the names of the Roman emperors, outlined above, the priests of the Great Oasis drew inspiration from the written form of the name of Tiberius in hieroglyphs and applied this to all subsequent emperors. Therefore, this particular part of the cultural identity may have been established during Tiberius' reign or not long afterwards.

Another aspect of the cultural identity of the oases is visible in the nature of the indigenous religion. The preference for male deities of a protective nature is strikingly prevalent throughout the oases, and this betrays a sense of insecurity among their inhabitants. The harsh circumstances in the Western Desert, with its scarcity of water, threatening sand dunes, and the overpowering heat of summer, make it understandable that a different outlook on life prevailed. In this case, the different physical surroundings led to cultural differences in the oases, as compared with the Nile Valley.

The recent excavations in the oases have started to show that the cultural identity of the oases was not determined by a backward, reactionary, provincial attitude. Rather, the oases were more independent of the Egyptian heartland than was at first suspected. The physical distance of the oases played a role in this, allowing more freedom from established traditions and decorum, while at the same time creating a specific need for the building of a new and distinct cultural identity.

Suggested Reading

A general introduction to the oases is Mills (2007); the history and monuments of the oases are the subject of Dunand and Lichtenberg (2008). The archaeological remains of the military presence in the Western Desert are described in Jackson (2002). The archaeological survey of the Dakhleh Oasis Project is published in Churcher and Mills (1999). The Roman period remains of Bahariya are included in Hawass (2000); those of Roman Siwa have been described in Kuhlmann (1998).

Bibliography

Aravecchia, N. Forthcoming. 'The Church Complex of Ain el-Gedida, Dakhleh Oasis', in *Acts of the 6th International Dakhleh Oasis Project Conference, Lecce, September 20–24, 2009*.

Assmann, J. 1992. *Das kulturelle Gedächtnis: Schrift, Erinnerung und politische Identität in frühen Hochkulturen*. Munich: Beck.

Bagnall, R. S., and G. Ruffini. 2012. *Amheida* I: *Ostraka from Trimithis* I. New York: NYU Press.

—— and K. A. Worp. Forthcoming. 'Family Papers from Second-Century A.D. Kellis', in O. E. Kaper et al. (eds), *Oasis Papers IV–V: Proceedings of the Conferences of the Dakhleh Oasis Project in Poznan (2002) and Cairo (2006)*. Oxford: Oxbow.

Birrell, M. 1999. 'Excavations in the Cemeteries of Ismant el-Kharab', in C. A. Hope and A. J. Mills (eds), *Dakhleh Oasis Project: Preliminary Reports on the 1992–1993 and 1993–1994 Field Seasons*. Oxford: Oxbow, 29–41.

Bongioanni, A., M. Sole Croce, and L. Accomazzo (eds) 2001. *The Illustrated Guide to the Egyptian Museum in Cairo*. Cairo: American University in Cairo Press.

Boozer, A. 2007. 'Housing Empire: The Archaeology of Daily Life in Roman Amheida, Egypt', doctoral dissertation, Columbia University.

Bousquet, B. 1996. *Tell-Douch et sa région: Géographie d'une limite de milieu à une frontière d'empire*. Cairo: Institut Français d'Archéologie Orientale.

Bowen, G. E. 2002. 'The Fourth Century Churches at Ismant el-Kharab', in C. A. Hope and G. E. Bowen (eds), *Dakhleh Oasis Project: Preliminary Reports of the 1994–1995 to 1998–1999 Field Seasons*. Oxford: Oxbow, 65–85.

—— and C. A. Hope (eds) 2003. *The Oasis Papers 3: Proceedings of the Third International Conference of the Dakhleh Oasis Project*. Oxford: Oxbow.

Churcher, C. S., and A. J. Mills (eds) 1999. *Reports from the Survey of the Dakhleh Oasis, Western Desert of Egypt 1977–1987*. Oxford: Oxbow.

Colin, F. 1997. 'Un ex-voto de pèlerinage auprès d'Ammon dans le temple dit "d'Alexandre", à Bahariya (désert libyque)', *Bulletin de l'Institut Français d'Archéologie Orientale* 97: 91–6.

Cribiore, R., P. Davoli, and D. M. Ratzan. 2008. 'A Teacher's Dipinto from Trimithis (Dakhleh Oasis)', *Journal of Roman Archaeology* 21: 170–91.

Darnell, J. C. 2007. 'The Antiquity of Ghueita Temple', *Göttinger Miszellen* 212: 29–40.

d'Auria, S., P. Lacovara, and C. H. Roehrig. 1988. *Mummies and Magic: The Funerary Arts of Ancient Egypt*. Boston: Museum of Fine Arts.

Davoli, P., and O. E. Kaper. 2006. 'A New Temple for Thoth in the Dakhleh Oasis', *Egyptian Archaeology* 28: 12–14.

Derda, T., and P. Janiszewski. 2002. 'Soterichus Oasites Revisited', in T. Derda, J. Urbanik, and M. Wecowski (eds), *Euergesias Charin: Studies Presented to Benedetto Bravo and Ewa Wipszycka by their Disciples*. Warsaw: Taubenschlag, 51–70.

Dils, P. 2000. *Der Tempel von Dusch: Publikation und Untersuchungen eines ägyptischen Provinztempels der römischen Zeit*, doctoral dissertation, University of Cologne. <http://kups.ub.uni-koeln.de/volltexte/2006/1614>.

Dobrowolski, J. 2002. 'Remarks on the Construction Stages of the Main Temple and Shrines I–II', in C. A. Hope and G. E. Bowen (eds), *Dakhleh Oasis Project: Preliminary Reports of the 1994–1995 to 1998–1999 Field Seasons*. Oxford: Oxbow, 121–8.

Dunand, F. 2004. 'Le mobilier funéraire des tombes d'el Deir (oasis de Kharga): Témoignage d'une diversité culturelle?', in P. C. Bol, G. Kaminski, and C. Maderna (eds), *Fremdheit—*

Eigenheit: Ägypten, Griechenland und Rom: Austausch und Verständnis. Stuttgart: Städelschen Museums-Verein, 565–79.

—— and R. Lichtenberg. 2006. *Mummies and Death in Egypt*. Ithaca, NY: Cornell University Press.

—— —— 2008. *Oasis égyptiennes: Les îles des Bienheureux*. Arles: Actes Sud.

—— J.-L. Heim, and R. Lichtenberg. 1998. 'La vie dans l'extrême: Douch, 1er s. è. chr.–IVe s. è. chr.', in O. E. Kaper (ed.), *Life on the Fringe: Living in the Southern Egyptian Deserts during the Roman and Early-Byzantine Periods*. Leiden: Research School CNWS, 95–138.

—— —— —— 2010. *El-Deir Nécropoles* I: *La nécropole Sud*. Paris: Cybele.

—— et al. 1992. *La nécropole: Exploration archéologique*. Cairo: Institut Français d'Archéologie Orientale.

—— et al. 2005. *Douch* V: *La nécropole de Douch: Exploration archéologique* II: *Monographie des tombes 73 à 92*. Cairo: Institut Français d'Archéologie Orientale.

El-Baz, F., and R. W. Wolfe. 1981. 'Wind Patterns in the Western Desert', *Annals of the Geological Survey of Egypt* 11: 119–39.

Fakhry, A. 1950. *The Egyptian Deserts: Bahria Oasis*, vol. 2. Cairo: Government Press.

Gallo, P. 2006. 'Ounamon, roi de l'oasis libyenne d'el-Bahreïn', *Bulletin de la Société Française d'Égyptologie* 166: 11–30.

Goyon, J.-C., et al. 2004. *La construction pharaonique du Moyen Empire à l'époque gréco-romaine: Contexte et principes technologiques*. Paris: Picard.

Grenier, J.-C. 1989. 'Traditions pharaoniques et realités imperiales: Le nom de couronnement du pharaon à l'époque romaine', in L. Criscuolo and G. Geraci (eds), *Egitto e storia antica dall'ellenismo all'età araba: Bilanco di un confronto*. Bologna: CLUEB, 403–20.

Grimal, N. 1995. 'Travaux de l'Institut Français d'Archéologie Orientale en 1994–1995', *Bulletin de l'Institut Français d'Archéologie Orientale* 95: 539–645.

Guermeur, I. 2005. *Les cultes d'Amon hors de Thèbes: Recherches de géographie religieuse*. Turnhout: Brepols.

Hagedorn, D. 1994. 'Zum ägyptischen Kalender unter Augustus', *Zeitschrift für Papyrologie und Epigraphik* 100: 211–22.

—— and K. A. Worp. 1994. 'Das Wandeljahr im römischen Ägypten', *Zeitschrift für Papyrologie und Epigraphik* 104: 243–55.

Hairy, I. 2009. 'Les machines de l'eau en Égypte et à Alexandrie', in Hairy (ed.), *Du Nil à Alexandrie: Histoires d'eaux*. Alexandria: Harpocrates, 550–71.

Hallof, J. 2010. *Hieroglyphische Schreibungen der Königsnamen der griechisch-römischen Zeit*, vol. 2: *Die römischen Kaiser*. Dettelbach: Röll.

Hawass, Z. 2000. *Valley of the Golden Mummies*. Cairo: American University in Cairo Press.

—— and P. Grossmann. 1993. 'Recent Discoveries in al-Haiz (Bahria Oasis)', *Bulletin de la Société d'Archéologie Copte* 32: 89–109.

Hickson, K. 2002. 'Excavations in Area C at Ismant el-Kharab in 1996–1997', in C. A. Hope and G. E. Bowen (eds), *Dakhleh Oasis Project: Preliminary Reports of the 1994–1995 to 1998–1999 Field Seasons*. Oxford: Oxbow, 157–66.

Hölbl, G. 2005. *Altägypten im römischen Reich: Der römische Pharao und seine Tempel* III. Mainz: von Zabern.

Hope, C. A. 1993. 'Pottery Kilns from the Oasis of el-Dakhla', in D. Arnold and J. Bourriau (eds), *An Introduction to Ancient Egyptian Pottery*. Mainz: von Zabern, 121–7.

—— 2002. 'Excavations in the Settlement of Ismant el-Kharab in 1995–1999', in C. A. Hope and G. E. Bowen (eds), *Dakhleh Oasis Project: Preliminary Reports of the 1994–1995 to 1998–1999 Field Seasons*. Oxford: Oxbow, 167–208.

—— 2003. 'The Excavations at Ismant el-Kharab from 2000 to 2002', in G. E. Bowen and C. A. Hope (eds), *The Oasis Papers 3: Proceedings of the Third International Conference of the Dakhleh Oasis Project*. Oxford: Oxbow, 207–89.
—— 2004. 'Ostraka and the Archaeology of Ismant el-Kharab', in K. A. Worp (ed.), *Greek Ostraka from Kellis: O. Kellis, Nos. 1–293*. Oxford: Oxbow.
—— 2009. 'Ismant el-Kharab: An Elite Roman Period Residence', *Egyptian Archaeology* 34: 20–4.
—— and G. E. Bowen (eds) 2002. *Dakhleh Oasis Project: Preliminary Reports of the 1994–1995 to 1998–1999 Field Seasons*. Oxford: Oxbow.
—— and H. Whitehouse. 2006. 'A Painted Residence at Ismant el-Kharab (Kellis) in the Dakhleh Oasis', *Journal of Roman Archaeology* 19: 313–28.
—— and K. A. Worp. 1998. 'A New Fragment of Homer', *Mnemosyne* 51: 206–10.
—— —— 2006. 'Miniature Codices from Kellis', *Mnemosyne* 59: 226–58.
—— et al. 1989. 'Dakhleh Oasis Project: Ismant e-Kharab 1991–92', *Journal of the Society for the Study of Egyptian Antiquities* 19: 1–26.
—— et al. 2006. 'Report on the Excavations at Ismant el-Kharab and Mut el-Kharab in 2006', *Bulletin of the Australian Centre for Egyptology* 17: 23–67.
—— et al. 2009. 'Report on the 2009 Season of Excavations at Mut el-Kharab, Dakhleh Oasis', *Bulletin of the Australian Centre for Egyptology* 20: 47–86.
Hussein, A. 2000. *Le sanctuaire rupestre de Piyris à Ayn al-Labakha*. Cairo: Institut Français d'Archéologie Orientale.
Ibrahim, B. A., et al. 2008. *Le matériel archéologique et les restes humains de la nécropole d'Aïn el-Labakha (Oasis de Kharga)*. Paris: Cybèle.
Ikram, S. 2008. 'The North Kharga Oasis Survey', *Bulletin of the American Research Center in Egypt* 193: 28–31.
Jackson, R. B. 2002. *At Empire's Edge: Exploring Rome's Egyptian Frontier*. New Haven: Yale University Press.
Kaper, O. E. 1987. 'How the God Amun-Nakht Came to Dakhleh Oasis', *Journal of the Society for the Study of Egyptian Antiquities* 17: 151–6.
—— 1997. 'Temples and Gods in Roman Dakhleh: Studies in the Indigenous Cults of an Egyptian Oasis', doctoral dissertation, University of Groningen.
—— 1998. 'Temple Building in the Egyptian Deserts during the Roman Period', in Kaper (ed.), *Life on the Fringe: Living in the Southern Egyptian Deserts during the Roman and Early-Byzantine Periods*. Leiden: Brill, 139–58.
—— 2002a. 'A Group of Priestly Dipinti in Shrine IV at Ismant el-Kharab', in C. A. Hope and G. E. Bowen (eds), *Dakhleh Oasis Project: Preliminary Reports of the 1994–1995 to 1998–1999 Field Seasons*. Oxford: Oxbow, 209–16.
—— 2002b. 'Pharaonic-Style Decoration in the Mammisi at Ismant el-Kharab: New Insights after the 1996–1997 Field Season', in C. A. Hope and G. E. Bowen (eds), *Dakhleh Oasis Project: Preliminary Reports of the 1994–1995 to 1998–1999 Field Seasons*. Oxford: Oxbow, 217–23.
—— 2003a. *The Egyptian God Tutu: A Study of the Sphinx-God and Master of Demons with a Corpus of Monuments*. Leuven: Peeters.
—— 2003b. 'The Decoration of North Tomb 1', in G. E. Bowen and C. A. Hope (eds), *The Oasis Papers 3: Proceedings of the Third International Conference of the Dakhleh Oasis Project*. Oxford: Oxbow, 323–30.
—— 2010. 'Galba's Cartouches at Ain Birbiyeh', in K. Lembke, M. Minas-Nerpel, and S. Pfeiffer (eds), *Tradition and Transformation: Egypt under Roman Rule*. Leiden: Brill, 181–201.

Kessler, D., and P. Brose. 2008. *Ägyptens letzte Pyramide: Das Grab des Seuta(s) in Tuna el-Gebel.* Haar: Brose.

Klotz, D. 2009. 'The Cult-Topographical Text of Qasr el-Zayyan', *Revue d'Égyptologie* 60: 17–40.

Kuhlmann, K. P. 1988. *Das Ammoneion: Archäologie, Geschichte und Kultpraxis des Orakels von Siwa.* Mainz: von Zabern.

—— 1998. 'Roman and Byzantine Siwa: Developing a Latent Picture', in O. E. Kaper (ed.), *Life on the Fringe: Living in the Southern Egyptian Deserts during the Roman and Early-Byzantine Periods.* Leiden: Research School CNWS, 159–80.

Kurth, D. 1991–2. 'Einige Anmerkungen zum oberen Tempel von Nadura in der Oase Charga', *Dielheimer Blätter zum Alten Testament* 27: 172–80.

Leahy, L. M. M. 1980. 'Dakhleh Oasis Project: The Roman Wall-Paintings from Amheida', *Journal of the Society for the Study of Egyptian Antiquities* 10: 331–78.

Miguélez Cavero, L. 2008. *Poems in Context: Greek Poetry in the Egyptian Thebaid 200–600 AD.* Berlin: de Gruyter.

Mills, A. J. 1983. 'The Dakhleh Oasis Project, Report on the Fifth Season of Survey: October 1982–January 1983', *Journal of the Society for the Study of Egyptian Antiquities* 13: 121–41.

—— 1999. 'Ein Birbiyeh', in C. A. Hope and A. J. Mills (eds), *Dakhleh Oasis Project: Preliminary Reports on the 1992–1993 and 1993–1994 Field Seasons.* Oxford: Oxbow, 23–4.

—— 2007. 'The Oases', in T. Wilkinson (ed.), *The Egyptian World.* London: Routledge, 49–56.

Molto, J. E. 2002a. 'Bio-Archaeological Research of Kellis 2: An Overview', in C. A. Hope and G. E. Bowen (eds), *Dakhleh Oasis Project: Preliminary Reports of the 1994–1995 to 1998–1999 Field Seasons.* Oxford: Oxbow, 239–55.

—— 2002b. 'Leprosy in Roman Period Skeletons from Kellis 2, Dakhleh, Egypt', in C. A. Roberts, M. E. Lewis, and K. Manchester (eds), *The Past and Present of Leprosy.* Oxford: Archaeopress, 179–92.

Naumann, R. 1938. 'Bauwerke der Oase Khargeh', *Mitteilungen des Deutschen Archäologischen Instituts, Abteilung Kairo* 8: 1–16.

Osing, J. 1990. 'Zur Anlage und Dekoration des Tempels von Hibis', in S. Israelit-Groll (ed.), *Studies in Egyptology Presented to Miriam Lichtheim*, vol. 2. Jerusalem: Magnes Press, 751–67.

—— et al. 1982. *Denkmäler der Oase Dachla: Aus dem Nachlass von Ahmed Fakhry.* Mainz: von Zabern.

Parlasca, K. 1995. 'Neue Beobachtungen zu den paganen Grabbauten in el-Bagawat (Kharga Oase) und ihre Funden', in N. Bonacasa (ed.), *Alessandria e il mondo ellinistico-romano*, vol. 1. Rome: 'L'Erma' di Bretschneider, 202–4.

Posener-Kriéger, P. 1992. 'Les tablettes en terre crue de Balat', in É. Lalou (ed.), *Les Tablettes à écrire de l'antiquité à l'époque moderne.* Turnhout: Brepols, 41–52.

Quaegebeur, J. 1975–6. 'Les appellations grecques des temples de Karnak', *Orientalia Lovaniensia Periodica* 6/7: 463–78.

Reddé, M. 1992. *Le Trésor: Inventaire des objets et essai d'interprétation.* Cairo: Institut Français d'Archéologie Orientale.

—— 1999. 'Sites militaries romains de l'oasis de Kharga', *Bulletin de l'Institut Français d'Archéologie Orientale* 99: 377–96.

—— et al. 2004. *Kysis: Fouilles de l'Ifao à Douch Oasis de Kharga (1985–1990).* Cairo: Institut Français d'Archéologie Orientale.

Rossi, C., and S. Ikram. 2006. 'North Kharga Oasis Survey 2003 Preliminary Report: Umm el-Dabadib', *Mitteilungen des Deutschen Archäologischen Instituts, Abteilung Kairo* 61: 279–306.

Ruffini, G., and R. S. Bagnall. 2004. 'Civic Life in Fourth-Century Trimithis: Two Ostraca from the 2004 Excavations', *Zeitschrift für Papyrologie und Epigraphik* 149: 143–52.

Salomons, R. P., and K. A. Worp. 2009. '*Onomasticon Oasiticum*: An Onomasticon of Personal Names Found in Documentary Texts from the Theban Oasis in Graeco-Roman Times', 2nd edn. <http://media.leidenuniv.nl/legacy/onomas_final.pdf>.

Schacht, I. 2003. 'A Preliminary Survey of the Ancient *Qanat* System of the Northern Kharga Oasis', *Mitteilungen des Deutschen Archäologischen Instituts, Abteilung Kairo* 59: 279–306.

Schweitzer, A. 2002. 'Les parures de cartonnage des momies d'une nécropole d'Ismant el-Kharab', in C. A. Hope and G. E. Bowen (eds), *Dakhleh Oasis Project: Preliminary Reports of the 1994–1995 to 1998–1999 Field Seasons*. Oxford: Oxbow, 269–76.

Tait, J. 2002. 'Demotic', in C. A. Hope and G. E. Bowen (eds), *Dakhleh Oasis Project: Preliminary Reports of the 1994–1995 to 1998–1999 Field Seasons*. Oxford: Oxbow, 297–8.

te Velde, H. 1977. *Seth, God of Confusion: A Study of his Role in Egyptian Mythology and Religion*, 2nd edn. Leiden: Brill.

Traunecker, C. 2009. 'Le monde funéraire et les temples', *Dossiers d'Archéologie hors série* 16: *Égypte: Les portes du ciel: Exposition au Musée du Louvre*, 70–7.

Verner, M., and H. Benesovska. 2008. *Unearthing Ancient Egypt: Fifty Years of the Czech Archaeological Exploration in Egypt*. Prague: Charles University.

Wagner, G. 1987. *Les oasis d'Égypte à l'époque grecque, romaine et byzantine d'après les documents grecs*. Cairo: Institut Français d'Archéologie Orientale.

Worp, K. A. 2002. 'Short Texts from the Main Temple', in C. A. Hope and G. E. Bowen (eds), *Dakhleh Oasis Project: Preliminary Reports of the 1994–1995 to 1998–1999 Field Seasons*. Oxford: Oxbow, 333–49.

—— 2003. 'A Mythological Ostrakon from Kellis', in G. E. Bowen and C. A. Hope (eds), *The Oasis Papers 3: Proceedings of the Third International Conference of the Dakhleh Oasis Project*. Oxford: Oxbow, 379–82.

—— and C. A. Hope. 2000. 'A Greek Account on a Clay Tablet from the Dakhleh Oasis', in H. Melaerts (ed.), *Papyri in Honorem Johannis Bingen Octogenarii (P. Bingen)*. Leuven: Peeters, 471–85.

—— —— 2002. 'Dedication Inscriptions from the Main Temple', in C. A. Hope and G. E. Bowen (eds), *Dakhleh Oasis Project: Preliminary Reports of the 1994–1995 to 1998–1999 Field Seasons*. Oxford: Oxbow, 323–31.

Wuttmann, M., et al. 1998. 'Ayn Manâwîr (oasis de Kharga): Deuxième rapport préliminaire', *Bulletin de l'Institut Français d'Archéologie Orientale* 98: 367–462.

Yamani, S. 2001. 'Roman Monumental Tombs in Ezbet Bashendi', *Bulletin de l'Institut Français d'Archéologie Orientale* 101: 393–414.

CHAPTER 44

THE EASTERN DESERT AND THE RED SEA PORTS

JENNIFER GATES-FOSTER

THE hyper-arid zone between the Nile Valley and the Red Sea known as the Arabian, or Eastern, Desert was a hive of activity during the Roman era. Despite its harsh climate and its challenging and diverse topography, it supported a dispersed, but surprisingly substantial, population throughout the first three centuries of Roman rule. Since the 1980s archaeological work in this region has proliferated, producing a vast corpus of documents and materials that rival the Fayum for the range of observations they offer on life in the marginal regions of Roman Egypt. Unlike the Fayum, however, the archaeological sites yielding this material are not, for the most part, agricultural towns and villages, but specialized installations constructed to shelter travellers, protect precious water resources, or house a seasonally resident population of workers and their families. The more substantial ports with their associated settlements were more likely occupied year-round, although the monsoon season that determined the viability of trade in the Red Sea and the Indian Ocean almost certainly dictated a cycle of low- and high-traffic periods throughout the year when there were probably fluctuating numbers of inhabitants present in the towns.

The special character of settlements and sites in the Eastern Desert is in part a reflection of its difficult climate; life in the desert was dependent on the water obtained from wells in the wadis (valleys) and the importation of most, if not all, foodstuffs (van der Veen 1998, 2004; Cappers 2006). The Eastern Desert receives less than 1 mm of rain annually and summer temperatures routinely reach 114 °F (45.5 °C). The landscape itself is divided between jagged volcanic mountain peaks that form a range running parallel with the coast and sandy wadis that cut through to a narrow coastal plain in the east (Fig. 44.1). The mountainous interior is flanked by a wide expanse of sandy plateau to the west leading into the Nile Valley. The geology of the region makes it a vast mineral storehouse, and the Roman era saw an intensification of mining operations at many sites, most famously at Mons Claudianus and Mons Porphyrites in the early first century CE. However, much of the activity taking place in the Eastern Desert during this time was the result of the burgeoning East African and Indian

FIG. 44.1 The Wadi Sikait

Author's photograph.

Ocean trade, which flowed along a series of desert tracks through the Eastern Desert to the Red Sea ports (Sidebotham 1986; Young 2001; Jackson 2002). Berenike Troglodytica, in particular, was a major hub for the trade in goods with India, Sri Lanka, and Yemen, and this is reflected in the extensive range of imported materials recovered at the site. Many of the Roman sites known from the desert were involved either directly or tangentially in the transport of materials from the ports to the Nile Valley, while others existed to support the mining operations.

The Roman army played a significant supporting role in these enterprises, as is increasingly clear from documents recovered from both the desert stations and the ports (Cuvigny 2003). The presence of the army is a testament both to the value of the commodities entering the Roman sphere through the region, but also to the anxiety caused by the presence of other groups in the desert, especially nomadic tribes such as the Blemmyes, whose presence was recorded by numerous authors and attested by documents from the desert itself as early as the first century CE. Thus far, the material culture of these nomadic groups remains largely obscure as archaeological work in the region has focused almost exclusively on the discovery and excavation of Graeco-Roman sites, especially those of Roman date. Nevertheless, these Bedouin were a significant factor in the eventual withdrawal of the Roman military from the Eastern Desert in the mid-third century, when the instability of the Thebaid, and weakening of the Roman regime, made supporting the desert infrastructure impractical.

While this narrative is relatively well developed and increasingly supplemented by further detail, synthetic scholarship on the Eastern Desert in this period remains largely in its infancy. Scholars working in the region continue to focus primarily on the documentation of remains and their speedy publication in detailed field reports, a tendency that is more than justified by ongoing threats from looting, adventure tourism, and development along the Red Sea coast, which have swallowed a number of important sites. As a result, material from the region is known primarily to specialists, while more synthetic treatments that attempt to contextualize the material from the Eastern Desert alongside that from other parts of the empire, or even to compare the Eastern Desert with other regions of Egypt, are few. The inclusion of the imperial stone quarries in treatments of Roman industrial and economic practices more generally is a notable exception (Maxfield 2001; Adams 2007a; Hirt 2010), and the Eastern Desert materials related to the Red Sea trade are appearing more frequently in discussions of Roman economic activity by scholars working outside Egypt (Young 2001). These welcome developments highlight the extraordinary richness of the Eastern Desert's material and historical record, but much remains to be done. Accordingly, this chapter aims both to offer an overview of current scholarship on the Eastern Desert and to highlight some of the contributions that this material makes to our understanding of Roman Egypt more generally.

Archaeological and Documentary Sources for the Eastern Desert

The Eastern Desert, like many other arid regions of Egypt, is blessed with a rich archaeological and documentary record. The wealth of materials recovered from the desert has much, however, to do with the extraordinary intensification of activity in the region from the late first century BCE and lasting into the seventh century CE, with some periods of relative abandonment. There is, for example, comparatively little evidence from the Eastern Desert during the Ptolemaic period, although, as knowledge of pottery chronologies improves and excavation increases, this will almost certainly change (Gates 2005). Likewise, the third century saw a general decline in the level of activity in the Eastern Desert, which remained depressed until a renaissance in the fourth century, which lasted until the early sixth century. For the Roman era, particularly for the first three centuries, there is quite simply much more to recover, and the preservation of these materials is a testimony both to their durability in the desert environment and to the sheer intensity of Roman activity.

The archaeological remains in the Eastern Desert have been known and recorded by European explorers for centuries and form part of the living landscape of the desert for the Bedouin tribes that still inhabit the land. Interest in the Eastern Desert intensified in the early nineteenth century, when a number of European scientists visited the region as part of their travels throughout Egypt. Most came because of interest in the region's mineral resources but were impressed above all else by the extraordinary quantity of visible archaeological remains in the landscape. John Gardner Wilkinson, best known for his work in the Valley of the Kings, also spent considerable time in the Eastern Desert making detailed drawings of many of the ruined buildings (Wilkinson 1835). His drawings, along with those of many others, are invaluable resources for understanding how the archaeological remains looked before many of the sites were destroyed by looters or damaged by natural processes. To these early visitors, the Eastern Desert offered a glimpse of a different type of ancient material from that found in the temple centres of the Nile Valley: houses, temples, mines, and, in some cases, whole villages belonging to the post-Pharaonic era lay abandoned in the landscape. It has only been relatively recently that systematic survey of these standing remains has been undertaken and that some sense of the range of site types present in the desert has been documented.

Most archaeological work in the region has understandably focused on recording in a more orderly way the same visible architectural remains that so fascinated early visitors to the desert. Regional survey has, for the most part, relied on extensive methods that record primarily large-scale remains and pass over sites without substantial visible material on the desert surface (Prickett 1979; Sidebotham and Zitterkopf 1995; Wright 2003). As a result, most of what is known about the archaeological profile of the Eastern Desert is constituted by intensive work on the Roman era fortifications, or *praesidia*, the port cities, such Berenike and Myos Hormos, and the imperial mining complexes. Smaller sites are generally only noted when located along an ancient roadway or near a larger installation. For practical reasons, the survey methods employed by teams working in the Eastern Desert have not been designed to detect other, less prominent remains, and as a result our sense of the material profile of the Eastern Desert is heavily skewed towards the more elaborate and monumental constructions that are associated with external initiatives and populations, especially the Roman army. The nomadic tribes, for example, which were almost certainly a fundamental part of the desert in all periods, are all but invisible in both the archaeological and historical record (Barnard 2009).

While survey archaeology has a long history in the Eastern Desert, systematic excavation is a much more recent arrival. In the 1970s and 1980s British and American archaeological teams in the region began the first systematic excavations at the sites of Myos Hormos (modern Quseir al-Qadim) (Whitcomb and Johnson 1979, 1982; Peacock and Blue 2005, 2011) and Mons Claudianus (Bingen et al. 1992, 1997; Peacock and Maxfield 1997; Cuvigny 2000; Maxfield and Peacock 2001a, 2006; Bülow-Jacobsen 2009). These excavations were soon followed by projects in the 1990s at other major sites of the Roman era, including Mons Porphyrites (Maxfield and Peacock 2001b; Peacock and Maxfield 2007), Berenike (Sidebotham et al. 1995; Sidebotham and Wendrich 1996, 1998, 1999, 2007), and the *praesidia* of the Koptos–Myos Hormos road (Cuvigny 2003). After a brief hiatus in the early 2000s, work in the desert began again in the new millennium with renewed urgency as development pressures along the coast and mineral mining threatens sites throughout the region. With the introduction of excavation, knowledge of the material profile of the desert settlements has expanded beyond architecture to include pottery, textiles, faunal and floral remains, cordage, and other categories of archaeological materials that reveal a much richer picture of the desert system, especially through its relationship to the Nile Valley and the lifeways of its inhabitants.

Not least among the categories of artefacts yielded by these excavations are the ostraca and papyri that are the best known sources of information about the Eastern Desert in the Roman era (Fig. 44.2). As in other parts of Roman Egypt, the overwhelming majority of the documents recovered in the Eastern Desert are written in Greek, although there are significant numbers of Latin examples, particularly at sites where the Roman army seems to have been present. At port sites, in particular, many foreign languages are represented. Some twelve written languages are attested at Berenike alone, including Tamil, Palmyrene, and a variety of other Semitic languages (Sidebotham and Zych 2010).

FIG. 44.2 Early Roman ostraca and reed pen from Berenike

Photo courtesy of S. Sidebotham.

The *sebakh*, or rubbish dumps, of the Eastern Desert settlements have proven to be rich with inscribed materials. Ostraca—sherds of broken pottery used as a writing surface—are by far the most commonly recovered category of inscribed material recovered from the Eastern Desert. Most archaeological sites of the Roman period yield a handful of these informative artefacts and some, like Mons Claudianus, Berenike, and Krokodilo, for example, yield hundreds or even thousands. Some 9,000 ostraca were recovered from Mons Claudianus alone (Bingen et al. 1992, 1997; Cuvigny 2000; Bülow-Jacobsen 2009). The durability and accessibility of the potsherd made it the preferred method of communication between desert settlements, as well as a useful means of keeping records in a difficult environment. The Customs House archive from the trash dump at Berenike, for example, includes texts detailing the passage of goods through the port destined for distant shores or for use on the ships taking part in the Indo-Roman trade of the first century CE (Bagnall et al. 2000, 2005).

In addition to the common ostraca, papyri have also been recovered from the Eastern Desert, but in fewer numbers. Papyri are inherently less durable than pottery sherds and the preservation of this material in the harsh desert environment is less likely. It seems, however, that papyri were also not as commonly used in the Eastern Desert as ostraca, being reserved, at least in some periods, for special communications (Cuvigny 2003) or letters. In any case, the papyri and ostraca offer considerable insight into the finer details of the administration of the Red Sea trade and the Eastern Desert mining industries, as well as information about the diet, personal relationships, and anxieties of the desert inhabitants.

Another important body of evidence from the Eastern Desert is that of the Roman era rock carvings—both figural and textual—that dot the desert landscape. These appear in a range of contexts; many are formal inscriptions like the Flavian inscription that was placed above the lintel of the *praesidium* at Siket near Berenike (Sidebotham and Wendrich 2007) or the inscribed altar (likely Trajanic) dedicated at the temple at Mons Claudianus to Zeus Helios Great Serapis (Maxfield and Peacock 2001a). Alongside these circumscribed accounts of personal piety and imperial ownership, however, are many more informal written responses to the desert. Proskynemata—expressions of personal piety or reverence—are found throughout the Eastern Desert. Many appear, for example, in the decorated galleries of the Wadi Hammamat between Koptos (modern Qift) and the Red Sea coast, where individuals added their own voice to a palimpsest of graffiti dating back to the Pharaonic period (Bernand 1972a; Cuvigny and Bülow-Jacobsen 1999; Gates-Foster 2012). Other well-known examples of this phenomenon are the inscriptions in the cave shelter at the Wadi Menih, also near Koptos, where individuals left detailed information about themselves as they travelled through the desert during the Roman era (Meredith 1953; de Romanis 1996; Adams 2007b). These inscriptions have received renewed attention as excavation and the study of documentary sources have enriched understanding of the desert context in novel ways.

The Early Roman Era: International Trade and Mining

The picture offered by this range of materials is an exciting one. A direct result of the renewed focus on the Eastern Desert has been a much more detailed understanding of the types of place that were important to or used by individuals in the Eastern Desert during the Roman period and the way that this changed over time. One of the benefits of this more detailed picture is the degree to which it is now possible to evaluate the relationship between Ptolemaic and early Roman practices in the Eastern Desert. Under the Ptolemies—as for the Roman emperors—the Eastern Desert was a place from which to extract mineral resources. In the Ptolemaic period, gold from the mines in the southern half of the desert was the primary focus and Ptolemaic installations at Barramiyya, Samut, and other sites seem to have been part of an early attempt on the part of the Ptolemies to establish gold works (Burstein 1989; Klemm et al. 2002; Gates 2005).

The importation of elephants for the Ptolemaic army was also of considerable interest to the Ptolemaic kings, and the creation of an infrastructure during the early third century BCE to support this network is now clearly substantiated not only by papyrological evidence from other parts of Egypt but also from the Eastern Desert itself (Burstein 1993; Sidebotham and Zych 2010). The primary route through the desert for the transport of the elephants was along a roadway, largely unmarked, from the port at Berenike to Apollinopolis Magna (Edfu), although other roadways have been documented from Marsa Nakari on the coast and there are numerous sites with Ptolemaic remains that lie off these main routes (Sidebotham 2002; Gates 2005). In addition to the trade in elephants and ivory, other commodities likely passed through the Red Sea ports, but much less is known about the trade contacts with the East established during this time than in the centuries to follow (Hölbl 2001).

In the late first century BCE, official attention to the region had waned considerably, and it was not until the last decade of the millennium that a resurgence took place. The change was stimulated by a number of factors, not least of which was a renewed interest in the Red Sea trade, which was dramatically expanded in the years following the annexation of Egypt by Rome (Young 2001). Under the Romans, trade contacts with India and other Far Eastern locales intensified as luxuries such as pepper and pearls were highly sought after for the Mediterranean market. There are a number of ancient authors who discuss the Red Sea trade in these early years, including Strabo, Pliny, and the anonymous author of the *Periplus of the Erythraean Sea*, which was likely written sometime in the first century CE (Casson 1989). In the Eastern Desert, Myos Hormos and Berenike were the primary ports of the early Roman era (Sidebotham and Wendrich 2001–2; Peacock and Blue 2005, 2011; Sidebotham and Zych 2010). Ostraca recovered from the Customs House archive at Berenike indicate that much of the trade was in particular varieties of Mediterranean wine, which was exported to the Indian Ocean and other parts of the Red Sea in return for luxury items. Likewise, the Nikanor Archive from Koptos offers details of the supplies meted out to the sailors and other labourers involved in the trade.

The early Roman levels excavated at Berenike have proven to be particularly rich sources for accessing a more complex picture of the international trade passing through Berenike. Not only has the site produced important documents that offer details of who was taking part in the trade and its organization, but it has also provided valuable information about the range of materials involved in these transactions. While Pliny and other authors discuss the commodities most highly prized in Rome, archaeologists working at Berenike have recovered a much wider array of materials that were also part of the picture. Wood from the genus of tree that produces frankincense, imported beads and wood, as well as a range of floral remains indicate that foodstuffs and other materials were also imported into the city during the Roman era (Sidebotham, Hense, and Nouwens 2008; Sidebotham and Zych 2010). The residents of early Roman Berenike also dined off a range of imported pottery types, including several types of Eastern Sigillata, as well as Indian rouletted wares.

The value of these items and the need to protect the caravans that transported them through the desert are the likely reasons that the first century CE also saw a surge in construction in the desert between the port cities and the Nile Valley (Fig. 44.3). During the late Ptolemaic period, Koptos (Qift) began functioning as the main entrepôt for the Red Sea trade, taking over from Apollonopolis Magna (Edfu) in the Ptolemaic period (Rathbone 2002). During this time, the routes between Berenike, Myos Hormos, and the Red Sea were fortified with elaborate *praesidia*, discussed above, many of which guarded wells or cisterns known as *hydreumata*. These impressive constructions were linked to the presence of the army quite early and remained so through the second century (Maxfield 2000). The desert roads and their associated settlements were overseen by the *praefectus Montis Berenicidis*, an equestrian military officer whose sphere of responsibilities extended to the imperial quarrying operations in the northern half of the Eastern Desert as well as the maintenance of the road installations and water supply (Bagnall et al. 2001). By the second century, the *praesidia* were garrisoned with small groups of soldiers who were responsible for the security of the road (Maxfield 1996). These soldiers were increasingly plagued by raids from nomadic *barbaroi* who threatened the commodities moving along the road and were presumably one of the threats that the fortifications were meant to guard against (Cuvigny 2003).

FIG. 44.3 The early Roman *praesidium* near ad-Dweig (ancient Phalacro)

Author's photograph.

This same period of flourishing commercial trade at the Red Sea ports was also the heyday of the mining and quarrying activities that took place in the Eastern Desert. The largest and most famous of these (although by no means the only ones) were the installations at Mons Porphyrites and Mons Claudianus, both established early in the first century CE. These operations, like many others in the Eastern Desert, were aimed at the procurement of decorative building stones meant for imperial building projects in other parts of the empire. Columns quarried at Mons Claudianus decorate the porch of the Pantheon, the Basilica of Trajan, and the Baths of Caracalla in Rome, while the purple porphyry of Mons Porphyrites was used to create the famous statue of the four tetrarchs, now in Venice.

These quarries were overseen by the same military official in charge of the roads in the region. Although it was thought for many years that these quarries were worked by slaves or convicts, documents recovered from Mons Claudianus indicate that the labourers—men, women, and children—were free Egyptian workers, and that their diet was surprisingly good (van der Veen and Hamilton-Dyer 1998). The presence of a bath building at Mons Claudianus, along with a large fortification, the temple to Serapis, and other buildings, gives the impression of a large, if not relatively comfortable, settlement. The quarrying and transportation of the stone from these remote quarries remains an impressive feat, and the system of ramps and slipways constructed to move these great monoliths is still readily visible and has been closely studied as part of the excavation and survey work at each of the quarries (Adams

1998, 2007a). The long tracks carved into the desert by the wheeled vehicles used to transport these quarried pieces to the Nile can still be seen in places and have been documented by numerous survey teams (Sidebotham, Hense, and Nouwens 2008).

While the instabilities of the second and early third centuries seem to have caused problems for the *praesidia* along the Myos Hormos–Koptos road, this period saw the addition of a new roadway with attendant installations. The Via Nova Hadriana was constructed in 137 CE and ran along the coast from Berenike to Antinoopolis, north of Koptos, effectively bypassing the desert interior in favour of a presumably safer route to the north (Bernand 1977; Boatwright 2000). This roadway represents the last of the major imperial projects in the region and was part of a Hadrianic initiative to connect Antinoopolis to all the Red Sea ports with a single road (Sidebotham et al. 2000). Like the other tracks in the region, the Via Hadriana was not marked by inscribed milestones, but rather by cairns built of desert cobbles and placed at irregular intervals along the road's course. The track itself seems only to have been a cleared area with no remnants of paving or other treatment visible along its course (Sidebotham and Zitterkopf 2006).

Current and Future Work in the Region

This chapter has undertaken to provide an overview of the incredible wealth of sources available to scholars working in the Eastern Desert, but by doing so, it also serves to highlight the fact that synthetic scholarship on the region is sorely lacking. Only in the last ten years or so have scholars working across multiple fields, including archaeology and papyrology, begun to articulate a research agenda for the Eastern Desert that extends beyond the recording and publication of materials limited to one site or period. This is, of course, in large part because of the urgency felt by many researchers as they watched endangered sites destroyed by looters and developers, but also because of the nature of the evidence. Almost every site in the Eastern Desert produces such a massive range of artefacts and texts that the process of publication and synthesis is remarkably complex, which in turn discourages studies that work across genres or places.

Thankfully, as these data sets mature and become more widely known, scholars are sure to begin to ask questions that demand that new methods and questions be deployed. One example of this phenomenon already taking place is the recent research on the role of nomadic tribes in the history of the Eastern Desert (Barnard 2009). By problematizing their material profile and asking new questions about the presence of these groups in the archaeological and historical record, scholars have begun to consider how methods might be improved to capture a greater range of evidence.

In a similar vein, the increasingly rich corpus of textual and archaeological material from the Eastern Desert is now ripe for more holistic and updated examination of topics such as death and burial, religious practices, and the presence and role of women in the Eastern Desert. Although each of these topics has been considered in a focused way by one or two researchers working with a particular body of evidence, there is a real need for more catholic studies that incorporate the wide range of newly published material. Finally, although papyrologists and archaeologists work alongside each other in the Eastern Desert, it still remains that much discussion of this material proceeds along parallel tracks, with little real conversation between disciplines. This is hardly a characteristic unique to the Eastern Desert, but the lack of conversation seems particularly egregious given the wealth and complexity of these sites, where material and text are found side by side.

Conclusion

While much remains to be done, the quantity and quality of research and publication of materials from the Roman Eastern Desert are enviable, making this region one of the most exciting new frontiers in Egyptian archaeology and history. As it was to the early European explorers who first recorded its remains, it continues to be the source of new discoveries and to challenge assumptions about the remoteness and isolation of Egypt's desert hinterlands. The Eastern Desert's connections to the farthest corners of Rome's international network of trade will likely help rewrite our picture of the way that Egypt functioned not only as a producer of the grain that fed Rome, but also as a conduit for Roman economic connections to lands very distant indeed.

Suggested Reading

Comprehensive works on the Eastern Desert are few, but the recent popular book *The Red Land: The Illustrated Archaeology of Egypt's Eastern Desert* (Sidebotham, Hense, and Nouwens 2008) offers an uneven but accessible introduction for the non-specialist to the material culture of the Eastern Desert during the Roman era. For the stone industry and quarries, see Hirt (2010). For the Red Sea–Indian Ocean trade, see Peacock and Williams (2007) and Tomber (2008). For the site of Berenike, Sidebotham's most recent book, *Berenike and the Ancient Maritime Spice Route* (Sidebotham 2011), provides a much-awaited synthesis, while for Myos Hormos, the recent volume on the excavations there is the best resource (Peacock and Blue 2005). André Bernand's publication of the epigraphic evidence from the Eastern Desert remains the best collection of these materials, while for the ostraca from the excavated sites, these are thoroughly published in the site reports mentioned in the text (Bernand 1972a, b, 1977, 1984). The many volumes of the Red Sea Project's *Proceedings* (all published as part of Archaeopress's BAR International Series) provide a wide range of focused, high-quality articles on various aspects of Eastern Desert and Red Sea history and are an excellent resource.

Bibliography

Adams, C. E. P. 1998. 'Who Bore the Burden? The Organisation of Stone Transport in Roman Egypt', in D. J. Mattingly and J. Salmon (eds), *Economies beyond Agriculture in the Classical World*. London: Routledge, 171–92.

—— 2007a. *Land Transport in Roman Egypt: A Study of Economics and Administration in a Roman Province*. Oxford: Oxford University Press.

Adams, C. E. P. 2007b. 'Travel and the Perception of Space in the Eastern Desert of Egypt', in M. Rathmann (ed.), *Wahrnehmung und Erfassung geographischer Räume in der Antike*. Mainz: von Zabern, 211–66.

Bagnall, R. S., et al. 2000. *Documents from Berenike*, vol. 1: *Greek Ostraka from the 1996–1998 Seasons*. Brussels: Fondation Égyptologique Reine Élisabeth.

—— et al. 2001. 'Security and Water on the Eastern Desert Roads', *Journal of Roman Archaeology* 14: 325–33.

—— et al. 2005. *Documents from Berenike*, vol. 2: *Greek Ostraka from the 1999–2001 Seasons*. Brussels: Fondation Égyptologique Reine Élisabeth.

Barnard, H. 2009. 'Archaeology of the Pastoral Nomads between the Nile and the Red Sea', in J. Szuchman (ed.), *Nomads, Tribes, and the Ancient State in the Near East*. Chicago: Oriental Institute, 15–41.

Bernand, A. 1972a. *De Koptos à Kosseir*. Leiden: Brill.

—— 1972b. *Le Paneion d'el-Kanaïs: Les inscriptions grecques*. Leiden: Brill.

—— 1977. *Pan du désert*. Leiden: Brill.

—— 1984. *Les portes du désert: Recueil des inscriptions grecques d'Antinooupolis, Tentyris, Koptos, Apollonopolis Parva et Apollonopolis Magna*. Paris: Centre National de la Recherche Scientifique.

Bingen, J., et al. (eds) 1992. *Mons Claudianus: Ostraca Graeca et Latina* I. Cairo: Institut Français d'Archéologie Orientale.

—— et al. (eds) 1997. *Mons Claudianus: Ostraca Graeca et Latina* II. Cairo: Institut Français d'Archéologie Orientale.

Boatwright, M. T. 2000. *Hadrian and the Cities of the Roman Empire*. Princeton: Princeton University Press.

Bülow-Jacobsen, A. (ed.) 2009. *Mons Claudianus: Ostraca Graeca et Latina* IV. Cairo: Institut Français d'Archéologie Orientale.

Burstein, S. M. 1989. *Agatharchides of Cnidus: On the Erythraean Sea*. London: Hakluyt Society.

—— 1993. 'The Hellenistic Fringe: The Case of Meroë', in P. Green (ed.), *Hellenistic History and Culture*. Berkeley: University of California Press, 38–66.

Cappers, R. T. J. 2006. *Roman Foodprints at Berenike: Archaeobotanical Evidence of Subsistence and Trade in the Eastern Desert of Egypt*. Los Angeles: Cotsen Institute of Archaeology.

Casson, L. 1989. *The Periplus Maris Erythraei: Text with Introduction, Translation, and Commentary*. Princeton: Princeton University Press.

Cuvigny, H. (ed.) 2000. *Mons Claudianus: Ostraca Graeca et Latina* III. Cairo: Institut Français d'Archéologie Orientale.

—— (ed.) 2003. *La route de Myos Hormos: L'armée romaine dans le désert oriental d'Égypte*. Cairo: Institut Français d'Archéologie Orientale.

—— and A. Bülow-Jacobsen. 1999. 'Inscriptions rupestres vues et revues dans le désert de Bérénice', *Bulletin de l'Institut Français d'Archéologie Orientale* 99: 133–93.

de Romanis, F. 1996. *Cassia, Cinnamomo, Ossidiana: Uomini e merci tra Oceano Indiano e Mediterraneo*. Rome: 'L'Erma' di Breitschneider.

Gates, J. E. 2005. 'Traveling the Desert Edge: The Ptolemaic Roadways and Regional Economy of Egypt's Eastern Desert in the Fourth through First Centuries BCE', doctoral dissertation, University of Michigan.

Gates-Foster, J. 2012. 'The Well-Remembered Path: Roadways and Cultural Memory in Ptolemaic and Roman Egypt', in S. E. Alcock, J. Bodel, and R. Talbert (eds), *Highways, Byways and Road Systems in the Pre-Modern World*. Malden, Mass.: Wiley-Blackwell, 202–21.

Hirt, A. M. 2010. *Imperial Mines and Quarries in the Roman World*. Oxford: Oxford University Press.

Hölbl, G. 2001. *A History of the Ptolemaic Empire*. London: Routledge.

Jackson, R. B. 2002. *At Empire's Edge: Exploring Rome's Egyptian Frontier*. New Haven: Yale University Press.

Klemm, D. D., et al. 2002. 'Ancient Gold Mining in the Eastern Desert of Egypt and the Nubian Desert of Sudan', in R. Friedman (ed.), *Egypt and Nubia: Gifts of the Desert*. London: British Museum Press, 215–31.

Maxfield, V. A. 1996. 'The Eastern Desert Forts and the Army in Egypt during the Principate', in D. M. Bailey (ed.), *Archaeological Research in Roman Egypt*. Ann Arbor: Journal of Roman Archaeology, 9–19.

—— 2000. 'The Deployment of the Roman Auxilia in Upper Egypt and the Eastern Desert during the Principate', in G. Alföldy, B. Dobson, and W. Eck (eds), *Kaiser, Heer and Gesellschaft in der römischen Kaiserzeit*. Stuttgart: Steiner, 407–42.

—— 2001. 'Stone Quarrying in the Eastern Desert with Particular Reference to Mons Claudianus and Mons Porphyrites', in D. J. Mattingly and J. Salmon (eds), *Economies beyond Agriculture in the Classical World*. London: Routledge, 143–70.

—— and D. P. S. Peacock. 2001a. *Mons Claudianus 1987–1993*, vol. 2, pt 1: *Excavation and Survey*. Cairo: Institut Français d'Archéologie Orientale.

—— —— 2001b. *The Roman Imperial Quarries: Survey and Excavations at Mons Porphyrites 1994–1998*, vol. 1: *Topography and Quarries*. London: Egypt Exploration Society.

Maxfield, V. A. and D. P. S. Peacock (eds) 2007. *Mons Claudianus: Survey and Excavation 1987–1993*, vol. 3: *Ceramic Vessels and Related Objects*. Cairo: Institut Français d'Archaéologie Orientale.

Meredith, D. 1953. '*Annius Plocamus*: Two Inscriptions from the Berenice Road', *Journal of Roman Studies* 43: 38–40.

Peacock, D. P. S., and L. Blue. 2005. *Myos Hormos—Quseir al-Qadim, Roman and Islamic Ports on the Red Sea*, vol. 1: *The Survey and Report on the Excavations*. Oxford: Oxbow.

—— —— 2011. *Myos Hormos—Quseir al-Qadim, Roman and Islamic Ports on the Red Sea*, vol. 2: *Finds from the Excavations 1999–2003*. Oxford: Archaeopress.

—— and V. A. Maxfield. 1997. *Mons Claudianus 1987–1993*, vol. 1: *Topography and Quarries*. Cairo: Institut Français d'Archéologie Orientale.

—— —— 2007. *The Roman Imperial Quarries: Survey and Excavation at Mons Porphyrites 1994–1998*, vol. 2: *The Excavations*. London: Egypt Exploration Society.

—— and D. F. Williams (eds) 2007. *Food for the Gods: New Light on the Ancient Incense Trade*. Oxford: Oxbow.

Prickett, M. 1979. 'Quseir Regional Survey', in D. Whitcomb and J. Johnson (eds), *Quseir al-Qadim 1978*. Cairo: American Research Center in Egypt Press, 255–352.

Rathbone, D. W. 2002. 'Koptos the Emporion: Economy and Society, I–III AD', in M.-F. Boussac (ed.), *Autour de Coptos: Actes du colloque organisée au Musée des Beaux Arts de Lyon (17–18 mars 2000)*. Lyon: Topoi, 179–98.

Sidebotham, S. E. 1986. *Roman Economic Policy in the Erythra Thalassa, 30 BC–AD 217*. Leiden: Brill.

—— 2002. 'From Berenike to Koptos: Recent Results of the Desert Route Survey', *Topoi*, suppl. 3: 415–38.

—— 2011. *Berenike and the Ancient Maritime Spice Route*. Los Angeles: University of California Press.

—— and W. Z. Wendrich. 1996. *Berenike 1995: Preliminary Report of the 1995 Excavations at Berenike (Egyptian Red Sea Coast) and the Survey of the Eastern Desert*. Leiden: Research School CNWS.

—— —— 1998. *Berenike 1996: Report of the 1996 Excavations at Berenike (Egyptian Red Sea Coast) and the Survey of the Eastern Desert*. Leiden: Research School CNWS.

Sidebotham, S. E. and W. Z. Wendrich, 1999. *Berenike 1997: Report of the 1997 Excavations at Berenike (Egyptian Red Sea Coast) and the Survey of the Eastern Desert*. Leiden: Research School CNWS.

—— —— 2001–2. 'Archaeological Fieldwork at a Ptolemaic–Roman Port on the Red Sea Coast of Egypt, 1999–2001', *Sahara* 13: 23–50.

—— —— 2007. *Berenike 1999/2000: Report on the Excavations at Berenike, including Excavations at Wadi Kalalat and Siket, and the Survey of the Mons Smaragdus Region*. Los Angeles: Cotsen Institute of Archaeology.

—— and R. E. Zitterkopf. 1995. 'Routes through the Eastern Desert of Egypt', *Expedition* 37: 39–52.

—— —— 2006. 'Surveying the Via Nova Hadriana: The Emperor Hadrian's Desert Highway in Egypt', *Minerva* 17/3: 34–5.

—— and I. Zych. 2010. 'Berenike: Archaeological Fieldwork at a Ptolemaic–Roman Port on the Red Sea Coast of Egypt 2008–2010', *Sahara* 21: 7–28.

—— M. Hense, and H. M. Nouwens. 2008. *The Red Land: The Illustrated Archaeology of Egypt's Eastern Desert*. Cairo: American University in Cairo Press.

—— et al. 1995. *Berenike 1994: Preliminary Report of the 1994 Excavations at Berenike (Egyptian Red Sea Coast) and the Survey of the Eastern Desert*. Leiden: Research School CNWS.

—— et al. 2000. 'Survey of the Via Hadriana: The 1998 Season', *Journal of the American Research Center in Egypt* 37: 115–26.

Tomber, R. S. 2008. *Indo-Roman Trade: From Pots to Pepper*. London: Duckworth.

van der Veen, M. 1998. 'Gardens in the Desert', in O. E. Kaper (ed.), *Life on the Fringe: Living in the Southern Egyptian Deserts during the Roman and Early-Byzantine Periods*. Leiden: Research School CNWS, 221–42.

—— 2004. 'The Merchants' Diet: Food Remains from Roman and Medieval Quseir al-Qadim, Egypt', in P. Lunde and A. Porter (eds), *Trade and Travel in the Red Sea Region*. Oxford: British Archaeological Reports, 123–30.

—— and S. Hamilton-Dyer. 1998. 'A Life of Luxury in the Desert? The Food and Fodder Supply to Mons Claudianus', *Journal of Roman Archaeology* 11: 101–16.

Whitcomb, D., and J. Johnson. 1979. *Quseir al-Qadim 1978*. Cairo: American Research Center in Egypt Press.

—— —— 1982. *Quseir al-Qadim 1980*. Malibu, Calif.: Undena.

Wilkinson, J. G. 1835. *Topography of Thebes and General View of Egypt*. London: Murray.

Wright, H. T. 2003. 'Archaeological Survey in the Eastern Desert Conducted by the University of Michigan and the University of Asiut: Interim Report', in S. C. Herbert and A. Berlin (eds), *Excavations at Coptos (Qift) in Upper Egypt, 1987–1992*. Portsmouth, RI: Journal of Roman Archaeology, 225–31.

Young, G. K. 2001. *Rome's Eastern Trade: International Commerce and Imperial Policy, 31 BC–AD 305*. London: Routledge.

CHAPTER 45

BETWEEN EGYPT AND MEROITIC NUBIA

The Southern Frontier Region

LÁSZLÓ TÖRÖK

Introduction: The Natural, Ethnic, and Symbolic Frontier

The First Nile Cataract, an outcrop of the granite bedrock, interrupts the course of the Nile and creates many small islands between Philae and Syene, ancient *Swnw* ('Trade'), modern Aswan. The swift rapids here make navigation almost impossible for a distance of about 6 km. In antiquity boats were hauled by ropes from each riverbank (Pomp. 1.9.51). Most cargoes travelling to the north or the south were, however, unloaded at one end of the Cataract, transported along the east bank on a portage road protected by a wall built in the Middle Kingdom (Jaritz and Rodziewicz 1993), and reloaded at the other end of the Cataract.

The First Cataract was a natural, ethnic, and symbolic frontier between Egypt and Nubia. The settlements of the Cataract region were inhabited by a mixed Egyptian and Nubian (in Greek texts: 'Ethiopian') population (Strabo 1.2.32, 17.1.49). The population of Lower Nubia south of Philae, albeit living for long periods of time under Egyptian domination, remained Meroitic-speaking Nubian (Rilly 2007) and included hardly any Egyptian ethnic element.

Egyptian religion localized the Nile's symbolic source as well as Egypt's symbolic frontier in the Cataract region (Locher 1999: 104–10, 159–77). Before it shifted to Philae in the Ptolemaic period, the symbolic frontier was identified with Syene and/or the island of Elephantine. The actual political frontier was more fluid. Its place changed many times between the early Dynastic period and the modern age. From the early third millennium onwards Egypt repeatedly invaded Nubia with the intention of fixing her southern frontier at the Second Cataract, i.e. the southern end of the Lower Nubian Nile Valley. The possession of Lower Nubia secured unlimited control over the river trade between Egypt and Upper Nubia. It also meant the ownership of the resources of the adjacent desert areas—above all the goldmines of the Eastern Desert—as well as control over the desert roads connecting Egypt with the interior of Africa. Egypt conquered Lower Nubia first around 2800 BCE. There existed independent native polities in Lower Nubia before *c.*2800 BCE and between *c.*2300 and 2050 BCE. The region was under Egyptian domination again between *c.*2050 and 1650 BCE. Between *c.*1650 and 1550 BCE it was occupied by the Upper Nubian kingdom of Kerma. Around 1550 BCE the whole of Nubia was conquered by Egypt. The New Kingdom domination (1550–1069 BCE) was followed by the rule of the 25th dynasty, which united Nubia with Egypt now from the south. After the disintegration of the Nubian pharaohs' double kingdom, Lower Nubia remained annexed to Egypt until the early fourth century BCE, when the successors of the 25th dynasty kings (referred to as Napatan rulers between the seventh and the fourth century BCE, and as kings of Meroe between the late fourth century BCE and the fourth century CE) extended their power to the First Cataract. Lower Nubia was reconquered from Meroe around 274 BCE by Ptolemy II. During the Upper Egyptian revolt (207/6–186 BCE), which was supported by the Meroitic rulers Arqamani and Adikhalamani, Lower Nubia was occupied by Meroe. After the revolt Lower Nubia came again under Ptolemaic rule, which became nominal, however, by the early first century BCE (Török 1997, 2009).

From the late third century BCE onwards Lower Nubia between the First and Second Cataracts appeared in official terminology as the 'Land of the Thirty Miles' (Greek: Triakontaschoinos; Egyptian: (*pꜣ ṯ-n-30*). The *c.*125 km-long northern section of the Land of the Thirty Miles between Syene and Hierasykaminos (Maharraqa) (or the nearby island of Tachompso) was distinguished as the 'Land of the Twelve Miles' (Greek: Dodekaschoinos; Egyptian: (*sḫt n ỉtrw 12*)) (Locher 1999: 230–56). The separate name indicated a special status. For example, in 157 BCE Ptolemy VI donated the

> 12 miles from Takompso to Syene on the west bank and 12 miles on the east bank, making together 24 miles, to Isis, so as they are with all their fields, ponds, islands, stones, plants, trees, flocks, cattle, fish, birds, all its oils, and all things which exist there, (including) all people... women together with the men. (Junker 1958; see Locher 1999: 341–2)

Isis of Philae also received royalties from the mines of the region and a 10 per cent tax levied on all wares transported on the Nile from Egypt to Nubia. The decree made the incomes of the Dodekaschoinos exempt from any taxes imposed elsewhere on temple land (Locher 1999: 341–2). Until the reign of Marcus Aurelius and Lucius Verus (161–9 CE), offering scene inscriptions in the temples of the Dodekaschoinos continued to refer to the Land of the Twelve Miles as a property of Isis, which did not mean, however, that the Philae temple continued to be the absolute owner of the Dodekaschoinos (Locher 1999: 345–6).

The Settlements

The settlements of the barren First Cataract region owed their prosperity to their role as trading centres (Syene, Elephantine), to their sanctuaries (Elephantine, Philae), and garrisons (Syene, Elephantine, Philae). The only fertile zone in the Dodekaschoinos (between Gerf Hussein and Korte) and the two Lower Nubian fertile zones south of the Dodekaschoinos (between Amada-Toshka and Abu Simbel-Ashkeit) had a limited subsistence potential. In the Ptolemaic and Roman periods they sustained a small population living in a few small urban settlements and scattered villages and hamlets (Williams 1985; Edwards 1996; Török 1997, 2009). The material culture and burial customs of the Nubian inhabitants of the Dodekaschoinos provide good evidence for the high degree of Egyptianization in the Ptolemaic and Roman periods (Adams 1977: 338–44; Williams 1985; Reisner 1910).

Elephantine was the centre of the ancient cults of the cataract gods Khnum and his consort, Satet. Their monumental temples were extended and rebuilt throughout the Ptolemaic and early Roman periods. The earliest sanctuary on the island of Philae was dedicated to Amun of Takompso by the 25th dynasty pharaoh Taharqo as a demonstration of the political and religious integration of the frontier area into Nubia. After the fall of the Nubian pharaohs the Amun cult was replaced by the cult of Isis. The monumental Isis temple (moved to the neighbouring island of Agilkia during the Unesco International Campaign to Save the Monuments of Nubia) has a long building history extending from Ptolemy II to Hadrian (Fig. 45.1). It opened towards the south, from where the life-bringing inundation arrived. The theology and cult of Isis of Philae was closely associated with Nubia and the Nile flood. Outside the enclosure of Isis smaller shrines were erected for the cults of the Egyptian national saint Imhotep (under Ptolemy V), Hathor (Ptolemy VI, Tiberius), Harendotes (Claudius?), the ancient Nubian god Arensnuphis (Ptolemy II and IV, Tiberius), and Mandulis, a deity associated with Lower Nubia and the Eastern Desert (Ptolemy VI?). The island of Abaton ('Pure Island', modern Biggeh), west of Philae, was the location of one of the sixteen mythical tombs of Osiris. In the Ptolemaic and Roman periods, Isis crossed over to the Pure Island every ten days to offer Osiris a milk libation (Haeny 1985; Vassilika 1989; Hölbl 2004).

The Roman Conquest of Lower Nubia

Although it may seem that the replacement of a Macedonian ruler by a Roman emperor went largely unnoticed in the Egyptian countryside (Bowman 1986: 37; Alston 2002: 198), the conquest of the land, the introduction of the Roman administration, and the establishment of Egypt's southern defence brought about a sharp, albeit in some respects only virtual, break in the life at the First Cataract and in Lower Nubia. Shortly after his appointment as the first Roman prefect of Egypt in the autumn of 30 BCE, the officer and poet C. Cornelius Gallus was confronted with a revolt in the Theban region against the tax collectors of Octavian (from January 27 BCE, called Augustus). After quelling the revolt, Gallus took his forces to Meroitic territory beyond the First Cataract. By 16 April 29 BCE, when he erected a trilingual, Egyptian, Latin, and Greek, triumphal stela at Philae, Cornelius Gallus reoccupied the whole Nile Valley from the First to the Second Cataract and established there a client state (*FHN* II, nos 163–5; Stickler 2002; Hoffmann, Minas-Nerpel, and Pfeiffer 2009).

The hieroglyphic text of Gallus' stela propagates the legitimacy of Octavian and the fiction of the unbroken continuity of pharaonic kingship. The Latin version follows the genre of the triumphal inscriptions of Roman generals and says that Gallus gave 'audience to the ambassadors from the king of the Ethiopians (i.e. Meroites) at Philae, received the same king under his protection (*tutela*), and installed a ruler (*tyrannus*) over the Triakontaschoinos on

FIG. 45.1 Lantern slide view of Philae in the nineteenth century, with the remains of mud-brick structures around the Isis temple

J. Levy & Cie Succrs. de Ferrier Père, Fils & Soulier, Paris. Vues Stéréoscopiques et Lanternes Magiques (n.d.). Brooklyn Museum Archives, S10|08 Philae, image 9659.

Ethiopian (i.e. Meroitic) territory'. In turn, the Greek inscription says that Gallus 'obtained from the king (of Meroe) the status of public friend (*proxenia*) and installed a ruler (*tyrannos*) over the Triakontaschoinos, one *toparkhia* (toparchy, district) of Ethiopia (= Meroe)'. The Latin version suggested to the Roman reader that the vanquished Meroitic king was taken into the victor's protection and the conquered territory became a political entity ruled now by a native *tyrannus*, who concluded an alliance (*foedus*) with Rome. By contrast, in the Greek text the relationship between the prefect of Egypt and the *tyrannos* of the Triakontaschoinos is represented as a consequence not of conquest but of the 'official friendship' concluded between the king of Meroe and Cornelius Gallus. Such a representation was meant to give the impression of an unusual legal arrangement, namely that the prefect obliged himself to protect the interests of Meroe's king in Rome. While 'Triakontaschoinos' and 'toparchy' were terms of the region's Ptolemaic administration, *proxenia* hinted at the ancient ties existing between the Napatan–Meroitic kingdom and Lower Nubia. Though the differences between the two versions reveal the deceptiveness of the victor's rhetoric, it cannot be doubted that Gallus indeed took into account the administrative traditions of the region as well as the ethnic composition of its population and its special relations with the Meroitic kingdom. But he was silent in either version about an important detail, namely, that by the establishment of the client state all inhabitants of Lower Nubia became obliged to pay poll tax to Rome.

In 27 BCE Augustus ordered Lucius Aelius Gallus, the second prefect of Egypt, to prepare a military expedition against Arabia Felix. The intention was to secure the trade route to India through the conquest of the South Arabian vassal of the Parthian ruler. As a first step Aelius Gallus regrouped the forces stationed in Egypt and decided to take to Arabia *c.*8,000 of the 16,800 men in the three legions and all of the 5,500 in the auxiliary forces. The expedition was carried out in 26–25 BCE (Stickler 2002). Not long after the news of the withdrawal of considerable forces from Upper Egypt, the inhabitants of the client Triakontaschoinos also received the news that the expedition had ended with Roman defeat. The popular revolt they started in summer 25 BCE was a reaction to this news. Their aim was to put an end to the client status and the obligation of paying poll tax to Rome.

The Lower Nubian rebels occupied Philae, Syene, and Elephantine, carried off the inhabitants, and pulled down the statues of Augustus (Strabo 17.1.54). At the same time an army set off from Upper Nubia under the command of King Teriteqas of Meroe with the aim of re-establishing Meroitic control in the Triakontaschoinos. The Meroitic army was met at Pselkis (Dakka) by Roman forces under the command of Publius Petronius, Egypt's newly appointed third prefect. The battle ended with Meroitic defeat. Roman rule over Lower Nubia was restored as far as the Second Cataract. In the winter of 25–24 BCE Petronius made a bold attempt at the conquest of the whole Meroitic kingdom. Although Augustus describes it as a victorious campaign in his *Res Gestae* (26.5), this undertaking failed. Only the territory between the First and Second Cataracts could be held: until 22 BCE Roman forces were stationed at Primis (Qasr Ibrim).

In early 22 BCE Meroitic forces appeared anew in Lower Nubia under the command of Teriteqas' successor Queen Amanirenas. It did not come to a battle, however. Realizing the superior force of Petronius' army, Amanirenas instead sent envoys to Augustus, who met with the emperor on Samos in the winter of 21–20 BCE. They learned that Augustus had decided to annex the Dodekaschoinos to Egypt and draw Egypt's southern frontier at Hierasykaminos (Burstein 2004; Török 2009: 427–42). The revolt in the Triakontaschoinos, Aelius Gallus' failure in Arabia, and Petronius' in Upper Nubia revealed to Augustus the impracticality of conquests beyond what experience proved to be defensible and economically rewarding.

The Frontier Garrison

The task of the Roman army stationed at the frontier was threefold: to secure the southern region of Egypt against internal enemies, defend the country against attacks from Meroe and incursions of the nomadic Blemmyes from the Eastern Desert, and control transfrontier trade. Three auxiliary cohorts were garrisoned in Syene, on Elephantine, and in a camp opposite Philae on the east bank. There were tactical outposts at Talmis, Pselkis, and Hierasykaminos. Watchtowers protected the portage road between Syene and Philae and the temples of the Dodekaschoinos (Speidel 1988).

We learn from second- and early third-century Greek ostraca found at Pselkis that the majority of the soldiers were of Egyptian origin. Many of them were born and raised in the garrison of Pselkis, and wrote letters to their relatives in Egypt in an idiomatic Greek characteristic of Upper Egypt (Préaux 1951). The military contributed to the mutual acculturation of the different ethnic groups living between Syene and Hierasykaminos, that is, the Nubian majority, the Egyptian priests and officials, and the soldiers originating from Egypt and other, more remote parts of the Roman empire. A remarkable case in point is the career of Paccius Maximus, a *decurio* apparently of Nubian descent. He is the author of four fine Greek inscriptions (Burstein 1998). In one of these, an adoration text in the temple of Talmis (Kalabsha), Maximus prays in verse for success in his military career in return for his faithful service to the god Mandulis. Towards the end of the first century CE he composed a thirty-six-line Greek metric hymn to the same god, whom he describes as the son of Leto, who 'charmed away the barbaric speech of the Ethiopians and urged me to sing in sweet Greek verse'. Paccius' eulogy to the god summarizes the composite cultural outlook of an ambitious Romanized 'Ethiopian': 'He (Mandulis) came with brilliant cheeks on the right hand of Isis, exulting in his greatness and the glory of the Romans, and uttering Pythian oracles like an Olympian god.'

The soldiers stationed in Lower Nubia turned with devotion to the gods of the land and also worshipped them at open-air cult places frequented by the local population. For example, Roman soldiers stationed at Pselkis invoked Thoth-Paotnuphis, the Romanized Nubian god of the Pselkis temple, in Greek adorations inscribed on the surface of the rocks of the hill above the temple (Maspero 1908). On nearby rocks Meroitic officials of the *tyrannos* of the client Triakontaschoinos inscribed their prayers in Meroitic cursive (*REM* 0091A–C). Greek graffiti in the Talmis temple show that the Graeco-Roman interpretation of Mandulis was dominant for visitors from Egypt just as for Nubians, who, like Paccius, were on their way towards being accepted by the Romanized provincial elite and tried to acquire and display the corresponding education. It was nevertheless the civil administration and the temples rather than the military that provided the most effective vehicles for mutual acculturation.

Administration

From 21/20 BCE the Dodekaschoinos was under the authority of the *strategos*, or governor, of the nome of Elephantine and Philae (*Peri Elephantinen kai Philas*). The *strategos* was answerable to the prefect of Egypt through the *epistrategos*, or regional administrator, of the Thebaid. A purely civil official responsible for administration and taxation, he was also concerned with judicial matters. There is sporadic evidence for the direct involvement of the prefect or the military in the case of violent conflicts. In the first and second centuries the administration of the nome of Elephantine and Philae was occasionally combined with an administrative authority over the vast Eastern Desert region between the Dodekaschoinos and the Red Sea (Locher 1999: 249–51, 283–6).

Second-century documents suggest that the nome of Elephantine and Philae was divided into two toparchies, or administrative districts, the northern one extending over the First Cataract region, the southern one over the Dodekaschoinos. In the third century the nome of Elephantine and Philae was incorporated into the nome of Ombos (Kom Ombo) and Elephantine. The Dodekaschoinos formed now one toparchy with the First Cataract region. *Strategoi* of the nome are continuously attested in the Cataract region and the Dodekaschoinos from the 20s BCE through the third century CE (Locher 1999: 201–27, 322–4).

Mentions of subordinate nome officials are sporadic and restricted to the Cataract region (a *komarchos*, the highest-ranking village official, Philae, 78 CE, and an *agoranomos*, the civic magistrate responsible for the supervision of markets and notarial records, Elephantine, 116 CE; Locher 1999: 323). The absence of lesser nome officials in the Dodekaschoinos is explained by a special feature of its administration. Namely, Demotic inscriptions dating from the period between the early 20s BCE and 57 CE, from 120 or 141 CE, and again from the mid-third century record the activity of native Nubian officials bearing the Demotic title *mr mšꜥ* (*FHN* II, nos 180–5; III, nos 229, 253). The title is usually translated as *strategos*. Here the approximate translation 'district commissioner' is preferred, for the *mr mšꜥ*, whose authority was limited to the Dodekaschoinos, must be clearly distinguished from the nome *strategos*.

The owners of the title were specially connected to the temple of Isis of Philae. All of them bore the title *pꜣ rt n ỉst*, 'agent of Isis', which defined a high, apparently not priestly, official responsible for temple administration. The earliest attested district commissioner also bore the title 'agent of Pharaoh'; another one was also 'agent of Thoth'. The high status of the district commissioners is indicated by the double-dating of one of their documents to the twentieth regnal year of Augustus *and* the year of the district commissioner (*FHN* II, no. 180). One of the district commissioners reported that the inner sanctuary of the temple of Pselkis was built on behalf of Augustus in his tenure and under his direction (*FHN* II, no. 181). Competences of this kind were usually reserved for the nome *strategos*. Like the nome *strategoi*, the district commissioners dealt with administrative as well as economic and juridical issues. They settled certain matters with the assistance of the priests of the temples and 'the elders and the agents' of the settlements (*FHN* II, no. 180). Their documents are close in content, form, and phraseology to the corpus of Upper Egyptian Demotic temple oaths from the Ptolemaic and Roman periods.

The delegation of important competences like the supervision of temple construction to the Nubian district commissioner obviously followed from a pragmatic consideration of the fact that the overwhelming majority of the population was Nubian. While the treatment of the Nubian population of the Dodekaschoinos as a sort of *natio* corresponded with the practice of incorporating defeated foreign communities into the Roman body politic, the actual case represents rather the continuation or the renewal of a Ptolemaic institution. For example, the Greek text of a granite stela from Philae (*FHN* II, no. 140) records that around 149/8 BCE the 'Ethiopians' of the Triakontaschoinos were under the authority of a native *eparchos* (governor), who was subordinate to the nome *strategos*. The association of the district commissioners with the temples of Isis and Thoth indicates the dominant role of temple personnel in civil administration. It does not necessarily mean, however, that the Dodekaschoinos was in its entirety composed of temple estates, especially since in the second century CE taxes were (also?) paid to the state at Pselkis (Locher 1999: 250).

Creating a Sacred Landscape

Together with a number of new sanctuaries founded by Augustus, the temples of Isis of Philae and Thoth of Pselkis served a comprehensive acculturation programme. The programme extended over all population groups living between Syene and Hierasykaminos. The various theological and cult associations established between the sanctuaries of northern Lower Nubia were intended to neutralize the actual political, ethnic, and cultural differences and tensions that were brought about by the Roman conquest. The cults of the region's shrines were interrelated. They constituted elements of a planned sacred landscape similarly to the New Kingdom temples of Thebes or the Roman period temples, for instance of the regions of Koptos and Esna and the Dakhla Oasis. The collective presence and fusions of the gods of Elephantine and Philae with other, Nubian, Graeco-Roman, and Egyptian deities brought to life a kind of regional religious identity the origins of which go back to the implantation of the cults of Arensnuphis and Mandulis in Ptolemaic Philae. The conception of religious unity with Meroe manifested itself through the prominent presence of Tefnut, the goddess 'returning from Nubia' in the iconographic programme of several sanctuaries (the temples of Isis and Hathor on Philae, the Thoth temple at Pselkis, the Mandulis temple at Talmis, and the temple dedicated at Dendur (Tutzis) to Amun of Debod, the gods of Philae, and the Lower Nubian saints Pediese and Pihor). Amun of Napata occupies an important place in the iconographic programme of the Pselkis temple. The living holy falcon 'enthroned' between the towers of the first pylon of the Isis temple was believed to have come from Nubia (Dijkstra 2002). As a rule, the iconographic programmes of the new temples were designed to display a well-balanced presence of the 'Nubian' and 'Egyptian' deities in both the northern ('Egyptian') and southern ('Nubian') halves of the temples (Török 2009: 443–56).

The Augustan temple building activity may be divided into three periods. Between 29 and 25 BCE works of unknown extent were started at Elephantine and in Philae. At Talmis the temenos gate of the Ptolemaic Mandulis chapel, the reliefs of which had been dominated by Osiris and Isis, was replaced by a monumental gateway with Mandulis at the centre of its iconographic programme. In the second period, between 25 and 22 BCE, the chapel as well as the temenos wall at Talmis were pulled down and the building of a new temple was started (Fig. 45.2). The monumental dimensions of the new temple and its iconographic programme equally indicate that Talmis was considered the most important settlement of the Dodekaschoinos and its temple was designed as a Nubian counterpart of the temple of Isis of Philae. Mandulis was declared the son of Horus and grandson of Osiris-Apollo and Isis. The syncretistic Mandulis appeared equally familiar to the native Lower Nubians, the Egyptian officials, the nomads of the Eastern Desert, and the soldiers recruited from Egypt, Lower Nubia, or other, more remote parts of the Roman empire.

FIG. 45.2 Detail of a screen wall from the pronaos of the Temple of Mandulis and Isis at Talmis, early first century CE

Photo: Christina Riggs.

In the third period, starting in 21/20 BCE, large-scale temple building and decoration works were carried out at Elephantine, Philae, Kertassi (Tzitzis) (Fig. 45.3), Tafis (Taifa), Talmis, Ajuala (Abu Hor East), Dendur, Pselkis, Korte, and Hierasykaminos (Griffith 1937; Arnold 1999; Hölbl 2004). Besides extensive decoration works, a magnificent colonnaded court was built in Philae in front of the first pylon of the Isis temple. Its irregular spatial organization may be compared to colonnaded squares in Hellenistic towns (Gilbert 1961). The court created a monumental festival scene connecting the temple of Isis with the Nile and the temples of Imhotep, Arensnuphis, and Mandulis. The court was framed in the west by a colonnade whose windows secured a visual contact with the Osiris sanctuary on the island of Biggeh. In 13/12 BCE Rubrius Barbarus, the fourth prefect of Egypt, erected to the north-east of the Isis sanctuary a classical-style temple dedicated to the cult of Augustus (McKenzie 2007: 166–8).

The gods worshipped in the temples of Lower Nubia regularly visited each other and were visited by Isis of Philae. The river voyages of the cult image of Isis to Lower Nubia and the oracular performances at the temples visited by the goddess continued until the fifth century (Priscus, fr. 21). The cult terraces in front of the temples were stages at which big crowds could gather to witness as the local god received his or her divine visitors arriving in their river barges, watch as the priests performed their offerings before the gods and/or the Nile, and turn to the deities for oracles. The voyages of the gods of Lower Nubia placed the settlements of the Dodekaschoinos in a perceivable sacred landscape. As feasts of the community's memory, they cyclically renewed a pluralistic Lower Nubian self-identity.

FIG. 45.3 Kiosk with Hathor head capitals at Kertassi, dating to the early first century CE, and used during visits from Isis of Philae

Photo: Christina Riggs.

The Arbiters of the Meroitic Reoccupation of the Dodekaschoinos

The brother of a district commissioner of the Dodekaschoinos, who was active in the second quarter of the second century CE (*FHN* II, no. 229), was in the service of the Meroitic ruler in the Meroitic part of Lower Nubia, where he was also buried (*REM* 0132). In 142 the Greek orator Aelius Aristides met an 'Ethiopian' (i.e. Nubian) official in Philae, who was 'in charge' there in the absence of the *hyparchos*, 'governor' (identical with the *komarchos* of Philae?). The institutionalization of the contacts between Meroitic Lower Nubia, the Dodekaschoinos, and the higher levels of Egypt's Roman administration is indicated by the frequent occurrence of the Meroitic titles *apote* (from Egyptian (*wpwtj*), 'envoy'; *apote Arome-li-se*, 'envoy to Rome (i.e. Egypt)'; *apote-lḫ Arome-li-se*, 'great envoy to Rome', in titularies of second- and third-century notables living in the Meroitic part of Lower Nubia. One of these Meroitic envoys was buried at Pselkis in the Roman Dodekaschoinos (*REM* 0130), and the title *apote* also occurs in the text of a Meroitic letter found at the same site (*REM* 0597).

The history of the Dodekaschoinos between the middle of the second and the latter half of the third centuries can best be followed in the Demotic documents of the Wayekiye family, an extended Nubian elite family known for eight generations. For six generations all senior members of the family occupied the administrative-economic office of the 'agent of Isis (of Philae)'. From the third generation they also bore high priestly titles at Philae and Pselkis. The family maintained close connections with the Meroitic part of Lower Nubia: two members of the fourth generation were buried on the Meroitic side of the Egyptian-Meroitic frontier, and several relatives lived farther south in the neighbourhood of Faras. Moreover, a member of the sixth generation was elevated in Meroitic Lower Nubia to the office of *peseto*, i.e. viceroy, of the king of Meroe (Török 2009: 456–73).

In the second third of the third century CE, two members of the family's fourth and one member of its fifth generation belonged to the learned priestly class of the 'writers of the sacred books'. They made repeated journeys to the Meroitic court, where they received high titles for introducing the methods of time reckoning in the form practised in Roman Egypt (Logan and Williams 2000). Their regular travels between Philae and the Meroitic capital and their Meroitic titles may give the impression that they were Meroitic subjects who visited Philae as pilgrims, participated in the festivals, and contributed to the financing of the sanctuaries on behalf of their king (thus, Dijkstra 2008: 137). This impression is misleading, however. The Demotic inscriptions of the family in general and the reports of these three members in particular, all inscribed at prominent places in the Isis temple (*FHN* III, nos 231–2, 245, 249–50, 252, 261–3) and the temple of Pselkis (*FHN* III, nos 244, 251, 254–5), leave no doubt whatsoever that their authors belonged to the personnel of these temples and were not pilgrims arriving from another country.

The aforementioned 'writers of the sacred books' travelled between Philae and Meroe as arbiters of political changes in the frontier region and not only as experts of astronomy. From the fourth generation onwards the inscriptions reflect marked changes in the political allegiances of the family and give an idea of the complex nature of their activities in Egypt and Meroe. In the second half of the second and the first third of the third centuries, the inscriptions of the Wayekiye family (and other Nubian officials) were dated with regnal years of Roman emperors. While still using the date year 7 of Severus Alexander in 227/8, Wayekiye (A) expressed his allegiance to both the Roman emperor and the king of Meroe (*FHN* II, no. 245, Philae). By the early 250s his brother-in-law Manitawawi and his son Hornakhtyotef II styled themselves as 'agents of the king of the land of Nubia (= Meroe)'. Moreover, they were 'princes of Takompso' and 'chiefs of the Triakontaschoinos' (*FHN* III, nos 249–50). It would be difficult to interpret these archaizing titles (Edel 1980) other than as evidence for an actual Meroitic political presence in the Dodekaschoinos, the principal vehicles of which were high priests and priestly officials of Nubian descent. The actual political status behind the titles of the 'princes of Takompso' and 'chiefs of the Triakontaschoinos' is also indicated by an inscription in which a member of the family prays for a safe journey to Meroe and favour with the king there, and also asks Thoth to grant the opportunity to deliver annual taxes in Meroe (*FHN* III, no. 254).

While at Pselkis in 253, Hornakhtyotef II dated an inscription (*FHN* II, no. 251) to the third regnal year of the Meroitic king Teqorideamani and reported that as high priest of Thoth he received royal decrees from Meroe, at Philae another Nubian dignitary dated an inscription in the same year by the third regnal year of Trebonianus Gallus (*FHN* III, no. 260). One may thus conclude that shortly after 248/9, when, according to a Greek inscription, Pselkis was still under the supreme authority of the *strategos* of Ombos and Elephantine (*FHN* II, no. 248), the Dodekaschoinos came under Meroitic rule. Philae remained under Roman authority, but the Wayekiye family and other priests and officials of Nubian descent retained their offices in the Isis temple, though not without being strictly controlled by the 'high priest of Alexandria and all Egypt' (the highest administrator of temple matters in Egypt), and by the commander of the frontier garrison. As indicated by several documents (*FHN* III, nos 261, 266–7), the civil administration of the Dodekaschoinos and the distribution of the taxes collected in the region repeatedly required high-level diplomatic negotiations, and the relations between Egypt and Meroe were usually strained. A Meroitic embassy including the viceroy of Lower Nubia and members of the Wayekiye family was recorded in the 250s in formal drawings and Meroitic inscriptions in an annexe room of the Isis temple. After concluding a peace agreement in 260, the envoy of the Meroitic ruler, an official of Nubian descent who had served Isis of Philae formerly as tax collector between *c.*240/1 and 249/50, installed a prophet in the Isis temple. He thus performed an official act that was originally the privilege of the high priest of Alexandria and all Egypt as a delegate of the prefect of Egypt. Continued Meroitic influence in the Isis temple is indicated by the Demotic inscriptions of two prophets who bear the title 'prince of Takompso' after around 260 (*FHN* II, nos 256, 262).

The unfolding of Meroitic political presence in the Dodekaschoinos coincided with the gradual withdrawal of the Roman forces. The last mention of the *cohors II Ituraeorum equitata* is from 205 (*FHN* III, no. 238), and of the *cohors I Flavia Cilicum equitata* from 217/18 (*FHN* III, no. 239). The latest Greek receipts for wine addressed to the troops stationed at Pselkis date from the 210s (Láda and Rubinstein 1996). Among the texts connected with works in the quarries of Kertassi, the latest inscription dated with the regnal year of a Roman emperor was written in 251 (Török 2009: 465). By 253 the Syene army no longer stationed permanent outposts south of Philae (Speidel 1988: 775).

In the last third of the third century CE, documents and literary works repeatedly mention conflicts between Egypt, Meroe, and the Blemmyes (*FHN* III, nos 272, 278–84). In 298 the emperor Diocletian visited the region of the First Cataract, officially withdrew Egypt's frontier from Hierasykaminos to Philae, refortified Philae as a frontier post, and concluded a treaty with Meroe and some groups of the Blemmyes (Procop. *Persian Wars* 1.19.27–37). It was now a task entirely for Meroe to deal in the Dodekaschoinos with the threat represented by the feared inhabitants of the Eastern Desert. As a first step, around the turn of the third to fourth century Meroe founded military settlements in the Talmis area and at Hierasykaminos and manned them with Blemmye warriors, following thus the contemporary Roman model of frontier defence provided by 'barbarian' enemies turned into federates (Török 2009: 522–3).

Conclusion

From the third century BCE onwards the Egyptian government of northern Lower Nubia encouraged the cult of Nubian deities, the existence of native institutions, and the functioning of indigenous people in local and temple administration as an effective means of legitimizing Ptolemaic rule over the conquered Meroitic population. The Augustan reorganization of the Dodekaschoinos relied largely on this Ptolemaic model. The coexistence of native Nubians, Egyptian officials, soldiers recruited from Egypt and other parts of the empire, and nomads of the Eastern Desert was cleverly supported by the syncretistic cults of the region. The maintenance of native institutions and the participation of the native elite in civil and temple administration proved to be useful in securing peace in the region annexed to Roman Egypt, but from the second century CE also facilitated increasingly aggressive Meroitic intervention into the matters of the estates of Isis of Philae and Thoth of Pselkis, which finally led to the withdrawal of the Roman frontier in 298 CE.

Suggested Reading

For an overview of this frontier, see Török (1997, 2009). For the kingdom of Meroe, the archaeological study by David N. Edwards (1996) is a useful starting point, as well as the well-illustrated catalogue of a recent British Museum exhibition on ancient Sudan (Welsby and Anderson 2004). Speidel (1988) discusses the Roman army garrison in Nubia. A recent study by Dijkstra (2008) examines social and religious changes at the island of Philae in late antiquity, extending beyond the chronological range of this chapter.

Bibliography

Adams, W. Y. 1977. *Nubia, Corridor to Africa*. London: Allen Lane.

Alston, R. 2002. *The City in Roman and Byzantine Egypt*. London: Routledge.

Arnold, D. 1999. *Temples of the Last Pharaohs*. New York: Oxford University Press.

Bowman, A. K. 1986. *Egypt after the Pharaohs, 332 BC–AD 642*. London: British Museum Press.

Burstein, S. M. 1998. 'Paccius Maximus: A Greek Poet in Nubia or a Nubian Greek Poet?', *Cahiers de Recherches de l'Institut de Papyrologie et d'Égyptologie de Lille* 17/3: 47–52.

—— 2004. 'Rome and Kush: A New Interpretation', in T. Kendall (ed.), *Nubian Studies 1998*. Boston: Northeastern University, 14–23.

Dijkstra, J. H. F. 2002. 'Horus on his Throne: The Holy Falcon of Philae in his Demonic Cage', *Göttinger Miszellen* 189: 7–10.

—— 2008. *Philae and the End of Ancient Egyptian Religion: A Regional Study of Religious Transformation (298–642 CE)*. Leuven: Peeters.

Edel, E. 1980. 'Der älteste Beleg für den Titel *ḥꜣty-pꜥt* und sein Weiterleben bis in römische Zeit hinein', *Sarapis* 6: 41–6.

Edwards, D. N. 1996. *The Archaeology of the Meroitic State: New Perspectives on its Social and Political Organisation*. Oxford: Tempus Reparatum.

Gilbert, P. 1961. 'Éléments hellénistiques de l'architecture de Philae', *Chronique d'Égypte* 36: 196–208.

Griffith, F. L. 1937. *Catalogue of the Demotic Graffiti of the Dodekaschoenus*. Oxford: Oxford University Press.

Haeny, G. 1985. 'A Short Architectural History of Philae', *Bulletin de l'Institut Français d'Archéologie Orientale* 85: 197–233.

Hoffmann, F., M. Minas-Nerpel, and S. Pfeiffer. 2009. *Die dreisprachige Stele des C. Cornelius Gallus: Übersetzung und Kommentar*. Berlin: de Gruyter.

Hölbl, G. 2004. *Altägypten im römischen Reich: Der römische Pharao und seine Tempel* II. Mainz: von Zabern.

Jaritz, H., and M. Rodziewicz. 1993. 'The Investigation of the Ancient Wall Extending from Aswan to Philae', *Mitteilungen des Deutschen Archäologischen Instituts, Abteilung Kairo* 49: 107–32.

Junker, H. 1958. *Der grosse Pylon des Tempels der Isis in Philae*. Vienna: Österreichische Akademie der Wissenschaften.

Láda, C., and L. Rubinstein. 1996. 'Greek Ostraca from Pselkis', *Zeitschrift für Papyrologie und Epigraphik* 110: 135–55.

Locher, J. 1999. *Topographie und Geschichte der Region am Ersten Nilkatarakt in griechisch-römischer Zeit*. Stuttgart: Teubner.

Logan, T. J., and B. B. Williams. 2000. 'On the Meroe Observatory', *Beiträge zur Sudanforschung* 7: 59–84.

McKenzie, J. 2007. *The Architecture of Alexandria and Egypt, 300 BC–AD 700*. New Haven: Yale University Press.

Maspero, G. 1908. 'Inscriptions romaines à Abou-Dourouah', *Annales du Service des Antiquités Égyptienne* 9: 267–70.

Préaux, C. 1951. 'Ostraca de Pselkis (Dakka) de la Bibliothèque Bodléenne', *Chronique d'Égypte* 51: 121–55.

Reisner, G. A. 1910. *The Archaeological Survey of Nubia, Report for 1907–1908*, vol. 1. Cairo: National Printing Department.

Rilly, C. 2007. *La langue du royaume de Méroé: Un panorama de la plus ancienne culture écrite d'Afrique subsaharienne*. Paris: Champion.

Speidel, M. P. 1988. 'Nubia's Roman Garrison', in H. Temporini (ed.), *Aufstieg und Niedergang der römischen Welt* II 10.1. Berlin: de Gruyter, 767–98.

Stickler, T. 2002. *'Gallus amore peribat'? Cornelius Gallus und die Anfänge der augusteischen Herrschaft in Ägypten*. Rahden: Leidorf.

Török, L. 1997. *The Kingdom of Kush: Handbook of the Napatan-Meroitic Civilization*. Leiden: Brill.

—— 2009. *Between Two Worlds: The Frontier Region between Ancient Nubia and Egypt, 3700 BC–AD 500*. Leiden: Brill.

Vassilika, E. 1989. *Ptolemaic Philae*. Leuven: Peeters.

Welsby, D. A., and J. Anderson (eds) 2004. *Sudan: Ancient Treasures: An Exhibition of Recent Discoveries from the Sudan National Museum*. London: British Museum Press.

Williams, B. B. 1985. 'A Chronology of Meroitic Occupation below the Fourth Cataract', *Journal of the American Research Center in Egypt* 22: 149–95.

Index

Bold entries refer to illustrations or figures.

Aaron of Alexandria 311–12
Abaton 751
Abinnaeus, Flavius 251
  and archive of 517
Abrasax 339, **340**, 346
Abydos:
  and Bes oracle 326, 343, 407, 408, 409, 411–12
  and graffiti at 702
  and Memnonion 353
  and Osiris 420–1
Acta Alexandrinorum 278, 538
  and Jewish revolt (115–17) 282
  and portrayal of Jews 284–5
Actium, battle of (31 BCE) 12, 431
Adams, J. N. 518, 519, 520, 522, 523
administration of Roman Egypt 3, 15–16
  and administrative units 16, 58, 64
  and assessments of officials 57
  and Diocletian's reforms 5
  and Dodekaschoinos 754–6
  and *epistrategoi* 58
  and First Cataract region 754–6
  and high priest of Alexandria and Egypt 92, 94, 760
  and indigenous elites 249–50, 255–6
  and liturgical system 5, 59
  and local authorities 58–9
  and nomes 16, 58
  and prefect as head of 4, 57
  and procurators 57
  and *strategoi* 16, 58
  and town councils 256
  and village level 59
  see also law; prefects of Egypt; taxation
Aelian 404
Aelinianus, Claudius 688
Africanus, Julius 475, 534
Agathos Daimon 320, 321, 439, 443
agriculture 22, 34–5
  and grain land 26–8
  and land fertility 28–9
  and land use and food production 29–33, 34–5
  and myth of unchanging nature of 38
  and orchards and gardens 28
  and private land 24–6
  and public land 26
Agrippa I 280
Ain Birbiya 376, 720, 722, **723**, 725, 730
Ain el-Gedida 720
Ain el-Labakha 667, 718, 719, 727
Ain el-Qurayshat 724
Ain Manawir 718, 722
Ajuala 374, 757
Akhmim, *see* Panopolis
Akhmimic dialect 582
Akoris 447, 448, 449
Alcock, S. E. 133
Alexander Mosaic 687
Alexander the Great 103
  as role model for Octavian 13
  and tomb of 109
Alexander, Tiberius Julius 4, 61, 104, 250–1, 253, 282
Alexandria 16, 56, **103**, 118–19, 123–4, 247
  and Alabaster Tomb 116–17
  and Christianity in 112–13, 475–7, 481
  and citizenship off 265
  and civic buildings 108–10
  and Column of Diocletian **106**
  and cultural role 526–7
  and domestic houses 115–16
  and economy of 107
  and foundation of 103
  and funerary practices 667–8

Alexandria (*cont.*)
and Great Catacomb at Kom el-Shuqafa **117**
and Greek characteristics of 103–4
and Greek-Jewish violence (38–41 CE) 279–82
and imperial temple in 86–7, 111
as intellectual and cultural centre 535–8, 539
and Isis 113, 422, 427
and Jewish Quarter 108
and Jewish revolt (115–17) 112, 282–4
and Jewish revolt (66–70) 282
and Jews in 112
and library of 109–10, 536
and monumental tombs 116–18
and Moustapha Pasha Tomb **116**
as multi-ethnic city 104
and museum of 109, 536
and officials of 253
and organization of 252–3
and the Pharos 108–9
and plan of **105**
and population size 125
and portrayal of Jews in *Acta Alexandrinorum* 284–5
and privileges of citizens 104, 252, 253
and religion 110–14
and Royal Quarter 109
and sanctuaries and temples to Greek gods 112
and the Sema (Alexander the Great's tomb) 109
and Serapeum 113–14, 422
and Serapeum library 115, 536
and Serapis 113–14
and social structure of 104
and status of Jews in 277–9, 286
and temples in 110–11
and terracottas 631
and Tigrane Tomb **118**
and topography of 107–8
and town council 256
Alföldy, G. 87
Alston, R. 452
Amanirenas, Queen of Meroe 753
Amarna East 163, 702
Amenemhat III 153–4
Amenhotep and Imhotep, and sanctuary of 180, 181
Amenhotep III 184, 371, 422, 437, 706
and temple of 177
Amenophis 183
Amheida (Trimithis), *see* Trimithis (Amheida)
Ammonius 425
Ammonius, Marcus Aurelius 209, 441
Ammonius Saccas 477
amphoras 655–7, **658**
'Amr ibn al-'Asi 109–10
amulets 338, 343, 344, 347–9
and language used 349
in mummification 672
and mummification 676
and object amulets 349
and papyrus amulet **348**
and written charms 349–**50**
Amun 173, 175, 443, 449
and cult of 179–80
and temple of 176, 180
Amun-Re 449, 465, 722
and temple of 175
Amunnakht 722
Anat 437, 441, 445
animal cults 180–1, 427
animal husbandry 32–3, 56
Ankhwennefer (Channophris) 173
Antaeopolis 386
Antinoe, *see* Antinoopolis
Antinoopolis 123, 124, 189, 744
and citizens of 253
and classical architecture 190–2
and founding of 4, 190
and map of **191**
and population of 190
and privileges of citizens 253–4
Antinoos 4, 189, 190, 253, 441, 537, 705
Antiochos IV 11
Antirhodos Island 113
Antonine Plague 4, 311, 312
Antoninus, Gaius Julius 176
Antoninus Pius, Emperor 190, 374
Antony (ascetic) 484
Antony, Mark 12, 111, 667
Anubion of Diospolis 534

Anubis 446
aphrodisiacs 352
Aphrodite 112, 428, 437, 439, 441, 443, 635
Apion 104, 260, 279
Apis 422, 446
Apis bull 13, 113, 422
 and Octavian's refusal to present offering 457
Apollo 112, 180, 198, 403, 408, 437, 440, 449
Apollonides 175
Apollonius (*strategos*) 58, 283–4
Apollonius Dyscolus 537
Apollonius Rhodius 533
Appianus, Aurelius 194, 196, 197, 265
apprenticeship system 44, 601–2
Apuleius 423, 425–6, 430, 431, 689
Aquila, Gaius Julius 93
Arabia, and trade with 48
Arabia Felix 753
archaeology of Roman Egypt:
 and identification of Roman period sites 141
 and infant state of 39
 and layout of Graeco-Roman settlements 162–6
archai 4
architecture:
 and Alexandrian houses 115
 and imperial temples in Egypt 95
 and monumental tombs 116
 and Roman period houses 166–7
 and temples in Western Oases 722–4
 see also classical architecture in Roman Egypt
archives:
 and archival practice 508
 and cache found at Karanis 510
 and document preservation 508
 and identification of 509–10
 and meaning of term 507, 509
 and reasons for keeping documents 511–13
 and reconstructed archives 508–9
 and replacement value of documents 513–14
Areius 537
Aretaios 311
Aristides, Aelius 533, 535, 705, 708, 710, 758
Aristophanes 533
Armant 362, 565
army, *see* Roman army in Egypt
Arnold, Dieter 160, 371
Arrian 533
Arsinoe 601, 615
art and artists, *see* funerary art/artists; nilotica; portraiture; pottery; sculpture; statues; terracottas
Artemidorus 604
asceticism 484
Assmann, J. 390, 424, 729–30
Astarte 437, 438, 441
Astrampsychos 404
astrology 345–6, 408
 and Egyptian literature 554
astronomy, and Egyptian literature 554
Aswan 426, 558
Asyut 392
Atargatis 440–1
Athanasius 331
Athena 198, 270, 427, 443, 449, 636
Athenaeus 538
Athenodoros 405
Athribis (Tell Atrib) 140, 143, 145, 190, 364, 449
 and excavations at 145–6
 and map of archaeological finds and excavations **148**
 and Roman villa at 145–6, **147**
Augustus, Emperor:
 and Alexandria 109, 536
 and annexation of Egypt 3–4, 11, 12–16
 and depiction as pharaoh 375–6
 and Egyptian religion 457
 and Horus name of 14–15
 and imperial cult 85
 and importing of obelisks to Rome 689–90
 and integration into Egyptian royal ideology 17
 and land reform 24
 and portraits of 614–15
 and refusal to present offerings to Apis bull 457
 and residency in Egypt 12–13

Augustus, Emperor (*cont.*)
  and silver denarius of **18**
  and temple-building 18, 373–4, 756
  and titles of 14–15
Aurelian, Emperor 5

Baal 437
Babrius 533
Bacchias 156, 161, 163
Badawy, Alexander 205, 207
Bagnall, Roger 305, 720
Bahariya Oasis 667, 717, 718, 721, 727
Bahr Yusuf 152, 153, 154
Bahrein Oasis 722
Baines, John 364
Balbilla, Julia 185, 571, 707
Balbillus, Tiberius Claudius 94, 281
bandagers, and funerary art 600
Banebdjeb 34
banks 47
bar Elias, Michael 110
Barb, Alphonse 325
Barbarus, Rubrius 88, 757
Barbarus, Rustius 520, 523, 524
barley cultivation 29
Barramiyya 741
Bárta, Miroslav 721
Bashendi 728, 729
Basilides 476
basilikos grammateus ('royal scribe') 16, 58
Bataille, André 183
bath houses 138–9
Bawiti 721, 722
Beck, R. L. 439
Bedouin 737
Behbeit el-Hagar 427
Beinlich, Horst 375
Bendis 112
Berenike 192, 737, 739, 740, 742, 744
Bes 446, 722
  and oracle of 326, 343, 407, 411
Biga 373
Bilad el-Rum 724
bilingualism 497–8, 516, 519
biology, and Egyptian literature 555
Bir el-Showish 721
Bir Shaghala 728
Birket Qarun 152
birth control 297–8
birth registration 251, 252, 299–300
Blemmyes 737, 753, 760
Blumenthal, F 85–6
Bohairic dialect 582
Book of Ba 388
Book of the Dead 384–5, 387–8, 389, 392, 460
Book of the Fayum 566
Book of the Temple 364, 460, 495, 557
Book of Thoth 460, 495, 551–2
Book of Traversing Eternity 387
Books of Transformation 387
Borchardt, Ludwig 158, 163
Boukoloi, revolt of the (172) 4
bouleutic class 265
Bourriau, Janine 648, 652
Bowman, Alan 1
breastfeeding 312
Bresciani, Edda 160
Brown, Peter 330
Brugsch, Heinrich 665–6
Bryaxis 113
bubonic plague 312
Bucheum (at Armant) 362
Buchis bulls 178, 180, 565
  and stela commemorating **181**
burial practices:
  and children 300
  and mortuary liturgies 423–4
  in Theban region 182–3
  and Tuna el-Gebel 219
  in Western Oases 727–8
  see also cemeteries; funerary art/artists; funerary religion; mummies and mummification
Busiris 420
Buto (Tell Fara'in) 140, 143, 420
  and excavations at 146–7

Caesar, Julius 12, 109, 110, 368
calendar reform 725
Callimachus 533
Canopus 90, 145, 408
  and sanctuary of Serapis 407

Canopus Decree 565
Canova, Antonio 692
Cape Lochias 109, 113
Capponi, L. 93
Caracalla, Emperor 4–5, 62, 183, 374, 536, 614, 615, 705
Carr, Hamzeh 233
Cassius, Avidius 4
Cavenaile, R. 517
cemeteries:
  at Alexandria 116
  at Karanis 240–1
  in Nile Delta 140
  at Terenouthis 139–40
  see also Tuna el-Gebel
census returns 305
central place theory 131
Cestius, Gaius 431
Chaeremon 104, 538, 571–2
Chairas 601
child-god, and terracotta figures of 633–5
child labour 299
children:
  and *apatores* 298–9
  and apprenticeships 44
  and breastfeeding 312
  and child labour 299
  and education of 528
  and fatherless children 298–9
  and funerary art 300
  and illegitimacy 294
  and legal status of 298
  and registration of 299–300
  and visibility in source 299
Chnoubis 339, **341**, 346
chora 4, 58
  and Christianity in 478–80, 481, 482–3
  and civic autonomy 255
  and imperial temples in 90–1
  and marriage in 289
  and Roman citizens in 251
Christianity 331–2, 485
  in Alexandria 112–13, 475–7, 481
  and asceticism 483–4
  in the *chora* 478–80, 481, 482–3
  and Christian literary papyri **478**, **479**, 483, **484**
  and Coptic 586–9
  and destruction of temples 467
  and development of organized Church in Egypt 480–1
  and divisions within 485
  and earliest documentary evidence 480
  and identity 271
  and Manichaeans 484
  and millenarianism 483, 484
  and origins in Egypt 475–6
  and persecution 5, 481–2
  and sources for study of 474–5
Chrysopolis 176
Chubb, J. Anthony 224–5
cities 123–4
  and central place theory 131
  and consumer city theory 130–1
  and definition of 125–8, 133
  and rank-size distributions 131–2
  and urban network theory 132
citizenship:
  and Alexandria 104
  and citizens of the Greek *poleis* 252–4, 262–3
  and classification of inhabitants 526
  and Constitutio Antoniniana (212) 4, 62, 256, 264–5
  and Jews 104
  and military service 266
  and non-citizens 254–7
  and *poleis* (cities) 247
  and privileges of 104, 252, 253–4
  and Ptolemaic period 249
  and Roman citizens 250–2, 262
  and soldiers 251
  and status 249, 257
Clarke, John 694
Clarysse, W. 179
classical architecture in Roman Egypt 189–90, 201–2
  and Antinoopolis 190–2
  and Herakleopolis Magna 200–1
  and Hermopolis Magna 192–8
  and Oxyrhynchus 199
Claudius, Emperor 87, 91, 109, 614
  and Alexandria 536
  and Alexandrian Jews 279–80, 281–2

Clauss, M. 84
clay tablets **726**–7, 729
Clement of Alexandria 474, 475, 477, 538
Cleopatra Canal 146
Cleopatra VII 12, 86, 111, 178, 368, 667
  and tomb of 117
'Cleopatra's needle' **111**
Coarelli, F. 688
coin hoards 140
collective identity 260–1
  and shifts in 265–6
Commodus, Emperor 374, 376
communications, and communication networks 46
Constantius II, Emperor 409
Constitutio Antoniniana (212) 4, 62, 256, 264–5
consumer city theory 130–1
Coptic Church 485
Coptic language/script 581, 589–90
  and Christian use of 586–9
  and Coptic literature 589–90
  and development of 582–3
  and dialects 582
  and emergence of 498, 499
  and Greek influence in 498, 499
  and monasticism 589
  and Old Coptic 582–6
  and pre-Christian Coptic 582–6
Cornutus 533
coronation of Ptolemaic rulers 13
cosmology 347
  and temples 375
crafts, *see* trades and crafts
credit system 47
Cribiore, Raffaella 528
crocodile gods 446–8, 450, 464
crocodile mummies 229
cryptography, and hieroglyphs 569–71
Cugusi, P. 517
cults, and expansion into the Mediterranean 427–9, 685
  see also imperial cult; imported cults; religion; temple cult
cultural identity:
  and language 497
  and Western Oases 729, 730
cultural memory 729–30
curse tablets 343, 344
custom duties 40, 61
  and paints 606
Cuvigny, Hélène 71
Cybele 112
Cyprian, bishop of Carthage 482

Daily Ritual 462–4, 465
Dakhla Oasis 311, 312, 343, 373, 376, 391, 439, 449, 528, 667, 675, 717, 718–19, 722, 726
Dakhleh Oasis Project 719, 720
Dakka 374, 753
Dal Pozzo, Cassiano 685–6
Damascius 329
Debod 373
Decius, Emperor 362, 466, 481–2
'Decree to the Nome of the Silent Land' 387, 389
Dedun 436
Deir el-Bahri 402, 405, 408, 412
  and mummies found at 674–5
Deir el-Hagar 564, 721
Deir el-Medina 177, 401, 499
Deir el-Shelwit 373, 427, 564
Delos 425, 428–9, 685
Demeter 320, 423, 439, 440, 441, 636
Demetrius, bishop of Alexandria 477, 480–1
Demetrius of Phaleron 109
Demetrius, Tiberius Claudius 250
demography:
  and age structure 305–7
  and causes of death 308–9
  and census returns 305
  and central place theory 131
  and consumer city theory 130–1
  and definition of cities 126–7
  and life expectancy 305–6, 337
  and modelling settlement patterns 130–2
  and mortality patterns 307–**8**
  and population size 4, 124–5
  and population structure 128–30
  and rank-size distributions of settlements 131–2
  and settlement patterns 122, 123

and urban graveyard theory 128–9
and urban network theory 132
see also settlements
Demosthenes 533
Demotic language/script 172, **544**
and competition from Greek 494
and decline of 494, 496, 527
and origins of 493, 543
in Roman period 545
and spread of 543
and temple texts 495
and transformation into Coptic 269
Demotic literature, *see* Egyptian literature in Roman period
Dendara, temple at 16, 353, 364–71, 427, 462, 564, 614
and connections with Edfu 366
and construction of 367
and crypts 368
and cult of Osiris 370
and enclosure wall 371
and festival of unification with the solar disk 369–70
and gateways **366**–7
and open court and *wabet* **369**–70
and outer walls **368**
and plan of temple complex **365**
and pronaos 370
and sanctuary 368–9
Dendur 374, 756, 757
Denon, Vivant 189, 199
dental health 312
Derchain, Philippe 364
Description de l'Égypte 156, 189, 201, 202
Diadumenianus, Emperor 377
Didymoi 408
Didymus 110, 537
Dime, *see* Soknopaiou Nesos
Dio, Cassius 13, 15, 16, 110, 457
Dio Chrysostom 104, 118, 119, 533, 535
Diocletian, Column of (Alexandria) **106**
Diocletian, Emperor 5, 56, 190, 485, 558, 760
and Maximum Price Edict (301) 5, 598, 605
Diodorus 177, 402, 423, 666, 677, 704
Dion **429**
Dionysias 156, 158–60, 163
and layout of 164
Dionysius, bishop of Alexandria 477, 481, 482, 484
Dionysius Periegetes 537
Dionysos 112, 423, 431, 439, 443, 636
Dios oracles 403, 408
Dioscoros, Antonios 480
Dioscoros (Roman official) 449
Dioscuri 320, 437, 440, 446–8, 449
Diospolis Magna 175, 190
Diospolis Parva (Tell el-Balamun) 145
diphtheria 311
disease 308, 309–12, 313
and sources for study of 309–10
divination 325–7, 338, 345–6
and ban on oracular activities 343, 409, 458
and competition among diviners 339
and diversification of divination media 407–9
and dramatization 399–400
and freelance diviners 345–6
and punishment for using 343
and regulation of social order 400
and *sortes* books 326–7, 400, 407
see also oracles
division of labour 43–4
and specialization 44–5
divorce 291–2
Djed-Thoth-iu-ef-ankh, tomb of 207, 209, 216
Djeme 176–7
Documents for Breathing 386, 387
Dodekaschoinos 17, 373, 702, 750, 760–1
and administration of 754–6
and annexation of 753
and creating a sacred landscape 756–7
and frontier garrison 753–4
and Meroitic political presence 758–60
and settlements 750–1
domestic religion 322–5
domestic structures, and stages in life of 510–11, **512**
Domitian, Emperor 536
Domitianus, Lucius Domitius 5
dovecotes, at Karanis 234–6
dowries, and marriage 289
dream books 556

dromoi:
at Dionysias 164
and Dromos of Hermes 194–5
at Hermopolis Magna 194–5
at Narmouthis 165, 166
at Soknopaiou Nesos 164, 165–6
at Tebtunis 164–5, 166
and urban layout 165–6
Dryton 179
Dunand, Françoise 86, 112, 405, 448, 719
Dundas, G. S. 86
Dush (Kysis) 564, 600, 667, 719

Eastern Desert 373, 736, 745
and archaeological sources 738–9
and climate 736
and documentary sources 739–41
and future research on 744–5
and geography of 736
and international trade 736–7, 741–3
and mining and quarrying 743–4
in Ptolemaic period 741
and rock carvings 741
and Roman army in 737, 742
and scholarship on 738
economy:
and agrarian nature of 46
and Alexandria 107
and associations of traders and craftsmen 41
and banks 47
and business taxes 60
and characteristics of 39–40, 49
and communication networks 46
and credit system 47
and division of labour 43–4
and economic growth 39
and integration into imperial economy 39
and land tenure reform 39–40
and markets 40, 45, 46, 49
and mistaken view of uniqueness of 38
and mobility 47
and monetized nature of 46–7
and myth of unchanging nature of agriculture 38
and organization of production 41
and problems with primary sources 38–9
and retail networks 45–6
and specialization 44–5
and taxation 40
and trade routes 40
and trades and crafts 40–1
see also manufacture; markets; production; taxation; trade
Edfu, temple at 363, 464
and connections with Dendara 366
education:
and citizenship in Ptolemaic Egypt 249
and Greek literary education 528–32, 539
and private organization of 528
and schoolroom 528, **529**
and women 531
Egypt:
and historical overview of Roman Egypt 3–5
and Ptolemaic empire 11–12
and Roman annexation of 3–4, 11, 12–16
Egypt Exploration Fund 201
Egypt Exploration Society Delta Survey 138, 141
Egyptian Antiquities Organization 138
Egyptian literature in Roman period 546, 558–9
and astrology 554
and astronomy 554
and belles-lettres 548–52
and biology 555
and Book of the Temple 557
and Book of Thoth 551–2
and cultic topography 556–7
and current state of research 548
and distinction between manuscript and text 547
and dream books 556
and end of pagan Egyptian literature 557–8
and future research on 558
and geography 556
and Inaros and Petubastis Cycle 549
and innovations in 547
and mathematics 554
and medicine 555
and Myth of the Sun's Eye 551

and mythological tales 550–1
and Nectanebo stories 550
and omen texts 556
and outward appearance of texts 546
and Petese stories 550
and philology 555–6
and poetry for cultic revelry 552
and prophetic literature 552
and religious texts 556–7
and scientific and scholarly texts 553–6
and tales of Setne 549–50
and translations of 557
and transmission of texts 547
and Western Oases 725–7
and wisdom literature 551
el-Abbadi, Mostafa 110
el-Bahnasa 199, **200**
el-Deir 667, 719, 727
el-Falaki, Mahmoud Bey 108
el-Gharaq basin 160
el-Gib 719
el-Haiz 718, 721
el-Lahun 153–4
el-Muzawwaqa 721
el-Qal'a, and temple at 16, 364, 373, 427, 564
el-Qusur 722
el-Sheikh Mansur 722
el-Zeitun 722
Elephantine 564, 702, 707, 749, 750, 751, 754, 755, 757
elephants, and trade in 741
elites, and religion 330–1
embalmers 608
and embalming techniques 668
and taxation 606–7
and wages 606
Empedocles 349
Empereur, Jean-Yves 110
emperor worship 83–5, 96
see also imperial cult
environment, and religious significance 35
Epidaurus 408, 412
epidemics 309, 312
Epiphanius 484
epistrategoi 16, 58
Eratosthenes 112
Eros 635
Esna 362, 364, 374, 496
ethnicity:
and artists and crafts-people 608–9
and ethnic identity of Egyptian Jews 270–1
and identity 268–70
Eudaimon 599
Euhemeria 156, 163
Eunapius 329
Euphorion 533
Euripides 529, 533
Eusebius 283, 474, 475, 477, 480
Euthenia 442
Eutychius, *Annals of* 480–1
exposure, and birth control 297

families, *see* children; households; marriage
Farasan 71
Favorinus 533
Fayum 23, 29, 35, 664
and archaeological discoveries and excavations in 155–62
and canal system 154, 155
and features of 152–3
and houses of Roman period 166–7
and land reclamation 153–5, 156
and layout of Graeco-Roman settlements 162–6
and satellite view of **153**
and terracottas 631
Fayum Survey Project 161
Fayumic dialect 582
Ferrari, G. 688
festivals:
and hieroglyphic inscriptions 565
and interaction of sacred and profane worlds 398–9
and patrons 330–1
and religion 320–1
Fish Mosaic 685, 686, 688
fishing 33, 34
Flaccus 280, 283
flax cultivation 32, 40
food production 29–33, 34–5
fountain houses 196
Frankfurter, D. 351, 377, 390, 406, 412, 441
Fraser, P. M. 112

Frier, Bruce 305
fruit cultivation 32
funerary art/artists 597
 and apprenticeships 601–2
 and bandagers 600
 and ethnicity 608–9
 and gender 609
 and gilders 599–600
 and gilding materials 604
 and guilds 607–8
 and linen costs 604
 and makers of coffins and mummy masks 597–9
 and materials used 603–5
 and painters 599
 and painting materials and dyes 603–4
 and premises/workshops 600–1
 and privileges of 607
 and taxation 606–7
 and wages 605–6
 and wood 604–5
 and working practices 602–3
funerary religion 383, 392–3
 and Book of Ba 388
 and Book of the Dead 384–5, 387–8, 389, 392
 and Book of Traversing Eternity 387
 and Books of Transformation 387
 and continuity in 385
 and continuity vs change 389–92
 and 'Decree to the Nome of the Silent Land' 387, 389
 and Documents for Breathing 386, 387
 and historical and economic context 390
 and longevity of 385
 and mummy breastplate 383, **384**, 385
 and Pyramid Texts 383–4, 385, 388–9
 and sources for study of 385–8
 and temple influence 388–9

Gabbari 668
Gabra, Sami 205, 209
Gaius, Emperor 279, 281
Galba, Emperor 376
Galen 110, 311, 535
Gallienus, Emperor 196, 482
Gallus, C. Cornelius 12, 493, 517, 709
 and appointed prefect 15
 and Lower Nubia 751–3
 and Meroe 751–3
 and stela of 13, 14, 17, 493, 501, 565, 751–2
 and suppression of revolts 16–17, 173
Gallus, Lucius Aelius 13, 183, 705, 753
Gardner, E. A. 143, 144
Gayet, Albert 192, 666
Geens, K. 263
Geertz, Clifford 398
Gellius, Aulus 109
gender:
 and artists and crafts-people 609
 and identity 266–7
 see also women
geography, and Egyptian literature 556
Germanicus 183, 458, 571, 705
Geta, Emperor 374
Ghueita 722, 730
gilding/gilders:
 and funerary art 599–600
 and materials used 604
 and mummification 675–7
 and wages 605–6
Giza, Sphinx at 702
Glare, P. 441
Gnostics/Gnosticism 476, 588, 589
goldsmiths 599–600
 and gilding materials 604
 and government control of industry 606
Gombert, A 205
Graeco-Roman, and meaning of term 3
Graf, F. 401
Graf, Theodor 664
graffiti **708**
 as evidence of travel 701–3, 704, 705, 707, **708**, 709, 710
 and hieroglyphic inscriptions 567
 in Latin 501, 516, 517
 and temple visitors 343, 353, 400, 407
Greek identity 526
 and classical past 533
 and *paideia* 526
Greek language 527–8
 and Egyptian adoption of 4, 179, 494
 and *koine* ('common' dialect) 527
 as language of administration 518, 526

and Latin loan-words 528
and literacy 500
and morphology 527
as professional language 498
and pronunciation of 527
Greek literary education 526, 528–32, 539
and benefits of 531–2, 539
and economically privileged character of 530–1
and first stage of 528–9
and methodological principles 528–9
and schoolroom 528, **529**
and second stage of 529–30
and third stage 530
and women 531
Greek literature 526
and literary papyri 532–5
Grenfell, Bernard 156–7, 199
Grimm, Günter 1
guilds 607–8
Gurna 671
Gurob 439
gymnasial class 263–4

Hadrian, Emperor 124, 176, 183, 253, 261, 374
and Alexandria 536–7
and tour of Egypt 4, 705
Hagedorn, Dieter 725
Hallof, Jochen 375
Hapy 33, 442
Harendotes 426
Haroeris 371
Harpocras 407
Harpocrates 34, 113, **323**, **330**, 339, 373, 446, 449, 465, 634
Harpocration, Valerius 537
Harris, J. R. 439
Harsomtus 366
Hartophnakhtes 391
Harwennefer (Haronnophris) 173
Hathor 180, 436, 437
and temple at Dendara 364–71, 564, 614
Hatmehyt 33–4, 35
Hatshepsut 371
Hawara 153–4, 156, 665–6
Hawara Canal 152
Hawass, Zahi 721
hay cultivation 32
Hayez, Francesco 692
healing 338, 352–4
and competition among healers 339
and curative charms 353
and engraved gems 353
health 313
and disease 309–12
Helena 447
Heliodorus of Emesa 707
Heliopolis 722
Helios 449
Hellenistic, and meaning of term 3
hellenistic, and meaning of term 3
Hephaesteion 537
Hera 441
Hera Teleia 112
Heraclas, bishop of Alexandria 477, 481
Herakleion 175
Herakleion-Thonis 145
Herakleopolis Magna 189
and classical architecture 200–1
and red granite columns **202**
Herakles 189, 722
Herakles Sotor 112
Hermaeus 425
Hermes 189, 192, 440
Hermonthis 178, 180
Hermonthites 171
Hermopolis Magna 189, 190, 192, 391, 441, 481
and Antinoe Street 195
and Christian churches 197
and Dromos of Hermes 194–5
and epitaph of impressiveness of architecture 195–6
and fountain houses 196
and four quarters of 195
and Great Basilica Church 197
and the Great Tetrastylon 194
and houses 195
and Jewish quarter 195
and the *komasterion* 193–4
and mosque in 197
and public buildings 197–8
and reconstructing layout of 197–**8**

Hermopolis Magna (*cont.*)
and 'repair papyrus' of Aurelius Appianus 196, 197
and Sacred Area 195
and Sphinx Gate 193
and temple of Thoth 192
Herodian 118, 537
Herodotus 152, 313, 422–3, 428, 437, 533, 543, 666, 677, 710
Heron 439, 440, 444–**5**, 446, **447**
Heroninus 156
Heroonpolis 140
Heros 444–5
Hesiod 533
Hibis 718, 719, 722, 730
Hierasykaminos (Maharraq) 17, 373, 374, 750, 753, 754, 757, 760
hieratic literature, *see* Egyptian literature in Roman period
hieratic script **544**
and origins of 543
in Roman period 545
and temple texts 495
and uses of 493, 543
hieroglyphs in Roman period 493
and common unilateral signs **570**
and contemporary interest in 571–2
and continued use of 563, 573
and cryptography 569–71
and decline of 496
and deterioration in workmanship 568
and development of 563
and fine examples of 567–**8**, **569**
and future research on 572–3
and graffiti 567
and grammatical errors 567
and language of 568–9
and last datable inscriptions 426, 545, 567
and obelisks 567
on papyri 566
and sign-list 571
and sources for study of 564–7
and statues 566
and stelae 565–6
as subject of study in Roman empire 563
and temple texts 363, 364, 495–6, 564–5
and tombs and mortuary equipment 567
and uses of 493
and writing of emperors' names 724–5
Himmelmann, N. 643
Hinterhöller, M. 688
hippodromes, and Antinoopolis 192
holy men 346
Homer 529, 532–3, 710
Homer Oracle 345
Honroth, Walter 205
Hope, Colin A. 719, 721
Horapollon 496, 572, 573
Hornbostel, W. 643
horoscopes 344, 345–6
horses 444–5
Horus 320, 366, **420**, 424, 443, 446, 449
and meanings of 465
and oracular statue of **406**
and temple at Edfu 363
Houroun 437
households, and size and composition 296–7
houses:
and Alexandria 115–16
and characteristics of 166–7, 295–6
and religious practice in 322–5
and sources for study of 295
and wall-niche altars 322, **323**
Hunt, Arthur 156–7, 199
husbandry 22, 32–3
Husson, G. 295

identity 5–6, 260, 272
and Christianity 271
and citizens of the Greek *poleis* 252, 262–3
and collective identity 260–1
and Constitutio Antoniniana (212) 264–5
and Egyptians 263–4
and ethnic identity of Egyptian Jews 270–1
and ethnicity 268–70
and gender 266–7
and Greek identity 526
and gymnasial class 263–4
and language 497
and metropolite class 4, 254–5, 263–4
and names 262, 264, 265, 271–2
and priesthood 263
and race 261

and Roman citizens 262
and shifts in collective identity 265–6
and social classes 262–5
and social mobility 265–6
and state identity 261–2
Idios Logos 57, 59
and Gnomon of the 64, 251, 252, 256–7, 262, 297, 458
Ihi 366, 371
Ikram, Salima 719
illegitimacy 294
Imhotep 177
immigration, and Graeco-Macedonian conquest 438
Imouthes-Petubastis III 14
imperial cult 83, 97
and characteristics of 84
and distinction from emperor worship 83–5
and high priest of Alexandria and Egypt 92–4
and impact in Egypt 96
and imperial temples in Egypt 86–91, 95, 111
and legitimization of Roman rule 96
and municipal imperial cult 85
and private imperial cult 85
in the provinces 85
and provincial imperial cult in Egypt 94–5
and regional high priesthood ('high priest of the city') 91–2
and type of cult in Egypt 85–6
imported cults:
and Graeco-Macedonian conquest 438–40
and impact of 452
and interactions with native pantheon 444–51
in Pharaonic Egypt 436–8
in Roman Egypt 436, 440–2, 450–1
and sources for study of 442–4
Inaros and Petubastis Cycle 549
incantation 460, 461
India, and trade with 48, 736–7, 742
infanticide 297
infectious diseases, *see* disease
ink 545
interpretatio Aegyptiaca 423, 439, 440, 452
interpretatio Graeca 422, 437, 446
interpretatio Romana 423, 446
Irenaeus 480
Iseum Campense 430
Isidora, Claudia 267
Isidoros, Flavius 599
Isidorus, Tiberius Claudius 250
Isis 33, 34, 320, 339, 373
and Alexandria 113, 427
and cult in Italy 430, 685, 687, 689
and depictions of 419, **420**
and ending of worship of 467
and expansion of cult into Mediterranean 427–9, 689
and festivals for 431
and hellenistic Isis in Roman Egypt 426–7
and Osiris 424
and Plutarch's *De Iside et Osiride* 425–6
and temple at Deir el-Shelwit 427
and temple at Dendara 367, 427
and temple at Philae 362, 363, 426, 751
and temples for 426–7
and terracotta figures of 635, **636**
and transformation into hellenistic goddess 422–3
as universal goddess 419, 423
and worship of 419
Ismant el-Kharab (Kellis), *see* Kellis (Ismant el-Kharab)
Isocrates 530, 533

Jews 256, 277
in Alexandria 104, 108, 112
and Alexandrian riots (38–41 CE) 279–82
and ethnic identity 270–1
and Jewish revolt (115–17) 4, 112, 270–1, 282–4
and Jewish revolt (132–5) 284
and Jewish revolt (66–70) 282
and Jewish tax 60, 270
and portrayal in *Acta Alexandrinorum* 284–5
and portrayal in the Oracle of the Potter 285–6
and privileges of 278–9
and Roman citizenship 279

Jews (*cont.*)
  and status of Alexandrian Jews 277–9, 286
Johnson, Barbara 233
Jomard, Edmé 189, 192, 194, 200–1
  and map of Antinoopolis **191**
Josephus 277, 533
  and Alexandrian riots (38–41 CE) 280
  and status of Alexandrian Jews 278
Julian, Emperor 292
Junker, Hermann 364
Jupiter Capitolinus 441–2
jurisdiction:
  and law 62
  and procurator in charge of 57
Justinian, Emperor 292
Juvenal 183, 705

Kahun 163
Kaiser, Werner 624
Kalabsha 17, 363, 374, 375
  and Mandulis shrine 408, 412
Kannenberg, John 238
Kaper, Olaf 376, 390–1, 439
Karanis 163, 452
  and animal remains found at 240
  and baskets found at 241–**2**
  and black basalt statue of priest 232, **233**
  and bronze bells 238, **239**
  and cemeteries at 240–1
  and Claudius Tiberianus archive 510, 518–19
  and dovecotes 234–6
  and excavations at (Cairo University 1967–75) 161
  and excavations at (University of Michigan 1924–35) 158, 223–42
  and housing 295
  and layout of 165
  and organic material found at 241–2
  and papyri finds at 231–2
  and photographs from Michigan expedition **224**, **226–41**
  and plant remains found at 238–40
  and pottery found at 233–4, **235–6**
  and *sebakhin* excavations **224**, 225, **226**
  and sensual experience of ancient world 238
  and temples at 229–31
  and toys found at **237–8**, **299**
  and wall paintings 233, **234**
Karnak 173, 176, 465
  and Amun temple 180
  and imperial temple in 89–**90**
  and temple of Ptah 402
Katzoff, R. 517
Kellis (Ismant el-Kharab) 719–20, 722, 725, 726, 729
  and mammisi of 723–**4**
Kelsey, Francis W. 224, 241
Kelsey Museum of Archaeology 223, 225
Kerameia 171, 178
Kerma 750
Kertassi 373, 757
Kerygma Petri ('Preaching of Peter') 474
Kessler, Dieter 205–6, 207
Kharga 373, 427, 675, 717, 718–19, 722, 726, 727, 730
Khnum 496, 751
  and temple of 320, 462
Khonsu 371
  and temple of 16, 175, 176
Kiman Fares 155, 156
Kircher, Athanasius 695
Kleon 154
Koinon of Asia 85
Kom Aushim, *see* Karanis
Kom Danial 160
Kom Doshen 139
Kom el-Ahmar **137**, 139
Kom el-Khamsin 161
Kom el-Shuqafa 391, 616–17
Kom Medinet Ghoran 161
Kom Ombo 702
  and temple at 16, 364, 371, **372**, 376–7, 462, 564
komai (villages) 123
komasteria, at Hermopolis Magna 193–4
Koptos 49, 174, 373
  and temple at 16, 427, 564
  and trade 48, 742
Korte 757
Krokodilopolis 152, 156, 173, 447, 740
Kronion, son of Apion 508, 509
Kurth, Dieter 364
Kysis 405, 722, 726, 727

land:
and fertility of 28–9
and grain land 26–8
and land reform 24
and land tenure reform 39–40
and land use and food production 29–33
and landownership 4
and orchards and gardens 28
and private land 24–6
and public land 26
and spirituality 33, 34
and state control 28
and taxation 24, 26–33, 60
and types of 23–4
land reclamation:
in the Fayum 153–5, 156
in Nile Delta 136
Landvatter, Thomas 240
language:
and bilingualism 497–8, 516, 519
and code switching 497
and cultural identity 497
and decline of indigenous scripts 496, 498
and diglossia 497, 498
and intercultural exchange 496–7
and language use 494–6
and literacy 499–500
and literary uses of indigenous scripts 494–5
and Roman policy 494
and use of Egyptian in temple texts 495–6
see also Coptic language/script; Demotic language/script; Greek language; hieratic script; hieroglyphs
in Roman period; Latin language
Latin language 493
and character of 519–22
and expressions of power 518
and functions in Egypt 518–19
and future research on 522–3
and limited use of 500–1, 516, 527
and military use of 519
and morphology 521–2
and non-standard form 519, 520–2
and political value of 518
and sources for study of 516–18
and standard form of 522
and syntax 521–2
and vocabulary 522
Latopolis 462, 702
Laubscher, H. P. 643
law 61–4, 251–2
and absence of legal policy 63
and edicts by prefect 63
and impact of Roman courts 62
and imperial interventions 63
and intercultural exchange 497
and jurisdiction 62
and persistence of customary forms 62, 63–4
and precedents 63
and Ptolemaic period 61–2
and trust in judicial institutions 63
Leemhuis, Fred 721
Lefebvre, Gustav 156, 158, 209
Leitz, Christian 364
Leontius, Aurelius 599
leprosy 311
Letter of Aristeas 109
Lewis, Naphtali 1, 362
Libanius 528
life expectancy 305–6, 337
linen production 40, 42–3
literacy 499–500
and Greek 500
literature:
and Egyptian language 494–5
and literary papyri 532–5
see also Egyptian literature in Roman period; Greek literary education; Greek literature
liturgical system 5, 59
and exemptions from 253, 607
and tax collection 60, 61
Livy 517
local authorities 58–9
lotus, and commercial exploitation of 33
Lower Egypt 309
Lower Nubia 17, 749–50, 760–1
and frontier garrison 753–4
and Land of the Thirty Miles 750
and Roman conquest of 751–3
Lucan 110
Lucian 533, 535

Lucius Verus, Emperor 374, 376, 377, 750
Lupus, Rutlius 282, 283
Luxor temple 173, **174**, 176, 427
Lykopolitan dialect 582
Lysimachus, Alexander 104

McKenzie, Judith 374, 375
Macrinus Augustus, Emperor 377
Magdola (Medinet el-Nehas) 157, 161, 440, 444, 446
magic 6, 325, 327–9
  and acquiring control 350–2
  and aphrodisiacs 352
  and attitude towards the divine 461
  and attraction rites 350, **351**
  and binding spells 350, 351
  and competition among magicians 339
  and contacting the divine 354–6
  and cult texts 462–5
  and curative charms 353
  and deities and spirits 346–7
  and favour charms 351
  and formularies 344
  and Graeco-Egyptian magic 346
  and Greek and Demotic Magical Papyri 326, 327, 328, 331, 344
  and healing 352–4
  and holy men 346
  and protection against misfortune 347–9
  and punishment for using 343
  and reliance on writing 346
  and religion 325, 327–9, 460–1
  and Roman Thebes 181
  and sources for study of 343–4
  and Theban Magical Library 344
  and theophany 354–5
  and wrath-restraining spells 351, **352**
  see also amulets; divination; rituals
Maharraqa (Hierasykaminos), *see* Hierasykaminos
malaria 308, 309, 310
Mandulis 449, 756
Manetho 425
Manichaeans 484, 588, 589, 720
manufacture:
  and associations of traders and craftsmen 41
  and division of labour 43–4
  and organization of production 41
  and premises/workshops 42–3
  and scale of 41–2
  and specialization 44–5
  and women 43
Marcellinus, Ammianus 109, 113, 119, 145, 411, 458, 572, 708, 709
Marcus Aurelius, Emperor 374, 376, 377, 496, 705, 750
Marisa 687, 688
Mark the Evangelist 475
markets 40, 45, 46, 49
  and communication networks 46
marriage:
  and age at marriage 291
  and birth control 297–8
  and demographic aspects of 291
  and divorce 291–2
  and dowries 289
  and form and legal aspects of 289
  and informality of 289
  and marriage document 289
  and matrimonial property 290–1
  and remarriage 291–2
  and sex 297
  and sibling marriage 266, 292–3, 312
  and soldiers 293–4
  and sources for study of 288
  and widows 290–1
Mars 441
Marsa Nakari 741
mathematics, and Egyptian literature 554
Maximinus Daia, Emperor 362, 496
Maximum Price Edict (301) 5, 598, 605
Maximus, bishop of Alexandria 482, 483
Maximus, Paccius 408, 754
medicine, and Egyptian literature 555
Medinet el-Fayum 152–3, 155
Medinet el-Nehas, *see* Magdola
Medinet Ghoran 157
Medinet Ghurob 154, 156
Medinet Habu 177, 564
Medinet Madi, *see* Narmouthis

Melitus, bishop of Lykopolis 485
Memmius, L. 704
Memnon colossi 177, **184**–5, 571, 710
 and travellers to 705–7
Memphis 13, 248, 430, 437, 438, 439, 441
 and Serapeum at 422
Menander 530, 533
Mendes 22, 33, 34
Mendesian nome 22–3
 and agriculture 34–5
 and categories of land 24
 and fishing 33, 34
 and grain land 26–8
 and Hatmehyt 33–4, 35
 and husbandry 32–3
 and land fertility 28–9
 and land use and food production 29–33, 34–5
 and orchards and gardens 28
 and private land 24–6
 and public land 26
Menouthis, and Isis temple 352, 466–7
Meroe 13, 17, 373, 557–8, 750, 751–3, 758–60
Mesobe 720
Mesokemic dialect 582
metalworking, and specialization 45
metropoleis 4, 123, 124
metropolis 16
metropolite class 4, 254–5, 263–4
Meyboom, P G P 688
Michigan University, and Karanis excavations (1924–35) 223–42
Mills, Anthony J. 719, 720
Min 436
mining, in Eastern Desert 743–4
Minshat Abu Omar 140
Mithras, cult of 439, 441
Mommsen, Theodor 248
monasticism 484, 589
money 46–7
 and coin hoards 140
moneylending 64
Mongos, Petros 466
Mons Claudianus **71**, 310, 408, 520, 736, 739, 740, 743
Mons Porphyrites 427, 736, 739, 743
Montsuef 671–2
Montu 175, 176, 179, 180
mortality:
 and causes of death 308–9
 and patterns of 307–**8**
mortuary liturgies 423–4
mosaics:
 and Alexander Mosaic 687
 in Alexandria 115, **116**
 and Fish Mosaic 685, 686, 688
 and Nile Mosaic 685–**6**, 687–9, 694
Mothis (Mut el-Kharab) 721, 722, 728, 730
mummies and mummification 6
 and amulets 672, 676
 and children's mummies 673, 675
 and classical authors on 666–7
 and cost of 670, 677
 and crocodile mummies 229
 and current state of research 666–7
 from Dakhla Oasis 675
 and damage to skeletons 670
 and decline in techniques 669
 and Deir el-Bahri group 674–5
 and destruction of 666
 and embalming techniques 668
 and eye and tongue plates **676**
 and fieldwork in Egypt and Roman Empire 667–8
 and gilding of the skin 675–7
 and high quality of workmanship 677–8
 with individually wrapped limbs 670–1
 from Kharga 675
 and mummies with similarities to Soter group 673–4
 and Pebos family group 300, 674
 and period of practice of 669
 and poor workmanship 669–70
 and research in museums 668–9
 from the Rhind Tomb (not preserved) 671–2
 and Soter family group 182, 300, 672–3
 as source of demographic and medical information 306, 307, 309, 310, 311
 in Theban region 182–3
 from Thebes 670–5
 see also embalmers; funerary art/artists; gilding/gilders
mummy masks 598–9, 620–1, **622**, 664

mummy portraits **78**, 192, 392, 597, **598**, 622, **623**, 624, 664, **665**
of children 300
and excavation and collection of 664–6
and separation from mummies 666
murals, at Karanis 233, **234**
museums, and mummy research 668–9
Mut 175–6, 721
Mut el-Kharab, *see* Mothis
Myos Hormos 739, 742
Myth of the Sun's Eye 465, 551
mythological tales 550–1

Nadura 568, 572, 722, 724
names:
and identity 262, 264, 265, 271–2
and intercultural exchange 497
in Western Oases 726
Napoleon I 692
Narmouthis (Medinet Madi) 157, 158, 160, 444, 495, 497, 702
and continuance of temple cult 466
and layout of 165
natron 668
Naukratis 16, 123, 247, 253, 437, 443, 526, 532
and archaeological work in 143–5
and intellectual and cultural life 538
and mapping of Roman pottery **144**
Naville, E. 201
Nearchus 711
necropolis, *see* cemeteries; Tuna el-Gebel
Nectanebo I 192, 194
and stories about 550
Nectanebo II 180
Neilos 33, 442
Neiloupolis 459
Neith 218, 270, 419, 449, 564
Neith cosmogony of Esna 465
Nemesis 112
Nephthys 34, 217, 218, 424, 427, 623
Nero, Emperor 371, 614
network theory, and settlements 132
New Testament 475, 476, 480, 582, 588
Nikagoras, son of Minoukianos 709
Nikanor 41, 48, 536
Nikopolis 70–1
Nile:
and First Nile Cataract 749
and religious significance 33
as trade route 40
and travellers to 707–8
Nile Delta 22
and animal husbandry 56
and annual flood 28
and archaeology in 136–49
and clusters of Roman sites in 141–3
and current archaeological work in 140–1
and excavations in 145–8
and idealized Roman image of 136
and identification of Roman period sites 141
and map of Roman period sites **142**
and previous archaeological work in 138–40
and problems of archaeological work in 137–8
and surveying and recording of Roman sites in 141–5
and topography of 136
Nile Mosaic 685–9, 694
and reconstruction of **686**
Nile Valley 29, 35
and agriculture 56
and trade routes 40
Nilos 481
nilotica:
and Isis cult in Italy 684, 687
and meaning of term 684
and Nile Mosaic 685–**6**, 687–9, 694
and obelisks imported to Rome 689–90
and post-conquest proliferation of 689–90
and pre-conquest Roman-Egyptian relations 684–5
and pygmy landscapes 691, **692**, 693–4, 695
and range and breadth of 690–1
and Roman attitudes to Egypt 684, 688–9, 693, 694–5
as scholarly construct 684
and significance of 684
and Vatican Nile **691**–4, 695
nomadic tribes 737, 739, 744
nomes 16, 58, 123
non-citizens 254–7

Nubia 17, 373, 749
  and Egyptian conquest of 750
  and graffiti in 702

Obbink, Dirk 161
obelisks:
  and hieroglyphic inscriptions 567
  and imported to Rome 689–90
  and Montecitorio obelisk **690**
Octavian, *see* Augustus, Emperor
oil crops 32
Old Testament 588
olive production 32
omen texts 556
Opet 16, 564
Oppian 533
Oracle of the Potter 285–6, 442–3
oracles 326, 345, 413
  and *astragaloi* oracles 403
  and astrology 408
  and ban on oracular activities 343, 409, 458
  and children and youths 404
  and consultation as drama 399–400
  and consultations 401–2
  and consultations in Roman Egypt 403–6
  and direct contact with the divine 409–10
  and distinction from prophecy 401
  and diversification of divination media 407–9
  and divine iconography 410
  and dreams 407
  and incubation 407–8
  and innovations in 406–11
  and judicial role of 399
  and marketing of 412
  and mediating role of 399
  and methodology in studying 401
  and participation in ritual system 398–9
  and personal piety 409
  and political role of 399, 409
  and priests 411–12
  and private oracles 409, 410–11
  and questions asked of 401
  and *Sortes Astrampsychi* **404**
  and *sortes* books 326–7, 400, 407, 413
  and sources for study of 400
  and speaking statues 405
  and textualization of 405–6
  and ticket oracles 401–2, 403
  and traditional Egyptian oracle 401–3
  and use of dice **402**–3
  and use of ostraca 403
  and voice oracles 405
  and written medium 405
Origen 474, 477, 484, 538
Osir-Apis 113
Osiris 33, 113, 370, 388
  and Abydos 420–1
  and death 419, 420, 421, 465
  and depictions of 419–20, **421**
  and fertility 419, 420, 421, 422
  as focus of funerary culture 421, 422
  and mortuary liturgies 423–4
  and myth of 423–4
  and origins of 420
  and Plutarch's *De Iside et Osiride* 425–6
  and resurrection 419, 420, 422, 465
  in Rome 430–1
  and worship as a national god 422
ostraca 172
  and astrological 342, 344
  from Eastern Desert 739–**40**
  and oracular consultations 401–2, 403
  and Roman army 71–2, 73, 76, 754
  and tax receipts 174, 176, 178
Oxyrhynchus 41, 42, 46, 189, **200**, **201**, 440, 441, 443, 728
  and classical architecture 199
  and housing 295–6

Padikam, tomb of 207, 209, 216
painters:
  and funerary art 599
  and paint pots **603**
  and painting materials and dyes 603–4
  and taxation 606
  and wages 605
  and working practices 602–3
palaeography 386
Palmyra 5
Pamphilus 536
Pan 112

Pancrates 537
Panebtawy 371
Panopolis (Akhmim) 265, 386, 388, 582, 601
Pantaenus 476–7
papyri:
 as archaeological artefacts 510, 514
 and archaeological context of 507, 509, 513, 514
 and archival practice 508
 and archives of 507, 509
 and cache found at Karanis 510
 and caches of 507
 and *cantina dei papyri* 509–10
 and dossiers of 509
 from Eastern Desert 740–1
 and literary papyri 532–5
 and reasons for keeping 511–13
 and reconstructed archives 508–9
 and replacement value of documents 513–14
 and stages in life of domestic structures 510–11, **512**
papyrus, and commercial exploitation of 33
Papyrus Jumilhac 375
Park, George K. 399
Parlasca, Klaus 1
Parthians 12
Pathyris 171, 173, 702
Pathyrites 171
patronage, and religion 330–1
Pausanias 173, 403, 705, 707
Pebos family mummies 300, 674
Pelusium 39, 190
Pentapolis 481
Pergamon, Red Hall at 430
Perithebas 171, 174
Petamenophis 672
Petaus 59, 500, 508
Peter, bishop of Alexandria 485
Petese stories 550
Petosiris, tomb of 205, 207, 209, 216, 391, 439
Petrie, W. M. F. 137–8, 143, 156, 199, 603, 648, 649, 665, 666
Petronius, Publius 753
Pharos Island 112
Pharos of Alexandria 108–9, 119, 701
Phatre 598, 599–600
Philadelphia 156, 157–8, **160**
 and layout of 163–4
 and plan of **159**
Philae 13, 190, 373, 462, 558, 564, 707, 750, 755, 757
 and continuance of temple cult 466
 and graffiti at 702
 and imperial temple on **88–9**
 and temple of Harendotes 362
 and temple of Isis 362, 363, 426, 751
Philip III Arrhidaeus 192
Philippi 430
Philo of Alexandria 86–7, 104, 108, 111, 277, 329, 476, 533
 and Alexandrian riots (38–41 CE) 280, 281
 and status of Alexandrian Jews 278, 279
philology, and Egyptian literature 555–6
Philostratus 538, 692, 705, 708, 711
Philoteris 163
pigeons, and dovecotes at Karanis 234–6
pilgrimage 703–4
Pindar 533
plague 309, 312
 and Antonine Plague 4, 311, 312
Plato 533
Pliny 192, 458, 685, 693, 742
Plutarch 113, 117, 321, 387, 404, 431, 533, 535, 704
 and *De Iside et Osiride* 423, 425–6, 571
 and library at Alexandria 110, 536
Pnepheros 444, 446
poleis (cities) 123–4, 133
 and citizenship 250, 252–4, 262–3
 and small number of 247
poll tax (*laographia*) 60
 and exemptions from 250, 252, 253
 and graduated system 254, 255
 and non-citizens 254
Pollio, Valerius 533, 537
Pollio, Vitrasius 281
Pollox, Julius 538
Polybius 112, 248
Pompeii 429, 689, 694
portraiture 613, 624–5
 and funerary monument **617**
 and imperial portraits 614–15
 and mummy decoration 620–4
 and mummy masks 620–1, **622**

and mummy portraits 622, **623**, 624
and private portraits 615–20
and relief sculpture 618–20
and statue of woman at Oxyrhynchus **616**
and statues 615–18
and styles during Hellenistic period 613–14
Poseidon 112
pottery 648–9, 657–8
and amphoras 655–7, **658**
and centrality in archaeological practice 649
and Egyptian early Roman finewares **656**
and fabric 652
and form 653
and important sites for study of **650–1**
and imported and domestic pottery of early Roman period 653–5
at Karanis 233–4, **235–6**
and pottery studies in Egypt 649–51
and production in Roman era 651–3
and publications on 649–51
and Roman sigillatas and Egyptian imitations **654**
and ware 653
see also terracottas
Praeneste 685
prefects of Egypt 56
and *conventus* 57, 63
and edicts of 63
and financial duties of 57
as head of administration 4, 57
and Hellenism 412
and powers of 56–7
and salary of 57
as springboard to higher office 57
Price Edict (301), *see* Maximum Price Edict (301)
priesthood:
and control over membership of 458, 459
and high priest of Alexandria and Egypt 92–4, 760
and integration of Augustus into royal ideology 17
and maintenance of indigenous tradition 16
and Octavian's title 14
and oracles 411–12
in Ptolemaic period 13
and recognition of Octavian's rule 14
and regional high priesthood ('high priest of the city') 91–2
and Roman relations with 14, 16, 17
and rules for priestly purity 460
as status group 257
Primis (Qasr Ibrim) 517, 753
processual archaeology 511
procurators 57
production:
and division of labour 43–4
and organization of 41
and premises/workshops 42–3
and scale of 41–2
and specialization 44–5
and women 43
prophetic literature 552
proskynemata 76–7, 180, 181, 408, 412, 497, 741
Pselkis 753, 754, 756, 759
Psenamun 14
Psenobastis 598, 599–600
Pseudo-Clementine writings 476
Ptah 13, 180, 402
and high priest of 13, 14
Ptolemais Euergetis 45, 190
Ptolemais Hermiou 16, 45, 104, 123, 124, 171, 247, 253, 262, 526
Ptolemy 110, 535
Ptolemy I Soter 109, 113, 154, 428
Ptolemy II Philadelphus 109, 113, 154, 688, 750
Ptolemy III Eurgetes 112, 114, 197
Ptolemy IV Philopator 113, 177
Ptolemy VI 177, 371, 750
Ptolemy VIII 177, 444, 535
Ptolemy IX 173
Ptolemy X 440
Ptolemy XII Neos Dionysos 11–12, 363, 367, 368, 444
Ptolemy XIII 12
Ptolemy XIV 12
Ptolemy XV Caesarion 12, 368
Puteoli 429
pygmy landscapes 691, **692**, 693–4, 695
Pyramid Texts 383–4, 385, 388–9, 424, 436
Pyramids at Giza, and travellers to 709
Pythagoras 349

Qadesh 437
Qaret el-Hamra 155
Qaret el-Rusas 155
Qasr Bahariya 722
Qasr el-Halaka 722
Qasr Ibrim (Primis) 517, 753
Qasr Qarun 158–60
Qattara Depression 718
Quack, Joachim F. 375, 390, 391, 402
Quintilian 528

race, and identity 261
Ramesses II 422
  and temple of 177, 192
Ramesses III, and temple of 177
Raphia Decree 565
Ras el-Soda 427
Rathbone, Dominic 161
Ray, J. D. C. 498
Red Hall at Pergamon 430
Red Sea, and trade routes 40
Red Sea ports 736, 737, 741–2
Reddé, Michel 719
religion 6
  and Alexandria 110–14
  and animal cults 180–1
  and Christianity 331–2
  and combination of local, pan-Egyptian and hellenistic 320
  and definition of 398
  and divination 325–7, 345–6
  in domestic sphere 322–5
  and Egyptian religion as cult religion 458–9
  and elites 330–1
  and the environment 33, 35
  and expansion of Egyptian gods into the Mediterranean 427–9
  and festivals 320–1
  and general commitment to 330
  and Hellenization 320
  and iconography 339
  and *interpretatio Aegyptiaca* 423, 439, 440, 452
  and *interpretatio Graeca* 422, 437, 446
  and *interpretatio Romana* 423, 446
  and local cults 320, 321–2
  and local practices 33
  and magic 325, 327–9, 460–1
  and nature of traditional 319
  and practitioners of 458–60
  and social classes 329–31
  and social dimension 319–20
  and soldiers 76–9
  and temple building 459
  in Theban region 179–81
  and theurgy 355–6
  and Western Oases 721–5
  see also Christianity; cults; divination; funerary religion; imperial cult; imported cults; magic; oracles; priesthood; rituals; temple cult; temples
religious associations 459
Reshep 437
retail networks 45–6
revolts and uprisings 5, 16–17
  and Jewish revolt (115–17) 4, 112, 270–1, 282–4
  and Jewish revolt (132–5) 284
  and Jewish revolt (66–70) 282
  and revolt of the Boukoloi (172) 4
Rhakotis 422
Rhind, Alexander Henry 182, 671
Rhodes 427, 428, 449, 685
ricin oil 32
Rifaud, J. J. 156
Rigsby, K. J. 86, 93
Rijksmuseum van Oudheden 669
rituals:
  and acquiring control 350–2
  and contacting the divine 354–6
  and Daily Ritual 462–4, 465
  and eclectic nature of 346
  and functions of 338
  and Graeco-Egyptian magic 346
  and healing 352–4
  and innovations in 339
  and manipulation of supernatural forces 346
  and nature of private ritual 342
  and participation in ritual system 398–9
  and private sphere 460
  and protection against misfortune 347–9

and relationship between temple and private ritual 339
and reliance on writing 346
and sources for study of 343–4
and theophany 354–5
Roberts, C. H. 479
rock carvings 741
Roman army in Egypt 68–9
and auxiliary units 69–70
and citizenship 251, 266
and distinctive features of 74–5
and Eastern Desert 737, 742
and frontier garrison 753–4
and the garrison 69–72
and integration of veterans 452
and language policy 519
and Latin language 519
and legions stationed in Egypt 69
and local recruitment 72
and marriage 293–4
and military centres 70–1
and military diplomas 69, **70**, 72–3
and mummy portrait of a soldier **78**
and officer class 68, 73–4
and origin of soldiers 72–3
and religious practice of soldiers 76–9
and similarity to formations in other regions 68
and smaller outposts 71–2
and a soldier's life 75–9
and *statores* 75
and Theban garrison 173–4
Roman citizens in Egypt 250–2, 262
Rome:
and Isis 430, 689
and Osiris 430–1
Römer, Cornelia 161
Rosetta Stone 493, 565
Rossi, Corinna 719
Rostovtzeff, M 158
Rowe, Alan 115
royal tombs, and travellers to 708–9
Rubensohn, Otto 157

Sabinus 599
Sabius, Aurelius **619**
Sahidic dialect 582
Sakaon 156
Salomons, Roger 726
Samos, Treaty of (21/20 BCE) 17, 373
Samut 741
Saqqara 385, 389, 407, 422, 427
Sarapammon, Aelius 251
Sarapion, Aelius 537, 538
Sassanids 5
Satet 751
Saturnalia 441
Saturninus, Quintus Aemilius 409, 458
Satyrus 112
Sauneron, Serge 719
Schedia 138, 139
and excavations at 146
schistosomiasis 311
Schwartz, J. 158, 160
Schweinfurth, G. 156
science, and Egyptian literature 553–6
scribes 523, 545–6
and assumptions about 563
sculpture:
and funerary monument **617**
and personified Nile 693
and portraiture 615–18
and relief sculpture 618–20
and statue of woman at Oxyrhynchus **616**
and Vatican Nile **691**–4, 695
see also terracottas
sebakhin 155, 156, 157, 158, 163
and Karanis site **224**, 225, **226**
Second Sophistic 535, 573
Sema (Alexander the Great's tomb) 109
Seneca the Elder 707–8
Senouy 446–7
Senwosret I 153
Senwosret II 153–4
Septuagint 479, 480, 582, 588
Serapion, Aurelius 403
Serapis 13, 77, 78, 91, 94, 320, 443
and Alexandria 113–14
and attestations outside Egypt 428
as consort of Isis 422
and origins of 422
and sanctuary at Canopus 407
and terracotta figures of 635

Sersena 139
Service des Antiquités de l'Égypte 156
Seth 285, 328, 354, 409, 419, 424, 437, 550, 722
Sethe, K. 389
Setne tales 549–50
settlements 122
and administrative status 123, 127, 133
and *cardo-decumanus* layout 190
and conventional typology of 123, 124, 133
and definition of cities 125–8, 133
and differentiation between 127–8
and *komai* (villages) 123
and layout of Graeco-Roman settlements in the Fayum 162–6
and *metropoleis* (towns) 123, 124
and modelling settlement patterns 130–2
and *poleis* (cities) 123–4
and population size 125
and population structure 128–30
and rank-size distributions 131–2
and spectrum of 123, 127–8
and urban network theory 132
and urbanization 125
Severus, Alexander, Emperor 615
Severus, Septimus, Emperor 4, 183, 252, 256, 261, 374, 466, 705
sex 297
Shabaka Stone 566
Shai 321, 322, 439, 445
Shanhur 364
and temple at 373, 427, 564
Shenhur, and temple at 16, 405
Shenoute of Atripe 322, 332, 461, 467, 590
Shu 384
Sibilla, Gaspare 692
sibling marriage 266, 292–3, 312
Siket 741
Siwa Oasis 717, 718, 721, 722, 724
and oracle of Zeus-Ammon 402
slavery 43
smallpox 309, 311–12
Smedley, A. 261
snakes 445
Sobek 320, 371, 450, **451**, 464, 465
social class:
and bouleutic class 265
and citizens of the Greek *poleis* 252, 262–3
and Constitutio Antoniniana (212) 264–5
and Egyptians 263–4
and gymnasial class 263–4
and metropolite class 4, 254–5, 263–4
and priesthood 263
and religion 329–31
and Roman citizens 262
and social mobility 265–6
social mobility 5–6, 265–6
Socrates of Karanis 532, 534
Soknebtunis 450
Soknopaios 161, 320, 403, 464
Soknopaiou Nesos (Dime) 156, 157, 161, 163, 386, 404, 459–60, 494, 495
and abandonment of 557
and cult practice in 464–5
and Daily Ritual 463–4
and layout of 164, 165–6
and plan of **162**
and ruins at **165**
solar rays, and depiction of gods 446–7, 449–50
Someira 719
Sostratos of Knidos 108
Sotas, bishop of Oxyrhynchus 483
Soter 174, 182
Soter family mummies 182, 300, 672–3
Soterichus the Oasite 534, 726
Sphinx at Giza, and travellers to 710
Sri Lanka 737
Stadler, M. A. 404
state identity 261–2
statues 139
and funerary monument **617**
and hieroglyphic inscriptions 566
and portraiture 615–18
and statue of woman at Oxyrhynchus **616**
status:
and Alexandrian Jews 277–9, 286
and citizens of the Greek *poleis* 252, 262–3
and citizenship 249, 262
and classification of inhabitants 526
and Egyptians 263–4
and gymnasial class 263–4
and metropolite class 4, 254–5, 263–4
and non-citizens 254–7

and priesthood 257, 263
and Roman policy 257
and social mobility 265–6
and status declarations 4, 252, 258
Steinmeyer-Schareika, Angela 688
Strabo 13, 16, 17, 47, 48, 116, 402, 407, 533, 535, 667, 705, 706, 708
and Alexandria 107, 108, 110, 112, 248–9
and animal cults 189
and Thebes 176, 183
strategoi 16, 58
succession, and law of 267
Successus 522
Suetonius 12–13, 112
supernatural 337–8
and protocol for survival 338
and psychological function of 338
see also amulets; divination; rituals
Supreme Council of Antiquities 138, 719
Swain, George R. 224
Syene 426, 749, 750, 754
Syringes (royal tombs) 708–9
Syrion, Aelius 251
Szymanska, H. 643

Tacitus 15, 248, 705
Tafa 373
Tafis 757
Tahta 362
Tallet, Gaëlle 719
Talmis 76–7, 412, 756, 757, 760
Tanaweruow 391
Tanis 138, 140
Tanuat 671
Taposiris Magna 108
Tasenetnofret 371
Tatius, Achilles 107, 108
taxation 59–61
and business taxes 60
and collection of taxes 60
and custom duties 40, 61
and funerary art and artists 606–7
and grain land 26–8
and Jewish tax 60, 270
and land fertility 28–9
and land types 24, 60
and land use and food production 29–33
and local taxes 60–1
and orchards and gardens 28
and poll tax (*laographia*) 60
and private land 24
and public land 26
and tax farmers 60, 61
and trade 40
Tebtunis 156, 157, 158, 161, 163, 386, 450, 459, 495, 601
and abandonment of 557
and *cantina dei papyri* 509–10
and Daily Ritual 462–3
and layout of 164–5
Teephibis 410
teeth 312
Tefnut 384, 756
Tell Atrib (Athribis), *see* Athribis (Tell Atrib)
Tell el-Khawalid (Phragonis) 138
Tell el-Ma'raka 160, 161
Tell el-Yahudiyeh 137
Tell Moqdam (Leontopolis) 139
Tell Timai (Thmuis) 137
temple cult:
and attitudes towards the divine 461
and continuance of 466
and cult texts 462–5
and Daily Ritual 462–4, 465
and end of the written tradition 465–8
and extinction of 468
and group participation in 459
and holistic character of 459
and incantation 460, 461
and magic 460–1
and practitioners of 458–60
and private participation in 459
and religious associations 459
in Roman Egypt 462–5
and Roman rule 457–8
and temple building 459
temples:
in Alexandria 110–11, 112
and architectural variations 371–3
and Book of the Temple 364, 460
and characteristics of 339
and civic ceremony 321

temples: (*cont.*)
and construction of 16, 17, 18, 370, 373–4, 459, 614, 756–7
and cosmological associations 375
and decoration of 363, 374–7
at Dendara 364–71
and depiction of Roman emperor as pharaoh 375–6
and destruction by Christians 467
and divination 325–7, 345
and Egyptian language 495–6
and Egyptian scripts 495
and festivals 320–1
and financing of construction 370
and funerary religion 388–9
and healing 352–3
and hieroglyphic inscriptions 363, 364, 564–5
and impact of Roman decline 321
and imperial temples in Egypt 86–91, 95
at Karanis 229–31
and layout of Graeco-Roman settlements in the Fayum 164–6
and loss of economic power 457
and nationalization of lands 457
and relationship with private ritual 339
as repositories of native Egyptian culture 374
and scriptorium (House of Life) 345, 460
and Sphinx Gate temple 193
and temple grammar 364
and temple guardians (*neokoroi*) 87
and texts and writing systems 363–4
in Theban region 175–8
and theological variations 371–3
in Western Oases 721–5
Terenouthis 138, 139, 241, 308, 309
Terentianus, Claudius 77, 510, 518–19
and archive of 520–1, 522, 523
Teriteqas, King of Meroe 753
terracottas 644
and animal figures 642–3
and child-god figure **633**, **634**–5
and dating of 632–3
and definition of 630
and discovery sites 631–2
and Egyptian god figures 633–5
and female dancer figures **639**
and figures with raised arms 638–9
and Greek god figures 635–7
and grotesque figures 640–1
and high point of production 633
and human figures 641–**2**
and inscriptions on 631
and manufacturing technique 630–1
and 'naked goddess' figures 637–8
and *pataikoi* figures 639–40
and 'phallus men' figures 638
and pseudo-Baubo figures 638
and scholarly assessments of 643
and uses of 632
tetrastyla:
and Antinoopolis 191
at Hermopolis Magna 194
textile production 601
and specialization 45
Thaumaturgus, Gregory 477
Theadelphia 156, 157, 158, 163, 444, 446, 448
Thebaid 16, 17, 386
Thebais 171
Theban Magical Library 344
Theban region:
and burial practices 182–3
and extent of 171
and Graeco-Roman tourists 183–5
and historical background of 173–5
and map of **172**
and religion 179–81
and Roman garrison 173–4
and settlements 178
and sources for study of 171–3
and temples of 175–8
Thebes 462, 667
and administrative divisions 175
and building activity 178
and funerary religion 387–8
and Graeco-Roman tourists 183–5
and graffiti at 702
and mummies from 670–5
and population of 179
in pre-Roman Egypt 173
and residential quarters 176, 178
in Roman period 174
and sacred precincts 175–6

and temples of 175–8, 373
Theodorus, Aurelius 47
Theodosius, Emperor 109
Theognostos, Pappos 615
Theon, Aelius 110, 322, 538
Theon, Gaius Julius 93, 110
Theonas, bishop of Alexandria 482, 483, 484, 485
Theones, Julii 250
Theophilos 604
Theophilus, bishop of Alexandria 109, 112, 114
Thermouthis 427
Thessalos of Tralles 704
theurgy 355–6
Thmuis 22, **23**
and carbonized archives from 23, 24, 29, 33, 137
Thoeris 443
Thoth 189, 410, 722
and temple of 176, 177–8, 180, 192
Thracian mercenaries 439
Thucydides 533
Tiberianus, Claudius, and archive of 77, 510, 518–19, 520, 522–3
Tiberianus, Titus Egnatius 449
Tiberius, Emperor 366, 458, 614, 705
Tneferos 14
Tod 564
tombs:
and Alabaster Tomb 116–17
in Alexandria 116–18
and Great Catacomb at Kom el-Shuqafa **117**
and house-tombs 205
and Moustapha Pasha Tomb **116**
in Theban region 182
and Tigrane Tomb **118**
see also cemeteries; Tuna el-Gebel
tourism, and Theban region 183–5
see also travel to Roman Egypt
town councils 256
towns 123
toys, at Karanis **237–8**, **299**
trade:
and Alexandria 107
with Arabia and India 48
and communication networks 46
and custom duties 40, 61
and Eastern Desert 736–7, 741–3
and markets 40, 45, 46, 49
and mobility 47
and pre-Roman conquest period 685
and retail networks 45–6
and scale of 41–2, 48
and spread of Egyptian cults 685
and taxation 40
and trade routes 40
trades and crafts 40–1
and apprenticeships 44, 600–1
and associations of traders and craftsmen 41
and business taxes 60
and guilds 607–8
and mobility of people 47
and organization of production 41
and premises/workshops 42–3, 600–1
and specialization 44–5
and women 43
see also funerary art/artists
traditions 6
Trajan, Emperor 374
transportation, and trade routes 40
travel to Roman Egypt 701
to Colossi of Memnon 705–7
and graffiti 701–3, **708**, 709, 710
and Greek influence on perceptions of 710–11
and identity of travellers 704–5
and motivations for 703–4
to the Nile cataracts 707–8
and pilgrimage 703–4
and Pyramids at Giza 709
and Roman emperors 705
to the royal tombs 708–9
and search for mystical knowledge 704
and sites visited 705–10
and sources for study of 701–3
and Sphinx at Giza 710
Triakontaschoinos 750, 751–2, 753
Trimithis (Amheida) 449, 720–1, 722, 725
and clay tablet from **726**
and pyramid superstructure **728**
triumphal arches, and Antinoopolis 191

Tryphon 110, 537
tuberculosis 310–11
Tuna el-Gebel, necropolis of 207–10, 220, 728
  and burial ceremonies 219
  and changes in construction techniques 209
  and changes in layout of tombs 209
  and cremation 211
  and decoration of tombs 216–19
  and development of urban structure in early Roman period 210–14
  and excavations at 205–7
  and family feasts at the tombs 219
  and general plan of **206**
  and house-tombs 210, 211–13, 214–**15**, **216**, **217**–18
  and mud-brick tombs 209, 210
  and plan of excavated area of the necropolis **208**
  and reuse of tombs 209–10, 219
  and site details 207
  and temple tombs 207–9, 210–**11**, **212**, 218
  and tomb of Djed-Thoth-iu-ef-ankh 207, 209, 216
  and tomb of Padikam 207, 209, 216
  and tomb of Petosiris 205, 207, 209, 216
  and tomb pillars 210, 213–14
  and tombs of second and third centuries CE 214–16
Turranius, C. 458
Tutu **410**, 446, 449, 722, 723
Tyche 440
Tzetzes 109

Umm el-Dabadib 718, 719
Upper Nubia 749, 750, 753
urbanization 122
  and central place theory 131
  and consumer city theory 130–1
  and definition of cities 125–8, 133
  and extent of 125, 247
  and levels of 123
  and modelling settlement patterns 130–2
  and population structure 128–30
  and rank-size distributions 131–2
  and urban graveyard theory 128–9
  and urban network theory 132

Vaballathus 5
Valentinian I, Emperor 607
Valentinus 476
Valerian, Emperor 482
Valley of the Kings, and travellers to 708–9
Vandorpe, K. 507, 511
Vassilika, Eleni 375
Vatican Nile **691**–4, 695
vegetable cultivation 32
Versluys, Miguel John 688, 694
Vespasian, Emperor 261, 270–1, 689, 705
  and proclaimed emperor 4
Vestinus, Julius 94, 536
Via Nova Hadriana 744
Villa of the Birds (Alexandria) 115, 116
villages 123
  and administration of 59
  and population size 125
Vindolanda Tablets 523
vineyards 32
visuality 6
Volpato, Giovanni 692

Wadi Fawakhir 520
Wadi Hammamat 373, 741
Wadi Menih 741
Wadi Sikait **737**
wages, and funerary artists 605–6
Wagner, Guy 717
water management, in Western Oases 718
Wayekiye family 758–60
Weber, W. 643
West Delta Regional Survey 143
Western Desert 373
Western Oases 717, 729–30
  and archaeological missions in 719–21
  and attachment to the past 729
  and cultural identity 729, 730
  and cultural innovation 729
  and cultural memory 729–30
  and economic importance of 717
  and geography of 717–19

and Greek culture 729
and literary culture 725–7
and mortuary culture 727–8
and population of 718
and religion in 721–5
and water management 718
and wind in 718
wheat cultivation 29, 34, 136
Wilcken, U. 92–3
Wilkinson, John Gardner 738–9
William of Boldensele 709
Wilson, Penelope 363, 364
Winter, Erich 363, 364
wisdom literature 551
Witt, R. E. 428
wizards 325, 328
women:
and age at marriage 291
and coming-of-age rites 300
and education 531
and involvement in business and trade 43
and law of succession 267
and legal capacity 267
and literacy 500
and matrimonial property 290–1
and property ownership 267
in public life 267
in Roman Egypt 266–7
and social mobility 265, 266
and widows 290–1
workshops 600–1
Worp, Klaas 725, 726
writing materials 545
writing systems, and temples 363–4

Xenophon 533
Xesebaieon 175
Xois (Kom Sakha) 139, 140, 143

Yemen 737

Zenobia, Queen of Palmyra 5, 706
Zenon of Caunos 437
Zeus 175, 440
Zeus-Ammon, oracle of 402
Zeus Basileus 437
Zeus Helios Megas Serapis 403, 408, 427, **448**–9
Zeus Ktesios 439
Zeus Megistos 449
Zeus Melchios 112
Zeus Orania 112
Zeus Soter 112

The manufacturer's authorised representative in the EU for product safety is Oxford University Press España S.A. of El Parque Empresarial San Fernando de Henares, Avenida de Castilla, 2 - 28830 Madrid (www.oup.es/en or product.safety@oup.com). OUP España S.A. also acts as importer into Spain of products made by the manufacturer.
Printed and bound by CPI Group (UK) Ltd, Croydon, CR0 4YY
15/03/2025
01833822-0011